P9-CEZ-150

ninth edition

Psychology Applied to Modern Life

ADJUSTMENT IN THE 21ST CENTURY

WAYNE WEITEN
University of Nevada, Las Vegas

MARGARET A. LLOYD
Georgia Southern University

DANA S. DUNN
Moravian College

ELIZABETH YOST HAMMER
Xavier University of Louisiana

WADSWORTH
CENGAGE Learning™

Australia • Brazil • Japan • Korea • Mexico • Singapore •
Spain • United Kingdom • United States

WADSWORTH
CENGAGE Learning™

***Psychology Applied to Modern Life: Adjustment in the 21st Century,* Ninth Edition**
Wayne Weiten, Margaret A. Lloyd, Dana S. Dunn, Elizabeth Yost Hammer

Publisher: Michele Sordi
Development Editor: Kristin Makarewycz
Assistant Editor: Magnolia Molcan
Editorial Assistant: Erin Miskelly
Technology Project Manager: Lauren Keyes
Marketing Manager: Kim Russell
Marketing Assistant: Melanie Cregger
Marketing Communications Manager: Linda Yip
Project Manager, Editorial Production: Jennie Redwitz
Creative Director: Rob Hugel
Art Director: Vernon Boes
Print Buyer: Karen Hunt
Permissions Editors: Linda L. Rill, Bob Kauser
Production Service: Tom Dorsaneo
Text Designer: Liz Harasymczuk
Photo Researcher: Linda L. Rill
Copy Editor: Jackie Estrada
Illustrator: Carol Zuber-Mallison
Cover Designer: Liz Harasymczuk
Cover Image: "Inner Peace" by Jennifer Main, mixed media on canvas, 2005 www.jennifermaingallery.com
Compositor: Thompson Type

© 2009, 2006 Wadsworth Cengage Learning

ALL RIGHTS RESERVED. No part of this work covered by the copyright herein may be reproduced, transmitted, stored, or used in any form or by any means graphic, electronic, or mechanical, including but not limited to photocopying, recording, scanning, digitizing, taping, Web distribution, information networks, or information storage and retrieval systems, except as permitted under Section 107 or 108 of the 1976 United States Copyright Act, without the prior written permission of the publisher.

For product information and technology assistance, contact us at
Cengage Learning Academic Resource Center, 1-800-423-0563
For permission to use material from this text or product, submit all requests online at **www.cengage.com/permissions.**
Further permissions questions can be e-mailed to
permissionrequest@cengage.com.

© 2009 Cengage Learning. All Rights Reserved. Cengage Learning WebTutor™ is a trademark of Cengage Learning.

Library of Congress Control Number: 2007930881

Student Edition:
ISBN-13: 978-0-495-55339-7
ISBN-10: 0-495-55339-5

Loose-leaf Edition:
ISBN-13: 978-0-495-50535-8
ISBN-10: 0-495-50535-8

Wadsworth Cengage Learning
10 Davis Drive
Belmont, CA 94002-3098
USA

Cengage Learning products are represented in Canada by Nelson Education, Ltd.

For your course and learning solutions, visit **academic.cengage.com.**

Purchase any of our products at your local college store or at our preferred online store **www.ichapters.com.**

Printed in the United States of America
1 2 3 4 5 6 7 12 11 10 09 08

To two pillars of stability in this era
of turmoil—my parents
W. W.

To the memory of my mother and
father—models of integrity and courage
M. A. L.

For Sarah
D. S. D.

To W. C. and M. C. G.
E. Y. H.

Cover Image: "Inner Peace" by Jennifer Main, mixed media on canvas, 2005
www.jennifermaingallery.com

About the Authors

WAYNE WEITEN is a graduate of Bradley University and received his Ph.D. in social psychology from the University of Illinois, Chicago in 1981. He currently teaches at the University of Nevada, Las Vegas. He has received distinguished teaching awards from Division Two of the American Psychological Association (APA) and from the College of DuPage, where he taught until 1991. He is a Fellow of Divisions 1 and 2 of the American Psychological Association. In 1991, he helped chair the APA National Conference on Enhancing the Quality of Undergraduate Education in Psychology and in 1996–1997 he served as President of the Society for the Teaching of Psychology. Weiten has conducted research on a wide range of topics, including educational measurement, jury decision-making, attribution theory, stress, and cerebral specialization. His recent interests have included pressure as a form of stress and the technology of textbooks. He is also the author of *Psychology: Themes & Variations* (2007) and the creator of an educational CD-ROM titled *PsykTrek: A Multimedia Introduction to Psychology.*

MARGARET (MARKY) A. LLOYD received her B.A. from the University of Denver and her M.A. and Ph.D. in psychology from the University of Arizona. She is the author of *Adolescence* (1985). She has served as chair of the psychology departments at Suffolk University and Georgia Southern University and is the founding Chair of the Council for Undergraduate Psychology Programs. She is a past President of the Society for the Teaching of Psychology (Division 2 of the American Psychological Association), past Executive Director of the Society's Office of Teaching Resources in Psychology, and currently serves on APA's Council of Representatives for the Society. She is a Fellow of Divisions 1 and 2 of the American Psychological Association. She is Emerita Professor and Chair of Psychology at Georgia Southern University and a recipient of that institution's Award for Excellence for Contributions to Instruction.

DANA S. DUNN earned his B.A. in psychology from Carnegie Mellon University and received his Ph.D. in social psychology from the University of Virginia. He is currently professor of psychology and director of the Learning in Common Curriculum at Moravian College, Bethlehem, PA. He chaired the psychology department at Moravian for 6 years. A Fellow of the American Psychological Association (APA), Dunn is active in the Society for the Teaching of Psychology and frequently presents at national and regional disciplinary conferences. Dunn has written numerous articles, chapters, and book reviews concerning his areas of research interest: the teaching of psychology, social psychology, and rehabilitation psychology. He is the author or editor of several books, including *Research Methods for Social Psychology* (in press) and *A Short Guide to Writing about Psychology* (2008).

ELIZABETH YOST HAMMER earned her B.S. in psychology from Troy State University and received her Ph.D. in social psychology from Tulane University. She is currently professor of psychology and director of the Center for the Advancement of Teaching at Xavier University of Louisiana in New Orleans. She is a Fellow of Division Two of the American Psychological Association (APA) and is a past President of Psi Chi, the National Honor Society in Psychology. Recently, she was elected as treasurer for the Society for the Teaching of Psychology. She is passionate about teaching and has published on collaborative learning, service learning, the application of social psychological theories to the classroom, and mentoring students. After her experience with Hurricane Katrina, she developed a Psychology of Disasters course and is currently co-authoring a book of the same title.

To the Instructor

Many students enter adjustment courses with great expectations. They've ambled through their local bookstores, and in the "Psychology" section they've seen numerous self-help books that offer highly touted recipes for achieving happiness for a mere $12.95. After paying far more money to enroll in a college course that deals with the same issues as the self-help books, many students expect a revelatory experience. However, the majority of us with professional training in psychology or counseling take a rather dim view of self-help books and the pop psychology they represent. Psychology professors tend to see this literature as oversimplified, intellectually dishonest, and opportunistic and often summarily dismiss the pop psychology that so many students have embraced. Instructors try to supplant pop psychology with more sophisticated academic psychology, which is more complex and less accessible.

In this textbook, we have tried to come to grips with this problem of differing expectations between student and teacher. Our goal has been to produce a comprehensive, serious, research-oriented treatment of the topic of adjustment that also acknowledges the existence of popular psychology and looks critically at its contributions.

In Chapter 1 we confront the phenomenon of popular self-help books. We try to take the student beneath the seductive surface of such books and analyze some of their typical flaws. Our goal is to make the student a more critical consumer of this type of literature.

While encouraging a more critical attitude toward self-help books, we do not suggest that all of them should be dismissed. Instead, we acknowledge that some of them offer authentic insights. In fact, we highlight some of the better books in Recommended Reading boxes sprinkled throughout the text. These recommended books tie in with the adjacent topical coverage and show the student the interface between academic and popular psychology.

Throughout the book we try to provide the student with a better appreciation of the merits of the empirical approach. This effort to clarify the role of research, which is rare for an adjustment text, appears in the first chapter.

Recognizing that adjustment students want to leave the course with concrete, personally useful information, we end each chapter with an application section. The Applications are "how to" discussions that address everyday problems. While they focus on issues that are relevant to the content of the particular chapter, they contain more explicit advice than the text proper.

In summary, we have tried to make this book both rigorous and applied. We hope that our approach will help students to better appreciate the value of scientific psychology.

Philosophy

A certain philosophy is inherent in any systematic treatment of the topic of adjustment. Our philosophy can be summarized as follows:

- We believe that an adjustment text should be a resource book for students. We have tried to design this book so that it encourages and facilitates the pursuit of additional information on adjustment-related topics. It should serve as a point of departure for more learning.
- We believe in theoretical eclecticism. This book will not indoctrinate your students along the lines of any single theoretical orientation. The psychodynamic, behavioral, and humanistic schools of thought are all treated with respect, as are cognitive, biological, evolutionary, and other perspectives.
- We believe that effective adjustment requires taking charge of one's own life. Throughout the book we try to promote the notion that active coping efforts are generally superior to passivity and complacency.

Changes in the Ninth Edition

One of the exciting things about psychology is that it is not a stagnant discipline. It continues to progress at what seems a faster and faster pace. A good textbook must evolve with the discipline. Although the professors and students who used the earlier editions of this book did not clamor for change, we have made countless content changes to keep up with new developments in psychology—adding and deleting some topics, condensing and reorganizing others, and updating everything (there are 1,082 new references). A brief overview of some of these changes, listed chapter by chapter, can be found on pages ix–xi following this introduction.

The most significant change in this edition is the addition of two new co-authors to the *Psychology Applied to Modern Life* team. Dana Dunn and Elizabeth Yost Hammer each contributed revisions of four chapters to this edition. We brought Dana and Elizabeth on board because Marky Lloyd intends to fully embrace retirement after this edition. This gradual transition in authorship has gone smoothly, as Dana and Elizabeth have brought fresh perspectives to the topics in their chapters, reenergizing the revision process and producing a great deal of new coverage.

Writing Style

This book has been written with the student reader in mind. We have tried to integrate the technical jargon of our discipline into a relatively informal and down-to-earth writing style. We use concrete examples extensively to clarify complex concepts and to help maintain student interest. Although we now have four authors, the original author of this book (Wayne Weiten) continues to do the final rewrite of all 16 chapters to ensure stylistic consistency.

Features

This text contains a number of features intended to stimulate interest and enhance students' learning. These special features include Applications, Recommended Reading boxes, Web Links, Practice Tests, a didactic illustration program, and cartoons.

Applications

The Applications should be of special interest to most students. They are tied to chapter content in a way that should show students how practical applications emerge out of theory and research. Although some of the material covered in these sections shows up frequently in adjustment texts, much of it is unique. Among the Application topics are

- Understanding Intimate Violence
- Monitoring Your Stress
- Understanding Eating Disorders
- Getting Ahead in the Job Game
- Building Self-Esteem
- Enhancing Sexual Relationships
- Bridging the Gender Gap in Communication

Recommended Reading Boxes

Recognizing students' interest in self-help books, we have sifted through hundreds of them to identify some that may be especially useful. These books are featured in boxes that briefly review some of the higher-quality books. These Recommended Reading boxes are placed where they are germane to the material being covered in the text. Some of the recommended books are well known, while others are obscure. Although we make it clear that we don't endorse every idea in every book, we think they all have something worthwhile to offer. This feature replaces the conventional suggested readings lists that usually appear at the ends of text chapters, where they are almost universally ignored by students.

Living in Today's World Boxes

The Living in Today's World boxes were originally developed to address issues that surfaced in the aftermath of the 9/11 terrorist attacks in the United States. Continuing in this vein, many of the boxes in this edition deal with concerns raised by the threat of terrorism in today's world. For example, we discuss how people tend to be affected by traumatic events, how people can cope more effectively with personal trauma, and how people can think more rationally about the threat of terrorism. However, we have broadened the scope of coverage in these boxes to include adjustment issues that are especially pertinent in light of current events, such as sexual interactions over the Internet, the controversy over whether the government should promote marriage, and difficulties coping with unemployment. We hope these digressions on pressing, contemporary issues prove helpful to students.

Web Links

The Internet is rapidly altering the landscape of modern life, and students clearly need help dealing with the information explosion in cyberspace. To assist them, we recruited web expert Vincent Hevern (Le Moyne College) to evaluate hundreds of psychology- and adjustment-related sites on the web and to come up with some recommended sites that appear to provide reasonably accurate, balanced, and empirically sound information. Short descriptions of these recommended websites are dispersed throughout the chapters, adjacent to related topical coverage. Because URLs change frequently, we have not included the URLs for the Web Links in the book. Insofar as students are interested in visiting these sites, we recommend that they do so through the *Psychology Applied to Modern Life* home page at the Wadsworth Psychology website (academic.cengage.com/psychology/weiten). Links to all the recommended websites are maintained there, and the Wadsworth webmaster periodically updates the URLs. Of course, students can also use search engines such as Google to locate the recommended websites.

Practice Tests

Each chapter ends with a ten-item multiple-choice Practice Test that should give students a fairly realistic assessment of their mastery of that chapter and valuable practice in taking the type of test that many of them will face in the classroom (if the instructor uses the *Test Bank*). This feature grew out of research on students' use of textbook pedagogical devices (see Weiten, Guadagno, & Beck, 1996). This research indicated that students pay scant attention to some standard pedagogical devices. When students were grilled to gain a better understanding of this perplexing finding, it quickly became apparent that students are pragmatic about pedagogy. Essentially, their refrain was, "We want study aids that will help us pass the next test." With this mandate in mind, we added the Practice Tests. They should be very realistic, as many of the items came from the *Test Bank* for previous editions (these items do not appear in the *Test Bank* for the current edition).

Didactic Illustration Program

The illustration program is once again in full color, and many new figures have been added along with extensive redrawing of many graphics. Although the illustrations are intended to make the book attractive and to help maintain student interest, they are not merely decorative: They have been carefully selected and crafted for their didactic value to enhance the educational goals of the text.

Cartoons

A little comic relief usually helps keep a student interested, so we've sprinkled numerous cartoons throughout the book. Like the figures, most of them have been chosen to reinforce ideas in the text.

Learning Aids

Because this book is rigorous, substantive, and sizable, a number of learning aids have been incorporated into the text to help the reader digest the wealth of material:

- The *outline* at the beginning of each chapter provides the student with a preview and overview of what will be covered.
- *Headings* are used extensively to keep material well organized.
- To help alert your students to key points, *learning objectives* are distributed throughout the chapters, after the first-level headings.
- *Key terms* are identified with ***blue italicized boldface type*** to indicate that these are important vocabulary items that are part of psychology's technical language.
- An *integrated running glossary* provides an on-the-spot definition of each key term as it is introduced in the text. Each formal definition is printed in **blue boldface** type.
- An *alphabetical glossary* is found in the back of the book, as key terms are usually defined in the integrated running glossary only when they are first introduced.
- *Italics* are used liberally throughout the text to emphasize important points.
- A *chapter review* is found at the end of each chapter. Each review includes a concise but thorough summary of the chapter's key ideas, a list of the key terms that were introduced in the chapter, and a list of important theorists and researchers who were discussed in the chapter.

Supplementary Materials

A complete teaching/learning package has been developed to supplement *Psychology Applied to Modern Life.* These supplementary materials have been carefully coordinated to provide effective support for the text. Supplements are available to qualified adopters. Please consult your local sales representative for details.

Personal Explorations Workbook

The *Personal Explorations Workbook* is a small booklet assembled by John Pulver of the College of Southern Nevada and Wayne Weiten. It contains experiential exercises for each text chapter, designed to help your students achieve personal insights. The questionnaires are psychological tests or scales that your students can administer and score for themselves. The "Personal Probes" consist of questions intended to help students think about themselves in relation to issues raised in the text. In addition to generating student interest, these exercises can be fruitful in stimulating class discussion. The *Personal Explorations Workbook* can be ordered shrinkwrapped with the text.

Instructor's Manual

The *Instructor's Manual,* revised by Lenore Frigo of Shasta College, is available as a convenient aid for your educational endeavors. It provides a thorough overview of each chapter, along with a list of relevant films and InfoTrac College Edition integration. It also includes a wealth of suggestions for lecture topics, class demonstrations, exercises, and discussion questions, organized around the content of each chapter in the text.

Test Bank

The *Test Bank,* revised by Joan Thomas-Spiegel of Los Angeles Harbor College, contains an extensive collection of multiple-choice questions for objective tests, all closely tied to the learning objectives found in the text chapters. We're confident that you will find this to be a dependable and usable test bank.

ExamView® Computerized Testing

Preloaded with all of the questions in the *Test Bank,* ExamView allows you to create, deliver, and customize tests and study guides (both print and online) in minutes. ExamView offers both a Quick Test Wizard and an Online Test Wizard that guides you step by step through the process of creating tests, while its unique "what you see is what you get" capability allows you to see the test you are creating onscreen exactly as it will print or display online. You can build tests of up to 250 questions using up to 12 question types. Using ExamView's complete word-processing capabilities, you can enter an unlimited number of new questions or edit existing questions.

PowerLecture with JoinIn™ and ExamView

This one-stop lecture and class preparation tool makes it easy for you to assemble, edit, publish, and present custom lectures for your course using Microsoft® PowerPoint®. PowerLecture lets you bring together text-specific lecture outlines written by Lisa Garner of Tallahassee Community College with art from the text, along with video and animations from the web or your own materials—culminating in powerful, personalized, media-enhanced presentations. The CD-ROM also contains the full *Instructor's Manual, Test Bank,* and other instructor resources. The CD-ROM also includes software that lets you pose book-specific questions and display students' answers seamlessly within the Microsoft® PowerPoint® slides of your own lecture, in conjunction with the "clicker" hardware of your choice, as well as the ExamView assessment and tutorial system, which guides you step by step through the process of creating tests.

Study Guide

The *Study Guide,* written by William Addison of Eastern Illinois University, is designed to help students master the information contained in the text. It contains a programmed review of learning objectives, quiz boxes, and a self-test for each chapter. Your students should find it helpful in their study efforts.

Culture and Modern Life

Culture and Modern Life is a small paperback intended to help your students appreciate how cultural factors moderate psychological processes and how the viewpoint of one's own culture can distort one's interpretation of the behavior of people from other cultures. Written by David Matsumoto (San Francisco State University), a leading authority on cross-cultural psychology, this supplementary book should greatly enhance your students' understanding of how culture can influence adjustment. *Culture and Modern Life* can be ordered shrinkwrapped with the text.

Critical Thinking Exercises

A set of critical thinking exercises can be found at the *Psychology Applied to Modern Life* website (academic.cengage.com/psychology/weiten). These exercises are intended to introduce students to specific critical thinking skills such as recognizing extraneous variables, sampling bias, and fallacies in reasoning. The exercises also challenge students to apply these skills to adjustment-related topics on a chapter-by-chapter basis.

Highlights of Content Changes in the Ninth Edition

To help professors who have used this book over many editions, we are providing an overview of the content changes in the current edition. The following list is not exhaustive, but it should alert faculty to most of the major changes in the book.

Chapter 1 Adjusting to Modern Life

In discussion of the paradox of progress, new material on how work follows people home and how the modern time crunch fosters an epidemic of sleep deprivation

In discussion of the paradox of progress, new material on compulsive buying syndrome

New discussion of modern "makeover culture," and the widespread obsession with self-improvement

New coverage of Salerno's critique and expose of self-help gurus.

New discussion of how self-help books often encourage a self-centered, exploitive approach to interpersonal relationships

New discussion of the surprisingly modest association between actual wealth and subjective perceptions of finances, and other new research on income and happiness

New coverage of the heritability of subjective well-being

New discussion of Gilbert's work on how people are surprisingly bad at predicting what will make them happy

New research on the degree to which the hedonic treadmill makes it difficult for people to enhance their happiness

Chapter 2 Theories of Personality

Discussion of trait models now includes explanation of the role of factor analysis

New research relating the Big Five traits to various aspects of behavior

Expanded coverage of relations between self-efficacy and specific behaviors

New discussion of Nettle's evolutionary analysis of the adaptive implications of the Big Five traits

New discussion of how hindsight bias presents problems for evolutionary theories of personality

New research on terror management theory and reactions to abstract art

New research relating terror management theory to psychological discomfort about bodily processes, including sexuality

New section on culture and personality examines the cross-cultural relevance of the five-factor model

New research on cultural variations in scores on Big Five traits and the inaccuracy of national character stereotypes

Revised, more critical evaluation of projective tests

Chapter 3 Stress and Its Effects

New discussion of recent research on the impact of stress appraisals, specifically on children's responses to the 9/11 terrorist attacks

Updated research using the City Stress Inventory as an index of urban environmental stress

New coverage of perceived discrimination as a source of stress

Discussion of acculturation as a form of stress

Streamlined coverage of conflict and vacillation

New description of the role of depleted self-control in test anxiety

Added description of posttraumatic shame and guilt

Expanded discussion of stress and memory

Coverage of new research on posttraumatic growth

Inclusion of 9/11 data on rescue workers and PTSD

Chapter 4 Coping Processes

New discussion of the importance of being flexible in choosing coping strategies

Expanded discussion of how exposure to media violence increases aggressive behavior

New data on the ramifications of self-blame as coping strategy

New, more contemporary introduction to using humor as a coping strategy

New discussion of cultural variations in the tendency to seek social support

New findings on personality factors related to procrastination

New discussion of the thinking underlying college students' procrastination on academic assignments

New coverage of the distinction between people who are future-oriented versus present-oriented in relation to time management

New section on exercise as an emotion-focused coping strategy

New advice on factors promoting effective exercise

Streamlined, reorganized coverage of meditation and relaxation

Chapter 5 The Self

New opening vignette illustrating self-reflection

Expanded discussion of efforts to cope with self-discrepancies

Expanded coverage of social comparison processes, including current versus past selves, reference group appraisal, and upward and downward comparisons

New section on the impact of social context as a factor shaping self-concept

New discussion of the self, cultural values, and focus on interpersonal agency

New discussion of trait versus state self-esteem

New material concerning secure high self-esteem and defensive high self-esteem

Broadened discussion of terror management theory and beliefs about terrorism in relation to self-esteem

New comparison drawn between self-handicapping and defensive pessimism

Additional details concerning predictors of self-handicapping

New Recommended Reading on defensive pessimism

Addition of negative acknowledgment as an impression management strategy

Chapter 6 Social Thinking and Social Influence

New opening vignette showing person perception in action

New discussion of how bad can be stronger than good in person perception

Extension of the confirmation bias to group behavior

Broader discussion of the attractiveness stereotype and its impact on romance

Added discussion regarding why the fundamental attribution error is hard to avoid

Additional discussion concerning why prejudice does not always lead to discrimination

Coverage of new topic, aversive racism

New material on a prejudiced personality style called the social dominance orientation

New discussion of mood and the need for cognition as receiver factors in persuasion

Additional consideration of the Asch study's impact

Introduction of how the foot-in-the-door technique can also be used for socially beneficial goals

Chapter 7 Interpersonal Communication

New material on net lingo and cyberspeak

New point about how nonverbal communication plays an important role in conveying emotions

New data on people's ability to detect deception in others

New material on nonverbal sensitivity, including gender differences

New discussion of the role of nonverbal communication in self-disclosure

Added visualization as a treatment for speech anxiety

New big-picture conclusion for the main body of the chapter

New box on communication in an adversarial culture

Chapter 8 Friendship and Love

New material on the use of online dating sites

New discussion of deception in online romantic interactions

New material on changing body ideals for men

New discussion of special friendship issues for gay males and lesbians

New data on Sternberg's triangular theory of love

Revised conceptualization of attachment styles in terms of continuous dimensions

New material on the contribution of increased social isolation to trends in loneliness

Added information on the emotional costs of receiving social support

Chapter 9 Marriage and Intimate Relationships

New discussion of polygamy

Expanded discussion of interracial marriages

Revised coverage of age at marriage as a predictor of marital success

New material on the importance of positive emotions in premarital interactions

New data on the most common problems in marriages in later life

Expanded discussion of positive and negative work-to-family spillover

New findings on maternal employment and child development

New material on adjusting to divorce

Increased discussion of same-sex relationships

Chapter 10 Gender and Behavior

New chapter introduction focuses on Harvard President Lawrence Summers' controversial remarks regarding gender differences in math and science

Expanded discussion of the concept of gender

New discussion of androcentrism in science literature

Added discussion of Hyde's gender similarities hypothesis

Streamlined coverage of gender differences in personality and social behavior

Added data of gender differences in PTSD

Expanded coverage of gender role socialization through children's literature

Expanded coverage of the role of TV in gender role socialization

New discussion of the role of new media (video games, software) in gender role socialization

New evidence on gender differences in pressure to succeed

Inclusion of the double jeopardy status for harassment of minority women in the workplace

New discussion of differentiated androgyny

Chapter 11 Development in Adolescence and Adulthood

New opening vignette illustrating the importance of developmental perspectives

Expanded discussion of adolescent autonomy and its positive impact on relations with parents

Lengthened discussion of parasuicide in adolescence

New material on the proposed stage of development known as emerging adulthood

New Recommended Reading on a book outlining research on emerging adulthood

More specific and up-to-date characterization of Erikson's concept of generativity

More on mid-life as a construct of modern cultures

Additional coverage of the "empty nest syndrome"

New discussion of belief in adaptive control in relation to mid-life adjustment

Additional coverage of women and the notion of the mid-life crisis

More detail on the role friendship and social support networks play in later life

Addition of new material on gender and ethnicity as risk factors for Alzheimer's disease

Supplementary discussion concerning adapting to grief across time

New Recommended Reading on the funeral industry and green burials

Chapter 12 Careers and Work

Revised chapter opener to be a more involving vignette

Extensive discussion of contemporary technological tools throughout

Streamlined coverage of Super's stages of vocational development

New material on sexual orientation disclosure and employment discrimination

New research on the glass ceiling for women, especially minority women

Updated discussion of family-friendly workplace policies

New findings on the benefits of leisure activities

New material on video résumés and on the perils of résumé padding

New Recommended Reading box profiles book on making the transition from college to career

Chapter 13 Development and Expression of Sexuality

Revised chapter opener to be a more engaging vignette

Updated material on peers as a socializing influence on sexual behavior

Revised discussion of how the media acts as a socializing influence on sexuality

Revised coverage of sexual identity development

New scheme for understanding motives for engaging in sex

New data on gender differences in comfort with "hooking up"

Revised discussion of constraints on effective contraception

Updated discussion of new contraceptive methods

Added information on the new vaccine for HPV

Chapter 14 Psychology and Physical Health

New opening vignette illustrating the connections between behavior and physical health

Expanded discussion of influential factors in the biopsychosocial model

Greater detail on how personality can be linked to physical health

New material on the interaction of race and hostility in relation to cardiovascular risk

Expanded discussion of the relation between low social support and heart disease

Discussion of problems in the prediction of heart disease posed by conceptual overlap of depression, anger, and anxiety

New description of the cancer prone or Type C personality

Updated discussion of stress and immune suppression

New research showing that merely thinking about alcohol can prime aggressive thoughts and behaviors

More detail on the link between sedentary lifestyle and weight gain

New material on demographic factors and obesity

Added detail regarding the benefits of exercise at any age

New discussion of age as a factor in treatment seeking

Chapter 15 Psychological Disorders

New discussion of how psychiatric views of homosexuality have changed over time, illustrating the value-laden nature of judgments of abnormality

New discussion of the process to develop DSM-V

New coverage of controversy surrounding recent high estimates of the prevalence of mental illness

New findings on personality and somatoform disorders

Updated discussion of diagnostic patterns for dissociative identity disorder

New discussion of genetic mapping findings in relation to the etiology of mood disorders

New coverage of innovative theory that attributes depression to suppressed neurogenesis in the hippocampus

Updated coverage of how interpersonal factors contribute to depressive disorders

New box on understanding and preventing suicide

Updated coverage of the prevalence of eating disorders

Application on eating disorders now includes description of binge-eating disorder

Chapter 16 Psychotherapy

Updated discussion of psychologists' efforts to obtain prescription privileges

New data on who seeks and receives professional treatment

New information on how hypnosis and dream interpretation may contribute to recovered memories of abuse in therapy

Coverage of cognitive therapy moved from section on insight therapies to section on behavioral treatments

Revised discussion of the effectiveness of insight therapies

New discussion of the cost effectiveness of newer atypical antipsychotics in comparison to conventional antipsychotics

New Recommended Reading box profiling the book *Crazy,* which provides a chilling and disturbing portrait of America's mental health system

Streamlined Application on looking for a therapist

Acknowledgments

This book has been an enormous undertaking, and we want to express our gratitude to the innumerable people who have influenced its evolution. To begin with, we must cite the contribution of our students who have taken the adjustment course. It is trite to say that they have been a continuing inspiration—but they have.

We also want to express our appreciation for the time and effort invested by the authors of various ancillary books and materials: Vinny Hevern (Le Moyne College), Bill Addison (Eastern Illinois University), Jeffry Ricker (Scottsdale Community College), John Pulver (Community College of Southern Nevada), David Matsumoto (San Francisco State University), Lenore Frigo (Shasta College), Lisa Garner (Tallahassee Community College), and Joan Thomas-Spiegel (Los Angeles Harbor College). In spite of tight schedules, they all did commendable work.

The quality of a textbook depends greatly on the quality of the prepublication reviews by psychology professors around the country. The reviewers listed on pages xiii–xiv have contributed to the development of this book by providing constructive reviews of various portions of the manuscript in this or earlier editions. We are grateful to all of them.

We would also like to thank Michele Sordi, who has served as editor of this edition. She has done a wonderful job following in the footsteps of Claire Verduin, Eileen Murphy, and Edith Beard Brady, to whom we remain indebted. We are also grateful to Jackie Estrada, who did an excellent job of copy editing and indexing; Tom Dorsaneo, who performed superbly as our production editor; Liz Harasymczuk, who created the colorful, inviting design; Linda Rill, who provided outstanding photo and permissions research; Carol Zuber-Mallison, who created the new graphics; Alma Bell of Thompson Type who oversaw the composition; and Fiorella Ljunggren, who shepherded previous editions into existence. Others who have made significant contributions to this project include Jennie Redwitz (project manager), Kristin Makarewycz (development editor), Magnolia Molcan (ancillaries editor), Kim Russell (marketing manager), Erin Miskelly (editorial assistant), Lauren Keyes (technology projects), and Vernon Boes (art director).

In addition, Wayne Weiten would like to thank his wife, Beth Traylor, who has been a steady source of emotional support despite the demands of her medical career, and his 14-year-old son, T. J., who adds a wealth of laughter to his dad's life. He is also grateful to his former colleagues at the College of DuPage and at Santa Clara University for their counsel and assistance, and to Melissa Lanctot for her assistance with the references. Marky Lloyd would like to thank Sarah Goss for her suggestions of popular songs and Judith A. Holleman for her assistance and support. Dana Dunn thanks his wife, editor Sarah Dunn, for making suggestions on drafts of the manuscript. As always, his children, Jake and Hannah, were happy distractions during the writing process. He also thanks one of his former students, Jessica Barkhausen, for suggesting and tracking down reference materials. Elizabeth Yost Hammer would like to thank Elliott Hammer—her constant source of inspiration, encouragement, and support—for far too much to list here. She is grateful to Samantha Hagler, Lyse Jackson, Alise Olivio, and Emily Santiago for their research assistance. She is also grateful to Kendall Eskine for his assistance with the reference list. Finally, she wishes to thank Wayne Weiten for inviting her to be part of this project.

Wayne Weiten
Margaret A. Lloyd
Dana S. Dunn
Elizabeth Yost Hammer

Reviewers

Bette Ackerman
Rhodes College
David W. Alfano
Community College of Rhode Island
Jeff Banks
Pepperdine University
Marsha K. Beauchamp
Mt. San Antonio College
John R. Blakemore
Monterey Peninsula College
Barbara A. Boccaccio
Tunxis Community College
Paul Bowers
Grayson County College
Tamara L. Brown
University of Kentucky
George Bryant
East Texas State University
James F. Calhoun
University of Georgia
Robert Cameron
Fairmont State College
Bernardo J. Carducci
Indiana University, Southeast
M. K. Clampit
Bentley College
Meg Clark
California State Polytechnic University-Pomona
Stephen S. Coccia
Orange County Community College
Dennis Coon
Santa Barbara City College
Katherine A. Couch
Eastern Oklahoma State College
Tori Crews
American River College
Salvatore Cullari
Lebanon Valley College
Kenneth S. Davidson
Wayne State University
Lugenia Dixon
Bainbridge College
Jean Egan
Asnuntuck Community College
Richard Fuhrer
University of Wisconsin-Eau Claire
R. Kirkland Gable
California Lutheran University
Lee Gills
Georgia College
Lawrence Grebstein
University of Rhode Island
Bryan Gros
Louisiana State University
Kyle Max Hancock
Utah State University
Barbara Hansen Lemme
College of DuPage
Robert Helm
Oklahoma State University
Barbara Hermann
Gainesville College
Jeanne L. Higbee
University of Minnesota
Robert Higgins
Central Missouri State University
Clara E. Hill
University of Maryland
Michael Hirt
Kent State University
Fred J. Hitti
Monroe Community College
William M. Hooper
Clayton College and State University
Joseph Horvat
Weber State University
Kathy Howard
Harding University
Teresa A. Hutchens
University of Tennessee-Knoxville
Jerry Jensen
Minneapolis Community & Technical College
Walter Jones
College of DuPage
Wayne Joose
Calvin College
Bradley Karlin
Texas A&M University
Margaret Karolyi
University of Akron
Lambros Karris
Husson College
Martha Kuehn
Central Lakes College
Susan Kupisch
Austin Peay State University
Robert Lawyer
Delgado Community College
Jimi Leopold
Tarleton State University
Harold List
Massachusetts Bay Community College
Corliss A. Littlefield
Morgan Community College
Louis A. Martone
Miami Dade Community College
Richard Maslow
San Joaquin Delta College
Sherri McCarthy
Northern Arizona University
William T. McReynolds
University of Tampa
Fred Medway
University of South Carolina-Columbia
Frederick Meeker
California State Polytechnic University-Pomona
Mitchell Metzger
Pennsylvania State University-Shenago Campus
John Moritsugu
Pacific Lutheran University
Jeanne O'Kon
Tallahassee Community College
Gary Oliver
College of DuPage
William Penrod
Middle Tennessee State University
Joseph Philbrick
California State Polytechnic University-Pomona
Barbara M. Powell
Eastern Illinois University
James Prochaska
University of Rhode Island
Megan Benoit Ratcliff
University of Georgia
Katherine Elaine Royal
Middle Tennessee State University
Joan Royce
Riverside Community College
Joan Rykiel
Ocean County College
John Sample
Slippery Rock University
Thomas K. Savill
Metropolitan State College of Denver
Patricia Sawyer
Middlesex Community College
Carol Schachat
De Anza College
Norman R. Schultz
Clemson University

Dale Simmons
Oregon State University
Sangeeta Singg
Angelo State University
Valerie Smead
Western Illinois University
Dolores K. Sutter
Tarrant County College-Northeast
Karl Swain
Community College of Southern Nevada
Diane Teske
Penn State Harrisburg
Kenneth L. Thompson
Central Missouri State University
David L. Watson
University of Hawaii
Deborah S. Weber
University of Akron
Clair Wiederholt
Madison Area Technical College
J. Oscar Williams
Diablo Valley College
Raymond Wolf
Moraine Park Technical College
Raymond Wolfe
State University of New York at Geneseo
Michael Wolff
Southwestern Oklahoma State University
Madeleine E. Wright
Houston Community College
Norbert Yager
Henry Ford Community College

Brief Contents

PART ONE The Dynamics of Adjustment

1 Adjusting to Modern Life 1
APPLICATION: IMPROVING ACADEMIC PERFORMANCE 24

2 Theories of Personality 32
THE NATURE OF PERSONALITY 33
APPLICATION: ASSESSING YOUR PERSONALITY 63

3 Stress and Its Effects 70
APPLICATION: MONITORING YOUR STRESS 97

4 Coping Processes 104
APPLICATION: ACHIEVING SELF-CONTROL 132

PART TWO The Interpersonal Realm

5 The Self 140
APPLICATION: BUILDING SELF-ESTEEM 167

6 Social Thinking and Social Influence 172
APPLICATION: SEEING THROUGH COMPLIANCE TACTICS 198

7 Interpersonal Communication 204
APPLICATION: DEVELOPING AN ASSERTIVE COMMUNICATION STYLE 229

8 Friendship and Love 236
APPLICATION: OVERCOMING LONELINESS 261

9 Marriage and Intimate Relationships 268
APPLICATION: UNDERSTANDING INTIMATE VIOLENCE 295

PART THREE Developmental Transitions

10 Gender and Behavior 302
APPLICATION: BRIDGING THE GENDER GAP IN COMMUNICATION 330

11 Development in Adolescence and Adulthood 336
APPLICATION: BECOMING AN EFFECTIVE PARENT 369

12 Careers and Work 372
APPLICATION: GETTING AHEAD IN THE JOB GAME 398

13 Development and Expression of Sexuality 406
APPLICATION: ENHANCING SEXUAL RELATIONSHIPS 433

PART FOUR Mental and Physical Health

14 Psychology and Physical Health 440
APPLICATION: UNDERSTANDING THE EFFECTS OF DRUGS 469

15 Psychological Disorders 478
APPLICATION: UNDERSTANDING EATING DISORDERS 507

16 Psychotherapy 514
APPLICATION: LOOKING FOR A THERAPIST 542

Contents

PART ONE

The Dynamics of Adjustment

CHAPTER 1 Adjusting to Modern Life 1

THE PARADOX OF PROGRESS 1

Living in Today's World *Life May Never Be the Same Again: Implications for Adjustment*

THE SEARCH FOR DIRECTION 4

Self-Help Books

The Approach of This Textbook

THE PSYCHOLOGY OF ADJUSTMENT 11

What Is Psychology?

What Is Adjustment?

THE SCIENTIFIC APPROACH TO BEHAVIOR 12

The Commitment to Empiricism

Advantages of the Scientific Approach

Experimental Research: Looking for Causes

Correlational Research: Looking for Links

THE ROOTS OF HAPPINESS: AN EMPIRICAL ANALYSIS 19

What Isn't Very Important?

What Is Somewhat Important?

What Is Very Important?

Conclusions

APPLICATION: IMPROVING ACADEMIC PERFORMANCE 24

Developing Sound Study Habits

Improving Your Reading

Getting More Out of Lectures

Applying Memory Principles

REVIEW 30

PRACTICE TEST 31

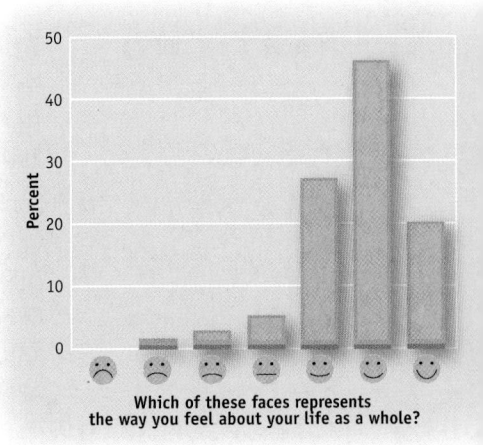

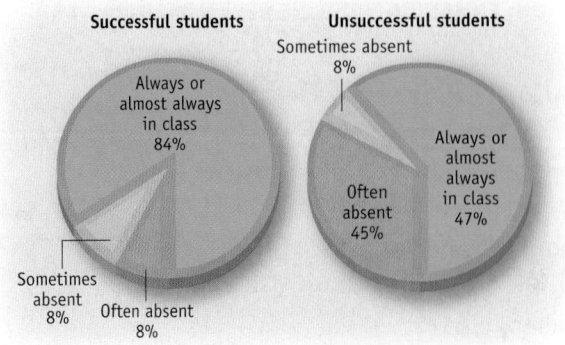

CHAPTER 2 Theories of Personality 32

THE NATURE OF PERSONALITY 33
- What Is Personality?
- What Are Personality Traits?
- The Five-Factor Model of Personality

PSYCHODYNAMIC PERSPECTIVES 35
- Freud's Psychoanalytic Theory
- Jung's Analytical Psychology
- Adler's Individual Psychology
- Evaluating Psychodynamic Perspectives

BEHAVIORAL PERSPECTIVES 43
- Pavlov's Classical Conditioning
- Skinner's Operant Conditioning
- Bandura's Social Cognitive Theory
- Evaluating Behavioral Perspectives

HUMANISTIC PERSPECTIVES 50
- Rogers's Person-Centered Theory
- Maslow's Theory of Self-Actualization
- Evaluating Humanistic Perspectives

BIOLOGICAL PERSPECTIVES 55
- Eysenck's Theory
- Recent Research in Behavioral Genetics
- The Evolutionary Approach to Personality
- Evaluating Biological Perspectives

A CONTEMPORARY EMPIRICAL APPROACH: TERROR MANAGEMENT THEORY 59
- Essentials of Terror Management Theory
- **Living in Today's World** *Understanding Reactions to Terrorist Attacks*
- Applications of Terror Management Theory

CULTURE AND PERSONALITY 62

APPLICATION: ASSESSING YOUR PERSONALITY 63
- Key Concepts in Psychological Testing
- Self-Report Inventories
- Projective Tests

REVIEW 68

PRACTICE TEST 69

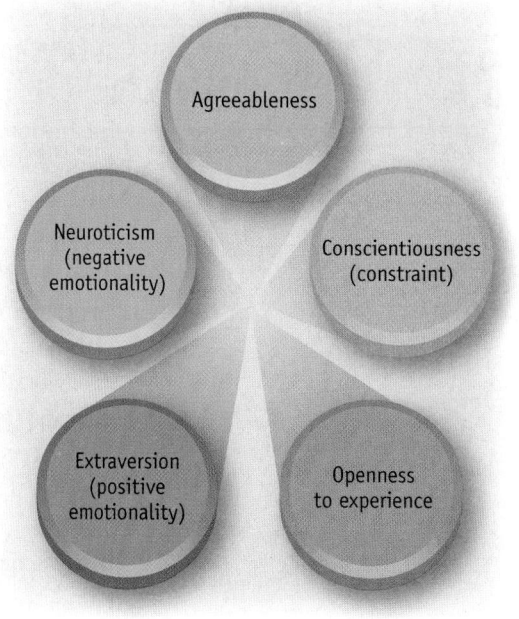

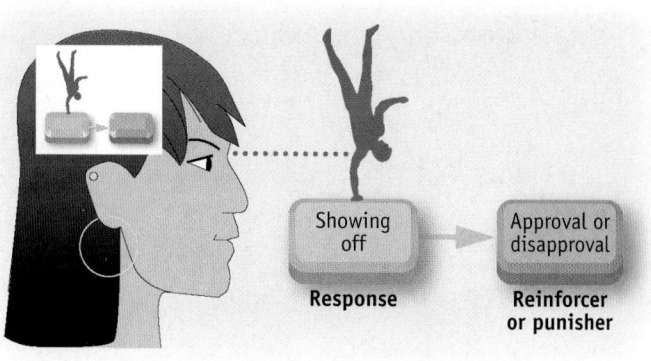

CHAPTER 3 Stress and Its Effects 70

THE NATURE OF STRESS 71
- Stress Is an Everyday Event
- Stress Lies in the Eye of the Beholder
- Stress May Be Embedded in the Environment
- Stress Is Influenced by Culture

MAJOR TYPES OF STRESS 75
- Frustration
- Conflict
- Change
- Pressure

RESPONDING TO STRESS 80
- Emotional Responses
- Physiological Responses
- Behavioral Responses

THE POTENTIAL EFFECTS OF STRESS 87
- Impaired Task Performance
- Disruption of Cognitive Functioning
- Burnout
- Posttraumatic Stress Disorder
- **Living in Today's World** *Common Reactions to Traumatic Events*
- Psychological Problems and Disorders
- Physical Illness
- Positive Effects

FACTORS INFLUENCING STRESS TOLERANCE 93
- Social Support
- Hardiness
- Optimism

APPLICATION: MONITORING YOUR STRESS 97
- Problems with the SRRS
- The Life Experiences Survey
- A Cautionary Note

REVIEW 102

PRACTICE TEST 103

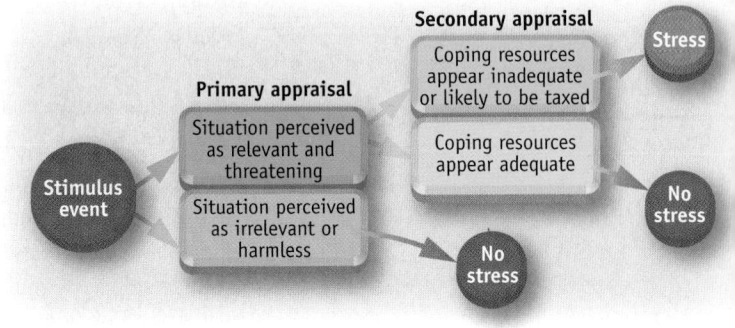

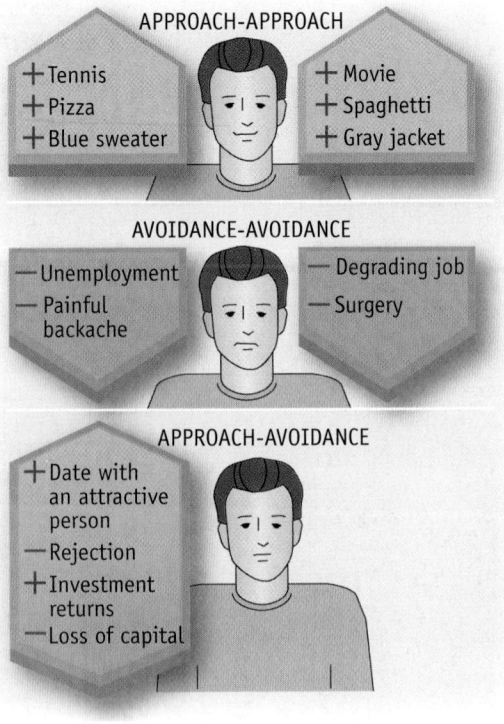

CHAPTER 4 Coping Processes 104

THE CONCEPT OF COPING 105

COMMON COPING PATTERNS OF LIMITED VALUE 106
- Giving Up
- Acting Aggressively
- Indulging Yourself
- Blaming Yourself
- Using Defensive Coping

THE NATURE OF CONSTRUCTIVE COPING 114

APPRAISAL-FOCUSED CONSTRUCTIVE COPING 115
- Ellis's Rational Thinking
- **Living in Today's World** *Thinking Rationally About the Threat of Traumatic Events*
- Humor as a Stress Reducer
- Positive Reinterpretation

PROBLEM-FOCUSED CONSTRUCTIVE COPING 120
- Using Systematic Problem Solving
- Seeking Help
- Using Time More Effectively

EMOTION-FOCUSED CONSTRUCTIVE COPING 126
- Enhancing Emotional Intelligence
- Expressing Emotions
- Managing Hostility and Forgiving Others
- Exercising
- Using Meditation and Relaxation

APPLICATION: ACHIEVING SELF-CONTROL 132
- Specifying Your Target Behavior
- Gathering Baseline Data
- Designing Your Program
- Executing and Evaluating Your Program
- Ending Your Program

REVIEW 138

PRACTICE TEST 139

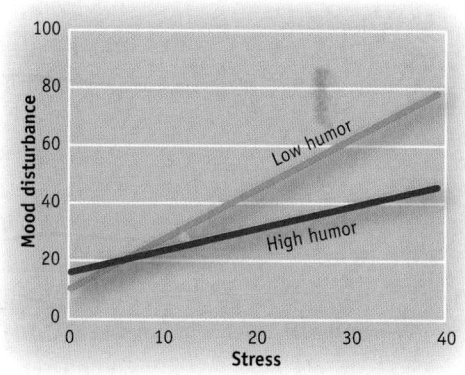

© Bruce Ayers/Stone/Getty Images

PART TWO

The Interpersonal Realm

CHAPTER 5 The Self 140

SELF-CONCEPT 141
- The Nature of the Self-Concept
- Self-Discrepancies
- Factors Shaping the Self-Concept

SELF-ESTEEM 148
- The Importance of Self-Esteem
- The Development of Self-Esteem
- **Living in Today's World** *Self-Esteem and Threats to Mortality*
- Ethnicity, Gender, and Self-Esteem

BASIC PRINCIPLES OF SELF-PERCEPTION 154
- Cognitive Processes
- Self-Attributions
- Explanatory Style
- Motives Guiding Self-Understanding
- Methods of Self-Enhancement

SELF-REGULATION 161
- Self-Efficacy
- Self-Defeating Behavior

SELF-PRESENTATION 164
- Impression Management
- Self-Monitoring

APPLICATION: BUILDING SELF-ESTEEM 167

REVIEW 170

PRACTICE TEST 171

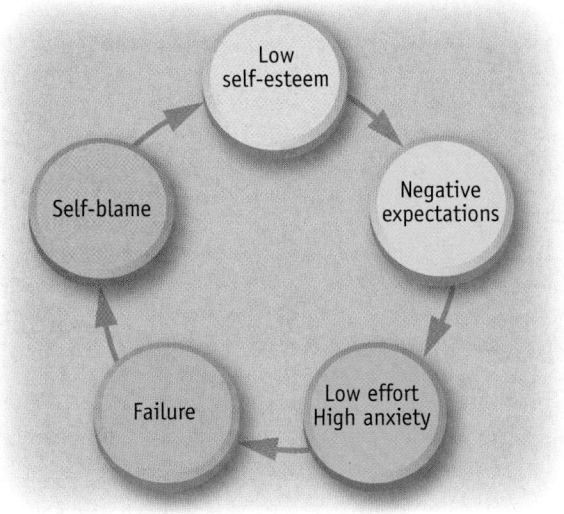

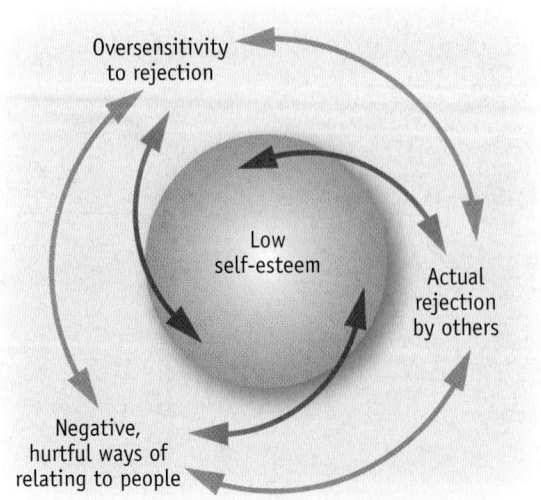

CHAPTER 6 Social Thinking and Social Influence 172

FORMING IMPRESSIONS OF OTHERS 173

Key Sources of Information
Snap Judgments Versus Systematic Judgments
Attributions
Perceiver Expectations
Cognitive Distortions

Living in Today's World *Beliefs, Revenge, and Intergroup Conflict*

Key Themes in Person Perception

THE PROBLEM OF PREJUDICE 182

"Old-Fashioned" Versus Modern Discrimination
Causes of Prejudice
Reducing Prejudice

THE POWER OF PERSUASION 188

The Elements of the Persuasion Process
The Whys of Persuasion

THE POWER OF SOCIAL PRESSURE 192

Conformity and Compliance Pressures
Pressure from Authority Figures

APPLICATION: SEEING THROUGH COMPLIANCE TACTICS 198

The Consistency Principle
The Reciprocity Principle
The Scarcity Principle

REVIEW 202

PRACTICE TEST 203

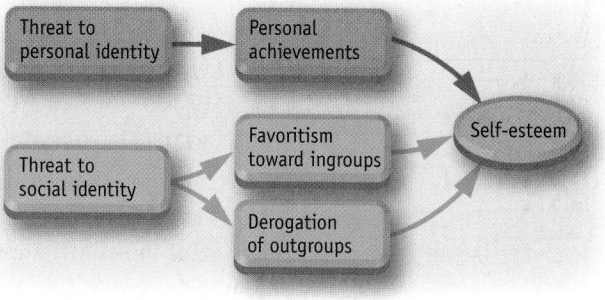

© Spencer Grant/PhotoEdit

CHAPTER 7 Interpersonal Communication 204

THE PROCESS OF INTERPERSONAL COMMUNICATION 205
- Components of the Communication Process
- Technology and Interpersonal Communication
- Communication and Adjustment

NONVERBAL COMMUNICATION 208
- General Principles
- Elements of Nonverbal Communication
- Detecting Deception
- The Significance of Nonverbal Communication

TOWARD MORE EFFECTIVE COMMUNICATION 216
- Creating a Positive Interpersonal Climate
- Conversational Skills
- Self-Disclosure
- Effective Listening

COMMUNICATION PROBLEMS 222
- Communication Apprehension
- Barriers to Effective Communication

INTERPERSONAL CONFLICT 224
- Beliefs About Conflict
- Types of Conflict
- **Living in Today's World** *Communication in an Adversarial Culture*
- Styles of Managing Conflict
- Dealing Constructively with Conflict

APPLICATION: DEVELOPING AN ASSERTIVE COMMUNICATION STYLE 229
- The Nature of Assertiveness
- Steps in Assertiveness Training

REVIEW 234

PRACTICE TEST 235

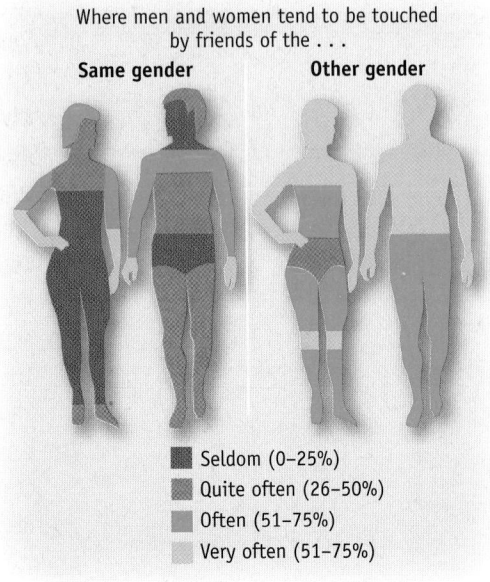

© Richard Flood/DK Stock/Getty Images

CHAPTER 8 Friendship and Love 236

PERSPECTIVES ON CLOSE RELATIONSHIPS 237
- The Ingredients of Close Relationships
- Culture and Relationships
- The Internet and Relationships

INITIAL ATTRACTION AND RELATIONSHIP DEVELOPMENT 240
- Initial Encounters
- Getting Acquainted
- Established Relationships

FRIENDSHIP 250
- What Makes a Good Friend?
- **Living in Today's World** *Social Support and Stress*
- Gender and Sexual Orientation Issues

ROMANTIC LOVE 252
- Sexual Orientation and Love
- Gender Differences
- Theories of Love
- The Course of Romantic Love

APPLICATION: OVERCOMING LONELINESS 261
- The Nature and Prevalence of Loneliness
- The Roots of Loneliness
- Correlates of Loneliness
- Conquering Loneliness

REVIEW 266

PRACTICE TEST 267

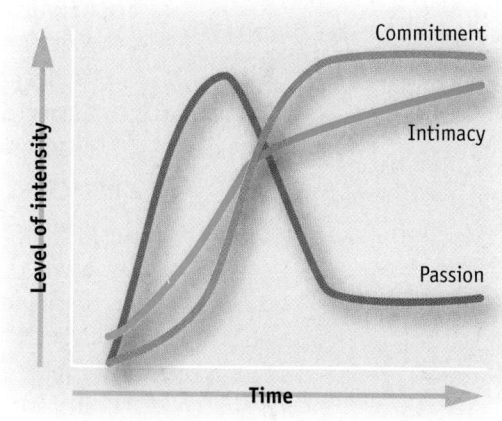

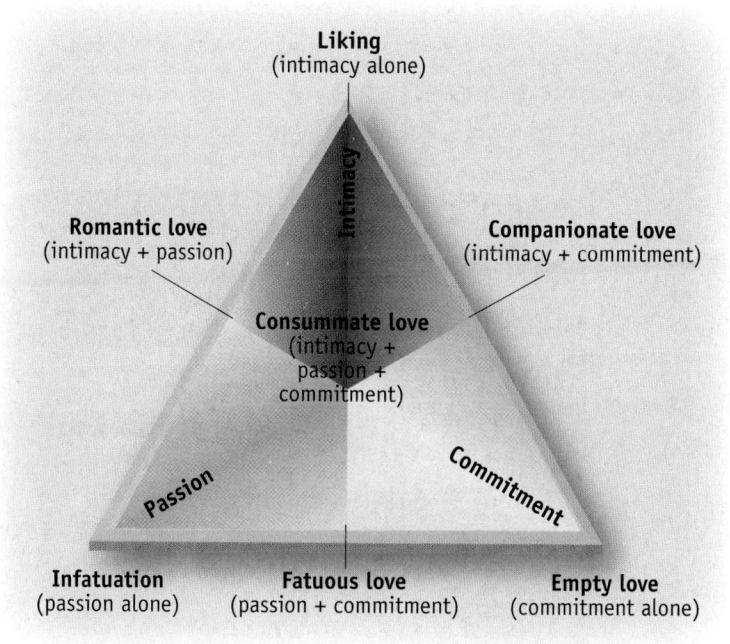

CHAPTER 9 Marriage and Intimate Relationships 268

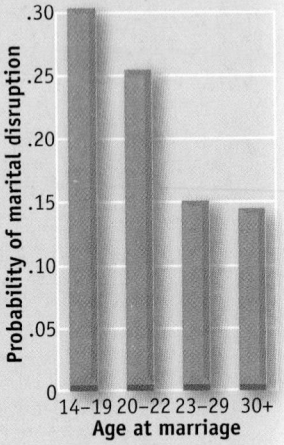

CHALLENGES TO THE TRADITIONAL MODEL OF MARRIAGE 269

MOVING TOWARD MARRIAGE 270
- The Motivation to Marry
- Selecting a Mate
- Predictors of Marital Success

MARITAL ADJUSTMENT ACROSS THE FAMILY LIFE CYCLE 274
- Between Families: The Unattached Young Adult
- Joining Together: The Newly Married Couple
- Family with Young Children
- Family with Adolescent Children
- Launching Children into the Adult World
- The Family in Later Life

VULNERABLE AREAS IN MARITAL ADJUSTMENT 279
- Gaps in Role Expectations
- Work and Career Issues
- Financial Difficulties
- Inadequate Communication

DIVORCE 284
- Divorce Rates
- **Living in Today's World** *Should the Government Promote Marriage?*
- Deciding on a Divorce
- Adjusting to Divorce
- Effects of Divorce on Children
- Remarriage

ALTERNATIVES TO MARRIAGE 290
- Remaining Single
- Cohabitation
- Gay Relationships

APPLICATION: UNDERSTANDING INTIMATE VIOLENCE 295
- Partner Abuse
- Date Rape

REVIEW 300

PRACTICE TEST 301

© Matthew McVay/Corbis Saba

PART THREE

Developmental Transitions

CHAPTER 10 Gender and Behavior 302

GENDER STEREOTYPES 303

GENDER SIMILARITIES AND DIFFERENCES 306
- Cognitive Abilities
- Personality Traits and Social Behavior
- Psychological Disorders
- Putting Gender Differences in Perspective

BIOLOGICAL ORIGINS OF GENDER DIFFERENCES 311
- Evolutionary Explanations
- Brain Organization
- Hormonal Influences

ENVIRONMENTAL ORIGINS OF GENDER DIFFERENCES 313
- Processes in Gender-Role Socialization
- Sources of Gender-Role Socialization

GENDER-ROLE EXPECTATIONS 318
- Role Expectations for Males
- Problems with the Male Role
- Role Expectations for Females
- Problems with the Female Role
- **Living in Today's World** *Gender Stereotypes and "Appearance Pressure"*
- Sexism: A Special Problem for Females

GENDER IN THE PAST AND IN THE FUTURE 327
- Why Are Gender Roles Changing?
- Alternatives to Traditional Gender Roles

APPLICATION: BRIDGING THE GENDER GAP IN COMMUNICATION 330
- The Clash of Two "Cultures"
- Instrumental and Expressive Styles
- Common Mixed-Gender Communication Problems
- Toward a "Shared Language"

REVIEW 334

PRACTICE TEST 335

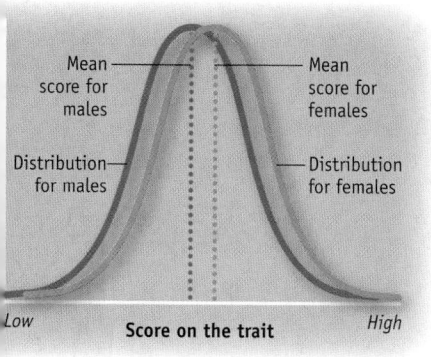

© Paul Wood/Alamy

CHAPTER 11 Development in Adolescence and Adulthood 336

THE TRANSITION OF ADOLESCENCE 337
- Physical Changes
- Cognitive Changes
- Personality Changes
- Adolescent Suicide

THE EXPANSE OF ADULTHOOD 345
- Early Adulthood (From About Age 20 to 40)
- Middle Adulthood (From About Age 40 to 65)
- Late Adulthood (After Age 65)

AGING: A GRADUAL PROCESS 353
- Physical Changes
- Cognitive Changes
- Personality Changes

DEATH AND DYING 359
- Attitudes About Death
- The Process of Dying
- Bereavement and Grieving

APPLICATION: BECOMING AN EFFECTIVE PARENT 369
- Dimensions of Childrearing
- Correlates of Parenting Styles
- **Living in Today's World** *Promoting Resilience in Children*
- Rearing Adolescents
- Toward Effective Parenting
- Using Punishment Effectively

REVIEW 370

PRACTICE TEST 371

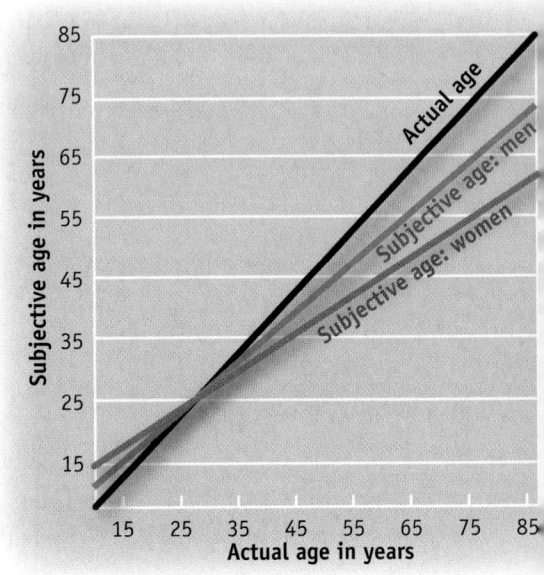

© Hill Street Studios/Blend Images/Getty Images

CHAPTER 12 Careers and Work 372

CHOOSING A CAREER 373
- Examining Personal Characteristics and Family Influences
- Researching Job Characteristics
- Using Psychological Tests for Career Decisions
- Taking Important Considerations into Account

MODELS OF CAREER CHOICE AND DEVELOPMENT 377
- Holland's Person-Environment Fit Model
- Super's Developmental Model
- Women's Career Development

THE CHANGING WORLD OF WORK 380
- Workplace Trends
- Education and Earnings
- The Changing Workforce

COPING WITH OCCUPATIONAL HAZARDS 386
- Job Stress
- Sexual Harassment
- Unemployment

Living in Today's World *Coping with Unemployment*

BALANCING WORK AND OTHER SPHERES OF LIFE 394
- Workaholism
- Work and Family Roles
- Leisure and Recreation

APPLICATION: GETTING AHEAD IN THE JOB GAME 398
- Putting Together a Résumé
- Finding Companies You Want to Work For
- Landing an Interview
- Polishing Your Interview Technique

REVIEW 404

PRACTICE TEST 405

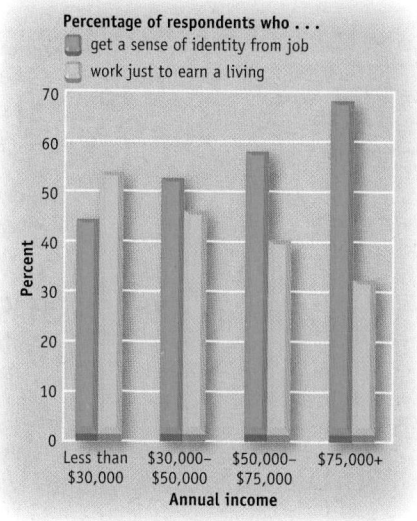

© Yellow Dog Productions/Stone/Getty Images

CHAPTER 13 Development and Expression of Sexuality 406

BECOMING A SEXUAL PERSON 407
- Key Aspects of Sexual Identity
- Physiological Influences
- Psychosocial Influences
- Gender Differences in Sexual Socialization
- **Living in Today's World** *Sex and the Internet*
- Sexual Orientation

INTERACTION IN SEXUAL RELATIONSHIPS 416
- Motives for Engaging in Sex
- Communicating About Sex

THE HUMAN SEXUAL RESPONSE 418
- The Sexual Response Cycle
- Gender Differences in Patterns of Orgasm

SEXUAL EXPRESSION 421
- Fantasy
- Kissing and Touching
- Self-Stimulation
- Oral and Anal Sex
- Intercourse

PATTERNS OF SEXUAL BEHAVIOR 423
- Sex in the Age of AIDS
- Early Sexual Experiences
- Sex in Committed Relationships
- Infidelity in Committed Relationships

PRACTICAL ISSUES IN SEXUAL ACTIVITY 427
- Contraception
- Sexually Transmitted Diseases

APPLICATION: ENHANCING SEXUAL RELATIONSHIPS 433
- General Suggestions
- Understanding Sexual Dysfunction
- Coping with Specific Problems

REVIEW 438

PRACTICE TEST 439

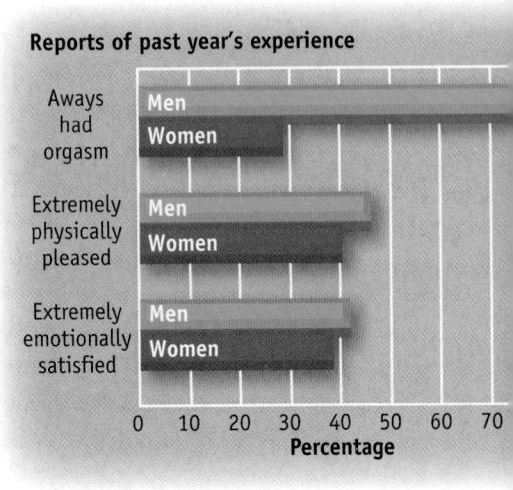

© Mario Tama/Getty Images

PART FOUR

Mental and Physical Health

CHAPTER 14 Psychology and Physical Health 440

STRESS, PERSONALITY, AND ILLNESS 443
- Personality, Emotions, and Heart Disease
- **Living in Today's World** *Coping with Traumatic Events*
- Stress and Cancer
- Stress and Other Diseases
- Stress and Immune Functioning
- Conclusions

HABITS, LIFESTYLES, AND HEALTH 450
- Smoking
- Drinking
- Overeating
- Poor Nutrition
- Lack of Exercise
- Behavior and AIDS

REACTIONS TO ILLNESS 467
- The Decision to Seek Treatment
- The Sick Role
- Communicating with Health Providers
- Adherence to Medical Advice

APPLICATION: UNDERSTANDING THE EFFECTS OF DRUGS 469
- Drug-Related Concepts
- Narcotics
- Sedatives
- Stimulants
- Hallucinogens
- Marijuana
- Ecstasy (MDMA)

REVIEW 476

PRACTICE TEST 477

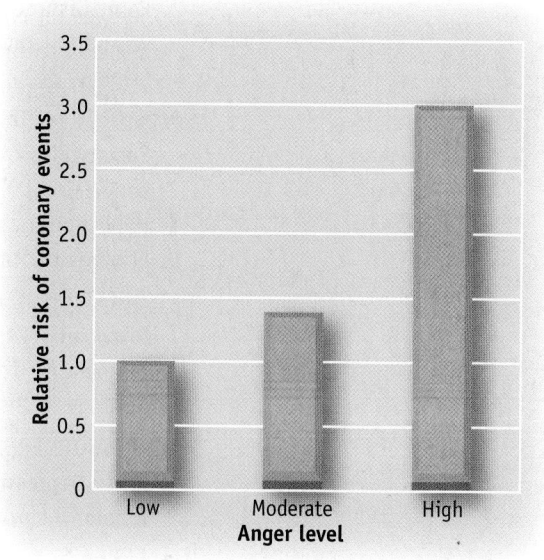

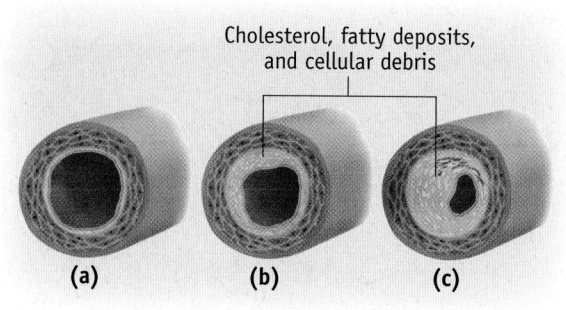

CHAPTER 15 Psychological Disorders 478

ABNORMAL BEHAVIOR: CONCEPTS AND CONTROVERSIES 479
- The Medical Model Applied to Abnormal Behavior
- Criteria of Abnormal Behavior
- Psychodiagnosis: The Classification of Disorders
- The Prevalence of Psychological Disorders

ANXIETY DISORDERS 485
- Generalized Anxiety Disorder
- Phobic Disorder
- Panic Disorder and Agoraphobia
- Obsessive-Compulsive Disorder
- Etiology of Anxiety Disorders

SOMATOFORM DISORDERS 489
- Somatization Disorder
- Conversion Disorder
- Hypochondriasis
- Etiology of Somatoform Disorders

DISSOCIATIVE DISORDERS 491
- Dissociative Amnesia and Fugue
- Dissociative Identity Disorder
- Etiology of Dissociative Disorders

MOOD DISORDERS 493
- Major Depressive Disorder
- Bipolar Disorder
- **Living in Today's World** *Understanding and Preventing Suicide*
- Etiology of Mood Disorders

SCHIZOPHRENIC DISORDERS 501
- General Symptoms
- Subtypes
- Course and Outcome
- Etiology of Schizophrenia

APPLICATION: UNDERSTANDING EATING DISORDERS 507
- Types of Eating Disorders
- History and Prevalence
- Etiology of Eating Disorders

REVIEW 512

PRACTICE TEST 513

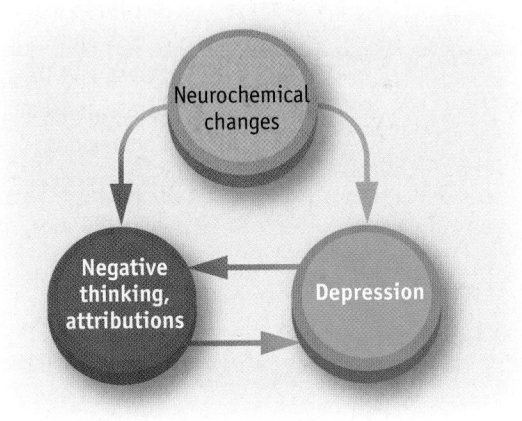

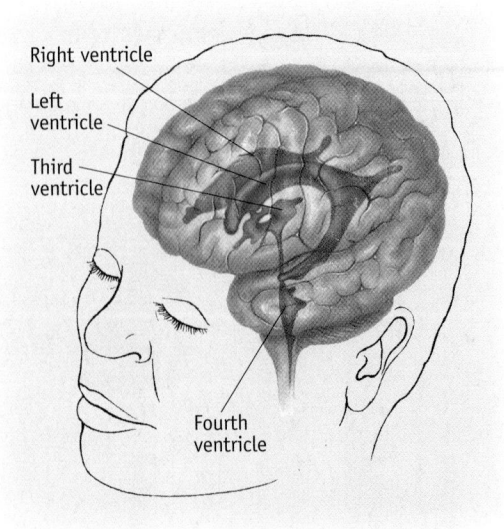

CHAPTER 16 Psychotherapy 514

THE ELEMENTS OF THE TREATMENT PROCESS 515
- Treatments: How Many Types Are There?
- Clients: Who Seeks Therapy?
- Therapists: Who Provides Professional Treatment?

INSIGHT THERAPIES 519
- Psychoanalysis
- Client-Centered Therapy
- Group Therapy
- Evaluating Insight Therapies
- Therapy and the Recovered Memories Controversy

BEHAVIOR THERAPIES 528
- Systematic Desensitization
- Aversion Therapy
- Social Skills Training
- Cognitive-Behavioral Treatments
- **Living in Today's World** *How Do Clinicians Treat Posttraumatic Stress Disorder?*
- Evaluating Behavior Therapies

BIOMEDICAL THERAPIES 533
- Treatment with Drugs
- Electroconvulsive Therapy (ECT)

CURRENT TRENDS AND ISSUES IN TREATMENT 539
- Grappling with the Constraints of Managed Care
- Blending Approaches to Treatment
- Increasing Multicultural Sensitivity in Treatment

APPLICATION: LOOKING FOR A THERAPIST 542
- Where Do You Find Therapeutic Services?
- Is the Therapist's Profession or Sex Important?
- Is Therapy Always Expensive?
- Is the Therapist's Theoretical Approach Important?
- What Is Therapy Like?

REVIEW 546

PRACTICE TEST 547

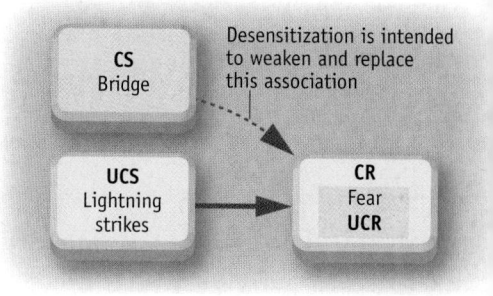

© Bruce Ayres/Stone/Getty Images

Glossary 549
References 555
Credits 612
Name Index 618
Subject Index 636

To the Student

In most college courses students spend more time with their textbooks than with their professors. Given this reality, it helps if you like your textbook. Making textbooks likable, however, is a tricky proposition. By its very nature, a textbook must introduce a great many new concepts, ideas, and theories. If it doesn't, it isn't much of a textbook, and instructors won't choose to use it—so you'll never see it anyway. Consequently, we have tried to make this book as likable as possible without compromising the academic content that your instructor demands. Thus, we have tried to make the book lively, informal, engaging, well organized, easy to read, practical, and occasionally humorous. Before you plunge into Chapter 1, let us explain some of the key features that can help you get the most out of the book.

Learning Aids

Mastering the content of this text involves digesting a great deal of information. To facilitate this learning process, we've incorporated a number of instructional aids into the book:

▶ *Outlines* at the beginning of each chapter provide you with both a preview and an overview of what will be covered. Think of the outlines as road maps, and bear in mind that it's easier to reach a destination if you know where you're going.

▶ *Headings* are used extensively to keep material well organized.

▶ To help alert you to key points, *learning objectives* are found throughout the chapters, immediately after the first-level headings.

▶ *Key terms* are identified with ***blue italicized boldface*** type to indicate that these are important vocabulary items that are part of psychology's technical language.

▶ An *integrated running glossary* provides an on-the-spot definition of each key term as it's introduced in the text. These formal definitions are printed in **blue boldface** type. It is often difficult for students to adapt to the jargon used by scientific disciplines. However, learning this terminology is an essential part of your educational experience. The integrated running glossary is meant to make this learning process as painless as possible.

▶ An *alphabetical glossary* is provided in the back of the book, as key terms are usually defined in the running glossary only when they are first introduced. If you run into a technical term that was introduced in an earlier chapter and you can't remember its meaning, you can look it up in the alphabetical glossary instead of backtracking to find the place where it first appeared.

▶ *Italics* are used liberally throughout the book to emphasize important points.

▶ A *chapter review* near the end of each chapter includes a thorough summary of the chapter and lists key terms and important theorists, with page references. Making use of these review materials can help ensure that you've digested the key points in the chapter.

▶ Each chapter ends with a ten-item *practice test* that should give you a realistic assessment of your mastery of that chapter and valuable practice taking multiple-choice tests that will probably be representative of what you will see in class (if your instructor uses the test bank designed for this book).

Recommended Reading Boxes

This text serves as a resource book. To facilitate this goal, particularly interesting self-help books on various topics are highlighted in boxes within the chapters. Each box provides a brief description of the book. We do not agree with everything in these recommended books, but all of them are potentially useful or intriguing. The main purpose of this feature is to introduce you to some of the better self-help books that are available.

Living in Today's World Boxes

These boxes were originally developed to address issues that surfaced in the aftermath of the 9/11 terrorist attacks in the United States. Continuing in this vein, many of the boxes in this edition deal with concerns raised by the threat of terrorism in today's world. For example, we discuss how people tend to be affected by traumatic events, how people can cope more effectively with personal trauma, and how people can think more rationally about the threat of terrorism. However, we have since broadened the scope of coverage in these boxes to include additional adjustment issues that are especially pertinent in light of current events, such as sexual interactions over the Internet, the controversy over whether government should promote marriage, and difficulties coping with unemployment. We hope ninth edition

Psychology Applied to Modern Life

ADJUSTMENT IN THE 21ST CENTURY

CHAPTER 1

Adjusting to Modern Life

The immense Boeing 747 lumbers into position to accept its human cargo. The eager passengers-to-be scurry on board. In a tower a few hundred yards away, air traffic controllers diligently monitor radar screens, radio transmissions, and digital readouts of weather information. At the reservation desks in the airport terminal, clerks punch up the appropriate ticket information on their computer terminals and quickly process the steady stream of passengers. Mounted on the wall are video terminals displaying up-to-the-minute information on flight arrivals, departures, and delays. Back in the cockpit of the plane, the flight crew calmly scans the complex array of dials, meters, and lights to assess the aircraft's readiness for flight. In a few minutes, the airplane will slice into the cloudy, snow-laden skies above Chicago. In a little over three hours its passengers will be transported from the piercing cold of a Chicago winter to the balmy beaches of the Bahamas. Another everyday triumph for technology will have taken place.

THE PARADOX OF PROGRESS

LIVING IN TODAY'S WORLD *Life May Never Be the Same Again: Implications for Adjustment*

THE SEARCH FOR DIRECTION
Self-Help Books
The Approach of This Textbook

THE PSYCHOLOGY OF ADJUSTMENT
What Is Psychology?
What Is Adjustment?

THE SCIENTIFIC APPROACH TO BEHAVIOR
The Commitment to Empiricism
Advantages of the Scientific Approach
Experimental Research: Looking for Causes
Correlational Research: Looking for Links

THE ROOTS OF HAPPINESS: AN EMPIRICAL ANALYSIS
What Isn't Very Important?
What Is Somewhat Important?
What Is Very Important?
Conclusions

APPLICATION: IMPROVING ACADEMIC PERFORMANCE
Developing Sound Study Habits
Improving Your Reading
Getting More Out of Lectures
Applying Memory Principles

REVIEW

PRACTICE TEST

The Paradox of Progress

LEARNING OBJECTIVES

- *Describe four examples of the paradox of progress.*
- *Explain what is meant by the paradox of progress and how theorists have explained it.*

We are the children of technology. We take for granted such impressive feats as transporting 300 people over 1500 miles in a matter of hours. After all, we live in a time of unparalleled progress. Our modern Western society has made extraordinary strides in transportation, energy, communication, agriculture, and medicine. Yet despite our technological progress, social problems and personal difficulties seem more prevalent and more prominent than ever before. This paradox is evident in many aspects of contemporary life, as seen in the following examples.

Point. Modern technology has provided us with countless time-saving devices—automobiles, telephones, vacuum cleaners, dishwashers, photocopiers, personal computers. Today, cell phones allow people to talk to friends or colleagues and battle rush hour at the same time. In a matter of seconds a personal computer can perform calculations that would take months if done by hand.

Counterpoint. Nonetheless, most of us complain about not having enough time. Our schedules overflow with appointments, commitments, and plans. Surveys suggest that a majority of people subjectively feel that they suffer from a *time famine*—that they have less and less time for themselves (Robinson & Godbey, 1997). Time has become such a precious commodity, one national survey found that 51% of the adult respondents would rather have more time than more money (Weil & Rosen, 1997). As social critic Jeremy Rifkin (1989) notes, "It is ironic in a culture so committed to saving time that we feel increasingly deprived of the very thing we value" (p. 19). Part of the problem is that in our modern society, work follows people home. Thus, Peter Whybrow (2005) comments, "citizens find themselves tethered to their jobs around the clock by the same nomadic tools—cell phones, pagers, wireless e-mail—that were heralded first as instruments of liberation" (p. 158). To deal with this time crunch, more and more people are cutting back on their sleep as they attempt to juggle work, family, and household responsibilities, leading noted sleep researcher William Dement to comment that "most Americans no longer know what it feels like to be fully alert" (Toufexis, 1990, p. 79). Sleep experts assert that American society suffers from an epidemic of sleep deprivation (Walsh, Dement, & Dinges, 2005). Unfortunately, research indicates that chronic sleep loss can have significant negative effects on individuals' daytime functioning, as well as their mental and physical health (Dinges, Rogers, & Baynard, 2005).

Point. Thanks in large part to technological advances, we live in extraordinary affluence. Undeniably, there are pockets of genuine poverty, but social critics, such as Paul Wachtel (1989), David Myers (2000), Gregg Easterbrook (2003), Paul Ransome (2005), and Peter Whybrow (2005) argue convincingly that in North America and Europe the middle and upper classes are larger and wealthier than ever before. Most of us take for granted things that were once considered luxuries, such as color television and air conditioning. People spend vast amounts of money on expensive automobiles, audio systems, computers, flat panel TVs, clothing, and vacations. In the late 1990s, the amount of money spent on luxury goods increased four times faster than overall spending (Frank, 1999). Wachtel quotes a New York museum director who asserts that "shopping is the chief cultural activity in the United States" (p. 23). Symptomatic of this trend, research suggests that many people in modern society are troubled by a *compulsive buying syndrome,* characterized by uncontrollable, impulsive, excessive shopping for things they don't need and often can't afford (Faber, 2003). One recent study estimated that 5%–6% of the U. S. population may have problems with this syndrome (Koran et al., 2006). Some clinical experts argue that compulsive buying should be viewed as a new psychiatric disorder (Hollander & Allen, 2006).

Counterpoint. In spite of this economic abundance, research suggests that most people do not feel very good about their financial well-being. For example, when one survey inquired about Americans' satisfaction with 13 aspects of their lives, the results showed that people were least satisfied with their finances (Myers, 2000). In his book titled *The High Price of Materialism,* Tim Kasser (2002) summarizes research showing that people who are especially concerned with money and possessions tend to report lower levels of happiness than others. Why are people so dissatisfied with their economic well-being? One problem is that advertising helps foster an insatiable thirst for consumption and the belief that material goods are the key to happiness (Kanner & Soule, 2004; Kasser et al., 2004). As Kasser

LIVING IN TODAY'S WORLD

Life May Never Be the Same Again: Implications for Adjustment

The citizens of the United States received a gigantic wake-up call on September 11, 2001, in the form of the horrific, tragic terrorist attacks on the World Trade Center and the Pentagon. Life in the United States and much of the Western world may never be quite the same again. The specter of terrorism has psychological repercussions for virtually everyone in the United States (Danieli, Engdahl, & Schlenger, 2004; McCauley, 2007). People are upset over losing many things that they used to take for granted but have lost, such as being able to fly to a business meeting without a second thought, to pick up mail without worrying about contamination, to walk into a tall building without being searched, and to interact with strangers without being suspicious. They are angry about the injustice of it all, disgusted by the senseless violence, and anxious about what future terrorist attacks might bring. Above all else, Americans have lost their sense of invulnerability.

In light of the fundamental ways in which our lives have been changed, you might wonder whether the principal premise of this book—that the basic challenge of modern life is the quest for meaning and direction—might suddenly seem irrelevant. In reality, the situation is quite the opposite. Perhaps more than before, because of the threat of terrorism, people are questioning the meaning of their lives. Americans are wondering whether what they do matters, whether what they cherish is important, and whether what they have worked for has been worth it. The terrorist-induced jolt to our collective psyche has made the search for a sense of direction even more relevant to contemporary life.

That said, the threat of terrorism raises some important issues that an adjustment textbook should attempt to address. Fortunately, the field of psychology has much to contribute to the battle against terrorism (Bongar,

© AP Images/Suzanne Plunkett

2007; Marsella, 2004). After all, terrorism is *psychological* warfare (Breckenridge & Zimbardo, 2007; Levant, Barbanel, & DeLeon, 2004). The goal of terrorism is to provoke psychological vulnerability and agitation in a population. The death, destruction, and havoc wreaked by terrorists is not an end in itself, but a means to an end—the creation of widespread anxiety, alarm, and panic.

In each chapter you will find boxes labeled "Living in Today's World" that address some of the adjustment issues raised by the threat of terrorism itself, related problems spawned by terrorism, and a variety of other challenges unique to our modern world. These boxes discuss such topics as how people tend to react to traumatic events, how people can cope more effectively with personal trauma, whether the government should promote marriage, how resilience can be enhanced in children, how workers can cope with unemployment, and other contemporary issues. We sincerely hope that this feature proves helpful.

(2004) puts it, "Everyday and in many ways people are bombarded with powerful, psychologically sophisticated proclamations that the good life is 'the goods life'" (p. 55). Thus, studies find that the gap between what people have and what they desire is greater in the material domain than in other areas of life (Solberg, Diener, & Robinson, 2004).

Point. The range of life choices available to people in modern societies has increased exponentially in recent decades. For example, Barry Schwartz (2004) describes how a simple visit to a local supermarket can require a consumer to choose from 285 varieties of cookies, 61 suntan lotions, 150 lipsticks, and 175 salad dressings. Although increased choice is most tangible in the realm of consumer goods and services, Schwartz argues that it also extends into more significant domains of life. Today, people tend to have unprecedented opportunities to make choices about how they will be educated (e.g., vastly more flexible college curricula are available), how and where they will work (e.g., telecommuting presents employees with all sorts of new choices about how to accomplish their work), how their intimate relationships will unfold (e.g., people have increased freedom to delay marriage, cohabit, not have children, and so forth), and even how they will look (advances in plastic surgery have made personal appearance a matter of choice).

Counterpoint. Although increased freedom of choice sounds attractive, Schwartz (2004) argues that the overabundance of choices in modern life has unexpected costs. He argues that people routinely make errors even when choosing among a handful of alternatives and that errors become much more likely when decisions become vastly more complex. And he explains how having more alternatives increases the potential for rumination, postdecision regret, and anticipated regret. Ultimately, he argues, the malaise associated with choice overload undermines individuals' happiness and contributes to depression. Consistent with this analysis, studies have found that the incidence of depressive disorders has increased dramatically—perhaps tenfold—over the last 50 years (Kessler, 2002). Average anxiety levels have also gone up substantially in recent decades (Twenge, 2000). It is hard to say whether choice overload is the chief culprit underlying these trends, but it is clear that increased freedom of choice has not resulted in enhanced tranquillity or improved mental health.

Point. Modern technology has gradually provided us with unprecedented control over the world around us. Advances in agriculture have dramatically increased food production, and biotechnology advocates claim that genetically modified crops will make our food supply more reliable that ever before. Elaborate water supply systems, made up of hundreds of miles of canals, tunnels, and pipelines, along with dams, reservoirs, and pumping stations, permit massive metropolitan areas to grow in inhospitable deserts. Thanks to progress in medicine, doctors can reattach severed limbs, use lasers to correct microscopic defects in the eye, and even replace the human heart.

Counterpoint. Unfortunately, modern technology has also had a devastating negative impact on the world around us, leading to environmental problems such as global warming, destruction of the ozone layer, deforestation, exhaustion of much of the world's fisheries, widespread air and water pollution, and extensive exposure of plants and animals to toxic chemicals (Oskamp, 2000). Many experts worry that in a few generations the earth's resources will be too depleted to sustain an adequate quality of life (Winter, 2004). To most people, these crises sound like technical problems that call for technological answers, but they are also behavioral problems in that they are fueled by overpopulation and overconsumption (Howard, 2000). In North America, the crucial problem is excessive consumption of the world's natural resources. For example, the United States houses 5% of the world's population but guzzles 25% of its commercial energy and fuel (Flavin & Dunn, 1999).

All these apparent contradictions reflect the same theme: *The technological advances of the past century, impressive though they may be, have not led to perceptible improvement in our collective health and happiness.* Indeed, many social critics argue that the quality of our lives and our sense of personal fulfillment have declined rather than increased. This is the paradox of progress.

© Carlos Spottorno/Taxi/Getty Images

Barry Schwartz argues that people in modern societies suffer from choice overload. He maintains that the endless choices people are presented with lead them to waste countless hours weighing trivial decisions and ruminating about whether their decisions were optimal.

What is the cause of this paradox? Many explanations have been offered. Erich Fromm (1963, 1981) has argued that the progress we value so much has scrambled our value systems and undermined our traditional sources of emotional security, such as family, community, and religion. Alvin Toffler (1970, 1980) attributes our collective alienation and distress to our being overwhelmed by rapidly accelerating cultural change. Robert Kegan (1994) maintains that the mental demands of modern life have become so complex, confusing, and contradictory that most of us are "in over our heads." Tim Kasser (2002) speculates that excessive materialism weakens the social ties that bind us, stokes the fires of insecurity, and undermines our collective sense of well-being. Micki McGee (2005) suggests that modern changes in gender roles, diminished job stability, and other social trends have fostered an obsession with self-improvement that ultimately undermines many individuals' sense of security and their satisfaction with their identity. According to McGee, our "makeover culture," nourishes the belief that we can all reinvent ourselves as needed, but this assumption can create tremendous pressures on people that "foster rather than quell their anxieties" (p. 17)).

Whatever the explanation, many theorists, working from varied perspectives, agree that *the basic challenge of modern life has become the search for meaning, a sense of direction, and a personal philosophy* (Dolby, 2005; Emmons, 2003; Naylor, Willimon, & Naylor, 1994; Sagiv, Roccas, & Hazan, 2004). This search involves struggling with such problems as forming a solid sense of identity, arriving at a coherent set of values, and developing a clear vision of a future that realistically promises fulfillment. Centuries ago, problems of this kind were probably much simpler. As we'll see in the next section, today it appears that many of us are floundering in a sea of confusion.

The Search for Direction

LEARNING OBJECTIVES

- *Provide some examples of people's search for direction.*
- *Describe four problems that are common to popular self-help books.*
- *Summarize advice about what to look for in quality self-help books.*
- *Summarize the philosophy underlying this textbook.*

We live in a time of unparalleled social and technological mutation. According to a number of social critics, the kaleidoscope of change that we see around us creates feelings of anxiety and uncertainty, which we try to alleviate by searching for a sense of direction. This search, which sometimes goes awry, manifests itself in many ways.

For example, we could discuss how hundreds of thousands of Americans have invested large sums of money to enroll in "self-realization" programs such as *est* training, Scientology, Silva Mind Control, John Gray's Mars and Venus relationship seminars, and Tony Robbins's Life Mastery seminars. These programs typically promise to provide profound enlightenment and quickly turn one's life around. Many participants claim that the programs have revolutionized their lives. However, most experts characterize such programs as intellectually bankrupt, and book and magazine exposés reveal them as simply lucrative money-making schemes (Behar, 1991; Pressman, 1993). In a particularly scathing analysis of these programs, Steve Salerno (2005) outlines the enormous financial benefits reaped by their inventors, such as Tony Robbins ($80 million in annual income), Dr. Phil ($20 million in annual income) and John Gray ($50,000 per speech). In his critique, Salerno also attacks the hypocrisy and inflated credentials of many leading self-help gurus. For example, he asserts that John Gray's doctorate came from a nonaccredited correspondence college; that Dr. Phil has a history of alleged marital infidelity and that some of his video segments are contrived to a degree that would make Jerry Springer proud; and that Dr. Laura is "a critic of premarital and extramarital sex who's indulged in both" (p. 44). More than anything else, the enormous success of these self-help gurus and self-realization programs demonstrates just how desperate some people are for a sense of direction and purpose in their lives.

We could also discuss how a host of unorthodox religious groups—commonly called *cults*—have attracted countless converts who voluntarily embrace a life of regimentation, obedience, and zealous ideology. One study suggested that more than 2 million young adults are involved with cults in the U.S. (Robinson, Frye, & Bradley, 1997). Most of these cults flourish in obscurity, unless bizarre incidents—such as the 1997 mass suicide of the Heaven's Gate cult near San Diego—attract public attention. It is widely believed that cults use brainwashing and mind control to seduce lonely outsiders, but in reality converts are a diverse array of normal people who are swayed by ordinary—albeit sophisticated—social-influence strategies (Baron, 2000;

© Christopher J. Morris/Corbis

© Reuters/Ho

There are many manifestations of our search for a sense of direction, including the emergence of cults, such as the Raelian UFO cult, and the astonishing popularity of "Dr. Laura."

Anthony, 1999; Zimbardo, 2002). According to Philip Zimbardo (1992), people join cults because these groups appear to provide simple solutions to complex problems, a sense of purpose, and a structured lifestyle that reduces feelings of uncertainty. Hunter (1998) emphasizes how alienation, identity confusion, and weak community ties make some people particularly vulnerable to seduction by cults.

And, if you would like a mundane, everyday example of people's search for direction, you need look no farther than your radio, where you will find that the hottest nationally syndicated personality is "Dr. Laura," who doles out advice to more than 15 million listeners a week over a network of nearly 300 stations. Even though only seven or eight people get through to her during each show, an astonishing 75,000 people call each day to seek her unique brand of blunt, outspoken, judgmental advice. Dr. Laura, who is not a psychologist or psychiatrist (her doctorate is in physiology), analyzes callers' problems in more of a moral than psychological framework. Unlike most therapists, she unabashedly preaches to her audience about how they ought to lead their lives. In many instances she is insulting and abusive to her callers, models remarkable intolerance, and provides terrible advice (Epstein, 2001). In an editorial in *Psychology Today,* Robert Epstein (2001) concludes that "no legitimate mental health professional would ever give the kind of hateful, divisive advice that Schlessinger doles out daily" (p. 5). Yet, the remarkable popularity of her highly prescriptive advice demonstrates once again that many people are eager for guidance and direction.

Although we might choose to examine any of these examples of people's search for a sense of direction, we will reserve our in-depth analysis for a manifestation of this search that is even more germane to our focus on everyday adjustment: the spectacular success of best-selling "self-help" books.

Self-Help Books

In 2003, Americans spent roughly $650 million on "self-help books" that offer do-it-yourself treatments for

Web Link 1.1 **Psychological Self-Help**

Clinical psychologist and professor Clayton E. Tucker-Ladd has spent some 25 years exploring how individuals can help themselves deal with personal issues and problems from a psychological perspective. Here he has assembled an online 12-chapter book, grounded in up-to-date research, that complements this textbook extremely well. **Note: The URLs (addresses) for the Web Links can be found on the website for this text (academic.cengage.com/psychology/weiten), or you can find them using a search engine such as Google.**

common personal problems (Arkowitz & Lilienfeld, 2006). If you include self-help audiotapes, CDs, DVDs, software, Internet sites, lectures, seminars, and life coaching, self-improvement appears to be a $2.5 billion-a-year industry (McGee, 2005). This fascination with self-improvement is nothing new. For decades American readers have displayed a voracious appetite for self-help books such as *I'm OK—You're OK* (Harris, 1967), *Your Erroneous Zones* (Dyer, 1976), *How to Be Awake and Alive* (Newman & Berkowitz, 1976), *Living, Loving & Learning* (Buscaglia, 1982), *The Seven Habits of Highly Effective People* (Covey, 1989), *Men Are from Mars, Women Are from Venus* (Gray, 1992), *Ageless Body, Timeless Mind* (Chopra, 1993), *Don't Sweat the Small Stuff . . . and It's All Small Stuff* (Carlson, 1997), *Life Strategies* (McGraw, 1999), *Making Peace with Your Past* (Bloomfield, 2000), *Self-Nurture* (Domar & Dreher, 2000), and *The Purpose Driven Life* (Warren, 2002). With their simple recipes for achieving happiness, these books have generally not been timid about promising to change the quality of the reader's life. Consider the following excerpt from the back cover of a self-help book titled *Self Creation* (Weinberg, 1979):

More than any book ever written, Self Creation *shows you who you are and reveals the secret to controlling your own life. It contains an action blueprint built around a clear-cut principle as basic and revolutionary as the law of gravity. With it you will discover how to conquer bad habits, solve sexual problems, overcome depression and shyness, deal with infuriating people, be decisive, enhance your career, increase creativity. And it will show you how to love and be loved. You created you. Now you can start to reap the boundless benefits of self-confidence, self-reliance, self-determination with* Self Creation.

If only it were that easy! If only someone could hand you a book that would solve all your problems! Unfortunately, it is not that simple. Merely reading a book is not likely to turn your life around. If the consumption of these literary narcotics were even remotely as helpful as their publishers claim, we would be a nation of serene, happy, well-adjusted people. It is clear, however, that serenity is not the dominant national mood. Quite the contrary, as already noted, in recent decades Americans' average anxiety level has moved upward (Twenge, 2000), and the prevalence of depression has increased as well (Kessler, 2002). The multitude of self-help books that crowd bookstore shelves represent just one more symptom of our collective distress and our search for the elusive secret of happiness.

The Value of Self-Help Books

It is somewhat unfair to lump all self-help books together for a critique, because they vary widely in quality (Fried & Schultis, 1995; Norcross et al., 2003). Surveys exploring psychotherapists' opinions of self-help books suggest that there are some excellent books that offer authentic insights and sound advice (Starker, 1990, 1992). Many therapists encourage their patients to read carefully selected self-help books (Campbell & Smith, 2003). A few books have even been tested in clinical trials with favorable results (Floyd, 2003; Gregory et al., 2004), although the studies have often had methodological weaknesses (Arkowitz & Lilienfeld, 2006). Thus, it would be foolish to dismiss all these books as shallow drivel. In fact, some of the better self-help books are highlighted in the Recommended Reading boxes that appear throughout this text. Unfortunately, however, the gems are easily lost in the

© AP Images/Stephen Chernin

The newest rage in self-help books is* The Secret*, written by Australian Rhonda Byrne, shown here at a* Time *magazine gala publicizing the magazine's selection of the 100 most influential people in the world. Byrne's (2006) book, DVD, and CDs have been flying off the shelves of American bookstores. The marketing campaign for the book has been absolutely brilliant (who can resist the opportunity to learn* the secret *to life?). What is Byrne's captivating thesis? The former television producer asserts that "Your current thoughts are creating your future life. What you think about the most or focus on the most will appear as your life" (p. 25). In other words, just think more about earning that "A" in Biochemistry, losing weight, or taking that expensive vacation, and events will go your way (no need to study, exercise, or save money). Characterized by psychologist John Norcross as "pseudoscientific, psychospiritual babble," (Adler, 2007),* The Secret *provides a remarkable demonstration of how seductive self-help books can be.

mountains of rubbish. A great many self-help books offer little of real value to the reader. Generally, they suffer from four fundamental shortcomings.

First, they are dominated by "psychobabble." The term *psychobabble,* coined by R. D. Rosen (1977), seems appropriate to describe the "hip" but hopelessly vague language used in many of these books. Statements such as "It's beautiful if you're unhappy," "You've got to get in touch with yourself," "You have to be up front," "You gotta be you 'cause you're you," and "You need a real high-energy experience" are typical examples of this language. At best, such terminology is ill-defined; at worst, it is meaningless. Consider the following example, taken from a question/answer booklet promoting *est* training:

The EST training doesn't change the content of anyone's life, nor does it change what anyone knows. It deals with the context or the way we hold the content. . . . Transformation occurs as a recontextualization. . . . "Getting it" means being able to discover when you have been maintaining (or are stuck with) a position which costs you more in aliveness than it is worth, realizing that you are the source of that position, and being able to choose to give up that position or hold it in a way that expands the quality of your life.

What exactly does this paragraph say? Who knows? The statements are so ambiguous and enigmatic that

Recommended READING

The Paradox of Choice: Why More Is Less
by Barry Schwartz (HarperCollins, 2004)

In *The Paradox of Choice,* Barry Schwartz argues that people in modern, affluent societies suffer a variety of negative consequences because they face an overabundance of choices in their personal lives (see pp. 2–3). Schwartz recognizes that his argument seems counterintuitive, as most people cherish their freedom of choice. But he maintains that "the fact that *some* choice is good doesn't necessarily mean that *more* choice is better" (p. 3). In perhaps the most interesting part of the book, Schwartz outlines the differences between *maximizers* and *satisficers.* Maximizers need to feel confident that virtually every decision they make yields the best possible outcome. In contrast, satisficers are frequently willing to settle for outcomes that are good enough. He emphasizes that satisficers try to meet certain standards—sometimes very high standards—in making their decisions, but they do not feel compelled to select the *best* possible printer, mattress, vacation, and so forth. Although maximizing sounds like an admirable goal, Schwartz reports that high maximization scores are associated with reduced optimism and happiness and increased depression—and he raises doubts about whether maximizing tends to lead to better decisions.

Does Schwartz have a solution for the problem of excessive choice? Yes, his final chapter offers advice for making the overabundance of choices in our modern world less painful. Among other things, he suggests that people should (1) decide which choices really matter, (2) satisfice more and maximize less, (3) avoid rumination about decisions, (4) let go of decision regrets, and (5) recognize that constraints on choice can sometimes be liberating. Schwartz's writing is clear, concise, and engaging. The book is loaded with charming anecdotes that provide real-life examples of the issues discussed, but Schwartz's conclusions are based on research rather than anecdotal evidence. In the final analysis, *The Paradox of Choice* delivers an enticing two-for-one bargain: It is a thought-provoking essay in social criticism and a sound, realistic self-help book.

you can read virtually any meaning into them. Therein lies the problem with psychobabble; it is often so obscure as to be unintelligible. Clarity is sacrificed in favor of a hip jargon that prevents, rather than enhances, effective communication.

A second problem is that self-help books tend to place more emphasis on sales than on scientific soundness. The advice offered in these books is far too rarely based on solid, scientific research (Ellis, 1993; Paul, 2001; Rosen, 1987, 1993). Instead, the ideas are frequently based on the authors' intuitive analyses, which may be highly speculative. Even when books are based on well-researched therapeutic programs, interventions that are effective in clinical settings with professional supervision may not be effective when self-administered without professional guidance (Rosen, Glasgow, & Moore, 2003). Moreover, even when responsible authors provide scientifically valid advice and are careful not to mislead their readers, sales-hungry publishers routinely slap outrageous, irresponsible promises on the books' covers, often to the dismay of the authors (Rosen et al., 2003).

The third shortcoming is that self-help books don't usually provide explicit directions about how to change your behavior. These books tend to be smoothly written and "touchingly human" in tone. They often strike responsive chords in the reader by aptly describing a common problem that many of us experience. The reader says, "Yes, that's me!" Unfortunately, when the book focuses on how to deal with the problem, it usually provides only a vague distillation of simple common sense, which could be covered in 2 rather than 200 pages. These books often fall back on inspirational cheerleading in the absence of sound, explicit advice.

Fourth, many of these books encourage a remarkably self-centered approach to life (Justman, 2005). Although there are plenty of exceptions, the basic message in many self-help books is "Do whatever you feel like doing, and don't worry about the consequences for other people." According to McGee (2005), this mentality began to creep into books in the 1970s, as "bald proposals that one ought to 'look out for #1' or 'win through intimidation' marked a new ruthlessness in the self-help landscape" (p. 50). This "me first" philosophy emphasizes self-determined ethics and an exploitive approach to interpersonal relationships.

Web Link 1.2 **Quackwatch**

Stephen Barrett, a retired psychiatrist, has sought to alert the public to "health-related frauds, myths, fads, and fallacies" for over 30 years. This site offers no-holds-barred evaluations of Internet-based medical resources that Barrett and his board of scientific and technical advisers judge to be dubious, fraudulent, or dangerous to one's health.

What to Look for in Self-Help Books

Because self-help books vary so widely in quality, it seems a good idea to provide you with some guidelines about what to look for in seeking genuinely helpful books. The following thoughts give you some criteria for judging books of this type.

1. Clarity in communication is essential. Advice won't do you much good if you can't understand it. Try to avoid drowning in the murky depths of psychobabble.

2. This may sound backward, but look for books that do not promise too much in the way of immediate change. The truly useful books tend to be appropriately cautious in their promises and realistic about the challenge of altering your behavior. As Arkowitz and Lilienfeld (2006, p. 79) put it, "Be wary of books that make promises that they obviously cannot keep, such as curing a phobia in five minutes or fixing a failing marriage in a week."

DOONESBURY © 1978 G. B. Trudeau. Reprinted with permission of UNIVERSAL PRESS SYNDICATE. All rights reserved.

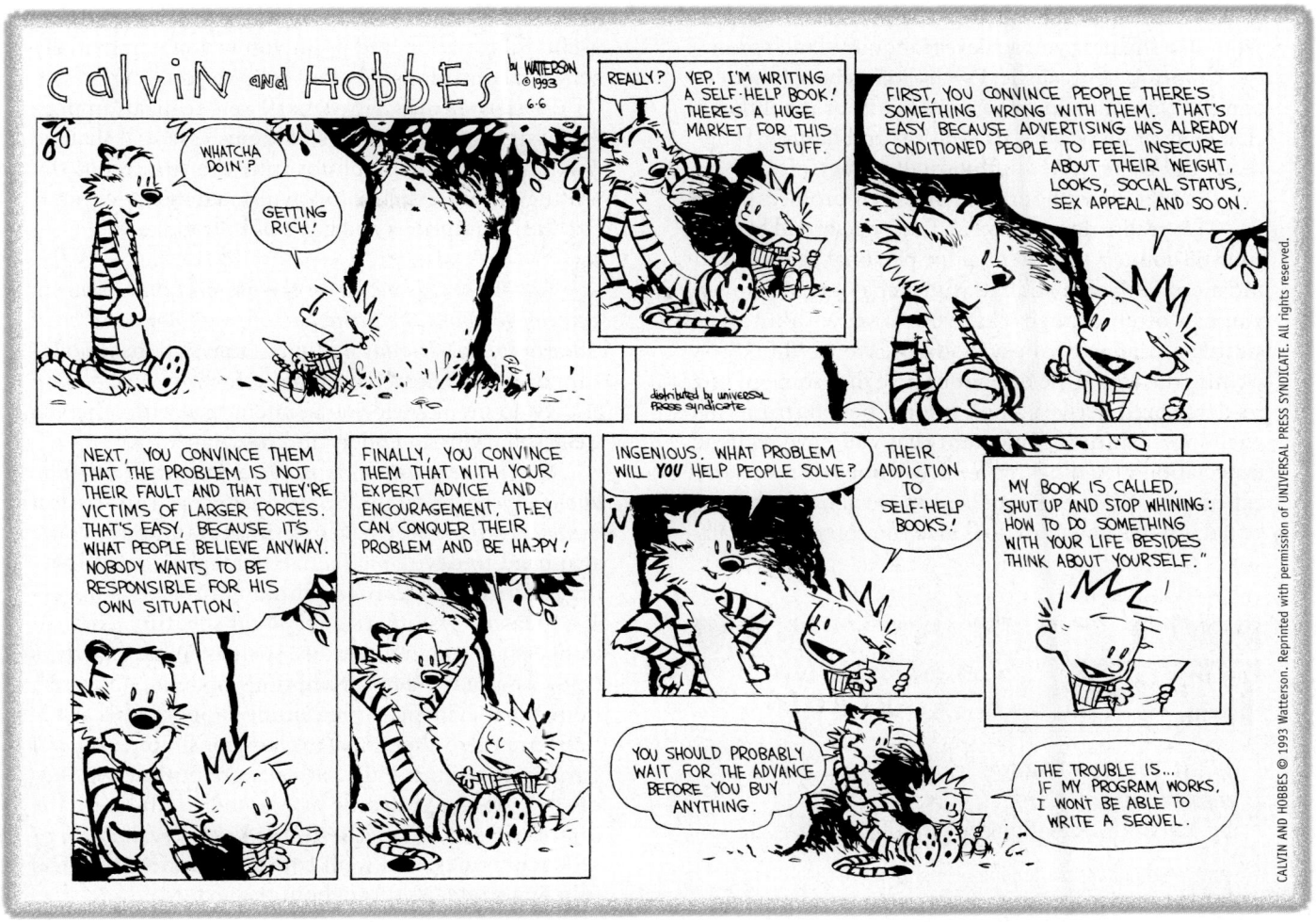

3. Try to check out the credentials of the author or authors. Book jackets will often exaggerate the expertise of authors, but these days a quick Internet search can often yield more objective biographical information and perhaps some perceptive reviews of the book.

4. Try to select books that mention, at least briefly, the theoretical or research basis for the program they advocate. It is understandable that you may not be interested in a detailed summary of research that supports a particular piece of advice. However, you should be interested in whether the advice is based on published research, widely accepted theory, anecdotal evidence, clinical interactions with patients, or pure speculation by the author. Books that are based on more than personal anecdotes and speculation should have a list of references in the back (or at the end of each chapter).

5. Look for books that provide detailed, explicit directions about how to alter your behavior. Generally, these directions represent the crucial core of the book. If they are inadequate in detail, you have been shortchanged.

6. More often than not, books that focus on a particular kind of problem, such as overeating, loneliness, or marital difficulties, deliver more than those that promise to cure all of life's problems with a few simple ideas. Books that cover everything are usually superficial and disappointing. Books that devote a great deal of thought to a particular topic tend to be written by authors with genuine expertise on that topic. Such books are more likely to pay off for you.

The Approach of This Textbook

Clearly, in spite of our impressive technological progress, we are a people beset by a great variety of personal problems. Living in our complex, modern society is a formidable challenge. This book is about that challenge. It is about you. It is about life. Specifically, it summarizes for you the scientific research on human behavior that appears relevant to the challenge of living effectively in contemporary society. It draws primarily, but not exclusively, from the science we call psychology.

This text deals with the same kinds of problems addressed by self-help books, self-realization programs, and Dr. Laura: anxiety, stress, interpersonal relationships, frustration, loneliness, depression, self-control. However, it makes no boldly seductive promises about solving your personal problems, turning your life around, or helping you achieve tranquility. Such promises simply aren't realistic. Psychologists have long recognized that changing a person's behavior is a difficult challenge, fraught with frustration and failure (Seligman, 1994). Troubled individuals sometimes spend years in therapy without resolving their problems.

This reality does not mean that you should be pessimistic about your potential for personal growth. You most certainly can change your behavior. Moreover, you can often change it on your own without consulting a professional psychologist. We would not be writing this text if we did not believe that some of our readers could derive some personal benefit from this encounter. But it is important that you have realistic expectations. Reading this book will not be a revelatory experience. No mysterious secrets are about to be unveiled. All this book can do is give you some potentially useful information and point you in some potentially beneficial directions. The rest is up to you.

In view of our criticisms of self-realization programs and self-help books, it seems essential that we explicitly lay out the philosophy that underlies the writing of this text. The following statements summarize the assumptions and goals of this book.

1. *This text is based on the premise that accurate knowledge about the principles of psychology can be of value to you in everyday life.* It has been said that knowledge is power. Greater awareness of why people behave as they do should help you in interacting with others as well as in trying to understand yourself.

2. *This text attempts to foster a critical attitude about psychological issues and to enhance your critical thinking skills.* Information is important, but people also need to develop effective strategies for evaluating information. Critical thinking involves subjecting ideas to systematic, skeptical scrutiny. Critical thinkers ask tough questions, such as: What exactly is being asserted? What assumptions underlie this assertion? What evidence or reasoning supports this assertion? Are there alternative explanations? Some general guidelines for thinking critically are outlined in **Figure 1.1**. We have already attempted to illustrate the importance of a critical attitude in our evaluation of self-help books, and we'll continue to model critical thinking strategies throughout the text.

3. *This text should open doors.* The coverage in this book is broad; we tackle many topics. Therefore, in some places it may lack the depth or detail that you would like. However, you should think of it as a resource book that can introduce you to other books or techniques or therapies, which you can then pursue on your own.

4. *This text assumes that the key to effective adjustment is to take charge of your own life.* If you are dissatisfied with some aspect of your life, it does no good to sit around and mope about it. You have to take an active role in attempting to improve the quality of your life. Doing so may involve learning a new skill or pursuing a particular kind of help. In any case, it is generally best to meet problems head-on rather than trying to avoid them.

Recommended **READING**

What You Can Change and What You Can't
by Martin E. P. Seligman (Knopf, 1994)

Martin Seligman is a prominent psychologist who has conducted influential research on learned helplessness, attributional style, optimism, depression, and phobias. He is also one of the chief architects of the new positive psychology movement (see Chapter 3). In this book he synthesizes research on a variety of issues to help people understand what they can and cannot change about themselves. Seligman points out that self-improvement programs of all types—from meditation, to self-help books, to professional therapy—are predicated on the assumption that people can permanently change themselves for the better. He notes, however, that recent, highly publicized research in biological psychiatry is at odds with this assumption. This research suggests that personality, intelligence, physique, and vulnerability to psychological disorders are predominantly determined by genetic inheritance and hence are largely unchangeable. Seligman asserts that both viewpoints are too extreme—that the architects of self-improvement programs are too optimistic while the authorities on biological psychiatry are too pessimistic about people's capacity for change. Thus, he sets out to review the empirical evidence on what can be modified with reasonable success, and what can't be. Seligman covers such wide-ranging topics as treatments for sexual difficulties, alcoholism, weight problems, anxiety, depression, obsessions, and posttraumatic stress syndrome. His discussions are lively, readable, objective, sophisticated, and thoroughly grounded in research.

Web Link 1.3 **Foundation for Critical Thinking**

How can students best develop those skills that go beyond merely acquiring information to actively weighing and judging information? The many resources of the Foundation for Critical Thinking at Sonoma State University are directed primarily toward teachers at every level to help them develop their students' critical thinking abilities.

Guidelines for Thinking Critically

1. **Ask questions; be willing to wonder.** To think critically you must be willing to think creatively—that is, to be curious about the puzzles of human behavior, to wonder why people act the way they do, and to question conventional explanations and examine new ones.
2. **Define the problem.** Identify the issues involved in clear and concrete terms, rather than vague generalities such as "happiness," "potential," or "meaningfulness." What does meaningfulness mean, exactly?
3. **Examine the evidence.** Consider the nature of the evidence that supports all aspects of the problem under examination. Is it reliable? Valid? Is it someone's personal assertion or speculation? Does the evidence come from one or two narrow studies, or from repeated research?
4. **Analyze biases and assumptions**—your own and those of others. What prejudices, deeply held values, and other personal biases do you bring to your evaluation of a problem? Are you willing to consider evidence that contradicts your beliefs? Be sure you can identify the bias of others, in order to evaluate their arguments as well.
5. **Avoid emotional reasoning** ("If I feel this way, it must be true"). Remember that everyone holds convictions and ideas about how the world should operate and that your opponents are as serious about their convictions as you are about yours. Feelings are important, but they should not substitute for careful appraisal of arguments and evidence.
6. **Don't oversimplify.** Look beyond the obvious. Reject simplistic, either-or thinking. Look for logical contradictions in arguments. Be wary of "arguments by anecdote."
7. **Consider other interpretations.** Before you leap to conclusions, think about other explanations. Be especially careful about assertions of cause and effect.
8. **Tolerate uncertainty.** This may be the hardest step in becoming a critical thinker, for it requires the ability to accept some guiding ideas and beliefs—yet the willingness to give them up when evidence and experience contradict them.

Figure1.1

Guidelines for thinking critically. Critical thinking should not be equated with criticism; it's not a matter of learning how to tear down others' ideas. Rather, critical thinkers carefully subject others' ideas—and their own—to careful, systematic, objective evaluation. The guidelines shown here, taken from Wade and Tavris (1990), provide a succinct overview of what it means to think critically.

From Wade, C., & Tavris, C. (1990). *Learning to Think Critically: A Handbook to Accompany Psychology.* New York: Harper & Row. Copyright © 1990 by Harper & Row Publishers, Inc. Reprinted by permission of Pearson Education, Inc.

The Psychology of Adjustment

LEARNING OBJECTIVES

- *Describe the two key facets of psychology.*
- *Explain the concept of adjustment.*

Now that we have spelled out our approach in writing this text, it is time to turn to the task of introducing you to some basic concepts. In this section, we'll discuss the nature of psychology and the concept of adjustment.

What Is Psychology?

***Psychology* is the science that studies behavior and the physiological and mental processes that underlie it, and it is the profession that applies the accumulated knowledge of this science to practical problems.** Psychology leads a complex dual existence as both a *science* and a *profession.* Let's examine the science first. Psychology is an area of scientific study, much like biology or physics. Whereas biology focuses on life processes and physics focuses on matter and energy, psychology focuses on *behavior* and *related mental and physiological processes.*

***Behavior* is any overt (observable) response or activity by an organism.** Psychology does *not* confine itself to the study of human behavior. Many psychologists believe that the principles of behavior are much the same for all animals, including humans. As a result, these psychologists often prefer to study animals—mainly because they can exert more control over the factors influencing the animals' behavior.

Psychology is also interested in the mental processes—the thoughts, feelings, and wishes—that accompany behavior. Mental processes are more difficult to study than behavior because they are private and not directly observable. However, they exert critical influence over human behavior, so psychologists have strived to improve their ability to "look inside the mind."

Finally, psychology includes the study of the physiological processes that underlie behavior. Thus, some psychologists try to figure out how bodily processes such as neural impulses, hormonal secretions, and genetic coding regulate behavior.

Practically speaking, all this means that psychologists study a great variety of phenomena. Psychologists are interested in maze running in rats, salivation in dogs, and brain functioning in cats, as well as visual perception in humans, play in children, and social interaction in adults.

As you probably know, psychology is not all pure science. It has a highly practical side, represented by the many psychologists who provide a variety of professional services to the public. Although the profession of psychology is quite prominent today, this aspect of psychology was actually slow to develop. Until the 1950s psychologists were found almost exclusively in the halls of academia, teaching and doing research. However, the demands of World War II in the 1940s stimulated rapid growth in psychology's first professional specialty—clinical psychology. ***Clinical psychology* is the branch of psychology concerned with the diagnosis and treatment of psychological problems and disorders.** During World War II, a multitude of academic psychologists were pressed into service as clinicians to screen military recruits and treat soldiers suffering from trauma. Many found their clinical work interesting and returned from the war to set up training programs to meet the continued high demand for clinical services. Soon, about half of the new Ph.D.'s in psychology were specializing in clinical work. Psychology had come of age as a profession.

What Is Adjustment?

We have used the term *adjustment* several times without clarifying its exact meaning. The concept of adjustment was originally borrowed from biology. It was modeled after the biological term *adaptation,* which refers to efforts by a species to adjust to changes in its environment. Just as a field mouse has to adapt to an unusually brutal winter, a person has to adjust to changes in circumstances such as a new job, a financial setback, or the loss of a loved one. Thus, ***adjustment* refers to the psychological processes through which people manage or cope with the demands and challenges of everyday life.**

The demands of everyday life are diverse, so in studying the process of adjustment we will encounter a broad variety of topics. In the first section of this book, "The Dynamics of Adjustment," we discuss general issues, such as how personality affects people's patterns of adjustment, how individuals are affected by stress, and how they use coping strategies to deal with stress. In the second section, "The Interpersonal Realm," we examine the adjustments that people make in their social relationships, exploring such topics as individuals' perceptions of others, interpersonal communication, behavior in groups, friendship, and intimate relationships. In the third section, "Developmental Transitions," we look at how individuals adjust to changing demands as they grow older. We discuss such topics as the development of gender roles, the emergence of sexuality, phases of adult development, and transitions in the world of work. Finally, in the fourth section, "Mental and Physical Health," we discuss how the process of adjustment influences a person's psychological and physical wellness.

As you can see, the study of adjustment delves into nearly every corner of people's lives, and we'll be discussing a diverse array of issues and topics. Before we begin considering these topics in earnest, however, we need to take a closer look at psychology's approach to investigating behavior—the scientific method.

The Scientific Approach to Behavior

LEARNING OBJECTIVES

- *Explain the nature of empiricism.*
- *Explain two advantages of the scientific approach to understanding behavior.*
- *Describe the experimental method, distinguishing between independent and dependent variables and between experimental and control groups.*
- *Distinguish between positive and negative correlation and explain what the size of a correlation coefficient means.*
- *Describe three correlational research methods.*
- *Compare the advantages and disadvantages of experimental versus correlational research.*

We all expend a great deal of effort in trying to understand our own behavior as well as the behavior of others. We wonder about any number of behavioral questions: Why am I so anxious when I interact with new people? Why is Sam always trying to be the center of attention at the office? Why does Joanna cheat on her wonderful husband? Are extraverts happier than introverts? Is depression more common during the Christmas holidays? Given that psychologists' principal goal is to explain behavior, how are their efforts different from everyone else's? The key difference is that psychology is a *science,* committed to *empiricism.*

The Commitment to Empiricism

***Empiricism* is the premise that knowledge should be acquired through observation.** When we say that scientific psychology is empirical, we mean that its conclusions are based on systematic observation rather than on reasoning, speculation, traditional beliefs, or common sense. Scientists are not content with having ideas that sound plausible; they must conduct research to *test* their ideas. Whereas our everyday speculations are informal, unsystematic, and highly subjective, scientists' investigations are formal, systematic, and objective.

In these investigations, scientists formulate hypotheses (the ideas they want to test), gather data (make observations) relevant to their hypotheses, use statistics to analyze these data, and report their results to the public and other scientists, typically by publishing their findings in a technical journal. The process of publishing scientific studies allows other experts to evaluate and critique new research findings.

Advantages of the Scientific Approach

Science is certainly not the only method that can be used to draw conclusions about behavior. We can also turn to logic, casual observation, and good old-fashioned common sense. Because the scientific method often requires painstaking effort, it seems reasonable to ask: What exactly are the advantages of the empirical approach?

The scientific approach offers two major advantages. The first is its clarity and precision. Commonsense notions about behavior tend to be vague and ambiguous. Consider the old truism "Spare the rod and spoil the child." What does this generalization about childrearing amount to? How severely should children be punished if parents are not to "spare the rod"? How do parents assess whether a child qualifies as "spoiled"? Such statements can have different meanings to different people. When people disagree about this assertion, it may be because they are talking about entirely different things. In contrast, the empirical approach requires that scientists specify *exactly* what they are talking about when they formulate hypotheses. This clarity and precision enhance communication about important ideas.

The second advantage offered by the scientific approach is its relative intolerance of error. Scientists subject their ideas to empirical tests. They also scrutinize one another's findings with a critical eye. They demand objective data and thorough documentation before they accept ideas. When the findings of two studies conflict, they try to figure out why the studies reached different conclusions, usually by conducting additional research. In contrast, common sense and casual observation often tolerate contradictory generalizations, such as "Opposites attract" and "Birds of a feather flock together." Furthermore, commonsense analyses involve little effort to verify ideas or detect errors, so that many myths about behavior come to be widely believed.

All this is not to say that science has a copyright on truth. However, the scientific approach does tend to yield more accurate and dependable information than casual analyses and armchair speculation. Knowledge of empirical data can thus provide a useful benchmark against which to judge claims and information from other kinds of sources.

Now that we have an overview of how the scientific enterprise works, we can look at some of the specific research methods that psychologists depend on most. The two main types of research methods in psychology are *experimental* and *correlational.* We discuss them separately because there is an important distinction between them.

Experimental Research: Looking for Causes

Does misery love company? This question intrigued social psychologist Stanley Schachter. When people feel anxious, do they want to be left alone, or do they prefer to have others around? Schachter's hypothesis was that increases in anxiety would cause increases in the desire to be with others, which psychologists call the *need for affiliation.* To test this hypothesis, Schachter (1959) designed a clever experiment. **The *experiment* is a research method in which the investigator manipulates one (independent) variable under carefully controlled conditions and observes whether any changes occur in a second (dependent) variable as a result.** Psychologists depend on this method more than any other.

Independent and Dependent Variables

An experiment is designed to find out whether changes in one variable (let's call it x) cause changes in another variable (let's call it y). To put it more concisely, we want to know how x affects y. In this formulation, we refer to x as the independent variable, and we call y the dependent variable. **An *independent variable* is a condition or event that an experimenter varies in order to see its impact on another variable.** The independent variable is the variable that the experimenter controls or manipulates. It is hypothesized to have some effect on the dependent variable. The experiment is conducted to verify this effect. **The *dependent variable* is the variable that is thought to be affected by the manipulations of the independent variable.** In psychology studies, the dependent variable usually is a measurement of some aspect of the subjects' behavior.

In Schachter's experiment, *the independent variable was the participants' anxiety level,* which he manipulated in the following way. Subjects assembled in his laboratory were told by a Dr. Zilstein that they would be participating in a study on the physiological effects of electric shock and that they would receive a series of shocks. Half of the participants were warned that the shocks would be very painful. They made up the *high-anxiety* group. The other half of the participants, assigned to the *low-anxiety* group, were told that the shocks would be mild and painless. These procedures were simply intended to evoke different levels of anxiety. In reality, no one was actually shocked at any time. Instead, the experimenter indicated that there would be a delay while he prepared the shock apparatus for use. The participants were asked whether they would prefer to wait alone or in the company of others. *This measure of the subjects' desire to affiliate with others was the dependent variable.*

Experimental and Control Groups

To conduct an experiment, an investigator typically assembles two groups of participants who are treated differently in regard to the independent variable. We call these groups the experimental and control groups. **The *experimental group* consists of the subjects who receive some special treatment in regard to the independent variable. The *control group* consists of similar subjects who do not receive the special treatment given to the experimental group.**

Let's return to the Schachter study to illustrate. In this study, the participants in the high-anxiety condition were the experimental group. They received a special treatment designed to create an unusually high level of anxiety. The participants in the low-anxiety condition were the control group.

It is crucial that the experimental and control groups be similar except for the different treatment they receive in regard to the independent variable. This stipulation brings us to the logic that underlies the experimental method. If the two groups are alike in all respects *except for the variation created by the manipulation of the independent variable,* then any differences between the two groups on the dependent variable *must be due to this manipulation of the independent variable.* In this way researchers isolate the effect of the independent variable on the dependent variable. In his experiment, Schachter isolated the impact of anxiety on need for affiliation. What did he find? As predicted, he found that increased anxiety led to increased affiliation. The percentage of people who wanted to wait with others was nearly twice as high in the high-anxiety group as in the low-anxiety group.

The logic of the experimental method rests heavily on the assumption that the experimental and control groups are alike in all important matters except for their different treatment with regard to the independent variable. Any other differences between the two groups cloud the situation and make it difficult to draw solid conclusions about the relationship between the independent variable and the dependent variable. To summarize our discussion of the experimental method, **Figure 1.2** provides an overview of the vari-

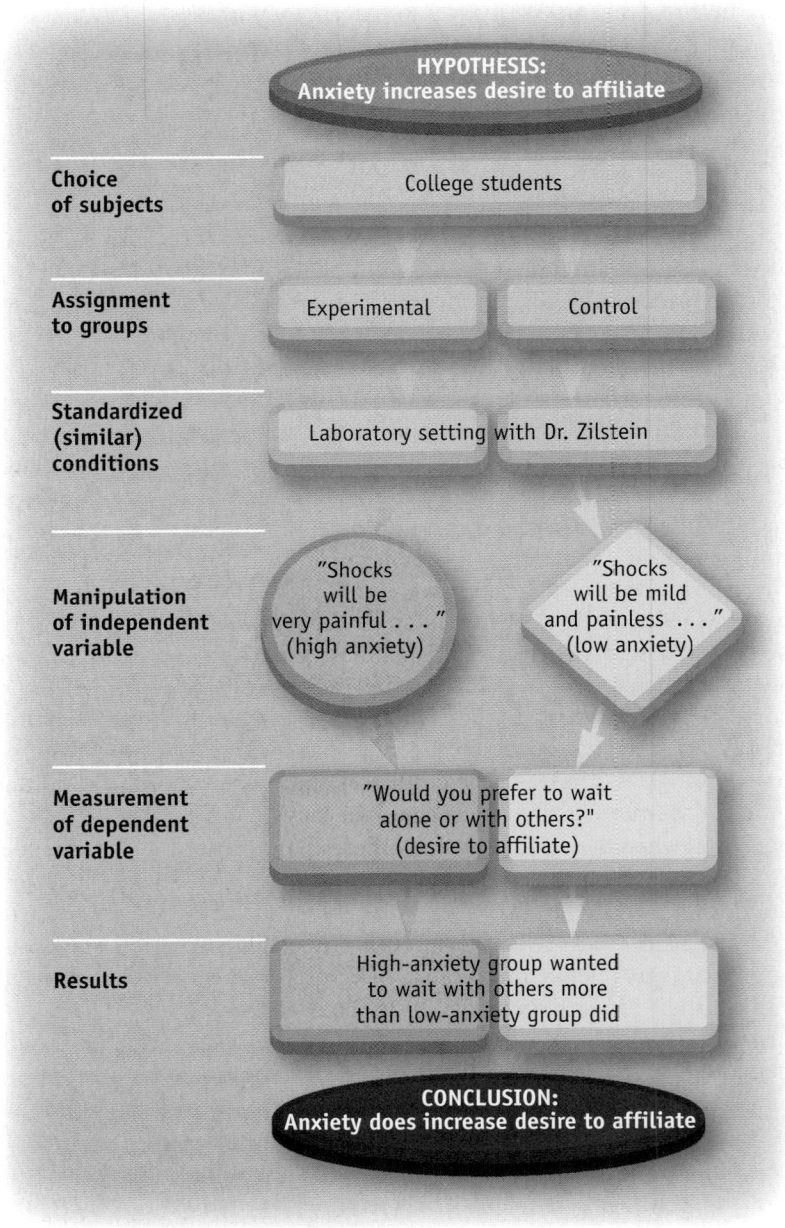

Figure 1.2

The basic elements of an experiment. This diagram provides an overview of the key features of the experimental method, as illustrated by Schachter's study of anxiety and affiliation. The logic of the experiment rests on treating the experimental and control groups alike except for the manipulation of the independent variable.

ous elements in an experiment, using Schachter's study as an example.

Advantages and Disadvantages

The experiment is a powerful research method. Its principal advantage is that it allows scientists to draw conclusions about cause-and-effect relationships between variables. Researchers can draw these conclusions about causation because the precise control available in the experiment permits them to isolate the relationship between the independent variable and the dependent variable. No other research method can duplicate this advantage.

For all its power, however, the experimental method has its limitations. One disadvantage is that researchers are often interested in the effects of variables that cannot be manipulated (as independent variables) because of ethical concerns or practical realities. For example, you might want to know whether being brought up in an urban area as opposed to a rural area affects people's values. A true experiment would require you to assign similar families to live in urban and rural areas, which obviously is impossible to do. To explore this question, you would have to use correlational research methods, which we turn to next.

Correlational Research: Looking for Links

As we just noted, in some situations psychologists cannot exert experimental control over the variables they want to study. In such situations, all a researcher can do is make systematic observations to see whether a link or association exists between the variables of interest. Such an association is called a correlation. **A *correlation* exists when two variables are related to each other.** The definitive aspect of correlational studies is that the researchers cannot control the variables under study.

Measuring Correlation

The results of correlational research are often summarized with a statistic called the *correlation coefficient.*

Web Link 1.4 **Research Methods Tutorials**

Bill Trochim's classes in research and program design at Cornell University have assembled tutorial guides for undergraduate and graduate students for more than 50 topics at this subpage of the Web Center for Social Research Methods. Students new to research design may find these tutorials particularly helpful.

We'll be referring to this widely used statistic frequently as we discuss studies throughout the remainder of this text. **A *correlation coefficient* is a numerical index of the degree of relationship that exists between two variables.** A correlation coefficient indicates (1) how strongly related two variables are and (2) the direction (positive or negative) of the relationship.

Two kinds of relationships can be described by a correlation. A *positive* correlation indicates that two variables co-vary in the same direction. This means that high scores on variable *x* are associated with high scores on variable *y* and that low scores on variable *x* are associated with low scores on variable *y.* For example, there is a positive correlation between high school grade point average (GPA) and subsequent college GPA. That is, people who do well in high school tend to do well in college, and those who perform poorly in high school tend to perform poorly in college (see **Figure 1.3**).

In contrast, a *negative* correlation indicates that two variables co-vary in the opposite direction. This means that people who score high on variable *x* tend to score low on variable *y,* whereas those who score low on *x* tend to score high on *y.* For example, in most college courses, there is a negative correlation between how frequently a student is absent and how well the student performs on exams. Students who have a high number of absences tend to earn low exam scores, while students who have a low number of absences tend to get higher exam scores (see **Figure 1.3**).

While the positive or negative sign indicates whether an association is direct or inverse, the *size* of the coefficient indicates the *strength* of the association between

Figure 1.3

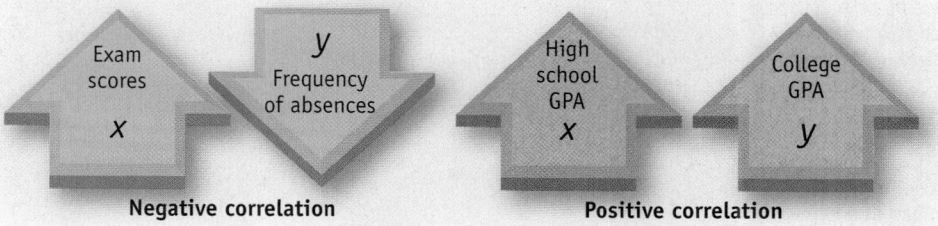

Positive and negative correlations. Variables are positively correlated if they tend to increase and decrease together and are negatively correlated if one variable tends to increase when the other decreases. Hence, the terms *positive correlation* and *negative correlation* refer to the *direction* of the relationship between two variables.

two variables. A correlation coefficient can vary between 0 and +1.00 (if positive) or between 0 and –1.00 (if negative). A coefficient near zero tells us there is no relationship between the variables. The closer the correlation to either –1.00 or +1.00, the stronger the relationship. Thus, a correlation of +.90 represents a stronger tendency for variables to be associated than a correlation of +.40 does (see **Figure 1.4**). Likewise, a correlation of –.75 represents a stronger relationship than a correlation of –.45. Keep in mind that the *strength* of a correlation depends only on the size of the coefficient. The positive or negative sign simply shows whether the correlation is direct or inverse. Therefore, a correlation of –.60 reflects a stronger relationship than a correlation of +.30.

Correlational research methods comprise a number of approaches, including naturalistic observation, case studies, and surveys. Let's examine each of these to see how researchers use them to detect associations between variables.

Naturalistic Observation

In *naturalistic observation* a researcher engages in careful observation of behavior without intervening directly with the subjects. This type of research is called *naturalistic* because behavior is allowed to unfold naturally (without interference) in its natural environment—that is, the setting in which it would normally occur.

As an example, consider a study by Stoffer, Davis, and Brown (1977), which sought to determine whether it is a good idea for students to reconsider and change answers on multiple-choice tests. The conventional wisdom is that "your first hunch is your best hunch," and it is widely believed that students should not go back and change their answers. To put this idea to an empirical test, Stoffer and his colleagues studied the answer changes made by college students on their regular exams in a psychology course. They simply examined students' answer sheets for evidence of response changes, such as erasures or crossing out of responses. As **Figure 1.5** shows, they found that changes that went from a wrong answer to a right answer outnumbered changes that went from a right answer to a wrong answer by a margin of nearly 3 to 1. The correlation between the number of changes students made and their net gain from answer changing was +.49, indicating that the more answer changing students engaged in, the more they improved their scores. These results, which have been replicated in a number of other studies (Benjamin, Cavell, & Shallenberger, 1984), show that popular beliefs about the harmful effects of answer changing are inaccurate.

Case Studies

A *case study* is an in-depth investigation of an individual participant. Psychologists typically assemble case studies in clinical settings where an effort is being made to diagnose and treat some psychological problem. To achieve an understanding of an individual, a clinician may use a variety of procedures, including interviewing the person, interviewing others who know the individual, direct observation, examination of records, and psychological testing. Usually, a single case

Figure 1.4

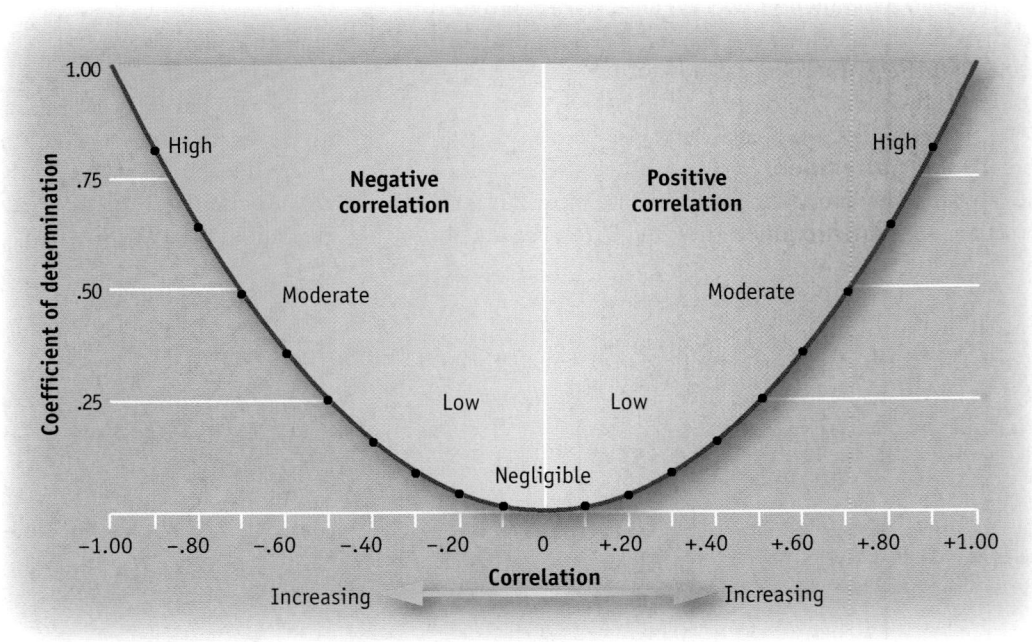

Interpreting correlation coefficients. The magnitude of a correlation coefficient indicates the strength of the relationship between two variables. The closer a correlation is to either +1.00 or –1.00, the stronger the relationship between the variables. The square of a correlation, which is called the *coefficient of determination,* is an index of a correlation's strength and predictive power. This graph shows how the coefficient of determination and predictive power goes up as the magnitude of a correlation increases.

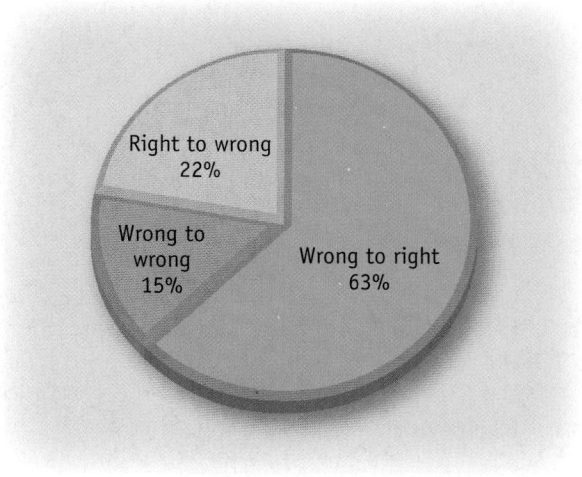

Figure1.5

The effects of answer changing on multiple-choice exams. In a study of answer changes, Stoffer et al. (1977) found that wrong-to-right changes outnumbered right-to-wrong changes by a sizable margin. These results are similar to those of other studies on this issue. However, these research results conflict with conventional wisdom, illustrating why it is prudent to test hypotheses empirically.

study does not provide much basis for deriving general laws of behavior. If researchers have a number of case studies available, however, they can look for threads of consistency among them, and they may be able to draw some general conclusions.

This was the strategy used by a research team (Farina et al., 1986) that studied psychiatric patients' readjustment to their community after their release from a mental hospital. The researchers wanted to know whether the patients' physical attractiveness was related to their success in readjustment. As we'll discuss in upcoming chapters, good-looking people tend to be treated better than homely people are, suggesting that attractive patients may have an easier time adjusting to life outside the hospital. To find out, the research team compiled case history data (and ratings of physical attractiveness) for patients just before their discharge from a mental hospital and six months later. A modest positive correlation (.38) was found between patients' attractiveness and their postdischarge social adjustment. Thus, the more-attractive patients were better off, suggesting that physical attractiveness plays a role in psychiatric patients' readjustment to community living.

Surveys

***Surveys* are structured questionnaires designed to solicit information about specific aspects of participants' behavior.** They are sometimes used to measure dependent variables in experiments, but they are mainly used in correlational research. Surveys are commonly used to gather data on people's attitudes and on aspects of behavior that are difficult to observe directly (marital interactions, for instance). As an example, consider a study by Alvin Cooper and his colleagues (1999) that examined people's Internet sexual pursuits. Cooper and his associates gathered data from an online questionnaire that was posted for seven weeks at the MSNBC website. The final sample consisted of 9,177 anonymous volunteers. The self-selected sample clearly was not representative of the general adult population in the United States, but the participants' demographic data suggested that they *were* reasonably representative of that portion of the population that visits sexually explicit websites.

What did the survey reveal? Male respondents outnumbered female respondents by about 6 to 1. Men reported mostly going to sites that featured visual erotica, whereas women were more likely to visit sexually themed chat rooms. Only 8%–9% of the respondents reported spending more than 10 hours per week in online sexual pursuits (see **Figure 1.6** on the next page). Although 87% of the subjects indicated that they never felt guilty about their behavior, 70% admitted keeping the extent of their online sexual activities secret from others. Among "heavy users" of Internet sex sites (more than 10 hours per week), about half admitted that their online activities were interfering with their lives. The authors conclude that "the vast majority of online users generally seem to use Internet sexual venues in casual ways that may not be problematic," but they emphasize that heavy users may be at risk for psychological difficulties.

Web Link 1.5 **American Psychological Association (APA)**

As the largest professional organization of psychologists, the APA continually publicizes the latest research findings for most topics discussed in this textbook. Students should consider using the excellent search engines at the APA's online site when looking for leads to new scientific research on adjustment issues.

Advantages and Disadvantages

Correlational research methods give psychologists a way to explore questions that they could not examine with experimental procedures. Consider the study of the association between attractiveness and adjustment in psychiatric patients. Obviously, Farina et al. (1986) could not manipulate the physical attractiveness of their subjects. But correlational methods allowed them to gather useful information on whether a link exists between attractiveness and adjustment. Thus, *correlational research broadens the scope of phenomena that psychologists can study.*

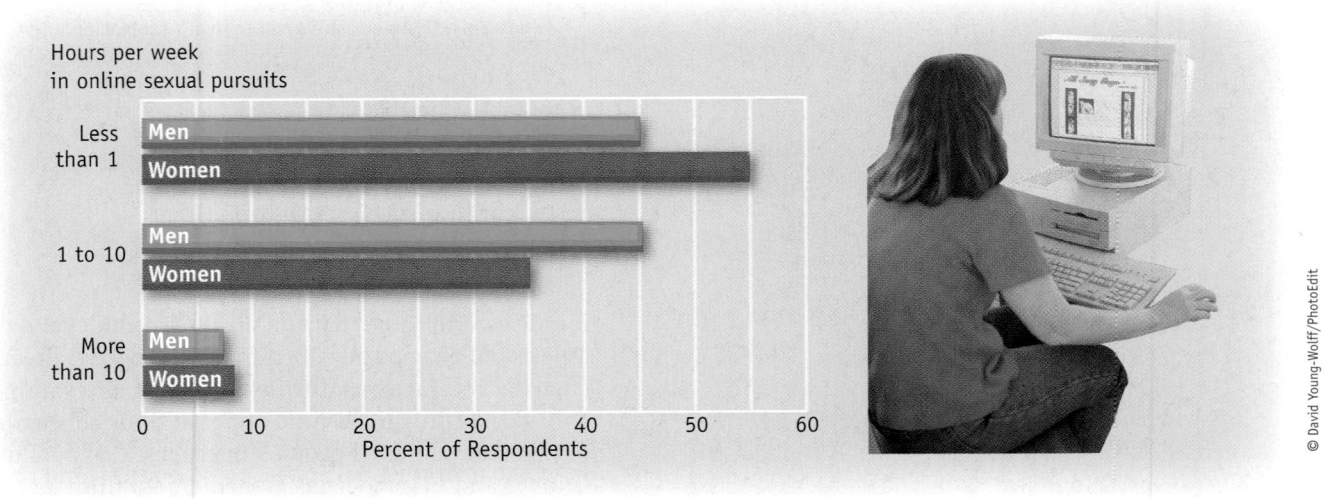

Figure 1.6

Time devoted to Internet sexual pursuits. In the online survey conducted by Cooper and his colleagues (1999), over 9,000 respondents provided information on how much time they spend weekly visiting sexually oriented websites. As you can see, the vast majority of participants reported that they spend 10 hours or less each week in online sexual pursuits. (Based on Cooper et al., 1999)

Unfortunately, correlational methods have one major disadvantage. The investigator does not have the opportunity to control events in a way to isolate cause and effect. *Consequently, correlational research cannot demonstrate conclusively that two variables are causally related.* The crux of the problem is that correlation is no assurance of causation.

When we find that variables *x* and *y* are correlated, we can safely conclude only that *x* and *y* are related. We do not know *how x* and *y* are related. We do not know whether *x* causes *y*, whether *y* causes *x*, or whether both are caused by a third variable. For example, survey studies show a positive correlation between marital satisfaction and sexual satisfaction (Christopher & Sprecher, 2000; Hunt, 1974). Although it's clear that good sex and a healthy marriage go hand in hand, it's hard to tell what's causing what. We don't know whether healthy marriages promote good sex or whether good sex promotes healthy marriages. Moreover, we can't rule out the possibility that both are caused by a third variable. Perhaps sexual satisfaction and marital satisfaction are both caused by compatibility in values. The plausible causal relationships in this case are diagrammed for you in **Figure 1.7**, which illustrates the "third-variable problem" in interpreting correlations. This problem occurs frequently in correlational research. Indeed, it will surface in the next section, where we review the empirical research on the determinants of happiness.

Figure 1.7

Possible causal relations between correlated variables. When two variables are correlated, there are several possible explanations. It could be that *x* causes *y*, that *y* causes *x*, or that a third variable, *z*, causes changes in both *x* and *y*. As the correlation between marital satisfaction and sexual satisfaction illustrates, the correlation itself does not provide the answer. This conundrum is sometimes referred to as the "third variable problem."

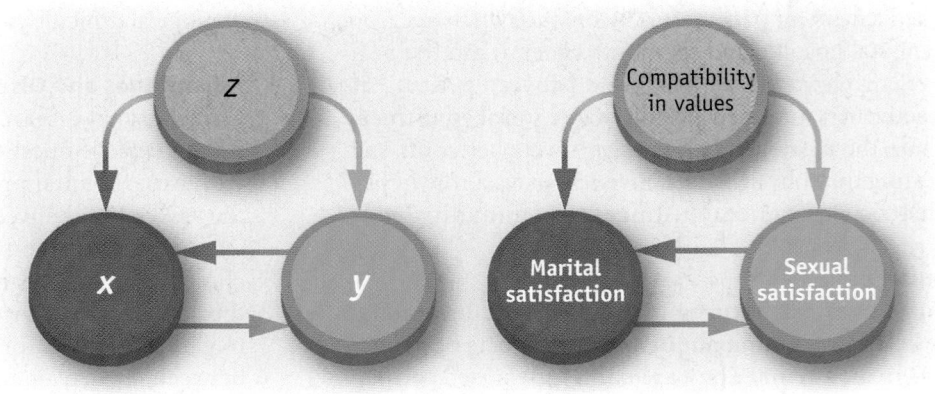

The Roots of Happiness: An Empirical Analysis

LEARNING OBJECTIVES

- *Discuss the prevalence of reported happiness in modern society.*
- *List the various factors that are surprisingly unrelated to happiness.*
- *Explain how health, social activity, and religion are related to happiness.*
- *Discuss how love, work, genetics, and personality are related to happiness.*
- *Summarize the conclusions drawn about the determinants of happiness.*

What exactly makes a person happy? This question has been the subject of much speculation. Commonsense hypotheses about the roots of happiness abound. For example, you have no doubt heard that money cannot buy happiness. But do you believe it? A television commercial says, "If you've got your health, you've got just about everything." Is health indeed the key? What if you're healthy but poor, unemployed, and lonely? We often hear about the joys of parenthood, the joys of youth, and the joys of the simple, rural life. Are these the factors that promote happiness?

In recent years, social scientists have begun putting these and other hypotheses to empirical test. Quite a number of survey studies have been conducted to explore the determinants of ***subjective well-being*—individuals' personal assessments of their overall happiness or life satisfaction.** The findings of these studies are quite interesting. We review this research because it is central to the topic of adjustment and because it illustrates the value of collecting data and putting ideas to an empirical test. As you will see, many commonsense notions about happiness appear to be inaccurate.

The first of these is the apparently widespread assumption that most people are relatively unhappy. Writers, social scientists, and the general public seem to believe that people around the world are predominantly dissatisfied, yet empirical surveys consistently find that the vast majority of respondents—even those who are poor or disabled—characterize themselves as fairly happy (Diener & Diener, 1996). When people are asked to rate their happiness, only a small minority place themselves below the neutral point on the various scales used (see **Figure 1.8**). When the average subjective well-being of entire nations is computed, based on almost 1000 surveys, the means cluster toward the positive end of the scale, as shown in **Figure 1.9** on the next page (Veenhoven, 1993). That's not to say that everyone is equally happy. Researchers have found substantial and thought-provoking disparities among people in subjective well-being, which we will analyze momentarily. But the overall picture seems rosier than anticipated.

What Isn't Very Important?

Let us begin our discussion of individual differences in happiness by highlighting those things that turn out to be relatively unimportant determinants of subjective well-being. Quite a number of factors that one might expect to be influential appear to bear little or no relationship to general happiness.

Money. Most people think that if they had more money, they would be happier. There *is* a positive correlation between income and feelings of happiness, but the association is surprisingly weak (Diener & Seligman, 2004). For example, one study found a correlation of just .13 between income and happiness in the United States (Diener et al., 1993), and another more recent investigation yielded an almost identical correlation of .12 (Johnson & Krueger, 2006). Admittedly,

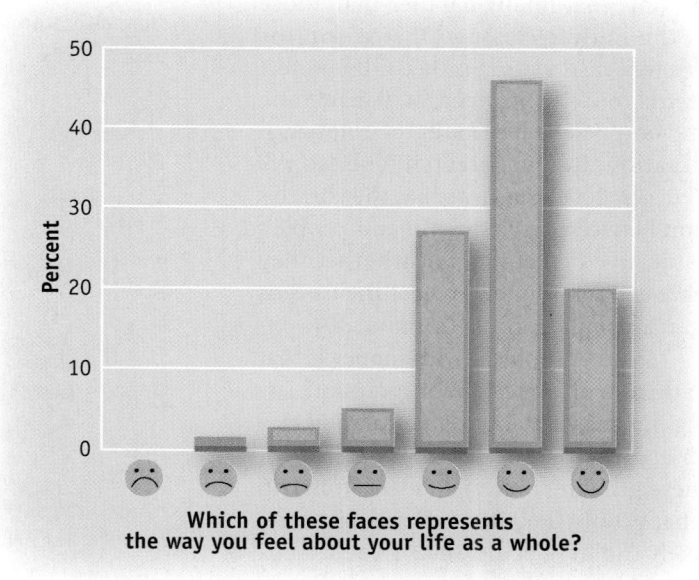

Figure1.8

Measuring happiness with a nonverbal scale. Researchers have used a variety of methods to estimate the distribution of happiness. For example, in one study in the United States, respondents were asked to examine the seven facial expressions shown and to select the one that "comes closest to expressing how you feel about your life as a whole." As you can see, the vast majority of participants chose happy faces. (Data adapted from Myers, 1992)

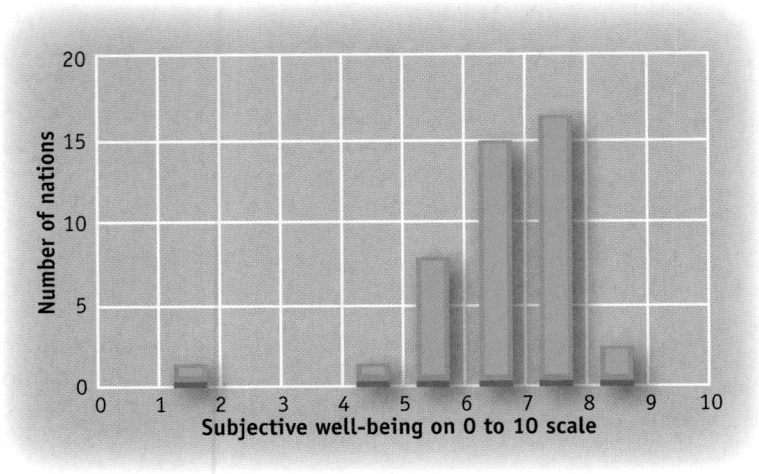

Figure1.9

The subjective well-being of nations. Veenhoven (1993) combined the results of almost 1000 surveys to calculate the average subjective well-being reported by representative samples from 43 nations. The mean happiness scores clearly pile up at the positive end of the distribution, with only two scores falling below the neutral point of 5. (Data adapted from Diener and Diener, 1996)

being very poor can make people unhappy, but once people ascend above the poverty level, there is little relation between income and happiness. On the average, even very wealthy people are only marginally happier than those in the middle classes. One reason for this weak association is that a disconnect seems to exist between actual income and how people feel about their financial situation. Recent research (Johnson & Krueger, 2006) suggests that the correlation between actual wealth and people's subjective perceptions of whether they have enough money to meet their needs is surprisingly modest (around .30).

Another problem with money is that in this era of voracious consumption, rising income contributes to escalating material desires (Frey & Stutzer, 2002). When these growing material desires outstrip what people can afford, dissatisfaction is likely (Solberg et al., 2002). Thus, complaints about not having enough money are routine even among people who earn hefty six-figure incomes. Interestingly, there is some evidence that people who place an especially strong emphasis on the pursuit of wealth and materialistic goals tend to be somewhat less happy than others (Ryan & Deci, 2001; Van Boven, 2005). Perhaps they are so focused on financial success that they derive less satisfaction from other aspects of their lives (Nickerson et al, 2003). Consistent with this view, a recent study (Kahneman et al., 2006) found that higher income was associated with working longer hours and allocating fewer hours to leisure pursuits (see **Figure 1.10**). Insofar as money does foster happiness, it appears to do so by reducing the negative impact of life's setbacks, allowing wealthier people to feel like they have a little more control over their lives (Johnson & Krueger, 2006; Smith et al., 2005).

Age. Age and happiness are consistently found to be unrelated (Lykken, 1999). Age accounts for less than 1% of the variation in people's happiness (Inglehart, 1990; Myers & Diener, 1997). The key factors influencing subjective well-being may shift some as people grow older—work becomes less important, health more so—but people's average level of happiness tends to remain remarkably stable over the life span.

Gender. Women are treated for depressive disorders about twice as often as men (Nolen-Hoeksema, 2002), so one might expect that women are less happy on the

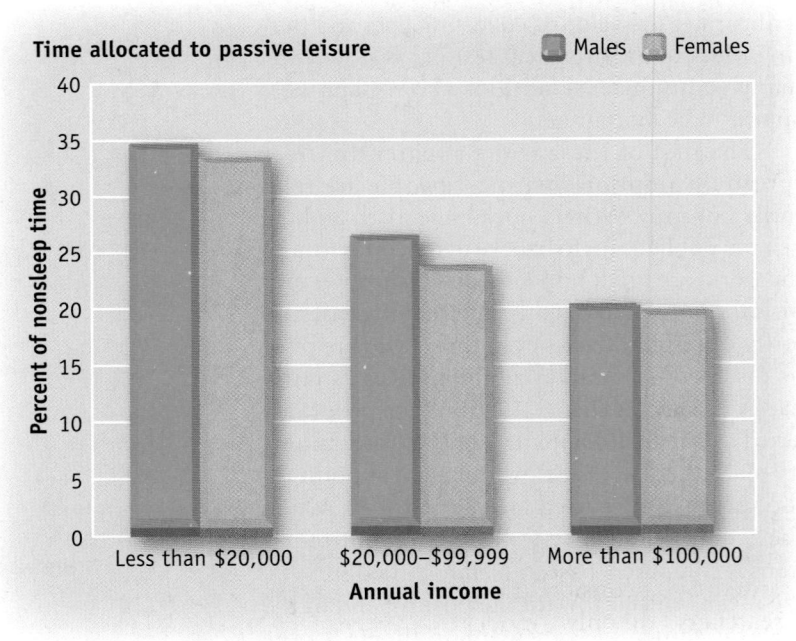

Figure1.10

Income and leisure. In an influential study of happiness, Nobel laureate Daniel Kahneman and his colleagues (2006) attempted to shed light on why the association between income and subjective well-being is so weak. One of their key findings was that as income goes up, the time devoted to work increases, and hence, the time left for leisure declines. This graph shows the percentage of nonsleep time devoted to passive leisure activities for three levels of income. (Data from Kahneman et al., 2006) average. And Lykken (1999) notes that "men still tend to have better jobs than women do, and get higher pay for the same jobs . . . but they [women] report well-being levels as high as those of men" (p. 181). Thus, like age, gender accounts for less than 1% of the variation in people's subjective well-being (Myers, 1992).

Parenthood. Children can be a tremendous source of joy and fulfillment, but they can also be a tremendous source of headaches and hassles. Compared to childless couples, parents worry more and experience more marital problems (Argyle, 1987). Apparently, the good and bad aspects of parenthood balance each other out, because the evidence indicates that people who have children are neither more nor less happy than people without children (Argyle, 2001).

Intelligence. Intelligence is a highly valued trait in modern society, but researchers have not found an association between IQ scores and happiness (Diener, 1984). Educational attainment also appears to be unrelated to life satisfaction (Ross & Van Willigen, 1997).

Physical attractiveness. Good-looking people enjoy a variety of advantages in comparison to unattractive people. Given that physical attractiveness is an important resource in Western society, we might expect attractive people to be happier than others, but the available data indicate that the correlation between attractiveness and happiness is negligible (Diener, Wolsic, & Fujita, 1995).

What Is Somewhat Important?

Research has identified three facets of life that appear to have a moderate impact on subjective well-being: health, social activity, and religious belief.

Health. Good physical health would seem to be an essential requirement for happiness, but people adapt to health problems. Research reveals that individuals who develop serious, disabling health conditions aren't as unhappy as one might guess (Myers, 1992; Riis et al., 2005). Good health may not, by itself, produce happiness, because people tend to take good health for granted. Such considerations may help explain why researchers find only a moderate positive correlation (average = .32) between health status and subjective well-being (Argyle, 1999).

Social activity. Humans are social animals, and people's interpersonal relations *do* appear to contribute to their happiness. People who are satisfied with their friendship networks and who are socially active report above-average levels of happiness (Diener & Seligman, 2004; Myers, 1999). And people who score as exceptionally happy tend to report greater satisfaction with their social relations than others (Diener & Seligman, 2002).

Religion. The link between religiosity and subjective well-being is modest, but a number of surveys suggest that people with heartfelt religious convictions are more likely to be happy than people who characterize themselves as nonreligious (Abdel-Khalek, 2006; Argyle, 1999; Ferriss, 2002). Researchers aren't sure how religious faith fosters happiness, but Myers (1992) offers some interesting conjectures. Among other things, he discusses how religion can give people a sense of purpose and meaning in their lives, help them accept their setbacks gracefully, connect them to a caring, supportive community, and comfort them by putting their ultimate mortality in perspective.

The Pursuit of Happiness
by David G. Myers (William Morrow, 1992)

The Pursuit of Happiness provides a thorough, accurate review of empirical research on the determinants of happiness, seasoned nicely with personal anecdotes and low-key, practical advice. Myers is a respected social psychologist and hard-nosed scientist who acknowledges that his reflections on happiness are "colored by Christian values and spirituality." Emphasizing the finding that objective circumstances have limited impact on happiness, Myers discusses how people might alter their subjective assessments of their lives to foster greater happiness. Working from the insight that happiness is relative, he offers suggestions for managing our comparisons to others and restraining our expectations to enhance our well-being.

Myers's book is a superb example of what self-help books could and should be, but rarely are. It is clearly written and appropriately cautious about the limits of our knowledge. It is carefully documented, and assertions are closely tied to research and theory. The author's conjectures—which are often fascinating—are accurately presented as learned speculation rather than scientific fact, and readers are encouraged to think for themselves. Complicated issues are not reduced to sound bites and bumper sticker slogans. Myers does not encourage a self-centered approach to life (quite the opposite!), nor does he offer simple prescriptions about how to live. Given these realities, *The Pursuit of Happiness* has not topped any best-seller lists, but it is well worth reading.

What Is Very Important?

The list of factors that turn out to be very important ingredients of happiness is surprisingly short. Only a few variables are strongly related to overall happiness.

Love and marriage. Romantic relationships can be stressful, but people consistently rate being in love as one of the most critical ingredients of happiness (Myers, 1999). Furthermore, although people complain a lot about their marriages, the evidence indicates that marital status is a key correlate of happiness. Among both men and women, married people are happier than people who are single or divorced (see **Figure 1.11**; Myers & Diener, 1995) and this relationship holds around the world in widely different cultures (Diener et al., 2000). However, the causal relations underlying this correlation are unclear. It may be that happiness causes marital satisfaction more than marital satisfaction promotes happiness. Perhaps people who are happy tend to have better intimate relationships and more stable marriages, while people who are unhappy have greater difficulty finding and keeping mates.

Work. Given the way people often complain about their jobs, we might not expect work to be a key source of happiness, but it is. Although less critical than love and marriage, job satisfaction is strongly associated with general happiness (Warr, 1999). Studies also show that unemployment has strong negative effects on subjective well-being (Lucas et al., 2004). It is difficult to sort out whether job satisfaction causes happiness or vice versa, but evidence suggests that causation flows both ways (Argyle, 2001).

Genetics and personality. The best predictor of individuals' future happiness is their past happiness (Diener & Lucas, 1999). Some people seem destined to be happy and others unhappy, regardless of their triumphs or setbacks. The limited influence of life events was highlighted in a fascinating study that found only modest differences in overall happiness between recent lottery winners and recent accident victims who became quadriplegics (Brickman, Coates, & Janoff-Bulman, 1978). Investigators were amazed that extremely fortuitous and horrible events like these didn't have a dramatic impact on happiness. Actually, *several* lines of evidence suggest that happiness does not depend on external circumstances—buying a nice house, getting promoted—as much as on internal factors, such as one's outlook on life (Lykken & Tellegen, 1996; Lyubomirsky, Sheldon, & Schkade, 2005).

With this reality in mind, researchers have investigated whether there might be a hereditary basis for variations in happiness. These studies suggest that people's genetic predispositions account for a substantial portion of the variance in happiness, perhaps as much as 50% (Lyubomirsky et al., 2005; Stubbe et al., 2005). How can one's genes influence one's happiness? Presumably, by shaping one's temperament and personality, which are known to be highly heritable. Hence, researchers have begun to look for links between personality and subjective well-being, and they have found some relatively strong correlations. For example, *extraversion* (sometimes referred to as *positive emotionality*) is one of the better predictors of happiness. People who are outgoing, upbeat, and sociable tend to be happier than others (Fleeson, Malanos, & Achille, 2002). Additional personality correlates of happiness include high

Figure1.11

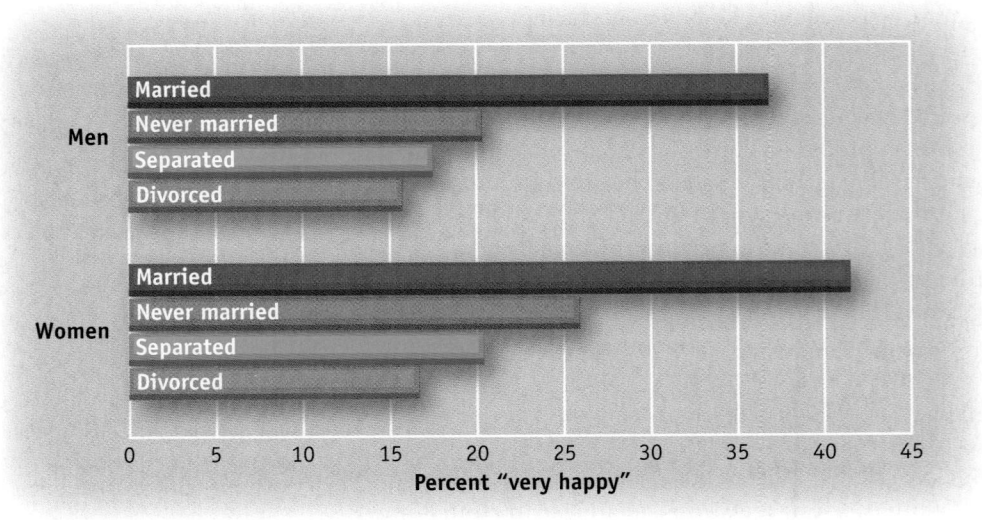

Happiness and marital status. This graph shows the percentage of adults characterizing themselves as "very happy" as a function of marital status. Among both women and men, happiness shows up more in those who are married as opposed to those who are separated, who are divorced, or who have never married. These data and many other findings suggest that marital satisfaction is a key ingredient of happiness.

Adapted from Myers, D. G. (1999). Close relationships and quality of life. In D. Kahneman, E. Diener, & N. Schwarz (Eds.), *Well-being: The foundations of hedonic psychology*. New York: Russell Sage Foundation. Copyright © 1999. Reprinted by permission of the Russell Sage Foundation.

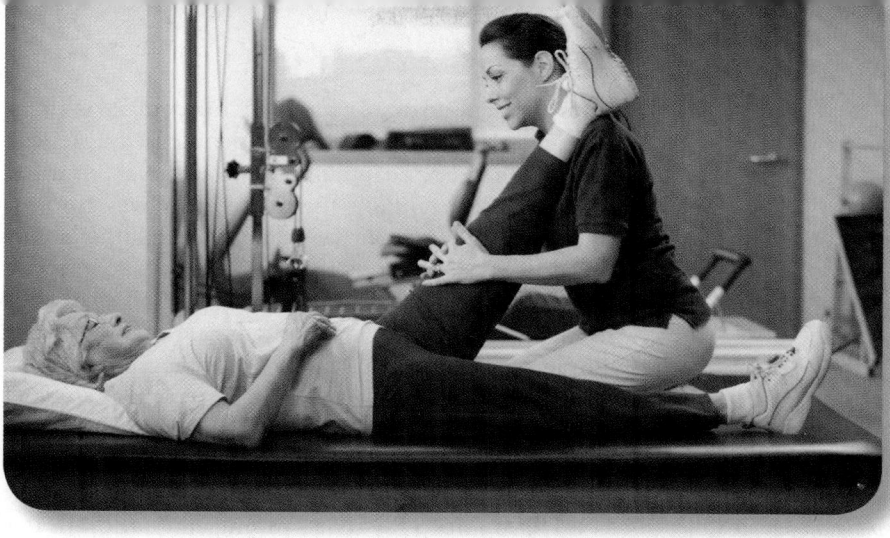

© Anderson Ross/Digital Vision/Getty Images

© Javier Pierini/Taxi/Getty Images

Research on the correlates of happiness suggests that two key ingredients of happiness are a rewarding work life and satisfaction in intimate relationships.

self-esteem and optimism (Lucas, Diener, & Suh, 1996; Lyubomirsky, Tkach, & DiMatteo, 2006).

Conclusions

We must be cautious in drawing inferences about the causes of happiness, because most of the available data are correlational data (see **Figure 1.12**). Nonetheless, the empirical evidence suggests that many popular beliefs about the sources of happiness are unfounded. The data also demonstrate that happiness is shaped by a complex constellation of variables. Despite this complexity, however, a number of worthwhile insights about human adjustment can be gleaned from research on the correlates of subjective well-being.

First, research on happiness demonstrates that the determinants of subjective well-being are precisely that: subjective. *Objective realities are not as important as subjective feelings.* In other words, your health, your wealth, your job, and your age are not as influential as how you *feel* about your health, wealth, job, and age (Schwarz & Strack, 1999).

Second, *when it comes to happiness, everything is relative* (Argyle, 1999; Hagerty, 2000). In other words, you evaluate what you have relative to what the people around you have. Thus, people who are wealthy assess what they have by comparing themselves with their wealthy friends and neighbors. This is one reason for the low correlation between wealth and happiness. You might have a lovely home, but if it sits next to a neighbor's palatial mansion, it might be a source of more dissatisfaction than happiness. People's evaluations are also made relative to their *expectations.* Research suggests that bad outcomes feel worse when unexpected than when expected, while good outcomes feel better when unexpected than when expected (Shepperd & McNulty, 2002). Thus, the same objective event, such as a pay raise of $2000 annually, may generate positive feelings in someone who wasn't expecting a raise and negative feelings in someone expecting a much larger increase.

Third, *research on happiness has shown that people are surprisingly bad at predicting what will make them happy.* We assume that we know what is best for us and that we can accurately forecast our emotional reactions to future events, but scores of studies suggest otherwise (Gilbert, 2006; Hsee & Hastie, 2005; Wilson & Gilbert, 2005). People routinely overestimate the pleasure that they will derive from buying an expensive automobile, taking an exotic vacation, earning an important promotion, moving to a beautiful coastal city, or building their dream home. Likewise, people tend to overestimate the misery and regret that they will experience if

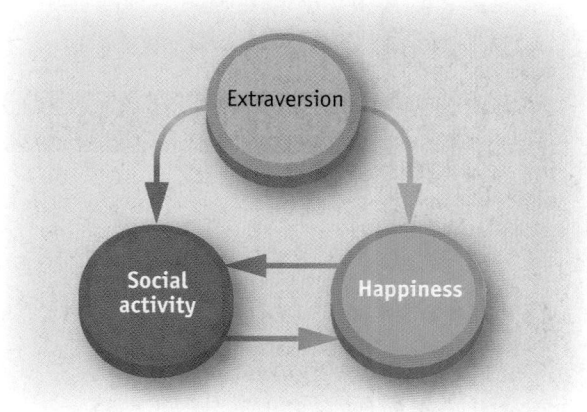

Figure1.12

Possible causal relations among the correlates of happiness. Although we have considerable data on the correlates of happiness, it is difficult to untangle the possible causal relationships. For example, we know that a moderate positive correlation exists between social activity and happiness, but we can't say for sure whether high social activity causes happiness or whether happiness causes people to be more socially active. Moreover, in light of the finding that a third variable—extraversion—correlates with both variables, we have to consider the possibility that extraversion causes both greater social activity and greater happiness.

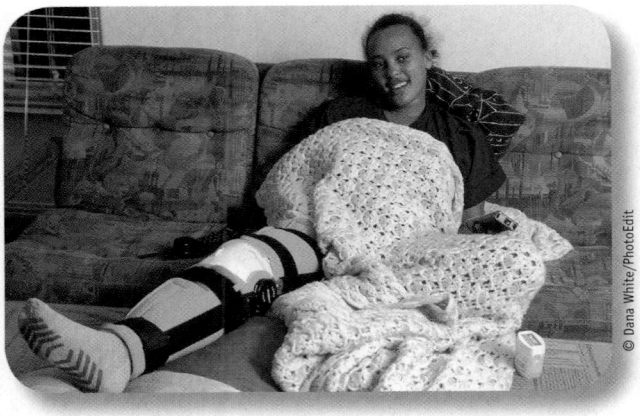

Research shows that happiness does not depend on people's positive and negative experiences as much as one would expect. Some people, presumably because of their personality, seem destined to be happy in spite of major setbacks, and others seem destined to cling to unhappiness even though their lives seem reasonably pleasant.

they experience a romantic breakup, don't get into the college they want, fail to get a promotion, or develop a serious illness. Thus, the roadmap to happiness is less clearly marked than widely assumed.

Fourth, *research on subjective well-being indicates that people often adapt to their circumstances.* This adaptation effect is one reason that an increase in income doesn't necessarily bring an increase in happiness. Thus, ***hedonic adaptation* occurs when the mental scale that people use to judge the pleasantness-unpleasantness of their experiences shifts so that their neutral point, or baseline for comparison, is changed.** Unfortunately, when people's experiences improve, hedonic adaptation may *sometimes* put them on a *hedonic treadmill*—their baseline moves upward, so that the improvements yield no real benefits (Kahneman, 1999). However, when people have to grapple with major setbacks, hedonic adaptation probably helps protect their mental and physical health. For example, people who are sent to prison and people who develop debilitating diseases are not as unhappy as one might assume because they adapt to their changed situations and evaluate events from a new perspective (Frederick & Loewenstein, 1999).

That's not to say that hedonic adaptation in the face of life's difficulties is inevitable or complete (Lucas et al., 2003). People who suffer major setbacks, such as the death of a spouse or serious illness, often are not as happy as they were before the setback, but generally they are not nearly as unhappy as they or others would have predicted (Diener & Oishi, 2005). The downside to the concept of hedonic adaptation is that it suggests that there is nothing people can do to increase their happiness. Fortunately, recent research on the hedonic treadmill is not as pessimistic as earlier research (Diener, Lucas, & Scollon, 2006). Although, this research has provided additional evidence that the hedonic treadmill is a genuine and common phenomenon, it has also shown that people vary considerably in the degree to which they experience hedonic adaptation and that enduring increases in individuals' set points for happiness can be achieved.

APPLICATION

Improving Academic Performance

LEARNING OBJECTIVES

- *List three steps for developing sound study habits.*
- *Describe the SQ3R method of effective reading.*
- *Summarize advice on how to get more out of lectures.*
- *Summarize how memory is influenced by practice, interference, depth of processing, and organization.*
- *Describe several verbal and visual mnemonic devices.*

Answer the following "true" or "false."

___ **1.** If you have a professor who delivers chaotic, hard-to-follow lectures, there is little point in attending class.

___ **2.** Cramming the night before an exam is an efficient way to study.

___ **3.** In taking lecture notes, you should try to be a "human tape recorder" (that is, take down everything exactly as said by your professor).

___ **4.** Outlining reading assignments is a waste of time.

As you will soon learn, all of these statements are false. If you answered them all correctly, you may already have acquired the kinds of skills and habits that lead to academic success. If so, however, you are not typical. Today, a huge number of students enter college with remarkably poor study skills and habits—and it's not entirely their fault. The U.S. educational system generally does not provide much in the way of formal instruction on good study techniques. In this first Application, we will try to remedy this deficiency to some extent by sharing some insights that psychology can provide on how to improve your academic performance. We will discuss how to promote better study habits, how to enhance reading efforts, how to get more out of lectures, and how to make your memory more effective.

Developing Sound Study Habits

Effective study is crucial to success in college. You may run into a few classmates who boast about getting good grades without studying, but you can be sure that if they perform well on exams, they study. Students who claim otherwise simply want to be viewed as extremely bright rather than as studious.

Learning can be immensely gratifying, but studying usually involves hard work. The first step toward effective study habits is to face this reality. You don't have to feel guilty if you don't look forward to studying. Most students don't. Once you accept the premise that studying doesn't come naturally, it should be clear that you need to set up an organized program to promote adequate study. Such a program should include the following three considerations (Siebert, 1995).

Set up a schedule for studying. Research on the differences between successful and unsuccessful college students suggests that successful students monitor and regulate their use of time more effectively (Allgood et al., 2000). If you wait until the urge to study hits you, you may still be waiting when the exam rolls around. Thus, it is important to allocate definite times to studying. Review your time obligations (work, housekeeping, and so on) and figure out in advance when you can study. In allotting certain times to studying, keep in mind that you need to be wide awake and alert. Be realistic, too, about how long you can study at one time before you wear down from fatigue. Allow time for study breaks; they can revive sagging concentration.

It's important to write down your study schedule. Doing so serves as a reminder and increases your commitment to the schedule. As shown in **Figure 1.13** on the next page, you should begin by setting up a general schedule for the quarter or semester. Then, at the beginning of each week, plan the specific assignments that you intend to work on during each study session. This approach should help you to avoid cramming for exams at the last minute.

In planning your weekly schedule, try to avoid the tendency to put off working on major tasks such as term papers and reports. Time management experts such as Alan Lakein (1996) point out that many of us tend to tackle simple, routine tasks first, saving larger tasks for later, when we supposedly will have more time. This common tendency leads many of us to delay working on major assignments until it's too late to do a good job. You can avoid this trap by breaking major assignments into smaller component tasks that you schedule individually.

Find a place to study where you can concentrate. Where you study is also important. The key is to find a place where distractions are likely to be minimal. Most people cannot study effectively while watching TV, listening to loud music, or overhearing conversations. Don't depend on willpower to carry you through these distractions. It's much easier to plan ahead and avoid the distractions altogether. Some learning theorists believe that it is wise to set up one or two specific places used solely for study (Hettich, 1998).

Reward your studying. One of the reasons it is so difficult to motivate oneself to study regularly is that the payoffs for studying often lie in the distant future. The ultimate reward, a degree, may be years away. Even shorter-term rewards, such as an A in the course, may be weeks or months off. To combat this problem, it helps to give yourself immediate rewards for studying. It is easier to motivate yourself to study if you reward yourself with a tangible payoff, such as a snack, TV show, or phone call to a friend, when you finish. Thus, you should set realistic study goals and then reward yourself when you meet them. This systematic manipulation of rewards involves harnessing the principles of *behavior modification,* which are described in some detail in the Chapter 4 Application.

Improving Your Reading

Much of your study time is spent reading and absorbing information. *These efforts must be active.* If you engage in passive reading, the information will pass right through you. Many students deceive themselves into thinking that they are studying if they run a marker through a few sentences here and there in their text. If such highlighting isn't done with thoughtful selectivity, the student is simply turning a textbook into a coloring book. Research suggests that highlighting selected textbook material *is* a useful strategy—if students are reasonably effective in identifying the main ideas in the material and if they subsequently review the main

Web Link 1.6 **Sites to Promote Academic Success**

This site provides links to a number of other sites that provide advice on a diverse array of study-related topics, such as time management, effective note taking, memory-improvement strategies, and test-taking skills. Developed by Linda Walsh, a psychology professor at the University of Northern Iowa, it is an invaluable resource for students seeking to improve their chances of academic success.

	Mon	Tues	Wed	Thurs	Fri	Sat	Sun
8 A.M.						Work	
9 A.M.	History	Study	History	Study	History	Work	
10 A.M.	Psych		Psych		Psych	Work	
11 A.M.	Study	French	Study	French	Study	Work	
Noon	Math	Study	Math	Study	Math	Work	Study
1 P.M.							Study
2 P.M.	Study		Study		Study		Study
3 P.M.	Study	English	Study	English	Study		Study
4 P.M.							
5 P.M.							
6 P.M.	Work	Study	Work				Study
7 P.M.	Work	Study	Work				Study
8 P.M.	Work	Study	Work				Study
9 P.M.	Work	Study	Work				Study
10 P.M.	Work		Work				

Figure1.13

Example of an activity schedule. One student's general activity schedule for a semester is shown here. Each week the student fills in the specific assignments to work on during the upcoming study sessions.

ideas they have highlighted (Caverly, Orlando, & Mullen, 2000).

You can choose from a number of methods for actively attacking your reading assignments. One of the more worthwhile strategies is Robinson's (1970) SQ3R method. ***SQ3R* is a study system designed to promote effective reading that includes five steps: survey, question, read, recite, and review.** Its name is an abbreviation for the five steps in the procedure:

Step 1: Survey

Before you plunge into the actual reading, glance over the topic headings in the chapter and try to get an overview of the material. Try to understand how the various chapter segments are related. If there is a chapter outline or summary, consult it to get a feel for the chapter. If you know where the chapter is going, you can better appreciate and organize the information you are about to read.

Step 2: Question

Once you have an overview of your reading assignment, proceed through it one section at a time. Take a look at the heading of the first section and convert it into a question. This is usually quite simple. If the heading is "Prenatal Risk Factors," your question should be "What are sources of risk during prenatal development?" If the heading is "Stereotyping," your question should be "What is stereotyping?" Asking these questions gets you actively involved in your reading and helps you identify the main ideas.

Step 3: Read

Only now, in the third step, are you ready to sink your teeth into the reading. Read only the specific section that you have decided to tackle. Read it with an eye toward answering the question that you just formulated. If necessary, reread the section until you can answer that question. Decide whether the segment addresses any other important questions and answer them as well.

Step 4: Recite

Now that you can answer the key question for the section, recite it out loud to yourself. Use your own words for the answer, because that requires understanding instead of simple memorization. Don't move on to the next section until you understand the main idea(s) of the current section. You may want to write down these ideas for review later. When you have fully digested the first section, go on to the next. Repeat steps 2 through 4 with the next section. Once you have mastered the crucial points there, you can continue. Keep repeating steps 2 through 4, section by section, until you finish the chapter.

Step 5: Review

When you have read the chapter, test and refresh your memory by going back over the key points. Repeat your questions and try to answer them without consulting your book or notes. This review should fortify your retention of the main ideas and alert you to any

© JFB/Stone/Getty Images

Although some students downplay the importance of study efforts, the reality is that effective study habits are crucial to academic success.

key ideas that you haven't mastered. It should also help you to see the relationships between the main ideas.

The SQ3R method does not have to be applied rigidly. For example, it is often wise to break your reading assignment into smaller segments than those separated by section headings. In fact, you should probably apply SQ3R to many texts on a paragraph by paragraph basis. Obviously, doing so will require you to formulate some questions without the benefit of topic headings. However, the headings are not absolutely necessary to use this technique. If you don't have enough headings, you can simply reverse the order of steps 2 and 3. Read the paragraph first and then formulate a question that addresses the basic idea of the paragraph. The point is that you can be flexible in your use of the SQ3R technique.

Using the SQ3R method does not automatically lead to improved mastery of textbook reading assignments. It won't be effective unless it is applied diligently and skillfully and it tends to be more helpful to students with low to medium reading ability (Caverly, Orlando, & Mullen, 2000). Any strategy that facilitates active processing of text material, the identification of key ideas, and effective review of these ideas should enhance your reading.

Getting More Out of Lectures

Although lectures are sometimes boring and tedious, it is a simple fact that poor class attendance is associated with poor grades. For example, in one study, Lindgren (1969) found that absences from class were much more common among "unsuccessful" students (grade average of C– or below) than among "successful" students (grade average of B or above), as is shown in **Figure 1.14**. Even when you have an instructor who delivers hard-to-follow lectures from which you learn virtually nothing, it is still important to go to class. If nothing else, you'll get a feel for how the instructor thinks. Doing so can help you anticipate the content of exams and respond in the manner your professor expects.

Fortunately, most lectures are reasonably coherent. Studies indicate that attentive note taking *is* associated with enhanced learning and performance in college classes (Titsworth & Kiewra, 2004; Williams & Eggert, 2002). However, research also shows that many students' lecture notes are surprisingly incomplete, with the average student often recording less than 40% of the crucial ideas in a lecture (Armbruster, 2000). Thus, the key to getting more out of lectures is to stay motivated, stay attentive, and expend the effort to make your notes as complete as possible. Books on study skills (Longman & Atkinson, 2005; Sotiriou, 2002) offer a number of suggestions on how to take good-quality lecture notes. These suggestions include:

- Use *active listening procedures.* With active listening, you focus full attention on the speaker. Try to anticipate what's coming and search for deeper meanings. Pay attention to nonverbal signals that may serve to further clarify the lecturer's intent or meaning.
- When course material is especially complex and difficult, it is a good idea to prepare for the lecture by reading ahead on the scheduled subject in your text. Then you have less information to digest that is brand new.
- Don't try to be a human tape recorder. Instead, try to write down the lecturer's thoughts in your own words. Doing so forces you to organize the ideas in a way that makes sense to you. In taking notes, look for subtle and not-so-subtle clues about what the instructor considers to be important. These clues may range from simply repeating main points to saying things like "You'll run into this again."
- Ask questions during lectures. Doing so keeps you actively involved and allows you to clarify points you may have misunderstood. Many students are more bashful about asking questions than they should be. They don't realize that most professors welcome questions.

Applying Memory Principles

Scientific investigation of memory processes dates back to 1885, when Hermann Ebbinghaus published a series

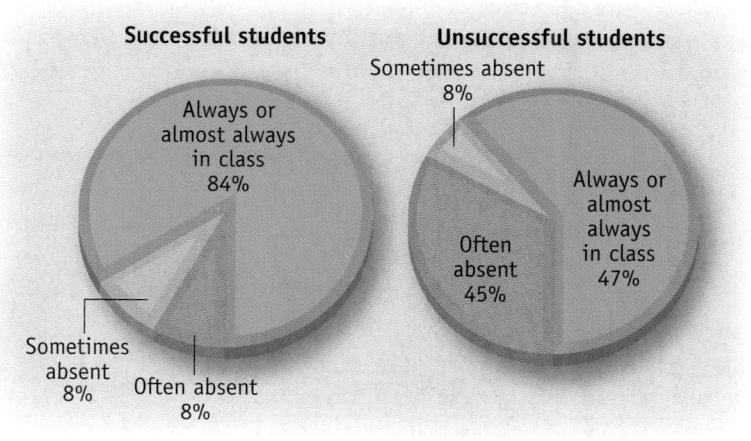

Figure 1.14

Successful and unsuccessful students' class attendance. Lindgren (1969) found that attendance was much better among successful students than unsuccessful students. (Data from Lindgren, 1969)

of insightful studies. Since then, psychologists have discovered a number of principles about memory that are relevant to helping you improve your study skills.

Engage in Adequate Practice

Practice makes perfect, or so you've heard. In reality, practice is not likely to guarantee perfection, but repeatedly reviewing information usually leads to improved retention. Studies show that retention improves with increased rehearsal (Greene, 1992). Continued rehearsal may also pay off by improving your *understanding* of assigned material (Bromage & Mayer, 1986). Although the benefits of practice are well known, people have a curious tendency to overestimate their knowledge of a topic and how well they will perform on a subsequent memory test of this knowledge (Koriat & Bjork, 2005). That's why it is a good idea to informally test yourself on information that you think you have mastered before confronting a real test (for example, by taking the Practice Tests in this text or additional tests available on the website for the book).

Evidence suggests that it even pays to overlearn material (Driskell, Wilis, & Copper, 1992). ***Overlearning* is continued rehearsal of material after you have first appeared to master it.** In one study, after participants mastered a list of nouns (they recited the list without error), Krueger (1929) required them to continue rehearsing for 50% or 100% more trials (repetitions). Measuring retention at intervals of up to 28 days, Kreuger found that overlearning led to better recall of the list. Modern studies have also shown that overlearning can enhance performance on an exam that occurs within a week, although the evidence on its long-term benefits (months later) is inconsistent (Peladeau, Forget, & Gagne, 2003; Rohrer et al., 2005).

Use Distributed Practice

Let's assume that you are going to study 9 hours for an exam. Is it better to "cram" all of your study into one 9-hour period (massed practice) or distribute it among, say, three 3-hour periods on successive days (distributed practice)? The evidence indicates that retention tends to be greater after distributed practice than massed practice (Payne & Wenger, 1996; Seabrook, Brown, & Solity, 2005). This advantage is especially apparent if the intervals between practice periods are fairly long, such as 24 hours (Zechmeister & Nyberg, 1982). The inefficiency of massed practice means that cramming is an ill-advised study strategy for most students (Dempster, 1996). Cramming will strain your memorization capabilities and tax your energy level. It may also stoke the fires of test anxiety.

Organize Information

Retention tends to be greater when information is well organized (Einstein & McDaniel, 2004). Hierarchical organization is particularly helpful when it is applicable (Tigner, 1999). Thus, it may be a good idea to *outline* reading assignments for school. Consistent with this reasoning, there is some empirical evidence that outlining material from textbooks can enhance retention of the material (McDaniel, Waddill, & Shakesby, 1996).

Emphasize Deep Processing

Research suggests that how *often* you go over material is less critical than the *depth* of processing that you engage in (Craik & Tulving, 1975). Thus, if you expect to remember what you read, you have to wrestle fully with its meaning (Einstein & McDaniel, 2004). Many students could probably benefit if they spent less time on rote repetition and devoted more effort to actually paying attention to and analyzing the meaning of their reading assignments. In particular, it is useful to make material *personally* meaningful. When you read your textbooks, try to relate information to your own life and experience. For example, if you're reading in your psychology text about the personality trait of assertiveness, you can think about which people you know who

DOONESBURY © G. B. Trudeau. Reprinted with permission of UNIVERSAL PRESS SYNDICATE. All rights reserved.

are particularly assertive and why you would characterize them as being that way.

Use Verbal Mnemonics

Of course, it's not always easy to make something personally meaningful. When you study chemistry, you may have a hard time relating to polymers at a personal level. This problem has led to the development of many ***mnemonic devices,* or strategies for enhancing memory,** that are designed to make abstract material more meaningful.

Acrostics and acronyms. *Acrostics* are phrases (or poems) in which the first letter of each word (or line) functions as a cue to help you recall the abstract words that begin with the same letter. For instance, you may remember the order of musical notes with the saying "Every good boy does fine" (or "deserves favor"). A variation on acrostics is the *acronym*—a word formed out of the first letters of a series of words. Students memorizing the order of colors in the light spectrum often store the name "Roy G. Biv" to remember red, orange, yellow, green, blue, indigo, and violet. Acrostics and acronyms that individuals create for themselves can be effective memory tools (Hermann et al., 2002).

Rhymes. Another verbal mnemonic that people often rely on is rhyming. You've probably repeated, "I before E except after C" thousands of times. Perhaps you also remember the number of days in each month with the old standby, "Thirty days hath September . . ." Rhyming something to remember it is an old and useful trick.

Use Visual Mnemonics

Memory can be improved through the use of visual imagery. One influential theory (Paivio, 1986) proposes that visual images create a second memory code and that two codes are better than one. Many popular mnemonic devices depend on visual imagery, including the link method and the method of loci.

Link method. The *link method* involves forming a mental image of items to be remembered in a way that links them together. For instance, suppose that you are going to stop at the drugstore on the way home and you need to remember to pick up a news magazine, shaving cream, film, and pens. To remember these items, you might visualize a public figure likely to be in the magazine shaving with a pen while being photographed. Some researchers suggest that the more bizarre the images, the better they will be remembered (Iaccino, 1996; Worthen, 1997).

Method of loci. The *method of loci* involves taking an imaginary walk along a familiar path where you have associated images of items you want to remember with certain locations. The first step is to commit to memory a series of loci, or places along a path. Usually these loci are specific locations in your home or neighborhood. Then envision each thing you want to remember in one of these locations. Try to form distinctive, vivid images. When you need to remember the items, imagine yourself walking along the path. The various loci on your path should serve as retrieval cues for the images that you formed (see **Figure 1.15**). The method of loci assures that items are remembered in their correct order because the order is determined by the sequence of locations along the pathway. Empirical studies have supported the value of this method for memorizing lists (Moe & De Beni, 2004).

Figure 1.15

The method of loci. In this example from Bower (1970), a person about to go shopping pairs items to be remembered with familiar places (loci) arranged in a natural sequence: (1) hot dogs/driveway; (2) cat food/garage; (3) tomatoes/front door; (4) bananas/coat closet; (5) whiskey/kitchen sink. As the last panel shows, the shopper recalls the items by mentally touring the loci associated with them.

Adapted from Bower, G. H. (1970). Analysis of a mnemonic device. *American Scientist, 58,* 496–499. Copyright © 1970 by Scientific Research Society. Reprinted by permission.

KEY IDEAS

The Paradox of Progress

▶ Although our modern era has seen great technological progress, personal problems have not diminished. In spite of many time-saving devices, people tend to have less free time. Although affluence is widespread, most people worry about economic decline, and materialism seems to undermine well-being.

▶ The life choices available to people have increased greatly, but Schwartz argues that choice overload undermines individuals' happiness. Although we have unprecedented control over the world around us, we seem to create as many problems as we solve. Thus, many theorists argue that technological progress has brought new, and possibly more difficult, adjustment problems.

The Search for Direction

▶ According to many theorists, the basic challenge of modern life has become the search for a sense of direction and meaning. This search has many manifestations, including the appeal of self-realization programs, religious cults, and media "therapists" such as Dr. Laura.

▶ The enormous popularity of self-help books is an interesting manifestation of people's struggle to find a sense of direction. Some self-help books offer worthwhile advice, but most are dominated by psychobabble and are not based on scientific research. Many also lack explicit advice on how to change behavior and some encourage a self-centered approach to interpersonal interactions.

▶ Although this text deals with many of the same issues as self-realization programs, self-help books, and other types of pop psychology, its philosophy and approach are quite different.

The Psychology of Adjustment

▶ Psychology is both a science and a profession that focuses on behavior and related mental and physiological processes.

▶ Adjustment is a broad area of study in psychology concerned with how people adapt effectively or ineffectively to the demands and pressures of everyday life.

The Scientific Approach to Behavior

▶ The scientific approach to understanding behavior is empirical. Psychologists base their conclusions on formal, systematic, objective tests of their hypotheses, rather than reasoning, speculation, or common sense. The scientific approach is advantageous in that it puts a premium on clarity and has little tolerance for error.

▶ Experimental research involves manipulating an independent variable to discover its effects on a dependent variable. The experimenter usually does so by comparing experimental and control groups, which must be alike except for the variation created by the manipulation of the independent variable. Experiments permit conclusions about cause-effect relationships between variables, but this method isn't usable for the study of many questions.

▶ Psychologists conduct correlational research when they are unable to exert control over the variables they want to study. The correlation coefficient is a numerical index of the degree of relationship between two variables. Correlational research methods include naturalistic observation, case studies, and surveys. Correlational research facilitates the investigation of many issues that are not open to experimental study, but it cannot demonstrate that two variables are causally related.

The Roots of Happiness: An Empirical Analysis

▶ A scientific analysis of happiness reveals that many commonsense notions about the roots of happiness appear to be incorrect, including the notion that most people are unhappy. Factors such as money, age, gender, parenthood, intelligence, and attractiveness are not correlated with subjective well-being.

▶ Physical health, social relationships, and religious faith appear to have a modest impact on feelings of happiness. The only factors that are clearly and strongly related to happiness are love and marriage, work satisfaction, and personality, which probably reflects the influence of heredity.

▶ Happiness is a relative concept mediated by people's highly subjective assessments of their lives. People are surprisingly bad at predicting what will make them happy. Individuals adapt to both positive and negative events in their lives, which creates a hedonic treadmill effect.

Application: Improving Academic Performance

▶ To foster sound study habits, you should devise a written study schedule and reward yourself for following it. You should also try to find places for studying that are relatively free of distractions.

▶ You should use active reading techniques, such as SQ3R, to select the most important ideas from the material you read. Good note taking can help you get more out of lectures. It's important to use active listening techniques and to record lecturers' ideas in your own words.

▶ Rehearsal, even when it involves overlearning, facilitates retention. Distributed practice and deeper processing tend to improve memory. Evidence also suggests that organization facilitates retention, so outlining reading assignments can be valuable.

▶ Meaningfulness can be enhanced through the use of verbal mnemonics such as acrostics and acronyms. The link method and the method of loci are mnemonic devices that depend on the value of visual imagery.

KEY TERMS

Adjustment p. 12
Behavior p. 11
Case study p. 16
Clinical psychology p. 12
Control group p. 14
Correlation p. 15
Correlation coefficient p. 15
Dependent variable p. 13
Empiricism p. 12
Experiment p. 13
Experimental group p. 14
Hedonic adaptation p. 24
Independent variable p. 13
Mnemonic devices p. 29
Naturalistic observation p. 16
Overlearning p. 28
Psychology p. 11
SQ3R p. 26
Subjective well-being p. 19
Surveys p. 17

KEY PEOPLE

David Myers p. 21
Barry Schwartz pp. 2–3, 7
Martin Seligman p. 10

PRACTICE TEST

1. Technological advances have not led to perceptible improvement in our collective health and happiness. This statement defines
   a. escape from freedom.
   b. the point/counterpoint phenomenon.
   c. modern society.
   d. the paradox of progress.

2. Kasser argues that the correlation between happiness and materialism (a strong focus on money and possessions) is
   a. positive.
   b. negative.
   c. zero.
   d. about +1.24.

3. Which of the following is *not* offered in the text as a criticism of self-help books?
   a. They are infrequently based on solid research.
   b. Most don't provide explicit directions for changing behavior.
   c. The topics they cover are often quite narrow.
   d. Many are dominated by psychobabble.

4. The adaptation of animals when environments change is similar to _____ in humans.
   a. orientation
   b. assimilation
   c. evolution
   d. adjustment

5. An experiment is a research method in which the investigator manipulates the _____ variable and observes whether changes occur in a (an) _____ variable as a result.
   a. independent; dependent
   b. control; experimental
   c. experimental; control
   d. dependent; independent

6. A researcher wants to determine whether a certain diet causes children to learn better in school. In the study, the independent variable is
   a. the type of diet.
   b. a measure of learning performance.
   c. the age or grade level of the children.
   d. the intelligence level of the children.

7. A psychologist collected background information about a psychopathic killer, talked to him and people who knew him, and gave him psychological tests. Which research method was she using?
   a. Case study
   b. Naturalistic observation
   c. Survey
   d. Experiment

8. The principal advantage of experimental research is that
   a. it has a scientific basis and is therefore convincing to people.
   b. experiments replicate real-life situations.
   c. an experiment can be designed for any research problem.
   d. it allows the researcher to draw cause-and-effect conclusions.

9. Research has shown that which of the following is moderately correlated with happiness?
   a. Income
   b. Intelligence
   c. Parenthood
   d. Social activity

10. A good reason for taking notes in your own words, rather than verbatim, is that
    a. most lecturers are quite wordy.
    b. "translating" on the spot is good mental exercise.
    c. it reduces the likelihood that you'll later engage in plagiarism.
    d. it forces you to assimilate the information in a way that makes sense to you.

Book Companion Website

Visit the Book Companion Website at **academic.cengage.com/psychology/weiten,** where you will find tutorial quizzes, flash cards, and web links for every chapter, a final exam, and more! You can also link to the Psychology Resource Center (accessible directly at **academic.cengage.com/login**) for a range of psychology-related resources.

Personal Explorations Workbook

The following exercises in your *Personal Explorations Workbook* may enhance your self-understanding in relation to issues raised in this chapter. **Questionnaire 1.1:** Testwiseness Scale. **Personal Probe 1.1:** What Are Your Study Habits Like? **Personal Probe 1.2:** What Factors Affect Your Current Adjustment in Life?

ANSWERS

1. d Pages 1–3
2. b Page 1
3. c Pages 7–8
4. d Page 12
5. a Page 13
6. a Pages 13–14
7. a Pages 16–17
8. d Page 15
9. d Pages 19–21
10. d Page 27

CHAPTER 2

Theories of Personality

THE NATURE OF PERSONALITY
What Is Personality?
What Are Personality Traits?
The Five-Factor Model of Personality

PSYCHODYNAMIC PERSPECTIVES
Freud's Psychoanalytic Theory
Jung's Analytical Psychology
Adler's Individual Psychology
Evaluating Psychodynamic Perspectives

BEHAVIORAL PERSPECTIVES
Pavlov's Classical Conditioning
Skinner's Operant Conditioning
Bandura's Social Cognitive Theory
Evaluating Behavioral Perspectives

HUMANISTIC PERSPECTIVES
Rogers's Person-Centered Theory
Maslow's Theory of Self-Actualization
Evaluating Humanistic Perspectives

BIOLOGICAL PERSPECTIVES
Eysenck's Theory
Recent Research in Behavioral Genetics
The Evolutionary Approach to Personality
Evaluating Biological Perspectives

A CONTEMPORARY EMPIRICAL APPROACH: TERROR MANAGEMENT THEORY
Essentials of Terror Management Theory

LIVING IN TODAY'S WORLD *Understanding Reactions to Terrorist Attacks*
Applications of Terror Management Theory

CULTURE AND PERSONALITY

APPLICATION: ASSESSING YOUR PERSONALITY
Key Concepts in Psychological Testing
Self-Report Inventories
Projective Tests

REVIEW

PRACTICE TEST

Imagine that you are hurtling upward in an elevator with three other persons when suddenly a power blackout brings the elevator to a halt 45 stories above the ground. Your three companions might adjust to this predicament differently. One might crack jokes to relieve tension. Another might make ominous predictions that "we'll never get out of here." The third might calmly think about how to escape from the elevator. These varied ways of coping with the same stressful situation occur because each person has a different personality. Personality differences significantly influence people's patterns of adjustment. Thus, theories intended to explain personality can contribute to our effort to understand adjustment processes.

In this chapter, we will introduce you to various theories that attempt to explain the structure and development of personality. Our review of personality theory will also serve to acquaint you with four major theoretical perspectives in psychology: the psychodynamic, behavioral, humanistic, and biological perspectives. These theoretical approaches are conceptual models that help explain behavior. Familiarity with them will help you understand many of the ideas that you will encounter in this book, as well as in other books about psychology.

The Nature of Personality

LEARNING OBJECTIVES

- *Explain the concepts of personality and traits.*
- *Describe the "Big Five" personality traits.*

To discuss theories of personality effectively, we need to digress momentarily to come up with a definition of personality and to discuss the concept of personality traits.

What Is Personality?

What does it mean if you say that a friend has an optimistic personality? Your statement suggests that the person has a fairly *consistent tendency* to behave in a cheerful, hopeful, enthusiastic way, looking at the bright side of things, across a wide variety of situations. In a similar vein, if you note that a friend has an "outgoing" personality, you mean that she or he consistently behaves in a friendly, open, and extraverted manner in a variety of circumstances. Although no one is entirely consistent in his or her behavior, this quality of *consistency across situations* lies at the core of the concept of personality.

Distinctiveness is also central to the concept of personality. Everyone has traits seen in other people, but each individual has her or his own distinctive *set* of personality traits. Each person is unique. Thus, as illustrated by our elevator scenario, the concept of personality helps explain why people don't all act alike in the same situation.

In summary, we use the idea of personality to explain (1) the stability in a person's behavior over time and across situations (consistency) and (2) the behavioral differences among people reacting to the same situation (distinctiveness). We can combine these ideas into the following definition: ***personality* refers to an individual's unique constellation of consistent behavioral traits.** Let's look more closely at the concept of traits.

What Are Personality Traits?

We all make remarks like "Melanie is very *shrewd*" or "Doug is too *timid* to succeed in that job" or "I wish I could be as *self-assured* as Antonio." When we attempt to describe an individual's personality, we usually do so in terms of specific aspects of personality, called traits. **A *personality trait* is a durable disposition to behave in a particular way in a variety of situations.** Adjectives such as *honest, dependable, moody, impulsive, suspicious, anxious, excitable, domineering,* and *friendly* describe dispositions that represent personality traits.

Most trait theories of personality assume that some traits are more basic than others. According to this notion, a small number of fundamental traits determine other, more superficial traits. For example, a person's tendency to be impulsive, restless, irritable, boisterous, and impatient might all derive from a more basic tendency to be excitable.

A number of psychologists have taken on the challenge of identifying the basic traits that form the core of personality. For example, Raymond Cattell (1950, 1966, 1990) used the statistical procedure of *factor analysis* to reduce a list of 171 personality traits compiled by Gordon Allport (1937) to just 16 basic dimensions of personality. In ***factor analysis,* correlations among many variables are analyzed to identify closely related clusters of variables.** If the measurements of a number of variables (in this case, personality traits) correlate highly with one another, the assumption is that a single factor is influencing all of them. Factor analysis is used to identify these hidden factors. Based on his factor analytic work, Cattell concluded that an individual's personality can be described completely by measuring just 16 traits. The 16 crucial traits are listed in **Figure 2.24**, which can be found in the Application, where we discuss a personality test that Cattell designed to assess these traits.

The Five-Factor Model of Personality

In recent years, Robert McCrae and Paul Costa (1987, 1997, 1999, 2003) have used factor analysis to arrive at an even simpler five-factor model of personality. They argue that the vast majority of personality traits derive from just five higher-order traits that have come to be known as the "Big Five": extraversion, neuroticism, openness to experience, agreeableness, and conscientiousness (see **Figure 2.1** on the next page). Let's take a closer look at these traits:

1. *Extraversion.* People who score high in extraversion are characterized as outgoing, sociable, upbeat,

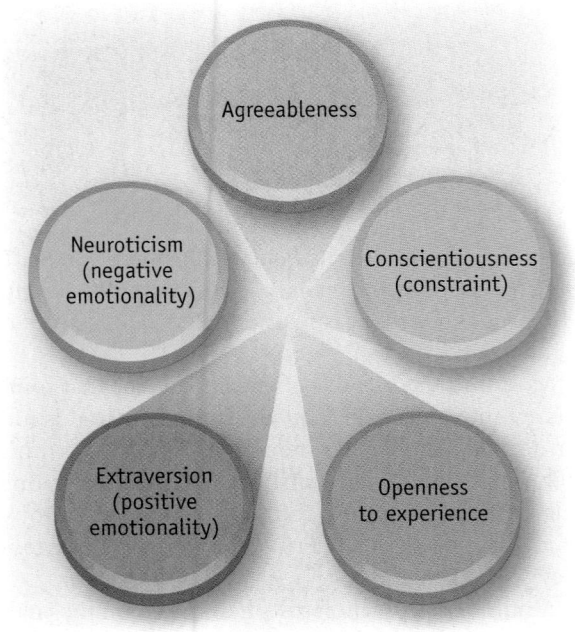

Figure 2.1

The five-factor model of personality. Trait models attempt to break down personality into its basic dimensions. McCrae and Costa (1987, 1997) maintain that personality can be described adequately with the five higher-order traits identified here, widely known as the Big Five traits.

friendly, assertive, and gregarious. Referred to as *positive emotionality* in some trait models, extraversion has been studied extensively in research for many decades (Watson & Clark, 1997).

2. *Neuroticism.* People who score high in neuroticism tend to be anxious, hostile, self-conscious, insecure, and vulnerable. Like extraversion, this trait has been the subject of thousands of studies. In some trait models it is called *negative emotionality.* Those who score high in neuroticism tend to overreact more in response to stress than others (Mroczek & Almeida, 2004).

3. *Openness to experience.* Openness is associated with curiosity, flexibility, vivid fantasy, imaginativeness, artistic sensitivity, and unconventional attitudes. McCrae (1996) maintains that the importance of this trait has been underestimated. Citing evidence that openness fosters liberalism, he argues that this trait is the key determinant of people's political attitudes and ideology.

4. *Agreeableness.* Those who score high in agreeableness tend to be sympathetic, trusting, cooperative, modest, and straightforward. People who score at the opposite end of this personality dimension are characterized as suspicious, antagonistic, and aggressive. Agreeableness may have its roots in childhood temperament and appears to promote altruistic (helping) behavior in social interactions (Graziano & Eisenberg, 1997).

5. *Conscientiousness.* Conscientious people tend to be diligent, disciplined, well organized, punctual, and dependable. Referred to as *constraint* in some trait models, conscientiousness is associated with higher productivity in a variety of occupational areas (Hogan & Ones, 1997) and with greater longevity (Bogg & Roberts, 2004).

Research shows that the Big Five traits are predictive of specific aspects of behavior, as one would expect (Paunonen, 2003). For example, extraversion correlates positively with popularity and dating a greater variety of people. Conscientiousness correlates with greater honesty, a higher grade point average in college, higher job performance ratings, and relatively low alcohol consumption. Openness to experience is associated with playing a musical instrument, whereas agreeableness correlates with honesty. Thousands of studies have been conducted exploring correlations between the Big Five traits and such other characteristics as self-esteem (Watson, Suls, & Haig, 2002), transformational leadership (Judge & Bono, 2000), and well-being at midlife (Siegler & Brummett, 2000).

McCrae and Costa maintain that personality can be described adequately by measuring the five basic traits they've identified. Their bold claim has been supported in many studies by other researchers, and the five-factor model has become the dominant conception of personality structure in contemporary psychology (John & Srivastava, 1999; McCrae, 2005). These traits have been characterized as the "latitude and longitude" along which personality should be mapped (Ozer & Reise, 1994, p. 361).

However, some theorists maintain that more than five traits are necessary to account for most of the variation seen in human personality (Ashton et al., 2004; Benet & Waller, 1995). The debate about how many dimensions are necessary to describe personality is likely to continue for many years to come. As you'll see throughout the chapter, the study of personality is an area in psychology that has a long history of "dueling theories." We'll begin our tour of these theories by examining the influential work of Sigmund Freud and his followers.

Psychodynamic Perspectives

LEARNING OBJECTIVES

- *Describe Freud's three components of personality and how they are distributed across levels of awareness.*
- *Explain the importance of sexual and aggressive conflicts in Freud's theory.*
- *Describe seven defense mechanisms identified by Freud.*
- *Outline Freud's stages of psychosexual development and their theorized relations to adult personality.*
- *Summarize Jung's views on the unconscious.*
- *Summarize Adler's views on key issues relating to personality.*
- *Evaluate the strengths and weaknesses of psychodynamic theories of personality.*

***Psychodynamic theories* include all the diverse theories descended from the work of Sigmund Freud that focus on unconscious mental forces.** Freud inspired many brilliant scholars who followed in his intellectual footsteps. Some of these followers simply refined and updated Freud's theory. Others veered off in new directions and established independent, albeit related, schools of thought. Today, the psychodynamic umbrella covers a large collection of related theories. In this section, we'll examine Freud's ideas in some detail and then take a brief look at the work of two of his most significant followers, Carl Jung and Alfred Adler. Another psychodynamic theorist, Erik Erikson, is covered in a later chapter on adolescent and adult development (see Chapter 11).

Freud's Psychoanalytic Theory

Born in 1856, Sigmund Freud grew up in a middle-class Jewish home in Vienna, Austria. He showed an early interest in intellectual pursuits and became an intense, hardworking young man. He dreamed of achieving fame by making an important discovery. His determination was such that in medical school he dissected 400 male eels to prove for the first time that they had testes. His work with eels did not make him famous. However, his later work with people made him one of the most influential and controversial figures of modern times.

National Library of Medicine

Sigmund Freud

Freud was a physician specializing in neurology when he began his medical practice in Vienna near the end of the 19th century. Like other neurologists in his era, he often treated people troubled by nervous problems such as irrational fears, obsessions, and anxieties. Eventually he devoted himself to the treatment of mental disorders using an innovative procedure he developed, called *psychoanalysis,* that required lengthy verbal interactions in which Freud probed deeply into patients' lives. Decades of experience with his patients provided much of the inspiration for Freud's theory of personality.

Although Freud's theory gradually gained prominence, most of Freud's contemporaries were uncomfortable with it, for at least three reasons. First, he argued that unconscious forces govern human behavior. This idea was disturbing because it suggested that people are not masters of their own minds. Second, he claimed that childhood experiences strongly determine adult personality. This notion distressed many, because it suggested that people are not masters of their own destinies. Third, he said that individuals' personalities are shaped by how they cope with their sexual urges. This assertion offended the conservative, Victorian values of his time. Thus, Freud endured a great deal of criticism, condemnation, and outright ridicule, even after his work began to attract more favorable attention. What were these ideas that generated so much controversy?

© Peter Aprahamian/Corbis

Freud's psychoanalytic theory was based on decades of clinical work. He treated a great many patients in the consulting room pictured here. The room contains numerous artifacts from other cultures—and the original psychoanalytic couch.

Web Link 2.1 **Sigmund Freud Museum, Vienna, Austria**

This online museum, in both English and German versions, offers a detailed chronology of Freud's life and explanations of the most important concepts of psychoanalysis. The highlights, though, are the rich audiovisual resources, including online photos, amateur movie clips, and voice recordings of Freud.

Structure of Personality

Freud (1901, 1920) divided personality structure into three components: the id, the ego, and the superego. He saw a person's behavior as the outcome of interactions among these three components.

The *id* is the primitive, instinctive component of personality that operates according to the pleasure principle. Freud referred to the id as the reservoir of psychic energy. By this he meant that the id houses the raw biological urges (to eat, sleep, defecate, copulate, and so on) that energize human behavior. The id operates according to the *pleasure principle,* which demands immediate gratification of its urges. The id engages in *primary process thinking,* which is primitive, illogical, irrational, and fantasy oriented.

The *ego* is the decision-making component of personality that operates according to the reality principle. The ego mediates between the id, with its forceful desires for immediate satisfaction, and the external social world, with its expectations and norms regarding suitable behavior. The ego considers social realities—society's norms, etiquette, rules, and customs—in deciding how to behave. The ego is guided by the *reality principle,* which seeks to delay gratification of the id's urges until appropriate outlets and situations can be found. In short, to stay out of trouble, the ego often works to tame the unbridled desires of the id. As Freud put it, the ego is "like a man on horseback, who has to hold in check the superior strength of the horse" (Freud, 1923, p. 15).

In the long run, the ego wants to maximize gratification, just like the id. However, the ego engages in *secondary process thinking,* which is relatively rational, realistic, and oriented toward problem solving. Thus, the ego strives to avoid negative consequences from society and its representatives (for example, punishment by parents or teachers) by behaving "properly." It also attempts to achieve long-range goals that sometimes require putting off gratification.

While the ego concerns itself with practical realities, **the *superego* is the moral component of personality that incorporates social standards about what represents right and wrong.** Throughout their lives, but especially during childhood, individuals receive training about what is good and bad behavior. Eventually they internalize many of these social norms, meaning that they truly *accept* certain moral principles, then *they* put pressure on *themselves* to live up to these standards. The superego emerges out of the ego at around 3 to 5 years of age. In some people, the superego can become irrationally demanding in its striving for moral perfection. Such people are plagued by excessive guilt.

According to Freud, the id, ego, and superego are distributed across three levels of awareness. He contrasted the unconscious with the conscious and preconscious (see **Figure 2.2**). **The *conscious* consists of**

Figure 2.2

Freud's model of personality structure. Freud theorized that people have three levels of awareness: the conscious, the preconscious, and the unconscious. To dramatize the size of the unconscious, it has often been compared to the portion of an iceberg that lies beneath the water's surface. Freud also divided personality structure into three components—id, ego, and superego—that operate according to different principles and exhibit different modes of thinking. In Freud's model, the id is entirely unconscious, but the ego and superego operate at all three levels of awareness.

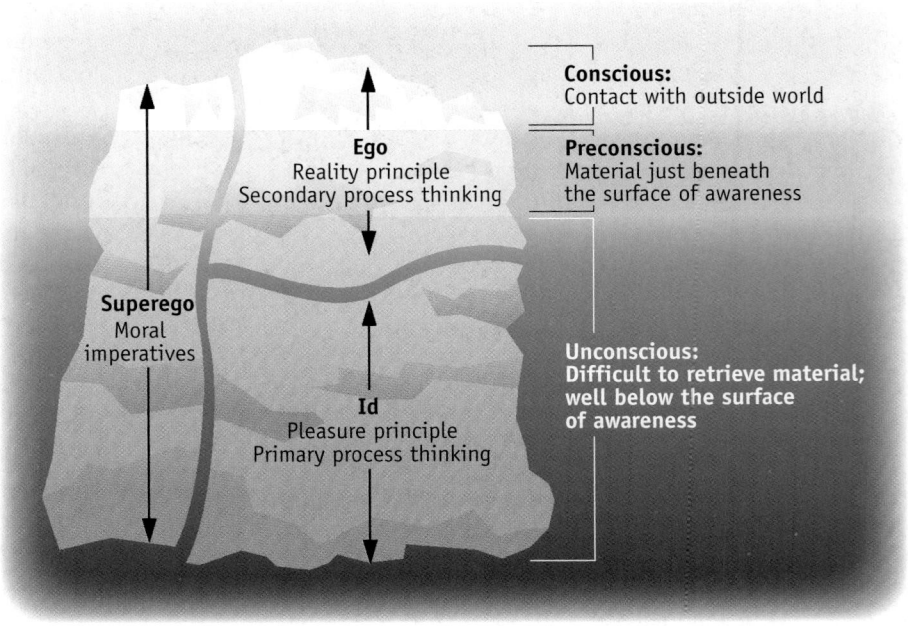

whatever one is aware of at a particular point in time. For example, at this moment your conscious may include the current train of thought in this text and a dim awareness in the back of your mind that your eyes are getting tired and you're beginning to get hungry. **The *preconscious* contains material just beneath the surface of awareness that can be easily retrieved.** Examples might include your middle name, what you had for supper last night, or an argument you had with a friend yesterday. **The *unconscious* contains thoughts, memories, and desires that are well below the surface of conscious awareness but that nonetheless exert great influence on one's behavior.** Examples of material that might be found in your unconscious would include a forgotten trauma from childhood or hidden feelings of hostility toward a parent.

Conflict and Defense Mechanisms

Freud assumed that behavior is the outcome of an ongoing series of internal conflicts. Battles among the id, ego, and superego are routine. Why? Because the id wants to gratify its urges immediately, but the norms of civilized society frequently dictate otherwise. For example, your id might feel an urge to clobber a coworker who constantly irritates you. However, society frowns on such behavior, so your ego would try to hold this urge in check, and you would find yourself in a conflict. You may be experiencing conflict at this very moment. In Freudian terms, your id may be secretly urging you to abandon reading this chapter so you can watch television or go online. Your ego may be weighing this appealing option against your society-induced need to excel in school (or at least pass your courses).

Freud believed that conflicts dominate people's lives. He asserted that individuals careen from one conflict to another. The following scenario provides a fanciful illustration of how the three components of personality interact to create constant conflicts.

Imagine your alarm clock ringing obnoxiously as you lurch across the bed to shut it off. It's 7 a.m. and time to get up for your history class. However, your id (operating according to the pleasure principle) urges you to return to the immediate gratification of additional sleep. Your ego (operating according to the reality principle) points out that you really must go to class since you haven't been able to decipher the stupid textbook on your own. Your id (in its typical unrealistic fashion) smugly assures you that you will get the A that you need. It suggests lying back to dream about how impressed your roommate will be. Just as you're relaxing, your superego jumps into the fray. It tries to make you feel guilty about the tuition your parents paid for the class that you're about to skip. You haven't even gotten out of bed yet—and there is already a pitched battle in your psyche.

Let's say your ego wins the battle. You pull yourself out of bed and head for class. On the way, you pass a donut shop and your id clamors for cinnamon rolls. Your ego reminds you that you're gaining weight and that you are supposed to be on a diet. Your id wins this time. After you've attended your history lecture, your ego reminds you that you need to do some library research for a paper in philosophy. However, your id insists on returning to your apartment to watch some sitcom reruns. It's only midmorning—and already you have been through a series of internal conflicts.

Freud believed that conflicts centering on sexual and aggressive impulses are especially likely to have far-reaching consequences. Why did he emphasize sex and aggression? Two reasons were prominent in his thinking. First, Freud thought that sex and aggression are subject to more complex and ambiguous social controls than other basic motives. The norms governing sexual and aggressive behavior are subtle, and people often get mixed messages about what is appropriate. Thus, he believed that these two drives are the source of much confusion.

Second, Freud noted that the sexual and aggressive drives are thwarted more regularly than other basic biological urges. Think about it: If you get hungry or thirsty, you can simply head for a nearby convenience store or a drinking fountain. But if a department store clerk infuriates you, you aren't likely to slug the clerk, because that isn't socially acceptable. Likewise, when you see an attractive person who inspires lustful urges, you don't normally walk up and propose a tryst in a nearby broom closet. There is nothing comparable to convenience stores or drinking fountains for the satisfaction of sexual and aggressive urges. Thus, Freud gave

great importance to these needs because social norms dictate that they are routinely frustrated.

Most psychic conflicts are trivial and are quickly resolved one way or the other. Occasionally, however, a conflict will linger for days, months, and even years, creating internal tension. Indeed, Freud believed that lingering conflicts rooted in childhood experiences cause most personality disturbances. More often than not, these prolonged and troublesome conflicts involve sexual and aggressive impulses that society wants to tame. These conflicts are often played out entirely in the unconscious. Although you may not be aware of these unconscious battles, they can produce *anxiety* that slips to the surface of conscious awareness. This anxiety is attributable to your ego worrying about the id getting out of control and doing something terrible.

The arousal of anxiety is a crucial event in Freud's theory of personality functioning (see **Figure 2.3**). Anxiety is distressing, so people try to rid themselves of this unpleasant emotion any way they can. This effort to ward off anxiety often involves the use of defense mechanisms. ***Defense mechanisms* are largely unconscious reactions that protect a person from painful emotions such as anxiety and guilt.** Typically, they are mental maneuvers that work through self-deception. A common example is ***rationalization*, which involves creating false but plausible excuses to justify unacceptable behavior.** You would be rationalizing if, after cheating someone in a business transaction, you tried to reduce your guilt by explaining that "everyone does it."

Characterized as "the flagship in the psychoanalytic fleet of defense mechanisms" (Paulhus, Fridhandler, & Hayes, 1997, p. 545), repression is the most basic and widely used defense mechanism. ***Repression* involves keeping distressing thoughts and feelings buried in the unconscious.** People tend to repress desires that make them feel guilty, conflicts that make them anxious, and memories that are painful. Repression is "motivated forgetting." If you forget a dental appointment or the name of someone you don't like, repression may be at work.

Self-deception can also be seen in the mechanisms of projection and displacement. ***Projection* involves attributing one's own thoughts, feelings, or motives to another.** For example, if your lust for a co-worker makes you feel guilty, you might attribute any latent sexual tension between the two of you to the *other person's* desire to seduce you. ***Displacement* involves diverting emotional feelings (usually anger) from their original source to a substitute target.** If your boss gives you a hard time at work and you come home and slam the door, yell at your dog, and lash out at your spouse, you are displacing your anger onto irrelevant targets. Unfortunately, social constraints often force people to hold back their anger until they end up expressing it toward the people they love the most.

Other prominent defense mechanisms include reaction formation, regression, and identification. ***Reaction formation* involves behaving in a way that is exactly the opposite of one's true feelings.** Guilt about sexual desires often leads to reaction formation. Freud theorized that many males who ridicule homosexuals are defending against their own latent homosexual impulses. The telltale sign of reaction formation is the exaggerated quality of the opposite behavior (such as trying to be ultra-nice to mask feelings of hostility).

***Regression* involves a reversion to immature patterns of behavior.** When anxious about their self-worth, some adults respond with childish boasting and bragging (as opposed to subtle efforts to impress others). For example, a fired executive having difficulty finding a new job might start making ridiculous statements about his incomparable talents and achievements. Such bragging is regressive when it is marked by massive exaggerations that anyone can see through.

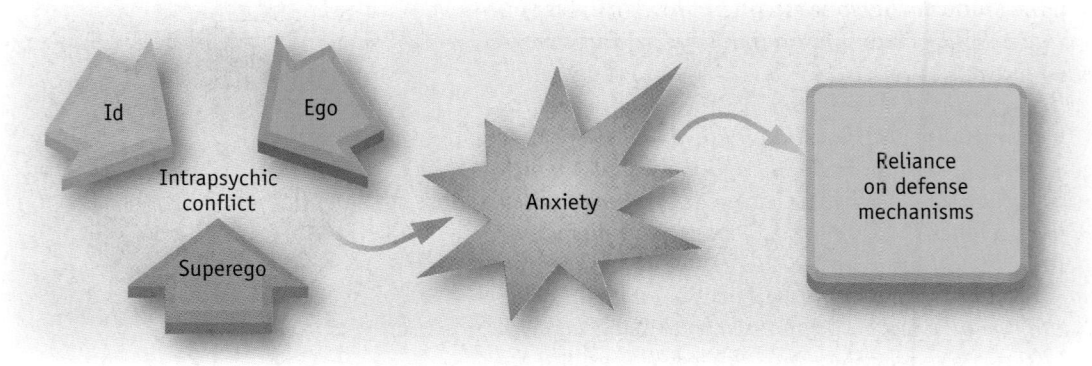

Figure 2.3

Freud's model of personality dynamics. According to Freud, unconscious conflicts among the id, ego, and superego sometimes lead to anxiety. This discomfort may lead to the use of defense mechanisms, which may temporarily relieve anxiety.

Defense Mechanisms, with Examples

Definition	Example
Repression involves keeping distressing thoughts and feelings buried in the unconscious.	A traumatized soldier has no recollection of the details of a close brush with death.
Projection involves attributing one's own thoughts, feelings, or motives to another person.	A woman who dislikes her boss thinks she likes her boss but feels that the boss doesn't like her.
Displacement involves diverting emotional feelings (usually anger) from their original source to a substitute target.	After a parental scolding, a young girl takes her anger out on her little brother.
Reaction formation involves behaving in a way that is exactly the opposite of one's true feelings.	A parent who unconsciously resents a child spoils the child with outlandish gifts.
Regression involves a reversion to immature patterns of behavior.	An adult has a temper tantrum when he doesn't get his way.
Rationalization involves the creation of false but plausible excuses to justify unacceptable behavior.	A student watches TV instead of studying, saying that "additional study wouldn't do any good anyway."
Identification involves bolstering self-esteem by forming an imaginary or real alliance with some person or group.	An insecure young man joins a fraternity to boost his self-esteem.

Figure 2.4

Defense mechanisms. According to Freud, people use a variety of defense mechanisms to protect themselves from painful emotions. Definitions of seven commonly used defense mechanisms are shown on the left, along with examples of each on the right. This list is not exhaustive; additional defense mechanisms are discussed in Chapter 4.

***Identification* involves bolstering self-esteem by forming an imaginary or real alliance with some person or group.** For example, youngsters often shore up precarious feelings of self-worth by identifying with rock stars, movie stars, or famous athletes. Adults may join exclusive country clubs or civic organizations with which they identify.

Additional examples of the defense mechanisms we've described can be found in **Figure 2.4**. If you see defensive maneuvers that you have used, you shouldn't be surprised. According to Freud, everyone uses defense mechanisms to some extent. They become problematic only when a person depends on them excessively. The seeds for psychological disorders are sown when defenses lead to wholesale distortion of reality.

Development: Psychosexual Stages

Freud made the startling assertion that the foundation of an individual's personality is laid down by the tender age of 5! To shed light on these crucial early years, Freud formulated a stage theory of development. He emphasized how young children deal with their immature, but powerful, sexual urges (he used the term "sexual" in a general way to refer to many urges for physical pleasure, not just the urge to copulate). According to Freud, these sexual urges shift in focus as children progress from one stage to another. Indeed, the names for the stages (oral, anal, genital, and so on) are based on where children are focusing their erotic energy at the time. Thus, ***psychosexual stages* are developmental periods with a characteristic sexual focus that leave their mark on adult personality.**

Freud theorized that each psychosexual stage has its own unique developmental challenges or tasks, as outlined in **Figure 2.5**. The way these challenges are handled supposedly shapes personality. The notion of *fixation* plays an important role in this process. ***Fixation* is a failure to move forward from one stage to another as expected.** Essentially, the child's development stalls for awhile. Fixation is caused by *excessive*

Freud's Stages of Psychosexual Development

Stage	Approximate ages	Erotic focus	Key tasks and experiences
Oral	0–1	Mouth (sucking, biting)	Weaning (from breast or bottle)
Anal	2–3	Anus (expelling or retaining feces)	Toilet training
Phallic	4–5	Genitals (masturbating)	Identifying with adult role models; coping with Oedipal crisis
Latency	6–12	None (sexually repressed)	Expanding social contacts
Genital	Puberty onward	Genitals (being sexually intimate)	Establishing intimate relationships; contributing to society through working

Figure 2.5

Freud's stages of psychosexual development. Freud theorized that people evolve through the series of psychosexual stages summarized here. The manner in which certain key tasks and experiences are handled during each stage is thought to leave a lasting imprint on one's adult personality.

process of striving for superiority (see **Figure 2.6**). He maintained that some people engage in *overcompensation* in order to conceal, even from themselves, their feelings of inferiority. Instead of working to master life's challenges, people with an inferiority complex work to achieve status, gain power over others, and acquire the trappings of success (fancy clothes, impressive cars, or whatever looks important to them). They tend to flaunt their success in an effort to cover up their underlying inferiority complex. The problem is that such people engage in unconscious self-deception, worrying more about *appearances* than *reality.*

Adler's theory stressed the social context of personality development (Hoffman, 1994). For instance, it was Adler who first focused attention on the possible importance of *birth order* as a factor governing personality. His theory stimulated hundreds of studies on the effects of birth order, but these studies generally failed to support his hypotheses and did not uncover any reliable correlations between birth order and personality (Ernst & Angst, 1983; Harris, 2000).

In recent years, however, Frank Sulloway (1995, 1996) has argued persuasively that birth order *does* have an impact on personality. Sulloway's reformulated hypotheses focus on how the Big Five traits are shaped by competition among siblings as they struggle to find a "niche" in their family environments. For example, he hypothesizes that firstborns should be more conscientious but less agreeable and open to experience than later-borns. In light of these personality patterns, he further speculates that firstborns tend to be conventional and achievement oriented, whereas later-borns tend to be liberal and rebellious. To evaluate his hypotheses, Sulloway reexamined decades of research on birth order. After eliminating many studies that failed to control for important confounding variables, such as social class and family size, he concluded that the results of the remaining, well-controlled studies provided impressive evidence in favor of his hypotheses. Some subsequent studies have provided additional support for Sulloway's analyses (Paulhus, Trapnell, & Chen, 1999; Rohde et al., 2003), but others have not (Freese, Powell, & Steelman, 1999; Harris, 2000; Skinner, 2003). More studies will be needed, as research on birth order is enjoying a bit of a renaissance.

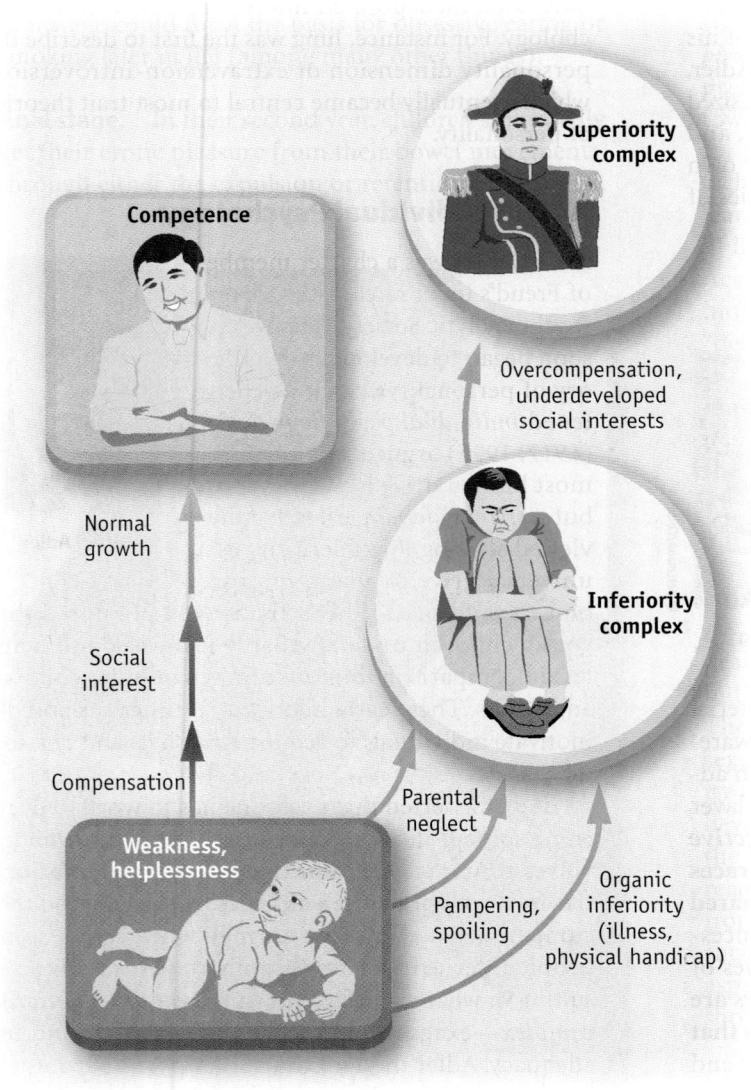

Figure 2.6

Adler's view of personality development. Like Freud, Adler believed that early childhood experiences exert momentous influence over adult personality. However, he focused on children's social interactions rather than on their grappling with their sexuality. According to Adler, the roots of personality disturbances typically lie in excessive parental neglect or pampering, which can lead to overcompensation.

Evaluating Psychodynamic Perspectives

The psychodynamic approach has given us a number of far-reaching theories of personality. These theories yielded some bold new insights for their time. Psychodynamic theory and research have demonstrated that (1) unconscious forces can influence behavior, (2) internal conflict often plays a key role in generating psychological distress, (3) early childhood experiences can exert considerable influence over adult personality, and (4) people do rely on defense mechanisms to reduce their experience of unpleasant emotions (Bornstein, 2003; Solms, 2004; Westen, 1998; Westen & Gabbard, 1999).

In a more negative vein, psychodynamic formulations have been criticized on several grounds, including the following (Crews,

2006; Fine, 1990; Kramer, 2006; Macmillan, 1991; Torrey, 1992):

1. *Poor testability.* Scientific investigations require testable hypotheses. Psychodynamic ideas have often been too vague to permit a clear scientific test. Concepts such as the superego, the preconscious, and collective unconscious are difficult to measure.

2. *Inadequate evidence.* The empirical evidence on psychodynamic theories has often been characterized as inadequate. The approach depends too much on case studies, in which it is easy for clinicians to see what they expect to see based on their theory. Recent reexaminations of Freud's own clinical work suggest that he sometimes distorted his patients' case histories to mesh with his theory (Esterson, 1993, 2001; Sulloway, 1991) and that a substantial disparity existed between Freud's writings and his actual therapeutic methods (Lynn & Vaillant, 1998). Insofar as researchers have accumulated evidence on psychodynamic theories, it has provided only modest support for the central hypotheses (Fisher & Greenberg, 1996; Westen & Gabbard, 1999).

3. *Sexism.* Many critics have argued that psychodynamic theories harbor a bias against women. Freud believed that females' penis envy made them feel inferior to males. He also thought that females tended to develop weaker superegos and to be more prone to neurosis than males. He dismissed female patients' reports of sexual molestation during childhood as mere fantasies. Admittedly, sexism isn't unique to Freudian theories, and the sex bias in modern psychodynamic theories has been reduced considerably. But the psychodynamic approach has generally provided a rather male-centered viewpoint (Lerman, 1986; Person, 1990).

It's easy to ridicule Freud for concepts such as penis envy and to point to ideas that have turned out to be wrong. Remember, though, that Freud, Jung, and Adler began to fashion their theories over a century ago. It is not entirely fair to compare these theories to other models that are only a few decades old. That's like asking the Wright brothers to race a supersonic jet. Freud and his psychodynamic colleagues deserve great credit for breaking new ground. Standing at a distance a century later, we have to be impressed by the extraordinary impact that psychodynamic theory has had on modern thought. No other theoretical perspective in psychology has been as influential, except for the one we turn to next—behaviorism.

Behavioral Perspectives

LEARNING OBJECTIVES

- *Describe Pavlov's classical conditioning and its contribution to understanding personality.*
- *Discuss how Skinner's principles of operant conditioning can be applied to personality development.*
- *Describe Bandura's social cognitive theory and his concept of self-efficacy.*
- *Evaluate the strengths and weaknesses of behavioral theories of personality.*

***Behaviorism* is a theoretical orientation based on the premise that scientific psychology should study observable behavior.** Behaviorism has been a major school of thought in psychology since 1913, when John B. Watson published an influential article. Watson argued that psychology should abandon its earlier focus on the mind and mental processes and focus exclusively on overt behavior. He contended that psychology could not study mental processes in a scientific manner because these processes are private and not accessible to outside observation.

In completely rejecting mental processes as a suitable subject for scientific study, Watson took an extreme position that is no longer dominant among modern behaviorists. Nonetheless, his influence was enormous, as psychology did shift its primary focus from the study of the mind to the study of behavior.

The behaviorists have shown little interest in internal personality structures such as Freud's id, ego, and superego, because such structures can't be observed. They prefer to think in terms of "response tendencies," which *can* be observed. Thus, most behaviorists view an individual's personality as a *collection of response tendencies that are tied to various stimulus situations.* A specific situation may be associated with a number of response tendencies that vary in strength, depending on an individual's past experience (see **Figure 2.7**).

Although behaviorists have shown relatively little interest in personality structure, they have focused extensively on personality *development.* They explain development the same way they explain everything else—through learning. Specifically, they focus on how children's response tendencies are shaped through classical conditioning, operant conditioning, and observational learning. Let's look at these processes.

Pavlov's Classical Conditioning

Do you go weak in the knees when you get a note at work that tells you to go see your boss? Do you get

Figure 2.7

A behavioral view of personality. Behaviorists devote little attention to the structure of personality because it is unobservable, but they implicitly view personality as an individual's collection of response tendencies. A possible hierarchy of response tendencies for a specific stimulus situation is shown here. In the behavioral view, personality is made up of countless response hierarchies for various situations.

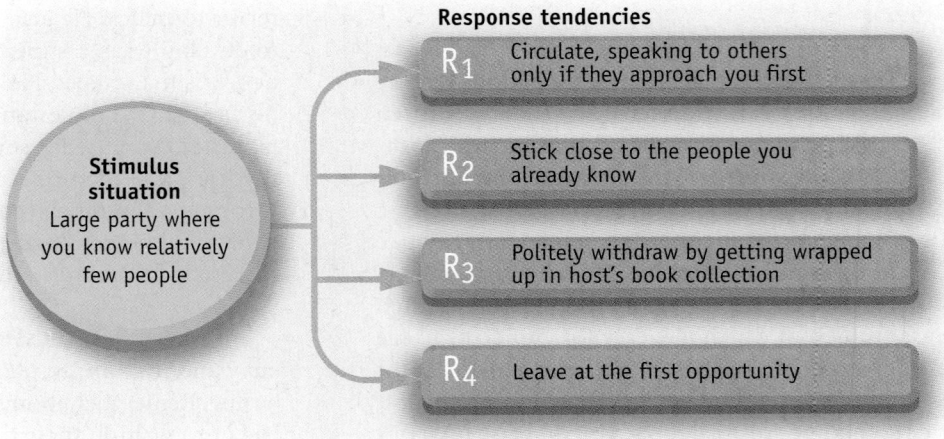

anxious when you're around important people? When you're driving, does your heart skip a beat at the sight of a police car—even when you're driving under the speed limit? If so, you probably acquired these common responses through classical conditioning. ***Classical conditioning* is a type of learning in which a neutral stimulus acquires the capacity to evoke a response that was originally evoked by another stimulus.** This process was first described back in 1903 by Ivan Pavlov.

Pavlov was a prominent Russian physiologist who did Nobel Prize–winning research on digestion. He was a dedicated scientist who was obsessed with his research. Legend has it that Pavlov severely reprimanded an assistant who was late for an experiment because he was trying to avoid street fighting in the midst of the Russian Revolution. The assistant defended his tardiness, saying, "But Professor, there's a revolution going on, with shooting in the streets!" Pavlov supposedly replied, "Next time there's a revolution, get up earlier!" (Fancher, 1979; Gantt, 1975).

© Bettmann/Corbis

Ivan Pavlov

The Conditioned Reflex

Pavlov (1906) was studying digestive processes in dogs when he discovered that the dogs could be trained to salivate in response to the sound of a tone. What was so significant about a dog salivating when a tone was presented? The key was that the tone started out as a *neutral* stimulus; that is, originally it did not produce the response of salivation (after all, why should it?). However, Pavlov managed to change that by pairing the tone with a stimulus (meat powder) that did produce the salivation response. Through this process, the tone acquired the capacity to trigger the response of salivation. What Pavlov had demonstrated was *how learned reflexes are acquired.*

At this point we need to introduce the special vocabulary of classical conditioning (see **Figure 2.8**). In Pavlov's experiment the bond between the meat powder and salivation was a natural association that was not created through conditioning. In unconditioned bonds, **the *unconditioned stimulus (UCS)* is a stimulus that evokes an unconditioned response without previous conditioning. The *unconditioned response (UCR)* is an unlearned reaction to an unconditioned stimulus that occurs without previous conditioning.**

In contrast, the link between the tone and salivation was established through conditioning. In conditioned bonds, **the *conditioned stimulus (CS)* is a previously neutral stimulus that has acquired the capacity to evoke a conditioned response through conditioning. The *conditioned response (CR)* is a learned reaction to a conditioned stimulus that occurs because of previous conditioning.** Note that the unconditioned response and conditioned response often involve the same behavior (although there may be subtle differences). In Pavlov's initial demonstration, salivation was an unconditioned response when evoked by the UCS (meat powder) and a conditioned response when evoked by the CS (the tone). The procedures involved in classical conditioning are outlined in **Figure 2.8**.

Web Link 2.3 **Behavior Analysis and Learning**

A multitude of annotated links, all focusing on learning through conditioning, have been compiled at the excellent Psychology Centre site at Athabasca University (Alberta, Canada).

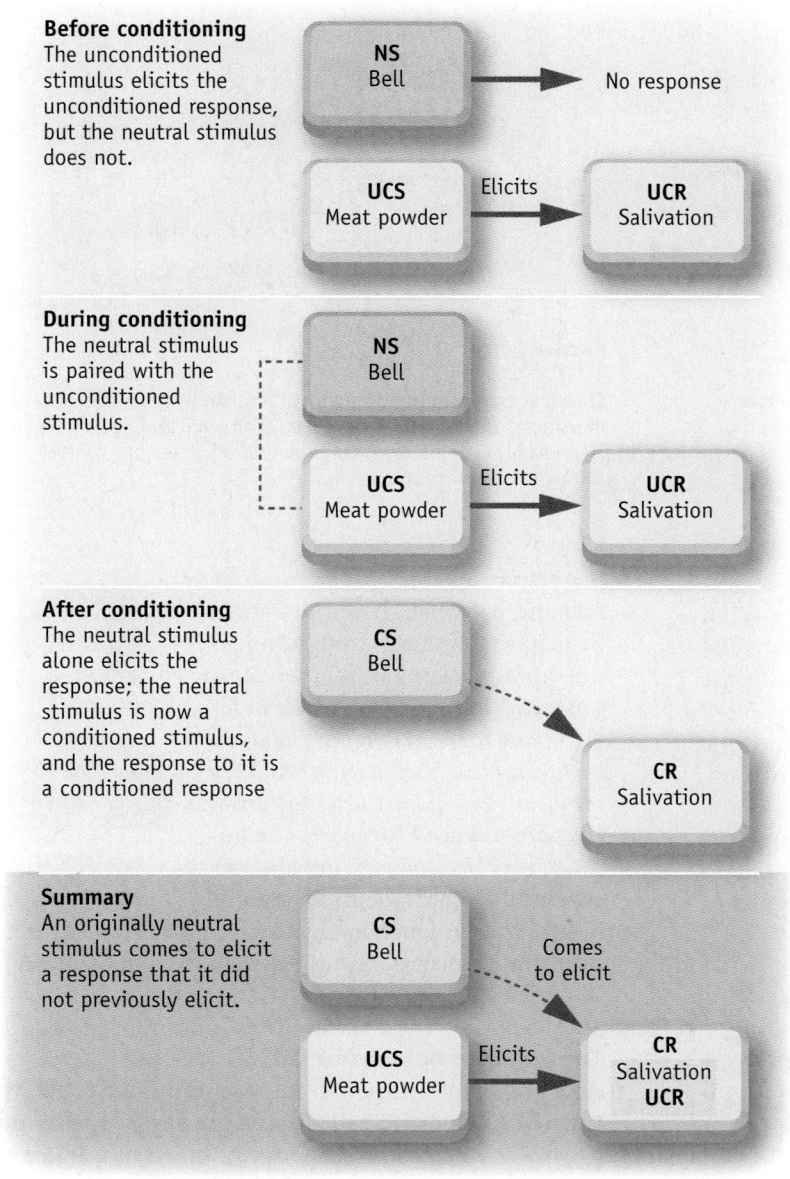

Figure 2.8

The process of classical conditioning. The sequence of events in classical conditioning is outlined here. As we encounter new examples of classical conditioning throughout the book, you will see diagrams like that shown in the bottom panel, which summarizes the process.

Pavlov's discovery came to be called the *conditioned reflex.* Classically conditioned responses are viewed as reflexes because most of them are relatively involuntary. Responses that are a product of classical conditioning are said to be *elicited.* This word is meant to convey the idea that these responses are triggered automatically.

Classical Conditioning in Everyday Life

What is the role of classical conditioning in shaping personality in everyday life? Among other things, it contributes to the acquisition of emotional responses, such as anxieties, fears, and phobias (Antony & McCabe, 2003; Ayres, 1998). This is a relatively small but important class of responses, as maladaptive emotional reactions underlie many adjustment problems. For example, one middle-aged woman reported being troubled by a bridge phobia so severe that she couldn't drive on interstate highways because of all the viaducts she would have to cross. She was able to pinpoint the source of her phobia. Back in her childhood, whenever her family would drive to visit her grandmother, they had to cross a little-used, rickety, dilapidated bridge out in the countryside. Her father, in a misguided attempt at humor, made a major production out of these crossings. He would stop short of the bridge and carry on about the enormous danger of the crossing. Obviously, he thought the bridge was safe or he wouldn't have driven across it. However, the naive young girl was terrified by her father's scare tactics, and the bridge became a conditioned stimulus eliciting great fear (see **Figure 2.9** on the next page). Unfortunately, the fear spilled over to all bridges, and 40 years later she was still carrying the burden of this phobia. Although a number of processes can cause phobias, it is clear that classical conditioning is responsible for many people's irrational fears.

Classical conditioning also appears to account for more realistic and moderate anxiety responses. For example, imagine a news reporter in a high-pressure job where he consistently gets negative feedback about his work from his bosses. The negative comments from his supervisors function as a UCS eliciting anxiety. These reprimands are paired with the noise and sight of the newsroom, so that the newsroom becomes a CS triggering anxiety, even when his supervisors are absent (see **Figure 2.10** on the next page). Our poor reporter might even reach a point at which the mere *thought* of the newsroom elicits anxiety when he is elsewhere.

Fortunately, not every frightening experience leaves a conditioned fear in its wake. A variety of factors influence whether a conditioned response is acquired in a particular situation. Furthermore, a newly formed stimulus-response bond does not necessarily last indefinitely. The right circumstances can lead

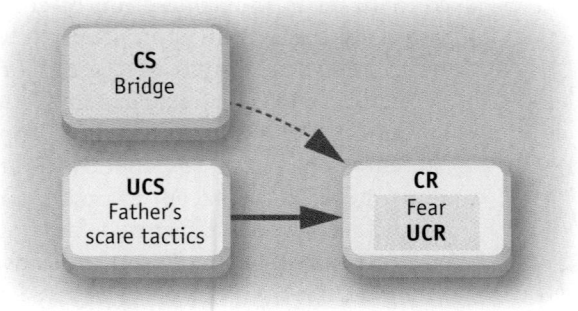

Figure 2.9

Classical conditioning of a phobia. Many emotional responses that would otherwise be puzzling can be explained as a result of classical conditioning. In the case of one woman's bridge phobia, the fear originally elicited by her father's scare tactics became a conditioned response to the stimulus of bridges.

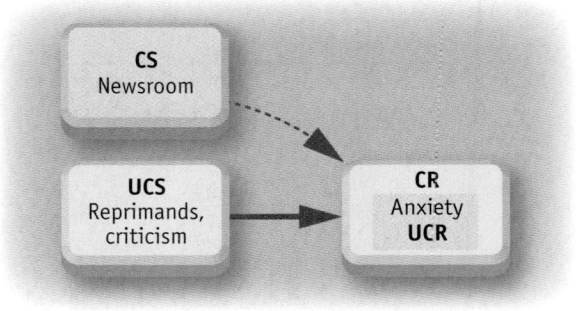

Figure 2.10

Classical conditioning of anxiety. A stimulus (in this case, a newsroom) that is frequently paired with anxiety-arousing events (reprimands and criticism) may come to elicit anxiety by itself, through classical conditioning.

to *extinction*—**the gradual weakening and disappearance of a conditioned response tendency.** What leads to extinction in classical conditioning? It is the consistent presentation of the CS *alone,* without the UCS. For example, when Pavlov consistently presented *only* the tone to a previously conditioned dog, the tone gradually stopped eliciting the response of salivation. How long it takes to extinguish a conditioned response depends on many factors. Foremost among them is the strength of the conditioned bond when extinction begins. Some conditioned responses extinguish quickly, while others are difficult to weaken.

Skinner's Operant Conditioning

Even Pavlov recognized that classical conditioning is not the only form of conditioning. Classical conditioning best explains reflexive responding controlled by stimuli that *precede* the response. However, both animals and humans make many responses that don't fit this description. Consider the response you are engaging in right now—studying. It is definitely not a reflex (life might be easier if it were). The stimuli that govern it (exams and grades) do not precede it. Instead, your studying response is mainly influenced by events that follow it—specifically, its *consequences.*

This kind of learning is called *operant conditioning.* ***Operant conditioning*** **is a form of learning in which voluntary responses come to be controlled by their consequences.** Operant conditioning probably governs a larger share of human behavior than classical conditioning, since most human responses are voluntary rather than reflexive. Because they are voluntary, operant responses are said to be *emitted* rather than *elicited.*

The study of operant conditioning was led by B. F. Skinner (1953, 1974, 1990), a Harvard University psychologist who spent most of his career studying simple responses made by laboratory rats and pigeons. The fundamental principle of operant conditioning is uncommonly simple. Skinner demonstrated that *organisms tend to repeat those responses that are followed by favorable consequences, and they tend not to repeat those responses that are followed by neutral or unfavorable consequences.* In Skinner's scheme, favorable, neutral, and unfavorable consequences involve reinforcement, extinction, and punishment, respectively. We'll look at each of these concepts in turn.

B. F. Skinner

Courtesy of B. F. Skinner

The Power of Reinforcement

According to Skinner, reinforcement can occur in two ways, which he called *positive reinforcement* and *negative reinforcement.* ***Positive reinforcement*** **occurs when a response is strengthened (increases in frequency) because it is followed by the arrival of a (presumably) pleasant stimulus.** Positive reinforcement is roughly synonymous with the concept of reward. Notice, however, that reinforcement is defined *after the fact,* in terms of its effect on behavior. Why? Because reinforcement is subjective. Something that serves as a reinforcer for one person may not function as a reinforcer for another. For example, peer approval is a potent reinforcer for most people, but not all.

Positive reinforcement motivates much of everyday behavior. You study hard because good grades are likely to follow as a result. You go to work because this behavior produces paychecks. Perhaps you work extra hard in the hopes of winning a promotion or a pay raise. In each of these examples, certain responses occur because they have led to positive outcomes in the past.

Positive reinforcement influences personality development in a straightforward way. Responses fol-

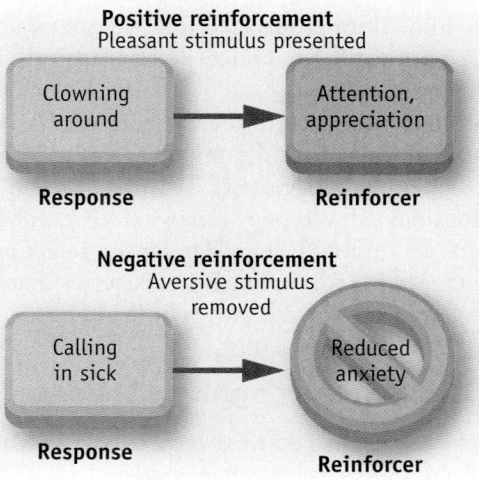

Figure 2.11

Positive and negative reinforcement in operant conditioning. Positive reinforcement occurs when a response is followed by a favorable outcome, so that the response is strengthened. In negative reinforcement, the removal (symbolized here by the "No" sign) of an aversive stimulus serves as a reinforcer. Negative reinforcement produces the same result as positive reinforcement: The person's tendency to emit the reinforced response is strengthened (the response becomes more frequent).

lowed by pleasant outcomes are strengthened and tend to become habitual patterns of behavior. For example, a youngster might clown around in class and gain appreciative comments and smiles from schoolmates. This social approval will probably reinforce clowning-around behavior (see **Figure 2.11**). If such behavior is reinforced with some regularity, it will gradually become an integral element of the youth's personality. Similarly, whether or not a youngster develops traits such as independence, assertiveness, or selfishness depends on whether the child is reinforced for such behaviors by parents and by other influential persons.

Negative reinforcement **occurs when a response is strengthened (increases in frequency) because it is followed by the removal of a (presumably) unpleasant stimulus.** Don't let the word *negative* here confuse you. Negative reinforcement *is* reinforcement. Like positive reinforcement, it strengthens a response. However, this strengthening occurs because the response gets rid of an aversive stimulus. Consider a few examples: You rush home in the winter to get out of the cold. You clean your house to get rid of a mess. Parents give in to their child's begging to halt his whining.

Negative reinforcement plays a major role in the development of avoidance tendencies. As you may have noticed, many people tend to avoid facing up to awkward situations and sticky personal problems. This personality trait typically develops because avoidance behavior gets rid of anxiety and is therefore negatively reinforced. Recall our imaginary newspaper reporter whose work environment (the newsroom) elicits anxiety (as a result of classical conditioning). He might notice that on days when he calls in sick, his anxiety evaporates, so this response is gradually strengthened—through negative reinforcement (shown in **Figure 2.11**). If his avoidance behavior continues to be successful in reducing his anxiety, it might carry over into other areas of his life and become a central aspect of his personality.

Extinction and Punishment

Like the effects of classical conditioning, the effects of operant conditioning may not last forever. In both types of conditioning, *extinction* refers to the gradual

The behavioral approach to personality centers around the principle of reinforcement—behaviors that are followed by favorable outcomes, such as attention, laughter, approval, and appreciation, tend to be strengthened and become more frequent.

weakening and disappearance of a response. In operant conditioning, extinction begins when a previously reinforced response stops producing positive consequences. As extinction progresses, the response typically becomes less and less frequent and eventually disappears.

Thus, the response tendencies that make up one's personality are not necessarily permanent. For example, the youngster who found that his classmates reinforced clowning around in grade school might find that his attempts at comedy earn nothing but indifferent stares in high school. This termination of reinforcement would probably lead to the gradual extinction of the clowning-around behavior. How quickly an operant response extinguishes depends on many factors in the person's earlier reinforcement history.

Some responses may be weakened by punishment. In Skinner's scheme, ***punishment* occurs when a response is weakened (decreases in frequency) because it is followed by the arrival of a (presumably) unpleasant stimulus.** The concept of punishment in operant conditioning confuses many students on two counts. First, it is often mixed up with negative reinforcement because both involve aversive (unpleasant) stimuli. Please note, however, that they are altogether different events with opposite outcomes! In negative reinforcement, a response leads to the removal of something aversive, and this response is strengthened. In punishment, a response leads to the arrival of something aversive, and this response tends to be weakened.

The second source of confusion involves the tendency to view punishment as only a disciplinary procedure used by parents, teachers, and other authority figures. In the operant model, punishment occurs whenever a response leads to negative consequences. Defined in this way, the concept goes far beyond actions such as parents spanking children or teachers handing out detentions. For example, if you wear a new outfit and your friends make fun of it and hurt your feelings, your behavior has been punished, and your tendency to wear this clothing will decline. Similarly, if you go to a restaurant and have a horrible meal, in Skinner's terminology your response has led to punishment, and you are unlikely to return.

The impact of punishment on personality development is just the opposite of reinforcement. Generally speaking, those patterns of behavior that lead to punishing (that is, negative) consequences tend to be weakened. For instance, if your impulsive decisions always backfire, your tendency to be impulsive should decline.

According to Skinner (1987), conditioning in humans operates much as it does in the rats and pigeons that he has studied in his laboratory. Hence, he assumes that conditioning strengthens and weakens people's response tendencies "mechanically"—that is, without their conscious participation. Like John Watson (1913) before him, Skinner asserted that we can explain behavior without being concerned about individuals' mental processes.

Skinner's ideas continue to be influential, but his mechanical view of conditioning has not gone unchallenged by other behaviorists. Theorists such as Albert Bandura have developed somewhat different behavioral models in which cognition plays a role. *Cognition* is another name for the thought processes that behaviorists have traditionally shown little interest in.

Bandura's Social Cognitive Theory

Albert Bandura is one of several theorists who have added a cognitive flavor to behaviorism since the 1960s. Bandura (1977), Walter Mischel (1973), and Julian Rotter (1982) take issue with Skinner's view. They point out that humans obviously are conscious, thinking, feeling beings. Moreover, these theorists argue that in neglecting cognitive processes, Skinner ignores the most distinctive and important feature of human behavior. Bandura and like-minded theorists originally called their modified brand of behaviorism *social learning theory.* Today, Bandura refers to his model as *social cognitive theory.*

Courtesy, Albert Bandura

Albert Bandura

Bandura (1986, 1999b) agrees with the basic thrust of behaviorism in that he believes that personality is largely shaped through learning. However, he contends that conditioning is not a mechanical process in which people are passive participants. Instead, he maintains that individuals actively seek out and process information about their environment in order to maximize their favorable outcomes.

Observational Learning

Bandura's foremost theoretical contribution has been his description of observational learning. ***Observational learning* occurs when an organism's responding is influenced by the observation of others, who are called models.** Bandura does not view observational learning as entirely separate from classical and operant conditioning. Instead, he asserts that both classical and operant conditioning can take place indirectly when one person observes another's conditioning (see **Figure 2.12**).

To illustrate, suppose you observe a friend behaving assertively with a car salesman. Let's say that her assertiveness is reinforced by the exceptionally good buy she gets on the car. Your own tendency to behave assertively with salespeople might well be strengthened as a result. Notice that the favorable consequence

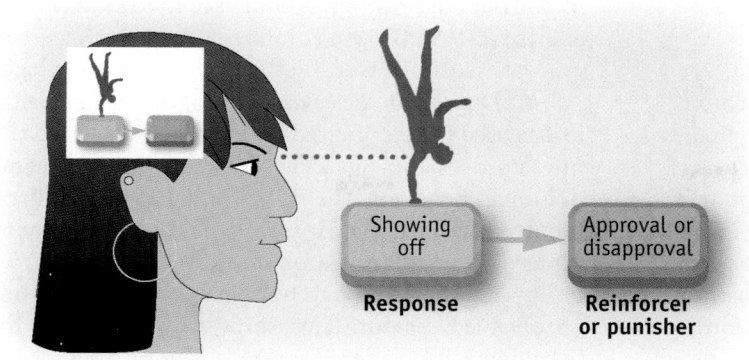

Figure 2.12

Observational learning. In observational learning, an observer attends to and stores a mental representation of a model's behavior (for example, showing off) and its consequences (such as approval or disapproval from others). According to social cognitive theory, many of our characteristic responses are acquired through observation of others' behavior.

is experienced by your friend, not you. Your friend's tendency to bargain assertively should be reinforced directly. But your tendency to bargain assertively may also be strengthened indirectly.

The theories of Skinner and Pavlov make no allowance for this type of indirect learning. After all, observational learning requires that you pay *attention* to your friend's behavior, that you *understand* its consequences, and that you store this *information* in *memory*. Obviously, attention, understanding, information, and memory involve cognition, which behaviorists used to ignore.

As social cognitive theory has been refined, it has become apparent that some models tend to be more influential than others (Bandura, 1986). Both children and adults tend to imitate people they like or respect more so than people they don't. People are also especially prone to imitate the behavior of those they consider attractive or powerful (such as celebrities). In addition, imitation is more likely when individuals see similarity between the model and themselves. Thus, children imitate same-sex role models somewhat more than other-sex models. Finally, as noted before, people are more likely to copy a model if they see the model's behavior leading to positive outcomes.

According to social cognitive theory, models have a great impact on personality development. Children learn to be assertive, conscientious, self-sufficient, dependable, easygoing, and so forth by observing others behaving in these ways. Parents, teachers, relatives, siblings, and peers serve as models for young children. Bandura and his colleagues have done extensive research showing how models influence the development of aggressiveness, gender roles, and moral standards in children (Bandura, 1973; Bussey & Bandura, 1984, 2004; Mischel & Mischel, 1976). Their research on modeling and aggression has been particularly influential.

Self-Efficacy

Bandura (1993, 1997, 2004) believes that *self-efficacy* is a crucial element of personality. ***Self-efficacy* is one's belief about one's ability to perform behaviors that should lead to expected outcomes.** When a person's self-efficacy is high, he or she feels confident in executing the responses necessary to earn reinforcers. When self-efficacy is low, the individual worries that the necessary responses may be beyond her or his abilities. Perceptions of self-efficacy are subjective and specific to different kinds of tasks. For instance, you might feel extremely confident about your ability to handle difficult social situations but doubtful about your ability to handle academic challenges.

Perceptions of self-efficacy can influence which challenges people tackle and how well they perform. Studies have found that feelings of greater self-efficacy are associated with reduced procrastination (Steel, 2007); greater success in giving up smoking (Boudreaux et al., 1998); greater adherence to an exercise regimen (Rimal, 2001); more effective weight-loss efforts (Linde et al., 2006); better outcomes in substance abuse treatment (Bandura, 1999a); more success in coping with medical rehabilitation (Waldrop et al., 2001); better self-care among diabetics (Williams & Bond, 2002); reduced disability from problems with chronic pain (Hadjistavropoulos et al., 2007); greater persistence and effort in academic pursuits (Zimmerman, 1995); higher levels of academic performance (Chemers, Hu, & Garcia, 2001); reduced vulnerability to anxiety and depression in childhood (Muris, 2002); less jealousy in romantic relationships (Hu, Zhang, & Li, 2005); enhanced performance in athletic competition (Kane et al., 1996); greater receptiveness to technological training (Christoph, Schoenfeld, & Tansky, 1998); greater success in searching for a new job (Saks, 2006); higher work-related performance (Stajkovic & Luthans, 1998); reduced strain from occupational stress (Grau, Salanova, Peiro, 2001); and greater resistance to stress (Jex et al., 2001), among many other things.

Evaluating Behavioral Perspectives

Behavioral theories are firmly rooted in empirical research rather than clinical intuition. Pavlov's model has shed light on how conditioning can account for people's sometimes troublesome emotional responses. Skinner's work has demonstrated how personality is shaped by the consequences of behavior. Bandura's social cognitive theory has shown how people's observations mold their characteristic behavior.

Behaviorists, in particular Walter Mischel (1973, 1990), have also provided the most thorough account of why people are only moderately consistent in their behavior. For example, a person who is shy in one context might be quite outgoing in another. Other models of personality largely ignore this inconsistency. The behaviorists have shown that this inconsistency occurs because people behave in ways they think will lead to reinforcement in the situation at hand. In other words, situational factors are important determinants of behavior. Thus, a major contribution of the behavioral perspective has been its demonstration that personality factors and situational factors jointly and interactively shape behavior (Fleeson, 2004; Roberts & Pomerantz, 2004)

Of course, each theoretical approach has its shortcomings, and the behavioral approach is no exception. Major lines of criticism include the following (Liebert & Liebert, 1998; Pervin & John, 2001):

1. *Dilution of the behavioral approach.* The behaviorists used to be criticized because they neglected cognitive processes, which clearly are important factors in human behavior. The rise of social cognitive theory blunted this criticism. However, social cognitive theory undermines the foundation on which behaviorism was built—the idea that psychologists should study only observable behavior. Thus, some critics complain that behavioral theories aren't very behavioral anymore.
2. *Overdependence on animal research.* Many principles in behavioral theories were discovered through research on animals. Some critics, especially humanistic theorists, argue that behaviorists depend too much on animal research and that they indiscriminately generalize from the behavior of animals to the behavior of humans.

Humanistic Perspectives

LEARNING OBJECTIVES

- *Discuss humanism as a school of thought in psychology.*
- *Explain Rogers's views on self-concept, development, and defensive behavior.*
- *Describe Maslow's hierarchy of needs, and summarize his findings on self-actualizing persons.*
- *Evaluate the strengths and weaknesses of humanistic theories of personality.*

Humanistic theory emerged in the 1950s as something of a backlash against the behavioral and psychodynamic theories (Cassel, 2000; DeCarvalho, 1991). The principal charge hurled at these two models was that they were dehumanizing. Freudian theory was criticized for its belief that primitive, animalistic drives dominate behavior. Behaviorism was criticized for its preoccupation with animal research. Critics argued that both schools view people as helpless pawns controlled by their environment and their past, with little capacity for self-direction. Many of these critics blended into a loose alliance that came to be known as "humanism" because of its exclusive interest in human behavior. ***Humanism* is a theoretical orientation that emphasizes the unique qualities of humans, especially their free will and their potential for personal growth.** Humanistic psychologists do not believe that we can learn anything of significance about the human condition from animal research.

Humanistic theorists take an optimistic view of human nature. In contrast to most psychodynamic and behavioral theorists, humanistic theorists believe that (1) human nature includes an innate drive toward personal growth, (2) individuals have the freedom to chart their courses of action and are not pawns of their environment, and (3) humans are largely conscious and rational beings who are not dominated by unconscious, irrational needs and conflicts. Humanistic theorists also maintain that one's subjective view of the world is more important than objective reality. According to this notion, if you *think* you are homely, or bright, or sociable, these beliefs will influence your behavior more than the actual realities of how homely, bright, or sociable you are.

The humanistic approach clearly provides a different perspective on personality than either the psychodynamic or behavioral approach. In this section we'll review the ideas of the two most influential humanistic theorists, Carl Rogers and Abraham Maslow.

Rogers's Person-Centered Theory

Carl Rogers (1951, 1961, 1980) was one of the founders of the human potential movement, which emphasizes personal growth through sensitivity training, encounter groups, and other exercises intended to help people get in touch with their true selves. Working at the University of Chicago in the 1940s, Rogers devised a major new approach to psychotherapy. Like Freud, Rogers based his personality theory on his extensive therapeutic interactions with many clients. Because of his emphasis on a person's subjective point of view, Rogers called his approach a *person-centered theory.*

Carl Rogers

Carl Rogers Memorial Library

The Self and Its Development

Rogers viewed personality structure in terms of just one construct. He called this construct the *self,* although it is more widely known today as the *self-concept.* **A *self-concept* is a collection of beliefs about one's own nature, unique qualities, and typical behavior.** Your self-concept is your mental picture of yourself. It is a collection of self-perceptions. For example, a self-concept might include such beliefs as "I am easygoing" or "I am pretty" or "I am hardworking."

Rogers stressed the subjective nature of the self-concept. Your self-concept may not be entirely consistent with your actual experiences. To put it more bluntly, your self-concept may be inaccurate. Most people are prone to distort their experiences to some extent to promote a relatively favorable self-concept. For example, you may believe that you are quite bright academically, but your grade transcript might suggest otherwise. Rogers used the term ***incongruence* to refer to the disparity between one's self-concept and one's actual experience.** In contrast, if a person's self-concept is reasonably accurate, it is said to be *congruent* with reality. Everyone experiences *some* incongruence; the crucial issue is how much (see **Figure 2.13**). Rogers maintained that a great deal of incongruence undermines a person's psychological well-being.

In terms of personality development, Rogers was concerned with how childhood experiences promote congruence or incongruence. According to Rogers, everyone has a strong need for affection, love, and acceptance from others. Early in life, parents provide most of this affection. Rogers maintained that some parents make their affection *conditional.* That is, they make it depend on the child's behaving well and living up to expectations. When parental love seems conditional, children often distort and block out of their self-concept those experiences that make them feel unworthy of love. At the other end of the spectrum, Rogers asserted that some parents make their affection *unconditional.* Their children have less need to block out unworthy experiences because they have been assured that they are worthy of affection no matter what they do.

Rogers believed that unconditional love from parents fosters congruence and that conditional love fosters incongruence. He further theorized that individuals who grow up believing that affection from others (besides their parents) is conditional go on to distort more and more of their experiences to feel worthy of acceptance from a wider and wider array of people, making the incongruence grow.

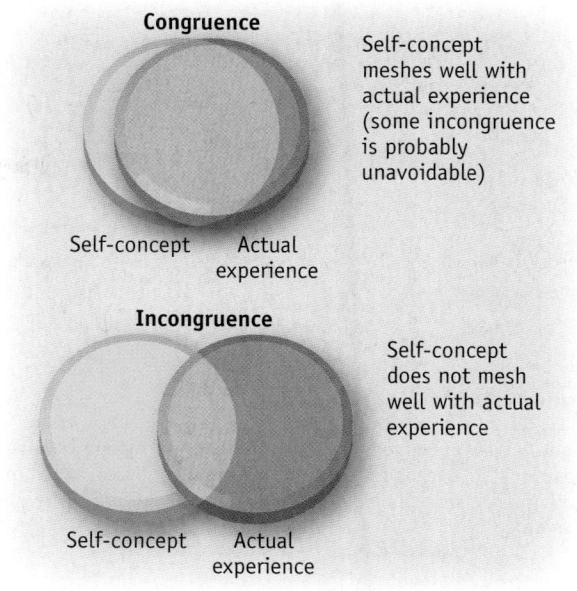

Figure 2.13

Rogers's view of personality structure. In Rogers's model, the self-concept is the only important structural construct. However, Rogers acknowledged that one's self-concept may not jell with the realities of one's actual experience—a condition called incongruence. Different people have varied amounts of incongruence between their self-concept and reality.

Anxiety and Defense

According to Rogers, experiences that threaten people's personal views of themselves are the principal cause of troublesome anxiety. The more inaccurate your self-concept, the more likely you are to have experiences that clash with your self-perceptions. Thus, people with highly incongruent self-concepts are especially likely to be plagued by recurrent anxiety (see **Figure 2.14** on the next page).

To ward off this anxiety, such people often behave defensively. Thus, they ignore, deny, and twist reality to protect their self-concept. Consider a young woman who, like most of us, considers herself a "nice person." Let us suppose that in reality she is rather conceited and selfish, and she gets feedback from both boyfriends and

Web Link 2.4 **Personality Theories**

C. George Boeree, who teaches personality theory at Shippensburg University, has assembled an online textbook that discusses more than 20 important personality theorists in depth. All of the important figures cited in this chapter (except for the behaviorists such as Skinner and Pavlov) receive attention at this valuable site.

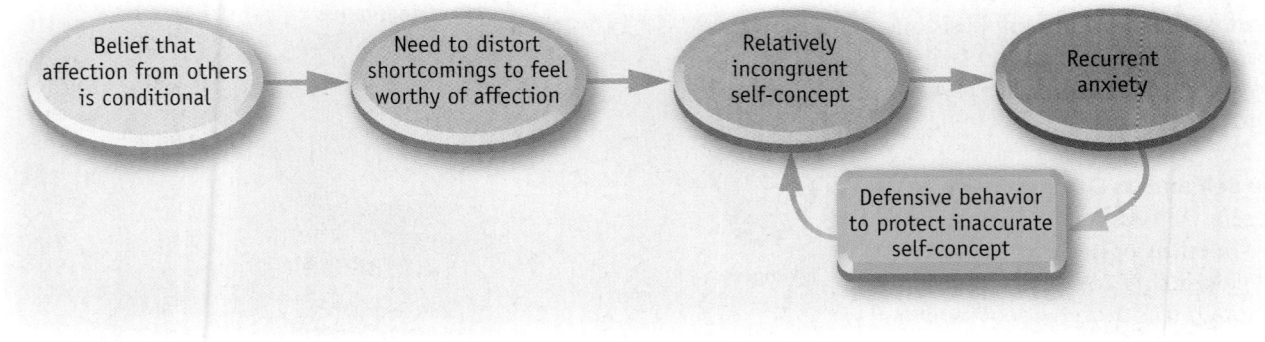

Figure 2.14

Rogers's view of personality development and dynamics. Rogers's theory of development posits that conditional love leads to a need to distort experiences, which fosters an incongruent self-concept. Incongruence makes one prone to recurrent anxiety, which triggers defensive behavior, which fuels more incongruence.

girlfriends that she is a "self-centered, snotty brat." How might she react to protect her self-concept? She might ignore or block out those occasions when she behaves selfishly and then deny the accusations by her friends that she is self-centered. She might also attribute her girlfriends' negative comments to their jealousy of her good looks and blame the boyfriends' negative remarks on their disappointment because she won't get more serious with them. Meanwhile, she might start doing some kind of charity work to show everyone (including herself) that she really is a nice person. As you can see, people often go to great lengths to defend their self-concept.

Rogers's theory can explain defensive behavior and personality disturbances, but he also emphasized the importance of psychological health. Rogers held that psychological health is rooted in a congruent self-concept. In turn, congruence is rooted in a sense of personal worth, which stems from a childhood saturated with unconditional affection from parents and others. These themes are similar to those emphasized by the other major humanistic theorist, Abraham Maslow.

Recommended **READING**

Three Psychologies: Perspectives from Freud, Skinner, and Rogers
by Robert D. Nye (Wadsworth, 2000)

One would be hard pressed to identify anyone who has had more influence over the evolution of psychology in the 20th century than the three theorists profiled in this book: Sigmund Freud, B. F. Skinner, and Carl Rogers. In this concise (159 pages), highly readable book, Robert Nye gives readers a simple—but not oversimplified—introduction to the theories of Freud, Rogers, and Skinner. After providing a brief overview of all three theories—the psychodynamic, behavioral, and humanistic—in the first chapter, Nye devotes a chapter to each theorist, attempting to present each man's ideas as convincingly as possible, holding criticisms until later. These chapters include short biographical sketches of each man and discuss practical examples and real-world implications of each theorist's provocative ideas. In the final chapter, Nye systematically compares the three theorists, reviews criticism of each, and adds his own personal comments. All in all, this is a superb introduction to the three major perspectives that have shaped contemporary psychology.

Maslow's Theory of Self-Actualization

Courtesy, Abraham Maslow

Abraham Maslow

Abraham Maslow grew up in Brooklyn and spent much of his career at Brandeis University, where he provided crucial leadership for the fledgling humanistic movement. Like Rogers, Maslow (1968, 1970) argued that psychology should take a greater interest in the nature of the healthy personality, instead of dwelling on the causes of disorders. "To oversimplify the matter somewhat," he said, "it is as if Freud supplied to us the sick half of psychology and we must now fill it out with the healthy half" (Maslow, 1968, p. 5). Maslow's key contributions were his analysis of how motives are organized hierarchically and his description of the healthy personality.

Hierarchy of Needs

Maslow proposed that human motives are organized into a ***hierarchy of needs*—a systematic arrangement**

Figure 2.15

Maslow's hierarchy of needs. According to Maslow, human needs are arranged in a hierarchy, and individuals must satisfy their basic needs first, before they progress to higher needs. In the diagram, higher levels in the pyramid represent progressively less basic needs. People progress upward in the hierarchy when lower needs are satisfied reasonably well, but they may regress back to lower levels if basic needs cease to be satisfied.

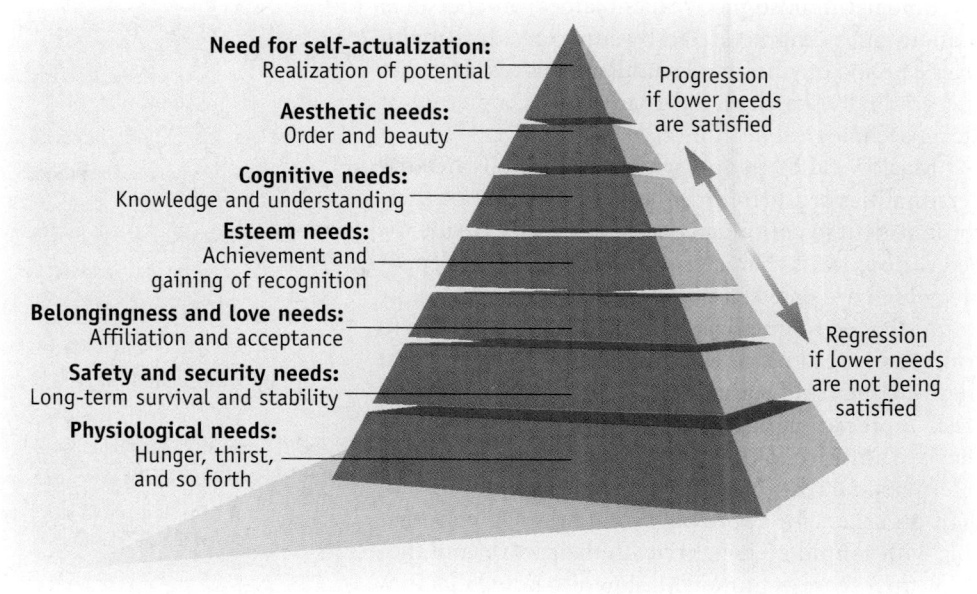

Web Link 2.5 **The Personality Project**

William Revelle, director of the graduate program in personality at Northwestern University's Psychology Department, has assembled a directory to many Internet-based resources in the study of personality.

of needs, according to priority, in which basic needs must be met before less basic needs are aroused. This hierarchical arrangement is usually portrayed as a pyramid (see **Figure 2.15**). The needs toward the bottom of the pyramid, such as physiological or security needs, are the most basic. Higher levels in the pyramid consist of progressively less basic needs. When a person manages to satisfy a level of needs reasonably well (complete satisfaction is not necessary), *this satisfaction activates needs at the next level.*

Like Rogers, Maslow argued that humans have an innate drive toward personal growth—that is, evolution toward a higher state of being. Thus, he described the needs in the uppermost reaches of his hierarchy as *growth needs.* These include the needs for knowledge, understanding, order, and aesthetic beauty. Foremost among the growth needs is the ***need for self-actualization,* which is the need to fulfill one's potential;** it is the highest need in Maslow's motivational hierarchy. Maslow summarized this concept with a simple statement: "What a man *can* be, he *must* be." According to Maslow, people will be frustrated if they are unable to fully utilize their talents or pursue their true interests. For example, if you have great musical talent but must work as an accountant, or if you have scholarly interests but must work as a sales clerk, your need for self-actualization will be thwarted.

The Healthy Personality

Because of his interest in self-actualization, Maslow set out to discover the nature of the healthy personality. He tried to identify people of exceptional mental health so that he could investigate their characteristics. In one case, he used psychological tests and interviews to sort out the healthiest 1 percent of a sizable population of college students. He also studied admired historical figures (such as Thomas Jefferson and

PEANUTS reprinted by permission of United Feature Syndicate, Inc.

psychologist-philosopher William James) and personal acquaintances characterized by superior adjustment. Over a period of years, he accumulated his case histories and gradually sketched, in broad strokes, a picture of ideal psychological health.

Maslow called people with exceptionally healthy personalities *self-actualizing persons* because of their commitment to continued personal growth. He identified various traits characteristic of self-actualizing people, which are listed in **Figure 2.16**. In brief, Maslow found that self-actualizers are accurately tuned in to reality and are at peace with themselves. He found that they are open and spontaneous and that they retain a fresh appreciation of the world around them. Socially, they are sensitive to others' needs and enjoy rewarding interpersonal relations. However, they are not dependent on others for approval, nor are they uncomfortable with solitude. They thrive on their work, and they enjoy their sense of humor. Maslow also noted that they have "peak experiences" (profound emotional highs) more often than others. Finally, he found that they strike a nice balance between many polarities in personality, in that they can be both childlike and mature, rational and intuitive, conforming and rebellious.

Characteristics of Self-Actualizing People

- Clear, efficient perception of reality and comfortable relations with it
- Spontaneity, simplicity, and naturalness
- Problem centering (having something outside themselves they "must" do as a mission)
- Detachment and need for privacy
- Autonomy, independence of culture and environment
- Continued freshness of appreciation
- Mystical and peak experiences
- Feelings of kinship and identification with the human race
- Strong friendships, but limited in number
- Democratic character structure
- Ethical discrimination between means and ends, between good and evil
- Philosophical, unhostile sense of humor
- Balance between polarities in personality

Figure 2.16

Characteristics of self-actualizing people. Humanistic theorists emphasize psychological health instead of maladjustment. Maslow's sketch of the self-actualizing person provides a provocative picture of the healthy personality.

Evaluating Humanistic Perspectives

The humanists added a refreshing perspective to the study of personality. Their argument that a person's subjective views may be more important than objective reality has proven compelling. Today, even behavioral theorists have begun to consider subjective personal factors such as beliefs and expectations. The humanistic approach also deserves credit for making the self-concept an important construct in psychology. Finally, one could argue that the humanists' optimistic, growth, and health-oriented approach laid the foundation for the emergence of the positive psychology movement that is increasingly influential in contemporary psychology (Sheldon & Kasser, 2001b; Taylor, 2001).

Of course, there is a negative side to the balance sheet as well. Critics have identified some weaknesses in the humanistic approach to personality, including the following (Burger, 2004; Carducci, 1998):

1. *Poor testability.* Like psychodynamic theorists, the humanists have been criticized for proposing hypotheses that are difficult to put to a scientific test. Humanistic concepts such as personal growth and self-actualization are difficult to define and measure.

2. *Unrealistic view of human nature.* Critics also charge that the humanists have been overly optimistic in their assumptions about human nature and unrealistic in their descriptions of the healthy personality. For instance, Maslow's self-actualizing people sound *perfect.* In reality, Maslow had a hard time finding self-actualizing persons. When he searched among the living, the results were so disappointing that he turned to the study of historical figures. Thus, humanistic portraits of psychological health are perhaps a bit unrealistic.

3. *Inadequate evidence.* Humanistic theories are based primarily on discerning but uncontrolled observations in clinical settings. Case studies can be valuable in generating ideas, but they are ill-suited for building a solid database. More experimental research is needed to catch up with the theorizing in the humanistic camp. This situation is precisely the opposite of the one you'll encounter in the next section, on biological perspectives, where more theorizing is needed to catch up with the research.

Biological Perspectives

LEARNING OBJECTIVES

- *Describe Eysenck's views on personality structure and development.*
- *Summarize recent twin studies that support the idea that personality is largely inherited.*
- *Summarize evolutionary analyses of why certain personality traits appear to be important.*
- *Evaluate the strengths and weaknesses of biological theories of personality.*

Like many identical twins reared apart, Jim Lewis and Jim Springer found they had been leading eerily similar lives. Separated four weeks after birth in 1940, the Jim twins grew up 45 miles apart in Ohio and were reunited in 1979. Eventually, they discovered that both drove the same model blue Chevrolet, chain-smoked Salems, chewed their fingernails, and owned dogs named Toy. Each had spent a good deal of time vacationing at the same three-block strip of beach in Florida. More important, when tested for such personality traits as flexibility, self-control, and sociability, the twins responded almost exactly alike. (Leo, 1987, p. 63)

So began a *Time* magazine summary of a major twin study conducted at the University of Minnesota, where investigators have been exploring the hereditary roots of personality. The research team has managed to locate and complete testing on 44 rare pairs of identical twins separated early in life. Not all the twin pairs have been as similar as Jim Lewis and Jim Springer, but many of the parallels have been uncanny (Lykken et al., 1992). Identical twins Oskar Stohr and Jack Yufe were separated soon after birth. Oskar was sent to a Nazi-run school in Czechoslovakia, while Jack was raised in a Jewish home on a Caribbean island. When they were reunited for the first time during middle age, they both showed up wearing similar mustaches, haircuts, shirts, and wire-rimmed glasses. A pair of previously separated female twins both arrived at the Minneapolis airport wearing seven rings on their fingers. One had a son named Richard Andrew, and the other had a son named Andrew Richard!

Could personality be largely inherited? These anecdotal reports of striking resemblances between identical twins reared apart certainly raise this possibility. In this section we'll discuss Hans Eysenck's theory, which emphasizes the influence of heredity, and look at behavioral genetics and evolutionary perspectives on personality.

Eysenck's Theory

Courtesy, Hans Eysenck, photo by Mark Gerson

Hans Eysenck

Hans Eysenck was born in Germany but fled to London during the era of Nazi rule. He went on to become one of Britain's most prominent psychologists. According to Eysenck (1967), "Personality is determined to a large extent by a person's genes" (p. 20). How is heredity linked to personality in Eysenck's model? In part, through conditioning concepts borrowed from behavioral theory. Eysenck (1967, 1982, 1991) theorizes that some people can be conditioned more readily than others because of inherited differences in

© Michael Nichols/Magnum Photos

© Michael Nichols/Magnum Photos

Is personality largely inherited? The story of these identical twins would certainly suggest so. Although they were reared apart from 4 weeks after their birth, Jim Lewis (left) and Jim Springer (right) exhibit remarkable correspondence in personality. Some of the similarities in their lives—such as the benches built around trees in their yards—seem uncanny.

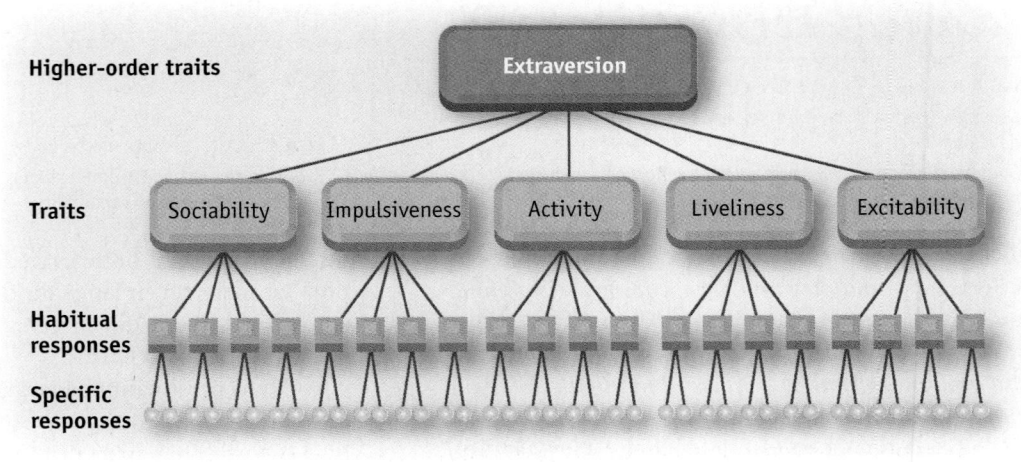

Figure 2.17

Eysenck's model of personality structure. Eysenck describes personality structure as a hierarchy of traits. In this scheme, a few higher-order traits (such as extraversion) determine a host of lower-order traits (such as sociability), which determine one's habitual responses (such as going to lots of parties).

From Eysenck, H. J. (1967). *The biological basis of personality,* p. 36. Springfield, IL: Charles C. Thomas. Courtesy of Charles C. Thomas.

their physiological functioning (specifically, their level of arousal). These variations in "conditionability" are assumed to influence the personality traits that people acquire through conditioning.

Eysenck views personality structure as a hierarchy of traits. Numerous superficial traits are derived from a smaller number of more basic traits, which are derived from a handful of fundamental higher-order traits, as shown in **Figure 2.17**. Eysenck has shown a special interest in explaining variations in *extraversion-introversion,* the trait dimension first described years earlier by Carl Jung. He has proposed that introverts tend to have higher levels of physiological arousal than extraverts. This higher arousal purportedly motivates them to avoid social situations that will further elevate their arousal and makes them more easily conditioned than extraverts. According to Eysenck, people who condition easily acquire more conditioned inhibitions than others. These inhibitions, coupled with their relatively high arousal, make them more bashful, tentative, and uneasy in social situations. This social discomfort leads them to turn inward. Hence, they become introverted.

Recent Research in Behavioral Genetics

Recent twin studies have provided impressive support for Eysenck's hypothesis that personality is largely inherited. **In *twin studies* researchers assess hereditary influence by comparing the resemblance of identical twins and fraternal twins on a trait.** The logic underlying this comparison is as follows. *Identical twins* emerge from one egg that splits, so that their genetic makeup is exactly the same (100% overlap). *Fraternal twins* result when two eggs are fertilized simultaneously; their genetic overlap is only 50%. Both types of twins *usually* grow up in the same home, at the same time, exposed to the same relatives, neighbors, peers, teachers, events, and so forth. Thus, both kinds of twins normally develop under similar environmental conditions, but identical twins share more genetic kinship. Hence, if sets of identical twins exhibit more personality resemblance than sets of fraternal twins, this greater similarity is probably attributable to heredity rather than to environment. The results of twin studies can be used to estimate the heritability of personality traits and other characteristics. **A *heritability ratio* is an estimate of the proportion of trait variability in a population that is determined by variations in genetic inheritance.** Heritability can be estimated for any trait. For example, the heritability of height is estimated to be around 90% (Plomin, 1994), whereas the heritability of intelligence appears to be about 50%–70% (Petrill, 2005; Plomin & Spinath, 2004).

The accumulating evidence from twin studies suggests that heredity exerts considerable influence over many personality traits (Livesley, Jang, & Vernon, 2003; Rowe & van den Oord, 2005). For instance, in research on the Big Five personality traits, identical twins have been found to be much more similar than fraternal twins on all five traits (Loehlin, 1992). Some skeptics still wonder whether identical twins might exhibit more personality resemblance than fraternal twins because they are raised more similarly. In other words, they wonder whether environmental factors (rather than heredity) could be responsible for identical twins' greater similarity. This nagging question can be answered only by studying identical twins who have been reared apart. Which is why the twin study at the University of Minnesota has been so important.

The Minnesota study (Tellegen et al., 1988) was the first to administer the same personality test to identical and fraternal twins reared together as well as apart. Most of the twins reared apart were separated quite early in life (median age of 2.5 months) and remained separated for a long time (median period of almost 34 years). Nonetheless, on all three of the higher-order traits examined, the identical twins reared apart displayed more personality resemblance than fraternal twins reared together. Based on the pattern of correlations observed, the researchers estimated that the heritability of personality is around 50%. Another large-scale twin study of the Big Five traits conducted in Germany and Poland yielded similar conclusions (Riemann, Angleitner, & Strelau, 1997). The heritability estimates based on the data from this study, which are shown in **Figure 2.18**, are in the same range as the estimates from the Minnesota study.

Research on the genetic bases of personality has inadvertently turned up another interesting finding that is apparent in the data shown in **Figure 2.18**. A number of recent studies have found that shared family environment has surprisingly little impact on personality (Beer, Arnold, & Loehlin, 1998; Rowe & van den Oord, 2005). This finding is surprising in that social scientists have long assumed that the family environment shared by children growing up together led to some personality resemblance among them. *These findings have led some theorists to conclude that parents don't matter—that they wield very little influence over how their children develop* (Cohen, 1999; Harris, 1998; Rowe, 1994).

Web Link 2.6 **Great Ideas in Personality**

At this site, personality psychologist G. Scott Acton demonstrates that scientific research programs in personality generate broad and compelling ideas about what it is to be a human being. He charts the contours of 12 research perspectives, including behaviorism, behavioral genetics, and sociobiology, and supports them with extensive links to published and online resources associated with each perspective.

Although the assertion that "parents don't matter" seems premature and overstated (Collins et al., 2000; Maccoby, 2000; Turkheimer & Waldron, 2000), the perplexing findings in behavioral genetics studies of personality have led researchers to investigate why children from the same family are often so different. Thus far, the evidence suggests that children in the same family experience home environments that are not nearly as homogeneous as previously assumed (Hetherington, Reiss, & Plomin, 1994; Pike et al., 2000). Children in the same home may be treated quite differently, because gender and birth order can influence parents' approaches to childrearing. Temperamental differences between children may also evoke differences in parenting. Focusing on how environmental factors vary *within* families represents a promising new way to explore the determinants of personality.

The Evolutionary Approach to Personality

In the realm of biological approaches to personality, the most recent development has been the emergence

Figure 2.18

Heritability and environmental variance for the Big Five traits. Based on the twin study data of Riemann et al. (1997), Plomin and Caspi (1999) estimated the heritability of each of the Big Five traits. The data also allowed them to estimate the amount of variance on each trait attributable to shared environment and nonshared environment. As you can see, the heritability estimates hovered in the vicinity of 40%, with two exceeding 50%. As in other studies, the influence of shared environment was very modest.

Based on Plomin, R., & Caspi, A. (1999). Behavioral genetics and personality. In L. A. Pervin & O. P. John (Eds.), *Handbook of Personality: Theory and Research*. New York: The Guilford Press. Adapted by permission.

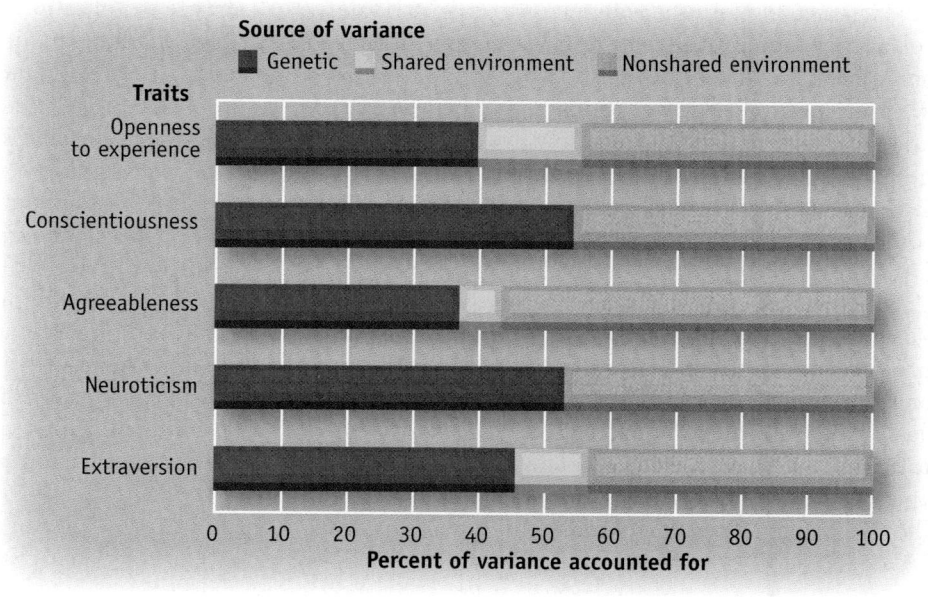

of an evolutionary perspective. Evolutionary psychologists assert that the patterns of behavior seen in a species are products of evolution in the same way that anatomical characteristics are. ***Evolutionary psychology* examines behavioral processes in terms of their adaptive value for members of a species over the course of many generations.** The basic premise of evolutionary psychology is that natural selection favors behaviors that enhance organisms' reproductive success—that is, passing on genes to the next generation. Evolutionary theorists assert that personality has a biological basis because natural selection has favored certain personality traits over the course of human history (Figueredo et al., 2005). Thus, evolutionary analyses of personality focus on how various traits—and the ability to recognize these traits in others—may have contributed to reproductive fitness in ancestral human populations.

For example, David Buss (1991, 1995, 1997) has argued that the Big Five personality traits stand out as important dimensions of personality across a variety of cultures because those traits have had significant adaptive implications. Buss points out that humans have historically depended heavily on groups, which afford protection from predators or enemies, opportunities for sharing food, and a diverse array of other benefits. In the context of these group interactions, people have had to make difficult but crucial judgments about the characteristics of others, asking such questions as: Who will make a good member of my coalition? Who can I depend on when in need? Who will share their resources? Thus, Buss (1995) argues, "Those individuals able to accurately discern and act upon these individual differences likely enjoyed a considerable reproductive advantage" (p. 22). According to Buss, the Big Five emerge as fundamental dimensions of personality because humans have evolved special sensitivity to variations in the ability to bond with others (extraversion), the willingness to cooperate and collaborate (agreeableness), the tendency to be reliable and ethical (conscientiousness), the capacity to be an innovative problem solver (openness to experience), and the ability to handle stress (low neuroticism). In a nutshell, Buss argues that the Big Five reflect the most salient features of others' adaptive behavior over the course of evolutionary history.

Daniel Nettle (2006) takes this line of thinking one step further, asserting that the traits themselves (as opposed to the ability to recognize them in others) are products of evolution that were adaptive in ancestral environments. For example, he discusses how extraversion could have promoted mating success, how neuroticism could have fueled competitiveness and avoidance of dangers, how agreeableness could have fostered the effective building of coalitions, and so forth. Nettle also discusses how each of the Big Five traits may have had adaptive costs (extraversion, for example, is associated with risky behavior) as well as benefits. Thus, he argues that evolutionary analyses of personality need to weigh the *trade-offs* between the adaptive advantages and disadvantages of the Big Five traits.

Evaluating Biological Perspectives

Recent research in behavioral genetics has provided convincing evidence that biological factors help shape personality. Evolutionary theorists have developed thought-provoking hypotheses about how natural selection may have sculpted the basic architecture of personality. Nonetheless, we must take note of some weaknesses in biological approaches to personality:

1. *Problems with estimates of hereditary influence.* Efforts to carve personality into genetic and environmental components with statistics are ultimately artificial. The effects of heredity and environment are twisted together in complicated interactions that can't be separated cleanly (Funder, 2001; Sternberg et al., 2005). Although heritability ratios sound precise, they are estimates based on a complicated chain of inferences that are subject to debate.

2. *Hindsight bias in evolutionary theory.* ***Hindsight bias*—the common tendency to mold one's interpretation of the past to fit how events actually turned out**—presents thorny problems for evolutionary theorists, who generally work backward from known outcomes to reason out how adaptive pressures in humans' ancestral past may have led to those outcomes (Cornell, 1997). Evolutionary theorists' assertion that the Big Five traits had major adaptive implications over the course of human history seems plausible, but what would have happened if other traits, such as dominance or sensation seeking, had shown up in the Big Five? With the luxury of hindsight, evolutionary theorists surely could have constructed plausible explanations for how these traits promoted reproductive success in the distant past. Thus, some critics have argued that evolutionary explanations are post-hoc, speculative accounts contaminated by hindsight bias.

3. *Lack of adequate theory.* At present there is no comprehensive biological theory of personality. Eysenck's model does not provide a systematic overview of how biological factors govern personality development (and it was never intended to). Evolutionary analyses of personality are even more limited in scope. Additional theoretical work is needed to catch up with recent empirical findings on the biological basis for personality.

A Contemporary Empirical Approach: Terror Management Theory

LEARNING OBJECTIVES

- *Explain the chief concepts and hypotheses of terror management theory.*
- *Describe how reminders of death influence people's behavior.*

So far, our coverage has been largely devoted to grand, panoramic theories of personality. In this section we'll examine a new approach to understanding personality functioning that has a narrower focus than the classic theories of personality. *Terror management theory* emerged as an influential perspective in the 1990s. Although the theory borrows from Freudian and evolutionary formulations, it provides its own unique analysis of the human condition. Developed by Sheldon Solomon, Jeff Greenberg, and Tom Pyszczynski (1991, 2004b), this fresh perspective is currently generating a huge volume of research, much of which seems especially relevant to contemporary adjustment issues.

Essentials of Terror Management Theory

One of the chief goals of terror management theory is to explain why people need self-esteem (Solomon, Greenberg, & Pyszczynski, 1991). The theory begins with the assumption that humans share an evolutionary heritage with other animals that includes an instinctive drive for self-preservation. However, unlike other animals, humans have evolved complex cognitive abilities that permit self-awareness and contemplation of the future. These cognitive capacities make humans keenly aware of the inevitability of death—they appreciate that life can be snuffed out unpredictably at any time. The collision between humans' self-preservation instinct and their awareness of the inevitability of death creates the potential for experiencing anxiety, alarm, and terror when people think about their mortality (see **Figure 2.19**).

How do humans deal with this potential for terror? According to terror management theory, "What saves us is culture. Cultures provide ways to view the world—worldviews—that 'solve' the existential crisis engendered by the awareness of death" (Pyszczynski, Solomon, & Greenberg, 2003, p. 16). Cultural worldviews diminish anxiety by providing answers to universal questions such as Why am I here? and What is the meaning of life? Cultures create stories, traditions, and institutions that give their members a sense of being part of an enduring legacy through their contributions to their families, tribes, schools, churches, professions, and so forth. Thus, faith in a cultural worldview can give people a sense of order, meaning, and context that can soothe their fear of death.

Where does self-esteem fit into the picture? Self-esteem is viewed as a sense of personal worth that depends on one's confidence in the validity of one's cultural worldview and the belief that one is living up to the standards prescribed by that worldview. "It is the feeling that one is a valuable contributor to a meaningful universe" (Pyszczynski, Solomon, & Greenberg, 2004, p. 437). Hence, self-esteem buffers people from the profound anxiety associated with the awareness that they are transient animals destined to die. In other words, self-esteem serves a *terror management* function (refer to **Figure 2.19**).

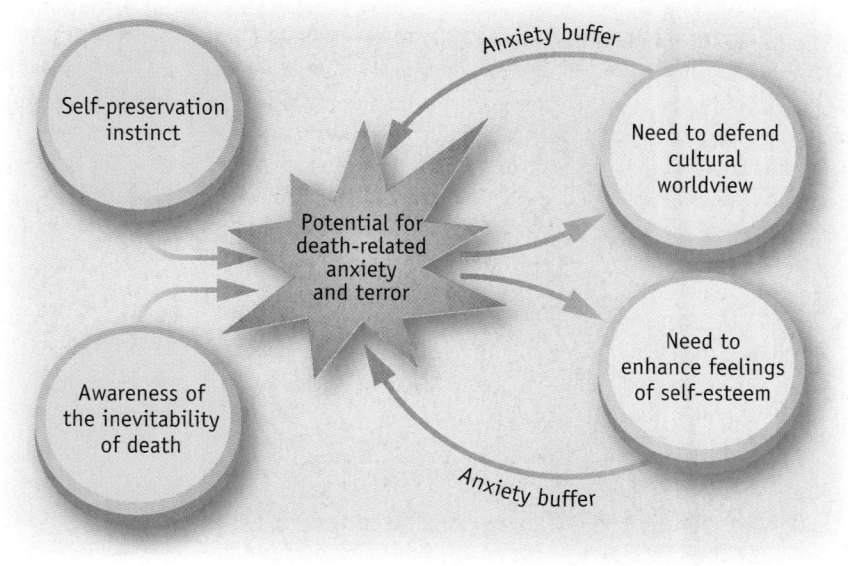

Figure 2.19

Overview of terror management theory. This graphic maps out the relations among the key concepts proposed by terror management theory. The theory asserts that humans' unique awareness of the inevitability of death fosters a need to defend one's cultural worldview and one's self-esteem, which serve to protect one from mortality-related anxiety.

LIVING IN TODAY'S WORLD

Understanding Reactions to Terrorist Attacks

Although its name might suggest otherwise, terror management theory was not developed to deal with the phenomenon of terrorism in the aftermath of 9/11. Terror management theory has been around since the mid-1980s, and as the text explains, it is a wide-ranging theory that analyzes the many ramifications of humans' existential struggle with the inevitability of death (see pp. 59–62). Nonetheless, given its central focus on the effects of reminding people of their mortality, the theory can help us understand the psychological impact of terrorist attacks in today's world.

In their book *In the Wake of 9/11,* Tom Pyszczynski, Sheldon Solomon, and Jeff Greenberg (2003) point out that the tragic events of 9/11 produced a powerful, nationwide manipulation of mortality salience. The televised images of death and destruction seen that day made most Americans feel extremely vulnerable. According to the architects of terror management theory, many of the reactions seen across the country after 9/11 were exactly what one would expect based on their theory. These reactions included the following:

Reaffirmation of cultural worldviews. When mortality salience is elevated, terror management theory predicts that people will embrace their cultural worldviews even more strongly than before. Consistent with this prediction, in the months following 9/11, church attendance and the sale of bibles both increased dramatically. Thus, people reaffirmed their faith in organized religion, which represents the foundation of many individuals' cultural worldview. People also became much more overtly patriotic. Flags flew everywhere, patriotic songs were all over the radio, and corporate logos were redesigned in red, white, and blue. Thus, people proudly proclaimed their faith in the American way.

Reduced tolerance. Research has shown that when death anxiety is heightened, people become less tolerant of opposing views and more prejudiced against those who are different. Consistent with this analysis, in the aftermath of 9/11 individuals who questioned government policies met more hostility than usual.

Increased altruism. Altruism, which consists of unselfish concern for the welfare of others, is a highly respected virtue in most cultures. Behaving in an altruistic manner makes people feel like they are good citizens, thus reaffirming their commitment to their cultural worldview and enhancing their self-esteem. Terror management theory would anticipate that increased mortality salience would stimulate increased altruism, which clearly was seen in the months after the terrorist assaults. Many people traveled to New York or Washington to help in whatever way they could after the attacks. Blood donations reached unprecedented levels, and charitable giving skyrocketed.

Intensified need for heroes. Research indicates that reminders of mortality increase the tendency to admire those who uphold cultural standards. More than ever, people need heroes who personify cultural values. This need was apparent in the aftermath of 9/11 in the way the media made firefighters into larger-than-life heroes. This analysis is not meant to suggest that firefighters did not deserve to be characterized as heroic. Rather, the point is that firefighters had a long history of heroic behavior that largely went unrecognized until a massive increase in mortality salience created an urgent need for uplifting heroes.

Admittedly, some of the reactions to 9/11 predicted by terror management theory could also be explained by other theoretical perspectives. Nonetheless, terror management theory seems to provide a perspective that is uniquely well suited to understanding some of the effects of terrorism on our collective psyche.

The notion that self-esteem functions as an *anxiety buffer* has been supported by numerous studies (Pyszczynski et al., 2004). In many of these experiments, researchers have manipulated what they call *mortality salience* (the degree to which subjects' mortality is prominent in their minds), usually by asking participants to briefly think about their own future death. Consistent with the anxiety buffer hypothesis, reminding people of their mortality leads subjects to engage in a variety of behaviors that are likely to bolster their self-esteem, thus reducing anxiety (see Chapter 5 for more on the terror management function of self-esteem).

Applications of Terror Management Theory

Increasing mortality salience also leads people to work harder at defending their cultural worldview (Arndt, Cook, & Routledge, 2004). For instance, after briefly pondering their mortality, research participants (1) hand out harsher penalties to moral transgressors, (2) respond more negatively to people who criticize their country, (3) give larger rewards to people who uphold cultural standards, and (4) show more respect for cultural icons, such as a flag (Greenberg et al., 1990; Rosenblatt et al., 1989). This need to defend one's cultural worldview may even fuel prejudice and aggression. Reminding subjects of their mortality leads to (1) more negative evaluations of people from different religious or ethnic backgrounds, (2) more stereotypic thinking about minority group members, and (3) more aggressive behavior toward people with opposing political views (McGregor et al., 1998; Schimel et al., 1999).

Terror management theory asserts that much of our behavior is motivated by the overlapping needs to defend our cultural worldview and to preserve our self-esteem. This perspective yields novel hypotheses regarding many phenomena. For instance, Solomon, Greenberg, and Pyszczynski (2004a) explain excessive materialism in terms of the anxiety-buffering function of self-esteem. Specifically, they argue that "conspicuous possession and consumption are thinly veiled efforts to assert that one is special and therefore more than just an animal fated to die and decay" (p. 134). Terror management theory has also been used to explain depressive disorders. According to Arndt et al. (2000), depression occurs when individuals' anxiety buffer fails and they lose faith in the cultural worldview that gave their life meaning. One fascinating study even applied terror management theory to the political process. Cohen et al. (2004) found that mortality salience increases subjects' preference for "charismatic" candidates who articulate a grand vision that makes people feel like they are part of an important movement of lasting significance. Yet another study showed that terror management processes can have an impact on people's reactions to certain types of art (Landau, Greenberg, et al., 2006). When mortality salience is elevated, people's need for a clear, meaningful view of reality is increased, leading them to have more negative reactions to abstract paintings that frustrate their need for meaning.

In another thought-provoking analysis, Jamie Goldenberg (2005, p. 224) argues that "uneasiness surrounding the body stems in part from existential concerns associated with human awareness that the physical body is the vehicle through which life passes unto death." In other words, bodily concerns remind people of their animal nature and hence their ultimate mortality. Based on this analysis, Goldenberg and colleages have predicted and found that mortality salience can increase individuals' ambivalence about the physical aspects of sexuality and lead to the suppression of some sexual urges (Goldenberg et al., 2002; Landau, Goldenberg, et al., 2006). Mortality salience can also inhibit health-protective behaviors, such as breast self-exams by women, when these behaviors highlight the frailty of the human body. Thus, terror management processes may contribute to psychological discomfort about bodily processes, including sexual desires.

Although terror management theory is narrower in scope than psychoanalytic, behavioral, and humanistic theories, it has wide-ranging implications and is being applied to more and more aspects of human behavior. At first glance, a theory that explains everything

© Jack Carey/Alamy

© Joe Raedle/Getty Images

Terror management theory has been applied to a remarkably diverse array of phenomena. For example, it has been used to explain conspicuous consumption and to predict people's voting preferences.

from prejudice to sexual ambivalence to compulsive shopping in terms of death anxiety may seem highly implausible. After all, most people do not appear to walk around all day obsessing about the possibility of their death. The architects of terror management theory are well aware of this reality. They explain that the defensive reactions uncovered in their research generally occur when death anxiety surfaces on the fringes of conscious awareness and that these reactions are automatic and subconscious (Pyszczynski, Greenberg, & Solomon, 1999). They also assert that people experience far more reminders of their mortality than most of us appreciate. They point out that people may be reminded of their mortality by a variety of everyday events, such as driving by a cemetery or funeral home, reading about an auto accident, visiting a doctor's office, hearing about a celebrity's heart attack, learning about alarming medical research, skipping over the obituaries in the newspaper, and so forth. Thus, the processes discussed by terror management theory may be more commonplace than one might guess.

Culture and Personality

LEARNING OBJECTIVES

- *Discuss whether the five-factor model has any relevance in non-Western cultures.*
- *Explain how researchers have found both cross-cultural similarities and disparities in personality.*
- *Summarize recent research on the accuracy of perceptions of national character.*

Are there connections between culture and personality? The investigation of this question dates back to the 1930s and 1940s, when researchers set out to identify various cultures' *modal personality* (Kardiner & Linton, 1945) or *national character* (Kluckhohn & Murray, 1948). These investigations sought to describe the *prototype* or *typical* personality in various cultures. For example, Ruth Benedict (1934) concluded that American Pueblo Indians were sober, orderly, conventional, and cooperative. Largely guided by Freud's psychoanalytic theory, this line of research generated interest for a couple decades, but ultimately met with little success (Bock, 2000; LeVine, 2001). Part of the problem may have been the rather culture-bound, Eurocentric nature of Freudian theory, but the crux of the problem was that it was unrealistic to expect to find a single, dominant personality profile in each culture.

Studies of the links between culture and personality dwindled to almost nothing for many decades. However, in recent decades psychology has become more interested in cultural factors, sparking a renaissance in culture-personality research. This research has sought to determine whether Western personality constructs are relevant to other cultures and whether cultural differences can be seen in the strength of specific personality traits. These studies have found evidence of both continuity and variability across cultures.

For the most part, continuity has been apparent in cross-cultural comparisons of the *trait structure* of personality. When English language personality scales have been translated and administered in other cultures, the predicted dimensions of personality have emerged from the factor analyses (Paunonen & Ashton, 1998). For example, when scales that tap the Big Five personality traits have been administered and subjected to factor analysis in other cultures, the usual five traits have typically emerged (Katigbak et al., 2002; McCrae et al., 2005b). Thus, research tentatively suggests that the basic dimensions of personality trait structure may be universal.

On the other hand, some cross-cultural variability is seen when researchers compare the average trait scores of samples from various cultural groups. For example, in a study comparing 51 cultures, McCrae et al. (2005a) found that Brazilians scored relatively high in neuroticism, Australians in extraversion, Germans in openness to experience, Czechs in agreeableness, and Malaysians in conscientiousness, to give but a handful of examples. These findings should be viewed as very preliminary, as more data are needed from larger and more carefully selected samples. Nonetheless, the findings suggest that genuine cultural differences may exist in some personality traits. That said, the observed cultural disparities in average trait scores were modest in size.

The availability of the data from the McCrae et al. (2005a) study allowed Terracciano et al. (2005) to revisit the concept of *national character.* Terracciano and his colleagues asked subjects from many cultures to describe the *typical* member of *their* culture on rating forms guided by the five-factor model. Generally, subjects displayed substantial agreement on these ratings of what was typical for their culture. The averaged ratings, which served as the measures of each culture's national character, were then correlated with the actual mean trait scores for various cultures compiled in the McCrae et al. (2005a) study. The results were definitive—the vast majority of the correlations were extremely low and often even negative. In other words, there was little or no relationship between perceptions of national character and actual trait scores for various cultures (see **Figure 2.20**). People's beliefs about national character, which often fuel cultural prejudices, turned out to be profoundly inaccurate stereotypes (McCrae & Terracciano, 2006).

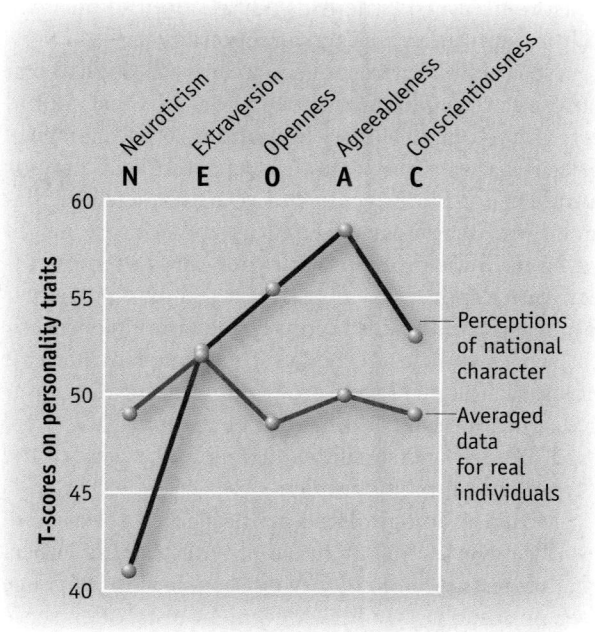

Figure 2.20

An example of inaccurate perceptions of national character. Terracciano et al. (2005) found that perceptions of national character (the prototype or typical personality for a particular culture) are largely inaccurate. The data shown here for one culture—Canadians—illustrates this inaccuracy. Mean scores on the Big Five traits for a sample of real individuals from Canada are graphed in red. Averaged perceptions of national character for Canadians are graphed in blue. The discrepancy between perception and reality is obvious. Terracciano et al. found similar disparities between views of national character and actual trait scores for a majority of the cultues they studied. (Adapted from McCrae & Terracciano, 2006)

APPLICATION

Assessing Your Personality

LEARNING OBJECTIVES

- *Explain the concepts of standardization, test norms, reliability, and validity.*
- *Discuss the value and the limitations of self-report inventories.*
- *Discuss the value and limitations of projective tests.*

Answer the following "true" or "false."

___ **1.** Responses to personality tests are subject to unconscious distortion.

___ **2.** The results of personality tests are often misunderstood.

___ **3.** Personality test scores should be interpreted with caution.

___ **4.** Personality tests may be quite useful in helping people to learn more about themselves.

If you answered "true" to all four questions, you earned a perfect score. Yes, personality tests are subject to distortion. Admittedly, test results are often misunderstood, and they should be interpreted cautiously. In spite of these problems, however, psychological tests can be very useful.

We all engage in efforts to size up our own personality as well as that of others. When you think to yourself that "this salesman is untrustworthy," or when you remark to a friend that "Howard is too timid and submissive," you are making personality assessments. In a sense, then, personality assessment is part of daily life. However, psychological tests provide much more systematic assessments than casual observations do.

The value of psychological tests lies in their ability to help people form a realistic picture of their personal qualities. In light of this value, we have included a variety of personality tests in the *Personal Explorations Workbook* that is available to accompany this text, and we have sprinkled a number of short tests throughout the text itself. Most of these questionnaires are widely used personality tests. We hope that you may gain some insights by responding to these scales. But it's important to understand the logic and limitations of such tests. To facilitate your use of these and other tests, this Application discusses some of the basics of psychological testing.

Key Concepts in Psychological Testing

A *psychological test* is a standardized measure of a sample of a person's behavior. Psychological tests are measurement instruments. They are used to measure abilities, aptitudes, and personality traits.

Note that your responses to a psychological test represent a *sample* of your behavior. This fact should alert you to one of the key limitations of psychological tests: It's always possible that a particular behavior sample is not representative of your characteristic behavior. We all have our bad days. A stomachache, a fight with a friend, a problem with your car—all might affect your responses to a particular test on a particular day. Because of the limitations of the sampling process, test scores should always be interpreted *cautiously.* Most psychological tests are sound measurement devices, but test results should not be viewed as the "final word" on one's personality and abilities because of the everpresent sampling problem.

Most psychological tests can be placed in one of two broad categories: (1) mental ability tests, and (2) personality tests. *Mental ability tests,* such as intelligence tests, aptitude tests, and achievement tests, often serve as gateways to schooling, training programs, and jobs. *Personality* tests measure various aspects of personality, including motives, interests, values, and attitudes. Many psychologists prefer to call these tests personality *scales,* since the questions do not have right and wrong answers as do those on tests of mental abilities.

Standardization and Norms

Both personality scales and tests of mental abilities are *standardized* measures of behavior. ***Standardization* refers to the uniform procedures used to administer and score a test.** All subjects get the same instructions, the same questions, the same time limits, and so on, so that their scores can be compared meaningfully.

The standardization of a test's scoring system includes the development of test norms. ***Test norms* provide information about where a score on a psychological test ranks in relation to other scores on that test.** Why do we need test norms? Because in psychological testing, everything is relative. Psychological tests tell you how you score *relative to other people.* They tell you, for instance, that you are average in impulsiveness, or slightly above average in assertiveness, or far below average in anxiety. These interpretations are derived from the test norms.

Reliability and Validity

Any kind of measuring device, whether it's a tire gauge, a stopwatch, or a psychological test, should be reasonably consistent. That is, repeated measurements should yield reasonably similar results. To appreciate the importance of reliability, think about how you would react if a tire pressure gauge gave you several very different readings for the same tire. You would probably conclude that the gauge was broken and toss it into the garbage, because you know that consistency in measurement is essential to accuracy.

***Reliability* refers to the measurement consistency of a test.** A reliable test is one that yields similar results upon repetition of the test (see **Figure 2.21**). Like most other types of measuring devices, psychological tests are not perfectly reliable. They usually do not yield the exact same score when repeated. A certain amount of inconsistency is unavoidable because human behavior is variable. Personality tests tend to have lower reliability than mental ability tests because daily fluctuations in mood influence how people respond to such tests.

Even if a test is quite reliable, we still need to be concerned about its validity. ***Validity* refers to the ability of a test to measure what it was designed to measure.** If we develop a new test of assertiveness, we have to provide some evidence that it really measures assertive-

Figure 2.21

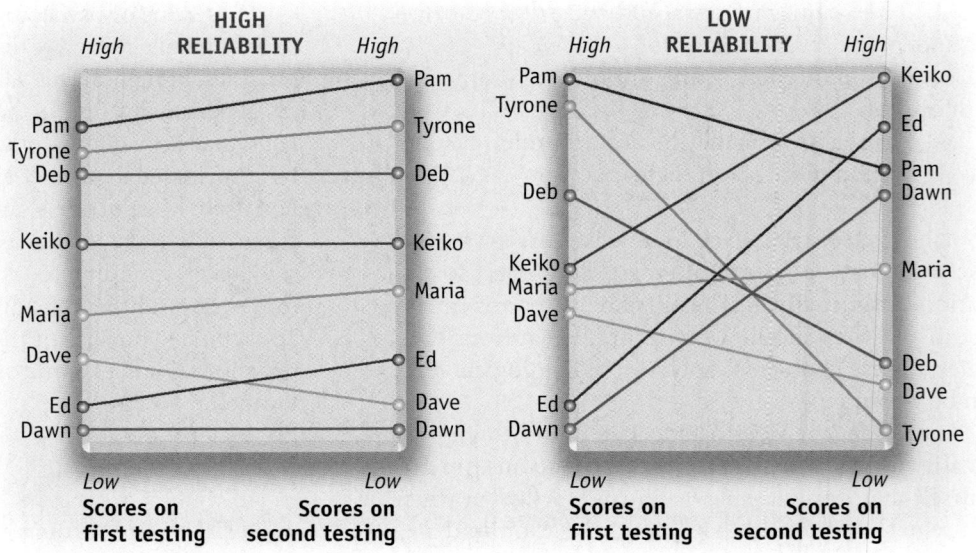

Test reliability. Subjects' scores on the first administration of an assertiveness test are represented on the left, and their scores on a second administration (a few weeks later) are represented on the right. If subjects obtain similar scores on both administrations, the test measures assertiveness consistently and is said to have high reliability. If subjects get very different scores when they take the assertiveness test a second time, the test is said to have low reliability.

Web Link 2.7 **Finding Information About Psychological Tests**

Maintained by the American Psychological Association, this FAQ site answers all sorts of questions about the availability of various kinds of tests. It explains how to find specific tests, how to get information on tests, and outlines information on the proper use of tests.

ness. Validity can be demonstrated in a variety of ways. Most of them involve correlating scores on a test with other measures of the same trait, or with related traits.

Self-Report Inventories

The vast majority of personality tests are self-report inventories. ***Self-report inventories* are personality scales that ask individuals to answer a series of questions about their characteristic behavior.** When you respond to a self-report personality scale, you endorse statements as true or false as applied to you, you indicate how often you behave in a particular way, or you rate yourself with respect to certain qualities. For example, on the Minnesota Multiphasic Personality Inventory, people respond "true," "false," or "cannot say" to 567 statements such as the following:

I get a fair deal from most people.
I have the time of my life at parties.
I am glad that I am alive.
Several people are following me everywhere.

The logic underlying this approach is simple: Who knows you better than you do? Who has known you longer? Who has more access to your private feelings?

The entire range of personality traits can be measured with self-report inventories. Some scales measure just one trait dimension, such as the measure of sensation seeking shown in **Figure 2.22**. Others

Measuring Sensation Seeking

Answer true or false to each of the items listed below. A "T" means that the item expresses your preference most of the time. An "F" means that you do not agree that the item is generally true for you. After completing the test, score your responses according to the instructions that follow the test items.

T	F	**1.** I would really enjoy skydiving.
T	F	**2.** I can imagine myself driving a sports car in a race and loving it.
T	F	**3.** My life is very secure and comfortable—the way I like it.
T	F	**4.** I usually like emotionally expressive or artistic people, even if they are sort of wild.
T	F	**5.** I like the idea of seeing many of the same warm, supportive faces in my everyday life.
T	F	**6.** I like doing adventurous things and would have enjoyed being a pioneer in the early days of this country.
T	F	**7.** A good photograph should express peacefulness creatively.
T	F	**8.** The most important thing in living is fully experiencing all emotions.
T	F	**9.** I like creature comforts when I go on a trip or vacation.
T	F	**10.** Doing the same things each day really gets to me.
T	F	**11.** I love snuggling in front of a fire on a wintry day.
T	F	**12.** I would like to try several types of drugs as long as they didn't harm me permanently.
T	F	**13.** Drinking and being rowdy really appeals to me on the weekend.
T	F	**14.** Rational people try to avoid dangerous situations.
T	F	**15.** I prefer Figure A to Figure B.

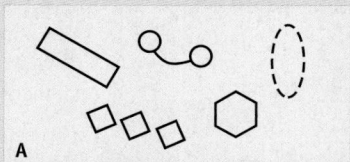

Give yourself 1 point for answering "T" to the following items: 1, 2, 4, 6, 8, 10, 12, and 13. Also give yourself 1 point for answering "F" to the following items: 3, 5, 7, 9, 11, 14, and 15. Add up your points, and compare your total to the following norms: 11–15, high sensation seeker; 6–10, moderate sensation seeker; 0–5, low sensation seeker. Bear in mind that this is a shortened version of the Sensation Seeking Scale and that it provides only a rough approximation of your status on this personality trait.

Figure 2.22

A brief scale to assess sensation seeking as a trait. First described by Marvin Zuckerman (1979, 1995), *sensation seeking* is a personality trait characterized by a generalized preference for high or low levels of sensory stimulation. People who are high in sensation seeking need a high level of stimulation. They are easily bored and they like activities that may involve some physical risk. They may satisfy their appetite for stimulation by experimenting with drugs, numerous sexual partners, and novel experiences. Follow the instructions for this version of the Sensation Seeking Scale to obtain a rough estimate of your sensation seeking tendencies. (Adapted from Grasha & Kirschenbaum, 1986) simultaneously assess a multitude of traits. The Sixteen Personality Factor Questionnaire (16PF), developed by Raymond Cattell and his colleagues (Cattell, Eber, & Tatsuoka, 1970), is a representative example of a multitrait inventory. The 16PF is a 187-item scale that measures 16 basic dimensions of personality, called source traits, which are shown in **Figure 2.23**.

As we noted earlier, some theorists believe that only five trait dimensions are required to provide a full description of personality. The five-factor model led to the creation of the NEO Personality Inventory. Developed by Paul Costa and Robert McCrae (1985, 1992), the NEO Inventory is designed to measure the Big Five traits: neuroticism, extraversion, openness to experience, agreeableness, and conscientiousness. The NEO Inventory is widely used in research and clinical work.

To appreciate the strengths of self-report inventories, consider how else you might assess your personality. For instance, how assertive are you? You probably have some vague idea, but can you accurately estimate how your assertiveness compares to others? To do that, you need a great deal of comparative information about others' usual behavior—information that all of us lack. In contrast, a self-report inventory inquires about your typical behavior in a wide variety of circumstances requiring assertiveness and generates an exact comparison with the typical behavior reported by many other respondents for the same circumstances. Thus, self-report inventories are much more thorough and precise than casual observations are.

However, these tests are only as accurate as the information that the test-takers provide (Ben-Porath, 2003). Deliberate deception can be a problem with these tests (Rees & Metcalfe, 2003), and some people are unconsciously influenced by the social desirability or acceptability of the statements (Kline, 1995; Paulhus, 1991). Without realizing it, they endorse only those statements that make them look good. This problem provides another reason why personality test results should always be regarded as suggestive rather than definitive.

Projective Tests

Projective tests, which all take a rather indirect approach to the assessment of personality, are used extensively in clinical work. ***Projective tests* ask people to respond to vague, ambiguous stimuli in ways that may reveal the respondents' needs, feelings, and personality traits.** The Rorschach test, for instance, consists of a series of ten inkblots. Respondents are asked to describe what they see in the blots. In the Thematic Apperception Test (TAT), a series of pictures of simple scenes is presented to subjects who are asked to tell stories about what is happening in the scenes and what the characters are feeling (see **Figure 2.24**). For instance, one TAT card shows a young boy contemplating a violin resting on a table in front of him.

The assumption underlying projective testing is that ambiguous materials can serve as a blank screen

Figure 2.23

The Sixteen Personality Factor Questionnaire (16PF). Cattell's 16PF is designed to assess 16 basic dimensions of personality. The pairs of traits listed across from each other in the figure define the 16 factors measured by this self-report inventory. The profile shown is the average profile seen among a group of airline pilots who took the test.

Adapted from Cattell, R. B. (1973, July). Personality pinned down. *Psychology Today,* 40–46. Reprinted by permission of Psychology Today Magazine. Copyright © 1973 Sussex Publishers, Inc.

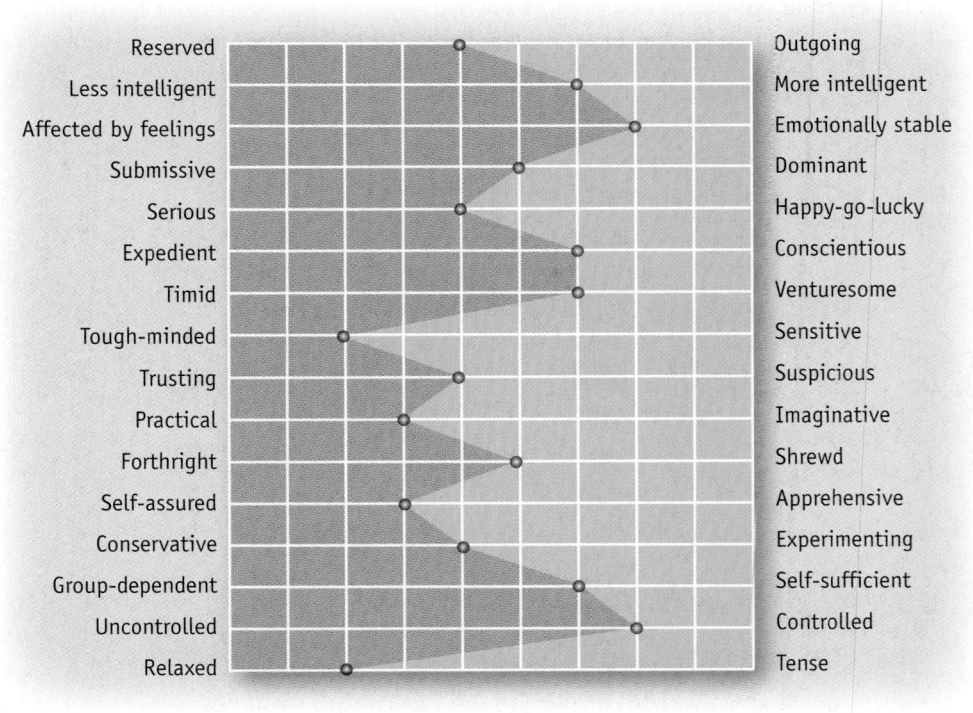

Figure 2.24

The Thematic Apperception Test (TAT). In taking the TAT, a respondent is asked to tell stories about scenes such as this one. The themes apparent in each story can be scored to provide insight about the respondent's personality.

From Murray. H. A. (1971). *Thematic Apperception Test.* Cambridge, MA: Harvard University Press. Copyright © 1943 by The President and Fellows of Harvard College, Copyright © 1971 by Henry A. Murray. Reprinted by permission of the publisher.

onto which people project their characteristic concerns, conflicts, and desires. Thus, a competitive person who is shown the TAT card of the boy at the table with the violin might concoct a story about how the boy is contemplating an upcoming musical competition at which he hopes to excel. The same card shown to a person high in impulsiveness might elicit a story about how the boy is planning to sneak out the door to go dirt-bike riding with friends.

Proponents of projective tests assert that the tests have two unique strengths. First, they are not transparent to subjects. That is, the subject doesn't know how the test provides information to the tester. Hence, it may be difficult for people to engage in intentional deception (Groth-Marnat, 1997). Second, the indirect approach used in these tests may make them especially sensitive to unconscious, latent features of personality.

Unfortunately, the scientific evidence on projective measures is unimpressive (Garb, Florio, & Grove, 1998; Hunsley, Lee, & Wood, 2003). In a thorough review of the relevant research, Lillienfeld, Wood, and Garb (2000) conclude that projective tests tend to be plagued by inconsistent scoring, low reliability, inadequate test norms, cultural bias, and poor validity estimates. They also assert that, contrary to advocates' claims, projective tests are susceptible to some types of intentional deception (primarily, faking poor mental health). Based on their analysis, Lillienfeld and his colleagues argue that projective tests should be referred to as projective "techniques" or "instruments" rather than tests because "most of these techniques as used in daily clinical practice do not fulfill the traditional criteria for psychological tests" (p. 29). In spite of these problems, projective tests continue to be used by many clinicians. Although the questionable scientific status of these techniques is a very real problem, their continued popularity suggests that they yield subjective information that many clinicians find useful (Viglione & Rivera, 2003).

KEY IDEAS

The Nature of Personality

▶ The concept of personality explains the consistency in individuals' behavior over time and situations while also explaining their distinctiveness. Personality traits are dispositions to behave in certain ways. Some theorists suggest that the complexity of personality can be reduced to just five basic traits: extraversion, neuroticism, openness to experience, agreeableness, and conscientiousness.

Psychodynamic Perspectives

▶ Freud's psychoanalytic theory emphasizes the importance of the unconscious. Freud described personality structure in terms of three components (id, ego, and superego), operating at three levels of awareness, that are involved in internal conflicts, which generate anxiety.

▶ According to Freud, people often ward off anxiety and other unpleasant emotions with defense mechanisms, which work through self-deception. Freud believed that the first five years of life are extremely influential in shaping adult personality. He describes five psychosexual stages that children undergo in their personality development.

▶ Jung's analytical psychology stresses the importance of the collective unconscious. Adler's individual psychology emphasizes how people strive for superiority to compensate for feelings of inferiority.

Behavioral Perspectives

▶ Behavioral theories view personality as a collection of response tendencies shaped through learning. Pavlov's classical conditioning can explain how people acquire emotional responses.

▶ Skinner's model of operant conditioning shows how consequences such as reinforcement, extinction, and punishment shape behavior. Bandura's social cognitive theory shows how people can be conditioned indirectly through observation. He views self-efficacy as an especially important personality trait.

Humanistic Perspectives

▶ Humanistic theories take an optimistic view of people's conscious, rational ability to chart their own courses of action. Rogers focused on the self-concept as the critical aspect of personality. He maintained that incongruence between one's self-concept and reality creates anxiety and leads to defensive behavior.

▶ Maslow theorized that needs are arranged hierarchically. He asserted that psychological health depends on fulfilling the need for self-actualization.

Biological Perspectives

▶ Eysenck believes that inherited individual differences in physiological functioning affect conditioning and thus influence personality. Recent twin studies have provided impressive evidence that genetic factors shape personality.

▶ Behavioral genetics research also suggests that the family has surprisingly little influence over personality. Evolutionary psychologists maintain that natural selection has favored the emergence of the Big Five traits as crucial dimensions of personality.

A Contemporary Empirical Approach: Terror Management Theory

▶ Terror management theory proposes that self-esteem and faith in a cultural worldview shield people from the profound anxiety associated with their mortality. Consistent with this analysis, increasing mortality salience leads people to make efforts to bolster their self-esteem and defend their worldviews. These defensive reactions are automatic and subconscious, but they influence many aspects of everyday behavior.

Culture and Personality

▶ Research suggests that the basic trait structure of personality may be much the same across cultures, as the Big Five traits usually emerge in cross-cultural studies. Cultural variations have been found in average trait scores on the Big Five traits, but the differences are modest. People's perceptions of national character appear to be remarkably inaccurate.

Application: Assessing Your Personality

▶ Psychological tests are standardized measures of behavior—usually mental abilities or aspects of personality. Test norms indicate what represents a high or low score. Psychological tests should produce consistent results upon retesting, a quality called reliability. Validity refers to the degree to which a test measures what it was designed to measure.

▶ Self-report inventories, such as the 16PF and NEO Personality Inventory, ask respondents to describe themselves. Self-report inventories can provide a better snapshot of personality than casual observations can, but they are vulnerable to deception and social desirability bias.

▶ Projective tests, such as the Rorschach and TAT, assume that people's responses to ambiguous stimuli reveal something about their personality. Projective tests' reliability and validity appear to be disturbingly low.

KEY TERMS

Archetypes p. 41
Behaviorism p. 43
Classical conditioning p. 44
Collective unconscious p. 41
Compensation p. 41
Conditioned response (CR) p. 44
Conditioned stimulus (CS) p. 44
Conscious pp. 36–37
Defense mechanisms p. 38
Displacement p. 38
Ego p. 36
Evolutionary psychology p. 58
Extinction p. 46
Factor analysis p. 33
Fixation p. 39
Heritability ratio p. 56
Hierarchy of needs pp. 52–53
Hindsight bias p. 58
Humanism p. 50
Id p. 36
Identification p. 39
Incongruence p. 51
Need for self-actualization p. 53
Negative reinforcement p. 47
Observational learning p. 48
Oedipal complex p. 40
Operant conditioning p. 46
Personality p. 33
Personality trait p. 33
Positive reinforcement p. 46
Preconscious p. 37
Projection p. 38
Projective tests p. 66
Psychodynamic theories p. 35
Psychological test p. 63
Psychosexual stages p. 39
Punishment p. 48
Rationalization p. 38
Reaction formation p. 38
Regression p. 38
Reliability p. 64
Repression p. 38
Self-concept p. 51
Self-efficacy p. 49
Self-report inventories p. 65
Standardization p. 64
Superego p. 36
Test norms p. 64
Twin studies p. 56
Unconditioned response (UCR) p. 44
Unconditioned stimulus (UCS) p. 44
Unconscious p. 37
Validity p. 64

KEY PEOPLE

Alfred Adler pp. 41–42
Albert Bandura pp. 48–49
Hans Eysenck pp. 55–56
Sigmund Freud pp. 35–41
Carl Jung p. 41
Abraham Maslow pp. 52–54
Ivan Pavlov pp. 43–46
Carl Rogers pp. 50–52
B. F. Skinner pp. 46–48

PRACTICE TEST

1. Which of the following is *not* included in McCrae and Costa's five-factor model of personality?
   a. Neuroticism
   b. Extraversion
   c. Conscientiousness
   d. Authoritarianism

2. You're feeling guilty after your third bowl of ice cream. You tell yourself it's all right because yesterday you skipped lunch. Which defense mechanism is at work?
   a. Conceptualization
   b. Displacement
   c. Rationalization
   d. Identification

3. According to Adler, _____ is a universal drive to adapt, improve oneself, and master life's challenges.
   a. compensation
   b. striving for superiority
   c. avoiding inferiority
   d. social interest

4. The strengthening of a response tendency by virtue of the fact that the response leads to the removal of an unpleasant stimulus is
   a. positive reinforcement.
   b. negative reinforcement.
   c. primary reinforcement.
   d. punishment.

5. Self-efficacy is
   a. the ability to fulfill one's potential.
   b. one's belief about one's ability to perform behaviors that should lead to expected outcomes.
   c. a durable disposition to behave in a particular way in a variety of situations.
   d. a collection of beliefs about one's nature, unique qualities, and typical behavior.

6. According to Rogers, disparity between one's self-concept and actual experience is referred to as
   a. a delusional system.
   b. dissonance.
   c. conflict.
   d. incongruence.

7. According to Maslow, which of the following is *not* characteristic of self-actualizing persons?
   a. Accurate perception of reality
   b. Being open and spontaneous
   c. Being uncomfortable with solitude
   d. Sensitivity to others' needs

8. If identical twins exhibit more personality resemblance than fraternal twins, it's probably due mostly to
   a. similar treatment from parents.
   b. their greater genetic overlap.
   c. their strong identification with each other.
   d. others' expectations that they should be similar.

9. Research on terror management theory has shown that increased mortality salience leads to all of the following except:
   a. increased striving for self-esteem.
   b. more stereotypic thinking about minorities.
   c. more aggressive behavior toward people with opposing views.
   d. reduced respect for cultural icons.

10. In psychological testing, consistency of results over repeated measurements refers to
    a. standardization.
    b. validity.
    c. statistical significance.
    d. reliability.

Book Companion Website

Visit the Book Companion Website at **academic.cengage.com/psychology/weiten,** where you will find tutorial quizzes, flash cards, and web links for every chapter, a final exam, and more! You can also link to the Psychology Resource Center (accessible directly at **academic.cengage.com/login**) for a range of psychology-related resources.

Personal Explorations Workbook

The following exercises in your *Personal Explorations Workbook* may enhance your self-understanding in relation to issues raised in this chapter. **Questionnaire 2.1:** Desirability of Control Scale. **Personal Probe 2.1:** Who Are You? **Personal Probe 2.2:** How You See Personality.

ANSWERS

1. d Pages 33–34
2. c Pages 38–39
3. b Page 41
4. b Page 47
5. b Page 49
6. d Page 51
7. c Page 54
8. b Page 56
9. d Pages 59–61
10. d Page 64

CHAPTER 3

Stress and Its Effects

THE NATURE OF STRESS
Stress Is an Everyday Event
Stress Lies in the Eye of the Beholder
Stress May Be Embedded in the Environment
Stress Is Influenced by Culture

MAJOR TYPES OF STRESS
Frustration
Conflict
Change
Pressure

RESPONDING TO STRESS
Emotional Responses
Physiological Responses
Behavioral Responses

THE POTENTIAL EFFECTS OF STRESS
Impaired Task Performance
Disruption of Cognitive Functioning
Burnout
Posttraumatic Stress Disorder

LIVING IN TODAY'S WORLD *Common Reactions to Traumatic Events*
Psychological Problems and Disorders
Physical Illness
Positive Effects

FACTORS INFLUENCING STRESS TOLERANCE
Social Support
Hardiness
Optimism

APPLICATION: MONITORING YOUR STRESS
Problems with the SRRS
The Life Experiences Survey
A Cautionary Note

REVIEW

PRACTICE TEST

You're in your car headed home from school with a classmate. Traffic is barely moving. A radio report indicates that the traffic jam is only going to get worse. You groan as you fiddle impatiently with the radio. Another motorist nearly takes your fender off trying to cut into your lane. Your pulse quickens as you shout insults at the driver, who cannot even hear you. You think about the term paper that you have to work on tonight. Your stomach knots up as you recall all the crumpled drafts you tossed into the wastebasket last night. If you don't finish the paper soon, you won't be able to find any time to study for your math test, not to mention your biology quiz. Suddenly you remember that you promised the person you're dating that the two of you would get together tonight. There's no way. Another fight looms on the horizon. Your classmate asks how you feel about the tuition increase the college announced yesterday. You've been trying not to think about it. You're already in debt up to your ears. Your parents are bugging you about changing schools, but you don't want to leave your friends. Your heartbeat quickens as you contemplate the debate you'll have to wage with your parents. You feel wired with tension as you realize that the stress in your life never seems to let up.

As this example shows, many circumstances can create stress in people's lives. Stress comes in all sorts of packages: large and small, pretty and ugly, simple and complex. All too often, the package is a surprise. In this chapter, we try to sort out these packages. We analyze the nature of stress, outline the major types of stress, and discuss how people respond to stressful events at several levels.

In a sense, stress is what a course on adjustment is all about. Recall from Chapter 1 that adjustment essentially deals with how people manage to cope with various demands and pressures. These demands or pressures represent the core of stressful experience. Thus, the central theme in a course such as this is: How do people adjust to stress, and how might they adjust more effectively?

The Nature of Stress

LEARNING OBJECTIVES

- *Describe the nature of stress and discuss how common it is.*
- *Distinguish between primary and secondary appraisal of stress.*
- *Summarize the evidence on ambient stress.*
- *Explain how culture and ethnicity are related to stress.*

Over the years, the term *stress* has been used in different ways by different theorists. Some have viewed stress as a *stimulus* event that presents difficult demands (a divorce, for instance), while others have viewed stress as the *response* of physiological arousal elicited by a troublesome event (Cooper & Dewe, 2004). However, the emerging consensus among contemporary researchers is that stress is neither a stimulus nor a response but a special stimulus-response transaction in which one feels threatened or experiences loss or harm (Carver, 2007; McEwen, 2000). Hence, we will define ***stress* as any circumstances that threaten or are perceived to threaten one's well-being and thereby tax one's coping abilities.** The threat may be to one's immediate physical safety, long-range security, self-esteem, reputation, or peace of mind. Stress is a complex concept—so let's dig a little deeper.

Stress Is an Everyday Event

The term *stress* tends to spark images of overwhelming, traumatic crises. People think of hijackings, floods, military combat, and nuclear accidents. Undeniably, these are extremely stressful events. Studies conducted in the aftermath of tornadoes, hurricanes, earthquakes, terrorist attacks, and the like typically find elevated rates of psychological problems and physical illness in the communities affected by these disasters (Raphael & Dobson, 2000; van Griensven et al., 2007; Weisler, Barbee, & Townsend, 2007). However, these unusual and infrequent events represent the tip of the iceberg. Many everyday events, such as waiting in line, having car trouble, shopping for Christmas presents, misplacing your checkbook, and staring at bills you can't pay, are also stressful. Of course, major and minor stressors are not entirely independent. A major stressful event, such as going through a divorce, can trigger a cascade of minor stressors, such as looking for an attorney, taking on new household responsibilities, and so forth (Pillow, Zautra, & Sandler, 1996).

Richard Lazarus

Courtesy of Richard Lazarus

You might guess that minor stressors would produce minor effects, but that isn't necessarily true. Research shows that routine hassles may have significant negative effects on a person's mental and physical health (Delongis, Folkman, & Lazarus, 1988). Richard Lazarus and his colleagues have devised a scale to measure stress in the form of daily hassles. Their scale lists 117 everyday problems, such as misplacing things, struggling with rising prices, dealing with delays, and so forth. When they compared their hassles scale against another scale that assessed stress in the form of major life events, they found that scores on their hassles scale were more strongly related to subjects' mental health than the scores on the other scale were (Kanner et al., 1981). Other investigators, working with different types of samples and different measures of hassles, have also found that everyday hassles are predictive of mental and physical health (Klumb & Baltes, 2004; Sher, 2003).

Why would minor hassles be more strongly related to mental health than major stressful events? The answer isn't entirely clear yet, but many theorists believe that stressful events can have a *cumulative* or *additive* impact (Seta, Seta, & McElroy, 2002). In other words, stress can add up. Routine stresses at home, at school, and at work might be fairly benign individually, but collectively they could create great strain. Whatever the reason, it is evident that daily hassles are distinct and make unique contributions to psychological distress (Serido, Almeida, & Wethington, 2004).

Stress Lies in the Eye of the Beholder

The experience of feeling threatened depends on what events you notice and how you choose to appraise or interpret them (Monroe & Kelley, 1995). Events that are stressful for one person may be "ho-hum" routine for another. For example, many people find flying in an airplane somewhat stressful, but frequent fliers may not even raise an eyebrow. Some people enjoy the excitement of going out on a date with someone new; others find the uncertainty terrifying.

In discussing appraisals of stress, Lazarus and Folkman (1984) distinguish between primary and secondary appraisal (see **Figure 3.1**). ***Primary appraisal* is an initial evaluation of whether an event is (1) irrelevant to you, (2) relevant but not threatening or (3) stressful.** When you view an event as stressful, you are likely to make a ***secondary appraisal,* which is an evaluation of your coping resources and options for dealing with the stress.** Thus, your primary appraisal would determine whether you saw an upcoming job interview as stressful. Your secondary appraisal would determine how stressful the interview appeared, in light of your assessment of your ability to deal with the event.

It should come as no surprise that people's beliefs about stressful events alter the impact of the events themselves (Daniels, Hartley, & Travers, 2006). Recent research has demonstrated that negative interpretations of events are often associated with increased distress surrounding these events (Boelen, van den Bout & van den Hout, 2003). In fact, when studying a sample of children after the 9/11 terrorist attacks, Lengua and her colleagues (2006) found that children's appraisals of the event as threatening predicted their stress symptoms as much as factors such as their coping style or pre-attack stress load.

Interestingly, people are rarely objective in their appraisals of potentially stressful events. A classic study of hospitalized patients awaiting surgery showed only a slight correlation between the objective seriousness of a person's upcoming surgery and the amount of fear the person experienced (Janis, 1958). Clearly, some people are more prone to feel threatened by life's difficulties than others. A number of studies have shown that anxious, neurotic people are more likely to make threat appraisals as well as to report more stress than others (Cooper & Bright, 2001; Schneider, 2004). Thus, stress lies in the eye (actually, the mind) of the beholder, and people's appraisals of stressful events are highly subjective.

Stress May Be Embedded in the Environment

Although the perception of stress is a highly personal matter, many kinds of stress come from the environmental circumstances that individuals share with others. ***Ambient stress* consists of chronic environmental conditions that, although not urgent, are negatively valued and that place adaptive demands on people.** Features of the environment such as excessive noise, traffic, and pollution can threaten well-being and leave their mark on mental and physical health.

For example, investigators have found an association between chronic exposure to high levels of noise and elevated blood pressure among children attending school near Los Angeles International Airport (Cohen et al., 1980). Similarly, studies of children living near Munich International Airport (Evans, Hygge, & Bullinger, 1995; Hygge, Evans, & Bullinger, 2002) have found elevated stress hormones, reading and memory deficits, and poor task persistence in samples of schoolchildren (see **Figure 3.2**).

Crowding is another source of environmental stress. Temporary experiences of crowding, such as being packed into a rock concert venue with thousands of other fans, can be stressful. Even being crowded in a laboratory setting is related to an increase in reported

Figure 3.1

Primary and secondary appraisal of stress. *Primary appraisal* is an initial evaluation of whether an event is (1) irrelevant to you, (2) relevant, but not threatening, or (3) stressful. When you view an event as stressful, you are likely to make a *secondary appraisal,* which is an evaluation of your coping resources and options for dealing with the stress. (Based on Lazarus & Folkman, 1994)

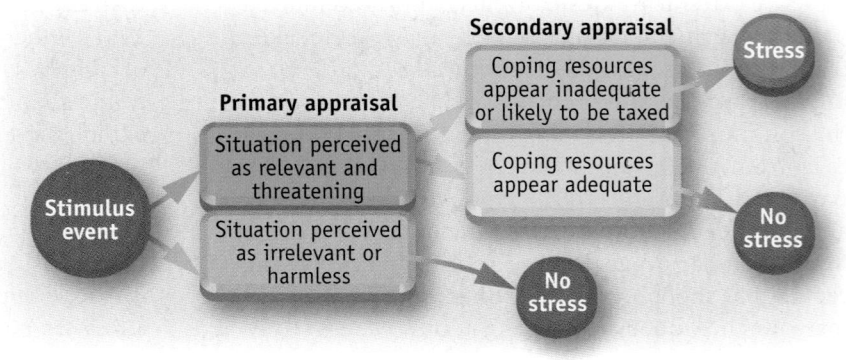

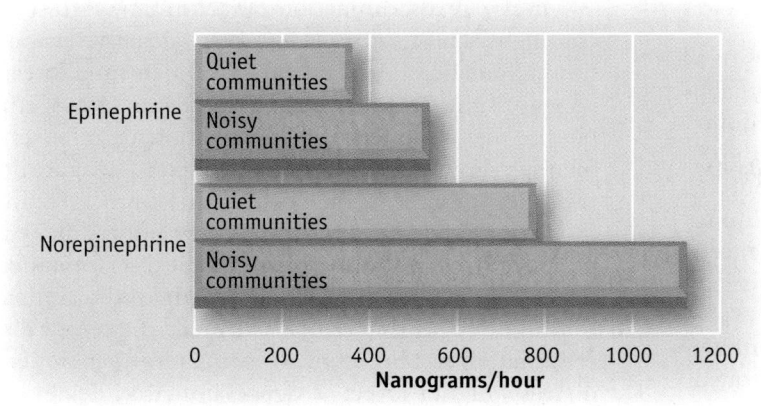

Figure 3.2

Excessive noise and stress hormones. Evans, Hygge, and Bullinger (1995) compared children from noisy areas near Munich International Airport with similar children from quiet neighborhoods in Munich. They found elevated levels of two hormones associated with stress reactions in the children exposed to the high noise of the airport. (Adapted from Evans, Hygge, & Bullinger, 1995)

stress (Martimportugués-Goyenechea & Gomez-Jacinto, 2005). However, most of the research on crowding has focused on the effects of residential density. Generally, studies suggest an association between high density and increased physiological arousal, psychological distress, and social withdrawal (Evans, 2001; Evans, LePore, & Schroeder, 1996). Siddiqui and Pandey (2003) found crowding to be one of the most critical stressors for urban residents in Northern India, indicating that this is an important issue that goes well beyond Western cities.

Psychologists have also explored the repercussions of living in areas that are at risk for disaster. For instance, studies suggest that people who live near nuclear power plants, hazardous waste sites, or polluting industrial facilities experience higher levels of distress (Downey & van Willigen, 2005). Similarly, residents in an area prone to earthquakes or hurricanes may experience increased stress (Carr, 2000; Dougall & Baum, 2000).

Recently, investigators have examined urban poverty and violence as a source of environmental stress. Ewart and Suchday (2002) developed a scale called the City Stress Inventory (CSI) to measure participants' exposure to street crime, gang activity, drug dealing, neighborhood decay, and unruly behavior. They found that scores on the CSI correlated (modestly) with measures of subjects' depressive symptoms, hostility, and irritability. More recently, Suchday and colleagues (2006) found that CSI scores were associated with high blood pressure and negative health habits such as alcohol use. Other studies have found that exposure to community violence, whether as a victim or as a witness, is associated with behavioral problems, anxiety, depression, and anger among urban youth (Foster, Kuperminc, & Price, 2004; Thompson & Massat, 2005).

© AP Images/Reed Saxon

© Richard Lord/PhotoEdit

Stress can be caused by environmental circumstances such as pollution, excessive noise, crowding, traffic jams, and urban decay.

Stress Is Influenced by Culture

Although certain types of events (such as the loss of a loved one) are probably viewed as stressful in virtually all human societies, cultures vary greatly in the predominant forms of stress their people experience. Obviously, the challenges of daily living encountered in modern, Western cities like Montreal or Philadelphia are quite different from the day-to-day difficulties experienced in indigenous societies in Africa or South America. Indeed, culture sets the context in which people experience and appraise stress (Chun, Moos, & Cronkite, 2006). The potential importance of culture is illustrated by the substantial body of evidence which suggests that *cultural change*—such as increased modernization and urbanization and shifting values and customs—has been a major source of stress in many societies around the world (Dessler, 2000). In some cases, a specific cultural group may be exposed to pervasive stress that is unique to that group (Berry & Ataca, 2000). For example, the ethnic cleansing of Albanians in Kosovo in 1999 and the devastating and widespread destruction from the tsunami in Indonesia and regions of Southeast Asia in 2004 were extraordinary forms of stress distinctive to these societies. Our discussion of stress will largely focus on the types of stressors confronted in everyday life in contemporary, Western society, but you should be aware that life in our society is not necessarily representative of life around the world.

Moreover, even within the modern, Western world, disparities can be found in the constellation of stressors experienced by specific cultural groups (Mino, Profit, & Pierce, 2000). In recent years, researchers have shown a new interest in the effects of ethnicity-related sources of stress experienced by African Americans, Hispanic Americans, Asian Americans, and other minority groups (Contrada et al., 2000). Social scientists interested in ethnicity have traditionally focused their attention on the causes of institutional racism, such as discrimination in hiring and in access to health care. But their focus has been shifting to the effects of subtle discrimination in day-to-day living. Although overt racial discrimination in America clearly has declined in recent decades, covert expressions of ethnic prejudice continue to be commonplace (Dovidio & Gaertner, 1999). For example, in one study of 520 African Americans, 96 percent of the respondents reported experiencing some type of racist discrimination in the most recent year—and 95 percent of these subjects indicated that they found this discrimination to be stressful (Klonoff & Landrine, 1999).

Everyday discrimination can take many forms, including verbal insults (ethnic slurs), negative evaluations, avoidance, denial of equal treatment, and threats of aggression. Feldman-Barrett and Swim (1998) emphasize that these acts of discrimination are often ambiguous (examples: "The clerk seemed to be ignoring me," "The teacher seemed disdainful of me"). Hence, theorists assert that minority group members may experience stress not only from explicit discrimination but also from the subjective perception of discrimination in ambiguous situations. In fact, perceived discrimination has been linked to greater psychological distress, higher levels of depression, and decreased well-being for a variety of minority groups, including sexual minorities such as lesbians (Lewis et al., 2006; Moradi & Risco, 2006; Sellers et al., 2006).

In addition to discrimination, members of ethnic minorities experience stress because they are keenly aware of negative racial stereotypes and often worry that others will interpret their behavior in ways that confirm these derogatory stereotypes (Steele, 1997). So the threat of *stereotype confirmation* can become a source of chronic apprehension. At the other extreme, individuals are often chastised by members of their own group for "acting white" or abandoning their cultural heritage (Contrada et al., 2000). Thus, ethnic minorities may be under constant pressure to conform to the expectations and values of their own group. In fact, for immigrants, ***acculturation*, or changing to adapt to a new culture,** is a major source of stress related to reduced well-being (Moradi & Risco, 2006; Ying & Han, 2006). Lopez (2005) surveyed Latino freshman during their first year at a predominately white college and found that they reported stress from their own Latino community (shown through statements such as "pressures to show loyalty to my race") as well as from experiencing discrimination ("being treated rudely due to race").

It seems likely that the extra layers of stress experienced by minority group members takes its toll on them. Scientists are still exploring the degree to which ethnicity-related stress may have detrimental effects on individuals' mental and physical health.

Web Link 3.1 **Centre for Stress Management**

This British website houses a diverse collection of brief online articles concerned with many aspects of the stress process. It also features links to many other sites around the world that provide information on stress.

Major Types of Stress

LEARNING OBJECTIVES

- *Distinguish between acute and chronic stressors.*
- *Describe frustration as a form of stress.*
- *Outline the three types of conflict, and discuss typical reactions to conflicts.*
- *Summarize evidence on life change as a form of stress.*
- *Discuss evidence on pressure as a form of stress.*

An enormous variety of events can be stressful for one person or another. To achieve a better understanding of stress, theorists have tried to analyze the nature of stressful events and divide them into subtypes. One sensible distinction involves differentiating between *acute stressors* and *chronic stressors* (Dougall & Baum, 2001). ***Acute stressors* are threatening events that have a relatively short duration and a clear endpoint.** Examples would include having a difficult encounter with a belligerent drunk, waiting for the results of a medical test, or having your home threatened by severe flooding. ***Chronic stressors* are threatening events that have a relatively long duration and no readily apparent time limit.** Examples would include persistent financial strains produced by huge credit card debts, ongoing pressures from a hostile boss at work, or the demands of caring for a sick family member over a period of years. Of course, this distinction is far from perfect. It is hard to decide where to draw the line between a short-lived versus lengthy stressor, and even brief stressors can have long-lasting effects.

None of the proposed schemes for classifying stressful events has turned out to be altogether satisfactory. Classifying stressful events into nonintersecting categories is virtually impossible. Although this problem presents conceptual headaches for researchers, it need not prevent us from describing four major types of stress: frustration, conflict, change, and pressure. As you read about each of them, you'll surely recognize some familiar situations.

Frustration

"It has been very frustrating to watch the rapid deterioration of my parents' relationship. Over the last year or two they have argued constantly and have refused to seek any professional help. I have tried to talk to them, but they kind of shut me and my brother out of their problem. I feel very helpless and sometimes even very angry, not at them, but at the whole situation."

This scenario illustrates frustration. As psychologists use the term, ***frustration* occurs in any situation in which the pursuit of some goal is thwarted.** In essence, you experience frustration when you want something and you can't have it. Everyone has to deal with frustration virtually every day. Traffic jams, long daily commutes, and annoying drivers, for instance, are a routine source of frustration that can elicit anger and increase levels of stress (Evans & Wener, 2006; Hennessy & Wiesenthal, 1999). Even artificially induced frustration in a laboratory setting leads to increased aggression (Verona & Curtin, 2006). Fortunately, most frustrations are brief and insignificant. You may be quite upset when you go to the auto shop to pick up your car and find that it hasn't been fixed as promised. However, a few days later you'll probably have your precious car back, and all will be forgotten.

Of course, some frustrations can be sources of significant stress. *Failures* and *losses* are two common kinds of frustration that are often very stressful. All people fail in at least some of their endeavors. Some make failure almost inevitable by setting unrealistic goals for themselves. People tend to forget that for every newly appointed vice-president in the business world, there are dozens of middle-level executives who don't get promoted. Losses may be especially frustrating when people are deprived of something they are accustomed to having. For example, there are few things that are more painful and frustrating than losing a dearly loved friend or family member.

More often than not, frustration appears to be the culprit at work when people feel troubled by environmental stress (Graig, 1993). Excessive noise, heat, pollution, and crowding are most likely stressful because they frustrate the desire for quiet, a comfortable body temperature, clean air, and adequate privacy. Interestingly, frustration in the workplace often results in burnout (Lewandowski, 2003), a specific effect of stress that we will discuss later in this chapter.

Conflict

"Should I or shouldn't I? I became engaged at Christmas. My fiancé surprised me with a ring. I knew if I refused the ring he would be terribly hurt and our relationship would suffer. However, I don't really know whether or not I want to marry him. On the other hand, I don't want to lose him either."

Like frustration, conflict is an unavoidable feature of everyday life. That perplexing question "Should I or shouldn't I?" comes up countless times on a daily basis. ***Conflict* occurs when two or more incompatible motivations or behavioral impulses compete for expression.** As we discussed in Chapter 2, Sigmund Freud proposed over a century ago that internal conflicts generate considerable psychological distress. This link between conflict and distress was measured with precision in studies by Laura King and Robert Emmons (1990, 1991). They used an elaborate questionnaire to assess the overall amount of internal conflict experienced by subjects. They found higher levels of conflict to be associated with higher levels of psychological distress.

Conflicts come in three types, which were originally described by Kurt Lewin (1935) and investigated extensively by Neal Miller (1944, 1959). These types—approach-approach, avoidance-avoidance, and approach-avoidance—are diagrammed in **Figure 3.3**.

Courtesy, Neal Miller

Neal Miller

In an ***approach-approach conflict* a choice must be made between two attractive goals.** The problem, of course, is that you can choose just one of the two goals. For example, you have a free afternoon; should you play tennis or go to the movies? You're out for a meal; do you want to order the pizza or the spaghetti? You can't afford both; should you buy the blue sweater or the gray jacket? Among the three kinds of conflict, the approach-approach type tends to be the least stressful. People don't usually stagger out of restaurants, exhausted by the stress of choosing which of several appealing entrees to eat. In approach-approach conflicts you typically have a reasonably happy ending, whichever way you decide to go. Nonetheless, approach-approach conflicts centering on important issues may sometimes be troublesome. If you are torn between two appealing college majors or two attractive boyfriends, you may find the decision-making process quite stressful.

In an *avoidance-avoidance conflict* a choice must be made between two unattractive goals. Forced to choose between two repelling alternatives, you are, as they say, "caught between a rock and a hard place." For example, let's say you have painful backaches. Should you submit to surgery that you dread, or should you continue to live with the pain? Obviously, avoidance-avoidance conflicts are most unpleasant and highly stressful. Typically, people keep delaying their decision as long as possible, hoping that they will somehow be able to escape the conflict situation. For example, you might delay surgery in the hope that your backaches will disappear on their own.

In an *approach-avoidance conflict* a choice must be made about whether to pursue a single goal that has both attractive and unattractive aspects. For instance, imagine that you're offered a career promotion that will mean a large increase in pay. The catch is that you will have to move to a city that you hate. Approach-avoidance conflicts are common, and they can be highly stressful. Any time you have to take a risk to pursue some desirable outcome, you are likely to find yourself in an approach-avoidance conflict. Should you risk rejection by asking out that attractive person in class? Should you risk your savings by investing in a new business that could fail? Approach-avoidance conflicts often produce *vacillation.* That is, people go back and forth, beset by indecision that can create stress. Fortunately we are equipped to focus on the positive aspects of our decision once it has been made (Brehm, 1956).

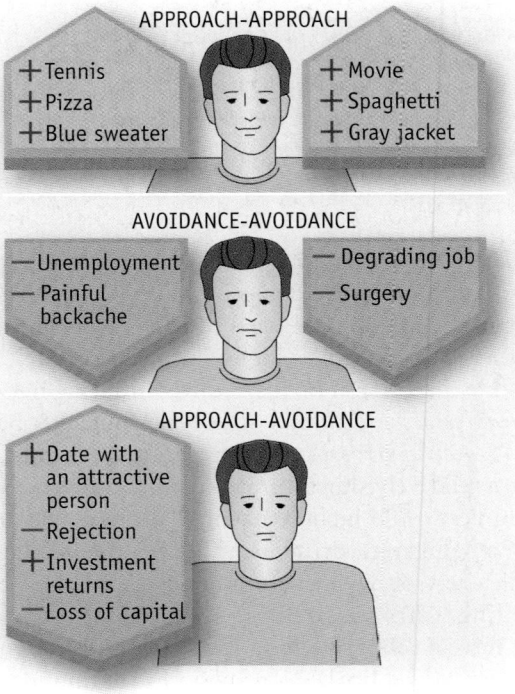

Figure 3.3

Types of conflict. Psychologists have identified three basic types of conflict. In approach-approach and avoidance-avoidance conflicts, the person is torn between two goals. In an approach-avoidance conflict only one goal is under consideration, but it has both positive and negative aspects.

Change

"After graduation, I landed my dream job and moved to another state. For the first time, I am living alone, far away from my friends and family. My biggest stress is getting used to my new life. Everything is different. I am learning how to do my new job, trying to make friends, and navigating my way around my new city. I love my job and my

new location, but I am having difficulties dealing with all these changes at once."

Life changes may represent a key type of stress. ***Life changes* are any noticeable alterations in one's living circumstances that require readjustment.** Research on life change began when Thomas Holmes, Richard Rahe, and their colleagues set out to explore the relation between stressful life events and physical illness (Holmes & Rahe, 1967; Rahe & Arthur, 1978). They interviewed thousands of tuberculosis patients to find out what kinds of events preceded the onset of their disease. Surprisingly, the frequently cited events were not uniformly negative. The list included plenty of aversive events, as expected, but patients also mentioned many seemingly positive events, such as getting married, having a baby, or getting promoted.

Why would positive events, such as moving to a nicer home, produce stress? According to Holmes and Rahe, it is because they produce *change.* Their thesis is that disruptions of daily routines are stressful. According to their theory, changes in personal relationships, changes at work, changes in finances, and so forth can be stressful even when the changes are welcomed.

Based on this analysis, Holmes and Rahe (1967) developed the Social Readjustment Rating Scale (SRRS) to measure life change as a form of stress. The scale assigns numerical values to 43 major life events that are supposed to reflect the magnitude of the readjustment required by each change (see **Figure 3.4** on the next page). In responding to the scale, respondents are asked to indicate how often they experienced any of these 43 events during a certain time period (typically, the past year). The person then adds up the numbers associated with each event checked. This sum is an index of the amount of change-related stress the person has recently experienced.

The SRRS and similar scales have been used in thousands of studies by researchers all over the world. Overall, these studies have shown that people with higher scores on the SRRS tend to be more vulnerable to many kinds of physical illness—and many types of psychological problems as well (Lynch et al., 2005; Rahe et al., 2000; Scully, Tosi, & Banning, 2000). These results have attracted a great deal of attention, and the SRRS has been reprinted in many newspapers and popular magazines. The attendant publicity has led to the widespread conclusion that life change is inherently stressful.

More recently, however, experts have criticized this research, citing problems with the methods used and raising questions about the meaning of the findings (Hobson & Delunas, 2001; Jones & Kinman, 2001; Monroe & McQuaid, 1994). At this point, it is a key interpretive issue that concerns us. Many critics have argued that the SRRS does not measure *change* exclusively. The list of life changes on the SRRS is dominated by events that are clearly negative or undesirable (marital separation, fired at work, and so on). These negative events probably generate great frustration. So even though the scale contains some positive events, it could be that frustration (generated by negative events), rather than change, creates most of the stress assessed by the scale.

To investigate this possibility, researchers came up with ways to take into account the desirability and undesirability of subjects' life changes. Participants were asked to indicate the desirability of the events that they checked off on the SRRS and similar scales. The findings in these studies clearly indicated that life change is *not* the crucial dimension measured by the SRRS and that in fact undesirable or negative life events cause most of the stress tapped by the scale (McLean & Link, 1994; Turner & Wheaton, 1995).

Should we discard the notion that change is stressful? Not entirely. Other lines of research, independent of work with the SRRS, support the hypothesis that change is an important form of stress. For instance, researchers have found associations between geographic mobility and impaired mental and physical health that

Social Readjustment Rating Scale

Life event	Mean value	Life event	Mean value
Death of a spouse	100	Son or daughter leaving home	29
Divorce	73	Trouble with in-laws	29
Marital separation	65	Outstanding personal achievement	28
Jail term	63	Spouse begins or stops work	26
Death of close family member	63	Begin or end school	26
Personal injury or illness	53	Change in living conditions	25
Marriage	50	Revision of personal habits	24
Fired at work	47	Trouble with boss	23
Marital reconciliation	45	Change in work hours or conditions	20
Retirement	45	Change in residence	20
Change in health of family member	44	Change in school	20
Pregnancy	40	Change in recreation	19
Sex difficulties	39	Change in church activities	19
Gain of a new family member	39	Change in social activities	18
Business readjustment	39	Loan for lesser purchase (car, TV, etc.)	17
Change in financial state	38	Change in sleeping habits	16
Death of a close friend	37	Change in number of family get-togethers	15
Change to a different line of work	36	Change in eating habits	15
Change in number of arguments with spouse	35	Vacation	13
Mortgage or loan for major purchase	31	Christmas	12
Foreclosure of mortgage or loan	30	Minor violations of the law	11
Change in responsibilities at work	29		

Figure 3.4

Social Readjustment Rating Scale (SRRS). Devised by Holmes and Rahe (1967), this scale is designed to measure the change-related stress in one's life. The numbers on the right are supposed to reflect the average amount of stress (readjustment) produced by each event. Respondents check off the events that have occurred to them recently and add up the associated numbers to arrive at their stress scores. See the Application for a detailed critique of the SRRS.

Adapted from Holmes, T. H., & Rahe, R. (1967). The Social Readjustment Rating Scale. *Journal of Psychosomatic Research, 11,* 213–218. Copyright © 1967 by Elsevier Science Publishing Co. Reprinted by permission.

presumably reflect the impact of change (Brett, 1980; Shuval, 1993). A study by Brown and McGill (1989) suggests that desirable life changes may be stressful for some people but not for others. More research is needed, but it is quite plausible that change constitutes a major type of stress in people's lives. However, we have little reason to believe that change is *inherently* or *inevitably stressful.* Some life changes may be quite challenging, while others may be quite benign.

Web Link 3.2 **Psychological Self-Tools: Anxiety and Worry**

The Mental Help Net website exists "to promote mental health and wellness education and advocacy." Basically, this site provides a comprehensive online self-help book with a particularly fine discussion of the nature of stress and its relationship to psychological and physical disorders.

Pressure

"My father questioned me at dinner about some things I did not want to talk about. I know he doesn't want to hear my answers, at least not the truth. My father told me when I was little that I was his favorite because I was 'pretty near perfect' and I've spent my life trying to keep that up, even though it's obviously not true. Recently, he has begun to realize this and it's made our relationship very strained and painful."

At one time or another, most of us have probably remarked that we were "under pressure." What does that expression mean? ***Pressure* involves expectations or**

demands that one behave in a certain way. Pressure can be divided into two subtypes: the pressure to *perform* and the pressure to *conform.* You are under pressure to perform when you are expected to execute tasks and responsibilities quickly, efficiently, and successfully. For example, salespeople are usually under pressure to move lots of merchandise. Professors at research institutions are often under pressure to publish in prestigious journals. Comedians are under pressure to be amusing. Secretaries are often under pressure to complete lots of clerical work in very little time. Pressures to conform to others' expectations are also common. Businessmen are expected to wear suits and ties. Suburban homeowners are expected to keep their lawns manicured. Teenagers are expected to adhere to their parents' values and rules. Young adults are expected to get themselves married by the time they're 30.

Although widely discussed by the general public, the concept of pressure has received scant attention from researchers. However, one scale has been developed to measure pressure as a form of life stress (Weiten, 1988). Studies with this scale have found a strong relationship between pressure and a variety of psychological symptoms and problems (Weiten, 1988, 1998). In fact, pressure has turned out to be more strongly related to measures of mental health than the SRRS and other established measures of stress (see **Figure 3.5**). Recent research suggests that stress resulting from academic pressure may actually impede academic performance and lead to problematic escape behaviors such as drinking (Kaplan, Liu, & Kaplan, 2005; Kieffer, Cronin, & Gawet, 2006).

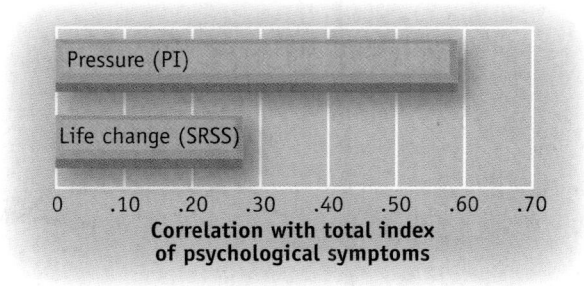

Figure 3.5

Pressure and psychological symptoms. A comparison of pressure and life change as sources of stress suggests that pressure may be more strongly related to mental health than change is. In one study, Weiten (1988) found a correlation of .59 between scores on the Pressure Inventory (PI) and symptoms of psychological distress. In the same sample, the correlation between SRRS scores and psychological symptoms was only .28.

We tend to think of pressure as something imposed on us from outside forces. However, studies of high school and college students find that pressure is often self-imposed (Kouzma & Kennedy, 2004; Misra & Castillo, 2004). For example, you might sign up for extra classes to get through school quickly. Or you might actively seek additional leadership positions to impress your family. People frequently put pressure on themselves to get good grades or to rapidly climb the corporate ladder. Many people create stress by embracing unrealistic expectations for themselves. In short, people might have more control over their stress than they realize.

© Allen Birnbach/Masterfile

© Kelvin Murray/Stone/Getty Images

Pressure comes in two varieties: pressure to perform and pressure to conform. For example, workers on assembly lines are often expected to maintain high productivity with few mistakes (performance pressure) and suburban homeowners are typically expected to maintain well-groomed exteriors (conformity pressure).

Responding to Stress

LEARNING OBJECTIVES

- *List three categories of negative emotions commonly elicited by stress.*
- *Discuss the role of positive emotions in the stress process.*
- *Explain the effects of emotional arousal on coping efforts, and describe the inverted-U hypothesis.*
- *Describe the fight-or-flight response and contrast it with the tend-and-befriend response.*
- *Describe the three stages of the general adaptation syndrome.*
- *Distinguish between the two major pathways along which the brain sends signals to the endocrine system in response to stress.*
- *Explain the concept of coping.*

The human response to stress is complex and multidimensional. Stress affects people at several levels. Consider again the chapter's opening scenario, in which you're driving home in heavy traffic, thinking about overdue papers, tuition increases, and parental pressures. Let's look at some of the reactions we mentioned. When you groan in reaction to the traffic report, you're experiencing an *emotional response* to stress—in this case, annoyance and anger. When your pulse quickens and your stomach knots up, you're exhibiting *physiological responses* to stress. When you shout insults at another driver, your verbal aggression is a *behavioral response* to the stress at hand. Thus, we can analyze people's reactions to stress at three levels: (1) their emotional responses, (2) their physiological responses, and (3) their behavioral responses. **Figure 3.6** depicts these three levels of response.

Emotional Responses

Emotion is an elusive concept. Psychologists debate about how to define emotion, and many conflicting theories purport to explain emotion. However, everybody has had extensive personal experience with emotions. Everyone has a good idea of what it means to be anxious, elated, gloomy, jealous, disgusted, excited, guilty, or nervous. So rather than pursue the technical debates about emotion, we'll rely on your familiarity with the concept and simply note that ***emotions* are powerful, largely uncontrollable feelings, accompanied by physiological changes.** When people are under stress, they often react emotionally. More often than not, stress tends to elicit unpleasant emotions (Lazarus, 1993), a fact that seems to transcend time and cul-

Web Link 3.3 **American Psychological Association: Stress**

The American Psychological Association is the largest professional organization for psychologists. This website presents up-to-date coverage of stress research, including recent press releases and psychological research in the news. This site provides a nice peek into stress research currently being published.

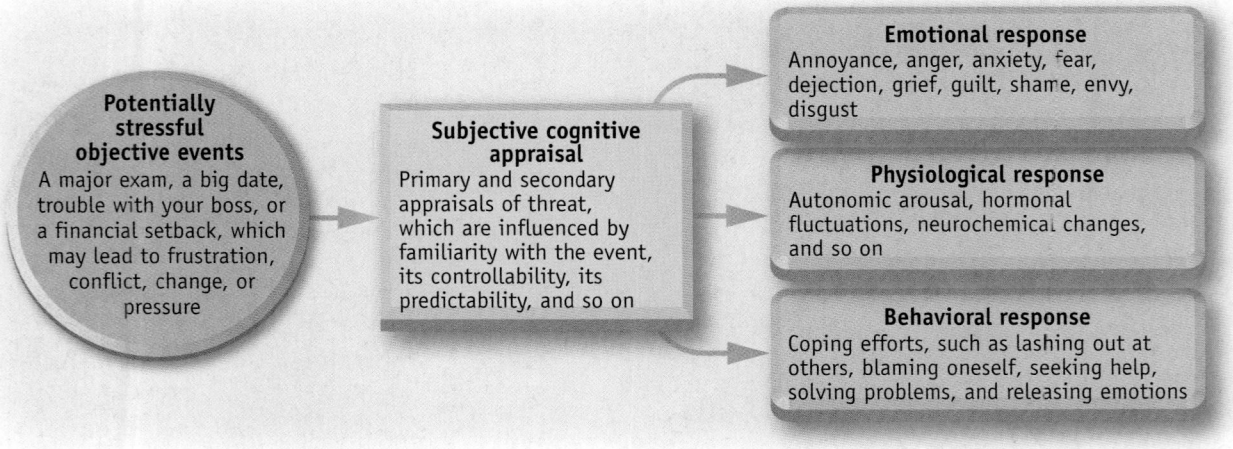

Figure 3.6

The multidimensional response to stress. A potentially stressful event, such as a major exam, will elicit a subjective, cognitive appraisal of how threatening the event is. If the event is viewed with alarm, the stress may trigger emotional, physiological, and behavioral reactions. The human response to stress is multidimensional.

ture. Recently, a historical researcher, examining texts from 2100–2000 B.C., found evidence that these core negative emotional reactions to trauma have not really changed over the millennia (Ben-Ezra, 2004).

Negative Emotions

There are no simple one-to-one connections between certain types of stressful events and particular emotions, but researchers *have* begun to uncover some strong links between specific *cognitive reactions to stress (appraisals)* and specific emotions (Smith & Lazarus, 1993). For example, self-blame tends to lead to guilt, helplessness to sadness, and so forth. Although stressful events can evoke many negative emotions, some are certainly more likely than others. Common negative emotional responses to stress include (Lazarus, 1993):

Annoyance, anger, and rage. Stress often produces feelings of anger ranging in intensity from mild annoyance to uncontrollable rage. Frustration is particularly likely to generate anger.

Apprehension, anxiety, and fear. Stress probably evokes anxiety and fear more frequently than any other emotions. As we saw in Chapter 2, Freudian theory has long recognized the link between conflict and anxiety. However, anxiety can also be elicited by the pressure to perform, the threat of impending frustration, or the uncertainty associated with change.

Dejection, sadness, and grief. Sometimes stress—especially frustration—simply brings one down. Routine setbacks, such as traffic tickets and poor grades, often produce feelings of dejection. More profound setbacks, such as deaths and divorces, typically leave one grief-stricken.

Of course, the above list is not exhaustive. In his insightful analyses of stress-emotion relations, Richard Lazarus (1991, 1993) mentions five other negative emotions that often figure prominently in reactions to stress: guilt, shame, envy, jealousy, and disgust.

Positive Emotions

Although investigators have tended to focus heavily on the connection between stress and negative emotions, research shows that positive emotions also occur during periods of stress (Folkman, 1997). This finding may seem counterintuitive, but researchers have found that people experience a diverse array of pleasant emotions even while enduring the most dire of circumstances. Consider, for example, the results of a five-year study of coping patterns in 253 caregiving partners of men with AIDS (Folkman et al., 1997). Surprisingly, over the course of the study, the caregivers reported experiencing positive emotions about as often as they experienced negative ones—except during the time immediately surrounding the death of their partners.

Similar findings have been observed in some other studies of serious stress that made an effort to look for positive emotions. The most interesting was a recent study that examined subjects' emotional functioning early in 2001 and then again in the weeks following the 9/11 terrorist attacks in the United States (Fredrickson et al., 2003). Like most U.S. citizens, these subjects reported many negative emotions in the aftermath of 9/11, including anger, sadness, and fear. However, within this "dense cloud of anguish" positive emotions also emerged. For example, people felt gratitude for the safety of their loved ones, many took stock and counted their blessings, and quite a few reported renewed love for their friends and family. Fredrickson et al. (2003) also found that the frequency of pleasant emotions correlated positively with a measure of subjects' resilience, whereas unpleasant emotions correlated negatively with resilience (see **Figure 3.7**). Based on their analyses, the researchers concluded that "positive emotions in the aftermath of crises buffer resilient people against depression and fuel thriving" (p. 365). Thus, contrary to common sense, positive emotions do *not* vanish during times of severe stress. Moreover, these positive emotions appear to play a key role in helping people bounce back from the negative emotions associated with stress (Ong et al., 2006; Tugade & Fredrickson, 2004).

Correlation Between Resilience and the Frequency of Selected Emotions in the Aftermath of 9/11

Specific emotions	Correlation with resilience
Negative emotions	
Angry/irritated/annoyed	−.44*
Sad/downhearted/unhappy	−.29*
Scared/fearful/afraid	−.19
Disgust/distate/revulsion	−.09
Positive emotions	
Grateful/appreciative/thankful	.13
Glad/happy/joyful	.52*
Hopeful/optimistic/encouraged	.40*
Content/serene/peaceful	.47*

*Statistically significant

Figure 3.7

Positive and negative emotions as correlates of resilience. Fredrickson et al. (2003) asked subjects to rate the frequency with which they experienced 20 different emotions in the aftermath of 9/11. The frequency ratings for specific emotions were then correlated with a measure of participants' resiliency. Representative results (for 8 of the 20 emotions studied) are shown here. As you can see, the frequency of pleasant emotions correlated positively with resiliency, whereas the opposite was true for negative emotions. (Adapted from Fredrickson et al., 2003)

How do positive emotions promote resilience in the face of stress? Susan Folkman and Judith Moskowitz (2000) argue that positive emotions experienced while under duress can promote creativity and flexibility in problem solving, facilitate the processing of important information about oneself, and reduce the adverse physiological effects of stress. Recent evidence suggests that these healthy outcomes occur because positive emotions broaden the scope of our attention, leading to broad-minded coping and positive *re*appraisals of a stressful situation (Fredrickson & Branigan, 2005). Positive emotions can also enhance immune system functioning, increase valuable social support available from friends and family, and promote proactive coping efforts (Salovey et al., 2000).

Courtesy, Susan Folkman

Susan Folkman

Simply put, positive emotions can contribute to building social, intellectual, and physical resources that can be helpful in dealing with stress and allow one to experience flourishing mental health (Fredrickson, 1998, 2001; Fredrickson & Losada, 2005). In fact, the benefits of positive emotions are so strong, Fredrickson (2006) argues that people should "cultivate positive emotions in themselves and in those around them as means to achieving psychological growth and improved psychological and physical well-being over time" (p. 85).

Effects of Emotional Arousal

Emotional responses are a natural and normal part of life. Even unpleasant emotions serve important purposes. Like physical pain, painful emotions can serve as warnings that one needs to take action. However, strong emotional arousal can also hamper efforts to cope with stress. For example, research has found that high emotional arousal can sometimes interfere with attention and memory retrieval and can impair judgment and decision making (Janis, 1993; Mandler, 1993).

The well-known problem of *test anxiety* illustrates how emotional arousal can hurt performance. Often students who score poorly on an exam will nonetheless insist that they know the material. Many of them are probably telling the truth. Several researchers have found a negative correlation between test-related anxiety and exam performance. That is, students who display high test anxiety tend to score low on exams (Hancock, 2001; Naveh-Benjamin et al., 1997). Test anxiety can interfere with test taking in several ways, but one critical consideration appears to be the disruption of attention to the test (Keough et al., 2004). Many test-anxious students waste too much time worrying about how they're doing and wondering whether others are having similar problems. In addition, there is evidence that test anxiety may deplete one's capacity for self-control, increasing the chance for poor performance (Oaten & Cheng, 2005). In other words, once distracted, test-anxious students might not have the self-control to get themselves back on course. This tendency is related to a concept called *ego depletion* that we will discuss in Chapter 5.

Although emotional arousal may hurt coping efforts, this isn't *necessarily* the case. The *inverted-U hypothesis* predicts that task performance should improve with increased emotional arousal—up to a point, after which further increases in arousal become disruptive and performance deteriorates (Anderson, 1990; Mandler, 1993). This idea is referred to as the inverted-U hypothesis because plotting performance as a function of arousal results in graphs that approximate an upside-down U (see **Figure 3.8**). In these graphs, the level of arousal at which performance peaks is characterized as the *optimal level of arousal* for a task.

This optimal level of arousal appears to depend in part on the complexity of the task at hand. The conventional wisdom is that *as tasks become more complex, the optimal level of arousal (for peak performance) tends to decrease.* This relationship is depicted in **Figure 3.8**. As you can see, a fairly high level of arousal should be optimal on simple tasks (such as driving eight hours to help a friend in a crisis). However, performance should peak at a lower level of arousal on complex tasks (such as making a major decision in which you have to weigh many factors).

The research evidence on the inverted-U hypothesis is inconsistent and subject to varied interpretations (Neiss, 1988, 1990). The original formulation of this hypothesis was more related to animal learning than to human performance in stressful situations (Hancock & Ganey, 2003). Hence, it may be risky to generalize this principle to the complexities of everyday coping efforts. Nonetheless, the inverted-U hypothesis provides a plausible model of how emotional arousal could have either beneficial or disruptive effects on coping, depending on the nature of the stressful demands.

Physiological Responses

As we have seen, stress frequently elicits strong emotional responses. These responses bring about important physiological changes. Even in cases of moderate stress, you may notice that your heart has started beating faster, you have begun to breathe harder, and you are perspiring more than usual. How does all this (and much more) happen? Let's see.

The "Fight-or-Flight" Response

The *fight-or-flight response* is a physiological reaction to threat that mobilizes an organism for attacking (fight) or fleeing (flight) an enemy. First described by Walter Cannon (1932), the fight-or-flight response

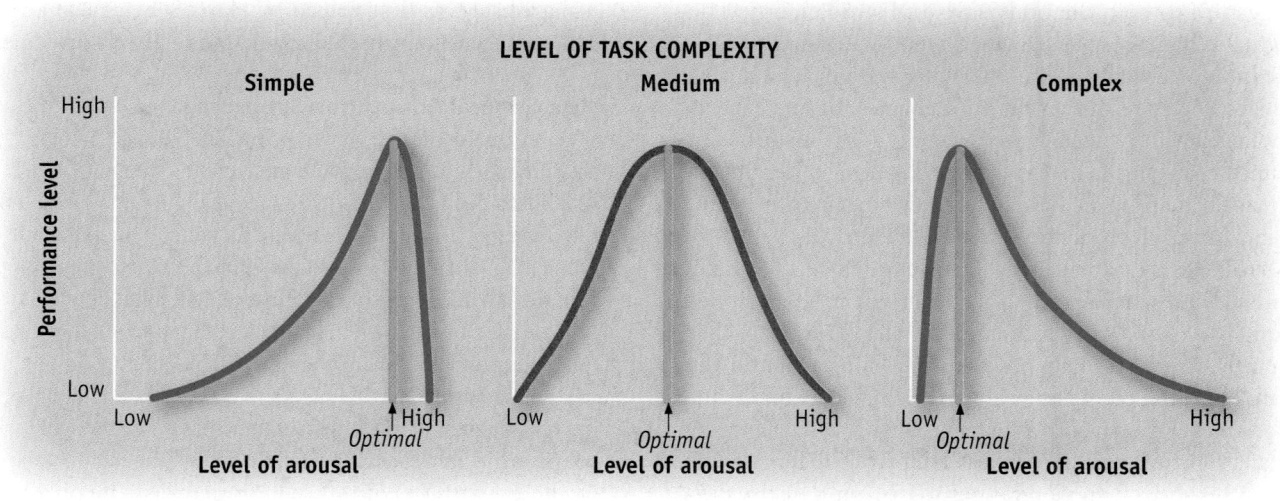

Figure 3.8

Arousal and performance. Graphs of the relationship between emotional arousal and task performance tend to resemble an inverted U, as increased arousal is associated with improved performance up to a point, after which higher arousal leads to poorer performance. The optimal level of arousal for a task depends on the complexity of the task. On complex tasks, a relatively low level of arousal tends to be optimal. On simple tasks, however, performance may peak at a much higher level of arousal.

occurs in the body's autonomic nervous system. **The *autonomic nervous system (ANS)* is made up of the nerves that connect to the heart, blood vessels, smooth muscles, and glands.** As its name hints, the autonomic nervous system is somewhat *autonomous.* That is, it controls involuntary, visceral functions that people don't normally think about, such as heart rate, digestion, and perspiration.

The autonomic nervous system can be broken into two divisions (see **Figure 3.9**). The *parasympathetic division* of the ANS generally conserves bodily resources. For instance, it slows heart rate and promotes

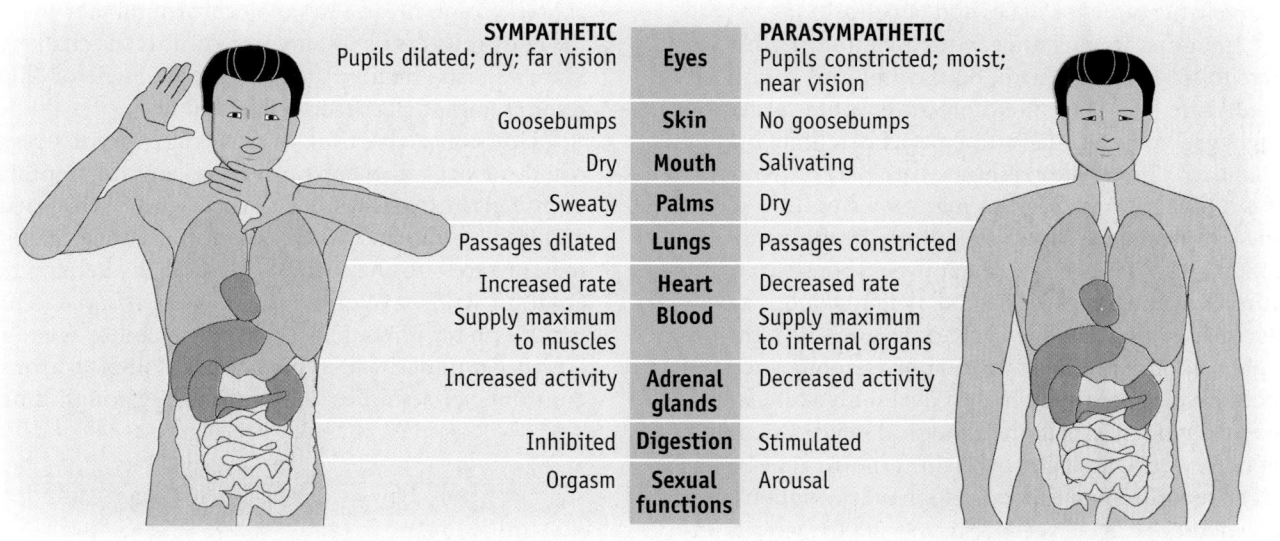

Figure 3.9

The autonomic nervous system (ANS). The ANS is composed of the nerves that connect to the heart, blood vessels, smooth muscles, and glands. The ANS is subdivided into the *sympathetic division,* which mobilizes bodily resources in times of need, and the *parasympathetic division,* which conserves bodily resources. Some of the key functions controlled by each division of the ANS are summarized in the center of the diagram.

digestion to help the body save and store energy. The fight-or-flight response is mediated by the *sympathetic division* of the autonomic nervous system, which mobilizes bodily resources for emergencies. In one experiment, Cannon studied the fight-or-flight response in cats by confronting them with dogs. Among other things, he noticed an immediate acceleration in breathing and heart rate and a reduction in digestive processes.

Shelley Taylor and her colleagues (2000) have questioned whether the fight-or-flight model applies equally well to both males and females. They note that in most species females have more responsibility for the care of young offspring than males do. Using an evolutionary perspective, they argue that this disparity may make fighting and fleeing less adaptive for females, as both responses may endanger offspring and thus reduce the likelihood of an animal passing on its genes. Taylor and colleagues maintain that evolutionary processes have fostered more of a "tend and befriend" response to stress in females. According to this analysis, in reacting to stress, females allocate more effort to the care of offspring and to seeking help and support. Consistent with this theory, David and Lyons-Ruth (2005) found gender differences in how infants respond to threat. Females infants showed more approach behaviors to frightening mothers (for example, mothers who suddenly loomed over the infant or assumed an attack posture) than male infants did. More research is needed to evaluate this provocative analysis. Even though they hypothesize gender differences in behavioral responses to stress, Taylor and her colleagues are quick to note that the "basic neuroendocrine core of stress responses" is largely the same for males and females.

Imagine, for instance, your reaction if your car were to spin out of control on the highway. Your heart would race, and your blood pressure would surge. You might get "goosebumps" and experience a "knot in your stomach." These reflex responses are part of the fight-or-flight syndrome seen in many species. In a sense, this automatic reaction is a leftover from our evolutionary past. It is clearly an adaptive response for many animals, as the threat of predators often requires a swift response of fighting or fleeing. Likewise, the fight-or-flight response probably was adaptive among ancestral humans who routinely had to deal with acute stressors involving threats to their physical safety. But in our modern world, the fight-or-flight response may be less adaptive for human functioning than it was thousands of generations ago (Neese & Young, 2000). Most modern stressors cannot be handled simply through fight or flight. Work pressures, marital problems, and financial difficulties require far more complex responses. Moreover, these chronic stressors often continue for lengthy periods of time, so that the fight-or-flight response leaves one in a state of enduring physiological arousal. Concern about the effects of prolonged physical arousal was first voiced by Hans Selye, a Canadian scientist who conducted extensive research on stress.

The General Adaptation Syndrome

© Bettmann/Corbis

Hans Selye

The concept of stress was popularized in both scientific and lay circles by Hans Selye (1936, 1956, 1982). Although born in Vienna, Selye spent his entire professional career at McGill University in Montreal, Canada. Beginning in the 1930s, Selye exposed laboratory animals to a diverse array of both physical and psychological stressors (heat, cold, pain, mild shock, restraint, and so on). The patterns of physiological arousal he observed in the animals were largely the same, regardless of the type of stress. Thus, Selye concluded that stress reactions are *nonspecific.* In other words, they do not vary according to the specific type of stress encountered. Initially, Selye wasn't sure what to call this nonspecific response to a variety of noxious agents. In the 1940s, he decided to call it *stress,* and his influential writings gradually helped make the word part of our everyday vocabulary (Cooper & Dewe, 2004).

Selye (1956, 1974) formulated a seminal theory of stress reactions called the general adaptation syndrome (see **Figure 3.10**). **The *general adaptation syndrome* is a model of the body's stress response, consisting of three stages: alarm, resistance, and exhaustion.** In the first stage of the general adaptation syndrome, an *alarm reaction* occurs when an organism recognizes the existence of a threat. Physiological arousal increases as the body musters its resources to combat the challenge. Selye's alarm reaction is essentially the fight-or-flight response originally described by Cannon.

However, Selye took his investigation of stress a couple of steps further by exposing laboratory animals to *prolonged stress,* similar to the chronic stress often endured by humans. If stress continues, the organism may progress to the second phase of the general adaptation syndrome, called the *stage of resistance.* During this phase, physiological changes stabilize as coping efforts get under way. Typically, physiological arousal continues to be higher than normal, although it may

Web Link 3.4 **The American Institute of Stress**

The American Institute of Stress is a nonprofit organization established in 1978 at the request of stress pioneer Hans Selye. Its Board of Trustees reads like a who's who of stress research. The resources available online are a bit limited, as one has to send for the information packets published by the institute. But the site contains an interesting tribute to Selye.

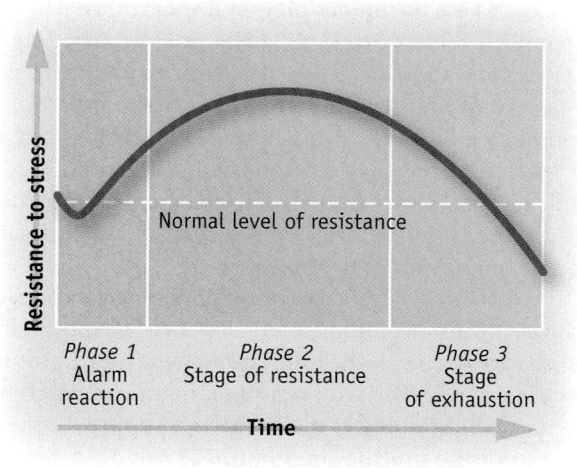

Figure 3.10

The general adaptation syndrome. According to Selye, the physiological response to stress can be broken into three phases. During the first phase, the body mobilizes its resources for resistance after a brief initial shock. In the second phase, resistance levels off and eventually begins to decline. If the third phase of the general adaptation syndrome is reached, resistance is depleted, leading to health problems and exhaustion.

level off somewhat as the organism becomes accustomed to the threat.

If the stress continues over a substantial period of time, the organism may enter the third stage, called the *stage of exhaustion.* According to Selye, the body's resources for fighting stress are limited. If the stress cannot be overcome, the body's resources may be depleted, and physiological arousal will decrease. Eventually, the individual may collapse from exhaustion. During this phase, the organism's resistance declines. This reduced resistance may lead to what Selye called "diseases of adaptation," such as ulcers or high blood pressure.

Selye's theory and research forged a link between stress and physical illness. He showed how prolonged physiological arousal that is meant to be adaptive could lead to diseases. His theory has been criticized because it ignores individual differences in the appraisal of stress (Lazarus & Folkman, 1984), and his belief that stress reactions are nonspecific remains the subject of debate (Kemeny, 2003; McCarty & Pacak, 2000). However, his model provided guidance for generations of researchers who worked out the details of how stress reverberates throughout the body. Let's look at some of those details.

Brain-Body Pathways

When you experience stress, your brain sends signals to the endocrine system along two major pathways (Clow, 2001; Dallman, Bhatnagar, & Viau, 2000; Felker & Hubbard, 1998). **The *endocrine system* consists of glands that secrete chemicals called hormones into the bloodstream.** The major endocrine glands, such as the pituitary, pineal, thyroid, and adrenal glands, are shown in **Figure 3.11**.

The hypothalamus, a small structure near the base of the brain, appears to initiate action along both pathways. The first pathway (shown on the right in **Figure 3.12** on the next page) is routed through the autonomic nervous system. The hypothalamus activates the sympathetic division of the ANS. A key part of this activation involves stimulating the central part of the adrenal glands (the adrenal medulla) to release large amounts of *catecholamines* into the bloodstream. These hormones radiate throughout your body, producing many important physiological changes. The net result of catecholamine elevation is that your body is mobilized for action (Lundberg, 2000). Heart rate and blood flow increase, pumping more blood to your brain and muscles. Respiration and oxygen consumption

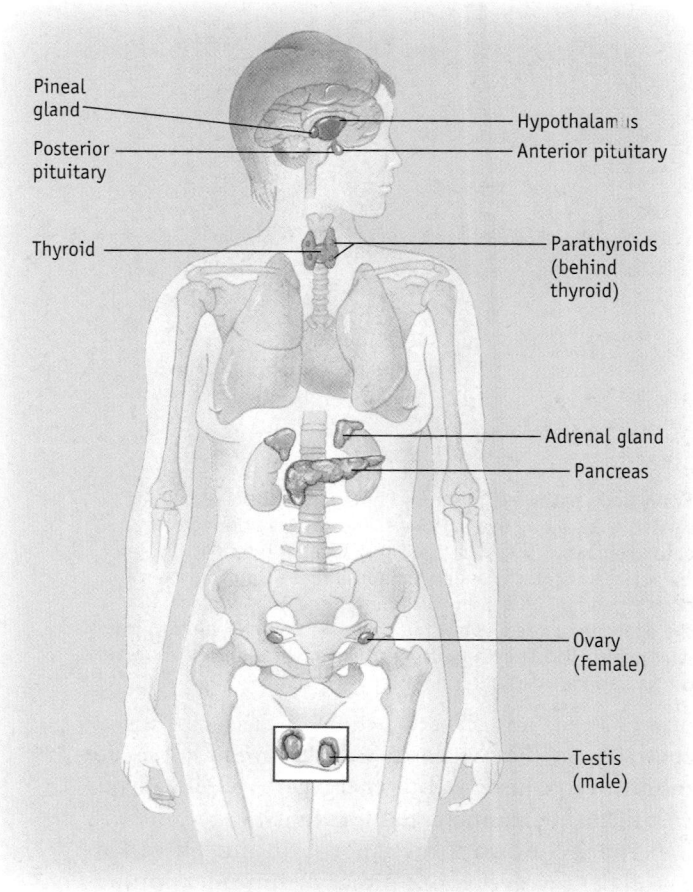

Figure 3.11

The endocrine system. The endocrine glands secrete hormones into the bloodstream. The locations of the principal endocrine glands are shown here. The hormones released by these glands regulate a variety of physical functions and play a key role in the physiological response to stress.

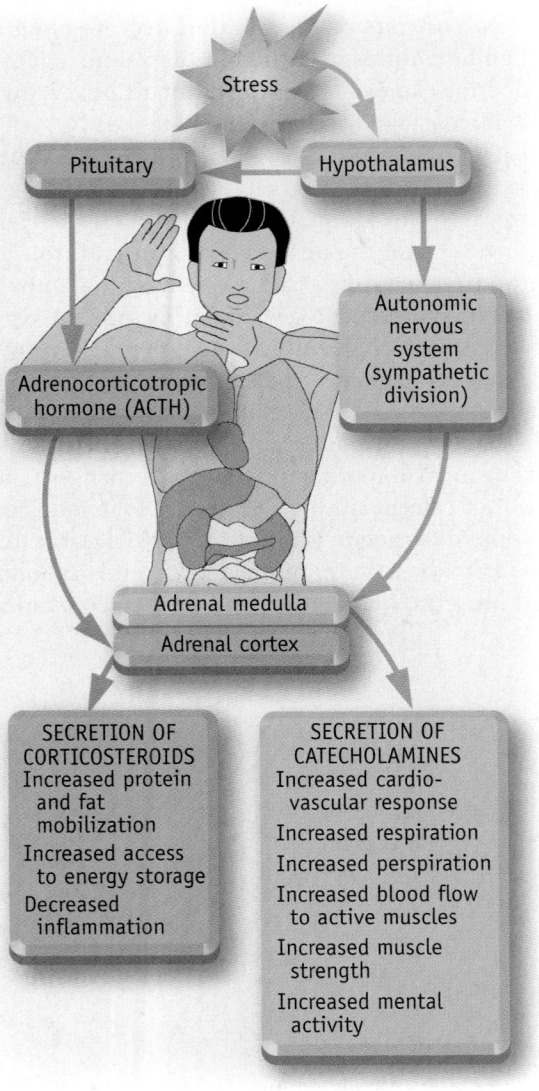

Figure 3.12

Brain-body pathways in stress. In times of stress, the brain sends signals along two pathways. The pathway through the autonomic nervous system (shown in blue on the right) controls the release of catecholamine hormones that help mobilize the body for action. The pathway through the pituitary gland and the endocrine system (shown in brown on the left) controls the release of corticosteroid hormones that increase energy and ward off tissue inflammation.

speed up, facilitating alertness. Digestive processes are inhibited to conserve your energy. The pupils of your eyes dilate, increasing visual sensitivity.

The second pathway (shown on the left in **Figure 3.12**) involves more direct communication between the brain and the endocrine system. The hypothalamus sends signals to the so-called master gland of the endocrine system, the pituitary gland. The pituitary secretes a hormone (ACTH) that stimulates the outer part of the adrenal glands (the adrenal cortex) to release another important set of hormones—*corticosteroids.* These hormones play an important role in the response to stress (de Kloet, Joels, & Holsboer, 2005). They stimulate the release of chemicals that help increase your energy and help inhibit tissue inflammation in case of injury (Munck, 2000). *Cortisol* is a type of corticosteroid that is often used as a physiological indicator of stress in humans. In fact, many of the studies discussed in this chapter used cortisol as a measure of subjects' response to stress.

Stress can also produce other physiological changes that we are just beginning to understand. The most critical changes occur in the immune system. Your immune system provides you with resistance to infections. However, evidence indicates that stress can suppress certain aspects of the multifaceted immune response, reducing its overall effectiveness in repelling invasions by infectious agents (Chiappelli & Hodgson, 2000; Kemeny, 2007). The exact mechanisms underlying immune suppression are complicated, but it appears likely that both sets of stress hormones (catecholamines and corticosteroids) contribute (Dantzer & Mormede, 1995). In any case, it is becoming clear that physiological responses to stress extend into every corner of the body. Moreover, some of these responses may persist long after a stressful event has ended (Esterling et al., 1994). As you will see, these physiological reactions can have an impact on both mental and physical health.

Behavioral Responses

Although people respond to stress at several levels, their behavior is the crucial dimension of these reactions. Emotional and physiological responses to stress—which are often undesirable—tend to be largely automatic. However, dealing effectively with stress at the behavioral level may shut down these potentially harmful emotional and physiological reactions.

Most behavioral responses to stress involve coping. ***Coping* refers to active efforts to master, reduce, or tolerate the demands created by stress.** Notice that this definition is neutral as to whether coping efforts are healthy or maladaptive. The popular use of the term often implies that coping is inherently healthy. When we say that someone "coped with her problems," we imply that she handled them effectively.

In reality, coping responses may be either healthy or unhealthy (Moos & Schaefer, 1993). For example, if you were flunking a history course at midterm, you might cope with this stress by (1) increasing your study efforts, (2) seeking help from a tutor, (3) blaming your professor for your poor grade, or (4) giving up on the class. Clearly, the first two coping responses would be healthier than the second two.

People cope with stress in an endless variety of ways. Because of the complexity and importance of coping processes, we'll devote all of the next chapter

to ways of coping. At this point, it is sufficient to note that coping strategies help determine whether stress has any positive or negative effects on an individual. In the next section, we'll see what some of those effects can be as we discuss the possible outcomes of people's struggles with stress.

The Potential Effects of Stress

LEARNING OBJECTIVES

- *Explain the phenomenon of choking under pressure.*
- *Summarize evidence on how stress can affect cognitive functioning.*
- *Describe the symptoms and causes of burnout.*
- *Discuss the prevalence, symptoms, and causes of posttraumatic stress disorder.*
- *Discuss the potential impact of stress on mental and physical health.*
- *Describe positive psychology and three ways in which stress might lead to beneficial effects.*

People struggle with many stressors every day, most of which come and go without leaving any enduring imprint. However, when stress is severe or when demands pile up, stress may have long-lasting effects. These effects, often called "adaptational outcomes," are relatively long-lasting (though not necessarily permanent) consequences of exposure to stress. Although stress can have beneficial effects, research has focused mainly on possible negative outcomes, so you'll find our coverage slanted in that direction.

Impaired Task Performance

Frequently, stress takes its toll on the ability to perform effectively on a task at hand. For instance, Roy Baumeister (1984) theorized that pressure to perform often makes people self-conscious and that this elevated self-consciousness disrupts their attention, thereby interfering with performance. He theorizes that attention may be distorted in two ways. First, elevated self-consciousness may divert attention from the demands of the task, creating distractions. Second, on well-learned tasks that should be executed almost automatically, the self-conscious person may focus *too* much attention on the task. Thus, the person thinks too much about what he or she is doing.

Baumeister (1984) found support for his theory in a series of laboratory experiments in which he manipulated the pressure to perform on a simple perceptual-motor task. His theory also garnered some support in a pair of studies of the past performance of professional sports teams in championship contests (Baumeister, 1995; Baumeister & Steinhilber, 1984). These findings were particularly impressive in that gifted professional athletes are probably less likely to choke under pressure than virtually any other sample one might assemble. Perhaps to reach that level, athletes must thrive under pressure and therefore simply don't feel performance pressure the way that we assume they do (Wallace, Baumeister, & Vohs, 2005). Laboratory research on "normal" subjects is more pertinent to the issue, and it suggests that choking under pressure is fairly common (Butler & Baumeister, 1998; Lewis & Linder, 1997).

Disruption of Cognitive Functioning

An interesting experimental study suggests that Baumeister is on the right track in looking to *attention* to explain how stress impairs task performance. In a study of stress and decision making, Keinan (1987) was able to measure subjects' attention under stressful and nonstressful conditions. Keinan found that stress disrupted two specific aspects of attention. Stress increased subjects' tendency (1) to jump to a conclusion too quickly without considering all their options and (2) to do an unsystematic, poorly organized review of their available options.

The results of some studies also suggest that stress can have detrimental effects on certain aspects of memory functioning (Kellogg, Hopko, & Ashcraft, 1999; Shors, 2004). In order to affect memory, stressors do not have to be major; even minor day-to-day stressors can have a negative impact (Neupert et al., 2006). Recent evidence suggests that stress can reduce the efficiency of the "working memory" system that allows people to juggle information on the spot (Beilock et al., 2004; Markman, Maddox, & Worthy, 2006). Thus, under stressful situations, people may not be able to process, manipulate, or integrate new information as effectively as normal. Ironically, simply being in a situation where you need cognitive resources the most (studying for a final exam, traveling in a foreign country) can produce this cognitive-sapping stress effect.

Severe stress may leave people dazed and confused, and perhaps even in a state of shock (Valent, 2000; Weisaeth, 1993). In such states, people report feeling emotionally numb, and they respond in a flat, apathetic fashion to events around them. They often stare off into space and have difficulty maintaining a coherent train of thought. Their behavior frequently has an automatic, rigid, stereotyped quality. Fortunately, this disorientation usually occurs only in extreme situations involving overwhelming stress, such as surviving a fire, a flood, or a tornado.

Burnout

Burnout is an overused buzzword that means different things to different people. Nonetheless, a few researchers have described burnout in a systematic way that has facilitated scientific study of the syndrome (Maslach & Leiter, 1997; Pines, 1993). ***Burnout* involves physical and emotional exhaustion, cynicism, and a lowered sense of self-efficacy that is attributable to work-related stress.** Exhaustion, which is central to burnout, includes chronic fatigue, weakness, and low energy. Cynicism is manifested in highly negative attitudes toward oneself, one's work, and life in general. Reduced self-efficacy involves declining feelings of competence at work that give way to feelings of hopelessness and helplessness.

What causes burnout? According to Leiter and Maslach (2001), "Burnout is a cumulative stress reaction to ongoing occupational stressors" (p. 418). The conventional wisdom is that burnout occurs because of some flaw or weakness within the person, but Christina

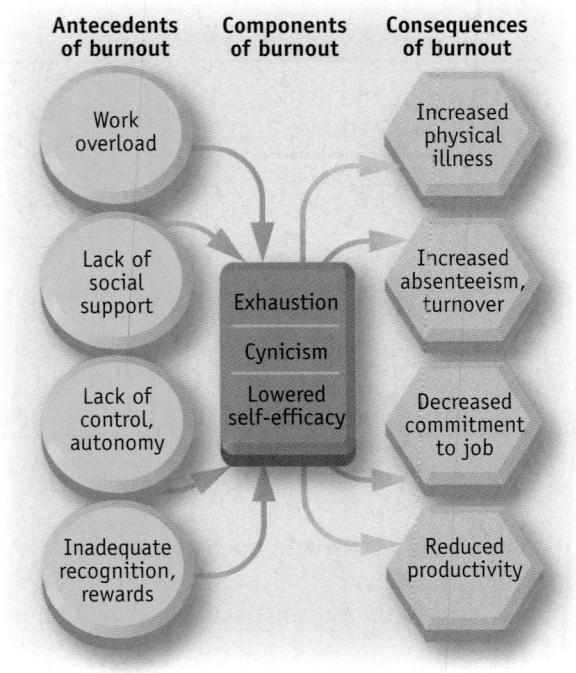

Figure 3.13

The antecedents, components, and consequences of burnout. Christina Maslach and Michael Leiter have developed a systematic model of burnout that specifies its antecedents, components, and consequences. The antecedents on the left in the diagram are the stressful features of the work environment that cause burnout. The burnout syndrome itself consists of the three components shown in the center of the diagram. Some of the unfortunate results of burnout are listed on the right. (Based on Leiter & Maslach, 2001)

Maslach (2003) asserts that "the research case is much stronger for the contrasting argument that burnout is more a function of the situation than of the person" (p. 191). Factors in the workplace that appear to promote burnout include work overload, interpersonal conflicts at work, lack of control over responsibilities and outcomes, and inadequate recognition for one's work (see **Figure 3.13**). As you might expect, burnout is associated with increased absenteeism and reduced productivity, as well as increased vulnerability to a variety of health problems (Grossi et al., 2003; Maslach & Leiter, 2000).

Posttraumatic Stress Disorder

Extremely stressful, traumatic incidents can leave a lasting imprint on victims' psychological functioning. ***Posttraumatic stress disorder (PTSD)* involves enduring psychological disturbance attributed to the experience of a major traumatic event.** Researchers began to appreciate the frequency and severity of posttraumatic stress disorder after the Vietnam war ended in 1975 and a great many psychologically scarred veterans returned home. These veterans displayed a diverse

LIVING IN TODAY'S WORLD

Common Reactions to Traumatic Events

Given recent high-profile disasters, both natural and human-made, social scientists and the lay public are increasingly interested in understanding people's reactions to traumatic events. The 2001 terrorist attacks on the World Trade Center and the Pentagon exposed millions of television viewers to death and destruction of unprecedented magnitude in real time. Similarly, the world witnessed scenes of desperation and despair in the aftermath of Hurricane Katrina, and virtually everyone saw the horrific images replayed again and again in the ensuing weeks. Moreover, the threat of additional terrorist attacks or hurricanes lingers. In light of these unpleasant realities, what can psychological research tell us about how people respond to traumatic events? There is a rich research literature on reactions to major disasters (such as earthquakes and floods) and to personal trauma (such as automobile accidents and armed robberies). Based on this research, common reactions to traumatic events include the following (Danieli, Engdahl, & Schlenger, 2004; Flannery, 1999; Foa et al., 2001; Wilson, Drozdek, & Turkovic, 2006):

Fear and anxiety. Anxiety is a normal response to threatening events. Many people find that certain cues associated with a traumatic event repeatedly trigger their anxiety.

Reexperiencing the trauma. Many people are troubled by unwanted thoughts of the traumatic event that they are unable to control. Some experience flashbacks in which they vividly relive the traumatic moments. Nightmares about traumatic experiences are also common.

Increased arousal. In the aftermath of traumatic events people tend to feel jumpy, jittery, and physically on edge. This physiological arousal may make sleep difficult.

Avoidance. Many people try to avoid situations or cues that remind them of their trauma. People also tend to suppress painful thoughts and feelings. This coping strategy sometimes results in feelings of emotional numbness.

Anger and irritability. Anger is a normal response to the perceived injustice of disastrous events. Coupled with increased arousal, this anger makes many people highly irritable. Ironically, some people get angry with themselves about their irritability.

Grief and depression. In the wake of traumatic events, people often experience sadness, despair, and hopelessness. Future plans that once were important seem trivial. Activities that were once enjoyable seem empty. People understandably grieve for what they have lost.

Shame and guilt. It is not uncommon for survivors of trauma to experience feelings of shame or guilt. This is especially likely if people feel that their behavior was somehow responsible for the traumatic event. As you might imagine, these feelings of self-blame are usually irrational.

Increased sense of vulnerability. Traumatic events often lead to negative changes in one's view of the world. People come to believe that the world is a dangerous place and that others cannot be trusted. One's sense of self-efficacy may be undermined by feelings of helplessness, vulnerability, and the perception that events are uncontrollable.

These reactions are normal short-term responses to traumatic events. Experiencing such reactions does not mean that you are weak or that you are "losing it." For most people these reactions usually dissipate within three months, although others may recover more slowly. If reactions such as these persist indefinitely and interfere with one's social, occupational, or family functioning, a diagnosis of *posttraumatic stress disorder* may be applicable (see pp. 89–91). If your reactions to a traumatic event are especially severe, persistent, and disabling, it may be wise to seek professional help (see Chapter 16).

array of psychological problems and symptoms that in many cases lingered much longer than expected. Studies suggest that nearly a half million Vietnam veterans were still suffering from PTSD over a decade after the end of the war (Schlenger et al., 1992). PTSD did not become an official psychological diagnosis until 1980, and since that time researchers have studied the disorder extensively to better understand the long-term impact of exposure to trauma (Yehuda, 2003). Currently, PTSD is being examined in military returnees from the

Major disasters, such as Hurricane Katrina, which devastated New Orleans and the Gulf Coast region, are just one of about a half-dozen types of calamitous events that frequently lead to posttraumatic stress disorders.

Afghanistan and Iraq wars. Similar to Vietnam veterans, these U.S. troops are showing elevated rates of PTSD upon returning home (Friedman, 2006).

Although posttraumatic stress disorder is widely associated with the experiences of veterans, it is seen in response to other cases of traumatic stress as well, and it appears to be much more common than originally believed. Research suggests that 7%–8% of people have suffered from PTSD at some point in their lives, with prevalence higher among women (10 percent) than men (5 percent) (Ozer et al., 2003). PTSD is seen in children as well as adults (La Greca, 2000). In some instances, PTSD does not surface until many months or years after a person's exposure to severe stress (Holen, 2000).

What types of stress besides combat are severe enough to produce PTSD? The syndrome is frequently seen after a rape, a serious automobile accident, a robbery or assault, or the witnessing of someone's death (Koren, Arnon, & Klein, 1999; Stein et al., 1997b). Studies indicate that PTSD is also common in the wake of major disasters, such as floods, hurricanes, earthquakes, fires, and so forth (Koopman, Classen, & Spiegel, 1994; Vernberg et al., 1996). Unfortunately, research by Stein et al. (1997b) suggests that the various types of traumatic events that can cause PTSD are more common than most people realize (see **Figure 3.14**).

Vulnerability to PTSD is not limited to victims, survivors, and witnesses of traumatic events. Rescue workers and cleanup crews who have to grapple with the gruesome carnage of major disasters, dangerous working conditions, and tremendous fatigue also have an elevated risk for PTSD and often are "forgotten victims" of disasters (Ursano et al., 1999). When examining disaster workers who responded to the events of 9/11, researchers found elevated levels of PTSD, depression, and general psychological distress, even over

Figure 3.14

The prevalence of traumatic events. We tend to think that traumatic events are relatively unusual and infrequent, but research by Stein et al. (1997b) suggests otherwise. When they interviewed over 1000 people in Winnipeg, they found that 74.2 percent of the women and 81.3 percent of the men reported having experienced at least one highly traumatic event. The percentage of respondents reporting specific types of traumatic events are summarized in this graph.

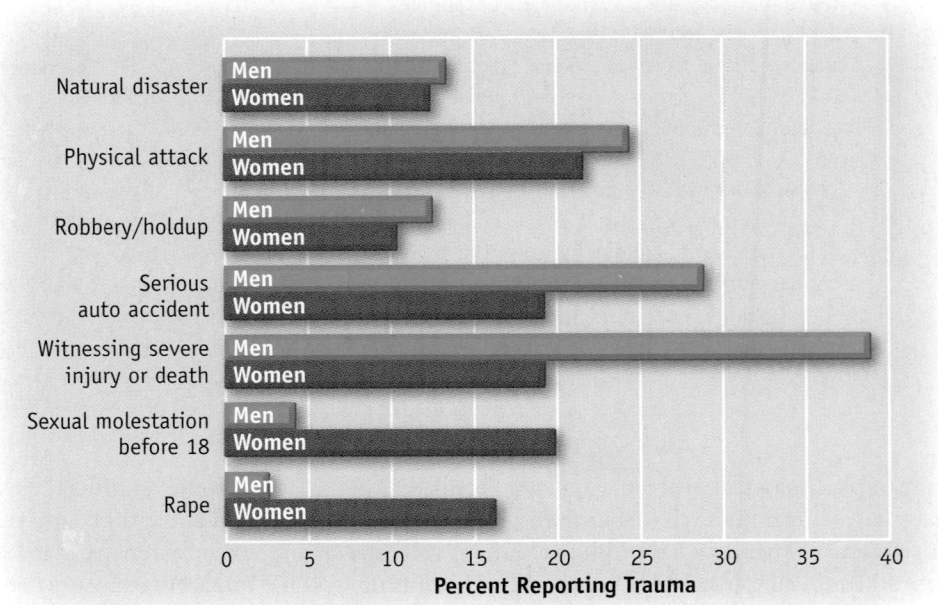

Web Link 3.5 **National Center for PTSD**

Maintained by the U.S. Department of Veterans Affairs, this exceptionally rich site is devoted to the understanding and treatment of posttraumatic stress disorder. The site has well-organized materials for both professionals and the public and includes a wealth of new postings related to the psychological consequences of terrorism.

a year later (Alvarez & Hunt, 2005; Fullerton, Ursano, & Wang, 2004). Psychologists have the opportunity to make an important contribution to society by identifying protective and proactive interventions that would make rescue and relief workers less vulnerable to the negative effects of trauma (see **Figure 3.15**).

What are the symptoms of posttraumatic stress disorder? Common symptoms include reexperiencing the traumatic event in the form of nightmares and flashbacks, emotional numbing, alienation, problems in social relations, and elevated arousal, anxiety, and guilt (Flannery, 1999; Shalev, 2001). PTSD is also associated with an elevated risk for substance abuse, depression, and anxiety disorders, as well as a great variety of physical health problems (Brady, Back, & Coffey, 2004; Fairbank, Ebert, & Caddell, 2001). The frequency and severity of posttraumatic symptoms usually decline gradually over time, but in many cases the symptoms never completely disappear.

Although PTSD is fairly common in the wake of traumatic events, the vast majority of people who experience such events do *not* develop PTSD (Bonanno et al., 2006; Ozer & Weiss, 2004). Thus, a current focus of research is to determine what factors make certain people more (or less) susceptible than others to the ravages of severe stress (Bonanno, 2004). According to McKeever and Huff (2003), this vulnerability probably depends on complex interactions among a number of biological and environmental factors. One key predictor that emerged in a recent review of the relevant research is the *intensity of one's reaction at the time of the traumatic event* (Ozer et al., 2003). Individuals who have especially intense emotional reactions during or immediately after the traumatic event go on to show elevated vulnerability to PTSD. Vulnerability seems to be greatest among people whose reactions are so intense that they report *dissociative experiences* (a sense that things are not real, that time is stretching out, that one is watching oneself in a movie). You can consult Chapter 15 for a fuller discussion of PTSD risk factors.

Psychological Problems and Disorders

Posttraumatic stress disorders are caused by an acute episode of extreme stress. Of greater relevance to most of us are the effects of chronic, prolonged, everyday stress. On the basis of clinical impressions, psychologists have long suspected that chronic stress might contribute to many types of psychological problems and mental disorders. Since the late 1960s, advances in the measurement of stress have allowed researchers to verify these suspicions in empirical studies. In the domain of common psychological problems, studies indicate that stress may contribute to poor academic performance (Akgun & Ciarrochi, 2003), insomnia and other sleep disturbances (Vgontzas, Bixler, & Kales, 2000), sexual difficulties (Lemack, Uzzo, & Poppas, 1998), alcohol abuse (Colder, 2001; Edwards et al., 2006), and drug abuse (Goeders, 2004).

Above and beyond these everyday problems, research reveals that stress often contributes to the onset of full-fledged psychological disorders, including depression (Rehm, Wagner, & Ivens-Tyndal, 2001), schizophrenia (McGlashan & Hoffman, 2000), anxiety disorders (Falsetti & Ballenger, 1998), and eating disorders (Cooper, 1995). We'll discuss the complex relations between stress and mental disorders in detail in Chapter 15.

Selected Effects of Trauma

Function	Effect
Cognitive processes	Impaired
Emotional expression	Suppressed
Memory for prior stressors	Increased
Ruminations on trauma	Increased
Vulnerability to gastric ulcers	Increased
Vulnerability to inflammatory bowel disease	Increased

Figure 3.15

The effects of trauma on psychological and physical functioning. Scientists have discovered many negative effects of experiencing extreme stress. This table presents only a limited set of ways that the experience of trauma can affect us psychologically and physically.

Adapted from Overmier, J. B., & Murison, R. (2005). Trauma and resulting sensitization effects are modulated by psychological factors. *Psychoneuroendocrinology, 30*(10), 965–973, Table 2. Copyright © 2005 Elsevier Ltd. All rights reserved. Adapted by permission.

Physical Illness

Stress can also have an impact on one's physical health. The idea that stress can contribute to physical ailments

Web Link 3.6 **David Baldwin's Trauma Information Pages**

This site has long been recognized as the premier repository for web-based and other resources relating to emotional trauma, traumatic stress, and posttraumatic stress disorder. David Baldwin has assembled more than 1000 links to information about these issues.

is not entirely new. Evidence that stress can cause physical illness began to accumulate back in the 1930s. By the 1950s, the concept of psychosomatic disease was widely accepted. ***Psychosomatic diseases* were defined as genuine physical ailments thought to be caused in part by stress and other psychological factors.** The classic psychosomatic illnesses were high blood pressure, peptic ulcers, asthma, skin disorders such as eczema and hives, and migraine and tension headaches (Kaplan, 1989; Rogers, Fricchione, & Reich, 1999). Please note, these diseases were not regarded as *imagined* physical ailments. The term *psychosomatic* has often been misused to refer to physical ailments that are "all in one's head," but that is an entirely different syndrome (see Chapter 15). Rather, psychosomatic diseases were viewed as authentic organic maladies that were heavily stress related.

Since the 1970s, the concept of psychosomatic disease has gradually fallen into disuse because research has shown that stress can contribute to the development of a diverse array of other diseases previously believed to be purely physiological in origin. Although there is room for debate on some specific diseases, stress may influence the onset and course of heart disease, stroke, tuberculosis, multiple sclerosis, arthritis, diabetes, leukemia, cancer, various types of infectious disease, and probably many other types of illnesses (Brummett et al., 2004; Critelli & Ee, 1996; Dougall & Baum, 2001; see Chapter 14). Thus, it has become apparent that there is nothing unique about the psychosomatic diseases that requires a special category. Modern evidence continues to demonstrate that the classic psychosomatic diseases are influenced by stress, but so are numerous other diseases (Levenson et al., 1999). Of course, stress is only one of many factors that may contribute to the development of physical illness. Nonetheless, it is sobering to realize that stress can have an impact on one's physical health.

Positive Effects

The effects of stress are not entirely negative. Recent years have brought increased interest in positive aspects of the stress process, including favorable outcomes that follow in the wake of stress (Folkman & Moskowitz, 2000). To some extent, the new focus on the possible benefits of stress reflects a new emphasis on "positive psychology." Some influential theorists have argued that the field of psychology has historically devoted too much attention to pathology, weakness, and damage and how to heal suffering (Seligman, 2003). This approach has yielded valuable insights and progress, but it has also resulted in an unfortunate neglect of the forces that make life worth living. The positive psychology movement seeks to shift the field's focus away from negative experiences. As Martin Seligman and Mihaly Csikszentmihalyi (2000) put it, "The aim of positive psychology is to begin to catalyze a change in the focus of psychology from preoccupation with only repairing the worst things in life to also building positive qualities" (p. 5). The advocates of positive psychology argue for increased research on well-being, contentment, hope, courage, perseverance, nurturance, tolerance, and other human strengths and virtues (Aspinwall & Staudinger, 2003; Peterson & Seligman, 2004). One of these strengths is resilience in the face of stress. The beneficial effects of stress may prove more difficult to pinpoint than the harmful effects because they may be more subtle. However, there appear to be at least three ways in which stress can have positive effects.

First, stress can promote positive psychological change, or what Tedeschi and Calhoun (1996) call *posttraumatic growth.* Experiences of posttraumatic growth are now well documented, and it appears that this phenomenon is evident in people facing a variety of stressful circumstances, including bereavement, cancer, sexual assault, and combat (Tedeschi & Calhoun, 2004). Stressful events sometimes force people to develop new skills, reevaluate priorities, learn new insights, and acquire new strengths. In other words, the adaptation process initiated by stress may lead to personal changes for the better. Confronting and conquering a stressful challenge may lead to improvements in specific coping abilities and to an enhanced self-concept. For example,

The End of Stress as We Know It
by Bruce McEwen with Elizabeth Norton Lasley (Joseph Henry Press, 2002)

The title of this book is a bit misleading, as it suggests that the author will provide some stunning new secret that will permit readers to end the stress in their lives. In reality, one of the principal points that McEwen makes is that stress is normal, inevitable, and not necessarily bad. McEwen is a renowned stress researcher whose main focus has been on neuroendocrine responses to stress. In keeping with his background, what he provides in this book is an exceptionally lucid account of how stress affects brain function and cardiovascular and immune system processes. This potentially difficult material is presented in a lively and understandable fashion. The coverage of "how not to be stressed out" is relatively modest. The author's advice is empirically sound but fairly conventional and not overly detailed. In sum, this book provides an outstanding overview of the physiology of stress, but it offers less than you might expect—given its title—on coping with stress.

a breakup with a boyfriend or a girlfriend may lead individuals to change aspects of their behavior that they find unsatisfactory. Moreover, even if people do not conquer stressors, they may be able to learn from their mistakes. In a review of recent research on posttraumatic growth, Helgeson, Reynolds, and Tomich (2006) found that it is related to lower levels of depression and enhanced well-being. In contrast, it is also related to increased intrusive thoughts about the stressful event. They note that these thoughts do not necessarily indicate distress. It could be that people are working through the stressful event and that in this process the growth happens.

Second, stressful events help satisfy the need for stimulation and challenge. Studies suggest that most people prefer an intermediate level of stimulation and challenge in their lives (Sutherland, 2000). Although we think of stress in terms of stimulus overload, underload can be stressful as well (Goldberger, 1993). Thus, most people would experience a suffocating level of boredom if they lived a stress-free existence. In a sense, then, stress fulfills a basic need of the human organism.

Third, today's stress can inoculate and psychologically prepare individuals so that they are less affected by tomorrow's stress. Some studies suggest that exposure to stress can increase stress tolerance—as long as the stress isn't overwhelming (Meichenbaum, 1993). Further, by dealing with a stressful event people will be better prepared for subsequent stress (Janoff-Bulman, 2004). Thus, a woman who has previously endured business setbacks may be much better prepared than most people to deal with a bank foreclosure on her home. In light of the negative effects that stress can have, improved stress tolerance is a desirable goal. We'll look next at the factors that influence the ability to tolerate stress.

Factors Influencing Stress Tolerance

LEARNING OBJECTIVES

- *Explain how social support moderates the impact of stress.*
- *Describe the hardiness syndrome and how it influences stress tolerance.*
- *Discuss how optimism is related to stress tolerance.*

Some people seem to be able to withstand the ravages of stress better than others (Holahan & Moos, 1990, 1994). Why? Because a number of *moderator variables* can soften the impact of stress on physical and mental health. To shed light on differences in how well people tolerate stress, we'll look at a number of key moderator variables, including social support, hardiness, and optimism. As you'll see, these factors influence people's emotional, physical, and behavioral responses to stress. These complexities are diagrammed in **Figure 3.16** on the next page, which builds on **Figure 3.6** (on page 80) to provide a more complete overview of the factors involved in individual reactions to stress.

Social Support

Friends may be good for your health! This startling conclusion emerges from studies on social support as a moderator of stress. ***Social support* refers to various types of aid and succor provided by members of one's social networks.** In fact, social support is regarded as such an important factor influencing stress tolerance that over 1,100 articles are published on the topic each year (Taylor, 2007). For example, Jemmott and Magloire (1988) examined the effect of social support on immune response in a group of students going through the stress of final exams. They found that students who reported stronger social support had higher levels of an antibody that plays a key role in warding off respiratory infections. Positive correlations between high social support and greater immunal functioning have been observed in quite a number of studies with diverse samples (Uchino, Cacioppo, & Kiecolt-Glaser, 1996).

Over the last two decades, a vast body of studies have found evidence that social support is favorably related to physical health (Taylor, 2007; Wills & Fegan, 2001). Social support seems to be good medicine for the mind as well as the body, as most studies also find an association between social support and mental health (Davis, Morris, & Kraus, 1998; Sarason, Pierce, & Sarason, 1994). It appears that social support serves as a protective buffer during times of high stress, reducing the negative impact of stressful events—and that social support has its own positive effects on health, which may be apparent even when people aren't under great stress (Peirce et al., 1996; Wills & Fegan, 2001). The stress-buffering effects of social support were apparent in a study that found strong social support to be a key factor reducing the likelihood of posttraumatic stress disorders among Vietnam veterans (King et al., 1998).

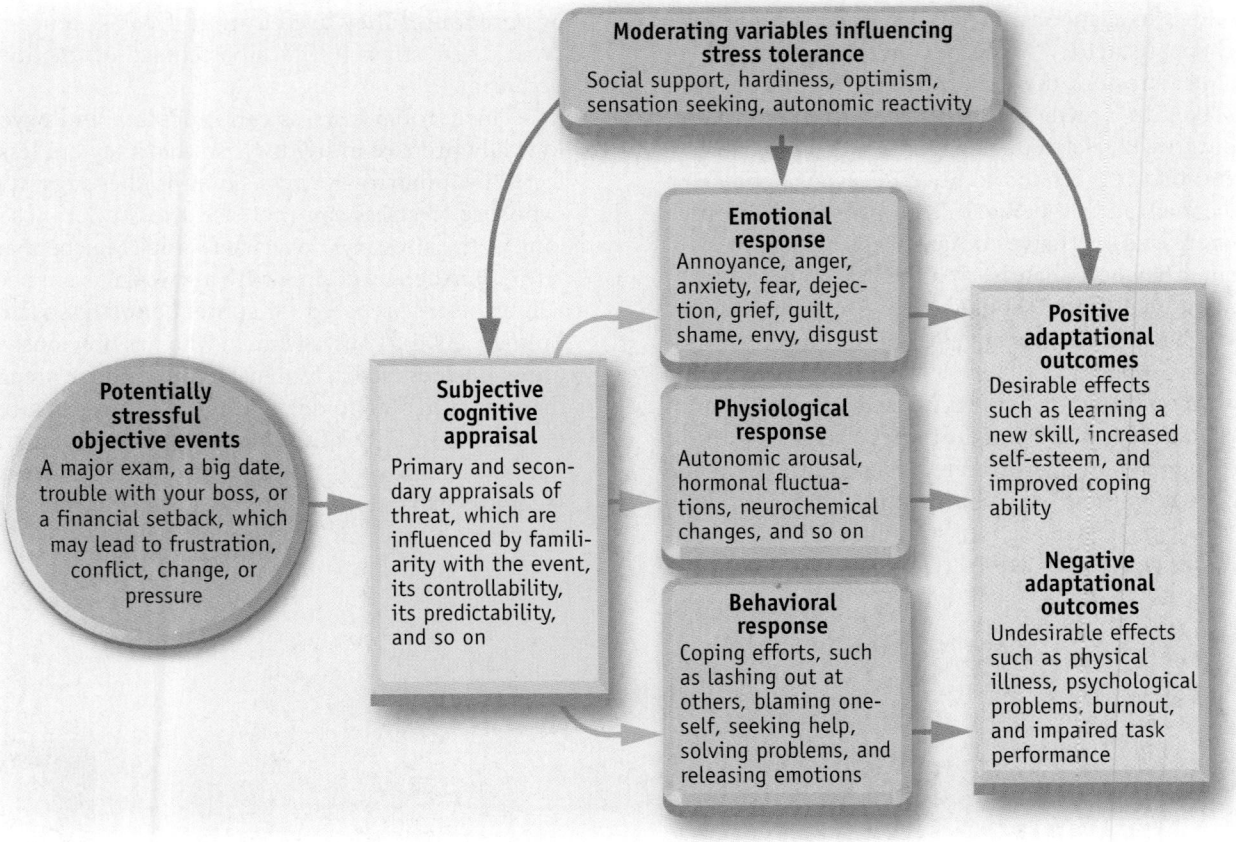

Figure 3.16

Overview of the stress process. This diagram builds on Figure 3.6 (the multidimensional response to stress) to provide a more complete overview of the factors involved in stress. This diagram adds the potential effects of stress (seen on the far right) by listing some of the positive and negative adaptational outcomes that may result from stress. It also completes the picture by showing moderating variables (seen at the top) that can influence the effects of stress (including some variables not covered in the chapter).

The mechanisms underlying the connection between social support and wellness have been the subject of considerable debate (Hobfoll & Vaux, 1993). A variety of mechanisms may be at work. Among other things, social support could promote wellness by making appraisals of stressful events more benign, dampening the intensity of physiological reactions to stress, reducing health-impairing behaviors such as smoking and drinking, encouraging preventive behaviors such as regular exercise and medical checkups, and fostering more constructive coping efforts (Taylor, 2007; Wills & Fegan, 2001).

Interestingly, recent studies suggest that *providing* social support to others can also have both psychological benefits (lower depression and perceived stress) and physical benefits (lower blood pressure) (Brown et al., 2003; Piferi & Lawler, 2006). Another study found that the personality trait of *sociability* (being friendly and agreeable), which certainly helps people build supportive social networks, is independently associated with reduced susceptibility to infectious disease (Cohen et al., 2003). Yet another study has demonstrated that many pet owners view their pets as sources of support in their lives, with resultant health benefits (Allen, Blascovich, & Mendes, 2002). Thus, it appears that there are many aspects of social support that have some bearing on our wellness.

Hardiness

Another line of research indicates that a syndrome called *hardiness* may moderate the impact of stressful events. Suzanne (Kobasa) Ouellette reasoned that if stress affects some people less than others, some people must be *hardier* than others. Hence, she set out to determine what factors might be the key to these differences in hardiness.

Courtesy, Suzanne Ouellette

Suzanne Ouellette

The availability of social support is a key factor influencing stress tolerance. Decades of research have shown that social support reduces the negative effects of stress and has positive effects of its own.

Kobasa (1979) used a modified version of the Holmes and Rahe (1967) stress scale (SRRS) to measure the amount of stress experienced by a group of executives. As in most other studies, she found a modest correlation between stress and the incidence of physical illness. However, she carried her investigation one step further than previous studies. She compared the high-stress executives who exhibited the expected high incidence of illness against the high-stress executives who stayed healthy. She administered a battery of psychological tests and found that the hardier executives "were more committed, felt more in control, and had bigger appetites for challenge" (Kobasa, 1984, p. 70). These traits have also shown up in many other studies of hardiness (Maddi, 2002, 2006; Ouellette, 1993).

Thus, ***hardiness* is a disposition marked by commitment, challenge, and control that is purportedly associated with strong stress resistance.** Hardiness may reduce the effects of stress by altering stress appraisals or fostering more active coping (Crowley, Hayslip, & Hobdy, 2003; Maddi, 2006; Maddi & Hightower, 1999). The benefits of hardiness showed up in a study of Vietnam veterans, which found that higher hardiness was related to a lower likelihood of developing posttraumatic stress disorders (King et al., 1998). Although the research on hardiness is promising, debate continues about how to measure hardiness and about its key elements (Klag & Bradley, 2004; Oullette & DiPlacido, 2001; Younkin & Betz, 1996).

Optimism

Everyone knows someone whose glass is half full, who sees the world through rose-colored glasses, who is an

Recommended READING

Why Zebras Don't Get Ulcers: The Acclaimed Guide to Stress, Stress-Related Diseases, and Coping
by Robert M. Sapolsky (W. H. Freeman, 2004)

This book provides a superb, wide-ranging discussion of the nature and effects of stress. The author is a neuroscientist at Stanford University whose research focuses on such issues as the relationship between stress and the cellular and molecular events underlying neural decay in the hippocampal area of the brain. That is not the type of résumé that you would normally associate with lively, witty discourse, but the book is written with flair and humor. Sapolsky's basic thesis is that the physiological response to stress is a remnant of evolution that is no longer adaptive for the majority of stressful situations that humans face. He outlines in detail how neuroendocrine responses to stress can cause or worsen a host of physical and psychological afflictions, including cardiovascular disease, ulcers, colitis, diarrhea, infectious diseases, and depression. Sapolsky does an excellent job of making complicated research understandable. Although opinionated, his overviews of research are scientifically sound and thoroughly documented in notes at the back of the book. This is not a coping manual, yet it is probably the most insightful and interesting dissection of the stress response available today and is highly worthwhile reading.

CALVIN AND HOBBES © Watterson. Reprinted with permission of UNIVERSAL PRESS SYNDICATE. All rights reserved.

optimist. ***Optimism* is a general tendency to expect good outcomes.** Pioneering research in this area by Michael Scheier and Charles Carver (1985) found a correlation between optimism as measured by the Life Orientation Test (see **Figure 3.17**) and relatively good physical health in a sample of college students. In another study that focused on surgical patients, optimism was found to be associated with a faster recovery and a quicker return to normal activities after coronary artery bypass surgery (Scheier et al., 1989). Yet another study found optimism to be associated with more effective immune functioning (Segerstrom et al., 1998). More recently, optimism was inversely related to PTSD symptoms for college students who knew a victim of the 9/11 terrorist attacks (Ai, Santangelo, & Cascio, 2006). Twenty years of research with the Life Orientation Test has consistently shown that optimism is associated with better mental and physical health (Carver & Scheier, 2005; Scheier, Carver, & Bridges, 2001).

In a related line of research, Christopher Peterson and Martin Seligman have studied how people explain bad events (personal setbacks, mishaps, disappointments, and such). These researchers identified a *pessimistic explanatory style,* in which people tend to blame setbacks on their own personal shortcomings, versus an *optimistic explanatory style,* which leads people to attribute setbacks to temporary situational factors. In two retrospective studies of people born many decades ago, they found an association between this optimistic explanatory style and relatively good health (Peterson,

Figure 3.17

The Life Orientation Test (LOT). The personality trait of optimism, which appears to foster resilience in the face of stress, can be measured by the Life Orientation Test (LOT) developed by Scheier and Carver (1985). Follow the instructions for this scale to obtain an estimate of your own optimism. High and low scores are based on scoring three-fifths of a standard deviation above or below the mean.

Adapted from Scheier, M. F., & Carver, C. S. (1985). Optimism, coping, and health: Assessment and implications of generalized outcome expectancies. *Health Psychology, 4,* 219–247. Copyright © 1985 Lawrence Erlbaum & Associates. Adapted by permission of the publisher and authors.

Measuring Optimism

In the following spaces, mark how much you agree with each of the items, using the following scale:

4 = strongly agree
3 = agree
2 = neutral
1 = disagree
0 = strongly disagree

_____ **1.** In uncertain times, I usually expect the best.
_____ **2.** It's easy for me to relax.
_____ **3.** If something can go wrong for me, it will.
_____ **4.** I always look on the bright side of things.
_____ **5.** I'm always optimistic about my future.
_____ **6.** I enjoy my friends a lot.
_____ **7.** It's important for me to keep busy.
_____ **8.** I hardly ever expect things to go my way.
_____ **9.** Things never work out the way I want them to.
_____ **10.** I don't get upset too easily.
_____ **11.** I'm a believer in the idea that "every cloud has a silver lining."
_____ **12.** I rarely count on good things happening to me.

Scoring

Cross out and ignore the responses you entered for items 2, 6, 7, and 10, which are "filler" items. For items 3, 8, 9, and 12, you need to reverse the numbers you entered. If you entered a 4, change it to 0. If you entered a 3, change it to 1. If you entered a 2, leave it unchanged. If you entered a 1, change it to 3. If you entered a 0, change it to 4. Now add up the numbers for items 1, 3, 4, 5, 8, 9, 11, 12, using the new numbers for the reversed items. This sum is your score on the Life Orientation Test. For college students, approximate norms are as follows: High score (25–32), intermediate score (18–24), low score (0–17).

Seligman, & Vaillant, 1988) and increased longevity (Peterson et al., 1998). Many other studies have linked the optimistic explanatory style to superior physical health (Peterson & Bossio, 2001), as well as higher academic achievement, increased job productivity, enhanced athletic performance, and higher marital satisfaction (Gillham et al., 2001).

Why does optimism promote a host of desirable outcomes? Above all else, research suggests that optimists cope with stress in more adaptive ways than pessimists (Aspinwall, Richter, & Hoffman, 2001; Carver & Scheier, 2002; Chang, 1996). Optimists are more likely to engage in action-oriented, problem-focused, carefully planned coping and are more willing than pessimists to seek social support. In comparison, pessimists are more likely to deal with stress by avoiding it, giving up, or engaging in denial. We will be discussing these specific types of coping styles in the next chapter.

APPLICATION

Monitoring Your Stress

LEARNING OBJECTIVES

- *List five problems with the SRRS.*
- *Summarize how the LES corrects some of the problems that are characteristic of the SRRS.*
- *Explain why one should be cautious in interpreting scores on stress scales.*

Rank the following five events in terms of how stressful they would be for you (1 = most stressful, 5 = least stressful):

___ **1.** Change in residence
___ **2.** Fired at work
___ **3.** Death of a close family member
___ **4.** Pregnancy
___ **5.** Personal injury or illness

All five events appear on the Social Readjustment Rating Scale (SRRS), developed by Holmes and Rahe (1967), which we described earlier (see **Figure 3.4** on page 78). If you ranked them in the same order as Holmes and Rahe's subjects, the rankings would be 5, 3, 1, 4, and 2. If you didn't rank them in that order, don't worry about it. That merely shows that the perception of stress is personal and subjective. Unfortunately, the SRRS fails to take this subjectivity into account. That is just one of a number of basic problems with the SRRS.

The SRRS and the research associated with it have received a great deal of publicity. The scale has been reprinted in many popular newspapers and magazines. In these articles, readers have been encouraged to attribute great significance to their scores. They have sometimes been told that they should reduce or minimize change in their lives if their scores are high (Cohen, 1979). Such bold advice could be counterproductive and needs to be qualified carefully. Therefore, in this application section we'll elaborate on some of the problems with the SRRS as a measurement scale, introduce you to an improved scale for measuring stress, and explain why scores on any stress scale should be interpreted with caution.

Problems with the SRRS

Courtesy, Eleanor Holmes Williams

Thomas Holmes

As you learned earlier in this chapter, the SRRS was developed in the early 1960s by Thomas Holmes and Richard Rahe (1967). They designed the scale to measure the amount of change-related stress that people experience. In a host of studies, these scores have been found to be related to the likelihood of developing an intimidating array of physical illnesses and psychological problems (Dougall & Baum, 2001; Lynch et al., 2005; Turner & Wheaton, 1995).

Before we discuss the shortcomings of the SRRS, we should emphasize that Holmes and Rahe deserve enormous credit for recognizing the potential importance of stress and for developing a scale that would permit its measurement. They pioneered a new area of research that has turned out to be extremely productive. However, their groundbreaking foray into the assessment of stress was not without its flaws, and their scale has been improved on. So, borrowing from the analyses of a number of critics (Derogatis, 1982; Rabkin, 1993; Schroeder & Costa, 1984), let's look at some of the major problems with the SRRS. Although our list is not exhaustive, we highlight the key problems.

First, as already discussed, the assumption that the SRRS measures change exclusively has been shown to be inaccurate. We now have ample evidence that the desirability of events affects adaptational outcomes more than the amount of change that they require (Turner & Wheaton, 1995). Thus, it seems prudent to view the SRRS as a measure of diverse forms of stress, rather than as a measure of change-related stress (McLean & Link, 1994).

Second, the SRRS fails to take into account differences among people in their subjective perception of how stressful an event is. For instance, while divorce may deserve a stress value of 73 for *most* people, a particular person's divorce might generate much less stress and merit a value of only 25.

Third, many of the events listed on the SRRS and similar scales are highly ambiguous, leading people to be inconsistent as to which events they report experiencing (Monroe & McQuaid, 1994). For instance, what qualifies as "trouble with boss"? Should you check that because you're sick and tired of your supervisor? What constitutes a "change in living conditions"? Does your purchase of a great new sound system qualify? As you can see, the SRRS includes many "events" that are described inadequately, producing considerable ambiguity about the meaning of one's response. Problems in recalling events over a period of a year also lead to inconsistent responding on stress scales, thus lowering their reliability (Klein & Rubovits, 1987).

Fourth, the SRRS does not sample from the domain of stressful events very thoroughly. Do the 43 events listed on the SRRS exhaust all the major stresses that people typically experience? Studies designed to explore that question have found many significant omissions (Dohrenwend et al, 1993; Wheaton, 1994).

Fifth, the correlation between SRRS scores and health outcomes may be inflated because subjects' neuroticism affects both their responses to stress scales and their self-reports of health problems. Neurotic individuals have a tendency to recall more stress than others and to recall more symptoms of illness than others (Watson, David, & Suls, 1999). These tendencies mean that some of the correlation between high stress and high illness may simply reflect the effects of subjects' neuroticism (Critelli & Ee, 1996). This is another case of the third variable problem in correlation that we introduced in Chapter 1 (see **Figure 3.18**). The possible contaminating effects of neuroticism obscure the meaning of scores on the SRRS and similar measures of stress.

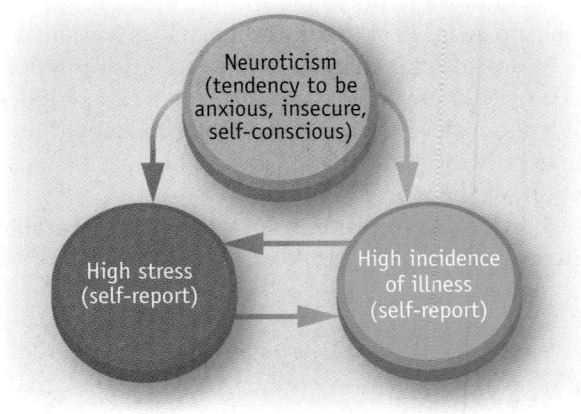

Figure 3.18

Neuroticism as a possible factor underlying the stress-illness correlation. Many studies have found a correlation between subjects' scores on self-report stress scales, such as the SRRS, and their reports of how much illness they have experienced. However, neurotic subjects, who are anxious, insecure, and self-conscious, tend to recall more stress *and* more illness than others. Although there is a great deal of evidence that stress contributes to the causation of illness, some of the stress-illness correlation may be due to neuroticism causing high recall of both stress and illness.

The Life Experiences Survey

In light of these problems, a number of researchers have attempted to develop improved versions of the SRRS. For example, the Life Experiences Survey (LES), assembled by Irwin Sarason and colleagues (1978), has become a widely used measure of stress in contemporary research (for examples see Ames et al., 2001; Denisoff & Endler, 2000; Malefo, 2000). The LES revises and builds on the SRRS in a variety of ways that correct, at least in part, most of the problems just discussed (see Hobson & Delunas, 2001 and Rahe et al., 2000 for other modernized versions of the SRRS).

Specifically, the LES recognizes that stress involves more than mere change and asks respondents to indicate whether events had a positive or negative impact on them. This strategy permits the computation of positive change, negative change, and total change scores, which helps researchers gain much more insight into which facets of stress are most crucial.

The LES also takes into consideration differences among people in their appraisal of stress, by dropping the normative weights and replacing them with personally assigned weightings of the impact of relevant events. Ambiguity in items is decreased by providing more elaborate descriptions of many items to clarify their meaning. The scale still contains some ambiguity, but there is no complete solution for this problem.

The LES deals with the failure of the SRRS to sample the full domain of stressful events in several ways. First, some significant omissions from the SRRS have been added to the LES. Second, the LES allows the respondent to write in personally important events that are not included on the scale. Third, the LES reprinted here (in **Figure 3.19**) has an extra section just for students. Sarason and colleagues (1978) suggest that special, tailored sections of this sort be added for specific populations whenever it is useful.

Arriving at your scores on the LES is very simple. Respond to the items in **Figure 3.19** and add up all the positive impact ratings on the right side. The total is

Figure 3.19

The Life Experiences Survey (LES). Like the SRRS, the LES is designed to measure change-related stress. However, Sarason, Johnson, and Siegel (1978) corrected many of the problems apparent in the SRRS. Follow the instructions to determine your positive, negative, and total change scores.

The Life Experiences Survey (LES)

Instructions. Listed below are a number of events that sometimes bring about change in the lives of those who experience them and that necessitate social readjustment. Examine each event on the list and if that event has occurred in your life during the past year please indicate the extent to which you viewed the event as having either a positive or negative impact on your life at the time the event occurred. That is, circle a number on the appropriate line to indicate the type and extent of impact that the event had. A rating of –3 would indicate an extremely negative impact. A rating of 0 suggests no impact, either positive or negative. A rating of +3 would indicate an extremely positive impact.

	Extremely negative	Moderately negative	Somewhat negative	No impact	Slightly positive	Moderately positive	Extremely positive
Section 1							
1. Marriage	−3	−2	−1	0	+1	+2	+3
2. Detention in jail or comparable institution	−3	−2	−1	0	+1	+2	+3
3. Death of spouse	−3	−2	−1	0	+1	+2	+3
4. Major change in sleeping habits	−3	−2	−1	0	+1	+2	+3
5. Death of a close family member	−3	−2	−1	0	+1	+2	+3
a. Mother	−3	−2	−1	0	+1	+2	+3
b. Father	−3	−2	−1	0	+1	+2	+3
c. Brother	−3	−2	−1	0	+1	+2	+3
d. Sister	−3	−2	−1	0	+1	+2	+3
e. Grandmother	−3	−2	−1	0	+1	+2	+3
f. Grandfather	−3	−2	−1	0	+1	+2	+3
g. Other (specify)	−3	−2	−1	0	+1	+2	+3
6. Major change in eating habits (much more or much less food intake)	−3	−2	−1	0	+1	+2	+3
7. Foreclosure on mortgage or loan	−3	−2	−1	0	+1	+2	+3
8. Death of a close friend	−3	−2	−1	0	+1	+2	+3
9. Outstanding personal achievement	−3	−2	−1	0	+1	+2	+3
10. Minor law violations	−3	−2	−1	0	+1	+2	+3
11. Male: Wife/girlfriend's pregnancy	−3	−2	−1	0	+1	+2	+3
12. Female: Pregnancy	−3	−2	−1	0	+1	+2	+3
13. Changed work situation (different work responsibility, major change in working conditions, working hours, etc.)	−3	−2	−1	0	+1	+2	+3
14. New job	−3	−2	−1	0	+1	+2	+3
15. Serious illness or injury of close family member:							
a. Mother	−3	−2	−1	0	+1	+2	+3
b. Father	−3	−2	−1	0	+1	+2	+3
c. Brother	−3	−2	−1	0	+1	+2	+3
d. Sister	−3	−2	−1	0	+1	+2	+3
e. Grandmother	−3	−2	−1	0	+1	+2	+3
f. Grandfather	−3	−2	−1	0	+1	+2	+3
g. Spouse	−3	−2	−1	0	+1	+2	+3
h. Other (specify)	−3	−2	−1	0	+1	+2	+3
16. Sexual difficulties	−3	−2	−1	0	+1	+2	+3
17. Trouble with employer (in danger of losing job, being suspended, being demoted, etc.)	−3	−2	−1	0	+1	+2	+3
18. Trouble with in-laws	−3	−2	−1	0	+1	+2	+3
19. Major change in financial status (a lot better off or a lot worse off)	−3	−2	−1	0	+1	+2	+3

(continued)

Adapted from Sarason, I. G., Johnson, J. H., & Siegel, J. M. (1978). Assessing the impact of life changes. *Journal of Consulting and Clinical Psychology, 46,* 932–946. Copyright © 1978 by the American Psychological Association. Reprinted by permission of the publisher and author.

The Life Experiences Survey (LES) *(continued)*

	Extremely negative	Moderately negative	Somewhat negative	No impact	Slightly positive	Moderately positive	Extremely positive
20. Major change in closeness of family members (increased or decreased closeness)	−3	−2	−1	0	+1	+2	+3
21. Gaining a new family member (through birth, adoption, family member moving in, etc.)	−3	−2	−1	0	+1	+2	+3
22. Change in residence	−3	−2	−1	0	+1	+2	+3
23. Marital separation from mate (due to conflict)	−3	−2	−1	0	+1	+2	+3
24. Major change in church activities (increased or decreased attendance)	−3	−2	−1	0	+1	+2	+3
25. Marital reconciliation with mate	−3	−2	−1	0	+1	+2	+3
26. Major change in number of arguments with spouse (a lot more or a lot fewer)	−3	−2	−1	0	+1	+2	+3
27. Married male: Change in wife's work outside the home (beginning work, ceasing work, changing to a new job, etc.)	−3	−2	−1	0	+1	+2	+3
28. Married female: Change in husband's work (loss of job, beginning new job, retirement, etc.)	−3	−2	−1	0	+1	+2	+3
29. Major change in usual type and/or amount of recreation	−3	−2	−1	0	+1	+2	+3
30. Borrowing for a major purchase (buying a home, business, etc.)	−3	−2	−1	0	+1	+2	+3
31. Borrowing for a smaller purchase (buying a car or TV, getting school loan, etc.)	−3	−2	−1	0	+1	+2	+3
32. Being fired from job	−3	−2	−1	0	+1	+2	+3
33. Male: Wife/girlfriend having abortion							
34. Female: Having abortion	−3	−2	−1	0	+1	+2	+3
35. Major personal illness or injury	−3	−2	−1	0	+1	+2	+3
36. Major change in social activities, e.g., parties, movies, visiting (increased or decreased participation)	−3	−2	−1	0	+1	+2	+3
37. Major change in living conditions of family (building new home, remodeling, deterioration of home or neighborhood, etc.)	−3	−2	−1	0	+1	+2	+3
38. Divorce	−3	−2	−1	0	+1	+2	+3
39. Serious injury or illness of close friend	−3	−2	−1	0	+1	+2	+3
40. Retirement from work	−3	−2	−1	0	+1	+2	+3
41. Son or daughter leaving home (due to marriage, college, etc.)	−3	−2	−1	0	+1	+2	+3
42. End of formal schooling	−3	−2	−1	0	+1	+2	+3
43. Separation from spouse (due to work, travel, etc.)	−3	−2	−1	0	+1	+2	+3
44. Engagement	−3	−2	−1	0	+1	+2	+3
45. Breaking up with boyfriend/girlfriend	−3	−2	−1	0	+1	+2	+3
46. Leaving home for the first time	−3	−2	−1	0	+1	+2	+3
47. Reconciliation with boyfriend/girlfriend	−3	−2	−1	0	+1	+2	+3
Other recent experiences that have had an impact on your life. List and rate.							
48. _____	−3	−2	−1	0	+1	+2	+3
49. _____	−3	−2	−1	0	+1	+2	+3
50. _____	−3	−2	−1	0	+1	+2	+3

(continued)

The Life Experiences Survey (LES) *(continued)*

	Extremely negative	Moderately negative	Somewhat negative	No impact	Slightly positive	Moderately positive	Extremely positive
Section 2. Students only							
51. Beginning a new school experience at a higher academic level (college, graduate school, professional school)	−3	−2	−1	0	+1	+2	+3
52. Changing to a new school at the same academic level (undergraduate, graduate, etc.)	−3	−2	−1	0	+1	+2	+3
53. Academic probation	−3	−2	−1	0	+1	+2	+3
54. Being dismissed from dormitory or other residence	−3	−2	−1	0	+1	+2	+3
55. Failing an important exam	−3	−2	−1	0	+1	+2	+3
56. Changing a major	−3	−2	−1	0	+1	+2	+3
57. Failing a course	−3	−2	−1	0	+1	+2	+3
58. Dropping a course	−3	−2	−1	0	+1	+2	+3
59. Joining a fraternity/sorority	−3	−2	−1	0	+1	+2	+3
60. Financial problems concerning school (in danger of not having sufficient money to continue)	−3	−2	−1	0	+1	+2	+3

your positive change score. Your negative change score is the sum of all of the negative impact ratings that you made on the left. Adding these two values yields your total change score. Approximate norms for all three of these scores are listed in **Figure 3.20** so that you can get some idea of what your score means.

Research to date suggests that the negative change score is the crucial one; positive change has not been found to be a good predictor of adaptational outcomes. Thus far, research has shown that negative change scores are related to a variety of negative adaptational outcomes.

Norms for LES

Score category	Negative change	Positive change	Total change
High	14 and above	16 and above	28 and above
Medium	4–13	7–15	12–27
Low	0–3	0–6	0–11

Figure 3.20

Norms for the Life Experiences Survey (LES). Approximate norms for college students taking the LES are shown for negative, positive, and total change scores. These norms are based on 345 undergraduates studied by Sarason, Johnson, and Siegel (1978). Data for males and females were combined, as gender differences were negligible. Negative change scores are the best predictor of adaptational outcomes.

Adapted from Sarason, I. G., Johnson, J. H., & Siegel, J. M. (1978). Assessing the impact of life changes. *Journal of Consulting and Clinical Psychology, 46,* 932–946. Copyright © 1978 by the American Psychological Association. Reprinted by permission of the publisher and author.

A Cautionary Note

There is merit in getting an estimate of how much stress you have experienced lately, but scores on the LES or any measure of stress should be interpreted with caution. You need not panic if you add up your negative change score and find that it falls in the "high" category. Although it is clear that a connection exists between stress and a variety of undesirable adaptational outcomes, a high score shouldn't cause undue concern.

For one thing, the strength of the association between stress and adaptational problems is modest. Most of the correlations observed between stress scores and illness have been low to moderate in magnitude, often less than .30 (Monroe & McQuaid, 1994). For researchers and theorists, it is interesting to find any relationship at all. However, the link between stress and adaptational problems is too weak to permit us to make confident predictions about individuals. Many people endure high levels of stress without developing significant problems.

Second, stress is only one of a multitude of variables that affect susceptibility to various maladies. Stress interacts with many other factors, such as lifestyle, coping skills, social support, hardiness, and genetic inheritance, in influencing one's mental and physical health.

It's important to remember that stress is only one actor on a crowded stage. In light of these considerations, you should evaluate the potential meaning of SRRS or LES scores with caution. A high score should be food for thought, but not reason for alarm.

KEY IDEAS

The Nature of Stress

▶ Stress involves transactions with the environment that are perceived to be threatening. Stress is a common, everyday event, and even routine hassles can be problematic. To a large degree, stress lies in the eye of the beholder. According to Lazarus and Folkman, primary appraisal determines whether events appear threatening, while secondary appraisal assesses whether one has the resources to cope with challenges. How one appraises an event can alter the impact of the event.

▶ Some of the stress that people experience comes from their environment. Examples of environmental stimuli that can be stressful include excessive noise, crowding, community violence, and urban decay. Stress can vary with culture. Within Western culture, ethnicity can be a source of stress in a variety of ways.

Major Types of Stress

▶ Stress can be acute or chronic. Major types of stress include frustration, conflict, change, and pressure. Frustration occurs when an obstacle prevents one from attaining some goal. There are three principal types of conflict: approach-approach, avoidance-avoidance, and approach-avoidance.

▶ A large number of studies with the SRRS suggest that change is stressful. Although that may be true, it is now clear that the SRRS is a measure of general stress rather than just change-related stress.

▶ Pressure (to perform and to conform) also appears to be stressful. Often this pressure is self-imposed.

Responding to Stress

▶ Emotional reactions to stress typically involve anger, fear, or sadness. However, people also experience positive emotions while under stress and these positive emotions may promote resilience. Emotional arousal may interfere with coping. As tasks get more complex, the optimal level of arousal declines.

▶ Physiological arousal in response to stress was originally called the fight-or-flight response by Cannon. Taylor has proposed an alternative response ("tend and befriend") that might be more applicable to females. Selye's general adaptation syndrome describes three stages in the physiological reaction to stress: alarm, resistance, and exhaustion. Diseases of adaptation may appear during the stage of exhaustion.

▶ In response to stress, the brain sends signals along two major pathways to the endocrine system. Actions along these paths release two sets of hormones into the bloodstream, catecholamines and corticosteroids. Stress can also lead to suppression of the immune response. Behavioral responses to stress involve coping, which may be healthy or maladaptive. If people cope effectively with stress, they can short-circuit potentially harmful emotional and physical responses.

The Potential Effects of Stress

▶ Common negative effects of stress include impaired task performance, disruption of attention and other cognitive processes, pervasive emotional exhaustion known as burnout, posttraumatic stress disorder, a host of everyday psychological problems, full-fledged psychological disorders, and varied types of damage to physical health.

▶ However, stress can also have positive effects, including posttraumatic growth. Stress fulfills a basic human need for challenge and can lead to personal growth and self-improvement. Stress can also have an inoculation effect, preparing us for the next stressful event.

Factors Influencing Stress Tolerance

▶ People differ in how much stress they can tolerate without experiencing ill effects. A person's social support can be a key consideration in buffering the effects of stress. The personality factors associated with hardiness—commitment, challenge, and control—may increase stress tolerance. People high in optimism also have advantages in coping with stress.

Application: Monitoring Your Stress

▶ It can be useful to attempt to measure the amount of stress in one's life, but the much-used SRRS is marred by a variety of shortcomings. It does not really measure change exclusively, and it fails to account for the subjective nature of stress. Some of the items on the SRRS are ambiguous, and the scale does not sample the domain of stress thoroughly.

▶ In contrast, the LES is an improved measure of stress that recognizes the subjectivity of stress and the importance of the desirability of life events. The LES also samples the domain of stressful events a little more thoroughly and has less ambiguity than the SRRS. Negative change scores on the LES have been found to be predictive of a variety of adaptational outcomes. Even still, individual results should be interpreted with caution.

KEY TERMS

Acculturation p. 74
Acute stressors p. 75
Ambient stress p. 72
Approach-approach conflict p. 76
Approach-avoidance conflict p. 76
Autonomic nervous system (ANS) p. 83
Avoidance-avoidance conflict p. 76
Burnout p. 88
Chronic stressors pp. 75
Conflict p. 76
Coping pp. 86
Emotions p. 80
Endocrine system p. 85
Fight-or-flight response p. 82
Frustration p. 75
General adaptation syndrome p. 84
Hardiness p. 95
Life changes p. 77
Optimism p. 96
Posttraumatic stress disorder (PTSD) p. 89
Pressure pp. 78–79
Primary appraisal p. 72
Psychosomatic diseases p. 92
Secondary appraisal p. 72
Social support p. 93
Stress p. 71

KEY PEOPLE

Susan Folkman pp. 81–82
Barbara Fredrickson p. 81
Thomas Holmes and Richard Rahe pp. 77, 97
Suzanne (Kobasa) Ouellette pp. 94–95
Richard Lazarus p. 71
Neal Miller p. 76
Hans Selye pp. 84–85
Shelley Taylor p. 84

PRACTICE TEST

1. Concerning the nature of stress, which statement is *not* accurate?
   a. Stress is an everyday event.
   b. Stress lies in the eye of the beholder.
   c. Stress may be embedded in the environment.
   d. Stress is always imposed on us by others.

2. Secondary appraisal refers to:
   a. second thoughts about what to do in a stressful situation.
   b. second thoughts about whether an event is genuinely threatening.
   c. initial evaluation of an event's relevance, threat, and stressfulness.
   d. evaluation of coping resources and options for dealing with a stressful event.

3. Kelli is having a hard time deciding whether she should buy a coat. On the one hand, it is a name brand coat on sale for a great price. On the other hand, it is an ugly mold-green color. Kelli is experiencing what type of conflict?
   a. approach-approach
   b. avoidance-aviodance
   c. approach-avoidance
   d. life change

4. José just completed writing an 8-page term paper. When he went to save it, the computer crashed and he lost all his work. What type of stress is José experiencing?
   a. Frustration
   b. Conflict
   c. Life change
   d. Pressure

5. The optimal level of arousal for a task appears to depend in part on:
   a. one's position on the optimism/pessimism scale.
   b. how much physiological change an event stimulates.
   c. the complexity of the task at hand.
   d. how imminent a stressful event is.

6. The fight-or-flight response is mediated by the:
   a. sympathetic division of the autonomic nervous system.
   b. sympathetic division of the endocrine system.
   c. visceral division of the peripheral nervous system.
   d. parasympathetic division of the autonomic nervous system.

7. Selye exposed lab animals to various stressors and found that:
   a. each type of stress caused a particular physiological response.
   b. each type of animal responded to stress differently.
   c. patterns of physiological arousal were similar, regardless of the type of stress.
   d. patterns of physiological arousal were different, even when stressors were similar.

8. Stress can _____ the functioning of the immune system.
   a. stimulate
   b. destroy
   c. suppress
   d. enhance

9. Salvador works as a security guard at a shopping center. His boss overloads him with responsibility but never gives him any credit for all his hard work. He feels worn down, disillusioned, and helpless at work. Salvador is probably experiencing:
   a. an alarm reaction.
   b. burnout.
   c. posttraumatic stress disorder.
   d. a psychosomatic disorder.

10. A personal disposition marked by commitment, challenge, and control and that appears to be related to stress resistance is called:
   a. hardiness.
   b. optimism.
   c. courage.
   d. conscientiousness.

Book Companion Website

Visit the Book Companion Website at **academic.cengage.com/psychology/weiten,** where you will find tutorial quizzes, flash cards, and web links for every chapter, a final exam, and more! You can also link to the Psychology Resource Center (accessible directly at **academic.cengage.com/login**) for a range of psychology-related resources.

Personal Explorations Workbook

The following exercises in your *Personal Explorations Workbook* may enhance your self-understanding in relation to issues raised in this chapter. **Questionnaire 3.1:** Sensation-Seeking Scale. **Personal Probe 3.1:** Where's the Stress in Your Life? **Personal Probe 3.2:** Stress—How Do You Control It? **Personal Probe 3.3:** Working Through and Assessing the Impact of a Stressful Event.

ANSWERS

1. d Pages 71–73
2. d Page 72
3. c Page 76
4. a Page 75
5. c Page 82
6. a Pages 82–84
7. c Page 84
8. c Page 86
9. b Page 88
10. a Pages 94–95

CHAPTER 4

Coping Processes

THE CONCEPT OF COPING

COMMON COPING PATTERNS OF LIMITED VALUE
Giving Up
Acting Aggressively
Indulging Yourself
Blaming Yourself
Using Defensive Coping

THE NATURE OF CONSTRUCTIVE COPING

APPRAISAL-FOCUSED CONSTRUCTIVE COPING
Ellis's Rational Thinking

LIVING IN TODAY'S WORLD *Thinking Rationally About the Threat of Traumatic Events*
Humor as a Stress Reducer
Positive Reinterpretation

PROBLEM-FOCUSED CONSTRUCTIVE COPING
Using Systematic Problem Solving
Seeking Help
Using Time More Effectively

EMOTION-FOCUSED CONSTRUCTIVE COPING
Enhancing Emotional Intelligence
Expressing Emotions
Managing Hostility and Forgiving Others
Exercising
Using Meditation and Relaxation

APPLICATION: ACHIEVING SELF-CONTROL
Specifying Your Target Behavior
Gathering Baseline Data
Designing Your Program
Executing and Evaluating Your Program
Ending Your Program

REVIEW

PRACTICE TEST

"I have begun to believe that I have intellectually and emotionally outgrown my husband. However, I'm not really sure what this means or what I should do. Maybe this feeling is normal and I should ignore it and continue my present relationship. This seems to be the safest route. Maybe I should seek a lover while continuing with my husband. Then again, maybe I should start anew and hope for a beautiful ending with or without a better mate."

The woman quoted above is in the throes of a thorny conflict. Although it is hard to tell just how much emotional turmoil she is experiencing, it's clear that she is under substantial stress. What should she do? Is it psychologically healthy to remain in an emotionally hollow marriage? Is seeking a secret lover a reasonable way to cope with this unfortunate situation? Should she just strike out on her own and let the chips fall where they may? These questions have no simple answers. As you'll soon see, decisions about how to cope with life's difficulties can be incredibly complex.

In the previous chapter we discussed the nature of stress and its effects. We learned that stress can be a challenging, exciting stimulus to personal growth. However, we also saw that stress can prove damaging to people's psychological and physical health because it often triggers physiological responses that may be harmful. These responses to stress tend to be largely automatic. Controlling them depends on the coping responses people make to stressful situations. Thus, a person's mental and physical health depends, in part, on his or her ability to cope effectively with stress.

This chapter focuses on how people cope with stress. We begin with a general discussion of the concept of coping. Then we review some common coping patterns that tend to have relatively little value. After discussing these ill-advised coping techniques, we offer an overview of what it means to engage in healthier, "constructive" coping. The remainder of the chapter expands on the specifics of constructive coping. We hope our discussion provides you with some new ideas about how to deal with the stresses of modern life.

The Concept of Coping

LEARNING OBJECTIVES

- *Describe the variety of coping strategies that people use.*
- *Discuss the role of flexibility in coping.*

In Chapter 3, you learned that ***coping* refers to efforts to master, reduce, or tolerate the demands created by stress.** Let's take a closer look at this concept and discuss some general points about coping.

People cope with stress in many ways. A number of researchers have attempted to identify and classify the various coping techniques that people use in dealing with stress. Their work reveals quite a variety of coping strategies. For instance, in a review of the literature, Skinner et al. (2003) found over 400 distinct coping techniques. Carver, Scheier, and Weintraub (1989) found that they could sort their participants' coping tactics into 14 categories, which are listed in **Figure 4.1**. Thus, in grappling with stress, people select their coping tactics from a large and varied menu of options.

It is most adaptive to use a variety of coping strategies. Even with a large menu of coping tactics to choose from, most people come to rely on some strategies more than others (Carver & Scheier, 1994; Shiota, 2006). Of course, an individual's coping strategies are

Types of Coping Strategies

Coping strategy	Example
Active coping	I take additional action to try to get rid of the problem.
Planning	I come up with a strategy about what to do.
Suppression of competing activities	I put aside other activities in order to concentrate on this.
Restraint coping	I force myself to wait for the right time to do something.
Seeking social support for instrumental reasons	I ask people who have had similar experiences what they did.
Seeking social support for emotional reasons	I talk to someone about how I feel.
Positive reinterpretation and growth	I look for the good in what is happening.
Acceptance	I learn to live with it.
Turning to religion	I seek God's help.
Focus on and venting of emotions	I get upset and let my emotions out.
Denial	I refuse to believe that it has happened.
Behavioral disengagement	I give up the attempt to get what I want.
Mental disengagement	I turn to work or other substitute activities to take my mind off things.
Alcohol-drug disengagement	I drink alcohol or take drugs in order to think about it less.

Figure 4.1

Classifying coping strategies. Carver, Scheier, and Weintraub (1989) sorted their subjects' coping responses into 14 categories. The categories are listed here (column 1) with a representative example from each category (column 2). As you can see, people use quite a variety of coping strategies.

From Carver, C. S., Scheier, M. F., & Weintraub, J. K. (1989). Assessing coping strategies: A theoretically based approach. *Journal of Personality and Social Psychology, 56*(2), 267–283. Copyright 1989 by the American Psychological Association. Reprinted by permission of the publisher and author.

also influenced by situational demands, and Cheng (2001, 2003) has argued that flexibility in coping is more desirable than consistently relying on the same strategy. Cheng and Cheung (2005) identified a key difference between individuals with high and low coping flexibility. Flexible copers can differentiate among stressful events in terms of controllability and impact, important information to know when choosing a coping strategy. Indeed, the ability to select a specific coping strategy to meet a specific adversity helps people avoid becoming stuck in a rut with a problematic strategy (Carbonell, Reinherz, & Beardslee, 2005). While everyone has an individual style of coping with life's difficulties, this need for flexibility may explain why people's coping strategies show only moderate stability across varied situations (Schwartz et al., 1999).

Coping strategies vary in their adaptive value. In everyday terms, when we say that someone "coped with her problems," we imply that she handled them effectively. In reality, however, all strategies are not created equal. Coping processes range from the helpful to the counterproductive (Carver et al., 1989; Vaillant, 2000). For example, coping with the disappointment of not getting a good grade by plotting to sabotage your professor's computer would be a negative way of coping. Hence, we will distinguish between coping patterns that tend to be helpful and those that tend to be maladaptive. Bear in mind, however, that our generalizations about the adaptive value of various coping strategies are based on trends or tendencies identified by researchers. Unlike what many self-help books and talk show hosts would have you believe, no coping strategy can guarantee a successful outcome. Furthermore, the adaptive value of a coping technique depends on the exact nature of the situation. As you'll see in the next section, even ill-advised coping strategies may have adaptive value in some instances.

Common Coping Patterns of Limited Value

LEARNING OBJECTIVES

- *Analyze the adaptive value of giving up as a response to stress.*
- *Describe the adaptive value of aggression as a response to stress.*
- *Evaluate the adaptive value of indulging yourself as a response to stress.*
- *Discuss the adaptive value of negative self-talk as a response to stress.*
- *Explain how defense mechanisms work.*
- *Evaluate the adaptive value of defense mechanisms, including recent work on healthy illusions.*

"Recently, after an engagement of 22 months, my fiancée told me that she was in love with someone else, and that we were through. I've been a wreck ever since. I can't study because I keep thinking about her. I think constantly about what I did wrong in the relationship and why I wasn't good enough for her. Getting drunk is the only way I can get her off my mind. Lately, I've been getting plastered about five or six nights a week. My grades are really hurting, but I'm not sure that I care."

This young man is going through a difficult time and does not appear to be handling it very well. He's blaming himself for the breakup with his fiancée. He's turning to alcohol to dull the pain that he feels, and it sounds like he may be giving up on school. These coping responses aren't particularly unusual in such situations, but they're only going to make his problems worse.

In this section, we'll examine some relatively common coping patterns that tend to be less than optimal. Specifically, we'll discuss giving up, aggression, self-indulgence, blaming yourself, and defense mechanisms. Some of these coping tactics may be helpful in certain circumstances, but more often than not, they are counterproductive.

Giving Up

Martin Seligman

Courtesy of Martin E. P. Seligman

When confronted with stress, people sometimes simply give up and withdraw from the battle. This response of apathy and inaction tends to be associated with the emotional reactions of sadness and dejection. Martin Seligman (1974, 1992) has developed a model of this giving-up syndrome that appears to shed light on its causes. In Seligman's original research, animals were subjected to electric shocks they could not escape. The animals were then given an opportunity to learn a response that would allow them to escape the shock. However, many of the animals became so apathetic and listless they didn't even try to learn the escape response. When researchers made similar manipulations with *human* subjects using inescapable noise (rather than shock) as the stressor, they observed parallel results (Hiroto & Seligman, 1975). This syndrome is referred to as learned helplessness. ***Learned helplessness* is passive behavior produced by exposure to unavoidable aver-**

sive events. Unfortunately, this tendency to give up may be transferred to situations in which one is not really helpless. Hence, some people routinely respond to stress with fatalism and resignation, passively accepting setbacks that might be dealt with effectively. Interestingly, Evans and Stecker (2004) argue that environmental stressors, such as excessive noise, crowding, and traffic (see Chapter 3), often produce a syndrome that resembles learned helplessness.

Seligman originally viewed learned helplessness as a product of conditioning. However, research with human participants has led Seligman and his colleagues to revise their theory. Their current model proposes that people's *cognitive interpretation* of aversive events determines whether they develop learned helplessness. Specifically, helplessness seems to occur when individuals come to believe that events are beyond their control. This belief is particularly likely to emerge in people who exhibit a pessimistic explanatory style. Among other things, such people tend to attribute setbacks to personal inadequacies instead of situational factors (Abramson, Seligman, & Teasdale, 1978; Seligman, 1990). As discussed in Chapter 3, this explanatory style is associated with poorer physical health and increased depression and anxiety (Wise & Rosqvist, 2006).

Overall, giving up is not a highly regarded method of coping. Carver and his colleagues (1989, 1993) have studied this coping strategy, which they refer to as *behavioral disengagement,* and found that it is associated with increased rather than decreased distress. A recent study of college students after the September 11 terrorist attacks supports this assertion, finding that behavioral disengagement was associated with increased anxiety shortly after the attack, even for those indirectly affected (see **Figure 4.2**; Liverant, Hafmann, & Litz, 2004). Furthermore, many studies suggest that learned helplessness can contribute to depression (Seligman & Isaacowitz, 2000). However, giving up could be adaptive in some instances. For example, if you were thrown into a job that you were not equipped to handle, it might be better to quit rather than face constant pressure and diminishing self-esteem. There is something to be said for recognizing one's limitations, avoiding unrealistic goals, and minimizing self-imposed stress.

Correlation Between Selected Coping Strategies and Anxiety

Specific coping strategy	Correlation with anxiety
Behavioral disengagement	.28
Mental disengagement	.38
Denial	.37
Focus on distressing emotions	.25

Figure 4.2

The relationship among methods of coping and anxiety. Approximately two months after the 9/11 terrorist attacks, Liverant and colleagues (2004) administered a coping inventory and a measure of anxiety to college students living in Boston who were indirectly affected by the attacks. Just 4 out of 13 coping strategies (those listed here) were significant predictors of participants' anxiety. As you can see, strategies that reflect giving up (such as behavioral and mental disengagement) were among the most maladaptive coping responses for this sample.

Adapted from Liverant, G. I., Hofmann, S. G., & Litz, B. T. (2004). Coping and anxiety in college students after the September 11th terrorist attacks. *Anxiety, Stress, & Coping, 17*(2), 127–139. (Table III). Copyright © 2004 by Routledge. Adapted by permission of Taylor & Francis.

Acting Aggressively

A young man, aged 17, cautiously edged his car into traffic on the Corona Expressway in Los Angeles. His slow speed apparently irritated the men in a pickup truck behind him. Unfortunately, he angered the wrong men—they shot him to death. During that same weekend there were six other roadside shootings in the Los Angeles area; all of them triggered by minor incidents or "fender benders." Frustrated motorists are attacking each other more and more frequently, especially on the overburdened highways of Los Angeles.

These tragic incidents of highway violence—so-called "road rage"—exemplify maladaptive ways in which drivers cope with the stress, anxiety, and hostility experienced while driving. These incidents have unfortunately become common enough that some professionals are calling for road rage to become an official psychiatric diagnosis (Ayar, 2006). Road rage vividly illustrates that people often respond to stressful events by acting aggressively. ***Aggression* is any behavior intended to hurt someone, either physically or verbally.** Snarls, curses, and insults are much more common than shootings or fistfights, but aggression of any kind can be problematic.

Many years ago, a team of psychologists (Dollard et al., 1939) proposed the *frustration-aggression hypothesis,* which held that aggression is always due to frustration. Decades of research eventually showed that there isn't an inevitable link between frustration and aggression, but this research also supported the basic idea that frustration *does* frequently elicit aggression (Berkowitz, 1989).

People often lash out aggressively at others who had nothing to do with their frustration, especially when they can't vent their anger at the real source of their frustration. Thus, you'll probably suppress your anger rather than lash out verbally at a police officer who gives you a speeding ticket. Twenty minutes later, however, you might be downright brutal in rebuking a waiter who is slow in serving your lunch. As

© Paul Thomas/The Image Bank/Getty Images

Lashing out at others with verbal aggression tends to be an ineffective coping tactic that often backfires, creating additional stress.

we discussed in Chapter 2, this diversion of anger to a substitute target was noticed long ago by Sigmund Freud, who called it *displacement.* Unfortunately, research suggests that when people are provoked, displaced aggression is a common response (Hoobler & Brass, 2006; Marcus-Newhall et al., 2000).

Freud theorized that behaving aggressively could get pent-up emotion out of one's system and thus be adaptive. He coined the term ***catharsis* to refer to this release of emotional tension.** The Freudian notion that it is a good idea to vent anger has become widely disseminated and accepted in modern society. Books, magazines, and self-appointed experts routinely advise that it is healthy to "blow off steam" and thereby release and reduce anger.

However, experimental research generally has *not* supported the catharsis hypothesis. Indeed, *most studies find just the opposite: behaving in an aggressive manner tends to fuel more anger and aggression* (Bushman, 2002; Bushman, Baumeister, & Stack, 1999). Moreover, Carol Tavris (1982, 1989) points out that aggressive behavior frequently backfires because it elicits aggressive responses from others that generate more anger. She asserts, "Aggressive catharses are almost impossible to find in continuing relationships because parents, children, spouses and bosses usually feel obliged to aggress back at you" (1982, p. 131). Hurting someone, especially someone irrelevant to the situation, is not likely to alleviate frustration. Moreover, the interpersonal conflicts that often emerge from aggressive behavior may produce additional stress.

Conventional wisdom holds that watching violent media or playing violent video games can be cathartic—that watching a murder on a TV show or killing a fictional character in a game can release pent-up anger and hostility. However, the research evidence strongly suggests that this is simply not true. Craig Anderson and Brad Bushman (2001) conducted a groundbreaking review of the research on violent video games and found that playing these games was related to increased aggression, physiological arousal, and aggressive thoughts, and decreased prosocial behavior. In fact, they found that the relationship between media violence and aggressive behavior was almost as strong as the relationship between smoking and cancer (Bushman & Anderson, 2001; see **Figure 4.3**). Exposure to media violence not only desensitizes people to violent acts, it also encourages aggressive self-views and automatic aggressive responses (Bartholow, Bushman, & Sestir, 2006; Uhlmann & Swanson, 2004). Experimental studies using an array of violent media, diverse laboratory conditions, and many kinds of samples continue to find convergent evidence that video games and other forms of violent media do not provide cathartic effects; rather, they increase aggressive tendencies (Anderson, 2004).

Anger: The Misunderstood Emotion
by Carol Tavris (Simon & Schuster, 1989)

With the possible exception of anxiety, anger is the emotion elicited by stress more than any other. It's a powerful emotion that can be harnessed to achieve admirable goals. The work of some of the world's great reformers and leaders has been fueled by moral outrage. However, anger also lies at the center of many human woes—wrecked friendships, destroyed marriages, murders, and wars. Hence, anger is a profoundly important emotion. Carol Tavris analyzes virtually every facet of anger in her book. She carefully scrutinizes common beliefs about anger and concludes that many of them are inaccurate. For instance, she argues convincingly against the idea that aggression can drain off anger through catharsis and the idea that anger and aggression are overpowering, instinctual responses. Tavris's book is a delight to read. It's witty, lively, practical, thought provoking, and frequently eloquent.

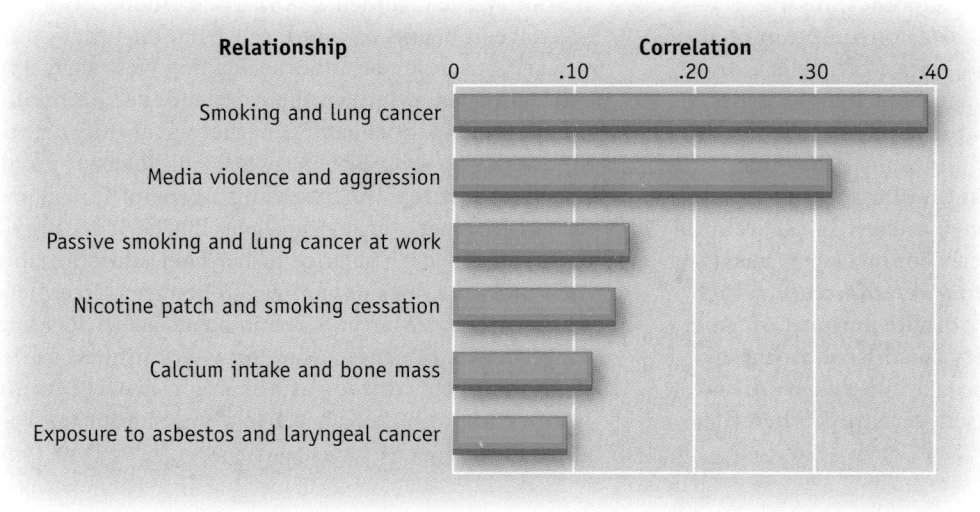

Figure 4.3

Comparison of the relationship between media violence and aggression to other correlations. Many studies have found a correlation between exposure to media violence and aggression. However, some critics have argued that the correlation is too weak to have any practical significance in the real world. In a rebuttal of this criticism, Bushman and Anderson (2001) note that the average correlation in studies of media violence and aggression is .31. They argue that this association is almost as strong as the correlation between smoking and the probability of developing lung cancer, which is viewed as relevant to real-world issues and notably stronger than a variety of other correlations shown here that are assumed to have practical importance.

Adapted from Bushman, B. J., & Anderson, C. A. (2001). Media violence and the American public: Scientific facts versus media misinformation. *American Psychologist, 56*(6-7), 477–489. (Figure 2). Copyright © 2001 American Psychological Association. Reprinted by permission of the publisher and author.

Indulging Yourself

Stress sometimes leads to reduced impulse control, or *self-indulgence* (Tice, Bratslavsky, & Baumeister, 2001). For instance, after an exceptionally stressful day, some people head for their kitchen, a grocery store, or a restaurant in pursuit of something chocolate. In a similar vein, others cope with stress by making a beeline for the nearest shopping mall for a spending spree. Still others respond to stress by indulging in injudicious patterns of drinking, smoking, gambling, and drug use.

In their classification of coping responses, Moos and Billings (1982) list *developing alternative rewards* as a common response to stress. It makes sense that when things are going poorly in one area of your life, you may try to compensate by pursuing substitute forms of satisfaction. Thus, it is not surprising that there is evidence relating stress to increases in eating

CATHY © Cathy Guisewite Reprinted with permission of UNIVERSAL PRESS SYNDICATE. All rights reserved.

(Barker, Williams, & Galambos, 2006), smoking (Kassel, Stroud, & Paronis, 2003), and consumption of alcohol and drugs (Goeders, 2004; Spada & Wells, 2006). In fact, Ng and Jeffery (2003) speculate that the general relationship between stress and poor physical health might be due in part to these unhealthy behaviors.

A more recent manifestation of this coping strategy is the tendency to immerse oneself in the online world of the Internet. Kimberly Young (1998) has described a syndrome called ***Internet addiction,* which consists of spending an inordinate amount of time on the Internet and inability to control online use** (see **Figure 4.4**). People who exhibit this syndrome tend to feel anxious, depressed, or empty when they are not online (Kandell, 1998). Their Internet use is so excessive, it begins to interfere with their functioning at work, at school, or at home, leading victims to start concealing the extent of their dependence on the Internet. Some people exhibit pathological Internet use for one particular purpose, such as online sex or online gambling, whereas others exhibit a general, global pattern of Internet addiction (Davis, 2001). It is difficult to estimate the prevalence of Internet addiction, but the syndrome does *not* appear to be rare (Greenfield, 1999; Morahan-Martin & Schumacher, 2000). Research suggests that Internet addiction is not limited to shy, male computer whizzes, as one might expect (Young, 1998). Although there is active debate about the wis-

Internet Addiction Test

To assess your level of addiction, answer the following questions using this scale:

1 = Not at all 2 = Rarely 3 = Occasionally 4 = Often 5 = Always

1. How often do you find that you stay online longer than you intended?	1	2	3	4	5
2. How often do you neglect household chores to spend more time online?	1	2	3	4	5
3. How often do you prefer the excitement of the Internet to intimacy with your partner?	1	2	3	4	5
4. How often do you form new relationships with fellow online users?	1	2	3	4	5
5. How often do others in your life complain to you about the amount of time you spend online?	1	2	3	4	5
6. How often do your grades or school work suffer because of the amount of time you spend online?	1	2	3	4	5
7. How often do you check your e-mail before something else that you need to do?	1	2	3	4	5
8. How often does your job performance or productivity suffer because of the Internet?	1	2	3	4	5
9. How often do you become defensive or secretive when anyone asks you what you do online?	1	2	3	4	5
10. How often do you block out disturbing thoughts about your life with soothing thoughts of the Internet?	1	2	3	4	5
11. How often do you find yourself anticipating when you will go online again?	1	2	3	4	5
12. How often do you fear that life without the Internet would be boring, empty, and joyless?	1	2	3	4	5
13. How often do you snap, yell, or act annoyed if someone bothers you while you are online?	1	2	3	4	5
14. How often do you lose sleep due to late-night log-ins?	1	2	3	4	5
15. How often do you feel preoccupied with the Internet when off-line, or fantasize about being online?	1	2	3	4	5
16. How often do you find yourself saying "just a few more minutes" when online?	1	2	3	4	5
17. How often do you try to cut down the amount of time you spend online and fail?	1	2	3	4	5
18. How often do you try to hide how long you've been online?	1	2	3	4	5
19. How often do you choose to spend more time online over going out with others?	1	2	3	4	5
20. How often do you feel depressed, moody, or nervous when you are off-line, which goes away once you are back online?	1	2	3	4	5

After you've answered all the questions, add the numbers you selected for each response to obtain a final score. The higher your score, the greater your level of addiction and the problems your Internet usage causes. Here's a general scale to help measure your score.

20–39 points: You are an average online user. You may surf the Web a bit too long at times, but you have control over your usage.

40–69 points: You are experiencing frequent problems because of the Internet. You should consider their full impact on your life.

70–100 points: Your Internet usage is causing significant problems in your life. You need to address them now.

Figure 4.4

Measuring addiction to the Internet. The questions on Young's (1998) Internet Addiction Test highlight the traits that make up this syndrome. You can check to see whether you exhibit any signs of Internet addiction by responding to the items and computing your score.

From Young, K. S. (1998). *Caught in the Net: How to recognize the signs of Internet addiction—and a winning strategy for recovery.* New York: John Wiley. Copyright ©1998 John Wiley & Sons, Inc. This material is used by permission of John Wiley & Sons, Inc.

© Rachel Epstein/The Image Works

Experts disagree about whether excessive Internet use should be characterized as an addiction, but the inability to control online use appears to be an increasingly common syndrome.

dom of characterizing excessive Internet surfing as an *addiction* (Goldsmith & Shapira, 2006), it is clear that this coping strategy can result in a disruption of time, ultimately increasing one's stress levels (Chou, Condron, & Belland, 2005).

There is nothing inherently maladaptive about indulging oneself as a way of coping with life's stresses. If a hot fudge sundae, some new clothes, or chatting online can calm your nerves after a major setback, who can argue? However, if a person consistently responds to stress with excessive self-indulgence, obvious problems are likely to develop. Excesses in eating may produce obesity. Excesses in drinking and drug use may endanger one's health and affect work quality. Given the risks associated with self-indulgence, it has rather marginal adaptive value.

Blaming Yourself

In a postgame interview after a tough defeat, a prominent football coach was brutally critical of himself. He said that he had been outcoached, that he had made poor decisions, and that his game plan was faulty. He almost eagerly assumed all the blame for the loss himself. In reality, he had taken some reasonable chances that didn't go his way and had suffered the effects of poor execution by his players. Looking at it objectively, the loss was attributable to the collective failures of 50 or so players and coaches. However, the coach's unrealistically negative self-evaluation was a fairly typical response to frustration. When confronted by stress (especially frustration and pressure), people often become highly self-critical.

The tendency to engage in "negative self-talk" in response to stress has been noted by a number of influential theorists. As we will discuss in greater detail later in this chapter, Albert Ellis (1973, 1987) calls this phenomenon "catastrophic thinking" and focuses on how it is rooted in irrational assumptions. Aaron Beck (1976, 1987) analyzes negative self-talk into specific tendencies. Among other things, he asserts that people often (1) unreasonably attribute their failures to personal shortcomings, (2) focus on negative feedback from others while ignoring favorable feedback, and (3) make unduly pessimistic projections about the future. Thus, if you performed poorly on an exam, you might respond to this stress by blaming it on your woeful stupidity, dismissing a classmate's comment that the test was unfair, and hysterically predicting that you will flunk out of school.

According to Ellis, catastrophic thinking causes, aggravates, and perpetuates emotional reactions to stress that are often problematic. Along even more serious lines, researchers have found that self-blame is associated with increased distress and depression for individuals who have experienced a variety of traumas such as sexual assault, war, and natural disasters (Frazier, Mortensen, & Steward, 2005, Jeney-Gammon et al., 1993; Kraaij & Garnefski, 2006). Although being realistic and recognizing one's weaknesses has value, Ellis and Beck agree that self-blame as a coping strategy can be enormously counterproductive. We cover Ellis's advice on more constructive thinking later in this chapter and we discuss Beck's recommendations for more effective coping in our chapter on psychotherapy (Chapter 16).

Using Defensive Coping

Defensive coping is a common response to stress. We noted in Chapter 2 that the concept of defense mechanisms was originally developed by Sigmund Freud. Though rooted in the psychoanalytic tradition, this concept has gained acceptance from psychologists of most persuasions (Cramer, 2000). Building on Freud's initial insights, modern psychologists have broadened the scope of the concept and added to Freud's list of defense mechanisms.

The Nature of Defense Mechanisms

***Defense mechanisms* are largely unconscious reactions that protect a person from unpleasant emotions**

Web Link 4.1 **American Self-Help Clearinghouse Sourcebook**

This online clearinghouse provides contact information for hundreds of self-help groups and organizations across the United States. For individuals trying to cope with specific problems or challenging life situations, one of these groups may be particularly helpful with focused advice and suggestions.

Common Defense Mechanisms

Mechanism	Example
Denial of reality. Protecting oneself from unpleasant reality by refusing to perceive or face it.	A smoker concludes that the evidence linking cigarette use to health problems is scientifically worthless.
Fantasy. Gratifying frustrated desires by imaginary achievements.	A socially inept and inhibited young man imagines himself chosen by a group of women to provide them with sexual satisfaction.
Intellectualization (isolation). Cutting off emotion from hurtful situations or separating incompatible attitudes in logic-tight compartments.	A prisoner on death row awaiting execution resists appeal on his behalf and coldly insists that the letter of the law be followed.
Undoing. Atoning for or trying to magically dispel unacceptable desires or acts.	A woman who feels guilty about insulting her co-worker excessively praises her after each insult.
Overcompensation. Covering up felt weaknesses by emphasizing some desirable characteristic, or making up for frustration in one area by overgratification in another.	A dangerously overweight woman goes on eating binges when she feels neglected by her husband.

Figure 4.5

Additional defense mechanisms. Like the seven defense mechanisms described in our discussion of Freudian theory in Chapter 2 (see **Figure 2.4** on page 39), these five defenses are frequently used in our efforts to cope with stress.

Adapted from Carson, R. C., Butcher, J. N., & Coleman, J. C. (1988). *Abnormal psychology and modern life.* Published by Allyn & Bacon, Boston, MA. Copyright © 1988 by Pearson Education. Adapted by permission of the publisher.

such as anxiety and guilt. A number of coping strategies fit this definition. For example, Laughlin (1979) lists 49 different defenses. In our discussion of Freud's theory in Chapter 2, we described seven common defenses. **Figure 4.5** introduces another five defenses that people use with some regularity. Although widely discussed in the popular press, defense mechanisms are often misunderstood. We will use a question-answer format to elaborate on the nature of defense mechanisms in the hopes of clearing up any misconceptions.

What do defense mechanisms defend against? Above all else, defense mechanisms shield the individual from the *emotional discomfort* elicited by stress. Their main purpose is to ward off unwelcome emotions or to reduce their intensity. Foremost among the emotions guarded against is anxiety. People are especially defensive when the anxiety is the result of some threat to their self-esteem. They also use defenses to prevent dangerous feelings of anger from exploding into acts of aggression. Guilt and dejection are two other emotions that people often try to evade through defensive maneuvers.

How do they work? Defense mechanisms work through *self-deception.* They accomplish their goals by distorting reality so it does not appear so threatening.

CALVIN AND HOBBES © Watterson. Reprinted with permission of UNIVERSAL PRESS SYNDICATE. All rights reserved.

Let's say you're doing poorly in school and are in danger of flunking out. Initially, you might use *denial* to block awareness of the possibility that you could flunk out. This tactic might temporarily fend off feelings of anxiety. If it becomes difficult to deny the obvious, you might resort to *fantasy,* daydreaming about how you will salvage adequate grades by getting spectacular scores on the upcoming final exams, when the objective fact is that you are hopelessly behind in your studies. Thus, defense mechanisms work their magic by bending reality in self-serving ways (Bowins, 2004).

Are they conscious or unconscious? Mainstream Freudian theory originally assumed that defenses operate entirely at an unconscious level. However, the concept of defense mechanisms has been broadened to include maneuvers that people may have some awareness of. Thus, defense mechanisms operate at varying levels of awareness and can be conscious or unconscious (Erdelyi, 2001).

Are they normal? Definitely. Everyone uses defense mechanisms on a fairly regular basis. They are entirely normal patterns of coping. The notion that only neurotic people use defense mechanisms is inaccurate.

Can Defense Mechanisms Ever Be Healthy?

The most critical question concerning defense mechanisms is: *Are they healthy?* This is a complicated question. More often than not, the answer is no. Generally, defense mechanisms are poor ways of coping for a number of reasons. First, defensive coping is an avoidance strategy, and avoidance rarely provides a genuine solution to our problems. In fact, Holahan and his colleagues (2005) found that avoidance coping is associated with increased chronic and acute life stressors as well as increased depressive symptoms. Second, defenses such as denial, fantasy, and projection represent "wishful thinking," which is likely to accomplish little. In a study of how students coped with the stress of taking the Medical College Admissions Test (MCAT), Bolger (1990) found that students who engaged in a lot of wishful thinking experienced greater increases in anxiety than other students as the exam approached. Third, a repressive coping style has been related to poor health, in part because repression often leads people to delay facing up to their problems (Weinberger, 1990). For example, if you were to block out obvious warning signs of cancer or diabetes and fail to obtain needed medical care, your defensive behavior could be fatal. Although illusions may protect us from anxiety in the short term, they can create serious problems in the long term.

Courtesy, Shelley Taylor

Shelley Taylor

Most theorists used to regard accurate contact with reality as the hallmark of sound mental health (Jahoda, 1958; Jourard & Landsman, 1980). However, Shelley Taylor and Jonathon Brown (1988, 1994) have reviewed several lines of evidence suggesting that defensive "illusions" may be adaptive for mental health and well-being. First, they note that "normal" people tend to have overly favorable self-images. In contrast, depressed subjects exhibit less favorable—but more realistic—self-concepts. Second, normal subjects overestimate the degree to which they control chance events. In comparison, depressed participants are less prone to this illusion of control. Third, normal individuals are more likely than depressed subjects to display unrealistic optimism in making projections about the future.

A variety of other studies have also provided support for the hypothesis that positive illusions promote well-being. For example, studies of individuals diagnosed with AIDS show that those with unrealistically optimistic expectations of the likely course of their disease actually experience a less rapid course of illness (Reed et al., 1999). In a laboratory study, Taylor et al. (2003) found that subjects who tended to exhibit positive illusions showed lower cardiovascular responses to stress, quicker cardiovascular recovery from stress, and lower levels of a key stress hormone. Further, a study of retirees found that those who held an exaggerated youthful bias reported higher self-esteem, better perceived health, and less boredom than those who held an accurate perception of their age (Gana, Alaphilippe, & Bailly, 2004).

As you might guess, critics have expressed considerable skepticism about the idea that illusions are adaptive. For example, Colvin and Block (1994) make an eloquent case for the traditional view that accuracy and realism are healthy. Moreover, they report data showing that overly favorable self-ratings are correlated with maladaptive personality traits (Colvin, Block, & Funder, 1995). One possible resolution to this debate is Roy Baumeister's (1989) theory that it's all a matter of degree and that there is an "optimal margin of illusion." According to Baumeister, extreme self-deception is maladaptive, but small illusions may often be beneficial.

The Nature of Constructive Coping

LEARNING OBJECTIVES

- *Describe the nature of constructive coping.*
- *Distinguish among the three categories of constructive coping.*

Our discussion thus far has focused on coping strategies that tend to be less than ideal. Of course, people also exhibit many healthful strategies for dealing with stress. We will use the term ***constructive coping* to refer to efforts to deal with stressful events that are judged to be relatively healthful.** No strategy of coping can guarantee a successful outcome. Even the healthiest coping responses may turn out to be ineffective in some cases. Thus, the concept of constructive coping is simply meant to convey a healthy, positive connotation, without promising success.

What makes a coping strategy constructive? Frankly, in labeling certain coping responses constructive or healthy, psychologists are making value judgments. It's a gray area in which opinions will vary to some extent. Nonetheless, some consensus emerges from the burgeoning research on coping and stress management. Key themes in this literature include the following:

1. Constructive coping involves confronting problems directly. It is task relevant and action oriented. It involves a conscious effort to rationally evaluate your options in an effort to solve your problems.

2. Constructive coping is based on reasonably realistic appraisals of your stress and coping resources. A little self-deception may sometimes be adaptive, but excessive self-deception and highly unrealistic negative thinking are not.

3. Constructive coping involves learning to recognize and manage potentially disruptive emotional reactions to stress.

4. Constructive coping involves learning to exert some control over potentially harmful or destructive habitual behaviors. It requires the acquisition of some behavioral self-control.

These points should give you a general idea of what we mean by constructive coping. They will guide our discourse in the remainder of this chapter as we discuss how to cope more effectively with stress. To organize our discussion, we will use a classification scheme proposed by Moos and Billings (1982) to divide constructive coping techniques into three broad categories: *appraisal-focused coping* (aimed at changing one's interpretation of stressful events), *problem-focused coping* (aimed at altering the stressful situation itself), and *emotion-focused coping* (aimed at managing potential emotional distress). **Figure 4.6** shows common coping strategies that fall under each category. It is important to note that many strategies could fall under more than one category. For instance, one could seek social support for practical purposes (problem focused) or emotional purposes (emotion focused).

Figure 4.6

Overview of constructive coping tactics. Coping tactics can be organized in several ways, but we will use the classification scheme shown here, which consists of three categories: appraisal-focused strategies, problem-focused strategies, and emotion-focused strategies. The list of coping tactics in each category is not exhaustive. We will discuss most, but not all, of the listed strategies in our coverage of constructive coping.

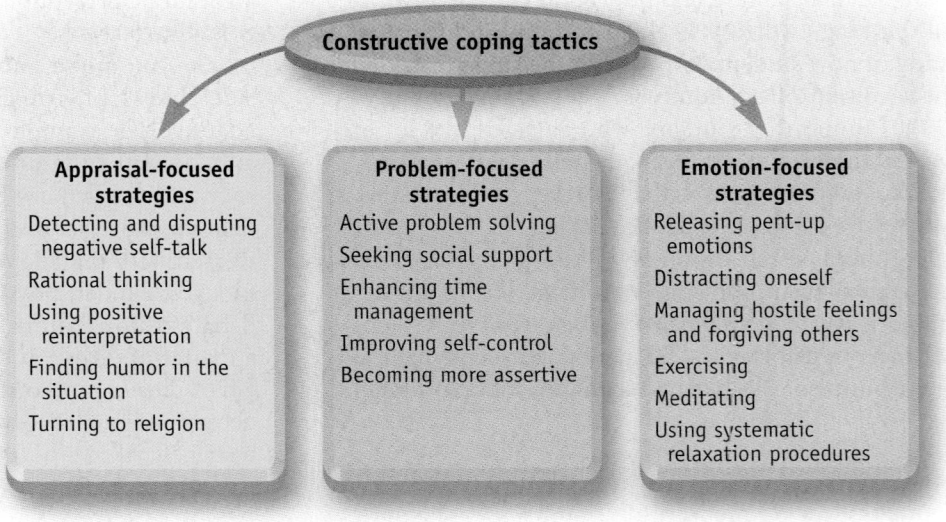

Sally Forth, Copyright © 1984 News Group Chicago, reprinted by permission of North American Syndicate.

Appraisal-Focused Constructive Coping

LEARNING OBJECTIVES

- *Explain Ellis's analysis of the causes of maladaptive emotions.*
- *Describe some assumptions that contribute to catastrophic thinking.*
- *Describe some ways to reduce catastrophic thinking.*
- *Discuss the merits of humor and positive reinterpretation as coping strategies.*

People often underestimate the importance of the appraisal phase in the stress process. They fail to appreciate the highly subjective feelings that color the perception of threat to one's well-being. A useful way to deal with stress is to alter your appraisal of threatening events. In this section, we'll examine Albert Ellis's ideas about reappraisal and discuss the value of using humor and positive reinterpretation to cope with stress.

Ellis's Rational Thinking

Albert Ellis (1977, 1985, 1996, 2001a, 2001b) is a prominent theorist who believes that people can short-circuit their emotional reactions to stress by altering their appraisals of stressful events. Ellis's insights about stress appraisal are the foundation for his widely used system of therapy. ***Rational-emotive behavior therapy* is an approach to therapy that focuses on altering clients' patterns of irrational thinking to reduce maladaptive emotions and behavior.**

Courtesy, Albert Ellis Institute

Albert Ellis

Ellis maintains that *you feel the way you think.* He argues that problematic emotional reactions are caused by negative self-talk, which, as we mentioned earlier, he calls catastrophic thinking. ***Catastrophic thinking* involves unrealistic appraisals of stress that exaggerate the magnitude of one's problems.** Ellis uses a simple A-B-C sequence to explain his ideas (see **Figure 4.7** on the next page):

A. *Activating event.* The A in Ellis's system stands for the activating event that produces the stress. The activating event may be any potentially stressful transaction. Examples might include an automobile accident, the cancellation of a date, a delay while waiting in line at the bank, or a failure to get a promotion you were expecting.

B. *Belief system.* B stands for your belief about the event. This represents your appraisal of the stress. According to Ellis, people often view minor setbacks as disasters, engaging in catastrophic thinking: "How awful this is. I can't stand it!" "Things never turn out fairly for me." "I'll be in this line forever." "I'll never get promoted."

C. *Consequence.* C stands for the consequence of your negative thinking. When your appraisals of stressful events are highly negative, the consequence tends to be emotional distress. Thus, you feel angry, outraged, anxious, panic stricken, disgusted, or dejected.

Ellis asserts that most people do not understand the importance of phase B in this three-stage sequence. They unwittingly believe that the activating event (A) *causes* the consequent emotional turmoil (C). However, Ellis maintains that A does *not* cause C. It only appears to do so. Instead, Ellis asserts that B causes C. Emotional

Figure 4.7

Albert Ellis's A-B-C model of emotional reactions. Most people are prone to attribute their negative emotional reactions (C) directly to stressful events (A). However, Ellis argues that emotional reactions are really caused by the way individuals think about these events (B).

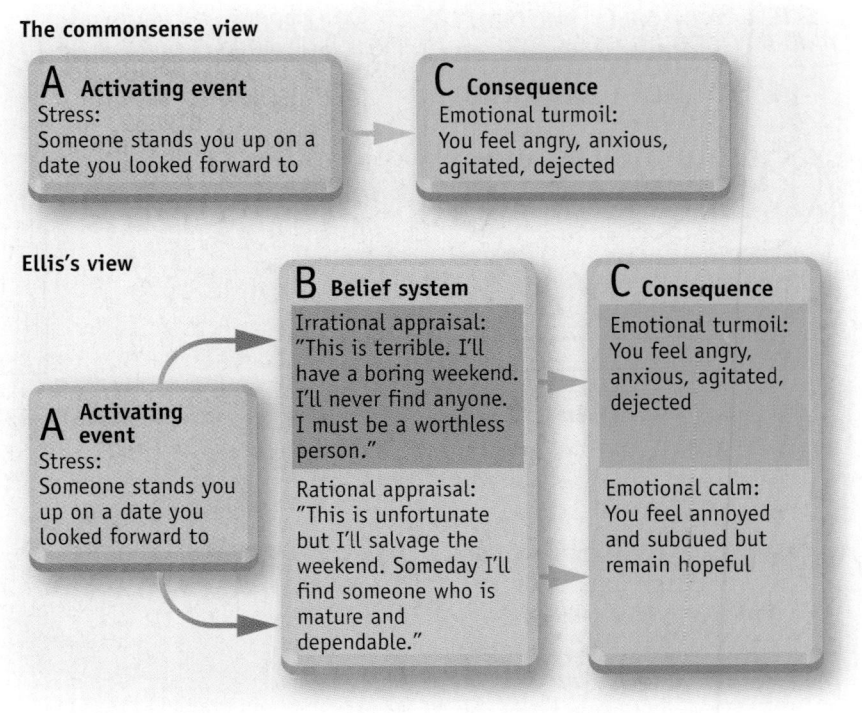

distress is actually caused by one's catastrophic thinking in appraising stressful events.

According to Ellis, it is common for people to turn inconvenience into disaster and make "mountains out of molehills." For instance, imagine that someone stands you up on a date that you were eagerly looking forward to. You might think, "Oh, this is terrible. I'm going to have another boring weekend. People always mistreat me. I'll never find anyone to fall in love with. I must be an ugly, worthless person." Ellis would argue that such thoughts are irrational. He would point out that it does not follow logically from being stood up that you (1) must have a lousy weekend, (2) will never fall in love, or (3) are a worthless person. Thinking this way does nothing but increase distress. Indeed, recent research indicates that the tendency toward catastrophic thinking is a risk factor for developing posttraumatic stress disorder (see Chapter 3) (Bryant & Guthrie, 2005).

Web Link 4.2 **The Albert Ellis Institute**

Albert Ellis developed rational-emotive behavior therapy in the mid-1950s as an effective alternative to psychoanalytically inspired treatment approaches. This site demonstrates the growth of Ellis's approach over the subsequent decades.

The Roots of Catastrophic Thinking

Ellis (1994, 1995, 2004) theorizes that unrealistic appraisals of stress are derived from the irrational assumptions that people hold. He maintains that if you scrutinize your catastrophic thinking, you will find that your reasoning is based on an unreasonable premise, such as "I must have approval from everyone" or "I must perform well in all endeavors." These faulty assumptions, which most people hold unconsciously, generate catastrophic thinking and emotional turmoil. To facilitate emotional self-control, it is important to learn to spot irrational assumptions and the unhealthy patterns of thought that they generate. Here are four particularly common irrational assumptions:

1. *I must have love and affection from certain people.* Everyone wants to be liked and loved. There is nothing wrong with that. However, many people foolishly believe that they should be liked by everyone they come into contact with. If you stop to think about it, that's clearly unrealistic. Once individuals fall in love, they tend to believe that their future happiness depends absolutely on the continuation of that one, special relationship. They believe that if their current love relationship were to end, they would never again be able to achieve a comparable one. This is an unrealistic view of the future. Such views make the person anxious during a relationship and severely depressed if it comes to an end.

LIVING IN TODAY'S WORLD

Thinking Rationally About the Threat of Traumatic Events

Some traumatic events, whether natural (such as earthquakes) or human-made (such as war) can provoke psychological instability in an entire population. For instance, the death, destruction, and havoc wreaked by terrorists is not an end in itself, but a means to an end—the creation of widespread anxiety, fear, and alarm (Everly & Mitchell, 2001). Unfortunately, a normal feature of human mental processing makes it much too easy for terrorists to achieve their goal. However, being aware of this cognitive tendency can help people to be more rational about the threat of traumatic events. To introduce you to this cognitive tendency, consider the following problem:

Various causes of death are paired up below. For each pairing, decide which is the more likely cause of death.

Asthma or tornadoes?
Syphilis or botulism (food poisoning)?
Tuberculosis or floods?

Would you believe that the first choice in each pair causes at least 18 times as many deaths as the second choice? If your guesses were wrong, don't feel bad. Most people tend to greatly overestimate the likelihood of dramatic and vivid—but infrequent—events that receive heavy media coverage. Thus, the number of fatalities caused by tornadoes, floods, and food poisonings is usually overestimated (Slovic, Fischhoff, & Lichtenstein, 1982), whereas fatalities caused by asthma and other run-of-the-mill diseases tend to be underestimated. This tendency to overestimate the improbable reflects the operation of the *availability heuristic,* which involves basing the estimated probability of an event on the ease with which relevant instances come to mind.

Relying on the availability heuristic is a normal cognitive tendency. However, to the extent that certain events occur infrequently but are easily available in memory, your estimates will be biased. Instances of hurricanes, tornadoes, and terrorists attacks are readily available in memory because these events receive a great deal of media attention. The result is that people tend to greatly exaggerate the likelihood that they might be a victim of such adverse events, and such overestimates fuel fear. Ironically, experiencing fear results in greater perceptions of being at risk (Keller, Siegrist, & Gutscher, 2006), which then makes one feel more fear—creating a vicious cycle of anxiety and alarm.

Admittedly, no one knows what the future might bring in the way of disasters or terrorist attacks. However, based on what has happened in recent years, your chances of being harmed by a terrorist are microscopic in comparison to your chances of perishing in an automobile accident (Myers, 2001). Since 9/11, many Americans have been reluctant to fly because the airplane hijackings that occurred on 9/11 remain salient in their minds. But think about it: Even if you knew in advance that terrorists planned to blow up a commercial flight next week, your chances of choosing that specific flight would only be about 1 in 173,000.

In sum, it is wise to be mindful of the natural tendency to overestimate the likelihood that you might be affected by a traumatic event. Thinking more rationally about the probability of being victimized can reduce people's collective sense of alarm.

2. *I must perform well in all endeavors.* We live in a highly competitive society. We are taught that victory brings happiness. Consequently, we feel that we must always win. For example, many sports enthusiasts are never satisfied unless they perform at their best level. However, by definition, their best level is not their typical level, and they set themselves up for inevitable frustration.

3. *Other people should always behave competently and be considerate of me.* People are often angered by others' stupidity and selfishness. For example, you may become outraged when a mechanic fails to fix your car properly or when a salesperson treats you rudely. It would be nice if others were always competent and considerate, but you know better—they are not! Yet many people go through life unrealistically expecting others' efficiency and kindness in every situation.

4. *Events should always go the way I like.* Some people simply won't tolerate any kind of setback. They assume that things should always go their way. For

Recommended READING

How to Stubbornly Refuse to Make Yourself Miserable About Anything—Yes, Anything!
by Albert Ellis (Citadel, 2006)

This is one of the better "popular" books by Albert Ellis, the world-renowned architect of rational-emotive behavior therapy. At last count, Ellis has written around 50 books, about evenly divided between popular books intended for a general audience and technical books intended for mental health professionals. This book doesn't break any new ground for Ellis, but it does bring his ideas together in one succinct, readable summary, complete with exercises. Ellis is a bit prone to overstatement, asserting that his book "will help you achieve a profound philosophic change and a radically new outlook on life." Whether it does so or not, his ideas can clearly be helpful in coping with stress more effectively. If you tend to fall into the trap of overly negative thinking, this book is worth reading. Other recent self-help titles from Ellis that cover much of the same ground include *Feeling Better, Getting Better, Staying Better: Profound Self-Help Therapy for Your Emotions* (2001), *Anger: How to Live With and Without It* (2002), *Ask Albert Ellis: Straight Answers and Sound Advice from America's Best-Known Psychologist* (2003), and *The Road to Tolerance: The Philosophy of Rational Emotive Behavior Therapy* (2004).

example, some commuters become tense and angry each time they get stuck in a rush-hour traffic jam. They seem to believe that they are entitled to coast home easily every day, even though they know that rush hour rarely is a breeze. Such expectations are clearly unrealistic and doomed to be violated. Yet few people recognize the obvious irrationality of the assumption that underlies their anger unless it is pointed out to them.

Reducing Catastrophic Thinking

How can you reduce your unrealistic appraisals of stress? Ellis asserts that you must learn (1) how to detect catastrophic thinking and (2) how to dispute the irrational assumptions that cause it. Detection involves acquiring the ability to spot unrealistic pessimism and wild exaggeration in your thinking. Examine your self-talk closely. Ask yourself why you're getting upset. Force yourself to verbalize your concerns, covertly or out loud. Look for key words that often show up in catastrophic thinking, such as *should, ought, always, never,* and *must.*

Disputing your irrational assumptions requires subjecting your entire reasoning process to scrutiny. Try to root out the assumptions from which your conclusions are derived. Most people are unaware of their assumptions. Once these thoughts are unearthed, their irrationality may be quite obvious. If your assumptions seem reasonable, ask yourself whether your conclusions follow logically. Try to replace your catastrophic thinking with more low-key, rational analyses. These strategies should help you to redefine stressful situations in ways that are less threatening. Strangely enough, another way to defuse such situations is to turn to humor.

Humor as a Stress Reducer

In a New Orleans suburb in the aftermath of Hurricane Katrina, "the grimy residue of receded floodwater covered the blue Chevrolet pickup parked outside a shattered two-story house, but the offer spray-painted on the vehicle in white overflowed with enthusiasm: 'For Sale. Like New. Runs Great'" (Associated Press. 2005). Obviously, the hurricane didn't destroy this vic-

Copyright © by Dan Piraro. Reprinted by permission of King Features Syndicate.

© Radhika Chalasani/Getty Images

People often turn to humor to help themselves cope during difficult times, as this photo taken in the aftermath of Hurricane Katrina illustrates. Research suggests that humor can help to reduce the negative impact of stressful events.

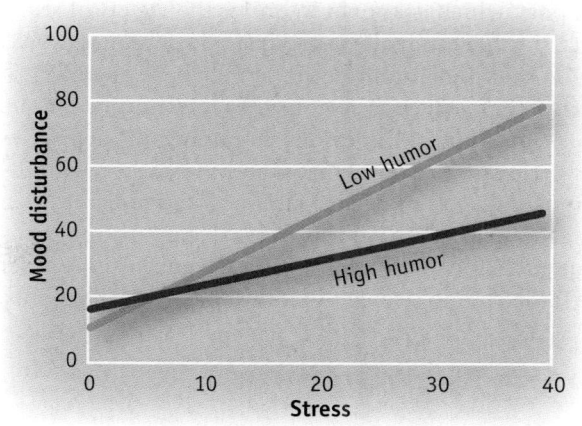

Figure 4.8

Humor and coping. Martin and Lefcourt (1983) related stress to mood disturbance in subjects who were either high or low in their use of humor. Increased stress led to smaller increases in mood disturbance in the high-humor group, suggesting that humor has some value in efforts to cope with stress.

Adapted from Martin, R. A., & Lefcourt, H. M. (1983). Sense of humor as a moderator of the relation between stressors and moods. *Journal of Personality and Social Psychology, 45* (6), 1313–1324. Copyright © 1983 by the American Psychological Association. Adapted by permission of the publisher and author.

tim's sense of humor. When the going gets tough, finding some humor in the situation is not uncommon and is often beneficial. In a study of coping styles, McCrae (1984) found that 40 percent of his subjects reported using humor to deal with stress.

Empirical evidence showing that humor moderates the impact of stress has been accumulating over the last 25 years (Lefcourt, 2001, 2005). For instance, in one influential study, Martin and Lefcourt (1983) found that a good sense of humor functioned as a buffer to lessen the negative impact of stress on mood. Some of their results are presented in **Figure 4.8**, which shows how mood disturbance increased as stress went up in two groups of participants—those who were high or low in their use of humor. Notice how higher stress leads to a smaller increase in mood disturbance in the high-humor group. Similar findings have been observed in other studies (Abel, 1998; Martin, 1996). Further, there is increasing evidence that humor is associated with enhanced immune functioning (Godfrey, 2004; Lefcourt, 2005).

How does humor help reduce the effects of stress and promote wellness? Several explanations have been proposed (see **Figure 4.9**). One possibility is that humor affects appraisals of stressful events (Abel, 2002). Jokes can help people put a less-threatening spin on their trials and tribulations. Another possibility is that humor increases the experience of positive emotions (Martin, 2002). As we discussed in Chapter 3, positive emotions can help people bounce back from stressful events (Tugade & Fredrickson, 2004). A recent study comparing types of constructive coping strategies found that those that increase positive emotions were most strongly associated with well-being (Shiota, 2006). Another hypothesis is that a good sense of humor facilitates positive social interactions, which promote social

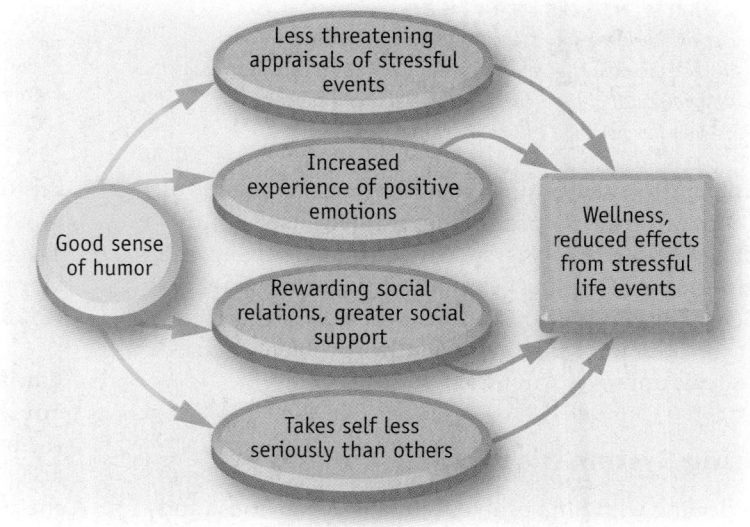

Figure 4.9

Possible explanations for the link between humor and wellness. Research suggests that a good sense of humor buffers the effects of stress and promotes wellness. Four hypothesized explanations for the link between humor and wellness are outlined in the middle column of this diagram. As you can see, humor may have a variety of beneficial effects.

support, which is known to buffer the effects of stress (Martin, 2002). Finally, Lefcourt and colleagues (1995) argue that high-humor people may benefit from not taking themselves as seriously as low-humor people do. As they put it, "If persons do not regard themselves too seriously and do not have an inflated sense of self-importance, then defeats, embarrassments, and even tragedies should have less pervasive emotional consequences for them" (p. 375). Thus, humor is a rather versatile coping strategy that may have many benefits.

Positive Reinterpretation

When you are feeling overwhelmed by life's difficulties, you might try the commonsense strategy of recognizing that "things could be worse." No matter how terrible your problems seem, you probably know someone who has even bigger troubles. That is not to say that you should derive satisfaction from others' misfortune. However, comparing your own plight with others' even tougher struggles can help you put your problems in perspective. Research suggests that this strategy of making positive comparisons with others is a common coping mechanism that can result in improved mood and self-esteem (Wills & Sandy, 2001). Moreover, this strategy does not depend on knowing others who are clearly worse off. You can simply imagine yourself in a similar situation with an even worse outcome (example: two broken legs after a horse-riding accident instead of just one). One healthy aspect of positive reinterpretation is that it can facilitate calming reappraisals of stress without the necessity of distorting reality.

Another way to engage in positive reinterpretation is to search for something good in a bad experience. Distressing though they may be, many setbacks have positive elements. After experiencing divorces, illnesses, firings, and the like, many people remark that "I came out of the experience better than I went in," or "I grew as a person." Studies of victims of natural disasters, heart attacks, and bereavement have found an association between this type of *benefit finding* under duress and relatively sound psychological and physical health (Nolen-Hoeksema & Davis, 2005; Tennen & Affleck, 2002, 2005). Further, benefit finding is associated with personal growth following adversity (Linley & Joseph, 2004). Of course, the positive aspects of a personal setback may be easy to see after the stressful event is behind you. The challenge is to recognize these positive aspects while you are still struggling with the setback, so that it becomes less stressful.

Problem-Focused Constructive Coping

LEARNING OBJECTIVES

- *List and describe four steps in systematic problem solving.*
- *Discuss the adaptive value of seeking help as a coping strategy.*
- *Describe cultural differences in seeking social support.*
- *Explain five common causes of wasted time.*
- *Describe evidence on the causes and consequences of procrastination.*
- *Summarize advice on managing time effectively.*

Problem-focused coping includes efforts to remedy or conquer the stress-producing problem itself. In this category, we'll discuss systematic problem solving, the importance of seeking help, and effective time management. The application section at the end of this chapter includes information on another problem-focused strategy, improvement of self-control.

Using Systematic Problem Solving

In dealing with life's problems, the most obvious (and often most effective) course of action is to tackle them head-on. In fact, problem solving has been linked to better psychological adjustment, lower levels of depression, reduced alcohol use, and fewer health complaints (Heppner & Lee, 2005). Obviously, people vary in their problem-solving skills. However, evidence suggests that problem-solving skills can be enhanced through training (Heppner & Lee, 2002, 2005). With this thought in mind, we will sketch a general outline of how to engage in more systematic problem solving. The plan described here is a synthesis of observations by various experts, especially Mahoney (1979), Miller (1978), and Chang and Kelly (1993).

Clarify the Problem

You can't tackle a problem if you're not sure what the problem is. Therefore, the first step in any systematic problem-solving effort is to clarify the nature of the problem. Sometimes the problem will be all too obvious. At other times the source of trouble may be quite difficult to pin down. In any case, you need to arrive at a specific concrete definition of your problem.

Two common tendencies typically hinder people's efforts to get a clear picture of their problems. First, they often describe their problems in vague generalities ("My life isn't going anywhere" or "I never have enough time"). Second, they tend to focus too much on negative feelings, thereby confusing the consequences of problems ("I'm so depressed all the time" or "I'm so nervous I can't concentrate") with the problems themselves ("I don't have any friends at my new school" or "I have taken on more responsibilities than I can realistically handle").

Generate Alternative Courses of Action

The second step in systematic problem solving is to generate alternative courses of action. Notice that we did not call these alternative *solutions.* Many problems do not have a readily available solution that will completely resolve the problem. If you think in terms of searching for complete solutions, you may prevent yourself from considering many worthwhile courses of action. Instead, it is more realistic to search for alternatives that may produce some kind of improvement in your situation.

Besides avoiding the tendency to insist on solutions, you need to avoid the temptation to go with the first alternative that comes to mind. Many people are a little trigger-happy. They thoughtlessly try to follow through on the first response that occurs to them. Various lines of evidence suggest that it is wiser to engage in brainstorming about a problem. ***Brainstorming* is generating as many ideas as possible while withholding criticism and evaluation.** In other words, you generate alternatives without paying any attention to their apparent practicality. This approach facilitates creative expression of ideas.

Evaluate Your Alternatives and Select a Course of Action

Once you generate as many alternatives as you can, you need to start evaluating the possibilities. There are no simple criteria for judging the relative merits of your alternatives. However, you will probably want to address three general issues. First, ask yourself whether each alternative is realistic. In other words, what is the probability that you can successfully execute the intended course of action? Try to think of any obstacles you may have failed to anticipate. In making this assessment, it is important to try to avoid both foolish optimism and unnecessary pessimism.

Second, consider any costs or risks associated with each alternative. The "solution" to a problem is sometimes worse than the problem itself. Assuming you can successfully implement your intended course of action, what are the possible negative consequences? Third, compare the desirability of the probable outcomes of each alternative. In making your decision, you have to ask yourself "What is important to me? Which outcomes do I value the most?"

Web Link 4.3 **Mind Tools**

James Manktelow's site in England offers practical techniques to help people deal with the world more efficiently and effectively. The site houses useful information on several of the topics discussed in this chapter, including stress management, time management, and effective problem solving.

Take Action While Maintaining Flexibility

After you have chosen your course of action, you should follow through in implementing your plan. In so doing, try to maintain flexibility. Do not get locked into a particular course of action. Few choices are truly irreversible. You need to monitor results closely and be willing to revise your strategy.

In evaluating your course of action, try to avoid the simplistic success/failure dichotomy. You should simply look for improvement of any kind. If your plan doesn't work out too well, consider whether it was undermined by any circumstances that you could not have anticipated. Finally, remember that you can learn from your failures. Even if things did not work out, you may now have new information that will facilitate a new attack on the problem.

Seeking Help

In Chapter 3, we learned that social support can be a powerful force that helps buffer the deleterious effects of stress and that has positive effects of its own (Taylor, 2007; Wills & Fegan, 2001). In trying to tackle problems directly, it pays to keep in mind the value of seeking aid from friends, family, co-workers, and neighbors. So far, we discussed social support as if it were a stable, external resource available to different people in varying degrees. In reality, social supports fluctuate over time and evolve out of individuals' interactions with others (Newcomb, 1990). Some people have more support than others because they have personal characteristics that attract more support or because they make more effort to seek support.

Interestingly, cultural factors seem to play a role in who seeks social support. Taylor and colleagues (2004) found that Asians and Asian Americans are less likely to seek social support in times of stress than European Americans. When examined closely, this difference appears to be rooted in cultural concerns about relationships. That is, individuals from cultures high in collectivism (see Chapter 5) don't want to risk straining relationships or disrupting group harmony by calling on others for help in times of stress (Kim, Sherman, & Ko, 2006; Taylor, 2004). Of course, broad cultural *similarities* exist in how people from different cultures react to stress. For example, individuals from both collectivistic and individualistic cultures view receiving comfort as an effective coping strategy. There appear to be cultural differences, however, in actively *seeking* that help (Mortenson, 2006). Given that social support is such an important resource, researchers will no doubt continue to examine it within a cultural context.

Using Time More Effectively

Do you constantly feel that you have too much to do, and too little time to do it in? Do you feel overwhelmed by your responsibilities at work, at school, and at home? Do you feel like you're always rushing around, trying to meet an impossible schedule? If you answered yes to some of these questions, you're struggling with time pressure, a huge source of stress in modern life. You can estimate how well you manage time by responding to the brief questionnaire in **Figure 4.10**. If the results suggest that your time is out of your control, you may be able to make your life less stressful by engaging in problem-focused coping and learning sound time-management strategies.

R. Alec Mackenzie (1997), a prominent time-management researcher, points out that time is a nonrenewable resource. It can't be stockpiled like money, food, or other precious resources. You can't turn back the clock. Furthermore, everyone, whether rich or poor, gets an equal share of time—24 hours per day, 7 days a week. Although time is our most equitably distributed

Time Management from the Inside Out: The Foolproof System for Taking Control of Your Schedule—and Your Life
by Julie Morgenstern (Henry Holt, 2000)

If you're locked in a perennial struggle with time—and if you're losing the battle—this book may be worth your time. Julie Morgenstern, whose first book dealt with improving personal organization, offers insightful analyses of why most of us never have enough time. She begins by describing a host of barriers to effective time use, such as unrealistic workloads, interruption-rich environments, unclear priorities, fear of failure, and perfectionism. She then discusses how to evaluate your use of time and how to prioritize your goals. She devotes quite a bit of attention to scheduling and planning and to modern devices intended to aid these processes (datebooks, computerized calendar programs, personal digital assistants, and so forth). This discussion is followed by a wealth of advice on how to be more efficient and make better choices in allocating your time. *Time Management from the Inside Out* is succinct, entertaining, and practical. Don't have time to read this book? It is now available on audio CD.

How Well Do You Manage Your Time?

Listed below are ten statements that reflect generally accepted principles of good time management. Answer these items by circling the response most characteristic of how you perform your job. Please be honest. No one will know your answers except you.

1. Each day I set aside a small amount of time for planning and thinking about my job.
   0. Almost never 1. Sometimes 2. Often 3. Almost always
2. I set specific, written goals and put deadlines on them.
   0. Almost never 1. Sometimes 2. Often 3. Almost always
3. I make a daily "to do list," arrange items in order of importance, and try to get the important items done as soon as possible.
   0. Almost never 1. Sometimes 2. Often 3. Almost always
4. I am aware of the 80/20 rule and use it in doing my job. (The 80/20 rule states that 80 percent of your effectiveness will generally come from achieving only 20 percent of your goals.)
   0. Almost never 1. Sometimes 2. Often 3. Almost always
5. I keep a loose schedule to allow for crises and the unexpected.
   0. Almost never 1. Sometimes 2. Often 3. Almost always
6. I delegate everything I can to others.
   0. Almost never 1. Sometimes 2. Often 3. Almost always
7. I try to handle each piece of paper only once.
   0. Almost never 1. Sometimes 2. Often 3. Almost always
8. I eat a light lunch so I don't get sleepy in the afternoon.
   0. Almost never 1. Sometimes 2. Often 3. Almost always
9. I make an active effort to keep common interruptions (visitors, meetings, telephone calls) from continually disrupting my work day.
   0. Almost never 1. Sometimes 2. Often 3. Almost always
10. I am able to say no to others' requests for my time that would prevent my completing important tasks.
    0. Almost never 1. Sometimes 2. Often 3. Almost always

To get your score, give yourself

3 points for each "almost always"
2 points for each "often"
1 point for each "sometimes"
0 points for each "almost never"

Add up your points to get your total score.

If you scored

0–15	Better give some thought to managing your time.
15–20	You're doing OK, but there's room for improvement.
20–25	Very good.
25–30	You cheated!

Figure 4.10

Assessing your time management. The brief questionnaire shown here is designed to evaluate the quality of one's time management. Although it is geared more for working adults than college students, it should allow you to get a rough handle on how well you manage your time.

From Le Boeuf, M. (1980, February). Managing time means managing yourself. *Business Horizons Magazine*, p. 45. Copyright © by the Foundation for the School of Business at Indiana University. Used with permission from Elsevier.

resource, some people spend it much more wisely than others. Let's look at some of the ways in which people let time slip through their fingers without accomplishing much.

The Causes of Wasted Time

When people complain about "wasted time," they're usually upset because they haven't accomplished what they really wanted to do with their time. Wasted time is time devoted to unnecessary, unimportant, or unenjoyable activities. Why waste time on such activities? There are many reasons.

Inability to set or stick to priorities. Time consultant Alan Lakein (1996) emphasizes that it's often tempting to deal with routine, trivial tasks ahead of larger and more difficult tasks. Thus, students working on a major term paper (or professors working on a manuscript) often read their e-mail, do the dishes, fold the laundry, or reorganize their desk instead of concentrating on the paper. Routine tasks are easy, and working on them allows people to rationalize their avoidance of more important tasks. Unfortunately, many of us spend too much time on trivial pursuits, leaving our more important tasks undone.

Inability to say no. Other people are constantly making demands on our time. They want us to exchange gossip in the hallway, go out to dinner on Friday night, cover their hours at work, help with a project, listen to their sales pitch on the phone, join a committee, or coach Little League. Clearly, we can't do everything that everyone wants us to. However, some people just can't say no to others' requests for their time. Such people end up fulfilling others' priorities instead of their own. Thus, McDougle (1987) concludes, "Perhaps the most successful way to prevent yourself from wasting time is by saying *no*" (p. 112).

Inability to delegate responsibility. Some tasks should be delegated to others—assistants, subordinates, fellow committee members, partners, spouses, children, and so on. However, many people have difficulty delegating work to others. Barriers to delegation include unwillingness to give up any control, lack of confidence in subordinates, fear of being disliked, the need to feel needed, and the attitude that "I can do it better myself" (Mitchell, 1987). The problem, of course, is that people who can't delegate waste a lot of time on trivial work or others' work.

Inability to throw things away. Some people are pack rats who can't throw anything into the wastebasket. Their desks are cluttered with piles of mail, newspapers, magazines, reports, and books. Their filing cabinets overflow with old class notes or ancient memos. At home, their kitchen drawers bulge with rarely used utensils and their closets bulge with old clothes that are never worn. Pack rats waste time in at least two ways. First, they lose time looking for things that have disappeared among all the chaos. Second, they end up reshuffling the same paper, rereading the same mail, resorting the same files, and so on. According to Mackenzie (1997), they would be better off if they made more use of their wastebaskets.

© Bruce Ayres/Stone/Getty Images

For many people, an inability to throw things away is a key factor promoting wasted time.

Inability to accept anything less than perfection. High standards are admirable, but some people have difficulty finishing projects because they expect them to be flawless. They can't let go. They dwell on minor problems and keep making microscopic changes in their papers, projects, and proposals. They are caught in what Emanuel (1987) calls the "paralysis of perfection." They end up spinning their wheels, redoing the same work over and over instead of moving on to the next task.

The Problem of Procrastination

Another time-related problem is ***procrastination*—the tendency to delay tackling tasks until the last minute.** Almost everyone procrastinates on occasion. For example, 70%–90% of college students procrastinate before beginning academic assignments (Knaus, 2000). However, research suggests that about 20 percent of adults are chronic procrastinators (Ferrari, 2001). Procrastination is more likely when people have to work on aversive tasks or when they are worried about their performance being evaluated (Milgram, Marshevsky, & Sadeh, 1995; Senecal, Lavoie, & Koestner, 1997).

Why do people procrastinate? In a recent review of the literature Steel (2007) found that procrastination was strongly related to low self-efficacy, low conscientiousness, lack of self-control, poor organization, low achievement motivation, and high distractibility. The type of irrational thinking described by Albert Ellis also seems to foster procrastination (Bridges & Roig, 1997), as do a strong fear of failure (Lay, 1992) and excessive perfectionism (Flett, Hewitt, & Martin, 1995).

Other factors besides personality can affect procrastination. Schraw and colleagues (2007) identified six general principles related to academic procrastination, including these three:

1. *Desire to minimize time on a task.* As you know, the modern student is busy—studying, working, socializing, and maintaining a personal life. Time is at a premium. Sometimes delaying as much academic work as possible seems to be a way to safeguard some personal time. As one student reported, "The truth is, I just don't have time *not* to procrastinate. If I did everything the way it could be done, I wouldn't have a life" (Schraw et al., 2007, p. 21).
2. *Desire to optimize efficiency.* Procrastination can be viewed as allowing one to be optimally efficient, concentrating academic work into focused time frames. Students reported that being pressed for time means that there is less opportunity for busywork, boredom, or false starts.
3. *Close proximity to reward.* Schraw et al. (2007) found that students often procrastinate because they are rewarded for it. By putting off academic work until the last minute, students not only get more immediate feedback (the grade), but they also get a sudden release of stress. In this way, procrastination is similar to other thrill-seeking behaviors.

Although these principles seem reasonable and many people rationalize their delaying tactics by claiming that "I work best under pressure" (Ferrari, 1992; Lay, 1995), the empirical evidence suggests otherwise. Studies show that procrastination tends to have a negative impact on the quality of task performance (Ferrari, Johnson, & McCown, 1995; Tice & Baumeister, 1997). In fact, Britton and Tesser (1991) found that time management was a better predictor of college GPA than SAT scores! Procrastinators may often underestimate how much time will be required to complete a task effectively, or they experience unforeseen delays and then run out of time because they didn't allow any "cushion." Another consideration is that waiting until the last minute may make a task more stressful—and while the release of this built-up stress might be exciting, performance often declines under conditions of high stress (as we saw in Chapter 3).

Moreover, work quality may not be the only thing that suffers when people procrastinate. Studies indicate that as a deadline looms, procrastinators tend to experience elevated anxiety and increased health problems (Lay et al., 1989; Tice & Baumeister, 1997). People who recognize that they need to alter their eating behavior or start an exercise regimen routinely put off these commitments, promising themselves that they will start tomorrow, or next week, or next month. In a similar vein, many people procrastinate about getting health checkups or even seeking medical treatment for existing maladies (Sirois, Melia-Gordon, & Pychyl, 2003).

People who struggle with procrastination often impose deadlines and penalties on themselves. This practice can be helpful, but self-imposed deadlines are not as effective as externally imposed deadlines (Ariely & Wertenbroch, 2002). Let's discuss some effective ways to manage your time.

Time-Management Techniques

Individuals vary in their time perspectives. Some people are *future oriented,* able to see the consequences of immediate behavior for future goals, whereas others are *present oriented,* focused on immediate events and not worried about consequences. These orientations influence how they manage their time and meet their time-related commitments. Future-oriented individuals, for example, are less likely to procrastinate and are more reliable in meeting their commitments (Harber, Zimbardo, & Boyd, 2003). Regardless of orientation, most people could benefit from more effectively managing their time.

What's the key to better time management? Most people assume that it's increased *efficiency*—that is, learning to perform tasks more quickly. Improved efficiency may help a little, but time-management experts maintain that efficiency is overrated. They emphasize that the key to better time management is increased *effectiveness*—that is, learning to allocate time to your most important tasks. This distinction is captured by a widely quoted slogan in the time-management literature: "Efficiency is doing the job right, while effectiveness is doing the right job." Here are some suggestions for using your time more effectively (based on Lakein, 1996; Mackenzie, 1997; Morgenstern, 2000):

1. *Monitor your use of time.* The first step toward better time management is to monitor your use of time to see where it all goes (Douglass & Douglass, 1993). Doing so requires keeping a written record of your activities, similar to that shown in **Figure 4.11**. At the end of each week, you should analyze how your time was allocated. Based on your personal roles and responsibilities, create categories of time use such as studying, child care, housework, commuting, working at the office, working at home, going online, eating, and sleeping. For each day, add up the hours allocated to each category. Record this information on a summary sheet like that in **Figure 4.12** (on p. 126). Two weeks of recordkeeping should allow you to draw some con-

clusions about where your time goes. Your records will help you make informed decisions about reallocating your time. When you begin your time-management program, these records will also give you a baseline for comparison, so that you can see whether your program is working.

2. *Clarify your goals.* You can't wisely allocate your time unless you decide what you want to accomplish. Lakein (1996) suggests that you ask yourself, "What are my lifetime goals?" Write down all the goals that you can think of, even relatively frivolous things like going deep-sea fishing or becoming a wine expert. Some of your goals will be in conflict. For instance, you can't become a vice-president at your company in Wichita and still move to the West Coast. Thus, the tough part comes next. You have to wrestle with your goal conflicts. Figure out which goals are most important to you, and order them in terms of priority. These priorities should guide you as you plan your activities on a daily, weekly, and monthly basis.

3. *Plan your activities using a schedule.* People resist planning because it takes time, but in the long run planning saves time. Thorough planning is essential to effective time management (McGee-Cooper & Trammell, 1994). At the beginning of each week, you should make up a list of short-term goals. This list should be

	Monday	Tuesday	Wednesday	Thursday	Friday	Saturday	Sunday
7 a.m.	Wake-up, jogging, shower, breakfast with family					Sleep in	Sleep in
8							
9	Bus to campus	Molly to daycare	Bus to campus	Molly to daycare	Bus to campus	Walk at beach with Vic	Waffles for family. Read Sunday paper
10	Medical Anthropology	Prepare lecture	Medical Anthropology	Prepare lecture	Medical Anthropology		
11		Teach class		Teach class		Clean house	
12 noon	lunch	lunch	lunch	lunch and shopping with Barbara	lunch		Hiking and picnic with family and Tom
1 p.m.	Biology seminar	pick up Molly at daycare	writing at home		pick up Molly at daycare	Work in garden	
2		writing at home		Lab work	writing at home		
3		Drive Florrie to piano lesson					
4					Molly to dentist		
5			Grocery shopping			Practice guitar	
6	Dinner at home	Dinner at home	Dinner at home	Dinner at home	Dinner out with Vic	Pick up babysitter	
7	Spend time with Vic and kids			Spend time with Vic and kids		Party at Reid's	Call mother
8	Guitar lesson		Women's meeting	Band rehearsal			
9		Practice guitar	Practice guitar				Watch TV
10	Reading and journal						
11	Sleep						
12							
1 a.m.							

Figure 4.11

Example of a time log. Experts recommend keeping a detailed record of how you use your time if you are to improve your time management. This example shows the kind of recordkeeping that should be done.

Figure 4.12

Time use summary. To analyze where your time goes, you need to review your time log and create a weekly time use summary, like the one shown here. The exact categories to be listed on the left depend on your circumstances and responsibilities.

Time Use Summary Form

Activity	Mon.	Tues.	Wed.	Thurs.	Fri.	Sat.	Sun.	Total	%
1. Sleeping	8	6	8	6	8	7	9	52	31
2. Eating	2	2	3	2	3	2	3	17	10
3. Commuting	2	2	2	2	2	0	0	10	6
4. Housework	0	1	0	3	0	0	2	6	4
5. In class	4	2	4	2	4	0	0	16	9
6. Part-time job	0	5	0	5	0	3	0	13	8
7. Studying	3	2	4	2	0	4	5	20	12
8. Relaxing	5	4	3	2	7	8	5	34	20
9.									
10.									

translated into daily "to do" lists of planned activities. To avoid the tendency to put off larger projects, break them into smaller, manageable components, and set deadlines for completing the components. Your planned activities should be allocated to various time slots on a written schedule. Schedule your most important activities into the time periods when you tend to be most energetic and productive.

4. *Protect your prime time.* The best-laid plans can quickly go awry because of interruptions. There isn't any foolproof way to eliminate interruptions, but you may be able to shift most of them into certain time slots while protecting your most productive time. The trick is to announce to your family, friends, and co-workers that you're blocking off certain periods of "quiet time" when visitors and phone calls will be turned away. Of course, you also have to block off periods of "available time" when you're ready to deal with everyone's problems.

5. *Increase your efficiency.* Although efficiency is not the key to better time management, it's not irrelevant. Time-management experts do offer some suggestions for improving efficiency, including the following (Klassen, 1987; Schilit, 1987):

- *Handle paper once.* When e-mails, letters, reports, and such cross your desk, they should not be stashed away to be read again and again before you deal with them. Most paperwork can and should be dealt with immediately.
- *Tackle one task at a time.* Jumping from one problem to another is inefficient. Insofar as possible, stick with a task until it's done. In scheduling your activities, try to allow enough time to complete tasks.
- *Group similar tasks together.* It's a good idea to bunch up small tasks that are similar. This strategy is useful when you're paying bills, replying to e-mails, returning phone calls, and so forth.
- *Make use of your downtime.* Most of us endure a lot of "downtime," waiting in doctors' offices, sitting in needless meetings, or riding on buses and trains. In many of these situations, you may be able to get some of your easier work done—if you think ahead and bring it along.

Emotion-Focused Constructive Coping

LEARNING OBJECTIVES

- *Describe the nature and value of emotional intelligence.*
- *Analyze the adaptive value of expressing emotions.*
- *Discuss the importance of managing hostility and forgiving others' transgressions.*
- *Explain how exercise can foster improved emotional functioning.*
- *Summarize the evidence on the effects of meditation.*
- *Describe the requirements and procedure for Benson's relaxation response.*

Let's be realistic: There are going to be occasions when appraisal-focused coping and problem-focused coping are not successful in warding off emotional turmoil. Some problems are too serious to be whittled down much by reappraisal, and others simply can't be "solved." Moreover, even well-executed coping strategies may take time to work before emotional tensions begin to subside. Thus, it is helpful to be able to recognize and modulate one's emotions. In this section, we will discuss a variety of coping abilities and strategies that relate mainly to the regulation of emotions.

Enhancing Emotional Intelligence

According to some theorists, *emotional intelligence* is the key to being resilient in the face of stress (Slaski & Cartwright, 2003). The concept of emotional intelligence was originally formulated by Peter Salovey and John Mayer (1990). ***Emotional intelligence* consists of the ability to perceive and express emotion, assimilate emotion in thought, understand and reason with emotion, and regulate emotion.** Emotional intelligence includes four essential components (Salovey, Mayer, & Caruso, 2002, 2005). First, people need to be able to accurately perceive emotions in themselves and others and have the ability to express their own emotions effectively. Second, people need to be aware of how their emotions shape their thinking, decision making, and coping with stress. Third, people need to be able to understand and analyze their emotions, which may often be complex and contradictory. Fourth, people need to be able to regulate their emotions so that they can dampen negative emotions and make effective use of positive emotions.

Several tests have been developed to measure the concept of emotional intelligence. The test that has the strongest empirical foundation is the Mayer-Salovey-Caruso Emotional Intelligence Test (2002). The authors have strived to make this test a performance-based measure of the ability to deal effectively with emotions rather than a measure of personality or temperament. Preliminary results suggest that they have made considerable progress toward this goal, as evidenced by the scale's ability to predict intelligent management of emotions in real-world situations (Ciarrochi, Dean, & Anderson, 2002; Lam & Kirby, 2002; Mayer et al., 2001). It has been found to reliably predict the quality of subjects' social interactions (Lopes et al., 2004), leadership effectiveness (Antoniou, 2005), and even physical health (Schutte et al., 2007). At present, ways to cultivate emotional intelligence are being explored in classrooms and workplaces. In fact, a recent study found that positive emotional expression can lead to an increase in emotional intelligence (Wing, Schutte, & Byrne, 2006). That leads us to our next topic.

Web Link 4.4 **International Society for Traumatic Stress Studies**

This site offers a vast storehouse of information relating to coping with traumatic events. The resources are divided into those for the general public, for professionals, and for the news media.

***Emotional Intelligence: Why It Can Matter More Than IQ* (10th Anniversary Edition)**
by Daniel Goleman (Bantam Books, 2006)

It's great to see a book like this make the best-seller lists. It is a serious, scholarly, yet readable analysis of how emotional functioning is important in everyday life. Daniel Goleman is both a psychologist and a journalist who writes about the behavioral sciences for the *New York Times*. In this book, he synthesizes the research of many investigators as he argues that emotional intelligence may be more important to success than high IQ. The concept of emotional intelligence, as originally developed by Peter Salovey and John Mayer (1990), languished in relative obscurity until Goleman's book attracted attention. He views emotional intelligence more broadly than Salovey and Mayer, who focused primarily on people's ability to access, monitor, and express their own emotions and to interpret and understand others' emotions. Goleman includes all of their ingredients but adds social poise and skill, strong motivation and persistence, and some desirable personality traits, such as optimism and conscientiousness. One can argue that Goleman's concept of emotional intelligence is too much of a hodgepodge of traits to be measureable or meaningful, but his broad view yields a wide-ranging book that discusses innumerable examples of how social finesse and emotional sensitivity can foster career success, marital satisfaction, and physical and mental health. In the course of this analysis, Goleman discusses research on a diverse array of topics in an exceptionally lucid manner.

Expressing Emotions

Try as you might to redefine or resolve stressful situations, you no doubt still go through times when you feel wired with stress-induced tension. When this happens, there's merit in the commonsense notion that you should try to release the emotions welling up inside. Why? Because the physiological arousal that accompanies emotions can become problematic. For example, research suggests that people who inhibit the expression of anger and other emotions are somewhat more likely than other people to have elevated blood pressure (Jorgensen et al., 1996). Moreover, research suggests that efforts to actively suppress emotions result in increased stress and autonomic arousal (Butler et al., 2003; Gross, 2001). Please note that such findings do not mean you should act aggressively (a coping strategy of limited value discussed earlier in the chapter). Instead, we are focusing on appropriate expression of emotions.

One interesting study looked at the repercussions of "psychological inhibition" in gay men who conceal their homosexual identity (Cole et al., 1996). Many gay individuals inhibit the public expression of their homosexuality to avoid stigmatization, discrimination, and even physical assault. Although hiding one's gay identity may be a sensible strategy, it entails vigilant inhibition of one's true feelings. To investigate the possible effects of this inhibition, Cole et al. (1996) tracked the incidence of cancer, pneumonia, bronchitis, sinusitis, and tuberculosis in a sample of 222 HIV-negative gay and bisexual men over a period of five years. As you can see in **Figure 4.13**, they found that the overall incidence of these diseases was noticeably higher among the men who concealed their homosexual identity. The investigators speculate that psychological inhibition may be detrimental to people's health, a position that has been supported in more recent research (Eisenberger, Kemeny, & Wyatt, 2003)

If inhibition is bad, perhaps expression is good. James Pennebaker and his colleagues have shown that talking or writing about traumatic events can have beneficial effects. For example, in one study of college students, half the subjects were asked to write three essays about their difficulties in adjusting to college. The other half wrote three essays about superficial topics. The participants who wrote about their personal problems and traumas enjoyed better health in the following months than the other subjects did (Pennebaker, Colder, & Sharp, 1990). Several subsequent studies have replicated the finding that emotional disclosure, or "opening up," is associated with improved mood, more positive self-perceptions, fewer visits to physicians, and enhanced immune functioning (Hemenover, 2003; Niederhoffer & Pennebaker, 2005;Smyth & Pennebaker, 2001). Summarizing this research, Smyth and Pennebaker (1999) assert that "when people put their emotional upheavals into words, their physical and mental health seems to improve markedly." They conclude that "the act of disclosure itself is a powerful therapeutic agent" (p. 70).

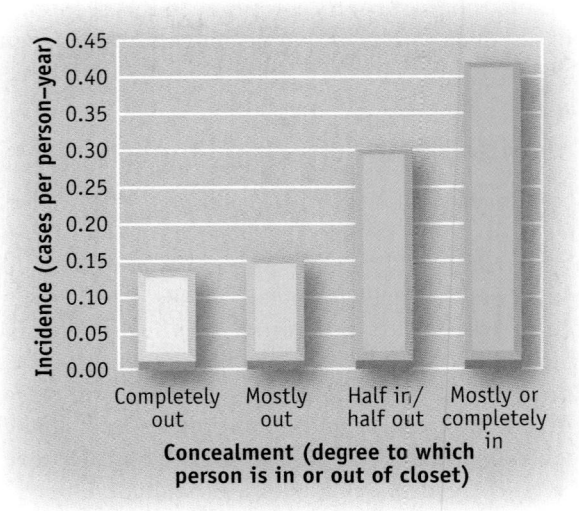

Figure 4.13

Elevated health risk among gay men who conceal their homosexual identity. In a sample of gay and bisexual men, Cole et al. (1996) found that the more the men concealed their homosexual identity, the more likely they were to experience various diseases. The investigators speculate that the elevated incidence of disease may reflect the costs of inhibiting one's true feelings. (Data from Cole et al., 1996)

In times of stress, seeking support from one's friends is a very useful coping strategy. Releasing pent-up emotions by talking about one's difficulties appears to be a particularly beneficial coping mechanism.

© Altrendo Images/Getty Images

Guidelines for Writing About Emotional Experiences

- Find a location where there will be no disturbances (from others, the phone, etc.).
- Set aside about 30 minutes each day: 20 minutes for writing, with a few minutes afterward to compose yourself if necessary.
- Write for three or four days, usually consecutively.
- Explore your deepest thoughts and feelings about any experiences or topics that are weighing heavily upon you.
- Explore how this topic is related to a variety of issues in your life: your childhood, your relationships, who you are, who you would like to be, and so forth.
- Write continuously, without regard for spelling or grammar.
- Remember that the writing is for you, not someone else.

Figure 4.14

Using writing about emotional experiences as a coping strategy. Many studies have shown that writing about traumatic experiences and sensitive issues can have beneficial effects on mental and physical health. These guidelines can help you to use this coping strategy.

From Smyth, J. M. & Pennebaker, J. W. (1999). Sharing one's story. In C. R. Snyder (Ed.), *Coping: The psychology of what works.* New York: Oxford. Copyright © 1999 by Oxford University Press. Reprinted by permission.

The research on emotional disclosure indicates that both writing and talking about important personal issues can be beneficial (Smyth & Pennebaker, 2001). Thus, if you can find a good listener, it may be wise to let your secret fears, misgivings, and suspicions spill out in a candid conversation. Of course, confiding in others about one's problems can be awkward and difficult. Therein lies the beauty and appeal of the writing approach, which can be kept private. **Figure 4.14** summarizes some guidelines for writing about personal issues and trauma that should make this coping strategy more effective.

Managing Hostility and Forgiving Others

Scientists have compiled quite a bit of evidence that hostility is related to increased risk for heart attacks and other types of illness (Williams, 2001; see Chapter 14). So how can individuals effectively regulate negative emotions that include anger and hostility? The goal of hostility management is not merely to suppress the overt expression of hostility that may continue to seethe beneath the surface, but to actually reduce the frequency and intensity of one's hostile feelings. The first step toward this goal is to learn to quickly recognize one's anger. A variety of strategies can be used to decrease hostility, including reinterpretation of annoying events, distraction, and the kind of rational self-talk advocated by Ellis (Williams & Williams, 1993). Efforts to increase empathy and tolerance can also contribute to hostility management, as can forgiveness, which has become the focus of a new line of research in psychology.

People tend to experience hostility and other negative emotions when they feel "wronged"—that is, when they believe that the actions of another person were harmful, immoral, or unjust. People's natural inclination is either to seek revenge or to avoid further contact with the offender (McCullough & Witvliet, 2005). *Forgiving* someone involves counteracting these natural tendencies and releasing the person from further liability for his or her transgression. Research suggests that forgiving is an effective emotion-focused coping strategy that is associated with better adjustment and well-being (McCullough & Witvliet, 2002; Worthington & Scherer, 2004). For example, in one study of divorced or permanently separated women reported by McCollough (2001), the extent to which the women had forgiven their former husbands was positively related to several measures of well-being and was inversely related to measures of anxiety and depression. In another study, when participants were instructed to

© Acey Harper/Time Life Pictures/Getty Images

In September 1994, Reg and Maggie Green were vacationing in Italy when their seven-year-old son Nicholas was shot and killed during a highway robbery. In an act of forgiveness that stunned Europe, the Greens chose to donate their son's organs, which went to seven Italians. The Greens, shown here five years after the incident, have weathered their horrific loss better than most, perhaps in part because of their willingness to forgive.

actively think about a grudge they had nursed and to think about forgiving the grudge, forgiving thoughts were associated with more positive emotions and reduced physiological arousal (Witvliet, Ludwig, & Vander Laan, 2001). Research also shows that vengefulness is correlated with more rumination and negative emotion and with lower life satisfaction (McCullough et al., 2001). Further, researchers have identified certain personality characteristics such as narcissistic entitlement as barriers to forgiveness (Exline et al., 2004). Although this area is still relatively new and there is more work to be done, findings to date suggest that it may be healthful for people to learn to forgive others more readily.

Exercising

Another healthy way to deal with overwhelming emotions is to engage in physical exercise. In fact, a recent study found that people who participated in a two-month program of regular exercise showed an increase in emotional control and a decrease in emotional distress (Oaten & Cheng, 2006). Exercise is an ideal coping strategy because it provides multiple benefits—an outlet for frustration, a distraction from the stressor, and benefits to physical and psychological health (Sapolsky, 2004). Regular exercise is related to decreases in depression, anxiety, and hostility, as well as increases in self-esteem and energy (Puetz, O'Connor, & Dishman, 2006; Spencer, 1990). Exercise is also associated with improved well-being, especially with regard to mood, stress, and coping (Edwards, 2006).

Although it is well documented that physical activity promotes overall mental health (Saxena et al., 2005), exercise can also help those who are dealing with physical and mental health issues (Faulkner & Carless, 2006). For instance, in a recent longitudinal study of long-term breast cancer survivors, increased activity following diagnosis predicted a higher quality of life and improved physical health, even 10 years after the diagnosis (Kendall et al. 2005). Of course these findings must be interpreted with caution. Although it appears likely that exercise increases quality of life, it could be that those with higher quality of life are more likely to exercise. While researchers continue to search for the causal mechanisms between physical activity and mental health, exercise is still an effective coping strategy.

Sapolosky (2004) asserts that in order to get maximal benefits from physical exercise, you should consider three rules. First, you must *want* to exercise. Forcing yourself to do something you don't want to do, even if that something is good for you, can be stressful in and of itself. Second, you should engage in aerobic exercise (such as jogging, swimming, or bicycling) because most of the positive effects come from this type of exercise. Third, you should exercise on a regular basis. Of course, regular exercise requires discipline and self-control. One of the main predictors of exercise maintenance is self-efficacy, a belief that you can do it (Sullum, Clark, & King 2000). If you are not currently as physically active as you would like, perhaps you could use the self-modification techniques covered in the Application section at the end of this chapter to improve your exercise habits. Advice on devising an effective exercise program can also be found in Chapter 14.

Using Meditation and Relaxation

Recent years have seen an explosion of interest in meditation as a method for modulating negative emotions caused by stress. ***Meditation* refers to a family of mental exercises in which a conscious attempt is made to focus attention in a nonanalytical way.** There are many approaches to meditation. In the United States, the most widely practiced approaches are those associated with yoga, Zen, and transcendental meditation (TM). However, meditation has been practiced throughout history as an element of all religious and spiritual traditions, including Judaism and Christianity. Moreover, the practice of meditation can be largely divorced from religious beliefs. In fact, most Americans who meditate have only vague ideas regarding its religious significance. Of interest to us is the possibility that meditation can calm inner emotional turmoil.

Advocates of meditation claim that it can improve learning, energy level, work productivity, physical health, mental health, and general happiness while reducing tension and anxiety caused by stress (Andresen, 2000; Shapiro, Schwartz, & Santerre, 2005). These are not exactly humble claims. Let's examine the scientific evidence on meditation.

What are the immediate physical effects of going into the meditative state? Most studies find decreases in participants' heart rate, respiration rate, oxygen consumption, and carbon dioxide elimination. Taken together, these physical changes suggest that meditation can lead to a potentially beneficial physiological state characterized by relaxation and suppression of arousal (Carrington, 1993; Fenwick, 1987; Travis, 2001).

What about the long-term psychological benefits that have been claimed for meditation? Research suggests that meditation may have some value in reducing the effects of stress (Anderson et al., 1999; Winzelberg

Web Link 4.5 **Stress Management and Emotional Wellness Links**

This website functions as a gateway to several other sites that may be relevant to the subject of coping with stress. Included are links to sites that deal with humor, relaxation, meditation, increasing social support, crisis intervention, and stress management for college students.

& Luskin, 1999). In particular, regular meditation is associated with lower levels of some stress hormones (Infante et al., 2001). Research also suggests that meditation can improve mental health while reducing anxiety and drug abuse (Alexander et al., 1994). Other studies report that meditation may have beneficial effects on blood pressure (Barnes, Treiber, & Davis, 2001), self-esteem (Emavardhana & Tori, 1997), mood and one's sense of control (Easterlin & Cardena, 1999), happiness (Smith, Compton, & West, 1995), and overall physical health and well-being (Reibel et al., 2001).

At first glance these results are profoundly impressive, but they need to be viewed with some caution. Critics wonder whether placebo effects, sampling bias, and other methodological problems may contribute to some of the reported benefits of meditation (Bishop, 2002; Shapiro et al., 2005). In a recent and relatively enthusiastic review of meditation research, Shapiro, Schwartz, & Santerre (2002) acknowledge that many meditation studies "do not use rigorous research design (including lack of randomization, lack of follow-up, and imprecise measurement of constructs) and sometimes are based on small samples" (p. 634). In addition, at least some of these beneficial effects may be just as attainable through other mental focusing procedures such as systematic relaxation (Shapiro, 1984; Smith, 1975). Ample evidence suggests that systematic relaxation procedures can soothe emotional turmoil and reduce stress-induced physiological arousal (Lehrer & Woolfolk, 1984, 1993; Smyth et al., 2001). There are a number of worthwhile approaches to achieving beneficial relaxation. We'll discuss one approach that is so simple that virtually anyone can learn to use it.

After studying various approaches to meditation, Herbert Benson, a Harvard Medical School cardiologist, concluded that elaborate religious rituals and beliefs are not necessary for someone to profit from meditation. He also concluded that what makes meditation beneficial is the relaxation it induces. After "demystifying" meditation, Benson (1975) set out to devise a simple, nonreligious procedure that could provide similar benefits. He calls his procedure the "relaxation response." According to Benson, four factors are critical to effective practice of the relaxation response:

1. *A quiet environment.* It is easiest to induce the relaxation response in a distraction-free environment. After you become skilled at the relaxation response, you may be able to accomplish it in a crowded subway. Initially, however, you should practice it in a quiet, calm place.

2. *A mental device.* To shift attention inward and keep it there, you need to focus it on a constant stimulus, such as a sound or word that you recite over and over. You may also choose to gaze fixedly at a bland object, such as a vase. Whatever the case, you need to focus your attention on something.

3. *A passive attitude.* It is important not to get upset when your attention strays to distracting thoughts. You must realize that such distractions are inevitable. Whenever your mind wanders from your attentional focus, calmly redirect attention to your mental device.

4. *A comfortable position.* Reasonable body comfort is essential to avoid a major source of potential distraction. Simply sitting up straight works well for most people. Some people can practice the relaxation response lying down, but for most people such a position is too conducive to sleep.

Benson's deceptively simple procedure for inducing the relaxation response is described in **Figure 4.15**. For full benefit, it should be practiced daily.

1 Sit quietly in a comfortable position.

2 Close your eyes.

3 Deeply relax all your muscles, beginning at your feet and progressing up to your face. Keep them relaxed.

4 Breathe through your nose. Become aware of your breathing. As you breathe out, say the word "one" silently to yourself. For example, breathe in . . . out "one"; in . . . out "one"; and so forth. Breathe easily and naturally.

5 Continue for 10 to 20 minutes. You may open your eyes to check the time, but do not use an alarm. When you finish, sit quietly for several minutes, at first with your eyes closed and later with your eyes opened. Do not stand up for a few minutes.

6 Do not worry about whether you are successful in achieving a deep level of relaxation. Maintain a passive attitude and permit relaxation to occur at its own pace. When distracting thoughts occur, try to ignore them by not dwelling on them, and return to repeating "one." With practice, the response should come with little effort. Practice the technique once or twice daily but not within two hours after any meal, since digestive processes seem to interfere with the elicitation of the relaxation response.

Figure 4.15

Benson's relaxation response. The relaxation procedure advocated by Herbert Benson is a simple one that should be practiced daily.

From Benson, H., & Klipper, M. Z. (1975, 1988). *The relaxation response.* New York: Morrow. Copyright © 1975 by William Morrow & Co. Reprinted by permission of HarperCollins Publishers.

APPLICATION

Achieving Self-Control

LEARNING OBJECTIVES

- *Explain why traits cannot be target behaviors in self-modification programs.*
- *Describe the three kinds of information you should pursue in gathering your baseline data.*
- *Discuss how to use reinforcement to increase the strength of a response.*
- *Explain how to use reinforcement, control of antecedents, and punishment to decrease the strength of a response.*
- *Analyze issues related to fine-tuning and ending a self-modification program.*

Answer the following "yes" or "no."

___ **1.** Do you have a hard time passing up food, even when you're not hungry?

___ **2.** Do you wish you studied more often?

___ **3.** Would you like to cut down on your smoking or drinking?

___ **4.** Do you experience difficulty in getting yourself to exercise regularly?

___ **5.** Do you wish you had more willpower?

If you answered "yes" to any of these questions, you have struggled with the challenge of self-control. This Application discusses how you can use the techniques of behavior modification to improve your self-control. If you stop to think about it, self-control—or rather a lack of it—underlies many of the personal problems that people struggle with in everyday life.

***Behavior modification* is a systematic approach to changing behavior through the application of the principles of conditioning.** Advocates of behavior modification assume that behavior is a product of learning, conditioning, and environmental control. They further assume that *what is learned can be unlearned.* Thus, they set out to "recondition" people to produce more desirable patterns of behavior.

The technology of behavior modification has been applied with great success in schools, businesses, hospitals, factories, child-care facilities, prisons, and mental health centers (Goodall, 1972; Kazdin, 1982, 2001; Rachman, 1992). Moreover, behavior modification techniques have proven particularly valuable in efforts to improve self-control. Our discussion will borrow liberally from an excellent book on self-modification by David Watson and Roland Tharp (2007). We will discuss five steps in the process of self-modification, which are outlined in **Figure 4.16**.

Specifying Your Target Behavior

The first step in a self-modification program is to specify the target behavior(s) that you want to change. Behavior modification can only be applied to a clearly defined, overt response, yet many people have difficulty pinpointing the behavior they hope to alter. They tend to describe their problems in terms of unobservable personality *traits* rather than overt behaviors. For example, asked what behavior he would like to change, a man might say, "I'm too irritable." That may be true, but it is of little help in designing a self-modification program. To use a behavioral approach, you need to

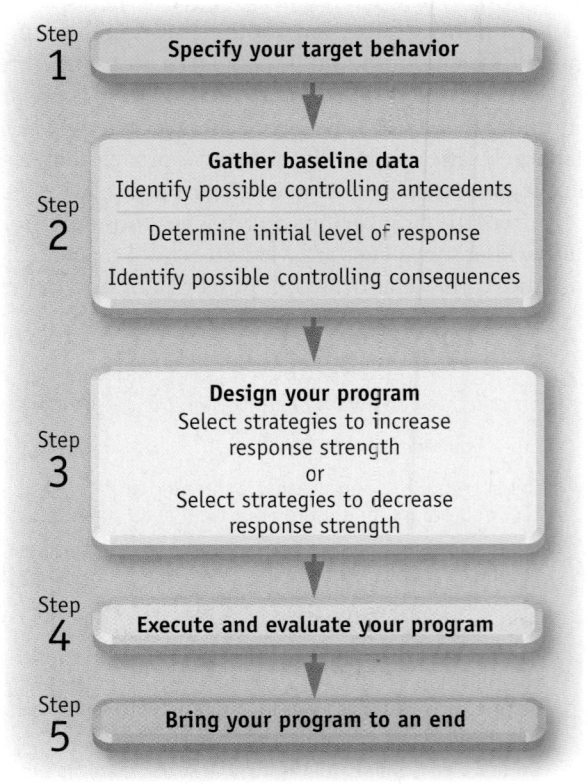

Figure 4.16

Steps in a self-modification program. This flowchart provides an overview of the steps necessary to execute a self-modification program.

translate vague statements about traits into precise descriptions of specific target behaviors.

To identify target responses, you need to think about past behavior or closely observe future behavior and list specific *examples* of responses that lead to the trait description. For instance, the man who regards himself as "too irritable" might identify two overly frequent responses, such as arguing with his wife and snapping at his children. These are specific behaviors for which he could design a self-modification program.

Gathering Baseline Data

The second step in behavior modification is to gather baseline data. You need to systematically observe your target behavior for a period of time (usually a week or two) before you work out the details of your program. In gathering your baseline data, you need to monitor three things.

First, you need to determine the initial response level of your target behavior. After all, you can't tell whether your program is working effectively unless you have a baseline for comparison. In most cases, you would simply keep track of how often the target response occurs in a certain time interval. Thus, you might count the daily frequency of snapping at your children, smoking cigarettes, or biting your fingernails. If studying is your target behavior, you will probably monitor hours of study. If you want to modify your eating, you will probably keep track of how many calories you consume. Whatever the unit of measurement, *it is crucial to gather accurate data.* You should keep permanent written records, preferably in the form of some type of chart or graph (see **Figure 4.17**).

Second, you need to monitor the antecedents of your target behavior. ***Antecedents* are events that typically precede the target response.** Often these events play a major role in evoking your target behavior. For example, if your target is overeating, you might discover that the bulk of your overeating occurs late in the evening while you watch TV. If you can pinpoint this kind of antecedent-response connection, you may be able to design your program to circumvent or break the link.

Third, you need to monitor the typical consequences of your target behavior. Try to identify the reinforcers that are maintaining an undesirable target behavior or the unfavorable outcomes that are suppressing a desirable target behavior. In trying to identify reinforcers, remember that avoidance behavior is usually maintained by negative reinforcement (see Chapter 2). That is, the payoff for avoidance is usually the removal of something aversive, such as anxiety or a threat to self-esteem. You should also take into account the fact that a response may not be reinforced every time, as most behavior is maintained by intermittent reinforcement.

Designing Your Program

Once you have selected a target behavior and gathered adequate baseline data, it is time to plan your intervention program. Generally speaking, your program will be designed either to increase or to decrease the frequency of a target response.

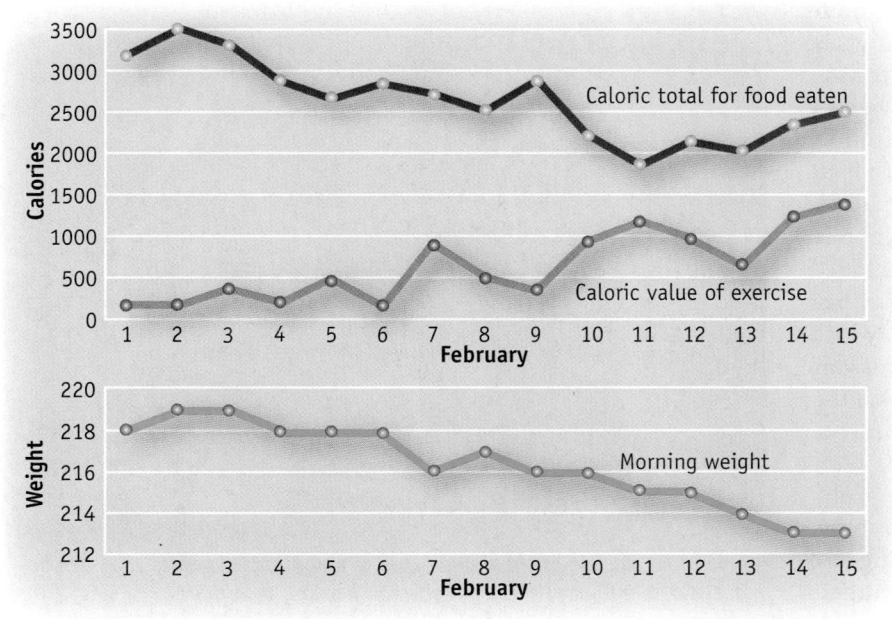

Figure 4.17

Example of record keeping in a self-modification program for losing weight. Graphic records are ideal for tracking progress in behavior modification efforts.

Increasing Response Strength

Efforts to increase the frequency of a target response depend largely on the use of positive reinforcement. In other words, you reward yourself for behaving properly. Although the basic strategy is quite simple, doing it skillfully involves a number of considerations.

Selecting a reinforcer. To use positive reinforcement, you need to find a reward that will be effective for you. Reinforcement is subjective—what is reinforcing for one person may not be reinforcing for another. **Figure 4.18** lists questions you can ask yourself to help you determine your personal reinforcers. Be sure to be realistic and choose a reinforcer that is really available to you.

You don't have to come up with spectacular new reinforcers that you've never experienced before. *You can use reinforcers that you are already getting.* However, you have to restructure the contingencies so that you get them only if you behave appropriately. For example, if you normally watch your favorite television show on Thursday nights, you might make this viewing contingent on studying a certain number of hours during the week. Making yourself earn rewards that you used to take for granted is often a useful strategy in a self-modification program.

Arranging the contingencies. Once you have chosen your reinforcer, you have to set up reinforcement contingencies. These contingencies will describe the exact behavioral goals that must be met and the reinforcement that may then be awarded. For example, in a program to increase exercise, you might make spending $40 on clothes (the reinforcer) contingent on having jogged 15 miles during the week (the target behavior).

Try to set behavioral goals that are both challenging and realistic. You want your goals to be challenging so that they lead to improvement in your behavior. However, setting unrealistically high goals—a common mistake in self-modification—often leads to unnecessary discouragement.

You also need to be concerned about doling out too much reinforcement. If reinforcement is too easy to get, you may become *satiated,* and the reinforcer may lose its motivational power. For example, if you were to reward yourself with virtually all the compact discs you wanted, this reinforcer would lose its incentive value.

One way to avoid the satiation problem is to put yourself on a token economy. **A *token economy* is a system for doling out symbolic reinforcers that are exchanged**

What Are Your Reinforcers?

1. What will be the rewards of achieving your goal?
2. What kind of praise do you like to receive, from yourself and others?
3. What kinds of things do you like to have?
4. What are your major interests?
5. What are your hobbies?
6. What people do you like to be with?
7. What do you like to do with those people?
8. What do you do for fun?
9. What do you do to relax?
10. What do you do to get away from it all?
11. What makes you feel good?
12. What would be a nice present to receive?
13. What kinds of things are important to you?
14. What would you buy if you had an extra $20? $50? $100?
15. On what do you spend your money each week?
16. What behaviors do you perform every day? (Don't overlook the obvious or commonplace.)
17. Are there any behaviors you usually perform instead of the target behavior?
18. What would you hate to lose?
19. Of the things you do every day, which would you hate to give up?
20. What are your favorite daydreams and fantasies?
21. What are the most relaxing scenes you can imagine?

Figure 4.18

Selecting a reinforcer. The questions listed here may help you to identify your personal reinforcers.

Adapted from Watson, D. L., & Tharp, R. G. (1997). *Self-directed behavior: Self-modification for personal adjustment.* Belmont, CA: Wadsworth. Reprinted by permission.

© Nicola Sutton/Life File/Photodisc Green/Getty Images

Smoking is just one of the many types of maladaptive habits that can be reduced or eliminated through self-modification techniques.

later for a variety of genuine reinforcers. Thus, you might develop a point system for exercise behavior, accumulating points that can be spent on compact discs, movies, restaurant meals, and so forth. You can also use a token economy to reinforce a variety of related target behaviors, as opposed to a single, specific response. The token economy in **Figure 4.19**, for instance, is set up to strengthen three different, though related, responses (jogging, tennis, and sit-ups).

Shaping. In some cases, you may want to reinforce a target response that you are not currently capable of making, such as speaking in front of a large group or jogging ten miles a day. This situation calls for ***shaping,* which is accomplished by reinforcing closer and closer approximations of the desired response.** Thus, you might start jogging two miles a day and add a half-mile each week until you reach your goal. In shaping your behavior, you should set up a schedule spelling out how and when your target behaviors and reinforcement contingencies should change. Generally, it is a good idea to move forward gradually.

Decreasing Response Strength

Let's turn now to the challenge of reducing the frequency of an undesirable response. You can go about this task in a number of ways. Your principal options are reinforcement, control of antecedents, and punishment.

Responses Earning Tokens

Response	Amount	Number of Tokens
Jogging	1/2 mile	4
Jogging	1 mile	8
Jogging	2 miles	16
Tennis	1 hour	4
Tennis	2 hours	8
Sit-ups	25	1
Sit-ups	50	2

Redemption Value of Tokens

Reinforcer	Tokens required
Purchase one compact disc of your choice	30
Go to movie	50
Go to nice restaurant	100
Take special weekend trip	500

Figure 4.19

Example of a token economy to reinforce exercise. This token economy was set up to strengthen three types of exercise behavior. The person can exchange tokens for four types of reinforcers.

Reinforcement. Reinforcers can be used in an indirect way to decrease the frequency of a response. This may sound paradoxical, since you have learned that reinforcement strengthens a response. The trick lies in how you define the target behavior. For example, in the case of overeating you might define your target behavior as eating more than 1600 calories a day (a response that you want to decrease) or eating less than 1600 calories a day (a response that you want to increase). You can choose the latter definition and reinforce yourself whenever you eat less than 1600 calories in a day. Thus, you can reinforce yourself for not emitting a response, or for emitting it less, and thereby decrease a response through reinforcement.

Control of antecedents. A worthwhile strategy for decreasing the occurrence of an undesirable response may be to identify its antecedents and avoid exposure to them. This strategy is especially useful when you are trying to decrease the frequency of a consummatory response, such as smoking or eating. In the case of overeating, for instance, the easiest way to resist temptation is to avoid having to face it. Thus, you might stay away from enticing restaurants, minimize time spent in your kitchen, shop for groceries just after eating (when willpower is higher), and avoid purchasing favorite foods. **Figure 4.20** (on the next page) lists a variety of suggestions for controlling antecedents to reduce overeating. Control of antecedents can also be helpful in a program to increase studying. The key often lies in *where* you study. You can reduce excessive socializing by studying somewhere devoid of people. Similarly, you can reduce loafing by studying someplace where there is no TV, stereo, or phone to distract you.

Punishment. The strategy of decreasing unwanted behavior by punishing yourself for that behavior is an obvious option that people tend to overuse. The biggest problem with punishment in a self-modification effort is the difficulty in following through and punishing oneself. Nonetheless, there may be situations in which your manipulations of reinforcers need to be bolstered by the threat of punishment. If you're going to use punishment, keep two guidelines in mind. First, do not use punishment alone. Use it in conjunction with positive reinforcement. If you set up a program in which you can earn only negative consequences, you probably won't stick to it. Second, use a relatively mild punishment so that you will actually be able to administer it to yourself. Nurnberger and Zimmerman (1970) developed a creative method of self-punishment. They had subjects write out a check to an organization they hated (for instance, the campaign of a political candidate whom they despised). The check was held by a third party who mailed it if subjects failed to meet their

Controlling the Antecedents of Overeating

A. Shopping for food

1. Do not purchase problematic foods. These include
   a. very fattening, high-calorie foods
   b. your favorite foods, unless they have very low caloric values (you will be tempted to overconsume favorite foods)
   c. foods requiring little preparation (they make it too easy to eat)
2. To facilitate the above, you should
   a. use a shopping list from which you do not deviate
   b. shop just after eating (your willpower is reduced to jelly when you're hungry)
   c. carry only enough money to pay for items on your list

B. In your kitchen

1. Don't use your kitchen for anything other than food preparation and consumption.
2. Keep food stock stored out of sight.
3. If you have problematic foods in your kitchen (for other household members, of course), arrange cupboards and the refrigerator so that these foods are out of reach or in the rear.
4. Don't hover over cooking food. It will cook itself.
5. Prepare only enough food for immediate consumption.

C. While eating

1. Don't do anything besides eating. Watching TV or reading promotes mindless consumption.
2. Leave serving dishes on the kitchen counter or stove. Don't set them right in front of you.
3. Eat from a smaller dish. It will make a quantity of food appear greater.
4. Slow the pace of eating. Relax and enjoy your food.

D. After eating

1. Quickly put away or dispose of leftover foods.
2. Leave the kitchen as soon as you are through.

E. In regard to restaurants

1. Insofar as possible, do not patronize restaurants. Menus are written in a much too seductive style.
2. If social obligations require that you eat out, go to a restaurant that you don't particularly like.
3. When in restaurants, don't linger over the menu, and don't gawk at the food on other tables.
4. Avoid driving down streets and going to shopping centers that are loaded with alluring fast-food enterprises.

F. In general

1. Try to avoid boredom. Keep yourself busy.
2. Try to avoid excessive sleep loss and fatigue. Your self-control diminishes when you are tired.
3. Avoid excessive fasting. Skipping meals often leads to overeating later.

Figure 4.20

Control of antecedents. Controlling antecedents that trigger overeating is often a crucial part of behavioral programs for weight loss. The tips listed here have proven useful to many people.

behavioral goals. Such a punishment is relatively harmless, but it can serve as a strong source of motivation.

Executing and Evaluating Your Program

Once you have designed your program, the next step is to put it to work by enforcing the contingencies that you have carefully planned. During this period, you need to continue to accurately record the frequency of your target behavior so you can evaluate your progress. The success of your program depends on your not "cheating." The most common form of cheating is to reward yourself when you have not actually earned it.

You can do two things to increase the likelihood that you will comply with your program. One is to make up a ***behavioral contract*—a written agreement outlining a promise to adhere to the contingencies of a behavior modification program** (see **Figure 4.21**). The formality of signing such a contract in front of friends or family seems to make many people take their program more seriously. You can further reduce the likelihood of cheating by having someone other than yourself dole out the reinforcers and punishments.

Behavior modification programs often require some fine-tuning. So don't be surprised if you need to make a few adjustments. Several flaws are especially common in designing self-modification programs. Among those that you should look out for are (1) depending on a weak reinforcer, (2) permitting lengthy delays between appropriate behavior and delivery of reinforcers, and (3) trying to do too much too quickly by setting unrealistic goals. Often, a small revision or two can turn a failing program around and make it a success.

Ending Your Program

Doing so involves setting terminal goals such as reaching a certain weight, studying with a certain regularity, or going without cigarettes for a certain length of time. Often, it is a good idea to phase out your program by

I, _____, do hereby agree to initiate my self-change strategy as of (date) _____ and to continue it for a minimum period of _____ weeks—that is, until (date) _____.

My specific self-change strategy is to _____

_____

_____

I will do my best to execute this strategy to my utmost ability and to evaluate its effectiveness only after it has been honestly tried for the specified period of time.

Optional Self-Reward Clause: For every _____ day(s) that I successfully comply with my self-change contract, I will reward myself with _____

_____

In addition, at the end of my minimum period of personal experimentation, I will reward myself for having persisted in my self-change efforts. My reward at that time will be _____

_____

I hereby request that the witnesses who have signed below support me in my self-change efforts and encourage my compliance with the specifics of this contract. Their cooperation and encouragement throughout the project will be appreciated.

Signed _____

Date _____

Witness:

Witness:

Figure 4.21

Figure A behavioral contract. Behavior modification experts recommend the use of a formal, written contract similar to that shown here to increase commitment to one's self-modification program.

planning a gradual reduction in the frequency or potency of your reinforcement for appropriate behavior.

If your program is successful, it may fade away without a conscious decision on your part. Often, new, improved patterns of behavior become self-maintaining. Responses such as eating right, exercising regularly, and studying diligently may become habitual. Whether you end your program intentionally or not, you should always be prepared to reinstitute the program if you find yourself slipping back to your old patterns of behavior.

© Mark Richards/PhotoEdit

Overeating is another type of maladaptive behavior that can be changed with a self-modification program.

KEY IDEAS

The Concept of Coping

▶ Coping involves behavioral efforts to master, reduce, or tolerate the demands created by stress. People cope with stress in many ways, but most have certain styles of coping. Coping strategies vary in their adaptive value, and flexibility is important when choosing a strategy.

Common Coping Patterns of Limited Value

▶ Giving up, possibly best understood in terms of learned helplessness, is a common coping pattern that tends to be of limited value. Another is engaging in aggressive behavior. Frequently caused by frustration, aggression tends to be counterproductive because it often creates new sources of stress.

▶ Indulging oneself is a common coping strategy that is not inherently unhealthy, but it is frequently taken to excess and thus becomes maladaptive. Internet addiction is a relatively new form of self-indulgence. Blaming yourself with negative self-talk is associated with depression.

▶ Defensive coping is common and may involve any of a number of defense mechanisms. However, the adaptive value of defensive coping tends to be less than optimal. Although some illusions may be healthful, extreme forms of self-deception are maladaptive.

The Nature of Constructive Coping

▶ Constructive coping involves efforts to deal with stress that are judged as relatively healthful. Constructive coping is rational, realistic, and action oriented. It also involves managing emotions and learning self-control.

Appraisal-Focused Constructive Coping

▶ Appraisal-focused constructive coping is facilitated by Ellis's suggestions on how to reduce catastrophic thinking by digging out the irrational assumptions that cause it. Other valuable strategies include using humor to deal with stress and looking for the positive aspects of setbacks and problems.

Problem-Focused Constructive Coping

▶ Systematic problem solving can be facilitated by following a four-step process: (1) clarify the problem, (2) generate alternative courses of action, (3) evaluate your alternatives and select a course of action, and (4) take action while maintaining flexibility.

▶ A problem-focused coping tactic with potential value is seeking social support. There appear to be cultural differences in who seeks social support. Improving time management can also aid problem-focused coping. Effective time management doesn't depend on increased efficiency so much as on setting priorities and allocating time wisely. It is also helpful to avoid the common tendency to procrastinate on aversive tasks.

Emotion-Focused Constructive Coping

▶ Emotional intelligence may help people to be more resilient in the face of stress. Inhibition of emotions appears to be associated with increased health problems. Thus, it appears that expressing emotions is adaptive. Research shows that writing about traumatic events or sensitive issues is associated with enhanced wellness.

▶ Research suggests that it is wise for people to learn how to manage their feelings of hostility. New evidence also suggests that forgiving people for their offenses is healthier than nursing grudges.

▶ Exercise is a healthy way to deal with emotional distress. Physical activity provides an outlet for frustration, can distract one from the stress, and is related to improved physical and mental health.

▶ Meditation can be helpful in soothing emotional turmoil. Meditation is associated with lower levels of stress hormones, improved mental health, and other indicators of wellness. Although less exotic, systematic relaxation procedures, such as Benson's relaxation response, can also be effective in reducing troublesome emotional arousal.

Application: Achieving Self-Control

▶ In behavior modification, the principles of learning are used to change behavior directly. Behavior modification techniques can be used to increase one's self-control. The first step in self-modification is to specify the overt target behavior to be increased or decreased.

▶ The second step is to gather baseline data about the initial rate of the target response and identify any typical antecedents and consequences associated with the behavior. The third step is to design a program. If you are trying to increase the strength of a response, you'll depend on positive reinforcement. A number of strategies can be used to decrease the strength of a response, including reinforcement, control of antecedents, and punishment.

▶ The fourth step is to execute and evaluate the program. Self-modification programs often require some fine-tuning. The final step is to determine how and when you will phase out your program.

KEY TERMS

Aggression p. 107
Antecedents p. 133
Behavior modification p. 132
Behavioral contract p. 136
Brainstorming p. 121
Catastrophic thinking p. 115
Catharsis p. 108
Constructive coping p. 114
Coping p. 105
Defense mechanisms pp. 111–112
Emotional intelligence p. 127
Internet addiction p. 110
Learned helplessness pp. 106–107
Meditation p. 130
Procrastination p. 123
Rational-emotive therapy p. 115
Shaping p. 135
Token economy pp. 134–135

KEY PEOPLE

Herbert Benson p. 131
Albert Ellis pp. 111, 115–118
Sigmund Freud pp. 108, 111–113
James Pennebaker pp. 128–129
Peter Salovey p. 127
Martin Seligman pp. 106–107
Shelley Taylor p. 113

PRACTICE TEST

1. Which of the following assertions is *not* supported by research on the cathartic effects of media violence?
   a. Playing violent video games releases pent-up hostility.
   b. Playing violent video games is related to decreased prosocial behavior.
   c. Exposure to media violence desensitizes individuals to violent acts.
   d. Exposure to media violence encourages aggressive responses.

2. Bill feels sure that he failed his calculus exam and that he will have to retake the course. He is very upset. When he gets home, he orders himself a jumbo-size pizza and drinks two six-packs of beer. Bill's behavior illustrates which of the following coping strategies?
   a. Catastrophic thinking
   b. Defensive coping
   c. Self-indulgence
   d. Positive reinterpretation

3. Defense mechanisms involve the use of _____ to guard against negative _____.
   a. self-deception; behaviors
   b. self-deception; emotions
   c. self-denial; behaviors
   d. self-denial; emotions

4. Taylor and Brown found that "normal" people's self-images tend to be _____; depressed people's tend to be _____.
   a. accurate; inaccurate
   b. less favorable; more favorable
   c. overly favorable; more realistic
   d. more realistic; overly favorable

5. According to Albert Ellis, people's emotional reactions to life events result mainly from:
   a. their arousal level at the time.
   b. their beliefs about events.
   c. congruence between events and expectations.
   d. the consequences following events.

6. Which of the following is *not* listed in your text as a cause of wasted time?
   a. Inability to set priorities
   b. Inability to work diligently
   c. Inability to delegate responsibility
   d. Inability to throw things away

7. Keysha works at a software firm. Today her boss unfairly blamed her for the fact that a new program is way behind schedule. The unjustified public criticism really had an impact on Keysha. Later that evening, she went for a long run to get her anger under control. Keysha is engaging in which category of coping?
   a. Self-focused coping
   b. Appraisal-focused coping
   c. Problem-focused coping
   d. Emotion-focused coping

8. Research by James Pennebaker and his colleagues suggests that wellness is promoted by:
   a. depending on more mature defense mechanisms.
   b. strong self-criticism.
   c. writing about one's traumatic experiences.
   d. inhibiting the expression of anger.

9. The first step in a self-modification program is:
   a. design your program.
   b. gather baseline data.
   c. specify your target behavior.
   d. any of the above; it doesn't matter.

10. A system providing for symbolic reinforcers is called a(n):
   a. extinction system.
   b. token economy.
   c. endocrine system.
   d. symbolic reinforcement system.

Book Companion Website

Visit the Book Companion Website at **academic.cengage.com/psychology/weiten,** where you will find tutorial quizzes, flash cards, and web links for every chapter, a final exam, and more! You can also link to the Psychology Resource Center (accessible directly at **academic.cengage.com/login**) for a range of psychology-related resources.

Personal Explorations Workbook

The following exercises in your *Personal Explorations Workbook* may enhance your self-understanding in relation to issues raised in this chapter. **Questionnaire 4.1:** Barnes-Vulcano Rationality Test. **Personal Probe 4.1:** Can You Detect Your Irrational Thinking? **Personal Probe 4.2:** Analyzing Coping Strategies. **Personal Probe 4.3:** Recognizing Coping Tactics

ANSWERS

1. a Page 108
2. c Page 109
3. b Page 112
4. c Page 113
5. b Pages 115–116
6. b Page 123
7. d Page 130
8. c Pages 128–129
9. c Page 132
10. b Pages 134–135

CHAPTER 5

The Self

SELF-CONCEPT
The Nature of the Self-Concept
Self-Discrepancies
Factors Shaping the Self-Concept

SELF-ESTEEM
The Importance of Self-Esteem
The Development of Self-Esteem

LIVING IN TODAY'S WORLD *Self-Esteem and Threats to Mortality*
Ethnicity, Gender, and Self-Esteem

BASIC PRINCIPLES OF SELF-PERCEPTION
Cognitive Processes
Self-Attributions
Explanatory Style
Motives Guiding Self-Understanding
Methods of Self-Enhancement

SELF-REGULATION
Self-Efficacy
Self-Defeating Behavior

SELF-PRESENTATION
Impression Management
Self-Monitoring

APPLICATION: BUILDING SELF-ESTEEM

REVIEW

PRACTICE TEST

At last you are in college and on your own, away from home. You are a little nervous but excited about your new life and its challenges. Today is your first official day of college and psychology is your first class. You arrive early. You take a seat near the front of the lecture hall and immediately feel conspicuous. You don't know anyone in the class; in fact, you suddenly realize you don't know anyone at the university except for your roommate, who is still more or less a stranger. Many students seem to know one another. They are laughing, talking, and catching up while you just sit there, quiet and alone. They seem friendly, so why won't they talk to you? Should you speak to them first? Are you dressed okay—what about your hair? You begin to question yourself: Will you ever make any friends in this class or at the university? Oh, here comes the professor. She seems nice enough, but you wonder what she expects. Will this class be difficult? Well, you do plan to work hard and study a lot, but how will psychology help you in the future? Perhaps you should be taking a more practical class, maybe accounting, which will lead right to a career. Wait a minute: What if the professor calls on you in front of all these strangers who already know each other? Will you sound intelligent or look foolish? As the professor begins to take the class roll, your mind is racing. You feel tense and your stomach gets a little queasy as she gets closer in the alphabet to your name.

This scenario illustrates the process of self-perception and the effects it can have on emotions, motivation, and goal setting. People engage in this sort of self-reflection constantly, especially when they are trying to understand the causes of their own behavior.

In this chapter, we highlight the self and its important role in adjustment. We begin by looking at two major components of the self: self-concept and self-esteem. Then we review some key principles of the self-perception process. Next, we turn to the important topic of self-regulation. Finally, we focus on how people present themselves to others. In this chapter's Application, we offer some suggestions for building self-esteem.

Self-Concept

LEARNING OBJECTIVES

- *Describe some key aspects of the self-concept.*
- *Cite two types of self-discrepancies and describe their effects.*
- *Describe two ways of coping with self-discrepancies.*
- *Discuss important factors that help form the self-concept.*
- *Discuss how individualism and collectivism influence the self-concept.*

If you were asked to describe yourself, what would you say? You'd probably start off with some physical attributes such as "I'm tall," "I'm of average weight," or "I'm blonde." Soon you'd move on to psychological characteristics: "I'm friendly," "I'm honest," "I'm reasonably intelligent," and so forth. People usually identify whatever makes them unique in a particular situation. These distinctive qualities fit into their self-definitions. American schoolchildren, for example, define themselves by highlighting how they are different from their classmates (McGuire & Pawader-Singer, 1978). You probably do the same thing. How did you develop these beliefs about yourself? Have your self-views changed over time? Read on.

The Nature of the Self-Concept

Although we usually talk about the self-concept as a single entity, it is actually a multifaceted structure (Mischel & Morf, 2003). That is, the ***self-concept* is an organized collection of beliefs about the self.** These beliefs, also called *self-schemas,* shape social perception (Green & Sedikides, 2001), are developed from past experience, and are concerned with one's personality traits, abilities, physical features, values, goals, and social roles (Campbell, Assanand, & DiPaula, 2000). People have self-schemas on dimensions that are important to them, including both strengths and weaknesses. **Figure 5.1** on the next page depicts the self-concepts of two hypothetical individuals.

Each self-schema is characterized by relatively distinct thoughts and feelings. For instance, you might have considerable information about your social skills and feel quite self-assured about them but have limited information and less confidence about your physical skills. Current thinking is that only a portion of the total self-concept operates at any one time. The self-concept that is accessible at any given moment has been termed the *working self-concept* by Hazel Markus, a leading researcher in this area (Markus & Wurf, 1987).

Stanford University News Service, photo by L. A. Cicero

Hazel Markus

Beliefs about the self influence not only current behavior but also future behavior. ***Possible selves* are one's conceptions about the kind of person one might become in the future** (Markus & Nurius, 1986). If you have narrowed your career choices to personnel manager and psychologist, they would represent two possible selves in the career realm. Possible selves are developed from past experiences, current behavior, and future expectations. They make people attentive to goal-related information and role models and mindful of the need to practice goal-related skills. As such, they help individuals not only to envision desired future goals but also to achieve them (Cross & Markus, 1991; Hock, Deshler, & Schumaker, 2006). Interestingly, it has been found that, for individuals who have experienced traumatic events, psychological adjustment is best among those who are able to envision a variety of positive selves (Morgan & Janoff-Bulman, 1994). Possible selves are useful when encouraging constructive change during psychotherapy (Dunkel, Kelts, & Coon, 2006). Sometimes, however, possible selves are negative and represent what you fear you might become—such

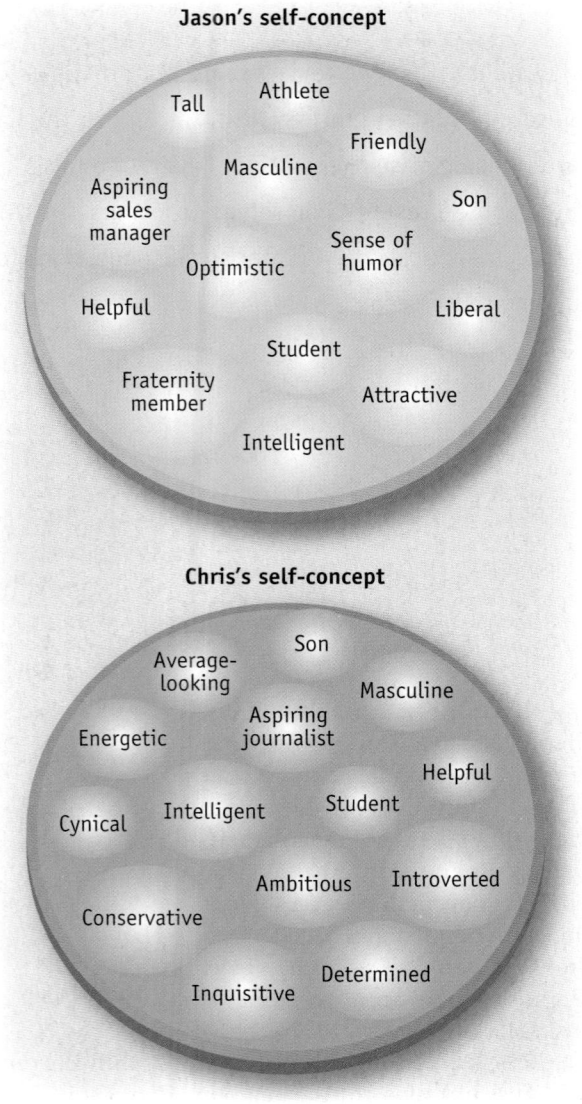

Figure 5.1

The self-concept and self-schemas. The self-concept is composed of various self-schemas, or beliefs about the self. Jason and Chris have different self-concepts, in part, because they have different self-schemas.

as an alcoholic like Uncle George or an adult without an intimate relationship like your next-door neighbor. In these cases, possible selves function as images to be avoided (Norman & Aron, 2003).

Individuals' beliefs about themselves are not set in concrete—but neither are they easily changed. People are strongly motivated to maintain a consistent view of the self across time and situations. Thus, once the self-concept is established, the individual has a tendency to preserve and defend it. In the context of this stability, however, self-beliefs do have a certain dynamic quality (Markus & Wurf, 1987). When coupled with educational strategies, for example, "academic possible selves" led to positive changes in planning, test scores, grades, and attendance in a sample of low-income minority youth (Oyserman, Bybee, & Terry, 2006). Self-concepts seem to be most susceptible to change when people shift from an important and familiar social setting to an unfamiliar one—for example, when moving off to college or to a new city for one's first "real" job. This flexibility clearly underscores the social foundations of the self-concept.

Web Link 5.1 **Research Sources: Concepts of Person and Self**

Over the past century psychologists, philosophers, and many others have wondered what is meant by terms like "person" and "self." Professor Shaun Gallagher of the University of Central Florida's Philosophy and Cognitive Science Department provides visitors with a variety of resources to explore these concepts.

Self-Discrepancies

Some people perceive themselves pretty much the way they'd like to see themselves. Others experience a gap between what they actually see and what they'd like to see. For example, Nathan describes his actual self as "shy" but his ideal self as "outgoing." According to E. Tory Higgins (1987), individuals have several organized self-perceptions: an *actual self* (qualities you believe you *actually* possess), an *ideal self* (characteristics you would *like* to have), and an *ought self* (traits you believe you *should* possess). The ideal and ought selves serve as personal standards or self-guides that direct behavior. ***Self-discrepancy* consists of a mismatch between the self-perceptions that make up the actual self, ideal self, and ought self.**

Self-Discrepancies and Their Effects

The differences among one's actual, ideal, and ought selves influence how one feels about oneself and can create some particular emotional vulnerabilities (Higgins, 1999). According to Higgins, when people live up to their personal standards (ideal or ought selves), they experience high self-esteem; when they don't meet their own expectations, their self-esteem suffers (Moretti & Higgins, 1990). In addition, he says, certain types of self-discrepancies are associated with specific emotions (see **Figure 5.2**). One type of self-discrepancy occurs when the *actual* self is at odds with the *ideal* self. Such instances trigger *dejection-related* emotions (sadness, disappointment). As actual-ideal discrepancies outnumber actual-ideal congruencies,

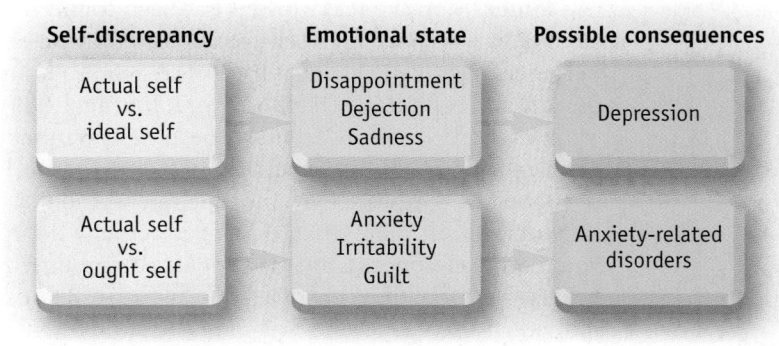

Figure 5.2

Types of self-discrepancies, their effects on emotional states, and possible consequences. According to E. Tory Higgins (1989), discrepancies between actual and ideal selves produce disappointment and sadness, whereas discrepancies between actual and ought selves result in irritability and guilt. Such self-discrepancies can make individuals vulnerable to more serious psychological problems, such as depression and anxiety-related disorders.

sadness increases and cheerfulness decreases (Higgins, Shah, & Friedman, 1997). Consider Tiffany's situation: She knows that she's attractive, but she is also overweight and would like to be thinner. Self-discrepancy theory predicts that she would feel dissatisfied and dejected. Interestingly, research has shown an association between discrepant actual/ideal views of body shape and eating disorders (Strauman et al., 1991).

A second type of discrepancy involves a mismatch between *actual* and *ought* selves. Let's say you don't stay in touch with your grandparents as often as you feel you should. According to Higgins, actual/ought self-discrepancies produce *agitation-related* emotions (irritability, anxiety, and guilt). As actual-ought discrepancies outnumber actual-ought congruencies, anxiety increases and calm emotions decrease (Higgins, Shah, & Friedman, 1997). Extreme discrepancies of this type can result in anxiety-related psychological disorders.

Everyone experiences self-discrepancies, yet most people manage to feel reasonably good about themselves. How is this possible? Three factors seem to be important: the amount of discrepancy you experience, your awareness of the discrepancy, and whether the discrepancy is actually important to you (Higgins, 1999). Thus, a pre-med major who gets a C in calculus will probably feel a lot worse than an English major who gets a C in the course.

Although people use both ideal and ought selves as personal standards, they usually rely on just one of these self-guides. These "preferences" are rooted in parent-child interactions and individual temperament (Higgins, 1987). If Kyle's parents typically communicate with him in terms of what they would *like* him to do, he will probably develop a strong *ideal* self-guide. If their communications usually take the form of what they think he *ought* to do, Kyle will probably develop a strong *ought* self-guide.

Coping with Self-Discrepancies

Can individuals do anything to blunt the negative emotions and blows to self-esteem associated with self-discrepancies? Yes! For one thing, people can *change their behavior* to bring it more in line with their ideal or ought selves. For instance, if your ideal self is a person who gets above-average grades and your actual self just got a D on a test, you can study more effectively for the next test to improve your grade. But what about the times you can't match your ideal standards? Perhaps you had your heart set on making the varsity tennis team but didn't make the cut. Maybe you had planned to go to medical school but barely managed to eke out C's in your science courses. One way to ease the discomfort associated with such discrepancies is to bring your ideal self a bit more in line with your actual abilities. You may not achieve your ideal self right away, if ever, but by behaving in ways that are consistent with that self, you will get closer to it and be more content (Haidt, 2006; Wilson, 2002). Alternatively, subtle encouragement to consider ways to approach an ideal self (perhaps a constructive, friendly suggestion from a friend or a teacher) is apt to raise your spirits in a positive way (Shah & Higgins, 2001).

Another, less positive, approach is to *blunt your self-awareness,* or how much you focus on what you like or dislike about yourself, your self-perceived strengths and shortcomings, and so on. You can do so by avoiding situations that increase your self-awareness—if you don't want to appear to be shy, don't attend a party where you expect to spend a miserable evening talking to yourself. If your weight is bothering you, you might avoid shopping for new clothes (as well as gazing into full-length mirrors).

Some people use alcohol to blunt self-awareness. In one study, college students were first put into either a high or a low self-awareness group based on test scores (Hull & Young, 1983). Then, both groups were given a brief version of an intelligence test as well as false feedback on their test performance. Half of the high self-awareness group were told that they had done quite well on the test and the other half were told that they had done quite poorly. Next, supposedly as part of a separate study, these participants were asked to taste and evaluate various wines for 15 minutes. The

When people don't live up to their personal standards, self-esteem suffers, and some turn to alcohol to blunt their awareness of the discrepancy.

experimenters predicted that the high self-awareness participants who had been told that they had done poorly on the IQ test would drink more than the other groups, and this is precisely what the study found (see **Figure 5.3**). Those who couldn't escape negative information about themselves drank more alcohol to reduce their self-awareness.

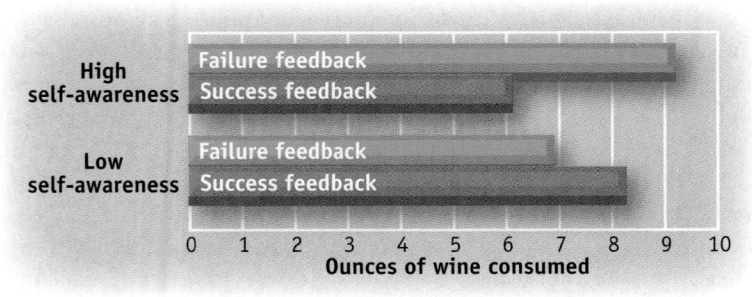

Figure 5.3

Self-awareness and alcohol consumption. Individuals who were high in self-awareness drank significantly more wine in a 15-minute period if they believed that they had performed poorly on an IQ test than did any other group. This finding shows how people sometimes try to blunt self-awareness to cope with self-discrepancies.

From Hull, J. G., & Young, R. D. (1983), Self-consciousness, self-esteem, and success-failure as determinants of alcohol consumption in male social drinkers. *Journal of Personality and Social Psychology, 44,* 1097–1109. Copyright © 1983 American Psychological Association. Reprinted by permission of the publisher and author.

Similarly, in the real world it has been found that alcoholics who have high self-awareness and who experience negative or painful life events relapse more quickly and completely (Hull, Young, & Jouriles, 1986).

Heightened self-awareness doesn't always make people focus on self-discrepancies and negative aspects of the self. If that were true, most people would feel a lot worse about themselves than they actually do. As you recall, self-concepts are made up of numerous self-beliefs—many of them positive, some negative. Because individuals have a need to feel good about themselves, they tend to focus on their positive features rather than their "warts" (Tesser, 2001). In fact, when a person's self-concept is threatened (a job interview doesn't go well), the individual can recover by affirming competence in an unrelated domain (focusing on extraordinary talent as a salsa dancer) (Aronson, Cohen, & Nail, 1999; Steele, 1988).

Factors Shaping the Self-Concept

A variety of sources influence one's self-concept. Chief among them are one's own observations, feedback from others, and cultural values.

One's Own Observations

Individuals begin observing their own behavior and drawing conclusions about themselves early in life. Children will make statements about who is the tallest, who can run fastest, or who can swing the highest. Leon Festinger's (1954) ***social comparison theory* proposes that individuals compare themselves with others in order to assess their abilities and opinions.** People compare themselves to others to determine how attractive they are, how they did on the history exam, how their social skills stack up, and so forth. In short, social comparisons can be ego enhancing (Helgeson & Michelson, 1995).

Although Festinger's original theory claimed that people engage in social comparison for the purpose of accurately assessing their abilities, research suggests that they also engage in social comparison to improve their skills and to maintain their self-image (Wheeler & Suls, 2005; Wood & Wilson, 2003). Sometimes social comparison is self-focused, such as when a successful professional woman compares her "current self" to the passive, withdrawn "past self" of high school (Ross & Wilson, 2002; Wilson & Ross, 2000). Generally, however, people compare themselves against others with particular qualities. **A *reference group* is a set of people who are used as a gauge in making social comparisons.** We choose our reference groups strategically.

For example, if you want to know how you did on your first test in social psychology (ability appraisal), your reference group would likely be the entire class. In terms of acquiring accurate self-knowledge about your performance, this sort of comparison is a good one if you are confident your classmates are similar to you (Wheeler, Koestner, & Driver, 1982).

What happens when people compare themselves to others who are better or worse off than them? For instance, if you want to improve your tennis game (skill development), your reference group should be limited to superior players, whose skills give you a goal to pursue. Such *upward social comparisons* can motivate you and direct your future efforts (Blanton et al., 1999). On the other hand, if your self-esteem needs bolstering, you will probably make a *downward social comparison,* looking to those whom you perceive to be worse off, thereby enabling you to feel better about yourself (Aspinwall & Taylor, 1993; Lockwood, 2002). We have more to say about downward social comparison a little later in the chapter.

People's observations of their own behavior are not entirely objective. The general tendency is to distort reality in a positive direction (see **Figure 5.4**). In other words, most people tend to evaluate themselves in a more positive light than they really merit (Taylor & Brown, 1988, 1994). The strength of this tendency was highlighted in a large survey of high school seniors conducted as part of the Scholastic Aptitude Test (SAT) (Myers, 1980). By definition, 50 percent of students must be "above average" and 50 percent "below average" on specific questions. However, 100 percent of the respondents saw themselves as above average in "ability to get along with others." And 25 percent of the respondents thought that they belonged in the top 1 percent!

© Pat Bruno/Positive Images

Figure 5.4

Distortions in self-images. How people see themselves may be different from how others see them. These pictures and text illustrate the subjective quality of self-concept and people's perception of others. Generally, self-images tend to be distorted in a positive direction.

Although the general tendency is to distort reality in a positive direction, most people make both positive and negative distortions. For example, you might overrate your social skill, emotional stability, and intellectual ability while underrating your physical attractiveness. Also, a minority of people consistently evaluate themselves in an unrealistically negative way. Thus, the tendency to see oneself in an overly favorable light is strong but not universal.

Web Link 5.2 **Identity and Self**

Professor Andy Lock at Massey University in New Zealand has posted the outline of a possible upper-level course that would explore contemporary psychological conceptions of the self and identity development, particularly from the social constructivist and cultural viewpoints. His site includes a full set of bibliographical and topical guides.

Feedback from Others

Individuals' self-concept is shaped significantly by the feedback they get from important people in their lives. Early on, parents and other family members play a dominant role. Parents give their children a great deal of direct feedback, saying such things as "We're so proud of you" or "If you just tried harder, you could do a lot better in math." Most people, especially when young, take this sort of feedback to heart. Thus, it comes as no surprise that studies find a link between parents' views of a child and the child's self-concept (Berne & Savary, 1993; Burhans & Dweck, 1995). There is even stronger evidence for a relationship between children's *perceptions* of their parents' attitudes toward them and their own self-views (Felson, 1989, 1992).

Teachers, Little League coaches, Scout leaders, classmates, and friends also provide feedback during childhood. In later childhood and adolescence, parents and classmates are particularly important sources of feedback and support (Harter, 2003). Later in life, feedback from close friends and marriage partners assumes importance. In fact, there is evidence that a close partner's support and affirmation can bring the loved one's actual self-views and behavior more in line with his or her ideal self (Drigotas et al., 1999). For this situation to happen, the partner needs to hold views of the loved one that match the target person's ideal self and behave in ways to bring out the best in the person. If the target person's behavior can closely match the ideal self, then self-views can move nearer to the ideal self. Researchers have labeled this process the *Michelangelo phenomenon* to reflect the partner's role in "sculpting" into reality the ideal self of a loved one.

Keep in mind that people filter feedback from others through their existing self-perceptions. That is, individuals don't see themselves exactly as others see them but rather as they *believe* others see them (Baumeister & Twenge, 2003; Tice & Wallace, 2003). Thus, feedback from others usually reinforces people's self-views.

Social Context

Receiving feedback from others reveals that the self-concept does not develop in isolation. Of course, it's not only people that matter; so do the social contexts where interactions occur. Think about it: You're much more boisterous (and less self-conscious) when you are out with friends at a dance or a diner than when you are sitting in class. Similarly, attending a funeral encourages you to think about yourself differently and to monitor your actions more carefully than going to a raucous Super Bowl party. Social context affects how people think and feel about others, as well. In office settings, for example, a superior will act and feel like a leader with subordinates but will quickly change demeanor and outlook in the presence of an equal (Moskowitz, 1994). Social contexts can affect self-concept indirectly, too. When a situation triggers a bad mood—you rarely play croquet, don't particularly care about the game, and lose a round to a friend—even those aspects of your self that are not central to who you are can suddenly seem negative (Sedikides, 1995). The resulting thoughts and

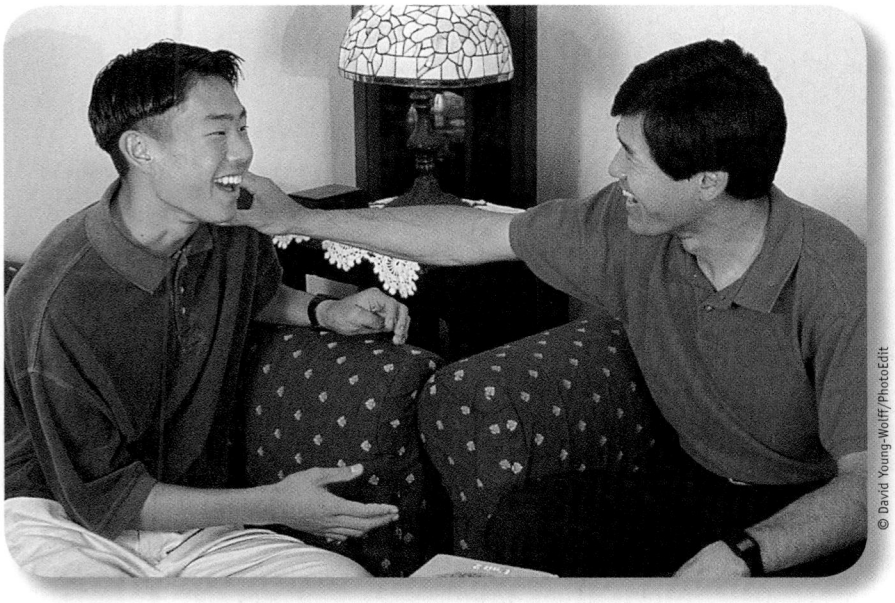

© David Young-Wolff/PhotoEdit

Whether positive or negative, feedback from others plays an important role in shaping a youngster's self-concept.

feelings caused by the situation can compel you to engage in more critical self-evaluations than usual.

Cultural Values

Self-concept is also shaped by cultural values. Among other things, the society in which one is reared defines what is desirable and undesirable in personality and behavior. For example, American culture puts a high premium on individuality, competitive success, strength, and skill. When individuals meet cultural expectations, they feel good about themselves and experience increases in self-esteem and vice versa (Cross & Gore, 2003).

Cross-cultural studies suggest that different cultures shape different conceptions of the self (Cross & Markus, 1999; Cross & Gore, 2003). One important way cultures differ is on the dimension of individualism versus collectivism (Hofstede, 1983; Triandis, 1989, 2001). ***Individualism* involves putting personal goals ahead of group goals and defining one's identity in terms of personal attributes rather than group memberships.** In contrast, ***collectivism* involves putting group goals ahead of personal goals and defining one's identity in terms of the groups one belongs to** (such as one's family, tribe, work group, social class, caste, and so on). Although it's tempting to think of these perspectives in either-or terms, it is more appropriate to view them as points along a continuum. Thus, it is more accurate to say that certain cultures are more or less individualistic (or collectivist) than others rather than seeing them as either one or the other.

Here is a clever but telling example illustrating the difference between individualist and collectivist cultures where simple choice is concerned. American students and Indian students selected a pen from a group composed of one blue pen and four red ones. American students consistently picked the singular blue pen, while the Indian students always chose the common red pen (Nicholson, 2006). In Western culture, we need to remember that "agency," or how people express their sense of power or influence in the social world, is not always found in other cultures or cultural contexts (Markus & Kitayama, 2004). In a follow-up study, once the students made their choice, some were told "Actually, you can't have that pen. Here, take this one instead." All students were then told to try their new pen, either one "chosen" or one "given" to them, and to rate it. The Americans preferred the pens they originally chose, so that those who were "given" a different pen devalued it. How did the Indian students react? They showed no preference for either the pen they freely chose or the one that was given to them. Individualistic cultures promote freedom and choice, and people who live in these cultures do not like to have either threatened.

A variety of factors influence societies' tendencies to cherish individualism or collectivism. Among other things, increases in a culture's affluence, education, urbanization, and social mobility tend to foster more individualism (Triandis, 1994). Many contemporary societies are in transition, but generally speaking North American and Western European cultures tend to be individualistic, whereas Asian, African, and Latin American cultures tend to be collectivist (Hofstede, 1980, 1983).

Individuals reared in individualistic cultures usually have an *independent view of the self,* perceiving themselves as unique, self-contained, and distinct from others. In contrast, individuals reared in collectivist cultures typically have an *interdependent view of the self.* They see themselves as inextricably connected to others and believe that harmonious relationships with others are of utmost importance. Thus, in describing herself, a person living in an individualistic culture might say, "I am kind," whereas someone in a collectivist culture might respond, "My family thinks I am kind" (Triandis, 2001). **Figure 5.5** depicts the self-conceptions of individuals from these contrasting cultures.

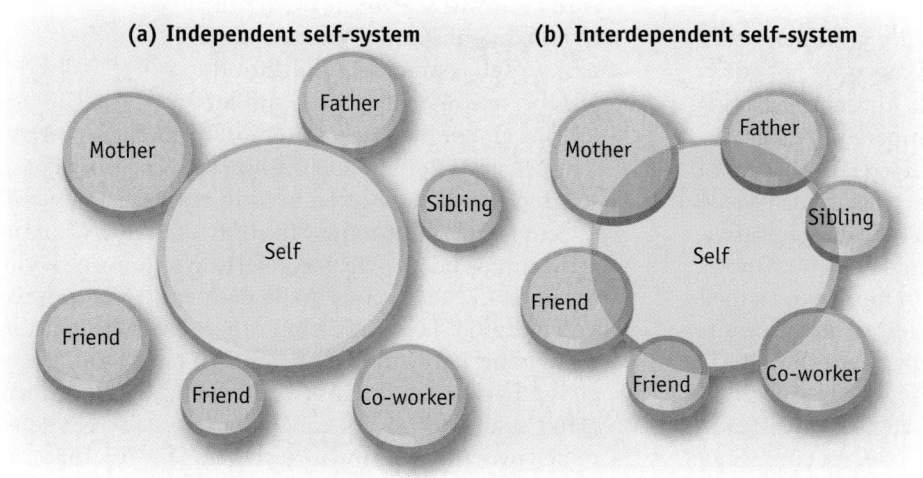

Figure 5.5

Independent and interdependent views of the self. (a) Individuals in cultures that support an independent view perceive the self as clearly separated from significant others. (b) Individuals in cultures that support an interdependent view perceive the self as inextricably connected to others.

Adapted from Markus, H. R., & Kitayama, S. (1991). Culture and the self: Implications for cognition, emotion, and motivation. *Psychological Review, 98,* 224–253. Copyright © 1991 American Psychological Association. Adapted by permission of the publisher and author.

Individuals with an independent view of the self are socialized to maintain their sense of self as a separate person—to "look out for number one," claim more than their share of credit for group successes, and disavow responsibility for group failure. Those with an interdependent view of the self are taught to adjust themselves to the needs of the groups to which they belong and to maintain the interdependence among individuals. In this situation, social duties and obligations assume great importance and people are likely to see themselves as responsible for group failures (Cross & Gore, 2003).

Researchers have noted parallels between the self-views promoted by individualistic and collectivist cultures and the self-views of some groups. For example, women usually have more interdependent self-views than men (Cross & Madson, 1997). But don't take this finding to mean that men are less social than women; rather, it means that men and women get their social needs met in different ways (Baumeister & Sommer, 1997). Thus women are usually involved in close relationships involving intimate friends and family members (*relational* interdependence), while men tend to interact in social groups such as clubs and sports teams (*collective* interdependence) (Gabriel & Gardner, 1999). These gender differences in self-views may explain other observed gender differences, such as women being more likely than men to share their feelings and thoughts with others.

Cultural values are also responsible for various stereotypes that can mold people's self-perceptions and behavior. And stereotypes—about gender, ethnicity, class, sexual orientation, and religion—can influence self-conceptions.

Self-Esteem

LEARNING OBJECTIVES

- *Describe the implications of self-concept confusion and self-esteem instability.*
- *Discuss how high and low self-esteem are related to adjustment.*
- *Distinguish between high self-esteem and narcissism, and discuss narcissism and aggression.*
- *Discuss some key influences in the development of self-esteem.*
- *Summarize the findings on ethnicity and gender regarding self-esteem.*

One of the functions of the self-concept is to evaluate the self; the result of this self-evaluation is termed *self-esteem.* ***Self-esteem* refers to one's overall assessment of one's worth as a person.** Do you think of yourself in primarily positive or negative terms? Self-esteem is a global self-evaluation that blends many specific evaluations about one's adequacy as a student, an athlete, a worker, a spouse, a parent, or whatever is personally relevant. **Figure 5.6** shows how specific elements of the self-concept may contribute to self-esteem. If you feel basically good about yourself, you probably have high self-esteem.

People with high self-esteem are confident, taking credit for their successes in various ways (Blaine & Crocker 1993) while seeking venues for demonstrating their skills (Baumeister, 1998). Compared to individuals with low self-esteem, they are also relatively sure of who they are (Campbell, 1990). In reality, the self-views of people with low self-esteem are not more negative; rather, they are more confused and tentative (Campbell, 1990; Campbell & Lavallee, 1993). In other words, their self-concepts seem to be less clear, less complete, more self-contradictory, and more susceptible to short-term fluctuations than the self-views of high-self-esteem individuals. According to Roy Baumeister (1998), an eminent researcher on the self, this "self-concept confusion" means that individuals with low self-esteem simply don't know themselves well enough to strongly endorse many personal attributes on self-esteem tests, which results in lower self-esteem scores.

Courtesy, Roy Baumeister

Roy Baumeister

Self-esteem can be construed in two ways: as trait or state. *Trait self-esteem* refers to the ongoing sense of confidence people possess regarding their abilities (athletic, assertive) and characteristics (friendliness, helpfulness). People's traits tend to stay with them and to remain constant; if one has high or low self-esteem in childhood, chances are one will have a similar level as an adult (Block & Robins, 1993; Trzesniewski, Donnellan, & Robins, 2003). **Figure 5.7** presents a basic self-report measure often used in research when self-esteem is studied as a trait. In contrast, *state self-esteem* is dynamic and changeable, referring to how individuals feel about themselves in the moment (Heatherton & Polivy, 1991). Feedback from others, self-observation, one's point in the life span, moods, a temporary financial setback, even the loss of one's alma mater's team (Hirt et al., 1992)—all can lower one's current sense of self-worth. Those whose self-esteem fluctuates in

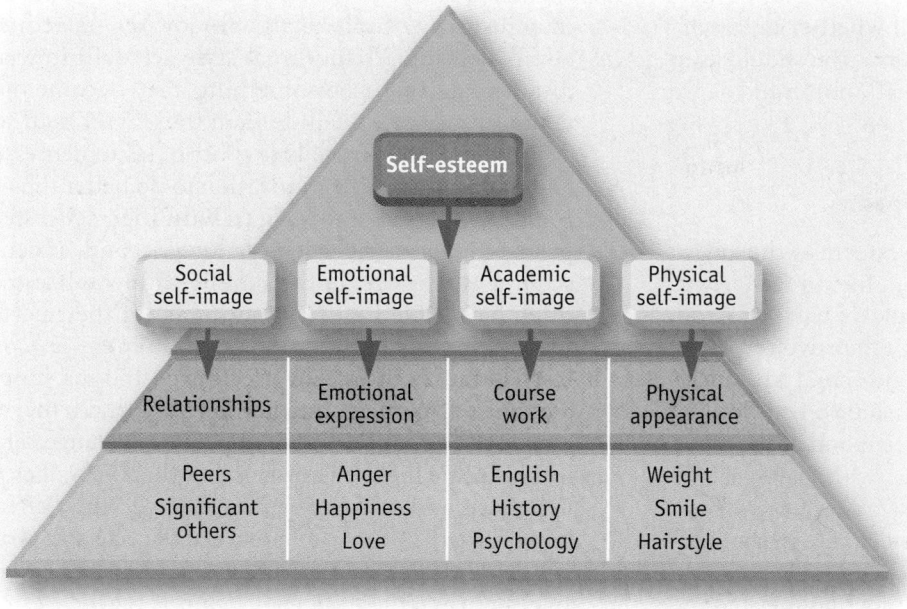

Figure 5.6

The structure of self-esteem. Self-esteem is a global evaluation that combines assessments of various aspects of one's self-concept, each of which is built up from many specific behaviors and experiences. (Adapted from Shavelson, Hubner, & Stanton, 1976)

response to daily experiences are highly sensitive to interactions and events that have potential relevance to their self-worth, and they may even mistakenly view irrelevant events as having significance (Kernis & Goldman, 2002). They always feel their self-worth is on the line. As we will shortly learn, such tendencies have important implications for adjustment.

Investigating self-esteem is challenging for several reasons. For one thing, obtaining accurate measures of self-esteem is difficult. The problem is that researchers tend to rely on self-reports from subjects, which obviously may be biased. As you've seen, most individuals typically hold unrealistically positive views about themselves; moreover, some people may choose not to disclose their actual self-esteem on a questionnaire. (What about you? Did you answer the questions in **Figure 5.7** truthfully and without any self-enhancing biases? How can you be sure?) Second, in probing self-esteem it is often quite difficult to separate cause from effect. Thousands of correlational studies report that high and low self-esteem are associated with various behavioral characteristics. For instance, you saw in

The Rosenberg (1965) Self-Esteem Scale

Using the scale below, indicate your agreement with each of the following statements.

1	2	3	4
Strongly disagree	Disagree	Agree	Strongly agree

___ 1. I feel that I am a person of worth, at least on an equal basis with others.
___ 2. I feel that I have a number of good qualities.
___ 3. All in all, I am inclined to feel that I am a failure.
___ 4. I am able to do things as well as most other people.
___ 5. I feel I do not have much to be proud of.
___ 6. I take a positive attitude toward myself.
___ 7. On the whole, I am satisfied with myself.
___ 8. I wish I could have more respect for myself.
___ 9. I certainly feel useless at times.
___ 10. At times I think I am no good at all.

To calculate your score, first reverse the scoring for the five negatively worded items (3, 5, 8, 9, and 10) as follows: 1 = 4, 2 = 3, 3 = 2, 4 = 1. Then, sum your scores across the 10 items. Your total score should fall between 10 and 40. A higher score indicates higher self-esteem.

Figure 5.7

A popular measure of self-esteem: Rosenberg Self-Esteem Scale. The scale shown here is a widely used research instrument that taps respondents' feelings of general self-esteem.

Adapted from Rosenberg, M. (1965). *Society and the adolescent self-image.* Princeton, NJ: Princeton University Press. Copyright © 1965 by Princeton University Press.

Chapter 1 that self-esteem is a good predictor of happiness. However, it is hard to tell whether high self-esteem causes happiness or vice versa. You should keep this problem in pinpointing causation in mind as we zoom in on this fascinating topic.

The Importance of Self-Esteem

Popular wisdom holds that self-esteem is the key to practically all positive outcomes in life. In fact, its actual benefits are much fewer—but, we hasten to add, not unimportant. A recent comprehensive review of research looked at the purported and actual advantages of self-esteem (Baumeister et al., 2003). Let's look at the findings that relate to self-esteem and adjustment.

Self-Esteem and Adjustment

The clearest advantages of self-esteem are in the *emotional sphere.* Namely, self-esteem is strongly and consistently related to happiness. In fact, Baumeister and his colleagues are persuaded that high self-esteem actually leads to greater happiness, although they acknowledge that research has not clearly established the direction of causation. On the other side, low self-esteem is more likely than high self-esteem to lead to depression.

In the area of *achievement,* high self-esteem has not been shown to be a reliable cause of good academic performance. In fact, it may actually be the (weak) result of doing well in school. Baumeister and his colleagues speculate that other factors may underlie both self-esteem and academic performance. Regarding job performance, the results are mixed. Some studies find that high self-esteem is linked to better performance, but others find no difference. And it may be that occupational success leads to high self-esteem.

In the *interpersonal realm,* Baumeister and his colleagues report that people with high self-esteem claim to be more likable and attractive, to have better relationships, and to make better impressions on others than people with low self-esteem. Interestingly, these advantages seem to exist mainly in the minds of the beholders because objective data (ratings of peers) do not support these views. In fact, Mark Leary's *sociometer theory* suggests that self-esteem is actually a subjective measure of one's interpersonal popularity and success (Leary et al., 1995; Leary & Baumeister, 2000). Regarding romantic relationships, those with low self-esteem are more likely to distrust their partners' expressions of love and support and to worry about rejection compared to high-self-esteem individuals. Still there is no evidence that self-esteem (high or low) is related to how quickly relationships end. When it comes to working in groups, high-self-esteem people are more likely to speak up and to criticize the group's approach. And they are perceived as contributing more to groups.

What about self-esteem and *coping,* a key aspect of adjustment? Individuals with low self-esteem *and* a self-blaming attributional style are definitely at a disadvantage here. For one thing, they become more demoralized after a failure than those with high self-esteem do. For them, failure contributes to depression and undermines their motivation to do better the next time. By contrast, individuals with high self-esteem persist longer in the face of failure. Second, as can be seen in **Figure 5.8**, individuals with low self-esteem often have negative expectations about their performance (in a social situation, at a job interview, on a test). Because self-esteem affects expectations, it operates in a self-perpetuating fashion. As a result, they feel anxious and may not prepare for the challenge. Then, if they blame themselves when they do poorly, they feel depressed and deliver one more blow to their already battered self-esteem. Of course, this cycle also works (in the opposite way) for those with high self-esteem. In either case, the important point is that self-esteem can affect not only the present, but also the future.

Finally, all may not be well for all high-self-esteem individuals; some may be more secure in their self-evaluations than others. Some researchers distinguish between people with *secure high self-esteem* and those with *defensive high self-esteem* (Jordan, Spencer, & Zanna, 2003; Jordan et al., 2003; Kernis & Paradise, 2002). Both groups demonstrate similarly high scores

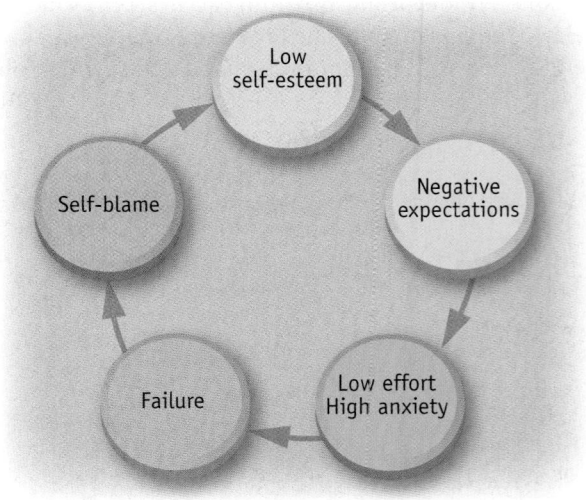

Figure 5.8

The vicious circle of low self-esteem and poor performance. Low self-esteem is associated with low or negative expectations about performance. These low expectations often result in inadequate preparation and high anxiety, which heighten the likelihood of poor performance. Unsuccessful performance triggers self-blame, which feeds back to lower self-esteem.

Adapted from Brehm, S. S., & Kassin, S. M. (1993). *Social psychology.* Boston: Houghton Mifflin. Copyright © 1993 by Houghton Mifflin Company. Adapted with permission.

on self-esteem measures. However, those with secure levels of esteem are quite confident in their positive self-views, neither needing nor seeking reassurance from others. Persons with defensive high self-esteem, on the other hand, have more delicate self-views undergirded by feelings of uncertainty, self-doubt, and insecurity, which can compel them to overreact to any unfavorable evaluation. Unfortunately, these folks need to be coddled and praised all the time, leading them to lash out at virtually any criticism, even when it is mild and intended to be helpful.

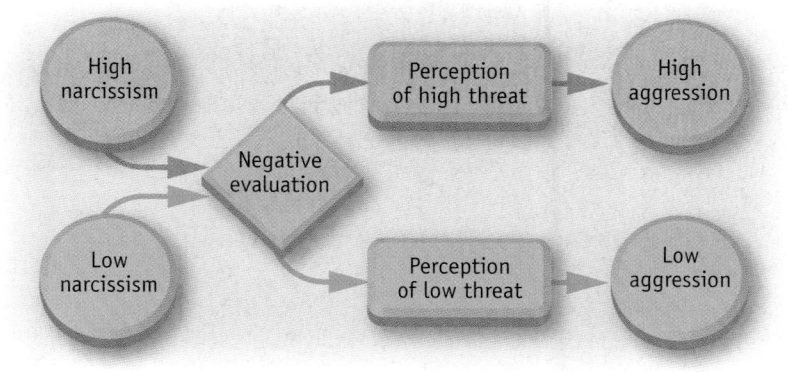

Figure 5.9

The path from narcissism to aggression. Individuals who score high on narcissism perceive negative evaluations by others to be extremely threatening. This experience of ego threat triggers strong hostile feelings and aggressive behavior toward the evaluator in retaliation for the perceived criticism. Low scorers are less likely to perceive negative evaluations as threatening and, therefore, behave much less aggressively toward evaluators. (Adapted from Bushman & Baumeister, 1998).

High Self-Esteem Versus Narcissism

Although feeling good about oneself is desirable, problems arise when people's self-views are inflated and unrealistic. Indeed, high self-esteem may not be all it's cracked up to be (Crocker & Park, 2004). ***Narcissism* is the tendency to regard oneself as grandiosely self-important.** Narcissistic individuals passionately want to think well of themselves and are highly sensitive to criticism (Twenge & Campbell, 2003). They are preoccupied with fantasies of success, believe that they deserve special treatment, and react aggressively when they experience threats to their self-views (ego threats). Those with fragile (unstable) self-esteem also respond in this manner (Kernis, 2003a, 2003b). On the other hand, individuals whose positive self-appraisals are secure or realistic are not so susceptible to ego threats and are less likely to resort to hostility and aggression in the face of them. Note that narcissists' aggression must be provoked; without provocation, they are no more likely to aggress than non-narcissists (Baumeister, Bushman, & Campbell, 2000; Twenge & Campbell, 2003).

Baumeister and his colleagues speculate that narcissists who experience ego threats have an elevated propensity to engage in aggression such as partner abuse, rape, gang violence, individual and group hate crimes, and political terrorism (Baumeister, 1999; Baumeister, Smart, & Boden, 1996; Bushman et al., 2003). Is there any evidence to support this idea? In a series of studies, researchers gave participants the opportunity to aggress against someone who had either insulted or praised an essay they had written (Bushman & Baumeister, 1998). The narcissistic participants reacted to their "insultors" with exceptionally high levels of aggression (see **Figure 5.9**). Another study compared male prisoners and college men on narcissism and self-esteem. Violent offenders scored significantly higher in narcissism, but their self-esteem scores were similar to those of the college men (Bushman & Baumeister, 2002).

These findings have important practical implications (Baumeister et al., 1996). Most rehabilitation programs for spousal abusers, delinquents, and criminals are based on the faulty belief that these individuals suffer from low self-esteem. In opposition to this view, current research suggests that efforts to boost (already inflated) self-esteem are misguided; a better approach is to help such individuals develop more self-control and more realistic views of themselves. Keep in mind, too, that narcissism cannot account for all problems associated with self-esteem. One recent series of studies found that low self-esteem among adolescents, not narcissism, predicted the incidence of aggression and of antisocial and delinquent behavior (Donnellan et al., 2005).

Web Link 5.3 **Self-Esteem vs. Narcissism: Implications for Teachers of Young Children**

Self-esteem in early childhood can be undermined by well-intentioned but ill-informed teachers who misunderstand how self-esteem is developed. Lilian G. Katz explores durable foundations for a child's self-worth in this online book from ERIC, the Education Resources Information Center.

The Development of Self-Esteem

Although people's sense of self-worth emerges in early childhood, individual differences in self-esteem begin to stand out in middle childhood and remain across the lifespan (Harter, 2006). The typical pattern found involves high self-esteem in childhood, an observed fall in adolescence (especially among girls), a gradual return

Self-Esteem and Threats to Mortality

One consequence of living in a post–9/11 world is that people experience anxiety about the possibility of terrorist attacks in the United States, as well as elsewhere. As explained in Chapter 2, *terror management theory (TMT)* is an influential new theoretical perspective asserting that self-esteem plays a pivotal role in people's efforts to deal with the threats to mortality posed by modern terrorism (Greenberg, Solomon, & Pyszczynski, 1997). As you may recall, terror management theory notes that human beings are the only creatures that live with the knowledge that they will die. According to TMT, the instinctive desire to live is juxtaposed against the inevitability of death, which produces the potential for paralyzing terror (Pyszczynski, Greenberg, & Goldenberg, 2003). To diminish the existential terror resulting from the awareness of their mortality, people are thought to rely on two defenses: efforts aimed at validating one's cultural worldview and those that bolster self-esteem.

First, belonging to a culture supposely reduces the fear of death because it provides a sense of meaning beyond oneself and a sense of belonging to a larger entity that will live beyond one's own lifetime. This idea has considerable support. Compared to participants who are not reminded about their own death, those for whom death is made salient are more likely to endorse negative evaluations of outgroup members (Schimel et al., 1999) and to endorse harsh punishments for those who violate cultural values (Greenberg et al., 1990).

More relevant to the current discussion is the second terror management mechanism, which ascribes great importance to self-esteem. Terror management theory proposes that the principal function of self-esteem is to serve as a buffer against death-related anxiety. The idea is that people can reduce or ward off their fear of death by focusing on thoughts and experiences that help them feel good about themselves. This idea was supported in a series of experiments in which people were shown graphic scenes of death aimed at building anxiety about their own mortality (Greenberg et al., 1992). Prior to viewing these scenes, half of the participants were given positive feedback to temporarily increase their self-esteem. Interestingly, the group that got the "self-esteem boost" showed less anxiety and less defensiveness in viewing the gruesome scenes than a control group that didn't receive the prior positive feedback.

A worldview implicit in TMT, that goodness must triumph heroically over evil, poses problems because it focuses on the transient nature of life (Pyszczynski, Solomon, & Greenberg, 2003). Specifically, to transcend death and find self-worth, people on both sides feel they must fight and, if necessary, kill others to eradicate wickedness; people are either saints or demons (Haidt & Algoe, 2004). Terror management theory has some interesting implications for thinking about terrorism and promoting peace. First, TMT theorists argue that the emphasis on mortality must be reduced. Second, fundamentalist belief systems in places like the Middle East must be constructively changed so as not to emphasize that self-worth and meaning can be achieved only by harming or eliminating groups or even nations (Pyszczynski et al., 2003).

People's reactions to terror have also been considered in light of TMT. One study, which focused on how interpersonal communication can reduce existential terror, interviewed young adults on a large Midwest university's campus two weeks after the fall of the World Trade Center Towers (Yum & Schenck-Hamlin, 2005). Participants reported initially feeling shock and disbelief on September 11, 2001. In the hours and days following the event, however, many reported looking for purpose or value in living, engaging in meaningful conversations with others, searching for or giving out information, and (unfortunately) making intolerant or prejudiced comments about Arab Muslims, all acts related to self-esteem. Another study looked at the effects of homegrown terrorism to discern whether existential terror maintains marital ties. Analyzing divorce rates in Oklahoma between 1985 and 2000, Nakonezny and colleagues found a decrease in divorces following the Oklahoma City bombing in April 1995 (Nakonezny, Reddick, & Rodgers, 2004). Perhaps awareness of mortality and the fragility of life encouraged some people to stay together.

Although TMT offers an intriguing perspective on the function of self-esteem, key aspects of the theory have not been tested (Crocker & Nuer, 2004), and alternative explanations can account for existing results (Leary, 2004). That said, there is quite a bit of empirical support for the specific idea that high self-esteem counteracts anxiety (Baumeister et al., 2003). This anxiety-buffering function of high self-esteem seems particularly relevant in these troubled times.

and rise in adulthood, and a precipitous decline once more during old age (Robins & Trzesniewski, 2005). Because the foundations of self-esteem are laid early in life (Harter, 2003), psychologists have focused much of their attention on the role of parenting in self-esteem development. Indeed, there is ample evidence that parental involvement, acceptance, support, and exposure to clearly defined limits have marked influence on children's self-esteem (Felson, 1989; Harter, 1998).

Two major dimensions underlie parenting behavior: acceptance and control (Maccoby & Martin, 1983). Diana Baumrind (1967, 1971, 1978) identified four distinct parenting styles as interactions between these two dimensions (see **Figure 5.10**). *Authoritative parenting* uses high emotional support and firm, but reasonable limits (high acceptance, high control). *Authoritarian parenting* entails low emotional support with rigid limits (low acceptance, high control). *Permissive parenting* uses high emotional support with few limits (high acceptance, low control), and *neglectful parenting* involves low emotional support and few limits (low acceptance, low control). Baumrind and others have found correlations between these parenting styles and children's traits and behaviors, including self-esteem (Furnham & Cheng, 2000; Maccoby & Martin, 1983). Authoritative parenting is associated with the highest self-esteem scores, and this finding holds true across different ethnic groups (Wissink, Dekovic, & Meijer, 2006). Authoritarian parenting, permissive parenting, and neglectful parenting are second, third, and fourth in line. These studies were correlational, so keep in mind they don't demonstrate that parenting style *causes* high or low self-esteem.

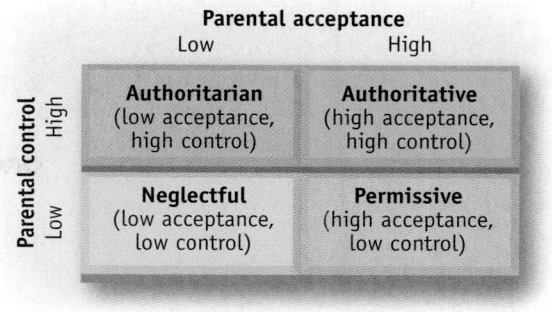

Figure 5.10

Baumrind's four parenting styles. Four parenting styles result from the interactions of parental acceptance and parental control, as theorized by Diana Baumrind.

Adapted from Baumrind, D. (1971). Current patterns of parental authority [Monograph]. *Developmental Psychology, 4*(1, Part 2), 1–103. Copyright © 1971 American Psychological Association. Adapted by permission of the publisher and author.

© Blend Images/Alamy

Significant others play a key role in shaping self-esteem.

Of course, parents are not the only significant people in a person's life: teachers, classmates, and close friends also play important roles. As you would expect, children who perceive they have the most support from the key people in their lives have the highest self-esteem, whereas those who have the lowest perceived support have the lowest self-esteem (Harter, 2003). For older children and adolescents, approval from parents and approval from classmates are the two strongest predictors of high self-esteem; by college age, peers have much more impact on self-esteem than parents do (Harter, 1993).

Children (and adults) also make their own judgments about themselves. Perceiving oneself as successful in domains that are highly valued is important in these self-evaluations (Harter, 2003; MacDonald, Saltzman, & Leary, 2003). For instance, if Maria values success in the academic and social areas and sees herself as competent in these arenas, she will have higher self-esteem than Heather, who also values these domains but rates herself low on one or both of them. An important basis for self-judgments is how well one "stacks up" against a selected reference group (recall social comparison theory).

Ethnicity, Gender, and Self-Esteem

Because prejudice and discrimination are still pervasive in the United States, people commonly assume that members of minority groups have lower self-esteem than members of the majority group. Research both supports and contradicts this assumption. On the one hand, the self-esteem of Asians, Hispanics, and Native Americans is lower than that of whites, although the differences are small (Twenge & Crocker, 2002). On the other hand, the self-esteem of blacks is higher than that of whites (Gray-Little & Hafdahl, 2000; Twenge & Crocker, 2002). Adding gender to the mix complicates the picture even more. White males have higher self-esteem than white females, but minority males have lower self-esteem than minority females (Twenge & Crocker, 2002).

Thus, ethnicity and gender interact in complex ways in self-esteem. The role of cultural differences in the self-concept may provide some insight here. Recall our earlier discussion of individualism and collectivism. Note that differences on this dimension are found not only between nations but also within a given country. And here's another fact: High individualism is associated with high self-esteem. What's interesting here is that the pattern of ethnic differences in individualism closely mirrors the pattern of ethnic differences in self-esteem (Twenge & Crocker, 2002). That is, blacks score higher than whites, whites do not differ significantly from Hispanics, and Hispanics score higher than Asian Americans. Thus, the ethnic differences in self-esteem are likely rooted in how the different groups view themselves, based on cultural messages.

Although females are not a minority group, they resemble ethnic minorities in that they tend to have lower status and less power than males. The popular press abounds with reports of low self-esteem in adolescent girls and women (Orenstein, 1994; Pipher, 1994). Is there any empirical basis for this assertion? In a massive undertaking, researchers examined gender differences in self-esteem by statistically summarizing the results of several hundred studies (with respondents ranging from 7 to 60 years of age) as well as the data from three nationally representative surveys of adolescents and young adults (Kling et al., 1999). In both analyses, males scored higher on self-esteem than females, although the differences were small for the most part. The largest difference occurred in the 15- to 18-year-old age group. Also, white girls have lower self-esteem than minority girls do. The fact that white girls tend to have more negative body images than minority girls may be a factor in their lower self-esteem (Twenge & Crocker, 2002).

Basic Principles of Self-Perception

LEARNING OBJECTIVES

- *Distinguish between automatic and controlled processing.*
- *Define self-attributions, and identify the key dimensions of attributions.*
- *Explain how optimistic and pessimistic explanatory styles are related to adjustment.*
- *Discuss four motives that guide self-understanding.*
- *Describe four strategies people use to maintain positive feelings about the self.*

Now that you're familiar with some of the major aspects of the self, let's consider how people construct and maintain a coherent and positive view of the self. First we'll look at the basic cognitive processes involved and then at the fascinating area of self-attributions. Then we will move on to discussions of explanatory style and the key motives guiding self-understanding, with a special emphasis on self-enhancement techniques.

Cognitive Processes

People are faced with an inordinate number of decisions on a daily basis. How do they keep from being overwhelmed? The key lies in how people process information. According to Shelley Taylor (1981a), people are "cognitive misers." In this model, cognitive resources (attention, memory, and so forth) are limited, so the mind works to "hoard" them by taking cognitive short-cuts. For example, you probably have the same morning routine—shower, drink coffee, read the paper as you eat breakfast, check e-mail, and so forth. Because you do these things without a lot of thought, you can conserve your attentional, decision-making, and memory capacities for important cognitive tasks. This example illustrates the default mode of handling information: *automatic processing.* On the other hand, when important decisions arise or when you're trying to understand why you didn't get that job you wanted, you spend those precious cognitive resources. This mode is termed *controlled processing.* Ellen Langer (1989) describes these two states as *mindlessness* and *mindfulness,* respectively. Mindfulness promotes cognitive flexibility, which in turn can lead to self-acceptance (Carson & Langer, 2006) and well-being (Langer, 2002). In contrast, mindlessness leads to rigid thinking.

Another way that cognitive resources are protected is through *selective attention,* with high priority given to information pertaining to the self (Bargh, 1997). An example of this tendency is a phenomenon known as the "cocktail party effect" —the ability to pick out the mention of your name in a roomful of chattering people (Moray, 1959; Wood & Cowan, 1995).

Another principle of self-cognition is that people strive to understand themselves. One way they do so, as you saw in our discussion of social comparison theory, is to compare themselves with others (Wood & Wilson, 2003). Yet another is to engage in attributional thinking, our next topic.

Self-Attributions

Let's say that you win a critical match for your school's tennis team. To what do you attribute your success? Is your new practice schedule starting to pay off? Did you have the home court advantage? Perhaps your opponent was playing with a minor injury? This example from everyday life illustrates the nature of the self-attribution process. ***Self-attributions* are inferences that people draw about the causes of their own behavior.** People routinely make attributions to make sense out of their experiences. These attributions involve inferences that ultimately represent guesswork on each person's part.

Fritz Heider (1958) was the first to assert that people tend to locate the cause of a behavior either within a person, attributing it to personal factors, or outside of a person, attributing it to environmental factors. He thus established one of the crucial dimensions along which attributions are made: internal versus external. The other two dimensions are stable—unstable and controllable—uncontrollable. Let's discuss these different types of attributions in greater detail.

Internal or external. Elaborating on Heider's insight, various theorists have agreed that explanations of behavior and events can be categorized as internal or external attributions (Jones & Davis, 1965; Kelley, 1967; Weiner, 1974, 2006). ***Internal attributions* ascribe the causes of behavior to personal dispositions, traits, abilities, and feelings. *External attributions* ascribe the causes of behavior to situational demands and environmental constraints.** For example, if you credit your poor statistics grade to your failure to prepare adequately for the test or to getting overly anxious during the test, you are making internal attributions. An external attribution could be that the course is simply too hard, that the teacher is unfair, or that the book is incomprehensible.

Whether one's self-attributions are internal or external can have a tremendous impact on one's personal adjustment. Studies suggest that people who attribute their setbacks to internal, personal causes while discounting external, situational explanations may be more prone to depression than people who display opposite tendencies (Riso et al., 2003).

Stable or unstable. A second dimension people use in making causal attributions is the stability of the causes underlying behavior (Weiner, 1986, 1994). A stable cause is one that is more or less permanent and unlikely to change over time. A sense of humor and intelligence are *stable internal* causes of behavior. *Stable external* causes of behavior include such things as laws and rules (speed limits, no smoking areas). Unstable causes of behavior are variable or subject to change. *Unstable internal* causes of behavior include such things as mood (good or bad) and motivation (strong or weak). *Unstable external* causes could be the weather and the presence or absence of other people. According to Bernard Weiner (1986, 1994), the stable-unstable dimension in attribution cuts across the internal-external dimension, creating four types of attributions for success and failure, as shown in **Figure 5.11**.

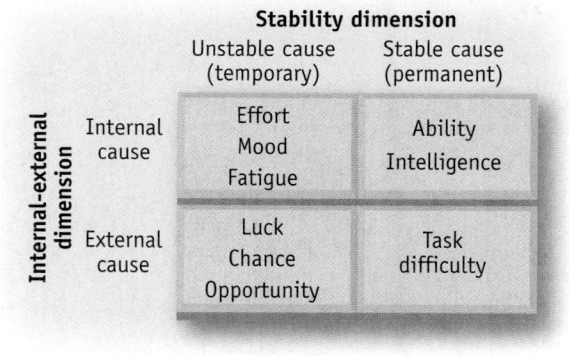

Figure 5.11

Key dimensions of attributional thinking. Weiner's model assumes that people's explanations for success and failure emphasize internal versus external causes and stable versus unstable causes. For example, if you attribute an outcome to great effort or to lack of effort, you are citing causes that lie within the person. Since effort can vary over time, the causal factors at work are unstable. Other examples of causal factors that fit into each of the four cells in Weiner's model are shown in the diagram.

From Weiner, B., Frieze, I., Kukla, A., Reed, L.. & Rosenbaum, R. M. (1972). Perceiving the causes of success and failure. In E. E. Jones, D. E. Kanouse, H. H. Kelly, R. E. Nisbett, S. Valins, & B. Weiner (Eds.), *Perceiving causes of behavior.* Morristown, NJ: General Learning Press. Reprinted by permission of the author.

Let's apply Weiner's model to a concrete event. Imagine that you are contemplating why you just landed the job you wanted. You might credit your situation to internal factors that are stable (excellent ability) or unstable (hard work on your eye-catching résumé). Or you might attribute the outcome to external factors that are stable (lack of top-flight competition) or unstable (luck). If you didn't get the job, your explanations would fall in the same four categories: internal-stable (lack of ability), internal-unstable (inadequate effort on your résumé), external-stable (too much competition in your field), and external-unstable (bad luck).

Controllable or uncontrollable. A third dimension in the attribution process acknowledges the fact that sometimes events are under one's control and sometimes they are not (Weiner, 1986, 1994). For example, the amount of effort you expend on a task is typically perceived as something under your control, whereas an aptitude for music is viewed as something you are born with (beyond your control). Controllability can vary with each of the other two factors.

These three dimensions appear to be the central ones in the attribution process. Research has documented that self-attributions are motivational, guiding one toward or away from possible courses of action. Thus, one's self-beliefs can influence future expectations (success or failure) and emotions (pride, hopelessness, guilt), and these expectations and emotions can combine to influence subsequent performance (Weiner, 1986, 1994, 2006). Self-attributions, then, play a key role in one's feelings, motivational state, and behavior.

Explanatory Style

Julio and Josh are freshmen who have just struck out trying to get their first college dates. After this disappointment, they reflect on the possible reasons for it. Julio speculates that his approach was too subtle. Looking back, he realizes that he wasn't very direct because he was nervous about asking the woman out. When she didn't reply, he didn't follow up for fear that she didn't really want to go out with him. On further reflection, he reasons that she probably didn't respond because she wasn't sure of his intentions. He vows to be more direct the next time. Josh, on the other hand, mopes, "I'll never have a relationship. I'm a total loser." On the basis of these comments, who do you think is likely to get a date in the future? If you guessed Julio, you are probably correct. Let's see why.

According to Martin Seligman (1991), people tend to exhibit, to varying degrees, an *optimistic explanatory style* or a *pessimistic explanatory style* (see **Figure 5.12**). As we saw in Chapter 3, ***explanatory style* refers to the tendency to use similar causal attributions for a wide variety of events in one's life.** The person with an optimistic explanatory style usually attributes setbacks to external, unstable, and specific factors. A person who failed to get a desired job, for example, might attribute this misfortune to factors in the interview situation ("The room was really hot," "The questions were

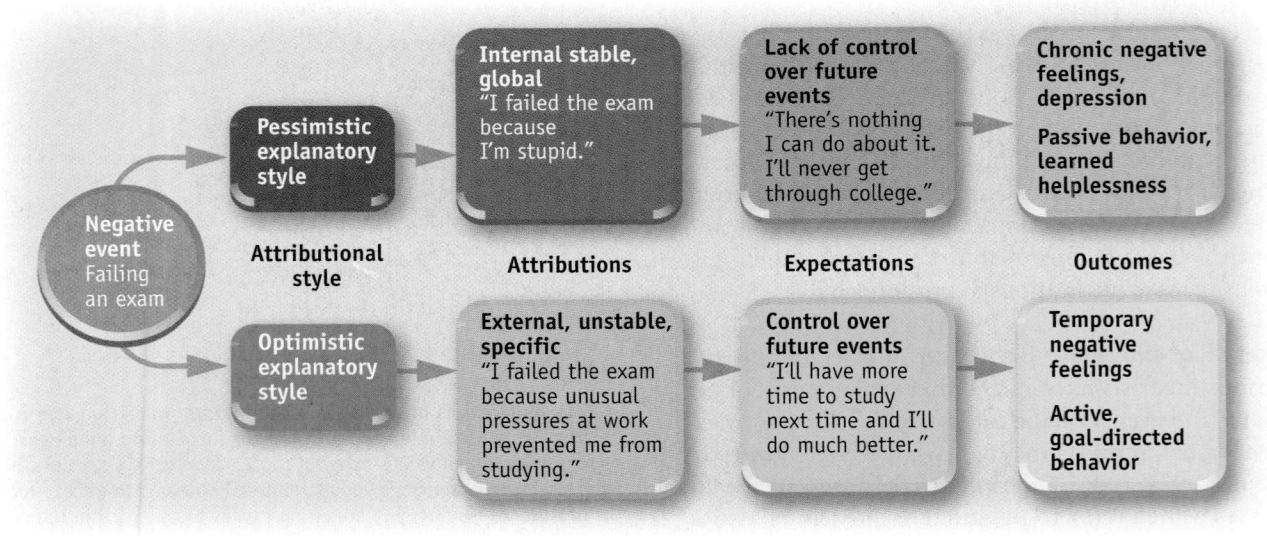

Figure 5.12

The effects of attributional style on expectations, emotions, and behavior. The pessimistic explanatory style is seen in the top row of boxes. This attributional style, which attributes setbacks to internal, stable, and global causes, tends to result in an expectation of lack of control over future events, depressed feelings, and passive behavior. A more adaptive, optimistic attributional style is shown in the bottom row of boxes.

slanted") rather than to personal shortcomings. This style can be psychologically protective (Wise & Rosqvist, 2006), helping people to discount their setbacks and thus maintain a favorable self-image. It also helps people bounce back from failure. One study found that optimistic students had more confidence and performed better than pessimistic students after a sports failure (Martin-Krumm et al., 2003).

In contrast, people with a pessimistic explanatory style tend to attribute their setbacks to internal, stable, and global (or pervasive) factors. These attributions make them feel bad about themselves and pessimistic about their ability to handle challenges in the future. Such a style can foster passive behavior and make people more vulnerable to learned helplessness and depression (Peterson, Maier, & Seligman, 1993), especially when they expect that things won't work out in their favor (Peterson & Vaidya, 2001). Of more concern is some suggestive evidence from a longitudinal sample of people that "catastrophizing"—attributing negative events to global causes—predicted accidental and violent deaths (Peterson et al., 1998). Luckily, cognitive-behavioral therapy appears to be successful in helping depressed individuals change their pessimistic explanatory style (Seligman et al., 1999).

Motives Guiding Self-Understanding

Whether people evaluate themselves by social comparisons, attributional thinking, or other means, they are highly motivated to pursue self-understanding. In seeking self-understanding, people are driven by four major motives: assessment, verification, improvement, and enhancement (Biernat & Billings, 2001; Sedikides & Strube, 1997).

Self-Assessment

The *self-assessment motive* is reflected in people's desire for truthful information about themselves (Trope, 1983, 1986). Unfortunately, many of these self-assessments are quite flawed; the only good news is that the person is typically unaware of this fact (Dunning, Heath, & Suls, 2004). Still, there is some hope. Individuals do seek accurate feedback about many types of information, including their personal qualities, abilities, physical features, and so forth. It's obvious why people look for accurate information. After all, it helps them set realistic goals and behave in appropriate ways (Oettingen & Gollwitzer, 2001). Still, the bald truth is not always welcome. Accordingly, people are also motivated by other concerns.

Self-Verification

The *self-verification motive* drives people toward information that matches what they already believe about themselves, whether it is positive or negative. This tendency to strive for a consistent self-image ensures that individuals' self-concepts are relatively stable. Individuals maintain consistent self-perceptions in a number of subtle ways and are often unaware of doing so (Schlenker & Pontari, 2000). For example, people maintain consistency between their past and present behavior by erasing past memories that conflict with present ones. To illustrate, people who were once shy and who later became outgoing have been shown to recall memories about themselves that indicate that they perceive themselves as always having been outgoing (Ross & Conway, 1986).

Another way people maintain self-consistency is by seeking out feedback and situations that will confirm their existing self-perceptions and avoiding potentially disconfirming situations or feedback. According to William Swann's ***self-verification theory,*** **people prefer to receive feedback from others that is consistent with their own self-views.** Thus, people with positive self-concepts should prefer positive feedback from others and those with negative self-concepts should prefer negative feedback. Research usually finds this to be the case (Swann, Rentfrow, & Guinn, 2003). In one study, college men were divided into a positive self-concept group or a negative self-concept group based on test scores. They were then asked to choose a partner for a subsequent 2- to 3-hour interaction. Participants were led to believe that one of the prospective partners held views of him that were consistent with his self-view and that the other held views of him that were inconsistent with his self-view. As predicted, subjects with positive self-views preferred partners who viewed them positively, whereas those with negative self-views chose partners who viewed them negatively (Swann, Stein-Seroussi, & Geisler, 1992). Among depressed persons, the persistent self-views predicted by self-verification processes may account for treatment setbacks or ongoing dysphoria (Petit & Joiner, 2006).

Self-Improvement

What is your current self-improvement project? To study more? To get more exercise? When people seek to better themselves, the *self-improvement motive* comes into play. In trying to improve, individuals typically look to successful others for inspiration (Collins, 1996). Advertisers of personal care products (tooth whiteners, exercise machines, and so forth) tap into this motive by showing before-and-after photographs of individuals who have used the products.

Self-Enhancement

Finally, people are motivated by the *self-enhancement motive.* ***Self-enhancement*** **is the tendency to maintain positive feelings about oneself.** One example of self-enhancement is the tendency to hold flattering views of one's personal qualities, a tendency termed the *better-than-average effect* (Alicke, 1985; Buckingham & Alicke, 2002). You've already seen an example of this effect in our earlier report that 100 percent of students who took the SAT rated themselves above average in the ability to get along with others—a mathematical impossibility. Students can take perverse pleasure in knowing that faculty also succumb to this bias: 94 percent of them regard their teaching as above average (Cross, 1977)!

A second example of self-enhancement concerns *illusions of control* (Langer, 1975), in which people overestimate their degree of control over outcomes. Thus, individuals who pick their own "lucky" numbers on lottery tickets falsely believe that they can influence the outcome of such random events, an act and inference that makes them feel good (Dunn & Wilson, 1990). A third form of self-enhancement is the tendency to have *unrealistic optimism about future events* (Weinstein, 1980). For example, most people believe that they will have a brighter future and experience fewer negative events than others (Helweg-Larsen & Shepperd, 2001), especially where health and safety are concerned (Weinstein, 1982).

The four self-motives of assessment, verification, improvement, and enhancement permit flexibility in making self-evaluations. Although you would think that accurate information would be the most useful to people, that doesn't seem to be the case. In a series of studies that pitted self-assessment, self-verification, and self-enhancement against each other, the self-enhancement motive was found to be the strongest, the self-verification motive a distant second, and the self-assessment motive an even more distant third (Sedikides, 1993).

Methods of Self-Enhancement

The powerful self-enhancement motive drives individuals to seek positive (and reject negative) information about themselves. Let's examine four cognitive strategies people commonly use in this process.

Downward Comparisons

We've already mentioned that people routinely compare themselves to others as a means of learning more about themselves (social comparison). However, once a threat to self-esteem enters the picture, people often adjust their strategy and choose to compare themselves with those who are worse off than they are (Wood, 1989). ***Downward social comparison* is a defensive tendency to compare oneself with someone whose troubles are more serious than one's own.** Why do people change strategies under threat? Because they need to feel better. Research shows that downward social comparisons are associated with increases in both mood and self-esteem (Reis, Gerrard, & Gibbons, 1993).

A dramatic example of downward comparison can be found in the aftermath of the terrorist attacks on the World Trade Center and the Pentagon in September 2001. Compared to the devastating losses suffered by the victims and families, most people's problems suddenly appeared insignificant. There are also more common examples. If you have ever been in a serious traffic accident in which your car was "totaled," you probably reassured yourself by reflecting on the fact that at least no one was seriously injured. Similarly, people with chronic illnesses may compare themselves with those who have life-threatening diseases.

Self-Serving Bias

Suppose that you and three other individuals apply for a part-time job in the parks and recreation department and you are selected for the position. How do you explain your success? Chances are, you tell yourself that you were hired because you were the most qualified for the job. But how do the other three people interpret their negative outcome? Do they tell themselves that you got the job because you were the most able? Un-

PEANUTS reprinted by permission of United Feature Syndicate, Inc.

likely! Instead, they probably attribute their loss to "bad luck" or to not having had time to prepare for the interview. These different explanations for success and failure reflect **the *self-serving bias,* or the tendency to attribute one's successes to personal factors and one's failures to situational factors** (Miller and Ross, 1975).

For example, in one experiment, two strangers jointly took a test. They then received bogus success or failure feedback about their test performance and were asked to assign responsibility for the test results. Successful participants claimed credit, but those who failed blamed their partners (Campbell et al., 2000). Still, people don't always rush to take credit. In another experiment in the just-cited study, participants were actual friends. In this case, participants shared responsibility for both successful and unsuccessful outcomes. Thus, friendship places limits on the self-serving bias.

Although the self-serving bias has been documented in a variety of cultures (Fletcher & Ward 1988), it seems to be particularly prevalent in individualistic, Western societies, where the emphasis on competition and high self-esteem motivates people to try to impress others, as well as themselves. In contrast, Japanese subjects exhibit a *self-effacing bias* in explaining successes (Akimoto & Sanbonmatsu, 1999; Markus & Kitayama, 1991), as they tend to attribute their successes to the help they receive from others or to the ease of the task, while downplaying the importance of their ability. When they fail, Japanese subjects tend to be more self-critical than subjects from individualistic cultures (Heine & Renshaw, 2002). They are more likely to accept responsibility for their failures and to use their setbacks as an impetus for self-improvement (Heine et al., 2001). When Japanese students' apprehension at being evaluated is reduced, however, one study found they make more internal attributions for success than failure (Kudo, 2003). Studies have also failed to find the usual self-serving bias in Nepalese and Chinese samples (Lee & Seligman, 1997; Smith & Bond, 1999).

© GDT/Stone/Getty Images

People frequently claim association with others who are successful (basking in reflected glory) to maintain positive feelings about the self.

Basking in Reflected Glory

When your favorite sports team won the national championship last year, did you make a point of wearing the team cap? And when Ben, your best friend, won that special award, do you remember how often you told others the good news about him? If you played a role in someone's success, it's understandable that you would want to share in the recognition; however, people often want to share recognition even when they are on the sidelines of an outstanding achievement. ***Basking in reflected glory* is the tendency to enhance one's image by publicly announcing one's association with those who are successful.**

Robert Cialdini and his colleagues (1976) studied this phenomenon on college campuses with nationally ranked football teams. The researchers predicted that, when asked how their team had fared in a recent football game, students would be more likely to say, "We won" (in other words, to bask in reflected glory, or to "BIRG"—pronounced with a soft "g") when the home team had been successful than to respond "We lost" when it had been defeated. Indeed, the researchers found that students were more likely to BIRG when their team won than when it lost. Also, subjects who believed that they had just failed a bogus test were more likely to use the words "we won" than those who believed they had performed well.

A related self-enhancement strategy is "CORFing," or *cutting off reflected failure.* Because self-esteem is partly tied to an individual's associations with others, people often protect their self-esteem by distancing themselves from those who are unsuccessful (Boen, VanBeselaere, & Feys, 2002; Cialdini et al., 1976). Thus, if your cousin is arrested for drunk driving, you may tell others that you don't really know him very well. Interestingly, BIRGing and CORFing are apparently not limited to the U.S. or only to public settings. Websites

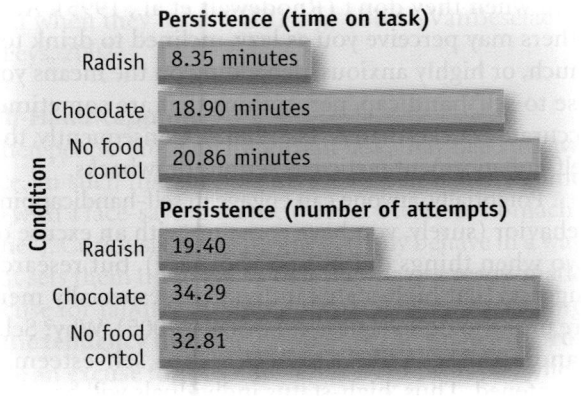

Figure 5.14

Persistence on unsolvable puzzles. Participants who were instructed to eat radishes and not to eat chocolate chip cookies or chocolate candy used more self-control resources than participants who were instructed to eat the chocolate and not to touch the radishes or participants in the no-food control group. Because the radish-eaters had relatively few self-control resources to help them persist at a difficult task (unsolvable puzzles), they persisted for the shortest time and made the fewest attempts to solve the puzzles compared to the other two groups. (Adapted from Baumeister et al., 1998)

terms of both academic performance and social competence some ten years later (Mischel, Shoda, & Peake, 1988; Shoda, Mischel, & Peake, 1990). Recent evidence suggests that self-regulation is malleable and can be strengthened like a muscle, which means that with regular "exercise," people can become less vulnerable to ego depletion effects (Baumeister et al., 2006). In this section, we examine self-efficacy, a key aspect of self-regulation, and then discuss self-defeating behavior, a case of self-control failure.

Self-Efficacy

Courtesy, Albert Bandura

Albert Bandura

As explained in Chapter 2, ***self-efficacy* refers to one's belief about one's ability to perform behaviors that should lead to expected outcomes.** Self-efficacy represents people's conviction that they can achieve specific goals. According to Albert Bandura (1997, 2000), efficacy beliefs vary according to the person's skills. You may have high self-efficacy when it comes to making friends but low self-efficacy when it comes to speaking in front of a group. However, simply having a skill doesn't guarantee that you will be able to put it into practice. Like the Little Engine That Could, you must also *believe* that you are capable of doing so ("I *think* I can, I *think* I can . . ."). In other words, self-efficacy is concerned not with the skills you have, but with your *beliefs about what you can do* with these skills.

Correlates of Self-Efficacy

A number of studies have shown that self-efficacy affects individuals' commitments to goals, their performance on tasks, and their persistence toward goals in the face of obstacles (Maddux & Gosselin, 2003). Self-efficacy is related to health promotion (Bandura, 2004), academic success (Schunk, 2003), career choice (Betz & Klein, 1996), and job performance (Stajkovic & Luthans, 1998). Because of the importance of self-efficacy in psychological adjustment, it is worth keeping in mind that self-efficacy is learned and can be changed. Research shows that increasing self-efficacy is an effective way to improve health (losing weight, stopping smoking) (Maddux & Gosselin, 2003) and to treat a variety of psychological problems, including test anxiety (Smith, 1989), fear of computer use (Wilfong, 2006), phobias (Williams, 1995), fear of sexual assault (Ozer & Bandura, 1990), eating disorders (Goodrick et al., 1999), and substance abuse (DiClemente, Fairhurst, & Piotrowski, 1995), including marijuana dependence (Lozano, Stephens, & Roffman, 2006).

Developing Self-Efficacy

Self-efficacy is obviously a valuable quality. How does one acquire it? Bandura (1997, 2000) identifies four sources of self-efficacy: mastery experiences, vicarious experiences, persuasion/encouragement, and interpretation of emotional arousal.

1. *Mastery experiences.* The most effective path to self-efficacy is through mastering new skills. Sometimes new skills come easily—learning how to use the copy machine in the library, for instance. Some things are harder to master, such as learning how to use a spreadsheet program or how to play the piano. In acquiring more difficult skills, people usually make mistakes. How they handle these failure experiences is the key to learning self-efficacy. If you give up when you make mistakes, your failure instills self-doubts or low self-efficacy. On the other hand, if you persist through failure experiences to eventual success, you learn the lesson of self-efficacy: I *can* do it!

2. *Vicarious experiences.* Another way to improve self-efficacy is by watching others perform a skill you want to learn. It's important that you choose a model who is competent at the task, and it helps if the model is similar to you (in age, gender, and ethnicity). For example, if you're shy about speaking up for yourself, observing someone who is good at doing so can help you develop the confidence to do it yourself. Picking successful role models is important—watching unsuccessful ones can undermine self-efficacy.

Ironically, difficulties and failures can ultimately contribute to the development of a strong sense of self-efficacy. Self-efficacy tends to improve when youngsters learn to persist through difficulties and overcome failures.

3. *Persuasion and encouragement.* Although it is less effective than the first two approaches, a third way to develop self-efficacy is through the encouragement of others. For example, if you're having a hard time asking someone for a date, a friend's encouragement might give you just the push you need. Of course, persuasion doesn't always work. And, unless encouragement is accompanied by specific and concrete suggestions, this tactic is unlikely to be successful.

4. *Interpretation of emotional arousal.* The physiological responses that accompany feelings and one's interpretations of these responses are another source of self-efficacy. Let's say you're sitting in class waiting for your professor to distribute an exam. You notice that your palms are moist and your heart is pounding. If you attribute these behaviors to fear, you can temporarily dampen your self-efficacy, thus decreasing your chances of doing well. Alternatively, if you attribute your sweaty palms and racing heart to the arousal everyone needs to perform well, you may be able to boost your self-efficacy and increase your chances of doing well. Of course, self-regulation doesn't always succeed. That's the case in self-defeating behavior, our next topic.

Self-Defeating Behavior

People typically act in their own self-interest. But sometimes they knowingly do things that are bad for them—such as smoking, having unprotected sex, and completing important assignments at the last minute. ***Self-defeating behaviors* are seemingly intentional actions that thwart a person's self-interest.** According to Roy Baumeister (1997; Baumeister & Scher, 1988), there are three categories of intentional self-defeating behaviors: deliberate self-destruction, tradeoffs, and counterproductive strategies. The key difference among these three behaviors lies in how intentional they are. As you can see in **Figure 5.15**, attempts at deliberate self-destruction involve the most intent; counterproductive strategies are the least intentional, and trade-offs fall in between.

In *deliberate self-destruction,* people want to harm themselves and they choose courses of action that will forseeably lead to that result. Although this type of behavior may occur in individuals with psychological disorders, deliberate self-destruction appears to be infrequent in normal populations.

In *tradeoffs,* people foresee the possibility of harming themselves but accept it as a necessary accompaniment to achieving a desirable goal. Overeating, smoking, and drinking to excess are examples that come

Three Categories of Self-Defeating Behavior

Type of self-defeating behavior	Harm foreseen?	Harm desired?
Deliberate self-destruction	Yes	Yes
Tradeoffs	Yes	No
Counterproductive strategies	No	No

Figure 5.15

Three categories of self-defeating behavior. Roy Baumeister and Steven Scher (1988) distinguished three categories of self-defeating behaviors, based on how intentional the behaviors are. Intentionality is determined by two factors: an individual's awareness that a behavior could bring possible harm and an individual's desire to harm himself or herself. Deliberate self-destruction is the most intentional, followed by tradeoffs, then counterproductive strategies. (Based on Baumeister & Scher, 1988)

© Marc Vaughn/Masterfile

Self-defeating behaviors come in many forms with many underlying motivations. Overeating is a matter of* tradeoffs. *People realize that excessive eating may be harmful in the long run, but it is enjoyable at the time.

readily to mind. Other examples include procrastinating (putting off tasks feels good in the short run, but the struggle to meet looming deadlines results in poor performance and increased stress and illness), failing to follow prescribed health care advice (it's easier to slack off now, but doing so leads to future problems), shyness (avoiding social situations protects against anxiety but makes loneliness more likely), and self-handicapping (getting drunk before an exam explains poor performance but increases the chances of failure). People engage in tradeoffs because they bring immediate, positive, and reliable outcomes, not because they want to hurt themselves in the short or the long run.

In *counterproductive strategies,* a person pursues a desirable outcome but misguidedly uses an approach that is bound to fail. Of course, you can't always know in advance if a strategy will pay off. Thus, people must *habitually* use this strategy for it to qualify as self-defeating. For example, some people tend to persist in unproductive endeavors, such as pursuing an unreachable career goal or an unrequited love. People persist in these behaviors because they erroneously believe they'll be successful, not because they are intent on self-defeat.

To conclude, although most people engage in self-defeating behavior at some time, there is little evidence that they deliberately try to harm themselves or to fail at a task. Instead, self-defeating behavior appears to be the result of people's distorted judgments or strong desires to escape from immediate, painful feelings.

Self-Presentation

LEARNING OBJECTIVES

- *Explain why and when individuals engage in impression management.*
- *Cite some strategies people use to make positive impressions on others.*
- *Describe how high self-monitors are different from low self-monitors.*

Whereas your self-concept involves how you see yourself, your public self involves how you want others to see you. **A *public self* is an image presented to others in social interactions.** This presentation of a public self may sound deceitful, but it is perfectly normal, and everyone does it (Schlenker, 2003). Many self-presentations (ritual greetings, for example) take place automatically and without awareness. But when it really counts (job interviews, for example), people consciously strive to make the best possible impression.

Typically, individuals have a number of public selves that are tied to certain situations and certain people. For instance, you may have one public self for your parents and another for your peers. You may have still others for your teachers, your boss, your co-workers, and so forth. Also, people differ in the degree of overlap or congruence among their various public selves (see **Figure 5.16**). Does it matter whether you perceive yourself to be essentially the same person in different situations? It seems so. People who see themselves as being similar across different social roles (with friends, at work, at school, with parents, with romantic partners) are better adjusted than those who perceive less integration in their self-views across these roles (Donahue et al., 1993; Lutz & Ross, 2003; but see Baird, Le, & Lucas, 2006).

Impression Management

Interestingly, people think others notice and evaluate them more than is the actual case (Gilovich, Kruger, &

Medvec, 2002). This common tendency is aptly termed *the spotlight effect.* People also normally strive to make a positive impression on others to be liked, respected, hired, and so forth (Baumeister & Twenge, 2003). The sociologist Erving Goffman (1959) used the term *face* to describe the idealized image of ourselves we try to create in the minds of others. ***Impression management* refers to usually conscious efforts by people to influence how others think of them.** To see impression management in operation, let's look at a study of behavior in simulated job interviews (von Baeyer, Sherk, & Zanna, 1981). In this study, female job applicants were led to believe that the man who would interview them held either traditional, chauvinistic views of women or just the opposite. The researchers found that applicants who expected a chauvinist presented themselves in a more traditionally feminine manner than subjects in the other condition. Their self-presentation efforts extended to both their appearance (they wore more makeup) and their communication style (they talked less and gave more traditional answers to a question about marriage and children). In a job interview, people are particularly attentive to making a good impression, but impression management also operates in everyday interactions, although individuals may be less aware of it (Schlenker, 2003). Let's look at some common impression management strategies.

Impression Management Strategies

One reason people engage in impression management is to claim a particular identity (Baumeister, 1998). Thus, you select a type of dress, hairstyle, and manner of speech to present a certain image of yourself. Tattoos and body piercings also create a specific image. A second motive for impression management is to gain liking and approval from others—by editing what you say about yourself and by using various nonverbal cues such as smiles, gestures, and eye contact. Because self-presentation is practiced so often, people usually do it automatically. At other times, however, impression management may be used intentionally—to get a job, a date, a promotion, and so forth. Some common self-presentation strategies include ingratiation, self-promotion, exemplification, intimidation, and supplication (Jones, 1990). To this list, we add a rarely recognized strategy, negative acknowledgment.

1. *Ingratiation.* Of all the self-presentation strategies, ingratiation is the most fundamental and most frequently used. ***Ingratiation* is behaving in ways to make oneself likable to others.** For example, *giving compliments* is effective, as long as you are sincere (people dislike insincerity and can often detect it). *Doing favors for others* is also a common tactic, as long as your gestures aren't so spectacular they leave others feeling indebted (Gordon, 1996). Other ingratiation tactics include *expressing liking for others* and *going along with others* (to get others to like you, it helps to do the things that they want to do).

2. *Self-promotion.* The motive behind self-promotion is earning respect. You do so by playing up your strong points so you will be perceived as competent. For instance, in a job interview, you might find ways to mention that you earned high honors at school and that you were president of the student body and a member of the soccer team. To keep from coming across as a braggart, you shouldn't go overboard with self-promotion. For this reason, false modesty often works well.

3. *Exemplification.* Because most people try to project an honest image, you have to demonstrate exemplary behavior to claim special credit for integrity or character. Occupations fraught with danger, such as those in the military or law enforcement, provide obvious opportunities to exemplify moral virtue. A less dramatic, but still effective, strategy is to behave consistently according to high ethical standards—as long as you don't come across as self-righteous. Also, your words and deeds need to match unless you want to be labeled a hypocrite.

4. *Negative acknowledgment.* Can confessing you've made a relatively minor error motivate people to like

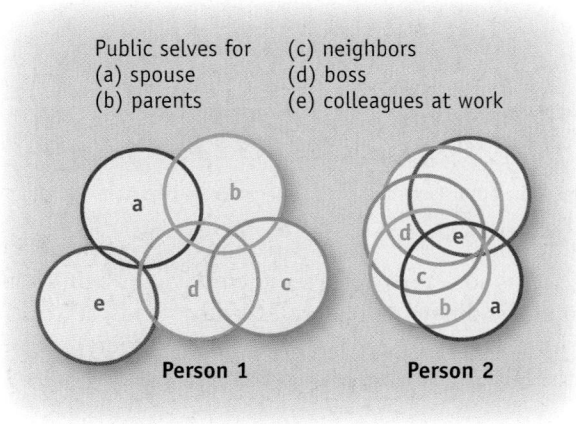

Figure 5.16

Public selves and adjustment. Person 1 has divergent public selves with relatively little overlap among them. Person 2, whose public selves are more congruent with each other, is likely to be better adjusted than Person 1.

Web Link 5.4 **Impression Management**

This short article at TheFreeDictionary.com explains impression management and provides a number of links to other articles on related issues.

you a bit more? Ward and Brenner (2006) found that making negative acknowledgments—candidly admitting to possessing some negative quality—triggered positive responses. In one study, when a hypothetical college student divulged that his high school record was by no means an outstanding one, his grades were judged more favorably than when he did not comment on his academic history. In another study, a speaker from another country was evaluated as having a clearer voice when he pointed out his strong accent than when he failed to do so. Perhaps negative acknowledgment leads people to see one as honest. As long as the quality does not define the person, admitting that one is not perfect, that everyone makes small mistakes, may sometimes be an advantage.

5. *Intimidation.* This strategy sends the message, "Don't mess with me." Intimidation usually works only in nonvoluntary relationships—for instance, when it's hard for workers to find another employer or for an economically dependent spouse to leave a relationship. Obvious intimidation tactics include threats and the withholding of valuable resources (salary increases, promotions, sex). A more subtle tactic is emotional intimidation—holding over a person's head the threat of an aggressive outburst if you don't get your way. The other self-presentation strategies work by creating a favorable impression; intimidation usually generates dislike. Nonetheless, it can work.

6. *Supplication.* This is usually the tactic of last resort. To get favors from others, individuals try to present themselves as weak and dependent—as in the song, "Ain't Too Proud to Beg." Students may plead or break into tears in an instructor's office in an attempt to get a grade changed. Because of the social norm to help those in need, supplication may work; however, unless the supplicator has something to offer the potential benefactor, it's not an effective strategy.

Individuals tailor their use of self-presentation strategies to match the situation. For instance, it's unlikely that you'd try intimidating your boss; you'd be more likely to ingratiate or promote yourself with him or her. As you can see in **Figure 5.17**, all of these strategies carry risks. Thus, to make a good impression, you must use these strategies skillfully.

Perspectives on Impression Management

Curiously, almost all research on self-presentation has been conducted on first meetings between strangers, yet the vast majority of actual social interactions take place between people who already know each other. Noting the gap between reality and research, Dianne Tice and her colleagues (1995) investigated whether self-presentation varied in these two situations. They found that people strive to make positive impressions when they interact with strangers but shift toward modesty and neutral self-presentations when they are with friends. Why the difference? Because strangers don't know you, you want to give them positive information so they'll form a good impression of you. Besides, strangers have no way of knowing whether you are bending the truth. On the other hand, your friends already know your positive qualities. Thus, belaboring them is unnecessary and may make you seem immodest. Likewise, your friends know you well enough to know whether you are grandstanding, so you don't bother. The best approach to managing impressions may be a balanced one. Robinson, Johnson, and Shields (1995) found that people who presented themselves using a mix of self-promoting and self-deprecating comments were viewed as more genuine and likeable than those who relied exclusively on either type of descriptions.

How good are people at discerning the results of their impression management attempts? As we noted earlier, individuals are much better judges of how peo-

Strategic Self-Presentation Strategies

Presentation Strategy	Impression Sought	Emotion to Be Aroused in Target	Negative Impressions Risked
Ingratiation	Likable	Affection	Boot-licker, conformist
Self-promotion	Competent	Respect	Conceited, defensive
Exemplification	Morally superior	Guilt	Hypocrite, sanctimonious
Intimidation	Dangerous	Fear	Blusterer, ineffectual
Supplication	Helpless	Obligation	Undeserving, lazy

Figure 5.17

Strategic self-presentation strategies. Individuals rely on a variety of self-presentation strategies to present a certain image of themselves to others. Five strategies described by Jones (1990) are compared here. A sixth strategy (negative acknowledgment) is also discussed in the text. To avoid the risks associated with the strategies, it's important to use the tactics skillfully. (Based on Jones, 1990) ple, in general, view them than they are of how specific persons evaluate them.

Self-Monitoring

Mark Snyder

Courtesy, Mark Snyder

According to Mark Snyder (1979, 1986; Gangestad & Snyder, 2000), people vary in their awareness of how they are perceived by others. ***Self-monitoring* refers to the degree to which people attend to and control the impressions they make on others.** People who are high self-monitors seem to be very sensitive to their impact on others. Low self-monitors, on the other hand, are less concerned about impression management and behave more spontaneously.

Compared to low self-monitors, high self-monitors want to make a favorable impression and try to tailor their actions accordingly; they are skilled at deciphering what others want to see. In fact, high self-monitors manage their social relations well, earning status from others by offering them aid while avoiding asking for assistance themselves (Flynn et al., 2006). Because they control their emotions well and deliberately regulate nonverbal signals, they are talented at self-presentation (Gangestad & Snyder, 2000). In contrast, low self-monitors are more likely to express their true beliefs or, possibly, to try to convey the impression that they are sincere and genuine individuals.

As you might infer, these two personality types view themselves differently (Gangestad & Snyder, 2000). Low self-monitors see themselves as having strong principles and behaving in line with them, whereas high self-monitors perceive themselves as flexible and pragmatic. Because high self-monitors don't see a necessary connection between their private beliefs and their public actions, they aren't troubled by discrepancies between beliefs and behavior.

In the upcoming Application, we redirect our attention to the critical issue of self-esteem and outline seven steps for boosting it.

APPLICATION

Building Self-Esteem

LEARNING OBJECTIVES

- *Explain when it is inadvisable to increase one's self-esteem and why this is so.*
- *List seven ways to build self-esteem.*

Answer the following "yes" or "no."

___ **1.** I worry that others don't like me.

___ **2.** I have very little confidence in my abilities.

___ **3.** I often feel awkward in social situations and just don't know how to take charge.

___ **4.** I have difficulty accepting praise or flattery.

___ **5.** I have a hard time bouncing back from failure experiences.

If you answered "yes" to most of these questions, you may suffer from low self-esteem. As we noted earlier, people with low self-esteem are less happy and more prone to depression, become demoralized after failures, and are anxious in relationships. Moreover, even people with high global self-esteem may have pockets of low self-esteem. For example, you may feel great about your "social self" but not so good about your "academic self." Thus, this Application can be useful to many people.

We have one caveat, however: It is possible for self-esteem to be too high—recall our earlier discussion about narcissism, ego threats, and violence. Better adjustment is associated with realistically high (and stable) self-esteem. Thus, our suggestions are directed to those whose self-esteem could use a legitimate boost, not to those whose self-esteem is inflated. The latter group can benefit from developing more realistic self-views.

As you saw in our discussion of self-efficacy, there is ample evidence that efforts at self-improvement can

Web Link 5.5 **Building Self-Esteem**

The Counseling Center at the University of Florida offers tips on how to build self-esteem and self-confidence at this website.

pay off by boosting self-esteem. Following are seven guidelines for building self-esteem. These suggestions are distilled from the advice of many experts, including Baumeister et al. (2003), Ellis (1989), McKay and Fanning (2000), Rogers (1977), and Zimbardo (1990).

1. Recognize That You Control Your Self-Image

The first thing you must do is recognize that *you* ultimately control how you see yourself. You *do* have the power to change your self-image. True, we have discussed at length how feedback from others influences your self-concept. Yes, social comparison theory suggests that people need such feedback and that it would be unwise to ignore it completely. However, the final choice about whether to accept or reject such feedback rests with you. Your self-image resides in your mind and is a product of your thinking. Although others may influence your self-concept, you are the final authority.

2. Learn More About Yourself

People with low self-esteem don't seem to know themselves in as much detail as those with high self-esteem. Accordingly, to boost your self-esteem, you need to take stock of yourself. The Recommended Reading titled *Self-Esteem* (McKay & Fanning, 2000) contains a self-concept inventory that includes areas such as physical appearance, personality characteristics, relating to others, school and job performance, intellectual functioning, and sexuality. In taking inventory, you may discover that you're fuzzy about certain aspects of yourself. To get a clearer picture, pay careful attention to your thoughts, feelings, and behavior and utilize feedback from others.

© Jo Hale/Getty Images

If you like singing star Beyoncé, that's fine, but she is not a sensible benchmark for evaluating your attractiveness or success. Some people distort the social comparison process.

Recommended **READING**

Self-Esteem

by Matthew McKay and Patrick Fanning
(New Harbinger Publications, 2000)

If you want to assess, raise, and maintain your self-esteem, this book can help you. The authors work from the premise that everyone has a "pathological critic," an inner voice that is judgmental and fault finding. Some people have an overly active and harsh pathological critic that, over time, erodes self-esteem. The reader is shown how to deal with these destructive self-statements through the use of cognitive restructuring. This book is easily understood, is written in an interesting style, and packs a lot of information in a few pages. It is most useful for those whose self-esteem problems are limited to a specific area (work, parenting, sex, etc.). While the book is also helpful to those whose esteem problems are more serious, the authors suggest that it will be most effective for this group when used along with psychotherapy.

3. Don't Let Others Set Your Goals

A common trap that many people fall into is letting others set the standards by which they evaluate themselves. Others are constantly telling you that you should do this or you ought to do that. Thus, you hear that you "should study computer science" or "ought to lose weight." Most of this advice is well intentioned and may contain good ideas. Still, it is important that you make your *own* decisions about what you will do and what you will believe in. Think about the source of and basis for your personal goals and standards. Do they really represent ideals that *you* value? Or are they beliefs that you have passively accepted from others without thinking?

4. Recognize Unrealistic Goals

Even if you truly value certain ideals and sincerely want to achieve certain goals, another question remains. Are your goals realistic? Many people demand too much of themselves. They want to always perform at their best, which is obviously impossible. For instance, you may have a burning desire to achieve national acclaim as an actress. However, the odds against such an achievement are enormous. It is important to recognize this reality

FRANK AND ERNEST

FRANK & ERNEST reprinted by permission of Newspaper Enterprise Association, Inc.

so that you do not condemn yourself for failure. Some overly demanding people pervert the social comparison process by always comparing themselves against the *best* rather than against similar others. They assess their looks by comparing themselves with famous models, and they judge their finances by comparing themselves with the wealthiest people they know. Such comparisons are unrealistic and almost inevitably undermine self-esteem.

5. Modify Negative Self-Talk

How you think about your life influences how you see yourself (and vice versa). People who are low in self-esteem tend to engage in various counterproductive modes of thinking. For example, when they succeed, they may attribute their success to good luck, and when they fail, they may blame themselves. Quite to the contrary, you should take credit for your successes and consider the possibility that your failures may not be your fault. As discussed in Chapter 4, Albert Ellis has pointed out that people often think irrationally and draw unwarranted negative conclusions about themselves. If someone breaks off a romantic relationship with you, do you think, "He doesn't love me. I must be a worthless, unlovable person?" The conclusion that you are a "worthless person" does *not* follow logically from the fact of the break-up. Such irrational thinking and negative self-talk breed poor self-esteem. Recognize the destructive potential of negative self-talk and bring it to a halt.

6. Emphasize Your Strengths

This advice may seem trite, but it has some merit. People with low self-esteem often derive little satisfaction from their accomplishments and virtues. They pay little heed to their good qualities while talking constantly about their defeats and frailties. The fact is that everyone has strengths and weaknesses. You should accept those personal shortcomings that you are powerless to change and work on those that are changeable, without becoming obsessed about it. At the same time, you should take stock of your strengths and learn to appreciate them.

7. Approach Others with a Positive Outlook

Some people with low self-esteem try to cut others down to their (subjective) size through constant criticism. This faultfinding and negative approach does not go over well. Instead, it leads to tension, antagonism, and rejection. This rejection lowers self-esteem still further (see **Figure 5.18**). You can boost your esteem-building efforts by recognizing and reversing this self-defeating tendency. Cultivate the habit of maintaining a positive, supportive outlook when you approach people. Doing so will promote rewarding interactions and help you earn others' acceptance. There is probably nothing that enhances self-esteem more than acceptance and genuine affection from others.

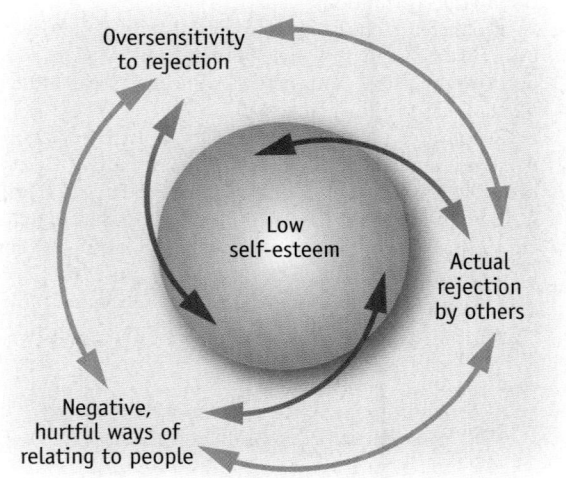

Figure 5.18

The vicious circle of low self-esteem and rejection. A negative self-image can make expectations of rejection a self-fulfilling prophecy, because people with low self-esteem tend to approach others in negative, hurtful ways. Real or imagined rejections lower self-esteem still further, creating a vicious circle.

KEY IDEAS

Self-Concept

▶ The self-concept is composed of a number of beliefs about what one is like, and it is not easily changed. It governs both present and future behavior. Discrepancies between one's ideal self and one's actual or ought self can produce negative emotions and lowered self-esteem. To cope with these negative states, individuals may bring their behavior in line with their ideal selves or blunt their awareness of self-discrepancies.

▶ The self-concept is shaped by several factors, including individuals' observations of their own behavior, which often involve social comparisons with others. Self-observations tend to be biased in a positive direction. In addition, feedback from others shapes the self-concept; this information is also filtered to some extent. Cultural guidelines also affect the way people see themselves. Members of individualistic cultures usually have an independent view of the self, whereas those in collectivist cultures often have an interdependent view of the self.

Self-Esteem

▶ Self-esteem is a person's global evaluation of his or her worth. Like the self-concept, it tends to be stable, but it can fluctuate in response to daily ups and downs.

▶ Compared to those with high self-esteem, individuals with low self-esteem are less happy, are more likely to be depressed, are more prone to giving up after failure, and are less trusting of others.

▶ Narcissistic individuals are prone to aggression when their self-esteem is threatened. Self-esteem develops through interactions with significant others. Self-esteem, ethnicity, and gender interact in complex ways.

Basic Principles of Self-Perception

▶ To avoid being overwhelmed with information, people use automatic processing; for important decisions, they use controlled processing. To explain the causes of their behavior, individuals make self-attributions. Generally, people attribute their behavior to internal or external factors and to stable or unstable factors. Controllability-uncontrollability is another key dimension of self-attributions.

▶ People tend to use either an optimistic explanatory style or a pessimistic explanatory style to understand various events that occur in their lives, and these attributional styles are related to psychological adjustment.

▶ People are guided by four distinct motives in seeking to understand themselves. The self-assessment motive directs people toward accurate feedback about the self. The self-verification motive drives people toward information that matches their current self-views, even though doing so may involve some distortion of reality. The self-improvement motive underlies people's attempts to better themselves. The self-enhancement motive enables people to maintain positive views of themselves.

▶ Common self-enhancement strategies include downward comparisons, the self-serving bias, basking in reflected glory, and self-handicapping.

Self-Regulation

▶ Self-regulation involves setting goals and directing behavior to meet those goals. A key aspect of self-regulation is self-efficacy—an individual's belief that he or she can achieve specific goals. Engaging in self-control can temporarily deplete what appears to be a limited underlying resource. Self-efficacy plays a key role in adjustment and can be learned through mastery experiences, vicarious experiences, persuasion, and positive interpretations of emotional arousal.

▶ Sometimes normal people knowingly do things that are bad for them. These self-defeating actions fall into three categories: deliberate self-destruction, tradeoffs, and counterproductive strategies.

Self-Presentation

▶ Public selves are the various images that individuals project to others. Generally, people try to manage the impressions they make by using a variety of strategies, including ingratiation, self-promotion, negative acknowledgment, exemplification, intimidation, and supplication. High self-monitors seem to be more concerned about making favorable impressions than low self-monitors are.

Application: Building Self-Esteem

▶ The seven building blocks to higher self-esteem are (1) recognize that you control your self-image, (2) learn more about yourself, (3) don't let others set your goals, (4) recognize unrealistic goals, (5) modify negative self-talk, (6) emphasize your strengths, and (7) approach others with a positive outlook.

KEY TERMS

Basking in reflected glory p. 159
Collectivism p. 147
Downward social comparison p. 158
Explanatory style p. 156
External attributions p. 155
Impression management p. 165
Individualism p. 147
Ingratiation p. 165
Internal attributions p. 155
Narcissism p. 151
Possible selves p. 141
Public self p. 164
Reference group p. 144
Self-attributions p. 155
Self-concept p. 141
Self-defeating behaviors p. 163
Self-discrepancy p. 142
Self-efficacy p. 162
Self-enhancement p. 157
Self-esteem p. 148
Self-handicapping p. 160
Self-monitoring p. 167
Self-regulation p. 161
Self-serving bias p. 159
Self-verification theory p. 157
Social comparison theory p. 144

KEY PEOPLE

Albert Bandura pp. 162–163
Roy Baumeister pp. 148, 151
Hazel Markus p. 141
Mark Snyder p. 167

PRACTICE TEST

1. Which of the following statements about the self-concept is false?
   a. It is composed of one dominant belief about the self.
   b. It is composed of many self-beliefs.
   c. It is relatively stable over time.
   d. It influences present as well as future behavior.

2. Mismatches between one's actual and ought selves result in lower self-esteem and:
   a. dejection-related feelings.
   b. agitation-related feelings.
   c. feelings of self-enhancement.
   d. no particular feelings.

3. A person reared in a collectivist culture is likely to have a(n) _____ self-view, whereas a person reared in an individualistic culture is likely to have a(n) _____ self-view.
   a. self-discrepant; self-consistent
   b. self-consistent; self-discrepant
   c. independent; interdependent
   d. interdependent; independent

4. Low self-esteem is associated with:
   a. happiness.
   b. high trust of others.
   c. self-concept confusion.
   d. recovering after failure experiences.

5. Aggression in response to self-esteem threats is more likely to occur in people who are:
   a. high in self-esteem.
   b. low in self-esteem.
   c. narcissistic.
   d. self-defeating.

6. Which of the following is *not* a basic principle of self-perception?
   a. People are "cognitive spenders."
   b. People's explanatory style is related to adjustment.
   c. People want to receive information that is consistent with their self-views.
   d. People want to maintain positive feelings about the self.

7. Keisha is upset when a textbook is stolen, but she feels better after she hears that a classmate's book bag, including her cell phone, was stolen. This is an example of:
   a. the self-serving bias.
   b. basking in reflected glory.
   c. downward comparison.
   d. self-handicapping.

8. Which of the following statements about self-efficacy is true?
   a. It can be developed by persevering through failure until one achieves success.
   b. It is something that one is born with.
   c. It refers to a person's general self-confidence.
   d. It refers to conscious efforts to make a certain impression on others.

9. The self-presentation strategy of ingratiation involves trying to make others:
   a. respect you.
   b. fear you.
   c. feel sorry for you.
   d. like you.

10. Which of the following will *not* help you build higher self-esteem?
   a. Minimizing negative self-talk
   b. Comparing yourself with those who are the best in a given area
   c. Working to improve yourself
   d. Approaching others with positive expectations

Book Companion Website

Visit the Book Companion Website at **academic.cengage.com/psychology/weiten,** where you will find tutorial quizzes, flash cards, and web links for every chapter, a final exam, and more! You can also link to the Psychology Resource Center (accessible directly at **academic.cengage.com/login**) for a range of psychology-related resources.

Personal Explorations Workbook

The following exercises in your *Personal Explorations Workbook* may enhance your self-understanding in relation to issues raised in this chapter. **Questionnaire 5.1:** Self-Monitoring Scale. **Personal Probe 5.1:** How Does Your Self-Concept Compare to Your Self Ideal? **Personal Probe 5.2:** Examining Your Self Evaluation. **Personal Probe 5.3:** Analyzing Your Emerging Self.

ANSWERS

1. a Pages 141–142
2. b Page 143
3. d Pages 147–148
4. c Page 148
5. c Page 151
6. a Pages 154–158
7. c Page 158
8. a Pages 162–163
9. d Page 165
10. b Pages 167–169

CHAPTER 6

Social Thinking and Social Influence

FORMING IMPRESSIONS OF OTHERS
Key Sources of Information
Snap Judgments Versus Systematic Judgments
Attributions
Perceiver Expectations
Cognitive Distortions

LIVING IN TODAY'S WORLD *Beliefs, Revenge, and Intergroup Conflict*
Key Themes in Person Perception

THE PROBLEM OF PREJUDICE
"Old-Fashioned" Versus Modern Discrimination
Causes of Prejudice
Reducing Prejudice

THE POWER OF PERSUASION
The Elements of the Persuasion Process
The Whys of Persuasion

THE POWER OF SOCIAL PRESSURE
Conformity and Compliance Pressures
Pressure from Authority Figures

APPLICATION: SEEING THROUGH COMPLIANCE TACTICS
The Consistency Principle
The Reciprocity Principle
The Scarcity Principle

REVIEW

PRACTICE TEST

You have a new boss at work. Your old boss was let go because of poor performance. The new boss looks very serious. He always wears a white shirt and a conservative tie, and he rarely smiles. Unlike your old boss, who was friendly and joked around a lot, this fellow is very reserved. He rarely even says hello to you when your paths cross in the halls or out in the parking lot. You wonder whether he doesn't like you or just treats everyone that way. Maybe he's just driven by his work. You resolve to ask around the office to see how he acts around your co-workers. You do know that he fired a woman who worked a few doors down the hall. You're not sure why; she seemed nice, always smiling and saying hello. She sure looked like a hard worker. Maybe he thought she was too friendly? The new boss is also not much older than you—in fact, he might be your age. What if he thinks you are not working hard enough? Maybe he feels you should have advanced farther in the company, that you are too nice? Could he be thinking about firing you?

This situation illustrates the process of person perception in everyday life. Everyone asks and answers "why" questions about the people around them. Individuals constantly form impressions to try to make sense of the people they encounter, not only to understand them but also to predict how they will behave. This chapter explores how people form impressions of others, as well as how and why such judgments can be incorrect. Our consideration of social cognition then broadens to examine the problems posed by prejudice. We then look at how others try to influence our beliefs and behavior. To do so, we explore the power of persuasive messages and the social pressures to conform and obey. As you will learn, social thinking and social influence play important roles in personal adjustment.

Forming Impressions of Others

LEARNING OBJECTIVES

- *Cite the five sources of information people use to form impressions of others.*
- *Describe the key differences between snap judgments and systematic judgments.*
- *Define attributions and explain when people are likely to make them.*
- *Describe two expectancies that can distort observer's perceptions.*
- *Describe four important cognitive distortions and how they operate.*
- *Describe some ways in which the process of creating perceptions of others is efficient, selective, and consistent.*

Do you recall the first time you met your roommate? She seemed friendly but a little shy, and perhaps a bit on the neat side, so much so that you wondered whether you two would get along. You like things less structured; not messy, but decidedly lived-in or comfortable. You were worried that you'd have to change your ways, straightening up your space all the time. Happily, once you got to know her better, she warmed up to you and your clutter—now you are close friends. As people interact with others, they constantly engage in ***person perception,* the process of forming impressions of others.** Because impression formation is usually such an easy and automatic process, people are unaware that it is taking place. Nonetheless, the process is a complex one. Let's review some of its essential aspects.

Key Sources of Information

Because you can't read other people's minds, you are dependent on *observations* of others to determine what they are like. In forming impressions of others, people rely on five key sources of observational information: appearance, verbal behavior, actions, nonverbal messages, and situational cues.

1. *Appearance.* Despite the admonition, "You can't judge a book by its cover," people frequently do exactly that. Physical features such as height, weight, skin color, and hair color are some of the cues used to "read" other people. Regardless of their accuracy, beliefs about physical features are used to form impressions of others (Hellström & Tekle, 1994). For example, Americans learn to associate the wearing of eyeglasses with studiousness. Style of dress, clothing or jewelry that designates religious beliefs, body piercings, and tattoos also provide clues about others. Failing to dress appropriately for a job interview can reduce the chances of being hired (Turner-Bowker, 2001).

2. *Verbal behavior.* Another obvious source of information about others is what they say. People form impressions based on what and how much others self-disclose, how often they give advice and ask questions, and how judgmental they are (Berry et al., 1997). If Tanisha speaks negatively about most of the people she knows, you will probably conclude that she is a critical person.

3. *Actions.* Because people don't always tell the truth, you have to rely on their behavior to provide insights about them. For instance, when you learn that Jamal volunteers five hours a week at the local homeless shelter, you are likely to infer that he is a caring person. In impression formation, actions speak louder than words.

4. *Nonverbal messages.* Another key source of information about others is nonverbal communication: facial expressions, eye contact, body language, and gestures (DePaulo & Friedman, 1998; Forrest & Feldman, 2000; Frank & Ekman, 1997). These nonverbal cues provide information about people's emotional states and dispositions. For example, in our culture a bright smile and good eye contact signal friendliness and openness. Also, because people know that verbal behavior is easily manipulated, they often rely on nonverbal cues to determine the truth of what others say (Frank & Ekman, 1997).

5. *Situations.* The setting in which behavior occurs provides crucial information about how to interpret a person's behavior (Ross & Nisbett, 1991; Trope & Gaunt, 2003). For instance, without situational cues (such as being at a wedding versus a funeral), it would be hard to know whether a person crying was happy or sad.

© Spencer Grant/PhotoEdit

In forming impressions of others, people rely on cues such as appearance, actions, and verbal and nonverbal messages, as well as the nature of the situation.

When it comes to drawing inferences about people, one bad piece of information can outweigh or undo a collection of positive characteristics. Social psychological research repeatedly demonstrates that the presence of a trait perceived to be negative (e.g., "untrustworthy") can have more influence on forming people's impressions than several positive qualities ("warm," "open," "friendly," "clever") (Skowronski & Carlston, 1989; Vonk, 1993). When an immoral act is performed, other good or virtuous behaviors cannot undo the damage to people's perceptions of the offender's character (Riskey & Birnbaum, 1974). In fact, a single bad deed can eliminate a good reputation, but one good deed cannot redeem an otherwise bad standing in the eyes of others (Skowronski & Carlston, 1992). Thus, in the realm of person perception *bad tends to be stronger than good.*

Snap Judgments Versus Systematic Judgments

In their interactions with others, people are bombarded with more information than they can possibly handle. To avoid being overwhelmed, they rely on alternative ways to process information. *Snap judgments* about others are those made quickly and based on only a few bits of information and preconceived notions. Thus, they may not be particularly accurate. Nevertheless, people can get by with superficial assessments of others quite often. As Susan Fiske (2004) puts it, "good-enough accuracy in forming impressions allows us to navigate our social seas and not collide or run aground too often" (p. 132). Often, interactions with others are so fleeting or inconsequential that it makes little difference that such judgments are imprecise. Does it really matter that you mistakenly infer that the blonde postal clerk is a fun-loving person, or that your bespectacled restaurant server is an intellectual? You may never interact with them again, and even if you do, your interactions are not likely to be significant to either of you.

Courtesy, Susan Fiske

Susan Fiske

On the other hand, when it comes to selecting a friend, a mate, a boss, or an employee, it's essential that your impressions be as accurate as possible. Thus, it's not surprising that people are motivated to take more care in these assessments. In forming impressions of those who can affect their welfare and happiness, people make *systematic judgments* rather than snap decisions (see **Figure 6.1**). That is, they take the time to observe the person in a variety of situations and to compare that person's behavior with that of others in similar situations.

In assessing what a significant individual is like, people are particularly interested in learning why the person behaves in a certain way. This deeper level of understanding is vital if one is to make accurate predictions about the person's future behavior. After all, when you're choosing a partner for an important group project, you want to choose the right person so that you don't end up doing all the work yourself. How do people make such decisions? What information do they consider? To determine the cause of others' behavior, people engage in the process of causal attribution.

Attributions

As we have noted in earlier chapters, ***attributions* are inferences that people draw about the causes of their own behavior, others' behavior, and events.** In Chapter 5, we focused on self-attributions. Here, we'll apply attribution theory to the behavior of *other people.* For example, suppose that your boss bawls you out for

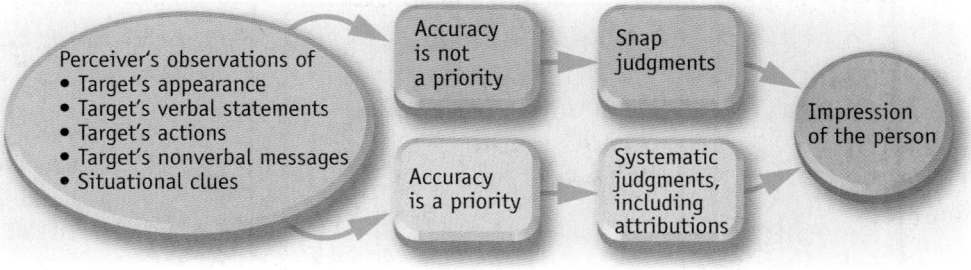

Figure 6.1

The process of person perception. In forming impressions of others, perceivers rely on various sources of observational information. When it's important to form accurate impressions of others, people are motivated to make systematic judgments, including attributions. When accuracy isn't a priority, people make snap judgments about others.

Adapted from Brehm, S. S., & Kassin, S. M. (1993) *Social psychology*. Boston: Houghton Mifflin. Copyright © 1993 by Houghton Mifflin Company. Adapted with permission.

doing a sloppy job on an insignificant project. To what do you attribute this tongue lashing? Was your work really that bad? Is your boss just in a grouchy mood? Is your boss under too much pressure?

In Chapter 5, we noted that attributions have three key dimensions: internal versus external, stable versus unstable, and controllable versus uncontrollable (Jones & Davis, 1965; Kelley, 1950; Weiner, 1974). For this discussion, we focus only on the internal/external dimension (Heider, 1958). When people ascribe the causes of someone's behavior to personal dispositions, traits, abilities, or feelings, they are making *internal* attributions. When they impute the causes of their behavior to situational demands and environmental constraints, they are making *external* attributions. For example, if a friend's business fails, you might attribute the failure to your friend's lack of business skills (an internal factor) or to negative trends in the economy (an external factor).

The types of attributions people make about others can have a tremendous impact on everyday social interactions. For example, blaming a friend's business failure on poor business "smarts" rather than on a poor economy will obviously affect how you view your friend—not to mention whether you'll lend her money! In fact, there is evidence that spouses' attributions for each other's behavior can affect their marital satisfaction (Fletcher & Thomas, 2000; Karney & Bradbury 2000).

Obviously, people don't make attributions about every person they meet. Research suggests that people are relatively selective in this process (Jones, 1990; Malle, 2004; Malle & Knobe, 1997). It seems that people are most likely to make attributions (1) when others behave in unexpected or negative ways, (2) when events are personally relevant, and (3) when they are suspicious about another person's motives. For example, if Serena laughs loudly at the local student hangout, no one bats an eye. But if she does so in the middle of a serious lecture, it raises eyebrows and generates speculation about why she behaved this way.

Some aspects of the attribution process are logical (Trope & Gaunt, 2003). Nonetheless, research also shows that the process of person perception is sometimes illogical and unsystematic, as in the case of snap judgments. Other sources of error also creep into the process, a topic we take up next.

Perceiver Expectations

Remember Evan, that bully from the fourth grade? He made your life miserable—constantly looking for opportunities to poke fun at you and beat you up. Now when you meet someone named Evan, your initial reaction is negative, and it takes a while to warm up to him (Andersen & Chen, 2002). Why? Your negative past experiences with an Evan have led you to expect the worst, whether or not it's warranted (Andersen, Reznik, & Manzella, 1996). This is just one example of how *perceiver expectations* can influence the perception of others. Let's look at two of the principles governing perceiver expectations: confirmation bias and self-fulfilling prophecy.

Confirmation Bias

Shortly after you begin interacting with someone, you start forming hypotheses about what the person is like. In turn, these hypotheses can influence your behavior toward that person in such a way as to confirm your ex-

Web Link 6.1 **Social Psychology Network**

Wesleyan University social psychologist Scott Plous offers a broad collection of more than 5,000 web links related to all aspects of social and general psychology, including how people understand and influence each other interpersonally.

DILBERT © Scott Adams. Distributed by permission of United Feature Syndicate, Inc.

pectations. Thus, if on your first encounter with Xavier he has a camera around his neck, you will probably hypothesize that he has an interest in photography and question him selectively about his shutterbug activities. You might also neglect to ask more wide-ranging questions that would give you a more accurate picture of him. ***Confirmation bias* is the tendency to seek information that supports one's beliefs while not pursuing disconfirming information.**

Confirmation bias is a well-documented phenomenon (Dougherty, Turban, & Callendar, 1994; Nickerson, 1998; Snyder & Swann, 1978). It occurs in casual social interactions as well as in job interviews and in courtrooms, where the interviewer or attorney may ask leading questions (Fiske & Taylor, 1991). When it comes to forming first impressions of others, the principle is not so much that "seeing is believing" but rather that "believing is seeing" (see **Figure 6.2**).

Confirmation bias also occurs because individuals selectively recall facts to fit their views of others. In one experiment (Cohen, 1981), participants watched a videotape of a woman engaging in a variety of activities, including listening to classical music, drinking beer, and watching TV. Half of them were told that the woman was a waitress and the other half were told that she was a librarian. When asked to recall the woman's actions on the videotape, participants tended to remember activities consistent with their stereotypes of waitresses and librarians. Thus, those who thought that the woman was a waitress recalled her drinking beer; those who thought she was a librarian recalled her listening to classical music.

Can a confirmation bias be used to characterize perceptions of group behaviors as well as individual actions? Apparently so. A recent study considered whether confirmation bias is linked to the pervasive belief in a sexual double standard, namely that men are rewarded for sexual activity while women are derogated for it (Marks & Fraley, 2006). Think about it: In our culture, isn't promiscuity sometimes praised (or at least ignored) when men engage in it? However, women run the risk of losing their reputations if they become known to have a variety of sexual partners. Participants in the study by Marks and Fraley (2006) read brief accounts about either a target male or female that contained an equal number of positive and negative observations about the individual's sexual behavior. Despite perceived advances in sexual equality and living in a society that is increasingly open-minded about sexual behavior, people were more likely to recall information that "confirmed" the double standard (pro-male, anti-female) than contradicted it. In other words, "boys will be boys" and they can get away with being promiscuous, but women cannot without sullying their reputations.

Normally, people remain unaware of the biases in their perceptions. They go blithely along, assuming that their version of reality is accurate. And, most of the time, this approach works (Fiske, 1993). It's only when someone disagrees that a perceiver is brought up short.

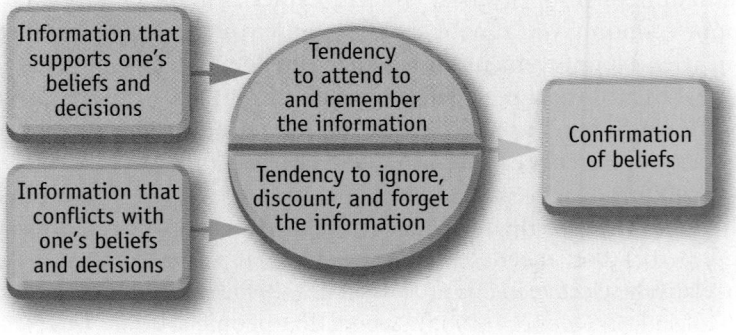

Figure 6.2

Confirmation bias. Confirmation bias is a two-pronged process in which people seek and remember information that supports their beliefs while discounting and forgetting information that is inconsistent with their beliefs. This common cognitive slant often distorts the process of person perception, leading to inaccurate impressions of people.

When this happens, the individual may alter his or her views, conclude that the other person's perception is "off," or look for another satisfactory explanation for the difference in perceptions.

Self-Fulfilling Prophecies

Sometimes a perceiver's expectations can actually change another person's behavior. **A *self-fulfilling prophecy* occurs when expectations about a person cause the person to behave in ways that confirm the expectations.** This term was originally coined by sociologist Robert Merton (1948) to explain such phenomena as "runs" on banks that occurred during the Depression. That is, when unfounded rumors would circulate that a bank couldn't cover its deposits, people would rush to the bank and withdraw their funds, thereby draining the deposits from the bank and making real what was initially untrue.

Figure 6.3 depicts the three steps in the self-fulfilling prophecy. First, the perceiver has an initial impression of someone. (A teacher believes that Jennifer is highly intelligent.) Then the perceiver behaves toward the target person in line with his or her expectations. (He asks her interesting questions and praises her answers.) The third step occurs when the target person adjusts his or her behavior to the perceiver's actions, which confirms the perceiver's hypothesis about the target person. (Jennifer performs well in class.) Note that both individuals are unaware that this process is operating. Also note that because perceivers are unaware of their expectations and of the effect they can have on others, they mistakenly attribute the target person's behavior to an internal cause (Jennifer is smart), rather than an external one (their own expectations).

The best-known experiments on the self-fulfilling prophecy have been conducted in classroom settings, looking at the effect of teachers' expectations on students' academic performance (Rosenthal, 1985). A review of 400 studies of this phenomenon over a period of 30 years reported that teacher expectations significantly influenced student performance in 36% of the experiments. When found in the classroom, however, the effect is typically relatively small, and its broader impact (Is it ever a bad thing? Does it enhance intelligence?) remains unclear (Jussim & Harber, 2005). The self-fulfilling prophecy also operates with adults and in noneducational settings such as the military, factories and businesses, courtrooms, and physicians' offices (Ambady et al., 2002; Halverson et al., 1997; Kierein & Gold, 2000; Rosenthal, 2003).

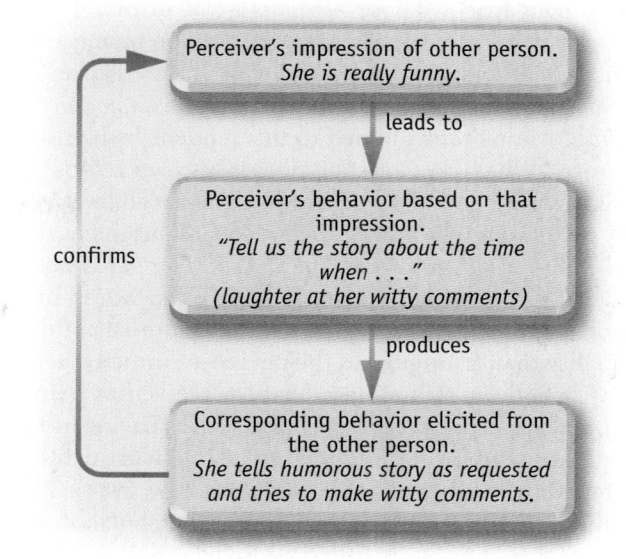

Figure 6.3

The three steps of the self-fulfilling prophecy. Through a three-step process, your expectations about a person can cause that person to behave in ways that confirm those expectations. First, you form an impression of someone. Second, you behave toward that person in a way that is consistent with your impression. Third, the person exhibits the behavior that you encourage, which confirms your initial impression.

Adapted from Smith, E. R., & Mackie, D. M. (1995). *Social psychology*. New York: Worth, p. 103. Copyright © 1995 Worth Publishing. Reprinted with permission.

Cognitive Distortions

Another source of error in person perception comes from distortions in the minds of perceivers. These errors in judgment are most likely to occur when a perceiver is in a hurry, is distracted, or is not motivated to pay careful attention to another person.

Social Categorization

One of the ways people efficiently process information is to classify objects (and people) according to their distinctive features (Fiske, 1998). Thus, people quite often categorize others on the basis of nationality, race, ethnicity, gender, age, religion, sexual orientation, and so forth (Crisp & Hewstone, 2006). People frequently take the easy path of categorizing others to avoid expending the cognitive effort that would be necessary for a more accurate impression.

People perceive others who are similar to them to be members of their *ingroup* ("us") and those who are dissimilar to them, in the *outgroup* ("them"). Such categorizing has three important results. First, people usually have less favorable attitudes toward outgroup members than ingroup members (Brewer & Brown, 1998), such that empathic reactions to those perceived to be in their ingroup are often exaggerated (Brown, Bradley, & Lang, 2006). Second, individuals usually see outgroup members as being much more alike than they really are, whereas they see members of their ingroup as unique individuals (Oakes, 2001). In other words, people frequently explain the behavior of outgroup members on the basis of the characteristic that sets them apart ("Those *Nerdians* are *all* drunks"), but attribute the same behavior by an ingroup member to individual personality traits ("*Brett* is a heavy drinker"). This phenomenon is termed the *outgroup homogeneity effect.* Anne Frank alluded to this tendency when she wrote, "What one Christian does is his own responsibility, what one Jew does is thrown back at all Jews."

A third result of categorizing is that it heightens the visibility of outgroup members when there are only a few of them within a larger group. In other words, minority group status in a group makes more salient the quality that distinguishes the person—ethnicity, gender, whatever. When people are perceived as being unique or distinctive, they are also seen as having more influence in a group, and their good and bad qualities are given extra weight (Crocker & McGraw, 1984). Significantly, distinctiveness—some quality that makes one person stand out from others—also triggers stereotyping when it becomes linked with particular behaviors. This phenomenon explains why many people notice assertive women (but not men), noisy blacks (but not whites), and jolly fat (but not thin) people.

Stereotypes

***Stereotypes* are widely held beliefs that people have certain characteristics because of their membership in a particular group.** For example, many people assume that Jews are shrewd and ambitious, that African Americans have special athletic and musical abilities, and that Muslims are religious fanatics. Although a kernel of truth may underlie some stereotypes, it should be readily apparent that not all Jews, African Americans, Muslims, and so forth behave alike. If you take the time to think about it, you recognize that there is enormous diversity in behavior within any group.

The most prevalent stereotypes in America are those based on gender, age, and ethnicity (Fiske, 1993). Gender stereotypes, although in transition, remain pervasive. For example, in a study of gender stereotypes in 30 countries, males were typically characterized as adventurous, powerful, and independent, while females were characterized as sentimental, submissive, and superstitious (Williams & Best, 1982, 1990). Because of their wide-ranging significance, we cover gender stereotypes in detail in Chapter 10, on gender.

Stereotypes may also be based on physical appearance. In particular, there is plenty of evidence that physically attractive people are believed to have desirable personality traits. This widespread perception is termed the *"what-is-beautiful-is-good" stereotype* (Dion, Berscheid, & Walster, 1972). Specifically, beautiful people are usually viewed as more socially competent, more assertive, better adjusted, and more intellectually competent than those who are less attractive (Eagly et al., 1991). Yet most of these perceptions have little basis in fact.

Web Link 6.2 **Social Cognition Paper Archive and Information Center**

Eliot R. Smith at Indiana University maintains a popular site that includes information about papers (abstracts, mostly) and people and that links to the wider social psychological research community.

Attractive people *do* have an advantage in the social arena. For example, they have better social skills, are more popular, are less socially anxious (especially about interactions with the other gender), are less lonely, and are more sexually experienced (Feingold, 1992b). However, they are not any different from others in intelligence, happiness, mental health, or self-esteem (Feingold, 1992b; Langlois et al., 2000). Thus, attractive people are perceived in a more favorable light than is actually justified. Unfortunately, the positive biases toward attractive people also operate in reverse. Thus, unattractive people are unjustifiably seen as less well adjusted and less intellectually competent than others. Most Americans believe that good looks are an advantage in everyday life (see **Figure 6.4**).

How does the attractiveness stereotype affect most people, including you and me? First, the bad news: Highly attractive people end up with one another (all else being equal, a perfect "10" might marry a "9," for example, but is unlikely to pair off with a "4" or a "5"). If there is any solace we can take, it's this: Most of us pair up with people who match our own level of attractiveness ("2s" find each other—and hopefully happiness—as do "7s"). Thus, we are likely to date those who match our own level of attractiveness (Berscheid et al., 1971). In fact, the correlation between lovers' respective levels of attractiveness is fairly robust (Feingold, 1988). Interestingly, close to the same level of association in rated appearance is found between male friends. Thus, we may not know it, but the attractiveness stereotype already has an effect in our lives—or it will at some point.

Stereotypes can be spontaneously triggered when people encounter members of commonly stereotyped groups—even in those who are not prejudiced (Devine, 1989; Dunning & Sherman, 1997). Worse still, racially based stereotypes can cause regrettable—and potentially dangerous—split-second decisions where people see a weapon when none is actually there (Payne, 2006). Stereotypes can exist outside a person's awareness (Bodenhausen, Macrae, & Hugenberg, 2003; Greenwald & Banaji, 1995). Because stereotyping is automatic, some psychologists are pessimistic about being able to control it (Bargh, 1999); others take a more optimistic view (Uleman et al., 1996). For example, a recent study found less automatic race bias when people were surreptitiously induced to smile while looking at photo-

Most Americans Believe Good Looks Are an Advantage

Poll Question	"Fairly important" or "Very important" answers			
"How important do you think a person's physical attractiveness is in our society today in terms of his or her happiness, social life, and ability to get ahead?"	Year	Men	Women	Total
	1990	82%	85%	84%
	1999	76%	76%	76%

Figure 6.4

Physical attractiveness as a social advantage. A Gallup poll reported that a large majority of men and women believe that physical attractiveness is an advantage when it comes to happiness, social life, and the ability to get ahead. Affirmative responses to the poll question decreased a little between 1990 and 1999, but it is clear that most people continue to believe that good looks are advantageous.

Data from Newport, F. (1999, September 15), *Americans agree that being attractive is a plus in American society.* Retrieved June 10, 2001 from http://gallup.com/poll/releases/pr990915.

graphs of blacks (Ito et al., 2006). If people put forth effort to respond in a friendly and open manner to individuals who are different from them on some important dimension (race, sexual orientation), perhaps the positive behaviors will lead to a reduction in automatic biases when reacting to others.

Why do stereotypes persist? For one thing, they are cognitively functional (Quinn, Macrae, & Bodenhausen, 2003). Recall that people are "cognitive misers." Because they are deluged with much more information than they can process, the tendency is to reduce complexity to simplicity. But, as we noted earlier, the tradeoff for simplification is inaccuracy. Stereotypes also endure because of confirmation bias. Thus, when individuals encounter members of groups that they view with prejudice, they are likely to see what they expect to see. The self-fulfilling prophecy is a third reason stereotypes persist: Beliefs about another person may actually elicit the anticipated behavior and confirm biased expectations.

The Fundamental Attribution Error

When explaining the causes of others' behavior, people invoke personal attributions and discount the importance of situational factors. Although this tendency is not universal (Choi, Nisbett, & Norenzayan, 1999; Miyamoto & Kitayama, 2002), it is strong enough that Lee Ross (1977) called it the "*fundamental* attribution error." **The *fundamental attribution error* refers to the tendency to explain other people's behavior as the result of personal, rather than situational, factors.**

This tendency (sometimes termed *correspondence bias;* Jones, 1990) differs from stereotyping in that inferences are based on actual behavior. Nonetheless, those inferences may still be inaccurate. If Jeremy leaves class early, you may be correct in inferring that he is inconsiderate, but he might also have had a previously scheduled job interview. Thus, a person's behavior at a given time may or may not reflect his or her personality—but observers tend to assume that it does. The situations people encounter can have profound effects on their behavior, often overpowering the influence of their dispositions—they just don't realize it (Ross & Ward, 1996).

What's behind this tendency to discount situational influences on people's behavior? Once again, the culprit is people's tendency to be cognitive misers. It seems that making attributions is a two-step process (Gilbert & Malone, 1995). As you can see in **Figure 6.5** (on the next page), in the first step, which occurs automatically, observers make an internal attribution because they are focusing on the person rather than the situation. (At your bank, if you observe the man ahead of you yell at the teller, you might infer that he is a hostile person.) In the second step, observers weigh the impact of the situation on the target person's behavior and adjust their inference. (If you overhear the customer say that this is the third time in three weeks that the bank has made the same error in his account, you're likely to temper your initial judgment about his hostile tendencies.)

The first step in the attribution process occurs spontaneously, but the second step requires cognitive effort and attention. Thus, it is easy to stop after step one—especially, if one is in a hurry or distracted. Failure to take the effortful second step can result in the fundamental attribution error. However, when people are motivated to form accurate impressions of others (Webster, 1993) or when they are suspicious about another's motives (Fein, 1996), they do expend the effort to complete the second step. In these cases, they are more likely to make accurate attributions. Some evidence suggests that these two steps may be related to different types of brain activity (Lieberman et al., 2004). Unfortunately, much of the time people are busy with their work and social lives, as well as preoccupied with their own thoughts, plans, and actions, which severely limits opportunities for attributional corrections while perceiving the intentions and behavior of others (Geeraert et al., 2004; Gilbert, 2002). Only when people are forced or seriously motivated to do a thorough analysis of possible causes for the behavior of another or others can they reduce the impact of the fundamental attribution error.

Cultural values seem to promote different attributional errors. In *individualistic* cultures, where independence is valued, it is assumed that people are responsible for their actions. In *collectivist* societies, conformity and obedience to group norms are valued, so it is assumed that one's behavior reflects adherence to group norms (see Chapter 5). Some experts specu-

Figure 6.5

Explaining the fundamental attribution error. People automatically take the first step in the attribution process (making a personal attribution). However, they often fail to take the second step (considering the possible influence of situational factors on a person's behavior) because that requires extra effort. The failure to consider situational factors causes observers to exaggerate the role of personal factors in behavior—that is, they make the fundamental attribution error. (Adapted from Brehm, Kassin, & Fein, 2002)

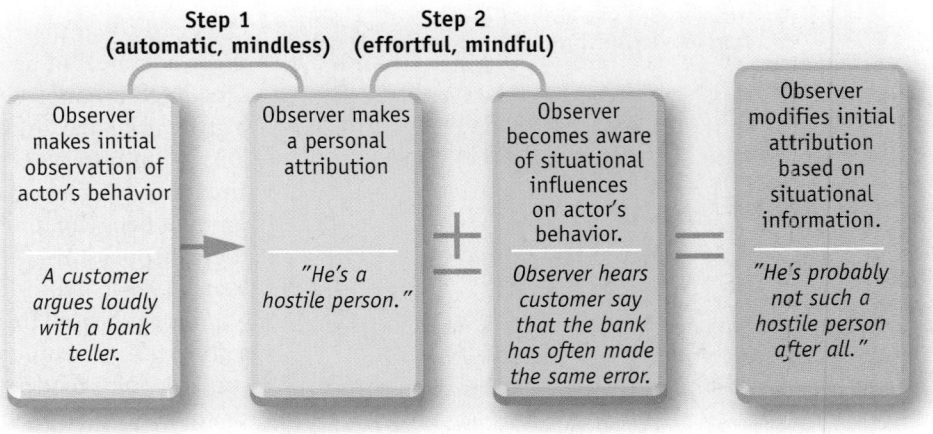

late that different styles of thinking underlie cultural differences in attributional styles (Nisbett et al., 2001; Nisbett & Miyamoto, 2005). They suggest that the Western mentality is *analytical* (attention is focused on an object, and causality is ascribed to it), whereas the East Asian mentality is *holistic* (attention is focused on the field surrounding an object, and causality is understood to reside in the relationship between the object and its field) (Masuda & Nisbett, 2006; Miyamoto, Nisbett, & Masuda, 2006). Consistent with both of these views, researchers have found that Americans explain others' behavior in terms of internal attributions more often than Hindus (Miller, 1984), Chinese (Chua, Leu, & Nisbett, 2005; Morris & Peng, 1994), Japanese (Weisz, Rothbaum, & Blackburn, 1984), or Koreans (Choi et al., 2003; Norenzayan, Choi, & Nisbett, 2002).

Defensive Attribution

Observers are especially likely to make internal attributions in trying to explain the calamities and tragedies that befall other people. Examples easily come to mind. When a woman is abused by a boyfriend or husband, people frequently blame the victim by remarking how stupid she is to stay with the man, rather than condemning the aggressor for his behavior (Summers & Feldman, 1984). Similarly, rape victims are often judged to have "asked for it" (Abrams et al., 2003).

***Defensive attribution* is a tendency to blame victims for their misfortune, so that one feels less likely to be victimized in a similar way.** Blaming victims for their calamities also helps people maintain their belief that they live in a "just world" where people get what they deserve and deserve what they get (Lerner, 1980, 1998). Acknowledging that the world is not just—that unfortunate events can happen as a result of chance factors—would mean having to admit the frightening possibility that the catastrophes that happen to others could also happen to oneself (Lambert, Burroughs, & Nguyen, 1999), especially when the victim is perceived to be like oneself (Correia, Vala, & Aguiar, 2007). Defensive attributions are a self-protective, but irrational, strategy that allows people to avoid such unnerving thoughts and helps them feel in control of their lives (Hafer, 2000; Lipkus, Dalbert, & Siegler, 1996). Unfortunately, when victims are blamed for their setbacks, people unfairly attribute undesirable traits to them, such as incompetence, foolishness, and laziness.

© Andrew Holbrooke/The Image Works

A common example of defensive attribution is the tendency to blame the homeless for their plight.

LIVING IN TODAY'S WORLD

Beliefs, Revenge, and Intergroup Conflict

Knowing that terrorist attacks could come at any time and in any location in the country disturbs Americans' sense of control over their own and their loved ones' safety (Unger, 2006). This experience strikes at a fundamental need to see one's world as stable and predictable (Greenberg, Solomon, & Pyszczynski, 1997). A foundation of this need for order is the *belief in a just world (BJW)*. As we discuss elsewhere in this chapter, this belief is the idea that good things happen to good people and bad things happen to bad people. Individuals differ on how strongly they endorse BJW. Compared to weak endorsers, strong endorsers are more likely to have an internal locus of control (believe that their fate is under their own control versus chance), to espouse the Protestant work ethic, and to be more authoritarian and more politically conservative (Furnham & Procter, 1989).

Having to face incontrovertible evidence that the world is not just (the 9/11 attacks, for example) triggers fear, stress, and vulnerability, especially among strong endorsers of BJW. One way for people to deal with these painful feelings is to restore justice cognitively—by persuading themselves that the victims of tragedies actually deserve their fate (because they are "bad" people). These defensive attributions help individuals maintain the comforting, but false, belief that nothing bad will happen to them (because they are "good" people). "Blaming the victim" is reduced when individuals identify with the victim. For example, because the 9/11 attacks were perceived as an attack against the United States (versus an individual or a group), Americans identified and sympathized with the victims of the 9/11 attacks rather than blaming them.

A second response to challenges to BJW is to seek revenge—to punish those responsible for the perceived injustice (and for threatening their BJW). If the perpetrators can be punished, justice can be restored (when bad things do happen to good people, the perpetrators will get what they deserve). A recent study investigated the psychological dynamics involved in BJW after the 9/11 events (Kaiser, Vick, & Major, 2004). Prior to the 9/11 attacks, participants (college students) completed a measure of BJW. Several months after 9/11, the subjects were assessed on a number of measures, including terrorism-related distress and the desire for revenge. The more strongly participants endorsed BJW, the more distressed they were about the attacks and the more they desired revenge against the terrorists.

Contrary to popular opinion, most terrorists are not deranged; rather, they are usually enraged young males seeking revenge for perceived injustices (Silke, 2003). Therefore, it seems likely that some terrorists would have strong beliefs in a just world. Although we deplore the acts of terrorists, it is possible to understand their actions as attempts to seek revenge for perceived injustices perpetrated by other countries.

When some people feel vulnerable, they engage in aggression (revenge) to feel less vulnerable. The shocking acts committed by American soldiers at the Abu Ghraib prison in Iraq are regrettable evidence that ordinary people can commit evil actions when situational pressures are present (Fiske, Harris, & Cuddy, 2004). Unfortunately, large-scale military strikes against terrorism can actually increase terrorist behavior when they "unwittingly reinforce terrorists' views of their enemies as aggressive, make it easier for terrorist groups to recruit new members, and strengthen alliances among terrorist organizations" (Plous & Zimbardo, 2004, p. B9). Ironically and tragically, engaging in vengeful aggression to reduce feelings of vulnerability may actually increase vulnerability when it perpetuates intergroup conflict.

Key Themes in Person Perception

The process of person perception is a complex one. Nonetheless, we can detect three recurrent themes in this process: efficiency, selectivity, and consistency.

Efficiency

In forming impressions of others, people prefer to exert no more cognitive effort or time than is necessary. Thus, much social information is processed automatically and effortlessly. According to Susan Fiske (1993), people are like government bureaucrats, who "only bother to gather information on a 'need to know' basis" (p. 175). Efficiency has two important advantages: People can make judgments quickly, and it keeps things simple. The big disadvantage is that judgments are error-prone. Still, on balance, efficiency works pretty well as an operating principle.

Selectivity

The old saying that "people see what they expect to see" has been confirmed repeatedly by social scientists. In a classic study, Harold Kelley (1950) showed how a person is preceded by his or her reputation. Students in a class at the Massachusetts Institute of Technology were told that a new lecturer would be speaking to them that day. Before the instructor arrived, the students were given a short description of him, with one important variation. Half the students were led to expect a "warm" person, while the other half were led to expect a "cold" one (see **Figure 6.6**). All the participants were exposed to exactly the same 20 minutes of lecture and interaction with the new instructor. However, those who were led to expect a warm person rated the instructor as significantly more considerate, sociable, humorous, good-natured, informal, and humane than those who were led to expect a cold person.

Mr. Blank is a graduate student in the Department of Economics and Social Science here at M.I.T. He has had three semesters of teaching experience in psychology at another college. This is his first semester teaching Ec. 70. He is 26 years old, a veteran, and married. People who know him consider him to be a rather cold person, industrious, critical, practical, and determined.	Mr. Blank is a graduate student in the Department of Economics and Social Science here at M.I.T. He has had three semesters of teaching experience in psychology at another college. This is his first semester teaching Ec. 70. He is 26 years old, a veteran, and married. People who know him consider him to be a very warm person, industrious, critical, practical, and determined.

Figure 6.6

Descriptions of the guest lecturer in Kelley's (1950) study. These two descriptions, provided to two groups of students before the lecturer spoke, differ by only an adjective. But this seemingly small difference caused the two groups to form altogether different perceptions of the lecturer.

Consistency

How many times did your parents remind you to be on your best behavior when you were meeting someone for the first time? As it turns out, they were onto something! Considerable research supports the idea that first impressions are powerful (Asch, 1956; Belmore, 1987). **A *primacy effect* occurs when initial information carries more weight than subsequent information.** We risk being labeled a hypocrite, for example, if we say one thing and then do another (such as claiming to have an open mind and then make a cutting, judgmental remark about someone) rather than the reverse (Barden, Rucker, & Petty, 2005). Initial negative impressions may be especially hard to change (Mellers, Richards, & Birnbaum, 1992). Thus, getting off on the wrong foot may be particularly damaging. As noted earlier in this chapter, negative information can outweigh positive factors; bad can indeed be stronger than good. Only if people are motivated to form an accurate impression and are not tired will they be less likely to lock in their initial impressions (Webster, Richter, & Kruglanski, 1996).

Why are primacy effects so potent? Because people find comfort in cognitive *consistency;* cognitions that contradict each other tend to create tension and discomfort. This principle applies to people's perceptions of others. Hence, once people believe that they have formed an accurate picture of someone, they tend to tune out or discount subsequent information that seems to contradict that picture (Belmore, 1987). It is not impossible to override an initial impression, but the built-in preference for consistency makes it more difficult than most people realize.

To conclude, although the process of person perception is highly subjective, people are relatively accurate perceivers of others (Fiske, 1998). Even when misperceptions occur, they are often harmless. However, there clearly are occasions when such inaccuracies are problematic. This is certainly true in the case of prejudice, which we consider next.

The Problem of Prejudice

LEARNING OBJECTIVES

- *Explain how "old-fashioned" and modern discrimination differ.*
- *Describe some of the key determinants of prejudice, and explain how they work.*
- *Describe the operation of several strategies for reducing prejudice.*

The terrorist attacks of September 11, 2001 were an extreme demonstration of the destructive power of prejudice—hatred of one group by another. Unfortunately, antagonism between groups continues to be a problem, both on the international scene and at home. For example, after the September 11 attacks, hate crimes increased against Americans presumed to be Muslims or Arabs. Why is it so hard for members of different groups to get along?

Let's begin our discussion by clarifying a couple of terms that are often confused. ***Prejudice* is a negative attitude toward members of a group; *discrimination***

Discrimination	Prejudice: Absent	Prejudice: Present
Absent	No relevant behavior	A restaurant owner who is bigoted against Hispanics treats them fairly because she needs their business.
Present	An executive with favorable attitudes toward blacks doesn't hire them because he would get in trouble with his boss.	A professor who is hostile toward women grades his female students unfairly.

Figure 6.7

Prejudice and discrimination. Prejudice and discrimination are highly correlated, but they don't necessarily go hand in hand. As the examples in the blue cells show, there can be prejudice without discrimination and discrimination without prejudice.

involves behaving differently, usually unfairly, toward the members of a group. Prejudice and discrimination do tend to go together, but that is not always the case (see **Figure 6.7**). One classic social psychology study found almost no discriminatory behavior aimed at a Chinese couple traveling around the country with a white professor in the 1930s. Before making the trips, the professor anticipated that they would encounter some prejudice about where they could stay or dine, but they were only declined service a few times. When the professor wrote to all the establishments they visited months later to ask whether Chinese guests were welcome, however, the majority of the responses were, in fact, prejudiced and rather uninviting, showing that attitudes don't always predict behavior (LaPiere, 1934). Why can people respond in discriminatory ways sometimes but not always? It is possible that a restaurant owner would be prejudiced against Chicanos and yet treat them like anyone else because he needed their business. This is an example of prejudice without discrimination. Although it is probably less common, discrimination without prejudice may also occur. For example, an executive who has favorable attitudes toward blacks may not hire them because he thinks his boss would be upset.

"Old-Fashioned" Versus Modern Discrimination

Over the past 40 years, prejudice and discrimination against minority groups have diminished in the United States. Racial segregation is no longer legal, and discrimination based on race, ethnicity, gender, and religion is much less common than it was in the 1950s and 1960s. Thus, the good news is that overt, or *"old-fashioned," discrimination* against minority groups has declined. The bad news is that a more subtle form of prejudice and discrimination has emerged (Dovidio & Gaertner, 1996; Gaertner & Dovidio, 1986). That is, people may privately harbor racist or sexist attitudes but express them only when they feel that such views are justified or that it's safe to do so. This new phenomenon has been termed *modern discrimination* (also called "modern racism"). Modern discrimination is also operating when people endorse equality as an abstract principle but oppose concrete programs intended to promote equality on the grounds that discrimination against minority groups no longer exists (Wright & Taylor, 2003). In **Figure 6.8**, you can see the kinds of items used to measure old-fashioned and modern sexism.

While modern racists do not wish to return to the days of segregation, they also feel that minority groups should not push too fast for advancement or receive special treatment by the government. Individuals who endorse statements that favor "modern" discrimination ("Blacks are getting too demanding in their push for equal rights") are much

Items Related to Old-Fashioned Sexism

1. Women are generally not as smart as men.
2. It is more important to encourage boys than to encourage girls to participate in athletics.

Items Related to Modern Sexism

1. Discrimination against women is no longer a problem in the United States.
2. Over the past few years, the government and news media have been showing more concern about the treatment of women than is warranted by women's actual experiences.

Scoring: Possible responses to the statements range from "strongly agree" to "strongly disagree." Individuals who moderately or strongly agree with the above items reflect old-fashioned or modern sexism, respectively.

Figure 6.8

Measuring old-fashioned and modern sexism. Research shows similarities between old-fashioned and modern beliefs about both racism and sexism. Janet Swim and colleagues (1995) have developed a scale to measure the presence of both types of sexism. Four items from the 13-item scale are shown here. Old-fashioned sexism is characterized by endorsement of traditional gender roles and acceptance of stereotypes that portray females as less competent than males. In contrast, subtle, modern sexism is characterized by denial of continued discrimination and rejection of policies intended to help women.

From Swim, J. K., Aikin, K. J., Hall, W. S., & Hunter, B. A. (1995). Sexism and racism: Old-fashioned and modern prejudices. *Journal of Personality and Social Psychology, 68,* 199–214. Copyright © 1995 American Psychological Association. Adapted by permission of the publisher and author.

more likely to vote against a black political candidate, to oppose school busing, and to favor tax laws that benefit whites at the expense of blacks, compared to those who do not endorse such views (Murrell et al., 1994). Interestingly, endorsing statements such as "I do not like black people" ("old-fashioned" racism) does *not* reliably predict an individual's political actions (because many people who might personally agree with such a statement are reluctant to publicly endorse it).

One important trend in the study of prejudice is the recognition that most white people consider the possibility that they might hold racist views to be very upsetting; indeed, they are conflicted about it. As a result, they avoid acting in any way that might be construed as racist to others or even to themselves. The upshot is that well-intentioned whites can engage in *aversive racism,* an indirect, subtle, ambiguous form of racism that occurs when their conscious endorsement of egalitarian ideals is in conflict with unconscious, negative reactions to minority group members (Dovidio & Gaertner, 2004; Dovidio, Gaertner, & Pearson, 2005). An aversive racist might act in a racist manner when a nonracist excuse is available (e.g., "I interviewed several qualified blacks for the job but I had to hire the best candidate, who happened to be white"). Fortunately, researchers are seeking ways to combat such unintended but real bias toward others (Gaertner & Dovidio, 2005). When people cannot reconcile the conflict between their expressed attitudes and how they act, for example, their prejudice decreases (Son Hing, Li, & Zanna, 2002).

Causes of Prejudice

Prejudice is obviously a complex issue and has multiple causes. Although we can't thoroughly examine all of the causes of prejudice, we'll examine some of the major psychological and social factors that contribute to this vexing problem.

Authoritarianism

In some of the earliest research on prejudice, Robert Adorno and his colleagues (1950) identified the *authoritarian personality,* a personality type characterized by prejudice toward *any* group perceived to be different from oneself. Subsequent research found serious methodological weaknesses in the study, calling into question the validity of the personality type.

Over the past 50 years, both the definition and measurement of authoritarianism have evolved (Dion, 2003). The construct is now termed *right-wing authoritarianism* (RWA) (Altemeyer, 1988a, 1988b), and it is characterized by authoritarian submission (exaggerated deference to those in power), authoritarian aggression (hostility toward targets sanctioned by authorities), and conventionalism (strong adherence to values endorsed by authorities). Because authoritarians tend to support established authority, RWA is more commonly found among political conservatives than among political liberals (who are more likely to challenge the status quo).

What causes RWAs to be prejudiced? According to Robert Altemeyer (1998), there are two key factors. First, they organize their social world into ingroups and outgroups, and they view outgroups as threatening their cherished traditional values. Second, they tend to be self-righteous: They believe that they are more moral than others, and they feel justified in derogating groups that authority figures define as less moral than themselves. RWAs have typically been reared in highly religious and socially homogeneous groups, with little exposure to minority groups and unconventional behavior. They feel unduly threatened by social change—a fear picked up from their parents who believe that "the world is a dangerous and hostile place" (Altemeyer, 1988b, p. 38). Altemeyer also notes that fearful attitudes are reinforced by the mass media's emphasis on crime and violence. Exposure to various kinds of people and perspectives can reduce RWA (Peterson & Lane, 2001).

Authoritarian behavior has been linked with other types of antisocial personalities. Recently, a related personality type, *social dominance orientation* (SDO), has received much research attention (Sidanius & Pratto, 1999; Son Hing, Bobocel, & Zanna, 2007). People high in SDO prefer inequality among social groups, believing in a hierarchy where some are destined to dominate others, such as men over women, majorities over minorities, or heterosexuals over homosexuals (Pratto et al., 1994). Those low in SDO are less likely to think in terms of a social pecking order where society's "haves" should control what happens to the "have nots." **Figure 6.9**

Sample Items from the Social Dominance Orientation Scale

- Some groups of people are simply inferior to other groups.
- It's okay if some groups have more of a chance in life than others.
- If certain groups stayed in their place, we would have fewer problems.
- It's probably a good thing that certain groups are at the top and other groups are at the bottom.
- Sometimes other groups must be kept in their place.

Figure 6.9

A preference for social hierarchies. Social dominance orientation (SDO) refers to a person's preference for maintaining inequality among different groups (e.g., race, gender, religion, social class) in society, so that some groups dominate the others. These five sample items are from the longer 16-item SDO test. Responses are scored on a 9-point scale ranging from "very negative" to "very positive."

From Pratto, F., Sidanius, J., Stallworth, L. M., & Malle, B. F. (1994). Social dominance orientation: A personality variable predicting social and political attitudes. *Journal of Personality and Social Psychology, 67,* 741–763. Copyright © 1994 American Psychological Association. Adapted by permission of the publisher and author.

illustrates some sample items from a scale designed to assess SDO.

Cognitive Distortions and Expectations

Much of prejudice is rooted in cognitive processes that kick in automatically and operate without conscious intent (Wright & Taylor, 2003). As you recall, *social categorization* predisposes people to divide the social world into ingroups and outgroups. This distinction can trigger negativity toward outgroup members.

Perhaps no factor plays a larger role in prejudice than *stereotyping* (Schneider, 2004). Many people subscribe to derogatory stereotypes of various ethnic groups. Although racial stereotypes have declined over the last 50 years, they're not entirely a thing of the past (Dovidio et al., 2003). Racial profiling, in which law enforcement officers stop motorists, pedestrians, or airline passengers solely on the basis of skin color, is a case in point. Similarly, the events of September 11, 2001 caused some Americans to view all Muslims and Arabs as potential terrorists.

It seems that people are particularly likely to make the *fundamental attribution error* when evaluating targets of prejudice (Hewstone, 1990; Levy, Stroessner, & Dweck, 1998). Thomas Pettigrew (2001) suggests that perceiving negative characteristics as being dis-

Which man looks guilty? If you picked the man on the right, you're wrong. Wrong for judging people based on the color of their skin. Because if you look closely, you'll see they're the same man. Unfortunately, racial stereotyping like this happens every day. On America's highways, police stop drivers based on their skin color rather than for the way they are driving. For example, in Florida 80% of those stopped and searched were black and Hispanic, while they constituted only 5% of all drivers. These humiliating and illegal searches are violations of the Constitution and must be fought. Help us defend your rights. Support the ACLU. www.aclu.org **american civil liberties union**

© Bill Aaron/PhotoEdit

This clever poster, sponsored by the American Civil Liberties Union, focuses a spotlight on the sensitive issue of racial profiling. Racial profiling, which is a manifestation of modern racism, reflects the influence of stereotyping. The phenomenon of racial profiling shows how simple, often automatic, cognitive distortions can have unfortunate consequences in everyday life.

positional (personality based) and due to group membership is the *ultimate attribution error.* Thus, when people take note of ethnic neighborhoods dominated by crime and poverty, they blame these problems on the residents (they're lazy and ignorant) and downplay or ignore situationally based explanations (job discrimination, poor police service, and so on). The old saying, "They should pull themselves up by their own bootstraps" is a blanket dismissal of how situational factors may make it especially difficult for minorities to achieve upward mobility. Similarly, in trying to understand why individuals in some countries hold negative views of the United States, many Americans depict such people as "crazy" or "evil" rather than looking at possible situational causes, such as the negative effects of American foreign policy on their countries or the negative portrayal of the United States in their media.

Defensive attributions, in which people unfairly blame victims of adversity to reassure themselves that the same thing won't happen to them, can also contribute to prejudice. For example, individuals who claim that people who contract AIDS deserve it may be trying to reassure themselves that they won't suffer a similar fate.

Expectations can also foster and maintain prejudice. You already know that once people have formed impressions, they are invested in maintaining them. For instance, people note and recall behavior that confirms their stereotypes better than information that is inconsistent with their beliefs (Bodenhausen, 1988). Also, when an outgroup member's behavior contradicts a stereotype, people often "explain away" such behavior to leave their stereotype intact (Ickes et al., 1982). Unfortunately, the fact that social thinking is automatic, selective, and consistent means that people usually see what they expect to see when they look through prejudiced eyes, even when viewing objective presentations from media sources (Vallone, Ross, & Lepper, 1985).

Competition Between Groups

Back in 1954, Muzafer Sherif and his colleagues conducted a now-classic study at Robbers' Cave State Park in Oklahoma to look at competition and prejudice (Sherif et al., 1961). In this study, 11-year-old white boys were invited, with parental permission, to attend a three-week summer camp. What the boys didn't know was that they were participants in an experiment. The boys were randomly assigned to one of two groups; at camp, they went directly to their assigned campsites and had no knowledge of the other group's presence. During the first week, the boys got to know the other members of their own group through typical camp activities (hiking, swimming, and camping out); each group also chose a name (the Rattlers and the Eagles).

In the second week, the Rattlers and Eagles were introduced to each other through intergroup competitions. Events included a football game, a treasure hunt, and a tug of war, with medals, trophies, and other desirable prizes for the winning team. Almost immediately after competitive games were introduced, hostile feelings erupted between the two groups and quickly escalated to highly aggressive behavior: Food fights broke out in the mess hall, cabins were ransacked, and group flags were burned.

This experimental demonstration of the effects of competition on prejudice is often mirrored in the real world. For example, disputes over territory often provoke antagonism, as is the case in the former Yugoslavia and in the Israeli-Palestinian conflict. The lack of jobs or other important resources can also create competition between social groups. Still, competition does not always breed prejudice. In fact, the *perception* of threats to one's ingroup (loss of status, for example) is much more likely to cause hostility between groups than actual threats to the ingroup are (Brown et al., 2001; Dovidio et al., 2003). Unfortunately, such perceptions are quite common, because ingroup members usually assume that outgroup members are competitive and will try to thwart the ingroup's success (Fiske & Ruscher, 1993). To conclude, there is ample evidence that conflict over actual and perceived scarce resources can prejudice individuals toward outgroup members.

Threats to Social Identity

Although group membership provides individuals with a sense of identity and pride, it can also foster prejudice and discrimination, as we just noted. Members' individual psychologies become merged with group and even societal processes (Turner & Reynolds, 2004). To explore a different facet of this idea, we turn to *social identity theory,* developed by Henri Tajfel (1982) and John Turner (1987). According to this theory, self-esteem is partly determined by one's *social identity,* or collective self, which is tied to one's group memberships (nationality, religion, gender, major, occupation, and so forth) (Luhtanen & Crocker, 1992; Sidanius, Van Laar, & Levin, 2004). Whereas your personal self-esteem is elevated by individual accomplishments (you got an A on a history exam), your collective self-esteem is boosted when an ingroup is successful (your team wins the football game, your country wins a war). Likewise, your self-esteem can be threatened on both the personal level (you didn't get called for that job interview) and the collective level (your football team loses the championship game, your country is defeated in a war).

Threats to both personal and social identity motivate individuals to restore self-esteem, but threats to social identity are more likely to provoke responses that foster prejudice and discrimination (Crocker & Luhtanen, 1990). When collective self-esteem is threatened, individuals react in two key ways to bolster it. The most common response is to show *ingroup favoritism*—for example, tapping an ingroup member for a job opening or rating the performance of an ingroup member higher than that of an outgroup member (Branscombe et al., 1993; Stroebe, Lodewijkx, & Spears, 2005). In fact, when individuals become wrapped up in identifying with a group, they respond to group criticism as if it were a critique of the self (McCoy & Major, 2003). The second way to deal with threats to social identity is to engage in *outgroup derogation*—in other words, to "trash" outgroups that are perceived as threatening. This latter tactic is more often used by individuals who identify especially strongly with an ingroup (Perreault & Bourhis, 1999). **Figure 6.10** depicts the various elements of social identity theory.

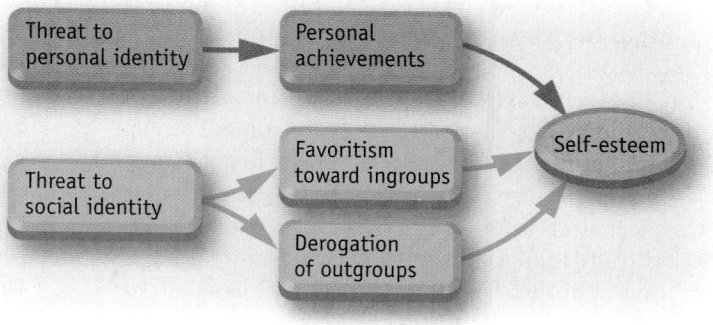

Figure 6.10

Social identity theory. According to Tajfel (1982) and Turner (1987), individuals have both a personal identity (based on a unique sense of self) and a social identity (based on group memberships). When social identity is threatened, people are motivated to restore self-esteem by either showing favoritism to ingroup members or derogating outgroup members. These tactics contribute to prejudice and discrimination.

Adapted from Brehm, S. S., & Kassin, S. M. (1993). *Social psychology.* Boston: Houghton Mifflin. Copyright © 1993 by Houghton Mifflin Company. Adapted with permission.

Significantly, it is "ingroup love," not "outgroup hate" that underlies most discrimination (Brewer, 1999). In other words, ingroups reward their own members and withhold rewards from outgroups, rather than deliberately blocking outgroups from desired resources (Fiske, 2002).

Reducing Prejudice

For decades, psychologists have searched for ways to reduce prejudice. Such a complicated problem requires solutions on a number of levels. Let's look at a few interventions that have been shown to work.

Cognitive Strategies

Because stereotypes are part of the social air that people breathe, practically everyone learns stereotypes about various groups. This means that stereotyped thinking about others becomes a mindless habit—even for individuals who have been taught to be tolerant of those who are different from themselves (Devine, 1989; Fiske, 2002).

Although it's true that stereotypes kick in automatically, unintentionally, and unconsciously, individuals *can* override them—with some cognitive effort (Fiske, 2002). Thus, if you meet someone who speaks with an accent, your initial, automatic reaction might be negative. However, if you believe that prejudice is wrong and if you are aware that you are stereotyping, you can intentionally inhibit such thoughts. According to Patricia Devine's (1989) model of prejudice reduction, this process requires an intentional shift from *automatic processing* to *controlled processing,* or from *mindlessness* to *mindfulness,* in Ellen Langer's terms (see Chapter 5). Thus, you can reduce prejudice if you are motivated to pay careful attention to what and how you think.

Intergroup Contact

Let's return to the Robbers' Cave study. When we left them, the Rattlers and Eagles were engaged in food fights and flag burning. Understandably, the experimenters were eager to restore peace. First, they tried speaking with each group, talking up the other group's good points and minimizing their differences. They also made the Eagles and the Rattlers sit together at meals and "fun" events like movies. Unfortunately, these tactics fell flat.

Next, the experimenters designed intergroup activities based on the principle of *superordinate goals*—goals that require two or more groups to work together to achieve mutual ends. For example, each boy had to contribute in some way (building a fire, preparing the food) on a cookout so that all could eat. After the boys had participated in a variety of such activities, the hostility between the two groups was much reduced. In fact, at the end of the three-week camping period, the Eagles and the Rattlers voted to ride the same bus back home.

Researchers have identified four necessary ingredients in the recipe for reducing intergroup hostility (Brewer & Brown, 1998). First, groups must *work together for a common goal*—merely bringing hostile groups into contact is not an effective way to reduce intergroup antagonism and may in fact worsen it. Second, cooperative efforts must have *successful outcomes*—if groups fail at a cooperative task, they are likely to blame each other for the failure. Third, group members must have the opportunity to establish *meaningful connections* with one another and not merely go through the motions of interacting. The fourth factor of *equal status contact* requires bringing together members of different groups in ways that ensure that everyone has equal status. A large meta-analysis demonstrated clear support for intergroup contact that meets these conditions as a means of reducing prejudice (Pettigrew & Tropp, 2000, 2006).

The "jigsaw classroom" uses these principles to reduce prejudice in schoolchildren (Aronson & Patnoe, 1997). In this intervention, six children are first assigned to an "expert group" in which they help each other learn specialized information prepared by the teacher about a study topic. Thus, each child becomes an "expert" on a subtopic. Then the children are assigned to ethnically mixed groups of six where they teach each other their school lessons. This arrangement puts all children on an equal footing (equal-status contact) and reduces competition for the teacher's attention and grades (scarce resources).

Children taught in a jigsaw classroom learn as much as peers taught in a traditional classroom setting. In addition, "jigsaw" children get an important bonus: Prejudice is replaced with positive feelings for ethnically different children, and the self-esteem of minority kids gets a big boost. The jigsaw concept may have broader societal applications, as well. Elliot Aronson, the social psychologist who pioneered the jigsaw classroom, suggests that the concept can be used to prevent violence in schools, even that rising to the horrific level of the Columbine massacre (Aronson, 2001).

To conclude, although prejudice remains a complex and distressing social problem, a number of effective strategies are available to combat it.

The Power of Persuasion

LEARNING OBJECTIVES

- *Cite the key elements in the persuasion process.*
- *Describe several source factors that influence persuasion.*
- *Discuss the evidence on one-sided versus two-sided messages and the value of arousing fear or positive feelings in persuasion.*
- *Describe several receiver factors that influence persuasion.*
- *Explain how the two cognitive routes to persuasion operate.*

Every day you are bombarded by attempts to alter your attitudes through persuasion. You may not even be out of bed before you start hearing radio advertisements that are meant to persuade you to buy specific toothpastes, cell phones, and athletic shoes. When you watch the morning news, you hear statements from numerous government officials, all of which have been carefully crafted to shape your opinions. On your way to school, you see billboards showing attractive models draped over cars in the hopes that they can induce positive feelings that will transfer to the vehicles. Walking to class, a friend tries to get you to vote for his candidate for student body president. "Does it ever let up?" you wonder.

When it comes to persuasion, the answer is "no." As Anthony Pratkanis and Elliot Aronson (2000) note, Americans live in the "age of propaganda." In light of this reality, let's examine some of the factors that determine whether persuasion works.

***Persuasion* involves the communication of arguments and information intended to change another person's attitudes.** What are attitudes? For the purposes of our discussion, we'll define ***attitudes* as beliefs and feelings about people, objects, and ideas.** Let's look more closely at two of the terms in this definition. We use the term *beliefs* to mean thoughts and judgments about people, objects, and ideas. For example, you may *believe* that equal pay for equal work is a fair policy or that capital punishment is not an effective deterrent to crime. The "feeling" component of attitudes refers to the positivity and negativity of one's feelings about an issue as well as how strongly one feels about it. For example, you may *strongly favor* equal pay for equal work but only *mildly disagree* with the idea that capital punishment reduces the crime rate. Psychologists assume that attitudes predict behavior—if you are favorably disposed toward some new product, you are likely to buy it; if not, you won't (Eagly & Chaiken, 1998). Of course, there is more to the persuasion side of the attitude-behavior relation: Read on.

The Elements of the Persuasion Process

The process of persuasion includes four basic elements (see **Figure 6.11**). The ***source* is the person who sends a communication, and the *receiver* is the person to whom the message is sent.** Thus, if you watched a presidential address on TV, the president would be the source, and you and millions of other viewers would be the receivers in this persuasive effort. **The *message* is the information transmitted by the source; the *channel* is the medium through which the message is sent.** In examining communication channels, investigators have often compared face-to-face interaction against appeals sent via mass media (such as television and radio). Although the research on communication channels is interesting, we'll confine our discussion to source, message, and receiver variables.

Recommended READING

Age of Propaganda: The Everyday Use and Abuse of Persuasion
by Anthony R. Pratkanis and Elliot Aronson
(W. H. Freeman, 2000)

The two social psychologists who wrote this book did so out of their concern about the harmful consequences of the increased use of propaganda in contemporary American society. Propaganda discourages careful reasoning and scrutiny, and the authors see its use by contemporary political leaders and the advertising industry as particularly problematic in a democracy. According to Pratkanis and Aronson, for a democratic form of government to survive in an age of propaganda, it must have "communicators who know how to present their message clearly and fairly, coupled with an informed electorate that knows the difference between a fair presentation and a con job" (p. xv). The authors have written the book to help Americans understand how their attitudes are being manipulated. Using an engaging writing style, they do an excellent job of applying research evidence to historical events (Nazi Germany, the Vietnam war, Iran-Contra, and the Persian Gulf War) and contemporary situations (political incidents and campaigns, televangelism, and commercials).

Source Factors

Persuasion tends to be more successful when the source has high *credibility* (Petty, Wegener, & Fabrigar, 1997). Two subfactors make a communicator credible: expertise and trustworthiness. People try to convey their *expertise* by mentioning their degrees, their training, and their experience, or by showing an impressive grasp of the issue at hand (Wood & Kallgren, 1988). As to *trustworthiness,* whom would you believe if you were told that your state needs to reduce corporate taxes to stimulate its economy—the president of a huge corporation in your state or an economics professor from out of state? Probably the latter. Trustworthiness is undermined when a source, such as the corporation president, appears to have something to gain. In contrast, trustworthiness is enhanced when people appear to argue against their own interests (Petty et al., 2001). This effect explains why salespeople often make remarks like "Frankly, my snowblower isn't the best and they have a better brand down the street if you're willing to spend a bit more . . ."

Likability is a second major source factor and includes a number of subfactors (Petty et al., 1997). A key consideration is a person's *physical attractiveness* (Petty et al., 1997). For example, one researcher found that attractive students were more successful than less attractive students in obtaining signatures for a petition (Chaiken, 1979). People also respond better to sources who are *similar* to them in ways that are relevant to the issue at hand (Mackie, Worth, & Asuncion, 1990). Thus, politicians stress the values they and their constituents hold in common.

Source variables are used to great effect in advertising. Many companies spend a fortune to obtain a spokesperson such as George Foreman, who combines trustworthiness, likability, and a knack for connecting with the average person. Companies quickly abandon spokespersons whose likability declines. For example, McDonald's and Sprite cancelled advertising contracts with basketball star Kobe Bryant after he was accused of rape. On the other hand, sometimes celebrities whose careers are in trouble can be used: Kevin Federline, who was married to pop-singer Britney Spears, was portrayed in a 2007 Super Bowl commercial as having to deal with his decline in popularity by taking a job in a fast food restaurant. Federline was shown flipping burgers in the ad, which quickly caused a controversy because viewers presumed he was poking fun at the lives and livelihoods of food service workers. Federline apologized,

Figure 6.11

Overview of the persuasion process. The process of persuasion essentially boils down to *who* (the source) communicates *what* (the message) *by what means* (the channel) *to whom* (the receiver). Thus, four sets of variables influence the process of persuasion: source, message, channel, and receiver factors. The diagram lists some of the more important factors in each category (including some that are not discussed in the text due to space limitations).

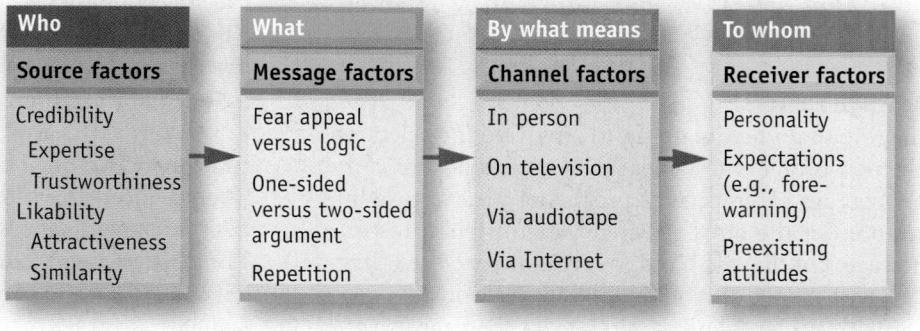

© Mychal Watts/WireImage/Getty Images

Advertisers frequently employ well-liked celebrities such as Ashley Judd to pitch their products, hoping that the positive feelings of the audience toward the source will transfer to the product.

which gave his fall from grace an air of authenticity and gave him more exposure (however short-lived) in the media. His sponsor did not appear to lose any profits as a result of his appearance in the ad. Indeed, there is an old advertising claim that even "bad press is good press." Thus, source variables are extremely important factors in persuasion.

Message Factors

Imagine that you are going to advocate the selection of a high-profile entertainer as the speaker at your commencement ceremony. In preparing your argument, you ponder the most effective way to structure your message. On the one hand, you're convinced that having a well-known entertainer on campus would be popular with students and would boost the image of your university in the community and among alumni. Still, you realize that this performer would cost a lot and that some people believe that an entertainer is not an appropriate commencement speaker. Should you present a *one-sided argument* that ignores the possible problems? Or should you present a *two-sided argument* that acknowledges concern about the problems and then downplays them?

In general, two-sided arguments seem to be more effective (Crowley & Hoyer, 1994). In fact, just mentioning that there are two sides to an issue can increase your credibility with an audience (Jones & Brehm, 1970). One-sided messages work only when your audience is uneducated about the issue or when they already favor your point of view.

Persuaders also use emotional appeals to shift attitudes. Insurance companies show scenes of homes on fire to arouse fear. Antismoking campaigns emphasize the threat of cancer. Deodorant ads prey on the fear of embarrassment. Does *fear arousal* work? Yes, studies involving a wide range of issues (nuclear policy, auto safety, and dental hygiene among others) have shown that the arousal of fear often increases persuasion (Perloff, 1993). However, there are limiting conditions (Rogers & Prentice-Dunn, 1997). Fear appeals are most likely to work when your listeners view the dire consequences that you describe as exceedingly unpleasant, as fairly probable if they don't take your advice, and as avoidable if they do (Das, deWit, & Stroebe, 2003). If you induce strong fear in your audience without providing a workable solution to the problem (such as a surefire stop-smoking or weight-loss program), you may make your audience defensive, causing them to tune you out (Petty & Wegener, 1998).

Generating *positive feelings* is also an effective way to persuade people. Familiar examples of such tactics include the use of music and physically attractive actors in TV commercials, the use of laugh tracks in TV programs, and the practice of wining and dining prospective customers. Shortly after the terrorist attacks on America, you probably noticed that patriotic themes and images in ads increased dramatically. Producing positive feelings to win people over *can* be effective—provided they don't care too much about the issue. If people do care about the topic, it takes more than good feelings to move them. For example, one study showed that the use of music in TV commercials was effective in persuading viewers, but only when the message concerned a trivial topic (Park & Young, 1986).

Receiver Factors

What about the receiver of the persuasive message? Are some people easier to persuade than others? Yes, but the answer is complicated. For instance, receptivity to a message can sometimes depend on people's *moods:* optimistic people process uplifting messages better than pessimists, who are drawn to counter-attitudinal communications, or those opposing their current views (Wegener & Petty, 1994). Other people want to think deeply about issues, having a so-called

need for cognition, **the tendency to seek out and enjoy effortful thought, problem solving activities, and in-depth analysis.** Such people, who truly relish intellectual give-and-take as well as debate, are more likely to be convinced by high-quality arguments than those who prefer more superficial analyses (Cacioppo et al., 1996).

Transient factors also matter in receptivity to persuasive messages. *Forewarning* the receiver about a persuasive effort and a receiver's initial position on an issue, for instance, seem to be more influential than a receiver's personality. When you shop for a new TV, you expect salespeople to work at persuading you. To some extent, this forewarning reduces the impact of their arguments (Petty & Wegener, 1998). When receivers are forewarned about a persuasion attempt on a personally important topic, it is harder to persuade them than when they are not forewarned (Wood & Quinn, 2003). But when they are told to expect a persuasive message on an unimportant topic, their attitudes shift in the direction of the persuasive appeal even before it occurs—to avoid appearing gullible! Thus, the old saying, "To be forewarned is to be forearmed" is often, but not always, true.

Understandably, receivers are harder to persuade when they encounter a position that is incompatible with their existing beliefs. In general, people display a *disconfirmation bias* in evaluating such arguments (Edwards & Smith, 1996). Also, people from different cultures respond to different themes in persuasive messages. In one study, participants from an individualistic culture (the United States) preferred magazine ads that stressed the theme of uniqueness, while those from a collectivist culture (Korea) preferred ads that stressed conformity (Kim & Markus, 1999).

The Whys of Persuasion

Why do people change their attitudes in response to persuasive messages? Thanks to the work of Richard Petty and John Cacioppo (1986), psychologists have a good understanding of the cognitive processes that underlie attitude change.

Richard Petty

Courtesy, Richard E. Petty

John Cacioppo

Courtesy, John T. Cacioppo

According to the ***elaboration likelihood model,*** **an individual's thoughts about a persuasive message (rather than the actual message itself) will determine whether attitude change will occur** (Petty & Cacioppo, 1986). As we have noted, at some times people make quick, sloppy decisions (automatic processing, mindlessness, snap judgments), whereas at other times they process information carefully (controlled processing, mindfulness, systematic judgments). These processes also operate in persuasion, with messages sometimes persuading receivers through a *peripheral* route and sometimes through a *central* route.

When people are distracted, tired, or uninterested in a persuasive message, they fail to key in on the true merits of the product or issue. They process information, but not mindfully. Being in a happy mood can produce the same effect (Sinclair, Mark, & Clore, 1994). Surprisingly, even when people do not carefully evaluate a message, attitude change can occur (Petty & Cacioppo, 1990). What happens is that the receiver is persuaded by cues that are peripheral to the message—thus the term *peripheral route* (see **Figure 6.12**). Just because you're not mindfully analyzing a TV commercial for a new fruit drink doesn't mean that you're totally tuned out. You may not be paying attention to the substance of the commercial, but you are aware of superficial aspects of the ad—you like the music, your favorite basketball player is pitching the product, and so forth.

Although persuasion usually occurs via the peripheral route, senders can also use another route to attitude change—the *central route* (see **Figure 6.12**). In this case, receivers process persuasive messages mindfully, by thinking about the logic and merits of the pertinent (or central) arguments. In other words, the

Figure 6.12

The peripheral and central routes to persuasion. Persuasion can occur via two different routes. The central route, which results in high elaboration, tends to produce longer-lasting attitude change.

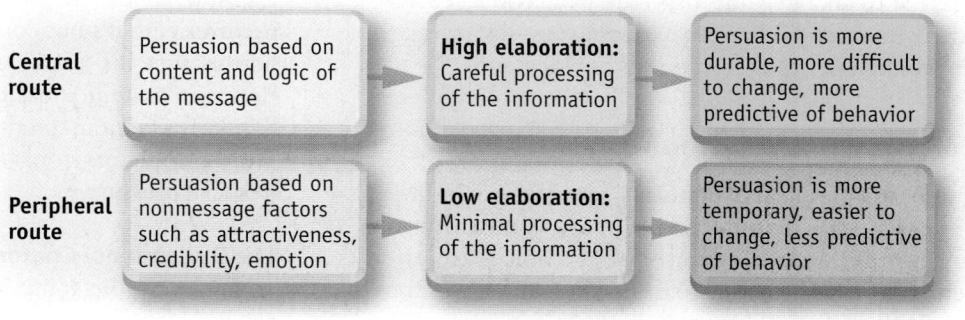

Political candidates use music, flags, and slogans to persuade via the peripheral route; when they present their views on an issue, they are going for the central route.

receiver cognitively *elaborates* on the persuasive message—hence, the name of the model. If people have a favorable reaction to their thoughtful evaluation of a message, positive attitude change occurs; an unfavorable reaction results in negative attitude change.

For the central route to override the peripheral route, there are two requirements. First, receivers must be *motivated* to process the persuasive message carefully. Motivation is triggered when people are interested in the issue, find it personally relevant, and have time and energy to think about it carefully. For example, if your university is considering changing its grading system, you will probably make a point of thinking carefully about the various options and their implications. Second, receivers must have the *ability* to grasp the message—that is, the message must be comprehensible, and individuals must be capable of understanding it. If people are distracted, tired, or find the message uninteresting or irrelevant, they will not pay careful attention to it, and superficial cues will become salient.

Ultimately, the two routes to persuasion are not equally effective. Attitudes formed via the central route are longer lasting and more resistant to challenge than those formed via the peripheral route (Petty & Wegener, 1998). They are also better predictors of a person's behavior (Petty, Priester, & Wegener, 1994).

To conclude, although we can't stem the tide of persuasive messages bombarding you every day, we hope we've alerted you to the need to be a vigilant recipient of persuasion attempts. Of course, persuasion is not the *only* method through which people try to influence you, as you'll see in the next section.

The Power of Social Pressure

LEARNING OBJECTIVES

- *Summarize what Asch discovered about conformity.*
- *Discuss the difference between normative and informational influence.*
- *Describe some conformity pressures in everyday life and how people can resist them.*
- *Describe Milgram's research on obedience to authority.*
- *Cite an important factor in resisting inappropriate demands from authority figures.*

In the previous section, we showed you how others attempt to change your *attitudes.* Now you'll see how others attempt to change your *behavior*—by trying to get you to agree to their requests and demands.

Conformity and Compliance Pressures

If you extol the talent of popular singer Beyoncé Knowles or keep a well-manicured lawn, are you exhibiting conformity? According to social psychologists, it depends on whether your behavior is freely chosen or the result of group pressure. ***Conformity* occurs when people yield to real or imagined social pressure.** For example, if you like Beyoncé because you truly enjoy her music, that's not conformity. However, if you like her because it's "cool" and your friends would question your taste if you didn't, then you're conforming. Similarly, if you maintain a well-groomed lawn just to avoid complaints from your neighbors, you're yielding to social pressure.

The Dynamics of Conformity

To introduce this topic, we'll re-create a classic experiment devised by Solomon Asch (1955). The partici-

Recommended READING

Influence: Science and Practice
by Robert B. Cialdini (Collins, 2007)

Cialdini, a social psychologist, has conducted extensive empirical research on influence tactics such as the door-in-the-face technique and lowballing (see the Application). As you might expect, Cialdini's book is based on his studies and his review of other scientific research on the topic. However, what makes his book unique is that he went far beyond laboratory research in his effort to better understand the ins and outs of social influence. For three years, he immersed himself in the real world of influence artists, becoming a "spy of sorts." As he puts it, "When I wanted to learn about the compliance tactics of encyclopedia (or vacuum cleaner, or portrait photography, or dance lessons) sales organizations, I would answer a newspaper ad for sales trainees and have them teach me their methods. Using similar but not identical approaches, I was able to penetrate advertising, public relations, and fund-raising agencies to examine their techniques" (from the preface). The result is an insightful book that bolsters scientific data with anecdotal accounts of how influence artists ply their trade. Familiarity with their strategies can help you avoid being an easy mark, or "patsy."

pants are male undergraduates recruited for a study of visual perception. A group of seven participants are shown a large card with a vertical line on it and asked to indicate which of three lines on a second card matches the original "standard line" in length (see **Figure 6.13**). All seven participants are given a turn at the task, and each announces his choice to the group. The subject in the sixth chair doesn't know it, but everyone else in the group is an accomplice of the experimenter.

Figure 6.13

Stimuli used in Asch's conformity studies. Subjects were asked to match a standard line (top) with one of three other lines displayed on another card (bottom). The task was easy—until experimental accomplices started responding with obviously incorrect answers, creating a situation in which Asch evaluated subjects' conformity.

Adapted from illustration on p. 35 by Sarah Love in Asch, S. (1955, November). Opinions and social pressure. *Scientific American, 193*(5), 31–35. Copyright © 1955 by Scientific American, Inc.

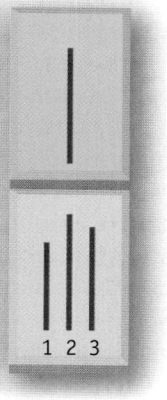

The accomplices give accurate responses on the first two trials. On the third trial, line 2 clearly is the correct response, but the first five participants all say that line 3 matches the standard line. The genuine subject can't believe his ears. Over the course of the experiment, the accomplices all give the same incorrect response on 12 out of 18 trials. Asch wanted to see how the subject would respond in these situations. The line judgments are easy and unambiguous. Without group pressure, people make matching errors less than 1% of the time. So, if the subject consistently agrees with the accomplices, he isn't making honest mistakes—he is

© Royalty Free-Masterfile

Conformity is far more common than most people appreciate. We all conform to social expectations in an endless variety of ways. There is nothing inherently good or bad about conforming to social pressures, it all depends on the situation. However, it is prudent to be aware of how social expectations can sometimes have a profound influence on our behavior.

conforming. Will the subject stick to his guns, or will he go along with the group? Averaging across 123 participants, Asch (1955) found that the men conformed (made mistakes) on 37% of the 12 trials. However, the participants varied considerably in their tendency to conform: 25% never caved in to the group, while 75% conformed on at least one trial. The point is not the relative amount of conformity behavior, of course, rather that any occurred at all in the situation (Friend, Rafferty, & Bramel, 1990; Harris, 1985). Ask yourself: Would you be willing to publicly agree with an untruth in order to comply with everyone else? Most of us would say no, but clearly a minority would comply even when the truth—which line is the same as which other line—is obvious. Although a meta-analysis of 133 Asch-type studies reported that conformity has declined over the past 50 years, it also concluded that majority influence remains a powerful force (Bond & Smith, 1996).

In subsequent studies, Asch (1956) determined that group size and group unanimity are key determinants of conformity. To examine group size, Asch repeated his procedure with groups that included 1 to 15 accomplices. Little conformity was seen when a subject was pitted against just one accomplice. Conformity increased rapidly as group size went from 2 to 4, peaked at a group size of 7, and then leveled off (see **Figure 6.14**). Thus, Asch concluded that as group size increases, conformity increases—up to a point. Significantly, Asch found that group size made little difference if just one accomplice "broke" with the others, wrecking their unanimous agreement. The presence of another dissenter lowered conformity to about one-quarter of its peak, even when the dissenter made inaccurate judgments that happened to conflict with the majority view. Apparently, the participants just needed to hear a second person question the accuracy of the group's perplexing responses.

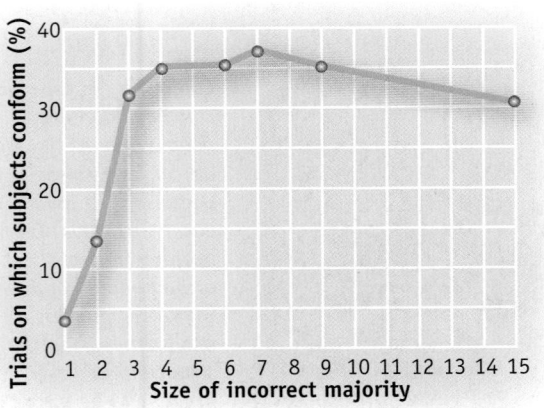

Figure 6.14

Conformity and group size. This graph shows the percentage of trials on which subjects conformed as a function of the number of individuals with an opposing view. Asch found that conformity became more frequent as group size increased, up to about 7 persons, and then leveled off.

Adapted from illustration on p. 32 by Sarah Love in Asch, S. (1955, November). Opinions and social pressure. *Scientific American, 193*(5), 31–35. Copyright © 1955 by Scientific American, Inc.

Conformity Versus Compliance

Did the conforming participants in Asch's study really change their beliefs in response to social pressure, or did they just pretend to change them? Subsequent studies asked participants to make their responses privately, instead of publicly (Deutsch & Gerard, 1955; Insko et al., 1985). Conformity declined dramatically when participants wrote down their responses. Thus, it is likely that Asch's participants did not really change their beliefs. Based on this evidence, theorists concluded that Asch's experiments evoked a particular type of conformity, called compliance. ***Compliance* occurs when people yield to social pressure in their public behavior, even though their private beliefs have not changed.** For example, many people comply with modest group pressure daily—they "dress up" for work by wearing suits, ties, dresses, and so on—when they would prefer to wear more casual clothing.

The Whys of Conformity

People often conform or comply because they are afraid of being criticized or rejected. ***Normative influence* operates when people conform to social norms for fear of negative social consequences.** Compliance often results from subtle, implied pressure. For example, for fear of making a negative impression, you may remove your eyebrow ring for a job interview. However, compliance also occurs in response to explicit rules, requests, and commands. Thus, you'll probably follow your boss's directions even when you think they're lousy ideas.

People are also likely to conform when they are uncertain how to behave (Cialdini, 2001; Sherif, 1936). Thus, if you're at a nice restaurant and don't know which fork to use, you may watch others to see what they're doing. ***Informational influence* operates when people look to others for how to behave in ambiguous situations.** In situations like this, using others as a source of information about appropriate behavior is a good thing. But relying on others to know how to behave in unfamiliar situations can sometimes be problematic, as you'll see shortly.

Resisting Conformity Pressures

Sometimes conforming is just harmless fun—such as participating in Internet-generated "flash mobs." At other times, people conform on relatively trivial matters—such as dressing up for a nice restaurant. In this

ZITS © ZITS Partnership. Reprinted by permission of King Features Syndicate.

case, conformity and compliance minimize the confusion and anxiety people experience in unfamiliar situations. However, when individuals feel pressured to conform to antisocial norms, tragic consequences may result. Negative examples of "going along with the crowd" include drinking more than one knows one should because others say, "C'mon, have just one more" and driving at someone's urging when under the influence of alcohol or drugs. Other instances include refusing to socialize with someone simply because the person isn't liked by one's social group and failing to come to another's defense when it might make one unpopular.

The above examples all concern normative influence, but pressure can come from informational influence as well. A useful example concerns a paradox called **the *bystander effect*—the tendency for individuals to be less likely to provide help when others are present than when they are alone.** Numerous studies have confirmed that people are less helpful in emergency situations when others are around (Latané and Nida, 1981; Levine et al., 1994). This effect even shows up on the Internet, when members of different-sized chat groups receive requests for assistance (Markey, 2000). Thankfully, the bystander effect is less likely to occur when the need for help is very clear (Fischer, Greitemeyer, & Pollozek, 2006).

What accounts for the bystander effect? A number of factors are at work, and conformity is one of them. The bystander effect is most likely to occur in *ambiguous situations,* because people look around to see whether others are acting as if there's an emergency (Harrison & Wells, 1991). If everyone hesitates, this inaction (informational influence) suggests that help isn't needed. So the next time you witness what you think might be an emergency, don't automatically give in to the informational influence of inaction.

To resist conformity pressures, we offer these suggestions: First, make an effort to pay more attention to the social forces operating on you. Second, if you find yourself in a situation where others are pressuring you, try to identify someone in the group whose views match yours. Recall that just one dissenter in Asch's groups significantly reduced conformity pressures. And, if you know in advance that you're heading into this kind of situation, consider inviting a friend with similar views to go along.

Pressure from Authority Figures

***Obedience* is a form of compliance that occurs when people follow direct commands, usually from someone in a position of authority.** In itself, obedience isn't good or bad; it depends on what one is being told to do. For example, if the fire alarm goes off in your classroom building and your instructor "orders" you to leave, obedience is a good idea. On the other hand, if your boss asks you to engage in an unethical or illegal act, *disobedience* is probably in order.

The Dynamics of Obedience

© 1981 Eric Kroll, courtesy of Alexandra Milgram
Stanley Milgram

Like many other people after World War II, social psychologist Stanley Milgram was troubled by how readily the citizens of Germany had followed the orders of dictator Adolf Hitler, even when the orders required morally repugnant actions, such as the slaughter of millions of Jews, as well as Russians, Poles, Gypsies, and homosexuals. This was Milgram's motivation to study the dynamics of obedience. Milgram's (1963) participants were a diverse collection of 40 men from the local community who volunteered for a study on the effects of punishment on learning. When they arrived at the lab, they drew slips of paper from a hat to get their assignments. The drawing was rigged so that the subject always be-

Web Link 6.3 **Stanley Milgram**

This site provides a wealth of accurate information about the work of Stanley Milgram, arguably one of the most controversial and creative social psychologists in the field's history. The site is maintained by Thomas Blass, a psychology professor at the University of Maryland (Baltimore County), who has published many articles and books on the life and work of Milgram.

came the "teacher" and an experimental accomplice (a likable 47-year-old accountant) became the "learner."

The teacher watched while the learner was strapped into a chair and as electrodes were attached to his arms (to be used to deliver shocks whenever he made a mistake on the task). The subject was then taken to an adjoining room that housed the shock generator that he would control in his role as the teacher. Although the apparatus looked and sounded realistic, it was a fake, and the learner was never shocked. The experimenter played the role of the authority figure who told the teacher what to do and who answered any questions that arose.

The experiment was designed such that the learner would make many mistakes, and the teacher was instructed to increase the shock level after each wrong answer. At 300 volts, the learner began to pound on the wall between the two rooms in protest and soon stopped responding to the teacher's questions. From this point forward, participants frequently turned to the experimenter for guidance. Whenever they did so, the experimenter (authority figure) firmly stated that the teacher should continue to give stronger and stronger shocks to the now-silent learner. Milgram wanted to know the maximum shock the teacher was willing to administer before refusing to cooperate.

As **Figure 6.15** shows, 65% of the subjects administered all 30 levels of shock. Although they tended to obey the experimenter, many participants voiced and displayed considerable distress about harming the learner. They protested, groaned, bit their lips, trembled, and broke into a sweat—but they continued administering the shocks. Based on these findings, Milgram concluded that obedience to authority was even more common than he or others had anticipated.

The Causes of Obedience

After his initial demonstration, Milgram (1974) tried about 20 variations on his experimental procedure, looking for factors that influenced participants' obedience. For instance, he studied female participants to look at gender differences in obedience (he found no

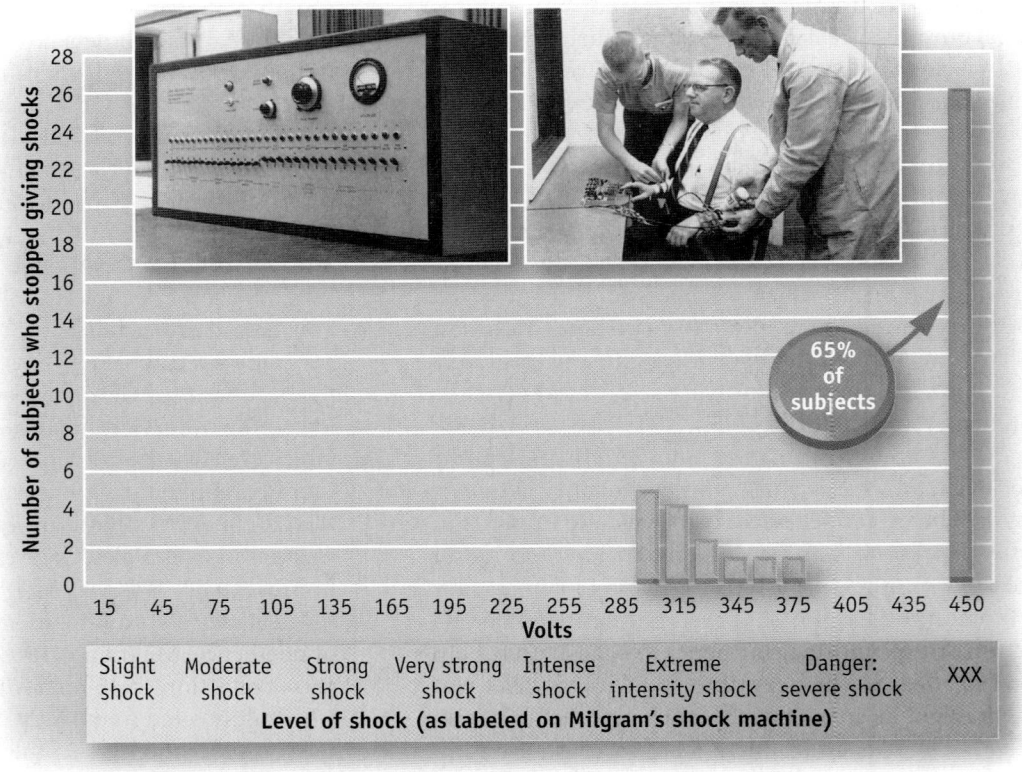

Figure 6.15

Milgram's (1963) experiment on obedience. The photos show the fake shock generator and the "learner" being connected to the shock generator during an experimental session. The results of the study are summarized in the bar graph. The vast majority of subjects (65%) delivered the entire series of shocks to the learner.

Photos copyright 1965 by Stanley Milgram. From the film *Obedience,* distributed by The Pennsylvania State University. Reprinted by permission of Alexandra Milgram.

evidence of such differences). In another condition, two confederates played the role of teachers who defied the experimenter's demands to continue, one at 150 volts and one at 210 volts. In this condition, only 10% of the subjects shocked at the maximum level.

What caused the obedient behavior observed by Milgram? First, the demands on the participants (to shock the learner) escalated gradually so that very strong shocks were demanded only after the participant was well into the experiment. Second, participants were told that the authority figure, not the teacher, was responsible if anything happened to the learner. Third, subjects evaluated their actions in terms of how well they lived up to the authority figure's expectations, not by their harmful effects on the victim. Taken together, these findings suggest that human behavior is determined not so much by the *kind of person* one is as by the *kind of situation* one is in. Applying this insight to Nazi war crimes and other atrocities, Milgram made a chilling assertion: Inhuman and evil visions may originate in the disturbed mind of an authority figure like Hitler, but it is only through the obedient actions of normal people that such ideas can be turned into frightening reality.

Milgram's study has been consistently replicated for many years, in diverse settings, with a variety of participants and procedural variations (Blass, 1999, 2000). Overall, the weight of evidence supports Milgram's results. Of course, critics have questioned the ethics of Milgram's procedure (Baumrind, 1964). Today, at most universities it would be difficult to obtain permission to replicate Milgram's study—an ironic epitaph for what may be psychology's best-known experiment.

To Obey or Not to Obey?

The findings of obedience research confront us with the chilling fact that most people can be coerced into engaging in actions that violate their morals and values. Perhaps you've heard of the 1968 My Lai incident, an American "crime of obedience," in which U.S. military forces killed 400–500 Vietnamese women, children, and elderly men (Kelman & Hamilton, 1989). The Abu Ghraib prison scandal in Iraq is a more recent reminder that strong social pressures can produce morally repugnant behavior. Nonetheless, some individuals *are* able to resist pressure from authority figures. A dramatic example is Karen Silkwood, who probably died because she tried to report unsafe practices at the nuclear power plant where she worked. Thankfully, disobedience to authority is usually less dramatic and less dangerous, but "ethical resisters" also risk the loss of credibility, friends, and jobs for the sake of important principles (Glazer & Glazer, 1990). Examples of "whistleblowers" include Erin Brockovich, who helped expose hazardous-waste dangers, and Sherron Watkins, who initially warned Ken Lay, her boss at Enron Corporation, about accounting irregularities that eventually led to the collapse of the company.

Web Link 6.4 **Stanford Prison Experiment**

The Stanford Prison Simulation is one of psychology's most renowned studies. Like Milgram's study of obedience, Phil Zimbardo's study provided a dramatic demonstration of the power of situational factors and how they can promote conformity and obedience. At this site, Zimbardo provides a fascinating slide show explaining the study in depth. The site also includes discussion questions, reflections on the study 30 years after it was conducted, and links to a host of related materials. The links include recent writings by Zimbardo that analyze the Abu Ghraib prison scandal.

In keeping with Milgram's finding that participants in the condition with two disobedient confederates found it easier to defy authority, it seems that social support plays a critical role in disobedient behavior. The findings of a study on college students' decisions to ride with an intoxicated driver are relevant here (Powell & Drucker, 1997). Participants were randomly assigned to one of four conditions: (1) driver with one beer, (2) intoxicated driver, (3) intoxicated driver and confederate who enters the car, and (4) intoxicated driver and confederate who refuses to enter the car. Participants consistently chose to enter the car in all conditions except when the confederate refused. Especially when disobedience involves risk, aligning oneself with supportive others (family, friends, labor unions, for example) can decrease anxiety and increase safety.

In dealing with pressure from authority figures, remember that social influence is a two-way street: You are not merely a helpless victim. Being mindful of how obedience pressures operate and of some strategies that make it easier to resist these pressures should make you a stronger player in these situations.

In the Application, we'll alert you to some social influence strategies that people use to get you and others to agree to their requests.

APPLICATION

Seeing Through Compliance Tactics

LEARNING OBJECTIVES

- *Describe two compliance strategies based on the principles of commitment and consistency.*
- *Describe some compliance strategies based on the principle of reciprocity.*
- *Discuss how the principle of scarcity can increase a person's desire for something.*

Which of the following statements is true?

___ **1.** It's a good idea to ask for a small favor before soliciting the larger favor that you really want.

___ **2.** It's a good idea to ask for a large favor before soliciting the smaller favor that you really want.

Courtesy, Robert Cialdini

Robert Cialdini

Would you believe that *both* of the statements are true? Although the two approaches work for different reasons, both can be effective ways to get people to do what you want. It pays to understand these and other social influence strategies because advertisers, salespeople, and fundraisers (not to mention friends and neighbors) use them frequently to influence people's behavior. So you can see the relevance of these strategies to your own life, we've grouped them by the principles that make them work. Much of our discussion is based on the work of Robert Cialdini (2007), a social psychologist who spent several years observing social influence tactics used by salespeople, fundraisers, advertisers, and other compliance professionals. His book, *Influence: Science and Practice,* is an excellent and entertaining discussion of social influence principles in action.

The Consistency Principle

Once people agree to something, they tend to stick with their initial commitment (Cialdini, 2007). This consistency is used to gain compliance in two ways. Both involve a person getting another individual to commit to an initial request and then changing the terms of the agreement to the requestor's advantage. Because people often stay with their initial commitments, the target will likely agree to the revised proposal, even though it may not be to his or her benefit.

The Foot-in-the-Door Technique

Door-to-door salespeople have long recognized the importance of gaining a *little* cooperation from sales targets (getting a "foot in the door") before hitting them with the real sales pitch. **The *foot-in-the-door* (FITD) *technique* involves getting people to agree to a small request to increase the chances that they will agree to a larger request later** (see **Figure 6.16a**). This technique is widely used. For example, groups seeking donations often ask people to simply sign a petition first. Salespeople routinely ask individuals to try a product with "no obligations" before they launch their hard sell. In a similar vein, a wife might ask her husband to get her a cup of coffee, and when he gets up to fetch it say, "While you're up, would you fix me a peanut butter sandwich?"

The FITD technique was first investigated by Jonathon Freedman and his colleagues. In one study (Freedman & Fraser, 1966), the large request involved telephoning homemakers to ask whether a team of six men doing consumer research could come into their home to classify all their household products. Imagine six strangers tramping through your home, pulling everything out of your closets and cupboards, and you can understand why only 22% of the subjects in the control group agreed to this outlandish request. Subjects in the experimental group were contacted three days before the unreasonable request was made and were asked to answer a few questions about the soaps used in their home. When the large request was made three days later, 53% of the experimental group complied with that request.

Of course, no strategy works all the time. A review of research reported that the FITD tactic increases compliance rates, on the average, about 13% (Burger, 1999). The technique may be ineffective if the second request follows too quickly on the heels of the first one (Chartrand, Pinckert, & Burger, 1999), if the initial request is too trivial to register, or if the second request is so large it is unreasonable (Burger, 1999). When this influence technique does work, however, it can be used in socially beneficial ways, such as increasing people's willingness to consider organ donation (Fabian, 2002) or to enhance teen participation rates in smoking cessation programs (Bloom, McBride, & Pollack, 2006).

Figure 6.16

The fioot-in-the-door and door-in-the-face techniques. These two influence techniques are essentially the reverse of each other, but both can work. (a) In the foot-in-the-door technique, you begin with a small request and work up to a larger one. (b) In the door-in-the-face technique, you begin with a large request and work down to a smaller one.

Why does this strategy work? The best explanation is rooted in Daryl Bem's *self-perception theory* or the idea that people sometimes infer their attitudes by observing their own behavior (Burger & Caldwell, 2003; Burger & Guadagno, 2003). When Joe agrees to sign a petition, he infers that he is a helpful person. So when he is confronted with a second, larger request to collect petition signatures, "helpful person" comes to mind, and Joe complies with the request.

The Lowball Technique

A second commitment-based strategy is the ***lowball technique,*** **which involves getting someone to commit to an attractive proposition before its hidden costs are revealed.** The name for this technique derives from a common practice in automobile sales, in which a customer is offered a terrific bargain on a car. The bargain price gets the customer to commit to buying, but soon after, the dealer starts revealing some hidden costs. Typically, the customer discovers that options apparently included in the original price are actually going to cost extra. Once they have committed to buying a car, most customers are unlikely to cancel the deal. Car dealers aren't the only ones who use this technique. For instance, a friend might ask if you want to spend a week with him at his charming backwoods cabin. After you accept this seemingly generous offer, he may add, "Of course, there's a little work to do. We need to paint the doors, repair the pier, and . . ." You might think that people would become angry and back out of a deal once its hidden costs are revealed. Sometimes this does happen, but once people make a public commitment, lowballing is a surprisingly effective strategy (Burger & Cornelius, 2003).

The Reciprocity Principle

Most people have been socialized to believe in the ***reciprocity principle*****—the rule that one should pay back in kind what one receives from others.** Charities frequently make use of this principle. Groups seeking donations for people with disabilities, homeless individuals, and so forth routinely send "free" address labels, key rings, and other small gifts with their pleas for donations. The belief that we should reciprocate others' kindness is a powerful norm; thus, people often feel obliged to reciprocate by making a donation in return for the gift. According to Cialdini (2007), the reciprocity norm is so powerful that it often works even when (1) the gift is uninvited, (2) the gift comes from someone you dislike, or (3) the gift results in an uneven exchange. Let's review some reciprocity-based influence tactics.

The lowball technique is a standard ploy that car dealers use to get customers to commit to buying a specific car. This unethical manipulation, which is also used in many other types of interactions, is surprisingly effective, in spite of its simplicity.

© Bob Daemmrich/PhotoEdit

The Door-in-the-Face Technique

The door-in-the-face technique reverses the sequence of requests employed with the foot-in-the-door technique. **The *door-in-the-face (DITF) technique* involves making a large request that is likely to be turned down in order to increase the chances that people will agree to a smaller request later** (see **Figure 6.16b**). The name for this strategy is derived from the expectation that an initial request will be quickly rejected. For example, a wife who wants to coax her frugal husband into agreeing to buy a $25,000 sports car might begin by proposing that they purchase a $35,000 sports car. By the time he has talked his wife out of the pricier car, the $25,000 price tag may look quite reasonable to him. For the DITF to work, there must be no delay between the two requests (O'Keefe & Hale, 2001). Interestingly, the effect has been shown to increase solicited donations online and in the absence of face-to-face interaction (Gueguen, 2003).

Other Reciprocity-Based Techniques

Salespeople who distribute free samples to prospective customers are also using the reciprocity principle. Cialdini (2007) describes the procedures used by the Amway Corporation, which sells such household products as detergent, floor wax, and insect spray. Amway's door-to-door salespeople give homemakers many bottles of their products for a "free trial." When they re-

CALVIN AND HOBBES © Watterson. Reprinted with permission of UNIVERSAL PRESS SYNDICATE. All rights reserved.

Web Link 6.5 **Influence at Work**

This website, created by researchers Robert Cialdini and Kelton Rhodes, offers an intriguing set of pages that explore a wide variety of social influence phenomena: persuasion, propaganda, brainwashing, and the tactics of various types of cults.

turn a few days later, most of the homemakers feel obligated to buy some of the products.

The reciprocity norm is meant to promote fair exchanges in social interactions. However, when people manipulate the reciprocity rule, they usually give something of minimal value in the hopes of getting far more in return. For example, a person selling large computer systems may treat a potential customer at an exclusive restaurant in an effort to close a deal worth hundreds of thousands of dollars.

The Scarcity Principle

It's no secret that telling people they can't have something only makes them want it more. According to Cialdini (2007), this principle derives from two sources. First, people have learned that items that are hard to get are of better quality than items that are easy to get. From there, they often assume, erroneously, that anything that is scarce must be good. Second, when people's choices (of products, services, romantic partners, job candidates) are constrained in some way, they often want what they can't have even more (Brehm & Brehm, 1981; Williams et al., 1993). The psychological term for this is *reactance* (Brehm, 1966).

© Tony Freeman/PhotoEdit

Advertisers often try to artificially create scarcity to make their products seem more desirable.

Companies and advertisers frequently use the scarcity principle to drive up the demand for their products. Thus, you constantly see ads that scream "limited supply available," "for a limited time only," "while they last," and "time is running out." Perhaps the scarcity principle accounts for the reason so many antique and "vintage" items on eBay generate so much interest and auction dollars.

In summary, people use a variety of methods to coax compliance from one another. Despite the fact that many of these influence techniques are more or less dishonest, they're still widely used. There is no way to completely avoid being hoodwinked by influence strategies. However, being alert to them can reduce the likelihood that you'll be a victim of influence artists. As we noted in our discussion of persuasion, "to be forewarned is to be forearmed."

KEY IDEAS

Forming Impressions of Others

▶ In forming impressions of other people, individuals rely on appearance, verbal behavior, actions, nonverbal messages, and situational cues. Individuals usually make snap judgments about others unless accurate impressions are important. To explain the causes of other people's behavior, individuals make attributions (either internal or external).

▶ People often try to confirm their expectations about what others are like, which can result in biased impressions. Self-fulfilling prophecies can actually change a target person's behavior in the direction of a perceiver's expectations. Cognitive distortions are caused by categorizing, stereotyping, the fundamental attribution error, and defensive attributions. The process of person perception is characterized by the themes of efficiency, selectivity, and consistency.

The Problem of Prejudice

▶ Prejudice is a particularly unfortunate outcome of the tendency to view others inaccurately. Blatant ("old-fashioned") discrimination occurs relatively infrequently today, but subtle expressions of prejudice and discrimination ("modern discrimination") have become more common.

▶ Common causes of prejudice include right-wing authoritarianism, cognitive distortions, competition between groups, and threats to social identity. Strategies for reducing prejudice are rooted in social thinking and collaborative intergroup contact.

The Power of Persuasion

▶ The success of persuasive efforts depends on several factors. A source of persuasion who is expert, trustworthy, likable, physically attractive, and similar to the receiver tends to be relatively effective. Although there are some limitations, two-sided arguments, arousal of fear, and generation of positive feelings are effective elements in persuasive messages. Persuasion is undermined when receivers are forewarned or have beliefs that are incompatible with the position being advocated.

▶ Persuasion takes place via two processes. The central route to persuasion requires a receiver to be motivated to process persuasive messages carefully (elaboration). A favorable reaction to such an evaluation will result in positive attitude change. When a receiver is unmotivated or unable to process persuasive messages carefully, persuasion may take place via the peripheral route (on the basis of simple cues such as a catchy tune).

The Power of Social Pressure

▶ Asch found that subjects often conform to the group, even when the group reports inaccurate judgments. Asch's experiments may have produced public compliance while subjects' private beliefs remained unchanged. Both normative and informational influence can produce conformity. Being mindful of social pressures and getting support from others with similar views are ways to resist conformity pressures.

▶ In Milgram's landmark study of obedience to authority, subjects showed a remarkable tendency to follow orders to shock an innocent stranger. Milgram's findings highlight the influence of situational pressures on behavior. Although people often obey authority figures, sometimes they are disobedient, usually because they have social support.

Application: Seeing Through Compliance Tactics

▶ Although they work for different reasons, all compliance tactics have the same goal: getting people to agree to requests. The foot-in-the-door and the lowball technique are based on the principle of consistency, while the door-in-the-face technique and the tactic of offering "giveaway" items rely on the principle of reciprocity. When advertisers suggest that products are in short supply, they are using the scarcity principle. Understanding these strategies can make you less vulnerable to manipulation.

KEY TERMS

Attitudes p. 188
Attributions p. 174
Bystander effect p. 195
Channel p. 188
Compliance p. 194
Confirmation bias p. 176
Conformity p. 192
Defensive attribution p. 180
Discrimination pp. 182–183
Door-in-the-face technique p. 200
Elaboration likelihood model p. 191
Foot-in-the-door technique p. 198
Fundamental attribution error p. 179
Informational influence p. 194
Lowball technique p. 199
Message p. 188
Need for cognition p. 191
Normative influence p. 194
Obedience p. 195
Person perception p. 173
Persuasion p. 188
Prejudice p. 182
Primacy effect p. 182
Receiver p. 188
Reciprocity principle p. 199
Self-fulfilling prophecy p. 177
Source p. 188
Stereotypes p. 178

KEY PEOPLE

Solomon Asch pp. 192–194
Robert Cialdini pp. 193, 198–201
Susan Fiske p. 174
Stanley Milgram pp. 195–197
Richard Petty and John Cacioppo pp. 191–192
Muzafer Sherif p. 186

PRACTICE TEST

1. Mindfulness operates when people:
   a. make snap judgments.
   b. are on "cognitive automatic pilot."
   c. make systematic judgments.
   d. are not concerned about forming accurate impressions.

2. Which of the following is *not* a type of cognitive distortion in perception?
   a. Categorizing
   b. The bystander effect
   c. Stereotypes
   d. Defensive attribution

3. Which of the following is *not* a theme in person perception?
   a. Efficiency
   b. Selectivity
   c. Consistency
   d. Mindfulness

4. "Old-fashioned" discrimination is _____; modern discrimination is _____.
   a. blatant; subtle
   b. legal; illegal
   c. common; rare
   d. race-based; gender-based

5. Which of the following is a cause of prejudice?
   a. Mindfulness
   b. Right-wing authoritarianism
   c. Jigsaw classrooms
   d. Activities based on superordinate goals

6. Receivers who are forewarned that someone will try to persuade them will most likely
   a. be very open to persuasion.
   b. get up and stomp out of the room.
   c. not be very open to persuasion.
   d. heckle the persuader.

7. Compared to attitudes formed via the peripheral route, those formed via the central route
   a. operate subliminally.
   b. are hard to change.
   c. last only a short time.
   d. are poor predictors of behavior.

8. When people change their outward behavior but not their private beliefs, _____ is operating.
   a. conformity
   b. persuasion
   c. obedience
   d. compliance

9. The results of Milgram's (1963) study imply that:
   a. situational factors can exert tremendous influence over behavior.
   b. in the real world, most people resist pressures to act in harmful ways.
   c. most people are willing to give obviously wrong answers on rigged perceptual tasks.
   d. disobedience is far more common than obedience.

10. When charities send prospective donors free address labels and the like, which of the following social influence principles are they using?
   a. The consistency principle
   b. The scarcity principle
   c. The reciprocity principle
   d. The foot-in-the-door principle

Book Companion Website

Visit the Book Companion Website at **academic.cengage.com/psychology/weiten,** where you will find tutorial quizzes, flash cards, and web links for every chapter, a final exam, and more! You can also link to the Psychology Resource Center (accessible directly at **academic.cengage.com/login**) for a range of psychology-related resources.

Personal Explorations Workbook

The following exercises in your *Personal Explorations Workbook* may enhance your self-understanding in relation to issues raised in this chapter. **Questionnaire 6.1:** Argumentativeness Scale. **Personal Probe 6.1:** Can You Identify Your Prejudicial Stereotypes? **Personal Probe 6.2:** How Do You Operate in a Group?

ANSWERS

1. c Page 174
2. b Pages 177–180
3. d Pages 181–182
4. a Pages 183–184
5. b Page 184
6. c Page 191
7. b Page 192
8. d Page 194
9. a Page 197
10. c Page 199

CHAPTER 7

Interpersonal Communication

THE PROCESS OF INTERPERSONAL COMMUNICATION
Components of the Communication Process
Technology and Interpersonal Communication
Communication and Adjustment

NONVERBAL COMMUNICATION
General Principles
Elements of Nonverbal Communication
Detecting Deception
The Significance of Nonverbal Communication

TOWARD MORE EFFECTIVE COMMUNICATION
Creating a Positive Interpersonal Climate
Conversational Skills
Self-Disclosure
Effective Listening

COMMUNICATION PROBLEMS
Communication Apprehension
Barriers to Effective Communication

INTERPERSONAL CONFLICT
Beliefs About Conflict
Types of Conflict

LIVING IN TODAY'S WORLD *Communication in an Adversarial Culture*
Styles of Managing Conflict
Dealing Constructively with Conflict

APPLICATION: DEVELOPING AN ASSERTIVE COMMUNICATION STYLE
The Nature of Assertiveness
Steps in Assertiveness Training

REVIEW

PRACTICE TEST

"Why don't you wear your new tie?" Robin suggests to Brian, as they are dressing to go out. "There you go again, telling me what to wear!" Brian retorts. To which Robin zings back with, "Oh, wear whatever you want. I don't care if you want to look like you're colorblind!" Could this couple have side-stepped the bad feelings and fight that are brewing? You bet! The keys to managing such encounters are recognizing the pitfalls of interpersonal communication and honing one's skills to deal effectively with them—two things you'll learn about in this chapter.

Communication skills are highly relevant to adjustment because they can be critical to happiness and success in life. In this chapter, we begin with an overview of the communication process and then turn to the important topic of nonverbal communication. Next, we discuss ways to communicate more effectively and examine common communication problems. Finally, we look at interpersonal conflict, including constructive ways to deal with it. In the Application, we consider ways to develop an assertive communication style.

The Process of Interpersonal Communication

LEARNING OBJECTIVES

- *List and explain the six components of the communication process.*
- *List several important differences between face-to-face and electronically mediated communication.*
- *Discuss how interpersonal communication is important to adjustment.*

Communication can be defined as the process of sending and receiving messages that have meaning. Your personal thoughts have meaning, of course, but when you "talk to yourself," you are engaging in *intra*personal communication. In this chapter, we will focus on *inter*personal communication—the transmission of meaning between two or more people. For the most part, we'll concentrate on two-person interactions.

We define ***interpersonal communication*** **as an interactional process in which one person sends a message to another.** Note several points about this definition. First, for communication to qualify as *interpersonal,* at least two people must be involved. Second, interpersonal communication is a *process.* By this, we simply mean that it usually involves a series of actions: Kelli talks/Jason listens, Jason responds/Kelli listens, and so on. Third, this process is *interactional.* Communication is generally not a one-way street: Both participants send as well as receive information when they're interacting. A key implication of this fact is that you need to pay attention to both *speaking* and *listening* if you want to be an effective communicator.

Components of the Communication Process

Let's take a look at the essential components of the interpersonal communication process. The key elements are (1) the sender, (2) the receiver, (3) the message, (4) the channel through which the message is sent, (5) noise or interference, and (6) the context in which the message is communicated. As we describe these components, refer to **Figure 7.1** to see how they work together.

The *sender* is the person who initiates the message. In a typical two-way conversation, both people serve as senders (as well as receivers). Keep in mind that each person brings a unique set of expectations and understandings to each communication situation. **The *receiver* is the person to whom the message is targeted.**

The *message* refers to the information or meaning that is transmitted from the sender to the receiver. The message is the *content* of the communication—that is, the ideas and feelings conveyed to another person. Two important cognitive processes underlie the transmission of messages: Speakers *encode* or transform their ideas and feelings into symbols and organize them into a message; receivers *decode* or translate a speaker's message into their own ideas and feelings (see **Figure 7.1**). Generally, fluent speakers of a language are unaware of these processes. If you've ever learned a new language, however, you have consciously experienced encoding (groping for the right word to express an idea) and decoding (trying to discover a word's meaning by how it is used).

The primary means of sending messages is language, but people also communicate to others nonverbally, through the facial expressions, gestures, and vocal inflections used to supplement (and sometimes entirely change) the meaning of verbal messages. For example, when you say, "Thanks a lot," your inflection can convey either sincere gratitude or heavy sarcasm.

The *channel* refers to the sensory channel through which the message reaches the receiver. Typically, people receive information from multiple channels simultaneously. They not only hear what the other person says, they also see the person's facial expressions, observe his or her gestures, experience eye contact, and sometimes feel the person's touch. Note that the messages in the various channels may be consistent or

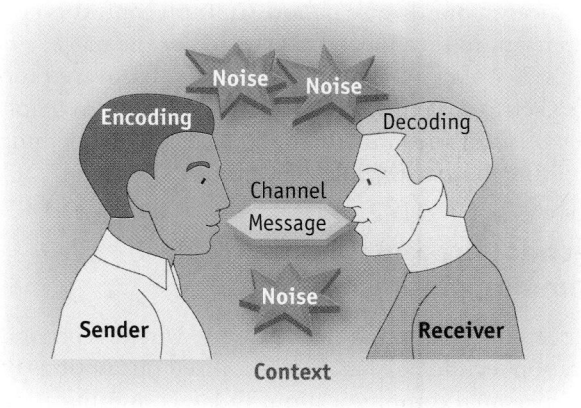

Figure 7.1

A model of interpersonal communication. Interpersonal communication involves six elements: the sender, the receiver, the message, the channel through which the message is transmitted, distorting noise, and the context in which the message is sent. In conversations, both participants function as sender and receiver.

inconsistent with each other, making their interpretation more or less difficult. Sometimes sound is the only channel available for receiving information—when you talk on the telephone, for instance. Through sound, people hear both the literal content of messages and vocal inflections. In computer-mediated communication (e-mail, chat rooms, and so on), only the visual channel is called into play, as individuals communicate in writing.

Whenever two people interact, miscommunication can occur. ***Noise* refers to any stimulus that interferes with accurately expressing or understanding a message.** Sources of noise include environmental factors (street traffic, loud music) and physical factors (poor hearing, poor vision). Noise can also have semantic origins (Verderber et al., 2008). For instance, profanity, ethnic slurs, or sexist language can cause a listener to disregard the larger message. In addition, psychological factors such as defensiveness and anxiety can contribute to noise, a topic we'll consider later in the chapter.

All social communication occurs in and is influenced by a ***context*, the environment in which communication takes place.** Context includes the *physical environment* (location, time of day, and noise level). Another aspect of the physical environment is how a conversation takes place: face to face, in a telephone call, or via the Internet. Other important aspects of context include the nature of the participants' *relationship* (work associates, friends, family), their *history* (previous interactions), their current *mood* (happy, stressed), and their *cultural backgrounds* (Verderber et al., 2008). Culture is especially important in the United States because of the varieties of subcultures, many with different rules of communication. The Recommended Reading *Multicultural Manners* is an excellent guide to the cultural variety in communication practices in our diverse nation. Cultural context is also important in the global marketplace, as the marketers of Coca-Cola in China unfortunately discovered too late (Petras & Petras, 1993). It seems that the symbols they used for the brand name translated to something like "Bite the wax tadpole" in Chinese!

Technology and Interpersonal Communication

The recent explosion in electronic and wireless communication technology has revolutionized our notions of interpersonal communication. Today, communication via e-mail, mailing lists (LISTSERVs), text messaging, instant messaging, chat rooms, and videoconferencing must be considered along with face-to-face interactions. ***Electronically mediated communication* is interpersonal communication that takes place via technology** (cell phones, computers, and hand-held devices). Even a new type of slang ("netlingo") has developed to facilitate quick and easy communication for use in text messaging, e-mail messages, and chat rooms (Ellis, 2006). **Figure 7.2** provides some examples of this slang.

Cell phones have both advantages and disadvantages. On the positive side, they are a convenient way to keep in touch with others, provide a sense of security, and can summon aid in an emergency. On the down side, they tie people to their jobs, can disrupt classrooms and public events, and bring private conversations into public places. Who hasn't been forced to listen to a loudmouth yelling his or her personal business into a cell phone in a public place? By now, most people are familiar with the basic rules of etiquette for

Multicultural Manners: New Rules of Etiquette for a Changing Society
by Norine Dresser (John Wiley & Sons, 2005)

This interesting book seeks to help Americans interact more comfortably and effectively as the nation becomes increasingly ethnically diverse. Written with humor, the book covers a wealth of practical issues that arise in a variety of settings: business, social, educational, and medical. The majority of the book addresses issues and situations that can result in miscommunication: body language, childrearing practices, classroom behavior, gift giving, male/female relations, verbal expressions, and so on. Each chapter includes real-life incidents of miscommunication, explanations of what happened in the situation, and verbal and behavioral guidelines for avoiding such problems. In two smaller sections of the book, Dresser explores the diversity in rules for holidays and worship (to help people feel comfortable when they visit unfamiliar places of worship) as well as multicultural health practices (some of which are benign, others of which are dangerous). Examples involve African Americans, Native Americans, Caribbean Islanders, Asians, Latinos, and recently arriving groups of immigrants. The author also provides information about the practices of a number of diverse religious groups.

Web Link 7.1 **NetLingo**

This unusual and informative site is the place to go to stay abreast of the latest terms related to cyberspace and technology. Visitors will find an Internet Dictionary containing thousands of technology terms and guides to the meaning of hundreds of text messaging acronyms as well as various emoticons (or smileys). Among the site's "Top 20" lists is one titled "Top 20 Internet Acronyms Every Parent Needs to Know."

Examples of Netlingo

Acronymn	Meaning
B4N or BFN	Bye For Now
CYM	Check Your Mail
GTG	Got To Go
IDK	I Don't Know
LOL	Laughing Out Loud
NBD	No Big Deal
PAL	Parents Are Listening
RUOK	Are You OK?
TY	Thank You
WKEWL	Way Cool

Figure 7.2

Cyberspace slang. A new type of slang has developed that allows quick and easy communication in e-mail messages, cell phone text messages, and chat rooms. These text messaging acronyms are variously termed netlingo, techspeak, or e-talk. Here you can see some frequently used text messaging acronyms and their meanings. Although netlingo is obviously useful for cybercommunication, its use in more formal settings (school, work) is problematic.

Copyright © 1994–2006. Netlingo™ The Internet Dictionary at http://www.netlingo.com

cell phone use in public: (1) turn off your phone (or put it on "vibrate" mode) when the ringing will disturb others, (2) keep your calls short, and (3) make and receive calls unobtrusively or out of earshot from others.

In the area of computer-mediated communication, e-mail is by far the most popular application, but chat rooms are also popular, especially among teens and those in their early and mid-20s (Nie & Erbring, 2002). As we have noted, face-to-face communication relies on the spoken word while Internet communication depends on the written word. You can see other important differences in **Figure 7.3** on the next page. The absence of nonverbal cues in computer-mediated communication means that you need to take special care that the other person understands your intended meaning. Thus, you should choose your words carefully, provide clarifying details, and describe your feelings, if necessary. It's also a good idea to review what you have written before you send it! The lack of nonverbal cues and the anonymous nature of computer-mediated communication also have important implications for relationship development (Bargh & McKenna, 2004), an issue we will take up in Chapter 8.

Communication and Adjustment

Before we plunge further into the topic of interpersonal communication, let's take a moment to emphasize its significance. Communication with others—friends, lovers, parents, spouses, children, employers, workers—is such an essential and commonplace aspect of everyday life that it's hard to overstate its role in adjustment. Many of life's gratifications (and frustrations and heartaches, as well) hinge on one's ability to communicate effectively with others. Numerous studies have shown that good communication can enhance satisfaction in relationships (Cordova, Gee, & Warren, 2005; Egeci & Gençöz, 2006) and that poor communication ranks high as a cause of breakups among both straight and gay couples (Kurdek, 1994, 1998).

© Richard Flood/DK Stock/Getty Images

Cell phone etiquette in public places calls for turning off your phone or putting it on vibrate mode, keeping your voice low and your calls short.

Dimension	Face-to-Face	Internet
Physical distance	People need to be in the same place at the same time to meet.	People can meet and develop a relationship with someone thousands of miles away.
Anonymity	One can't be anonymous in real-life interactions.	People take greater risks in disclosing personal information than they otherwise do. Thus, feelings of intimacy can develop more quickly.
Richness of communication	People have access to nonverbal cues such as facial expressions and tone of voice to detect nuances in meaning or deception.	In cyberspace, these cues are absent, making social and status cues, such as gender, age, social class, race, and ethnicity less discernible.
Visual cues	Physical appearance and visual cues play a big role in attraction in face-to-face relationships.	These cues are generally absent on the Internet (although people can exchange photographs online).
Time	Two people have to connect at the same time.	Although instant messaging and chat room conversations take place in real time, there is no need for an immediate response, so time becomes relatively unimportant. On the Internet, you can take as long as you like to craft a response so you can more completely explain yourself.

Figure 7.3

Differences between face-to-face and electronically mediated communication. Electronically mediated communication applications (cell phone text messaging, e-mail, chat rooms, news groups, and so forth) have dramatically changed the ways people interact and develop relationships. These two types of communication differ from each other in five important ways. (Adapted from Bargh & McKenna, 2004; Boase & Wellman, 2006; Verderber & Verderber, 2004)

Nonverbal Communication

LEARNING OBJECTIVES

- *List five general principles of nonverbal communication.*
- *Discuss personal space and display rules.*
- *Discuss what can be discerned from facial cues and eye contact.*
- *Describe the roles of body movement, posture, and gestures in communication.*
- *Summarize the research findings on touching and paralanguage.*
- *Discuss the difficulty of detecting deception and the nonverbal cues linked to deception.*
- *Describe the significance of nonverbal sensitivity in interpersonal interactions.*

You're standing at the bar in your favorite hangout, gazing across a dimly lit room filled with people drinking, dancing, and talking. You signal to the bartender that you'd like another drink. Your companion comments on the loudness of the music, and you nod your head in agreement. You spot an attractive stranger across the bar; your eyes meet for a moment and you smile. In a matter of seconds, you have sent three messages without uttering a syllable. To put it another way, you have just sent three *nonverbal* messages. ***Nonverbal communication* is the transmission of meaning from one person to another through means or symbols other than words.** Communication at the nonverbal level takes place through a variety of behaviors: interpersonal distance, facial expression, eye contact, body posture and movement, gestures, physical touch, and tone of voice.

Clearly, a great deal of information is exchanged through nonverbal channels—more than most people realize. You can significantly enhance your communication skills by learning more about this important aspect of communication.

General Principles

Let's begin by examining some general principles of nonverbal communication.

1. *Nonverbal communication conveys emotions.* People can communicate their feelings without saying a word—for example, "a look that kills." Nonverbal demonstrations of positive feelings include sitting or standing close to those you care for, touching them often, and looking at them frequently. Still, nonverbal signals, on their own, are not the precise indicators of emotional states that they were once believed to be (Samovar, Porter, & McDaniel, 2007), so you should be cautious in making inferences.

2. *Nonverbal communication is multichanneled.* Nonverbal communication typically involves simultaneous messages sent through a number of channels. For instance, information may be transmitted through gestures, facial expressions, eye contact, and vocal tone at the same time. In contrast, verbal communication is limited to a single channel: speech. If you have ever tried to follow two people speaking at once, you understand how difficult it is to process multiple inputs of information. This means that many nonverbal transmissions can sail by the receiver unnoticed.

3. *Nonverbal communication is ambiguous.* A shrug or a raised eyebrow can mean different things to different people. Moreover, receivers may have difficulty determining whether nonverbal messages are being sent intentionally. Although some popular books on body language imply otherwise, few nonverbal signals carry universally accepted meanings, even within the same culture. Thus, nonverbal cues are informative, but they are most reliable when accompanied by verbal messages and embedded in a familiar cultural and social context (Samovar et al., 2007).

4. *Nonverbal communication may contradict verbal messages.* How often have you seen people proclaim "I'm not angry" even though their bodies shout that they are positively furious? When confronted with such an inconsistency, which message should you believe? Because of their greater spontaneity, you're probably better off heeding the nonverbal signs. Research shows that when someone is instructed to tell a lie, deception is most readily detected through nonverbal signals (DePaulo, LeMay, & Epstein, 1991; Sporer & Schwandt, 2007).

5. *Nonverbal communication is culture-bound.* Like language, nonverbal signals are different in different cultures (Samovar et al., 2007). Sometimes cultural differences can be quite dramatic. For example, in Tibet people greet their friends by sticking out their tongues (Ekman, 1975).

The power of nonverbal communication was dramatically illustrated during the first Presidential Debate of the 2004 election. President Bush's poor performance during the debate was attributed, in part, to facial expressions that conveyed a variety of negative emotions.

Web Link 7.2 **Nonverbal Communication Research Page**

Social psychologist Marvin A. Hecht, this site's editor, has amassed numerous resources for those interested in nonverbal communication: major researchers, relevant journals, important news, the latest books, and helpful information about teaching and training. Although the page is of greatest interest to professionals, the links can introduce students and others to this fascinating field.

Elements of Nonverbal Communication

Nonverbal signals can provide a great deal of information in interpersonal interactions. As we discuss specific nonverbal behaviors, we will focus on what they communicate about interpersonal attraction and social status.

Personal Space

***Proxemics* is the study of people's use of interpersonal space. *Personal space* is a zone of space surrounding a person that is felt to "belong" to that person.** Personal space is like an invisible bubble you carry around with you in your social interactions. The size of this mobile zone is related to your cultural background, social status, personality, age, and gender.

The amount of interpersonal distance people prefer depends on the nature of the relationship and the situation (J. A. Hall, 1990). The appropriate distance between people is also regulated by social norms and varies by culture (J. A. Hall, 1990; Samovar et al., 2007). For instance, people of Northern European heritage tend to engage in less physical contact and keep a greater distance between themselves than people of Latin or Middle Eastern heritage. The United States is usually characterized as a medium-contact culture, but there is a lot of variability among ethnic groups.

Anthropologist Edward T. Hall (1966) has described four interpersonal distance zones that are appropriate for middle-class encounters in American culture (see **Figure 7.4** on the next page). The general rule is that the more you like someone, the more comfortable you feel being physically close to that person. Of course, there are obvious exceptions, such as in crowded subways and elevators, but these situations are often experienced as stressful. Women seem to have smaller personal-space zones than men do (Holland et al., 2004). When talking, women sit or stand closer together than men do.

Personal distance can also convey information about status. People generally stand farther away from

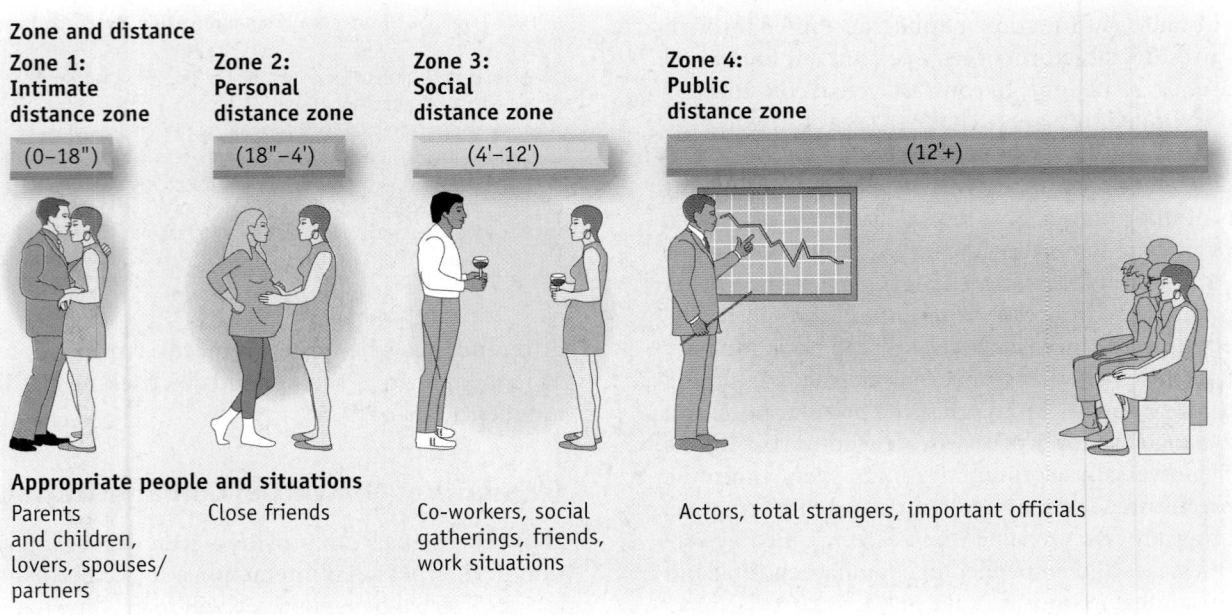

Figure 7.4

Interpersonal distance zones. According to Edward Hall (1966), people like to keep a certain amount of distance between themselves and others. The distance that makes one feel comfortable depends on whom one is interacting with and the nature of the situation.

high-status communication partners versus partners of lower power (Holland et al., 2004). Moreover, it is the prerogative of the more powerful person in an interaction to set the "proper" distance (Henley, 1986).

Invasions of personal space usually produce discomfort and stimulate attempts to restore your privacy zone. To illustrate, if someone stands too close, you may back up. Or, if a stranger sits down at "your" table in the library and forces you to share it, you may reorient your body away from the intruder, place a barrier (for example, a stack of books) between you and the invader, or move to a different table. Invasions of personal space rarely go unnoticed, and they usually elicit a variety of reactions.

Facial Expression

More than anything else, facial expressions convey emotions (Horstmann, 2003). Paul Ekman and Wallace Friesen have identified six distinctive facial expressions that correspond with six basic emotions: anger, disgust, fear, happiness, sadness, and surprise (Ekman, 1994; Ekman & Friesen, 1984). Early research involving participants from many countries supported the idea that these six emotions are universally recognized (Ekman, 1972). In such studies, researchers show photographs depicting different emotions to subjects from a variety of Western and non-Western cultures and ask them to match the photographs with an emotion. Some representative results from this research are depicted in **Figure 7.5**.

© AP Images/Greg Baker

Display rules require unsuccessful contestants in beauty pageants to suppress the display of resentful, envious, or angry feelings.

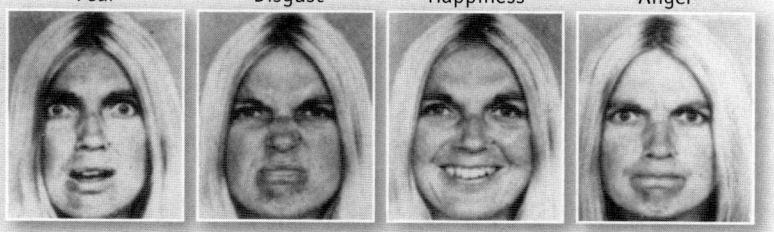

Country	Fear	Disgust	Happiness	Anger
	Emotion displayed			
	Agreement in judging photos (%)			
United States	85	92	97	67
Brazil	67	97	95	90
Chile	68	92	95	94
Argentina	54	92	98	90
Japan	66	90	100	90
New Guinea	54	44	82	50

Figure 7.5

Facial expressions and emotions. Ekman and Friesen (1984) found that people in highly disparate cultures showed fair agreement on the emotions portrayed in these photos. This consensus across cultures suggests that the facial expressions associated with certain emotions may have a biological basis.

Photos from *Unmasking the Face,* © 1975 by Paul Ekman, photographs courtesy of Paul Ekman

A more recent meta-analysis of 97 studies (over 42 countries) looked at whether these six emotions are universally recognized or are culturally specific (Elfenbein & Ambady, 2002). Interestingly, there was evidence for both perspectives. In support of the universal view, individuals do accurately recognize emotions in photographs of people from other cultures. Favoring cultural specificity, there was evidence of an "ingroup advantage." Thus, observers are better at recognizing the emotions in photographs from their own cultural groups than from cultural outgroups. A few basic facial expressions are universally recognizable, but other emotional expressions vary from culture to culture—as we noted in the earlier example of Tibetans sticking out their tongues to greet their friends.

Each society has rules that govern whether and when it is appropriate to express one's feelings (Zaalberg, Manstead, & Fischer, 2004). ***Display rules* are norms that govern the appropriate display of emotions in a culture.** In the United States, for instance, it is considered bad form to gloat over one's victories or to show envy or anger in defeat.

Besides cultural differences, there are gender differences in facial expression (LaFrance, Hecht, & Paluck, 2003). For example, men typically show less facial expression than women do, a finding linked to social pressures for males to inhibit such displays (Kilmartin, 2007). Also, as you might expect, high self-monitors are better than low self-monitors at managing their facial expressions (Gangestad & Snyder, 2000).

Is it possible to deliberately deceive others through facial expression? Absolutely. In fact, people are better at sending deceptive messages with their faces than with other areas of their bodies (Ekman & O'Sullivan, 1991). You are no doubt familiar with the term "poker face," an allusion to poker players who are experts at controlling their excitement about a good hand of cards (or their dismay about a bad one).

Eye Contact

Eye contact (also called mutual gaze) is another major channel of nonverbal communication. The duration of eye contact is its most meaningful aspect. Because there is considerable research on "eye communication," we will summarize the most relevant findings.

Among European Americans, people who engage in high levels of eye contact are usually judged to have effective social skills and credibility. Similarly, speakers, interviewers, and experimenters receive higher ratings of competence when they maintain high rather than low eye contact with their audience. As a rule, people engage in more eye contact when they're listening than when they're talking (Bavelas, Coates, & Johnson, 2002).

Gaze also communicates the *intensity* (but not the positivity or negativity) of feelings. For example, couples who say they are in love spend more time gazing at each other than other couples do (Patterson, 1988). Also, maintaining moderate (versus constant or no) eye contact with others typically generates positive feelings in them.

In a negative interpersonal context, a steady gaze becomes a stare that causes most people to feel uncomfortable (Kleinke, 1986). Moreover, like threat displays among nonhuman primates such as baboons and rhesus monkeys, a stare can convey aggressive intent (Henley, 1986). Thus, if you want to avoid road rage incidents, avoid making eye contact with hostile motorists. People also communicate by *reducing* eye contact with others. Unpleasant interactions, embarrassing situations, or invasions of personal space usually trigger this behavior (Kleinke, 1986).

© Walter Hodges/Corbis

© Tony Freeman/PhotoEdit

The eyes can be used to convey either very positive or very negative feelings.

Culture strongly affects patterns of eye contact (Samovar et al., 2007). For example, Americans should be sensitive to the fact that direct eye contact is perceived as an insult in Mexico, Latin America, Japan, and Africa, and in some Native American tribes. By contrast, people from Arab countries look directly into the eyes of their conversational partners for longer periods than Americans are used to.

In the United States, gender and racial differences have been found in eye contact. For instance, women tend to gaze at others more than men do (Briton & Hall, 1995). However, the patterning of eye contact also reflects status, and gender and status are often confounded. Higher-status individuals look at the other person more when speaking than when listening, while lower-status people behave just the opposite. Women usually show the lower-status visual pattern because they are typically accorded lower status than men. As you can see in **Figure 7.6**, when women are in high-power positions, they show the high-status visual pattern to the same extent that men do (Dovidio et al., 1988). African Americans use more continuous eye contact than European Americans when speaking, but less when listening (Samovar & Porter, 2004). Misunderstandings can arise if eye-gaze behaviors that are intended to convey interest and respect are interpreted as being disrespectful or dishonest.

Body Language

Body movements—those of the head, trunk, hands, legs, and feet—also provide nonverbal avenues of communication. ***Kinesics* is the study of communication through body movements.** By noting a person's body movements, observers may be able to tell an individual's level of tension or relaxation. For instance, frequent touching or scratching suggests nervousness (Harrigan et al., 1991).

Posture also conveys information. Leaning back with arms or legs arranged in an asymmetrical or "open" position conveys a feeling of relaxation. Posture can also indicate someone's attitude toward you (McKay, Davis, & Fanning, 1995). A body leaning toward you typically indicates interest and a positive attitude. Conversely, a body angled away from you or crossed arms may indicate a negative attitude or defensiveness.

Posture can also convey status differences. Generally, a higher-status person will look more relaxed. By contrast, a lower-status person will tend to exhibit a more rigid body posture, often sitting up straight with feet together, flat on the floor, and arms close to the body (a "closed" position) (J. A. Hall, 1984; Vrugt & Luyerink, 2000). Again, status and gender differences are frequently parallel. That is, men are more likely to exhibit the high-status "open" posture and women the lower-status "closed" posture (Cashdan, 1998).

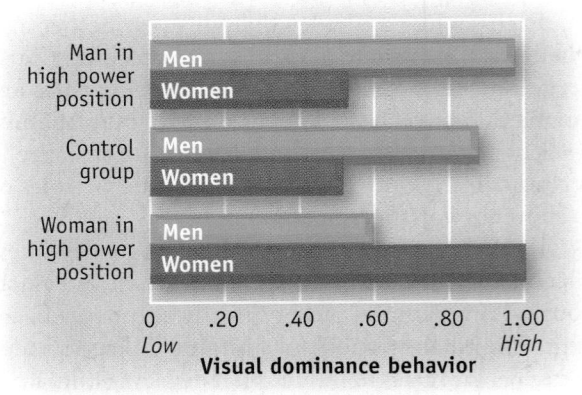

Figure 7.6

Visual dominance, status, and gender. Women typically show low visual dominance (see control condition) because they are usually accorded lower status than men (Dovidio et al. 1988). However, when researchers placed women in a high-power position and measured their visual behavior, women showed the high visual dominance pattern and men showed the low visual dominance pattern. When men were placed in the high-power position, the visual dominance patterns reversed. Thus, visual dominance seems to be more a function of status than of gender.

People use *hand gestures* to describe and emphasize the words they speak. You might point to give directions or slam your fist onto a desk to emphasize an assertion. As travelers frequently discover, the meaning of gestures is not universal (Samovar et al., 2007). For instance, a circle made with the thumb and forefinger means that everything is "OK" to an American but is considered an obscene gesture in some countries.

People in higher-status positions tend to adopt an "open" body posture, and those in lower-status roles usually adopt a "closed" position.

Touch

Touch takes many forms and can express a variety of meanings: support, consolation, and sexual intimacy. Touch can also convey messages of status and power. In the United States, people typically "touch downward"—i.e., higher-status individuals are freer to touch subordinates than vice versa (Henley & Freeman, 1995). How people interpret the possible messages communicated by touch depends on the age and gender of the individuals involved, the setting in which the touching takes place, and the relationship between the toucher and recipient, among other things (Major, Schmidlin, & Williams, 1990). Also, there are strong norms about *where* people are allowed to touch friends. These norms are quite different for same-gender as opposed to cross-gender interactions, as can be seen in **Figure 7.7**.

Other findings about touching behavior come from an observational study of 4,500 pairs of Bostonians interacting in a variety of public places, such as shopping malls, hotel lobbies, and subway stations (Hall & Veccia, 1990, 1991). For one thing, female-female pairs touched each other significantly more than male-male pairs. Second, in younger pairs, men touched women more, but in older pairs, the pattern was reversed. Comparable age changes were not found for same-gender pairs.

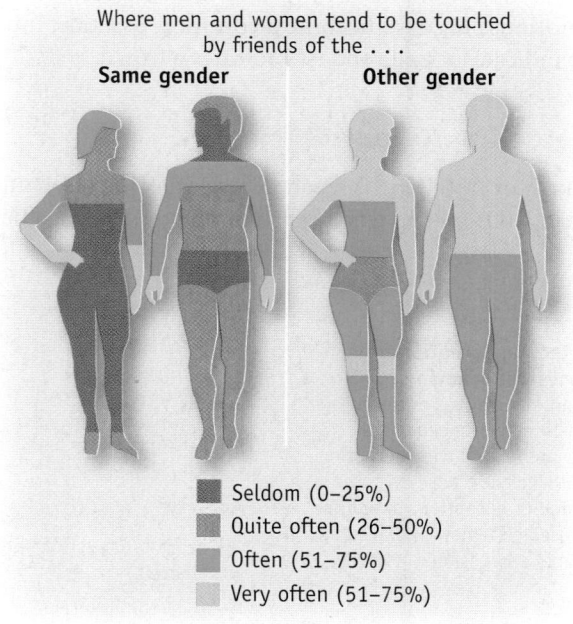

Figure 7.7

Where friends touch each other. Social norms govern where friends tend to touch each other. As these figures show, the patterns of touching are different in same-gender as opposed to cross-gender interactions.

Adapted from Marsh, P. (Ed.). (1988). *Eye to eye: How people interact.* Topsfield, MA: Salem House. Copyright © 1988 by Andromeda Oxford Ltd. Reprinted by permission of HarperCollins, Publishers, Inc. and Andromeda Oxford Ltd.

Paralanguage

The term *paralanguage* refers to *how* something is said rather than to *what* is said. Thus, ***paralanguage* includes all vocal cues other than the content of the verbal message itself.** These cues include how loudly or softly people speak, how fast they talk, and the pitch, rhythm, and quality of their speech. Each of these vocal characteristics can affect the message being transmitted.

Variations in vocal emphasis can give the same set of words very different meanings. Consider the sentence "I really enjoyed myself." By varying the word that is accented, you can speak this sentence in three ways, each resulting in a different meaning:

- ► *I* really enjoyed myself! (Even though others may not have had a good time, I did.)
- ► I *really* enjoyed myself! (My enjoyment was exceptional.)
- ► I really *enjoyed* myself! (Much to my surprise, I had a great time.)

As you can see from these examples, you can actually reverse the literal meaning of a verbal message by how you say it (such as with sarcasm).

Aspects of vocalization can also communicate emotions (Banse & Scherer, 1996). For example, rapid speech may mean that a person is happy, frightened, or nervous. Slower speech might be used when people are uncertain or when they want to emphasize a point. Loud vocalization often signals anger. A relatively high pitch may indicate anxiety. Slow speech, low volume, and low pitch are often associated with sadness. Thus, vocal quality provides another window on someone's true feelings. Keep in mind, however, that it is easy to assign meanings to voice quality that aren't valid, such as associating a deep voice with masculinity and maturity and a high, breathy voice with femininity and youth.

In cyberspace communication, e-mailers use various substitutes for the paralanguage cues used in spoken communication. For instance, capital letters are used for emphasis ("I had a GREAT vacation"); however, using capital letters throughout a message is viewed as shouting and considered rude behavior. Using *emoticons* (punctuation marks arranged to indicate the writer's emotions) has also become a common practice; thus, :-) indicates a smile and :-(indicates a frown.

Detecting Deception

Like it or not, lying is a part of everyday life (DePaulo et al., 2003). People typically tell one to two lies a day (DePaulo et al., 1997). Most of these everyday lies are inconsequential "white lies," such as claiming to be better than one actually is or lying to avoid hurting someone's feelings.

Courtesy, Bella DePaulo

Bella DePaulo

Is it possible to catch people in a lie? Yes, but it's difficult—even for experts (Bond & DePaulo, 2006). Some studies have found that professionals whose work involves detecting lies (police officers, FBI agents, and psychiatrists, for example) are more accurate judges of liars than nonexperts are (Ekman, O'Sullivan, & Frank, 1999), Still, even these individuals have accuracy rates around 57%—not much better than chance (50%). Moreover, a recent meta-analysis found no significant differences in the accuracy rates of experts and non-experts (Bond & DePaulo, 2006). Regardless, people overestimate their ability to detect liars (DePaulo et al., 1997).

The popular stereotypes about how liars give themselves away don't necessarily correspond to the actual clues related to dishonesty. For example, observers tend to focus on the face (the least revealing channel) and to ignore more useful information (Burgoon, 1994). In **Figure 7.8**, you can review the research findings on the nonverbal behaviors actually associated with deception (based on DePaulo, Stone, & Lassiter, 1985). By comparing the second and third columns in the figure, you can see which cues are actually associated with deception and which are erroneously linked with decep-

Figure 7.8

Detecting deception from nonverbal behaviors. This chart summarizes evidence on which nonverbal cues are *actually* associated with deception and which are *believed* to be a sign of deception, based on a research review by DePaulo, Stone, and Lassiter (1985).

Nonverbal Cues and Deceptions

Kind of Cue	Are cues associated with actual deception?	Are cues believed to be a sign of deception?
Vocal cues		
Speech hesitations	YES: Liars hesitate more	YES
Voice pitch	YES: Liars speak with higher pitch	YES
Speech errors (stutters, stammers)	YES: Liars make more errors	YES
Speech latency (pause before starting to speak or answer)	NO	YES: People think liars pause more
Speech rate	NO	YES: People think liars talk slower
Response length	YES: Liars give shorter answers	NO
Visual cues		
Pupil dilation	YES: Liars show more dilation	(No research data)
Adapters (self-directed gestures)	YES: Liars touch themselves more	NO
Blinking	YES: Liars blink more	(No research data)
Postural shifts	NO	YES: People think liars shift more
Smile	NO	YES: People think liars smile less
Gaze (eye contact)	NO	YES: People think liars engage in less eye contact

tion. Contrary to popular belief, lying is *not* associated with slow talking, long pauses before speaking, excessive shifting of posture, reduced smiling, or lack of eye contact. A meta-analysis of over 300 studies generally supported these findings, concluding that liars say less, tell less-compelling stories, make a more negative impression, are more tense, and include less unusual content in their stories than truth tellers do (DePaulo et al., 2003).

So, how *do* liars give themselves away? As you may have noted in **Figure 7.8**, many of the clues "leak" from nonverbal channels, because speakers have a harder time controlling these channels (DePaulo & Friedman, 1998; Ekman and Friesen, 1974). Vocal cues include speaking with a higher pitch, giving relatively short answers, and excessive hesitations. Visual cues include dilation of the pupils. It's also helpful to look for inconsistencies between facial expressions and lower body movements. For example, a friendly smile accompanied by a nervous shuffling of feet could signal deception.

Bella DePaulo (1994), a noted researcher in this area, isn't too optimistic about the prospects of teaching people to spot lies, because the cues are usually subtle. If she's correct, perhaps *machines* can do better. **The *polygraph* is a device that records fluctuations in physiological arousal as a person answers questions.** Although called a "lie detector," it's really an emotion detector. The polygraph monitors key indicators of autonomic arousal such as heart rate, blood pressure, respiration rate, and perspiration, or galvanic skin response (GSR). The assumption is that when people lie, they experience emotion that produces noticeable changes in these physiological indicators (see **Figure 7.9**).

Polygraph experts claim that lie detector tests are 85%–90% accurate and that there is research support for the validity of polygraph testing (Honts, Raskin, & Kircher, 2002). These claims are clearly not supported by the evidence. Methodologically sound research on this question is surprisingly sparse (largely because the research is difficult to do), and the limited evidence available is not very impressive (Branaman & Gallagher, 2005; Fiedler, Schmid, & Stahl, 2002). One problem is that when people respond to incriminating questions, they may experience emotional arousal even when they are telling the truth. Thus, polygraph tests often lead to accusations against the innocent. Another problem is that some people can lie without experiencing physiological arousal. Thus, because of high error rates, polygraph results are not admitted as evidence in most types of courtrooms. Yet, many companies require prospective and current employees to take lie detector tests to weed out thieves. Obviously, it would be extremely useful to have a test or a machine that could easily and accurately detect deception. Thus, researchers continue to search for such a device.

To summarize, deception is potentially detectable, but the nonverbal behaviors that accompany lying are subtle and difficult to spot.

© Bob Daemmrich/The Image Works

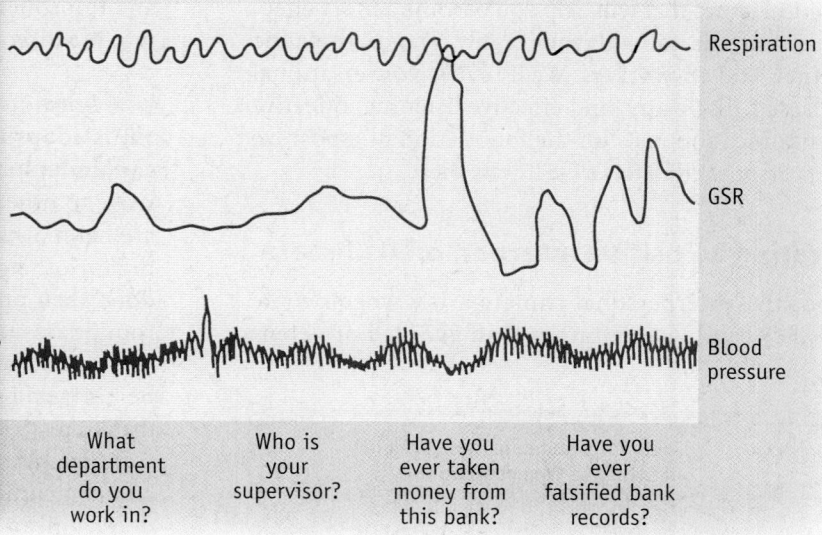

Figure 7.9

The polygraph measures emotional reactions. A lie detector measures the physiological arousal that most people experience when they tell a lie. After using nonthreatening questions to establish a baseline, a polygraph examiner looks for signs of arousal (such as the sharp change in GSR shown here) on incriminating questions.

The Significance of Nonverbal Communication

Good nonverbal communication skills are associated with good social adjustment and with relationship satisfaction (Schachner, Shaver, & Mikulincer, 2005). Experts give particular attention to ***nonverbal sensitivity*—the ability to accurately encode (express) and decode (understand) nonverbal cues.** Nonverbal sensitivity is related to social and academic competence even in children (Hubbard & Coie, 1994; Izard et al., 2001).

In a study of college students' romantic relationships, nonverbal sensitivity was correlated with relationship well-being (Carton, Kessler, & Pape, 1999). And it's been found that spouses with poor nonverbal communication skills are more dissatisfied with their marriages (Noller, 1987). Since these are correlational studies, we can't tell whether nonverbal insensitivity leads to marital dissatisfaction or whether unhappy relationships cause couples to make less effort at communicating. No doubt both possibilities are correct. And nonverbal insensitivity and dissatifaction can set up a vicious cycle that spirals downward (Miller, Perlman, and Brehm, 2007).

Generally women are better encoders and decoders of nondeceptive messages than men (Hall, 1998). It is not that women are innately better at these skills or that they have lower status than men. Rather, it seems that women are more motivated than men to exert effort at these skills (Hall, Coats, & LeBeau, 2005; Hall & Matsumoto, 2004). The good news is that men (and women) who are willing to exert some effort can improve their nonverbal communication skills—and enjoy happier and more satisfying relationships.

Toward More Effective Communication

LEARNING OBJECTIVES

- *List five suggestions for creating a positive interpersonal climate.*
- *Give five steps involved in making small talk.*
- *Explain how self-disclosure is important to adjustment.*
- *Cite some ways to reduce the risks of self-disclosure.*
- *Describe the role of self-disclosure in relationship development.*
- *Discuss cultural and gender differences in self-disclosure.*
- *Cite four points good listeners need to keep in mind.*

If you are like most people, you probably overestimate how effectively you communicate with others (Keysar & Henly, 2002). In this section, we'll turn to some practical issues that will help you become a more effective communicator with your family, friends, romantic partner, and co-workers. We'll review conversational skills, self-disclosure, and effective listening. Effective communication rests on the foundation of a positive interpersonal climate, so we'll start there.

Creating a Positive Interpersonal Climate

A positive interpersonal climate exists when people feel they can be open rather than guarded or defensive in their communication. Nonverbal sensitivity is one important ingredient in creating a positive atmosphere. You can also help create (and maintain) such an atmosphere by putting the following suggestions into practice.

Web Link 7.3 **Tools for Communication: A Model of Effective Communication**

Communicating effectively is essential to success in most aspects of life, including relationships and work. This online manual provides helpful advice on key issues related to effective communication. It is one of many online manuals on coping with various life stresses at Coping.org, a site maintained by James J. Messina, Ph.D. and Constance M. Messina, Ph.D.

▶ *Learn to feel and communicate empathy.* ***Empathy* is adopting another's frame of reference so you can understand his or her point of view.** Being sensitive to others' needs and accepting of their feelings are hallmarks of empathy. Note that showing empathy for others doesn't require you to condone or endorse their problematic behavior. For example, if your roommate confides his concerns about his drinking, you can support him as a person by continuing to be his friend—without encouraging him to continue drinking.

▶ *Practice withholding judgment.* You can promote an open climate by trying to be nonjudgmental. That doesn't mean that you can't express opinions and make judgments. It merely means that you should strive to interact with people in ways that don't make them feel inadequate or that put them down.

▶ *Strive for honesty.* Mutual trust and respect thrive on authenticity and honesty. So-called hidden agendas don't stay hidden for long. Even if others don't know exactly what your underlying motives are, they often can sense that you're not being entirely honest. Of course, striving for honesty does not require you to communicate everything to everyone. For those conversations that are unavoidably painful—such as breaking up with a romantic partner—you should strive to be honest without being needlessly hurtful.

▶ *Approach others as equals.* Most people don't like to be reminded of another's higher status or greater ability. When you have the higher status, it helps to approach people on equal terms.

▶ *Express your opinions tentatively.* Instead of coming across as a know-it-all, let others know that your beliefs and attitudes are flexible and subject to revision. Using qualifying words or phrases is helpful. For instance, instead of announcing, "Here's the plan," you might say, "There seem to be several options; I lean toward . . . What do you think?"

Conversational Skills

When it comes to meeting strangers, some people launch right into a conversation, while others break into a cold sweat as their minds go completely blank. If you fall into the second category, don't despair! The art of conversation is actually based on conversational *skills.* And these skills can be learned. To get you started, we'll offer a few general principles, gleaned primarily from *Messages: The Communication Skills Book* by McKay and associates (1995). If you want to explore this topic in greater depth, this book is an excellent source of practical advice.

First, follow the Golden Rule: Give to others what you would like to receive from them. In other words, give others your attention and respect and let them know that you like them. Second, focus on the other person instead of yourself. Concentrate on what the person is saying, rather than on how you look, what you're going to say next, or winning the argument. Third, as we have noted, use nonverbal cues to communicate your interest in the other person. Like you, others also find it easier to interact with a person who signals friendliness. A welcoming smile can make a big difference in initial contacts.

Now, how do you actually get the conversational ball rolling? Psychologist Bernardo Carducci (1999) suggests five steps for making successful small talk. We'll use his template and fill in with additional suggestions:

1. *Indicate that you are open to conversation by commenting on your surroundings.* ("This line sure is slow.") Of course, you can begin with other topics, too, but you should be careful about your opening line. In one study, participants viewed videotapes of a man or a woman approaching an other-gender stranger and initiating a conversation using a cute/flippant, an innocuous, or a direct opening line (Kleinke, Meeker, & Staneski, 1986). The preferred openers were either innocuous ("Where are you from?") or direct ("Hi, I'm a little embarrassed about this, but I'd like to get to know you"). In contrast, the least preferred openers were of the cute/flippant variety ("Hi, I'm easy—are you?"). Because cute lines often backfire, your best bet is probably the conventional approach.

2. *Introduce yourself.* Do this early in the conversation and use specifics to give the other person information to help find common ground. ("I'm Jeremy Jackson. I'm a psychology major at the university.")

3. *Select a topic others can relate to.* ("I heard a great band last night.") Keep an eye out for similarities and differences between you and your conversational partner (McKay et al., 1995). Thus, look for things you have in common—a tattoo, a class, a hometown—and build a conversation around that. Alternatively, work off of your differences. ("How did you get interested in science fiction? I'm a mystery fan myself.")

4. *Keep the conversational ball rolling.* You can keep things going by elaborating on your initial topic. ("After the band finished, a bunch of us walked to the new coffee house and tried their death-by-chocolate dessert special.") Alternatively, you can introduce a related topic or start a new one.

5. *Make a smooth exit.* Politely end the conversation. ("Well, I've got to be going. I enjoyed talking with you.")

Messages: The Communication Skills Book
by Matthew McKay, Martha Davis, and Patrick Fanning (New Harbinger Publications, 1995)

In this short book, you will find a wealth of information by which to improve your communication skills in a wide variety of situations. *Messages* is organized according to six types of communication skills: basic, advanced, conflict, social, family, and public. Within each of these sections, chapters address important issues. For example, the section on family skills includes chapters on sexual communication, parent effectiveness, and family communications; the section on public skills addresses communication in small groups and public speaking; and "advanced skills" deals with hidden agendas, transactional analysis, and the role of culture and gender in communication. The authors have a breezy writing style and use lots of examples to illustrate their points. They have also included numerous exercises to help you assess your communication skills and practice more effective ways of interacting with others.

After you've learned a little about another person, you may want to move the relationship to a deeper level. This is where self-disclosure comes into play, the topic we'll address next.

Self-Disclosure

***Self-disclosure* is the act of sharing information about yourself with another person.** In other words, self-disclosure involves opening up about yourself to others. The information you share doesn't have to be a deep, dark secret, but it may be. Conversations with strangers and acquaintances typically start with superficial self-disclosure—your opinion of the TV show you saw last night or your views on who will win the World Series. Typically, only when people have come to like and trust each other do they begin to share private information—such as self-consciousness about one's weight, or jealousy of one's brother (Greene, Derlega, & Mathews, 2006). **Figure 7.10** illustrates how self-disclosure varies according to type of relationship.

In discussing self-disclosure, we will focus on verbal communication. But keep in mind that *non*verbal communication plays an equally important role in self-disclosure (Laurenceau & Kleinman, 2006). For example, you have already seen how nonverbal cues can support or completely change the meaning of the words they accompany. Also, nonverbal behaviors can determine whether interactions have positive, neutral, or negative outcomes. Thus, if you tell a friend about a very distressing experience and she signals her concern via sympathtic nonverbal cues (eye contact, leaning forward, intent facial expression), your feelings about the interaction will be positive. But if she conveys a lack of interest (looking around the room, bored facial expression), you will walk away with negative feelings.

Self-disclosure is critically important to adjustment for several reasons. First, sharing fears and problems (as well as good news) with others who are trustworthy and supportive plays a key role in mental health

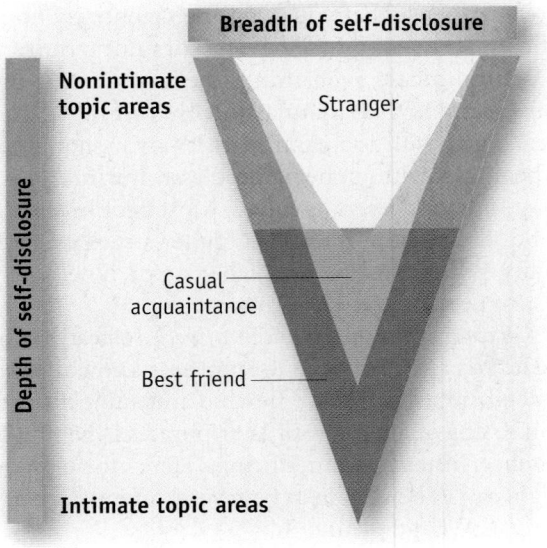

Figure 7.10

Breadth and depth of self-disclosure. Breadth of self-disclosure refers to how many topics one opens up about; depth refers to how far one goes in revealing private information. Both the breadth and depth of one's disclosures are greater with best friends as opposed to casual acquaintances or strangers. (Adapted from Altman & Taylor, 1973)

(Greene et al., 2006). Recall from Chapter 4 that sharing your feelings can reduce stress. And after mutual self-disclosures, people experience a boost in positive feelings (Vittengl & Holt, 2000). Second, emotional (but not factual) self-disclosures lead to feelings of closeness, as long as disclosers feel that listeners are understanding and accepting (Laurenceau & Kleinman 2006; Reis & Shaver, 1988). And, as you saw in Chapter 1, having close relationships is an important ingredient of happiness.

Third, self-disclosure in romantic relationships correlates positively with relationship satisfaction (Greene

DAVE © 1993. Dave Miller. Reprinted with permission of the artist. All rights reserved.

© Mary Kate Denny/PhotoEdit

Self-disclosure can be a risky business. In many instances self-disclosure can lead to increased intimacy, but that depends on the nature of the relationship and the disclosure. Hence, when making disclosures it is important to pay attention to others' nonverbal reactions.

et al., 2006). More specifically, *equity* in self-disclosure, rather than high self-disclosure, may be the critical factor that helps couples avoid stress (Bowers, Metts, & Duncanson, 1985).

Reducing the Risks of Self-Disclosure

Let's face it: Disclosing private information to others is a risky business. When you reveal private things about yourself to others, they might reject you or divulge your confidences to someone else. A study of European college students reported that they revealed others' personal emotional disclosures to third parties in 66%–78% of the cases (Christophe & Rime, 1997). Although the researchers did not ask the students if they had been sworn to secrecy, in 85 percent of the cases the students were intimates (versus acquaintances) of the self-disclosers. Moreover, more emotionally intense disclosures were more likely to be shared—and with more people—than less emotionally intense revelations. Thus, if you have a secret you cannot risk others knowing but that is troubling you, it is probably safer to share it with a trained counselor. Alternatively, writing about an issue, such as in a journal, can help you feel better (Pennebaker, 1997; Sloan & Marx, 2004). Lab studies have also shown that written disclosures in e-mail form can have beneficial effects (Sheese, Brown, & Graziano, 2004).

While it pays to be discriminating about sharing private business, limiting your conversations to superficial topics won't deepen a relationship. To safely steer the conversation toward more intimate topics, we advise using the strategy of *gradual* self-disclosure. Moving gradually gives you the chance to observe how the other person responds to your self-disclosures. Of course, the principle of gradual self-disclosure doesn't always hold. Many people can tell, early on, which relationships they want to remain relatively superficial and which they would like to become more intimate. But, for most situations, we advise gradual self-disclosure as the optimal route to close relationships because it entails less risk and stress.

How can you gauge whether it's safe to share personal information with someone? It should reassure you to know that self-disclosure is *usually* reciprocated in depth and topic (Collins & Miller, 1994). Thus, a good strategy is to monitor your partners' verbal and nonverbal cues for their reactions to your disclosures. If you make a personal disclosure and the other person reciprocates with a parallel disclosure, this reciprocity ordinarily signals comfort with more intimacy. Of course, some people who aren't comfortable engaging in self-disclosure themselves are sincerely willing to listen to you anyway. Thus, you can't depend on reciprocity alone as an indicator of another's interest.

That's why tuning in to nonverbal signals is of crucial importance (Laurenceau & Kleinman, 2006). When people are uncomfortable, they will usually send you a nonverbal message to that effect to avoid the awkwardness of an obvious verbal warning. "Stop" cues include reduced eye contact and a puzzled, apprehensive, or pained facial expression. Your partner may angle his or her body away from you, increase the distance between you, or shuffle his or her feet impatiently. In contrast, when listeners lean forward, appear relaxed, and maintain good eye contact, they are likely interested in your self-disclosure.

What about the risk of self-disclosure in computer-mediated communication? Because of the relative anonymity of the Internet, self-disclosure in e-mail and chat rooms involves less face-to-face risk (Bargh & McKenna, 2004). Still, electronically mediated communication has risks of its own, including your e-mail messages being passed on without your knowledge and predators taking adavantage of you. We'll explore the implications of electronically mediated communication for relationship development in Chapter 8.

Self-Disclosure and Relationship Development

Earlier, we noted that self-disclosure leads to feelings of intimacy. Actually, the process is a little more complicated than that. Research suggests that only certain types of disclosures lead to feelings of closeness (Laurenceau, Barrett, & Rovine, 2005). For instance, emotional-evaluative self-disclosures (how you feel about your sister, for instance) do, but factual-descriptive self-disclosures (that you have three siblings, for example) do not. Moreover, for intimacy to develop in a relationship, a discloser must feel understood and cared for (Reis & Patrick, 1996; Lin & Huang, 2006). In other words, self-disclosure alone doesn't lead to intimacy.

Self-disclosure varies over the course of relationships. At the beginning of a relationship, high levels of mutual disclosure prevail (Taylor & Altman, 1987). Once a relationship is well established, the level of disclosure tapers off, although responsiveness remains high (Reis & Patrick, 1996). Also, in established relationships, people are less likely to reciprocate disclosures in the same conversation. Thus, when a lover or a good friend reveals private information, you frequently respond with words of sympathy and understanding rather than a like disclosure. This movement away from equal exchanges of self-disclosure appears to be based on twin needs that emerge as intimate relationships develop: (1) the need for connection (via openness) and (2) the need for autonomy (via privacy) (Planalp, Fitness, & Fehr, 2006). By reciprocating support (versus information), individuals can strengthen relationships while maintaining a sense of privacy. In fact, successfully balancing these contradictory needs seems to be an important factor in relationship satisfaction (Finkenauer & Hazam, 2000).

When relationships are in distress, self-disclosure patterns change. For example, one or both individuals may decrease the breadth and depth of their self-disclosures, indicating that they are emotionally withdrawing (Baxter, 1988).

Culture, Gender, and Self-Disclosure

Americans generally assume that personal sharing is essential to close friendships and happy romantic partnerships. This view is consistent with an individualistic culture that emphasizes the individual and the expression of each person's unique feelings and experiences. In collectivist cultures such as China and Japan, people are open about their group memberships and status because these factors guide social interactions; however, sharing personal information is reserved for established relationships (Samovar et al., 2007).

Web Link 7.4 **Cross-Cultural Communication Strategies**

Citizens of the 21st century are challenged to communicate sensitively with individuals from other cultural groups both within the United States and around the world. This site, maintained by the Conflict Research Consortium at the University of Colorado, provides commentaries by experts on a variety of intercultural communication settings.

In the United States, it has been found that females tend to be more openly self-disclosing than males, although the disparity seems smaller than once believed (Fehr, 2004). This gender difference is strongest in *same-gender* friendships, with female friends sharing more personal information than male friends (Reis, 1998; Wright, 2006). In *other-gender* relationships, self-disclosure is more equal, although men with traditional gender-role attitudes are less likely to self-disclose, because they view sharing personal information as a sign of weakness. Also, women share more personal information and feelings, whereas men share more nonpersonal information, both in conversations and e-mail messages (Boneva, Kraut, & Frohlich, 2001; Kilmartin, 2007).

Gender disparities in self-disclosure are attributed to socialization. In American culture, most men are taught to conceal tender emotions and feelings of vulnerability, especially from other men (Athenstaedt, Haas, & Schwab, 2004; Kilmartin, 2007). But different gender patterns are found in other countries (Reis & Wheeler, 1991). For example, in Jordan and Japan, where early intimacy between male and female friends is discouraged, close contacts between same-gender friends is encouraged.

And, in the early stages of other-gender relationships, American men often disclose more than women (Derlega et al., 1985). This finding is consistent with the traditional expectations that males should initiate relationships and females should encourage males to talk. Thus, it is an oversimplification to say that American women are always more open than men. We will take up other aspects of gender and communication in the Chapter 10 Application.

Effective Listening

Effective listening is a vastly underappreciated skill. There's a lot of truth in the old saying, "We have two ears and only one mouth, so we should listen more than we speak." Because listeners process speech much more rapidly than people speak (between 500 and 1,000 words per minute versus 125–175 words per minute), it's easy for them to become bored, distracted, and inattentive (Hanna, Suggett, & Radtke, 2008). Fatigue and preoccupation with one's own thoughts are other factors that interfere with effective listening.

To be a good listener, you need to keep four points in mind. First, *signal your interest in the speaker by using nonverbal cues.* Face the speaker squarely and lean toward him or her (rather than slouching or leaning back in a chair). This posture shows that you are interested in what the other person has to say. Try not to cross your arms and legs, as this posture can signal defensiveness. Maintaining eye contact with the speaker also conveys your attentiveness. (You know how annoy-

Being a good listener is an essential skill that contributes to success in relationships and on the job.

ing it is to talk with someone whose eyes are roaming around the room.) Communicate your feelings about what the speaker is saying by nodding your head or raising your eyebrows.

Second, *hear the other person out before you respond.* Listeners often tune out or interrupt a conversational partner when (1) they know someone well (because they believe that they already know what the speaker will say), (2) a speaker has mannerisms listeners find frustrating (stuttering, mumbling, speaking in a monotone), and (3) a speaker discusses ideas (abortion, politics) that generate strong feelings or uses terms (*welfare cheat, redneck*) that push "hot buttons." Although it is challenging not to tune out a speaker or lob an insult in these situations, you'll be better able to formulate an appropriate response if you allow the speaker to complete his or her thought.

Third, *engage in active listening* (Verderber et al., , 2008). Pay attention to what the speaker is saying and mindfully process the information. Active listening also involves the skills of clarifying and paraphrasing. Inevitably, a speaker will skip over an essential point or say something that is confusing. When this happens, you need to ask for clarification. "Was Bill her boyfriend or her brother?" Clarifying ensures that you have an accurate picture of the message and also tells the speaker that you are interested. Paraphrasing takes clarifying another step. To paraphrase means to state concisely what you believe the speaker said. You might say, "Let me see if I've got this right . . ." or "Do you mean . . .?" It's obviously silly to paraphrase every single thing the speaker says; you need to paraphrase only when the speaker says something important. Paraphrasing has a number of benefits: It reassures the speaker that you are "with" him or her, it derails misinterpretations, and it keeps you focused on the conversation.

Paraphrasing can take several forms (Verderber et al., , 2008). In *content paraphrasing,* you focus on the literal meaning of the message. In *feelings paraphrasing,* you focus on the emotions connected to the content of the message. If your friend declares, "I just can't believe he showed up at the party with his old girlfriend!," a feelings paraphrase is obviously in order ("You were really hurt by that").

To develop your skill at paraphrasing, try practicing it with a friend. Have the friend tell you about something; your job is to paraphrase from time to time to be sure that you really understand what your friend is trying to communicate. After each paraphrase, your friend can tell you whether he or she agrees with your interpretation. Don't be surprised if you have to reparaphrase several times. Keep trying until you get it right. You may discover that paraphrasing is harder than you think!

Finally, *pay attention to the other person's nonverbal signals.* Listeners use a speaker's words to get the "objective" meaning of a message, but they rely on nonverbal cues for the emotional and interpersonal meanings of a message. Your knowledge of body language, tone of voice, and other nonverbal cues can give you deeper understanding of what others are communicating. Remember that these cues are available not only

DILBERT © 2004 Scott Adams. Distributed by permission of United Feature Syndicate, Inc.

when the other person is speaking but also when you are talking. If you often get signals that your listener is drifting away, you might be going overboard on irrelevant details or, perhaps, hogging the conversation. The antidote is active listening.

Most people are inadequate listeners because they are unaware of the elements of effective listening—information you now have. Also, effective listening hinges largely on your attitude. If you're willing to work at it, you can become a good listener fairly quickly.

Communication Problems

LEARNING OBJECTIVES

- *Discuss four responses to communication apprehension.*
- *Describe four barriers to effective communication.*

In this section, we focus on two problems that can interfere with effective communication: anxiety and communication barriers.

Communication Apprehension

It's the first day of your child psychology class and you have just learned that 30-minute oral presentations are a course requirement. Do you welcome this requirement as an opportunity to polish your public speaking skills or, panic-stricken, do you race to the nearest computer station to drop the class? If you opted for the latter, you may suffer from ***communication apprehension,* or anxiety caused by having to talk with others.** Some people experience communication apprehension in all speaking situations (including one-on-one encounters), but most people who have the problem notice it only when they have to speak before groups.

Bodily experiences associated with communication apprehension can range from "butterflies" in the stomach to cold hands, dry mouth, and a racing heart rate. These physiological effects are stress-induced "fight or flight" responses of the autonomic nervous system (see Chapter 3). The physiological responses themselves aren't the root of communication apprehension; rather, the problem lies in the speaker's *interpretation* of these bodily responses. That is, high scorers on measures of communication apprehension frequently interpret the bodily changes they experience in public speaking situations as indications of fear. In contrast, low scorers often chalk up these reactions to the normal excitement in such a situation (Richmond & McCroskey, 1995).

Researchers have identified four responses to communication apprehension (Richmond & McCroskey, 1995). The most common is *avoidance,* or choosing not to participate when confronted with a voluntary communication opportunity. If people believe that speaking will make them uncomfortable, they will typically avoid the experience. *Withdrawal* occurs when people unexpectedly find themselves trapped in a communication situation they can't escape. Here they may clam up entirely or say as little as possible. *Disruption* refers to the inability to make fluent oral presentations or to engage in appropriate verbal or nonverbal behavior. Of course, inadequate communication skills can produce this same behavioral effect, and it isn't always possible for the average person to identify the actual cause of the problem. *Overcommunication* is a relatively unusual response to high communication apprehension, but it does occur. An example would be someone who attempts to dominate social situations by talking nonstop. Although such individuals are seen as poor communicators, they are not usually perceived as having communication apprehension. That's because we expect to see this problem only in those who talk very little. Of course, overcommunication may be caused by other factors as well.

Obviously, avoidance and withdrawal tactics are merely short-term strategies for coping with communication apprehension (Richmond & McCroskey, 1995). Because it is unlikely that you can go though life without having to speak in front of a group, it is important to learn to cope with this stressful event rather than avoid it time and again. Allowing the problem to get out of hand can result in self-limiting behavior, such as refusing a job promotion that entails public speaking. People with high communication apprehension are likely to have difficulties in relationships, at work, and at school (Richmond & McCroskey, 1995).

Happily, there are effective ways to reduce speech anxiety. With the technique of visualization, for ex-

Web Link 7.5 **Effective Presentations**

Students often tell teachers that they are terrified of making a presentation in front of a class. Professor Jeff Radel (University of Kansas Medical Center) has crafted an excellent set of guides to show the best ways of communicating by means of oral presentations, visual materials, and posters.

Being able to speak effectively before a group is a highly useful skill, so it is important to overcome communication apprehension.

ample, you picture yourself successfully going through all of the steps involved in preparing for and making a presentation. Research shows that people who practice visualization have less anxiety and fewer negative thoughts when they actually speak compared to previsualization levels (Ayres, Hopf, & Ayres, 1994). Both *cognitive restructuring* (Chapter 4) and *systematic desensitization* (Chapter 16) are also highly effective methods for dealing with this problem.

Barriers to Effective Communication

Earlier in the chapter, we discussed noise and its disruptive effects on interpersonal communication. Now we want to check out some psychological factors that contribute to noise. These barriers to effective communication can reside in the sender, in the receiver, or sometimes in both. Common obstacles include defensiveness, motivational distortion, self-preoccupation, and game playing.

Defensiveness

Perhaps the most basic barrier to effective communication is ***defensiveness*—an excessive concern with protecting oneself from being hurt.** People usually react defensively when they feel threatened, such as when they believe that others are evaluating them or trying to control or manipulate them. Defensiveness is also triggered when others act in a superior manner. Thus, those who flaunt their status, wealth, brilliance, or power often put receivers on the defensive. Dogmatic people who project "I'm always right" also breed defensiveness. A threat need not be real to elicit defensive behavior. If you persuade yourself that Brandon won't like you, your interactions with him will probably not be very positive. And, if the self-fulfilling prophecy kicks in, you may produce the negative reaction you fear. Strive to cultivate a communication style that minimizes defensiveness in others. At the same time, keep in mind that you don't have complete control over others' perceptions and reactions.

Motivational Distortion

In Chapter 6, we discussed distortions and expectancies in person perception. These same processes operate in communication. That is, motivational distortion occurs when people hear what they want to hear instead of what is actually being said. Each person has a unique frame of reference—certain attitudes, values, and expectations—that can influence what he or she hears. Information that contradicts an individual's own views often produces emotional distress. One way people avoid such unpleasant feelings is to engage in *selective attention,* or actively choosing to attend to information that supports their beliefs and ignoring information that contradicts them. Similarly, an individual may read unintended meanings into statements or jump to erroneous conclusions. This tendency to distort information occurs most often when people are discussing issues they feel strongly about, such as politics, racism, sexism, homosexuality, or abortion.

Self-Preoccupation

Who hasn't experienced the frustration of trying to communicate with someone who is so self-focused as to make two-way conversation impossible? These annoying individuals seem to talk to hear themselves talk. If you try to slip in a word about *your* problems, they cut you off by proclaiming, "That's nothing. Listen to what happened to me!" Further, self-preoccupied people are poor listeners. When someone else is talking, they're mentally rehearsing their next comments. Because they are self-focused, these individuals are usually oblivious to their negative impact on others. Self-preoccupied people arouse negative reactions in others for several reasons. First, their remarks are usually so self-serving (seeking to impress, to gain unwarranted sympathy, and so on) that others find it offensive. Another problem is that they consistently take up more than their fair share of conversation time. After a "conversation" with such a person, listeners feel ignored. No wonder people try to avoid these individuals if they can. If they can't, they usually respond only minimally to end the conversation quickly. Needless to say, you risk alienating others if you ignore the norm that conversations should involve a mutual sharing of information.

Game Playing

"Game playing" is another barrier to effective communication. Game playing was first described by Eric Berne (1964), who originated *transactional analysis,* a theory of personality and interpersonal relations that emphasizes patterns of communication. In Berne's scheme, ***games* are manipulative interactions with predictable outcomes, in which people conceal their real motives.** For instance, Yvonne knows that Carlos gets upset when she mentions her former boyfriend. So when they're out with others, she "innocently" inquires, "Say, has anyone seen Rodrigo lately?" Here, the hidden agenda is to make Carlos feel bad. If Yvonne's behavior produces the desired response, she "wins." In the broadest sense, game playing can include the deliberate (or sometimes unintentional) use of ambiguous, indirect, or deceptive statements. Some game playing involves "verbal fencing" to avoid having to make clear one's meaning or intent. Particularly problematic are repetitive games that result in bad feelings and that erode the trust and respect that are essential to good relationships.

Interpersonal Conflict

LEARNING OBJECTIVES

- *Cite some positive outcomes associated with constructive interpersonal conflict.*
- *Describe five types of conflicts.*
- *Describe five personal styles of dealing with interpersonal conflict.*
- *List seven tips for coping effectively with interpersonal conflict.*

People do not have to be enemies to be in conflict, and being in conflict does not make people enemies. ***Interpersonal conflict* exists whenever two or more people disagree.** By this definition, conflict occurs between friends and lovers as well as between competitors and enemies. The discord may be caused by a simple misunderstanding, or it may be a product of incompatible goals, values, attitudes, or beliefs. Because conflict is an unavoidable aspect of interactions, knowing how to deal constructively with it is essential. Many studies report associations between effective conflict management and relationship satisfaction (Gill, Christensen, & Fincham, 1999; Kline et al., 2006).

Beliefs About Conflict

Many people assume that any kind of conflict is bad and that it should be suppressed if at all possible. In reality, conflict is neither inherently bad nor inherently good. It is a natural phenomenon that may lead to either good or bad outcomes, depending on how people deal with it. When people see conflict as negative, they tend to avoid dealing with it. Of course, sometimes avoiding conflict can be good. If a relationship or an issue is of little importance to you, or if you believe that the costs of confrontation are too high (your boss might fire you), avoidance might be the best way to handle a conflict. Also, cultures differ in how conflict should be handled. Collectivist cultures (such as China and Japan) often avoid conflict, whereas individualistic cultures tend to encourage direct confrontations (Samovar et al., 2007). In individualistic cultures, the consequences of avoiding conflict depend on the nature of the relationship. When relationships and issues are important to you, avoiding conflict is generally counterproductive. For one thing, it can lead to a self-perpetuating cycle (see **Figure 7.11**).

When dealt with openly and constructively, interpersonal conflict can lead to a variety of valuable outcomes (Clark & Grote, 2003). Among other things, constructive confrontation may (1) bring problems out into the open where they can be solved, (2) put an

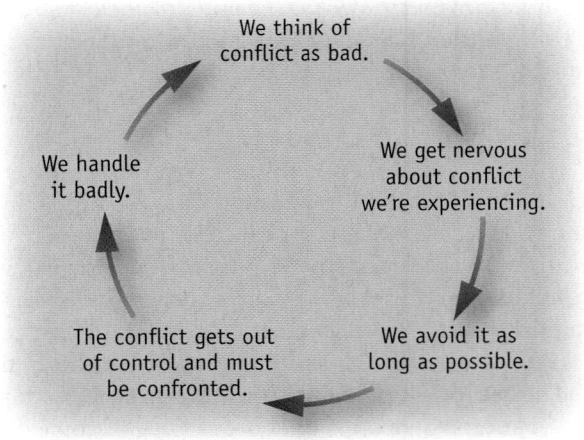

Figure 7.11

The conflict avoidance cycle. Avoiding conflict can lead to a self-perpetuating cycle: (1) People think of conflict as bad, (2) they get nervous about a conflict they are experiencing, (3) they avoid the conflict as long as possible, (4) the conflict gets out of control and must be confronted, and (5) they handle the confrontation badly. In turn, this negative experience sets the stage for avoiding conflict the next time—usually with the same negative outcome. (Adapted from Lulofs, 1994)

Disagreements are a fact of everyday life, so effective communicators need to learn how to deal with them constructively.

end to chronic sources of discontent in a relationship, and (3) lead to new insights through the airing of divergent views.

Types of Conflict

To manage conflict effectively, you need to know what you're dealing with. A useful scheme categorizes conflicts into five types: pseudoconflicts, factual conflicts, policy conflicts, value conflicts, and ego conflicts (Verderber, Verderber, & Berryman-Fink, 2007).

A *pseudoconflict* is just what it says: a false conflict. The game playing between Yvonne and Carlos is one type of pseudoconflict. The goal of the game is to "hook" the other person so that an unresolved issue comes out. The "fight" between Brian and Robin that introduced the chapter is another example of a pseudoconflict. Brian's retort, "There you go again, telling me what to wear," was intended to draw Robin into a fight about power issues in their relationship. Robin's comeback that Brian looked like he was colorblind was an acceptance of Brian's invitation to fight. Had Robin been able to identify the interchange as a pseudoconflict, she could have declined his invitation using a nondefensive tone of voice ("I was just making a suggestion. Wear what you like"). The key to managing such encounters is being able to recognize the game and not allowing yourself to be drawn in.

A second type of conflict occurs when people disagree about issues of a factual nature. For instance, Keisha and DeWayne disagree about whether they are supposed to meet another couple at the restaurant or be picked up so they can all drive in one car. The way to deal with such *fact-based conflicts* is to check the facts and then not dwell on who was right and who was wrong. But, note that either party can escalate the disagreement into an argument with insulting comments ("Can't you ever get anything straight?").

Recommended **READING**

The Argument Culture: Moving from Debate to Dialogue
by Deborah Tannen (Random House, 1998)

In this thought-provoking work, Tannen claims that public interchanges in America are increasingly framed as battles or games. Hence, the focus has become trying to win arguments rather than trying to understand what is being said. While acknowledging that opposition can be useful and necessary, Tannen is concerned with what she sees as a trend for Americans to use an adversarial approach to the exclusion of other ways of communicating in public. And living in "the argument culture" is having negative effects on Americans and the larger society. With an easy-going style, Tannen brings in research and wide-ranging examples from politics, the media, the legal profession, the classroom, and the Internet to bolster her thesis.

To halt the growth of the argument culture, Tannen advocates using nonadversarial ways to negotiate disagreements and mediate conflicts. For instance, she urges people to start looking for ways that both sides can win disagreements (as opposed to thinking in terms of one side "winning" and the other "losing"). In addition, she urges people to get out of the "dualism trap." Instead of asking, "What is the other *side*?" individuals can ask, "What are the other *sides*?" Tannen recommends setting up discussions with three or more people rather than using the debate-prone two-person format. She also suggests reducing the use of war metaphors (the battle of the sexes, the war on drugs, "annihilating" the other team, and so forth) and replacing them with less combative figures of speech.

Communication in an Adversarial Culture

Political attack ads, vicious reality TV shows, hate-generating Internet sites, road rage—hostile incidents assault Americans on a daily basis. A 2005 Associated Press-Ipsos poll reported that nearly 70 percent of American adults believe that people are ruder today than they were 20 or 30 years ago (Cassata, 2005). In fact, some universities have instituted speech and behavior codes to counteract hate speech and disrespectful behavior. Vulgarities in the workplace have become so commonplace that some employers have instituted anti-swearing policies (DuFrene & Lehman, 2002). Ominously, aggression among nonemotionally disturbed kindergartners is on the rise, including hitting, biting, and swearing at teachers; assaulting peers; and even carrying weapons (Wallis, 2003).

Sociolinguist Deborah Tannen (1998) characterizes contemporary America as "the argument culture." Hostile public debates confuse and frustrate listeners, inflame emotions, and alienate Americans from each other and their leaders. Tannen worries that this constant exposure to public arguments is having a "corrosive" effect on Americans' spirit and is creating serious social problems.

Photo by Sara Barrett, courtesy, Random House

Deborah Tannen

What lies behind all this social contentiousness? For starters, the United States is a strongly individualistic culture. Thus, Americans are predisposed to be adversarial because the self is perceived to be an isolated entity and in opposition to society. Second, Americans (and those in other Western cultures) have a dualistic view of nature and tend to see things in terms of opposites—good *versus* bad, strong *versus* weak, and so on (Tannen, 1998). By contrast, most Eastern cultures have a nondualistic perspective, in which opposites are seen as complementary partners, both essential to a larger whole (good *and* bad, strong *and* weak).

A third factor is that face-to-face communication is on the decline, fed by economic pressures and advances in technology. Whereas families used to gather around a single radio or television, now family members each have their own radios and TVs (as well as MP3 players, cell phones, and computers). To accommodate busy schedules, family members each pop frozen dinners into the microwave rather than gather regularly for family meals. When individuals spend more time on their own, they have fewer opportunities to learn good interaction skills.

Excessive exposure to the high levels of verbal and physical aggression, especially in the media, is a fourth factor. By the time a child finishes grade school, he or she will have witnessed approximately 8,000 murders and 100,000 other acts of violence on TV (Huston et al., 1992). Aggression also appears in other types of media: video games, the Internet, music videos, and music lyrics. Over time, excessive exposure to these various forms of media violence takes its toll. Numerous studies suggest that extensive exposure to media violence contributes to the development of aggressiveness in some children (Anderson et al., 2003), and aggressive children grow up to be aggressive adults (Broidy et al., 2003; Huesmann et al., 2003). Repeated exposure to aggression also causes viewers to become numb or *desensitized* to violence and its effects on victims (Anderson et al., 2003); this means that viewers become more accepting of it. Furthermore, some people who are exposed to considerable TV violence come to believe that society is more hostile and dangerous than it actually is. Then they become more distrustful, view aggression as an acceptable way to solve problems, and are more likely to carry a weapon (Nabi & Sullivan, 2001).

Must Americans resign themselves to living this way, or can we reduce public hostility? Social institutions—the government, media, and schools, for instance—could address this situation in a variety of ways (Anderson et al., 2003). Politicians could stop their hostile campaign rhetoric, and governments could enact legislation to reduce access to weapons and reduce poverty. Newspapers could minimize sensationalism and emphasize substance in their reporting, while media producers could reduce the amount of gratuitous violence portrayed on television and in films and increase nonviolent and prosocial messages. Schools could teach children social skills and nonviolent ways of resolving conflicts (Aber, Brown, & Jones, 2003).

Individuals can also help. Parents have a special role to play because efforts to reduce aggression are most effective with young children (Anderson & Huesmann, 2003). They can limit their children's exposure to physical and verbal aggression—on television, in movies, in video games, in books, and on the Internet. And they

Communication in an Adversarial Culture (continued)

can expose their kids to TV programs and movies that model helpful and cooperative interactions with others (Huston & Wright, 1998). Parents can also encourage and reward nonaggressive ways to resolve childhood conflicts (especially in boys). And they can avoid disciplinary methods that model aggressive behavior (for more information, see the Application for Chapter 11, on effective parenting).

You can do your part by minimizing the amount of media violence you watch and hear—be selective about the TV programs, movies, video games, and music you expose yourself to. And strive to apply the principles of effective interpersonal communication discussed in this chapter—in face-to-face interactions and when you're on the phone or Internet or in your car.

Policy conflicts arise when people disagree about how to handle a particular situation. Take the case of Brad and Julia, who are planning a summer vacation. Brad earns more than Julia. Should they split the expenses down the middle, or should they share the expenses based on the proportion of their incomes? Obviously, there is no right or wrong answer here. Successfully resolving a policy conflict depends on finding a solution that addresses the problem and the feelings of both people. Policy conflicts can reerupt when two people agree on a policy but one or both fail to follow through on it.

Differing personal values can also lead to conflicts. *Values* are beliefs people use to evaluate the worth of various aspects of life—religion, politics, and various social and aesthetic issues. Some values are obviously more important to people than others, and higher-ranked values usually have more influence on behavior. Thus, if you believe that your family's happiness is more important than your work, you may opt for a career with minimal stress and time demands. *Value-based conflicts* are a particular problem in intimate relationships. If couples can recognize conflicts as value based, they can understand that an issue is important to the other person and that he or she is not just being stubborn. When conflicts can't be resolved, two people may be willing to take turns obliging each other to maintain the relationship. For example, they might alternate going to each other's favorite hangout. Sometimes people can agree to disagree. Nonetheless, when unresolvable conflicts become an ongoing source of distress in relationships, they can lead to breakups. You can minimize value-based conflicts by matching up with a person who has similar values.

The most difficult conflicts to manage are those in which one or both parties view the outcome as a measure of self-worth—how competent one is, how much one knows, how much power one has, and so forth. In these *ego-based conflicts*, "winning" becomes more important than finding a fair solution to the problem. Ego-based conflicts often arise when one or both parties lapse into negative personal judgments about a content- or value-based issue under discussion. People most often slip into judgmental statements when they have expertise or a special stake in the discussion. Before they realize it, they are hooked by their emotions, lose the ability for rational thought, and find themselves saying things they can't take back. Because individuals perceive so much to be at stake, ego-based conflicts are difficult to manage. Thus, the best way to handle them is to recognize them early on and to move the conflict back to a content level. Unfortunately, even minor disagreements can erupt into aggressive confrontations. Clearly, learning how to manage conflict is an essential skill in today's world.

Styles of Managing Conflict

How do you react to conflict? Most people have a habitual way or personal style of dealing with dissension. Studies have consistently revealed five distinct patterns of dealing with conflict: avoiding/withdrawing, accommodating, competing/forcing, compromising, and collaborating (Lulofs & Cahn, 2000). Two dimensions underlie these different styles: interest in satisfying one's own concerns and interest in satisfying others' concerns (Rahim & Magner, 1995). You can see the location of these five styles on these two dimensions in **Figure 7.12** on the next page. As you read about these styles, try to determine where you fit:

► *Avoiding/withdrawing* (low concern for self and others). Some people simply find conflict extremely distasteful. When a conflict emerges, the avoider will change the subject, deflect discussion with humor, make a hasty exit, or pretend to be preoccupied with something else. Usually, people who prefer this style hope that ignoring a problem will make it go away. For minor problems, this tactic is often a good one—there's no need to react to every little annoyance. For bigger conflicts, avoiding/withdrawing is not a good strategy; it usually just delays the inevitable clash. If Maria tries

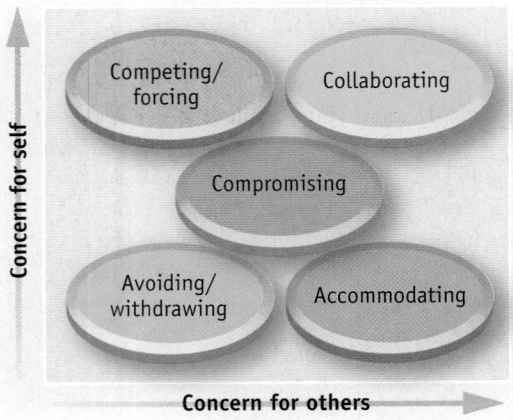

Figure 7.12

Five styles of handling interpersonal conflict. In dealing with discord, individuals typically prefer one of five styles. The two dimensions of *concern for self* and *concern for others* underlie each of the five styles.

repeatedly to discuss a problem and Tony refuses to do so, relationship difficulties can arise. A particular problem occurs when an avoider has greater power in a relationship (parent, supervisor, romantic partner). This situation prevents the less powerful person from airing his or her concerns and breeds frustration and resentment. Of course, in some cases it is good to postpone a discussion, especially if one or both individuals are tired or rushed or need time to cool off. Postponing qualifies as avoiding only if the promised discussion never takes place.

▸ *Accommodating* (low concern for self, high concern for others). Like the avoider, the accommodator feels uncomfortable with conflict. However, instead of ignoring the disagreement, this person brings the conflict to a quick end by giving in easily. People who are overly concerned about acceptance and approval from others commonly use this strategy of surrender. Habitual accommodating is a poor way of dealing with conflict because it does not generate creative thinking and effective solutions. Moreover, feelings of resentment (on both sides) may develop because the accommodator often likes to play the role of a martyr. Of course, when you don't have strong preferences (for instance, where to eat out), occasional accommodating is perfectly appropriate. Also, in some cultures (such as Japan), it is the preferred style of dealing with conflict (Samovar et al., 2007).

▸ *Competing/forcing* (high concern for self, low concern for others). The competitor turns every conflict into a black-and-white, win-or-lose situation. Competitors will do virtually anything to emerge victorious from confrontations; thus, they can be deceitful and aggressive—including using verbal attacks and physical threats. They rigidly adhere to one position and will use threats and coercion to force the other party to submit. This style is undesirable because, like accommodation, it fails to generate creative solutions to problems. Moreover, this approach is especially likely to lead to postconflict tension, resentment, and hostility.

▸ *Compromising* (moderate concern for self and others). Compromising is a pragmatic approach to conflict that acknowledges the divergent needs of both parties. Compromisers are willing to negotiate and to meet the other person halfway. With this approach, each person gives up something so both can have partial satisfaction. Because both parties gain some satisfaction, compromising is a fairly constructive approach to conflict, especially when the issue is moderately important.

▸ *Collaborating* (high concern for self and others). Whereas compromising simply entails "splitting the difference" between positions, collaborating involves a sincere effort to find a solution that will optimally satisfy both parties. In this approach, conflict is viewed as a mutual problem to be solved as effectively as possible. Collaborating thus encourages openness and honesty. It also stresses the importance of criticizing the other person's *ideas* in a disagreement rather than the other *person.* To collaborate, you have to work on clarifying differences and similarities in positions so that you can build on the similarities. Generally, this is the most productive approach for dealing with conflict. Instead of resulting in a postconflict residue of tension and resentment, collaborating tends to produce a climate of trust.

Dealing Constructively with Conflict

As you have seen, the most effective approach to conflict management is collaborating. To help you implement such an approach, we will offer some specific suggestions. But, before we get down to specifics, there are a few principles to keep in mind (Alberti & Emmons, 2001; Verderber et al., 2007). First, in a conflict situation, try to give the other person the benefit of the doubt; don't automatically assume that those who disagree with you are ignorant or mean-spirited. Show respect for their position, and do your best to empathize with, and fully understand, their frame of reference. Second, approach the other person as an equal. If you have a higher status or more power (parent, supervisor), try to set this difference aside. Third, define the conflict as a mutual problem to be solved cooperatively, rather than as a win-lose proposition. Fourth, choose a mutually acceptable time to sit down and work on resolving the conflict. It is not always best to tackle the conflict when and where it first arises. Finally, communicate your flexibility and willingness to modify your position.

Here are some explicit guidelines for dealing effectively with interpersonal conflict (Alberti & Emmons, 2001; Verderber et al., 2007):

▶ *Make communication honest and open.* Don't withhold information or misrepresent your position. Avoid deceit and manipulation.

▶ *Use specific behaviors to describe another person's annoying habits rather than general statements about their personality.* You'll probably get further with your roommate if you say something like, "Please throw your clothes in the hamper" rather than "You're such an inconsiderate slob." Remarks about specific actions are less threatening and are less likely to be taken personally. They also clarify what you hope will change.

▶ *Avoid "loaded" words.* Certain words are "loaded" in the sense that they tend to trigger negative emotional reactions in listeners. For example, you can discuss politics without using terms such as "right-winger" and "knee-jerk liberal."

▶ *Use a positive approach and help the other person save face.* Saying "I love it when we cook dinner together" will go over better than "You never help with dinner, and I resent it." Similarly, you can increase your chances of having a request accepted if you say, "I realize that you are very busy, but I'd really appreciate it if you would look at my paper again. I've marked the places I'd like you to reconsider."

▶ *Limit complaints to recent behavior and to the current situation.* Dredging up past grievances only rekindles old resentments and distracts you from the current problem. And avoid saying things like "You *always* say you're too busy" or "You *never* do your fair share of the housework." Such categorical statements are bound to put the other person on the defensive.

▶ *Assume responsibility for your own feelings and preferences.* Rather than "*You* make me mad," say "*I* am angry." Or, try "I'd appreciate it if you'd water the garden" instead of "Do you think the garden needs watering?"

▶ *Use an assertive (as opposed to submissive or aggressive) communication style.* This approach will make it easier to head off and deal constructively with conflict situations. In our upcoming Application, we elaborate on *assertive communication* and its usefulness in a wide variety of interpersonal communication situations—for example, making acquaintances, developing relationships, and resolving conflicts.

Web Link 7.6 **The Conflict Resolution Information Source**

This excellent resource on conflict management is provided by the University of Colorado's Conflict Research Consortium. The site is actually a gateway to a huge variety of resources on conflict management and is easy to navigate.

We'll close this section with some food for thought. Think of relationships as having a "bank account" (Notarius & Markman, 1993). People make both deposits to (kindnesses, compliments) and withdrawals from (negative interactions, hostile comments) these accounts. Happy couples know that to avoid being overdrawn, it's important to make frequent deposits to offset the unavoidable withdrawals (Kline, et al., 2006).

APPLICATION

Developing an Assertive Communication Style

LEARNING OBJECTIVES

- *Differentiate assertive communication from submissive and aggressive communication.*
- *List five steps that lead to more assertive communication.*

Answer the following questions "yes" or "no."

___ **1.** When someone asks you for an unreasonable favor, is it difficult to say no?

___ **2.** Do you feel timid about returning flawed merchandise?

___ **3.** Do you have a hard time requesting even small favors from others?

___ **4.** When a group is hotly debating an issue, are you shy about speaking up?

___ **5.** When a salesperson pressures you to buy something you don't want, is it hard for you to resist?

If you answered "yes" to several of these questions, you may need to increase your assertiveness. Many people have a hard time being assertive; however, this problem is more common among females because they are socialized to be more submissive than males—for example, to "be nice." Consequently, assertiveness training is especially popular among women. Men, too, find assertiveness training helpful, both because some have been socialized to be passive and because others want to learn to be less aggressive and more assertive. In this Application we elaborate on the differences between assertive, submissive, and aggressive behavior and discuss some procedures for increasing assertiveness.

Keep in mind that our views reflect an individualistic perspective. Other cultures may have different perspectives on submissiveness, assertiveness, and aggressiveness (Samovar et al., 2007). For instance, some Native American tribes disdain both assertiveness and aggression. Similarly, such collectivist societies as China, Japan, Thailand, and the Philippines place a high value on interpersonal harmony. By contrast, Israelis and members of the Jewish culture tend to have a confrontational interactional style in which vigorous debate is expected.

The Nature of Assertiveness

***Assertiveness* involves acting in your own best interests by expressing your thoughts and feelings directly and honestly.** Essentially, assertiveness involves standing up for your rights when someone else is about to infringe on them. To be assertive is to speak out rather than pull your punches.

The nature of assertive communication can best be clarified by contrasting it with other types of communication. *Submissive communication* involves consistently giving in to others on points of possible contention. Submissive people often let others take advantage of them. Typically, their biggest problem is that they cannot say no to unreasonable requests. A common example is the college student who can't tell her roommate not to borrow her clothes. Submissive people also have difficulty voicing disagreement with others and making requests themselves. In traditional trait terminology, they are timid.

Although the roots of submissiveness have not been investigated fully, they appear to lie in excessive concern about gaining the social approval of others. However, the strategy of "not making waves" is more likely to garner others' contempt than their approval. Moreover, individuals who use this style often feel bad about themselves (for being "pushovers") and resentful of those whom they allow to take advantage of them. These feelings often lead the submissive individual to try to punish the other person by withdrawing, sulking, or crying (Bower & Bower, 1991, 2004). These manipulative attempts to get one's own way are sometimes referred to as "passive aggression" or "indirect aggression."

At the other end of the spectrum, *aggressive communication* focuses on saying and getting what you want at the expense of others' feelings and rights. With assertive behavior, however, you strive to respect others' rights and defend your own. The problem in real life is that assertive and aggressive behaviors *may* overlap. When someone is about to infringe on their rights, people often lash out at the other party (aggression) while defending their rights (assertion). The challenge, then, is to be firm and assertive without becoming aggressive. Advocates of assertive communication argue that it is much more adaptive than either submissive or aggressive communication (Alberti & Emmons, 2001; Bower & Bower, 1991, 2004). They maintain that submissive behavior leads to poor self-esteem, self-denial, emotional suppression, and strained interpersonal relationships. Conversely, aggressive communication tends to promote guilt, alienation, and disharmony. In contrast, assertive behavior is said to foster high self-esteem, satisfactory interpersonal relationships, and effective conflict management.

The essential point with assertiveness is that you are able to state what you want clearly and directly. Being able to do so makes you feel good about yourself and will usually make others feel good about you, too. And, although being assertive doesn't guarantee your chances for getting what you want, it certainly enhances them.

Steps in Assertiveness Training

Numerous assertiveness training programs are available in book form, on CDs or DVDs, or through seminars. Some recommendations about books appear in the Recommended Reading box in this section. Most of the programs are behavioral and emphasize gradual improvement and reinforcement of appropriate behavior. Here we will summarize the key steps in assertiveness training.

1. Understand What Assertive Communication Is

To produce assertive behavior, you need to understand what it looks and sounds like. Thus, most programs begin by clarifying the nature of assertive communication. Assertiveness trainers often ask clients to imagine situations calling for assertiveness and compare hypothetical submissive (or passive), assertive, and aggressive responses. Let's consider one such comparison. In

Web Link 7.7 **Assertiveness**

In an online brochure, this site clarifies the nature of assertiveness and describes specific techniques for becoming more assertive. The site is maintained by the Counseling Center at the University of Illinois at Urbana-Champaign.

KUDZU © Tribune Media Services, Inc. All Rights Reserved. Reprinted with permission.

this example, a woman in assertiveness training is asking her roommate to cooperate in cleaning their apartment once a week. The roommate, who is uninterested in the problem, is listening to music when the conversation begins. In this example, the roommate is playing the role of the antagonist—called a "downer" in the following scripts (excerpted from Bower & Bower, 2004, pp. 8, 9, 11).

The Passive Scene

SHE: *Uh, I was wondering if you would be willing to take time to decide about the housecleaning.*

DOWNER: *(listening to the music) Not now, I'm busy.*

SHE: *Oh, okay.*

The Aggressive Scene

SHE: *Listen, I've had it with you not even talking about cleaning this damn apartment. Are you going to help me?*

DOWNER: *(listening to the music) Not now, I'm busy.*

SHE: *Why can't you look at me when you turn me down? You don't give a damn about the housework or me! You only care about yourself!*

DOWNER: *That's not true.*

SHE: *You never pay any attention to the apartment or to me. I have to do everything around here!*

DOWNER: *Oh, shut up! You're just neurotic about cleaning all the time. Who are you, my mother? Can't I relax with my stereo for a few minutes without you pestering me? This was my apartment first, you know!*

The Assertive Scene

SHE: *I know housework isn't the most fascinating subject, but it needs to be done. Let's plan when we'll do it.*

DOWNER: *(listening to music) Oh, c'mon—not now! I'm busy.*

SHE: *This won't take long. I feel that if we have a schedule, it will be easier to keep up with the chores.*

DOWNER: *I'm not sure I'll have time for all of them.*

SHE: *I've already drawn up a couple of rotating schedules for housework, so that each week we have an equal division of tasks. Will you look at them? I'd like to hear your decisions about them, say, tonight after supper?*

DOWNER: *[indignantly] I have to look at these now?*

SHE: *Is there some other time that's better for you?*

DOWNER: *Oh, I don't know.*

SHE: *Well, then let's discuss plans after supper for 15 minutes. Is that agreed?*

Recommended READING

Asserting Yourself: A Practical Guide for Positive Change
by Sharon Anthony Bower and Gordon H. Bower (Perseus, 1991, 2004)

Bower and Bower put the problem of nonassertiveness into perspective, relating it to self-esteem and anxiety. They then lay out a systematic program for increasing assertive behavior. The book makes extensive use of probing questions to help you work out a personally relevant plan of action. The authors also provide sample verbal scripts for numerous common situations that typically call for assertive behavior. Among other topics covered are requesting a raise, saying "no" to unreasonable demands, protesting unjust criticism, dealing with a substance abuser, protesting annoying habits, and dealing with the silent treatment. The Bowers devote a full chapter to the role of assertive behavior in developing friendships—initiating and ending conversations, keeping conversations going, making dates, self-disclosure, listening, and coping with social anxieties.

Among other books on assertiveness, we highly recommend *Your Perfect Right,* by Robert E. Alberti and Michael L. Emmons (2001), which is now in its eighth edition. Many assertiveness books target women, focusing on the communication problems women tend to encounter. *The Assertive Woman,* by Stanlee Phelps and Nancy Austin (2002) is particularly useful.

DOWNER: *I guess so.*

SHE: *Good! It won't take long, and I'll feel relieved when we have a schedule in place.*

A helpful way to distinguish among the three types of communication is in terms of how people deal with their own rights and the rights of others. Submissive people sacrifice their own rights. Aggressive people tend to ignore the rights of others. Assertive people consider both their own rights *and* the rights of others.

As we have noted, the nonverbal aspect of communication is extremely important. To ensure that your assertive words have impact, it is important to back them up with congruent nonverbal messages. Thus, you'll come across as more assertive if you face the person you're talking with, look directly at him or her, and maintain eye contact, rather than looking away from the other person, fidgeting, slouching, and shuffling your feet (Bower & Bower, 1991, 2004). You'll find some additional guidelines for behaving assertively in **Figure 7.13**.

2. Monitor Your Assertive Communication

Most people's assertiveness varies from one situation to another. In other words, they may be assertive in some social contexts and timid in others. Consequently, once you understand the nature of assertive communication, you should monitor yourself and identify when

Figure 7.13

Guidelines for assertive behavior. Gordon and Sharon Bower (1991, 2004) outline a four-step program intended to help readers create successful assertive scripts for themselves. The four steps are (1) *describe* the unwanted behavior from another person (called your "Downer") that is troubling you, (2) *express* your feelings about the behavior to the other person, (3) *specify* the changes needed, and (4) try to provide rewarding *consequences* for the change. Using this framework, the table shown here provides some useful dos and don'ts for achieving effective assertive behavior.

Adapted from Bower, S. A., & Bower, G. H. (1991). *Asserting yourself: A practical guide for positive change* (2nd ed.). Reading, MA: Addison-Wesley. Copyright © 2004, 1991 by Sharon Anthony Bower and Gordon H. Bower. Reprinted by permission of Perseus DA CAPO PRESS, a member of Perseus Books.

Rules for Assertive Scripts

Do	Don't
Describe	
■ Describe the other person's behavior objectively.	Describe your emotional reaction to it.
■ Use concrete terms.	Use abstract, vague terms.
■ Describe a specified time, place, and frequency of the action.	Generalize for "all time."
■ Describe the action, not the "motive."	Guess at your Downer's motives or goals.
Express	
■ Express your feelings.	Deny your feelings.
■ Express them calmly.	Unleash emotional outbursts.
■ State feelings in a positive manner, as relating to a goal to be achieved.	State feelings negatively, making Downer attack.
■ Direct yourself to the specific offending behavior, not to the whole person.	Attack the entire character of the person.
Specify	
■ Ask explicitly for change in your Downer's behavior.	Merely imply that you'd like a change.
■ Request a small change.	Ask for too large a change.
■ Request only one or two changes at one time.	Ask for too many changes.
■ Specify the concrete actions you want to see stopped and those you want to see performed.	Ask for changes in nebulous traits or qualities.
■ Take account of whether your Downer can meet your request without suffering large losses.	Ignore your Downer's needs or ask only for your satisfaction.
■ Specify (if appropriate) what behavior you are willing to change to make the agreement.	Consider that only your Downer has to change.
Consequences	
■ Make the consequences explicit.	Be ashamed to talk about rewards and penalties.
■ Give a positive reward for change in the desired direction.	Give only punishments for lack of change.
■ Select something that is desirable and reinforcing to your Downer.	Select something that only you might find rewarding.
■ Select a reward that is big enough to maintain the behavior change.	Offer a reward you can't or won't deliver.
■ Select a punishment of a magnitude that "fits the crime" of refusing to change behavior.	Make exaggerated threats.
■ Select a punishment that you are actually willing to carry out.	Use unrealistic threats or self-defeating punishment.

Assertive Responses to Some Common Putdowns

Nature of Remark	Put-Down Sentence	Suggested Assertive Reply
Nagging about details	"Haven't you done this yet?"	"No, when did you want it done?" (Answer without hedging, and follow up with a question.)
Prying	"I know I maybe shouldn't ask, but . . ."	"If I don't want to answer, I'll let you know." (Indicate that you won't make yourself uncomfortable just to please this person.)
Putting you on the spot socially	"Are you busy Tuesday?"	"What do you have in mind?" (Answer the question with a question.)
Pigeonholing you	"That's a woman for you!"	"That's one woman, not *all* women." (Disagree—assert your individuality.)
Using insulting labels for your behavior	"That's a dumb way to . . ."	"I'll decide what to call my behavior." (Refuse to accept the label.)
Basing predictions on an amateur personality analysis	"You'll have a hard time. You're too shy."	"In what ways do you think I'm too shy?" (Ask for clarification of the analysis.)

Figure 7.14

Assertive responses to common put-downs. Having some assertive replies at the ready can increase your confidence in difficult social interactions.

Adapted from Bower, S. A., & Bower, G. H. (1991). *Asserting yourself: A practical guide for positive change* (2nd ed.). Reading, MA: Addison-Wesley. Copyright © 2004, 1991 by Sharon Anthony Bower and Gordon H. Bower. Reprinted by permission of Perseus DA CAPO PRESS, a member of Perseus Books.

you are nonassertive. In particular, you should figure out *who* intimidates you, on *what topics,* and in *which situations.*

3. Observe a Model's Assertive Communication

Once you have identified the situations in which you are nonassertive, think of someone who communicates assertively in those situations and observe that person's behavior closely. In other words, find someone to model yourself after. This is an easy way to learn how to behave assertively in situations crucial to you. Your observations should also allow you to see how rewarding assertive communication can be, which should strengthen your assertive tendencies. If an assertive model isn't available, you can adapt the relevant scenarios in most self-help books on assertiveness.

4. Practice Assertive Communication

The key to achieving assertive communication is to practice it and work toward gradual improvement. Your practice can take several forms. In *covert rehearsal,* you imagine a situation requiring assertion and the dialogue that you would engage in. In *role playing,* you ask a friend or therapist to play the role of an antagonist. Then practice communicating assertively in this artificial situation.

Eventually, of course, you want to transfer your assertiveness skills to real-life situations. Most experts recommend that you use *shaping* to increase your assertive communication gradually. As we discussed in the Chapter 4 Application, shaping involves rewarding yourself for making closer and closer approximations of a desired behavior. For example, in the early stages of your behavior-change program, your goal might be to make at least one assertive comment every day, while toward the end you might be striving to make at least eight such comments a day. Obviously, in designing a shaping program, it is important to set realistic goals for yourself.

5. Adopt an Assertive Attitude

Most assertiveness training programs have a behavioral orientation and focus on specific responses for specific situations (see **Figure 7.14**). However, it's obvious that real-life situations only rarely match those portrayed in books. Thus, some experts maintain that acquiring a repertoire of verbal responses for certain situations is not as important as developing a new attitude that you're not going to let people push you around (or let yourself push others around, if you're the aggressive type) (Alberti & Emmons, 2001). Although most programs don't talk explicitly about attitudes, they do appear to instill a new attitude indirectly. A change in attitude is probably crucial to achieving flexible, assertive behavior.

KEY IDEAS

The Process of Interpersonal Communication

▶ Interpersonal communication is the interactional process that occurs when one person sends a message to another. Communication takes place when a sender transmits a message to a receiver either verbally or nonverbally. The widespread use of electronic communication devices has raised new issues in interpersonal communication. Although people often take it for granted, effective communication contributes to their adjustment in school, in relationships, and at work.

Nonverbal Communication

▶ Nonverbal communication conveys emotions, above all. It tends to be more spontaneous than verbal communication, and it is more ambiguous. Sometimes it contradicts what is communicated verbally. It is often multichanneled and, like language, is culturally bound. Elements of nonverbal communication include personal space, facial expression, eye contact, body language, touch, and paralanguage.

▶ Certain nonverbal cues are associated with deception, but many of these cues do not correspond to popular beliefs about how liars give themselves away. Discrepancies between facial expressions and other nonverbal signals may suggest dishonesty. The vocal and visual cues associated with lying are so subtle, however, that the detection of deception is difficult. Machines used to detect deception (polygraphs) are not particularly accurate.

▶ Nonverbal communication, particularly nonverbal sensitivity, plays an important role in adjustment, especially in the quality of interpersonal relationships. Women are typically more nonverbally sensitive than men because they exert more effort at it.

Toward More Effective Communication

▶ Effective communication rests on a foundation of a positive interpersonal climate. To promote a positive interpersonal climate, it helps to show empathy, treat people as equals, withhold judgment, strive for honesty, and express opinions tentatively. To be an effective communicator, it's important to develop good conversational skills, including knowing how to make small talk with strangers.

▶ Self-disclosure—opening up to others—is associated with good mental health, happiness, and satisfying relationships. To reduce the risks of self-disclosure, it's best to self-disclose gradually. The receiver's nonverbal signals help the speaker know whether to continue or stop disclosing.

▶ Self-disclosure can foster emotional intimacy in relationships. Emotional-evaluative self-disclosures lead to feelings of closeness, but factual-descriptive disclosures do not. The level of self-disclosure varies over the course of relationships. Cultures vary in the preferred level of self-disclosure. American women tend to self-disclose more than men, but this disparity is not so large as it once was. Effective listening is an essential aspect of interpersonal communication.

Communication Problems

▶ A number of problems can arise that interfere with effective communication. Individuals who become overly anxious when they talk with others suffer from communication apprehension. This difficulty can cause problems in relationships and in work and educational settings. Sometimes communication can produce negative interpersonal outcomes. Barriers to effective communication include defensiveness, motivational distortion, self-preoccupation, and game playing.

Interpersonal Conflict

▶ Dealing constructively with interpersonal conflict is an important aspect of effective communication. Individualistic cultures tend to encourage direct confrontations, whereas collectivist cultures often avoid them. Nonetheless, many Americans have negative attitudes about conflict.

▶ Conflicts can be classified as one of five types: pseudoconflicts, fact-based conflicts, policy conflicts, value conflicts, or ego conflicts. In dealing with conflict, most people have a preferred style: avoiding/withdrawing, accommodating, competing, compromising, or collaborating. This last style is the most effective in managing conflict.

Application: Developing an Assertive Communication Style

▶ An assertive style enables individuals to stand up for themselves and to respect the rights of others. To become more assertive, individuals need to understand what assertive communication is, monitor assertive communication, observe a model's assertive communication, practice being assertive, and adopt an assertive attitude.

KEY TERMS

Assertiveness p. 230
Channel p. 205
Communication apprehension p. 222
Context p. 206
Defensiveness p. 223
Display rules p. 211
Electronically mediated communication p. 206
Empathy p. 216
Games p. 224
Interpersonal communication p. 205
Interpersonal conflict p. 224
Kinesics p. 212
Message p. 205
Noise p. 206
Nonverbal communication p. 208
Nonverbal sensitivity p. 216
Paralanguage p. 213
Personal space p. 209
Polygraph p. 215
Proxemics p. 209
Receiver p. 205
Self-disclosure p. 218
Sender p. 205

KEY PEOPLE

Sharon Anthony Bower and Gordon Bower pp. 230–233
Bella DePaulo pp. 214–215
Paul Ekman and Wallace Friesen pp. 210–211
Edward T. Hall pp. 209–210
Deborah Tannen pp. 226–227

PRACTICE TEST

1. Which of the following is *not* a component of the interpersonal communication process?
   a. The sender
   b. The receiver
   c. The channel
   d. The monitor

2. Research shows that individuals from a variety of cultures:
   a. agree on the facial expressions that correspond with all emotions.
   b. agree on the facial expressions that correspond with 15 basic emotions.
   c. agree on the facial expressions that correspond with 6 basic emotions.
   d. do not agree on the facial expressions that correspond with any emotions.

3. Which of the following is *not* an aspect of nonverbal communication?
   a. Facial expressions
   b. Homogamy
   c. Posture
   d. Gestures

4. According to research, which of the following cues is associated with dishonesty?
   a. Speaking with a higher-than-normal pitch
   b. Speaking slowly
   c. Giving relatively long answers to questions
   d. Lack of eye contact

5. With regard to self-disclosure, it is best to:
   a. share a lot about yourself when you first meet someone.
   b. share very little about yourself for a long time.
   c. gradually share information about yourself.
   d. give no personal information on a first encounter, but share a lot the next time.

6. Paraphrasing is an important aspect of
   a. nonverbal communication.
   b. active listening.
   c. communication apprehension.
   d. assertiveness.

7. When people hear what they want to hear instead of what is actually said, _____ is operating.
   a. assertiveness
   b. self-preoccupation
   c. motivational distortion
   d. game playing

8. The most difficult conflicts to manage are:
   a. pseudoconflicts.
   b. content-based conflicts.
   c. value-based conflicts.
   d. ego-based conflicts.

9. Generally, the most productive style for managing conflict is:
   a. collaboration.
   b. compromise.
   c. accommodation.
   d. avoidance.

10. Expressing your thoughts directly and honestly without trampling on other people is a description of which communication style?
   a. Aggressive
   b. Empathic
   c. Submissive
   d. Assertive

Book Companion Website

Visit the Book Companion Website at **academic.cengage.com/psychology/weiten,** where you will find tutorial quizzes, flash cards, and web links for every chapter, a final exam, and more! You can also link to the Psychology Resource Center (accessible directly at **academic.cengage.com/login**) for a range of psychology-related resources.

Personal Explorations Workbook

The following exercises in your *Personal Explorations Workbook* may enhance your self-understanding in relation to issues raised in this chapter. **Questionnaire 7.1:** Opener Scale. **Personal Probe 7.1:** How Do You Feel about Self-Disclosure? **Personal Probe 7.2:** Reflections on Your Communication Style and Feelings about Conflict.

ANSWERS

1. d Pages 202–203
2. c Pages 210–211
3. b Pages 208–214
4. a Pages 214–215
5. c Page 219
6. b Page 221
7. c Page 223
8. d Pages 225, 227
9. a Pages 227–228
10. d Page 230

CHAPTER 8

Friendship and Love

PERSPECTIVES ON CLOSE RELATIONSHIPS
The Ingredients of Close Relationships
Culture and Relationships
The Internet and Relationships
INITIAL ATTRACTION AND RELATIONSHIP DEVELOPMENT
Initial Encounters
Getting Acquainted
Established Relationships
FRIENDSHIP
What Makes a Good Friend?
LIVING IN TODAY'S WORLD *Social Support and Stress*
Gender and Sexual Orientation Issues
ROMANTIC LOVE
Sexual Orientation and Love
Gender Differences
Theories of Love
The Course of Romantic Love
APPLICATION: OVERCOMING LONELINESS
The Nature and Prevalence of Loneliness
The Roots of Loneliness
Correlates of Loneliness
Conquering Loneliness
REVIEW
PRACTICE TEST

Antonio was so keyed up, he tossed and turned all night. When morning finally arrived, he was elated. In less than two hours, he would be meeting Sonia for coffee! In his first class that morning, thoughts and images of Sonia constantly distracted him from the lecture. When class was finally over, he had to force himself not to walk too fast to the Student Union, where they had agreed to meet. Sound familiar? Chances are that you recognize Antonio's behavior as that of someone falling in love.

Friendship and love play a major role in psychological adjustment. Recall from Chapter 1 that the strongest predictor of happiness, after personality, is social connectedness. And, social isolation is associated with poor physical and mental health and antisocial behavior (Baumeister & Leary, 1995; Loving, Heffner, & Kiecolt-Glaser, 2006). We begin this chapter by defining close relationships, including a discussion of how culture and the Internet influence relationships. Next, we consider why people are attracted to each other and why they stay in or leave relationships. Following that, we probe more deeply into friendship and romantic love. In the Application section, we focus on the painful problem of loneliness and how to overcome it.

Perspectives on Close Relationships

LEARNING OBJECTIVES

- *Define close relationships and give some examples.*
- *Describe how people from individualistic cultures and collectivist cultures view love and marriage.*
- *Describe how differences between Internet and face-to-face interactions affect relationship development.*

Before diving into the fascinating topic of romantic love, it is helpful to have some background information. Let's examine the variety of close relationships, how culture influences people's views of relationships, and how the Internet affects relationships.

The Ingredients of Close Relationships

Typically, ***close relationships*** **are those that are important, interdependent, and long lasting.** In other words, people in close relationships spend a lot of time and energy maintaining the relationship, and what one person says and does affects the other. As you are aware, close relationships can arouse intense feelings—both positive (passion, concern, caring) and negative (rage, jealousy, despair). This phenomenon is termed the *paradox of close relationships* (Rook & Pietromonaco, 1987).

Close relationships come in many forms: family relationships, friendships and work relationships, romantic relationships, and marriage. Although many close relationships are based on mutual, intimate self-disclosure, many are not. When college students were asked to identify the person to whom they felt closest, 47% named a romantic partner, 36% listed a friend, 14% mentioned a family member, and 3% named another individual such as a co-worker (Berscheid, Snyder, & Omoto, 1989). Thus, not all close relationships are characterized by emotional intimacy.

Culture and Relationships

Cross-cultural research on close relationships is largely limited to romantic relationships, so we'll focus on them. Although it appears that romantic love is experienced in most cultures (Jankowiak & Fischer, 1992), cultures do vary in their emphasis on romantic love as a prerequisite for marriage. Interestingly, love as the basis for marriage goes back only to the 18th century of Western culture (Stone, 1977). According to Elaine Hatfield and Richard Rapson (1993), "Marriage-for-love represents an ultimate expression of individualism" (p. 2). By contrast, marriages arranged by families and other go-betweens remain common in cultures high in collectivism, including India (Gupta, 1992), Japan (Iwao, 1993), China (Xiaohe & Whyte, 1990), and West African countries (Adams, Anderson, & Adonu, 2004). This practice is declining in some societies as a result of Westernization. Still, when people in collectivist societies contemplate marriage, they weigh strongly the impact a relationship will have on their family rather than rely solely on what their heart says (Triandis, 1994). Studies show that attitudes about love in India, Pakistan, Thailand, and West African countries reflect these cultural priorities (Adams et al., 2004; Levine et al., 1995; Medora et al., 2002).

© Earl & Nazima Kowalt/Corbis

© Royalty-Free/Masterfile

Marriages based on romantic love are the norm in Western cultures, whereas arranged marriages prevail in collectivist cultures.

Cultural views of love and marriage are linked to both a country's values and its economic health. In one study, researchers asked college students in 11 countries the following question: "If a man (woman) had all the other qualities you desired, would you marry this person if you were not in love with him (her)?" (Levine et al., 1995). Students in countries with more individualistic values and higher standards of living were significantly less likely to answer "yes" to the question than were those in countries with more collectivist values and lower standards of living (see **Figure 8.1**). Another cross-cultural investigation of the meaning of various emotions found that Italians and Americans equated love with happiness, whereas Chinese respondents associated it with sadness and envisioned unrequited love (Shaver, Wu, & Schwartz, 1991).

People from Western societies are often dumbfounded by collectivist cultures' deemphasis of romantic love and their penchant for arranged marriages. Most Westerners assume that the modern conception of romantic love as the basis for marriage must result in better marital relationships than collectivist cultures' "antiquated" beliefs and practices. However, there is little empirical support for this ethnocentric view (Dion & Dion, 1993; Triandis, 1994). Take, for example, a study of couples in India, which found that love grew over the years in arranged marriages, whereas it declined among couples who married for romantic love (Gupta & Singh, 1982). Also, the expectation that marriage will fill diverse psychological needs places greater pressure on marital relationships in individualistic societies than on those in collectivist cultures (Dion & Dion, 1993). These high expectations for personal fulfillment in marriage may be linked to the rapidly escalating divorce rates in these societies (Dion & Dion, 1993). The dearth of cross-cultural research on love means that we can only speculate on these matters. But smug assumptions about the superiority of Western ways are unwise, given our extremely high divorce rates.

Cross-Cultural Views on Love and Marriage

Country	Yes	No	Undecided
Japan	2.3	62.0	35.7
United States	3.5	85.9	10.6
Brazil	4.3	85.7	10.0
Australia	4.8	80.0	15.2
Hong Kong	5.8	77.6	16.7
England	7.3	83.6	9.1
Mexico	10.2	80.5	9.3
Philippines	11.4	63.6	25.0
Thailand	18.8	33.8	47.5
India	49.0	24.0	26.9
Pakistan	50.4	39.1	10.4

Figure 8.1

Cross-cultural views on love and marriage. College students in ten countries and Hong Kong responded to the following question: "If a man (woman) had all the other qualities you desired, would you marry this person if you were not in love with him (her)?" Generally, students in countries with higher standards of living and more individualistic values were significantly less likely to answer "yes" to the question than those in countries with lower standards of living and more collectivist values.

Adapted from Levine, R., Sato, S., Hashimoto, T., & Verma, J. (1995). Love and marriage in eleven cultures. *Journal of Cross-Cultural Psychology 26*(5), pp. 561, 564. Copyright © 1995 by Sage Publications, Inc. Adapted by permission of Sage Publications.

Web Link 8.1 **The Student Counseling Virtual Pamphlet Collection**

The Student Counseling office at the University of Chicago had a great idea: gather together links to the best online information from other counseling centers for the problems and issues faced by students. The section on relationships provides advice on a diverse array of topics, including advice on getting along with a roommate, online dating, fighting fair, preventing violence, and dealing with loneliness.

The Internet and Relationships

To meet prospective friends and romantic partners, people used to be limited to school, work, and church settings. Then came the "bar scene," personal ads in newspapers, singles mixers, and video dating services. More recently, the Internet has dramatically expanded opportunities for people to meet and develop relationships through social networking services (Myspace, Friendster), online dating services, e-mail, chat rooms, and news groups.

Critics see these trends as leading to the demise of face-to-face interactions, widespread loneliness and alienation, and millions being lured into dangerous liaisons by unscrupulous people. But research to date generally paints a positive picture of the Internet's impact on people's connections with one another. For example, the web offers a wealth of opportunities to interact for those normally separated because of geography, physical infirmity, or social anxiety (McKenna & Bargh, 2000). Also, Internet groups provide a safer venue than real life for individuals with stigmatized identities (for example, gay people) to interact and receive support. Similarly, Internet groups for those with grave illnesses (cancer, multiple sclerosis, diabetes, AIDS) provide important support and information to their subscribers (Bargh & McKenna, 2004). Of course, the anonymous nature of Internet communication *does* make it easy for dishonest individuals to take advantage of others, so it's smart to be cautious about revealing personal information online.

© David Young-Wolff/Photo/Edit

The Internet is playing a larger and larger role in the formation and maintenance of interpersonal relationships.

Dating-Related Activities Online

Online Activities	Single and Looking Internet Users (%)
Flirt with someone	40
Go to an online dating website	37
Ask someone out on a date	28
Find a place offline, like a nightclub or singles event, where you might meet someone to date	27
Been introduced to a potential date by a third party using e-mail or instant messaging	21
Participate in an online group where you hope to meet people to date	19
Search for information about someone you dated in the past	18
Maintain a long-distance relationship	18
Search for information about someone you are currently dating or are about to meet for a first date	17
Break up with someone you are dating	9

Figure 8.2

Dating-related activities online. Researchers asked Internet users who were single and looking for a romantic partner how they used the Internet (including e-mail and instant messaging) for dating (Madden & Lenhart, 2006). Flirting and going to an online dating website were most frequently mentioned. Most respondents engaged in three or fewer of these activities.

Adapted from Madden, M. & Lenhart, A. (2006). "Online dating," retrieved April 29, 2007 from http://www.pewinternet.org/pdfs/PIP_Online_Dating.pdf (Dating-Related Activities Online table, p. 5.) Reprinted by permission of PEW Internet & American Life Project. Washington, D.C.

In a short period of time, the Internet has become an indispensable vehicle for making acquaintances and developing relationships. One survey based on a nationally representative sample of American adults reported that 31% (representing 63 million people) knew someone who had used a dating website, and 11% (representing 16 million adults) had visited such a site to meet people (Madden & Lenhart, 2006). Among those who used online dating sites, a majority (52%) reported "mostly positive" experiences, although a sizeable number (29%) had "mostly negative" experiences. This report also asked the Internet users who said they were single and looking for a romantic partner to identify how they used the Internet for dating. You can see their responses in **Figure 8.2**.

Although critics are concerned that Internet relationships are superficial, research suggests that virtual relationships are just as intimate as face-to-face ones and are sometimes even closer (Bargh, McKenna, & Fitzsimons, 2002), for reasons we will discuss shortly. Regardless, many virtual relationships migrate to face-to-face interactions (Boase & Wellman, 2006). When people do decide to move beyond an Internet-based relationship, they typically first exchange letters via "snail mail" or talk on the telephone. Actual meetings usually take place only after telephone contact. Researchers find that romantic relationships that begin on the Internet seem to be just as stable over two years as traditional relationships ((McKenna, Green, & Gleason, 2002). This same study reported that 22% of the participants said that they were living with, had become engaged to, or were married to someone they had first met on the Internet.

The Internet has also assumed importance in maintaining established relationships. In a poll of 1,000 Internet users, 94% reported that the Internet made it easier for them to communicate with friends and family who live far away, and 87% said that they use it regularly for that purpose (D'Amico, 1998). Although some social critics have predicted that Internet use will reduce face-to-face interactions, but in fact Internet users typically maintain their social involvements while cutting back on TV time (Boase & Wellman, 2006).

The differences between Internet and face-to-face communication (see **Figure 7.2** in the previous chapter) require psychologists to reexamine the established theories and principles of relationship development that we discuss in this chapter (Bargh & McKenna, 2004).

For example, good looks and close physical proximity are powerful factors in initial attraction in the real world. On the Internet, where people form relationships sight unseen, these factors are irrelevant. Online, similarity of interests and values kicks in earlier and assumes more power than it does in face-to-face relationships. One study found that pairs of strangers who chatted on the Internet liked each other more than if they had talked face-to-face (McKenna et al., 2002). But in another study of pairs randomly assigned to either face-to-face or Internet chat conversations, the face-to-face group felt more satisfied with the experience and felt a higher degree of closeness and self-disclosure with their partners (Mallen, Day, & Green, 2003).

Self-disclosure is another relationship issue affected by the differences in the two types of communication. Because the Internet is shrouded in the cloak of anonymity, people take greater risks in self-disclosure. Thus, feelings of intimacy can develop more quickly (McKenna & Bargh, 2000). Sometimes this experience can set up a false sense of intimacy, which can create uncomfortable feelings if a face-to-face meeting ensues—that is, meeting with a stranger who knows "too much" about you (Hamilton, 1999). Of course, face-to-face meetings can also go smoothly.

Anonymity also allows people to construct a virtual identity. Obviously, this can be a problem if one person adopts a fictional persona and another assumes that it is authentic and begins to take the relationship seriously. A related concern is truthfulness. In one survey, 25% of online daters admitted to using deception (Byrm & Lenton, 2001), yet a whopping 86% of participants in an online dating site felt that others misrepresented their physical appearance (Gibbs, Ellison, & Heino, 2006). How do we explain this huge discrepancy? For one thing, some people rationalize lying because it has practical advantages: Men who claim to earn high salaries receive more replies than those who say they earn less money (Epstein, 2007). Second, there are semantic misunderstandings: One person's "average" may be another person's "plump." Third, some people "stretch the truth" to work around frustrating constraints imposed by the technological design of dating websites (such as age cutoffs). Finally, creating an accurate online representation of oneself is a complex process: Individuals need to put their best self forward to attract potential dates, but they also need to present themselves authentically—especially if they expect to meet a person face to face (Gibbs, et al. 2006). One study found that online daters dealt with this tension by constructing profiles that reflected their "ideal self" rather than their "actual self" (Ellison, Heino, & Gibbs, 2006). The most common factors that online daters misrepresent are age, appearance, and marital status (Byrm & Lenton, 2001).

Additional research in this fascinating area will not only provide valuable information about virtual relationships but will also reveal interesting new perspectives on face-to-face relationships.

Web Link 8.2 **Online Dating Magazine**

This independent and privately owned online magazine is a source of wide-ranging information about online dating: reviews of dating services, tips on online safety, tactics used by some dating services to gain members, and advice (from a psychologist) on how to form better social relationships.

Initial Attraction and Relationship Development

LEARNING OBJECTIVES

- *Discuss the roles of proximity and familiarity in initial attraction.*
- *Summarize the findings on physical attractiveness in initial attraction.*
- *Discuss the role of reciprocal liking and similarity in getting acquainted.*
- *Describe the personality qualities that people like in others.*
- *Give some commonly used relationship maintenance strategies, and explain what is meant by "minding" relationships.*
- *Summarize interdependence theory and explain how rewards, costs, and investments influence relationship satisfaction and commitment.*

Individuals use a multitude of factors to assess another person's appeal as a mate or a friend. Furthermore, because attraction is a two-way street, intricate interactions occur between variables. To simplify this complex issue, we'll divide our coverage into four segments. First, we'll review the factors that operate in initial encounters. Then we'll consider elements that come into play as relationships begin to develop. Next, we'll review what's involved in maintaining relationships. Finally, we'll look at what influences people to stay in or get out of relationships.

Our review of research in this section pertains to both friendships and romantic relationships. In some cases, a particular factor (such as physical attractiveness) may play a more influential role in love than in friendship, or vice versa. However, all the factors dis-

CATHY © 1993 by Cathy Guisewite. Reprinted with permission of UNIVERSAL PRESS SYNDICATE. All rights reserved.

cussed in this section enter into both types of relationships. These factors also operate the same in the friendships and romantic relationships of gay and straight individuals (Peplau & Fingerhut, 2007). But we should note that homosexuals face three unique dating challenges (Peplau & Spaulding, 2003): They have a small pool of potential partners, they are often under pressure to conceal their sexual orientation, and they have limited ways to meet prospective partners. Also, fears of hostility may cause them to guard their self-disclosures to acquaintances and friends.

Initial Encounters

Sometimes initial encounters begin dramatically with two strangers' eyes locking across a room. More often, two people become aware of their mutual interest, usually triggered by each other's looks and conversations. What draws two strangers together? Three factors stand out: proximity, familiarity, and physical attractiveness.

Proximity

Attraction usually depends on proximity: People have to be in the same place at the same time. ***Proximity* refers to geographic, residential, and other forms of spatial closeness.** Of course, proximity is not an issue in cyberspace interactions. But in everyday life people become acquainted with, and attracted to, someone who lives, works, shops, and plays nearby.

The importance of proximity was apparent in a study of Maryland state police trainees (Segal, 1974). At the training academy, both dormitory rooms and classroom seats were assigned on the basis of alphabetical order. Six months after their arrival, participants were asked to name their three closest friends among the group of trainees. The trainees whose last names were closer together in the alphabet were much more likely to be friends than trainees whose names were widely separated in the alphabet. Proximity effects may seem self-evident, but it is sobering to realize that your friendships and love interests are shaped by seating charts, apartment availability, shift assignments, and office locations (Berscheid & Reis, 1998).

Familiarity

You probably walk the same route to your classes several times a week. As the term progresses, you begin to recognize some familiar faces on your route. Have you also found yourself nodding or smiling at these people? If so, you've experienced the ***mere exposure effect,* or an increase in positive feelings toward a novel stimulus (person) based on frequent exposure to it** (Zajonc, 1968). Note that the positive feelings arise just on the basis of seeing someone frequently—not because of any interaction.

The implications of the mere exposure effect on initial attraction should be obvious. Generally, the more familiar someone is, the more you will like him or her. And greater liking increases the probability that you will strike up a conversation and, possibly, develop a relationship with the person. There is, however, an important exception to the familiarity principle: If your initial reaction to someone is negative, increased exposure will only intensify your dislike (Swap, 1977). Of course, people can be attracted to total strangers, so familiarity isn't the only factor involved in initial attraction (Fitness, Fletcher, & Overall, 2007).

Physical Attractiveness

Physical attractiveness plays a major role in initial face-to-face encounters (Peretti & Abplanalp, 2004). In other words, most people pay no mind to statements such as "Beauty is only skin deep" and "You can't judge a book by its cover." Among American college students, physical attractiveness in a dating partner has increased in importance over the past 50 years—for both sexes, but especially for men (Buss et al., 2001).

The role of physical beauty in attraction has been studied in settings ranging from college dances to get-acquainted dates to commercial dating services

(Sprecher & Duck, 1994; Walster et al., 1966). All show that attractiveness is a key factor in dating. Good looks play a role in friendships as well. People, especially males, prefer attractiveness in their same- and other-gender friends (Aboud & Mendelson, 1996; Fehr, 2000).

Do gays and straights differ in the importance they place on the physical attractiveness of prospective dating partners? It seems not (Peplau & Spaulding, 2000). In fact, researchers often find gender rather than sexual orientation to be the more important factor in partner preferences. For example, in the wording of gay and straight personal advertisements in newspapers, both heterosexual and homosexual men are more likely to request physically attractive partners than either heterosexual or homosexual women are (Bailey et al., 1997; Deaux & Hanna, 1984).

The emphasis on beauty may not be quite as great as the evidence reviewed thus far suggests. **Figure 8.3** summarizes the results of a cross-cultural study conducted with 37 cultural groups on the characteristics commonly sought in a mate (Buss, 1989). As you can see, personal qualities, such as kindness and intelligence, were ranked higher than physical attractiveness by both genders. Similarly, a 1997 survey of American college students' most preferred qualities in a mate reported that both men and women ranked "mutual attraction/love," "dependable character," and "emotional stability/maturity," respectively, the highest (Buss et al., 2001). "Good looks" was ranked only 8th by men and 13th by women (out of 18 total qualities). These results are reassuring, although we know that verbal reports don't always predict people's actual priorities and behavior.

What makes someone attractive? Although people can hold different views about what makes a person attractive, they tend to agree on the key elements of good looks. Researchers who study attractiveness focus almost exclusively on facial features and physique. Both are important in perceived attractiveness, but an unattractive body is seen as a greater liability than an unattractive face (Alicke, Smith, & Klotz, 1986). Males, whether gay or straight, place more emphasis on body build.

Even across different ethnic groups and countries, there seems to be strong agreement on attractive *facial features* (Cunningham et al., 1995; Langlois et al., 2000). Women who have "baby-faced" features such as large eyes, prominent cheekbones, a small nose, and full lips get high ratings (Jones, 1995). In particular, the combination of these youthful features with "mature" features (prominent cheekbones, narrow cheeks, wide smile) seems to be the winning ticket—picture Julia Roberts and Angelina Jolie (Cunningham, Druen, & Barbee, 1997). Men who have a strong jaw and a broad forehead get high ratings on attractiveness (George Clooney and Denzel Washington come to mind) (Cunningham, Barbee, & Pike, 1990). On the other hand, softer- and finer-featured male faces are also rated attractive (Leonardo DiCaprio, for example) (Perrett et al., 1998).

When it comes to *physique,* males who have broad shoulders, slim waists and legs, and small buttocks receive high attractiveness ratings (Singh, 1995). In recent years, the ideal body shape for males has become more muscular (Martins, Tiggeman, & Kirkbride, 2007). Tall men are also considered attractive (Lynn & Shurgot, 1984). Women of average weight with an "hourglass" figure and medium-sized breasts are rated high in attractiveness (Franzoi & Herzog, 1987; Singh, 1993). African American men and women prefer a larger body type than European American men and women do (Jackson & McGill, 1996; Rosenfeld et al., 1999).

Figure 8.3

Characteristics sought in a mate. Buss (1989) surveyed individuals from 37 cultural groups on the characteristics they sought in a mate. Kindness/understanding and intelligence were ranked higher than physical attractiveness by both males and females. Statistically significant gender differences in rankings were found for a variety of characteristics, which are shown in italics. For example, males ranked physical attractiveness higher than females did.

From Buss, D. M. (1989). Sex differences in human mate preferences: Evolutionary hypotheses tested in 37 cultures. *Behavioral and Brain Sciences, 12,* 1–14. Copyright © 1989 by Cambridge University Press. Reprinted with the permission of Cambridge University Press and the author.

Characteristics Commonly Sought in a Mate

Rank	Characteristics Preferred by Men	Characteristics Preferred by Women
1	Kindness and understanding	Kindness and understanding
2	Intelligence	Intelligence
3	*Physical attractiveness*	Exciting personality
4	Exciting personality	Good health
5	Good health	Adaptability
6	Adaptability	*Physical attractiveness*
7	Creativity	Creativity
8	Desire for children	*Good earning capacity*
9	College graduate	College graduate
10	Good heredity	Desire for children
11	*Good earning capacity*	Good heredity
12	Good housekeeper	Good housekeeper
13	Religious orientation	Religious orientation

Nonetheless, being considerably overweight is viewed very negatively in the United States, despite the increasing incidence of obesity (Hebl & Mannix, 2003).

Currently in the United States, thinness is given heightened emphasis, especially for girls and women. Many studies show that repeated exposure to media portrayals of the thin ideal are associated with body dissatisfaction (Groesz, Levine, & Murnen, 2002; Stice, Spangler, & Agras, 2001). Thus, it is not surprising that high school girls underestimate the body size that boys find attractive (Paxton, et al., 2005). Also, many college women perceive themelves to be heavier than they actually are and wish to be thinner (Vartanian, Giant, & Passino, 2001). This emphasis on thinness likely lies behind the high incidence of eating disorders found among European American, Asian American, and Hispanic adolescent girls (Halpern et al., 1999). Mexican American women who are oriented toward Anglo American culture are significantly more likely to have eating disorders than those oriented toward Mexican culture, illustrating the role of acculturation (Cachelin et al., 2006). Eating disorders are less common among African American females because the ideal physique for this group is larger than that for European females (Polivy & Herman, 2002).

Gay males also live in a subculture that emphasizes physical appearance. A study that experimentally induced self-objectification (wearing a swimsuit versus a turtleneck sweater) showed that gay males felt more body shame, had more body dissatisfaction, and ate less when given the opportunity than the straight males (Martins et al., 2007). These findings match the results of a similar study where women wore a swimsuit (Fredrickson, et al., 1998). As American culture increasingly objectifies male bodies, and as men feel greater pressure to meet the ideals of male body shape, appearance may become more central to the self-concept of heterosexual men, leading to greater body dissatisfaction and more eating disorders in this group (Martins et al., 2007). We explore the important issue of eating disorders in the Chapter 15 Application.

Another response to "attractiveness pressure" is the increased rate of cosmetic surgery, especially among younger people. Between 2003 and 2004, the number of cosmetic surgeries performed on Americans 18 and younger increased a whopping 48% (Springen, 2004). Most such surgeries are nose jobs and breast augmentations. The popularity of television shows like *Extreme Makeover* or *The Swan* no doubt account for some of this increase.

Because our culture particularly values attractiveness in females, physical attractiveness appears to be a more valued relationship quality for women than for men (Aubrey, 2006; Regan, 2003). This gender gap was apparent in a study of the tactics heterosexual individuals used in pursuing romantic relationships. David

© Ephraim Ben-Shimon/Corbis

According to the matching hypothesis, we tend to wind up with someone similar to ourselves in attractiveness. However, other factors such as personality, intelligence, and social status also influence attraction.

Buss (1988) asked 208 newlywed individuals to describe the things they did when they first met their spouse, and during the remainder of their courtship, to make themselves more appealing to their partner. Buss found that men were more likely than women to emphasize their material resources by doing such things as flashing lots of money, buying nice gifts, showing off expensive possessions, and bragging about their importance at work (see **Figure 8.4** on the next page). In contrast, women were more likely than men to work at enhancing their appearance by dieting, wearing stylish clothes, trying new hairstyles, and getting a tan. Although there were relative differences between the genders in emphasis on physical attractiveness, the data in **Figure 8.4** show that both genders relied on tactics intended to enhance or maintain good looks.

Matching up on looks. Thankfully, people can enjoy rewarding social lives without being spectacularly good looking. In the process of dating and mating, people apparently take into consideration their own level of attractiveness. **The *matching hypothesis* proposes that people of similar levels of physical attractiveness gravitate toward each other.** This hypothesis is supported by findings that both dating and married heterosexual couples tend to be similar in physical attractiveness (Feingold, 1988). There is some debate, however,

Tactics of Attraction

	Mean Frequency	
Tactics used significantly more by males	**Men (N = 102)**	**Women (N = 106)**
Display resources	0.67	0.44
Brag about resources	0.73	0.60
Display sophistication	**1.18**	0.88
Display strength	0.96	0.44
Display athleticism	**1.18**	0.94
Show off	0.70	0.47
Tactics used significantly more by females		
Wear makeup	0.02	**1.63**
Keep clean and groomed	**2.27**	**2.44**
Alter appearance—general	0.39	**1.27**
Wear stylish clothes	**1.22**	**2.00**
Act coy	0.54	0.73
Wear jewelry	0.25	**2.21**
Wear sexy clothes	0.68	0.91
Tactics for which no significant gender differences were found		
Act provocative	0.77	0.90
Flirt	**2.13**	**2.09**
Keep hair groomed	**2.20**	**2.31**
Increase social pressure	0.89	0.90
Act nice	**1.77**	**1.86**
Display humor	**2.24**	**2.28**
Act promiscuous	0.30	0.21
Act submissive	**1.24**	**1.11**
Dissemble (feign agreement)	**1.26**	1.09
Touch	**2.26**	**2.16**

Figure 8.4

Similarities and differences between the genders in the tactics of attraction. Buss (1988) asked newlywed subjects to rate how often they had used 23 tactics of attraction to make themselves more appealing to their partner. The tactics used by one gender significantly more often than the other are listed in the first two sections of the figure. Although there were significant differences between the genders, there were also many similarities. The 11 tactics used most frequently by each gender (those above the median) are boldfaced, showing considerable overlap between males and females in the tactics they used most. (Note: Higher means in the data reflect higher frequency of use, but the numbers do not indicate frequency per day or week.)

Adapted from Buss, D. M. (1988). The evolution of human intrasexual competition: Tactics of mate attraction. *Journal of Personality and Social Psychology, 54*(4), 616–628. Copyright © 1988 by the American Psychological Association. Adapted by permission of the publisher and author.

about whether people match up by their own choice (Aron, 1988; Kalick & Hamilton, 1986). Some theorists believe that individuals mostly pursue highly attractive partners and that their matching is the result of social forces beyond their control, such as rejection by more attractive others. Researchers have also found evidence for matching effects in friendships between men, but not between women (Duck, 1994). The reasons for this gender difference are not readily apparent.

Attractiveness and resource exchange. Contradicting the matching hypothesis, a number of studies have shown that, in heterosexual dating, males "trade" occupational status for youth and physical attractiveness in females, and vice versa (Fletcher, Overall, & Friesen, 2006; Fletcher et al., 2004). This finding also holds true in many other cultures. As you already saw in the cross-cultural study summarized in **Figure 8.3**, men in most countries rate physical attractiveness in a prospective mate as more important than women do, whereas women rate "good financial prospects" and "ambitious and industrious" as more important characteristics than men do (Buss, 1989). In reviewing the content of personal ads in newspapers and magazines, Wiederman (1993) reported that women advertisers sought financial resources in prospective partners 11 times as often as men did.

David Buss

Courtesy of David M. Buss

Evolutionary social psychologists such as David Buss (1988) believe that these findings on age, status, and physical attractiveness reflect gender differences in inherited reproductive strategies that have been sculpted over thousands of generations by natural selection. Their thinking has been guided by ***parental investment theory,*** **which maintains that a species' mating patterns depend on what each sex has to invest—in the way of time, energy, and survival risk—to produce and nurture offspring.** According to this model, members of the gender that makes the smaller investment will compete with each other for mating opportunities with the gender that makes the larger investment, and the gender with the larger investment will tend to be more discriminating in selecting its partners.

How does this analysis apply to humans? Like many mammalian species, human males are required to invest little in the production of offspring beyond the act of copulation, so their reproductive potential is maximized by mating with as many females as possible. As well, males should prefer young and attractive females because these qualities are assumed to signal fertility, which should increase the chances of conception and passing genes on to the next generation. The situation for females is quite different. Females have to invest nine months in pregnancy, and our female ancestors typically had to devote at least several additional years to nourishing offspring through breastfeeding. These realities limit the number of offspring women can produce, regardless of how many males they mate with. Hence, females have little or no incentive for mating with many males. Instead, females can optimize their reproductive potential by selectively mating with reliable partners who have greater material resources (Buss, 1994). These preferences should increase the likelihood that a male partner will be committed to a long-term relationship and will be able to support the woman and their children, thus ensuring that her genes will be passed on.

Thus, in humans, males are thought to compete with other males for the relatively scarce and valuable "commodity" of reproductive opportunities. Parental investment theory predicts that in comparison to women, men will show more interest in sexual activity, more desire for variety in sexual partners, and more willingness to engage in uncommitted sex (see **Figure 8.5**). In contrast, females are thought to be the conservative, discriminating gender that is highly selective in choosing partners. This selectivity supposedly entails seeking partners who have more material resources that can be invested in feeding and caring for offspring.

Are there alternatives to the evolutionary explanation for patterns of mate selection and resource exchange in heterosexual relationships? Yes, sociocultural models can also provide plausible explanations which center on traditional gender-role socialization and men's greater economic power (Sprecher, Sullivan, & Hatfield, 1994). Some theorists argue that women have learned to value men's economic clout because their own economic potential has been severely limited in virtually all cultures by a long history of discrimination. Consistent with this hypothesis, it is women in countries with limited educational and career opportunities for females who show the strongest preferences for men with high incomes (Eagly & Wood, 1999). Moreoever, when women's economic power increases, so does their preference for a physically attractive mate (Gangestad, 1993). Thus, environmental factors may also contribute to gender differences in mate selection strategies (Fletcher et al., 2006; Wood & Eagly, 2002).

© Hepp/Stone/Getty Images

Although most couples are similar in age and attractiveness, sometimes men exchange occupational status for physical attractiveness in women, and vice versa.

Getting Acquainted

After several initial encounters, people typically begin the dance of getting to know each other. Is it possible to predict which budding relationships will flower and which will die on the vine? We'll examine three

	Biological reality	Evolutionary significance	Behavioral outcomes
Males	Reproduction involves minimal investment of time, energy, and risk	Maximize reproductive success by seeking more sexual partners with high reproductive potential	More interest in uncommitted sex, greater number of sex partners over lifetime, look for youth and attractiveness in partners
Females	Reproduction involves substantial investment of time, energy, and risk	Maximize reproductive success by seeking partners willing to invest material resources in your offspring	Less interest in uncommitted sex, smaller number of sex partners over lifetime, look for income, status, and ambition in partners

Figure 8.5

Parental investment theory and mating preferences. Parental investment theory suggests that basic differences between males and females in parental investment have great adaptive significance and lead to gender differences in mating propensities and preferences, as outlined here.

BIZARRO © by Dan Piraro. Reprinted by special permission of King Features Syndicate.

factors that can keep the ball rolling: reciprocal liking, perceived similarity, and desirable personality characteristics.

Reciprocal Liking

An old adage advises, "If you want to *have* a friend, *be* a friend." This suggestion captures the idea of the reciprocity principle in relationships. ***Reciprocal liking* refers to liking those who show that they like you.** Many studies show that if you believe another person likes you, you will like him or her (Aron, Fisher, & Strong, 2006; Berscheid & Walster, 1978). Think about it. Assuming that others are sincere, you respond positively when they flatter you, do favors for you, and use nonverbal behavior to signal their interest in you (eye contact, leaning forward). Moreover, you usually reciprocate such behavior.

You can see the self-fulfilling prophecy at work here. If you believe that someone likes you, you behave in a friendly manner toward that person. Your behavior encourages him or her to respond positively, which confirms your initial expectation. A study by Rebecca Curtis and Kim Miller (1986) shows the self-fulfilling prophecy in action. College students who were strangers were divided into pairs for a 5-minute "get acquainted" conversation. Afterward, one member of each pair was led to believe that the other student either did or didn't like him or her. Then the pairs met again and talked about current events for 10 minutes. Raters, blind to the experimental condition of the participants, listened to tape recordings of the 10-minute interactions and rated the participants on a number of behaviors. As predicted, the individuals who believed that they were liked were rated as disclosing more about themselves, behaving more warmly, disagreeing less, and having a more positive tone of voice and general attitude than those who believed that they were disliked (see **Figure 8.6**).

The strategy of "playing hard to get" (nonreciprocity) seems at odds with the reciprocity principle. Is there any evidence that it works? You should probably avoid this tactic. People are usually turned off by others who reject them (Wright & Contrada, 1986). It also seems that individuals prefer those who are *moderately* selective in their liking for others. By contrast, people who like everyone are seen as having no standards, while those who like very few are perceived as arrogant.

Similarity

Do "birds of a feather flock together," or do "opposites attract"? Research offers far more support for the first adage than for the second (Surra, et al., 2006). Despite the increasing diversity in the United States, similarity continues to play a key role in attraction (Macionis, 1997), and the similarity principle operates in both friendships and romantic relationships regardless of sexual orientation (Aubé & Koestner, 1995; Peplau & Fingerhut, 2006). Likewise, people who meet others via the Internet often narrow down prospects in advance by selecting individuals who are like them in key respects (sexual orientation, age, religion, and so forth).

Heterosexual married and dating couples tend to be similar in *demographic characteristics* (age, race, religion, socioeconomic status, and education), *physical attractiveness, intelligence,* and *attitudes* (Kalmijn, 1998; Watson et al., 2004). Support for similarity in *personality* as a factor in attraction is weaker and mixed (Kloh-

Figure 8.6

Reciprocal liking. Research participants were led to believe that their research partner either did or did not like them. The participants who believed that their partners liked them liked their partners more than the participants who believed that their partners did not like them. These results illustrate how reciprocity and the self-fulfilling prophecy can influence attraction to others. (Adapted from Curtis & Miller, 1986)

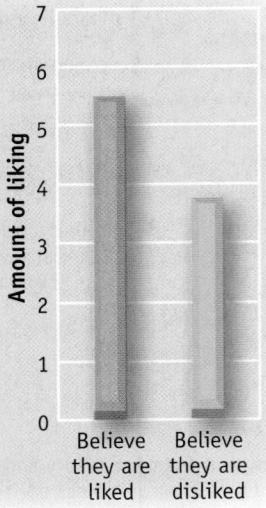

nen & Luo, 2003; Luo & Klohnen, 2005). However, once people are in committed relationships, similarity in personality is associated with relationship satisfaction (Luo & Klohnen, 2005). We've already explored similarity in physical attractiveness. Now, let's consider attitudes.

That similarity in attitudes promotes liking is a well-documented principle (Byrne, 1971; Byrne, Clore, & Smeaton, 1986). According to Donn Byrne's two-stage model, people first "sort" for dissimilarity, avoiding those who appear to be different. Then, from among the remaining group, individuals gravitate toward those who are most similar (Byrne, Clore, & Smeaton, 1986). Here's a typical laboratory experiment that demonstrates the impact of similarity on attraction. Subjects who have previously provided information on their own attitudes are led to believe that they will be meeting a stranger. They are given information about the stranger's views that has been manipulated to show various degrees of similarity to their own views. As attitude similarity increases, subjects' ratings of the likability of the stranger increase (see **Figure 8.7**). And, once two people start dating, a phenomenon termed *attitude alignment* enhances attitudinal similarity. That is, when dating partners discover that they disagree on important values, one or both people typically modify their attitudes so they are more congruent (Davis & Rusbult, 2001).

What is the appeal of similarity? For one thing, you assume that a similar person will probably like you (Condon & Crano, 1988). Second, when others share your beliefs, it validates them (Byrne & Clore, 1970). Finally, interacting with a similar person reduces the chances for conflicts and hassles.

Figure 8.7

Attitude similarity and attraction. When asked to rate the likability of a hypothetical stranger, subjects give progressively higher ratings to people who they are told share more attitudes with them.

Adapted from Gonzales, M. H., Davis, J. M., Loeny, G. L., Lukens, C. K., & Junghans, C. H. (1983). Interactional approach to interpersonal attraction. *Journal of Personality and Social Psychology, 44,* 1191–1197. Copyright © 1983 by the American Psychological Association. Adapted by permission of the publisher and author.

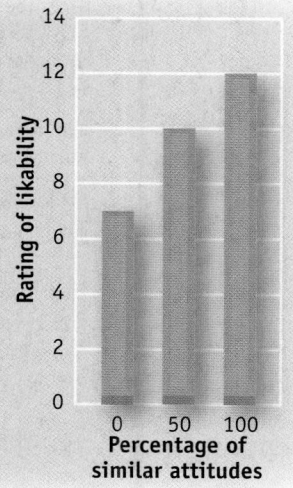

Desirable Personality Characteristics

As you might expect, personal qualities are more important than physical characteristics for a future spouse or life partner, and the reverse is true for casual relationships. As you can see in **Figure 8.8**, for a marriage partner, both male and female college students highly ranked a good overall personality, honesty and trustworthiness, and kindness and compassion (Regan & Berscheid, 1997). For a sexual partner, both men and women ranked "attractive appearance" the highest. Other desirable personality qualities in relationship partners include warmth, friendliness, good sense of humor, and social assertiveness (Hatfield & Rapson, 1993; Regan, 2003).

	Sexual partner	Marriage partner
Women	Physically attractive	Honest or trustworthy
	Healthy	Sensitive/compassionate
	Attentive to my needs	Overall personality
	Sense of humor	Intelligent
	Overall personality	Attentive to my needs
Men	Physically attractive	Overall personality
	Healthy	Honest or trustworthy
	Overall personality	Physically attractive
	Attentive to my needs	Intelligent
	Self-confident	Healthy

Figure 8.8

Characteristics men and women consider most important for a sexual partner and a marriage partner. Both men and women emphasize good looks when judging a sexual partner. When judging a marriage partner, both stress desirable personal qualities, although men also consider physical attractiveness to be important in a marriage partner. (Adapted from Regan & Berscheid, 1997)

Established Relationships

Over time, some acquaintanceships evolve into established relationships. Through conversation and shared activities, individuals mutually determine the desired level of intimacy they want in a relationship. Not all relationships need to be highly intimate to be satisfying. For others, intimacy is an essential ingredient of relationship satisfaction. In either case, to continue, relationships need to be maintained.

Maintenance of Ongoing Relationships

***Relationship maintenance* involves the actions and activities used to sustain the desired quality of a relationship.** In **Figure 8.9** on the next page, you can see a list of commonly used relationship maintenance behaviors. Often, these behaviors occur spontaneously (calling on the phone to check in, eating meals together); at other times, behaviors are more intentional

Relationship Maintenance Strategies	
Strategy	**Behavioral Example**
Positivity	Try to act nice and cheerful
Openness	Encourage him/her to disclose thoughts and feelings to me
Assurances	Stress my commitment to him/her
Social networking	Show that I am willing to do things with his/her friends and family
Task sharing	Help equally with tasks that need to be done
Joint activities	Spend time hanging out
Mediated communication	Use e-mail to keep in touch
Avoidance	Respect each other's privacy and need to be alone
Antisocial behaviors	Act rude to him/her
Humor	Call him/her by a funny nickname
No flirting	Do not encourage overly familiar behavior (relevant in cross-gender friendships)

Figure 8.9

Relationship maintenance strategies. College students were asked to describe how they maintained three different personal relationships over a college term. Their responses were grouped into 11 categories. You can see that, ironically, some people behave negatively in an attempt to enhance relationships. Openness was the most commonly nominated strategy. (Adapted from Canary & Stafford, 1994)

and require more planning (traveling to visit family and friends) (Canary & Stafford, 2001). People use most of these strategies in their various relationships. Obviously, strategies vary depending on the nature of a relationship (familial, friendship, romantic) and its stage of development (new, developing, mature). For example, married couples engage in more assurances and social networking than dating partners do (Stafford & Canary, 1991). Both spontaneous and routine maintenance activities are correlated with relationship satisfaction and commitment (Canary & Dainton, 2006). Of the behaviors in **Figure 8.9**, the best predictors of marital satisfaction are positivity, assurances, and sharing tasks (Canary, Stafford, & Semic, 2002). Also, when the frequency of one partner's maintenance activities compares favorably with the other's expectations, relationship satisfaction is higher (Dainton, 2000). Gay and lesbian couples generally use the same maintenance behaviors as heterosexual couples (Hass & Stafford, 1998).

Another approach to relationship maintenance involves the process of "minding" relationships (Harvey & Omarzu, 1997). *Minding* is an active and ongoing process that involves continuing mutual self-disclosure and maintaining relationship-enhancing beliefs and attributions about one's partner. This model asserts that a high level of minding is associated with satisfying and intimate long-term relationships, and vice versa. To elaborate, a high degree of minding involves using good listening skills, having detailed knowledge about your partner's opinions, making generally positive attributions for your partner's behaviors, expressing feelings of trust and commitment, recognizing your partner's support and effort, and having an optimistic view of the future of the relationship. By contrast, a low degree of minding is characterized by a lack of interest in your partner's self-disclosures, generally negative attributions for your partner's behavior, dwelling on your partner's faults, and a pessimistic view of the future of the relationship. As you can see, this model has a strong cognitive flavor. Although Harvey and Omarzu focus on committed romantic relationships, they suggest that their model likely applies to family and friendship relationships as well.

Relationship Satisfaction and Commitment

How do you gauge your satisfaction in a relationship? What determines whether you will stay in or get out of a relationship? ***Interdependence* or *social exchange theory* postulates that interpersonal relationships are governed by perceptions of the rewards and costs exchanged in interactions.** Basically, this model predicts that interactions between acquaintances, friends, and lovers will continue as long as the participants feel that the benefits they derive from the relationship are reasonable in comparison to the costs of being in the relationship. Harold Kelley and John Thibaut's interdependence theory (Kelley & Thibaut, 1978; Thibaut & Kelley, 1959) is based on B. F. Skinner's principle of reinforcement, which assumes that individuals try to maximize their rewards in life and minimize their costs (see Chapter 2).

Rewards include such things as emotional support, status, and sexual gratification (in romantic relationships); costs are such things as the time and energy that a relationship requires, emotional conflicts, and the inability to engage in other rewarding activities because of relationship obligations. According to interdependence theory, people assess a relationship by its *outcome*—their subjective perception of the rewards of the relationship minus its costs (see **Figure 8.10**).

Web Link 8.3 **SUNY Buffalo Counseling Center: Relationships Page**

The Counseling Center at SUNY–Buffalo is recognized for its excellent guides to interpersonal relationships and to improving communication among college students. The online materials here focus on important questions and issues stemming from people relating intimately to each other.

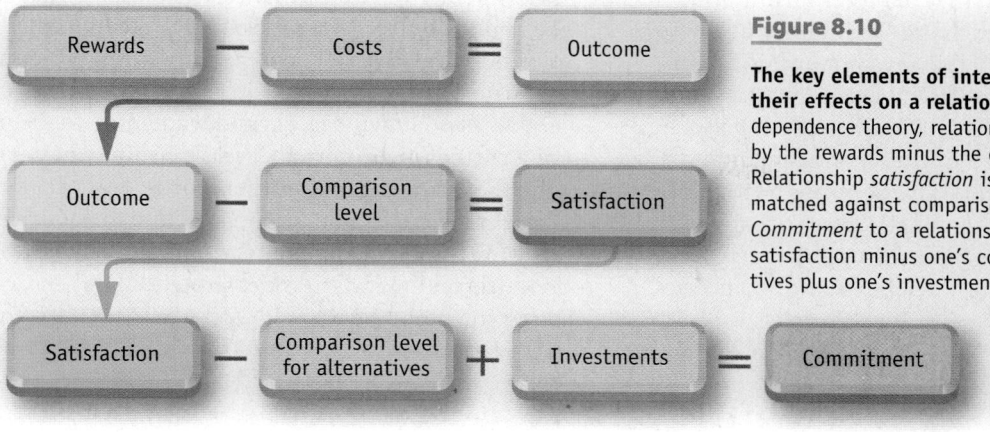

Figure 8.10

The key elements of interdependence theory and their effects on a relationship. According to interdependence theory, relationship *outcome* is determined by the rewards minus the costs of a relationship. Relationship *satisfaction* is based on the outcome matched against comparison level (expectations). *Commitment* to a relationship is determined by one's satisfaction minus one's comparison level for alternatives plus one's investments in the relationship.

Adapted from Brehm, S. S., & Kassin, S, M. (1993). *Social psychology.* Boston: Houghton Mifflin. Copyright © 1993 by Houghton Mifflin Company. Adapted with permission.

Individuals assess their *satisfaction* with a relationship by comparing the relationship outcomes (rewards minus costs) to their subjective expectations. **A *comparison level* is a personal standard of what constitutes an acceptable balance of rewards and costs in a relationship.** It is based on the outcomes you have experienced in previous relationships and the outcomes you have seen others experience in their relationships. Your comparison level may also be influenced by your exposure to fictional relationships, such as those you have read about or seen on television. Consistent with the predictions of interdependence theory, research shows that relationship satisfaction is higher when rewards are perceived to be high and costs are viewed as relatively low.

To understand the role of *commitment* in relationships, we need to consider two additional factors. The first is the ***comparison level for alternatives,* or one's estimation of the available outcomes from alternative relationships.** In using this standard, individuals assess their current relationship outcomes in comparison to the potential outcomes of other similar relationships that may be available to them. This principle helps explain why many unsatisfying relationships are not terminated until another love interest actually appears. The second factor that figures in relationship commitment is ***investments,* or things that people contribute to a relationship that they can't get back if the relationship ends.** Investments include past costs (time, money) that they can never recover if the relationship fails. Understandably, putting investments into a relationship strengthens one's commitment to it.

But what happens if individuals feel that they have invested a lot in a relationship that starts to have problems? Because they're unwilling to forfeit their investments, some people put even *more* into such a relationship. Others decide that they will probably have to forfeit their investment sooner or later, so they choose not to wait—especially if an attractive alternative comes into the picture.

Here's how interdependence theory works: If both members of a couple feel that they are getting a lot out of the relationship (lots of strokes, high status) compared to its costs (a few arguments, occasionally giving up preferred activities), they will probably perceive the relationship as satisfactory and will keep it going. However, if either one begins to feel that the ratio of rewards to costs is falling below his or her comparison level, dissatisfaction is likely to occur. The dissatisfied person may attempt to alter the balance of costs and rewards or try to ease out of the relationship. The likelihood of ending the relationship depends on the number of important investments a person has in the relationship and whether the person believes that an alternative relationship is available that could yield greater satisfaction.

Research generally supports interdependence theory and its extensions (Le & Agnew, 2003; Noller, 2006). Social exchange principles seem to operate in a similar fashion regardless of a couple's sexual orientation (Peplau & Fingerhut, 2007). Moreover, heterosexual and homosexual couples seem quite similar with regard to important aspects of relationships (Peplau & Spaulding, 2003). For example, studies of heterosexual males and females, gay males, and lesbians found that all groups report high satisfaction with their relationships (Duffy & Rusbult, 1986; Kurdek, 2005), as well as moderately high investments in their relationships, moderately poor alternatives, and strong commitment (Duffy & Rusbult, 1986).

This theory of an "interpersonal marketplace" provides a useful model for analyzing many relationships, particularly those in highly individualistic societies. The usefulness of interdependence theory appears more limited for people in collectivist cultures or those with interdependent self-views (Chapter 5).

Even in individualistic cultures, many people resist the idea that close relationships operate according to an economic model. Much of this resistance probably comes from discomfort with the idea that self-interest plays such an important role in the maintenance of relationships. Resistance may also stem from doubts about how well social exchange principles apply to close relationships. In fact, there is some empirical support for this position (Harvey & Wenzel, 2006). Margaret Clark and Judson Mills (1993) distinguish between *exchange relationships* (with strangers, acquaintances, co-workers) and *communal relationships* (with close friends, lovers, family members). Research suggests that in exchange relationships, the usual principles of social exchange dominate. Social exchange principles also operate in communal relationships but seem to be applied differently. For example, in communal relationships, rewards are usually given freely, without any expectation of prompt reciprocation (Clark & Mills, 1993). Also, individuals pay more attention to the needs of a partner in a communal relationship than in an exchange relationship. In other words, you use a need-based norm with people who are close to you and help them without calculating whether and when they will reward you in kind (Clark & Grote, 2003).

Friendship

LEARNING OBJECTIVES

- *Summarize the research on what makes a good friend.*
- *Describe some key gender and sexual orientation differences in friendships.*

It's hard to overestimate the importance of friends. They give help in times of need, advice in times of confusion, consolation in times of failure, and praise in times of achievement. Friends clearly are important to individuals' adjustment. College students with strong friendships are more optimistic and deal better with stressful life events (Brissette, Scheirer, & Carver, 2002). Same-gender friendships between women are linked to positive mental and physical health (Knickmeyer, Sexton, & Nishimura, 2002). Also, developing friendships with people who are different from oneself—in terms of ethnicity or sexual orientation, for example—can break down prejudice (Herek & Capitanio, 1996; Levin, van Laar, & Sidanius, 2003). Intimate and stable friendships are associated with less stress in adulthood and less troublesome behavior among teens (Hartup & Stevens, 1999).

Recommended READING

Friendshifts: The Power of Friendship and How It Shapes Our Lives
by Jan Yager (Hannacroix Creek Books, 1999)

The author of this useful self-help manual has coined the word "friendshifts" to make the point that friendships change over the life span. In this readable book, sociologist Jan Yager traces the nature and role of friendships for children, teens, and adults (in both personal life and the workplace). At all ages, friendships play a vital role in mental health; thus the author urges readers to look carefully at the balance of positives and negatives in their various friendships. Drawing on psychological and sociological research as well as her own interviews, Yager offers excellent advice on making, keeping, and improving friendships. The book also includes a helpful resource section with websites and a bibliography.

What Makes a Good Friend?

Exactly what makes a good friend? One approach to this question comes from a cross-cultural study of students in England, Italy, Japan, and Hong Kong (Argyle & Henderson, 1984). Interestingly, there was enough agreement on how friends should conduct themselves in this diverse sample to identify six informal rules governing friendships. As **Figure 8.11** shows, the common thread running through these rules seems to be providing emotional and social support to friends.

We can also look at the common themes that underlie friendships of all ages to understand the nature of friendship. Researchers have identified three such themes (de Vries, 1996). The first involves the emotional dimension of friendship (self-disclosure, expressing

The Rules of Friendship
Share news of success with a friend
Show emotional support
Volunteer help in time of need
Strive to make a friend happy when in each other's company
Trust and confide in each other
Stand up for a friend in his or her absence

Figure 8.11

Vital behaviors in friendship. A cross-cultural inquiry into the behaviors that are vital to friendship identified these six rules of friendship. (Adapted from Argyle & Henderson, 1984)

LIVING IN TODAY'S WORLD

Social Support and Stress

When Americans think of highly stressful events, September 11 and Hurricane Katrina quickly come to mind. Other frightening events include tornadoes and floods as well as life-threatening accidents and illnesses. Death, divorce, and romantic breakups are also difficult to deal with. Regardless of the type of traumatizing event, people seek out their friends and family to help them cope. As we noted in Chapter 3, this coping strategy can be very adaptive. Social support can serve as a protective buffer that reduces the negative effects of stress (Loving et al., 2006). For example, the survivors of Hurricanes Hugo and Andrew who best coped with the disasters were those who felt that they had the most social support (Norris & Kaniasty, 1996). Also, individuals with post-traumatic stress disorder reported less severe symptoms when they perceived more support from friends (Haden et al., 2007).

Another example of the importance of social support comes from a study of breast cancer patients (Spiegel et al., 1989). Women with advanced breast cancer were randomly assigned to a social support or control condition. Those in the social support condition met weekly for 90 minutes with other patients and doctors to discuss their problems and fears; those in the control group had no access to this support system. Those in the social support condition showed improved moods and reduced fears, and, amazingly, they also lived an average of 18 months longer than those in the no-support condition!

Social support also helps with everyday adjustment. Those who have a network of close relationships are happier and more satisfied with life than those who have fewer social connections (Diener et al., 1999). One study showed that those who have strong social support during medical exams had a stronger immune response than those with weak social support (Glaser et al., 1992). Also, those with close social ties have better physical health and are less likely to die early (Cohen et al., 2002; Uchino, Cacioppo, & Kiecolt-Glaser, 1996).

Although people desire support, receiving it sometimes entails emotional costs such as feelings of indebtedness or loss of self-esteem (Bolger, Zuckerman, & Kessler, 2000). Studies show that invisible support (not obvious to the recipient) can be especially effective in helping people cope with significant stress because it does not undermine self-efficacy (Bolger & Amarel, 2007). People obviously need the reassurance that comes from seeing that others provide help, so visible and invisible support need to be balanced.

Why is social support beneficial in times of stress? Although researchers are still working out definitive answers to this question, a number of factors are likely to come into play. At the cognitive level, sharing a stressful event with others helps individuals interpret the event as less overwhelming than if they had to face it on their own. Emotional support in the form of sympathy and reassurance also figures in. And social support also reduces the physiological impact of stress (Loving et al., 2006).

In these stressful times, individuals' connections to their families, friends, lovers, mates, and co-workers form a life-sustaining web of interconnectedness. There is much truth in the Beatles lyrics, "I get by with a little help from my friends" (and other supportive people).

affection and support, and so forth). A second theme concerns the communal nature of friendship (participating in or supporting each other in mutually shared activities). The third dimension entails sociability and compatibility (friends are sources of fun and recreation). These studies and others show that the most important element of friendship is emotional support (Collins & Madsen, 2006).

Gender and Sexual Orientation Issues

Men's and women's same-gender friendships have a lot in common (Wright, 2006), but there are some interesting differences that appear rooted in traditional gender roles and socialization. In the United States, women's friendships are more often emotionally based, whereas men's tend to be activity based. Although some researchers have challenged this characterization (Walker, 1994), the current belief is that men's friendships are typically based on shared interests and doing things together, while women's friendships more often focus on talking—usually about personal matters (Fehr, 1996, 2004).

We can also compare American men's and women's friendships on *preferred topics* of conversation. Women are far more likely than men to discuss personal problems, people, relationships, and feelings (Fehr, 2004). Men, on the other hand, are much more likely to talk about sports, work, vehicles, and computers than personal concerns. E-mail communications also reflect this gender difference (Colley & Todd, 2002). Whose friendships are more intimate, men's or women's? Currently, there is controversy over this question. The most widely accepted view is that women's friendships are closer and more satisfying—because they involve more self-disclosure (Fehr, 2004; Reis, 1998).

In some countries, men's same-gender friendships are more intimate (Reis, 1998). What short-circuits intimate connections between American men? Several factors stand out (Kilmartin, 2007; Bank & Hansford, 2000). First, men are socialized to be self-sufficient, which inhibits self-disclosure. Second, fear of homosexuality, which is stronger in males than females, is a barrier to intimacy between male friends. Third, traditional gender-role expectations encourage men to see each other as competitors. Why reveal weaknesses to someone who might take advantage of you?

The boundaries between the friendship and romantic or sexual relationships of gay men and lesbians appear to be more complex than those of heterosexuals (Peplau & Fingerhut, 2007; Diamond & Dubé, 2002). Many intimate relationships among lesbians begin as friendships and progress to romance and then to a sexual relationship (Peplau & Spaulding, 2003). Obviously, discerning and negotiating these shifts can be difficult. Also, both lesbians and gay men are much more likely than heterosexuals to maintain social contacts with former sexual partners (Solomon, Rothblum, & Balsam, 2004). One possible explanation for this phenomenon is the small size of some gay and lesbian social networks (Peplau & Fingerhut, 2007). Also, compared to heterosexual couples, gay and lesbian couples have less support from families and societal institutions (Kurdek, 2005). So, maintaining close connections with friends is especially important.

Romantic Love

LEARNING OBJECTIVES

- *Summarize the research findings on the experience of love in gay and straight couples.*
- *Discuss some gender differences regarding love.*
- *Define passion, intimacy, and commitment, and describe Sternberg's eight types of love.*
- *Discuss adult attachment styles, including their correlates and stability.*
- *Discuss the course of romantic love over time.*
- *Explain why relationships end and what couples can do to help relationships last.*

Wander through a bookstore and you'll see an overwhelming array of titles such as *Men Who Can't Love, Women Who Love Too Much,* and *How to Survive the Loss of a Love.* Turn up your radio and you'll hear the refrains of "This Love," "Like I Love You," and "I Will Always Love You." Although there are other forms of love, such as parental love and platonic love, these books and songs are all about *romantic love,* a subject of consuming interest for almost everyone.

Love is difficult to define, difficult to measure, and frequently difficult to understand. Nonetheless, psychologists have conducted thousands of studies and developed a number of interesting theories on love and romantic relationships.

Sexual Orientation and Love

***Sexual orientation* refers to a person's preference for emotional and sexual relationships with individuals of the same gender, the other gender, or either gender.** *Heterosexuals* seek emotional-sexual relationships with members of the other gender. *Homosexuals* seek emotional-sexual relationships with members of the same gender. *Bisexuals* seek emotional-sexual relationships with members of both genders. In recent years, the terms *gay* and *straight* have become widely used to refer to homosexuals and heterosexuals, respectively. *Gay* can refer to homosexuals of either gender, but most homosexual women prefer to call themselves *lesbians.*

Most studies of romantic love and relationships suffer from ***heterosexism,* or the assumption that all individuals and relationships are heterosexual.** For instance, most questionnaires on romantic love and romantic relationships fail to ask participants about their sexual orientation. Thus, when data are analyzed, there is no way to know whether subjects are referring to same- or other-gender romantic partners. Assuming that their subjects are all heterosexuals, researchers proceed to describe their findings without any mention of homosexuals. Because most people identify themselves as heterosexual, heterosexism in research isn't likely to distort conclusions about heterosexuals; however, it renders homosexual relationships invisible. Consequently, psychologists don't know as much about homosexual relationships as they would like to. Researchers are now devoting much more attention to this issue.

We discuss gay and lesbian relationships more in Chapter 9, so we will just touch on the basics here. We *do* know that homosexual romances and relationships

© AP Images/Winslow Townson

The experience of romantic love seems to be the same regardless of a person's sexual orientation.

are essentially the same as those of heterosexuals. Both groups experience romantic and passionate love and make commitments to relationships (Diamond, 2006; Kurdek, 1994, 1998). Both heterosexual and homosexual couples say they want their partners to have characteristics similar to theirs, hold similar values about relationships, report similar levels of relationship satisfaction, and perceive their relationships to be loving and satisfying (Peplau & Fingerhut, 2007). When relationship differences are found, they are much more likely to be rooted in gender than in sexual orientation, as we'll see next.

Gender Differences

The stereotype holds that women are more romantic than men. Nonetheless, much of the research evidence suggests just the opposite—that men are the more romantic gender (Dion & Dion, 1988). For example, men hold more romantic beliefs ("Love lasts forever" or "There is one perfect love in the world for everyone") (Peplau, Hill, & Rubin, 1993). In addition, men fall in love more easily than women, whereas women fall out of love more easily than men (Hill, Rubin, & Peplau, 1976; Rubin, Peplau, & Hill, 1981). Also, women are more likely than men to say that they would marry someone they didn't love (Peplau & Gordon, 1985).

Thus, much of the evidence—which admittedly is limited—suggests that men are more romantic than women. However, there are some ways in which women seem more romantic. For one thing, women are more likely to report physical symptoms associated with being in love—for instance, feeling like they are "floating on a cloud" (Peplau & Gordon, 1985). Second, women are somewhat more likely to verbalize and display tender emotions (Dindia & Allen, 1992).

Research also supports the view that women are more selective in choosing a partner than men are (Kenrick et al., 1990). Evolutionary social psychologists would explain women's tendency to be more "picky" in terms of the parental investment model we discussed earlier. The sociocultural explanation is based on the fact that heterosexual women are still more economically dependent on their partners than vice versa. This means that choosing a potential partner solely for romantic reasons may be a luxury that men (gay or straight) can more easily afford than heterosexual women. Support for this perspective comes from a previously mentioned study showing that women who prefer men with high incomes are those in countries with limited opportunities for females (Eagly & Wood, 1999).

Theories of Love

Can the experience of love be broken down into certain key components? How are romantic love relationships similar to other types of close relationships? These are the kinds of questions that two current theories of love address.

Triangular Theory of Love

Robert Sternberg's (1986, 1988) *triangular theory of love* posits that all love experiences are made up of three components: intimacy, passion, and commitment. Each of the components is represented as a point of a triangle, from which the theory derives its name (see **Figure 8.12** on the next page).

Michael Marsland/Yale University

Robert Sternberg

***Intimacy* refers to warmth, closeness, and sharing in a relationship.** Signs of intimacy include giving and receiving emotional support, valuing the loved one, wanting to promote the welfare of the loved one, and sharing one's self and one's possessions with another. As we've already discussed, self-disclosure is necessary to achieve and maintain feelings of intimacy in a relationship, whether platonic or romantic.

***Passion* refers to the intense feelings (both positive and negative) experienced in love relationships, including sexual desire.** Passion is related to drives that lead to romance, physical attraction, and sexual consummation. Although sexual needs may be dominant in many close relationships, other needs also figure

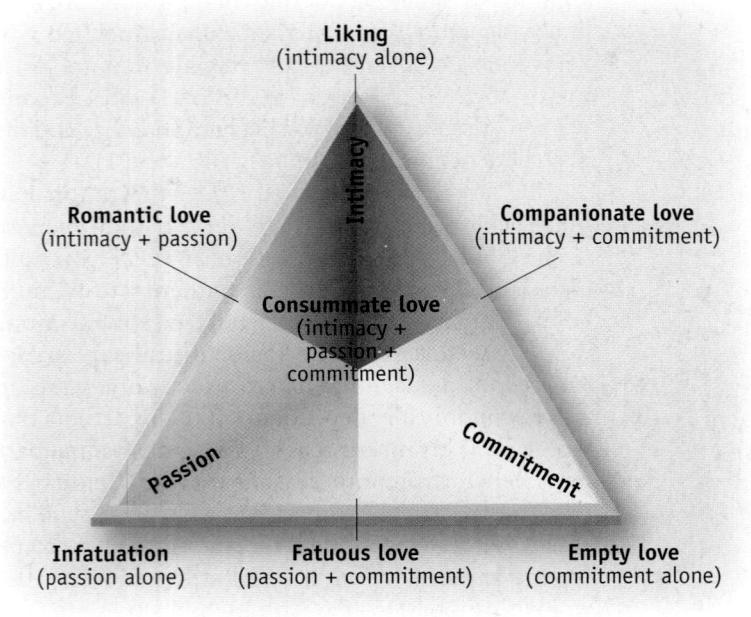

Figure 8.12

Sternberg's triangular theory of love. According to Robert Sternberg (1986), love includes three components: intimacy, passion, and commitment. These components are portrayed here as points on a triangle. The possible combinations of these three components yield the seven types of relationships mapped out here. The absence of all three components is called nonlove, which is not shown in the diagram.

From Sternberg, R. J. (1986). A triangular theory of love. *Psychological Review, 93,* 119–135. Copyright © 1986 by the American Psychological Association. Adapted by permission of the publisher and author.

in the experience of passion, including the needs for nurturance, self-esteem, dominance, submission, and self-actualization. For example, self-esteem is threatened when one experiences jealousy. Passion obviously figures most prominently in romantic relationships.

***Commitment* involves the decision and intent to maintain a relationship in spite of the difficulties and costs that may arise.** According to Sternberg, commitment has both short-term and long-term aspects. The short-term aspect concerns the conscious decision to love someone. The long-term aspect reflects the determination to make a relationship endure. Although the decision to love someone usually comes before commitment, that is not always the case (in arranged marriages, for instance).

Web Link 8.4 **Love Page**

James Park, an existentialist philosopher and advocate of freedom and authenticity in relationships, offers a distinctive challenge to more traditional notions of romantic love at this site. Park provides bibliographies on a number of topics, such as jealousy, sexual scripts, and the decision to have children.

Sternberg has described eight types of relationships that can result from the presence or absence of each of the three components of love, as depicted in **Figure 8.12**. One of these relationship types, *nonlove,* is not pictured in the diagram because it is defined as the absence of any of the three components. Most casual interactions are of this type. When all three components are present, *consummate love* is said to exist.

Sternberg's model has generated considerable interest and some research. In support of his theory, researchers report that Sternberg's three components characterize not only how people think about love in general but also how they personally experience love (Aron & Westbay, 1996). Also, measures of commitment and intimacy were found to be among the best predictors of whether dating couples continued their relationships (Hendrick, Hendrick, & Adler, 1988). Another study looked at changes in passion, intimacy, and commitment scores over time (Lemieux & Hale, 2002). Participants aged 18 to 75 were classified as casually dating, exclusively dating, engaged, or married. Passion and intimacy scores were lower for casual daters, higher for engaged participants, and lower for married subjects, while commitment scores increased from casually dating participants to married participants. A cross-cultural sudy of Chinese and American heterosexual couples in their 20s used questionnaires to measure intimacy, passion, and commitment (Gao, 2001). Scores on these three components of love increased as relationships became more serious. Although there were no significant differences between the two groups on intimacy and commitment scores, Americans scored significantly higher on the passion scale than the Chinese.

Romantic Love as Attachment

In a groundbreaking theory of love, Cindy Hazan and Phillip Shaver (1987) asserted that romantic love can be conceptualized as an attachment process, with similarities to the bond between infants and their caregivers. According to these theorists, adult romantic love and infant attachment share a number of features: intense fascination with the other person, distress at separation, and efforts to stay close and spend time together. Of course, there are also differences: Infant-caregiver relationships are one-sided, whereas caregiving in roman-

Photo by Bill Warren/*Ithaca Journal*

Cindy Hazan

tic relationships works both ways. A second difference is that romantic relationships usually have a sexual component, whereas infant-caregiver relationships do not.

Hazan and Shaver's ideas build on earlier work in attachment theory by John Bowlby (1980) and Mary Ainsworth (Ainsworth et al., 1978). Researchers who study attachment are keenly interested in the nature and development of ***attachment styles*, or typical ways of interacting in close relationships.** Their interest is fueled by the belief that attachment styles develop during the first year of life and strongly influence individuals' interpersonal interactions from then on.

Photo provided by Phillip Shaver

Phillip Shaver

Infant attachment. Based on actual observations of infants and their primary caregivers, earlier researchers identified three attachment styles (Ainsworth et al., 1978). Over half of infants develop a *secure attachment style* (see **Figure 8.13**). However, other infants develop insecure attachments. Some infants are very anxious when separated from their caretaker, a response characterized as an *anxious-ambivalent attachment style.* A third group of infants never connect very well with their caretaker and are classified in the *avoidant attachment style.* How do attachments in infancy develop? As you can see in **Figure 8.13**, three parenting styles have been identified as likely determinants of attachment quality. A *warm/responsive* approach seems to promote secure attachments, while a *cold/rejecting* style is associated with avoidant attachments. An *ambivalent/*

Figure 8.13

Infant attachment and romantic relationships. According to Hazan and Shaver (1987), romantic relationships in adulthood are similar in form to attachment patterns in infancy, which are determined in part by parental caregiving styles. The theorized relations between parental styles, attachment patterns, and intimate relations are outlined here. Hazan and Shaver's (1987) study sparked a flurry of follow-up research, which has largely supported the basic premises of their groundbreaking theory, although the links between infant experiences and close relationships in adulthood appear to be somewhat more complex than those portrayed here. (Based on Hazan and Shaver, 1986, 1987; Shaffer, 1989)

Parent's caregiving style	Infant attachment	Adult attachment style
Warm/responsive— She/he was generally warm and responsive; she/he was good at knowing when to be supportive and when to let me operate on my own; our relationship was always comfortable, and I have no major reservations or complaints about it.	**Secure attachment—** An infant-caregiver bond in which the child welcomes contact with a close companion and uses this person as a secure base from which to explore the environment.	**Secure—**I find it relatively easy to get close to others and am comfortable depending on them and having them depend on me. I don't often worry about being abandoned or about someone getting too close to me.
Cold/rejecting—She/he was fairly cold and distant, or rejecting, not very responsive; I wasn't her/his highest priority, her/his concerns were often elsewhere; it's possible that she/he would just as soon not have had me.	**Avoidant attachment—** An insecure infant-caregiver bond, characterized by little separation protest and a tendency for the child to avoid or ignore the caregiver.	**Avoidant—**I am somewhat uncomfortable being close to others; I find it difficult to trust them, difficult to allow myself to depend on them. I am nervous when anyone gets too close, and often love partners want me to be more intimate than I feel comfortable being.
Ambivalent/ inconsistent— She/he was noticeably inconsistent in her/his reactions to me, sometimes warm and sometimes not; she/he had her/his own agenda, which sometimes got in the way of her/his receptiveness and responsiveness to my needs; she/he definitely loved me but didn't always show it in the best way.	**Anxious/ambivalent attachment—**An insecure infant-caregiver bond, characterized by strong separation protest and a tendency of the child to resist contact initiated by the caregiver, particularly after a separation.	**Anxious/ambivalent—** I find that others are reluctant to get as close as I would like. I often worry that my partner doesn't really love me or won't want to stay with me. I want to merge completely with another person, and this desire sometimes scares people away.

inconsistent style seems to result in anxious-ambivalent attachments.

Adult attachment. What do these attachment styles look like in adulthood? To answer this question, we'll summarize the findings of a number of studies (Mickelson, Kessler, & Shaver, 1997; Shaver & Hazan, 1993). You can also see capsule summaries of adult attachment styles in **Figure 8.13.**

▸ *Secure adults* (about 55% of subjects). These people trust others, find it easy to get close to them, and are comfortable with mutual dependence. They rarely worry about being abandoned by their partner. Secure adults have the longest-lasting relationships and the fewest divorces. They describe their parents as behaving warmly toward them and toward each other.

▸ *Avoidant adults* (about 25% of subjects). These individuals both fear and feel uncomfortable about getting close to others. They are reluctant to trust others and prefer to maintain emotional distance from others. They have the lowest incidence of positive relationship experiences of the three groups. Avoidant adults describe their parents as less warm than secure adults do and see their mothers as cold and rejecting.

▸ *Anxious-ambivalent adults* (about 20% of subjects). These adults are obsessive and preoccupied with their relationships. They want more relationship closeness than their partners do and suffer extreme feelings of jealousy, based on fears of abandonment. Their relationships have the shortest duration of the three groups. Ambivalent adults describe their relationship with their parents as less warm than secure adults do and feel that their parents had unhappy marriages.

Cross-cultural studies in Australia and Israel have confirmed that people are distributed across the three attachment styles with similar percentages in those countries (Feeney & Noller, 1990; Mikulincer, Florian, & Tolmacz, 1990). Also, males and females are distributed similarly across the three styles, and the proportions of gay men and lesbians in the different attachment styles match those of straight men and women (Ridge & Feeney, 1998).

Expanding on earlier work, researchers subsequently expanded the three attachment styles to four: secure, preoccupied (anxious-ambivalent), avoidant-dismissing, and avoidant-fearful (Bartholomew & Horowitz, 1991; Brennan, Clark & Shaver, 1998). You are already familiar with the secure style, and "preoccupied" is just a different label for the anxious-ambivalent style. The dismissing and fearful styles are two variations of the avoidant style. We will elaborate on these styles shortly, but first we need to provide some background information.

The latest thinking assumes that attachment style is determined by where people fall on two continuous dimensions (Brennan, et al., 1998; Mikulincer, 2006). *Attachment anxiety* reflects how much a person worries that a partner will not be available when needed. This fear of abandonment stems, in part, from a person's doubts about his or her lovability. *Attachment avoidance* reflects the degree to which a person distrusts a partner's good will and has tendencies to maintain emotional and behavioral distance from a partner. People's scores on these two dimensions are measured by self-report scales.

As you can see in **Figure 8.14**, securely attached individuals (low on both anxiety and avoidance) enjoy close relationships and are not worried that others will leave them. Those in the *preoccupied* category (high on anxiety, low on avoidance) desire closeness with others but fear rejection. Those with an *avoidant-dismissing* style (high on avoidance, low on anxiety) prefer to maintain their distance from others and are not concerned about rejection, while those with an *avoidant-fearful* style (high on both avoidance and anxiety) are uncomfortable being close to others but still worry about rejection.

Although it might appear from **Figure 8.14** that the four attachment styles are distinctly different categories or typologies, that is not the case (Shaver & Miikulincer, 2006). Recall that the two underlying dimensions of anxiety and avoidance are distributed along a continuum (as indicated by the arrows in the figure) from low to high. This means that people are *more or less* anxious (or avoidant) versus totally con-

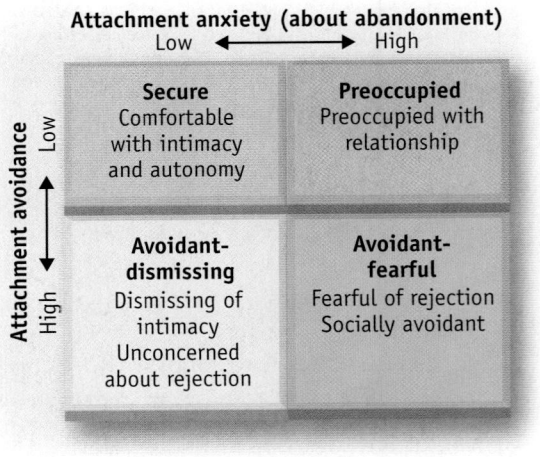

Figure 8.14

Attachment styles and their underlying dimensions. Attachment styles are determined by where people fall along two continuous dimensions that range from low to high: attachment avoidance and attachment anxiety (about abandonment). This system yields four attachment styles, which are described here. (Adapted from Brennan, Clark, & Shaver, 1998; Fraley & Shaver, 2000) sumed by anxiety or totally without anxiety. So, as you read about the four attachment styles, keep in mind that they are "convenient labels for sets of anxiety and avoidance scores rather than distinctly different categories that have nothing in common" (Miller, Perlman, & Brehm, 2007).

Correlates of attachment styles. The idea of adult attachment styles has stimulated a huge body of research. Among other findings, studies consistently show that securely attached individuals have more committed, satisfying, interdependent, and well-adjusted relationships compared to those who are insecurely attached (Banse, 2004; Mikulincer & Shaver, 2003). Also, having an anxious-ambivalent style is associated with not being in a relationship and with being in relationships of shorter duration, and an avoidant style is associated with shorter relationships (Shaver & Brennan, 1992).

When researchers subject couples to stress to study the connection between attachment style and relationship health, the findings generally support attachment theory predictions (Feeney, 2004). That is, securely attached individuals both seek out and provide support under stress. By contrast, avoidant people withdraw from their partners and may become angry either when they are asked for support or when they don't receive the support they want. Anxious individuals become fearful and sometimes exhibit hostility.

In terms of psychological adjustment, secure people typically have better mental health than insecure people (Meyers & Landsberger, 2002). Individuals who are insecurely attached are more vulnerable to a number of problems, including low self-esteem, low self-confidence, self-consciousness, anger, resentment, anxiety, loneliness, and depression (Cooper et al., 2004; Mikulincer & Shaver, 2003). Finally, attachment patterns exert influence far beyond romantic relationships. For instance, correlations have been found between attachment styles and friendships (Weimer, Kerns, & Oldenburg, 2004), gender roles (Schwartz, Waldo, & Higgins, 2004), health habits (Huntsinger & Luecken, 2004), religious beliefs (Kirkpatrick, 2005), and job satisfaction (Schirmer & Lopez, 2001).

Stability of attachment styles. A number of studies have demonstrated that early bonding experiences do influence relationship styles later in life. For example, a meta-analysis of longitudinal studies concluded that attachment styles are moderately stable over the first 19 years of life (Fraley, 2002). Also, across adulthood, stability appears to increase to some degree (Fraley & Brumbaugh, 2004). However, despite the relative stability of attachment styles, they are not set in stone. In childhood, changes from secure to insecure attachment are typically related to negative life events (divorce or death of parents, parental substance abuse, maltreatment) (Waters et al., 2000; Weinfield, Sroufe, & Egeland, 2000). Experiences later in life may also lead to shifts in attachment style (Davila & Cobb, 2003; Davila & Sargent, 2003). One study reported that about 30% of individuals had changed their attachment style over a period of four years (Kirkpatrick & Hazan, 1994). In another, a significant number of individuals (aged 26–64 years) in short-term psychotherapy shifted from an insecure to a secure attachment style (Travis et al., 2001). Thus, psychotherapy may be a helpful option for those with attachment difficulties.

The Course of Romantic Love

Most people find being in love exhilarating and wish the experience could last forever. Must passion fade? Regrettably, the answer to this question seems to be "yes." Consistent with this view, Sternberg's (1986) theory holds that passion peaks early in a relationship and then declines in intensity. In contrast, both intimacy and commitment increase as time progresses, although they develop at different rates (see **Figure 8.15**). Research supports the idea that the intense attraction and arousal one feels for a lover does tend to subside over time—for both gays and straights (Aron et al., 2006; Kurdek, 2005).

Why does passion fade? It seems that three factors kick into high gear early, then fade in the stretch: fantasy, novelty, and arousal (Miller et al., 2007). At first, love is "blind," so individuals usually develop a fantasy picture of their lover (often a projection of their own needs). However, as time passes, the intrusion of reality undermines this idealized view. Also, the novelty of a new partner fades with increased interactions

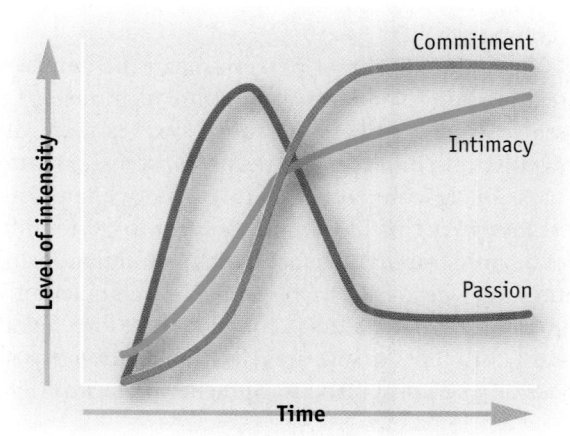

Figure 8.15

The course of love over time. According to Sternberg (1986), the three components of love typically progress differently over time. He theorizes that passion peaks early in a relationship and then declines. In contrast, intimacy and commitment are thought to build gradually.

Recommended READING

The Mating Game: A Primer on Love, Sex, and Marriage
by Pamela Regan (Sage Publications, 2003)

Pamela Regan, a social psychologist and respected researcher on interpersonal relationships, has put together a highly readable primer on love, sex, and marriage. Although designed as a supplemental textbook, the book's informal writing style makes it an informative read for anyone interested in relationships. The first three sections address relevant theories and empirical research on love, sex, and marriage. A fourth section looks at individual differences in relationship orientation: gender, personality, and interpersonal beliefs (attachment style, rejection sensitivity, and romanticism). *The Mating Game* includes a number of relevant scales along with their scoring information. Unfortunately, Regan has not provided norms by which to interpret one's scores, making the scales less useful than they could be. Readers can obtain the norms by reading the articles in which the scales were originally published, and Regan has provided the citations for these articles.

and knowledge. Finally, people can't exist in a state of heightened physical arousal forever.

Might the loss of passion be a function of age? After all, people who stay in long relationships are also older. Some evidence argues against the age explanation. For example, people who change partners and remarry show an increase in the frequency of sex (Call, Sprecher, & Schwartz, 1995). So, while age probably plays some role, it isn't the sole explanation of this phenomenon.

Does the decline of passion mean the demise of a relationship? Not necessarily. Some relationships do dissolve when early passion fades. However, many others evolve into different, but deeply satisfying, mixtures of passionate-companionate love. And while passion *does* fade over time, it's important not to overemphasize or oversimplify this fact. Long-term relationships (and sexual feelings, as well) seem to be a complex amalgam of both passionate and companionate love. Significantly, both types of love are related to relationship satisfaction and commitment (Sprecher & Regan, 1998).

Why Relationships End

The question of why some relationships last while others end is a popular issue in relationship research. Nonetheless, the matter is complex, so easy answers have not been forthcoming.

If we were to follow seriously dating couples over several years, what proportion of them would split up over that period? If you guessed about half, you'd be right. According to three longitudinal studies (all on heterosexual couples), 58% of dating or engaged college couples broke up over a four-year period (Sprecher, 1994), 51% of "steady or serious" dating couples had split at the end of three years (Kirkpatrick & Davis, 1994), and 45% of dating couples had ended their relationships by the end of two years (Hill, Rubin, & Peplau, 1976).

Honing in on our key question as to why some relationships stand the test of time and some don't, let's take a closer look at the Boston Couples Study, one of the studies just cited (Hill et al., 1976). Here, 200 couples (predominantly college students in Boston) were followed over two years. To participate, couples had to be "going steady" and believe that they were in love. If couples split, researchers asked them to give their reasons (see **Figure 8.16**). The results of this and other studies (Buss, 1989; Miller et al., 2007; Sprecher, 1994) suggest that four prominent factors contribute to romantic breakups:

1. *Premature commitment.* Virtually all the reasons for breakups involved things that could only be known by interacting over time. Hence, it seems that many couples make romantic commitments without taking the time to get to know each other. These individuals may find out later that they don't really like each other

For Better or For Worse®

© 1988 Lynn Johnston Productions, Inc. Distributed by Universal Press Syndicate, Inc. Reprinted with permission. All rights reserved.

What Causes Couples to Break Up?

Factors	Women's Reports (%)	Men's Reports (%)
Interactive factors		
Becoming bored with relationship	77	77
Differences in interests	73	61
Differences in backgrounds	44	47
Differences in intelligence	20	10
Conflicting sexual attitudes	48	43
Conflicting marriage ideas	43	29
Noninteractive factors		
Woman's desire to be independent	74	50
Man's desire to be independent	47	61
Woman's interest in someone else	40	31
Man's interest in someone else	18	29
Living too far apart	28	41
Pressure from woman's parents	18	13
Pressure from man's parents	10	9

Figure 8.16

Factors contributing to breakups. Couples who broke up after dating steadily were asked why by Hill, Rubin, and Peplau (1976). The factors commonly cited are listed here. The researchers distinguished between interactive factors, which consisted of problems that emerged out of the partners' ways of relating to each other, and noninteractive factors.

Adapted from Hill, C. T., Rubin, Z., & Peplau, L. A. (1976). Breakups before marriage: The end of 103 affairs. *Journal of Social Issues, 32,* 147–168. © Society for the Psychological Study of Social Issues. Adapted by permission of the author. All rights reserved.

or that they have little in common. For these reasons, "whirlwind courtships" are risky. Intimacy needs to be combined with commitment if relationships are to survive.

2. *Ineffective communication and conflict management skills.* The vast majority of couples have disagreements. Not surprisingly, disagreements increase as couples learn more about each other and become more interdependent (Buss, 1989). Poor conflict management skills are a key factor in relationship distress and can lead to romantic breakups (Kline et al., 2006). They are also associated with a greater likelihood of relationship aggression (see the Chapter 9 Application on intimate violence). As we discussed in Chapter 7, the solution to this problem is not to stifle all disagreements, because conflict can be helpful to relationships. The key is to manage conflict constructively.

3. *Becoming bored with the relationship.* Couples who break up rank "boredom with the relationship" high on the list of reasons for splitting. As we have noted, novelty usually fades as people get to know each other, and boredom can set in. Individuals have needs for both novelty and predictability in close relationships (Sprecher, 1994). Balancing the two can be tricky for couples.

4. *Availability of a more attractive relationship.* Whether a deteriorating relationship actually ends depends, in great part, on the availability of a more attractive alternative (Felmlee, Sprecher, & Bassin, 1990; South & Lloyd, 1995). We all know of individuals who remained in unsatisfying relationships only until they met a more appealing prospect.

Helping Relationships Last

How can couples increase the likelihood that their relationships will last? Amazingly, researchers have only recently addressed this critical question. Still, there is enough research to support a few suggestions:

1. *Take plenty of time to get to know the other person before you make a long-term commitment.* Research based on Sternberg's theory found that the best predictors of whether dating couples' relationships would continue were their levels of intimacy and commitment (Hendrick et al., 1988). Regarding intimacy, we have already noted that self-disclosures that lead individuals to feel understood, cared for, and validated are crucial (Green, Derlega, & Matthews, 2006; Reis & Patrick, 1996). Other advice comes from long-married couples who were asked why they thought their relationship had lasted (Lauer & Lauer, 1985). The most frequently cited responses of 351 couples who had been married for 15 years or more were (1) friendship ("I like my spouse as a person"); (2) commitment to the relationship ("I want the relationship to succeed"); (3) similarity in values and relationship issues ("We agree on how and how often to show affection"); and (4) positive feelings about each other ("My spouse has grown more interesting"). Thus, early attention to the intimacy foundations of a relationship and ongoing, mutual efforts to build a commitment can foster more enduring love. **Figure 8.17** on the next page offers some key questions for couples to discuss before they decide to marry or partner (in the case of gay and lesbian couples).

2. *Emphasize the positive qualities in your partner and relationship.* It is essential to communicate more positive feelings than negative ones to your partner. Early in a relationship, this is easy to do, but it gets harder as relationships continue. Once the initial glow of the relationship wears off, a common attributional error comes into play. **The *actor-observer effect* is the tendency to attribute one's own behavior to situational factors and the behavior of others to personal factors.** This tendency can set up the destructive habit of chronically blaming the other person for problems and not taking responsibility when one should. Ironically, married couples generally make more negative and fewer positive statements to their spouse than

Engaging in novel activities together, like traveling to interesting destinations, contributes to long-term relationship satisfaction.

to strangers, and we presume this situation holds for those in other types of committed relationships as well (Fincham, 2001; Fincham & Beach, 2006). This tendency is more prevalent among distressed than among nondistressed couples (Gottman, 1993). Unfortunately, when one partner engages in this behavior, the other often responds in kind, which can set in motion a pattern of reciprocal negativity that makes things worse. Hence, as the old song advises, it helps to "accentuate the positive and eliminate the negative." Similarly, married couples who seek and grant forgiveness have better chances for longer and more satisfying relationships than those who avoid each other or retaliate in kind for a partner's negative behavior (Fincham, 2003).

3. *Find ways to bring novelty to long-term relationships.* As romantic partners learn more about each other and develop feelings of intimacy, they also become more predictable to each other. But, too much predictability can translate into loss of interest and, possibly, boredom. One way "to keep the bloom on the rose" is to engage in novel activities together (Aron et al., 2000; Baumeister & Bratslavsky, 1999). For example, one study reported that couples who participated in exciting activities together (versus just spending time together) showed increases in relationship satisfaction over a 10-week period (Reissman, Aron, & Bergen, 1993).

4. *Develop effective conflict management skills.* Conflicts arise in all relationships, so it's essential to handle them well. For one thing, it's helpful to distinguish between minor annoyances and significant problems. You need to learn to see minor irritations in perspective and recognize how little they matter. With big problems, however, it's usually best to avoid the temptation to sweep them under the rug in the hope that they'll disappear. Important issues rarely vanish on their own, and if you postpone the inevitable discussion, the "sweepings" will have accumulated, making it harder to sort out the various issues. An interaction pattern common to dissatisfied couples is "demand-withdraw" (Roberts & Krokoff, 1990). Typically, this pattern involves the woman pressing the man to discuss a relationship problem and the man avoiding or withdrawing from the interaction. This pattern is associated with the "closeness versus separateness dilemma," in which one partner wants more intimacy and closeness and the other wants more privacy and independence (Sagrestano, Heavey, & Christensen, 2006). For more specific suggestions on handling conflict, refer to our discussion in Chapter 7.

Should We Marry?

1. What are our separate professional goals in terms of positions or jobs desired? One year from now? Five years? Fifteen years?
2. How do we decide to spend our money? Is there an amount ($50? $500? $5,000?) over which we need to discuss a purchase before committing to it?
3. Who is responsible for grocery shopping, cooking, and other tasks connected with meals? Do we eat out? A lot? A little?
4. Am I comfortable giving and receiving love, sexually? In sex, does my partner feel my love for him or her?
5. Who will take care of our child if we both work? How does each partner feel about day care?

Figure 8.17

Key questions for dating couples to discuss before deciding to marry. To increase their chances for satisfying and long-lasting marriages and partnerships, experts advise dating couples to get to know each other well. Author Susan Piver (2000) has developed a list of 100 essential questions for couples to discuss before they make long-term commitments. The questions cover home, money, work, sex, health and food, family, children, community and friends, and spiritual life. Here is a sample of five questions to consider. (From Piver, 2000)

APPLICATION

Overcoming Loneliness

LEARNING OBJECTIVES

- *Describe various types of loneliness.*
- *Discuss the prevalence of loneliness.*
- *Explain how early experiences and current social trends contribute to loneliness.*
- *Describe how shyness, poor social skills, and self-defeating attributions contribute to loneliness.*
- *Summarize the suggestions for conquering loneliness.*

Answer the following "true" or "false."

___ **1.** Adolescents and young adults are the loneliest age group.

___ **2.** Many people who are lonely are also shy.

___ **3.** The seeds of loneliness are often sown early in life.

___ **4.** Effective social skills can be learned relatively easily.

All of the above are true, as you'll learn shortly. But let's start with a couple of general points. First, being alone doesn't necessarily produce feelings of loneliness. In these fast-paced times, solitude can provide needed down time to recharge your batteries. Also, people need time alone to deepen self-understanding, wrestle with decisions, and contemplate important life issues. Second, people can feel lonely even when surrounded by others (at a party or concert, for instance). Similarly, it's possible to have a large social network but not feel close to anyone in particular.

The Nature and Prevalence of Loneliness

***Loneliness* occurs when a person has fewer interpersonal relationships than desired or when these relationships are not as satisfying as desired.** Of course, people vary in their needs for social connections. Thus, if you're not distressed by the quantity or quality of your social and emotional ties, you wouldn't be considered lonely.

We can think about loneliness in several ways. One approach is to look at the type of relationship deficit involved (Weiss, 1973). *Emotional loneliness* stems from the absence of an intimate attachment figure. For a child, this figure is typically a parent; for an adult, it is usually a spouse or partner or an intimate friend. *Social loneliness* results from the lack of a friendship network (typically provided in school and work settings and in community groups). For example, a married couple who move to a new city will experience social loneliness until they make new social connections; however, because they have each other, they should not experience emotional loneliness. On the other hand, a recently divorced person will probably feel emotional loneliness but should not experience social loneliness, assuming that work and friendship networks remain intact (which is not always the case).

Emotional loneliness seems to be tied to the absence of a romantic partner in both college students and senior adults (Green et al., 2001). Social loneliness, however, seems to spring from different roots, depending on age. In college students, it's the *quantity* of friendship contacts that counts; among the older group, it's the *quality* of contacts. It's also worth noting that social support can't compensate for emotional loneliness—for example, the presence of friends and family cannot substitute for a loved one who has died (Stroebe et al., 1996). Of course, this is not to say that social support is unimportant. The point is that different types of loneliness require different responses; therefore, you need to pinpoint the exact nature of your social deficits to cope effectively with loneliness.

A second way to look at loneliness is in terms of its duration (Young, 1982). *Transient loneliness* involves brief and sporadic feelings of loneliness, which many people may experience even when their social lives are reasonably adequate. *Transitional loneliness* occurs when people who have had satisfying social relationships in the past become lonely after experiencing a disruption in their social network (the death of a loved one, say, or divorce or moving to a new locale). *Chronic loneliness* is a condition that affects people who have been unable to develop a satisfactory interpersonal network over a period of years. We'll focus on chronic loneliness for the most part.

How many people are tormented by loneliness? Although we don't have a precise answer to this question, anecdotal evidence suggests that the number of people plagued by loneliness is substantial. Telephone hotlines for troubled people report that complaints of loneliness dominate their calls. No doubt some of the popularity of cell phone calls, instant messaging, and chat rooms can be traced to loneliness.

The prevalence of loneliness in specific age groups actually contradicts stereotypes. For example, many assume that the loneliest age group is the elderly, but this "distinction" actually belongs to adolescents and young adults (Rokach, 2001). Gay and lesbian adolescents are particularly likely to be lonely (Westefeld et al., 2001). Another vulnerable group is beginning college students. One study reported that 75% of those in this group experienced loneliness in their first few weeks on campus (Cutrona, 1982). It is likely that frequent changes of schools, jobs, and relationships during adolescence and young adulthood all contribute to the high rates of loneliness for this age group. A second surprising finding is that loneliness decreases with age, at least until the much later years of adulthood when one's friends begin to die (Pinquart & Sörensen, 2001).

In line with expectations, people who live alone are more lonely than those who live with a partner (Pinquart, 2003), although some married people do feel lonely (Stack, 1998). Also, divorce often disrupts the relationship between parents and children, especially fathers, and adds to the burden of loneliness (Kaufman & Uhlenberg, 1998). Across the life span, good friends provide emotional support and a buffer against stress (Yager, 1999). Women are found to be lonelier than men, but only on measures that use words such as "lonely" or "loneliness" (Borys & Perlman, 1985). Thus, it is likely that this apparent gender difference is really men's reluctance to admit to feeling lonely.

© Royalty-Free/Masterfile

Thanks to automation and online technology, people today are able to take care of many of life's necessities without interacting with other human beings. These reduced opportunities for social interaction help to fuel increased loneliness.

The Roots of Loneliness

Any event that ruptures the social fabric of a person's life may lead to loneliness, so no one is immune. We'll consider the roles of early experience and social trends.

Early Experiences

The seeds for chronic loneliness are likely sown early in life. A key problem seems to be early negative social behavior that leads to rejection by peers (Asher & Paquette, 2003). Children who are aggressive or withdrawn are likely to suffer peer rejection even in preschool (Ray et al., 1997). What prompts inappropriate social behavior in young children? One factor is insecure attachment styles. Because of difficult early parent-infant interactions, children often develop social behaviors (aggression, aloofness, competitiveness, overdependence) that "invite" rejection by adults and peers (Bartholomew, 1990; Duggan & Brennan, 1994). You can see how a vicious cycle gets set up. A child's inappropriate behavior prompts rejection by others, which in turn triggers negative expectations about social interactions in the child, along with more negative behavior, and so on. To help break this self-defeating cycle (and head off the loneliness that can result), it is crucial to help children learn appropriate social skills early in life. Without intervention, this vicious cycle can continue and eventuate in chronic loneliness.

Social Trends

Social isolation appears to be on the rise, according to a study based on national surveys in 1985 and 2004 (McPherson, Smith-Lovin, & Brashears, 2006). Among the troubling findings the researchers reported were that the number of people who said they had no one with whom to discuss important matters almost tripled during this period. Also, in 1985, the average American had three confidants, yet by 2004 that number had dropped to two. Further, 25% of the respondents in 2004 said that they had no one to confide in.

Some social commentators and social scientists are concerned that recent trends are undermining social connections in our culture (Putnam, 1996; McPherson et al., 2006). A number of factors come into play. Parents (especially if they are single) may be so pressed for time that they have little time to cultivate adult relationships. Because of busy schedules, face-to-face interactions at home are reduced as family members eat on the run, on their own, or in front of the TV. And the fact that people watch television so much tends to diminish meaningful family conversation. While technology makes life easier in some respects and does provide opportunities for meaningful relationships, it has its down sides. For example, superficial social interactions become prevalent as people order their meals and do their banking at drive-up windows, purchase their groceries via automated check-out stations, and so forth. Finally, people are spending more time alone at computers in their offices and homes, which may reduce opportunities for face-to-face interactions.

Correlates of Loneliness

For people who are chronically lonely, painful feelings are a fact of life. Three factors that figure prominently in chronic loneliness are shyness, poor social skills, and a self-defeating attributional style. Of course, the link between these factors and loneliness could go either way. Feeling lonely might cause you to make negative attributions about others, but making negative attributions can also lead to loneliness.

Shyness

Shyness is commonly associated with loneliness (Jackson et al., 2002). ***Shyness* refers to discomfort, inhibition, and excessive caution in interpersonal relations.** Specifically, shy people tend to (1) be timid about expressing themselves, (2) be overly self-conscious about how others are reacting to them, (3) embarrass easily, and (4) experience physiological symptoms of their anxiety, such as a racing pulse, blushing, or an upset stomach. In pioneering research on shyness, Philip Zimbardo (1977, 1990) and his associates report that 60% of shy people indicated that their shyness was *situationally specific.* That is, their shyness is triggered only in certain social contexts, such as asking someone for help or interacting with a large group of people (see **Figure 8.18**).

Poor Social Skills

Studies have found that lonely people evaluate others negatively (Duck, Pond, & Leatham, 1995; Wittenberg & Reis, 1986), although this is not always the case (Christensen & Kashy, 1998). Either way, people who suffer from chronic loneliness typically have casual acquaintances rather than close friends, and they date infrequently (Bell, 1991). They spend much of their time in solitary activities such as listening to music or reading (Rubenstein & Shaver, 1982).

Often, these individuals are adults who were unable to break out of self-defeating patterns of social behavior developed early in life. A variety of problematic social skills are associated with loneliness (Gierveld, van Tilburg, & Dykstra, 2006). A common finding is that lonely people show lower responsiveness to their conversational partners and are more self-focused (Rook, 1998). Similarly, researchers report that lonely people are relatively inhibited and unassertive, speaking less than nonlonely people. They also seem to disclose less about themselves than those who are not lonely. This (often unconscious) tendency has the effect of keeping people at an emotional distance and limits interactions to a relatively superficial level. These interactional problems are based, in part, on heightened fears of rejection (Jackson et al., 2002). It seems that people with "rejection anxiety" believe that their signaled interest is obvious to others when it is not (Vorauer et al., 2003). Thus, unaware that their signal was invisible, those with rejection anxiety may perceive rejection where none exists.

Web Link 8.5 **The Shyness Homepage**

The Shyness Institute (Portola Valley, CA) offers a "gathering of network resources for people seeking information and services for shyness." The Institute is co-directed by psychologists Lynne Henderson and Philip Zimbardo.

"What Makes You Shy?"

Sources	Percentage of Shy Students
Other people	
Strangers	70
Opposite sex	64
Authorities by virtue of their knowledge	55
Authorities by virtue of their role	40
Relatives	21
Elderly people	12
Friends	11
Children	10
Parents	8
Situations	
Where I am focus of attention—large group (as when giving a speech)	73
Large groups	68
Of lower status	56
Social situations in general	55
New situations in general	55
Requiring assertiveness	54
Where I am being evaluated	53
Where I am focus of attention—small group	52
Small social groups	48
One-to-one different-sex interactions	48
Of vulnerability (need help)	48
Small task-oriented groups	28
One-to-one same-sex interactions	14

Figure 8.18

The situational determinants of shyness. Zimbardo (1977) asked subjects about the people and circumstances that made them feel shy. The results of his survey showed that shyness depends to a large degree on situational factors.

From Zimbardo, P. (1977). *Shyness: What is it, what to do about it.* Reading, MA: Addison-Wesley. Copyright © 1977 by Philip Zimbardo, Inc. Reprinted by permission of DA CAPO PRESS, a member of Perseus Books Publishers.

Self-Defeating Attributional Style

It's easy to see how repeated rejections can foster negative expectations about social interactions. Thus, lonely

Recommended READING

Shyness
by Philip G. Zimbardo
(Addison Wesley, 1977, 1990)

Zimbardo, a noted social psychologist, focuses his keen insight on the frustrations of being shy. A lack of jargon and ample use of actual case histories make this book highly readable. In Part I, Zimbardo explores the roots of shyness. Here he discusses various types of shyness and how shyness affects people, especially their social and intimate relationships. He also examines the origins of shyness and how family and school experiences can breed shyness. In Part II, Zimbardo turns to the practical question of how to cope with various types of shyness. Dealing with some forms of shyness requires examining and changing one's thinking about shyness and oneself. Other types require changes in behavior, especially social skills. The book includes numerous exercises and lots of sound advice to help readers implement the changes they need to make. For parents, teachers, and friends of shy individuals, Zimbardo includes a chapter on helping others to overcome their shyness.

Other helpful books on shyness written by mental health professionals include *Living Fully with Shyness and Social Anxiety,* by Erika Hilliard (2005); *Shyness: A Bold New Approach,* by Bernardo Carducci and Susan Golant (2000); and *The Shy Single* by Bonnie Jacobson and Sandra Gordon (2004).

people are prone to irrational thinking about their social skills, the probability of their achieving intimacy, the likelihood of being rejected, and so forth. Unfortunately, once people develop these negative ideas, they often behave in ways to confirm their expectations, setting up a vicious cycle of behavior.

Jeffrey Young (1982) points out that lonely people engage in *negative self-talk* that prevents them from pursuing intimacy in an active and positive manner. He has identified some clusters of ideas that foster loneliness. **Figure 8.19** gives examples of typical thoughts from six of these clusters of cognitions and the overt behaviors that result. As you can see, several of the cognitions in **Figure 8.19** are stable, internal self-attributions. This tendency to attribute loneliness to stable, internal causes constitutes a self-defeating attributional style (Anderson et al., 1994). That is, lonely people tell themselves that they're lonely because they're basically unlovable individuals. Not only is this a devastating belief, it is also self-defeating because it offers no way to change the situation. Happily, it *is* possible to reduce loneliness, as you'll see.

Conquering Loneliness

The personal consequences associated with chronic loneliness can be painful and sometimes overwhelming: low self-esteem, hostility, depression, alcoholism, psychosomatic illness, and, possibly, suicide (McWhirter, 1990). Chronic loneliness is also associated with immune system deficits and is a predictor of a number of diseases, including cardiovascular disease and cancer (Loving et al., 2006). Although there are no simple solutions to loneliness, there are some effective ones. Let's look at four useful strategies.

One option is to use the Internet to overcome loneliness, although this approach can be a two-edged sword (McKenna & Bargh, 2000). On the plus side, the Internet is an obvious boon to busy people, those with stigmatized social identities, and those who find physical mobility difficult (the infirm and people with se-

Figure 8.19

Patterns of thinking underlying loneliness. According to Young (1982), negative self-talk contributes to loneliness. Six clusters of irrational thoughts are illustrated here. Each cluster of cognitions leads to certain patterns of behavior (right) that promote loneliness.

From a paper presented at the annual convention of the American Psychological Association (1979, September). An expanded version of this paper appears in G. Emery, S. D. Hollan, & R. C. Bedrosian (Eds.) (1981). *New directions in cognitive therapy.* New York: Guilford Press and in L. A. Peplau & D. Perlman (Eds.) (1982). *Loneliness: A sourcebook of current theory, research and therapy.* New York: Wiley. Copyright © 1982 by John Wiley & Sons, Inc. and Jeffrey Young.

Clusters of Cognitions Typical of Lonely People

Clusters	Cognitions	Behaviors
A	1. I'm undesirable. 2. I'm dull and boring.	Avoidance of friendship
B	1. I can't communicate with other people. 2. My thoughts and feelings are bottled up inside.	Low self-disclosure
C	1. I'm not a good lover in bed. 2. I can't relax, be spontaneous, and enjoy sex.	Avoidance of sexual relationships
D	1. I can't seem to get what I want from this relationship. 2. I can't say how I feel, or he/she might leave me.	Lack of assertiveness in relationships
E	1. I won't risk being hurt again. 2. I'd screw up any relationship.	Avoidance of potentially intimate relationships
F	1. I don't know how to act in this situation. 2. I'll make a fool of myself.	Avoidance of other people

rious medical conditions). Moreover, shy people can interact without the anxiety involved in face-to-face communication. On the other hand, if lonely people spend a lot of time online, will they devote less time to face-to-face relationships? Will shy individuals develop the self-confidence to pursue relationships offline? The good news is that Internet use in the general population is associated with generally positive effects (Bargh & McKenna, 2004). Among lonely persons, Internet use is also associated with benefits such as reduced loneliness, improved social support, and formation of online friendships (Morahan-Martin & Schumacher, 2003; Shaw, & Gant, 2002). Still, one study found that lonely individuals more often reported that Internet use caused disturbances in their daily functioning (Morahan-Martin & Schumacher, 2003), raising concerns about Internet addiction (Nalwa & Anand, 2003: Yuen & Lavin, 2004). Clearer answers to these questions await further research.

A second suggestion is to resist the temptation to withdraw from social situations. A study that asked people what they did when they felt lonely found the top responses to be "read" and "listen to music" (Rubenstein & Shaver, 1982). These days, playing computer games and using the Internet are also options. If used occasionally, these activities can be constructive ways of dealing with loneliness. However, as long-term strategies, they do nothing to help a lonely person acquire new "real-world" friends. This situation is particularly relevant to those with an avoidant attachment style. The importance of staying active socially cannot be overemphasized. Recall that proximity is a powerful factor in the development of close relationships. To make friends, you have to be around people.

A third strategy is to break out of the habit of the self-defeating attributional style we just discussed ("I'm lonely because I'm unlovable"). Recall from Chapter 5 that there are *other* attributions a lonely person could make and that these alternative explanations point to solutions (see **Figure 8.20**). If a person says, "My conversational skills are weak" (unstable, internal cause), the solution would be: "I'll try to find out how to improve them." Or, if someone thinks, "It always takes time to meet people when you move to a new location" (unstable, external cause), this attribution suggests the solution of trying harder to develop new relationships and giving them time to work. The attribution "I've really searched, but I just can't find enough compatible people at my workplace" (stable, external cause) may lead to the decision, "It's time to look for a new job." As you can see, the last three attributions lead to active modes of coping rather than the passivity fostered by a self-defeating attributional style.

Finally, to thwart loneliness, people need to cultivate their social skills (DiTommaso et al., 2003). You'll find a wealth of information on this important topic in Chapter 7 (Interpersonal Communication). Lonely people, especially, should focus on attending to others' nonverbal signals, deepening the level of their self-disclosure, engaging in active listening, improving their conversational skills, and developing an assertive communication style.

Anyone who feels overwhelmed at the prospect of tackling loneliness on his or her own should consider paying a visit to the college counseling center. Dealing with loneliness and shyness usually involves work on two fronts. First, counselors help people improve social skills through *social skills training.* In this program, individuals learn and practice the skills involved in initiating and maintaining relationships. For example, they might watch videotapes of socially skilled models demonstrating appropriate social behavior in a variety of settings. They then practice these behaviors in the therapist's office. Sometimes these practice sessions are taped so people can actually see how they are coming across. Second, counselors use *cognitive therapy* (see Chapter 16) to help lonely and shy individuals break the habit of automatic negative thoughts and self-defeating attributions. Over a series of sessions, individuals learn to change their negative views of themselves ("I'm boring") and other people ("They're cold and unfriendly"). Both of these approaches have high success rates, and they can pave the way to more positive social interactions that are critical to adjustment.

Internal-external dimension	Stability dimension: Unstable cause (temporary)	Stability dimension: Stable cause (permanent)
Internal cause	I'm lonely now, but won't be for long. I need to get out and meet some new people.	I'm lonely because I'm unlovable. I'll never be worth loving.
External cause	My lover and I just split up. I guess some relationships work and some don't. Maybe I'll be luckier next time.	The people here are cold and unfriendly. It's time to look for a new job.

Figure 8.20

Attributions and loneliness. Lonely people often have a self-defeating attributional style, in which they attribute their loneliness to stable, internal causes (see upper right quadrant). Learning to make alternative attributions (see other quadrants) can bring to light ways to deal with loneliness and facilitate active coping.

Based on Shaver, P., & Rubenstein, C. (1980). Childhood attachment experience and adult loneliness. In L. Wheeler (Ed.), *Review of personality and social psychology* (Vol.1, pp. 42–73). Thousand Oaks, CA: Sage Publications.

KEY IDEAS

Perspectives on Close Relationships

▶ Close relationships are those that are important, interdependent, and long-lasting. They include friendships as well as work, family, and romantic relationships. People in individualistic cultures believe that romantic love is a prerequisite for marriage, whereas those in collectivist cultures are accustomed to arranged marriages.

▶ The Internet offers many new vehicles for meeting others and developing relationships. The differences between Internet and face-to-face communication have important implications for established psychological theories and principles of relationship development.

Initial Attraction and Relationship Development

▶ People are initially drawn to others who are nearby, who are seen often, and who are physically attractive. Although physical attractiveness plays a key role in initial attraction, people also seek other desirable characteristics, such as kindness, intelligence, dependable character, and maturity. Couples often match up on looks, but sometimes men trade status for physical attractiveness in women, and vice versa.

▶ As people get acquainted, they prefer others who like them and those who have desirable personality characteristics. Similarity is a key factor in relationship development. Couples tend to be similar in age, race, religion, education, and attitudes.

▶ Once relationships are established, people engage in various maintenance behaviors and actions to sustain them. Interdependence (social exchange) theory uses principles of reinforcement to predict relationship satisfaction and commitment. How individuals apply social exchange principles depends on whether they are in exchange or communal relationships.

Friendship

▶ The key ingredients of friendship are loyalty, emotional support, and letting friends be themselves. Women's same-gender friendships are usually characterized by self-disclosure and intimacy, whereas men's same-gender friendships typically involve doing things together. Some friendship issues are more complex for homosexuals than heterosexuals.

Romantic Love

▶ Research indicates that the experience of romantic love is the same for heterosexual and homosexual individuals. Contrary to stereotypes, men may be more romantic than women. In choosing a partner, women are more selective than men.

▶ Sternberg's triangular theory of love proposes that passion, intimacy, and commitment combine into eight types of love. Hazan and Shaver theorize that love relationships follow the form of attachments in infancy. Researchers subsequently expanded the number of attachment styles from three to four: secure, preoccupied, avoidant-dismissing, and avoidant-fearful. Each style has a characteristic profile. Although attachment styles show stability over time, it is possible for them to change.

▶ Initially, romantic love is usually characterized by passion, but strong passion appears to fade over time for a number of reasons. In relationships that continue, passionate love evolves into a less intense, more mature form of love.

▶ The chief causes of relationship failure are the tendency to make premature commitments, ineffective conflict management skills, boredom with the relationship, and the availability of a more attractive relationship. To help relationships last, couples should take the time to know each other very well, emphasize the positive qualities in their partner and relationship, engage in novel activities together, and develop effective conflict management skills.

Application: Overcoming Loneliness

▶ Loneliness involves discontent with the extent and quality of one's interpersonal network. A surprisingly large number of people in our society are troubled by loneliness. The age groups most affected by loneliness contradict stereotypes.

▶ The origins of chronic loneliness can often be traced to early negative behavior that triggers rejection by peers and teachers. Social trends may also promote loneliness. Loneliness is associated with shyness, poor social skills, and self-defeating attributions.

▶ The keys to overcoming loneliness include resisting the temptation to withdraw from social situations, avoiding self-defeating attributions, and working on one's social skills.

KEY TERMS

Actor-observer effect p. 259
Attachment styles p. 255
Close relationships p. 237
Commitment p. 254
Comparison level p. 249
Comparison level for alternatives p. 249
Heterosexism p. 253
Interdependence theory p. 248
Intimacy p. 253
Investments p. 249
Loneliness p. 261
Matching hypothesis p. 243
Mere exposure effect p. 241
Parental investment theory p. 244
Passion p. 253
Proximity p. 241
Reciprocal liking p. 246
Relationship maintenance p. 247
Sexual orientation p. 252
Shyness p. 263
Social exchange theory p. 248

KEY PEOPLE

David Buss pp. 244–245
Cindy Hazan and Philip Shaver pp. 254–256
Harold Kelley and John Thibaut pp. 248–250
Robert Sternberg pp. 253–254

PRACTICE TEST

1. Arranged marriages are most common in:
   a. individualistic cultures.
   b. collectivist cultures.
   c. unrequited cultures.
   d. both individualistic and collectivist cultures.

2. Which of the following is a relationship issue that operates differently in online versus face-to-face interactions?
   a. Physical proximity
   b. Physical attractiveness
   c. Self-disclosure
   d. All of the above

3. The mere exposure effect refers to an increase in positive feelings due to:
   a. seeing someone often.
   b. interacting with someone often.
   c. communicating via e-mail often.
   d. seeing someone only once.

4. The matching hypothesis suggests that people match up on the basis of:
   a. religion.
   b. personality.
   c. socioeconomic status.
   d. looks.

5. An individual's personal standard of what constitutes an acceptable balance of rewards and costs in a relationship is termed:
   a. social exchange.
   b. comparison level.
   c. proximity level.
   d. relationship satisfaction.

6. Women's same-gender friendships are typically based on ____; men's are typically based on ____.
   a. shopping together; hunting together
   b. attending sports events; attending sports events
   c. shared activities; intimacy and self-disclosure
   d. intimacy and self-disclosure; shared activities

7. If a researcher fails to determine the sexual orientation of her research participants and reports her findings without any mention of homosexuals, her study suffers from:
   a. homosexism.
   b. social exchange.
   c. heterosexism.
   d. romantic bias.

8. A sociocultural explanation for the finding that women are more selective than men in choosing partners is that women:
   a. have better vision than men.
   b. have less economic power than men.
   c. are less superficial than men.
   d. have to compensate for being more romantic than men.

9. Adults who tend to keep their distance from others and who are unconcerned about social rejection would be classified in which of the following attachment styles?
   a. Secure
   b. Preoccupied
   c. Avoidant-dismissing
   d. Avoidant-fearful

10. A self-defeating attributional style associated with loneliness involves attributing loneliness to:
   a. internal, stable factors.
   b. internal, unstable factors.
   c. external, stable factors.
   d. external, unstable factors.

Book Companion Website

Visit the Book Companion Website at **academic.cengage.com/psychology/weiten,** where you will find tutorial quizzes, flash cards, and web links for every chapter, a final exam, and more! You can also link to the Psychology Resource Center (accessible directly at **academic.cengage.com/login**) for a range of psychology-related resources.

Personal Explorations Workbook

The following exercises in your *Personal Explorations Workbook* may enhance your self-understanding in relation to issues raised in this chapter. **Questionnaire 8.1:** Social Avoidance and Distress Scale. **Personal Probe 8.1:** How Do You Relate to Friends? **Personal Probe 8.2:** Analyzing Your Views of Social Connectedness.

ANSWERS

1. b Pages 237–238
2. d Pages 239–240
3. a Page 241
4. d Pages 243–244
5. b Page 249
6. d Pages 251–252
7. c Page 252
8. b Page 253
9. c Page 256
10. a Pages 263–264

CHAPTER 9

Marriage and Intimate Relationships

"My hands are shaky. I want to call her again but I know it is no good. She'll only yell and scream. It makes me feel lousy. I have work to do but I can't do it. I can't concentrate. I want to call people up, go see them, but I'm afraid they'll see that I'm shaky. I just want to talk. I can't think about anything besides this trouble with Nina. I think I want to cry."—A recently separated man quoted in Marital Separation *(Weiss, 1975, p. 48)*

This man is describing his feelings a few days after he and his wife broke up. He is still hoping for a reconciliation. In the meantime, he feels overwhelmed by anxiety, remorse, and depression. He feels very alone and is scared at the prospect of remaining alone. His emotional distress is so great that he can't think straight or work effectively. His reaction to the loss of an intimate relationship is not all that unusual. Breakups are devastating for most people—a reality that illustrates the enormous importance of intimate relationships in people's lives.

In this chapter we take a look at marriage and other intimate relationships. We discuss why people marry and how they progress toward the selection of a mate. To shed light on marital adjustment, we describe the life cycle of the family, highlighting key vulnerable spots in marital relations. We also address issues related to divorce, cohabitation, remaining single, and being gay. Finally, in the Application we examine the tragic problem of violence in intimate relationships. Let's begin by discussing recent challenges to the traditional concept of marriage.

CHALLENGES TO THE TRADITIONAL MODEL OF MARRIAGE

MOVING TOWARD MARRIAGE
The Motivation to Marry
Selecting a Mate
Predictors of Marital Success

MARITAL ADJUSTMENT ACROSS THE FAMILY LIFE CYCLE
Between Families: The Unattached Young Adult
Joining Together: The Newly Married Couple
Family with Young Children
Family with Adolescent Children
Launching Children into the Adult World
The Family in Later Life

VULNERABLE AREAS IN MARITAL ADJUSTMENT
Gaps in Role Expectations
Work and Career Issues
Financial Difficulties
Inadequate Communication

DIVORCE
Divorce Rates

LIVING IN TODAYS' WORLD *Should the Government Promote Marriage?*
Deciding on a Divorce
Adjusting to Divorce
Effects of Divorce on Children
Remarriage

ALTERNATIVES TO MARRIAGE
Remaining Single
Cohabitation
Gay Relationships

APPLICATION: UNDERSTANDING INTIMATE VIOLENCE
Partner Abuse
Date Rape

REVIEW

PRACTICE TEST

Challenges to the Traditional Model of Marriage

LEARNING OBJECTIVES

- *Discuss recent trends relating to the acceptance of singlehood and cohabitation.*
- *Describe changing views on the permanence of marriage and gender roles.*
- *Explain how increased childlessness and the decline of the nuclear family have affected the institution of marriage.*

***Marriage* is the legally and socially sanctioned union of sexually intimate adults.** Traditionally, the marital relationship has included economic interdependence, common residence, sexual fidelity, and shared responsibility for children. Although the institution of marriage remains popular, it sometimes seems to be under assault from shifting social trends. This assault has prompted many experts to ask whether marriage is in serious trouble (Cherlin, 2004; Lewin, 2004). Although it appears that the institution of marriage will weather the storm, it's worth looking at some of the social trends that are shaking up the traditional model of marriage:

1. *Increased acceptance of singlehood.* An increasing proportion of the adult population under age 35 is remaining single (Teachman, Polonko, & Scanzoni, 1999). In part, this trend reflects longer postponement of marriage than before. The median age at which people marry has been increasing gradually since the mid-1960s, as **Figure 9.1** shows. In 2005, the median age at first marrige was 25.8 years for women and 27.1 years for men (U.S. Bureau of the Census, 2006a). Thus, remaining single is becoming a more acceptable lifestyle (DeFrain & Olson, 1999). Furthermore, the negative stereotype of people who remain single—which pictures them as lonely, frustrated, and unchosen—is gradually evaporating.

2. *Increased acceptance of cohabitation.* ***Cohabitation* is living together in a sexually intimate relationship without the legal bonds of marriage.** Negative attitudes toward couples living together have clearly declined (Cherlin, 2004), although many people continue to disapprove of the practice (Thornton & Young-DeMarco, 2001). The prevalence of cohabitation has increased dramatically in recent decades. In fact, recent census figures reveal that married couples are in the minority for the first time, with only 49.7% of households consisting of married couples (Roberts, 2006). Moreover, cohabiting relationships increasingly include children (Smock, 2000), as we will discuss more fully later in this chapter.

3. *Reduced premium on permanence.* Most people still view marriage as a permanent commitment, but an increasing number of people regard divorce as justifiable if their marriage fails to foster their interests as individuals (Bianchi & Casper, 2000). Accordingly, the social stigma associated with divorce has lessened, and divorce rates have risen. Some experts estimate that roughly 50% of marriages ultimately end in separation or divorce (Amato, 2004a).

4. *Transitions in gender roles.* The women's movement and economic pressures have led to substantial changes in the gender-role expectations of many people entering marriage today (Brewster & Padavic, 2000; Zuo & Tang, 2000). The traditional breadwinner and homemaker roles for the husband and wife are being discarded by many couples, as more and more married women enter the workforce (Halpern, 2005; see **Figure 9.2** on the next page). Role expectations for husbands and wives are becoming more varied, more flexible, and more ambiguous (Amato et al., 2003). Many people regard this trend as a step in the right direction. However, changing gender roles create new potential for conflict between marital partners (McGraw & Walker, 2004).

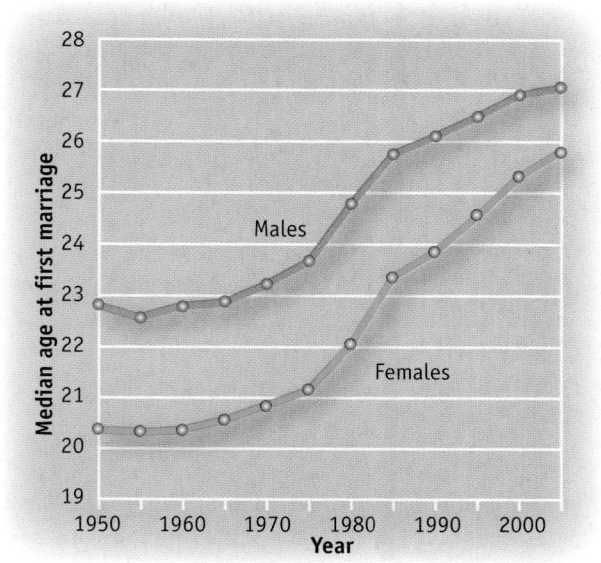

Figure 9.1

Median age at first marriage. The median age at which people in the United States marry for the first time has been creeping up for both males and females since the mid-1960s. This trend indicates that more people are postponing marriage. (Data from U.S. Bureau of the Census)

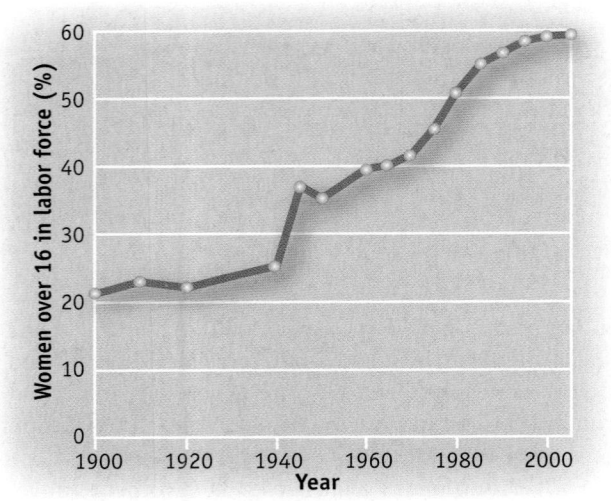

Figure 9.2

Women in the workforce. The percentage of women in the United States (over age 16) who work outside the home has been rising steadily, although it has leveled off in recent years. (Data from U.S. Bureau of Labor Statistics)

5. *Increased voluntary childlessness.* In the past two decades, the percentage of women without children has climbed in all age groups as an increasing number of married couples have chosen not to have children or to delay having children (Bulcroft & Teachman, 2004). This trend is a result of new career opportunities for women, the tendency to marry at a later age, and changing attitudes.

6. *Decline of the traditional nuclear family.* Thanks to endless reruns of television shows like *Leave It to Beaver, Father Knows Best, and Happy Days,* in the eyes of most American adults the ideal family should consist of a husband and wife married for the first time, rearing two or more children, with the man serving as the sole breadwinner (Coontz, 2000). As McGraw and Walker (2004) put it, "Many people today, both in academic settings and popular culture, continue to idealize the image of the traditional nuclear family—one consisting of a breadwinner father and a homemaker mother . . . Because this ideology remains strong, a dearth of support exists for families that do not conform to the image" (p. 177). In reality, this image was never all that accurate, and today only a small minority of American families are estimated to match this ideal (Coontz, 2000; Halpern, 2005). The increasing prevalence of single-parent households, stepfamilies, childless marriages, unwed parents, and working wives make the traditional nuclear family a highly deceptive mirage that does not reflect the diversity of family structures in America. Interestingly, this change is reflected in the fact that there are virtually no television shows with traditional family structure today.

In summary, the norms that mold marital and intimate relationships have been restructured in fundamental ways in recent decades. Traditional values have eroded as people have increasingly embraced more individualistic values (Bianchi & Casper, 2000; Popenoe, 1993). Thus, the institution of marriage is in a period of transition, creating new adjustment challenges for modern couples. Support for the concept of monogamy remains strong, but changes in the society are altering the traditional model of marriage. The impact of these changes can be seen throughout this chapter as we discuss various facets of married life.

Moving Toward Marriage

LEARNING OBJECTIVES

- *Discuss several factors influencing the selection of a mate.*
- *Outline Murstein's stage theory of mate selection.*
- *Summarize evidence on predictors of marital success.*

"I'm ashamed of being single, I have to admit it. I have grown to hate the word. The worst thing someone can say is, 'How come you're still not married?' It's like saying, 'What's wrong with you?' I look at women who are frumpy and physically undesirable and they're monochromatic and uninteresting and they don't seem unselfish and giving and I wonder, 'How did they become such an integral part of a man's life that he wanted to marry them and spend his life with them?' I'm envious. They're married and I date."—A woman quoted in Tales from the Front *(Kavesh & Lavin, 1988, p. 91)*

This woman desperately wants to be married. The intensity of her motivation for marriage may be a bit unusual, but otherwise she is fairly typical. Like most people, she has been socialized to believe that her life isn't complete until she finds a mate. Although alternatives to marriage are more viable than ever, experts project that over 90% of Americans will marry at least once. Some will do it several times! But why? What motivates people to marry? And how do individuals choose their partners? We'll address these questions as we discuss the factors that influence the movement toward marriage.

The Motivation to Marry

A great variety of motivational factors propel people into marriage. Foremost among them is the desire to participate in a socially sanctioned, mutually rewarding, intimate relationship. Another key factor is the social pressure exerted on people to marry. Getting married is still the norm in our society. Your parents, relatives, and friends expect you to marry eventually, and they often make this expectation abundantly clear with their comments and inquiries.

The popular view in our culture is that people marry because they have fallen in love. Although partially accurate, this view is oversimplified. A multitude of motivational factors are involved in the decision to marry. Peter Stein (1975, 1976) interviewed single men and women ages 22 to 45 who were judged to be neither unattractive nor socially inept. As you can see in **Figure 9.3**, he learned that many forces push and pull people toward marriage or singlehood.

Selecting a Mate

Modern Western cultures are somewhat unusual in permitting free choice of one's marital partner. Most societies rely on parental arrangements and severely restrict the range of acceptable partners along religious and class lines (Ingoldsby, 1995). Mate selection in American culture is a gradual process that begins with dating and moves on to sometimes lengthy periods of courtship. In this section, we will look at the impact of endogamy, homogamy, and gender on marital choice. We'll also discuss Bernard Murstein's S-V-R theory, which provides a good overview of the process of mate selection.

Monogamy

***Monogamy* is the practice of having only one spouse at a time.** In our society, monogamous marital relationships are the norm and the law. However, the recent HBO show *Big Love* has placed ***polygamy,* having more than one spouse at a time,** in the spotlight (Lee, 2006). This show features a fictional suburban, polygamous family. Though many cultures practice polygamy, it is typically associated with the Mormon religion, even though the Mormon Church officially denounced it in the late 18th century (White & White, 2005). Research suggests that polygamy in both well- and poorly functioning families is painful for wives.

The Decision to Marry

Pushes Toward Marriage	Pulls Toward Marriage	Pushes Toward Singlehood	Pulls Toward Singlehood
Economic security	Influence of parents	Restrictions	Career opportunities
Influence from mass media	Desire for family	Suffocating one-to-one relationships, feeling trapped	Variety of experiences
Pressure from parents	Example of peers	Obstacles to self-development	Self-sufficiency
Need to leave home	Romanticization of marriage	Boredom, unhappiness, anger	Sexual availability
Interpersonal and personal reasons	Love	Role playing and conformity to expectations	Exciting lifestyle
Fear of independence	Physical attraction	Poor communication with mate	Freedom to change and experiment
Loneliness	Emotional attachment	Sexual frustration	Mobility
Alternative did not seem feasible	Security, social status, prestige	Lack of friends, isolation, loneliness	Sustaining friendships
Cultural expectations, socialization		Limitations on mobility and available experience	Supportive groups
Regular sex		Influence of and participation in women's movement	Men's and women's groups
Guilt over singlehood			Group living arrangements
			Specialized groups

Figure 9.3

The decision to marry. Stein (1975) interviewed single people ages 22 to 45 to determine the motivational factors that influence the decision to marry. *Pushes toward marriage* involve deficits supposedly felt by single persons. *Pushes toward singlehood* involve deficits felt by married people. *Pulls* are positive factors associated with marriage or being single. The two lists on the left identify the factors favoring marriage, while the two lists on the right identify those favoring singlehood. Not everyone weighs all these factors, but this list illustrates the complexity of the decision to marry.

Adapted from Stein, P. J. (1975). Singlehood: An alternative to marriage. *The Family Coordinator, 24*(4), 500. Copyright © 1975 by the National Council on Family Relations. Reprinted by permission.

Common ways of dealing with the pain include acceptance that this way of life is God's will, allocating of household resources equally, and maintaining an attitude of respect for the other wives (Slonim-Nevo & Al-Krenawi, 2006). Although the Mormon Church is worried that *Big Love* perpetuates inaccurate stereotypes, many current polygamous wives report that it is a realistic view of polygamous family life (Lee, 2006).

Endogamy

***Endogamy* is the tendency of people to marry within their own social group.** Research demonstrates that people tend to marry others of the same race, religion, ethnic background, and social class (Kalmijn, 1998; McPherson, Smith-Lovin, & Cook, 2001). This behavior is promoted by cultural norms and by the way similarity fosters interpersonal attraction (see Chapter 8). Although endogamy appears to be declining, this decrease has been gradual. For example, in 2000, 6% of all households reported an interracial marriage, with races encompassing black, white, Asian, Native American, and so on (Simmons & O'Connell, 2003).

Although some people speculate that interracial relationships carry an extra burden, recent research suggests that there are no differences between interracial couples and same-race couples in terms of relationship quality, conflict patterns, and attachment. In fact, interracial couples tend to report higher relationship satisfaction than others (Troy, Lewis-Smith, & Laurenceau, 2006).

Homogamy

***Homogamy* is the tendency of people to marry others who have similar personal characteristics.** Among other things, marital partners tend to be similar in age and education (Jepsen & Jepsen, 2002), physical attractiveness (Feingold, 1988), attitudes and values (Kilby, 1993; Luo & Klohnen, 2005), marital history (Ono, 2006), and even vulnerability to psychological disorders (Matthews & Reus, 2001). Interestingly, homogamy *is* associated with longer-lasting and more satisfying marital relations (Gaunt, 2006; Heaton, 2002). Even in dating relationships, similarity on a variety of characteristics is related to stability and satisfaction (Peretti & Abplanalp, 2004).

Deviations from homogamy in age and education do not tend to be symmetrical, as husbands are usually older and better educated than their wives (South, 1991). In fact, men report believing that women with higher income and education levels than themselves will be less likeable and less faithful (Greitemeyer, 2006). The typical age gap between spouses is about three to four years. Cultural norms that discourage women from dating younger men may contribute to a "marriage squeeze" for women. Without the freedom to date younger men, women are likely to find their pool of potential partners dwindling more rapidly than men of similar age do.

Gender and Mate Selection Preferences

Research reveals that males and females exhibit both similarities and differences in what they look for in a marital partner. Many characteristics, such as physical attractiveness, similarity, emotional stability, dependability, and a pleasant disposition, are rated highly by both sexes (Buss et al., 2001; Peretti & Abplanalp, 2004). However, a few crucial differences between men's and women's priorities have been found, and these differ-

© Michael Newman/PhotoEdit

People tend to marry others who are similar in race, religion, social class, education, and other personal characteristics—a phenomenon called homogamy.

ences appear to be nearly universal across cultures. As we saw in Chapter 8, women tend to place a higher value than men on potential partners' socioeconomic status, intelligence, ambition, and financial prospects. In contrast, men consistently show more interest than women in potential partners' youthfulness and physical attractiveness (Buss & Kenrick, 1998).

Fletcher (2002) asserts that mate selection criteria can be grouped in three major categories: warmth/loyalty, vitality/attractiveness, and status/resources. Compared to men, women tend to place a greater emphasis on warmth/loyalty and status/resources and less of an emphasis on vitality/attractiveness. This gender difference is greater for long-term as opposed to short-term mate selection (Fletcher et al., 2004).

Most theorists explain these gender disparities in terms of evolutionary concepts (Archer, 1996; Buss, 1996; Fletcher, 2002). According to evolutionary theories, all organisms, including humans, are motivated to enhance their chances of passing on their genes to subsequent generations. Human females supposedly accomplish this end not by seeking larger or stronger partners, as in the animal kingdom, but by seeking male partners who possess or are likely to acquire more material resources that can be invested in children. Men, on the other hand, are assumed to maximize their reproductive outlook by seeking female partners with good breeding potential. Thus, men are thought to look for youth, attractiveness, good health, and other characteristics presumed to be associated with higher fertility. These evolutionary analyses of gender differences in mating are speculative, and there are alternative explanations (as we saw Chapter 8), but they fit with the evidence quite well.

Stimulus-Value-Role Theory

A number of theories have attempted to shed light on the *process* of mate selection and the development of premarital relationships. We'll focus on one particularly prominent model, Bernard Murstein's (1976, 1986) *stimulus-value-role (S-V-R) theory.* According to Murstein, couples generally proceed through three stages—the stimulus, value, and role stages—as they move toward marriage.

During the first stage, a person's attraction to members of the other gender depends mainly on their *stimulus* characteristics, such as physical attractiveness, social status, occupational success, and reputation. If a couple makes it to the *value* stage, further progress depends on compatibility in values. Typically, the pair will begin to explore each other's attitudes about religion, politics, sex, gender roles, leisure activities, and so forth. If fundamental incompatibilities are uncovered, the relationship may stall, or it may come to an end. However, if the two persons discover similarity in values, they might begin to think about making a more permanent commitment and enter the *role stage.* At this point people start evaluating whether the other person does a satisfactory job in the role of intimate companion. They consider issues such as the distribution of power in their relationship, the reliability of emotional support, and the quality of their sexual liaison (if they have formed one). Murstein maintains that marriage is generally delayed until couples are comfortable with role enactments in Stage 3.

Murstein's theory has been questioned on the grounds that courtship relationships do not really evolve through distinct stages. Critics argue that individuals in romantic relationships acquire information about each other's stimulus characteristics, values, and roles continuously rather than in discrete stages (Leigh, Holman, & Burr, 1984, 1987). Although there is merit to this criticism, S-V-R theory provides a useful overview of the factors that influence whether romantic relationships progress toward marriage. If people do choose the marriage route, what are some of the factors that influence marital success?

Predictors of Marital Success

Are there any factors that reliably predict marital success? A great deal of research has been devoted to this question. This research has been plagued by one obvious problem: How do you measure "marital success"? Some researchers have simply compared divorced and intact couples in regard to premarital characteristics. The problem with this strategy is that it only assesses commitment and not satisfaction. Many intact couples obviously do not have happy or successful marriages (Amato, 2007). Other researchers have used elaborate questionnaires to measure couples' marital satisfaction. Unfortunately, these scales are plagued by a number of problems. Among other things, they appear to measure complacency and lack of conflict more than satisfaction (Fowers et al., 1994).

Although research shows some thought-provoking correlations between couples' premarital characteristics and marital adjustment, most of the correlations are relatively small. Thus, there are no fool-proof predictors of marital success. Nevertheless, here are some of the factors that researchers have looked at.

Family background. The marital adjustment of partners is correlated with the marital satisfaction of their parents. People whose parents were divorced are more likely than others to experience divorce themselves (Amato & DeBoer, 2001). For a number of reasons, there appears to be an intergenerational "divorce cycle" (Wolfinger, 2005).

Age. The ages of the bride and groom are also related to the likelihood of success. Couples who marry young have higher divorce rates (Bramlett & Mosher, 2001), as **Figure 9.4** shows. Perhaps people who marry late have more carefully selected their mate, or are less likely to undergo dramatic personal change that would render them incompatible with their partners. Researchers speculate that as more individuals choose to marry later in life, divorce rates could actually decrease (Teachman, Tedrow, & Hall, 2006).

Length of courtship. Longer periods of courtship are associated with a greater probability of marital success (Cate & Lloyd, 1988). Longer courtships may allow couples to evaluate their compatibility more accurately. Alternatively, the correlation between courtship length and marital success may exist because people who are cautious about marriage have attitudes and values that promote marital stability.

Personality. Generally, studies have found that partners' specific personality traits are not strong predictors of marital success. That said, there are some traits that show modest correlations with marital adjustment. For example, two negative predictors of marital success are perfectionism (Haring, Hewitt, & Flett, 2003) and insecurity (Crowell, Treboux, & Waters, 2002). In terms of the Big Five personality traits, there is evidence for a negative association between neuroticism and marital satisfaction (Rogge et al., 2006), and some preliminary evidence suggests a weak positive association between marital adjustment and both agreeableness and conscientiousness (Bouchard, Lussier, & Sabourin, 1999).

Premarital interaction. As you might expect, the degree to which couples get along well during their courtship is predictive of their marital adjustment. The quality of premarital communication appears especially crucial. For example, the more that prospective mates are negative, sarcastic, insulting and unsupportive during courtship, the greater the likelihood of marital distress and divorce (Clements, Stanley, & Markman, 2004). Close relationships that include self-disclosure and acceptance of what is learned through disclosure are likely to be the most satisfying over long periods of time (Harvey & Omarzu, 1999). Although most research in the area of communication has focused on discussions of conflict, a recent study demonstrates that being understood and validated in conversation is strongly related to satisfaction, even when the conversation is about a positive event (Gable, Gonzaga, & Strachman, 2006). While this research focused on dating couples, Gable and his colleagues speculate that "positive emotional exchanges may serve as a foundation on which stable and satisfying relationships rest" (p. 916). In fact, playfulness and positive emotion in mundane, everyday interactions in couples seem to be emerging as important components in marital adjustment (Driver & Gottman, 2004).

Figure 9.4

Age at marriage and probability of marital disruption in the first five years. Martin and Bumpass (1989) estimated the likelihood of marital disruption (either divorce or separation) within five years for various groups. The data summarized here show that the probability of marital disruption is substantially higher among those who marry young.

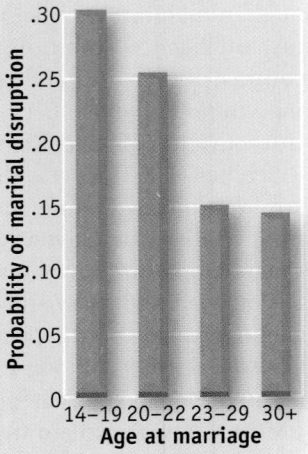

Marital Adjustment Across the Family Life Cycle

LEARNING OBJECTIVES

- *Explain what the family life cycle is.*
- *Describe the factors couples weigh in deciding whether to have children.*
- *Analyze the dynamics of the transition to parenthood.*
- *Identify common problems that surface as a family's children reach adolescence.*
- *Discuss the transitions that occur in the later stages of the family life cycle.*

"Jennifer has taken a lot of time away from us, the time that we normally spend doing things together or talking. It seems like maybe on a weekend when we would normally like to sleep in, or just have lazy sex, Jennifer wakes up and needs to be fed. . . . But I'm sure that will pass as soon as Jennifer gets a little older. We're just going through a phase."—A new mother quoted in American Couples *(Blumstein & Schwartz, 1983, p. 205)*

"We're just going through a phase." That statement highlights an important point: There are predictable patterns of development for families, just as there are for individuals. These patterns make up the ***family life cycle*, an orderly sequence of developmental stages that families tend to progress through.** The institutions of marriage and family are inevitably intertwined. With the advent of marriage, two persons create an entirely new family. Typically, this new family forms the core of one's life as an adult.

Sociologists have proposed a number of models to describe family development. Our discussion is organized around a six-stage model outlined by Carter and McGoldrick (1988, 1999). **Figure 9.5** provides an overview of their model. It spells out the developmental tasks during each stage of the life cycle for families that eventually have children and remain intact. Admittedly, not all families progress through the family life cycle in an orderly fashion, and some researchers find that marital problems are similar whether a couple is newly married, have young children, or have been married for many years (Miller et al., 2003). Nevertheless, the model does appear to be a useful predictive tool for the marriage experience (Kapinus & Johnson, 2003). Although Carter and McGoldrick have described variations on this basic pattern that are associated with remaining childless or going through a divorce, we will focus primarily on the basic pattern in this section.

Between Families: The Unattached Young Adult

As young adults become independent of their parents, they go through a transitional period during which they are "between families" until they form a new family through marriage. What is interesting about this stage is that it is being prolonged by more and more people. The percentage of young adults who are postponing marriage until their late twenties or early thirties has risen dramatically (DeFrain & Olson, 1999). The extension of this stage is probably due to a number of factors, including the availability of new career options for women, increased educational requirements in

The Family Life Cycle

Family life cycle stage	Emotional process of transition: Key developmental task	Additional changes in family status required to proceed developmentally
1. Between families: The unattached young adult	Accepting parent/offspring separation	a. Differentiation of self in relation to family of origin b. Development of intimate peer relationships c. Establishment of self in work
2. The joining of families through marriage: The newly married couple	Commitment to new system	a. Formation of marital system b. Realignment of relationships with extended families and friends to include spouse
3. The family with young children	Accepting new members into the system	a. Adjusting marital system to make space for child(ren) b. Taking on parenting roles c. Realignment of relationships with extended family to include parenting and grandparenting roles
4. The family with adolescents	Increasing flexibility of family boundaries to include children's independence	a. Shifting of parent-child relationships to permit adolescent to move in and out of system b. Refocus on midlife marital and career issues c. Beginning shift toward concerns for older generation
5. Launching children and moving on	Accepting a multitude of exits from and entries into the family system	a. Renegotiation of marital system as a dyad b. Development of adult-to-adult relationships between grown children and their parents c. Realignment of relationships to include in-laws and grandchildren d. Dealing with disabilities and death of parents (grandparents)
6. The family in later life	Accepting the shifting of generational roles	a. Maintaining own and/or couple functioning and interests in face of physiological decline; exploration of new familial and social role options b. Support for a more central role for middle generation c. Making room in the system for the wisdom and experience of the elderly; supporting the older generation without over-functioning for them d. Dealing with loss of spouse, siblings, and other peers and preparation for own death; life review and integrations

Figure 9.5

Stages of the family life cycle. The family life cycle can be divided into six stages, as shown here (based on Carter & McGoldrick, 1988). The family's key developmental task during each stage is identified in the second column. The third column lists additional developmental tasks at each stage.

the world of work, an increased emphasis on personal autonomy, and more positive attitudes about remaining single.

Joining Together: The Newly Married Couple

The next phase begins when the unattached adult becomes attached. The newly married couple gradually settle into their roles as husband and wife. For some couples, this phase can be quite troublesome, as the early years of marriage are often marred by numerous problems and disagreements (McGoldrick, 1999). When reporting on maritial satifaction, 8%–14% of newlyweds score in the distressed range, and the most commonly reported problems are balancing work and marriage and financial concerns (Schramm et al., 2005). *In general, however, this stage tends to be characterized by great happiness—the proverbial "marital bliss."* Spouses' satisfaction with their relationship tends to be relatively high early in marriage, before the arrival of the first child.

This prechildren phase used to be rather short for most newly married couples, as they quickly went about the business of having their first child. Traditionally, couples simply *assumed* that they would proceed to have children. Remaining childless by choice used to be virtually unthinkable for wives, as having a child was viewed as the ultimate fulfillment of womanhood (Ulrich & Weatherall, 2000). This value system meant that women who remained childless often felt incomplete (Morell, 2000) or were viewed by others as selfish (Letherby & Williams, 1999).

In recent decades, however, ambivalence about the prospect of having children has clearly increased (T. W. Smith, 1999), and the percentage of voluntarily childless couples has roughly doubled since 1980 (Bulcroft & Teachman, 2004). Thus, more and more couples find themselves struggling to *decide* whether to have children. Often, the decision to remain childless occurs after numerous postponements, when the couple finally acknowledge that "the right time" is never going to arrive. Intentions about having children are not as stable over time as one might expect. In one study that followed adult participants over a span of six years, about one-quarter of the respondents changed their plans (Heaton, Jacobson, & Holland, 1999). These subjects were almost evenly split between those who planned to remain childless but subsequently decided they wanted to have children and those who intended to have children but subsequently expressed a preference for remaining child-free.

Couples who choose to remain childless cite the great costs incurred in raising children. In addition to the financial burdens, they mention such costs as giving up educational or career opportunities, loss of time for leisure activities and each other, loss of autonomy, worry about the responsibility associated with childrearing, and concerns about overpopulation (Bulcroft & Teachman, 2004; Connidis & McMullin, 1999). Women especially cite career issues as playing a role in their decisions (Park, 2005), and voluntarily childless women tend to have higher incomes and more work experience than other women (Abma & Martinez, 2006).

Although voluntary childlessness is becoming more common, such couples are still in the minority. Couples who decide to have children cite many reasons for this choice, including the responsibility to procreate, the joy of watching youngsters mature, the sense of purpose that children create, and the satisfaction associated with emotional nurturance and the challenges of childrearing (Cowan & Cowan, 2000; Goetting, 1986). Clearly, parenthood is associated with both benefits and costs (Nomaguchi & Milkie, 2003). However, the vast majority of parents rate parenthood as a positive and satisfying experience and report no regret about their choice (Demo, 1992). Simlarily, most voluntarily childless couples do not regret their decision (Jeffries & Konnert, 2002).

Family with Young Children

Although most parents are happy with their decision to have children, the arrival of the first child represents a major transition, and the disruption of routines can be emotionally draining (Bost et al., 2002; Carter, 1999). The transition to parenthood tends to have more impact on mothers than fathers (Nomaguchi & Milkie, 2003). The new mother, already physically exhausted by the birth process, is particularly prone to postpartum distress, and about 10%–13% of new moms experience depression within the first 12 weeks after birth (Dennis & Ross, 2005; Formichelli, 2001). This disorder received increased national attention when the actress Brooke Shields went public with her struggle with postpartum depression after the birth of her daughter in 2003. Issues such as infants' sleeps patterns and crying are associated with mothers' depressive symptoms and martial satisfaction (Dennis & Ross, 2005; Meijer & van den Wittenboer, 2007).

The transition to parenthood is more difficult when a wife's expectations regarding how much the father will be involved in child care are not met (Fox, Bruce, & Combs-Orme, 2000). A review of decades of research on parenthood and marital satisfaction found that (1) parents exhibit lower marital satisfaction than comparable nonparents, (2) mothers of infants report the steepest decline in marital satisfaction, and (3) the more children couples have, the lower their marital satisfaction tends to be (Twenge, Campbell, & Foster, 2003).

© AP Images/Susan Walsh

Actress Brooke Shields, who suffered from postpartum depression after the birth of her daughter, has campaigned for increased awareness of this potentially dangerous illness. She is shown here at a 2007 press conference related to federal legislation that would improve government efforts to detect and treat postpartum depression.

Crisis during the transition to first parenthood is far from universal, however (Cox et al., 1999). Couples with high levels of affection and commitment prior to the first child's birth are likely to maintain a stable level of satisfaction after the child's birth (Shapiro, Gottman, & Carrère, 2000). The key to making this transition less stressful may be to have *realistic expectations* about parental responsibilities (Belsky & Kelly, 1994). Studies find that stress tends to be greatest in new parents who have overestimated the benefits and underestimated the costs of their new role. Reactions to parenthood may also depend on how a couple's marriage is going. Involvement in and satisfaction with parenting tends to be higher when marital quality is higher (Gavin et al., 2002; Rogers & White, 1998).

Web Link 9.1 **American Academy of Child and Adolescent Psychiatry (AACAP): Facts for Families**

Many new parents may need help coping with emerging problems in their children. The brochures here (in both English and Spanish) cover a wide range of psychological issues and psychiatric conditions.

Although children bring their share of trials and tribulations to a marriage, divorce rates are clearly higher for those who remain childless (Shapiro et al., 2000).

Family with Adolescent Children

Although the adolescent years have long been viewed as a period of great stress and turmoil, research from the past decade has led to the conclusion that adolescence is not as turbulent or difficult as once believed (Steinberg & Levine, 1997). Ironically, though, studies indicate that it is an especially stressful period for the parents, who overwhelmingly rate adolescence as the most difficult stage of parenting (Gecas & Seff, 1990).

As adolescent children seek to establish their own identities, parental influence tends to decline while the influence of peer groups tends to increase. Parents tend to retain more influence than peers over important matters, such as educational goals and career plans, but peers gradually gain more influence over less critical matters, such as style of dress and recreational plans (Gecas & Seff, 1990). Thus, conflicts between adolescent children and their parents tend to involve everyday matters such as chores and dress more than substantive issues such as sex and drugs (Barber, 1994). Conflict is particularly likely to surface between adolescents (of both sexes) and their mothers. Adolescents tend to exhibit better adjustment in families in which they are encouraged to participate in decision making but parents ultimately maintain control (Preto, 1999). Parents seem to learn from their experience in dealing with an adolescent child, as they report less conflict with their second adolescent child than their first (Whiteman, McHale, & Crouter, 2003).

In addition to worrying about their adolescent children, middle-aged couples often worry about the care of their aging parents. Adults caught between these conflicting responsibilities have been called the *sandwich generation* (Riley & Bowen, 2005). Based on national survey data from Great Britain and the United States, one-third of women between the ages of 55 and 69 simlutaneously provide help to both generations (Grundy & Henretta, 2006). Thanks to increased longevity and decreased family size, today's average married couple has more parents than children, and an increasing number of adults provide care to their aging parents (Starrels et al., 1997). Females tend to assume most of the responsibility for elderly relatives, and it is estimated that in the future women can expect to spend more years caring for their aging parents than for their dependent children (Bromley & Blieszner, 1997). Many theorists are concerned that these multigenerational caregiving responsibilities may prove burdensome. Supporting this concern, one study found that the number of hours spent caring for an aging parent was

Cathy © 1994 Cathy Guisewite. Reprinted with permission of UNIVERSAL PRESS SYNDICATE. All rights reserved.

correlated with wives' psychological distress (Voydanoff & Donnelly, 1999). For women, becoming a caregiver for a parent is associated with declines in happiness, autonomy, and personal growth and increases in financial difficulties later in life (Marks, Lambert, & Choi, 2002; Wakabayashi & Donato, 2006).

Launching Children into the Adult World

When children begin to reach their twenties, the family has to adapt to a multitude of exits and entries, as children leave and return, sometimes with their own spouses. This period, during which children normally progress from dependence to independence, brings a variety of transitions. In many instances, conflict subsides and parent-child relations become closer and more supportive (Aquilino, 1997).

One might argue that launching children into the adult world tends to be a lengthier and more difficult process today than it once was (Furstenberg, 2001). The percentage of young adults who live with their parents has climbed in recent decades. The rapidly rising cost of a college education and the shrinking job market have probably led many young adults to linger in their parents' homes. Moreover, crises such as separation, divorce, job loss, and pregnancy out of wedlock force many children who have ventured out on their own to return to their parents. Young adults who come home after living independently have been characterized as the *boomerang generation* (Mitchell, 2006). Children from intact, two-parent homes are more likely to return than those with stepparents (Goldscheider & Goldscheider, 1998). Interestingly, young adults have more negative attitudes about returning home than their parents do (Veevers, Gee, & Wister, 1996). Data suggest that living with one's parents during adulthood has a modest negative impact on parent-child relations (White & Rogers, 1997). Conflicts are particularly likely when returning children have been unsuccessful in moving into autonomous adult roles (Treas & Lawton, 1999).

When parents do manage to get all their children launched into the adult world, they find themselves faced with an "empty nest." This period was formerly thought to be a difficult transition for many parents, especially mothers who were familiar only with the maternal role. In recent decades, however, more women have experience with other roles outside the home and look forward to their "liberation" from child-rearing responsibilities. Most parents adjust effectively to the empty nest transition and are more likely to have problems if their children *return* to the once-empty nest (Blacker, 1999). Hence, researchers have found that the empty nest is associated with improved mood and well-being for most women (Dennerstein, Dudley, & Guthrie, 2002). Middle-aged parents who have launched their children into the adult world report more enjoyment of life and higher marital satisfaction than similar-aged parents who still have children at home (White & Edwards, 1990).

Web Link 9.2 **The Whole Family Center**

This lively site features reasonable advice and useful links for the issues that come up in families, such as rearing children and coping with family crises. A team of psychologists, social workers, educators, and marriage and family therapists, among others, serve as the experts at the center.

The Family in Later Life

Marital satisfaction tends to climb in the postparental period as couples find they have more time to devote attention to each other (Brubaker, 1990). Whether this trend is the result of reduced parental responsibilities, reduced work responsibilities, or other considerations remains unclear (Lee, 1988). In any case, many couples take advantage of their newfound freedom, traveling or developing new leisure interests. For many people this can be a period of increased intimacy. However, spouses do have to adapt to spending more time with each other and often need to renegotiate role expectations (Walsh, 1999). Of course, age-related considerations that are independent of the relationship, such as the increased likelihood of physical illness, can make the later years stressful. The three most commonly reported problems in late-life marriages are disagreements or disappointments about leisure activities, intimacy, and finances (Henry, Miller, & Giarrusso, 2005). Some gender differences in disappointments are apparent in older couples: Men are more likely to be disappointed about financial matters, whereas women are more likely to be disappointed about personal habits and health matters.

Vulnerable Areas in Marital Adjustment

LEARNING OBJECTIVES

- *Discuss how gaps in role expectations may affect marital adjustment.*
- *Summarize how spouses' work affects their marital satisfaction and their children.*
- *Describe how financial issues are related to marital adjustment.*
- *Summarize evidence on the relationship between communication quality and marital adjustment.*

"When we first got married, the first six months of conflicts were all about getting him to take account of what I had planned for him at home. . . . He would come waltzing in an hour and a half late for dinner, or cancel an evening with friends, because he had to close a deal. . . . We would argue and argue . . . not because I didn't want him to make a living . . . but because I thought he had to be more considerate."—A wife quoted in American Couples *(Blumstein & Schwartz, 1983, p. 174)*

An unavoidable reality of marriage is that couples must confront a legion of problems together. During courtship, couples tend to focus on pleasurable activities. But once couples are married, they deal with a variety of problems, such as arriving at acceptable role compromises, paying bills, and raising a family. Marital conflict is associated with several negative outcomes for partners and their family members, including increased depression, alcoholism, physical health problems, domestic violence, and divorce (Fincham, 2003). There is no such thing as a problem-free marriage. Successful marriages depend on couples' ability to handle their problems. In this section we will analyze the major kinds of difficulties that are likely to emerge. There are no simple solutions for these problems. However, in navigating your way through life, it helps to know where you're likely to encounter the most perilous reefs.

Gaps in Role Expectations

When a couple marry, they assume new roles—those of husband and wife. Each role comes with certain expectations that the partners hold about how wives and husbands should behave. These expectations may vary greatly from one person to another. Gaps between partners in their role expectations appear to have a negative effect on couples' marital satisfaction (Lye & Biblarz, 1993). Unfortunately, substantial differences in role expectations seem particularly likely in this era of transition in gender roles, a topic we will discuss in depth in Chapter 10.

The traditional role expectations for husbands and wives used to be fairly clear. A husband was supposed to act as the principal breadwinner, make the important decisions, and take care of certain household chores, such as car or yard maintenance. A wife was supposed to raise the children, cook, clean, and follow the leadership of her husband. Spouses had different spheres of influence. The working world was the domain of the husband, the home the domain of the wife. In recent decades, however, the women's movement and other forces of social change have led to new expectations about marital roles. Thus, modern couples need to negotiate and renegotiate role responsibilities throughout the family life cycle (Zvonkovic et al., 1996).

Women may be especially vulnerable to ambivalence about shifting marital roles. More and more women are aspiring to demanding careers. Yet research shows that husbands' careers continue to take priority over their wives' ambitions (Haas, 1999). It is wives who are expected to interrupt their career to raise young children, stay home when children are sick, and abandon their jobs when husbands' careers require relocation. Moreover, even when both spouses are employed, many husbands maintain traditional role expectations about housework, child care, and decision making. Research shows that couples in which the husband holds egalitarian attitudes have higher levels of marital happiness than those where the husband holds more traditional attitudes (Kaufman & Taniguchi, 2006).

Although men's contribution to housework has increased noticeably since the 1960s (Bianchi et al., 2000), wives are still doing the bulk of the household

Figure 9.6

Division of household labor. This chart breaks down the proportion of housework done by husbands and wives for specific tasks. The data show that wives continue to do a highly disproportionate share of most household tasks, especially the "core housework" tasks (cooking, cleaning, laundry) that are hard to ignore. Note also, that in spite of great changes in modern life, the division of labor in the household still largely meshes with traditional gender roles. (Data from Bianchi et al., 2000)

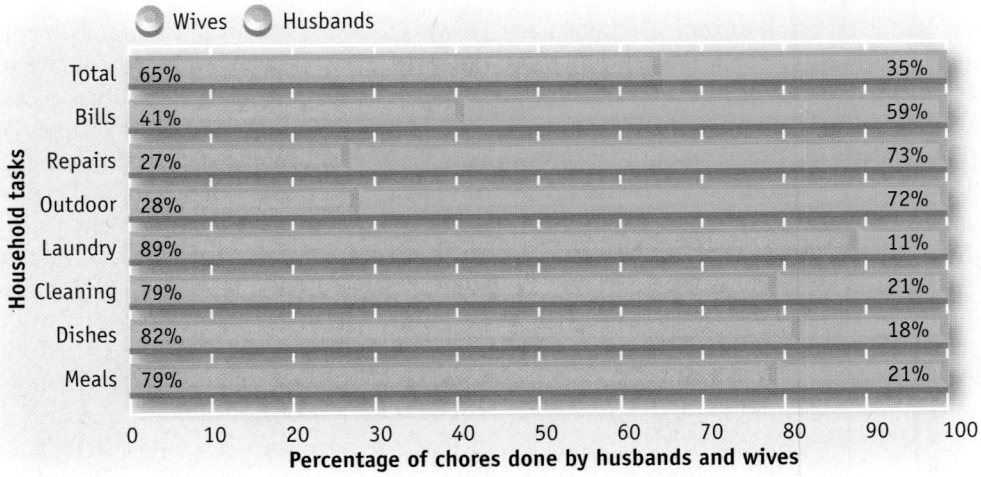

chores in America, even when they work outside the home (Coltrane, 2001; Sayer, 2005). For example, the data show that wives take responsibility for about 65% of total housework (not including child care), while husbands do the remaining 35% (see **Figure 9.6**). Moreover, wives still account for 78% of the essential "core housework" such as cooking, cleaning, and laundry, while men continue to handle more discretionary, traditional "male chores," such as yard or auto maintenance (Bianchi et al., 2000).

Although married women perform almost two-thirds of all housework, only about one-third of wives characterize their division of labor as unfair, because most women don't expect a 50-50 split (Coltrane, 2001). Although many couples accept these gender-driven expectations, the one-third of wives who perceive their division of labor as unfair constitute a sizable population of women for whom housework is a source of discontent. Research shows that women are more likely to perceive their share of housework as unfair when they have nontraditional attitudes about gender roles and when they work outside the home (Coltrane, 2001). As you might expect, wives who perceive their housework burden to be unfair tend to report lower levels of marital satisfaction (Haas, 1999).

In light of this reality, it is imperative that couples discuss role expectations in depth before marriage. If they discover that their views are divergent, they need to take the potential for problems seriously. Many people casually dismiss gender-role disagreements, thinking they can "straighten out" their partner later on. But assumptions about marital roles, whether traditional or not, may be deeply held and not easily changed.

Work and Career Issues

The possible interactions between one's occupation and one's marriage are numerous and complex. Although the data on the effect of income and employment on marital stability are inconsistent (Rodrigues, Hall, & Fincham, 2006), individuals' job satisfaction and involvement can affect their own marital satisfaction, their partner's marital satisfaction, and their children's development.

SALLY FORTH Reprinted with special permission of King Features Syndicate.

Work and Marital Adjustment

Many studies have compared the marital adjustment of male-breadwinner versus dual-career couples. The interest in this comparison arises from traditional views that regard men's *lack* of employment, but women's *employment,* as departures from the norm. Typically, these studies simply categorize women as working or nonworking and evaluate couples' marital satisfaction. Most of these studies find little in the way of consistent differences in the marital adjustment of male-breadwinner versus dual-career couples (Haas, 1999; Perry-Jenkins & Turner, 2004). Although dual-career couples do face special problems in negotiating career priorities, child-care arrangements, and other practical matters, their marriage need not be negatively affected.

Other studies have investigated the relationship between spouses' job satisfaction and their marital adjustment. We could speculate that these two variables might be either positively or negatively related. On the one hand, if a spouse is highly committed to a satisfying career, he or she may have less time and energy to devote to marriage and family. On the other hand, the frustration and stress of an unsatisfying job might *spill over* to contaminate one's marriage.

The research on this question suggests that both scenarios are realistic possibilities. Both husbands and wives struggle to balance the demands of work and family, and both report that work commitments often interfere with family responsibilities (Hochschild, 2001; Milkie & Peltola, 1999). When pressures increase at work, husbands and wives report more role conflicts and often feel overwhelmed by their multiple commitments (Crouter et al., 1999). Furthermore, studies find that spouses' stress at work can have a substantial negative effect on their marital and family interactions (Perry-Jenkins, Repetti, & Crouter, 2001). For example, after highly stressful days at work, spouses tend to withdraw from family interactions (Crouter & Bumpus, 2001). The stress associated with working night shifts appears to be especially tough on spouses and families (Presser, 2000), as does the experience of jobs that require travel (Zvonkovic et al., 2005).

Negative work-to-family spillover seems to be more common for mothers than for fathers and is especially problematic when preschool children are involved (Dilworth, 2004; Stevens et al., 2007). Perhaps this difference is due to the fact that even when working, women continue to do more household labor than do men (Sayer, 2005). Work demands that increase the likelihood of family conflict and stress include long commutes, bringing work home, and receiving job contacts at home (Voydanoff, 2005).

Although the difficulties involved in juggling work and family roles can be challenging, some theorists have argued that in the long run multiple roles are beneficial to both men and women. Barnett and Hyde (2001) assert that negative effects of stress in one role can be buffered by success and satisfaction in another role. They also note that multiple roles can increase sources of social support and opportunities to experience success. Moreover, when both spouses work outside the home, income tends to be greater and the spouses often find they have more in common. Typically, those who report positive home-work interactions have positive perceptions of their work and working conditions (Demerouti & Geurts, 2004)

Parents' Work and Children's Development

Another issue of concern has been the potential impact of parents' employment on their children. Virtually all

Web Link 9.3 **National Council on Family Relations (NCFR)**

The National Council on Family Relations has developed a site to reach out to families with practical advice from a cadre of experts on all sorts of family issues. Information is available on a variety of topics, from how to discuss terrorism with children to school violence, drugs, anger management, and so forth.

Reconcilable Differences
by Andrew Christensen and Neil S. Jacobson (Guilford Press, 2002)

Innumerable books attempt to tell couples how to make their relationships work. This entry in the market, written by two experts in marital and family therapy, appears to be superior to most of the others. Christensen and Jacobson argue that no matter how much spouses love each other, their differences will inevitably lead to some conflict. They further assert that the key to a healthy marriage is not to avoid conflict but to learn to accept each other's differences in an atmosphere of empathy and understanding. The early chapters describe the typical sources of conflict in intimate relationships, how arguments unfold, and how conflicts affect couples. Most of the remaining chapters outline concrete steps that couples can take to improve their communication, become more accepting of their differences, and learn to make changes to accommodate each other. The writing sometimes gets a little abstract for a "how to" book, but the wealth of interesting, real-life examples keeps the book moving along at a pleasant pace. The authors' advice is sound and sophisticated, and the book is filled with engaging exercises for the reader. In sum, this is a sensitive, practical guide for couples who want to enhance their relationship.

of the research in this area has focused on the effects of mothers' employment outside the home. In 2006, the U.S. Department of Labor reported that 70.9% of mothers with children under the age of 18 were employed. What does the research on maternal employment show? Although most Americans seem to believe that maternal employment is detrimental to children's development, the vast majority of empirical studies have found little evidence that a mother's working is harmful to her children (Bianchi, 2000; Haas, 1999; Perry-Jenkins et al., 2001). For instance, studies generally have not found a link between mothers' employment status and the quality of infant-mother emotional attachment (Etaugh, 1993; NICHD Early Child Care Research Network, 1997). Some studies have found that maternal employment in the first year after a child's birth may have negative effects on youngster's cognitive skills during early and middle childhood (Han, Waldfogel, & Brooks-Gunn, 2001; Hill et al., 2005), but these effects are modest and are inconsistent across ethnic groups (Han et al., 2001; Harvey, 1999).

Maternal employment has also been shown to have positive associations on children's development. Recent data from the Canadian National Longitudinal Survey of Children and Youth indicate that maternal employment is related to decreased hyperactivity, lower levels of anxiety, and increased prosocial behavior at age 4 (Nomaguchi, 2006). High-quality child care is also related to advanced language functioning (Belsky, 2006). Further, while maternal employment doesn't eliminate poverty, it does mean that fewer children are raised in poverty (Esping-Anderson, 2007; Lichter & Crowley, 2004). Children brought up in poverty exhibit poorer physical health, reduced mental health, lower academic performance, and increased delinquency in comparison to other children (Seccombe, 2001). However, experts are careful to note that any benefits of maternal employment also come at the cost of fewer positive interactions between the mother and child (Nomaguchi, 2006).

Financial Difficulties

How do couples' financial resources affect marital adjustment and family functioning? Neither financial stability nor wealth can ensure marital satisfaction. However, poverty can produce daunting challenges and serious problems for married couples (Rank, 2004). Without money, families live in constant dread of financial drains such as illness, layoffs, or broken appliances. Spontaneity in communication may be impaired by an understandable reluctance to talk about financial concerns. Thus, it is not surprising that serious financial worries among couples are associated with increased hostility in husbands, increased depression in wives, and lower marital happiness in both husbands and wives (White & Rogers, 2001). Similarly, husbands' job insecurity is predictive of wives' reports of marital conflict and their thoughts of divorce (Fox & Chancey, 1998). Moreover, evidence consistently demonstrates that the risk of separation and divorce increases as husbands' income declines (Ono, 1998; South & Lloyd, 1995).

Even when financial resources are plentiful, money can be a source of marital strain. Quarrels about how to spend money are common and are potentially damaging at all income levels. For instance, studies have found that perceptions of financial problems (regardless of a

Why Marriages Succeed or Fail . . . and How You Can Make Yours Last
by John Gottman (with Nan Silver)
(Simon & Schuster, 1995)

This book is about communication in intimate relationships—a subject that Gottman has studied intensively for over 20 years. A psychology professor at the University of Washington, Gottman is justifiably famous for his landmark research on the prediction of divorce. He has demonstrated that he can predict which couples will divorce with remarkable accuracy, based on careful examination of the couples' communication patterns. According to Gottman, the marriages that last are not those that appear to be free of conflict but those in which couples are able to resolve the conflicts that inevitably arise in intimate relationships. Gottman categorizes couples into three types based on their style of conflict resolution. In *validating marriages,* couples compromise often and work out their disagreements calmly. In *conflict-avoiding marriages,* couples rarely confront their disagreements openly. In *volatile marriages,* couples have frequent and passionate disputes. For all three types, the crucial consideration, according to Gottman, is the relative balance of positive versus negative interactions.

In this practical, readable analysis of marital communication, the author provides plenty of case histories to make ideas come alive. The book also includes many thought-provoking scales that readers can take to evaluate their own communication styles and tendencies. For example, there are scales to measure stonewalling, defensiveness, and the other communication tendencies Gottman characterizes as the "Four Horsemen of the Apocalypse." *Why Marriages Succeed or Fail* is an outstanding book loaded with exercises, quizzes, and tips that should help readers improve their marital communication. Gottman has written two other highly practical books on marriage that are worth consulting: *10 Lessons to Transform Your Marriage* (2006) and a more elaborate and detailed analysis titled *The Relationship Cure* (2001).

family's actual income) are associated with decreased marital satisfaction (Dean, Carroll, & Yang, 2007). In a study that examined how happily married couples handled their money in comparison to couples that eventually divorced, Schaninger & Buss (1986) found that the happy couples engaged in more joint decision making on finances. Thus, the best way to avoid troublesome battles over money is probably to engage in extensive planning of expenditures together.

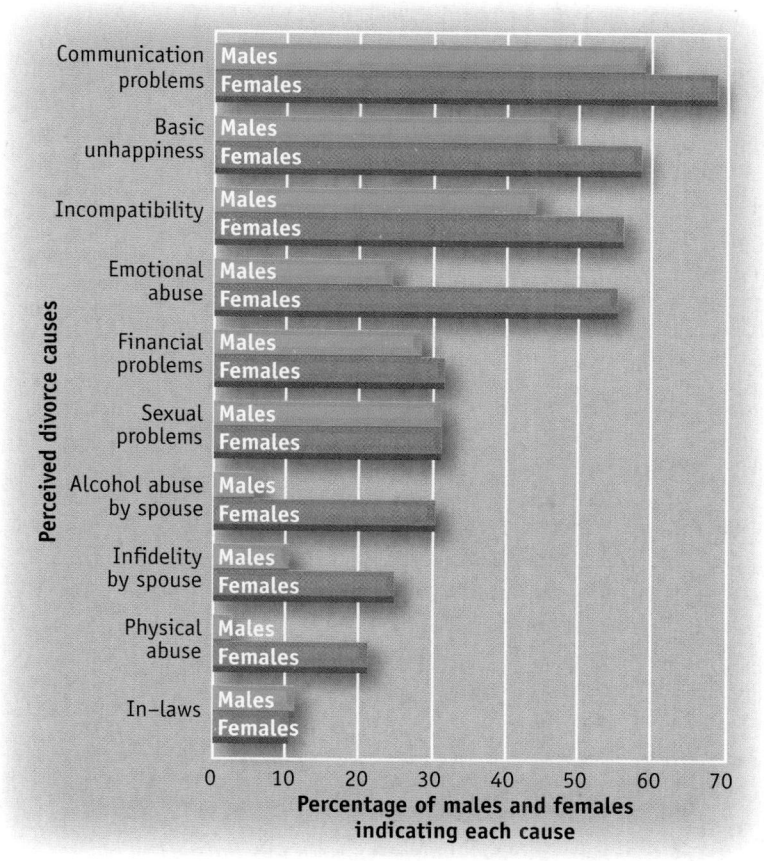

Figure 9.7

Causes of divorce. When Cleek and Pearson (1985) asked divorcing couples about their perceptions regarding the causes of their divorce, both men and women cited communication difficulties more than any other cause.

Inadequate Communication

Effective communication is crucial to the success of a marriage and is consistently associated with increased marital satisfaction (Litzinger & Gordon, 2005; Rogge et al., 2006). The damaging role that poor communication can play in marital relations was clearly demonstrated in a study of couples getting a divorce (Cleek & Pearson, 1985). In this study, communication difficulties were the most frequently cited problem among both husbands and wives (see **Figure 9.7**). Spouses' strategies for resolving conflicts may be particularly crucial to marital satisfaction (Crohan, 1992). Many partners respond to conflict by withdrawing and refusing to communicate—a pattern associated with deteriorating marital satisfaction over time (Heavey, Christensen, & Malamuth, 1995; Roberts, 2000). Couples need to feel safe discussing conflict; the ability to communicate emotions is associated with better marital adjustment (Cordova, Gee, & Warren, 2005).

A number of studies have compared communication patterns in happy and unhappy marriages. This research indicates that unhappily married couples (1) find it difficult to convey positive messages, (2) misunderstand each other more often, (3) are less likely to recognize that they have been misunderstood, (4) use more frequent, and more intense, negative messages, and (5) often differ in the amount of self-disclosure they prefer in the relationship (Noller & Fitzpatrick, 1990; Noller & Gallois, 1988; Sher & Baucom, 1993). Above all else, unhappy couples tend to get caught up in escalating cycles of conflict from which they cannot escape, whereas happy couples find ways to exit the cycles (Fincham, 2003).

The importance of marital communication was underscored in a widely cited study by John Gottman and his colleagues that attempted to predict the likelihood of divorce in a sample of 52 married couples (Buehlman, Gottman, & Katz, 1992). Each couple provided an oral history of their relationship and a 15-minute sample of their interaction style, during which they discussed two problem areas in their marriage. The investigators rated the spouses on a variety of factors that mostly reflected the subjects' ways of relating to each other. Based on these ratings, they were able to predict which couples would divorce within three years with 94% accuracy! Follow-up research has demonstrated that marital adjustment depends not on whether there is conflict (conflict is virtually inevitable) but rather on how conflict is handled when it occurs (Driver et al., 2003).

John Gottman

Photo by Sharon M. Fentiman

John Gottman, who is probably the world's foremost authority on marital communication, asserts that conflict and anger are normal in marital interactions and that they are not, in and of themselves, predictive of marital dissolution. Instead, Gottman (1994) identifies four other communication patterns, which he calls the "Four Horsemen of the Apocalypse," that are risk factors for divorce: contempt, criticism, defensiveness,

CATHY © 1996 Cathy Guisewite. Reprinted with permission of UNIVERSAL PRESS SYNDICATE. All rights reserved.

and stonewalling. *Contempt* involves communicating insulting feelings that one's spouse is inferior. *Criticism* involves constantly expressing negative evaluations of one's partner. *Defensiveness* involves responding to contempt and criticism with obstructive communication that escalates marital conflict. *Stonewalling* involves refusing to listen to one's partner, especially the partner's complaints. Gottman eventually added a fifth troublesome communication pattern, *belligerence,* which involves provocative, combative challenges to partners' power and authority (Gottman et al., 1998; Gottman, Gottman, & DeClaire, 2006). Given the importance of good communication, many approaches to marital therapy emphasize the development of better communication skills in partners (Gottman et al., 2002).

Divorce

LEARNING OBJECTIVES

- *Describe the evidence on changing divorce rates.*
- *Discuss how men and women tend to adjust to divorce.*
- *Analyze the evidence on the effects of divorce on children.*
- *Summarize data on the frequency and success of remarriage and its impact on children.*

"In the ten years that we were married I went from twenty-four to thirty-four and they were a very significant ten years. I started a career, started to succeed, bought my first house, had a child, you know, very significant years. And then all of a sudden, every goddamn thing, I'm back to zero. I have no house. I don't have a child. I don't have a wife. I don't have the same family. My economic position has been shattered. And nothing recoverable. All these goals which I had struggled for, every goddamn one of them, is gone."—A recently divorced man quoted in Marital Separation *(Weiss, 1975, p. 75)*

The dissolution of a marriage tends to be a bone-jarring event for most people, as this bitter quote illustrates.

Any of the problems discussed in the previous section might lead a couple to consider divorce. However, people appear to vary in their threshold for divorce, just as they do in their threshold for marriage. Some couples will tolerate a great deal of disappointment and bickering without seriously considering divorce. Other couples are ready to call their attorney as soon as it becomes apparent that their expectations for marital bliss were somewhat unrealistic. Typically, however, divorce is the culmination of a gradual disintegration of the relationship brought about by an accumulation of interrelated problems, which often date back to the beginning of couples' relationships (Huston, Niehuis, & Smith, 2001).

Divorce Rates

Although relatively accurate statistics are available on divorce rates, it is still difficult to estimate the percentage of marriages that end in divorce. It is clear that divorce rates increased dramatically between the 1950s and 1980s, but they appear to have stabilized and even declined slightly since the 1980s (Amato et al., 2003). When divorce rates were at their peak, the most widely cited estimates of future divorce risk were around 50% (Bumpass, Raley, & Sweet, 1995). However, the modest reductions in divorce rates in recent years appear to have lowered the risk of divorce to 40%–45% for today's couples (Bramlett & Mosher, 2001; Whitehead & Popenoe, 2001). The decline in divorce rates is encouraging, but the chances of marital dissolution remain quite high. In 2001, about one in five adults had been divorced (Kreider, 2005). Although most people realize that divorce rates are high, they have a curious tendency to underestimate the likelihood that they will personally experience a divorce. On the average, people peg their probability of divorce at about 10%–11%, which is far below the actual probability for the population as a whole (Fowers et al., 2001).

Divorce rates are higher among blacks than whites or Hispanics, among lower-income couples, among couples who cohabitated, among couples who do not have children, among people who marry at a relatively young age, and among those whose parents divorced (Faust & McKibben, 1999; Rodrigues et al., 2006). As **Figure 9.8** shows, the vast majority of divorces occur during the first decade of a marriage (Hiedemann, Suhomlinova, & O'Rand, 1998). What types of marital problems are predictive of divorce? The most frequently cited problems include communication difficulties (not talking; being moody, critical, and easy to anger), infidelity, jealousy, growing apart, foolish spending behavior, and substance abuse problems (Amato & Previti, 2003; Amato & Rogers, 1997).

A wide variety of social trends have probably contributed to increasing divorce rates (Amato et al., 2003; Giddens, 2001; Sabatelli & Ripoll, 2004). The stigma attached to divorce has gradually eroded. Many religious denominations are becoming more tolerant of divorce, and marriage has thus lost some of its sacred quality. The shrinking of families probably make divorce a more viable possibility. The entry of more women into the workforce has made many wives less

© Matthew McVay/Corbis Saba

The high divorce rate has led to some novel ways of dealing with its worrisome legal aspects. Attorney Robert Nordyke discovered that the drive-up window at his new office—a former savings and loan branch in Salem, Oregon—was perfect for serving legal papers on his clients' spouses.

Figure 9.8

Divorce rate as a function of years married. This graph shows the distribution of divorces in relation to how long couples have been married. As you can see, the vast majority of divorces occur in the early years, with divorce rates peaking between the fifth and tenth years of marriage. (Data from National Center for Health Statistics)

Should the Government Promote Marriage?

As noted in the main body of the chapter, research evidence suggests that marriage is good for one's health and happiness (Hawkins & Booth, 2005; Waite & Gallagher, 2000). And studies show that children whose parents divorce exhibit an increased risk for quite a variety of negative outcomes (Amato, 2003; Barber & Demo, 2006). These findings suggest that both adults and children are most likely to flourish in stable, loving families, but social trends are clearly moving in just the opposite direction. Marriage rates are down and divorce rates are up, cohabitation rates are skyrocketing, and more and more children are being born out of wedlock (Bianchi & Casper, 2000). Concerns about these trends have led some religious leaders and public officials to argue that government entities ought to do more to promote a culture of marriage (Hackstaff, 1999; Popenoe, 1999; Wagner, 1998). At first glance, this sounds like a sensible, enlightened policy that everyone ought to be able to agree on, but in reality this issue turns out to be surprisingly complex and controversial.

The pro-marriage movement has been gathering momentum since the early 1990s. The advocates of this movement argue that people today are overly focused on their personal happiness and are unwilling to endure hardship and show loyalty when the going gets rough in a marriage (Fowers, 2000). They also assert that the emergence of no-fault divorce laws since the 1970s has made it too easy to get a divorce. Hence, the pro-marriage advocates campaign for policies that would make divorces more difficult to obtain. For example, several states have enacted *covenant marriage* laws (Rosier & Feld, 2000). Couples who choose to enter into a covenant marriage agree to complete premarital education programs and pledge to divorce only in response to severe problems (such as spouse abuse or a lengthy prison term), and only after seeking extensive marriage counseling (Hawkins et al., 2002). Other advocated reforms have included waiting periods for divorces of up to five years and more demanding legal proceedings for divorces involving children. More proactive proposals have included mandating high school education programs touting the value of marriage, providing government subsidies for marriage counseling, and requiring couples to complete premarital relationship skills training (Amato, 2004b). Some pro-marriage proponents have also suggested giving married couples preferential treatment (over single, divorced, and cohabiting individuals) in regard to government benefits, such as welfare payments and housing subsidies (Murray, 2001).

Critics of the pro-marriage movement raise a variety of objections. First, they question the meaning of the research findings that serve as the rationale for this movement. Although they acknowledge that married people are somewhat healthier and happier than nonmarried adults, they point out that the data are correlational and that there is no solid evidence that being married *causes* this difference (Huston & Melz, 2004). They argue that causation probably runs the other way—that being healthy and happy causes people to have better marital opportunities and greater marital success. Indeed, there is empirical support for this notion (Lyubomirsky, King, & Diener, 2005). In a similar vein, they admit that experiencing divorce can be harmful for children but suggest that remaining in a home filled with bitter discord can be just as harmful (Booth & Amato, 2001).

Second, the critics express concern that restricting access to divorce could leave some spouses and children stranded in homes riddled with alcoholism, drug abuse, or domestic violence (Gelles, 1996). Third, critics point out that making divorces harder to get just may not be a realistic option in today's society (Coontz, 1997). Although a majority of adults agree—in the abstract—that divorce laws should be tougher, they do not want *their own* personal freedom in this area to be impeded. Consistent with this finding, only 3 percent of couples have chosen covenant marriage in the state (Louisiana) that first offered this option (Licata, 2002). Further, preliminary data suggest that choosing a convenant marriage might not reduce marital instability (Brown et al., 2006).

Fourth, critics argue that if the government wants to promote marital success, it should focus more on making it *easier to stay married,* as opposed to harder to get a divorce. In particular, they note that divorce rates tend to be high in lower social classes where families could be better strengthened by improving social services (such as child care and job training). Finally, critics maintain that the pro-marriage movement treats the traditional nuclear family as the only legitimate family form and that pro-marriage programs will unfairly discriminate against single parents, divorced persons, cohabiting couples, and gay and lesbian partners (Coltrane, 2001; Scanzoni, 2004).

financially dependent on the continuation of their marriage. New attitudes emphasizing individual fulfillment seem to have counterbalanced older attitudes that encouraged dissatisfied spouses to suffer in silence. Reflecting all these trends, the legal barriers to divorce have also diminished.

Web Link 9.4 **Divorce Central**

Divorce Central is one of a number of excellent sites that provide information and advice on legal, emotional, and financial issues for individuals contemplating or going through a divorce. Annotated links to the other outstanding divorce-related sites can also be found here.

Deciding on a Divorce

Divorces are often postponed repeatedly, and they are rarely executed without a great deal of agonizing forethought (Ahrons, 1999). Indecision is common, as roughly two out of five divorce petitions are eventually withdrawn (Donovan & Jackson, 1990). The decision to divorce is usually the outcome of a long series of smaller decisions or relationship stages that may take years to unfold, so divorce should be viewed as a process rather than a discrete event (Morrison & Cherlin, 1995; Rollie & Duck, 2006). Wives' judgments about the likelihood of their marriages ending in divorce tend to be more accurate than husbands' judgments (South, Bose, & Trent, 2004). This finding may be related to the fact that wives initiate two-thirds of divorce actions (Hetherington, 2003).

It is difficult to generalize about the relative merits of divorce as opposed to remaining in an unsatisfactory marriage. Extensive research clearly shows that people who are currently divorced suffer a higher incidence of both physical and psychological maladies and are less happy than those who are currently married (Amato, 2001; Waite & Gallagher, 2000). Furthermore, the process of getting divorced is stressful for both spouses. We might guess that as divorce becomes more commonplace, it should also become less traumatic, but available evidence does not support this supposition (Kitson, 1992). As painful as marital dissolution may be, remaining in an unhappy marriage is also potentially detrimental. Research has shown that in comparison to divorced individuals, unhappily married people tend to show poorer physical health, lower levels of happiness, less life satisfaction, and lower self-esteem (Hawkins & Booth, 2005; Wickrama et al., 1997). Moreover, like other stressful life events, divorce can lead to personal growth and positive changes in the self (Tashiro, Frazier, & Berman, 2006), so the picture is not entirely negative.

Adjusting to Divorce

Objectively speaking, divorce appears to be more difficult and disruptive for women than for men, especially in terms of finances (Clarke-Stewart & Bailey, 1989; Sayer, 2006). Women are more likely to assume the responsibility of raising the children, whereas men tend to reduce their contact with their children. Within the first year after divorce, half of fathers basically lose contact with their kids (Carter & McGoldrick, 1999). Another key consideration is that divorced women are less likely than their ex-husbands to have adequate income or a satisfying job (Smock, Manning, & Gupta, 1999). For example, one well-designed study found that custodial mothers experienced a 36% percent decrease in their standard of living, whereas noncustodial fathers experienced a 28% *increase* (Bianchi, Subaiya, & Kahn, 1999). The economic consequences of divorce clearly are more severe for women than for men, but in this era of two-income families, many men also experience a noticeable decline in their standard of living after going through a divorce (McManus & DiPrete, 2001).

Although divorce appears to impose greater stress on women than men, researchers do *not* find consistent gender differences in postdivorce adjustment (Amato, 2001). In the aggregate, the magnitude of the negative effects of divorce on individuals' psychological and physical well-being seems to be pretty similar for husbands and wives. Among both men and women, high preoccupation with one's ex-spouse is associated with poorer adjustment to divorce (Masheter, 1997). Factors associated with favorable postdivorce adjustment include having higher income, getting remarried, having more positive attitudes about divorce, and being the partner who initiated the divorce (Wang & Amato,

"That's right, Phil. A separation will mean—among other things—watching your own cholesterol."

2000). Forgiveness of the ex-spouse is also associated with increased well-being and lowered depression (Rye et al., 2004). Interestingly, research shows that the relationship between divorce and adjustment is also influenced by preexisting factors. That is, even before getting married, people who eventually divorce are less happy than people who remain married (Lucas, 2005).

Effects of Divorce on Children

Roughly half of all divorces involve children. When couples have children, decisions about divorce must take into account the potential impact on their offspring. Widely publicized research by Judith Wallerstein and her colleagues has painted a rather bleak picture of how divorce affects youngsters (Wallerstein & Kelly, 1980; Wallerstein & Blakeslee, 1989; Wallerstein, Lewis, & Blakeslee, 2000). This research has followed a sample of 60 divorced couples and their 131 children since 1971. At the 10-year follow-up, almost half of the participants were characterized as "worried, underachieving, self-deprecating, and sometimes angry young men and women" (Wallerstein & Blakeslee, 1989, p. 299). Even *25 years* after their parents' divorce, a majority of subjects were viewed as troubled adults who found it difficult to maintain stable and satisfying intimate relationships (Wallerstein, 2005). The enduring, long-term effects of divorce reported by Wallerstein were particularly disturbing and generated great interest from the media, resulting in an abundance of TV interviews, magazine articles, and so forth.

Although the lengthy follow-up in Wallerstein's research is commendable, critics point out that her study suffers from a variety of flaws (Amato, 2003; Cherlin, 1999; Kelly & Emery, 2003). It was based on a small sample of children from a wealthy area in California that clearly was not representative of the population at large. There was no comparison group, and conclusions were based on impressions from clinical interviews, in which it is easy for interviewers to see what they want to see. Further, critics caution against drawing causal conclusions from corrleational data (Gordon, 2005). Coltrane and Adams (2003) also note that Wallerstein is part of a conservative political-religious movement that favors traditional family arrangements and reforms that would make divorces more difficult to obtain. Hence, her conclusions may be shaped in part by a political agenda.

Are Wallerstein's findings consistent with other research? Yes and no. The results of another long-running study by E. Mavis Hetherington (1993, 1999, 2003), which used a larger and more representative sample, a control group, and conventional statistical comparisons, suggest that Wallerstein's conclusions are unduly pessimistic. According to Hetherington, divorce can be traumatic for children, but a substantial majority adjust reasonably well after two to three years, and only about 25% show serious psychological or emotional problems in adulthood (versus 10% in the control group).

Courtesy, E. Mavis Hetherington

E. Mavis Hetherington

Another complicated issue in assessing the effects of divorce is the choice of whom should be used as a baseline for comparison. One can argue that children of divorce should be compared to children from intact homes characterized by persistent marital discord, a group that also shows elevated rates of many types of adjustment problems (Morrison & Coiro, 1999; Papp, Cummings, & Schermerhorn, 2004).

Although Wallerstein's conclusions appear overly negative, *they differ from the results of other research only in degree* (Amato, 2003). After a divorce, many children exhibit depression, anxiety, nightmares, dependency, aggression, withdrawal, distractibility, lowered academic performance, reduced physical health, precocious sexual behavior and substance abuse (Barber & Demo, 2006; Kelly & Emery, 2003; Knox, 2000). Although these problems dissipate in most children after a few years, divorce can have a lasting impact that extends into adulthood. Experiencing divorce during childhood is a risk factor for many subsequent problems in one's adult years, including maladjustment, marital instability, and reduced occupational attainments (Amato, 1999). Children have more adjustment problems when their parents have a history of particularly bitter, acrimonious conflict (Amato, 2001).

So what can we conclude about the effects of divorce on children? *Overall, the weight of evidence suggests that divorce tends to have harmful effects on many children but can have beneficial effects for children if their parents' relationship is dominated by conflict* (Booth & Amato, 2001). However, the latter assertion is based on the assumption that the parents' divorce brings their bickering to an end. Unfortunately, the conflicts between divorcing spouses often continue for many years after they part ways (Hopper, 2001). This pattern has led to a recent interest in divorce education and intervention programs to ease the transition for families; such efforts still need to be scientifically evaluated (Blaisure & Geasler, 2006). It is also reasonable to conclude that *divorces have highly varied effects on children that depend on a complex constellation of interacting factors.* As Furstenberg and Kiernan (2001) put it, "Many researchers have become increasingly wary about public discussions of divorce that treat it as an undifferentiated and uniform occurrence resulting in similar outcomes for all children" (p. 446).

Remarriage

Evidence that adequate courtship opportunities exist for the divorced is provided by the statistics on remarriage: Roughly three-quarters of divorced people eventually remarry (Bramlett & Mosher, 2001). The mean length of time between divorce and remarriage is within three to four years (Kreider, 2005).

How successful are second marriages? The answer depends on your standard of comparison. Divorce rates *are* higher for second than for first marriages (of divorced people), though the average duration for second marriages is about the same as for first, about eight to nine years (Kreider, 2005; Mason, 1998). However, this statistic may simply indicate that this group of people see divorce as a reasonable alternative to an unsatisfactory marriage. Nonetheless, studies of marital adjustment suggest that second marriages are slightly less successful than first marriages (Brown & Booth, 1996). Of course, if you consider that in this pool of people *all* the first marriages ran into serious trouble, then the second marriages look rather good by comparison. As with first marriages, communication plays a major role in marital satisfaction for both spouses (Beaudry et al., 2004).

Although remarried couples tend to have more open communication, the evidence suggests that second marriages are slightly less successful than first marriages, on the average.

Another major issue related to remarriage is its effect on children. Adaptation to remarriage can be difficult for children. Evidence suggests that on the average, interaction in stepfamilies appears to be somewhat less cohesive and warm than interaction in first-marriage families, and stepparent-stepchild relations tend to be more negative and distant than parent-child relations in first marriages (Pasley & Moorefield, 2004). Stepfamily formation can be a negative experience for children who feel powerless or who undergo dramatic changes in living spaces, rules, and expectations (Stoll et al., 2005).

Taken as a whole, the evidence suggests that children in stepfamilies are a little less well adjusted than children in first marriages and are roughly similar in adjustment to children in single-parent homes (Coleman, Ganong, & Fine, 2001). In an analysis of 61 studies, Jeynes (2006) found that children in stepfamilies tend to show lower academic achievement and psychological well-being than those from intact or single-parent families. However, the differences between stepfamilies and other types of families in the adjustment of their children tend to be modest. For example, **Figure 9.9** highlights some representative results from one large-scale study (Acock & Demo, 1994).

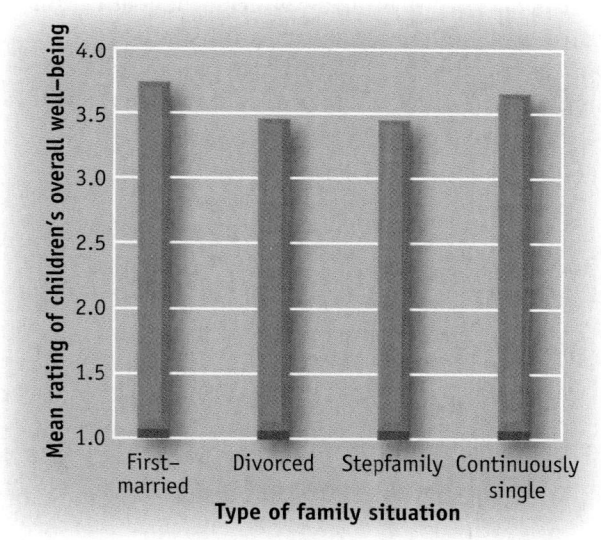

Figure 9.9

Children's adjustment in four types of families. Acock and Demo (1994) assessed children's adjustment in four types of family structures: first marriages, divorced single-parent homes, stepfamilies, and families in which the mother never married. The comparisons of 2,457 families did turn up some statistically significant differences, as children's overall well-being was highest in intact first marriages. However, as you can see, the differences were rather small, and the authors concluded that "family structure has a modest effect on children's well-being."

Alternatives to Marriage

LEARNING OBJECTIVES

- *Describe stereotypes of single life, and summarize evidence on the adjustment of single people.*
- *Discuss the prevalence of cohabitation and whether it improves the probability of marital success.*
- *Discuss the stability and dynamics of intimate relationships among homosexual couples.*
- *Outline some misconceptions about gay couples.*

So far we have been discussing the traditional model of marriage, which, as we noted at the beginning of the chapter, has been challenged by a variety of social trends. More and more people are choosing alternatives to marriage. In this section we examine some of these alternatives, including remaining single, cohabitation, and gay relationships.

Remaining Single

The pressure to marry is substantial in our society (Berliner, Jacob, & Schwartzberg, 1999). People are socialized to believe that they are not complete until they have found their "other half" and have entered into a partnership for life. And reference is often made to people's "failure" to marry. In spite of this pressure, an increasing proportion of young adults are remaining single (Teachman, Tedrow, & Crowder, 2001), as **Figure 9.10** shows.

Does the increased number of single adults mean that people are turning away from the institution of marriage? Perhaps a little, but for the most part, no. A variety of factors have contributed to the growth of the single population. Much of this growth is a result of the increase in the median age at which people marry and the increased rate of divorce. The vast majority of single, never-married people *do* hope to marry eventually. In one study of never-married men and women (South, 1993), 87.4% of the 926 respondents ages 19 to 25 agreed with the statement "I would like to get married someday," and in a recent study of unmarried parents, most expected to marry (Waller & McLanahan, 2005).

Singles continue to be stigmatized and plagued by two disparate stereotypes (Byrne & Carr, 2005; DeFrain & Olson, 1999). On the one hand, single people are sometimes portrayed as carefree swingers who are too busy enjoying the fruits of promiscuity to shoulder marital responsibilities. On the other hand, they are seen as losers who have not succeeded in snaring a mate, and they may be portrayed as socially inept, maladjusted, frustrated, lonely, and bitter. These stereotypes do a great injustice to the diversity that exists among those who are single. In fact, the negative stereotypes of singles have led some researchers to coin the term *singlism* to capture how single people can be victims of prejudice and discrimination (DePaulo & Morris, 2005, 2006).

Moving beyond stereotypes, what do scientists know about singlehood? It is true that single people exhibit poorer mental and physical health than married people (Joung et al., 1997; Waite, 1995), and they rate themselves as less happy than their married counterparts (Stack & Eshleman, 1998; Waite, 2000). However, the differences are modest, and the happiness gap has shrunk, especially among women. The physical health benefits of being married appear to be greater for men than for women (Waite, 2000; Wu & Hart, 2002). But most studies find that single women are more satisfied with their lives and less distressed than comparable single men, and various lines of evidence suggest that women get along without men better than men get along without women (Davies, 1995; Marker, 1996).

Why is being married associated with greater health and happiness? The *health benefits* of marriage may result because spouses provide emotional and social support that buffers the negative effects of

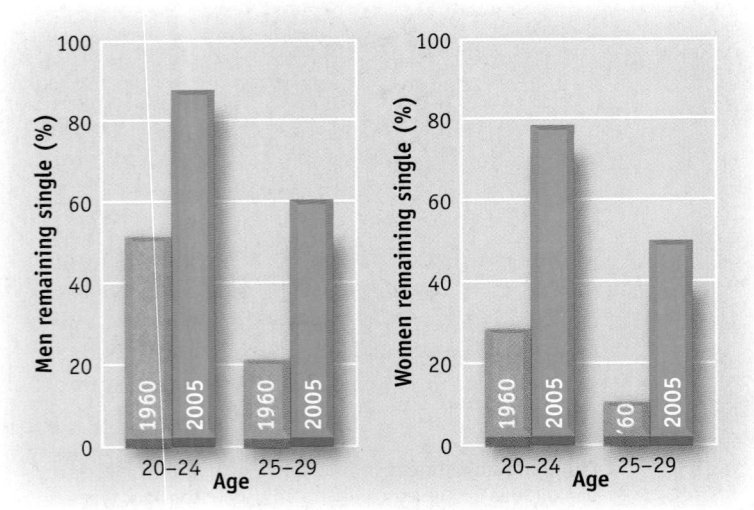

Figure 9.10

The proportion of young people who remain single. This graph shows the percentage of single men and women, ages 20–24 or 25–29, in 2005 as compared to 1960 (based on U.S. Census data). The proportion of people remaining single has increased substantially for both sexes, in both age brackets. Single men continue to outnumber single women in these age brackets.

stress and because they discourage their partners' unhealthy habits (Joung et al., 1997; Murphy, Glaser, & Grundy, 1997). Another consideration is that married people tend to have higher incomes (Hirschl, Altobelli, & Rank, 2003), and affluence is associated with better health (Adler & Snibbe, 2003). The *greater happiness* of married people has been attributed to the advantages they enjoy in social support, financial well-being, and physical health (Stack & Eshleman, 1998). However, when interviewing life-long single women between the ages of 65 and 77, Baumbusch (2004) found that these women expressed satisfaction with their decision to remain single and emphasized the importance of their independence.

Cohabitation

As we noted earlier in the chapter, *cohabitation* refers to living together in a sexually intimate relationship outside of marriage. Recent years have witnessed a tremendous increase in the number of cohabiting couples (see **Figure 9.11**). Although cohabitation is still illegal in six states (Florida, Michigan, Mississippi, North Carolina, Virginia, and West Virginia), over 55.2 million couples are living together unmarried in the United States (Roberts, 2006). Increasing rates of cohabitation are not unique to the United States and are even higher in many European countries (Kiernan, 2004). However, the percentage of couples living together at any one time does not accurately convey how widespread this phenomenon has become, because cohabitating unions tend to be short (Seltzer, 2004).

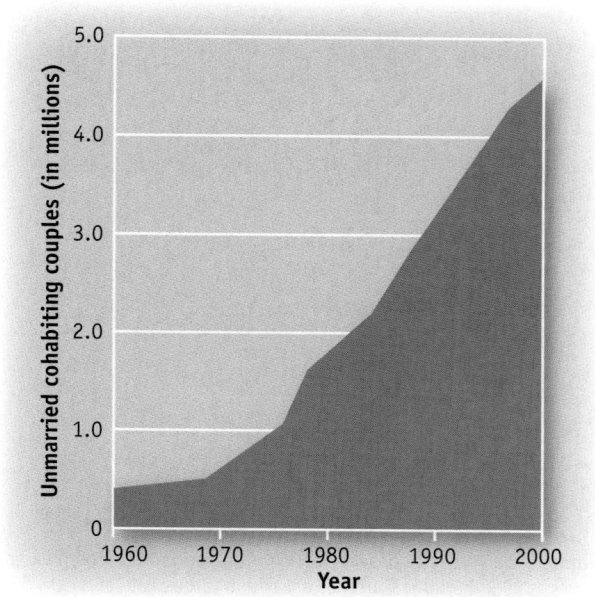

Figure 9.11

Cohabitation in the United States. The number of unmarried couples living together has been increasing rapidly since 1970 (based on U.S. Census data). This increase shows no signs of leveling off.

Cohabitation tends to conjure up images of college students or other well-educated young couples without children, but these images are misleading. In reality, cohabitation rates have always been higher in the less-educated and lower-income segments of the population (Bumpass & Lu, 2000). Moreover, many cohabitating couples have children: About half of previously married cohabitants and 35% of never-married cohabitants have children in their household (Smock, 2000).

Although many people see cohabitation as a threat to the institution of marriage, many theorists see it as a new stage in the courtship process—a sort of trial marriage. Consistent with this view, about three-quarters of female cohabitants expect to marry their current partner (Lichter, Batson, & Brown, 2004). In spite of these expectations, however, cohabitants report that they are less satisfied with their relationships than married couples (Brown & Booth, 1996; Nock, 1995). Moreover, cohabitating relationships are notably less durable than marital relationships (Seltzer, 2004). Conceiving a child during cohabitation tends to increase couples' chances of staying together (Manning, 2004).

As a prelude to marriage, cohabitation should allow people to experiment with marital-like responsibilities and reduce the likelihood of entering marriage with unrealistic expectations, suggesting that couples who cohabit before they marry should go on to more successful marriages than those who do not. Although this analysis sounds plausible, researchers have *not* found that premarital cohabitation increases the likelihood of subsequent marital success. In fact, studies have consistently found an association between premarital cohabitation and *increased* marital discord and divorce rates (Bumpass & Lu, 2000; Cohan & Kleinbaum, 2002; Teachman, 2003).

What accounts for this finding? Many theorists argue that this nontraditional lifestyle has historically attracted a more liberal and less conventional segment of the population with a weak commitment to the institution of marriage and relatively few qualms about getting divorced. This explanation has considerable empirical support (Hall, 1996; Smock, 2000; Stanley, Whitton, & Markman, 2004), but some support also exists for the alternative explanation—that the experience of cohabitation changes people's attitudes, values, or habits in ways that somehow increase their vulnerability to divorce (Kamp Dush, Cohan, & Amato, 2003; Seltzer, 2001).

Gay Relationships

Up until this point, we have, for purposes of simplicity, focused our attention on *heterosexuals,* those who seek

Despite the common stereotype that homosexuals rarely form long-term relationships, the fact is that they are similar to heterosexual couples in their attitudes and behaviors, and many enjoy long-term commitments in marriage-like arrangements.

© Ron Chapple/Thinkstock/Alamy

emotional-sexual relationships with members of the other gender. However, we have been ignoring a significant minority group: *homosexual* men and women, who seek emotional-sexual relationships with members of the same gender. (In everyday language, the term *gay* is used to refer to homosexuals of both genders, although many homosexual women prefer the term *lesbian* for themselves.)

How large is this minority group? No one knows for sure. Part of the problem is that this question is vastly more complex than it appears at first glance (LeVay, 1996; Gates & Sell, 2007). Sexual orientation is best represented as a continuum (as we will discuss in Chapter 13), so where do you draw the lines between heterosexuality, bisexuality, and homosexuality? Researchers distinguish among three components of sexual orientation: sexual attraction, overt behavior, and sexual identity (Savin-Williams, 2006). So where, for instance, do you put a person who is married and has never engaged in homosexual behavior but who reports homosexual fantasies and acknowledges being strongly drawn to members of the same sex? The other part of the problem is that many people have prejudicial attitudes about homosexuality, which makes gays cautious and reluctant to give candid information about their sexuality (Smith & Gates, 2001). Small wonder then that estimates of the portion of the population that is homosexual vary widely (Gonsiorek & Weinrich, 1991; Savin-Williams, 2006). A frequently cited statistic is 10%, but recent surveys suggest that this percentage may be an overestimate. Michaels (1996) has combined data from two of the better large-scale surveys to arrive at the estimates seen in **Figure 9.12**. As you can see, the numbers are open to varying interpretations, but as a

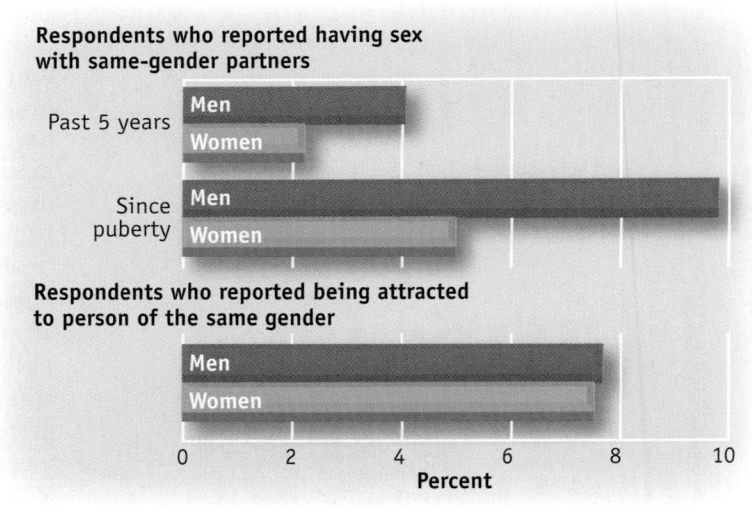

Figure 9.12

How common is homosexuality? The answer to this question is both complex and controversial. Michaels (1996) brought together data from large-scale surveys to arrive at the estimates shown here. If you look at how many people have actually had a same-sex partner in the last five years, the figures are relatively low, but if you count those who have had a same-sex partner since puberty, the figures more than double. Still another way to look at it is to ask people whether they are attracted to people of the same sex (regardless of their actual behavior). This approach suggests that about 8 percent of the population could be characterized as homosexual.

whole they suggest that about 5%–8% of the population could reasonably be characterized as homosexual.

Attitudes about gay relationships have become more favorable in recent years, but over half of Americans still condemn homosexual relations as morally wrong and oppose gay marriage and gays' right to adopt children (Herek, 2002). ***Homophobia,* a type of prejudice and discrimination against homosexuals,** is common, and gay men and lesbians continue to be victims of employment and housing discrimination, not to mention verbal and physical abuse and hate crimes (Herek, 2000; Herek, Cogan, & Gillis, 2002). African Americans, especially men, hold more negative attitudes toward gays than their white counterparts (Lemelle & Battle, 2004). With rare exceptions, gay couples cannot legally formalize their unions by getting married, and in fact, during the past decade many states passed laws prohibiting same-gender marriages. Gay couples are also denied many economic benefits available to married couples. For example, they can't file joint tax returns, and gay individuals often can't obtain employer-provided health insurance for their partner.

Comparisons to Heterosexual Couples

Devoting a separate section to gay couples may seem to imply that the dynamics of their close relationships are different from those seen in heterosexual couples. Actually, this assumption appears to be much less true than is widely thought. It is true that gays' close relationships unfold in a vastly different social context than heterosexuals' marital or cohabitating relationships. As Garnets and Kimmel (1991) point out, gay relationships "develop within a social context of societal disapproval with an absence of social legitimization and support; families and other social institutions often stigmatize such relationships and there are no prescribed roles and behaviors to structure such relationships" (p. 170).

Although gay relationships evolve in a different social context, research has documented that close relationships, gay or heterosexual, function in similar ways (Herek, 2006; Kurdek, 2006). Both types of couples report similar levels of love and commitment in their relationships, similar levels of overall satisfaction with their relationships, and similar levels of sexual satisfaction (Kurdek, 1998; Peplau, 1991). Resemblance is also apparent when researchers study what gays and heterosexuals want out of their relationships (Peplau, 1988; see **Figure 9.13**). Futhermore, homosexual and heterosexual couples are similar in terms of the factors that predict relationship satisfaction, the sources of conflict in their relationships, and their patterns of conflict resolution (Kurdek, 2004).

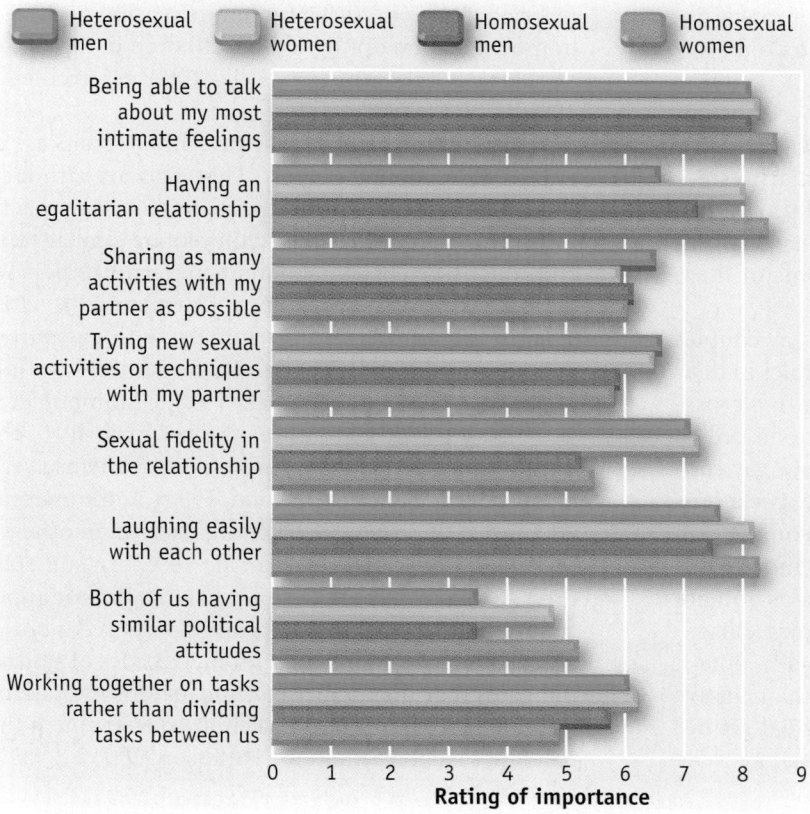

Figure 9.13

Comparing priorities in intimate relationships. Peplau (1981) asked heterosexual men and women and homosexual men and women to rate the significance (9 = high importance) of various aspects of their intimate relationships. As you can see, all four groups returned fairly similar ratings. Peplau concluded that gays and heterosexuals largely want the same things out of their relationships.

From Peplau, L. A. (1981, March). What homosexuals want. *Psychology Today, 3,* 28–38. Reprinted with permission from Psychology Today Magazine. Copyright © 1981 Sussex Publishers, Inc.

Web Link 9.5 **Parents, Families, and Friends of Lesbians and Gays (PFLAG)**

PFLAG is a national nonprofit organization dedicated to promoting the "health and well-being of gay, lesbian, bisexual and transgender persons, their families and friends." This site includes educational as well as advocacy information.

Given the lack of moral, social, legal, and economic supports for gay relationships, are gay unions less stable than marital unions? Researchers have not yet been able to collect adequate data on this question, but the limited data available suggest that gay couples' relationships *are* somewhat briefer and more prone to breakups than heterosexual marriages (Kurdek, 1998; Peplau, 1991). If that's the case, it's probably because gay relationships face fewer barriers to dissolution—that is, fewer practical problems that make breakups difficult or costly (Kurdek, 1998; Peplau & Cochran, 1990). Interestingly, Herek (2006) argues that (1) because gay and heterosexual relationships are simliar on psychosocial dimensions, (2) because sexual orientation is unrelated to an individual's ability to provide a healthy family environment, and (3) given that marriage is associated with improved psychological and physical health, perhaps gay couples and their children could benefit from recognized legal partnerships. Of course, this topic is currently the subject of much national debate, one that psychologists will no doubt follow closely.

Misconceptions About Gay Relationships

Although research indicates striking similarities between homosexual and heterosexual relationships, basic misconceptions about the nature of gay relationships remain widespread. Let's look at some of these inaccurate stereotypes.

First, many people assume that most gay couples adopt traditional masculine and feminine roles in their relationships, with one partner behaving in a cross-gendered manner. This appears to be true in only a small minority of cases. In fact, on the whole, gay couples appear to be more flexible about role expectations than heterosexuals (Reimann, 1997). In comparison to married couples, gay couples display a more equitable balance of power in their relationships and are less likely to adhere to traditional gender roles (Rosenbluth, 1997; Solomon, Rothblum, & Balsam, 2004). As with heterosexual relationships, there is a negative association between adherence to traditional gender roles and relationship satisfaction among gay male couples (Wester, Pionke, & Vogel, 2005).

Second, popular stereotypes suggest that gays only rarely get involved in long-term intimate relationships. In reality, most homosexual men, and nearly all homosexual women, prefer stable, long-term relationships, and at any one time roughly 40%–60% of gay males and 45%–80% of lesbians are involved in committed relationships (Kurdek, 2004). Lesbian relationships are generally sexually exclusive. About half of committed male couples have "open" relationships, allowing for the possibility of sexual activity (but not affection) with outsiders. While intimate relationships among gays appear to be less stable than marriages among straights, they may compare favorably with heterosexual cohabitation, which would be a more appropriate baseline for comparison. Both gays and heterosexual cohabitants may face opposition to their relationship from their families and from society in general, and neither enjoys the legal and social sanctions of marriage.

Third, lesbians and gay men tend to be thought of as individuals rather than as members of families. This thinking reflects a bias that homosexuality and family just don't mesh (Allen & Demo, 1995). In reality, gays are very much involved in families as sons and daughters, as parents and stepparents, as aunts, uncles, and grandparents (Johnson & Colluci, 1999). Although exact data are not available, far more are parents than most people realize. Many of these parental responsibilities are left over from previous marriages, as about 20%–30% of gays have been heterosexually married (Kurdek, 2004). But an increasing number of homosexuals are opting to have children in the context of their gay relationships (Falk, 1994; Gartrell et al., 1999).

What do we know about gays and lesbians as parents? The evidence suggests that gays are similar to their heterosexual counterparts in their approaches to parenting and that their children are similar to the children of heterosexual parents in terms of personal development and peer relations (Patterson, 2001, 2006). The overall adjustment of children with gay parents appears similar in quality to that of children of heterosexual parents (Chan et al., 1998; Golombok et al., 2003; Tasker, 2005). Moreover, the vast majority of children of gay parents grow up to identify themselves as heterosexual (Bailey & Dawood, 1998), and some studies suggest that they are no more likely than others to become homosexual (Flaks et al., 1995). In sum, children reared by gay and lesbian parents do not appear to suffer any special ill effects and do not seem noticeably different from other children. Decades of research indicates that the quality of child-parent interactions is much more important to a child's development than parental sexual orientation (Patterson, 2006).

APPLICATION

Understanding Intimate Violence

LEARNING OBJECTIVES

- *Discuss the incidence of partner abuse and the characteristics of batterers.*
- *Discuss why women stay in abusive relationships.*
- *Discuss the incidence and consequences of date rape.*
- *Explain the factors that contribute to date rape.*

Answer the following statements "true" or "false."

___ **1.** Most rapes are committed by strangers.

___ **2.** Research indicates that aggressive pornography does *not* contribute to sexual coercion.

___ **3.** Most women in abusive relationships are attracted to violent men.

___ **4.** Most men who have witnessed domestic violence as children will batter their intimate partners.

All of the above statements are false, as you will see in this Application, which examines the darker side of intimate relationships. Most of us assume that we will be safe with those whom we love and trust. Unfortunately, some people are betrayed by individuals to whom they feel closest. ***Intimate violence* is aggression toward those who are in close relationship to the aggressor.** Intimate violence takes many forms: psychological, physical, and sexual abuse. Tragically, this violence sometimes ends in homicide. In this Application, we'll focus on two serious social problems: partner abuse and date rape.

Partner Abuse

Cases such as the O. J. Simpson trial and the disappearance and murder of Laci Peterson have dramatically heightened public awareness of partner violence, particularly wife battering and homicide. ***Battering* encompasses physical abuse, emotional abuse, and sexual abuse** (Lundberg-Love & Wilkerson, 2006). *Physical abuse* can include kicking, biting, punching, choking, pushing, slapping, hitting with an object, and threatening with or using a weapon. Examples of *emotional abuse* include humiliation, name calling, controlling what the partner does and with whom the partner socializes, refusing to communicate, unreasonable withholding of money, and questioning of the partner's sanity. *Sexual abuse* is characterized as using sexual behavior to control, manipulate, or demean the other person (Nichols, 2006). We will focus primarily on physical abuse of partners.

Incidence and Consequences

As with other taboo topics, obtaining accurate estimates of physical abuse is difficult. Research suggests that about 25% of women and 7% of men have been physically assaulted by an intimate partner at some point in their lives (Tjaden & Thoennes, 2000). Wives attack their husbands more than most people realize (P. Pearson, 1998), but much of wives' aggression appears to be retaliation for abuse and women tend to inflict less physical damage than men (Johnson, 2000; Swan &

© AP Images/Ben Margot

The disappearance and murder of Californian Laci Peterson focused international attention on the problem of violence in intimate relationships. Laci's husband, Scott, was eventually convicted of murdering his wife and unborn child.

Snow, 2006). Thus, women are the principal victims of severe, dangerous abuse. A woman is the victim in 85% of nonfatal violent crimes committed by intimate partners and in 75% of murders by spouses (Rennison & Welchans, 2000). That said, women commit one-quarter of spousal murders, so it is an oversimplification to assume that partner abuse involves only male aggression against women. It is also inaccurate to assume that intimate violence is seen only in marital relationships. Partner abuse is also a significant problem for cohabiting heterosexual couples (DeMaris et al., 2003) and for gay and lesbian couples (Greenwood et al., 2002; Renzetti, 1995).

The effects of battering reverberate beyond the obvious physical injuries. Victims of partner abuse tend to suffer from severe anxiety, depression, feelings of helplessness and humiliation, stress-induced physical illness, symptoms of posttraumatic stress disorder, and increased vulnerability to suicide (Brewster, 2002; Lundberg-Love & Wilkerson, 2006). Children who witness marital violence also experience ill effects, such as anxiety, depression, reduced self-esteem, and increased delinquency (Johnson & Ferraro, 2001).

Characteristics of Batterers

Men who batter women are a diverse group, so a single profile has not emerged (Dixon & Browne, 2003. Some factors associated with an elevated risk for domestic violence include unemployment, drinking and drug problems, a tendency to anger easily, attitudes that condone aggression, and high stress (Stith et al., 2004). Males who were beaten as children or who witnessed their mothers being beaten are more likely to abuse their wives than other men are, although most men who grow up in these difficult circumstances do not become batterers (Stith et al., 2000). Battering appears to be somewhat more common in families of lower socioeconomic status, but no social class is immune (Roberts, 2002). Batterers tend to be jealous in relationships, have unrealistic expectations of their partners, blame others for their own problems, and have their feelings hurt easily (Lundberg-Love & Wilkerson, 2006). In many instances, the motivation for battering is to use it as a tool to exert control over women (Johnson & Ferraro, 2001). Other relationship factors that are associated with domestic violence include having frequent disagreements, exhibiting a heated style of dealing with disagreements, and pairing a man holding traditional gender role attitudes with a woman who has nontraditional views of gender roles (DeMaris et al., 2003).

Web Link 9.6 **Office on Violence Against Women**

This U.S. Department of Justice office was created in 1995 after federal legislation mandated national efforts to reduce domestic violence, sexual assault, and stalking. This site provides a wide variety of legal and social scientific resources in support of this mission.

Why Do Women Stay in Abusive Relationships?

Women leave abusive partners more often than popular stereotypes suggest (Johnson & Ferraro, 2001), but people are still perplexed by the fact that many women remain in abusive relationships that seem horrible and degrading. However, research shows that this phenomenon is not really that perplexing. A number of seemingly compelling reasons explain why many women feel that leaving is not a realistic option, and many of the reasons revolve around fear. Many fear economic hardship and believe that they won't be able to survive financially without their husband (Choice & Lamke, 1997). Many simply have no place to go and fear becoming homeless (Browne, 1993a). Many feel guilty and ashamed about their failing relationship and don't want to face disapproval from family and friends, who are likely to fall into the trap of blaming the victim (Barnett & La Violette, 1993). Above all else, many fear that if they try to leave, they may precipitate more brutal violence and even murder (DeMaris & Swinford, 1996; Grothues & Marmion, 2006). Unfortunately, this fear is not an unrealistic one, in that many men have shown remarkable persistence in tracking down, stalking, threatening, beating, and killing their ex-partners. Despite the many difficulties of leaving abusive relationships (see **Figure 9.14**), attention is still focused on why women stay rather than on why men batter and on what interventions can prevent women from being brutalized or killed when they do leave (Koss et al., 1994). Treatment programs for men who batter their wives can be helpful in decreasing further violence, but the effectiveness of these programs is rather modest (Babcock, Green, & Robie, 2004; Roberts, 2002).

Date Rape

Unfortunately, intimate violence is not limited to marital relations. ***Date rape* refers to forced and unwanted intercourse in the context of dating.** Date rape can occur on a first date, with someone you've dated for a while, or with someone to whom you're engaged. Many people confuse date rape with seduction. The latter occurs when a woman is persuaded *and agrees* to have sex. Date rape often occurs when seduction fails and the man goes on to have sex with the woman without her consent. The force used in date rape is typically

Perceived Reasons for Returning to Abusive Relationships

Reasons	Mean rating
Give the abuser one more chance	10.0
Lack of financial resources	9.1
Emotional dependency on the abuser	9.0
Lack of housing resources	8.7
Lack of job opportunities	7.7
Denial of cycle of violence	7.6
Lack of support or follow-through by the legal system	7.6
Lack of child-care resources	7.1
Lack of transportation	6.7
Fear that the abuser will find her and do her harm	6.7
Lack of support from other family members	6.6
Fear that the abuser will get custody of the children	5.8
Fear that the abuser will kidnap the children	5.8
Children miss the absent parent	5.6
Lack of professional counseling	5.1
Fear that the abuser will harm the children	4.6

Figure 9.14

Perceived reasons for returning to abusive relationships. Shelters for battered wives generally report that the majority of their clients return to their partners. In one study (Johnson, Crowley, & Sigler, 1992), workers at ten shelters in Alabama were asked to rate the reasons that women returned to abusive relationships. The most frequently cited reasons are listed here in order of rated importance. As you can see, a variety of factors appear to propel women back into abusive relationships.

From Johnson, I. M., Crowley, J., & Sigler, R. T. (1992). Agency response to domestic violence: Services provided to battered women. In E. C. Viano (Ed.), *Intimate violence: Interdisciplinary perspectives* (pp. 191–202, Table on p. 199). Philadelphia: Taylor & Francis. Copyright © 1992 Hemisphere Publishing. Reprinted with permission of Taylor & Francis, Inc.

© AP Images/Ed Andriesky

The rape allegations against basketball star Kobe Bryant focused a great deal of attention on the problem of date rape, which is far more common than most people realize.

verbal or physical coercion, but sometimes it involves a weapon.

Incidence and Consequences

How common is date rape? It's much more common than widely realized. Research suggests that 13%–30% of women are likely to be victimized by date rape or attempted sexual coercion at some point in their lives (Abbey et al., 2004; Koss & Cook, 1993; Spitzberg, 1999). Most people naively assume that the vast majority of rapes are committed by strangers who leap from bushes or dark alleys to surprise their victims. In reality, research indicates that strangers are responsible for only a small minority of rapes and that over half of all rapes occur in the context of dating relationships (see **Figure 9.15** on the next page). Most rape victims are between the ages of 16 and 24 (Sampson, 2003).

How are women affected by date rape? All rape is traumatic, but it is particularly shattering for a woman to be raped by someone she has trusted. In the aftermath of date rape, women typically experience a variety of emotional reactions, including fear, anger, anxiety, self-blame, and guilt (Kahn & Andrioli Mathie, 1999). Many rape victims suffer from depression, symptoms of posttraumatic stress disorder, and increased risk for suicide (Foa, 1998; Slashinski, Coker, & Davis, 2003; Ullman, 2004). Negative reactions can be exacerbated if the woman's family and friends are not supportive—particularly if family or friends blame the victim for the attack. In addition to the trauma of the rape, women also have to cope with the possibilities of pregnancy and sexually transmitted disease (Golding, 1996). Moreover, if the rape survivor presses charges against her attacker, she may have to deal with difficult legal proceedings, negative publicity, and social stigma.

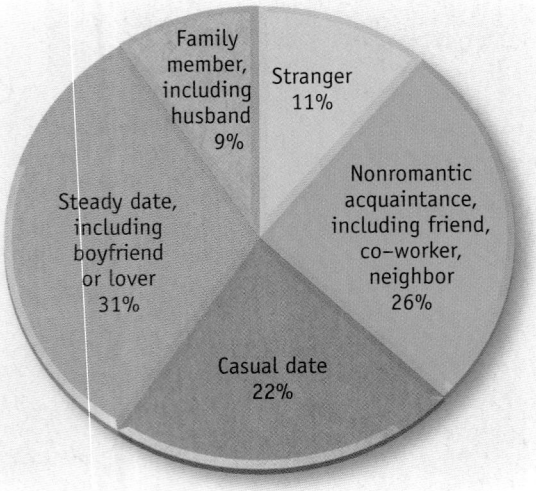

Figure 9.15

Rape victim–offender relationships. Based on a national survey of 3,187 college women, Mary Koss and her colleagues (1988) identified a sample of 468 women who indicated that they had been a victim of rape and who provided information on their relationship to the offender. Contrary to the prevailing stereotype, only a small minority (11%) had been raped by a stranger. As you can see, over half of rapes occur in the context of dating relationships. (Data based on Koss et al., 1988)

Contributing Factors

To understand the phenomenon of date rape, it's essential to know something about the factors that contribute to this behavior. It probably comes as no surprise to learn that alcohol contributes to about half of sexually aggressive incidents (Abbey et al., 2004; Sampson, 2003; Ward & Lundberg-Love, 2006). Alcohol impairs judgment and reduces inhibitions, making men more willing to use force. Drinking also undermines men's ability to interpret ambiguous social cues, making them more likely to overestimate their date's interest in sex. The more intoxicated perpetrators are, the more aggressive they tend to be (Abbey et al., 2003). Alcohol also increases women's vulnerability to sexual coercion. Drinking can cloud women's assessments of their risk and their ability to mount firm resistance or find a way to escape the situation.

Increasingly, so-called "date rape drugs" are a cause for concern (Pope & Shouldice, 2001; Ward & Lundberg-Love, 2006). Rohypnol ("roofies") and gamma hydroxybutyrate (GHB) are two drugs used to subdue dates. Although these drugs are colorless, odorless, and tasteless, their effects are anything but benign, and they can even be fatal. Victims typically pass out and have no recall of what happened while they were under the influence of the drug. To make it easier to spike a drink, predators typically look for individuals who are already intoxicated.

Gender differences in sexual standards also contribute to date rape. Society still encourages a double standard for males and females. Men are encouraged to have sexual feelings, to act on them, and to "score," whereas women are socialized to be coy about their sexual desires. This double standard can promote sexual aggression by men who come to view dating as a "battle of the sexes" in which they are supposed to persist in their pursuit of sexual conquests (Abbey et al., 2001a; Forbes, Adams-Curtis, & White, 2004; Sampson, 2003).

Many date rapes are the result of miscommunication (Lim & Roloff, 1999). Social norms encourage game playing as part of flirting, so dating partners may not always say what they mean or mean what they say. Whereas the majority of women say "no" and mean it, some women may say "no" to sexual activity when they actually mean "maybe" or "yes." Studies surveying the extent of token resistance among college women report that approximately 38% of them have acted this way (Muehlenhard & McCoy, 1991; Shotland & Hunter, 1995). Unfortunately, this behavior can backfire. For some men, it can cloud the issue of whether a woman has consented to sex (Osman, 2003).

In terms of personal characteristics, males who engage in sexual aggression tend to be relatively impulsive, low in empathy, hostile toward women, and heavy drinkers (Abbey et al., 2001b, 2004). They tend to endorse traditional gender stereotypes about male dominance and to have had more (consensual) sex partners than their age-mates. They also tend to have poor anger management skills (Lundeberg et al., 2004).

A variety of situational factors influence the likelihood of date rape. Sexual assault is more likely (1) the more the man knows the woman, (2) the more isolated the setting they are in, (3) the more they have had some consensual sexual activity previously, and (4) the longer the man has misperceived the woman's sexual interest (Abbey et al., 2001a). These factors can contribute to a man feeling that his date owes him sex because he has been "led on." He may then use his anger as an excuse to force the woman to have sex.

Reducing the Incidence of Date Rape

What can women do to reduce the likelihood of being victimized by date rape? Here are some suggestions: (1) Recognize date rape for what it is: an act of sexual aggression. (2) Become familiar with the characteristics of men who are likely to engage in date rape (see **Figure 9.16**) and be cautious about dating men who exhibit these traits. (3) Beware of excessive alcohol and drug use, which may undermine self-control and self-

Characteristics of Date Rapists			
Sexual entitlement	**Power and control**	**Hostility and anger**	**Acceptance of interpersonal violence**
Touching women with no regard for their wishes	Interrupting people, especially women	Showing a quick temper	Using threats in displays of anger
Sexualizing relationships that are appropriately not sexual	Being a bad loser	Blaming others when things go wrong	Using violence in borderline situations
Engaging in conversation that is inappropriately intimate	Exhibiting inappropriate competitiveness	Tending to transform other emotions into anger	Approving observed violence
Telling sexual jokes at inappropriate times or places	Using intimidating body language		Justifying violence
Making inappropriate comments about women's bodies, sexuality, and so on	Game playing		

Figure 9.16

Date rapists: Warning signs. According to Rozee, Bateman, and Gilmore (1991), four factors appear to distinguish date rapists: feelings of sexual entitlement, a penchant for exerting power and control, high hostility and anger, and acceptance of interpersonal violence. The presence of more than one of these characteristics is an important warning sign. When sexual entitlement is coupled with any other factor, special heed should be taken.

determination in sexual interactions. (4) When dating someone new, agree to go only to public places and always carry enough money for transportation back home. (5) Communicate feelings and expectations about sex by engaging in appropriate self-disclosure. (6) Finally, be prepared to act *aggressively* if assertive refusals fail to stop unwanted advances.

Although most of us would prefer not to think about this darker side of relationships, intimate violence is a reality we can ill-afford to ignore. It deeply touches the lives of millions of individuals. We can only hope that increased public awareness of intimate violence will help reduce its incidence and its tragic effects.

KEY IDEAS

Challenges to the Traditional Model of Marriage

▶ The traditional model of marriage is being challenged by the increasing acceptability of singlehood, the increasing popularity of cohabitation, the reduced premium on permanence, changes in gender roles, the increasing prevalence of voluntary childlessness, and the decline of the traditional nuclear family. Nonetheless, marriage remains quite popular.

Moving Toward Marriage

▶ A multitude of factors influence an individual's motivation to marry. The norm for our society is to select a mate and engage in a monogamous marriage. Mate selection is influenced by endogamy, homogamy, and gender. Women place more emphasis on potential partners' ambition and financial prospects, whereas men are more interested in a partner's youthfulness and physical attractiveness.

▶ According to Murstein, the process of mate selection goes through three stages, which emphasize the stimulus value of the potential partner, value compatibility, and adequacy of role enactments. There are some premarital predictors of marital success, such as family background, age, length of courtship, and personality, but the relations are weak. The nature of a couple's premarital interactions is a better predictor of marital adjustment.

Marital Adjustment Across the Family Life Cycle

▶ The family life cycle is an orderly sequence of developmental stages that families tend to progress through. Newly married couples tend to be very happy before the arrival of children. Today more couples are struggling with the decision about whether to have children. The arrival of children is a major transition that is handled best by parents who have realistic expectations about the difficulties inherent in raising a family.

▶ As children reach adolescence, parents should expect more conflict as their influence declines. They must learn to relate to their children as adults and help launch them into the adult world. Most parents no longer struggle with the empty nest syndrome. Adult children returning home may be more of a problem.

Vulnerable Areas in Marital Adjustment

▶ Gaps in expectations about marital roles may create marital stress. Disparities in expectations about gender roles and the distribution of housework may be especially common and problematic. Work concerns can clearly spill over to influence marital functioning, but the links between parents' employment and marital adjustment are complex.

▶ Wealth does not ensure marital happiness, but a lack of money can produce marital problems. Inadequate communication is a commonly reported marital problem, which is predictive of divorce.

Divorce

▶ Divorce rates have increased dramatically in recent decades, but they appear to be stabilizing. Deciding on a divorce tends to be a gradual process marred by indecision. Unpleasant as divorce may be, the evidence suggests that toughing it out in an unhappy marriage can often be worse.

▶ Wallerstein's research suggests that divorce tends to have extremely negative effects on children. Hetherington's research suggests that most children recover from divorce after a few years. The effects of divorce on children vary, but negative effects can be long-lasting.

▶ A substantial majority of divorced people remarry. These second marriages have a somewhat lower probability of success than first marriages.

Alternatives to Marriage

▶ An increasing proportion of the young population are remaining single, but this fact does not mean that people are turning away from marriage. Although singles generally have the same adjustment problems as married couples, evidence suggests that singles tend to be somewhat less happy and less healthy.

▶ The prevalence of cohabitation has increased dramatically. Logically, one might expect cohabitation to facilitate marital success, but research has consistently found an association between cohabitation and marital instability.

▶ Gay relationships develop in a starkly different social context than marital relationships. Nonetheless, studies have found that heterosexual and homosexual couples are similar in many ways. Gay relationships are characterized by great diversity. It is not true that gay couples usually assume traditional masculine and feminine roles, nor is it true that gays rarely get involved in long-term intimate relationships or family relations.

Application: Understanding Intimate Violence

▶ Research suggests that about 25% of women and 7% of men have been victims of partner abuse. Women are the principal victims of serious, dangerous abuse. Men who batter their partners are diverse, but control is often the central issue. Women stay in abusive relationships for a variety of compelling, practical reasons, including economic realities.

▶ Over half of rapes are committed in the context of dating. Estimates suggest that the chances of a woman being victimized by date rape at some time in her life range from 13% to 30%. Rape is a traumatic experience that has many serious consequences. Alcohol, drug use, and gender-based sexual standards all contribute to date rape. Miscommunication revolving around token resistance is particularly problematic.

KEY TERMS

Battering p. 295
Cohabitation p. 269
Date rape p. 296
Endogamy p. 272
Family life cycle p. 275
Homogamy p. 272
Homophobia p. 293
Intimate violence p. 295
Marriage p. 269
Monogamy p. 271
Polygamy p. 271

KEY PEOPLE

John Gottman pp. 283–284
E. Mavis Hetherington p. 288
Bernard Murstein p. 273
Judith Wallerstein p. 288

PRACTICE TEST

1. Which of the following is *not* one of the social trends that are undermining the traditional model of marriage?
   a. Increased acceptance of singlehood
   b. Increased voluntary childlessness
   c. Increased acceptance of cohabitation
   d. Increased premium on permanence in marriage

2. Endogamy refers to:
   a. the tendency to marry within one's social group.
   b. the tendency to marry someone with similar characteristics.
   c. the final marriage in serial monogamy.
   d. norms that promote marriage outside one's social unit.

3. Based on trends in the data, which of the following couples has the greatest likelihood of marital success?
   a. Stephanie and Barry whose parents are divorced.
   b. Jessica and Carlos who are both perfectionists.
   c. Gwen and Aaron who had a long courtship.
   d. Carla and Turk who married at a very young age.

4. The transition to parenthood tends to be easier when:
   a. the newborn child was planned for.
   b. the parents have realistic expectations.
   c. the new parents are relatively young.
   d. the father is not heavily involved in child care.

5. Which of the following characteristics in young children is related to maternal employment?
   a. increased hyperactivity
   b. higher anxiety
   c. decreased cognitive skills
   d. increased prosocial behavior

6. When financial resources are plentiful in a marriage, arguments about money:
   a. may still be a problem.
   b. don't occur.
   c. are a big problem only if the wife earns more than her husband.
   d. are unrelated to marital satisfaction.

7. The evidence suggests that the negative effects of divorce on former spouses' *psychological* adjustment are:
   a. exaggerated for both sexes.
   b. greater for men than women.
   c. greater for women than men.
   d. about the same for men and women.

8. What is the most probable reason for the increase in the proportion of young people who are single?
   a. Loss of faith in the institution of marriage
   b. Increased individualism and declining collectivism
   c. The median age at which people get married has increased
   d. An increase in the number of young people unwilling to undertake the financial burdens of marriage and family

9. Research on cohabitation indicates that:
   a. most cohabitants are just not interested in marriage.
   b. most cohabitants would eventually like to marry.
   c. cohabitation is declining.
   d. cohabitation experience improves the chances that one's marriage will be successful.

10. Which of the following has been supported by research on intimate relationships among gay men and lesbians?
   a. Gay couples adopt traditional male/female gender roles.
   b. Gays rarely become involved in long-term relationships.
   c. Gays have impoverished family relations.
   d. Gays want the same things out of intimate relationships that heterosexuals want.

Book Companion Website

Visit the Book Companion Website at **academic.cengage.com/psychology/weiten,** where you will find tutorial quizzes, flash cards, and web links for every chapter, a final exam, and more! You can also link to the Psychology Resource Center (accessible directly at **academic.cengage.com/login**) for a range of psychology-related resources.

Personal Explorations Workbook

The following exercises in your *Personal Explorations Workbook* may enhance your self-understanding in relation to issues raised in this chapter. **Questionnaire 9.1:** Self-Report Jeaelousy Scale. **Personal Probe 9.1:** How Do Behave in Intimate Relationships? **Personal Probe 9.2:** Thinking About Your Attitudes About Marriage and Cohabitations.

ANSWERS

1. d Pages 269–270
2. a Page 272
3. c Pages 273–274
4. b Pages 276–277
5. d Page 282
6. a Pages 282–283
7. d Page 287
8. c Page 290
9. b Page 291
10. d Pages 293–294

CHAPTER 10

Gender and Behavior

On January 14, 2005, Harvard University President Lawrence H. Summers spoke at a conference of the National Bureau of Economic Research about Harvard's policies regarding diversity. Dr. Summers focused his remarks on the issue of women's underrepresentation in tenured positions in science and engineering at top universities. He offered three broad hypotheses about this gender disparity. The one that attracted the most media attention was what he called "different availability of aptitude at the high end." While he acknowledged that there are differences in socialization and patterns of discrimination between men and women, he ranked innate gender differences in mathematical and scientific ability as having greater "importance" in explaining the disparity. Dr. Summers based much of his argument on standardized tests, even though, in his own words, "These tests are not a very good measure and are not highly predictive with respect to people's ability." He went on to say, "Because if my reading of the data is right—it's something people can argue about—that there are some systematic differences in variability in different populations. . . . So my sense is that the unfortunate truth—I would far prefer to believe something else, because it would be easier to address what is surely a serious social problem if something else were true—is that the combination of the [expectations for high-powered jobs] and the differing variances probably explains a fair amount of this problem" (Harvard Crimson, 2005).

GENDER STEREOTYPES

GENDER SIMILARITIES AND DIFFERENCES
Cognitive Abilities
Personality Traits and Social Behavior
Psychological Disorders
Putting Gender Differences in Perspective

BIOLOGICAL ORIGINS OF GENDER DIFFERENCES
Evolutionary Explanations
Brain Organization
Hormonal Influences

ENVIRONMENTAL ORIGINS OF GENDER DIFFERENCES
Processes in Gender-Role Socialization
Sources of Gender-Role Socialization

GENDER-ROLE EXPECTATIONS
Role Expectations for Males
Problems with the Male Role
Role Expectations for Females
Problems with the Female Role

LIVING IN TODAY'S WORLD *Gender Stereotypes and "Appearance Pressure"*
Sexism: A Special Problem for Females

GENDER IN THE PAST AND IN THE FUTURE
Why Are Gender Roles Changing?
Alternatives to Traditional Gender Roles

APPLICATION: BRIDGING THE GENDER GAP IN COMMUNICATION
The Clash of Two "Cultures"
Instrumental and Expressive Styles
Common Mixed-Gender Communication Problems
Toward a "Shared Language"

REVIEW

PRACTICE TEST

As you may recall, Lawrence Summers' remarks on this issue sparked a contentious debate among academics, scientists, and the public. The war of words lingered for months and eventually led to Summers' resignation as President of Harvard. This scenario demonstrates in a highly compelling way that gender research is relevant, important, and frequently controversial. Obviously, psychologists have a lot to offer in this area, and gender has been examined for many decades and from various perspectives. In this chapter, we explore some intriguing and controversial questions: Are there genuine behavioral and cognitive differences between males and females? If so, what are their origins? Are traditional gender-role expectations healthy or unhealthy? Why are gender roles in our society changing, and what does the future hold? After addressing those questions, in the Application we explore gender and communication styles.

Gender Stereotypes

LEARNING OBJECTIVES

- *Distinguish between sex and gender.*
- *Explain the nature of gender stereotypes and their connection with instrumentality and expressiveness.*
- *Discuss four important points about gender stereotypes.*
- *Describe androcentrism.*

Let's begin by clarifying some terms. Some scholars prefer to use the term *gender* to refer to male-female differences that are learned and *sex* to designate biologically based differences between males and females. However, as respected authority Janet Shibley Hyde (2004) points out, making this sharp distinction between sex and gender fails to recognize that biology and culture interact. Following this reasoning, we'll use ***gender* to mean the state of being male or female.** (When we use the term *sex*, we're referring to sexual behavior.) It's important to note that, as *we* use the term, *gender* says nothing about the *causes* of behavior. In other words, if we say that there are gender differences in aggressive behavior, we are simply stating that males and females differ in this area. This behavioral disparity might be caused by biological factors, by environmental factors, or by both. **Figure 10.1** sorts out a number of gender-related terms that we will use in our discussions.

Courtesy, Janet Shibley Hyde

Janet Shibley Hyde

Gender-Related Concepts

Term	Definition
Gender	The state of being male or female
Gender identity	An individual's perception of himself or herself as male or female
Gender stereotypes	Widely held and often inaccurate beliefs about males' and females' abilities, personality traits, and social behavior
Gender differences	Actual disparities in behavior between males and females, based on research observations
Gender roles	Culturally defined expectations about appropriate behavior for males and females
Gender-role identity	A person's identification with the traits regarded as masculine or feminine (one's sense of being masculine or feminine)
Sexual orientation	A person's preference for sexual partners of the other gender (heterosexual), the same gender (homosexual), or both genders (bisexual)

Figure 10.1

Terminology related to gender. The topic of gender involves many closely related ideas that are easily confused. The gender-related concepts introduced in this chapter are summarized here for easy comparison.

Obviously, males and females differ biologically—in their genitals and other aspects of anatomy, and in their physiological functioning. These readily apparent physical disparities between males and females lead people to expect other differences as well. Recall from Chapter 6 that *stereotypes* are widely held beliefs that people possess certain characteristics simply because of their membership in a particular group. Thus, ***gender stereotypes* are widely shared beliefs about males' and females' abilities, personality traits, and social behavior.** Research finds that beliefs about the typical attributes characteristic of men and women are widely shared (Desert & Leyens, 2006). For example, a survey of gender stereotypes in 25 countries revealed considerable similarity of views (Williams & Best, 1990; Williams, Satterwhite, & Best, 1999). Because of the widespread gains in educational and occupational attainment by American women since the 1970s, you might expect to find changes in contemporary gender stereotypes for both genders. However, gender stereotypes in this country have remained largely stable since the early 1970s, especially those for men (Diekman & Eagly, 2000; Spence & Buckner, 2000).

Gender stereotypes are too numerous to summarize here. Instead, you can examine **Figure 10.2**, which lists a number of characteristics people commonly link with femininity and masculinity. Note that the stereotyped attributes for males generally reflect the quality of ***instrumentality*, an orientation toward action and accomplishment,** whereas the stereotypes for females reflect the quality of ***expressiveness*, an orientation toward emotion and relationships** (Eagly, Wood, & Diekman, 2000; Parsons & Bales, 1955). There is considerable evidence that in the United States gender is a status characteristic, with higher overall status and competence being associated with masculinity (Ridgeway & Bourg, 2004).

Elements of Traditional Gender Stereotypes

Masculine	Feminine
Active	Aware of others' feelings
Adventurous	Considerate
Aggressive	Creative
Ambitious	Cries easily
Competitive	Devotes self to others
Dominant	Emotional
Independent	Enjoys art and music
Leadership qualities	Excitable in a crisis
Likes math and science	Expresses tender feelings
Makes decisions easily	Feelings hurt easily
Mechanical aptitude	Gentle
Not easily influenced	Home oriented
Outspoken	Kind
Persistent	Likes children
Self-confident	Neat
Skilled in business	Needs approval
Stands up under pressure	Tactful
Takes a stand	Understanding

Figure 10.2

Traditional gender stereotypes. Gender stereotypes are widely known and relate to many diverse aspects of psychological functioning. This is a partial list of the characteristics that college students associate with a typical man and a typical woman. Gender stereotypes have remained remarkably stable in spite of all the changes in modern societies in recent decades relating to gender issues.

Adapted from Ruble, T. L. (1983). Sex stereotypes: Issues of change in the 70s. *Sex Roles, 9,* 397–402. Copyright © 1983 Plenum Publishing Co. Adapted by permission of Springer Science and Business Media and the author.

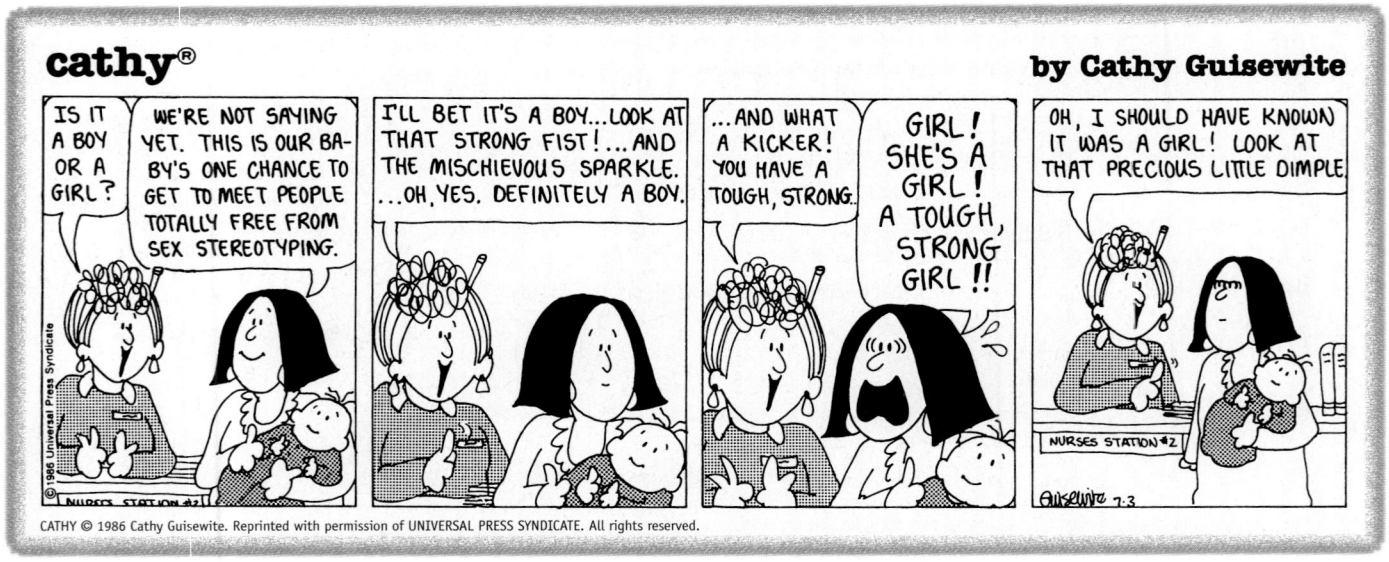

CATHY © 1986 Cathy Guisewite. Reprinted with permission of UNIVERSAL PRESS SYNDICATE. All rights reserved.

Six Chix © by Isabella Bannerman, Margaret Shulock, Rina Piccolo, Ann C. Teinaes, Kathryn LeMieux and Stephanie Piro. Reprinted by permission of King Features Syndicate.

When it comes to stereotypes, there are some important points to keep in mind. First, despite the general agreement on a number of gender stereotypes, variability also occurs (Williams & Best, 1990, Best & Thomas, 2004). The characteristics in **Figure 10.2** represent the prototypic American male or female: white, middle-class, heterosexual, and Christian. But it is obvious that not everyone fits this set of characteristics. For example, the stereotypes for African American males and females are more similar on the dimensions of competence and expressiveness than those for white American males and females (Kane, 2000). Also, the stereotypes of white and Hispanic women are more positive than those for African American women (Niemann et al., 1994).

A second point about gender stereotypes is that since the 1980s, the boundaries between male and female stereotypes have become less rigid (Deaux & Lewis, 1983, 1984). Earlier, the male and female stereotypes were seen as separate and distinct categories (for example, men are strong and women are weak). Now it seems that people perceive gender as a continuum as opposed to a dichotomy (Beall, Eagly, & Sternberg, 2004).

A third consideration is that the traditional male stereotype is more complimentary than the conventional female stereotype. This fact is related to ***androcentrism,* or the belief that the male is the norm** (Bem, 1993). In other words, our society is organized in a way that favors "masculine" characteristics and assumes maleness to be the norm. **Figure 10.3** provides some examples of how androcentrism can be manifested in the workplace. Ironically, this bias is evident even in the psychological science of gender. Hegarty and Buechel (2006) examined 388 articles on gender differences from journals published by the American Psychological Association and found evidence of androcentric reporting. Specifically, gender differences were reported in terms of *women* being different, as opposed to men. The implicit assumption, then, is that men are the norm from which women deviate. Look for evidence of this bias as you read about studies in this chapter.

Finally, keep in mind what you learned about stereotypes in Chapter 6: They can bias your perceptions and expectations of others as well as your interactions. Now, let's shift from gender stereotypes to what males and females are actually like. Keep in mind that our discussion focuses on modern Western societies; the story may be different in other cultures.

Web Link 10.1 **Women's Studies Database**

Established in 1992, this database at the University of Maryland has been recognized as one of the premier Internet guides to issues related to women's and gender studies.

Androcentrism in the Workplace

He's good on details.	She's picky.
He follows through.	She doesn't know when to quit.
He's assertive.	She's pushy.
He stands firm.	She's rigid.
He's a man of the world.	She's been around.
He's not afraid to say what he thinks.	She's outspoken.
He's close-mouthed.	She's secretive.
He exercises authority.	She's controlling.
He climbed the ladder of success.	She slept her way to the top.
He's a stern taskmaster.	She's difficult to work for.

Figure 10.3

Male bias on the job. In the world of work, women who exhibit traditional "masculine" characteristics are often perceived negatively. Thus, a man and a woman may display essentially the same behavior but elicit very different reactions.

Gender Similarities and Differences

LEARNING OBJECTIVES

- *Explain how meta-analyses have helped researchers who study gender.*
- *Describe the gender similarity hypothesis.*
- *Summarize the research findings on gender similarities and differences in verbal, mathematical, and spatial abilities.*
- *Summarize the research on gender similarities and differences in personality and social behavior.*
- *Summarize the research on gender and psychological disorders.*
- *Summarize the situation regarding overall similarities and differences between males and females.*
- *Give two explanations for why gender differences appear larger than they actually are.*

Are men more aggressive than women? Do more women than men suffer from depression? Hundreds of studies have attempted to answer these and related questions about gender and behavior. Moreover, new evidence is pouring in constantly, and many researchers report conflicting findings. To add to the confusion, gender differences are not clear cut; they are complex and subtle. It is an oversimplification, for instance, to say that women are verbal and men are spatial (Spelke, 2005).

Thus, it is almost an overwhelming task to keep up with the research in this area. Thankfully, a statistical technique called meta-analysis helps us to clarify this body of research. ***Meta-analysis* combines the statistical results of many studies of the same question, yielding an estimate of the size and consistency of a variable's effects.** This approach allows a researcher to assess the overall trends across all the previous studies of how gender is related to, say, math abilities or conformity. Meta-analysis has been a great boon to researchers, and quite a few meta-analyses on gender differences have now been conducted.

Keep in mind that many researchers disagree about gender differences and similarities. Janet Shibley Hyde has recently proposed the *gender similarities hypothesis.* Based on the results of over 46 meta-analyses, Hyde (2005) notes that that men and women are similar on most psychological variables and that most of the time when researchers report a difference, it is quite small. She further asserts that overinflated claims of gender differences have costs associated with them for the workplace and relationships. Critics of this hypothesis argue that Hyde omitted several important variables from her review and that methodological limitations led her to underestimate true gender differences (Davies & Shackelford, 2006; Lippa, 2006). It will be interesting to see where this dispute leads over the next several years.

In addition, there is much debate as to whether gender differences are largely attributable to environmental factors, as opposed to biological factors, and there is evidence on both sides of the question (Halpern, 2000; Hyde, Fennema, & Lamon, 1990; Nowell & Hedges, 1998). We'll examine the possible causes of these differences after we examine gender comparisons. First, let's thread our way through the available research in three areas: cognitive abilities, personality traits and social behavior, and psychological disorders.

Cognitive Abilities

Perhaps we should first point out that gender differences have *not* been found in *overall* intelligence. Of course, this fact shouldn't be surprising, because intelligence tests are intentionally designed to minimize differences between the scores of males and females. But what about gender differences in *specific* cognitive skills? Let's start with verbal abilities.

Verbal Abilities

Verbal abilities include a number of distinct skills, such as vocabulary, reading, writing, spelling, and grammar abilities. Girls and women generally have the edge in the verbal area, although the gender differences are small (Halpern, 2000; Hyde & Kling, 2001; Weiss et al., 2003). Among the findings worth noting are the fact that girls usually start speaking a little earlier, have larger vocabularies and better reading scores in grade school, and are more verbally fluent (on tests of writing, for instance). Boys seem to fare better on verbal analogies. However, they are three to four times more likely to be stutterers (Skinner & Shelton, 1985) and five to ten times more likely than girls to be dyslexic (Vandenberg, 1987). It is important to remember that while gender differences in verbal abilities generally favor females, these differences are small. The ovelap between males and females in verbal abilities is much greater than the gap (Weiss et al., 2003).

Mathematical Abilities

Researchers have also looked at gender differences in *mathematical abilities,* including performing computations and solving word and story problems. Meta-analyses of mathematical abilities show small gender differences favoring males (Hedges & Nowell, 1995; Hyde et al., 1990; Nowell & Hedges, 1998). Interestingly, research shows no such differences in the elementary school years (Aunola et al., 2004). Further, differences favoring males appear for European Americans but not for African Americans, Hispanic Americans, or Asian Americans (Hyde, 1994b); and in Canada, gender differences in mathematical abilities are less pronounced (Randhawa & Hunter, 2001).

Thus, the current view is that gender differences in mathematical abilities in the general population are essentially nil. However, this conclusion has a few exceptions. In mathematical *problem solving,* boys start to slightly outperform girls when they reach high school. This difference is attributable in part to the fact that boys take more high school math courses (Halpern, 2000). Still, because problem-solving ability is essential for success in scientific courses and careers (arenas currently underpopulated by women), this finding is a concern. Males also outperform females at the high end of the mathematical ability distribution (Dweck, 2007). For instance, when gifted seventh- and eighth-graders take the math subtest of the SAT, boys outnumber girls 17 to 1 in the group scoring over 700 (Benbow, 1988). Overall, when all students are compared, gender differences in mathematical ability are small but favor males.

Spatial Abilities

In the cognitive area, the most compelling evidence for gender differences is in *spatial abilities,* which include perceiving and mentally manipulating shapes and figures. Males typically outperform females in most spatial abilities, and gender differences favoring males are consistently found in the ability to perform mental rotations of a figure in three dimensions—a skill important in occupations such as engineering, chemistry, and the building trades (see **Figure 10.4**). This gender gap in the ability to handle mental rotations is relatively large and has been found repeatedly (Halpern, 2000, 2004;Voyer & Hou, 2006). However, experience and training can improve mental rotation in both girls and boys (Sanz de Acedo & Garcia Ganuza, 2003).

Web Link 10.2 **Voice of the Shuttle: Gender Studies**

The VOS maintains one of the broadest databases of web resources across many topics. The multiple links cited here cover the spectrum of gender-related issues from women's and men's studies to gay and lesbian identity resources.

Personality Traits and Social Behavior

Turning to personality and social behavior, let's examine those factors for which gender differences are reasonably well documented.

Self-Esteem

As we noted in Chapter 5, females typically score lower than males on tests of self-esteem, but the difference in scores is generally small, and Hyde (2005) argues that this difference has been exaggerated in the popular press. For example, a meta-analysis of several hundred studies that included respondents from 7 to 60 years of age found only a small difference in self-esteem that favored males (Kling et al., 1999). The authors found no support for claims that girls' self-esteem drops dramatically during adolescence (Brody, 1997; Orenstein, 1994). A second meta-analysis also reported only a small overall gender difference favoring males (Major et al., 1999). Recent research finds that women who have

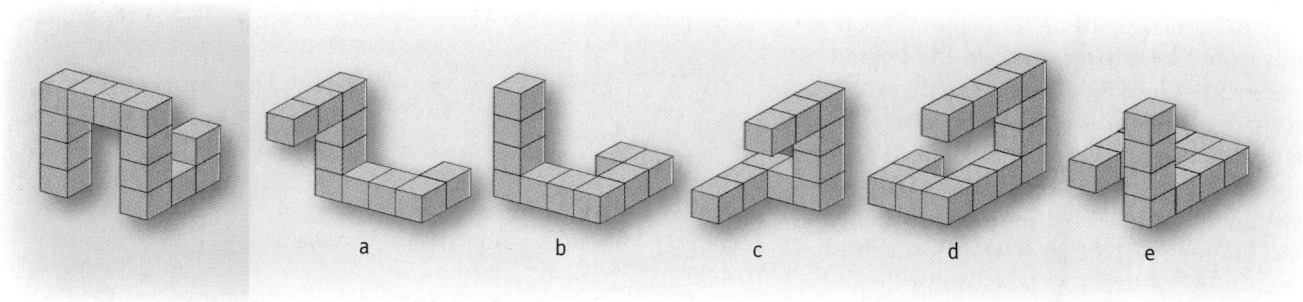

Figure 10.4

Mental rotation test. If you mentally rotate the figure on the left, which of the five figures on the right would match it? The answer is "d." This problem illustrates how spatial rotation skills are measured. Researchers have uncovered some interesting gender differences in the ability to mentally rotate figures in space.

Adapted from Shepard, R. N., & Metzler, J. N. (1971). Mental rotation of three-dimensional objects. *Science, 171,* 701–703. Copyright © 1971 by American Association for the Advancement of Science. Adapted by permission of the publisher and author.

lower levels of self-esteem at age 18 show faster increases in self-esteem than men by age 25 (Galambos, Barker, & Krahn, 2006).

As with other gender differences, the findings on self-esteem are complex and are influenced by context. For instance, socioeconomic status and ethnicity mediate gender differences in self-esteem (Major et al., 1999; Twenge & Crocker, 2002). Relatively large gender differences in self-esteem are found for lower- and middle-class males and females but not for upper-class males and females. Research consistently reports self-esteem differences between white men and women, but findings are mixed for other ethnic groups (Major et al., 1999; Twenge and Crocker, 2002).

Aggression

***Aggression* involves behavior that is intended to hurt someone, either physically or verbally** (see Chapter 4). Gender differences in aggression vary depending on the form aggression takes. A recent summary of cross-cultural meta-analyses reported that males consistently engage in more *physical aggression* than females (Archer, 2005). In the area of *verbal aggression* (insults, threats of harm), the findings are inconsistent (Geen, 1998; Harris, 1996). When it comes to *relational aggression,* such as giving someone the "silent treatment" to get one's way, talking behind another's back, or trying to get others to dislike someone, females are rated higher (Archer, 2005; Coyne, Archer, & Eslea, 2006). Experts believe that the higher rates of relational aggression among girls and women result from the importance that females attach to close relationships (Crick, Casas, & Nelson, 2002).

Indirect aggression overlaps to some degree with relational aggression; it involves covert behaviors in which the target is not directly confronted—spreading rumors, for instance. In a study of 8-, 11-, and 15-year-olds from Finland, Israel, Italy, and Poland, researchers looked at gender differences in three types of aggression: physical, verbal, and indirect (Oesterman et al., 1998). Across nations, boys were equally likely to use physical and verbal aggression and less likely to use indirect aggression. Girls most often used indirect aggression, followed by verbal aggression, then physical aggression. Even in a controlled laboratory setting where male and female participants are exposed to the same aggression-evoking stimulus, women are more likely than men to aggress indirectly (Hess & Hagen, 2006).

However, when you consider extreme forms of aggression, there is no getting around the fact that men commit a grossly disproportionate share of violent crimes. The U.S. Department of Justice (2007) reports that only 7% of all federal inmates are women and, based on self-reports of victims, women make up 14% of violent offenders. Further, the lifetime chances of going to prison are much higher for men (11.3%) than for women (1.8%). **Figure 10.5** shows the stark gender differences in such crimes as assault, armed robbery, rape, and homicide.

Sexual Attitudes and Behavior

In the sexual domain, meta-analyses have found men to have more permissive attitudes than women about casual, premarital, and extramarital sex (Hyde & Oliver, 2000; Oliver & Hyde, 1993). Again, it's important to note that the analyses have also revealed many similarities between men and women—for example, both men and women are somewhat negative toward sexual permissiveness. In a sample of 168 heterosexual adults, Yost and Zurbriggen (2006) found that for both men and women, the endorsement of casual sex was associated with earlier sexual experiences, a greater number of sexual partners, and more frequent sexual activity. For men only, this endorsement was also associated with acceptance of rape myths and conservative attitudes toward women, while for women it was associated with sexual fantasies of dominance and lower levels of sexual conservatism. Researchers also report that males are more sexually active and more likely to engage in masturbation than females (Hyde & Oliver, 2000).

In a summary of gender differences in sexuality, Letitia Anne Peplau (2003) reported four key differences that hold for both gays and straights. First, men

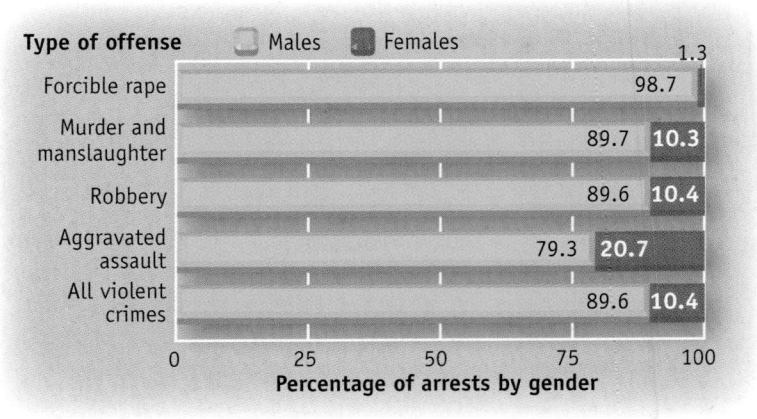

Figure 10.5

Gender differences in violent crimes. Males are arrested for violent crimes far more often than females, as these statistics show. These data support the findings of laboratory studies indicating that males are more physically aggressive than females. (Data from U.S. Department of Justice, 2003) have more interest in sex than women (they think about sex more often and prefer to have sex more often, for example). Second, the connection between sex and intimacy is more important for women than for men (women typically prefer sex in the context of a relationship). Third, aggression is more often linked to sexuality for men than for women (men engage in coercive sex much more often). Finally, women's sexuality is more easily shaped by cultural and situational factors (their sexual attitudes are easier to change, for instance).

Emotional Expression

Conventional wisdom holds that women are more "emotional" than men. Does research support this belief? If by being "emotional," we mean outwardly displaying one's emotions, the answer is yes. A number of studies have found that women express more emotion than men (Ashmore, 1990; Brody & Hall, 1993). Gender differences "favoring" women have been found on such emotions as sadness, disgust, fear, surprise, happiness, and anger. Similarly, women are better than men at recognizing emotions in others based on facial expressions or other nonverbal cues (Hampson, van Anders, & Mullin, 2006).

Do women actually *experience* more emotion? To answer this question, Ann Kring and Albert Gordon (1998) had college students view films selected to evoke sadness, happiness, and fear. The researchers videotaped the participants' facial expressions and asked the subjects to describe their emotional experiences. As expected, they found gender differences in the facial expression of emotion (see **Figure 10.6**). However, they failed to find any gender differences in *experienced* emotions. Thus, gender differences in emotional functioning may be limited to the outward expression of feelings and could stem from the different display rules parents teach their sons and daughters (DeAngelis, 2001).

Communication

Popular stereotypes have it that females are much more talkative than males. In fact, the opposite seems to be true: Men talk more than women (Gleason & Ely, 2002). Men also tend to interrupt women more than women interrupt men, although this difference is small (Eckert & McConnell-Ginet, 2003). Yet when women have more power in work or personal relationships, women interrupt more (Aries, 1998). Thus, this supposed gender difference is probably better seen as a status difference.

Most studies have found that women speak more tentatively ("I may be wrong, but") than men (Carli & Bukatko, 2000). One explanation attributes women's greater use of tentative and polite language to lower status; another, to gender-specific socialization (Athenstadt, Haas, & Schwab, 2004). For more on gender and communication, see this chapter's Application.

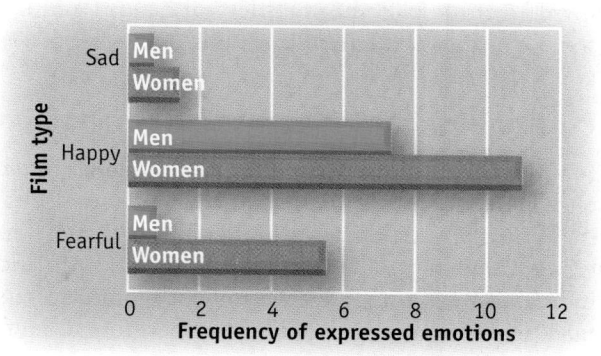

Figure 10.6

Gender differences in emotional expression. Researchers calculated how often men and women showed facial expressions of various emotions as they viewed films. Women were judged to be more emotionally expressive than men on all three emotions studied. However, men and women did not differ significantly in their reports of *experienced* emotion.

Adapted from Kring, A. M., & Gordon, A. H. (1998). Sex differences in emotions: Expression, experience and physiology. *Journal of Personality and Social Psychology, 74,* 686–703. Copyright © 1998 by the American Psychological Association. Adapted by permission of the publisher and author.

Psychological Disorders

In terms of the *overall* incidence of mental disorders, only minimal gender differences have been found. When researchers assess the prevalence of *specific* disorders, however, they do find some rather consistent gender differences (Klose & Jacobi, 2004; Nolen-Hoeksema & Keita, 2003). Antisocial behavior, alcoholism, and other drug-related disorders are far more prevalent among men than among women. On the other hand, women are about twice as likely as men to suffer from depression and anxiety disorders (phobias, for example). Even when comparing opposite-sex fraternal twins, females have a higher rate of mood disorders than males (Kendler, Myers, & Prescott, 2005).

Females also show higher rates of eating disorders (see the Chapter 15 Application). In addition, women *attempt* suicide more often than men, but men *complete* suicides (actually kill themselves) more frequently than women (Maris, Berman, & Silverman, 2001).

In Chapter 3, we discussed posttraumatic stress disorder (PTSD). In a meta-analysis including 290 studies over the past two decades, Tolin and Foa (2006) found that females are more likely than males to develop PTSD, even when the traumatic events are the same. Other researchers posit that this difference is attributable to females' typically experiencing trauma at a younger age than males, perceptions of threat and loss, insufficient social support networks, and gender-specific biological reactions to trauma (Olff et al., 2007).

Putting Gender Differences in Perspective

It pays to be cautious when interpreting gender differences. Although research has uncovered some genuine differences in behavior, remember that these are *group* differences. That is, they tell us nothing about individuals. Essentially, we are comparing the "average man" with the "average woman." Furthermore, as Hyde (2005) argues, the differences between these groups are usually relatively small. **Figure 10.7** shows how scores on a trait might be distributed for men and women. Although the group averages are detectably different, you can see that there is great variability within each group (gender) and huge overlap between the two group distributions. *Ultimately, the similarities between women and men greatly outweigh the differences.* Thus, a gender difference that shows up on the average does not by itself tell us anything about you or any other unique individual.

A second essential point is that gender accounts for only a minute proportion of the differences between individuals. Using complicated statistical procedures, it is possible to gauge the influence of gender (or other factors) on behavior. These tests show that gender accounts for a very small amount of the variation among people. Thus, factors other than gender (for example, the social context in which behavior occurs) are far more important determinants of differences between individuals (Yoder & Kahn, 2003).

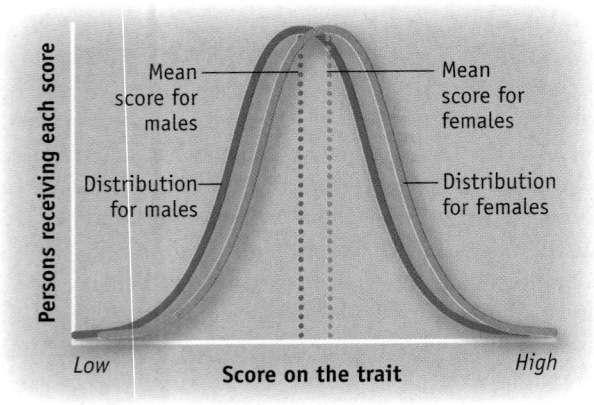

Figure 10.7

The nature of group differences. Gender differences are group differences that tell us little about individuals because of the great overlap between the groups. For a given trait, one gender may score higher on the average, but there is far more variation within each gender than between the genders.

Another point to keep in mind is that when gender differences are found, they do not mean that one gender is better than the other (Halpern, 2004). When certain qualities are deemed superior to others by a particular society or group, the tendency is to perceive the group that performs less well in these valued areas as deficient, rather than as different. As Diane Halpern (1997) humorously notes, "It is about as meaningful to ask 'Which is the smarter sex?' . . . as it is to ask 'Which has the better genitals?'" (p. 1092). The problem is not with gender differences, but with how these differences are evaluated by the larger society.

Courtesy, Alice Eagly

Alice Eagly

Although gender differences in personality and behavior are relatively few in number and small in size, sometimes it seems otherwise. How come? One explanation focuses on gender-based differences in social roles. Alice Eagly's (1987) ***social role theory* asserts that minor gender differences are exaggerated by the different social roles that males and females occupy.** For example, because women are assigned the role of caregiver, they learn to behave in nurturing ways. Over time, people come to associate such role-related behaviors with individuals of a given gender, not with the roles they play. In other words, people come to see nurturing as a female trait rather than a characteristic that anyone in a nurturing role would demonstrate. This is one way that gender stereotypes develop and persist.

Another explanation for discrepancies between beliefs and reality is that the differences actually reside in the eye of the beholder, not the beholdee. ***Social constructionism* asserts that individuals construct their own reality based on societal expectations, conditioning, and self-socialization** (Hyde, 1996; Marecek, 2001). According to social constructionists, people's specific beliefs about gender (as well as their tendency to look for gender differences) are rooted in the "gendered" messages and conditioning that permeate socialization experiences. To better understand these issues, we need to explore the role of biological and environmental factors as likely sources of gender differences.

Biological Origins of Gender Differences

LEARNING OBJECTIVES

- *Summarize evolutionary explanations for gender differences.*
- *Review the evidence linking gender differences in cognitive abilities to brain organization.*
- *Review the evidence relating hormones to gender differences.*

Are the gender differences that *do* exist biologically built in, or are they acquired through socialization? This is the age-old issue of nature versus nurture. The "nature" theorists concentrate on how biological disparities between the genders contribute to differences in behavior. "Nurture" theorists, on the other hand, emphasize the role of learning and environmental influences. Although we will discuss biological and environmental influences separately, keep in mind that most contemporary researchers and theorists in this area recognize that biological and environmental factors interact. First we'll look at three biologically based lines of inquiry on this topic: evolutionary explanations, brain organization, and hormonal influences.

Evolutionary Explanations

Evolutionary psychologists suggest that gender differences in behavior reflect different natural selection pressures operating on the genders over the course of human history (Archer, 1996). That is, natural selection favors behaviors that maximize the chances of passing on genes to the next generation (reproductive success).

To support their assertions, evolutionary psychologists look for gender differences that are consistent across cultures (Kenrick & Trost, 1993, Kenrick, Trost, & Sundie, 2004). Is there consistency across cultures for the better-documented gender differences? Despite some fascinating exceptions, gender differences in cognitive abilities, aggression, and sexual behavior *are* found in many cultures (Beller & Gafni, 1996; Halpern, 2000). According to evolutionary psychologists, these consistent differences have emerged because males and females have been confronted with different adaptive demands. For example, males supposedly are more *sexually active and permissive* because they invest less than females in the process of procreation and can maximize their reproductive success by seeking many sexual partners (Buss & Kenrick, 1998, Lippa, 2005). However, it is important to remember that even in cross-cultural work, there are more differences *within* each gender that *between* the genders, especially when it comes to cognitive abilities (Kenrick et al., 2004).

The gender gap in *aggression* is also explained in terms of reproductive fitness. Because females are more selective about mating than males are, males have to engage in more competition for sexual partners than females do. Greater aggressiveness is thought to be adaptive for males in this competition for sexual access because it should foster social dominance over other males and facilitate the acquisition of the material resources emphasized by females when they evaluate potential partners (Kenrick & Trost, 1993). Evolutionary theorists assert that gender differences in *spatial abilities* reflect the division of labor in ancestral hunting-and-gathering societies in which males typically handled the hunting and females the gathering. Males' superiority on most spatial tasks has been attributed to the adaptive demands of hunting (Eals & Silverman, 1994). However, when examining the research, there is very little support for this hypothesis for any species (Jones, Braithwaite, & Healy, 2003).

Evolutionary analyses of gender differences are interesting, but controversial. While it is eminently plausible that evolutionary forces could have led to some divergence between males and females in typical behavior, evolutionary hypotheses are highly speculative and difficult to test empirically (Fausto-Sterling, 1992; Halpern, 2000). In addition, evolutionary theory can be used to claim that the status quo in society is the inevitable outcome of evolutionary forces. Thus, if males have dominant status over females, natural selection must have favored this arrangement. The crux of the problem is that evolutionary analyses can be used to explain almost anything. For instance, if the situation regarding mental rotation were reversed—if females scored higher than males—evolutionary theorists might attribute females' superiority to the adaptive demands of gathering food, weaving baskets, and making clothes—and it would be difficult to prove otherwise.

Web Link 10.3 **Great Ideas in Personality: Evolutionary Psychology and Sociobiology**

Professor G. Scott Acton's excellent site in personality includes a major collection of resources supporting and opposing evolutionary psychology and sociobiology—the theory that human behavior is predominantly governed by biological forces, particularly those arising from one's genes.

Brain Organization

Some theorists propose that male and female brains are organized differently, which might account for gender differences in some gender-specific abilities

(Lippa, 2005). As you may know, the human brain is divided into two halves. **The *cerebral hemispheres* are the right and left halves of the cerebrum, which is the convoluted outer layer of the brain.** The largest and most complicated part of the human brain, the cerebrum is responsible for most complex mental activities.

Some evidence suggests that the right and left cerebral hemispheres are specialized to handle different cognitive tasks (Sperry, 1982; Springer & Deutsch, 1998). For example, it appears that the *left hemisphere* is more actively involved in *verbal and mathematical processing,* while the *right hemisphere* is specialized to handle *visual-spatial and other nonverbal processing.* This pattern is generally seen in both right-handed and left-handed people, although it is less consistent among those who are left-handed.

After these findings on hemispheric specialization surfaced, some researchers began looking for disparities between male and female brain organization as a way to explain the then-observed gender differences in verbal and spatial skills. Some thought-provoking findings have been reported. For instance, males exhibit more cerebral specialization than females (Bryden, 1988; Hines, 1990). In other words, males tend to depend more heavily than females on the left hemisphere in verbal processing and on the right hemisphere in spatial processing. Gender differences have also been found in the size of the ***corpus callosum,* the band of fibers connecting the two hemispheres of the brain** (Steinmetz et al., 1995). More specifically, some studies suggest that females tend to have a larger corpus callosum. This greater size might allow for better interhemispheric transfer of information, which in turn might underlie the more bilateral organization of female brains (Innocenti, 1994, Lippa, 2005). Thus, some theorists have argued that these differences in brain organization are responsible for gender differences in verbal and spatial ability (Clements et al. 2006; Kimura & Hampson, 1993).

Although this idea is intriguing, there are some important limitations in this line of reasoning. First, studies have not consistently found that males have more specialized brain organization than females (Fausto-Sterling, 1992; Kaiser et al., 2007), and the finding of a larger corpus callosum in females does not always show up (Hines, 1990). Second, because a significant amount of brain development occurs over the first five to ten years after birth, during which time males and females are socialized differently, it is possible that different life experiences may accumulate to produce slight differences in brain organization (Hood et al., 1987). In other words, the biological factors that supposedly cause gender differences in cognitive functioning may actually reflect the influence of environmental factors. Third, gender accounts for only a small amount of the variance in lateralization and is dependent on the type of task (Boles, 2005). Finally, it's important to remember that male and female brains are much more similar than they are different.

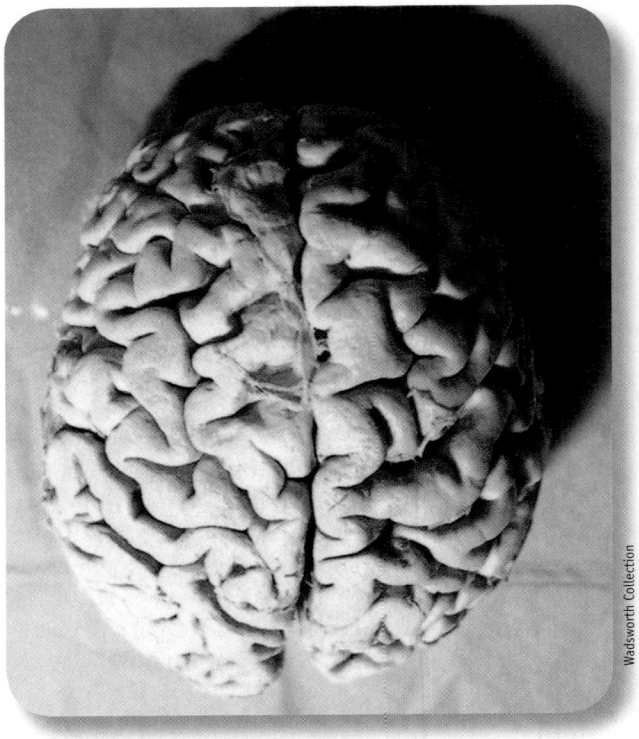

Studies have shown that the brain's cerebral hemispheres, shown here, are somewhat specialized in the kinds of cognitive tasks they handle and that such specialization is more pronounced in males than in females. Whether this difference bears any relation to gender differences in behavior is yet to be determined.

Consequently, even though the popular press has often touted the idea that there are "male brains" and "female brains" that are fundamentally different (Bleier, 1984), the notion that cerebral specialization is linked to gender differences in mental abilities is still under debate. As brain imaging techniques such as MRIs become more sophisticated, the research in this area will no doubt advance.

Hormonal Influences

Biological explanations of gender differences have also focused on the possible role of hormones. As we discussed in Chapter 3, ***hormones* are chemical substances released into the bloodstream by the endocrine glands.** In this section we'll examine the effect of hormones on prenatal sexual differentiation and on sexual and aggressive behavior.

Prenatal Gender Differentiation

Hormones play a key role in gender differentiation during prenatal development. Biological gender is determined by sex chromosomes: An XX pairing produces a female, and an XY pairing produces a male. However, both male and female embryos are essentially the same until about 8 to 12 weeks after conception. Around this time, male and female gonads (sex glands) begin to produce different hormonal secretions. The high level of *androgens* (male hormones) in males and the low level of androgens in females lead to the differentiation of male and female genital organs.

The influence of prenatal hormones on genitalia is clear; however, their influence on behavioral gender differentiation is harder to establish and becomes apparent only when something interferes with normal prenatal hormonal secretions (Hines, 2004). Scientists have studied children born to mothers given an androgen-like drug to prevent miscarriage. Two trends have been noted in this research (Collaer & Hines, 1995). First, females exposed prenatally to abnormally high levels of androgens exhibit more male-typical behavior than other females do. Second, males exposed prenatally to abnormally low levels of androgens exhibit more female-typical behavior than other males. For example, girls with *congenital adrenal hyperplasia* (elevated levels of androgens) tend to show increased interest in "male" toys, regardless of parental encouragement to play with "female" toys (Pasterski et al., 2005; Servin et al., 2003).

These findings suggest that prenatal hormones shape gender differences in humans. But there are a number of problems with this evidence (Basow, 1992; Fausto-Sterling, 1992). First, there is much more and much stronger evidence for females than for males. Second, behavior is always subject to social factors after birth. Third, it's always dangerous to draw conclusions about the general population based on small samples of people who have abnormal conditions. Fourth, most of the endocrine disorders studied have multiple effects (besides altering hormone level) that make it difficult to isolate actual causes. Finally, most of the research is necessarily correlational, and it is always risky to draw causal conclusions from correlational data.

Sexual and Aggressive Behavior

The hormone testosterone plays an important role in *sexual desire* for both men and women (Bancroft, 2002a). That is, when testosterone is reduced or eliminated, both men and women show decreases in sexual drive. A handful of studies have also reported associations between levels of male and female hormones and specific traits, but the results of these studies are inconsistent (Fausto-Sterling, 1992; Hines, 1982). For instance, testosterone has been linked with higher levels of *aggression* (impulsive and antisocial behavior) in humans, but the picture is complicated because aggressive behavior can produce increases in testosterone (Dabbs, 2000). In fact, a recent study demonstrated that simply interacting with a gun increased testosterone levels in males (Klinesmith, Kasser, & McAndrew, 2006).

The nature of the connection between hormones and gender-specific behaviors is not well understood. Hormones have less influence on human behavior than they do on animal behavior, because humans are more susceptible to environmental influences. We still have much to learn about the complicated ways in which hormones interact with social and psychological factors.

The overall evidence suggests that, aside from obvious physical differences, biological factors play a relatively minor role in gender differences. In contrast, efforts to link gender differences to disparities in the way males and females are socialized have proved more fruitful. We consider this perspective next.

Environmental Origins of Gender Differences

LEARNING OBJECTIVES

- *Define socialization and gender roles, and describe Margaret Mead's findings on the variability of gender roles and their implications.*
- *Explain how reinforcement and punishment, observational learning, and self-socialization operate in gender-role socialization.*
- *Describe how parents and peers influence gender-role socialization.*
- *Describe how schools and the media influence gender-role socialization.*

***Socialization* is the acquisition of the norms and roles expected of people in a particular society.** This process includes all the efforts made by a society to ensure that its members learn to behave in a manner that's considered appropriate. Teaching children about gender roles is an important aspect of the socialization process. ***Gender roles* are cultural expectations about what is appropriate behavior for each gender.** For example, in our culture women have been expected to rear children, cook meals, clean house, and do laundry. On the other hand, men have been expected to be the family breadwinner, do yardwork, and tinker with cars.

Are gender roles in other cultures similar to those seen in our society? Generally, yes—but not necessarily. Despite a fair amount of cross-cultural consistency in gender roles, some dramatic variability occurs as well (Gibbons, 2000). For instance, anthropologist Margaret Mead (1950) conducted a now-classic study of three tribes in New Guinea. In one tribe, *both* genders followed our masculine role expectations (the Mundugumor); in another, *both* genders approximated our feminine role (the Arapesh). In a third tribe, the male and female roles were roughly the *reverse* of our own (the Tchambuli). Such remarkable discrepancies between cultures existing within 100 miles of one another demonstrate that gender roles are not a matter of biological destiny. Instead, like other roles, gender roles are acquired through socialization.

Keep in mind that gender roles and gender stereotypes are intertwined, each fueling the other. As we noted earlier, Eagly's social role theory suggests that gender differences often occur (and seem bigger than they actually are) because males and females are guided by different role expectations. In the next section, we'll discuss how society teaches individuals about gender roles.

Processes in Gender-Role Socialization

How do people acquire gender roles? Several key learning processes come into play, including reinforcement and punishment, observational learning, and self-socialization.

Reinforcement and Punishment

In part, gender roles are shaped by the power of rewards and punishment—the key processes in operant conditioning (see Chapter 2). Parents, teachers, peers, and others often reinforce (usually with tacit approval) "gender-appropriate" behavior (Fagot & Hagan, 1991; Lippa, 2005). For example, a young boy who has hurt himself may be told that "big boys don't cry." If he succeeds in inhibiting his crying, he may get a pat on the back or a warm smile—both powerful reinforcers. Over time, a consistent pattern of such reinforcement will strengthen the boy's tendency to "act like a man" and suppress emotional displays.

Most parents take gender-appropriate behavior for granted and don't go out of their way to reward it. On the other hand, parents are much less tolerant of gender-inappropriate behavior, especially in their sons (Lytton & Romney, 1991; Sandnabba & Ahlberg, 1999). For instance, a 10-year-old boy who enjoys playing with dollhouses will probably elicit strong disapproval. Reactions usually involve ridicule or verbal reprimands rather than physical punishment.

Observational Learning

Younger children commonly imitate the behavior of a parent or an older sibling. This imitation, or *observational learning,* occurs when a child's behavior is influenced by observing others, who are called *models.* Parents serve as models for children, as do siblings, teachers, relatives, and others who are important in children's lives. Models are not limited to real people; television, movie, and cartoon characters can also serve as models.

Parents typically reward "gender-appropriate" behavior in their children.

According to *social cognitive theory* (see Chapter 2), young children are more likely to imitate people who are nurturant, powerful, and similar to them (Bussey & Bandura, 1984, 1999, 2004). Children imitate both genders, but most children are prone to imitate same-gender models. Thus, observational learning often leads young girls to play with dolls, dollhouses, and toy stoves. By contrast, young boys are more likely to tinker with toy trucks, miniature gas stations, and tool kits. Interestingly, same-gender peers may be even more influential models than parents are (Maccoby, 2002).

Self-Socialization

Children are not merely passive recipients of gender-role socialization. Rather, they play an active role in this process, beginning early in life (Lippa, 2005; Martin, Ruble, & Szkrybalo, 2002). Because society labels people, characteristics, behavior, and activities by gender, children learn that gender is an important social category. For example, they learn that females wear dresses and males don't. Around 2 to 3 years of age,

Children learn behaviors appropriate to their gender roles very early in life. According to social learning theory, girls tend to do the sorts of things their mothers do, while boys tend to follow in their fathers' footsteps.

children begin to identify themselves as male or female (Martin et al., 2002). In addition, they begin to organize the various pieces of gender-relevant information into gender schemas. ***Gender schemas* are cognitive structures that guide the processing of gender-relevant information.** Basically, gender schemas work like lenses that cause people to view and organize the world in terms of gender (Bem, 1993).

Self-socialization begins when children link the gender schema for their own gender to their self-concept. Once this connection is made, children are motivated to selectively attend to activities and information that are consistent with the schema for their own gender. For example, Terrance knows that he is a boy and also has a "boy" schema that he attaches to himself. Now his self-esteem is dependent on how well he lives up to his boy schema. In this way, children get involved in their own socialization. They are "gender detectives," working diligently to discover the rules that are supposed to govern their behavior (Martin & Ruble, 2004).

Sources of Gender-Role Socialization

Four major sources of gender-role messages are parents, peers, schools, and the media. Keep in mind that gender-role socialization varies depending on one's culture (Best & Thomas, 2004). For example, black families typically make fewer distinctions between girls and boys when compared to white families (Hill, 2002). By contrast, gender roles are relatively rigidly defined in Asian and Hispanic families (Chia et al., 1994; Comas-Diaz, 1987). Also, gender roles are changing, so the generalizations that follow may say more about how *you* were socialized than about how your children will be.

Parents

Although a meta-analysis of 172 studies of parental socialization practices suggests that parents don't treat girls and boys as differently as one might expect (Lytton & Romney, 1991), there are some important disparities. For one thing, there is a strong tendency for both mothers and fathers to emphasize and encourage *play activities* that are "gender appropriate." For example, studies show that parents encourage boys and girls to play with different types of toys (Wood, Desmarais, & Gugula, 2002). As **Figure 10.8** indicates, gender differences are found in toy preferences. Even in private child-care settings, the toys that are available for children are often gender stereotypic (Chick, Heilman-Houser, & Hunter, 2002). Generally, boys have less leeway to play with "feminine" toys than girls do with "masculine" toys. As children grow older, their leisure activities often vary by gender: Jaime plays in Little League and Alexis gets dancing lessons.

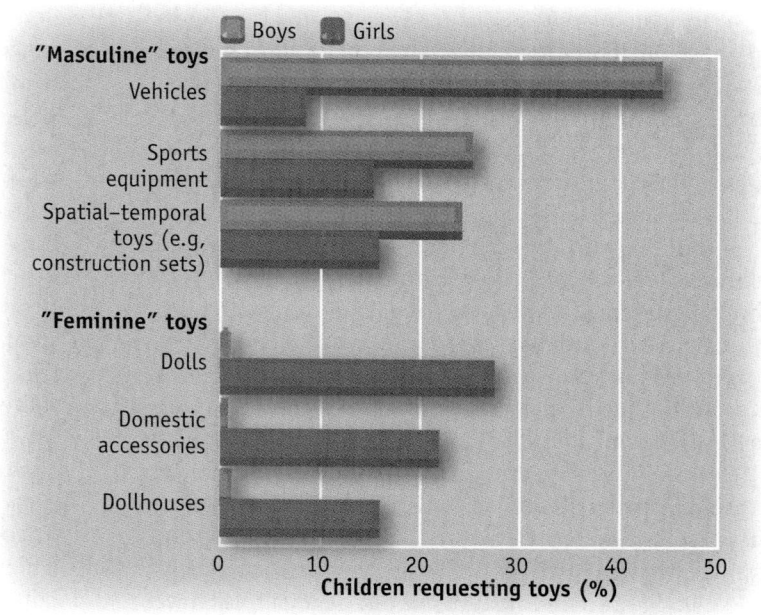

Figure 10.8

Toy preferences and gender. This graph depicts the percentage of boys and girls asking for various types of toys in letters to Santa Claus (adapted from Richardson & Simpson, 1982). Boys and girls differed substantially in their toy preferences, which probably reflects the effects of gender-role socialization.

Adapted from Richardson, J. G., & Simpson, C. H. (1982). Children, gender and social structure: An analysis of the contents of letters to Santa Claus. *Child Development, 53,* 429–436. Copyright © 1982 by the Society for Research in Child Development, Inc. Adapted by permission.

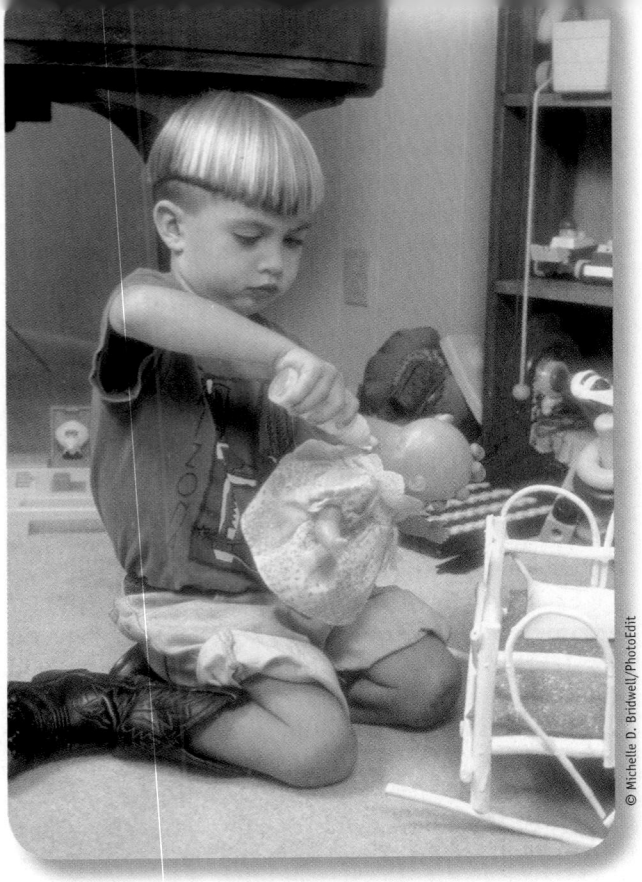

Boys are under more pressure than girls to behave in gender-appropriate ways. Little boys who show an interest in dolls are likely to be chastised by both parents and peers.

Too, the picture books parents buy for their children typically depict characters engaging in gender stereotypic activities (Gooden & Gooden, 2001). Even books that parents and teachers rate as "nonsexist" portray female characters with stereotypic personalities, chores, and leisure activities (Diekman & Murnen, 2004). Interestingly, this gender bias holds for representations of parents in these books as well. In a content analysis of 200 prominent children's picture books, Anderson and Hamilton (2005) found that fathers were underrepresented and, when they did appear, were withdrawn and ineffectual.

Another way parents emphasize gender is in the assignment of *household chores* (Lytton & Romney, 1991; Cunningham, 2001). Tasks are doled out on the basis of gender stereotypes: Girls usually do laundry and dishes, whereas boys mow the lawn and sweep the garage.

Finally, parents' attitudes about gender roles have been shown to influence the gender roles their children acquire (Fiese & Skillman, 2000). Gender expectations vary by ethnicity and socioeconomic status. African American families seem to place less emphasis on traditional gender roles than white American families do (Hill, 2002). By contrast, Hispanic families usually encourage traditional gender-role behavior, and Asian American families typically encourage subservience in their daughters (Tsai & Uemera, 1988). Also, middle-class parents may allow their children to deviate more from traditional gender roles than lower-class parents do (Reid & Paludi, 1993). Because social class cuts across ethnicity with regard to gender-role attitudes, the findings in this area are complex (Flannagan & Perese, 1998).

Peers

Children's' preferences for play activities are also highly influenced by peers (Lippa, 2005). Peers form an important network for learning about gender-appropriate and gender-inappropriate behavior. Between the ages of 4 and 6, children tend to separate into same-gender groups. From then to about age 12, boys and girls spend much more time with same-gender than other-gender peers. Moreover, according to Eleanor Maccoby (1998, 2002), over time boys' and girls' groups develop different "subcultures" (shared understandings and interests) that strongly shape youngsters' gender-role socialization (Maccoby, 1998, 2002).

Play among same-gender peers takes different forms for boys and girls (Maccoby, 1998, 2002). Boys play in larger groups and roam farther away from home, whereas girls prefer smaller groups and stay near the house. In addition, high status in boys' groups tends to be achieved by engaging in dominant behavior (telling others what to do and enforcing orders). In contrast, girls usually express their wishes as suggestions rather than demands. Also, boys engage in rough-and-tumble play much more frequently than girls do (Lippa, 2005).

Because both boys and girls are critical of peers who violate traditional gender norms, they perpetuate stereotypical behavior. Among children ages 3–11, boys are devalued more than girls for dressing like the other gender, whereas girls are evaluated more negatively than boys for playing like the other gender—for instance, loudly and roughly versus quietly and gently (Blakemore, 2003). Further, "gender atypical boys" more often report being a victim of bullying, more loneliness, and greater distress than their "typical" peers (Young & Sweeting, 2004).

Schools

The school environment figures importantly in socializing gender roles (Meece & Scantlebury, 2006; Sadker & Sadker, 1994). Children's grade-school *textbooks* have often ignored or stereotyped girls and women (AAUW Educational Foundation, 1992). Traditionally, these books have portrayed males as clever, heroic, and adventurous, whereas females have been shown performing domestic chores. Although the depiction of stereotypical gender roles has declined considerably since the 1970s, researchers still find significant differences in how males and females are portrayed, even in supposedly nonsexist books (Diekman & Murnen, 2004). Many high school and college textbooks also contain gender bias. The most common problems are using generic masculine language ("policeman" versus "police officer" and so forth) and portraying males and females in stereotypic roles. In addition, subtle word choices can reinforce stereotypes, such as passivity in females (for example, women were *given* the right to vote; Meece & Scantlebury, 2006).

Gender bias in schools also shows up in *teachers' treatment of boys and girls.* Preschool and grade-school teachers often reward gender-appropriate behavior in their pupils (Fagot et al., 1985). Teachers also tend to pay greater attention to boys—helping them, praising them, and scolding them more than females (Sadker & Sadker, 1994). By contrast, girls tend to be less visible in the classroom and to receive less encouragement for academic achievement from teachers. These findings have been replicated in other cultures as well (Best & Thomas, 2004). Overall, these teacher-student interactions reinforce the gender stereotype of male competence and dominance (Meece & Scantlebury, 2006). With regard to teacher training, many teacher education textbooks still give little attention to gender equity (Zittleman & Sadker, 2002).

Gender bias also shows up in *academic and career counseling.* Despite the fact that females obtain higher grades than males (on the average) in all subjects from elementary school through college (Halpern, 2004, 2006), many counselors continue to encourage male students to pursue high-status careers in medicine or engineering while guiding female students toward less prestigious careers (Read, 1991). Differential treatment by counselors and teachers can facilitate barriers to women's career choices (Betz, 2006; Halpern, 2006).

The Media

Television is yet another source of gender-role socialization (Luecke-Aleksa et al., 1995). American youngsters spend a lot of time watching TV (see **Figure 10.9**). A recent Nielsen Media Research report (2006) found that TV viewing is at an all-time high, with the average household watching 8 hours, 14 minutes of TV per day! A systematic review of the literature indicates that contemporary youth view an average of 1.8–2.8 hours of TV a day, with 28% watching more than 4 hours per day (Marshall, Gorely, & Biddle, 2006). Approximately 35% of children are raised in homes where the TV is on "always" or "most of the time," and these children have lower reading ability than their peers (Vandewater et al., 2005). African American children and adolescents spend more time in front of the tube than their white peers (Roberts et al., 1999).

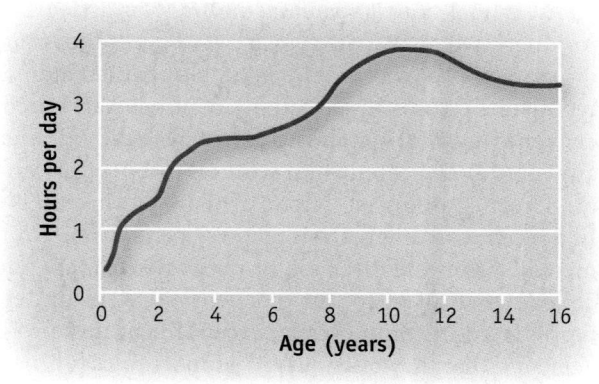

Figure 10.9

Television viewing habits. As children grow up, they spend more and more time watching TV until viewing time begins to decline slightly around age 12. Research shows that children's conceptions of gender roles are influenced to a considerable degree by what they watch on television.

Adapted from Liebert, R. M., & Sprafkin, J. (1988). *The early window: Effects of television on children and youth,* 3rd ed. Boston: Allyn & Bacon. Copyright © 1988 by Pearson Education. Adapted by permission of the publisher.

An analysis of male and female characters on prime-time *television programs* showed that the number and variety of roles of female TV characters have increased over the past 30 years but that these shifts lag behind the actual changes in women's lives (Glascock, 2001; Signorielli & Bacue, 1999). Compared to males, females appear less often, are less likely to be employed (especially in prestigious positions), are more likely to be younger, and are more likely to appear in secondary and comedy roles. As compared to female characters, males are still more likely to demonstrate competence-related behaviors such as reaching a goal, showing ingenuity, and answering questions (Aubrey & Harrison, 2004). In traditional children's adventure *cartoons* (as opposed to educational cartoons), male characters appear more often and engage in more physical aggression, whereas female characters are much more likely to show fear, act romantic, be polite, and act supportive (Leaper et al., 2002).

Television commercials are even more gender-stereotyped than TV programs (Furnham & Mak, 1999; Lippa 2005). Women are frequently shown worrying

Web Link 10.4 **Center for Screen-Time Awareness**

This site is the home of TV Turnoff Week. It "provides information so people can live healthier lives in functional families in vibrant communities by taking control of the electronic media in their lives, not allowing it to control them." It includes a thorough set of facts and figures based on recent Neilsen Media Research Group reports.

about trivial matters such as laundry and cleaning products, whereas men appear as bold outdoorsmen or energetic sports fans. In a study of gender stereotyping in TV commercials on five continents, researchers reported that, in all the countries studied, men appeared more often than women in both on- and off-screen announcer roles (Furnham & Mak, 1999). In a recent content analysis of 1,337 prime-time commercials from the three major networks, Ganahl and colleagues (2003) found that women were underrepresented in commercials (except for beauty products) and that they often played support roles for men.

Another manifestation of gender bias is television's inordinate *emphasis on women's physical appearance* (Lauzen & Dozier, 2002). Males on television may or may not be good-looking, but the vast majority of females are young, attractive, and sexy (Signorielli & Bacue, 1999). Overweight female characters are much more likely than male characters to receive negative comments about their weight (Fouts & Burggraf, 1999; Fouts & Vaughan, 2002). As you'll see in the Chapter 15 Application, these cultural expectations have been cited as a cause of the disproportionately high incidence of eating disorders in females and are related to the development of unhealthy body images (Smolak, 2006).

A meta-analysis reported a link between the number and type of television programs children watch and the acquisition of gender-stereotyped beliefs. Children who watched a lot of television held more stereotyped beliefs about gender than children who watched less TV (Herrett-Skjellum & Allen, 1996). Still, this research is correlational, so it is quite likely that other factors—such as parental values—come into play as well. Nonetheless, once gender stereotypes are learned, they are difficult to change.

Web Link 10.5 **Gender and Race in Media**

The University of Iowa's Communications Studies Program offers a focused guide to the ways in which gender and racial differences are expressed in various media, including an excellent set of materials dealing with gender and advertising.

TV is not the only medium that perpetuates gender stereotypes; gender-role socialization is a multimedia event. Most *video games* push a hypermasculine stereotype featuring search-and-destroy missions, fighter pilot battles, and male sports (Lippa, 2005). Of the few video games directed at girls, the great majority of them are highly stereotypic (shopping and Barbie games). Also, *music videos* frequently portray women as sex objects and men as dominating and aggressive (Sommers-Flanagan, Sommers-Flanagan, & Davis, 1993), and these portrayals appear to influence viewers' sexual attitudes (Kalof, 1999). As demonstrated in a content analysis of *educational software* for young children, most software programs had more male than female characters, portrayed males in more stereotypical ways, and focused more on gender-stereotypical appearance for females (Sheldon, 2004).

Gender-Role Expectations

LEARNING OBJECTIVES

- *List five elements of the traditional male role, and contrast it with the modern male role.*
- *Describe three common problems associated with the traditional male role.*
- *List three major expectations of the female role.*
- *Describe three common problems associated with the female role.*
- *Describe two ways in which women are victimized by sexism.*

Traditional gender roles are based on several unspoken assumptions: that all members of the same gender have basically the same traits, that the traits of one gender are very different from the traits of the other gender, and that masculine traits are more highly valued. In recent decades, many social critics and theorists in psychology and other fields have scrutinized gender roles, identifying the essential features and the ramifications of traditional roles. In this section, we review the research and theory in this area and note changes in gender roles over the past 30 to 40 years. We begin with the male role.

Role Expectations for Males

A number of psychologists have sought to pinpoint the essence of the traditional male role (Brannon, 1976; Levant, 1996, 2003; Pleck, 1995). Many consider *antifemininity* to be the central theme that runs through the male gender role. That is, "real men" shouldn't act in any way that might be perceived as feminine. For example, men should not publicly display vulnerable emotions, should avoid feminine occupations, and should not show obvious interest in relationships—especially homosexual ones. Five key attributes constitute the traditional male role (Brannon, 1976; Jansz, 2000):

1. *Achievement.* To prove their masculinity, men need to beat out other men at work and at sports. Having a high-status job, driving an expensive car, and making lots of money are aspects of this element.
2. *Aggression.* Men should be tough and fight for what they believe is right. They should aggressively defend themselves and those they love against threats.
3. *Autonomy.* Men should be self-reliant and not admit to being dependent on others.
4. *Sexuality.* Real men are heterosexual and are highly motivated to pursue sexual activities and conquests.
5. *Stoicism.* Men should not share their pain or express their "soft" feelings. They should be cool and calm under pressure.

Gender-role expectations for males have remained relatively stable for years. However, the male role may be undergoing some changes. According to Joseph Pleck (1995), who has written extensively on this issue, in the *traditional male role,* masculinity is validated by individual physical strength, aggressiveness, and emotional inexpressiveness. In the *modern male role,* masculinity is validated by economic achievement, organizational power, emotional control (even over anger), and emotional sensitivity and self-expression, but only with women.

Thus, in modern societies, the traditional male role coexists with some new expectations. Some theorists use the plural "masculinities" to describe these variations in the male gender role (Smiler, 2004). This flux in expectations means that males are experiencing role inconsistencies and pressures to behave in ways that conflict with traditional masculinity: to communicate personal feelings, to nurture children and share in housework, to integrate sexuality with love, and to curb aggression (Levant, 1996, 2003). Some psychologists believe that these pressures have shaken traditional masculine norms sufficiently that many men are experiencing a masculinity crisis and diminished pride in being a man (Levant, 1996, 2003). Indeed, college men who experience gender-role conflict report higher levels of internalized shame (Thompkins & Rando, 2003). The rise in popularity of men's groups and organizations such as the Promise Keepers may reflect this confusion. The good news is that boys and men are beginning to get more attention from psychological theorists, researchers, and clinicians.

"Norman won't collaborate."

© The New Yorker Collection 2002 Robert Weber from cartoonbank.com. All rights reserved.

Web Link 10.6 **American Men's Studies Association**

This site collects academic resources to advance "the critical study of men and masculinities." It includes links to many other sites and organizations interested in the male experience.

Problems with the Male Role

It is often assumed that only females suffer from the constricting binds of traditional gender roles. Not so. Increasingly, the costs of the male role are a cause for concern (Levant, 1996; Pleck, 1995). As we examine the relevant research, keep in mind that many variables besides gender factor into problems related to male roles. For instance, many researchers are calling for a closer examination of the influence of culture on gender-role stress (Carter et al., 2005; Wester et al. 2006).

Pressure to Succeed

Most men are socialized to be highly competitive and are taught that a man's masculinity is measured by the size of his paycheck and job status. As Christopher Kilmartin (2000) notes, "There is always another man who has more money, higher status, a more attractive partner, or a bigger house. The traditional man . . . must constantly work harder and faster" (p. 13). Small wonder, then, that so many men pursue success with a fervor that is sometimes dangerous to their health. The extent of this danger is illustrated by men's life expectancy, which is about six years shorter than women's (of course, factors besides gender roles contribute to this difference).

The majority of men who have internalized the success ethic are unable to fully realize their dreams. This is a particular problem for African American and Hispanic men, who experience more barriers to financial success than European American men do (Biernat & Kobrynowicz, 1997). How does this "failure" affect men? Although many are able to adjust to it, many are not. The men in this latter group are likely to suffer from shame and poor self-esteem (Kilmartin, 2000). Men's emphasis on success also makes it more likely that they will spend long hours on the job. This pattern in turn decreases the amount of time families can spend together and increases the amount of time partners spend on housework and child care.

Interestingly, younger men seem less inclined to embrace the success ethic than older men. A significantly smaller proportion of men between the ages of 18 and 37 are work focused (they want to spend more time with their families) compared to men age 38 and older (Families and Work Institute, 2004).

Gender differences in pressure to succeed might be more perceived than real. When asked about *perceptions,* college students rated the typical man as worrying about achievement more that the typical woman. However, when asked about their *own* worry, females reported more worry about achievement than male students did (Wood et al. 2005). Perhaps this finding reflects men's not wanting to express that they are worrying about anything.

The Emotional Realm

Most young boys are trained to believe that men should be strong, tough, cool, and detached (Brody, 2000; Jansz, 2000). Thus, they learn early to hide vulnerable emotions such as love, joy, and sadness because they believe that such feelings are feminine and imply weakness. Over time, some men become strangers to their own emotional lives (Levant, 1996). It seems that men with traditional views of masculinity are more likely to suppress outward emotions and to fear emotions, supposedly because such feelings may lead to a loss of composure (Jakupcak et al., 2003). Keep in mind, however, that this view is challenged by some researchers (Wong & Rochlen, 2005). As with many gender gaps, differences in emotionality tend to be small, inconsistent, and dependent on the situation. For instance, Robertson and colleagues (2001) found that males who were more traditionally masculine were more emotionally expressive in a structured exercise than when they were simply asked to talk about their emotions.

Males' difficulty with "tender" emotions has serious consequences. First, as we saw in Chapter 3, suppressed emotions can contribute to stress-related disorders. And worse, men are less likely than women to seek help from health professionals (Addis & Mahalik, 2003; Berger et al., 2005). Second, men's emotional inexpressiveness can cause problems in their relationships with partners and children. For example, men who endorse traditional masculine norms report lower relationship satisfaction, as do their female partners (Burn & Ward, 2005). Further, children whose fathers are warm, loving, and accepting toward them have higher self-esteem and lower rates of aggression and behavior problems (Rohner & Veneziano, 2001). On a positive note, fathers are increasingly involving themselves with their children. And 30% of fathers report that they take equal or greater responsibility for their children than their working wives do (Bond et al., 2003).

One emotion males are allowed to express is anger. Sometimes this anger translates into physical aggression or violence. Men commit nearly 90% of violent crimes in the United States and almost all sexual assaults (U.S. Department of Justice, 2003).

Sexual Problems

Men often experience sexual problems that derive partly from their gender-role socialization, which gives them

Recommended **READING**

The Masculine Self
by Christopher T. Kilmartin
(McGraw-Hill, 2000)

This small paperback, written for college courses on gender, is highly readable. Kilmartin's major purpose in writing the book was to help readers "understand the difference between being male and being a 'generic human being'" (p. xiv). The implication is that androcentrism may render invisible the uniqueness of the male experience.

Kilmartin, a psychologist, does an excellent job of blending classic and contemporary research findings to shed light on important questions. About half of the book is devoted to a thorough and research-based discussion of current problem areas for men: emotions, physical health, work, sexuality, violence, relationships, and mental health. He also addresses the important issues of race, ethnicity, sexual orientation, and age. In addition, he integrates male gender-role theory into the major perspectives on personality—psychoanalytic, social learning, humanistic, and biological. There is also a chapter on cultural influences.

The book closes with an enlightening discussion of contemporary men's movements, including the mythopoetic movement (Robert Bly and Sam Keen), profeminism, the men's rights movement (Robert Farrell), and Promise Keepers. Also included is an interesting discussion of men's studies, an emerging area of scholarly work.

Two other books, also written by psychologists, focus on helping *boys* deal with gender-role pressures: *Real Boys: Rescuing Our Sons from the Myths of Boyhood,* by William Pollack (1998), and *Raising Cain: Protecting the Emotional Life of Boys,* by Dan Kindlon and Michael Thompson (1999). Although Pollack's book could better address relationships between boys and their fathers, both books offer insightful first-person accounts of the challenges boys face, especially from male peers and in the school setting.

a "macho" sexual image to live up to. There are few things that men fear more than a sexual encounter in which they are unable to achieve an erection (Doyle, 1989). Unfortunately, these very fears often *cause* the dysfunction that men dread (see Chapter 13). The upshot is that men's obsession with sexual performance can produce anxiety that may interfere with their sexual responsiveness.

Another problem is that many men learn to confuse feelings of intimacy and sex. In other words, if a man experiences strong feelings of connectedness, he is likely to interpret them as sexual feelings. This confusion has a number of consequences (Kilmartin, 2000). For one thing, sex may be the only way some men can allow themselves to feel intimately connected to another. Thus, men's keen interest in sex may be driven, in part, by strong needs for emotional intimacy that don't get satisfied in other ways. The confusion of intimacy and sex may underlie the tendency for men (compared to women) to perceive eye contact, a compliment, an innocent smile, a friendly remark, or a brush against the arm as a sexual invitation (Kowalski, 1993). Finally, the sexualization of intimate feelings causes inappropriate anxiety when men feel affection for another man, thus promoting homophobia.

As we discussed in Chapter 9, ***homophobia* is the intense fear and intolerance of homosexuality.** Because homosexuality still has a social stigma attached to it, fear of being labeled homosexual keeps many people, who might otherwise be more flexible, adhering to traditional gender roles. This situation is particularly true for males. Indeed, endorsement of traditional gender roles and hypermasculinity are both related to negative attitudes toward homosexuality (Whitley, 2001). One reason that homophobia is more prevalent among males is that the male role is rooted in the fear of appearing feminine—and feminine characteristics are mistakenly associated with gay males (Maurer, 1999). Second, homophobia is much more common in men than in women because males feel more pressure to avoid any behavior characteristic of the other gender (Herek, 2003). Although they will tolerate "tomboyism" in girls, parents (especially fathers) are highly intolerant of any "sissy" behavior exhibited by their sons. This intense pressure against appearing feminine contributes not only to homophobia among heterosexual males but also to negative attitudes toward females (Friedman, 1989).

Role Expectations for Females

In the past 30 years, the role expectations for American women have undergone dramatic changes, especially with regard to work. Prior to the 1970s, a woman was expected to be a wife and a stay-at-home mother. Today, there are three major expectations:

1. *The marriage mandate.* Even though more women are choosing to remain single, there is still a stigma attached to singlehood in a society where marriage is the norm (Gordon, 2003). Most women are socialized to feel incomplete until they find a mate. Women attain adult status when they get married. In the context of marriage, women are expected to be responsible for cooking, cleaning, and other housework.

2. *The motherhood mandate.* The imperative of the female role is to have children. This expectation has been termed the "motherhood mandate" (Rice & Else-Quest, 2006; Russo, 1979). The prevailing ideology of today's motherhood mandate is that of "intensive mothering"—mothering should be wholly child-centered, and mothers should be self-sacrificing rather than persons who also have needs and interests (Arendell, 2000).

3. *Work outside the home.* Most of today's young women, especially those who are college educated, expect to work outside the home, and they also want a satisfying family life (Family and Work Institute, 2004; Konrad, 2003). As you can see in **Figure 10.10**, the percentage of women in the labor force has been steadily rising over the last 30 years.

The marriage and motherhood mandates fuel women's focus on *heterosexual success*—learning how

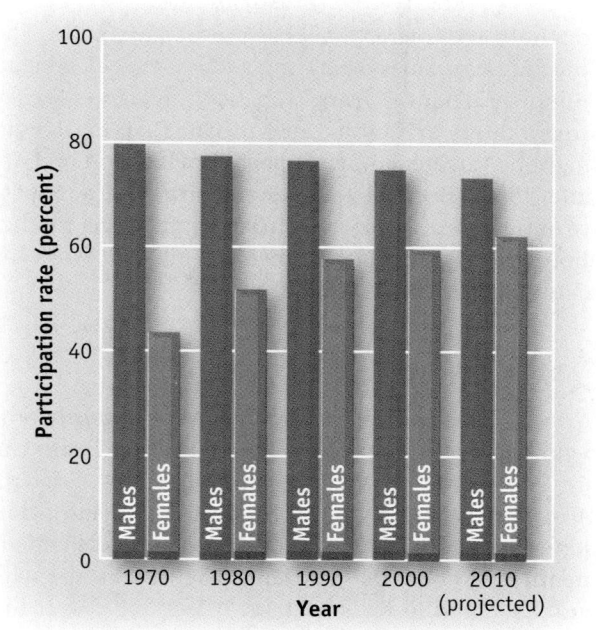

Figure 10.10

Increases in women's workforce participation. The percentage of women who work outside the home has increased steadily over the past century, especially since 1970. In 2010, close to two-thirds of women are projected to be in the labor force, about 10% fewer than men. (Data from U.S. Bureau of the Census, 2000, 2003, 2004a)

to attract and interest males as prospective mates. The resulting emphasis on dating and marriage can lead some women away from a challenging career—they worry about driving away a prospective mate who might be threatened by a high-achieving woman (Arnold, 1995). Because younger men are more supportive of their wives' working than older men, this conflict should ease for younger women (Family and Work Institute, 2004).

Problems with the Female Role

Writers in the feminist movement generated some compelling analyses of the problems associated with the pre-1970s traditional role of wife and mother (Friedan, 1964; Millett, 1970). Many criticized the assumption that women, unlike men, did not need an independent identity; it should be sufficient to be Jim Smith's wife and Jason and Robin's mother. Increasingly over the past 40 years, girls and women have been encouraged to develop and use their talents, and work opportunities for women have greatly expanded. Still, there are problems with the female role.

Web Link 10.7 **Feminist Majority Foundation**

This site brings together a massive set of resources dealing with issues from a feminist perspective.

Diminished Career Aspirations

Despite recent efforts to increase women's opportunities for achievement, young women continue to have lower career aspirations than young men with comparable backgrounds and abilities (Wilgosh, 2001). Also, they are more likely to underestimate their achievement than boys (who overestimate theirs) (Eccles, 2001). This thinking is especially likely when estimating performance on "masculine" tasks such as science and math versus "feminine" (social skills, language) or gender-neutral tasks. This is a problem because science and math are the foundations for many high-paying, high-status careers, and it is often the lack of math background (as opposed to ability) that contributes to the inferior performance for some women (Betz, 2006). Higher intelligence and good grades are generally associated with higher career aspirations, but this trend is less likely to hold true for girls than for boys (Kelly & Cobb, 1991).

The discrepancy between women's abilities and their level of achievement has been termed the *ability-achievement gap* (Hyde, 1996). The roots of this gap seem to lie in the conflict between achievement and

LIVING IN TODAY'S WORLD

Gender Stereotypes and "Appearance Pressure"

Currently in the United States, the ideal physique for women is an hourglass shape with medium-sized breasts packaged in a relatively thin body. For men, the ideal physique includes broad shoulders, narrow hips, narrow waist, and muscularity. Images of these gender ideals pervade "women's" and "men's" magazines as well as those that focus on fitness (Vartanian, Giant, & Passino, 2001). To make matters worse, many of the images are computer-enhanced and unrealistic. Physically attractive men and women dominate television programs and commercials. In an ironic use of the term, "reality" television shows such as *Extreme Makeover* and *Dr. 90210* depict real men and women undergoing extensive plastic surgery to improve their lives. The media message for today's women: thin is "in"; for men: you need "six-pack abs" to be attractive.

Weight is particularly important for women because men generally prefer thinner women to those who are heavier. For many years, this concern with thinness has existed among white and Asian Americans, but it has been a lesser concern among Hispanics and black Americans (Polivy & Herman, 2002). Unfortunately, some recent evidence suggests that the thin female ideal may be spreading to these two groups as well (Barnett, Keel, & Conoscenti, 2001; Bay-Cheng et al., 2002, but also see Schooler et al. 2004). Failure to live up to these ideals can create body dissatisfaction and lead to eating disorders (Smolak, 2006)

Today, males also seem to be experiencing "appearance pressure." Recent studies show that adolescent boys, college men, and adult males all prefer to be more muscular (Morrison, Morrison, & Hopkins, 2003; Olivardia, Pope, & Phillips, 2000). Pressure on males also appears to be coming from women, who prefer a large torso with narrow waist and hips (Maisey et al., 1999). More men are dieting, working out, and seeking surgery than has been true in the past (Olivardia et al., 2000).

Do televised images of body ideals have any impact on viewers? Unfortunately, it seems that they do—negative ones. For example, in one study, college men and women were exposed to either sexist ads, nonsexist ads, or no ads (Lavine, Sweeney, & Wager, 1999). (The sexist ads portrayed both men and women as sex objects as part of a bogus marketing research study.) The results showed that both the men and women who were exposed to sexist ads had greater body dissatisfaction than students in the other two conditions. In a correlational study, the amount of exposure to ideal body images of women on television (based on viewing habits) was measured. Women with a lot of exposure to these ideal images were more likely to prefer a smaller waist and hips and a medium-sized bust for themselves (Harrison, 2003). Further, both women and men who viewed ideal body images of women were more likely to approve of cosmetic surgery for women.

The current social pressures to attain an ideal body shape push many individuals into unhealthy eating behaviors. Experts say that eating disorders are at an all-time high (Gleaves et al., 2000). And some males may turn to dangerous anabolic steroids to build up their muscle mass (Courtenay, 2000). Another response to "attractiveness pressure" is the increased rate of cosmetic surgeries. Between 2003 and 2004, a 48 percent increase occurred in the number of cosmetic surgeries performed on Americans who were 18 and younger (Springen, 2004). Thus, the pressure to live up to an unrealistic, and sometimes unhealthy, ideal body shape is a significant adjustment challenge facing both males and females today.

femininity that is built into the traditional female role. Many women worry that they will be seen as unfeminine if they boldly strive for success. Of course, this is not a concern for all women. Still, gender discrimination remains a barrier for those who aim for prestigious careers.

Juggling Multiple Roles

Another problem with the female role is that societal institutions have not kept pace with the reality of women's lives. Women are able to successfully manage marriage and a career. But when children enter the picture, the emotional and time demands on women increase dramatically (Hoffnung, 2004).

Today 60% of married women with children under the age of 6 work outside the home (U.S. Bureau of the Census, 2004b). Yet the workplace (and many husbands and fathers) still operate as if women were stay-at-home moms and as if there were no single-parent families. This gap between policies based on outdated assumptions about women's lives and reality means that women who "want it all" experience burdens and conflicts that most men do not. That's because most men typically have *major* day-to-day responsibilities in only *one* role: worker. But most women have major day-to-day responsibilities in *three* roles: spouse, parent, and worker.

Although more men, and especially younger men, are giving additional time to household chores and child care, women still do most of this work (Family & Work Institute, 2004; Shapira-Berman, 2004). One way today's college-educated women deal with these conflicts is to postpone marriage and motherhood (and to have small families) to pursue more education or to launch their careers (Hoffnung, 2004). Women are more likely than men to expect childrearing to disrupt their careers (Singer, Cassin, & Dobson, 2005). Once women in high-powered careers are established, some are temporarily "stopping out" of the workforce to focus on childbearing and rearing their young children (Wallis, 2004). Given the three-role reality of their lives, they trade off the worker role and income for a slower pace and less stress to rear young children, although they miss the stimulation and recognition from their work. (But keep in mind that these women have husbands who can support the family.) Their strategy: "You can have it all, just not all at the same time" (Wallis, 2004, p. 53).

Of course multiple roles, in themselves, are not inherently problematic. In fact, there is some evidence that multiple roles can be beneficial for mental health, as you'll see in Chapter 12. Rather, the problem stems from the tensions among these roles and the unequal sharing of role responsibilities. Greater participation in household tasks and child-care by husbands or others as well as family-friendly workplaces and subsidized quality child-care programs would alleviate women's stress in this area. However, this issue is not clear cut. Goldberg and Perry-Jenkins (2004) note that women with traditional gender roles whose husbands did *more* child care after the birth of their first child experienced greater distress. Of course, this tendency can also be interpreted as women who did *less* child care than they expected, experiencing greater distress perhaps because they were not living up to their own gender-role expectations.

The Mismeasure of Woman
by Carol Tavris (Touchstone, 1993)

The title and thesis of this book refer to Protagoras's statement that "Man is the measure of all things." Tavris, a social psychologist, has written this book for the nonprofessional audience and uses her natural wit and humor to excellent advantage. She points out the fallacy of using a male-centered standard for evaluating "what is normal" for both men and women. Using research findings, she exposes numerous myths about males and females that are the source of misunderstanding and frustration for many. Tavris is not interested in replacing a male-centered view with a female-dominant view but rather in expanding our view of what it means to be human. She urges people to move away from the tendency to think in "us versus them" terms about gender issues. Instead, she suggests that men and women need to work together and rethink how they need to be to have the kind of relationships and work that are life enhancing.

Ambivalence About Sexuality

Like men, women may have sexual problems that stem, in part, from their gender-role socialization. For many women, the problem is difficulty in enjoying sex. Why? For one thing, many girls are still taught to suppress or deny their sexual feelings (Hyde & DeLamater, 2003). For another, they are told that a woman's role in sex is a passive one. In addition, girls are encouraged to focus on romance rather than on gaining sexual experience. As a result, many women feel uncomfortable (guilty, ashamed) with their sexual urges. The experience of menstruation (and its association with blood and pain) and the fear of pregnancy add another dimension of negativity to sex. And females' concerns about sexual exploitation and rape also foster negative emotions. Thus, when it comes to sexuality, women are likely to have ambivalent feelings instead of the largely positive feelings that men have (Tolman, 2002; Hyde, 2004). Unfortunately, this ambivalence is often viewed as sexual "dysfunction" for women, as opposed to an attitude resulting from narrow gender roles and beliefs (Drew, 2003).

Sexism: A Special Problem for Females

Intimately intertwined with the topic of gender roles is the issue of sexism. ***Sexism* is discrimination against people on the basis of their gender.** (Using our terminology, the term should be "genderism," but we'll stick with standard terminology for the sake of clarity.) Sexism usually refers to discrimination by men against women. However, sometimes *women* discriminate against other women and sometimes *men* are the victims of gender-based discrimination. In this section, we'll discuss two specific problems: economic discrimination and aggression toward women.

Economic Discrimination

Women are victimized by two forms of economic discrimination: differential access to jobs and differential treatment once on the job. Concerning *job access,* the

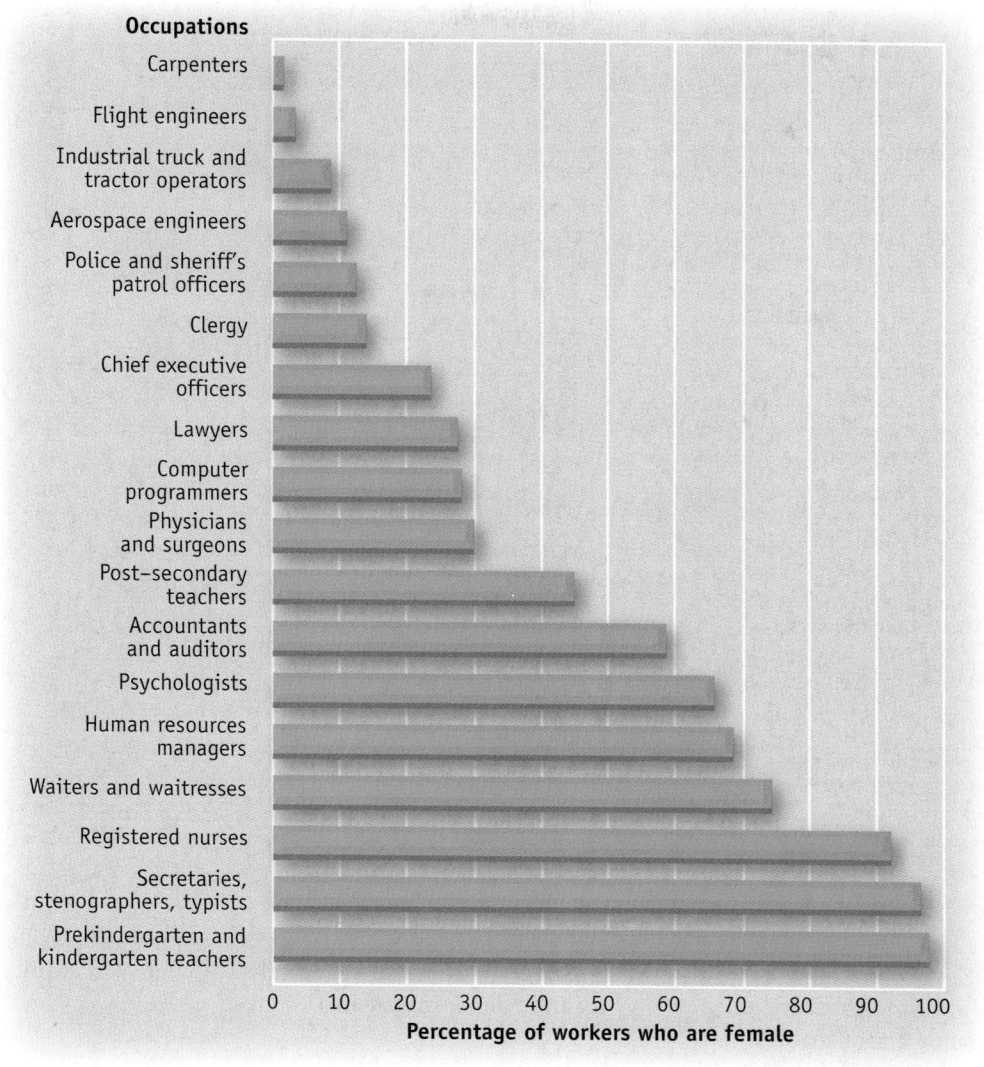

Figure 10.11

Women in the world of work. Career opportunities for women have expanded dramatically in the past 40 years. Nonetheless, women remain underrepresented in many traditionally masculine occupations and overrepresented in many traditionally feminine occupations. (Data from U.S. Bureau of the Census, 2004a)

problem is that women still lack the same employment opportunities as men. For example, in 2003, only 6% of mechanical engineers were women and only 30% of physicians and 14% of Congresspersons were women (U.S. Bureau of the Census, 2004a). Further, women hold only 27.5% of all computer and mathematical related jobs (U.S. Bureau of the Census, 2005). Ethnic minority women are even less likely than white women to work in these occupations. On the other hand, women are overrepresented in "pink-collar ghetto" occupations, such as secretary and preschool and kindergarten teacher (see **Figure 10.11**).

The second aspect of economic discrimination is *differential treatment* on the job. For example, women typically earn lower salaries than men in the same jobs (see **Figure 10.12** on the next page). And occupations that are male dominated typically pay more than those that are female dominated (Pratto & Walker, 2004). Further, when women demonstrate leadership qualities such as confidence, ambitiousness, and assertiveness, they are evaluated less favorably than men because this behavior contradicts the female gender stereotype (Eagly & Karau, 2002; Lyness & Heilman, 2006). There appears to be a *glass ceiling* that prevents most women and ethnic minorities from being advanced to top-level professional positions (Reid, Miller, & Kerr, 2004). For example, as of February 2005 there were only eight female CEOs of Fortune 500 companies (Inskeep, 2005). Ironically, men employed in traditionally female fields are promoted more quickly than their female counterparts, a phenomenon dubbed the *glass escalator* (Hultin, 2003; Williams, 1998).

Aggression Toward Females

Forms of aggression toward girls and women include rape, intimate violence, sexual harassment, sexual abuse, incest, and violent pornography. We've discussed a number of these problems elsewhere (in particular, consult the Application for Chapter 9), so we'll focus here on sexual harassment. *Sexual harassment* has be-

Figure 10.12

The gender gap in annual wages. Women continue to earn less than men in all occupational categories, as these 2005 data for selected occupations make clear. Many factors can contribute to this gender gap in earned income, but economic discrimination is probably a major consideration. (Data from U.S. Bureau of Labor Statistics, 2005)

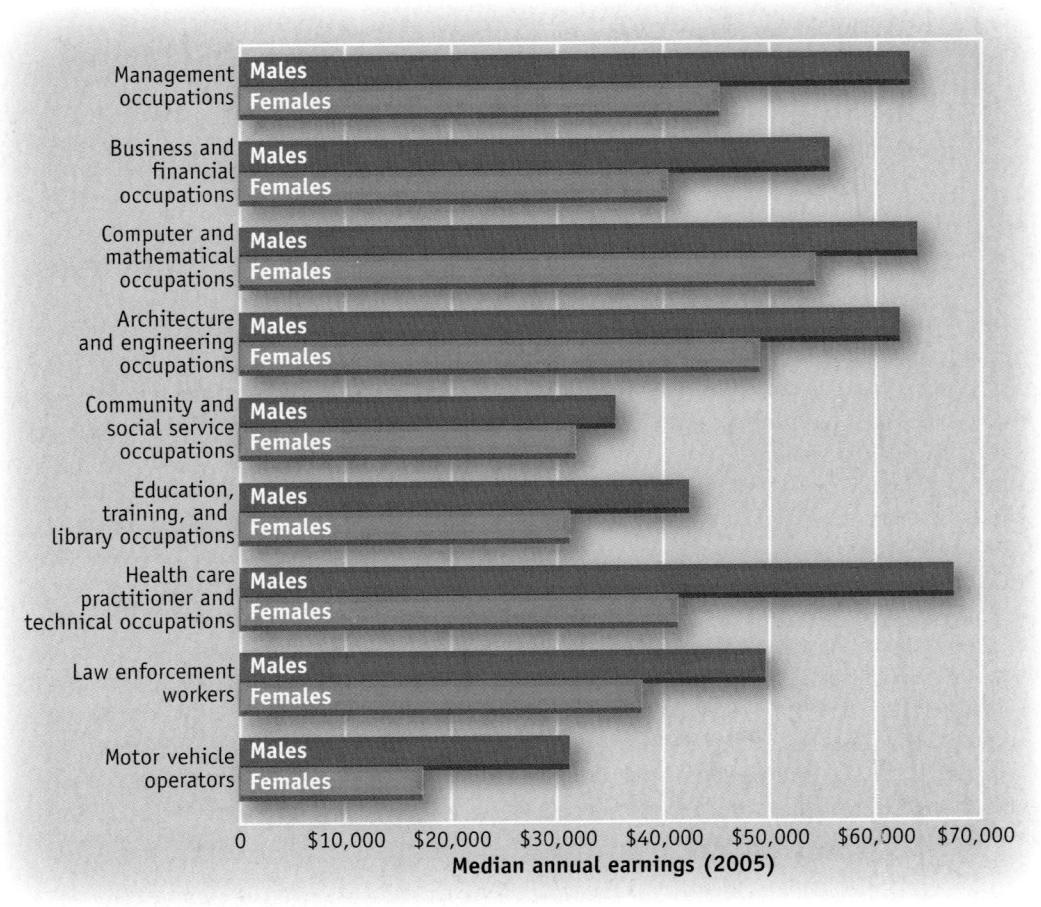

come recognized as a widespread problem that occurs not only on the job but also at home (obscene telephone calls), while walking outside (catcalls and whistles), and in medical and psychotherapy settings. It also takes place in schools and colleges (see **Figure 10.13**). Teachers and professors who pressure students for sexual favors in exchange for grades have been singled out for strong criticism.

Recent research shows that minority women experience a form of "double jeopardy" when it comes to workplace harassment. Berdahl and Moore (2006) surveyed employees from five ethnically diverse organizations and found that women experience more harassment than men, that minorities experience more harassment than whites, and that minority women experience more harassment than any other group. Betz (2006) distinguishes between two categories of sexual harassment in the workplace. In *quid pro quo harassment* employees are expected to give in to sexual demands in exchange for employment, raises, promotions, and so forth. In *hostile environment harassment* employees are exposed to sexist or sexually oriented comments, cartoons, posters, and so forth. Given that harassment continues to be a major problem in the workplace and is related to poorer job outcomes (Settles et al., 2006), future researchers will no doubt continue to examine the relationship between ethnicity and gender in this area.

Sexual Harassment in the Schools

Type of harassment	Percentage reporting
Received suggestive gestures, looks, comments, or jokes	89
Touched, pinched, or grabbed	83
Leaned over or cornered	47
Received sexual notes or pictures	28
Pressured to do something sexual	27
Forced to do something sexual	10
Other form of harassment	7

Note: Percentages do not add to 100 because readers could indicate more than one type of harassment.

Figure 10.13

Reported incidence of sexual harassment in the schools. This figure depicts common forms of sexual harassment in grades 2 through 12 and the percentage of girls reporting them. (Adapted from Stein, Marshall, & Tropp, 1993)

Adapted from Stein, N., Marshall, N. L., & Tropp, L.R. (1993). *Secrets in public: Sexual harassment in our schools,* p. 4. Copyright © 1993 Center for Research on Women at Wellesley College and the NOW Legal Defense and Education Fund. Adapted by permission.

Gender in the Past and in the Future

LEARNING OBJECTIVES

- *Explain the basis for traditional gender roles and why they are changing.*
- *Define gender-role identity and discuss two alternatives to traditional gender roles.*

In Western society, gender roles are in a state of transition. As we have noted, sweeping changes in the female role have already occurred. It's hard to imagine today, but less than 100 years ago, women were not allowed to vote or to manage their own finances. Only a few decades ago, it was virtually unheard of for a woman to initiate a date, manage a corporation, or run for public office. In this section, we'll discuss why gender roles are changing and what the future might bring.

Why Are Gender Roles Changing?

Many people are baffled as to why gender roles are changing. They can't understand why age-old traditions are being flouted and discarded. A number of theories attempt to explain why gender roles are in transition. Basically, these theories look at the past to explain the present and the future. A key consideration is that gender roles have always constituted a division of labor. In earlier societies, the division of labor according to gender was a natural outgrowth of some simple realities. In most hunting-and-gathering societies, as well as most herding societies, an economic premium was put on physical strength. Men tend to be stronger than women, so they were better equipped to handle such jobs as hunting and farming. In most societies they got those assignments, whereas women were responsible for gathering, home maintenance, and childrearing (Nielsen, 1990). Another consideration was that women had to assume responsibility for nursing young children. Thus, although people might have worked out other ways of doing things (and some cultures did), there were some basic reasons for dividing labor according to gender in premodern societies.

Traditional gender roles are a carryover from the past. Once traditions are established, they have a way of perpetuating themselves. Over the past century or so in Western society, these divisions of labor have become increasingly antiquated. Therein lies the prime reason for changes in gender roles. *Traditional gender roles no longer make economic sense.* The widespread use of machines to do work has rendered physical strength relatively unimportant. Furthermore, as we move toward a service economy, physical strength will become even less relevant.

The future is likely to bring even more dramatic shifts in gender roles. We can see the beginnings of these changes now. For example, although women still bear children, nursing responsibilities are now optional. Moreover, as women become more economically independent, they will have less need to get married solely for economic reasons. The possibility of developing a fetus outside the uterus may seem farfetched now, but some experts predict that it is only a matter of time. If so, both men and women could be "mothers." In light of these and other changes in modern society, it is safe to say that gender roles are likely to remain in flux for some time to come.

© Paul Wood/Alamy

A division of labor based on gender no longer makes economic sense in our society. Relatively few jobs require great physical strength; the rest call for skills possessed by both men and women.

that this emotional unresponsiveness is characteristic of many men and that it seems to figure importantly in marital dissatisfaction (Larson & Pleck, 1998).

Many studies indicate that women are more skilled than men in nonverbal communication—a key component of the expressive style. For example, they are better at reading and sending nonverbal messages (Hall, 1998; Hall & Matsumoto, 2004). And women tend to be better listeners (Miller, Berg, & Archer, 1983). But women engage in some "negative" expressive behaviors as well (Brehm, 1992). For example, during relationship conflicts, women are more likely to (1) display strong negative emotions (Noller, 1985, 1987); (2) use psychologically coercive tactics, such as guilt manipulations, verbal attacks, and power plays (Barnes & Buss, 1985); and (3) reject attempts at reconciliation (Barnes & Buss, 1985).

Common Mixed-Gender Communication Problems

Let's explore some common mixed-gender communication problems noted by Tannen. To keep things simple, we use "she" and "he" to illustrate various scenarios, but you should interpret these labels loosely for the reasons we have mentioned.

Cross-Purpose Communication

People expect their friends and partners to support and reassure them. When a mismatch occurs between their expectations and reality, they become confused, frustrated, and possibly hurt or angry. Consider a woman who tells her partner about a recurring problem she is having at work—not because she wants help with the problem but because she wants some sympathy. However, thinking that she is seeking a solution to the problem, he gives her advice. She is frustrated because she did not receive the consolation she sought. He is frustrated about her repeated complaining, because he has offered her the same advice in the past. Although neither wants to frustrate the other, that's exactly what happens because they are talking at cross-purposes. She wants him to commiserate with her, but he thinks she wants him to help her solve a problem. Each assumes the other knows what each wants, and neither does. Cross-purpose communication can crop up quite frequently in intimate relationships.

Talking About People Versus Things

Women's conversations frequently involve sharing the details of their personal lives or talking *about* people. Talking about people isn't necessarily destructive, although it can be if it turns into talking *against* people. As they did in childhood, women share secrets with one another as a way of being close. Men are interested in details, too, but those of a different kind: politics, news, and sports. Women fear being left out by not knowing what is going on in friends' lives; men fear being left out by not knowing what is going on in the world (Tannen, 1990).

Tannen suggests that both women and men need to extend their communication strategies by adding aspects of the other style to their own. Thus, some men may need to learn to be more comfortable talking about their personal lives, whereas some women could benefit by talking more about impersonal topics and talking in a more assertive manner.

Lecturing and Listening

In many mixed-gender conversations, particularly those in public settings, women often end up playing the listener to the man's "lecture." Are men self-centered big-mouths? Are women meek, passive creatures? Instead of these interpretations, Tannen suggests that men and women are playing different games that are rooted in their childhood experiences. Men are playing "Do you respect me?" and women, "Do you like me?"

As we noted, males use conversation to jockey for status and challenge the authority of others—both men and women. A woman who lacks experience defending herself against these challenges can easily misinterpret an assertive man's style as an attack on her credibility. Similarly, women have been taught to hand off the conversational ball and expect that others will do the same. While most women reciprocate, many men don't. When this happens, some women may feel awkward drawing the focus of the conversation back to themselves, because this style was frowned on during their childhood play with other girls.

To improve this kind of mixed-gender communication problem, Tannen suggests that women who tire of listening need to be more assertive and take some control of the conversation. Also, some men might be relieved to learn that they don't always have to talk. As we noted in Chapter 7, effective listening is a much-underrated communication skill.

Toward a "Shared Language"

Tannen asserts that many frustrations in personal and work relationships could be avoided if men and women were more aware of gender differences in communication styles. Many people misperceive style differences as the other's personal failings. Individuals who are able to see the style differences for what they are can eliminate a lot of negative feelings. As Tannen (1990) says, "Nothing hurts more than being told your intentions are bad when you know they are good, or being told that you are doing something wrong when you know you're just doing it your way" (pp. 297–298). People need to understand that there are different ways of listening, talking, and having conversations, not just their own way. For some hints on how to improve gender-based communication, see **Figure 10.15**.

Hints to Improve Communication

Hints for men

1. Notice whether or not you have a tendency to interrupt women. If you do, work on breaking this habit. When you catch yourself interrupting, say, "I'm sorry, I interrupted you. Go ahead with what you were saying."
2. Avoid responding to a woman's questions in monosyllables ("Yep," "Nope," "Uh-huh"). Give her more details about what you did and explain why.
3. Learn the art of conversational give and take. Ask women questions about themselves. And listen carefully when they respond.
4. Don't order women around. For example, don't say, "Get me the newspaper." First, notice whether it might be an inconvenience for her to do something for you. If it isn't, say, "Would you mind giving me the newspaper?" or "Would you please give me the newspaper?"
5. Don't be a space hog. Be more aware of the space you take up when you sit with others (especially women). Watch that you don't make women feel crowded out.
6. Learn to open up about personal issues. Talk about your feelings, interests, hopes, and relationships. Talking about personal things helps others know who you are (and probably helps you clarify your self-perceptions, too).
7. Learn to convey enthusiasm about things in addition to the victories of your favorite sports teams.
8. Don't be afraid to ask for help if you need it.

Hints for women

1. When others interrupt you, politely but firmly redirect the conversation back to you. You can say, for example, "Excuse me. I haven't finished my point."
2. Look the person you're talking with directly in the eye.
3. A lower-pitched voice gets more attention and respect than a higher-pitched one, which is associated with little girls. Keeping your abdominal muscles firm as you speak will help keep your voice low.
4. Learn to be comfortable claiming more space (without becoming a space hog). If you want your presence to be noted, don't fold yourself up into an unobtrusive object.
5. Talk more about yourself and your accomplishments. This isn't offensive as long as others are doing the same and the circumstances are appropriate. If the conversation turns to photography and you know a lot about the topic, it's perfectly OK to share your expertise.
6. Make a point of being aware of current events so you'll be knowledgeable about what others are discussing and have an opinion to contribute.
7. Resist the impulse to be overly apologetic. Although many women say "I'm sorry" to convey sympathy or concern (not apology), these words are likely to be interpreted as an apology. Because apologizing puts one in a lower-power position, women who use apologetic words inappropriately put themselves at a disadvantage.

Figure 10.15

Hints to improve communication between women and men. To have productive personal and work relationships in today's world demands that people be knowledgeable about gender and communication styles. Men and women may be able to benefit from the suggestions listed here. (Compiled by the authors based on insights from Tannen, 1990)

KEY IDEAS

Gender Stereotypes

▶ Many stereotypes have developed around behavioral differences between the genders, although the distinctions between the male and female stereotypes are less rigid than they used to be. Gender stereotypes may vary depending on ethnicity, and they typically favor males.

Gender Similarities and Differences

▶ Some contemporary researchers have adopted the gender similarity hypothesis, emphasizing the fact that males and females are similar on most psychological variables.

▶ There are no gender differences in general intelligence. When it comes to verbal abilities, gender differences are small, and they generally favor females. Gender differences in mathematical abilities are typically small as well, and they favor males. Males perform much better than females on the spatial ability of mental rotation.

▶ Research shows that males typically are somewhat higher in self-esteem and more physically aggressive than females. Females are higher in relational aggression. Males and females are similar in the experience of emotions, but females are more likely to outwardly display emotions. Males have more permissive attitudes about casual sex and are more sexually active than females. The genders are similar in overall mental health, but they differ in prevalence rates for specific psychological disorders.

▶ The gender differences that do exist are quite small. Moreover, they are group differences that tell us little about individuals. Nonetheless, some people still believe that psychological differences between the genders are substantial. Social role theory and social constructionism provide two explanations for this phenomenon.

Biological Origins of Gender Differences

▶ Biological explanations of gender differences include those based on evolution, brain organization, and hormones. Evolutionary psychologists explain gender differences on the basis of their purported adaptive value in ancestral environments. These analyses are speculative and difficult to test empirically.

▶ Regarding brain organization, some studies suggest that males exhibit more cerebral specialization than females. However, linking this finding to gender differences in cognitive abilities is questionable for a number of reasons.

▶ Efforts to tie hormone levels to gender differences have also been troubled by interpretive problems. Nonetheless, there probably is some hormonal basis for gender differences in aggression and in some aspects of sexual behavior.

Environmental Origins of Gender Differences

▶ The socialization of gender roles appears to take place through the processes of reinforcement and punishment, observational learning, and self-socialization. These processes operate through many social institutions, but parents, peers, schools, and the media are the primary sources of gender-role socialization.

Gender Role Expectations

▶ Five key attributes of the traditional male role include achievement, aggression, autonomy, sexuality, and stoicism. The theme of anti-femininity cuts across these dimensions. Problems associated with the traditional male role include excessive pressure to succeed, difficulty dealing with emotions, and sexual problems. Homophobia is a particular problem for men.

▶ Role expectations for females include the marriage mandate, the motherhood mandate, and working outside the home. Among the principal costs of the female role are diminished aspirations, juggling of multiple roles, and ambivalence about sexuality. In addition to these psychological problems, women also face sexist hurdles in the economic domain and may be victims of aggression.

Gender in the Past and in the Future

▶ Gender roles have always represented a division of labor. They are changing today, and they seem likely to continue changing because they no longer mesh with economic reality. Consequently, an important question is how to move beyond traditional gender roles. The perspectives of androgyny and gender-role transcendence provide two possible answers to this question.

Application: Bridging the Gender Gap in Communication

▶ Because of different socialization experiences, many males and females learn different communication styles. These differences in experience and style seem to underlie a number of mixed-gender communication problems. Men and women need to understand these style differences to reduce interpersonal conflicts and the frustrations they cause.

▶ Men are more likely to use an instrumental style of communication, whereas women tend toward an expressive style. Common mixed-gender communication problems include cross-purposes communication, differences in the tendency to talk about people versus things, and falling into the lecture and listen trap.

KEY TERMS

Aggression p. 308
Androcentrism p. 305
Androgyny p. 328
Cerebral hemispheres p. 312
Corpus callosum p. 312
Expressiveness p. 304
Gender p. 303
Gender-role identity p. 328
Gender-role transcendence perspective p. 329
Gender roles p. 313
Gender schemas p. 315
Gender stereotypes p. 304
Homophobia p. 321
Hormones p. 312
Instrumentality p. 304
Meta-analysis p. 306
Sexism p. 324
Social constructionism p. 310
Social role theory p. 310
Socialization p. 313

KEY PEOPLE

Sandra Bem pp. 328–329
Alice Eagly p. 310
Janet Shibley Hyde p. 303
Joseph Pleck p. 319
Deborah Tannen pp. 330–333

PRACTICE TEST

1. Taken as a whole, gender differences in verbal abilities are:
   a. small and favor females.
   b. large and favor females.
   c. nonexistent.
   d. small and favor males.

2. Among the following traits, the largest gender differences are found in:
   a. verbal abilities.
   b. mathematical abilities.
   c. physical aggression.
   d. conformity.

3. Which of the following statements about gender differences is false?
   a. Males have higher self-esteem than females.
   b. Males are more physically aggressive than females.
   c. Males have more permissive attitudes about sex than females.
   d. Women talk more than men.

4. The finding that males exhibit more cerebral specialization than females supports which of the following biologically based explanations for gender differences?
   a. Evolutionary theory
   b. Brain organization
   c. Hormones
   d. Social constructionism

5. Four-year-old Rachel seems to pay particular attention to what her mother and her older sister do, and she often imitates them. What is taking place?
   a. Sexism
   b. Observational learning
   c. Operant conditioning
   d. Androcentric bias

6. Parents tend to respond more negatively to _____ behavior, especially in _____.
   a. gender appropriate; boys
   b. gender appropriate; girls
   c. gender inappropriate; boys
   d. gender inappropriate; girls

7. Which of the following statements about peer socialization is true?
   a. Peer groups appear to influence gender-role socialization more in boys than girls.
   b. Girls play in smaller groups and boys in larger groups.
   c. High status in boys' groups is achieved by making suggestions to others.
   d. Peers have relatively little impact on gender-role socialization.

8. Which of the following is *not* a problem with the male role?
   a. Pressure to succeed
   b. Emotional inexpressiveness
   c. Sexual problems
   d. Androgyny

9. Which of the following is *not* a problem with the female role?
   a. Poor nonverbal communication skills
   b. Diminished aspirations
   c. Juggling multiple roles
   d. Ambivalence about sexuality

10. According to Deborah Tannen, men tend to use an _____ communication style, and women tend to use an _____ communication style.
   a. expressive; expressive
   b. expressive; instrumental
   c. instrumental; instrumental
   d. instrumental; expressive

Book Companion Website

Visit the Book Companion Website at **academic.cengage.com/psychology/weiten,** where you will find tutorial quizzes, flash cards, and web links for every chapter, a final exam, and more! You can also link to the Psychology Resource Center (accessible directly at **academic.cengage.com/login**) for a range of psychology-related resources.

Personal Explorations Workbook

The following exercises in your *Personal Explorations Workbook* may enhance your self-understanding in relation to issues raised in this chapter. **Questionnaire 10.1:** Personal Attributes Questionnaire. **Personal Probe 10.1:** How Do You Feel about Gender Roles? **Personal Probe 10.2:** Reflecting on the Power of Gender Roles.

ANSWERS

1. a Page 306
2. c Pages 306–308
3. d Page 309
4. b Pages 311–312
5. b Page 314
6. c Page 314
7. b Page 316
8. d Pages 319–321
9. a Pages 322–324
10. d Page 331

CHAPTER 11

Development in Adolescence and Adulthood

Teenage son or daughter: "All my parents ever ask me is whether my homework is done or how I'm doing in school. Am I studying hard enough? Do I know how hard it is to get into a good college? As if I don't know all that! Oh, sure, when I'm out with my friends they ask about where I'm going to be and who else is going to be there . . . but they don't see how important my social life is, that what I'm learning from my friends is just as important for life as the stuff I learn about in school. What they don't realize is that homework and school isn't really as important as who I'm with and what we're doing. The parties I go to, the teams I'm on, who my friends are matter as much or more than all those tests and quizzes. They have no idea how complicated my life is!"

Teen's mother or father: "Life is more complicated now than ever. I just want my child to realize how much I've sacrificed and saved and worked to make our lives as carefree as possible. I don't ask a lot, really, but grades really matter today—I wish I knew when I was a teen what I know now! I would have made many different decisions, let me tell you, and I don't want my child to have to learn the hard way or to make the same mistakes. What you do now, the habits you form, will help you in the long run. I know friends are important—I had a lot of friends at that age—but friends will be there. What you learn or don't learn now can affect you in the future. I hope my child understands that I am just trying to help."

THE TRANSITION OF ADOLESCENCE
Physical Changes
Cognitive Changes
Personality Changes
Adolescent Suicide

THE EXPANSE OF ADULTHOOD
Early Adulthood (From About Age 20 to 40)
Middle Adulthood (From About Age 40 to 65)
Late Adulthood (After Age 65)

AGING: A GRADUAL PROCESS
Physical Changes
Cognitive Changes
Personality Changes

DEATH AND DYING
Attitudes About Death
The Process of Dying
Bereavement and Grieving

APPLICATION: BECOMING AN EFFECTIVE PARENT
Dimensions of Childrearing
Correlates of Parenting Styles

LIVING IN TODAY'S WORLD *Promoting Resilience in Children*
Rearing Adolescents
Toward Effective Parenting
Using Punishment Effectively

REVIEW

PRACTICE TEST

Do these scripts sound a little familiar? Have you ever been frustrated by your parents' or your child's unwillingness to see things from your perspective, to understand life as you see it? What the teen and the teen's parents say in this scenario nicely illustrate different levels of cognitive and personality development responding to the same situation. They both see the same world, but they are experiencing that world in different ways because they are in different places in the arcs of their lives.

Until the 1970s, researchers assumed that psychological development slowed to a crawl as people reached adulthood. Now, however, psychologists realize that important developmental changes continue across adulthood, even up until the end of life. As a result, researchers are examining these changes in order to portray the crucial patterns and trends that occur. In this chapter, we review the major changes that take place during adolescence and adulthood. We also examine the topics of dying and death. Finally, this chapter's Application offers some suggestions for being an effective parent.

The Transition of Adolescence

LEARNING OBJECTIVES

- *Define and discuss pubescence and secondary sex characteristics.*
- *Define and discuss puberty and primary sex characteristics.*
- *Summarize the findings on early and late maturation in boys and girls.*
- *Describe the cognitive changes that occur during adolescence.*
- *Explain Erikson's psychosocial crisis of adolescence and Marcia's four identity statuses.*
- *Discuss whether adolescence is a period of emotional turmoil and describe recent trends in adolescent suicide.*

Adolescence is a transitional period between childhood and adulthood. Its age boundaries are not exact, but in our society adolescence begins at around age 13 and ends at about age 22. In some ways, adolescents resemble the children they were, yet the many changes they undergo during this stage ensure that they will be different from children in many respects. Similarly, we see glimpses of the adults that adolescents will become, but more often we observe that they don't behave much like adults. As adolescents mature, we see fewer resemblances to children and more similarities to adults.

Although most societies have at least a brief period of adolescence, this phenomenon is not universal across cultures (Schlegel & Barry, 1991). In some cultures, young people move almost directly from childhood to adulthood. A protracted period of adolescence is seen primarily in industrialized nations. In these societies, rapid technological progress has made lengthy education, and therefore prolonged economic dependence, the norm. Thus, in our own culture, middle school, high school, and college students often have a "marginal" status. They are capable of reproduction and are physiologically mature, yet they have not achieved the emotional and economic independence from their parents that are the hallmarks of adulthood. Globalization, immigration, and the emergence of new technologies, among other influences in daily life may alter our current conceptions of adolescence in the future (Larson, 2002). Let's begin our discussion of adolescent development with its most visible aspect: the physical changes that transform the body of a child into that of an adult.

Physical Changes

Do you remember your middle school days when your body grew so fast that your clothes just couldn't "keep up"? This phase of rapid growth in height and weight is called the *adolescent growth spurt*—"spurt" because of the relatively sudden increases in body height and weight. Brought on by hormonal changes, it typically starts at about age 11 in girls and about two years later in boys (Malina, 1990).

Psychologists use the term ***pubescence*** **to describe the two-year span preceding puberty during which the changes leading to physical and sexual maturity take place.** Besides growing taller and heavier during pubescence, children begin to take on the physical features that characterize adults of their respective genders. These bodily changes are termed ***secondary sex characteristics*—physical features that distinguish one gender from the other but that are not essential for reproduction.** For example, boys go through a voice change, develop facial hair, and experience greater skeletal and muscle growth in the upper torso, leading to broader shoulders and enhanced upper-body strength. Females experience breast growth and a widening of the pelvic bones, plus increased fat deposits in this area, resulting in wider hips (Dick et al., 2001; Susman, Dorn, & Schiefelbein, 2003). **Figure 11.1** details these physical changes in boys and girls.

The physical changes we've been describing are triggered by the pituitary gland. This "master gland" of the endocrine system sends signals to the adrenal glands (on top of the kidneys) and gonads (ovaries and testes), which in turn secrete the hormones responsible for the changes in physical characteristics that differentiate males and females.

Note that the capacity to reproduce is not attained in pubescence. This ability develops during ***puberty*, the stage that marks the beginning of adolescence and during which sexual functions reach maturity.** During puberty, the ***primary sex characteristics*—the structures necessary for reproduction**—develop fully. In the male, these structures include the testes, penis, and related internal structures; in females, they include the ovaries, vagina, uterus, and other internal reproductive structures (see **Figure 11.1**).

In females, the onset of puberty is typically signaled by ***menarche*—the first occurrence of menstruation.** American girls typically reach menarche between ages 12 and 13, with further sexual maturation continuing until approximately age 16 (Susman et al., 2003). Most girls are sterile for 12 to 18 months following menarche. (Nevertheless, pregnancy is a possibility for some girls at this age, so any girl who has begun to menstruate should assume that she can become pregnant.) Breast development and the presence of pubic hair serve as important social criteria of adolescence for girls.

In males, there is no clear-cut marker of the onset of sexual maturity, although the capacity to ejaculate is used as an index of puberty (the onset of sperm production not being a visible event). ***Spermarche*, or the first ejaculation,** usually occurs through masturbation, rather than nocturnal emissions (Hyde, 1994a). Experts note that ejaculation may not be a valid index of actual maturity, as early ejaculations may contain seminal fluid but not active sperm. The average age of spermarche in American boys is around age 13 (Halpern et al., 2000), with complete sexual maturation occurring at about 18 (Susman et al., 2003).

As we have noted, puberty arrives about two years later in boys than in girls. In fact, the major reason that adult males are taller than adult females is that males typically experience two additional years of development before the onset of the growth spurt (Graber, Petersen, & Brooks-Gunn, 1996). Generational changes have occurred in the timing of puberty, at least for girls in industrialized countries (Anderson, Dallal, & Must, 2003). (To date, no valid method has been found for establishing the existence of a comparable trend among boys.) Today's girls begin puberty earlier, and complete it more rapidly, than their counterparts in earlier generations. This trend apparently reflects improvements in nutrition and medical care (Brooks-Gunn, 1991). In the United States and some other industrialized countries, this trend appears to have leveled off, probably

Figure 11.1

Physical development during pubescence and puberty. During pubescence, the two years prior to puberty, a growth spurt occurs and secondary sex characteristics develop. During puberty, the primary sex characteristics mature. These various physical changes are caused by hormonal secretions.

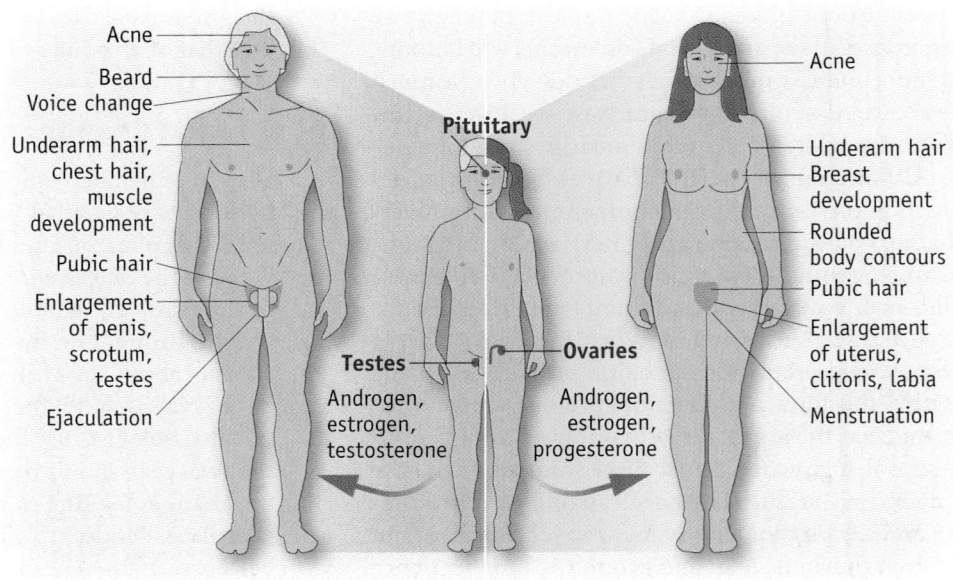

For Better or For Worse®

5-5 ©1988 Universal Press Syndicate

© 1988 Lynn Johnston Productions, Inc./Distributed by Universal Press Syndicate. Reprinted with permission. All rights reserved.

because of the high standard of living (Tanner, 1990). Thus, the onset of sexual maturation may have a genetically predetermined age "floor."

Puberty also brings important changes in other body organs. For instance, the heart and lungs increase considerably in size, and the heart rate drops. These changes are more marked for boys than for girls and are responsible, in part, for the superior performance of males in certain physical activities relative to females. Before about age 12, boys and girls are similar in physical strength, speed, and endurance. After puberty, boys have clear advantage in all three areas (Smoll & Schutz, 1990). After sexual maturation has been attained, adolescents continue to mature physically until their secondary sex characteristics are fully developed and their body has reached adult height and proportions. In girls, such growth continues until about 17 years of age; in boys, it goes on until about age 20.

Variation in the onset of pubescence and puberty is normal. Still, the timing of these physical changes figures importantly in adjustment. More specifically, research suggests that girls who mature early and boys who mature late seem to feel particularly anxious and self-conscious about their changing bodies (Graber et al., 1997; Sinkkonen, Anttila, & Siimes, 1998). The early-maturing girl is taller and heavier than most of the girls and nearly all of the boys her age. The late-maturing boy is shorter and slighter than most of the boys and nearly all of the girls his age. To make matters worse, both groups have body types that are at odds with the cultural ideals of extreme slenderness for females and muscular physique for males.

Compared to other girls, those who mature early fare more poorly in school, are less popular, have lower self-confidence, and have earlier sexual experiences and more unwanted pregnancies (Ge, Conger, & Elder, 1996; Stattin & Magnusson, 1990). They are also more likely to have tried alcohol, cigarettes, and marijuana (Lanza & Collins, 2002), to have more negative body images (Striegel-Moore et al., 2001), and to be depressed (Rierdan & Koff, 1991). Girls who mature early are often socially isolated from their peers who are maturing "on time," which propels the former to seek out older adolescent friends, thereby compounding their emotional distress (Ge et al., 2003). At age 24, early-maturing women have had more self-reported psychological disorders and current psychosocial symptoms compared to on-time maturers (Graber et al., 2004). Late-maturing boys have been found to feel more inadequate, to feel more insecure, and to think less of themselves than other boys do (Siegel, 1982). Still, early-maturing boys who were perceived by others to be well adjusted reported more emotional distress and hostile feelings than their less-developed peers (Ge, Conger, & Elder, 2001). At age 24, late-maturing males had engaged in significantly more deviant behavior and substance abuse than other men (Graber et al.,

© David Young-Wolff/Photographer's Choice/Getty Images

As they mature, adolescents look increasingly like adults, although boys typically lag two years behind girls in physical development.

2004). Optimal adjustment for girls is associated with puberty coming "on time," whereas optimal adjustment for boys is most often related to early puberty. Girls' and boys' *perceptions* of the timing of their puberty and their feelings of attractiveness follow this same pattern (see **Figure 11.2**).

Cognitive Changes

Around the time of early adolescence, major changes take place in thinking and problem solving (Eccles, Wigfield, & Byrnes, 2003). Compared to those who are younger, adolescents can think more abstractly and more efficiently. They also become more self-aware and self-reflective and can view problems from several perspectives rather than only one. Thus, the thinking of adolescents is qualitatively different from that of younger children (Fischer & Bidell, 1998; Flavell, Miller, & Miller, 2001). Whereas children go about solving problems on a trial-and-error basis, most adolescents are capable of solving problems by generating a number of possible hypotheses and systematically testing them. These sudden intellectual advances in early adolescence can have a down side: Teens sometimes miss obvious answers through overanalysis, making a reasoning task (such as organizing a potluck party and deciding who brings what type of dish) more complicated than it needs to be. Elkind (1978) refers to the resulting "Why didn't I think of that?" moments as *pseudostupidity.*

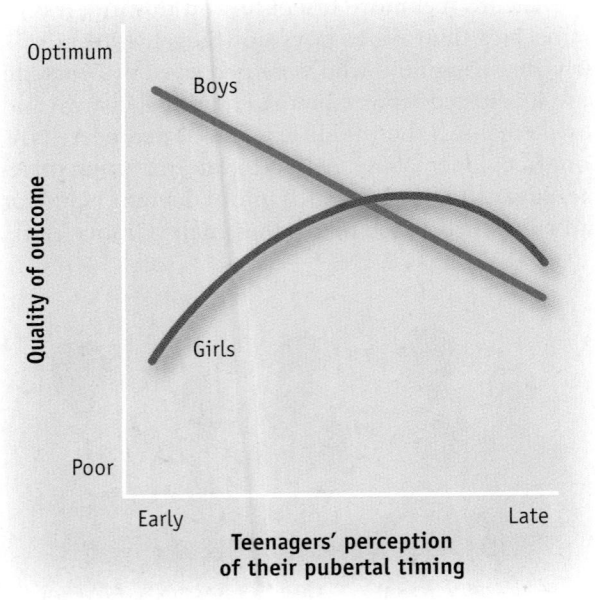

Figure 11.2

Perceived timing of puberty and optimal adjustment. For girls, feelings of attractiveness and a positive body image are associated with the perception that puberty arrives "on time"; for boys, these feelings are associated with the perception that puberty arrives early.

Adapted from Tobin-Richards, M. H., Boxer, A. A., & Petersen, A. C. (1983). The psychological significance of pubertal change: Sex differences in perceptions of self during early adolescence. In J. Brooks-Gunn & A. C. Petersen (Eds.), *Girls at puberty: Biological and psychosocial perspectives.* New York: Plenum Publishing. Copyright © 1983 Plenum Publishing Co. Adapted by permission of Springer Science and Business Media and the authors.

Web Link 11.1 **Adolescent Health and Mental Health**

Visitors at this website will find links to resources about adolescence that cover many of the pressing health and mental health issues important to this phase of development. The site is edited by Michael Fenichel, a prominent psychologist in the use of the Internet to distribute quality professional information to the public.

As would be expected, adolescents show increases across several spheres of knowledge compared to children. For example, as individuals age, they know more facts (declarative knowledge), have more skills (procedural knowledge), and have a greater understanding of why one problem-solving approach works better than another (conceptual knowledge) (Byrnes, 2001; Eccles et al., 2003).

Adolescents are also more skilled than children in deductive reasoning skills (Eccles et al., 2003). These skills involve the ability to reach logical conclusions when given certain information (including that which is contrary to fact). Age-related increases have also been found in mathematical, spatial, and scientific reasoning ability, as well as in some memory processes (Byrnes, 2001; Eccles et al., 2003).

Another facet of cognitive functioning involves decision making about taking risks . Numerous studies have looked at age differences in the tendency to engage in physically harmful risky behavior: smoking, drinking, and unprotected sex (Byrnes, Miller, & Schafer, 1999). Most research shows that older adolescents are more likely than younger adolescents and children to engage in such behavior (DiClemente, Hansen, & Ponton, 1995; Eccles et al., 2003). When researchers examine risky behavior by ethnic groups, they find that white teens are more likely to smoke or drink alcohol than Hispanics or blacks, while the latter group is more likely to have had sexual intercourse than either of the other two groups (Blum et al., 2000). Because "risky" adolescents are as knowledgeable about the possible negative outcomes of their behavior as "nonrisky" adolescents, psychologists speculate that the causes of risk-taking behavior are not cognitively rooted (Eccles et al., 2003). Instead, they probably involve other aspects of decision making, such as self-regulation (see Chapter 5).

Personality Changes

Adolescents are faced with a number of challenges in the realm of personality, including greater autonomy

(Noom, Dekovic, & Meeus, 2001) and "individuation," determining which attitudes, feelings, and beliefs are truly their own (Josselson, 1988). They must grapple with identity questions and deal with the stresses of moving from childhood to adulthood.

The Search for Identity

As adulthood looms closer, adolescents turn their attention to their place in the larger social order. Erik Erikson (1968), an influential psychoanalyst who followed in Sigmund Freud's footsteps, devised an elaborate theory of development over the lifespan that has been enormously influential in understanding how youngsters cope with identity issues in adolescence. Erikson's theory partitioned the life span into eight stages, each of which brings a *psychosocial crisis* involving transitions in important social relationships. **Figure 11.3** depicts all eight of Erikson's stages. We'll discuss the fifth stage in this section and subsequent stages in our upcoming coverage of adult development. According to Erikson, ***identity* refers to having a relatively clear and stable sense of who one is in the larger society.** Developing a sense of identity involves wrestling with such important issues as "Who am I?" "What do I stand for?" and "What kind of work do I want to do?" Gender, ethnicity, and sexual orientation are also important aspects of identity development.

© Ted Streshinsky/Corbis

Erik Erikson

According to Erikson, identity emerges out of an "identity crisis," or a period of personal questioning during which individuals reflect on and experiment with various occupational possibilities and value choices (political, religious, sexual, and so forth). For most people, an identity crisis is not a sudden or agonizing experience but rather the gradual evolution of a sense of who one is. An identity crisis usually ends with a commitment to a specific career and personal value system. According to James Marcia (1980), these two factors of crisis and commitment combine in various ways to produce four identity statuses (see **Figure 11.4** on the next page) instead of just the two outcomes shown in **Figure 11.3**. Note that these are not stages that people pass through, but rather statuses that characterize a person's identity orientation at any particular time. Thus, a person may never experience some of the statuses, including identity achievement. The point is that in the midst of all the biological, psychological, and social changes, adolescents try to maintain a connection to their past selves as they develop into their future selves (Chandler, et al., 2003).

The status of *identity foreclosure* is a premature commitment to visions, values, and roles prescribed by one's parents. *Moratorium* involves delaying commit-

Erikson's Stages of Psychosocial Development

Stage	Psychosocial crisis	Significant social relationships	Favorable outcome
1. First year of life	Trust versus mistrust	Mother or mother substitute	Trust and optimism
2. Second and third years	Autonomy versus doubt	Parents	A sense of self-control and adequacy
3. Fourth through sixth years	Initiative versus guilt	Basic family	Purpose and direction; ability to initiate one's own activities
4. Age 6 through puberty	Industry versus inferiority	Neighborhood, school	Competence in intellectual, social, and physical skills
5. Adolescence	Identity versus diffusion	Peer groups and outgroups; models of leadership	An integrated image of oneself as a unique person
6. Early adulthood	Intimacy versus isolation	Partners in friendship and sex; competition, cooperation	An ability to form close and lasting relationships, to make career commitments
7. Middle adulthood	Generativity versus stagnation	Divided labor and shared household	Concern for family, society, and future generations
8. The aging years	Integrity versus despair	"Humankind," "my kind"	A sense of fulfillment and satisfaction with one's life; willingness to face death

Figure 11.3

Overview of Erikson's stages. Building on earlier work by Sigmund Freud (see Chapter 2), Erik Erikson (1963) divided the life span into eight stages. Each stage involves a psychosocial crisis (column 2) that is played out in certain social relationships (column 3). If a crisis is handled effectively, a favorable outcome results (column 4).

Adapted from Erikson, E. H. (1963). *Childhood and society* (2nd ed.). New York: W. W. Norton. Copyright © 1950, 1963 by W. W. Norton & Co. Inc. Copyright renewed 1978, 1991 by Erik H. Erikson. Used by permission of W. W. Norton & Company, Inc. Futher permission from Hogarth Press (UK). Reprinted by permission of The Random House Group Ltd.

Marcia's Four Identity Statuses		
	Crisis present	**Crisis absent**
Commitment present	*Identity achievement* (successful achievement of a sense of identity)	*Identity foreclosure* (unquestioning adoption of parental or societal values)
Commitment absent	*Identity moratorium* (active struggling for a sense of identity)	*Identity diffusion* (absence of struggle for identity, with no obvious concern about this)

Figure 11.4

Marcia's four identity statuses. According to James Marcia, the experience of an identity crisis and the development of personal commitments can combine into four possible identity statuses, as shown in this diagram.

Adapted from Marcia, J. E. (1980). Identity in adolescence. In J. Adelson (Ed.), *Handbook of adolescent psychology* (pp. 159–210). New York: Wiley. Copyright © 1980 by John Wiley & Sons. Inc. Adapted by permission of John Wiley & Sons, Inc.

ment for a while to experiment with alternative ideologies. *Identity achievement* is arriving at a sense of self and direction after some consideration of alternative possibilities. Finally, *identity diffusion* is an inability to make identity commitments. In both identity achievement and foreclosure, the identity crisis is resolved because a sense of commitment is present. Of course, in foreclosure, the commitment is not an independently developed one, as is desirable. Individuals in both the moratorium and diffusion statuses have not resolved the identity crisis. While those experiencing identity diffusion have given up the search for identity, "moratoriums" are still pursuing it. As they move into their 20s, adolescents typically shift from the foreclosure and diffusion statuses to the moratorium or achievement statuses (Kroger, 1997; Meeus, 1996).

Considerable research has been done on identity statuses and their characteristics (Marcia, 1980, 1991; Marcia et al., 1993). Compared to those in other statuses, adolescents in identity foreclosure are strongly connected to their families, cognitively rigid, conventional, and conservative in their values. Those going through a moratorium are conflicted between conforming and rebelling, have ambivalent feelings toward their parents, and are perceived by others to be intense. The identity-diffused feel alienated from their parents, exhibit lower levels of moral reasoning, and show less emotional intimacy than those in the other statuses. Those who experience identity achievement are more cognitively flexible, function at higher levels of moral reasoning, and have more emotionally intimate relationships.

Time of Turmoil?

Is adolescence a period of emotional upheaval and turmoil? G. Stanley Hall (1904), the first psychologist

The Hurried Child: Growing Up Too Fast, Too Soon
by David Elkind (Perseus Publishing, 2006)

In this eye-opening book, psychologist David Elkind shows how recent changes in the structure of family life have altered views of children and their needs. Earlier generations saw children as needing adult protection and guidance, a view consistent with the "traditional" family structure, in which at least one parent was available to the children at all times. Today, in many stepfamilies, single-parent households, and dual-earner families, such nurturing is impossible for parents to provide. Many of these parents have alleviated their anxiety about parenthood by adopting a new conception of children as "superkids" who can take care of themselves.

This new view of children as "miniature adults" is mirrored in every facet of children's culture: education, television, movies, and music. Computer software for infants, video games for children, and the Internet also encourage the hurrying of intellectual and social development. Thus, society as a whole conspires with the parents to "hurry" children to outgrow their need for nurturance as quickly as possible.

According to Elkind, pressuring children to grow up fast can produce negative outcomes ranging from academic failure to psychosomatic illness to teenage suicide. Nevertheless, he maintains an attitude of optimism and hope that, with awareness of the pressures today's children face, parents can and will seek to alleviate their children's stress. Reading this book can help a concerned parent to do just that.

Web Link 11.2 **Erik Erikson Tutorial Homepage**

Margaret Anderson, who teaches at Cortland College in New York, has developed a set of tutorials on major figures of importance to educational psychology. Her Erik Erikson tutorial includes a summary of his eight stages of development, biographical details, some controversies regarding his theories, and links to other online sources.

to study adolescence, thought so. In fact, he specifically characterized adolescence as a period of "storm and stress." Hall attributed this turmoil to the conflicts between the physical changes of puberty and society's demands for social and emotional maturity.

Does research support Hall's idea? To answer this question, Jeffrey Arnett (1999) looked at the research on three relevant issues. First, there is evidence that *parent-adolescent conflicts* increase during (early) adolescence (Laursen, Coy, and Collins, 1998). Adolescents also experience more *volatile emotions and extremes of mood* than preadolescents or adults do (Larson & Richards, 1994). Finally, adolescents engage in more *risky behaviors:* delinquent and antisocial behavior, alcohol and substance abuse, careless sexual practices, and school failure (Perkins & Borden, 2003).

Increases in these areas are not found in more traditional (preindustrial) cultures (Suarez-Orozco & Suarez-Orozco, 1995). Thus, Arnett argues that there is support for a modified storm-and-stress view that takes into account individual differences and cultural variations. Studies focused on the experience of normal adolescents in Western culture, however, indicate that even when conflicts arise, most teens continue to enjoy close relationships with their parents (Larson et al., 1996; van Wel, Linssen, & Abma, 2000). In fact, those adolescents who behave most autonomously and display some independence are also likely to claim a close connection to their parents, who continue to be asked for advice and guidance about life (Fuligni & Eccles, 1993). So, where positive regard for parents is concerned, there is some calm and continuity in the eye of the adolescent storm (Offer, Ostrov, & Howard, 1981; van Wel et al., 2000). Still, even for adolescents who do experience turmoil, it is important not to exaggerate the phenomenon. Based on her extensive studies of adolescents, Anne Petersen (1987) has concluded, "The adolescent's journey toward adulthood is inherently marked by change and upheaval, but need not be fraught with chaos or deep pain" (p. 34).

As young people progress through adolescence, the differences between the vast majority who can cope with the transition to adulthood and the small minority who cannot become increasingly obvious. Emotionally, for example, the general trend between the ages of 6 to 18 is a downward one, such that children feel less competent on various dimensions each year (Jacobs et al., 2002). Those adolescents who have trouble coping are prone to depression, suicidal behavior, drug and alcohol abuse, and chronic delinquency (Petersen, 1988; Takanishi, 1993).

Adolescent Suicide

Adolescent suicide rates have risen alarmingly in recent decades. Suicide among 15- to 24-year-olds increased dramatically after 1960, while it rose only slightly in the general population during this time. Despite these increases, only a small minority of adolescents commit suicide (Meehan et al., 1992). Also, even with the increased rate in the 15–24 age group, the incidence of suicide in this group is about the same as or lower than that for any older age group.

Actually, the suicide crisis among teenagers involves *attempted suicide* more than *completed suicide.* Attempted suicides are technically called ***parasuicides,* a term referring to self-destructive behavior that is not fatal nor entirely intentional.** In other words, adolescents who act out in this manner are not consciously trying to end their lives (De Leo et al., 2004; Diekstra, Kienhorst, & de Wilde, 1996). Parasuicides can range from minor (e.g., inflicting small cuts or wounds on the wrist) to potentially deadly acts (e.g., jumping from a high ledge, ingesting a bottle of pills). Consistent themes accompanying parasucide, however, are excessive emotional turmoil, bewilderment, and nervous distress.

Experts estimate that when all age groups are lumped together, suicide attempts outnumber actual suicidal deaths by a ratio of about 8 to 1 (Cross & Hirschfeld, 1986). However, the ratio of attempted to completed suicides among adolescents is much higher than that for any other age group—anywhere from 100:1 to 200:1 (Maris, Berman, & Silverman, 2000). Suicide attempts by adolescents tend to be desperate cries for attention, help, and support. Gay and lesbian youth are much more likely to attempt suicide than their hetero-

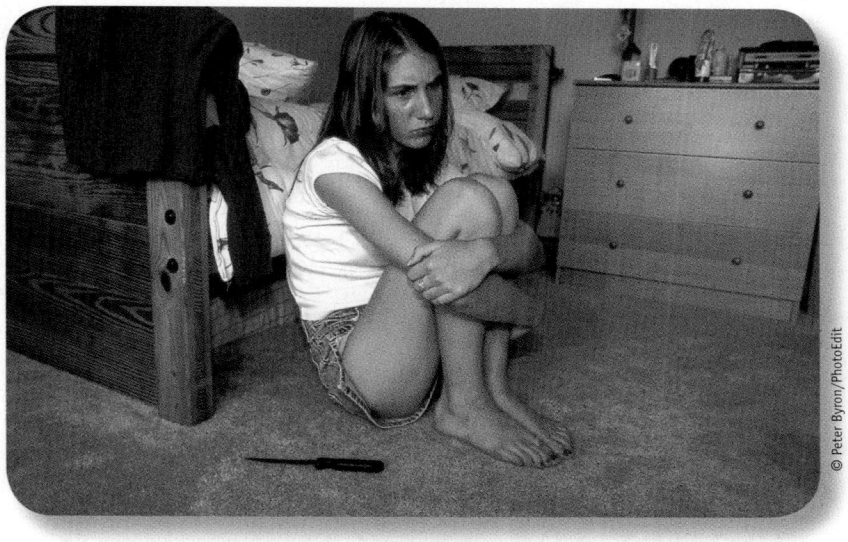

© Peter Byron/PhotoEdit

Most adolescents who attempt suicide have a long history of stress and personal problems and are socially isolated. A perceived failure at school or a perceived social slight can be the "final straw" that triggers a suicide attempt in such teens.

sexual peers. Experts estimate that 33% of homosexual youth have attempted suicide, compared to 13% of their heterosexual peers (Hershberger & D'Augelli, 2000). These high rates are not a result of homosexuality per se but are linked to other factors associated with psychological distress such as high stress, lack of social support, and so forth (Goldfried, 2001).

Girls are more likely to attempt suicide, and boys are more likely to complete suicide (Garland & Zigler, 1993). That's because girls use methods that are less lethal (overdosing on sleeping pills, for instance), whereas boys elect methods with a lower likelihood of survival (shooting or hanging). Another factor may be lower tolerance for the perceived weakness implied in suicide attempts by males (Canetto & Sakinofsky, 1998). White adolescents have higher suicide rates than African American and Hispanic youth. Sadly, Native American adolescents have a suicide rate that is more than twice the national average, a finding that is likely rooted in extreme poverty and a sense of hopelessness about the future (Strickland, 1997).

What drives an adolescent to such a dramatic, but dangerous, gesture? One researcher labeled suicide as a motivated means to escape from aversive self-awareness (Baumeister, 1990), so perhaps some adolescents hope to flee from what they perceive to be unbearable thoughts and feelings about themselves. What seems to be a drastic act to observers is construed as reasonable and acceptable to the teen actor. Consider these troubling facts: *Suicidal ideation*—thinking about committing suicide—is common among high school students, so common that it is almost a "normal" preoccupation (Diekstra, 1995). Around one-third of teen girls in the United States report feeling hopeless within a one-year period; about one quarter of them give suicide serious thought (Centers for Disease Control, 2002c). The "typical" suicidal adolescent has a long history of stress and personal problems extending back into childhood (de Wilde et al., 1992). Unfortunately, for some teenagers these problems—trouble at home, difficulties in school, problems with girlfriends and boyfriends—escalate during adolescence. As their efforts to cope with these problems fail, many teenagers rebel against parental authority, withdraw from social relationships, and make dramatic gestures such as running away from home. These actions often lead to progressive social isolation. The experience of a humiliating event such as an arrest, a conflict with or a rejection by a parent or romantic partner, or a perceived failure at school or work can be the final thread in a tapestry of frustration and distress (Garland & Zigler, 1993; King, 1997). Alcohol consumption and its effects on mood, risky behavior, and preexisting aggressive or impulsive traits is also a factor (Sher, Kandel, & Merrick, 2006). In **Figure 11.5**, we provide some suggestions for dealing with someone who tells you that he or she is contemplating suicide (consult Chapter 15 for more information on suicide).

Figure 11.5

Preventing suicide. If someone tells you that he or she is contemplating suicide, you should treat this information seriously. Here are some suggestions for dealing with that enormously difficult situation.

Based on American Foundation for Suicide Prevention (n.d.). *When you fear someone may take their life.* Retrieved January 10, 2005 from http://www.afsp.org/about/whattodo.htm

What to Do When You Fear Someone is Contemplating Suicide

Determine whether the person is in imminent danger:

Ask the following questions in a nonjudgmental way:

1. Do you have a plan?
2. Do you know when you would do it (today, next week)?
3. Do you have access to what you would use?

If you believe that the person is in imminent danger:

Call 911 or get the person to a hospital emergency room or to the campus or local police station. If you are with the person, do not leave him or her alone.

If you believe that the threat is not imminent:

1. Do not discount the threat by telling the person that his or her problems are not that bad, or that the person has everything to live for, or that he or she is silly to contemplate suicide.
2. Reassure the person that help is available, that depression is treatable, and that suicidal feelings are temporary.
3. Let the person know that he or she is very important to you and how devastated you and others would be if he or she followed through with suicide.
4. Emphasize that there are alternative ways to deal with problems other than suicide. Often people fail to see other solutions to their problems.
5. Offer to go with the person to your campus counseling center, or to help him or her find a doctor or mental health professional.
6. Understandably, you may be frightened and worried when you learn such information. Consider going to the campus counseling center and asking for advice.

The Expanse of Adulthood

LEARNING OBJECTIVES

- *Discuss Erikson's analysis of early adulthood and evidence on achieving intimacy.*
- *Summarize key developmental transitions in early adulthood, including work and family life.*
- *Discuss Erikson's analysis of personality development in middle adulthood.*
- *Summarize key developmental transitions in middle adulthood, including parenting, work and the midlife crisis.*
- *Discuss Erikson's analysis of personality development in late adulthood.*
- *Summarize key developmental transitions in late adulthood, including retirement and friendships.*

Have you ever wondered if you are "on track," if your life is unfolding as it is supposed to, and if certain key events and noteworthy personal milestones are happening "on schedule"? Many adults believe that certain events (e.g., love, marriage, career, first child) should happen at certain times (Keith, 1990; Settersten & Hagestad, 1996). As people progress through adulthood, they periodically ask themselves, "How am I doing for my age?" In pondering this question, they are likely to be influenced by their social clocks (Helson, Mitchell, & Moane, 1984; Helson & Moane, 1987). **A *social clock* is a person's notion of a developmental schedule that specifies what he or she should have accomplished by certain points in life.** For example, if you feel that you should be married by the time you're 30, that belief creates a marker on your social clock. Although social clocks are a product of socialization, they do show individual variations (see **Figure 11.6**).

Social clocks can exert considerable influence over decisions concerning education, career moves, marriage, parenting, and other life choices. Adhering to a social clock based on prevalent age norms brings social approval and is thus a way to evaluate one's own development. Important life events that come too early or too late according to one's social clock produce more stress than transitions that occur "on time" (Chiriboga, 1987). It is easy to imagine how an early marriage, delayed career promotion, or delayed retirement might be especially stressful. In particular, it seems that lagging behind one's personal schedule for certain achievements results in psychological distress (Antonucci & Akiyama, 1997). In short, most people listen carefully to their social clocks ticking in the background as they proceed through adulthood.

Early Adulthood (From About Age 20 to 40)

Between the ages of about 20 and 30, adults must learn a number of new and important roles. Take Jack, for example: He graduated from college at age 22, then left his family and moved to Atlanta to start work as a management trainee. Over the next four years, he was involved in several serious relationships (which later broke up), and he changed jobs several times. At age 26, Jack got engaged and married. At age 28, he and his wife had their first child and he again changed jobs. Based on Jack's scenario, you can see why the years from 20 to 30 have been described as "demographically dense," referring to the fact that more role changes occur during this period than any other (Rindfuss, 1991). For some, early adulthood brings additional stress because it is a time for sorting out sexual orientation. As we discuss in Chapter 13, gay males and lesbians take longer than heterosexuals to recognize their sexual orientation (Garnets & Kimmel, 2003a).

Telling (Life) Time on the Social Clock

Typical American clock	Atypical American clock
College (ages 18–22)	World travel (ages 18–20)
Begin career (ages 22–23)	Peace Corps (ages 20–22)
Marriage (age 25)	College (ages 22-26)
First child (age 27)	Begin career (age 26)
Second child (age 29)	Graduate school (ages 29–31)
Focus on career (ages 30–40)	Second career (ages 32–45)
New job (age 41)	Marriage; no children (age 35)
Focus on career (ages 42–65)	Third career (ages 46–70)
Retirement (ages 65+)	Full-time community volunteer work (ages 70+)

Figure 11.6

Taking the road more (or less) traveled. The column on the left shows a conventional developmental progression for American adults and the column on the right shows a less typical developmental sequence. People's social clocks—their views of how these timelines should unfold—have become much more variable in recent decades.

Recommended READING

Emerging Adulthood: The Winding Road from the Late Teens Through the Twenties
by Jeffrey Jensen Arnett
(Oxford University Press, 2006)

Is adolescence expanding so that young people are taking longer and longer to make mature decisions or to plan their lives? When do adults become adults? How do they do so? These sorts of questions are representative of the new stage, time of life, and research topic known as "emerging adulthood." According to Arnett, the years between 18 and 29 are radically different for the current generation than in generations past—the social clock seems to stop for a bit, allowing for self-focused exploration of possibilities relating to work, family, and future.

What makes the argument interesting is the experience and behavior of the people in this age group. At the same time they are exploring new horizons involving, for example, love and sex, they feel at sea, uncertain about what to do and what is to come. And yet, according to Arnett, emerging adults are quite able to reach a balance among their conflicting thoughts, feelings, and longings. Adolescents, parents, and emerging adults themselves (to which group do you belong?) will want to consider the thought-provoking possibilities for the twentysomething generation of Americans.

© Red Chopsticks/Getty Images

The positive outcome of Erikson's sixth stage is intimacy, or the capacity to relate openly to others and to make emotional commitments. Isolation, the negative outcome, is characterized by difficulties in forming relationships with others.

Arnett (2000, 2004) made the radical claim for "emerging adulthood," a period of time running from the late teen years through the 20s. Young adults are not necessarily marrying or having children as early as in past generations, for example, and their dependence on their own parents for emotional as well as financial support seems different from that of previous generations. Arnett suggests that young people are using this new time of growth to discover their identities more fully where career and family is concerned. The question for psychological research is whether emerging adulthood represents a real and new stage of development or whether its demographic reality is more historical (and potentially short term) than evolutionary. Research, too, needs to definitively determine whether emerging adulthood is limited to fast-paced, industrialized Western countries or whether the same pattern of development can be discerned in other cultures, as well.

Erikson's Theory: Intimacy Versus Isolation

In Erikson's sixth stage, the psychosocial crisis centers on whether a person can develop the capacity to share *intimacy* with others (refer back to **Figure 11.3**). Erikson was not concerned simply with the young adult's need to find a marriage partner. Rather, he was concerned with more subtle issues, such as whether one can learn to open up to others, truly commit to others, and give of oneself unselfishly. The person who can experience genuine intimacy is thought to be more likely to develop a mature and successful long-term relationship. Failure to favorably resolve this psychosocial crisis leads to difficulties in relating to others in an authentic fashion. The resulting sense of isolation can foster competitive interactions with friends and troublesome intimate relationships.

Jacob Orlofsky and his colleagues (1973) found support for five intimacy statuses, based on the quality of a person's relationships with others.

1. *Intimate.* Individuals in this status are capable of forming open and close relationships with both male and female friends and are involved in a committed relationship.
2. *Preintimate.* Although people in this category are capable of mature, reciprocal relationships, they

haven't yet experienced a committed relationship because they are ambivalent about making commitments.

3. *Stereotyped.* Men and women in this status have relationships that are superficial and not very close. They often see others as objects to manipulate rather than to share with.

4. *Pseudointimate.* These individuals are typically involved in a relatively permanent relationship, but it resembles the stereotyped relationship in quality.

5. *Isolate.* Isolates avoid social situations and appear to be loners whose social interactions consist of casual conversations with a few acquaintances.

According to Erikson, the ability to establish and maintain intimate relationships depends on having successfully weathered the identity crisis of adolescence. The rationale here is that without a clear sense of yourself before you enter into an intimate relationship, you risk becoming overly dependent on someone else for your identity. Researchers typically find that college males and females in the more advanced identity statuses (achievement and moratorium) are most likely to be in the more advanced intimacy statuses (intimate and preintimate) (Fitch & Adams, 1983). Similarly, those experiencing identity foreclosure or diffusion predominate in the less advanced intimacy statuses (stereotyped, pseudointimate, and isolate). A similar pattern has been found in adults up to 35 years of age (Raskin, 1986; Tesch & Whitbourne, 1982).

Going beyond Erikson's theory, two specific developmental tasks of early adulthood are adjusting to full-time work and adjusting to marriage and family life. After all, Sigmund Freud (1935) famously claimed that the healthy adult individual is one who can "love and work."

Adjusting to the World of Work

Young adults are confronted with several major challenges in their work lives (Super, 1957, 1985, 1988). To start, they need to complete their schooling and secure their first job. At this point in career development, many people are still only tentatively committed to their chosen occupational area. If their first experiences are not rewarding, they may shift to another area, where they continue to explore their work options.

Web Link 11.3 **Adult Development and Aging (APA Division 20)**

Psychological researchers interested in adulthood and aging form a distinct division within the American Psychological Association—Division 20. The division's homepage contains a wide range of educational, instructional, and clinical resources and references for this area of concern.

People in their twenties change jobs on the average of every two years (Peterson & Gonzales, 2005).

Once men begin working full-time, they tend to stay in the workforce until they retire (a continuous pattern). Women's work lives often have a discontinuous pattern—typically because women have greater child-care responsibilities. Thus, they may move in and out of the workforce at different points in their lives (Betz, 1993). Those women who maintain full-time careers nonetheless often end up working a veritable "second shift" by managing the household responsibilities and children (Hochschild, 1989). Equality and opportunity for women in the workplace does not necessarily mean equality on the home front. Although many couples share domestic duties, a large part of the traditional ones (e.g., child care, food preparation, housekeeping) seem to fall to women.

Adjusting to Marriage and Family Life

Although an increasing proportion of the population under 35 are remaining single (Teachman, Polonko, & Scanzoni, 1999), most people marry or become involved in committed relationships during early adulthood. Today, the average age of first marriage for women is about 25; for men, it is about 27 (U.S. Bureau, of the Census 2004a). As noted in Chapter 9, the first few years of married life tend to be very happy. The early years of committed gay and lesbian relationships also follow this pattern (Peplau & Spalding, 2003).

Compared to earlier generations, more of today's married couples are choosing not to have children (Bulcroft & Teachman, 2004), but the vast majority plan to do so. The arrival of the first child represents a major transition. Among other things, it triggers a shift toward traditional roles for husband and wife (Cowan & Cowan, 1997). This shift is significant because greater discrepancies between the responsibilities of husband and wife after childbirth are associated with more marital conflict as well as declines in marital satisfaction and mental health, particularly for women (Perry-Jenkins, Repetti, & Crouter, 2001).

As already noted, even in dual-earner families, women typically bear greater responsibilities in the realms of child care and housework (Bond et al., 2003). Thus, mothers experience more work-family conflicts than fathers do. After the first few years of married life, marital satisfaction typically declines and continues at a lower level until middle adulthood, when it rises again (Glenn, 1998).

Like heterosexual married couples, most gay and lesbian couples are in dual-worker relationships. Unlike married couples, however, committed homosexual couples are more likely to have a flexible division of labor, where the workload is shared and tasks are completed based on personal preference (Peplau & Spaulding, 2003).

Middle Adulthood (From About Age 40 to 65)

Compared to early adulthood, which requires learning so many new roles, middle adulthood is an easier period.

Erikson's Theory: Generativity Versus Stagnation

The challenge of middle adulthood is acquiring *generativity,* or a concern for the welfare of future generations (refer to **Figure 11.3**). According to Erikson and researchers who have used the construct (e.g., McAdams, 1997), generativity is a desire to "give back" to the people one loves or knows, or even to help the community where one resides. Such giving can take the form of sharing a talent or a skill, leading a youth group, organizing a charity event, or simply spending time doing activities that can promote the greater good, such as volunteer work. The important point is that being a "generative" person helps the self by establishing meaning and purpose at the same time it helps others in direct and literal ways. The desire to be generative motivates people to leave something behind that can represent the best of themselves while establishing connections to others.

Adults demonstrate generativity when they provide unselfish guidance to younger people. The recipients of this guidance are often their own children, but not necessarily. Generativity can often occur as a result of one's work (Wethington, 2002). For example, a middle-aged college professor may gain great satisfaction from working with students. Or a 50-year-old attorney might mentor a younger woman in her law firm. Thus, generativity and its opposite, stagnation, do not hinge on a person's having children. Stagnation is characterized by self-absorption and self-indulgent preoccupation with one's own needs.

A number of studies support Erikson's views on generativity and middle adulthood. For example, researchers have found that generativity increases between young adulthood and middle age (de St. Aubin, McAdams, & Kim, 2004; Stewart, Ostrove, & Helson, 2001). Studies also report that highly generative individuals are well adjusted (low levels of anxiety and depression) and high in life satisfaction (Ackerman, Zuroff, & Moskowitz, 2000; Grossbaum & Bates, 2002). More specific challenges of middle age include confronting the aging process and making transitions in work and family roles. Let's look at these issues.

Confronting the Aging Process

What does it mean to be "middle aged"? How do we know whether we are still a young adult or in our midyears? The middle years can begin around age 40 and continue to the mid-60s. But what happens if a 70-year-old feels and acts like someone who is 50? Is she no longer middle-aged? The conceptual and experiential difficulty people face is that the whole idea of middle age as a stage of life is a relatively new one. Prior to the 20th century, there was no "midlife" per se (Moen & Wethington, 1999). Great strides in health, wealth, and social well-being have expanded the life span dramatically over the last century (see **Figure 11.7**). As a result, the nature and fabric of middle age has changed (Willis & Reid, 1999). Around 1900, the outer

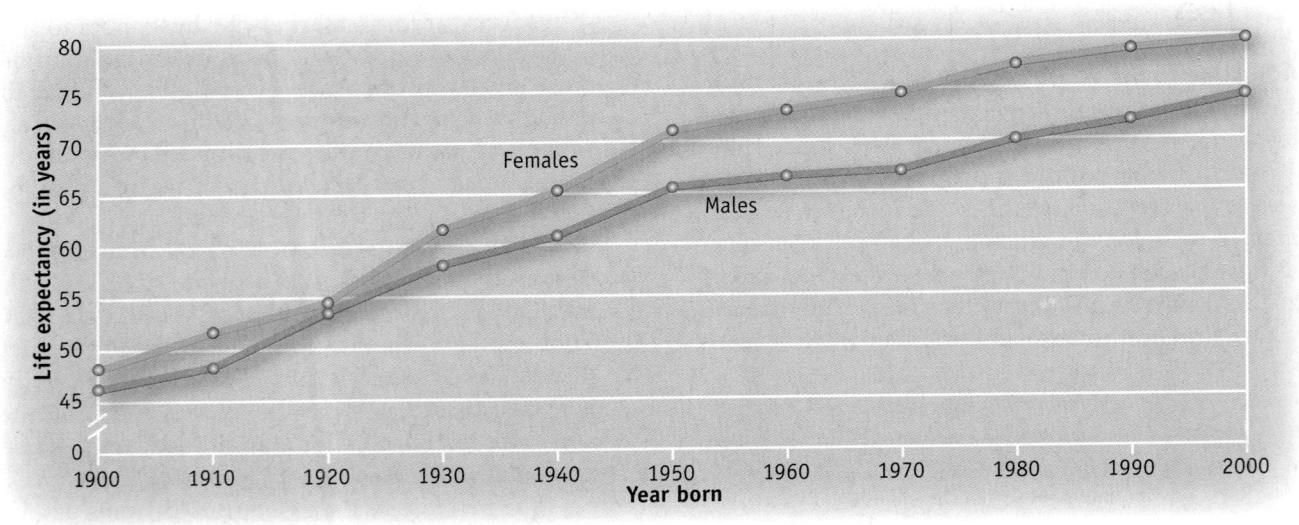

Figure 11.7

Trends in life expectancy. Average life expectancy at birth in the United States has increased dramatically since 1900, as this graph shows. Today, on average, people live about 30 years longer than their ancestors from a century ago. This increase in longevity has changed people's typical developmental trajectories and has altered the concept of aging. (Data from National Center for Health Statistics, 2006)

ZITS © Jerry Scott and Jim Borgman. Reprinted by permission of King Features Syndicate.

rim of people's life span was 50 years. Can you imagine being considered an elderly person at age 50? In our time, some might argue that 50 is an age where things are just getting interesting, where many adults are just hitting their strides (e.g., career is presumably on track, children are grown and soon to be out on their own). Of course, modern or not, midlife presents several challenges.

Chief among these challenges is coming to terms with the aging process. Middle-aged adults notice a number of physical transformations: changes in vision that often require glasses or bifocals for reading, the onset of wrinkles and sagging skin, weight gain, tooth and gum problems, and more bodily aches and pains and general "creakiness" (Lachman, 2004; Whitbourne, 2001). Even people's height decreases (around an inch on average) as the vertebrae in their spines compresses a bit (Merrill & Verbrugge, 1999). In addition, people are forced to acknowledge their mortality as they witness the deaths of parents, colleagues, and friends.

Actual chronological aging does affect everyone, but for many people, the perception of aging does not (Staudinger & Bluck, 2001). After early adulthood, people perceive themselves to be younger than they actually are (Montepare & Lachman, 1989). In **Figure 11.8**, you can see that the gap between actual and subjective age widens over time, especially among women, suggesting that women find it harder to accept growing older. This attitude no doubt reflects the "double standard of aging"—the perception that women's attractiveness declines more with age than men's does (Zebrowitz & Montepare, 2000). On a positive note, feeling younger than one's actual age is correlated with greater psychological adjustment and health (Lachman, 2004).

Transitions in the Parenting Role

As children grow up, parental influence tends to decline, and the early years of parenting—which once seemed so difficult—are often recalled with fondness. When children reach adolescence and seek to establish their own identities, gradual realignment occurs in parent-child relationships. As a result, conflicts over values are common, and power struggles frequently ensue (Arnett, 1999). Parents overwhelmingly rate adolescence as the most difficult stage of childrearing (Steinberg, 2001). Still, on balance, most parents have little regret about their decision to have children and rate parenthood as a positive experience (Demo, 1992).

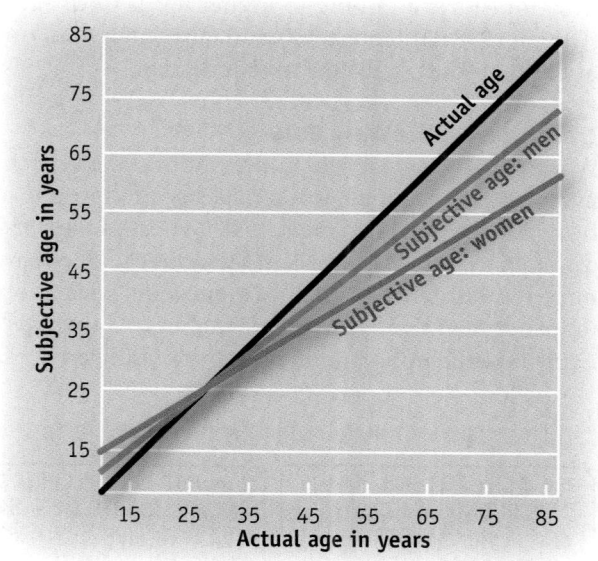

Figure 11.8

Discrepancies between actual and subjective age. After early adulthood, people see themselves as younger than they really are. This gap between reality and perception increases with age, especially among women. This graph also shows that adolescents perceive themselves to be older than they really are, while the age perceptions of young adults match reality fairly closely.

Adapted from Montepare, J., & Lachman, M. E. (1989). You're only as old as you feel: Self-perceptions of age, fears of aging, and life satisfaction. *Psychology and Aging*, 4, 73–78. Copyright © 1989 American Psychological Association. Adapted by permission of the publisher and author.

Although "emptying of the nest" is widely believed to be a traumatic event for parents, especially mothers, only about 25 percent of mothers and fathers report being very sad or unhappy when the last child leaves home (Lewis & Lin, 1996). Although its impact may be relatively minor, the "empty nest syndrome" may not be limited exclusively to parents. Interestingly, younger siblings who remain at home after their brothers or sisters leave report some sadness as a result (Rosen, Ackerman, & Zosky, 2002). For most women who are parents, the "empty nest" is associated with improved mood and well-being; however, when their young adult children return home for a time (as "emerging adults" often do), mothers' moods and the sexual relationships of the parents can suffer (Dennerstein, Dudley, & Guthrie, 2002). An interesting phenomenon is that in recent decades, the percentage of young adults who return home to live with their parents has increased. Returning home is due to a number of factors: inability to find a job, marital separation, divorce, or job loss. To date, research indicates that young adults living with their parents has a small negative impact on parent-child relationships (White & Rogers, 1997).

The postparental period often provides couples with more freedom and time to devote to each other, to travel, and to pursue new leisure interests. As offspring strike out on their own, couples' marital satisfaction starts climbing to higher levels once again (Glenn, 1998). It tends to remain fairly high until one of the spouses (usually the husband) dies.

Transitions in the Work Role

Work plays a central role in the midlife years (Lachman, 2004). At midlife, workers seem to follow one of two patterns (Papalia & Olds, 1995). Those in the *stable career pattern* are at the peak of their careers. They have more responsibility, earn more money, and wield more influence than their younger co-workers. As we noted, many take the opportunity to mentor younger workers, an expression of generativity. Some workers in this group continue to work at a frantic pace, struggling to accomplish their goals as they hear their social clocks ticking. Others seem content with their work achievements and begin to shift some of their attention and energy to family and leisure activities.

Workers in the *changing careers pattern* make up a more varied group. Whereas all are seeking to begin a different type of work, their reasons for doing so are quite varied. Some are looking for a new line of work because they have been forced out of a job by cutbacks. Others are seeking new careers because they want new challenges at this time in their lives. A third group is composed of women who are entering or reentering the workforce because family concerns now occupy less of their time and energy.

Is There a Midlife Crisis?

How well do people adjust to middle age? One important factor in people's midlife adjustment is whether they feel in control (Lachman & Firth, 2004; Wrosch, Heckhausen, & Lachman, 2006). Life areas in which such control can matter a great deal include psychological and social well-being, interpersonal relationships, and physical health. Having a sense or perception of control in midlife allows a person to constructively react to the challenges and demands of midlife, as well as the inevitable physical declines, such as being able to cope well with memory loss (Lachman, 2006). Perhaps perceiving such control even allows people to consider their own mortality and positive responses they can make (leading to generativity, for instance).

What happens if individuals feel out of control? Much has been made about whether most people go through a ***midlife crisis*—a turbulent period of doubts and reappraisal of one's life.** Two influential studies of adult development in the 1970s both concluded that a midlife crisis is a normal transition experienced by a majority of people. Daniel Levinson and his colleagues

CATHY © Cathy Guisewite. Reprinted with permission of UNIVERSAL PRESS SYNDICATE. All rights reserved.

Do most adults go through a midlife crisis in their 40s? The research on this question is contradictory, but overall, the evidence suggests that only a minority of people in their 40s struggle with a midlife crisis.

(1978) found that most of their subjects (all men) went through a midlife crisis around the ages of 40 to 45. This transition was marked by life reevaluation and emotional turmoil. Roger Gould (1978) found that people tended to go through a midlife crisis between the ages of 35 and 45. His subjects reported feeling pressed by time. They heard their social clocks ticking loudly as they struggled to achieve their life goals.

Since the landmark studies of Levinson and Gould, many other researchers have questioned whether the midlife crisis is a normal developmental transition. A number of studies have failed to detect an increase in emotional turbulence at midlife (Baruch, 1984; Eisler & Ragsdale, 1992; Roberts & Newton, 1987). How can we explain this discrepancy? Levinson and Gould both depended primarily on interview and case study methods to gather their data. However, when knitting together impressionistic case studies, it is easy for investigators to see what they expect to see. Given that the midlife crisis has long been a part of developmental folklore, Levinson and Gould may have interpreted their case study data in this light (McCrae & Costa, 1984). In any case, investigators relying on more objective measures of emotional stability have found signs of midlife crises in only a tiny minority (2%–5%) of subjects (Chiriboga, 1989; McCrae & Costa, 1990). Typically, these are individuals whose circumstances in early adulthood (family pressures, poverty, and so forth) severely limited their chances to achieve life satisfaction (McAdams, 1988). To summarize, midlife may bring a period of increased reflection as people contemplate the remainder of their lives, but it's clear that the fabled midlife crisis is not typical (Lemme, 1999).

The original research on "midlife crisis" was skewed toward the experience of men. What about women? How do they react to this stage of life? Instead of being a time of crisis, midlife can be a time of promise or rebirth for women (Heckhausen, 2001). What we might call "midcourse corrections"—new adventures, new relationships, new purpose—can occur (Stewart & Ostrove, 1998). If there is a "crisis" in the lives of women, it may be actually a constructive one. As one author put it, "It may be that part of the resilience of the midlife crisis [myth] lies in its benefit: to anticipate the worst at midlife and be pleasantly surprised by one's own comparatively smooth sail" (Heckhausen, 2001, p. 378). Of course, researchers find that such "turning points" are more often caused by unexpected events (divorce, job transfers, serious illness), which can occur at any time in adulthood (Lachman & Bertrand, 2001; Wethington, Kessler, & Pixley, 2004). In fact, some evidence exists for a "quarter-life" crisis (mid-20s and early 30s) involving the search for meaningful work and relationships (Lachman, 2004; Robbins & Wilner, 2001).

Late Adulthood (After Age 65)

Late adulthood also has its share of developmental transitions. These challenges include adjusting to retirement, adapting to changes in one's support network, coping with health problems, and confronting death. Let's begin by discussing Erikson's views of late adulthood.

Erikson's Theory: Integrity Versus Despair

The challenge of Erikson's last stage is to achieve *ego integrity* (refer to **Figure 11.3**). People who achieve integrity are able to look back on their lives with a sense of satisfaction and to find meaning and purpose there. The opposite, despair, is the tendency to dwell on the mistakes of the past, bemoan paths not chosen, and contemplate the approach of death with bitterness. Erikson asserts that it is better to face the future in a spirit of acceptance than to wallow in regret and resentment. In a test of Erikson's theory, researchers studied male and female adults over a 20-year span (Whitbourne et al., 1992). Among other things, they found that favorable resolutions of earlier stages lead to favorable resolutions of later stages. Another study of participants ages 17 to 82 reported that subjective well-being was correlated with increasing age and psychological maturity and that the factors of generativity and ego integrity accounted for most of the relationship between age and well-being (Sheldon & Kasser, 2001a). In addition to personality transitions, major developmental challenges in late adulthood include retirement and changes in support networks.

Retirement

Psychosocially, retirement is an especially interesting topic because most people associate it with old age when, in fact, this time of leaving the workforce happens to most people while in midlife. How so? The average age of retirement has been decreasing for some time and it is now 62. Still, this number is misleading because it falsely implies that retirement is an abrupt event. In fact, retirement these days is usually a gradual process during which people cut back on their work hours over some years rather than stopping work altogether (Mutchler et al., 1997).

Individuals approach retirement with highly variable attitudes. Generally, retirement is construed as something of a mixed blessing, yet most people welcome rather than reject it (Kim & Moen, 2001). Chief concerns include having adequate retirement income and being able to fill the hours previously devoted to paid work. Happily, many studies have shown that retirement has no adverse effect on overall health or life satisfaction (Bossé, Spiro, & Kressin, 1996). Retirement can pose a problem, however, for those who are forced to leave work because of ill health, mandatory retirement policies, or job elimination or whose incomes are inadequate. Those most likely to be so affected are blacks, Hispanics, and women (Flippen & Tienda, 2000). Retirement can also be stressful if it comes at the same time as other life changes, such as widowhood. Although retirement may result in decreased income, it also provides more time for travel, hobbies, and friends. Retirees who make the best adjustment have an adequate income, good health, and an extended social network of friends and family (Gall, Evans, & Howard, 1997).

Web Link 11.4 **American Geriatrics Society (AGS)**

This site contains a vast spectrum of resources—generated by the AGS itself or from other agencies on the Internet—regarding health and medical care, public policy, and many other issues related to the concerns of older adults.

Changes in Support Networks

As we noted, relationship satisfaction starts rising later in life and remains fairly high until one of the spouses or partners dies. In addition, most older adults maintain their ties to their children and grandchildren. In one large study of over 11,000 adults age 65 and over, 63 percent of the participants reported that they saw at least one of their children at least once a week, and another 16 percent saw a child one to three times a month. Only 20 percent indicated that they saw their

© Hill Street Studios/Blend Images/Getty Images

For older adults, friendships provide companionship and opportunities for shared activities.

children once a month or less often (Crimmins & Ingegneri, 1990). Surprisingly, elderly parents who see their children regularly or who report positive interactions with them don't describe themselves as happier than those who see their children less often or who have less positive relationships with their offspring (Markides & Krause, 1985; Seccombe, 1987).

Friends seem to play a more significant role in life satisfaction for older adults than family members do, at least for most white Americans (Pruchno & Rosenbaum, 2003). Friendships provide companionship, as well as opportunities for engaging in leisure activities and sharing thoughts and feelings. If there is a recipe for successful aging, older adults must learn to avoid social isolation by compensating for loss, carefully selecting their friends, and optimizing their existing or potential relationships (Baltes & Carstensen, 2003). Although the elderly have fewer friends than those who are younger, they are happier with their current number of friends than younger adults are (Lansford, Sherman & Antonucci, 1998). The elderly have fewer friends in part because they have lost friends through death, but also because they are more selective about their friends (Carstensen, 1995). Friendship quality matters more than the number of friendships, so that a strong bond with one person might matter more than several superficial connections (Charles & Carstensen, 1999). Even one close relationship can serve as a meaningful buffer against the changes of late adulthood, including shifting social roles (such as wife to widow) and loss of status (such as worker to retiree). Of course, each person's network will be somewhat different so that the nature of the buffering process and resulting adaptation will vary (Atchley, 1999). Interestingly, when distance or death reduces the membership of a person's social network, he or she is likely to seek new friends and bring them in as intimates.

In contrast to younger adults, older adults prefer friends who help them avoid stress and make them feel good. The gender differences in friendships we noted in Chapter 8 continue throughout adulthood. Thus, older men may have a larger network of friends than women do, but women's friendships are more intimate (Gurung, Taylor, & Seeman, 2003; Sherman, deVries, & Lansford, 2000). Men rely heavily on their wives for emotional support, whereas women derive support from children and friends, along with their spouse (Umberson, Wortman, & Kessler, 1992). This difference in social support puts husbands at greater risk than wives for health and adjustment problems when a spouse dies (Lee, Willetts, & Seccombe, 1998).

For African American elders, *ritual kin* are an important component of social support networks. In these relationships, certain neighbors or peers acquire the status of a close family member and render mutual aid and support (Taylor et al., 1990). Also, for elderly African Americans, participation in church activities plays a central role in psychological adjustment (Bryant & Rakowski, 1992).

Other significant challenges for older adults include coping with health problems, dealing with the deaths of friends and partners, and confronting one's own mortality. We'll address these issues in the last two sections of the chapter.

Aging: A Gradual Process

LEARNING OBJECTIVES

- *Discuss age-related changes in appearance and their psychological significance.*
- *Describe the sensory, neurological, and endocrine changes that accompany aging.*
- *Discuss health changes as people age.*
- *Describe age-related changes in intelligence, information processing, and memory.*
- *Summarize evidence on personality change and stability in adulthood.*

As an alternative to the ages-and-stages approach to adult development, many psychologists take the approach of identifying the physical, cognitive, and personality changes that occur throughout the expanse of adulthood. Whereas some of these age-related developments are quite obvious, others are very subtle. In either case, the changes take place gradually.

Physical Changes

The physical changes that occur in adulthood affect appearance, the nervous system, vision and hearing, hormone functioning, and health. Unless we indicate otherwise, the following summary of trends is based on the work of Susan Krauss Whitbourne (1996, 2001, 2002), a leading researcher in adult psychology and aging.

Courtesy, Susan Whitbourne

Susan Krauss Whitbourne

Changes in Appearance

As noted earlier, as the spinal column settles, an inch or so drop in height begins in midlife, usually

Web Link 11.5 **SeniorNet**

Research on Internet use has demonstrated an increasingly significant presence by older adults online. Perhaps some of that presence has been aided by this excellent site that links seniors (age 50 and up) to technology and many age-related resources, especially discussion groups and educational opportunities.

after age 55. Weight is more variable and tends to increase in most adults up through the mid-50s, when a gradual decline typically begins. Although weight often goes down late in life, the percentage of body weight that is fat tends to increase throughout adulthood, to the chagrin of many. The skin of the face and body tends to wrinkle and sag. The appearance of the face may change, as the nose and ears tend to become longer and wider, and the jaw appears to shrink. Hair tends to thin out and become gray in both genders, and many males have to confront receding hairlines and baldness.

The net impact of these changes is that many older people view themselves as less attractive. This unfortunate reality is probably aggravated by the media's obsession with youthful attractiveness. Older women suffer more than older men as a result of the decline in physical attractiveness because of the "double standard of aging." That is, because much of a woman's worth is determined by her physical attractiveness to men, her social status declines along with her attractiveness. In contrast, older men don't have to rely on their looks for social status; instead, they can use their occupational achievements and money.

Sensory Changes

The most important changes in sensory reception occur in hearing and vision. Hearing problems and visual impairments become common, with men exhibiting higher frequencies of both. Noticeable hearing losses do not usually show up until people reach their 50s. Whereas the vast majority of the elderly require corrective treatment for visual losses, only about one-third of older adults suffer hearing losses that require corrective treatment. Some researchers suggest that a straightforward means of deciding how much a person has aged mentally is by assessing his or her hearing, vision, and ability to smell (Lindenberger & Baltes, 1997).

The proportion of people with 20/20 vision declines steadily as age increases. From about age 30 to the mid-60s, most people become increasingly farsighted. After the mid-60s, the trend is toward greater nearsightedness. Depth perception begins to decline in the mid-40s. As well, older people commonly have difficulty adapting to darkness, experience poor recovery from glare, and have reduced peripheral vision. These changes in vision may be responsible for accidents in and outside the home, but they most seriously affect driving ability (particularly at night). Drivers over age 65 have a high proportion of car accidents (except compared to males under 25), which are typically caused by failing to obey traffic signs, not yielding the right of way, and making improper turns, rather than speeding (Kline et al., 1992).

Neurological Changes

The nervous system is composed of ***neurons*, individual cells that receive, integrate, and transmit information.** The number of active neurons in the brain declines steadily during adulthood. As neurons die, the brain decreases in both weight and volume, especially after age 50. Although this progressive neuronal loss sounds alarming, it is a normal part of the aging process. Its functional significance is the subject of some debate, but it doesn't appear to contribute to any of the age-related dementias. ***Dementia* is an abnormal condition marked by multiple cognitive deficits that include memory impairment.** Dementia can be caused by a variety of disorders, such as Alzheimer's disease, Parkinson's disease, and AIDS, to name just a few. Because some of these diseases are more prevalent in older adults, dementia is seen in about 15 percent of people over age 65 (Elias, Elias, & Elias, 1990). However, it is important to emphasize that dementia and "senility" are not part of the normal aging process. As Cavanaugh (1993) notes, "The term *senility* has no valid medical or psychological meaning, and its continued use simply perpetuates the myth that drastic mental decline is a product of normal aging" (p. 85).

Alzheimer's disease accounts for about 50%–60% of all cases of dementia. Some 5%–7% of adults over age 65 have the disease; this number grows to about 25% for those 85 and older (Gatz & Smyer, 2001; Gurland et al., 1999). Although the precise causes of Alzheimer's disease are not yet known, it is associated with changes in brain chemistry (Davis et al., 1999) and structure (Knowles et al., 1999). It is a vicious af-

Web Link 11.6 **The Nun Study**

Maintained by the Chandler Medical Center at the University of Kentucky, this site serves as a portal for information about the ongoing Nun Study on aging and Alzheimer's disease described in the text. The homepage provides a number of links, including frequently asked questions and publications that detail the findings from the continuing study.

fliction that can strike during middle age (40–65) or later in life (after 65). The disease is one of progressive deterioration, ending in death, and it takes from 8 to 10 years, on average, to run its course.

Are there particular risk factors associated with the onset of Alzheimer's disease? Advanced age is the most obvious factor, however, some people are diagnosed with early onset of the disease in their forties or fifties. Women are at slightly greater risk than men, perhaps because they tend to live longer. Ethnicity, too, is a predictor. Alzheimer's disease is less common in China or Japan than in Europe or the United States. Moreover, individuals of East Asian descent in the United States are diagnosed less frequently with the disease than are citizens who trace their lineage back to Europe (Jellinger, Schmidt, & Windlisch, 2002).

Although it will be many years before drugs and vaccines are available to safely slow or stop the disease, federally funded research programs around the country are making progress on the Alzheimer's puzzle (Siegler, Bosworth, & Poon, 2003). For example, older adults who engage frequently in cognitively stimulating activities may reduce their risk of Alzheimer's disease (Wilson & Bennett, 2003). One research project involves a group of elderly Catholic nuns in a Minnesota convent (Nash, 1997). About 20 years ago, these women agreed to serve as research subjects in a longitudinal study of Alzheimer's disease and, on death, to donate their brains to this scientific project. Among other findings from the ongoing Nun Study is a strong association between a high frequency of small strokes and severe confusion and memory loss (Snowdon, 2001). It also seems that folic acid (one of the B vitamins) may exert a protective effect against Alzheimer's disease (Sommer, Hoff, & Costa. 2003).

The beginnings of Alzheimer's disease are so subtle that they are difficult to detect. Individuals often forget common words, may report reduced energy, and may lose their temper. Early on, depression often appears (Espiritu et al., 2001). Later, obvious problems begin to emerge, including difficulties in speaking, comprehending, and performing complicated tasks. Individuals don't seem to have trouble with familiar activities. However, profound memory loss develops, especially for recent events. For example, patients may forget the time, date, current season of the year, and where they are. They may also fail to recognize familiar people, something particularly devastating to family and friends. Sometimes, they experience hallucinations, delusions, and paranoid thoughts. Later, victims become completely disoriented and lose control of bladder and bowel functions. At this point, they are unable to care for themselves at all. The disease is eventually fatal, with death occurring sometime between 10 and 15 years after the first sign of memory loss occurs (Fromholt & Bruhn, 1998)

Aging with Grace: What the Nun Study Teaches Us About Leading Longer, Healthier, and More Meaningful Lives
by David Snowdon (Bantam, 2001)

In this fascinating and inspiring book, the director of the Nun Study details the long-term research project that is tracking the effects of aging, with a special focus on Alzheimer's disease. David Snowdon, professor of neurology and director of the Nun Study at the Sanders-Brown Center on Aging at the University of Kentucky Medical Center, and his colleagues initiated the study in 1991, and it continues today.

The participants in the study are 678 elderly nuns of the School Sisters of Notre Dame order in Mankato, Minnesota. In a remarkable humanitarian gesture, the Catholic sisters agreed to share with Snowdon their medical and personal histories and, on their deaths, to donate their brains for research. As of December 2003, approximately 150 of the nuns were still alive, ranging in age from 87 to 100.

Snowdon's scientific account of the project is infused with affectionate biographies of the participants and compassionate personal observations. Readers will appreciate the book's inspirational messages and practical information. For example, aging successfully is positively correlated with maintaining an optimistic outlook, keeping up an exercise program, and consuming antioxidants such as lycopene, which is found in tomatoes and watermelon.

Hormonal Changes

Although age-related changes occur in hormonal functioning, their significance is not well understood. They do not appear to be the chief cause of declining sexual activity during the later years. Rather, this decline reflects the acceptance of social norms that older people don't have sexual desires and that sexual activity in the elderly is "inappropriate." For women, decreased sexual activity may simply reflect lack of opportunity, as the proportion of widows increases dramatically with age. The vast majority of older adults remain physically capable of engaging in rewarding sexual encounters, although arousal tends to be somewhat slower and less intense.

Among women, menopause is a key transition that typically occurs in the early 50s. ***Menopause* is the time when menstruation ceases.** It is tied to a decrease in the production of estrogen. Episodes of moderate physical discomfort ("hot flashes" and "night sweats") during the transitional phase are fairly common but are usually no more troublesome than menstruation itself. The decrease in estrogen is also tied to loss of bone density, which makes women more susceptible than men to osteoporosis and bone fractures (Masi & Bilezikian, 1997). Not so long ago, menopause was almost universally associated with severe emotional strain. However, it is now clear that women's reactions to menopause vary greatly, depending on their expectations (Matthews, 1992). Most women suffer little psychological distress (George, 2002). In fact, many feel liberated from menstrual periods, childbearing, and worrying about birth control (Walter, 2000).

Although the idea of a "male menopause" has generated much discussion in recent years, there really is no equivalent experience among men (Jacobs, 2001). Significant endocrine changes do occur in males in their later years, but these changes are gradual and are largely unrelated to physical or psychological distress. Although sperm production declines between the ages of 25 and 60, older men are still capable of fathering children (Morley, 2001). A more relevant issue is erectile dysfunction in males, an age-related condition (Rodger, 2004) that can sometimes be alleviated by some medications, such as Viagra (Marshall, 2006).

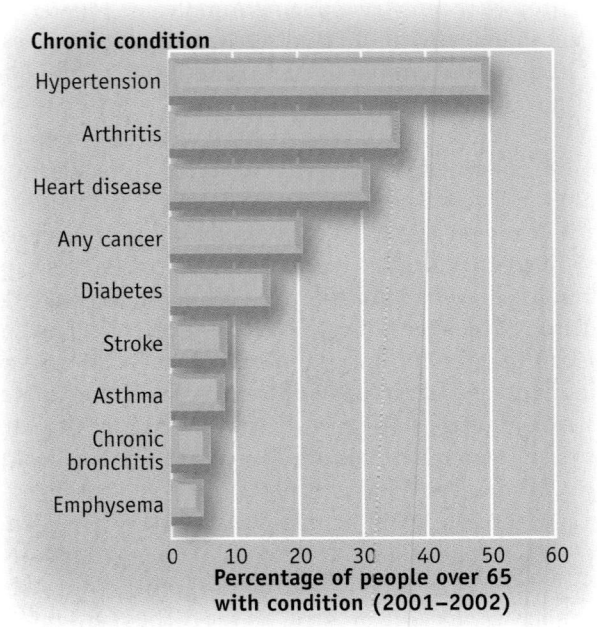

Figure 11.9

Chronic health problems in those over 65. Although most people over age 65 are in good health, they suffer from a number of chronic health problems. The data shown here refer only to noninstitutionalized individuals. (Federal Interagency Forum on Aging-Related Statistics, 2004)

Changes in Health Status

On average, the quality of health diminishes with increasing age. There are many reasons for this trend. Vital organ systems lose some of their functional capacity. Vulnerability to some diseases (such as heart disease) increases with age. For other diseases (such as pneumonia), the vulnerability may remain unchanged, but their effects may be more serious. In any case, the proportion of people with a chronic health problem climbs steadily with age. As you can see in **Figure 11.9**, common chronic health problems among those over 65 are hypertension, arthritis, heart disease, cancer, and diabetes.

Factors such as lifestyle differences and access to and affordability of health care obviously play an important role in maintaining good health. Among the elderly, the affluent have better health than the poor, and whites are healthier than African Americans (Berkman & Gurland, 1998). The health of elderly Hispanics seems to fall between that of whites and African Americans. Native Americans fare the worst.

Most older people live independently—at least until they reach 85. However, with "the graying of America" because of the aging of the baby boomer generation, the number of elderly individuals needing assistance with activities of daily living is expected to soar. Home health care and assisted living facilities are cost-effective alternatives to nursing homes (Maddox, 2001). They also have the important added advantage of permitting individuals to function somewhat independently. Although relatively few elderly Americans live in nursing homes, these numbers do increase with age (U.S. Bureau of the Census, 2004b). Nursing home use varies across ethnic groups, typically because of the availability of family members to care for the frail elderly. For instance, African American, Hispanic, and Asian American families are more likely to care for the elderly at home than white families are (Gabrel, 2000).

Cognitive Changes

It is commonly believed that intelligence drops during middle age and that memory lapses become more frequent in the later years. Are these notions accurate? Let's review the evidence.

Intelligence

Researchers have long been interested in whether general intelligence, as measured by IQ tests, remains stable throughout the adult years. The current evidence suggests that IQ is fairly stable throughout most of adulthood, with most declines beginning after age 60

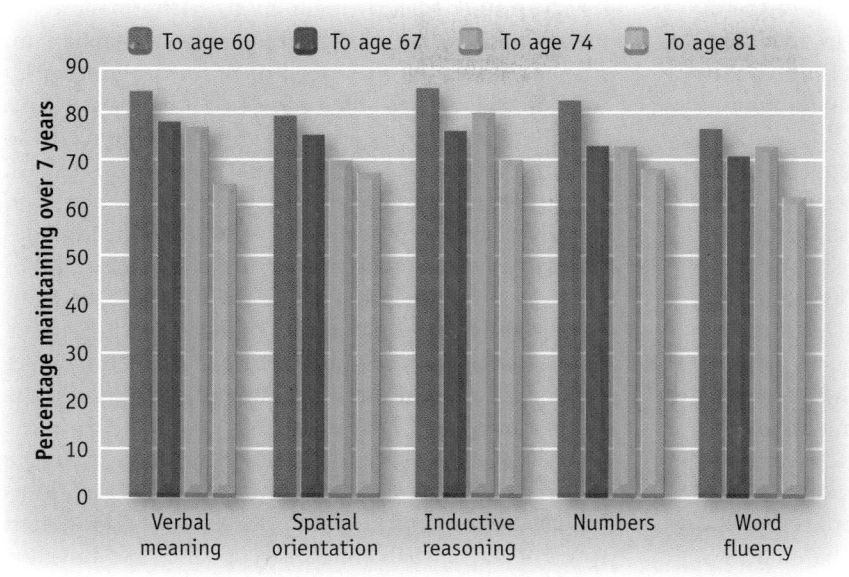

Figure 11.10

Age and stability of primary mental abilities. In his longitudinal study of cognitive performance begun in 1956, Schaie (1983, 1994) has repeatedly assessed the five basic mental abilities shown along the bottom of this chart. The data graphed here show the percentage of subjects who maintained stable levels of performance on each ability through various ages up to age 81. As you can see, even at the oldest ages, the majority of subjects show no significant decline on most abilities.

From Schaie, K. W. (1990). Intellectual development in adulthood. In J. E. Birren & K. W. Schaie (Eds.), *Handbook of the psychology of aging* (3rd ed). San Diego: Academic Press. Copyright © 1990, reproduced with permission of Elsevier.

(Schaie, 1994). Still, there are large individual differences in IQ fluctuations, and findings are typically based on *average* test scores, which can be dragged down by a small group of people who experience declines. When Schaie (1990) calculated the percentage of people who maintained stable performance on various mental abilities (see **Figure 11.10**), he found that about 80 percent showed no declines by age 60 and that about two-thirds were still stable through age 81. Older individuals who maintain higher levels of cognitive functioning have good physical health, have above-average education and occupations, enjoy plenty of intellectual and social stimulation, and are satisfied with their life accomplishments in midlife or early old age (Schaie, 1994).

Information Processing and Problem Solving

Although intelligence is more stable during adulthood than widely believed, some significant cognitive changes do take place. These changes are most apparent in specific aspects of information processing and problem solving.

There is ample evidence that the ability to narrow one's focus of attention diminishes somewhat with increasing age, as does the ability to handle simultaneous multiple inputs (Hartley & McKenzie, 1991; Kausler, 1994). These changes may be due to decreased efficiency in filtering out irrelevant stimuli. Most of the studies have simply compared extreme age groups (very young participants against very old participants). Thus, it's not clear at what age these changes tend to emerge.

In the cognitive domain, age seems to take its toll on speed first. Many studies indicate that speed in learning, solving problems, retrieving memories, and processing information tends to decline with age, probably beginning in middle adulthood (Salthouse, 2000, 2004). The general nature of this trend (across differing tasks) suggests that it may be a result of age-related changes in neurological functioning.

Overall success on both practical and laboratory problem-solving tasks appears to decrease as people grow older (Sinnott, 1989). For the most part, problem-solving ability is unimpaired if older people are given

© Siphiwe Sibeko/Reuters

Many people, such as Nelson Mandella, former president of South Africa, and Jimmy Carter, former president of the United States, remain active and productive in their 70s, 80s, and even beyond.

adequate time to compensate for their reduced speed in information processing. Furthermore, many of the age-related decrements in cognitive functioning can be partly compensated for by increases in older adults' knowledge.

It should be emphasized that many people remain capable of great intellectual accomplishment in their later years (Simonton, 1997). This fact was verified in a study of scholarly, scientific, and artistic productivity that examined lifelong patterns of work among 738 men who lived at least through the age of 79 (Dennis, 1966). **Figure 11.11** plots the percentage of professional works completed by these men in their 20s, 30s, 40s, 50s, 60s, and 70s. As you can see, in most professions the 40s decade was the most productive. However, in many areas productivity was remarkably stable through the 60s and even the 70s. Other researchers have focused on the quality, rather than the quantity, of output. They typically find that "masterpieces" occur at the same relative frequency among the works of creators of all ages (Simonton, 1997).

Memory

Many older people complain about problems with their memory. There is some good news, however: People tend to be poor judges of their own memories and, in any case, memory problems linked to aging are not as prevalent as anticipated (Lane & Zelinski, 2003; Petersen, 2003). In other words, the reality of the expected deficits may not turn out to be so severe; however, changes do occur. It does seem that the capacity of "working memory" decreases as people age (Dixon & Cohen, 2003). ***Working memory*** **refers to the short-term, limited capacity memory store that people use to juggle information they are currently focusing on.** Also, as we noted, the speed of processing information slows with age. This combination of less working memory capacity and slower processing seems to underlie older adults' poorer performance on complex tasks that demand considerable cognitive effort and resources. Older adults also experience frustrating declines in episodic memory (Dixon & Cohen, 2003). For example, sometimes they may have difficulties remembering individuals' names or where the car is parked. On tasks that don't require much mental effort (recognizing a familiar face, for example), age-related declines are minimal.

The memory losses associated with aging, then, are moderate and by no means universal. However, individuals' beliefs abut their memory abilities do matter; when negative, such beliefs can produce self-fulfilling prophecies. In one study, individuals who believed that memory gets worse with age estimated larger self-declines in memory compared to people who believed that memory declines only a little with age (Cavanaugh, Feldman, & Hertzog, 1998). Self-beliefs are also important because they are tied to the use of compensatory strategies (for example, investing extra time and effort in learning new skills) to offset memory problems (Cavanaugh, 2000).

A popular misconception is that older people have vivid recollections of events in the distant past while being forgetful about recent events. In actuality, there is no evidence that the elderly have more numerous, or more vivid, early memories (Ashok & Parkin, 1996; Kausler, 1994). In fact, memories of events long ago

Figure 11.11

Age trends in professional productivity. Dennis (1966) compiled the percentage of professional works completed in each decade of life by 738 men who lived to at least age 79. Productivity peaked in the 40s decade, but professional output remained strong through the 60s decade, and even lasted through the 70s decade for the humanities and sciences.

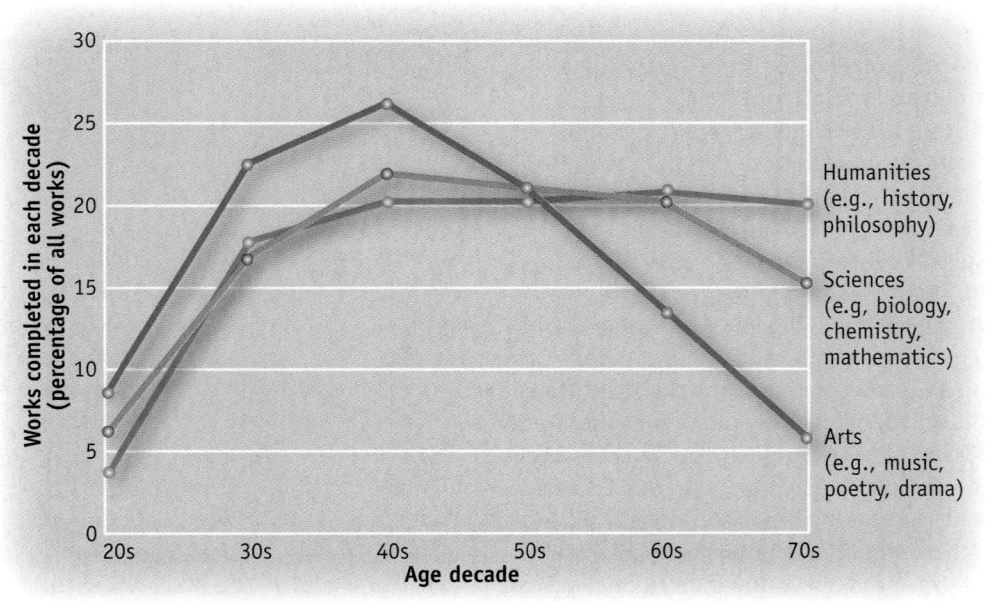

may be loose reconstructions that are less accurate than people assume.

Personality Changes

Is a grouchy 20-year-old destined to be crotchety at 40 or 65? Or can the cranky young adult become a mellow senior citizen? Psychologists have engaged in lively debate about whether personality remains stable in adulthood, and both sides have been able to cite supportive research. On the one hand, a number of large-scale longitudinal studies using objective assessments of personality traits provide evidence for long-term stability in personality. The general conclusion that emerges from these longitudinal studies is that personality tends to be quite stable over periods of 20 to 40 years (Costa & McCrae, 1994, 1997). A recent study, for example, suggests that people remain who they are after early midlife, which means that people's personalities remain relatively stable after age 30 (Terracciano, Costa, & McCrae, 2006). For example, Paul Costa and Robert McCrae (1988) conducted a six-year longitudinal study of 983 men who were ages 21 to 76 at the time of the first testing. Over this six-year period, the researchers looked at the stability of the traits in their five-factor model of personality (see Chapter 2). The stability of the participants' self-ratings on these five traits over six years was quite high. Costa and McCrae also asked the spouses of the participants to rate the subjects over the same six-year interval. They found that the stability of the spousal ratings closely matched that of the participants' self-ratings. Also, a recent meta-analysis of 150 studies, involving almost 50,000 participants, concluded that personality in early adulthood was a good predictor of personality in late adulthood and that the stability of personality increases with age up to about age 50 (Roberts & DelVecchio, 2000).

On the other hand, some studies suggest that substantial personality changes continue to occur throughout the life span (Haan, Millsap, & Hartka, 1986; Helson & Moane, 1987; Whitbourne et al., 1992). For example, in a study of women graduates of Mills College, few personality changes were found between the ages of 21 and 27; however, between the ages of 27 and 43, the women increased in dominance (including confidence) and independence (Helson and Moane, 1987; Helson, Mitchell, & Moane, 1984). According to Susan Krauss Whitbourne and her colleagues (1992), "There is a growing body of evidence indicating the existence of adult personality changes on a variety of . . . variables" (p. 268).

In sum, researchers assessing the stability of personality in adulthood have reached contradictory conclusions. How can they be reconciled? This appears to be one of those debates in which researchers are eyeing the same findings from different perspectives. Hence, some conclude that the glass is half full, whereas others conclude that it's half empty. In his discussion of this controversy, Lawrence Pervin (1994) concludes that personality is characterized by *both* stability and change.

Death and Dying

LEARNING OBJECTIVES

- *Discuss cultural and individual attitudes about death, including death anxiety.*
- *Describe Kübler-Ross's five stages of dying and research findings about the dying process.*
- *Describe cultural variations in mourning practices and discuss the grieving process.*
- *Discuss various types of loss and what helps people cope with bereavement.*

Life is indeed a journey and death is the ultimate destination. Dealing with the deaths of close friends and loved ones is an increasingly frequent adjustment problem as people move through adulthood. Moreover, the final challenge of life is to confront one's own death.

Attitudes About Death

Because death is a taboo topic in modern Western society, the most common strategy for dealing with it is *avoidance.* There is abundant evidence of Americans' inability to confront death comfortably. People often use euphemisms such as "passed away" to avoid even the word itself. To minimize exposure to the specter of death, individuals sometimes unnecessarily quarantine the dying in hospitals and nursing homes. Professionals take custody of the body at death and manage funeral arrangements for families. These are all manifestations of what Kastenbaum (2001) calls a ***death system*—the collection of rituals and procedures used by a culture to handle death.** Death systems vary from culture to culture. Ours happens to be rather negative and evasive. Some scholars even argue that our individual psychologies work to help us deny that death exists (Becker, 1997).

Negativism and avoidance are *not* universal features of death systems. In Mexican culture, death is discussed frequently and is even celebrated on a national

Web Link 11.7 **The End of Life: Exploring Death in America**

Since late 1997, National Public Radio (NPR) has regularly aired a range of programs relating to dying and death as experienced in American culture. This companion website at NPR offers not only printed and audio transcripts of each program but many bibliographical and organizational resources as well.

feast day, the Day of the Dead (DeSpelder & Strickland, 1983). Also, the Amish view death as a natural transition rather than a dreaded adversary (Bryer, 1979). Thus, some cultures and subcultures display less fear of death than others.

Death anxiety **is the fear and apprehension about one's own death.** In Chapters 2 and 5, we noted that terror management theory asserts that death anxiety stems from the conflict between humans' instinct for self-preservation and their awareness of the inevitability of death. According to terror management theory, cultures provide traditions and institutions to help people deal with death anxiety. In support of the theory, adults who have a strong faith in a higher force or being have lower death anxiety (Cicirelli, 1999, 2002). Having a well-formulated personal philosophy of death, rather than having a particular religious affiliation, is associated with lower death anxiety. For instance, one study found that both devout Christians and confirmed atheists were less anxious about death than those with ambivalent religious views (Moore, 1992). Also, individuals who haven't accomplished all that they had hoped are more likely to fear death, as are those who are anxious and depressed (Neimeyer & Van Brunt, 1995).

Death anxiety typically declines from early to late adulthood (Thorson & Powell, 2000). In fact, elderly adults are more likely to fear the period of uncertainty that comes before death than death itself. They worry about where they will live, who will take care of them, and how they will cope with the loss of control and independence they may experience before death.

Recommended **READING**

Grave Matters: A Journey through the Modern Funeral Industry to a Natural Way of Burial
by Mark Harris (Scribner, 2007)

The American way of death is not only a matter of grief and bereavement, it is also often a matter of great expense. The costs of burying a loved one can easily and all too routinely exceed $10,000. The costs are not just monetary, as contemporary burials also take a toll on our environment (e.g., loss of land, burial of hazardous chemicals). In this new book, environmental journalist and author Mark Harris offers thoughtful suggestions about how to have green (chemical free, environmentally friendly) burials that celebrate the life of the dead while preserving or even enhancing nature in the process.

Concerns about the cost of dying to families and to the environment are likely to increase as America's baby boomers begin to age and die. Harris offers interesting, even provocative, alternatives to traditional burial, everything from placing a loved one's ashes in an artificial reef under the sea to burial in "natural" cemeteries where no caskets or other containers are allowed. Other options—such as internment in a simple pine box—lie between these poles. If nothing else, *Grave Matters* will encourage readers to reflect on what sort of environmental legacy they and their loved ones want to leave behind once they go on that journey we must all eventually take.

The Process of Dying

Pioneering research on the experience of dying was conducted by Elisabeth Kübler-Ross (1969, 1970) during the 1960s. At first, her project met with immense resistance. Fellow physicians at the hospital where she worked were initially unresponsive to her requests to interview dying patients. Gradually, however, it became apparent that many such patients were enthusiastic about the discussions. They were frustrated by the "conspiracy of silence" that surrounds death and were relieved to get things out in the open. Eventually, Kübler-Ross interviewed over 200 terminally ill patients and developed a model of the process of dying. According to her model, people evolve through a series of five stages as they confront their own death:

© Ken Ross

Elisabeth Kübler-Ross

Stage 1: Denial. Denial, shock, and disbelief are the first reactions to being informed of a serious, life-terminating illness. According to Kübler-Ross, few patients maintain this stance to the end.

Stage 2: Anger. After denial, the patient often becomes nasty, demanding, difficult, and hostile. Asking and resolving the question "Why me?" can help the patient reduce resentment.

Stage 3: Bargaining. In this stage the patient wants more time and asks for favors to postpone death. The bargaining may be carried out with the physician or, more frequently, with God.

Stage 4: Depression. Depression is a signal that the acceptance process has really begun. Kübler-Ross has referred to this stage as "preparatory grief"—the sadness of anticipating an impending loss.

Stage 5: Acceptance. The person who achieves acceptance has taken care of unfinished business. The patient has stopped fighting the inevitable and is now ready to die. He or she will want to be with close family members, usually a spouse or partner and children; dying children want to be with their parents. Although patients desire the presence of someone warm, caring, and accepting at this time, verbal communication may be totally unnecessary.

Although Kübler-Ross asserted that people do not necessarily progress through these five stages in lock-step sequence, her use of the term "stages" implies otherwise. Thus, it is not surprising that her theory has been criticized on this confusing point (Kastenbaum, 1999). Systematic studies of dying patients have not always observed the same five emotions or the same progression of emotions she described (Corr, 1993). Instead of progressing though a common, five-stage process, dying people seem to show "a jumble of conflicting or alternating reactions running the gamut from denial to acceptance, with tremendous variation affected by age, sex, race, ethnic group, social setting, and personality" (Butler & Lewis, 1982, p. 370). Nonetheless, Kübler-Ross greatly improved our understanding of the process of dying and stimulated research that continues to add to our knowledge.

Bereavement and Grieving

When a friend, spouse, or relative dies, individuals must cope with ***bereavement,* or the painful loss of a loved one through death.** The death of someone close typically brings forth the painful and complex emotions of grief. ***Mourning* refers to the formal practices of an individual and a community in response to a death.** Many cultural and religious rituals help survivors adjust to and cope with their loss.

Cultural Variations

Considerable variation exists among and within cultures as to how this major life event is acknowledged. In America and Western European countries, the bereaved are typically encouraged to break their emotional ties with the deceased relatively quickly and to return to their regular routines. Nonetheless, research has found support for "continued bonds" with the deceased among American widows and widowers (Bonanno & Kaltman, 1999). Based on interviews of men and women during the first two months of bereavement, one study reported that 71 percent felt that their deceased spouses were still with them at times and that 61 percent felt that their deceased spouses were watching out for them (Shuchter & Zisook, 1993). Moreover, 39 percent reported that they talked regularly with their deceased spouses. In Asian, African, and Hispanic cultures, the bereaved are encouraged to maintain emotional ties to their dead loved ones (Bonanno, 1998). Almost all Japanese homes have altars dedicated to family ancestors, and family members routinely talk to the deceased and offer them food. Regardless of the particular form that mourning takes, all such rituals are designed to make death meaningful and to help the bereaved cope with the pain and disruption of death.

The Grieving Process

The common view of bereavement asserts that distress is an inevitable response to loss and that failure to experience distress is a sign that the individual has not grieved "properly" (Bonanno & Kaltman, 1999). As a result, the person is expected to suffer negative consequences later. In keeping with this view, John Bowlby (1980) characterized grieving as a four-stage process:

Stage 1: Numbness. In this initial phase, survivors are typically dazed and confused. They may experience physical reactions such as nausea or tightness in the chest or throat. This phase may last several days or, in cases when death has been unexpected, several weeks.

Stage 2: Yearning. Here, survivors try to recover the lost person. Individuals may report that they see the deceased and may wander as if they are searching for the loved one. They often feel frustration, anger, and guilt. In addition, they may experience intense feelings of sadness and may cry and sob uncontrollably. They may also suffer loss of appetite and insomnia.

Stage 3: Disorganization and despair. Searching for the loved one ceases as the loss is accepted as real. However, accepting the loss brings feelings of helplessness, despair, and depression. Survivors often experience extreme fatigue and a need to sleep much more than usual.

Stage 4: Reorganization. Individuals are able to resume their normal routines at home and at work. Depression lifts, regular sleeping habits return, and energy increases. Thoughts of the loved one may bring sadness, but these feelings are no longer overwhelming.

Although Bowlby's model is certainly plausible, research suggests that most grief reactions do not

The grieving process is more variable among people than is widely appreciated.

follow this straightforward path (Wortman & Boerner, 2007; Wortman, Wolff, & Bonanno, 2004). Just as people react differently to the experience of dying, they also show variable responses to bereavement. For instance, one study examined the patterns of change in depression in a sample of older adults prior to a spouse's death and at 6 and 18 months after spousal loss (Bonanno et al., 2002). By measuring depression both before and after a spouse's death, researchers could separate preloss depression from loss-induced depression. Participants' grief reactions could be categorized into five patterns. *Absent grief* or the *resilient pattern* is characterized by low levels of depression before and after the spouse's death. In *chronic grief,* depression exists before and after the spouse's death. *Common grief* is characterized by an increase in depression shortly after the spouse's death and a decrease in depression over time. The *depressed-improved* pattern reflects a decrease in depression after the spouse's death. *Chronic depression* describes those who are depressed both before and after spousal loss.

When you examine **Figure 11.12**, you may be surprised to find that common grief is *not* the most frequent pattern. In fact, absent grief occurs much more frequently—almost half of the participants follow this pattern. As we noted earlier, many (including some mental health professionals) believe that individuals who fail to engage in "grief work" will suffer long-term adjustment problems. However, this view is contradicted by many studies (Bonanno et al., 2002; Wortman et al., 2004). In Bonnano et al.'s (2002) study, resilience was found to be associated with preloss acceptance of death, whereas chronic grief was associated with preloss dependency on the spouse. To counter the traditional "negative" view of bereavement, some researchers have been investigating how positive emotions and laughter can ameliorate the stress of grieving (Bonanno & Keltner, 1997).

Other research examines grief reactions as time passes. The bulk of available studies track grief in the first year or years following the death of a spouse, and many are aimed at examining who is resilient versus

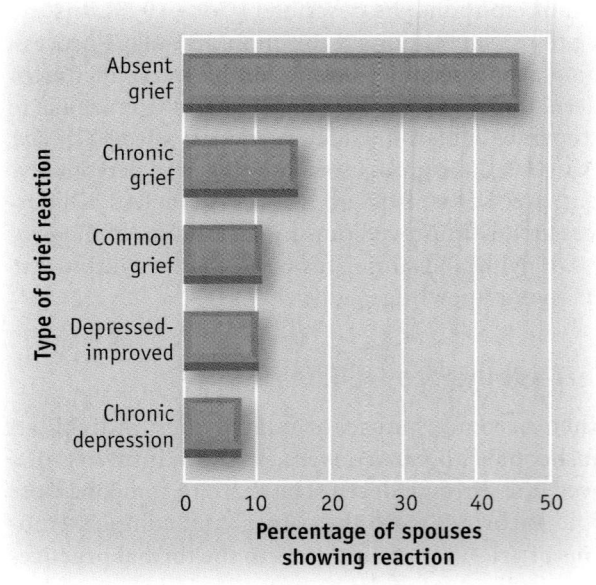

Figure 11.12

Five reactions to spousal loss. Researchers gathered data on 205 older individuals prior to spousal loss and 6 months and 18 months following spousal loss. Ninety percent of the subjects exhibited one of the five bereavement patterns shown in the figure. Contrary to popular belief, "absent grief" or the "resilient pattern" was the most frequently experienced reaction, while "common grief" occurred relatively infrequently. Traditional views of grief hold that the "common grief" reaction is the only healthy response to loss, but numerous studies contradict that view. (Adapted from Bonanno et al., 2002) being at risk for psychological distress (Boerner, Wortman, & Bonanno, 2005). A recent study involved a national, representative sample of widowed people whose spouses had been dead for many years (Carnelley et al., 2006). Even after 20 years, many widowed people reported thinking about their spouse every week or so and spoke about the person about once a month. Feelings of distress were found to dissipate after the first decade following the death, and most people did report being upset when recalling their loved one.

Coping with Various Types of Loss

The research we have been discussing looked only at the experiences of widows and widowers. The researchers would probably have obtained quite different findings if the subjects had been parents who had lost a child, the most difficult type of death adults must cope with (Stillion, 1995). Coping with miscarriage and stillbirth can also be painful (Klass, 1996). One study compared the grief reactions of 255 middle-aged women who had experienced the death of a spouse, a parent, or a child in the two years preceding the study (Leahy, 1993). As you might expect, mothers who had lost children had the highest levels of depression. And women whose husbands had died were significantly more depressed than women who had lost a parent. Other studies of bereaved persons (including men) have also found that they score higher on depression than the nonbereaved (Wortmann & Silver, 1990). They also score lower on life satisfaction and are at greater risk for illness. Thus, the death of an intimate is an adjustment challenge for most people, even though individuals' reactions to the experience may vary.

A particularly difficult bereavement situation occurs when a child or an adolescent loses a parent to death. In these cases, grieving typically involves frequent crying, angry outbursts, trouble concentrating at school, and sleep problems. These symptoms may last from several months to a year (Silverman & Worden, 1992). It is important for adults to take the time to talk with grieving children. In particular, children need to be assured that the parent did not leave out of anger and that the remaining parent will not disappear (Furman, 1984).

Bereavement overload occurs when individuals experience several deaths at the same time or in close succession. As an example, the tens of thousands of individuals who lost all or most of their families and friends during the December 26, 2004 earthquake and tsunami disaster in Southeast Asia come quickly to mind. On a less dramatic scale, other groups who are likely to suffer bereavement overload include members of the gay community, who have lost lovers and friends to AIDS, and the elderly, who must deal with the loss of spouses, friends, and siblings because of advancing years.

To cope with loss, people need the sympathy and support of family and friends as well as the passage of time. Still, the presence of friends and family can't substitute for a loved one who has died (Stroebe et al., 1996).

Now that we have looked at the ways in which development continues throughout adulthood, in the Application, we turn to some ways that parents can facilitate their children's development by providing optimal combinations of affection and discipline.

The Southeast Asian tsunami disaster was a rare and dramatic example of bereavement overload, the devastating experience of having to cope with several or more deaths at the same time.

APPLICATION

Becoming an Effective Parent

LEARNING OBJECTIVES

- *Discuss Baumrind's parenting styles and their effects on children's development.*
- *Discuss issues related to the effective parenting of adolescents.*
- *List five suggestions for more effective parenting.*
- *List five suggestions for the effective use of punishment.*

Are the following statements "true" or "false"?

___ **1.** Authoritarian parenting appears to be the most effective style of parenting.

___ **2.** Extensive use of punishment is the key to effective discipline.

___ **3.** Parents shouldn't have to explain their reasons for punishing their children.

All of these statements are false. They all represent popular myths about childrearing that we address in this Application. Many parents are eager to learn all they can about children's development. They search to find new and better ways to ensure optimal social, emotional, and cognitive development in their children. What kinds of answers can psychology provide?

Dimensions of Childrearing

As children grow from infancy into toddlerhood, the role of parenting broadens. How parents react to a child's actions communicates their standards of appropriate and inappropriate behavior. Parents fulfill this role with varying degrees of conscious awareness.

As we mentioned in Chapter 5, two major dimensions underlie parenting behavior (Maccoby & Martin, 1983). The first, and most important, is *parental acceptance.* Although most parents are at least moderately accepting of their children, some are indifferent or even hostile and rejecting. Parental acceptance and warmth appear to influence the degree to which children internalize the standards and expectations of their parents (Eccles et al, 1997). Children whose parents hold them in high regard develop high self-esteem and self-control (behave appropriately even if the parents are not present). In contrast, children whose parents are less accepting may develop lower self-esteem and less self-control. Thus, they may behave when the parents are around (out of fear of punishment) but misbehave when on their own.

The second dimension of parenting behavior is *parental control,* or strictness of parental standards. For example, a parent who is moderately controlling sets high performance standards and expects increasingly mature behavior. A parent who is uncontrolling expects little of the child. The absence of control is associated with maladjustment and high levels of aggression.

Diana Baumrind (1967, 1971, 1978) looked at specific parenting styles as interactions between the two dimensions of acceptance and control. In addition, she wanted to know the effects of these parenting styles on children's social and intellectual competence. In her initial study, Baumrind observed a sample of preschool children and their parents and rated both groups on a number of dimensions. Additional data were obtained through interviews with the parents. Baumrind was able to identify four distinct parenting styles: authoritarian, permissive, authoritative, and neglectful.

Courtesy, Diana Baumrind

Diana Baumrind

1. *Authoritative parents* (high acceptance, high control) set high goals for their children but are also accepting of their children and responsive to their needs. They also provide age-appropriate explanations that emphasize the consequences of "good" and "bad" behavior. They encourage verbal give-and-take and allow their children to question parental requests. Authoritative parents maintain firm control but take into account each child's unique and changing needs. They are willing to negotiate with their children, setting new and less restrictive limits when appropriate, particularly as children mature.

2. *Authoritarian parents* (low acceptance, high control) are highly demanding and controlling and use physical punishment or the threat of it with their children. By virtue of their higher status, they issue commands that are to be obeyed without question ("Do it because I said so"). These parents rigidly maintain tight control even as their children mature. They also tend to be somewhat emotionally distant and may be rejecting.

Web Link 11.8 **The ChildTrauma Academy**

Founded by Bruce Perry, a psychiatrist, The ChildTrauma Academy develops programs that seek to nurture, protect, and enrich children. Its website is rich with information on basic child development topics, such as attachment, curiosity, and language development. However, its foremost strength is its collection of materials on how to help children victimized by physical, psychological, or sexual abuse or other types of severe trauma.

3. *Permissive parents* (high acceptance, low control) make few or no demands of their children. They allow children free expression of impulses and set few limits on appropriate behavior. Permissive parents are responsive and warmly accepting and indulge their children's desires.

4. *Neglectful parents* (low acceptance, low control) provide for the basic physical and emotional needs of their children, but not much else. They convey the impression that they don't really care for their children. They are not particularly involved with or supportive of their children (no help with homework, minimal supervision, little time spent together).

Correlates of Parenting Styles

Baumrind and others have found that parenting styles are associated with different traits in children, as summarized in **Figure 11.13**. As you might expect, *authoritative* parenting is associated with the most positive outcomes. Children whose parents use this style do

© David Young-Wolff/PhotoEdit

Research has uncovered some interesting correlations between parents' disciplinary style and their children's personality traits. An authoritative parenting style seems to be associated with the most desirable traits.

Parenting Styles and Children's Traits

Parenting style	Authoritative	Authoritarian	Permissive
Children's behavioral profile	**Energetic-friendly**	**Conflicted-irritable**	**Impulsive-aggressive**
	Self-reliant	Fearful, apprehensive	Rebellious
	Self-controlled	Moody, unhappy	Low in self-reliance and self-control
	Cheerful and friendly	Easily annoyed	Impulsive
	Copes well with stress	Passively hostile	Aggressive
	Cooperative with adults	Vulnerable to stress	Domineering
	Curious	Aimless	Aimless
	Purposive	Sulky, unfriendly	Low in achievement
	Achievement-oriented		

Figure 11.13

Baumrind's findings on parenting styles and children's traits. Diana Baumrind (1978) has studied three styles of parenting and their relations to children's social and intellectual competence. As you can see, authoritative parenting is associated with the most desirable outcomes.

Promoting Resilience in Children

Peoples' coping abilities are overwhelmed when they are exposed to traumatic events such as the 9/11 terrorist attacks, a space shuttle explosion, a violent homicide or suicide, rape, or a natural disaster such as Hurricane Katrina. Other events that traumatize individuals include exposure to acts of war, domestic or community violence, and child abuse or neglect.

Psychologists are particularly interested in how children react to traumatic events to understand how to protect them from long-term damage. Children's reactions to traumatic events are likely to vary depending on their age (Gallagher & Chase, 2002; National Institute of Mental Health, 2001). The responses of children under the age of 6 tend to be muted unless their parents exhibit strong distress that disturbs the children. If children between the ages of 6 and 11 are troubled, parents may observe regressive or disruptive behaviors, nightmares, irrational fears, reluctance to go to school, and vague bodily complaints (stomachaches, headaches, and so forth). The responses of youngsters in the 12–17 age bracket tend to resemble the responses seen in adults, such as flashbacks, emotional numbing, and avoidance of any reminders of the traumatic event. Sleep disturbances and difficulties at school are also common. Adolescents may increase their use of alcohol or cigarettes.

Following a traumatic experience, most children return to their normal level of functioning after the acute phase of distress passes (Cloitre, Morin, & Lanares, 2004). Unfortunately, a few have difficulties getting back on track. Children and adolescents who have experienced at least one of the following risk factors are more likely to have long-term difficulties coping with a traumatic event (Cloitre, et al., 2004):

- Directly witnessed an event or have a family member who observed an event
- Survived the death of a parent or another important person
- Had mental health problems before the event
- Experienced an earlier traumatic event
- Lacked a strong support network
- Had a parent whose levels of stress and fear are on the increase

Although exposure to a traumatic event heightens the risk for psychological problems, many children have an amazing ability to overcome adversity. This ability to bounce back from traumatic experiences is termed *resilience.* Researchers have tracked the adjustment of children who have (1) been exposed to war, (2) lived in areas of high terrorist activity, (3) experienced traumatic events such as the 9/11 attacks, (4) lived in American slums, (5) lost loved ones through death, (6) witnessed life-threatening natural disasters, and (7) lived with a parent with a serious psychological disorder such as schizophrenia (Gallagher & Chase, 2002; Cloitre, et al., 2004).

According to Richard Gallagher and Ayana Chase (2002), "Many children who have experienced tragedy or witnessed life-threatening events emerge with a positive outlook on life, have a good capacity to form positive, fulfilling relationships, achieve a high level of personal success, and develop effective resources for dealing with future negative events" (p. 2). Parents, teachers, and others who work with children and adolescents can do a lot to foster such positive outcomes in the face of traumatic events. The following advice, adapted from Gallagher and Chase (2002), may be helpful:

- *Help children establish and maintain a close relationship with an adult.* Children who experience the harshest circumstances can do well if they have a relationship with at least one very supportive adult. Nonparental figures can fill this role if parents cannot.
- *Be sure that children and teens know ways to calm themselves.* Help children relax through play, talk, art activities, music, or physical comforting. Teens should be encouraged to engage in exercise, muscle relaxation, or deep breathing to reduce stress, as opposed to unhealthy stress-reduction methods such as smoking, drinking, and drugs.
- *Help children understand the real statistical probability of tragedy and disaster.* Children need to understand that traumatic events are very unlikely to happen to them or to their family members. A realistic outlook will help children remain alert to dangers, but free from constant worries that they are in danger.
- *Watch for negative reactions and provide early assistance, or treatment, when necessary.* Reactions to traumatic events may appear months after rather than immediately following the event. Chronic irritability, avoiding anxiety-inducing situations, fatigue, and inability to concentrate may signal problems, especially if these symptoms interfere with daily functioning and last for more than a week.
- *Keep children informed about related events.* Children may overhear information about a traumatic event and misinterpret it. Adults should provide age-appropriate

Promoting Resilience in Children (continued)

facts about frightening situations. Repeated exposure to violent images and those related to destruction and death is especially harmful to children.

- *Help children establish a set of values to guide their actions.* Children who have values for relating to the world show less depression and anxiety than others. Prosocial values help them feel connected to a larger social group and engage in positive behavior.
- *Help children develop a positive outlook for the future.* Traumatic events can shake children's natural optimism about the future. Parents can help children recover their optimism by reminding them that negative events are temporary. They can also help their kids develop self-efficacy (see Chapter 5) so that the children believe they are able to cope with stressful situations and can make contributions to better the world.

the best in school and tend to be self-reliant, friendly, cooperative, and autonomous (Mattanah, 2005). In contrast, the children of *authoritarian* parents tend to do less well in school and to have lower self-esteem and poorer social skills. *Permissive* parents often have children whose grades are lower and who are undisciplined, impulsive, and easily frustrated. Although Baumrind didn't report on children of *neglectful* parents, other researchers have found them to have low self-esteem and to be moody, impulsive, and aggressive (Maccoby & Martin, 1983). This style also predicts the most maladaptive outcomes of the four parenting styles (Baumrind, 1991; Patterson, DeBaryshe, & Ramsey, 1989). Problems include low academic and social competence, delinquency, and alcohol and substance abuse.

Of course, these data are correlational and do not establish that the parenting style is the *cause* of the children's traits. The direction of influence goes both ways (Cummings, Braungart-Rieker, & du Rocher-Schudlich, 2003). For instance, parents may become increasingly authoritarian *in response to* their child's increasing resentment and irritability. Even so, Baumrind's results imply that authoritative parenting is most likely to foster social and cognitive competence in children.

Rearing Adolescents

Adolescents' emerging cognitive abilities enable them to question parental values and to formulate a personal philosophy to guide their own behavior. Although this process is necessary, it often drives intergenerational conflicts. Parents seem to have a harder time dealing with these conflicts than adolescents do (Steinberg, 2001).

One of the undercurrents in parent-adolescent relationships is that the balance of power between parent and child is shifting. Younger children accept their parents' power as a legitimate source of authority, especially if they have a warm relationship. The increasing autonomy of adolescents, however, requires a more equal parent-child relationship. While this is a necessary step on the road to autonomous adulthood, negotiating such shifts in power can be difficult. Authoritative parents who are willing to respond to their teenagers' input are most likely to avoid such turmoil (Steinberg, 2001; Steinberg, Blatt-Eisengart, & Cauffman, 2006). Authoritarian parents who are unwilling to relinquish control promote hostility and rebellion in adolescents. Permissive and neglectful parents, who never exercised much control over their children, may find themselves faced with adolescents whose behavior is completely out of hand. Compared to the other parenting styles, authoritative parenting is also associated with greater resistance to unfavorable peer pressure (Masten, 2001).

Researchers who have studied parenting styles in adolescence have found essentially the same pattern of outcomes we noted earlier, although the differences among the four groups are not always dramatic (Baumrind, 1989; Steinberg, 2001). Authoritatively reared adolescents show the highest competence and adjustment, while neglectfully reared adolescents generally show the lowest. Adolescents reared with authoritarian or permissive styles generally fall between the other two groups. **Figure 11.14** depicts the high school grades and school misconduct of adolescents in these four groups. These findings are consistent across a number of ethnic groups, including African Americans, Hispanics, and Asian Americans (Steinberg, 2001).

Toward Effective Parenting

Are there some "basic rules" for effective parenting? We offer five key principles here. Of course, it's essential to tailor these suggestions to the age and developmental level of a specific child. For an additional perspective, see the Recommended Reading box on Laurence Steinberg's (2004) book on effective parenting.

Courtesy, Laurence Steinberg

Laurence Steinberg

Figure 11.14

Parenting styles, school performance, and school misconduct. Lamborn and colleagues (1991) classified the families of over 4,000 14- to 18-year-olds into four parenting styles, based on adolescents' ratings of their parents. They then compared the youths on a number of outcomes, including high school grade point average and frequency of school misconduct. Adolescents from authoritative families showed the highest competence and adjustment (higher grades, less misconduct), while those from neglectful families showed the lowest.

Data from Lamborn, S. D., Mounts, N. S., Steinberg, L., & Dornbusch, S. M. (1991). Patterns of competence and adjustment among adolescents from authoritative, authoritarian, indulgent, and neglectful families. *Child Development, 62,* 1049–1065. Copyright © 1991 by the Society for Research in Child Development. Used with permission of SRCD.

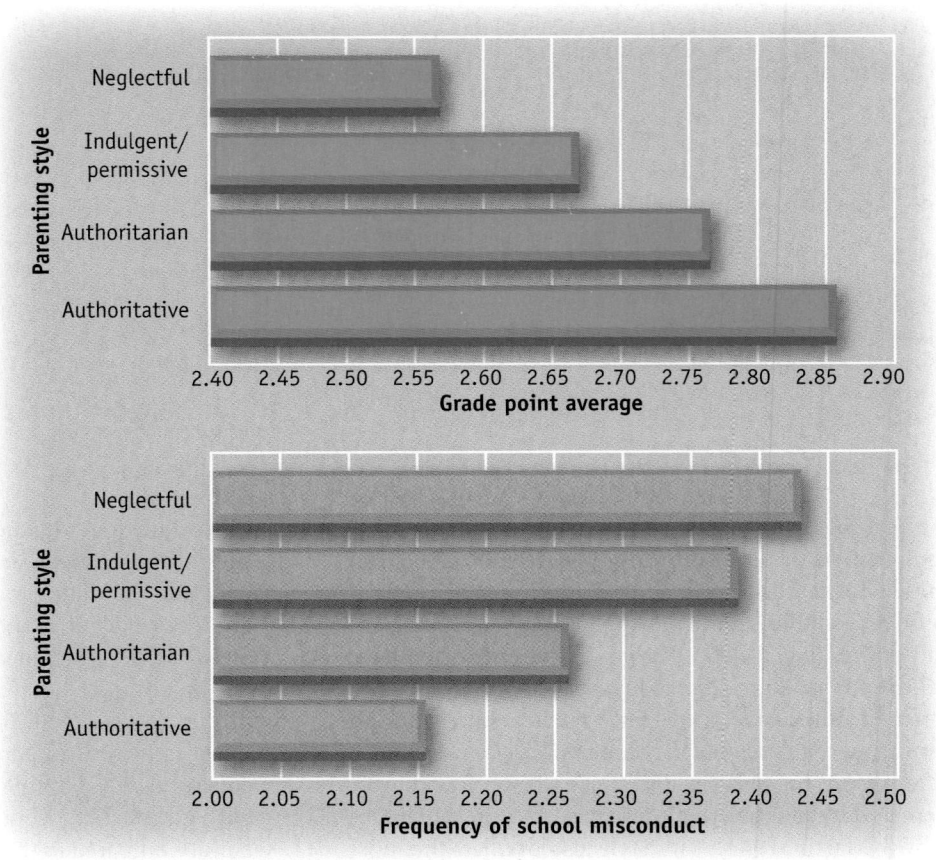

1. *Set high, but reasonable standards.* Children should be expected to behave in a socially appropriate manner for their age and to do as well as they can in school and in other activities. Parents who don't expect much from their children are teaching them not to expect much from themselves.

2. *Stay alert for "good" behavior and reward it.* Most parents pay attention to children when they are misbehaving and ignore them when they're being good. This approach is backward! Develop the habit of praising good behavior so a child knows what you want.

3. *Explain your reasons when you ask a child to do something.* Don't assume that a child can read your mind. Explaining the purpose of a request can transform what might appear to be an arbitrary request into a reasonable one. It also encourages self-control in a child.

4. *Encourage children to take the perspective of others.* Talk to children about the effects of their behavior on others ("How would you feel if Keisha did that to you?"). This role-playing approach fosters moral development and empathy in children.

5. *Enforce rules consistently.* Children need to have a clear idea about what is expected of them and to know that there will be consequences when they fail to meet your standards. This practice also fosters self-control in children.

Using Punishment Effectively

To use punishment effectively, most parents probably should use it less often. That's because punishment often has unintended, negative side effects. A recent meta-analysis of 88 studies on corporal punishment reported that it *is* associated with stopping the punished behavior (Gershoff, 2002). Still, the bad news is that punishment is also associated with a host of problematic outcomes: reduced quality of parent-child relationships, poorer mental health in childhood and adulthood, increased delinquency and aggression in childhood, and increased aggression and criminal behavior in adulthood.

Many professionals decry the use of physical punishment for these reasons. Others assert that occasional, mild spankings should not be conflated with harsher punishment (which was the case in Gershoff's meta-analysis). Advocates of this position argue that infrequent, mild spankings can reduce disobedience and fighting and are not associated with negative out-

Recommended READING

The 10 Basic Principles of Good Parenting
by Laurence Steinberg
(Simon & Schuster, 2004)

Laurence Steinberg, a respected researcher in developmental psychology, has consolidated the voluminous findings on child development and parenting into ten basic principles of effective parenting. Steinberg asserts that these principles can be universally applied—regardless of a family's income, race, or parental status (two-parent or single-parent). His principles are designed to foster competence, responsibility, security, and kindness in children and to help adults be happier and more confident parents.

Steinberg's ten principles are: "What You Do Matters," "You Cannot Be Too Loving," "Be Involved in Your Child's Life," "Adapt Your Parenting to Fit Your Child," "Establish Rules and Set Limits," "Help Foster Your Child's Independence," "Be Consistent," "Avoid Harsh Discipline," "Explain Your Rules and Decisions," and "Treat Your Child with Respect." For each principle, Steinberg elaborates on the concept, explains how the principle applies to children of different ages, and offers "dos and don'ts."

comes (Baumrind, Larzelere, & Cowan, 2002; Larzelere, 2000). The following guidelines summarize research evidence on how to make punishment effective while minimizing its side effects (Berkowitz, 1993):

1. *Punishment should not damage the child's self-esteem.* To be effective, punishment should get across the message that it is the behavior that is undesirable, not the child. Unduly harsh physical punishment, derogatory accusations, and other hurtful words erode the child's self-esteem.

2. *Punishment should be swift.* A delay in delivering punishment undermines its impact. A parent who says, "Wait until your father (or mother) gets home . . ." is making a fundamental mistake. (He or she is also unfairly setting up the other parent as the "heavy.") Quick punishment highlights the connection between the prohibited behavior and its negative outcome.

3. *Punishment should be consistent.* If you want to eliminate an undesirable behavior, you should punish it every time it occurs. When parents are inconsistent about punishing a particular behavior, they only create confusion in the child.

4. *Punishment should be explained.* When children are punished, the reason for their punishment should be explained as fully as possible, given the constraints of their age. The more children understand the reason they are punished, the more effective the punishment tends to be. These explanations, characteristic of the authoritative style, also foster the development of self-control.

5. *Point out alternative, positive ways for your child to behave and reinforce these actions.* One shortcoming of punishment is that it only tells a child what not to do. A better strategy is to punish an undesirable response and reward a positive alternative behavior. Children usually engage in undesirable behavior for a reason. Suggest another response that serves the same purpose and reward a child for doing it. For example, many troublesome behaviors exhibited by children are primarily attention-seeking devices. Punishment of these responses will be more effective if you can provide a child with more acceptable ways to gain attention.

KEY IDEAS

The Transition of Adolescence

▶ During pubescence, the adolescent growth spurt takes place and secondary sex characteristics develop. During puberty, which begins a few years later, the primary sex characteristics mature. The onset of puberty marks the beginning of adolescence. Girls typically mature two years earlier than boys. Boys who mature late and girls who mature early may find puberty particularly stressful.

▶ During adolescence, cognitive changes also occur, including development of the ability to apply logic to hypothetical situations, increases in knowledge, and greater skills in deductive reasoning. Despite greater cognitive sophistication, older adolescents are more likely to engage in physically harmful risky behavior, suggesting that this behavior is governed by noncognitive factors.

▶ In the realm of personality, adolescents must develop a clear sense of identity. Some theorists assert that adolescence is a period of turmoil, and there is research support for a modified storm-and-stress view that recognizes cultural and individual differences. Attention should be paid to youths who display symptoms of serious problems such as depression, suicidal behavior, drug and alcohol abuse, and chronic delinquency. Suicide among adolescents has greatly increased since 1960, but very few young people actually succeed in taking their lives.

The Expanse of Adulthood

▶ During early adulthood, individuals make more major role changes than in any other developmental stage. In Erikson's theory, the key psychosocial crisis for young adults is intimacy versus isolation. Specific developmental tasks of young adulthood include leaving one's family, entering the workplace and developing a career, finding a mate, having and rearing children, and adjusting to family life.

▶ In middle adulthood, the major psychosocial crisis is generativity versus stagnation, according to Erikson. Additional tasks for this group include confronting the aging process and dealing with transitions in the parental role as children mature and leave home. Midlife adults also experience changes in their work roles. Typically, they follow either the stable career pattern or the changing careers pattern. Few individuals seem to experience a midlife crisis.

▶ The key psychosocial crisis for older adults, according to Erikson, is integrity versus despair. Older adults must adjust to retirement, adapt to changes in their social networks, cope with health problems, and confront their own death.

Aging: a Gradual Process

▶ Physical development during adulthood leads to many obvious changes in physical appearance and sensory acuity. After age 30 there is a steady loss of active brain cells; however, this loss does not appear to underlie reductions in cognitive functioning. Similarly, hormonal changes appear to be only modestly related to midlife distress or declining sexual activity. Unfortunately, health does tend to decline with increasing age for a variety of reasons.

▶ Intelligence seems to remain fairly stable during most of adulthood. Attentional capacity, speed of learning, and success in problem solving all tend to decline slightly during old age. Memory processes also deteriorate but can be exacerbated by self-fulfilling prophecies. However, most people remain capable of sound intellectual functioning in their later years. The adult personality seems to be characterized by both stability and change.

Death and Dying

▶ Attitudes about death vary from one culture to another. Attitudes in this culture are characterized by negativism, avoidance, and fear. Kübler-Ross's research on the process of dying indicated that individuals progress through a sequence of five stages. Later research has called into question the idea that people's reactions to dying follow such a straightforward path.

▶ A wide variation exists between and within cultures regarding how death is acknowledged. Research has revealed a variety of patterns of grieving, calling into question traditional views of the process of mourning. The loss of a child is the most difficult type of death adults must cope with. In dealing with bereavement, people need the support of family and friends. Support groups can also be helpful.

Application: Becoming an Effective Parent

▶ According to Diana Baumrind, parenting styles can be classified as authoritative, authoritarian, permissive, and neglectful. Of Baumrind's four parenting styles, authoritative parenting is associated with the most positive outcomes in children.

▶ Intergenerational conflicts typically increase during adolescence, and parents seem to find these conflicts more difficult to deal with than adolescents do. Effective parenting involves following five key principles, as well as knowing how to use punishment effectively.

KEY TERMS

Bereavement p. 361
Death anxiety p. 360
Death system p. 359
Dementia p. 354
Identity p. 341
Menarche p. 338
Menopause p. 355
Midlife crisis p. 350
Mourning p. 361
Neurons p. 354
Parasuicide p. 343
Primary sex characteristics p. 338
Puberty p. 338
Pubescence p. 337
Secondary sex characteristics p. 338
Social clock p. 345
Spermarche p. 338
Working memory p. 358

KEY PEOPLE

Diana Baumrind pp. 364–367
Erik Erikson p. 341
Elisabeth Kübler-Ross pp. 360–361
Laurence Steinberg pp. 367–368
Susan Krauss Whitbourne p. 353

PRACTICE TEST

1. Primary sex characteristics develop during _____; secondary sex characteristics develop during _____.
   a. menarche, menopause
   b. puberty, pubescence
   c. the sexual stage; the physical stage
   d. adulthood; adolescence

2. Optimal adjustment is associated with puberty arriving ____ for girls and ____ for boys.
   a. late; on time
   b. early; on time
   c. on time; early
   d. late; early

3. Compared to those who are younger, adolescents:
   a. can think more abstractly.
   b. have greater knowledge.
   c. show greater self-awareness.
   d. do all of the above.

4. Which of the following statements about storm and stress in adolescence is false?
   a. Conflicts with parents increase during adolescence.
   b. Adolescents experience more volatile emotions than younger or older individuals do.
   c. Adolescents engage in more risky behaviors than children do.
   d. Heightened emotional turmoil in adolescence is found in all cultures.

5. The life stage that involves more role changes than any other is:
   a. adolescence.
   b. early adulthood.
   c. middle adulthood.
   d. later adulthood.

6. According to Erikson, the psychosocial conflict of middle adulthood is:
   a. identity versus identity diffusion.
   b. intimacy versus isolation.
   c. generativity versus stagnation.
   d. integrity versus despair.

7. Which of the following is a false statement about retirement?
   a. Retirement typically has a negative impact on overall health and life satisfaction.
   b. The best-adjusted retirees have an adequate income, good health, and a social network.
   c. Most older adults maintain their ties to their children.
   d. Retirement is typically a gradual process of cutting back on work hours over a period of years.

8. With regard to whether personality changes with age, it can be concluded that:
   a. a pattern of change is most typical.
   b. a pattern of stability is most typical.
   c. personality is characterized by both stability and change.
   d. no pattern can be discerned.

9. Less anxiety about death is found among those who:
   a. feel they haven't accomplished all that they had hoped.
   b. have a particular religious affiliation.
   c. have ambivalent religious views.
   d. have a well-formulated philosophy of death.

10. Baumrind's authoritative parenting style is characterized by:
   a. high acceptance and high control.
   b. low acceptance and high control.
   c. high acceptance and low control.
   d. low acceptance and low control.

Book Companion Website

Visit the Book Companion Website at **academic.cengage.com/psychology/weiten,** where you will find tutorial quizzes, flash cards, and web links for every chapter, a final exam, and more! You can also link to the Psychology Resource Center (accessible directly at **academic.cengage.com/login**) for a range of psychology-related resources.

Personal Explorations Workbook

The following exercises in your *Personal Explorations Workbook* may enhance your self-understanding in relation to issues raised in this chapter. **Questionnaire 11.1:** Death Anxiety Scale. **Personal Probe 11.1:** How Do You Feel about Age Roles? **Personal Probe 11.2:** How Flexible Is Development?

ANSWERS

1. b Pages 337–338
2. c Pages 339–340
3. d Page 340
4. d Pages 342–343
5. b Page 345
6. c Page 348
7. a Page 352
8. c Page 359
9. d Page 360
10. a Page 364

CHAPTER 12

Careers and Work

CHOOSING A CAREER
Examining Personal Characteristics and Family Influences
Researching Job Characteristics
Using Psychological Tests for Career Decisions
Taking Important Considerations into Account

MODELS OF CAREER CHOICE AND DEVELOPMENT
Holland's Person-Environment Fit Model
Super's Developmental Model
Women's Career Development

THE CHANGING WORLD OF WORK
Workplace Trends
Education and Earnings
The Changing Workforce

COPING WITH OCCUPATIONAL HAZARDS
Job Stress
Sexual Harassment
Unemployment

LIVING IN TODAY'S WORLD *Coping with Unemployment*

BALANCING WORK AND OTHER SPHERES OF LIFE
Workaholism
Work and Family Roles
Leisure and Recreation

APPLICATION: GETTING AHEAD IN THE JOB GAME
Putting Together a Résumé
Finding Companies You Want to Work For
Landing an Interview
Polishing Your Interview Technique

REVIEW

PRACTICE TEST

Ben and Sarah, both in their mid-twenties, meet at a party hosted by mutual friends. After exchanging names and describing their connections to the hosts, the next question is, "What do you do for a living?" Their replies to this crucial question will reveal information not only about each other's occupation but also about their social status, lifestyle, personality, interests, and aptitudes. Their responses might also influence whether Ben and Sarah see each other again. In other words, work plays a pivotal role in adult life. According to a recent Gallup poll, 73% Americans rated work as either "extremely" or "very important" in their life (Moore, 2003). In **Figure 12.1**, you can see that how people view their jobs is strongly correlated with their income.

Because work is such a significant aspect of life, psychologists take a great interest in it. ***Industrial/organizational (I/O) psychology* is the study of human behavior in the workplace.** Among other issues, I/O psychologists study worker motivation and satisfaction, job performance, leadership, personnel selection, and diversity in organizations. A recent concern is how individuals balance work and family life (Borman, Klimoski, & Ilgen, 2003).

We begin this chapter by reviewing some important considerations in choosing a career. Then we explore two models of career development and discuss women's career issues. Next, we examine how the workplace and workforce are changing and look at some occupational hazards such as job stress, sexual harassment, and unemployment. Finally, we address the important issues of balancing work, relationships, and leisure. In the Application, we offer some concrete suggestions for enhancing your chances of landing a desirable job.

Choosing a Career

LEARNING OBJECTIVES

- *Describe personal and family influences on job choice.*
- *Cite several helpful sources of career information.*
- *List some aspects of potential occupations that are important to know about.*
- *Explain the role of occupational interest inventories in career decisions.*
- *List five important considerations in choosing an occupation.*

One of your biggest decisions in life is choosing a career. The importance of this decision is enormous. It may determine whether you are employed or unemployed, financially secure or insecure, happy or unhappy. Rapidly advancing technology and the increased training and education required to break into most fields make it more important than ever to choose thoughtfully. In theory, what's involved in making a successful career choice is pretty straightforward. First, you need to have a clear grasp of your personal characteristics. Second, you need realistic information about potential careers. From there, it's just a matter of selecting an occupation that is a good match with your personal characteristics. In reality, the process is a lot more complicated. Let's take a closer look.

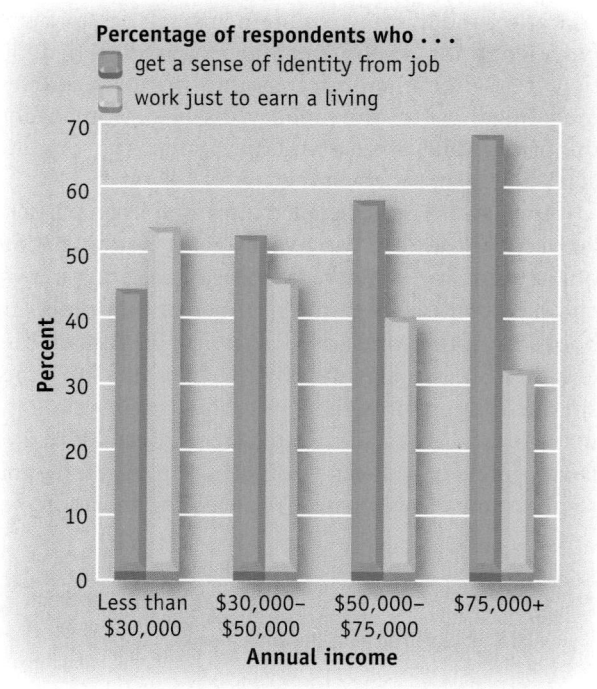

Figure 12.1

How workers view their jobs. The way workers view their jobs is strongly related to their income. Those who earn higher salaries are more likely to obtain a sense of identity from their work, whereas those who earn lower salaries typically see their jobs merely as a way to make a living. (Data from Moore, 2001)

Examining Personal Characteristics and Family Influences

People with limited job skills and qualifications have limited job options. As a result, they must usually take whatever job is available rather than a job that is well suited for them. In fact, *choosing* a career is a luxury usually afforded to the middle and upper classes. For those who *are* able to select a career, personal qualities and family influences come into play.

Personal Characteristics

Making career decisions can be scary. Individuals who exhibit *secure attachment* (see Chapter 8) and who have a sense of *self-efficacy* about career-relevant abilities (see Chapter 5) thus find it easier to make career choices (Fouad, 2007; Wolfe & Betz, 2004).

What other personal characteristics affect career choice? Although *intelligence* does not necessarily predict occupational success, it does predict the likelihood of entering particular occupations. That's because intelligence is related to academic success—the ticket required to enter certain fields. Professions such as law, medicine, and engineering are open only to those who can meet increasingly selective criteria as they advance from high school to college to graduate education and professional training. This relationship between intelligence and occupational level generally holds well for men, but an ability-achievement gap exists for women, as we noted in Chapter 10.

In many occupations, special talents are more important than general intelligence. *Specific aptitudes* that might make a person well suited for certain occupations include creativity, artistic or musical talent, mechanical ability, clerical skill, mathematical ability, and persuasive talents. A particularly crucial characteristic is *social skills,* since the use of teams to accomplish work tasks is increasingly important in a wide variety of organizations (Kozlowski & Bell, 2003).

As people travel through life, they acquire a variety of *interests.* Are you intrigued by the business world? the academic world? international affairs? the outdoors? physical sciences? music? athletics? human services? The list of potential interests is virtually infinite. Because interests underlie your motivation for work and your job satisfaction, they should definitely be considered in your career planning.

Finally, it is important to choose an occupation that is compatible with your *personality* (Swanson & D'Achiardi, 2005). We'll examine the relationship between personality types and career choice in a later section.

Family Influences

Individuals' career choices are strongly influenced by their family background (Whiston & Keller, 2004). That is, the jobs that appeal to people tend to be like those of their parents. For instance, people who grow up in middle-class homes are likely to aspire to high-paying professions in law, medicine, or engineering. On the other hand, individuals from low-income families often lean toward blue-collar jobs in construction work, office work, and food services.

Family background influences career choice for several reasons. For one thing, a key predictor of occupational status is the number of years of education an individual has completed (Arbona, 2005). And, because parents and children often attain similar levels of education, they are likely to have similar jobs. Second, career attainment is related to socioeconomic status. The factors that mediate this relationship are educational aspirations and attainment during the school years (Schoon & Parsons, 2002). This means that parents and teachers can help boost children's career aspirations and opportunities by encouraging them to do well in school. Although socioeconomic status seems to have more influence on career aspirations than ethnicity (Rojewski, 2005), ethnic differences in aspirations are still found. For example, a cross-cultural and multi-ethnic study reported that Chinese and Asian American college students more often choose investigative occupations, and their career decisions are more influenced by parents than European American college students' decisions are (Tang, 2002).

Finally, parenting practices come into play. As we noted in Chapter 11's Application on parenting, parenting styles are correlated with socioeconomic status. They also shape work-related values. Most children from middle-class homes are encouraged to be curious and independent, qualities that are essential to success in many high-status occupations. By contrast, children from lower-status families are often taught to conform and obey. As a result, they may have less opportunity to develop the qualities demanded in high-status jobs. As we noted in Chapter 10, parents' gender-role expectations also influence their children's aspirations and sometimes interact with socioeconomic status and ethnicity.

Researching Job Characteristics

The second step in selecting an occupation is seeking out information about jobs. Because the sheer number of jobs is overwhelming, you have to narrow the scope of your search before you can start gathering information.

Sources of Career Information

Once you have selected some jobs that might interest you, the next question is: Where do you get information on them? A helpful place to start is the *Occupational Outlook Handbook,* available in most libraries and on the World Wide Web (see Web Link 12.1). This government document, published every two years by the U.S. Bureau of Labor Statistics, is a comprehensive guide to occupations. It includes job descriptions, education and training requirements, salaries, and employment outlooks for over 800 occupations. In addition, it details numerous career information resources, including those for the military, disabled, women, and minorities. You can also find tips on locating jobs and accepting salary offers in this useful resource.

If you want more detailed information on particular occupations, you can usually get it by doing some online searching. If you're interested in a career in psychology, you can obtain a number of pamphlets or books from the American Psychological Association (APA). Also, the APA website provides links to other sites describing more than 50 subfields in psychology, many of which provide useful career information. Related professions (social work, school psychology, and so on) also have web pages. You will find the addresses

Web Link 12.1 **Occupational Outlook Handbook (OOH) Online**

Every two years the Bureau of Labor Statistics publishes the OOH, now available via the Internet. This guide to every occupation in the United States includes descriptions of the nature of each job and its working conditions, educational requirements, future employment, and earnings prospects. You can also find information about job and workforce trends here.

© AP Images/Richard Drew

© Bonnie Kamin/PhotoEdit

People vary in their preferences for work environments. Some like high-pressure work; others prefer more low-key jobs.

of these pages on Marky Lloyd's Careers in Psychology website (see Web Link 12.2).

After you've read the available literature about an occupation, it's helpful to talk to some individuals working in that area. People in the field can provide you with more down-to-earth information than you can get by reading. Keep in mind, though, that the people you talk to may not be a representative sample of those who work in an occupation. Don't reject a potentially satisfying career just because one person hates it.

Essential Information About Occupations

When you examine occupational literature and interview people, what kinds of information should you seek? To some extent, the answer depends on your unique interests, values, and needs. However, some things are of concern to virtually anyone. Workers typically give high ratings to good health insurance, retirement plans, limited job stress, and recognition for performing well (Saad, 1999). Some key issues you need to know about include:

▶ *The nature of the work.* What would your duties and responsibilities be on a day-to-day basis?

▶ *Working conditions.* Is the work environment pleasant or unpleasant, low key or high pressure?

▶ *Job entry requirements.* What education and training are required to break into this occupational area?

Web Link 12.2 **Marky Lloyd's Careers in Psychology Page**

For those who think they might want a job or career in psychology or allied fields, Professor Marky Lloyd, one of this textbook's authors, has put together a fine set of resources to help in both planning and making the choice. Many of the resources are helpful to any student seeking career guidance and employment tips.

▶ *Potential earnings.* What are entry-level salaries, and how much can you hope to earn if you're exceptionally successful? What does the average person earn? What are the fringe benefits?

▶ *Potential status.* What is the social status associated with this occupation? Is it personally satisfactory for you?

▶ *Opportunities for advancement.* How do you move up in this field? Are there adequate opportunities for promotion and advancement?

▶ *Intrinsic job satisfaction.* Apart from money and formal fringe benefits, what can you derive in the way of personal satisfaction from this job? Will it allow you to help people, to have fun, to be creative, or to shoulder responsibility?

▶ *Future outlook.* What is the projected supply and demand for this occupational area?

By the way, if you're wondering whether your college education will be worth the effort in terms of dollars and cents, the answer is yes. As we'll discuss shortly, the jobs that you can obtain with a college degree typically yield higher pay than those that require less education (Crosby & Moncarz, 2006). The experts also agree that the future belongs to those who are better educated (Gordon, 2006).

Using Psychological Tests for Career Decisions

If you are undecided about an occupation, you might consider taking some tests at your campus counseling center. ***Occupational interest inventories*** **measure your interests as they relate to various jobs or careers.**

Two widely used tests of this type are the Strong Interest Inventory (SII) and the Self-Directed Search (SDS) (Brown, 2007).

Occupational interest inventories do not attempt to predict whether you would be successful in various occupations. Rather, they focus more on the likelihood of job *satisfaction* than job *success*. When you take an occupational interest inventory, you receive many scores indicating how similar your interests are to the typical interests of people in various occupations. For example, a high score on the accountant scale of a test means that your interests are similar to those of the average accountant. This correspondence in interests does not ensure that you would enjoy a career in accounting, but it is a moderately good predictor of job satisfaction (Hansen, 2005).

Interest inventories like the SII can provide worthwhile food for thought about possible careers. The results may confirm your subjective guesses about your interests and strengthen already-existing occupational preferences. Additionally, the test results may inspire you to investigate career possibilities that you had never thought of before. Unexpected results may stimulate you to rethink your career plans.

Although interest inventories can be helpful in working through career decisions, several cautions are worth noting. First, you may score high on some occupations that you're sure you would hate. Given the sheer number of occupational scales on the tests, this can easily happen by chance. However, you shouldn't dismiss the remainder of the test results just because you're sure that a few specific scores are "wrong." Second, don't let the test make career decisions for you. Some students naïvely believe that they should pursue whatever occupation yields their highest score. That is not how the tests are meant to be used. They merely provide information for you to consider. Ultimately, you have to think things out for yourself.

Third, you should be aware that most occupational interest inventories have a lingering gender bias. Many of these scales were originally developed 40 to 50 years ago when outright discrimination or more subtle discouragement prevented women from entering many traditionally "male" occupations. Critics assert that interest inventories have helped channel women into gender-typed careers, such as nursing and teaching, while guiding them away from more prestigious "male" occupations, such as medicine and engineering. Undoubtedly, this was true in the past. Recently, progress has been made toward reducing gender bias in occupational tests, although it has not been eliminated (Hansen, 2005). Research suggests that ethnic bias on interest tests is less of a concern than gender bias (Hansen, 2005; Worthington, Flores, & Navarro, 2005). In interpreting interest inventory results, be wary of letting gender stereotypes limit your career options.

Taking Important Considerations into Account

As you contemplate your career options, here are some important points to keep in mind.

1. *You have the potential for success in a variety of occupations.* Career counselors stress that people have multiple potentials (Spokane & Cruza-Guet, 2005). Considering the huge variety of job opportunities, it's foolish to believe that only one career would be right for you. If you expect to find one job that fits you perfectly, you may spend your entire lifetime searching for it.

2. *Be cautious about choosing a career solely on the basis of salary.* Because of the tremendous emphasis on material success in America, people are often tempted to choose a career solely on the basis of income or status. Experts advise against this strategy (Pollack, 2007). When people ignore personal characteristics in choosing a career, they risk being mismatched. Such job mismatching can result in boredom, frustration, and unhappiness with one's work, and these negative feelings can spill over into other spheres of life.

3. *There are limits on your career options.* Entry into a particular occupation is not simply a matter of choosing what you want to do. It's a two-way street. You get to make choices, but you also have to persuade schools and employers to choose you. Your career options will be limited to some extent by factors beyond your control, including fluctuations in the economy and the job market.

4. *Career choice is a developmental process that extends throughout life.* Occupational choice involves not a single decision but a series of decisions. Although this process was once believed to extend only from prepuberty to the early 20s, authorities now recognize that the process continues throughout life. Some experts predict that the average person will have ten jobs over the course of his or her working life (Levitt, 2006). Nonetheless, middle-aged people may underestimate the options available to them and therefore miss opportunities to make constructive changes. We want to emphasize that making occupational choices is not limited to youth.

5. *Some career decisions are not easily undone.* Although it's never too late to strike out in new career directions, it is important to recognize that many decisions are not readily reversed. Once you invest time, money, and effort in moving along a particular career path, it may not be easy to change paths. And family responsibilities can make major career changes difficult. This potential problem highlights why it is important to devote careful thought to your occupational choice.

In the next section, we explore in greater detail how personal characteristics are related to career choice and career development.

Models of Career Choice and Development

LEARNING OBJECTIVES

- *Summarize Holland's model of career choice.*
- *Summarize Super's five-stage model of career development.*
- *Discuss women's career development.*

Psychologists have long been interested in understanding how individuals make career choices and how their careers evolve over time. Theorists have developed several approaches to these issues. Here we examine two influential models.

Holland's Person-Environment Fit Model

The most influential trait model of career choice is that developed by John Holland (1985, 1996). According to Holland, career choice is related to an individual's personality characteristics, which are assumed to be relatively stable over time. In Holland's system, people can be classified into one of six personality types, called *personal orientations.* Similarly, occupations can be classified into six ideal *work environments.* According to Holland, people flourish when their personality type is matched with a work environment that is congruent with their abilities, interests, and self-beliefs. A good match typically results in career satisfaction, achievement, and stability. Here are the six personal orientations and their optimal work environments:

▶ *Realistic* people describe themselves as good at mechanical tasks and weak in social skills. They prefer jobs with tasks that are physical or mechanical and that are clearly defined, such as farming, auto mechanics, and engineering. They tend to avoid tasks that involve social skills, abstract thinking, subjectivity, or verbal skill.

▶ *Investigative* people enjoy abstract thinking and logical analysis, preferring understanding to action. They like working with ideas rather than with things or people. Investigative individuals can often be found working in research laboratories or libraries.

▶ *Artistic* people see themselves as imaginative and independent. They tend to be impulsive, creative, and socially aloof. These individuals dislike structured tasks, preferring instead to rely on their subjective impressions in dealing with the environment. They have a high need for emotional expression and often seek careers in art, music, or drama.

▶ *Social* people describe themselves as being understanding and wanting to help others. They prefer to interact with people, and they have the necessary social skills to do so comfortably. They typically have greater verbal ability than mathematical ability. Social types are often found in the helping professions, such as teaching, nursing, and social work.

▶ *Enterprising* people perceive themselves as happy, self-confident, sociable, and popular. They like to use their social skills to lead or persuade others. They prefer sales or supervisory positions, in which they can express these characteristics.

▶ *Conventional* people are conforming, systematic, and orderly. They typically have greater clerical and

© Bill Aron/PhotoEdit

Those with a "social" personal orientation in Holland's theory are understanding and want to help others. Teachers typically score high on the "social" orientation.

mathematical ability than verbal ability. They prefer working environments that are structured and predictable and may be well suited to occupations in the business world.

Holland has developed several tests to measure the six basic personal orientations. One of them, the Self-Directed Search (SDS), is a self-scoring test. Once individuals identify their personality type on the SDS, they can match it with various relevant occupations. Studies have shown the SDS to be a useful career assessment tool (Spokane & Cruza-Guet, 2005).

Obviously, these six personal orientations are ideal types, and no one person will fit perfectly into any one type. In fact, most people are a combination of two or three types (Holland, 1996). You can take a rough stab at categorizing your own personal orientation by studying **Figure 12.2**. Look at the matching work environments to get some ideas for possible career options.

More research has been conducted on Holland's model than any other theory in vocational psychology, and much of this research is supportive (Spokane & Cruza-Guet, 2005). For instance, researchers report that Holland's model describes the career preferences of ethnically diverse male and female college students relatively accurately (Fouad & Mohler, 2004). On the other hand, people with good job-personality matches should be more satisfied with their jobs and likely to remain in these jobs longer than those who are less well matched, but research shows that job-personality fit contributes very little (5%) to job satisfaction (Fouad, 2007).

In contrast to trait models such as Holland's that view occupational choice as a specific event, stage theories view occupational choice as a developmental process. We look at that approach next.

Super's Developmental Model

A highly influential developmental model of career choice is that outlined by Donald Super (1957, 1985, 1988). He views occupational development as a process that begins in childhood, unfolds gradually across most of the life span, and ends with retirement. Super asserts that the person's *self-concept* is the critical factor in this process. In other words, decisions about work and career commitments reflect people's attempts to express

Holland's Personal Orientations and Related Work Environments

Themes	Personal orientations	Work environments
Realistic	Values concrete and physical tasks. Perceives self as having mechanical skills and lacking social skills.	*Settings:* concrete, physical tasks requiring mechanical skills, persistence, and physical movement *Careers:* machine operator, pilot, draftsperson, engineer
Investigative	Wants to solve intellectual, scientific, and mathematical problems. Sees self as analytical, critical, curious, introspective, and methodical.	*Settings:* research laboratory, diagnostic medical case conference, work group of scientists *Careers:* marine biologist, computer programmer, clinical psychologist, architect, dentist
Artistic	Prefers unsystematic tasks or artistic projects: painting, writing, or drama. Perceives self as imaginative, expressive, and independent.	*Settings:* theater, concert hall, library, radio or TV studio *Careers:* sculptor, actor, designer, musician, author, editor
Social	Prefers educational, helping, and religious careers. Enjoys social involvement, church, music, reading, and dramatics. Is cooperative, friendly, helpful, insightful, persuasive, and responsible.	*Settings:* school and college classrooms, psychiatrist's office, religious meetings, mental institutions, recreational centers *Careers:* counselor, nurse, teacher, social worker, judge, minister, sociologist
Enterprising	Values political and economic achievements, supervision, and leadership. Enjoys leadership control, verbal expression, recognition, and power. Perceives self as extraverted, sociable, happy, assertive, popular, and self-confident	*Settings:* courtroom, political rally, car sales room, real estate firm, advertising company *Careers:* realtor, politician, attorney, salesperson, manager
Conventional	Prefers orderly, systematic, concrete tasks with verbal and mathematical data. Sees self as conformist and having clerical and numerical skills.	*Settings:* bank, post office, file room, business office, Internal Revenue office *Careers:* banker, accountant, timekeeper, financial counselor, typist, receptionist

Figure 12.2

Overview of Holland's theory of occupational choice. According to John Holland (1985), people can be divided into six personality types (personal orientations) that prefer different work environments, as outlined here.

Adapted from Holland, J. L. (1985). *Making occupational choices: A theory of occupational personalities and work environments* (2nd ed.). Englewood Cliffs, NJ: Prentice-Hall. Adapted by permission of Prentice-Hall, Inc.

their changing views of themselves. To map these changes, Super breaks the occupational life cycle into five major stages and a variety of substages (see **Figure 12.3**).

Columbia University Archives, Columbia University

Donald Super

Growth Stage

The growth stage occurs during childhood, when youngsters fantasize about exotic jobs they would enjoy. Generally, they imagine themselves as detectives, airplane pilots, and brain surgeons rather than plumbers, salespersons, and bookkeepers. Until near the end of this period, children are largely oblivious to realistic considerations such as the abilities or education required for specific jobs.

Exploration Stage

Pressures from parents, teachers, and peers to develop a general career direction begin to intensify during high school. By the end of high school, individuals are expected to have narrowed a general career direction into a specific one. Young people try to get a real taste of their intended occupation through reading about it or part-time work. During the later part of this stage, youth typically seek full-time work. If their initial work experiences are gratifying, their tentative commitment will be strengthened. However, unrewarding early experiences may motivate individuals to shift to another occupation, where they will continue the exploration process.

Establishment Stage

Vacillation in career commitment continues to be common during the first part of the establishment stage. Once people make gratifying occupational choices, their career commitment is strengthened. With few exceptions, future job moves will take place *within* the preferred occupational area. Having made a commitment, the person now needs to demonstrate the ability to function effectively in the area. To succeed, individuals must use previously acquired skills, learn new skills, and display flexibility in adapting to organizational changes.

Maintenance Stage

As the years go by, opportunities for further career advancement and occupational mobility decline. Around their mid-40s, many people cross into the maintenance stage, during which they worry more about *retaining* their achieved status than *improving* it. Although middle-aged employees may need to update their skills to compete with younger workers, their primary goal is to protect the security, power, advantages, and perks that they have attained. With decreased emphasis on career advancement, many people shift energy and attention away from work in favor of family or leisure activities.

Stages of Occupational Development

Stage	Approximate ages	Key events and transitions
Growth stage	**0–14**	**A period of general physical and mental growth**
Prevocational substage	0–3	No interest or concern with vocations
Fantasy substage	4–10	Fantasy is basis for vocational thinking
Interest substage	11–12	Vocational thought is based on individual's likes and dislikes
Capacity substage	13–14	Ability becomes the basis for vocational thought
Exploration stage	**15–24**	**General exploration of work**
Tentative substage	15–17	Needs, interests, capacities, values, and opportunities become bases for tentative occupational decisions
Transition substage	18–21	Reality increasingly becomes basis for vocational thought and action
Trial substage	22–24	First trial job is entered after the individual has made an initial vocational commitment
Establishment stage	**25–44**	**Individual seeks to enter a permanent occupation**
Trial substage	25–30	Period of some occupational change due to unsatisfactory choices
Stabilization substage	31–44	Period of stable work in a given occupational field
Maintenance stage	**45–65**	**Continuation in one's chosen occupation**
Decline stage	**65+**	**Adaptation to leaving workforce**
Deceleration substage	65–70	Period of declining vocational activity
Retirement substage	71+	A cessation of vocational activity

Figure 12.3

Overview of Super's theory of occupational development. According to Donald Super, people go through five major stages (and a variety of substages) of occupational development over the life span.

Adapted from Zaccaria, J. (1970). *Theories of occupational choice and vocational development.* Boston: Houghton Mifflin. Copyright © 1970 by Time Share Corporation, New Hampshire.

Decline Stage

Deceleration involves a decline in work activity in the years prior to retirement. People redirect their energy and attention toward planning for this major transition. Super's original formulation, which was based on research in the 1950s, projected that deceleration ought to begin at around age 65. Since the 1970s, however, the large baby boom cohort has created an oversupply of skilled labor and professional talent. This social change has created pressures that promote early retirement. Because of these conditions, deceleration often begins earlier than Super initially indicated.

Retirement brings work activity to a halt. People approach this transition with highly varied attitudes. Many individuals look forward to it eagerly. Others approach it with apprehension, unsure about how they will occupy themselves and worried about their financial viability. Still others approach retirement with a combination of hopeful enthusiasm and anxious concern. Although retirement may mean less income, it can also mean more time to spend with friends and on hobbies, travel, and meaningful volunteer work.

As a stage theorist, Super deserves credit for recognizing that people follow different patterns in their career development. For example, he identified several patterns for both men and women that do not coincide with the conventional pattern we have described. In support of Super's model, it has been found that career maturity is correlated with self-esteem and self-efficacy (Creed, Prideaux, & Patton, 2005; Kornspan & Etzel, 2001). A more serious problem with Super's theory is that it assumes that people will remain in the same careers all of their working lives. But today's American workers will have many career changes, a reality that is incompatible with the assumptions of long-term models like Super's. The current thinking about career stages or cycles is that they are shorter and recur periodically over the course of a person's career (Greenhaus, 2003). To be useful, stage models must reflect today's workplace realities.

Women's Career Development

It is currently estimated that 59% of adult women (versus 73% of men) are in the labor force (U.S. Census Bureau, 2006b). Moreover, the odds that a woman will work outside the home during her adult life are greater than 90% (U.S. Department of Labor, 2003). Although women's labor force participation is approaching that of men's, important gender differences remain when it comes to career choice and development. For one thing, most women still subordinate their career goals to their husband's (Betz, 2005). This is even the case with academically gifted women (Arnold, 1995). If a married man wants or needs to move to another job, his wife typically follows him and takes the best job she can find in the new location. Hence, married women usually have less control over their careers than married men do. Also, the high divorce rate (45%) means that many women will have to provide for themselves and their children (Betz, 2006). One study reported that after a divorce, the woman's standard of living drops 27% (Weitzman, 1996). Today's women need to take these factors into account as they consider their career options.

Another gender difference concerns career paths. Men's career paths are usually *continuous,* whereas women's tend to be *discontinuous* (Betz, 1993). In other words, once men start working full-time, they usually continue to work. Women are more likely to interrupt their careers to concentrate on childrearing or family crises (Hynes & Clarkberg, 2005). Because women are having fewer children and are returning to work sooner, the amount of time they are out of the labor force is decreasing. Although labor force discontinuity is a factor in women's lower salaries and status, there is also evidence that women are simply paid less than men (Dey & Hill, 2007; U.S. General Accounting Office, 2003). Women who do not have children usually remain in the labor force and tend to have a pattern of career advancement similar to men's (Blair-Loy & DeHart, 2003).

The Changing World of Work

LEARNING OBJECTIVES

- *List six work-related trends.*
- *Describe the relationship between education and salary.*
- *Summarize important demographic changes that are transforming the workforce.*
- *Cite some problems that women and minorities face in today's workplace.*
- *Describe some challenges presented by workforce diversity to organizations and workers.*

Before you enter the working world, it's important to get your bearings. In this section we look at several important background issues: contemporary trends in the workplace, the relationship between education and earnings, and diversity in the workforce.

Workplace Trends

***Work* is an activity that produces something of value for others.** For some people, work is just a way to earn a living; for others, work is a way of life. For both types

The growth of technology is significantly changing the nature of work, with both positive and negative effects.

of workers, the nature of work is undergoing dramatic changes. Because such changes can affect your future job prospects, you need to be aware of six important trends:

1. *Technology is changing the nature of work.* Computers and electronic equipment have dramatically transformed the workplace. From the worker's point of view, these changes have both down sides and up sides. On the negative side, computers automate many jobs that people perform, eliminating jobs. The digital workplace also demands that employees have more education and skills than were previously required (Cetron & Davies, 2003). And workers have to keep upgrading their technology skills, which can be stressful. On the positive side, technological advances allow employees to work at home and to communicate with others in distant offices and while traveling. Another "plus" is that computer-driven machines require workers to design, manufacture, sell, and service them.

2. *New work attitudes are required.* Yesterday's workers could usually count on job security. Thus, many could afford a somewhat passive attitude in shaping their careers. But today's workers have job security only as long as they can add value to a company. This situation means that workers must take a more active role in shaping their careers (Smith, 2000). In addition, they must develop a variety of valuable skills, be productive workers, and skillfully market themselves to prospective employers. In the new work environment, the keys to job success are self-direction, self-management, up-to-date knowledge and skills, flexibility, and mobility (Smith, 2000).

3. *Lifelong learning is a necessity.* Experts predict that today's jobs are changing so rapidly that in many cases, work skills will become obsolete over a 10- to 15-year period (Lock, 2005a). Thus, lifelong learning and training will become essential for employees. Every year, nearly one-third of American workers take courses to improve their job skills (American Council on Education, 1997). In some cases, retraining occurs on the job; in others, community colleges and technical institutes provide continuing education. Distance learning courses and programs are also available, although you have to watch out for bogus programs (Mariani, 2001). For suggestions on how to evaluate the quality and accreditation claims of distance education programs, see Web Link 12.3. Workers who know "how to learn" will be able to keep pace with the rapidly changing workplace and will be highly valued. Those who cannot may be left behind.

4. *Independent workers are increasing.* Corporations are downsizing and restructuring to cope with the changing economy and to be competitive globally. In doing so, they are slashing thousands of permanent jobs and doling out the work to temporary employees or to workers in other countries, a practice termed "outsourcing." By reducing the number of regular workers, companies can chop their expenditures on payroll, health insurance, and pension plans, as temporary employees don't typically receive such benefits. A leaner workforce also enables organizations to respond quickly to fast-changing markets. According to Daniel Pink (2001), one way to survive in this new environment is to become a "free agent" and hire out

Web Link 12.3 **DegreeInfo.com**

If you need assistance evaluating distance learning programs, this site can help you. Its purpose is to disseminate accurate information about quality distance-based higher education programs. None of the writers for this site is currently affiliated with any school, although some of them are alumni of regionally accredited distance learning programs.

your skills to one or more organizations on a contract basis. To characterize the "free agent" work pattern, Pink suggests the metaphor of the "LEGO career" instead of the "career ladder." Just as you can construct a variety of structures by assembling LEGO blocks, "free agents" assemble and reassemble the building blocks of their work life (values, interests, aptitudes, and skills) in various combinations to match career opportunities that emerge over time. Many professionals thrive on contract work; they have freedom, flexibility, and high incomes. But for those who are short on skills and entrepreneurial spirit, this work can be stressful and risky. About a third of independent employees would prefer to work for someone else than to work for themselves (Bond et al., 2003).

5. *The boundaries between work and home are breaking down.* Today's technological advances allow people to work at home and stay in touch with the office via high-speed Internet, telephones, and fax machines. Working at home is convenient—workers save time (no commuting) and money (on gas, parking, clothes). Still, family members and friends may interrupt home-workers, necessitating setting rules to protect work time. With the advent of cell phones, pagers, and wireless modems, employees can be contacted any time and any place, making some workers feel as though they are on an "electronic leash." Looking at the flip side, the availability of onsite day care in some large companies means that a traditional home function has moved to the office (Drago, 2007). This development is largely a response to increases in the number of single-parent families and ***dual-earner households,* in which both partners are employed.** Quality onsite day care is a big draw to workers because it allows parents to interact with their children during the day.

6. *The highest job growth will occur in the professional and service occupations.* The United States, like many other industrialized nations, continues to shift from a manufacturing, or "goods-producing," economy to a service-producing one (U.S. Bureau of Labor Statistics, 2006). Whereas the bulk of yesterday's jobs were in manufacturing, construction, agriculture, and mining, the jobs of the next decade will be in the professional (and related technical) occupations and service occupations. Among the professional occupations, jobs in the computer and health care industries are expected to expand dramatically. In psychology, jobs in health, clinical, counseling, and school psychology are expected to show strong growth. In the service occupations, strong job growth should occur in education, health services, social services, professional services, and business services. **Figure 12.4** depicts 20 occupations expected to grow the most and pay the most between now and 2014.

Web Link 12.4 **U.S. Department of Labor**

With primary responsibility for many job- and work-related matters in the U. S. government, the Labor Department offers a site that can serve as a base to explore a variety of topics, including wages and compensation, worker productivity, and the legal rights of workers (such as protection from sexual harassment).

Education and Earnings

Although many jobs exist for individuals without a college degree, these jobs usually offer the lowest pay and benefits. In fact, all but 1 of the 50 highest-paying occupations require a college degree or higher (U.S. Bureau of Labor Statistics, 2004). (By the way, the high-paying job that doesn't require a college degree is air traffic controller.) In **Figure 12.5**, you can see that the more you

Figure 12.4

High-growth, high-salary occupations. According to the U.S. Department of Labor (2006), between 2004 and 2014 these 20 occupations will have the largest number of job openings and will provide the highest pay. Median annual salaries range from $145,600 (physicians and surgeons) to $30,710 (general maintenance and repair workers). (Adapted from *Occupational Outlook Quarterly,* Spring 2006)

"Best Bet" Occupations, 2004–2014

Registered nurses	Secondary school teachers, except vocational education
Postsecondary teachers	Carpenters
General and operations managers	First-line supervisors or managers of retail sales workers
Elementary school teachers	Automotive service technicians and mechanics
Sales representatives, wholesale and manufacturing, except technical and scientific products	Licensed practical and licensed vocational nurses
Truck drivers, heavy and tractor-trailer	Computer software engineers
Executive secretaries and administrative assistants	Police and sheriff's patrol officers
Accountants and auditors	Middle-school teachers
General maintenance and repair workers	Physicians and surgeons
First-line supervisors or managers of office and administration support workers	First-line supervisors/managers of construction workers

learn, the more you earn. This relationship holds for both males and females, although, as you can see, men are paid approximately $12,000 to $35,000 more than women with the same educational credentials.

On the other hand, a college diploma is no guarantee of a great job. In fact, many college graduates are underemployed. ***Underemployment* is settling for a job that does not fully utilize one's skills, abilities, and training.** About 18% of college graduates take jobs that don't usually require a college degree, and experts predict that this situation is unlikely to change in the near future (Lock, 2005a). And while it's true that the jobs you can obtain with a college degree pay more than those requiring less education, the higher-paying jobs go to college graduates with *college-level* reading, writing, and quantitative skills. College graduates without these skills more often end up in high-school-level jobs (Pryor & Schaffer, 1997).

Current employers are not very happy with the academic skills of many of their employees. According to a survey by the College Board's National Commission on Writing, a majority of U.S. employers say that about a third of their workers do not meet the writing requirements of their positions (College Entrance Examination Board, 2004). As new jobs develop, they will require more education and higher skill levels. International competition and technology are the two driving forces here (U.S. Department of Labor, 2000). Thus, computer literacy is an essential complement to a good basic education.

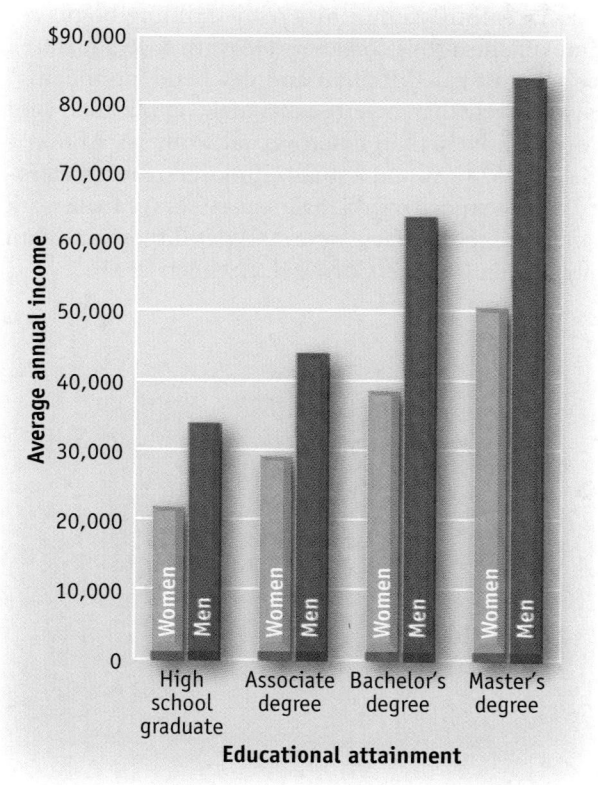

Figure 12.5

Education and income. This graph shows the average incomes of year-round, full-time workers age 18 and over, by gender and educational attainment. As you can see, the more education people have, the higher their income tends to be. However, at all levels women earn less than men with comparable education. (Data from U.S. Bureau of the Census, 2006)

Free Agent Nation: The Future of Working for Yourself
by Daniel H. Pink (Warner Books, 2001)

In this provocative book, Daniel Pink describes the workplace of the future for an increasing number of workers. The recent mega-changes in the workplace brought about by international competition and technological innovations have dramatically altered work patterns. People no longer work for the same company all of their adult lives but rather change (and, sometimes, lose) jobs regularly. To deal with these workplace changes, to gain more control over their lives, and to do work that is personally meaningful, many workers go into business for themselves. Pink describes three types of these free agents. Soloists (or freelancers or independent contractors) are the most common type; they work for themselves, selling their services as they move from project to project. Owners of microbusinesses (organizations with only two or three workers) are a second type of free agent. Temps (temporary workers) are free agents by default, as they would rather be working for someone else. In his engaging writing style, Pink details both the pros and cons of working as a free agent. The book also includes an excellent resource guide detailing the basics of self-employment (getting started, finding health insurance, and so forth).

The Changing Workforce

The ***labor force* consists of all those who are employed as well as those who are currently unemployed but are looking for work.** In this section, we look at some of the changes affecting the workforce and consider how women and other minorities fare in the workplace.

Demographic Changes

The workforce is becoming increasingly diverse, with regard to both gender and ethnicity. In 2005, 61% of married women worked, compared to 41% in 1970 (U.S. Bureau of the Census, 2006b). This increase holds even for women with very young children. For instance, in 1975 only 33% of women with children under the age of 3 worked outside the home. By 2005, this number had grown to 57% (U.S. Bureau of the Census, 2006b). These changes have implications not only for work and family life but also for men's and women's roles.

The workforce is also becoming more ethnically diversified (see **Figure 12.6**) (U.S. Bureau of Labor Statistics, 2006). High school graduation rates for Asian Americans about match those for European Americans, and college graduation rates for Asian Americans exceed those of European Americans. By contrast, the high school and college graduation rates of Hispanics and African Americans lag behind those of European Americans, although they have been improving in recent decades (Worthington et al., 2005). Consequently, both groups are at a disadvantage when it comes to competing for the better jobs.

John Browne, the long-time chief executive of British Petroleum and close associate of former British Prime Minister Tony Blair, had little choice but to resign after a judge cleared the way for a newspaper to publish allegations made by a former boyfriend. The exposé of Browne's private life ended his 41-year career at British Petroleum. The stunning demise of Browne's career demonstrates why many gay individuals choose to remain "closeted" in the workplace due to concern about recriminations.

Although gay, lesbian, and bisexual workers have been long-standing participants in the workplace, they are often "closeted" for fear of discrimination. Unfortunately, most of these workers do not have the same legal protections against employment discrimination as their heterosexual counterparts (Badgett, 2003). Thus, disclosing one's sexual orientation may cause a homophobic supervisor to fire, refuse to promote, or reduce the income of a gay or lesbian employee. Predictably, factors associated with the decision to disclose one's sexual orientation at work include employer policies and perceived gay supportiveness of the employer (Griffith & Hebl, 2002). Research on the effects of sexual orientation disclosure and employment discrimination are scarce. One laboratory study manipulated sexual orientation, gender, and masculinity/femininity while holding bogus résumé qualifications constant (Horvath & Ryan, 2003). Participants rated lesbian and gay male "applicants" less positively than heterosexual male "applicants" (but more positively than heterosexual women). And in a survey of 534 gay and lesbian employees, more heterosexism was reported with male supervisors or male work teams, and these effects were stronger for lesbians than for gay men (Ragins, Cornwell, & Miller, 2003).

Figure 12.6

Increasing diversity in the workforce. Women and minority group members are entering the workforce in greater numbers than before. This graph projects changes in the share of the labor force by gender and by ethnicity between 1990 and 2010. (Data from U.S. Bureau of Labor Statistics, 2002)

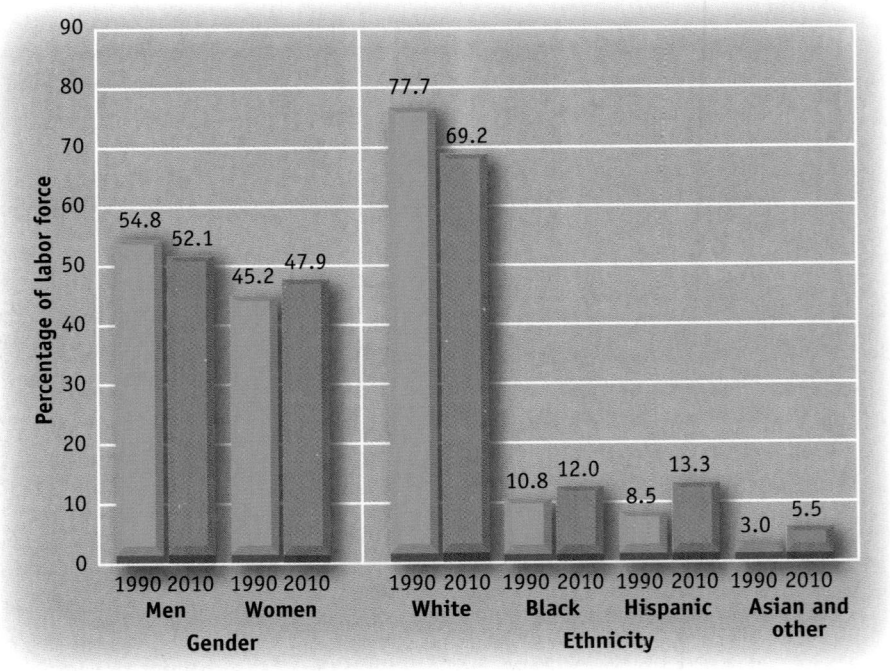

Today's Workplace for Women and Minorities

Recent years have seen a dramatic upsurge in the number of females and ethnic minorities in the workplace. Is today's workplace essentially the same for these groups as it is for white males? In many respects, the answer appears to be no. Although job discrimination on the basis of race and gender has been illegal for more than 40 years, women and minority group members continue to face obstacles to occupational success, as evidenced by relatively recent court decisions that found Wal-Mart and Morgan Stanley guilty of sex discrimination. Foremost among these obstacles is *job segregation.* Jobs are simultaneously typed by gender and by race. For example, skycaps are typically African American males and most hotel maids are minority females. Most white women and minority workers tend to be concentrated in jobs where there is little opportunity for advancement or increase in salary (U.S. Equal Employment Opportunity Commission, 2007). Also, as we discussed in Chapter 10, workers in female-dominated fields typically earn less than employees in male-dominated fields, even when the jobs require similar levels of training, skill, and responsibility.

More women and ethnic minorities are entering higher-status occupations, but they still face discrimination because they are frequently *passed over for promotion* in favor of white men (Whitley & Kite, 2006). This seems to be a problem especially at higher levels of management (Cotter et al., 2001). For example, in 2006, about 16% of corporate officer positions in Fortune 500 companies were held by women and only about 1.5% were held by women of color (Catalyst, 2007). There appears to be a ***glass ceiling,* or invisible barrier that prevents most women and ethnic minorities from advancing to the highest levels of occupations** (see **Figure 12.7**). The fact that very few black women are in managerial positions has caused some to term the glass ceiling a "concrete wall" for women of color (U.S. Department of Labor, 1992). Largely because of these reduced opportunities for career advancement, some female corporate managers are quitting their jobs and starting their own firms. In 2002, women owned 28% of nonfarm U.S. businesses (U.S. Small Business Administration, 2006). At the other end of the job spectrum, there seems to be a "sticky floor" that causes women and minorities to get stuck in low-paying occupations (Brannon, 2005).

When there is only one woman or minority person in an office, that person becomes a ***token*—or a symbol of all the members of that group.** Tokens are more distinctive or visible than members of the dominant majority. And, as we discussed in Chapter 6, distinctiveness makes a person's actions subject to intense scrutiny, stereotyping, and judgments. Thus, if a white male makes a mistake, it is explained as an *individual* problem. When a token woman or minority person makes a mistake, it is seen as evidence that *all* members of that group are incompetent. Hence, tokens experience a great deal of *performance pressure,* an added source of job stress (Thomas, 2005). Interestingly, if tokens are perceived as being "too successful," they may be labeled "workaholics" or may be accused of trying to "show up" members of the dominant majority. These unfavorable perceptions may be reflected in performance appraisals. The performance of successful white men is less likely to be interpreted in these negative ways.

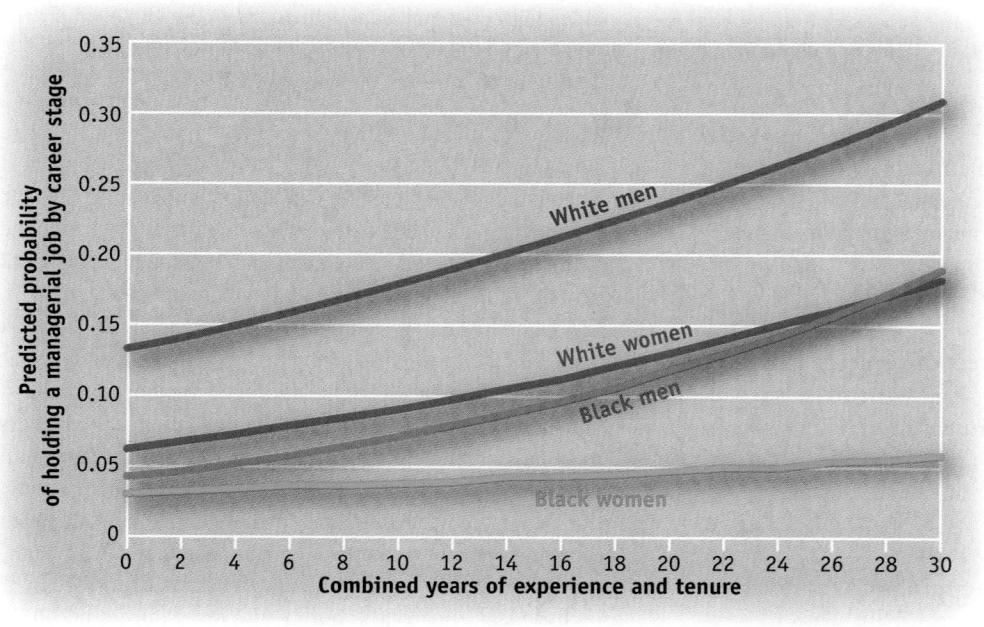

Figure 12.7

The glass ceiling for women and minorities. A longitudinal study looked at the chances of promotion to a managerial position in a sample of more than 26,000 adults over 30 years of career experience. This graph shows that promotion chances increased along with career experience for white men. By contrast, the promotion chances of white women and black men were much lower. As you can see, black women lagged far behind all groups. These trends are consistent with the existence of a glass ceiling for women and minorities.

From Maume, D. J. (2004). Is the glass ceiling a unique form of inequality? *Work and Occupations, 31*(2), 250–274. Figure 2, p. 266. Copyright © 2004 by Sage Publications, Inc. Adapted by permission of Sage Publications.

Another way the world of work is different for women, ethnic, and gay and lesbian minorities is that they have *less access to same-gender or same-group role models and mentors* (Murrell & James, 2001). Finally, *sexual harassment,* a topic we'll take up later, is much more likely to be a problem for working women than for working men. In sum, women and minority individuals must contend with discrimination on the job in a number of forms.

The Challenges of Change

The increasingly diverse workforce presents challenges to both organizations and workers. Important cultural differences exist in managing time and people, in identifying with work, and in making decisions (Thomas, 2005). These differences can contribute to conflict. Another challenge is that some individuals feel that they are personally paying the price of prejudice in the workplace, and this perception causes resentment. Recognizing the problem, some corporations offer diversity training programs for their employees. Ironically, these programs can make the problem worse if they take a blaming stance toward white males or if they stir up workers' feelings but provide no ongoing support for dealing with them. Thus, it is essential that such programs be carefully designed (Ocon, 2006). The strong support of top management is also critical to their success.

Many who advocate abandoning affirmative action programs that are intended to promote access to jobs for women and minorities argue that these programs promote "reverse discrimination" through the use of unfair hiring and promotion practices. For some, this perception may reflect a sense of *privilege,* an unquestioned assumption that white males should be guaranteed a place in society and that others should compete for the remaining jobs (Jacques, 1997). Some also argue that affirmative action undercuts the role of merit in employment decisions and sets up (supposedly) underprepared workers for failure. Many laboratory studies show that individuals have negative feelings about employees who may have been hired under affirmative action (Crosby et al., 2003). However, studies conducted with actual workers have not found this situation (Taylor, 1995). Regardless, this potential negative effect can be counteracted when workers know that decisions are based on merit as well as on group membership.

To minimize conflict and to maintain worker productivity and satisfaction, companies can provide well-designed diversity programs, and managers can educate themselves about the varied values and needs of their workers (Ocon, 2006). Similarly, both majority and minority employees must be willing to learn to work comfortably with those who come from other backgrounds.

Coping with Occupational Hazards

LEARNING OBJECTIVES

- *List some important sources of job stress.*
- *Summarize the effects of job stress on physical and mental health.*
- *Describe actions that organizations are taking to reduce job stress.*
- *Describe the prevalence and consequences of sexual harassment.*
- *Cite some ways that organizations and individuals can reduce sexual harassment.*
- *Describe some causes and effects of unemployment.*

Work can bring people deep satisfaction, but it can also be a source of frustration and conflict. In this section, we explore three challenges to today's workers: job stress, sexual harassment, and unemployment.

Job Stress

You saw in Chapter 3 that stress can emerge from any corner of your life. However, many theorists suspect that the workplace is the primary source of stress in modern society. Let's examine job stress and what employers and workers can do about it.

Sources of Stress on the Job

Between 2001 and 2004, the number of Americans claiming to feel overworked rose from 28% to 44% (Galinsky et al., 2005). Current estimates clock the average full-time workweek at 48 hours; in law and finance, 60-hour weeks are common (Hodge, 2002). According to a United Nations report, the average American worked 1,978 hours in 2000, up from 1,942 hours in 1990 (International Labour Office, 2002). That's an increase of nearly a full week over the past decade. Compare this situation to that in Canada, Japan, and Mexico, where the average worker put in about 100 hours, or 2.5 weeks, less than American workers in 2000. Germans worked nearly 12.5 weeks less than Americans in 2000. Also, among affluent nations, only the United States does not require a minimum number of sick days for workers (Heymann et al., 2004).

In addition to long hours, common job stressors include lack of privacy, high noise levels, unusual hours

CATHY © Cathy Guisewite. Reprinted with permission of UNIVERSAL PRESS SYNDICATE. All rights reserved.

(such as rotating shifts), the pressure of deadlines, lack of control over one's work, inadequate resources to do a job, and perceived inequities at work (Fairbrother & Warn, 2003). Fears of being "downsized," concerns about health care benefits (losing them or paying increasingly higher premiums), and worries about losing pension plans also dog workers in today's economy. Office politics and conflict with supervisors, subordinates, and co-workers also make the list of job stressors. Having to adapt to changing technology and automated offices is another source of work stress. Firefighters and miners face frequent threats to their physical safety. High-pressure jobs such as air traffic controller and surgeon demand virtually perfect performance, as errors can have disastrous consequences. Ironically, "underwork" (boring, repetitive tasks) can also be stressful.

Women may experience certain workplace stressors, such as sex discrimination and sexual harassment, at higher rates than men (Betz, 2006). African Americans and ethnic minorities must cope with racism and other types of discrimination on the job (Betz, 2006). Discrimination is also a problem for gay and lesbian employees (Badgett, 2003). Workers from lower socioeconomic groups typically work in more dangerous jobs than workers from higher socioeconomic status do.

Why are American workers so stressed out? According to Gwendolyn Keita and Joseph Hurrell (1994), four factors are the culprits:

1. *More workers are employed in service industries.* Workers in these jobs must interact with a variety of individuals on a daily basis. While most customers are

© AP Images/Steve Ruark

Firefighters obviously face a great deal of stress in their work, but so do people in many other jobs. Work stress is a major issue in a diverse array of occupations.

civil and easy to deal with, some are decidedly difficult. Nonetheless, even obnoxious and troublesome customers "are always right," so workers have to swallow their frustration and anger, and doing so is stressful.

2. *The economy is unpredictable.* In the age of restructuring, downsizing, takeovers, and bankruptcies, even excellent workers aren't assured of keeping their jobs like workers in the past. Thus, the fear of job loss may lurk in the back of workers' minds.

3. *Rapid changes in computer technology tax workers' abilities to keep up.* Computers have taken over some jobs, forcing workers to develop new skills and to do so quickly. In other jobs, the stress comes from rapid and ongoing advances in technology that force workers to keep pace with the changes.

4. *The workplace is becoming more diverse.* As more women and minority group members enter the workplace, individuals from all groups must learn to interact with those who are unfamiliar. Developing these skills takes time and may be stressful.

Taking a broader view, Robert Karasek contends that the two key factors in occupational stress are the *psychological demands* made on a worker and a worker's amount of *decision control* (Karasek, 1979; Karasek & Theorell, 1990). Psychological demands are measured by asking employees questions such as "Is there excessive work?" and "Must you work fast (or hard)?" To measure decision control, employees are asked such questions as "Do you have a lot of say in your job?" and "Do you have freedom to make decisions?" In Karasek's demand-control model, *stress is greatest in jobs characterized by high psychological demands and low decision control.* Based on survey data obtained from workers, he has tentatively mapped out where various jobs fall on these two key dimensions of job stress, as shown in **Figure 12.8**. The jobs thought to be most stressful are those with heavy psychological demands and little control over decisions (see the lower right area of the figure). Considerable research has been conducted on the demand-control model, most of which has been supportive (Sonnentag & Frese, 2003). Still, some criticize the model as being too simplistic (Ippolito et al., 2005).

Effects of Job Stress

As with other forms of stress, occupational stress is associated with numerous negative effects. In the work arena itself, job stress has been linked to an increased number of industrial accidents, increased absenteeism, poor job performance, and higher turnover rates (Colligan & Higgins, 2005). Experts estimate that stress-related reductions in workers' productivity may cost American industry hundreds of billions per year.

When job stress is temporary, as when important deadlines loom, workers usually suffer only minor and brief effects of stress, such as sleeplessness or anxiety. Prolonged high levels of stress are more problematic, as those who work in people-oriented jobs such as human services, education, and health care can attest (Maslach, 2005). As we noted in Chapter 3, prolonged stress can lead to *burnout,* characterized by exhaustion, cynicism, and poor job performance (Maslach, 2005).

Of course, the negative effects of occupational stress extend beyond the workplace. Foremost among these adverse effects are those on employees' *physical health.* Work stress has been related to a variety of physical maladies, including heart disease, high blood pressure, ulcers, arthritis, asthma, and cancer (Thomas, 2005). In a test of Karasek's model of work

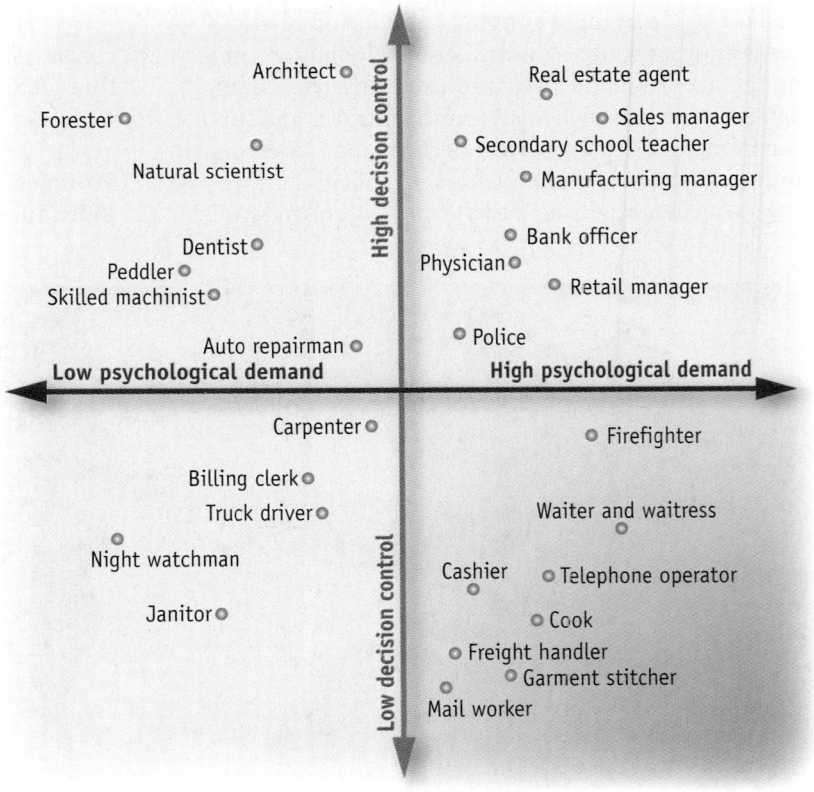

Figure 12.8

Karasek's model of occupational stress as related to specific jobs. Robert Karasek (1979) theorizes that occupational stress is greatest in jobs characterized by high psychological demands and low decision control. Based on survey data, this chart shows where various familiar jobs fall on these two dimensions. According to Karasek's model, the most stressful jobs are those shown in the shaded area on the lower right.

stress, symptoms of heart disease were more prevalent among Swedish men whose jobs were high in psychological demands and low in decision control (Karasek et al., 1981; see **Figure 12.9**). Job stress can also have a negative impact on workers' *psychological health.* Occupational stress has been related to distress, anxiety, and depression (Sonnentag & Frese, 2003).

Dealing with Job Stress

There are essentially three avenues of attack for dealing with occupational stress (Ivancevich et al., 1990). The first is to intervene at the *individual* level by modifying workers' ways of coping with job stress. The second is to intervene at the *organizational* level by redesigning the work environment itself. The third is to intervene at the *individual-organizational interface* by improving the fit between workers and their companies.

Interventions at the *individual* level are the most widely used strategy for managing work stress in the United States (Sonnenberg & Frese, 2003). Many companies have instituted programs designed to improve their employees' coping skills. These programs usually focus on relaxation training, time management, cognitive approaches to reappraising stressful events, and other constructive coping strategies that we discussed in Chapter 4. Also popular are *workplace wellness programs* that seek to improve employees' physical health (Nurminen et al., 2002). These programs usually focus on exercise and fitness training, health screening, nutritional education, and reduction of health-impairing habits, such as smoking and overeating.

Interventions at the *organizational* level are intended to make work environments less stressful. Some companies attempt to reduce occupational stress by reducing noise levels, instituting rest periods, making surroundings more attractive, and giving workers different tools or responsibilities. Decentralizing management and giving workers greater participation in decision making may also help reduce occupational stress (Wilpert, 1995).

Interventions at the *individual-organizational* interface can take many forms. Now and for the foreseeable future, the biggest challenge is probably to accommodate the changing nature of the workforce, which increasingly

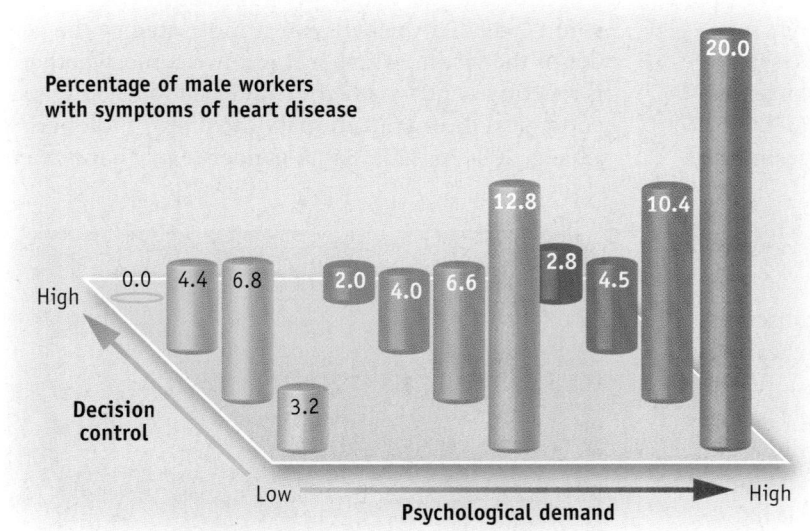

Figure 12.9

Job characteristics in Karasek's model and heart disease prevalence. Karasek et al. (1981) interviewed 1,621 Swedish men about their work and assessed their cardiovascular health. The vertical bars in this figure show the percentage of the men with symptoms of heart disease as a function of the characteristics of their jobs. The highest incidence of heart disease was found among men who had jobs high in psychological demands and low in decision control, just as Karasek's model of occupational stress predicts.

Redrawn from Karasek, R. A., Baker, D., Marxer, F., Ahlbom, A., & Theorell, T. (1981). Job decision latitude, job demand, and cardiovascular disease: A prospective study of Swedish men. *American Journal of Public Health, 71,* 694–705. Reprinted with permission from the American Public Health Association.

includes dual-earner couples and single parents rather than married men who are the sole wage earners in their families. What kinds of accommodations are companies making in response to the changing needs of their workers? In the important area of child care, the workplace has not been particularly responsive. Only 10% of full-time workers in private industry have access to on-site or off-site child care or receive funding for child care (U.S. Bureau of the Census, 2006b).

Another family-friendly employer policy is being able to set one's own starting and quitting times within some range of hours. In 2004, about 28% of full-time workers had flexible schedules (U.S. Bureau of Labor Statistics, 2005). Flexible schedules were more common among white workers than minority workers. Among other things, flexible work times help parents manage child care and other family responsibilities. Thus, it is not surprising that workers who have flexible work arrangements report better mental health as well as higher job satisfaction and company loyalty than employees whose jobs are less flexible (Bond et al., 2005; Cascio & Young, 2005). Interestingly, companies with a high proportion (half or more) of women in top slots are more likely to offer family-friendly policies (Murphy & Zagorski, 2005). We'll return to the issue of family-friendly work benefits in our discussion of work and family roles.

As we noted, workers from lower socioeconomic groups typically experience more work stress than those from higher-status groups. Ironically, these are the workers who receive less attention through stress management and other programs (Ilgen, 1990). Researchers are beginning to pay more attention to working-class and low-income families (Crosby & Sabattini, 2006). Perhaps their findings will encourage changes in the workplace.

Sexual Harassment

Sexual harassment burst into the American consciousness in 1991 during the televised confirmation hearings for the nomination of Clarence Thomas as a Justice of the U.S. Supreme Court. Although Justice Thomas survived the confirmation process, many would argue that his reputation was damaged by Anita Hill's public allegations of sexual harassment (while she was his assistant in the U.S. Department of Education a decade earlier), and so was Hill's. Allegations of sexual harassment also caused serious problems for President Bill Clinton. These highly publicized examples of sexual harassment charges have served as a wake-up call to individuals and companies, as both can be sued for harassment (regulations were instituted in 1980). Although most workers recognize that they need to take the problem of sexual harassment seriously, many people remain relatively naïve about what constitutes sexual harassment.

Sexual harassment **occurs when employees are subjected to unwelcome sexually oriented behavior.** According to law, there are two types of sexual harassment. The first is *quid pro quo* (from the Latin expression that translates as "something given or received in exchange for something else"). In the context of sexual harassment, quid pro quo involves making submission to unwanted sexual advances a condition of hiring, advancement, or not being fired. In other words, the worker's survival on the job depends on agreeing to engage in unwanted sex. The second type of harassment is *hostile environment,* or any type of unwelcome sexual behavior that creates hostile work situations that can inflict psychological harm and interfere with job performance.

Sexual harassment can take a variety of forms: unsolicited and unwelcome flirting, sexual advances, or propositions; insulting comments about an employee's appearance, dress, or anatomy; unappreciated dirty jokes and sexual gestures; intrusive or sexual questions about an employee's personal life; explicit descriptions of the harasser's own sexual experiences; abuse of familiarities such as "honey" and "dear"; unnecessary and unwanted physical contact such as touching, hugging, pinching, or kissing; catcalls; exposure of genitals; physical or sexual assault; and rape. As experts have pointed out, sexual harassment is an abuse of power by a person in authority. To determine what legally constitutes sexual harassment, the courts take into account "whether the behavior is motivated by the gender of the victim, whether it is unwelcome, whether it is repetitive, and whether it could lead to negative psychological or organizational outcomes" (Goldberg & Zhang, 2004, p. 823). Same-gender sexual harassment

© AP Images/Gregory Bull

Highly-publicized accusations of sexual harassment have become common in recent years. Here, Andrea Mackris appears with her attorney at a press conference to discuss allegations of sexual harassment lodged against Bill O'Reilly of the Fox News Channel.

also occurs and is tried according to the same standards applied in cross-sex sexual harassment although little research has been done on the topic.

Prevalence and Consequences

Sexual harassment in the workplace is more widespread than most people realize. A review of 18 studies suggested that approximately 42% of female workers in the United States report having been sexually harassed (Gruber, 1990). A liberal estimate for male workers is 15% (Gutek, 1993). The typical female victim is young, divorced or separated, in a nonsenior position, and in a masculine-stereotyped field (Davidson & Fielden, 1999). A review of studies on women in the military reported rates of sexual harassment ranging from 55% to 79% (Goldzweig, 2006). Women in blue-collar jobs are also at high risk, but sexual harassment also occurs in the professions. For example, in a survey of United Methodist clergywomen, 77% reported that they had experienced sexual harassment—with 41% of these incidents perpetrated by colleagues and other ministers ("Women Clerics," 1990).

Experiencing sexual harassment can have negative effects on psychological and physical health (Norton, 2002). Problematic reactions include anger, reduced self-esteem, depression, and anxiety. Victims may also have difficulties in their personal relationships and in sexual adjustment (loss of desire, for example). Increased alcohol consumption, smoking, and dependence on drugs are also reported (Davidson & Fielden, 1999). In addition, sexual harassment can produce fallout on the job: Women who are harassed may be less productive, less satisfied with their jobs, and less committed to their work and employer (Woodzicka & LaFrance, 2005).

Stopping Sexual Harassment

To predict the occurrence of sexual harassment, researchers have developed a two-factor model based on the person (prospective harasser) and the social situation (Pryor, Giedd, & Williams, 1995). According to this model, individuals vary in their proclivity for sexual harassment, and organizational norms regarding the acceptability of sexual harassment also vary. Sexual harassment is most likely to occur when individual proclivity is high and organizational norms are accepting. Thus, it follows that organizations can reduce the incidence of sexual harassment by promoting norms that are intolerant of it.

Acknowledging the prevalence and negative impact of sexual harassment, many organizations have taken steps to educate and protect their workers. Managers are publicly speaking out against sexual harassment, supporting programs designed to increase employees' awareness of the problem, issuing policies expressly forbidding harassment, and implementing formal grievance procedures for handling allegations of harassment.

Responses to sexual harassment may be personal as well as organizational. Researchers have developed a typology of possible responses to this problem (see **Figure 12.10**) and have studied their relative effectiveness (Bowes-Sperry & Tata, 1999; Knapp et al., 1997).

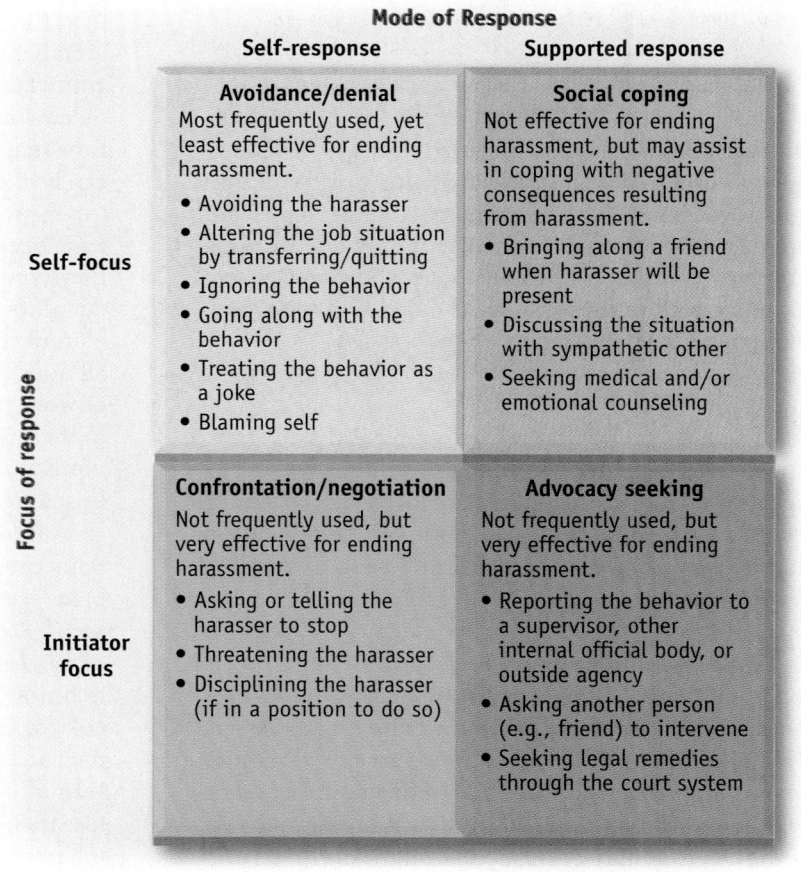

Figure 12.10

Effectiveness of responses to sexual harassment. Responses to sexual harassment can be classified into four categories based on the focus of the response (directed toward self or toward the harasser) and the mode of the response (involving the self or others). Unfortunately, the most frequent reactions turn out to be the least helpful. Effective strategies are available, but they are infrequently used.

From Bowes-Sperry, L., & Tata, J. (1999). A multiperspective framework of sexual harassment. In G. N. Powell (Ed.), *Handbook of gender and work* (pp. 263–280). Thousand Oaks, CA: Sage Publications. Copyright © 1999 by Sage Publications. Reprinted with permission of Sage Publications, Inc.

Sexual Harassment on the Job: What It Is and How to Stop It
by William Petrocelli and Barbara Kate Repa
(Nolo Press, 1998)

Employees and employers now recognize that they need to know what constitutes sexual harassment and what does not. In addition, those who believe that they are being sexually harassed want to know how to stop it. As the title of this book indicates, it addresses both issues. The authors clearly define the varieties of sexual harassment and provide examples from the workplace and from court cases to reinforce their points. Petrocelli and Repa view the solution to ending sexual harassment as a series of escalating steps, and they helpfully guide readers through their various options. For employers, there is a chapter on workplace policies and programs to reduce occurrences of sexual harassment.

Ironically, the most frequently used strategy—avoiding/denial—is also the least effective one. Confrontation and advocacy seeking are two effective strategies but are infrequently used. In the Recommended Reading box above, we describe a book that both employers and employees should find helpful in ridding the workplace of sexual harassment.

Unemployment

People with little education and training have always been vulnerable to unemployment. In today's economic market, however, even those with a good education and excellent job skills are not immune to unemployment. What's going on?

Causes of Unemployment

Unemployment today is caused primarily by the dramatic economic changes we have already discussed. First, the shift from a manufacturing to a service economy has significantly transformed the nature of work. On the positive side, this means that many new jobs are being created; on the negative side, it means that workers in high-paying manufacturing jobs are being laid off (robots now assemble cars, for instance). A second economic change is the globalization of the marketplace. For corporations, this means restructuring and downsizing to increase efficiency and profits—at the expense of workers, including those in white-collar jobs. Thus, a major consequence of these economic upheavals is ***displaced workers*—individuals who are unemployed because their jobs have disappeared.** Between 1999 and 2001, roughly 5 million workers with three or more years of experience were displaced as a result of plant closings, slack or insufficient work, or positions being eliminated (U.S. Bureau of the Census, 2006b).

Effects of Unemployment

Losing one's job is difficult at best and devastating at worst. Not only can it cause economic distress, it can also cause health problems and such psychological difficulties as loss of self-esteem, depression, and anxiety (Bobek & Robbins, 2005). Also, the rate of attempted and completed suicides increases with unemployment. Gender does not affect the amount of distress experienced due to job loss (Kulik, 2000).

While losing a job at any age is highly stressful, those who are laid off in middle age seem to find the experience most difficult (Breslin & Mustard, 2003). For one thing, they typically have more financial responsibilities than those in other age groups. Second, if other family members aren't able to provide health insurance, the entire family's health and welfare is jeopardized. Third, older workers typically remain out of work for a longer time than younger workers. Thus, economic hardship can be a real possibility and can threaten quality of life for the worker's family. Finally, middle-aged workers have been on the job for a number of years. Because they typically feel highly involved in their work, being cut off from this important source of life satisfaction is painful (Broomhall & Winefield, 1990). Of course, not all middle-aged workers are affected negatively by loss of work (Leana & Feldman, 1991). Individuals who are in their 50s and close to retirement and those who are motivated to try their hand at something new seem the least affected.

Occasionally the stress of job loss leads to violence. Sometimes, these violent episodes occur in the workplace itself (Sygnatur & Toscano, 2000). As you can see in **Figure 12.11** (on page 394), the leading cause of on-the-job homicides is robberies (67%). Of the remaining causes, the next highest is disputes between co-workers (15%). These situations often involve a displaced worker who lashes out in rage and desperation at a supervisor or co-workers. Employees who lose their jobs because of downsizing—instead of poor job performance—are likely to believe they have been treated arbitrarily and unfairly—a situation associated with increased aggression (LeBlanc & Barling, 2004). Workplace murderers are typically middle-aged white males who are loners at work, owners of gun collections, and fascinated by exotic weapons (Stuart, 1992). They are often angry and paranoid and may signal their intentions by making violent threats. Incidents of workplace violence and recent concerns about terror-

Coping with Unemployment

Mental health experts view job loss as a devastating life experience—similar to death, divorce, and serious illness or disability. Foremost, people are hit with the frightening prospect of loss of income and must deal with the stressful practicalities of how to live on less. Job loss also deals a psychological blow because it strikes at a key component of adult identity—having a job. And victims of downsizing must deal with the anger and resentment that stem from the unfairness of the situation. Understandably, job loss is associated with decreases in self-confidence, feelings of failure and rejection, and increases in anxiety and depression (Bobek & Robbins, 2005). Unfortunately, job loss also increases the likelihood of marital problems. Being aware of the psychological aspects of job loss can help you cope with the experience.

Some experts suggest that individuals' reactions to job loss are similar to what they experience when they confront their own death (Bobek & Robbins, 2005; Lock, 2005b). Both of these experiences involve coming to terms with loss (although the losses are obviously quite different). In contemplating one's death, Elisabeth Kübler-Ross (1969) asserted that people experience a series of reactions. These include *denial* ("I can't believe this is happening to me"), *anger* ("How could they do this to me?"), *bargaining* ("Maybe if I offer to work overtime for free, my boss will change her mind"), *depression* ("How can I look my kids in the eye?"), and *acceptance* ("I can learn from this painful experience and will be able to provide for myself and my family again"). As we noted in Chapter 11, people don't necessarily go through these five reactions in lockstep sequence. Individuals often move in and out of these emotional states as they strive to recover their psychological equilibrium. Interestingly, one author of a survival guide for the unemployed advises those who have been "downsized" to get angry—and then to move on (Laskoff, 2004).

For some practical suggestions for coping with job loss, we draw on the advice of career experts Michael Laskoff (2004) and Robert Lock (2005b).

Apply for unemployment benefits as soon as possible. The average length of unemployment in 2005 was 18 weeks (U.S. Bureau of the Census, 2006b). Thus you need to look into unemployment benefits, which you may be able to collect for 26 weeks (or longer in some cases). Contact the nearest office of your state's Employment Security Commission or Department of Labor.

Determine your income and expenses. Determine precisely your sources of income (unemployment benefits, spouse or partner's income, savings) and how much you can count on per week/month. Itemize your weekly/monthly expenses. Set up a realistic budget and stick to it. Talk with your creditors if you need to.

Lower your expenses and think of ways to bring in extra income. Cut out unnecessary expenses for now. Minimize your credit card purchases and pay the bills off every month to avoid building up huge debt and becoming a slave to high interest payments. For extra income, consider selling a car, having a garage sale, or putting items up for auction on eBay. Use your skills as a temporary worker.

Stay healthy. To save money on medical expenses, eat well-balanced meals and get adequate sleep. Use relaxation techniques to manage your stress (see Chapter 4). Keep yourself in a positive frame of mind by recalling past successes and imagining future ones.

Reach out for support. Although it is difficult to do, explain your situation to your family. You need their support and they need to know how your unemployment will affect them. If you are having relationship problems, consult a counselor. Let your friends know that you are looking for work; they may have job leads. Consider attending a support group or consulting a career counselor. Attend religious services or make time for daily meditation or spiritual reading.

Get organized and get going. Start by setting aside time and space to work on your job search. Then consider your situation. Can you find the same type of job or do you need to think about other options? Do you need to relocate? Do you need more education or retraining? Some people decide to go into business for themselves, so don't overlook this option (see the Recommended Reading, *Free Agent Nation*). Check out some of the excellent career planning books (*What Color Is Your Parachute?*, for example) and visit relevant websites. Once you're clear about your options, get busy. Expect to spend 15–25 hours a week on job-searching activities. Spend some time every week on volunteer activities in an area you would like to pursue.

Figure 12.11

Violence at work. Business-related disputes with work colleagues, such as retaliation for being fired, account for a relatively small portion of homicides at work, even though they are the second leading cause of on-the-job homicides. Homicides in the workplace are not the largest source of fatalities in the workplace (accidents are). Nonetheless, they occur often enough to be a source of concern to workers. (Data from U.S. Bureau of Labor Statistics, 1998)

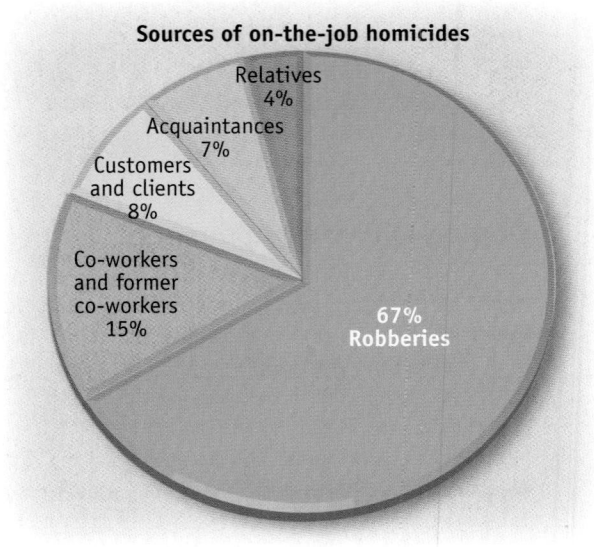

ism have prompted some organizations to make an effort to identify potentially dangerous individuals (Auerbach & Gramling, 1998). Workplace homicides in 2005 were at the lowest level since 1992, the year these data were first recorded (Pegula & Marsh, 2007). Job loss can also generate anger among people who are dependent on the displaced workers. For example, a study of over 800 employed individuals and their partners reported that job loss led partners to withdraw social support from each other and to be increasingly critical, insulting, and angry (Vinokur, Price, & Caplan, 1996).

Support from friends and family is essential in coping with unemployment. When a person is out of work for an extended period of time or has little social support, counseling may also be helpful. Some companies offer programs for laid-off workers. These programs typically teach employees how to search for jobs, manage stress, and cultivate social support. In the "Living in Today's World" box on page 393, we offer some specific suggestions for coping with unemployment.

Balancing Work and Other Spheres of Life

LEARNING OBJECTIVES

- *Summarize current perspectives on workaholism.*
- *Define work-family conflict, and discuss the benefits of multiple roles.*
- *List several types of leisure activities and summarize their benefits.*

A major challenge for individuals today is balancing work, family, and leisure activities in ways that are personally satisfying. We noted earlier that dual-earner families are becoming increasingly common and that the traditional boundaries between family and paid work life are breaking down. These two developments are related. Historically, traditional gender roles assigned women's work to the home and men's work outside the home. This division of labor created boundaries between family and work life. With more women entering the workforce, these boundaries have become blurred. The technology-based changes in the workplace are also eroding these distinctions between family and work life (Jackson, 2005). Here we examine three issues related to balancing various life roles.

Workaholism

Most people cherish their leisure activities and relationships with their families and friends. However, *workaholics* devote nearly all their time and energy to their jobs. They put in lots of overtime, take few vacations, regularly bring work home from the office, and think about work most of the time. They are energetic, intense, and ambitious. In addition to personal factors, situational forces can also promote workaholism (Murphy & Zagorski, 2005). Thus, workaholism is more common where the organizational climate supports imbalances between work and personal life (Burke, 2001).

Although workaholism has received considerable attention in the popular press, empirical research on the topic is relatively limited (Harpaz & Snir, 2003). A survey of 800 senior-level managers reported that nearly one in four considered themselves to be workaholics (Joyner, 1999). Psychologists are divided on the issue of whether workaholism is problematic. Should workaholics be praised for their dedication and encouraged in their single-minded pursuit of fulfillment through work? Or is workaholism a form of addiction,

a sign that an individual is driven by compulsions he or she cannot control? In support of the former view is evidence that some workaholics tend to be highly satisfied with their jobs and with their lives (Bonebright, Clay, & Ankenmann, 2000). They work hard simply because work is the most meaningful activity they know. Yet other evidence suggests that workaholics may have poorer emotional and physical well-being than nonworkaholics (Bonebright et al., 2000; Burke, 2000). How can these conflicting findings be reconciled?

It seems that there are two types of workaholics (Aziz & Zickar, 2006; Spence & Robbins, 1992). One type, the *enthusiastic workaholic,* works for the pure joy of it. Such people derive immense satisfaction from work and generally perform well in highly demanding jobs. The other type, the *nonenthusiastic workaholic,* feels driven to work but reports low job enjoyment. Moreover, these workaholics tend to report lower life satisfaction and less purpose in life than enthusiastic workaholics. Thus, it is not surprising that the nonenthusiastic group is more likely to develop *burnout* (Maslach, 2005).

Both types of workaholics experience an imbalance between work and personal time. Not surprisingly, this situation translates into a high degree of work-family conflict for both groups (Bonebright et al., 2000). Moreover, the families of both groups suffer (Robinson, Flowers, & Ng, 2006). So, although enthusiastic workaholics really love their work, their devotion to their jobs has a price, one often paid by their families.

Work and Family Roles

One of the biggest recent changes in the labor force has been the emergence of dual-earner households, now the dominant family form in the United States (U.S. Bureau of the Census, 2006b). Dual-earner couples are struggling to discover better ways of balancing family life and the demands of work. These changes in work and family life have sparked the interest of researchers in many disciplines, including psychology.

An important fact of life for dual-earner couples is that they juggle *multiple roles:* spouse or partner and employee. TICKS (two-income couples with kids) add a third role: parent. Thus, today's working parents experience ***work-family conflict,* or the feeling of being pulled in multiple directions by competing demands from the job and the family.** In heterosexual dual-earner families, men are taking on more household chores and child care, but most wives still have greater responsibilities in these areas (Drago, 2007). In gay and lesbian dual-earner households, responsibilities are more evenly divided (Kurdek, 2005; Patterson, 2003). Single parents are especially likely to have work-family conflicts.

Although employers are reducing their contributions to employee benefits such as pension and retirement plans, health care benefits, and the like, they do not seem to be cutting back on flexible work schedules, family leave, and child and elder care support (Bond et al., 2005). A key reason employers are retaining these programs is that they help to recruit and retain employees. Still, the fact is that most employees do not have access to such programs. Some believe that this situation is partly to blame for the downward drift in the percentage of mothers with infant children who are in the labor force (Stone & Lovejoy, 2004). In 1998, the participation rate for this group had reached a high of 59%; by 2005, it had fallen to 56%. According to Ellen Galinsky, president of the Families and Work Institute, "They're not fleeing work—they're fleeing the demanding way of work" (Armour, 2004). To gain more control over their lives, some women are temporarily opting out of the workforce; others are going into business for themselves.

To be fair, some of the decline in women's labor force participation rates can probably also be attributed to generational shifts in the views of the optimal

Generational Differences in Work and Family Priorities

Relative emphasis on work and family	2002 Ages Gen-X (23–37)	Boomers (38–57)
Family-centric	55%	46%
Dual-centric	33	35
Work-centric	13	20

Figure 12.12

Generational differences in work and family priorities. Gen-X parents are significantly more likely than Boomer parents to be family-centric (place more emphasis on family than work), whereas Boomer parents are significantly more likely than Gen-Xers to be work-centric (place greater emphasis on work than family). The fact that both groups have children under 18 living at home suggests that this is a generational, rather than a life cycle, difference.

From Families and Work Institute (2004, October). *Generation and gender in the workplace.* New York: Families and Work Institute.

balance of work and family roles. As you can see in **Figure 12.12**, more Gen-X employees with children endorse a family-centric view over a work-centric view compared to a comparable group of Boomers. Some suggest that these generational differences are due, in part, to many Gen-Xers seeing their hardworking parents lose their jobs due to downsizing (Families and Work Institute, 2004).

Although today's working parents may feel stressed, researchers find that multiple roles are beneficial for both men's and women's mental, physical, and relationship health, at least in middle-class couples (Barnett, 2005; Barnett & Hyde, 2001). For women, the benefits of multiple roles are attributed primarily to the effects of the employee role. For men, family involvement is important, especially in the area of relationship health. According to Rosalind Barnett and Janet Hyde (2001), a number of factors contribute to the positive outcomes associated with multiple roles, including added income, social support, opportunities to experience success, and buffering. The latter refers to the idea that successes and satisfactions in one role provide a buffer against the negative effects of stress or failure in another role. Of course, there are outside limits to the number of roles and the amount of work that people can take on before they sacrifice the benefits of multiple roles (Barnett & Hyde, 2001). Role overload likely causes psychological distress.

Leisure and Recreation

Most Americans are putting in 48-hour workweeks, and many work more hours than that. Some workers put in extra hours because their employers mandate it. Others choose to work more hours to maintain their standard of living, because real earning power, especially for low-wage workers, has fallen behind what it was 25 years ago (Joyner, 2001). And when workers arrive home, unpaid family work awaits them. Given the pace of contemporary American life, it's no surprise that almost 60% of Americans say that having leisure time is either "extremely important" or "very important" in their lives, according to a Gallup poll (Moore, 2003).

American workers take an average of 14 days of paid annual vacation. The paid vacation time of American workers lags far behind that of many European workers (see **Figure 12.13**). Moreover, workers in most European Union countries get four weeks of vacation time by law (Roughton, 2001). A generous number of public holidays pushes the average vacation time in the E.U. to about seven weeks!

We define ***leisure* as unpaid activities people choose to engage in because the activities are personally meaningful.** How might we distinguish activities that are meaningful from those that aren't? Although

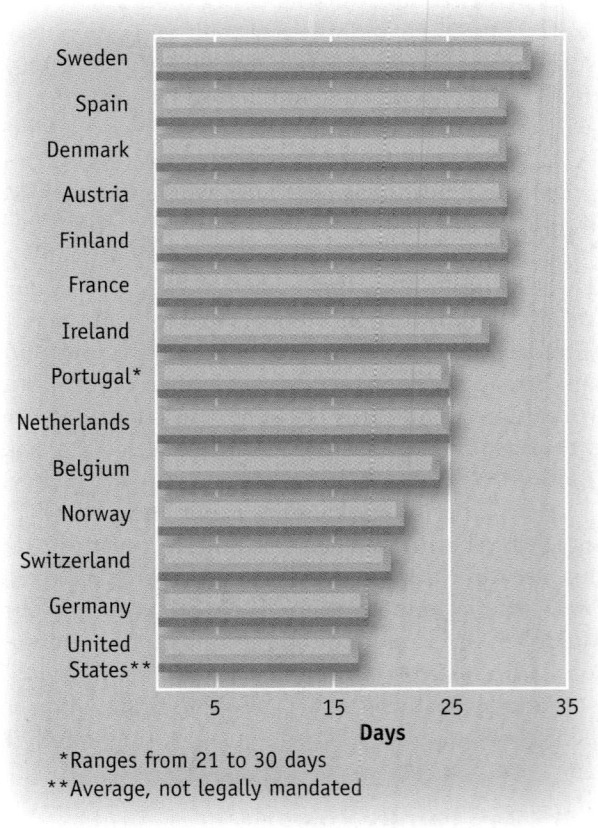

Figure 12.13

American and European vacation days. American workers average 16 paid vacation days a year. Most European workers get considerably longer vacations. Moreover, these are benefits mandated by law.

Adapted from Mischel, L., Bernstein, J., & Schmitt, J. (2001). *The state of working America 2000–2001.* Ithaca, NY: Cornell University Press. Copyright © 2001 by Cornell University Press. Adapted by permission of the publisher, Cornell University Press.

And people who are willing to volunteer information tend to be more liberal and more sexually experienced than the general population (Wiederman, 2004). In addition, respondents may shade the truth about their sex lives because of shame, embarrassment, boasting, or wishful thinking. Researchers also have difficulty getting representative samples, so most studies of American sexuality are overrepresented with white, middle-class volunteers. With this situation in mind, you need to evaluate the results of sex research with more than the usual caution.

Becoming a Sexual Person

LEARNING OBJECTIVES

- *List four key aspects of sexual identity.*
- *Discuss how hormones influence sexual differentiation and sexual behavior.*
- *Discuss how families, peers, schools, and the media shape sexual attitudes and behavior.*
- *Discuss gender differences in sexual socialization and how they affect individuals.*
- *Summarize the current thinking on the origins of sexual orientation and attitudes toward homosexuality.*
- *Discuss the identity development and adjustment of lesbians and gay males.*

People vary greatly in how they express their sexuality. While some eagerly reveal the intimate details of their sex lives, others can't even utter sexual words without embarrassment. Some people need to turn out the lights before they can have sex; others would like to be on camera with spotlights shining. To understand this diversity, we need to examine developmental influences on human sexual behavior.

Key Aspects of Sexual Identity

Identity refers to a clear and stable sense of who one is in the larger society (see Chapter 11). We'll use the term ***sexual identity* to refer to the complex of personal qualities, self-perceptions, attitudes, values, and preferences that guide one's sexual behavior.** In other words, your sexual identity is your sense of yourself as a sexual person. It includes four key features: sexual orientation, body image, sexual values and ethics, and erotic preferences:

1. *Sexual orientation.* Sexual orientation is an individual's preference for emotional and sexual relationships with individuals of one gender or the other. ***Heterosexuals* seek emotional-sexual relationships with members of the other gender. *Homosexuals* seek emotional-sexual relationships with members of the same gender. *Bisexuals* seek emotional-sexual relationships with members of both genders.** In recent years, the terms *gay* and *straight* have become widely used to refer to homosexuals and heterosexuals, respectively. Male homosexuals are called *gay,* whereas female homosexuals prefer to be called *lesbians.* Frequently, the term *LGB* is used to refer, collectively, to lesbians, gay men, and bisexuals. *Transgendered* individuals are "those whose appearance and/or behaviors do not conform to traditional gender roles" (Crooks & Baur, 2008, p. 62). Because the lesbian, gay male, bisexual, and transgendered communities often have intersecting interests, the term *LGBT* is used to refer, collectively, to these groups.

2. *Body image.* Your body image is how you see yourself physically. Your view of your physical self definitely affects how you feel about yourself in the sexual domain. A positive body image is correlated with greater sexual activity, higher sexual satisfaction, and fewer sexual problems (Nobre & Pinto-Gouveia, 2006; Weaver & Byers, 2006). While ultra-thinness for women has been a longtime media message, muscular body types for men are getting more promotion (Martins, Tiggeman, & Kirkbride, 2007). The increasing popularity of gym memberships and the recent dramatic increases in facelifts and breast enhancements testifies to the importance of body image (Springen, 2004).

3. *Sexual values and ethics.* All cultures impose constraints on how people are expected to behave sexually. People are taught that certain expressions of sexuality are "right" while others are "wrong." The nature of these sexual messages varies depending on gender, race, ethnicity, and socioeconomic status. For example, the sexual double standard encourages sexual experimentation in males, but not females. Individuals are faced with the daunting task of sorting through these often-conflicting messages to develop their own sexual values and ethics.

Recommended READING

Sex Matters for College Students: FAQ's in Human Sexuality
by Sandra L. Caron
(Pearson Prentice Hall, 2007)

This small paperback is designed around frequently asked questions the author gets in her college sexuality classes. Caron covers a wide range of topics and groups the many questions into sections based on traffic signs. For instance, the "Pass with Care" section addresses issues for which caution is advised: birth control, pregnancy testing, and abortion. The questions under "Traffic Circle Ahead" focus on sexual decisions and address gender roles, sexual orientation, and gender identity issues. "Do Not Enter" deals with questions on sexual assault, sexual abuse, and sexual harassment. The author answers the FAQs as if she were responding to questions in class. Her replies are informative, supportive, and free of jargon. The last two sections are devoted to lists of relevant websites and books, organized by topic.

4. *Erotic preferences.* Within the limits imposed by sexual orientation and values, people still differ in what they find enjoyable. Your erotic preferences encompass your attitudes about self-stimulation, oral sex, intercourse, and other sexual activities. They develop through a complex interplay of physiological and psychosocial influences—issues we take up next.

Physiological Influences

Among the various physiological factors involved in sexual behavior, hormones have been of particular interest to researchers.

Hormones and Sexual Differentiation

During prenatal development, a number of biological developments result in a fetus that is a male or a female. Hormones play an important role in this process, which is termed *sexual differentiation.* Around the third month of prenatal development, different hormonal secretions begin to be produced by male and female ***gonads*—the sex glands.** In males, the testes produce ***androgens,* the principal class of male sex hormones.** Testosterone is the most important of the androgens. In females, the ovaries produce ***estrogens,* the principal class of female sex hormones.** Actually, both classes of hormones are present in both genders, but in different proportions. During prenatal development, the differentiation of the genitals depends primarily on the level of testosterone produced—high in males, low in females.

At puberty, hormones reassert their influence on sexual development. As you saw in Chapter 11, adolescents attain reproductive capacity as hormonal changes trigger the maturation of the *primary sex characteristics* (sex organs). Hormonal shifts also regulate the development of *secondary sex characteristics* (physical features that distinguish the genders but are not directly involved in reproduction). In females, more estrogen leads to breast development, widened hips, and more rounded body contours. In males, more androgen results in developing facial hair, a deeper voice, and angular body contours.

Hormones and Sexual Behavior

Hormonal fluctuations clearly regulate sex *drive* in many species of animals. Hormones also play a role in human sexuality, but their influence is much more modest. *Androgen* levels appear to be related to sexual motivation in *both* men and women, although the effect is less strong in women (Apperloo et al., 2003; Freeman, Bloom, & McGuire, 2001). High levels of testosterone in female and male subjects correlate with higher rates of sexual activity (Morley & Perry, 2003). Curiously, *estrogen* levels among women do not correlate well with sexual interest. In summary, physiological factors have important effects on sexual development. Their influence on sexual *anatomy,* however, is much greater than their influence on sexual *activity.*

Psychosocial Influences

The principal psychosocial influences on sexual identity are essentially the same as the main sources of gender-role socialization discussed in Chapter 10. Sexual identity is shaped by families, peers, schools, and the media.

Families

Parents and the home environment are significant influences on sexual identity in the early years. Before they reach school age, children usually engage in some sex play and exploration, often under the guise of "playing doctor." They also display curiosity about sexual matters, asking questions such as "Where do babies come from?" Parents who punish innocent, exploratory sex play and who stutter and squirm when kids ask sexual questions convey the idea that sex is "dirty." As a result, children may begin to feel guilty about their sexual urges and curiosity.

According to a 2003 Gallup Youth Survey, 63% of teenagers (ages 13 to 17) reported that their parents talked to them about sex, while 36% said that their parents mostly left this discussion up to the schools

(Mazzuca, 2003). In another national survey of adolescents and young adults (ages 13 to 24), only 37% felt that they learned "a lot" of information about relationships and sexual health from their parents (see **Figure 13.1**). Adolescents who feel close to their parents and who believe that their parents support them are likely to adopt sexual attitudes similar to their parents' and to limit or delay their sexual activities (Maguen & Armistead, 2006; Sprecher, Christopher, & Cate, 2006). Parents who make sex a taboo topic reduce their influence on their kids' evolving sexual identity, as the children turn elsewhere for information.

Peers

As you can see in **Figure 13.1**, friends are a leading source of relationship and sexual health information. Only health care providers are rated higher, and only by females. Adolescents' sexual attitudes and behavior are positively associated with their *perceptions* of their friends' sexual attitudes and behavior (Kinsman et al., 1998; Sprecher et al., 2006). Unfortunately, peers can be a source of highly misleading information and often champion sexual ethics at odds with parents' views.

Schools

Surveys show that the vast majority of parents and other adults support sex education programs in the schools, despite the media attention given to isolated, vocal protests (SIECUS, 2004). Also, most teenagers want their schools to offer sex education (McKay & Holoway, 1997).

Main Sources of Sex Information Among Youth

	Percentage		
Source	**Male**	**Female**	**Total**
Friends	46	48	47
Sex education classes	42	39	40
Boyfriends, girlfriends, partners	40	39	39
Media (TV, movies, magazines, the Internet)	33	42	38
Parents	34	40	37
Doctors, other health care providers	21	50	36
Brothers and sisters	24	19	22

Figure 13.1

Main sources of sex information among youth. Adolescents and young adults (ages 13 to 24) said they had learned "a lot" from these sources, according to a national survey.

Adapted from Holt, T., Greene, L., & Davis, J. (2003). *National survey of adolescents and young adults: Sexual health knowledge, attitudes, and experience.* Menlo Park, CA: Henry J. Kaiser Family Foundation. (Question 2, p. 97)

Web Link 13.1 **SIECUS (Sexuality Information and Educational Council of the United States)**

This site is produced by one of the oldest organizations in the United States devoted to educating the public about matters of sexuality. It contains not only SIECUS-related information but an excellent annotated set of web-based links to a variety of topics related to sexuality.

Researchers who surveyed a nationally representative sample of American public, middle, junior, and senior high schools reported that 90% of schools offered *some* type of sex education (Kaiser Family Foundation, 2004). Among the surveyed schools, 30% offer "abstinence only" programs (no information about contraceptive methods), 47% offer "abstinence plus" programs (information about contraception and sexually transmitted diseases), and 20% offer comprehensive programs (information on such topics as contraception, abortion, sexually transmitted diseases, relationships, sexual orientation, and responsible decision making).

What is the effectiveness of these various programs? Unfortunately, "abstinence only" programs do not deter adolescents from engaging in sex, do not delay first intercourse, and do not reduce the number of sexual partners (U.S. Department of Health and Human Services, 2007). In contrast, comprehensive programs result in a wide range of positive outcomes: increased use of contraception, reduced pregnancies, and reduced high-risk sexual behavior (Kirby, 2001; Schaalma et al., 2004). Also, these programs do not promote (and may delay) having early sex and do not increase (and may decrease) the number of sexual partners.

The Media

Americans see thousands of sexual encounters a year on television, videos, DVDs, and computers. And the portrayal of sexual content appears to be on the rise (Kunkel et al., 2005b). As you can see in **Figure 13.2** (on the next page), the percentage of television shows containing sexual content increased between 1998 and 2005. Television portrayals of sexual behavior can influence adolescents' beliefs about typical sexual practices as well as their sexual intentions and behavior (L'Engle, Brown, & Kenneavy, 2006; Taylor, 2005). And hearing talk about casual sex has the same effect as viewing "permissive" sexual behavior. On the other hand, television can promote responsible sexual behavior and tolerance of homosexuality (Keller & Brown, 2002; Silver, 2002). Unfortunately, only 10% of the top 20 teen programs made references to sexual risks or responsibilities (Kunkel et al., 2005b).

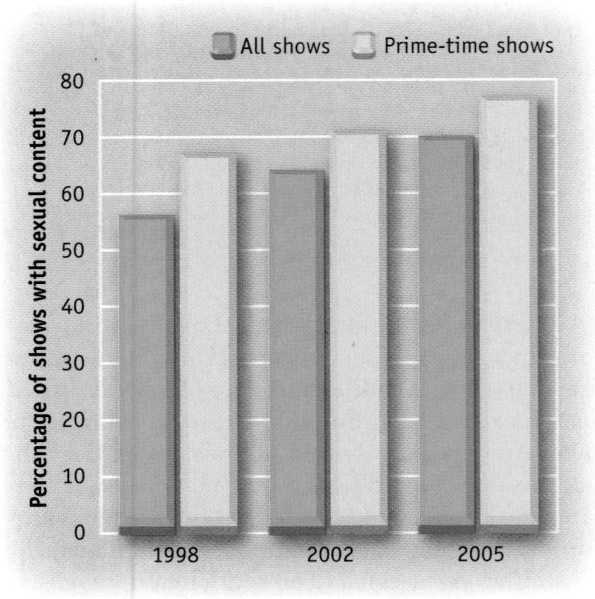

Figure 13.2

Sexual content in television programs continues to increase. Researchers reviewed a representative sample of more than 1,100 television programs (other than daily newscasts, sports events, and children's shows) in 1998, 2002, and 2005 and identified the proportion of shows that contained sexual content (talk about sex and sexual behaviors). The sexual content in all shows and in prime time shows has increased over the years.

From Kunkel, D., Eyal, K., Finnerty, K., Biely, E., & Donnerstein, E. (2005). *A Biennial Report of the Kaiser Family Foundation: Sex on TV 4, Executive Summary,* (#7399), The Henry J. Kaiser Family Foundation, November 2005. This information was reprinted with permission of the Henry J. Kaiser Family Foundation.

Books and magazines are another source of information on sex. Some 20% of adolescents and young adults reported that they had learned "a lot" about relationships and sexual health from magazines (Holt, Greene, & Davis, 2003). Some publications provide accurate and useful information, but many perpetuate myths about sex and miseducate young readers.

Music lyrics and music videos are additional vehicles of sexual socialization. For example, one study found that teens who listen to music lyrics containing explicit references to sex acts and depicting men as sexually aggressive and women as sex objects are significantly more likely to have sex sooner than teens who listen to music lyrics containing more subtle references to sex (Martino et al., 2006). This study also found that the highest proportion of negative sexual messages occurred in rap and rap-rock music.

Turning to cyberspace, experts estimate that there were 1.1 billion Internet users worldwide in 2007 (Internet World Stats, 2007). Newsgroups with sexually explicit images are extremely popular, especially among males. Parents are understandably alarmed about children having easy access to sexually explicit material online. Among 10- to 17-year-olds, 25% have encountered unwanted pornography, and 20% have been exposed to unwanted sexual solicitations (Finkelhor, Mitchell, & Wolak, 2000). On the up-side, the Internet provides easy and private access to useful information on a variety of sexual topics, including contraceptive methods and resources for the LGBT communities (Ross, 2005). The "Living in Today's World" sidebar expands on the issue of sex and the Internet.

To conclude, sexual identities are shaped by a number of intersecting influences. Thus, individuals bring highly diverse expectations to their sexual relationships. As you'll see, this variability can complicate sexual interactions.

Gender Differences in Sexual Socialization

To what degree are males and females socialized differently about sexual matters? Summarizing the research on gender differences in sexuality, Letitia Anne Peplau (2003; Impett & Peplau, 2006), a major researcher on gender and relationships, concludes that there are five key differences and that all but one of these hold for both gays and straights:

Courtesy, Letitia Anne Peplau

Letitia Anne Peplau

1. Men have more interest in sex than women (they think about and want to have sex more often).

2. The connection between sex and intimacy is more important for women than for men (women typically prefer sex in the context of a relationship).

3. Aggression is more often linked to sexuality for men than for women (men engage in coercive sex much more often).

4. Women's sexuality is more easily shaped by cultural and situational factors (their sexual attitudes are easier to change and they are more likely to change their sexual orientation over time).

5. Among heterosexual couples, men typically take the lead in initiating sexual intimacy, while women serve as "gate-keepers," determining whether and when a couple engages in sexual activities.

Societal values and gender roles obviously come into play here. American males are encouraged to experiment sexually, to initiate sexual activities, and to enjoy sex without emotional involvement (Kilmartin, 2007). They also get the message to be conquest oriented regarding sex ("scoring"). Thus, men may emphasize "sex for fun" in casual relationships and reserve "sex with love" for committed relationships (Oliver & Hyde, 1993).

Girls are typically taught to view sex in the context of a loving relationship (Impett & Peplau, 2006). They learn about romance and the importance of physical

LIVING IN TODAY'S WORLD

Sex and the Internet

The Internet is playing an increasingly important role in sexuality. In fact, some experts say that "the influence of the Internet on sexuality is likely to be so significant that it will ultimately be recognized as the next 'sexual revolution'" (Cooper et al., 2000). Researchers estimate that 20%–33% of Internet users engage in some form of online sexual activity (Egan, 2000).

Online sexual activity involves the use of the Internet for any activity (text, audio, or graphics) that involves sexuality (Cooper et al, 2002). These activities are quite diverse and include using the Internet for information or entertainment as well as for purchasing sexual materials, searching for sexual partners, and having sexually explicit discussions. Some people use the Internet to engage in forbidden fantasies by masquerading as a member of the other gender (Ross, 2005).

Cybersex, a subcategory of online sexual activity, involves the use of computerized content for sexual stimulation and gratification (Maheu & Subotnik, 2001). People look at erotic pictures (on computers, cell phones, and iPods), engage in sexual chat, and exchange sexually explicit e-mail messages. Some share mutual sexual fantasies while masturbating. In a large online survey, 39% of the respondents said that they had engaged in cybersex, although fewer than 3% engaged in it "often" or "all the time" (Cooper et al., 2002). Interestingly, 60% of people in this survey did not believe that cybersex violated a person's marriage vows. Other research disputes these findings (Whitty, 2005), and spouses of individuals who are involved in Internet sexual affairs say that online affairs are as emotionally painful as those offline (Schneider, 2003).

The large online survey also reported that 25% of respondents had had an in-person meeting for a date or sexual experience with someone whom they had met online (Cooper et al., 2002). More women than men reported engaging in this behavior, since women are more likely to use the Internet to explore online sexual relationships. Because people who make these arrangements are more likely to engage in risky sexual behavior, they expose themselves to potential sexual assault and STDs (McFarlane, Bull, & Reitmeijer, 2000).

Actual cybersex addiction or Internet sex addiction is a specific form of Internet addiction (see Chapter 4). People with this problem engage in online sex so often that it interferes with their personal and work life, they are unable to refrain from the activity (except temporarily), and they deny its negative effects on their lives. Most professionals view cybersex addiction as a type of compulsion (see Chapter 15). This behavior can have serious consequences for addicted individuals and their families (Cooper, 2002). Internet sex addicts may neglect their spouses and children, sow feelings of betrayal in their mates, and break up their marriages (Schneider, 2003). They can also lose their jobs if they neglect their work or are discovered engaging in cybersex at the office. Amazingly, about 20% of people who engage in online sex use an office computer for this activity, which is a risky proposition in that many organizations now monitor the online activities of their employees (Cooper, Safir, & Rosenmann, 2006).

Because Internet sexuality is a relatively new phenomenon, mental health professionals are still developing their views about it. Some see it as just another form of sexual expression. Others are alarmed that Internet sex addiction is a growing problem. To date, research supports both of these perspectives (Cooper et al., 1999; 2002). Online sex does seem to be a form of sexual expression for light users (less than 1 hour per week) and moderate users (1 to 10 hours per week). They typically use sexual material on the Internet for entertainment more than for sexual release—akin to reading *Playboy* or viewing TV programs with lots of "skin." These individuals make up about 92% of all Internet sex users. Unfortunately, it is quite a different story for high users (11 to 80 hours per week), who make up 8% of all those involved in online sexual activity. These people report significantly more psychological distress and score higher on measures of compulsivity and sensation seeking. They are at high risk for developing psychological problems. Research needs to substantiate these findings and to determine which activities increase risk for heavy users.

The Internet can obviously have a positive influence on sex. Among other things, it is an excellent source of helpful information. And gay, lesbian, bisexual, and transgendered individuals can use it to locate virtual support communities (Diamond, 2006). On the other hand, the anonymity, affordability, and accessibility of the Internet lead some individuals to become hooked on cybersex, resulting in serious negative consequences (Cooper & Sportolari, 1997). We look to researchers and mental health professionals for insights into this emerging and significant area of sexuality.

© Michael Newman/PhotoEdit

Because of gender differences in sexual socialization, females tend to begin seeing themselves as sexual persons at a later age than males.

attractiveness and catching a mate. Unlike males, they are not encouraged to experiment with sex or to have numerous sexual partners. It isn't until women actually begin having sexual experiences that they start to see themselves as sexual persons.

Sexual socialization usually takes longer for females than for males because women usually have more emotional baggage connected with sex than men do. One factor is the *fear of pregnancy.* Concerns about becoming pregnant inhibit a woman's enthusiasm for sex. Second, girls hear *negative messages about sex and men* ("Men only want one thing") from their mothers, siblings, and female peers. They are also aware of rape and incest. Third, women typically develop *negative associations about their genitals and sex* that males don't experience: blood and pain associated with menstruation and fears of penetration. A fourth factor is *sexual guilt.* Whereas social norms encourage males to be sexually active, these norms discourage such behavior in females—sexually active women may be looked on as "loose." All these negative associations with sex are combined with the positive rewards of dating and emotional intimacy. Hence, it's no surprise that many women feel ambivalent about sex (Hyde, 2004). These feelings can tilt in the negative direction if early sexual partners are unskilled, impatient, or selfish.

With differing views of sexuality and relationships, males and females can be out of sync with each other—particularly in adolescence and early adulthood. In adulthood, women become more comfortable with themselves as sexual persons, while males become more comfortable with emotional intimacy and commitment. These gender differences mean that communication is essential for mutually satisfying sexual relationships.

Because both members of *same-gender couples* have been socialized similarly, they are less likely than straight couples to have compatibility problems. Like heterosexual women, lesbians typically experience emotional attraction to their partners before experiencing sexual feelings (Peplau & Fingerhut, 2007). By contrast, gay men (like heterosexual men) tend to place much more importance on physical appearance and sexual compatibility in selecting partners and to then develop emotional relationships out of sexual ones (Diamond, 2006).

Sexual Orientation

Gay, straight, or in between? In this section, we'll explore the intriguing and controversial topic of sexual orientation.

Key Considerations

Most people view heterosexuality and homosexuality as two distinct categories: you're either one or the other. However, many individuals who define themselves as heterosexuals have had homosexual experiences, and vice versa (Kinsey et al., 1948, 1953; Laumann et al., 1994). Thus, it is more accurate to view heterosexuality and homosexuality as end points on a continuum. Indeed, Alfred Kinsey devised a seven-point scale, shown in **Figure 13.3**, to characterize sexual orientation.

AP Images/HO

Alfred Kinsey

How are people distributed on this scale? No one knows for sure, because it's hard to get accurate data. Furthermore, there's some debate about where to draw the lines between heterosexuality, bisexuality, and homosexuality on the Kinsey scale. A frequently cited estimate of the number of people who are predominantly homosexual is 10%; however, several influential surveys have reported lower estimates (ACFS Investigators, 1992; Johnson et al., 1992; Laumann et al., 1994). The overall evidence suggests that about 5%–8% of the population could reasonably be characterized as homosexual (Michaels, 1996; see Chapter 9).

Now let's complicate things a little more. Using Kinsey's model, where would you place a person who was married for 10 years, has children, is divorced, and is now involved in a committed homosexual relationship? And what about a person who is married but who has homosexual fantasies and engages in same-gender sex talk on the Internet? Clearly, we need more complex paradigms. One such model portrays sexual orientation as a cluster of seven factors that can be rated along Kinsey's seven-point scale: sexual behavior; emotional preference; sexual fantasies; sexual attraction; social preference; lifestyle, social world, and community; and self-identification (Klein, Sepekoff, & Wolf, 1986). In this view, individuals' ratings on the seven factors may or may not be congruent, and ratings may change over time to match shifts in people's understanding

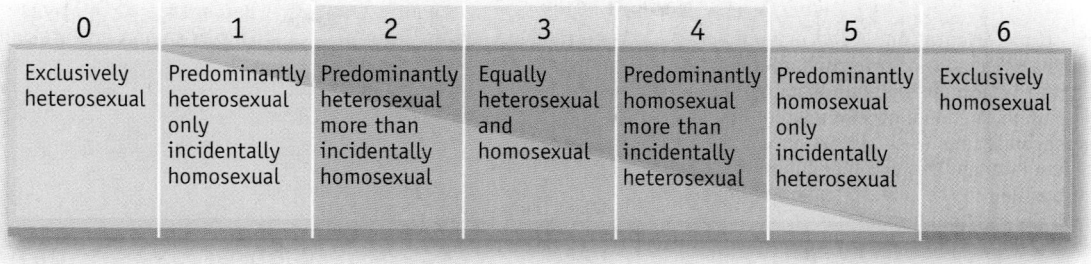

Figure 13.3

Heterosexuality and homosexuality as end points on a continuum. Kinsey and other sex researchers view heterosexuality and homosexuality as ends of a continuum rather than as all-or-none distinctions. Kinsey created this seven-point scale (from 0 to 6) for describing sexual orientation.

of their sexual orientation. Thus, research supports a complex and malleable view of sexual orientation (Diamond, 2003).

Origins

Why do some people become straight and others, gay? A number of *environmental explanations* have been suggested as causes of homosexuality. Freud believed that homosexuality originates from an unresolved Oedipus complex (see Chapter 2). That is, instead of coming to identify with the parent of the same gender, the child continues to identify with the parent of the other gender. Learning theorists assert that homosexuality results from early negative heterosexual encounters or early positive homosexual experiences. Sociologists propose that homosexuality develops because of poor relationships with same-gender peers or because being labeled a homosexual sets up a self-fulfilling prophecy. Surprisingly, a comprehensive review of the causes of sexual orientation found no compelling support for *any* of these explanations of homosexuality (Bell, Weinberg, & Hammersmith, 1981).

Similarly, there is no evidence that parents' sexual orientation is linked to that of their children (Patterson, 2003). That is, heterosexual parents are as likely to produce homosexual (or heterosexual) offspring as homosexual parents are. Children who grow up in gay or lesbian families are predominantly heterosexual.

Researchers have found that extremely feminine behavior in young boys and masculine behavior in young girls is correlated with subsequent homosexuality (Bailey, 2003; Bem, 2000). Consistent with this finding, many gay men and some gay women say they can trace their homosexual leanings back to their early childhood (Bailey, 2003). This connection is less strong in lesbians than it is in gay males, supporting the emerging view that female sexuality is more fluid than that of males (Diamond, 2003; Impett & Peplau, 2006).

Some theorists speculate that *biological factors* are involved in the development of homosexuality, because many gay men and some lesbians can recall having homosexual feelings in their childhood years (Bell, Weinberg, & Hammersmith, 1981; Garnets & Kimmel, 1991). Several lines of research suggest that hormonal secretions during prenatal development may shape sexual development, organize the brain in a lasting manner, and influence subsequent sexual orientation (Cohen-Bendahan, van de Beek, & Berenbaum, 2005; Rahman, 2005). To date, however, the research is inconclusive, so this theory must be viewed with caution. Other researchers have explored the relationship between circulating hormone levels in adults and sexual orientation, but there is no convincing evidence of an association (Bailey, 2003; Banks & Gartrell, 1995).

Genetic factors are also of interest. In an important study, investigators identified gay and bisexual men who had a twin brother or an adopted brother (Bailey & Pillard, 1991). They found that 52% of the subjects' identical twins were gay, that 22% of their fraternal twins were gay, and that 11% of their adoptive brothers were gay. A companion study of lesbian women with twin or adopted sisters reported a similar pattern of results (Bailey et al., 1993; see **Figure 13.4** on the next page). More recent twin studies, with larger and more representative samples, have provided further support for the conclusion that heredity influences sexual orientation, although these studies have yielded smaller estimates of genetic influence (Bailey, Dunne, & Martin, 2000; Kendler et al., 2000). Thus, there may be genetic links to homosexuality.

The bottom line is that it isn't yet clear what determines sexual orientation. Moreover, it appears that complex paradigms are needed to explain male and female homosexuality (Peplau & Garnets, 2000). It is likely that there are a variety of types of homosexuality—and heterosexuality—that will require a variety of explanations rather than a single account (Hyde &

Figure 13.4

Genetics and sexual orientation. A concordance rate indicates the percentage of twin pairs or other pairs of relatives that exhibit the same characteristic. If relatives who share more genetic relatedness show higher concordance rates than relatives who share less genetic overlap, this evidence suggests a genetic predisposition to the characteristic. Recent studies of both gay men and lesbian women have found higher concordance rates among identical twins than fraternal twins, who, in turn, exhibit more concordance than adoptive siblings. These findings are consistent with the hypothesis that genetic factors influence sexual orientation. If *only* genetic factors were responsible for sexual orientation, the identical twin concordance rates would push 100%; because they are much lower, environmental factors must also play a role. (Data from Bailey & Pillard, 1991; Bailey et. al., 1993)

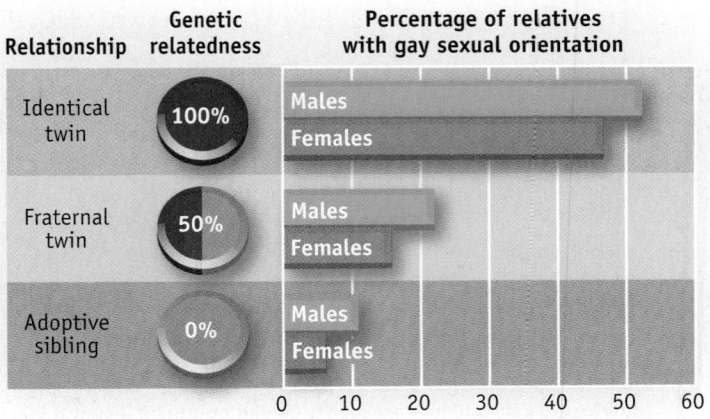

DeLamater, 2003). This issue is exceedingly complex and research is still in its infancy. The most we can conclude is that the explanations must lie in some complex interaction of biological and environmental factors.

Attitudes about homosexuality are gradually shifting towards greater acceptance of gays. For example, when comedian Ellen DeGeneres first came out of the closet in 1997, there was quite a bit of negative reaction from the general public. Today, however, she has a popular TV talk show and little was said when she was selected to host the movie industry's Academy Awards.

Attitudes Toward Homosexuality

The legalization of same-gender marriage in Massachusetts and the legal recognition of civil unions and domestic partnerships in seven other states have set off contentious public debates in the last few years. Fueling the controversy, constitutional amendments banning gay marriage have been introduced in the U.S. Congress and in many state legislatures. Although the public discussion of gay marriage can be divisive, some believe that it has value (Garnets & Kimmel, 2003a). First, it has allowed the gay community to educate straight citizens about the realities and diversity of same-gender couples and their family relationships. Second, it has helped raise the nation's awareness about the facets of discrimination against gays. Although many Americans are opposed to gay marriage, they are much more accepting of other issues related to homosexuality (see **Figure 13.5**). Greater acceptance is due, in part, to the increasing visibility of lesbians and gays in society, including likable gay characters (*Will and Grace*) and individuals (*Queer Eye for the Straight Guy*) on television (Schiappa, Gregg, & Hewes, 2006).

***Homophobia* is the intense fear and intolerance of homosexuals.** Because few people with negative attitudes toward homosexuals have the psychopathology that "phobia" implies, some psychologists believe that *sexual prejudice* is a more appropriate term (Herek, 2003). The lowest levels of sexual prejudice are associated with individuals who personally know someone who is gay (Herek & Capitanio, 1996). Higher levels of sexual prejudice are associated with being older, male, less educated, and living in the South or Midwest and in rural areas (Herek & Capitanio, 1996). Sexual prejudice is also correlated with such psychological factors as authoritarianism (see Chapter 6), traditional

Attitudes Toward Homosexuals

Poll question*	Percent endorsing
1. Homosexuals should have equal rights in terms of job opportunities.	89
2. Gay partners should have the same inheritance rights as married couples.	60
3. Gay partners should have the same health insurance and other employee benefits as married couples.	60
4. Gay partners should have the same social security benefits as married couples.	55
5. Gay and lesbian partners should have the same adoption rights as married couples.	45
6. Which of the following do you support for gay couples?	
a. Marriage rights	28
b. Civil unions	23
c. No legal recognition	43
d. Don't know	6

*Item 1 is based on a May 2–4, 2004 Gallup survey. Items 2–5 are based on a February 5–6, 2004 *Newsweek* survey. Item 6 is based on a May 13–14, 2004 *Newsweek* survey. All surveys are based on randomly selected national samples.

Figure 13.5

Attitudes toward homosexuals. Americans' attitudes toward gays are highly variable, depending on the specific issue. Women generally have more accepting attitudes than men.

gender-role attitudes, and conservative religious and political beliefs (Altemeyer, 1996; Herek & Capitanio, 1996; Whitley, 2001). Unfortunately, negative attitudes sometimes translate into hate crimes. Around a third of gay men and lesbians have been victims of hate crimes (Parrott & Zeichner, 2006).

Sexual Identity Development

Developing one's sexual identity is complicated and difficult when it must take place in a climate of sexual prejudice. In discussing that process, we draw heavily on the work of psychologists Linda Garnets and Douglas Kimmel (1991, 2003b). For gays, lesbians, and bisexuals, sexual identity development involves acknowledging, recognizing, and labeling one's sexual orientation; conceptualizing it in positive terms; and disclosing it to others. Compared with earlier generations, recent generations are becoming aware of and are disclosing gay, lesbian, or bisexual identities earlier in life (Floyd & Bakeman, 2006).

Courtesy, Linda Doris Garnets

Linda Garnets

Courtesy, Douglas C. Kimmel

Douglas C. Kimmel

© AP Images/Chris Pizzello

Popular television programs like **Queer Eye for the Straight Guy** *have contributed to the increased acceptance of gays and lesbians.*

Coming to terms with one's homosexuality in a hostile environment is difficult. And LGB people from some minority groups must contend with the additional stress of negative reactions to their sexual orientation in their cultural communities (Harper, Jernewall, & Zea, 2004). Some parents throw their gay children out of the house, and some teachers and peers harass and assault gay and lesbian youth. The quality of a parent-child relationship prior to disclosure may be the best predictor of how parents will initially react and adjust to their child's coming out (Savin-Williams, 2001). At least half of gay and lesbian teenagers reported that they had lost at least one friend because of their sexual orientation (Ryan & Futterman, 1997). High schools and colleges increasingly support groups for LGBT students. And the Internet offers a wealth of resources for LGBT people (see Web Link 13.2).

In deciding to disclose one's sexual orientation to others, people must balance the psychological and social benefits against the costs (losing friends, being fired, falling victim to hate crimes, and losing custody of children). A pragmatic solution to this conflict is *rational outness*—being "as open as possible, because it feels healthy to be honest, and as closed as necessary to protect against discrimination" (Bradford & Ryan, 1987, p. 77). People are more likely to disclose their sexual orientation to close heterosexual friends and siblings than to parents, co-workers, or employers.

Web Link 13.2 **Parents, Families, and Friends of Lesbians and Gays**

The mission of this national organization is to promote the health and well-being of gay, lesbian, bisexual, and transgendered people as well as that of their families and friends. The organization is involved in support, education, and advocacy efforts and has more than 500 chapters in every state and many cities.

Adjustment

The mental health community initially classified homosexuality as a psychological disorder. But researchers demonstrated that view to be a myth: Gays and straights do not differ on overall measures of psychological adjustment (Bell & Weinberg, 1978; Hooker, 1957; Rosen, 1974). As a result of research, changes in public attitudes, and political lobbying, homosexuality was deleted from the official list of psychological disorders in 1973. Since then, research continues to demonstrate comparable psychological adjustment in gay and straight individuals, couples, and parents (Gonsiorek, 1991; Patterson & Redding, 1996; Peplau & Spaulding, 2003). Similarly, there is no evidence of elevated psychopathology in nonclinical samples of bisexual men and women (Fox, 1996).

Although there is no reliable evidence that homosexual orientation per se impairs psychological functioning, exposure to sexual prejudice and discrimination can cause acute distress (Meyer, 2003). Some recent studies suggest that gay males and lesbians are at greater risk than their straight peers for anxiety, depression, self-injurious behavior, substance dependence, suicidal ideation, and suicide attempts (Balsam et al., 2005; Cochran, 2001).

According to the 2000 U.S. Census, 33% of female same-gender couples and 22% of male same-gender couples are rearing children. The children of some couples are their own from previous heterosexual relationships or artificial insemination; other children have been adopted. Studies show that children of gay or lesbian parents are no different than children of heterosexual parents in terms of self-esteem, gender roles, sexual orientation, peer group relationships, school outcomes, or social adjustment (Patterson, 2003, 2006; Tasker, 2005).

Recommended **READING**

Loving Someone Gay
by Don Clark (Celestial Arts, 2005)

Now in its fourth edition, this book speaks both to those who are gay and to those who know someone gay. The author, a clinical psychologist who is gay, writes in a personal and informal style that draws the reader in. He also easily weaves in real-life examples to illustrate his points. The first two sections address questions of special interest to homosexuals. For example, Clark discusses the impact of invisibility and oppression on one's self-concept, as well as the rewards of being gay. Other topics include coming out, meeting other gay people, the emotional and sexual aspects of relationships, and dealing with break-ups. The third section, "Loving Someone Gay," contains advice for people who know someone gay: parents, wives, husbands, sons, daughters, other relatives, friends, and neighbors. In "Professional Services," the fourth section, Clark provides suggestions for those who interact, often unknowingly, with gays (teachers, librarians, physicians, nurses, clergy, counselors, police, judges, legislators, and researchers).

Another excellent book in this area is *Positively Gay: New Approaches to Gay and Lesbian Life* edited by Betty Berzon (Celestial Arts, 2001). In this book, experts explore a variety of topics of interest to gay individuals: special issues in same-gender relationships, family relationships, children, aging, religion, work, and minorities. For a book that deals specifically with gays and their parents, try *Now That You Know: A Parents' Guide to Understanding their Gay and Lesbian Children* by Betty Fairchild and Nancy Hayward (Harvest Books, 1998).

Interaction in Sexual Relationships

LEARNING OBJECTIVES

- *List several approach and several avoidance sexual motives.*
- *Describe four common barriers in communicating about sex.*

Sexual relationships stir up intense emotions. When things are going well, one feels on top of the world; when they're not, one feels in the grip of despair. In this section, we'll briefly discuss the interpersonal dynamics of sexual relationships.

Motives for Engaging in Sex

What motivates individuals to engage in sexual encounters? Sexual motives are numerous and diverse. One conceptual framework for understanding sexual motives is to classify them as approach and avoidance motives (Cooper, Shapiro, & Powers, 1998; Impett, Peplau, & Gable, 2005). Approach motives focus on obtaining positive outcomes: (1) pursuing one's own sexual pleasure, (2) feeling good about oneself, (3) pleasing one's partner, (4) promoting intimacy in a relationship, and (5) expressing love for one's partner. Avoidance motives center on evading negative outcomes: (1) avoiding relationship conflict, (2) preventing a partner from becoming upset, (3) preventing a partner's anger, and (4) preventing a partner from losing interest. Researchers report that sexual encounters based on approach motives are positively associated with personal and relationship well-being. By contrast, sexual interactions based on avoidance motives are negatively associated with well-being and are especially detrimental to relationships' continuing (Impett et al., 2005).

On a related issue—the relationship between sex and love—men and women often have somewhat different views. Women are more likely than men to associate sex with love and to "romanticize" sexual desire (Impett & Peplau, 2006). These gender differences transcend sexual orientation, as they are observed in gays as well as straights (Peplau, Fingerhut, & Beals, 2004). Some experts speculate that these differences stem from gender-role socialization (Carroll, Volk, & Hyde, 1985). Others believe that they are a product of biological influences (Buss, 1998). It is possible that both influences play a role.

Communicating About Sex

Because individuals differ in sexual motives, attitudes, and appetites, disagreements about sex are to be expected. Couples have to negotiate whether, how often, and when they will have sex. They also have to decide what kinds of erotic activities will take place and what sexual behavior means to their relationship. This negotiation process may not be explicit, but it's there. Unresolved disparities can be an ongoing source of frustration in a relationship. Still, many people find it difficult to talk with their partner about sex. Couples can encounter four common barriers to sexual communication:

1. *Fear of appearing ignorant.* According to a Kinsey Institute/Roper poll, most Americans are woefully ignorant about sex. That is, on an 18-item test of basic sexual knowledge, 55% of adults responded incorrectly to at least half of the questions (Reinisch, 1990). (You can test your own knowledge about some aspects of sex by responding to the questions in **Figure 13.6**.) Because most people feel that they should be experts about sex and know that they are not, they feel ashamed. To hide their ignorance, they avoid talking about sex.

Web Link 13.3 **American Psychological Association: Psychology Topics**

APA's website offers information and resources on many important contemporary psychological issues. Under the heading of Psychology Topics, the site provides answers to common questions about sexuality and sexual orientation as well as links to additional web resources.

How Knowledgeable About Sex Are You?

1. Massage oil, petroleum jelly, and body lotions are good lubricants to use with a condom or diaphragm.
____ True ____ False ____ Don't know

2. Adult male homosexuals have lower than normal levels of male hormones.
____ True ____ False ____ Don't know

3. A teenage girl or woman can get pregnant during her menstrual period.
____ True ____ False ____ Don't know

4. Most cases of sexually transmitted diseases occur in people aged 26-50.
____ True ____ False ____ Don't know

5. In the United States, heterosexually-transmitted HIV infections rarely occur.
____ True ____ False ____ Don't know

Scoring: 1. False. (Oil-based creams, lotions, and jellies can produce microscopic holes in rubber products within 60 seconds of their application.) 2. False. (Research does not support this view.) 3. True. (While the chance of a woman's becoming pregnant during her menstrual period is lower than at other times, pregnancy can occur if she has unprotected sex during her period. Sperm can live for up to 8 days in a woman's reproductive tract, and if the menstrual cycle is irregular, as it is likely to be in adolescence, sperm may still be present in the reproductive tract a week later to fertilize a new egg.) 4. False. (Most cases of sexually transmitted diseases occur in the under-25 age group.) 5. False. (There is currently an upsurge in heterosexually-transmitted HIV infections in the U.S.)

Figure 13.6

How knowledgeable about sex are you? Check your basic sexual knowledge by answering these five questions. Information about each of the questions is discussed in this chapter.

2. *Concern about partner's response.* Both men and women say they want their partners to tell them what they want sexually (see **Figure 13.7** on the next page). Ironically, neither feels comfortable doing so. People usually hold back because they're afraid of hurting the other's feelings. Or they fear that their partner won't respect and love them if they are truthful. Research shows that more extensive disclosure of sexual likes and dislikes positively predicts sexual and relationship satisfaction in committed relationships (Sprecher et al., 2006). Individuals who keep their preferences to themselves are likely to remain frustrated and unsatisfied.

3. *Conflicting attitudes about sex.* Many people, particularly women, are burdened with the negative sexual messages they learned as children. Also, most individuals have contradictory beliefs about sex ("Sex is 'beautiful'" and "Sex is 'dirty'"), and this dissonance produces psychological conflicts.

4. *Early negative sexual experiences.* Some people have had negative sexual experiences that inhibit their enjoyment of sex. If these experiences are due to

Figure 13.7

What men and women want more of during sex. Dating and married couples were asked which sexual activities they wanted more of in their relationships. Men and women all agreed that they wanted more instructions from their partners. They also generally agreed that they wanted warmer, more involved sexual relationships and more experimentation. In terms of gender differences, men wanted their partners to take the initiative and to be wilder and sexier; women wanted more emotional reassurance.

From Hatfield, E., & Rapson, R. L. (1997). *Love, sex, and intimacy: Their psychology, biology, and history.* Boston: Allyn & Bacon. Copyright © 1997 by Pearson Education. Reprinted by permission of the publisher.

What Men and Women Want More of During Sex

Dating couples	
Men	**Women**
Wish their partners would:	
Be more experimental	Talk more lovingly
Initiate sex more often	Be more seductive
Try more oral-genital sex	Be warmer and more involved
Give more instructions	Give more instructions
Be warmer and more involved	Be more complimentary
Married couples	
Men	**Women**
Wish their partners would:	
Be more seductive	Talk more lovingly
Initiate sex more often	Be more seductive
Be more experimental	Be more complimentary
Be wilder and sexier	Be more experimental
Give more instructions	Give more instructions
	Be warmer and more involved

ignorant or inconsiderate sexual partners, subsequent positive sexual interactions will usually resolve the problem over time. If earlier sexual experiences have been traumatic, as in the case of rape or incest, counseling may be required to help a person view sex positively and enjoy it.

To communicate more easily and effectively about sex, you may want to review Chapter 7. Most of the advice on how to improve verbal and nonverbal communication can be applied to sexual relationships. Assertive communication and constructive conflict-resolution strategies can keep sexual negotiations healthy. A basic rule is to accentuate the positive ("I like it when you . . .") rather than the negative ("I don't like it when you . . .").

The Human Sexual Response

LEARNING OBJECTIVES

- *Describe the four phases of the human sexual response cycle.*
- *Discuss gender differences in patterns of orgasm and some reasons for them.*

When people engage in sexual activity, exactly how does the body respond? Surprisingly, until William Masters and Virginia Johnson conducted their groundbreaking research in the 1960s, little was known about the physiology of the human sexual response. Masters and Johnson used physiological recording devices to monitor the bodily changes of volunteers engaging in sex. Their observations and interviews with their subjects yielded a detailed description of the human sexual response that won them widespread acclaim.

The Sexual Response Cycle

Masters and Johnson's (1966, 1970) description of the sexual response cycle is a general one, outlining typical rather than inevitable patterns—people vary considerably. **Figure 13.8** shows how the intensity of sexual arousal changes as women and men progress through the four phases of the sexual response cycle.

Excitement Phase

During the initial phase of excitement, the level of arousal usually escalates rapidly. In both sexes, muscle tension, respiration rate, heart rate, and blood pressure increase quickly. In males ***vasocongestion*—engorgement of blood vessels**—produces penile erection, swollen testes, and the movement of the scrotum (the sac containing the testes) closer to the body. In females, vasocongestion leads to a swelling of the clitoris and vaginal lips, vaginal lubrication, and enlargement of the uterus. Most women also experience nipple erection and a swelling of the breasts.

Plateau Phase

The name given to the "plateau" stage is misleading because physiological arousal does not level off. Instead, it continues to build, but at a much slower pace. In women, further vasocongestion produces a tightening of the lower third of the vagina and a "ballooning" of

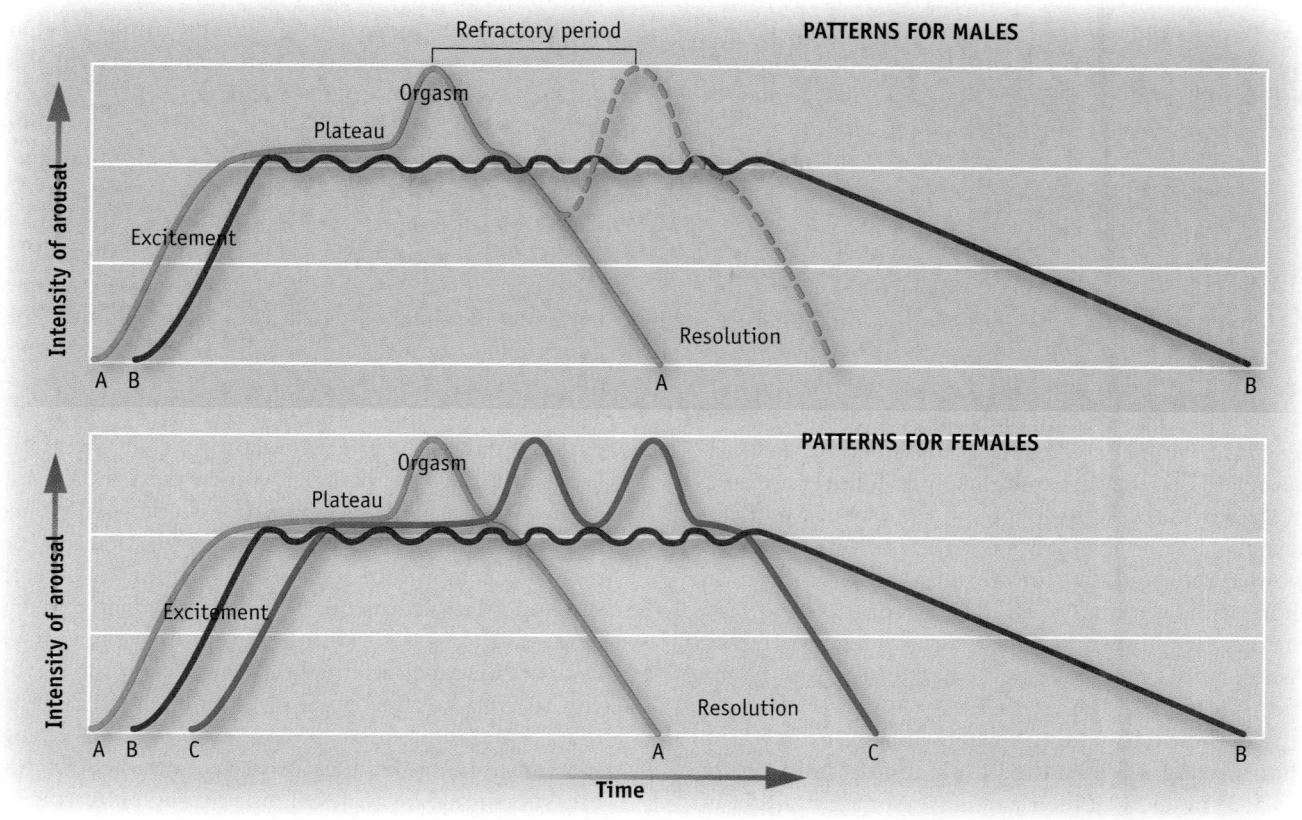

Figure 13.8

The human sexual response cycle. There are similarities and differences between men and women in patterns of sexual arousal. Pattern A, which culminates in orgasm and resolution, is the most typical sequence for both sexes. Pattern B, which involves sexual arousal without orgasm followed by a slow resolution, is also seen in both genders, but it is more common among women. Pattern C, which involves multiple orgasms, is seen almost exclusively in women, as men go through a refractory period before they are capable of another orgasm. (Based on Masters & Johnson, 1966)

the upper two-thirds, which lifts the uterus and cervix away from the end of the vagina. In men, the head of the penis may swell, and the testicles typically enlarge and move closer to the body. Many men secrete a bit of pre-ejaculatory fluid from the tip of the penis that may contain sperm.

Distractions during the plateau phase can delay or stop movement to the next stage. These include ill-timed interruptions like a telephone or doorbell ringing, or a child's knocking—or not!—on the bedroom door. Equally distracting can be such things as physical discomfort, pain, guilt, frightening thoughts, feelings of insecurity or anger toward one's partner, and anxiety about not having an orgasm.

Orgasm Phase

***Orgasm* occurs when sexual arousal reaches its peak intensity and is discharged in a series of muscular contractions that pulsate through the pelvic area.** Heart rate, respiration rate, and blood pressure increase sharply during this exceedingly pleasant spasmodic response. The male orgasm is usually accompanied by ejaculation of seminal fluid. Some women report that they ejaculate some kind of fluid at orgasm. The prevalence of female ejaculation and the source and nature of the fluid are matters still under debate (Alzate, 1990; Whipple, 2000). The subjective experience of orgasm appears to be essentially the same for men and women.

Resolution Phase

During the resolution phase, the physiological changes produced by sexual arousal subside. If one has not had an orgasm, the reduction in sexual tension may be relatively slow and sometimes unpleasant. After orgasm, men generally experience a ***refractory period*, a time following male orgasm during which males are largely unresponsive to further stimulation.** The refractory period varies from a few minutes to a few hours and increases with age.

Critics note that the Masters and Johnson model focuses entirely on genital changes during sex and ignores cognitive factors. An alternative is the three-stage model of noted sex therapist Helen Singer Kaplan (1979), which begins with desire, followed by excitement and then orgasm. Since people's thoughts and views about sex underlie many sexual problems, it is helpful to keep in mind that the sexual response involves more than just physical factors.

Gender Differences in Patterns of Orgasm

As a whole, the sexual responses of women and men parallel each other fairly closely. Nonetheless, there are some interesting differences between the genders in their patterns of experiencing orgasm. During *intercourse,* women are less likely than men to reach orgasm (that is, they are more likely to follow pattern B in **Figure 13.8**). According to one survey of American sexual behavior (Laumann et al., 1994), about 29% of women reported that they *always* reached orgasm in their primary sexual relationships, compared to 75% of men (see **Figure 13.9**). Apparently, about 10% of American women have never had an orgasm by any means (Spector & Carey, 1990).

In their laboratory, Masters and Johnson found that the men they studied took about 4 minutes to reach a climax with their partners. Women took about 10–20 minutes to reach orgasm with their partners, but they reached orgasm in about 4 minutes when they masturbated. Clearly, then, women are capable of reaching orgasm more quickly than they typically do. Our point here is not that men and women should race each other to the finish line but that physiological factors are not the likely cause of gender differences related to orgasm.

How do we account for these disparities? First, although most women report that they enjoy intercourse, it is not the optimal mode of stimulation for them. This is because intercourse provides rather indirect stimulation to the clitoris, the most sexually sensitive genital area in most women. Thus, more lengthy *foreplay,* including manual or oral stimulation of the clitoris, is usually the key to enhancing women's sexual pleasure. Many men mistakenly assume that women experience the same degree of pleasurable sensations that they do during sexual intercourse. But this is not the case, as the upper two-thirds of the vagina has relatively few nerve endings—a good thing, since the vagina serves as the birth canal! Manual or oral stimulation of the clitoris is more effective in producing female orgasm than sexual intercourse alone (Bancroft, 2002b). Unfortunately, many couples are locked into the idea that orgasms should be achieved only through intercourse. Even the word *foreplay* suggests that any other form of sexual stimulation is merely preparation for the "main event." Also, most women associate sex with affection, so they want to hear some tender words during a sexual encounter. Men who verbally express their love and affection usually find their partners more responsive.

Research suggests that lesbians have orgasms more often and more easily in sexual interactions than heterosexual women do (Diamond, 2006; Peplau et al., 2004). Kinsey (1953) attributed this difference to female partners' knowing more about women's sexuality and how to optimize women's sexual satisfaction than male partners do. Also, female partners are more likely to emphasize the emotional aspects of lovemaking than male partners (Peplau et al., 2004). Taken together, these facts support a socialization-based explanation of gender differences in orgasmic consistency.

Because women reach orgasm through intercourse less consistently than men, they are more likely than men to fake an orgasm. Surveys reveal that more than half of all adult women (straight and lesbian) have faked an orgasm (Elliott & Brantley, 1997). Men (straight and gay) also fake them, but much less frequently. People typically do so to make their partner feel better or to bring sexual activity to an end when they're tired. Frequent faking is not a good idea, because it can become a vicious cycle and undermine communication about sex (Crooks & Bauer, 2008).

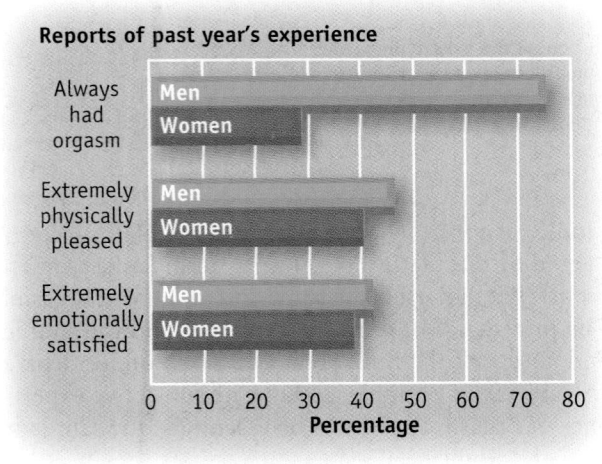

Figure 13.9

Sexual satisfaction with primary partner. A major survey of American sexual behavior showed large gender differences in the consistency of orgasm, a physical measure of sexual satisfaction. Men's and women's subjective evaluations of physical and emotional sexual satisfaction are much more similar. These data indicate that not everyone who has an orgasm every time has a blissful sex life and that factors other than orgasm contribute to a satisfying sex life.

From Laumann, E. O., Gagnon, J. H., Michael, R. T., & Michaels, S. (1994). *The social organization of sexuality: Sexual practices in the United States.* Chicago: University of Chicago Press. Copyright © 1994 by University of Chicago Press. Reprinted by permission.

Sexual Expression

LEARNING OBJECTIVES

- *Discuss fantasy as well as kissing and touching as aspects of sexual expression.*
- *Discuss the prevalence of self-stimulation and attitudes about it.*
- *Discuss oral and anal sex as forms of sexual expression.*
- *Discuss intercourse and the preferred sexual activities of gay males and lesbians.*

People experience and express sexuality in myriad ways. ***Erogenous zones* are areas of the body that are sexually sensitive or responsive.** The genitals and breasts usually come to mind when people think of erogenous zones, as these areas are particularly sensitive for most people. But it's worth noting that many individuals fail to appreciate the potential that lies in other areas of the body. Virtually any area of the body can function as an erogenous zone.

Indeed, the ultimate erogenous zone may be the mind. That is, an individual's mental set is extremely important to sexual arousal. Skillful genital stimulation by a partner may have absolutely no impact if a person is not in the mood. Yet fantasy in the absence of any other stimulation can produce great arousal. In this section, we'll consider the most common forms of sexual expression.

Fantasy

Have you ever fantasized about having sex with someone other than your partner? If so, you've had one of the most commonly reported fantasies (see **Figure 13.10**). In fact, a study of university students and employees reported that 98% of men and 80% of women had sexual fantasies involving someone other than their current partner (Hicks & Leitenberg, 2001). As you might expect, women's fantasies tend to be more romantic, while men's tend to contain more explicit imagery (Impett & Peplau, 2006). Most sex therapists view sexual fantasies as harmless ways to enhance sexual excitement and achieve orgasm either during masturbation or with a partner.

Recommended READING

Sexuality Now: Embracing Diversity
by Janell L. Carroll (Thomson Wadsworth, 2007)

Today, almost all colleges offer courses on sexuality. But if you can't enroll in a sexuality course, you may want to read one of the better textbooks. If so, *Sexuality Now* by Janell Carroll is an excellent candidate. Carroll's text is accurate, thorough, up to date, well organized, and written in an engaging, highly readable manner. In addition, the text is sprinkled with first-person accounts, useful questions and answers based on her students' questions, and fascinating multicultural and cross-cultural perspectives on sexuality. Moreover, the book is a paperback and thus more manageable than most heavy, hardcover texts on the topic.

Other sexuality texts of similar quality are *Our Sexuality* by Robert Crooks and Karla Baur (Thomson Wadsworth, 2008) and *Human Sexuality Today* by Bruce M. King (Pearson Prentice Hall, 2005). Any of these books can provide you with an excellent introduction to the realities of human sexual expression.

Fantasies During Intercourse

Theme	Subjects reporting fantasy (%)	
	Males	Females
A former lover	42.9	41.0
An imaginary lover	44.3	24.3
Oral-genital sex	61.2	51.4
Group sex	19.3	14.1
Being forced or overpowered into a sexual relationship	21.0	36.4
Others observing you engage in sexual intercourse	15.4	20.0
Others finding you sexually irresistible	55.2	52.8
Being rejected or sexually abused	10.5	13.2
Forcing others to have sexual relations with you	23.5	15.8
Others giving in to you after resisting you at first	36.8	24.3
Observing others engaging in sex	17.9	13.2
A member of the same sex	2.8	9.4
Animals	0.9	3.7

Note: For comparison, the responses of "frequently" and "sometimes" were combined for both males and females to obtain these percentages. The number of respondents answering for a specific fantasy ranged from 103 to 106 for males and from 105 to 107 for females.

Figure 13.10

Common sexual fantasies. The percentage of men and women reporting various sexual fantasies during intercourse is shown here. Sue (1979) concluded that people fantasize about experiences they wouldn't seek out in real life.

Adapted from Sue, D. (1979). The erotic fantasies of college students during coitus. *Journal of Sex Research, 15*(4), 299–305. Copyright © 1979 for the Society for the Scientific Study of Sexuality. Reprinted by permission.

As you saw in **Figure 13.10**, dominance and submission fantasies are not uncommon. Still, just because you fantasize about a particular encounter, such as forced sex, doesn't mean that you really want to have such an experience. Only one-tenth of 1% of women say that they enjoy forced sex, and only one-third of 1% of men say that they enjoy forcing a partner to have sex (Laumann et al., 1994).

Kissing and Touching

Most two-person sexual activities begin with kissing. Kissing usually starts at the lips but may be extended to almost any area of the partner's body. Mutual caressing is also an integral element of sexual stimulation for most couples. Like kissing, this tactile stimulation may be applied to any area of the body. Manual and oral stimulation of the other partner's genitals are related sexual practices.

Men often underestimate the importance of kissing and touching (including clitoral stimulation). It is not surprising, therefore, that heterosexual women commonly complain that their partners are in too much of a hurry (King, 2005). Partners who seek to learn about each other's preferences and who try to accommodate each other are much more likely to have mutually satisfying sexual experiences than those who don't.

Self-Stimulation

Masturbation, or the stimulation of one's own genitals, has traditionally been condemned as immoral because it is nonreproductive. Disapproval and suppression of masturbation were truly intense in the 19th and early 20th centuries, when people believed that the practice was harmful to physical and mental health. Because the term *masturbation* has acquired negative connotations, the preferred terminology is *self-stimulation* or *autoeroticism.* Sometimes people, more often women, use vibrators or other "sex toys" for self-stimulation.

Kinsey discovered over four decades ago that most people masturbate with no ill effects. Sexologists now recognize that self-stimulation is normal and healthy. In fact, sex therapists often prescribe masturbation to treat both male and female sexual problems (see this Chapter's Application). Nonetheless, nearly half of those who engage in the practice feel guilty about it (Laumann et al., 1994).

Self-stimulation is common in our society: By adulthood, nine out of ten males and eight out of ten females report having masturbated at least once (Atwood & Gagnon, 1987). African American males masturbate less than Asian, white, and Hispanic men. Also, masturbation is less common among those with less education (Laumann et al., 1994).

Web Link 13.4 **Kaiser Family Foundation**

This foundation sponsors multiple programs and educational efforts in the United States and South Africa to promote health generally, and its site provides a large set of resources regarding human sexuality, one major focus of its educational efforts.

Among married couples, 57% of husbands and 37% of wives report engaging in self-stimulation (Laumann et al., 1994). In fact, masturbation in marriage is often associated with a greater degree of marital and sexual satisfaction (Leitenberg, Detzer, & Srebnik, 1993). Still, couples usually don't talk about it, probably for fear that it will be viewed as a sign of sexual discontent.

Oral and Anal Sex

Oral sex refers to oral stimulation of the genitals. ***Cunnilingus* is oral stimulation of the female genitals; *fellatio* is oral stimulation of the penis.** Partners may stimulate each other simultaneously, or one partner may stimulate the other without immediate reciprocation. Oral-genital sex may be one of several activities in a sexual encounter, or it may be the main event. Oral sex is a major source of orgasms for many heterosexual couples, and it plays a central role in homosexual relationships. A positive aspect of oral sex is that it does not result in pregnancy. This fact partly accounts for the finding that younger teens are more likely to engage in oral sex than in sexual intercourse (Halpern-Felsher et al., 2005). However, some sexually transmitted diseases (human immunodeficiency virus or HIV, for example) can be contracted through mouth-genital stimulation, especially if there are small cracks in the mouth or if the mouth is exposed to semen (Guest, 2004). And a person with a cold sore can pass along the herpes virus during oral sex (or kissing) (Carroll, 2007).

Negative attitudes persist about oral sex, particularly among African Americans, Hispanics, religious conservatives, and those with less education (Laumann et al., 1994). About 80% of men and 70% of women (both gay and straight) report that they have either given or received oral sex at least once (Laumann et al., 1994). Oral sex is now a component in most couples' sexual relationships.

***Anal intercourse* involves insertion of the penis into a partner's anus and rectum.** Legally, it is termed *sodomy* (and is still considered illegal in some states). About 25% of men and women report that they have practiced anal sex at least once (Laumann et al., 1994). Anal intercourse is more popular among homosexual male couples than among heterosexual couples. However, even among gay men it ranks behind oral sex and mutual masturbation in prevalence. Anal sex is risky, as rectal tissues are easily torn, facilitating HIV transmission.

Intercourse

Vaginal intercourse, known more technically as ***coitus,* involves inserting the penis into the vagina and (typically) pelvic thrusting.** It is the most widely endorsed and widely practiced sexual act in our society. In the American sex survey, 95% of heterosexual respondents said that they had practiced vaginal sex the last time they had sex (Laumann et al., 1994). Inserting the penis generally requires adequate vaginal lubrication, or intercourse may be difficult and painful for the woman. This is another good reason for couples to spend plenty of time on mutual kissing and touching, since sexual excitement causes vaginal lubrication. In the absence of adequate lubrication, partners may choose to use artificial lubricants.

Couples use a variety of positions in intercourse and may use more than one position in a single encounter. The man-above, or "missionary," position is the most common, but the woman-above, side-by-side, and rear-entry positions are also popular. Each position has its advantages and disadvantages. Although people are fascinated by the relative merits of various positions, specific positions may not be as important as the tempo, depth, and angle of movements in intercourse. As with other aspects of sexual relations, the crucial consideration is that partners talk to each other about their preferences.

What kinds of sexual activities do homosexuals prefer in the absence of coitus (which is, by definition, a heterosexual act)? As is true with heterosexual couples, the preliminary activities of gay and lesbian couples include kissing, hugging, and petting. Gay men also engage in fellatio, mutual masturbation, and anal intercourse, in that order (Lever, 1994). Lesbians engage in cunnilingus, mutual masturbation, and *tribadism,* in which one partner lies on top of the other and makes thrusting movements so that both receive genital stimulation at the same time.

Patterns of Sexual Behavior

LEARNING OBJECTIVES

- *Describe how the fear of contracting AIDS has influenced sexual attitudes and practices.*
- *Summarize attitudes toward and prevalence of early sexual experiences.*
- *Summarize the findings on sex patterns in dating couples and married couples.*
- *Compare and contrast sexual behavior in married couples versus committed homosexual couples.*
- *Summarize the evidence on infidelity in committed relationships.*

In this section we consider whether fears of contracting acquired immune deficiency syndrome (AIDS) have influenced sexual attitudes and behaviors. Then we'll see how age and type of relationship are related to sexual behavior and then explore the issue of infidelity.

Sex in the Age of AIDS

Over the past 40 years, American sexual attitudes and behaviors have become much more liberal, although this trend has slowed since the 1990s (Christopher & Sprecher, 2000). While heralded by some, the liberal trends have had several serious drawbacks. Two troublesome problems are escalating teenage pregnancy rates and increases in sexually transmitted diseases (Trussell, Brown, & Hogue, 2004). The spread of HIV infection that leads to AIDS remains a special concern. (For a discussion of AIDS, see Chapter 14.) Has public awareness of AIDS put the brakes on the liberalizing trends?

For both pregnancy rates and sexually transmitted diseases, the news is mixed. Although in the United States the teenage birth rate declined 26% between 1991 and 2001, the rate remains one of the highest in the world (Trussell et al, 2004; U.S. Department of Health and Human Services, 2002). Regarding sexually transmitted diseases, rates of genital infections among adolescents remain at high levels. One-fourth of all cases of sexually transmitted diseases occur among teenagers and two-thirds are among people under 25 years of age (Trussell et al., 2004). The good news is that most young people are knowledgeable about HIV and AIDS. Also, between 1991 and 2005, the percentage of high school students who had ever had sexual intercourse decreased, the average number of sex partners decreased, and the incidence of condom use increased, as you can see in **Figure 13.11** (on the next page). Unfortunately, these positive patterns do not hold for all teens. Thus, in the age of AIDS, there is both good and bad news about patterns of sexual behavior.

Figure 13.11

Sexual risk behavior in high school students. In national surveys over a 14-year period, high school students reported on their sexual behavior: whether they had ever had sexual intercourse, the number of sex partners they had had, and whether they had used a condom during their last intercourse. Between 1991 and 2005, sexual risk behavior declined: Fewer students had sex, fewer had four or more sex partners, and more had used a condom during their last sexual encounter. Still, risky behavior increased as students progressed in school.

From Centers for Disease Control. (2006). Trends in sexual risk behaviors among high school students—United States, 1991–2005. *Morbidity and Mortality Weekly Report, 55*(31), 851-854. (Figure based on data in table on pp. 853–854)

Sexual Risk Behavior in High School Students

Grade	Survey year	Ever had intercourse (%)	Four or more sexual partners in lifetime (%)	Condom use during last sexual intercourse (%)
9	1991	39	13	53
	2005	34	9	75
10	1991	48	15	46
	2005	43	12	65
11	1991	62	22	49
	2005	51	16	62
12	1991	67	25	41
	2005	63	21	55

Note: Percentages are rounded to the nearest whole number.

Early Sexual Experiences

By age 22, 90% of Americans have had sexual intercourse. With the average age for marriage being 27 for men and 25 for women, it is obvious that most people are not virgins when they enter committed relationships. Thus, the term *premarital sex* is losing relevance. Another problem is that the term doesn't apply to homosexuals, who aren't permitted to marry under the law (except in Massachusetts as of 2007). Thus, we have chosen to characterize youthful sexual encounters as "early sexual experiences" instead of "premarital sex."

Attitudes

Compared to a generation ago, more people believe that sex before marriage is acceptable, especially if the two people are emotionally committed to each other. Nonetheless, a sexual double standard still exists (Crawford & Popp, 2003). Both men and women are less approving of sexual activity for women than men, especially in the early stages of relationships (Willets, Sprecher, & Beck, 2004).

© Mario Tama/Getty Images

Sexual encounters with casual acquaintances are common in today's society. Nonetheless, casual sex can be risky for a variety of reasons.

Prevalence

In **Figure 13.11**, you can see that the percentage of high school students who have had intercourse increases with age—from 34% in grade 9 to 63% in grade 12 (U.S. Department of Health and Human Services, 2006a). Early sexual activity is correlated with parents' lack of education, poor academic performance, and low educational expectations (Lammers et al., 2000). Also, surveys report that African American teenagers, on average, are likely to engage in sex earlier than their Hispanic or European American peers (U.S. Department of Health and Human Services, 2006b), but it is likely that these apparent ethnic differences are actually differences in socioeconomic status (Lammers et al., 2000).

"Hooking up," a phenomenon that has arisen since the late 1990s, involves two strangers or briefly acquainted people having a single sexual encounter. "Friends with benefits" is a related term that refers to friends who engage in sex but who don't have romantic feelings for each other . Unlike a one-night stand, hookups don't always involve intercourse (petting below the waist and oral sex are common). According to one study, 78% of college students have had at least one hookup (Paul, McManus, & Hayes, 2000). It seems that college students wrongly believe that their peers are significantly more comfortable with hooking up than they, themselves, are (Lambert, Kahn, & Apple, 2003). The researchers speculate that these false perceptions might influence students to override their own comfort level and engage in sexual behavior to be in step with the perceived peer norm. **Figure 13.12** depicts men's and women's comfort level with various hooking-up behaviors. Casual sex is risky: People don't always

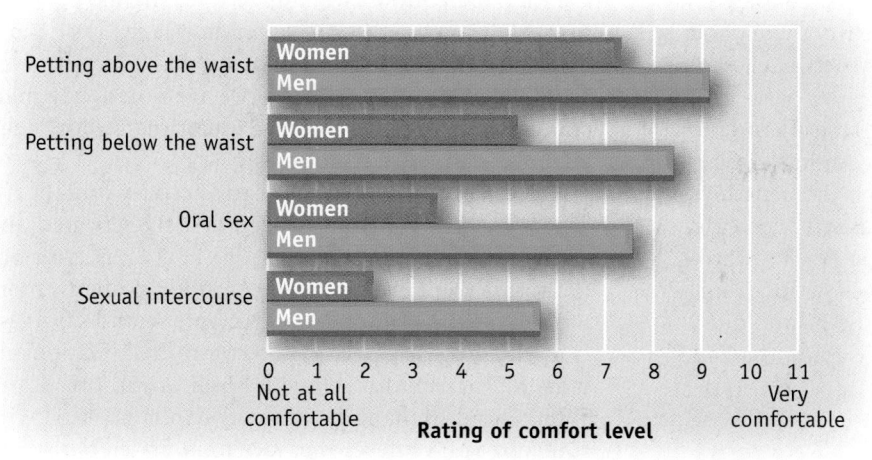

Figure 13.12

Gender differences in comfort level with hooking-up behaviors. College men and women were asked to rate their comfort level with four hooking-up behaviors. The ratings were made on an 11-point scale (11 = *Very comfortable;* 1 = *Not at all comfortable*). As you can see from the mean ratings shown here, men's comfort level significantly exceeded women's for all four behaviors.

From Lambert, T.A., Kahn, A. S., & Apple,,K. J. (2003). Pluralistic ignorance and hooking up. *The Journal of Sex Research, 40*(2) 129-133. Copyright © 2003 Society for the Scientific Study of Sexuality. Reprinted by permission.

practice safer sex, and the risk of contracting sexually transmitted diseases increases with multiple partners.

Sex in Committed Relationships

Sex is a key aspect of most committed, romantic relationships. In this section, we examine patterns of sexual activity in dating couples, married couples, and gay couples.

Sex Between Dating Partners

At some point, couples confront the question of whether or when they should have sex. Some worry that sex might adversely affect the relationship; others fear that not having sex will cause trouble. Is there evidence to support either view? As it turns out, sexual intimacy is a positive predictor of relationship stability (Sprecher & Cate, 2004). However, gender and sexual and relationship satisfaction are also part of this equation. For men, sexual (but not relationship) satisfaction is significantly correlated with relationship stability; for women, relationship (but not sexual) satisfaction is significantly associated with relationship stability (Sprecher, 2002).

Marital Sex

Couples' overall marital satisfaction is strongly related to their satisfaction with their sexual relationship (Sprecher et al., 2006). Of course, it is difficult to know whether good sex promotes good marriages or good marriages promote good sex. In all probability, it's a two-way street. Relationship satisfaction is also correlated with satisfaction in other areas of a relationship (fairness in distribution of household labor, for example) (Impett & Peplau, 2006).

Married couples vary greatly in how often they have sex (see **Figure 13.13**). *On the average,* couples in their 20s and 30s engage in sex about two or three times a week. The frequency of sex among married couples tends to decrease as the years pass (Sprecher et al., 2006). Biological changes play some role in this trend, but

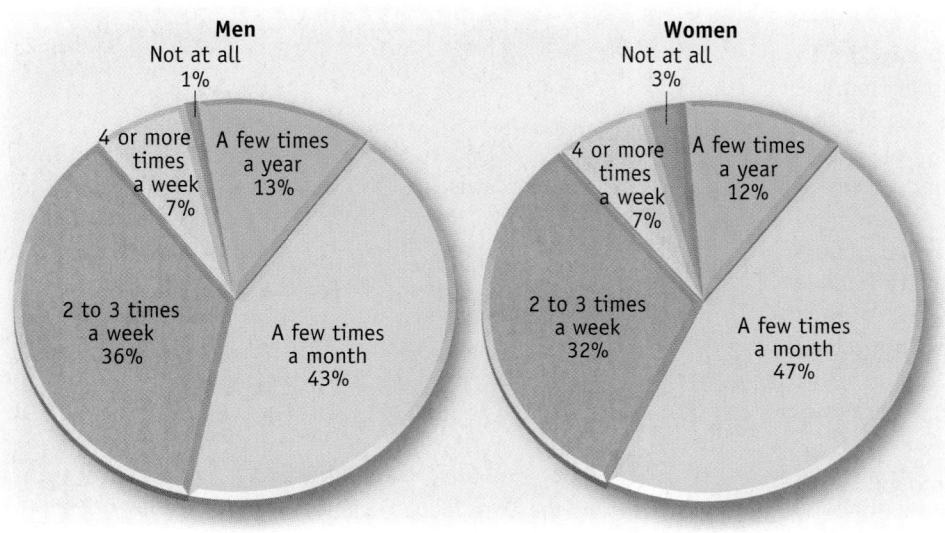

Figure 13.13

Frequency of sex among married men and women. A well-sampled survey asked Americans, "How often have you had sex in the past 12 months?" Married individuals' responses to the question were wide ranging. The most frequent response was "a few times per month" followed by "2 to 3 times a week."

From Michael, R. T., Gagnon, J. H., Laumann, E. O., & Kolata, G. (1994). *Sex in America: A definitive survey.* Boston: Little, Brown. Copyright © 1994 by CSG Enterprises, Inc. Edward O. Lauman, Robert T. Michael, and Gina Kolata. By permission of Little, Brown and Company, Inc., and Brockman, Inc.

social factors seem more compelling. Most couples attribute this decline to increasing fatigue from work and childrearing and to growing familiarity with their sexual routine.

As men and women age, sexual arousal tends to build more slowly and orgasms tend to diminish in frequency and intensity. Males' refractory periods lengthen, and females' vaginal lubrication and elasticity decrease. Nevertheless, older people remain capable of rewarding sexual encounters (Burgess, 2004). A national survey of couples reported that those in the 75 and older age group had sex slightly less than once a month (Call, Sprecher, & Schwartz, 1995).

Sex in Homosexual Relationships

What about the frequency of sex among lesbian, gay, and heterosexual couples? Peplau and her colleagues (2004) report three patterns. First, there is a general decline in the frequency of sexual behavior over time. Second, in the early stages of a relationship, gay males engage in sex more frequently than the other couples. For example, among couples who had been together for two years or less, 67% of gay men reported having sex three or more times a week, compared to 45% of married couples and 33% of lesbian couples (Blumstein & Schwartz, 1983). Third, lesbian couples have sex less often than the other couples.

Like heterosexual women, most lesbians believe that sex and love are intertwined. In contrast (and like straight males), gay men find casual sex more acceptable (Sanders, 2000). Comparative studies find comparable levels of sexual satisfaction in gay, lesbian, and heterosexual couples (Kurdek, 2005). And for both lesbians and gay men, sexual satisfaction is correlated with overall relationship satisfaction.

Infidelity in Committed Relationships

Sexual infidelity occurs when a person who is in a committed relationship engages in erotic activity with someone other than his or her partner. Among married couples, this behavior is also called "adultery" or "extramarital sex." Infidelity among couples in committed relationships (straight and gay) is termed "extradyadic sex." The vast majority of people (91%) in our society believe that extramarital sex is "always" or "almost always wrong" (Saad, 2007). Nonetheless, Americans are fascinated by infidelity, if the popularity of such TV series as *Desperate Housewives* is any gauge!

Although it's not common, extramarital sex can be consensual. Two examples include "swinging" and "open marriage." Swingers are married couples who agree to exchange partners for sex (Rubin, 2001). In "open marriage," both partners agree that it is okay for each to have sex with others (O'Neill & O'Neill, 1972). As we noted, gay male couples are more likely to have "open 'marriages'" than are lesbian or married couples.

Precisely what kind of erotic activity qualifies as "cheating" is debatable, especially between men and women, as you can see in **Figure 13.14**. Are you unfaithful if you develop a deep emotional involvement without sex? No doubt many people would say "yes." Is it "cheating" if a person in a committed relationship uses the Internet for sexual arousal or masturbation? What about exchanging sexually explicit e-mail with someone you've never met face to face? Therapists are seeing more couples for problems related to cyber affairs (Cooper & Griffin-Shelley, 2002).

Prevalence

Despite the fact that most people disapprove of infidelity, a number of people get involved in it. Because of the associated stigma and secrecy, accurate estimates of infidelity are difficult to come by. Surveys report that about 25% of married men and about 10% of married women had engaged in an extramarital affair at least once (Laumann et al., 1994; Wiederman, 1997).

In straight cohabiting relationships, about a third of men and women have engaged in extradyadic sex (Blumstein & Schwartz, 1983). As we noted, sexual openness is more common in committed gay male relationships, and the rates of extradyadic sex for this group are higher than for all other groups (Peplau & Fingerhut, 2007). Committed lesbian relationships are much

© AP Images/Seth Wenig

The popularity of the TV series **Desperate Housewives** *suggests that Americans are fascinated by infidelity.*

What Constitutes Infidelity?

Does this constitute cheating in a marriage?	Answered "yes" Married men	Married women
Kissing someone else	59%	75%
Having a sexually explicit conversation on the phone	64%	74%
Having a sexually explicit conversation on the Internet	62%	72%
Holding hands with someone else	40%	49%
Fantasizing about having sex with someone else	39%	43%
Casually flirting with someone else	32%	38%

Figure 13.14

What constitutes infidelity? A 1998 Time/CNN poll asked 397 married men and 431 married women whether various actions constituted cheating in a marriage. Men's responses were more liberal than women's, especially regarding "kissing someone else."

From Handy, B. (1998, August 3). How we really feel about infidelity. *Time*, pp. 52–53. Copyright © 1998 by Time Inc. Reprinted by permission.

more exclusive, in principle and in practice, than gay male relationships (Peplau & Fingerhut, 2007). Rates of lesbian extradyadic sex are also lower than those for married women.

Motivations

Why do people pursue extramarital sexual encounters? Common reasons include dissatisfaction with a relationship, anger toward a partner, and boredom (Willets et al., 2004). Sometimes people need to confirm that they are still desirable, or they want to trigger the end of an unsatisfying relationship. Then again, extramarital sexual activity can occur simply because two people are attracted to each other. Erotic reactions to people other than one's partner do not cease when one makes a permanent commitment. Most people suppress these sexual desires because they disapprove of adultery.

The gender differences in motivations for infidelity parallel the gender differences in sexual socialization. Men tend to engage in extradyadic affairs to obtain sexual variety or more frequent sex, while women usually seek an emotional connection (Buunk & Dijkstra, 2006). Age is also a factor. People between the ages of 18 and 30 are twice as likely to engage in sex outside a committed relationship than people over 50 (Treas & Giesen, 2000). Too, there is some evidence that insecure attachment styles are positively correlated with infidelity (Buunk & Dijkstra, 2006).

Impact

The impact of extramarital sexual activity on marriages has not been investigated extensively. Experts speculate that approximately 20% of all divorces are caused by infidelity (Reinisch, 1990). Still, it's hard to know in these cases whether extramarital sex is a symptom of a disintegrating relationship or its cause. Occasionally, extramarital affairs can have a positive effect on a marriage if they motivate a couple to resolve relationship problems. Participants in extramarital affairs, whether or not they are discovered, may experience loss of self-respect, guilt, stress, and complications of sexually transmitted diseases. Sexual fidelity is positively correlated with relationship satisfaction for lesbian and heterosexual couples, but not for gay male couples (Kurdek, 1991).

Practical Issues in Sexual Activity

LEARNING OBJECTIVES

- *Describe constraints on effective contraception and discuss the merits of hormone-based contraceptives and condoms.*
- *Describe the various types of STDs, and discuss their prevalence and means of transmission.*
- *List some suggestions for safer sexual practices.*

Regardless of the context of sexual activity, two practical issues are often matters of concern: contraception and sexually transmitted diseases. These topics are more properly in the domain of medicine than of psychology, but birth control and sex-related infections certainly do have their behavioral aspects.

Contraception

Most people want to control whether and when they will conceive a child, so they need reliable contraception. Despite the availability of effective contraceptive methods, however, many people fail to exercise much control.

Constraints on Effective Contraception

Effective contraception requires that intimate couples negotiate their way through a complex sequence of steps. First, both people must define themselves as sexually active. Second, both must have accurate knowledge about fertility and conception. Third, their chosen method of contraception must be readily accessible. Finally, both must have the motivation and skill to use the method correctly and consistently. Failure to meet even one of these conditions can result in an unintended pregnancy.

Given the difficulties surrounding effective contraception, it is extremely encouraging that teenage pregnancy rates declined dramatically between 1991 and 2003 (Santelli et al., 2006). The main reasons for this steep decline are improved use of contraceptives and delays in beginning sexual intercourse. Although these changes are heartening, many high school students (23% of girls and 16% of boys) use either withdrawal or no contraception at all (Santelli et al. 2006). These individuals are at high risk for pregnancy and sexually transmitted diseases. In addition, any couple who do not use condoms (even if they use another contraceptive method) can contract sexually transmitted diseases unless both partners have tested negatively for such infections.

© 1986 Wasserman, *The Boston Globe*. All rights reserved. Reprinted by permission of the Los Angeles Times Syndicate.

Why do some individuals and couples engage in risky sexual behavior? Of course, one cause is ignorance about preventing pregnancy and sexually transmitted diseases. Another factor is conflicting norms about gender and sexual behavior. Men are socialized to be the initiators of sexual activity, but when it comes to birth control, they often rely on women to take charge. It is hard for a woman to maintain an image of sexual naïveté and also be responsible for contraception. Telling her partner that she is "on the pill" or whipping out a condom conveys quite a different image. Unfortunately, a woman's decision to use a condom may be influenced more by concerns about how her partner might perceive her than her perceived susceptibility to infections and attitudes about condom use (Bryan, Aiken, & West, 1999). Finally, alcohol can undermine condom use, although this is not always the case (Cooper, 2006). Some individuals drink as a socially acceptable way to avoid potentially embarrassing discussions about sex.

Selecting a Contraceptive Method

If a couple is motivated to control their fertility, how should they go about selecting a technique? A rational choice requires accurate knowledge of the effectiveness, benefits, costs, and risks of the various methods. **Figure 13.15** summarizes information on most of the methods currently available. The *ideal failure rate* estimates the probability of conception when the technique is used correctly and consistently. The *actual failure rate* is what occurs in the real world, when users' negligence is factored in.

Besides being informed about contraceptive methods, couples must also put this information to use. Contraception is a joint responsibility. Hence, it's essential for partners to discuss their preferences, to decide what method(s) they are going to use, and to *act* on their decision. Let's look in more detail at the two most widely used birth control methods in the Western world: hormone-based contraceptives and condoms.

Hormone-based contraceptives contain synthetic forms of estrogen and progesterone (or progesterone only, in the minipill), which inhibit ovulation in women. Types of hormone-based contraceptives include "the pill," hormonal injectables (Depo-Provera), the transdermal patch (worn on the skin), the vaginal ring (inserted once a month), and contraceptive implants. Many couples prefer these birth control options because contraceptive use is not tied to the sex act. Only the intrauterine device (IUD) permits a similar degree of sexual spontaneity. But these contraceptives do not protect against sexually transmitted diseases.

Except for Depo-Provera, use of hormone-based contraceptives does not appear to increase a woman's overall risk for cancer (Trussell, 2004). Depo-Provera may increase the risk of cervical, liver, and/or breast cancers (Carroll, 2007). In fact, the likelihood of certain forms of cancer (such as uterine and ovarian cancer) is reduced in women who use low-dosage *oral* contra-

Web Link 13.5 **Sexual Health Network**

The health professionals who staff this Connecticut-based site have assemblied a comprehensive set of resources related to all aspects of human sexual health. Especially notable are materials discussing sexual functioning for persons with physical injuries or disabilities.

Contraceptive Methods				
Method	**Ideal failure rate (%)**	**Actual failure rate (%)**	**Advantages**	**Disadvantages**
Birth control pills (combination)	0.3	8	Highly reliable; coitus-independent; has some health benefits	Side effects; daily use; continual cost; health risks for some women; no protection against STDs
Minipill (progestin only)	0.3	8	Thought to have low risk of side effects; coitus-independent; has some health benefits	Breakthrough bleeding; daily use; continual cost; health risks for some women; no protection against STDs
Hormonal injectables (Depo-Provera)	0.3	3	Highly reliable; coitus independent; no memory or motivation required for use; reduces risk of endometrial and ovarian cancer	Side effects; use may increase risk of certain cancers; continual cost; injection every 3 months; no protection against STDs
Hormonal ring (NuvaRing)	0.3	8	Highly reliable; coitus independent; no memory or motivation required for use; may offer protection against endometrial and ovarian cancer	Side effects; no data on extended use; no protection against STDs
Subdermal implants (Implanon)	0.1	0.1	Highly reliable; coitus independent; no memory or motivation required for use	Side effects; painful removal; possible scarring at site; no protection from STDs
Transdermal patch	.03	8	No memory or motivation required to use; coitus-independent; very reliable; has some health benefits	Continual cost; skin irritation for some women; no protection against STDs
IUD	0.6	0.8	No memory or motivation required for use; very reliable; some health benefits	Cramping, bleeding, expulsion; risk of pelvic inflammatory disease; no protection against STDs
Diaphragm with spermicidal cream or jelly	6	16	No major health risks; inexpensive	Aesthetic objections; initial cost
Condom (male)	2	15	Protects against STDs; simple to use; male responsibility; no health risks; no prescriptions required	Unaesthetic to some; requires interruption of sexual activity; continual cost
Sponge	9	16	24-hour protection; simple to use; no taste or odor; inexpensive; effective with several acts of intercourse	Aesthetic objections; continual cost; no protection against STDs
Cervical cap with spermicidal cream or jelly	9	16	48-hour protection; no major health risks	May be difficult to insert; may irritate cervix; initial cost
Spermicides	18	29	No major health risks; no prescription required	Unaesthetic to some; must be properly inserted; continual cost; no protection against STDs
Fertility awareness (rhythm)	1–9	25	No cost; acceptable to Catholic church	Requires high motivation and periods of abstinence; unreliable; no protection against STDs
Withdrawal	4	27	No cost or health risks	Reduces sexual pleasure; unreliable; requires high motivation; no protection against STDs
No contraception	85	85	No immediate monetary cost	High risk of pregnancy and STDs

Note: STDs = Sexually transmitted diseases

Figure 13.15

A comparison of widely used contraceptive techniques. Couples can choose from a variety of contraceptive methods. This chart summarizes the advantages and disadvantages of each method. Note that the typical failure rate is much higher than the ideal failure rate for all methods, because couples do not use contraceptive techniques consistently and correctly. (Based on Carroll, 2007; Crooks & Baur, 2008; Hatcher et al., 2004)

ceptives. These methods do slightly increase the risk of certain cardiovascular disorders, such as heart disease and stroke. Thus, alternative methods of contraception should be considered by women who smoke, are over age 35, have any suspicion of cardiovascular disease, have liver disease, or have breast or uterine cancer.

A *condom* is a sheath worn over the penis during intercourse to collect ejaculated semen. The condom is the only widely available contraceptive device for use by males. A condom slightly reduces a man's sensitivity, but many men see this dulling as a plus because it can make sex last longer. Condoms can be purchased in any drugstore without a prescription. If used correctly, the condom is highly effective in preventing pregnancy (Warner, Hatcher, & Steiner, 2004). It must be placed over the penis after erection but before any contact with the vagina, and space must be left at the tip to collect the ejaculate. The man should withdraw before completely losing his erection and firmly hold the rim of the condom during withdrawal to prevent any semen from spilling into the vagina.

Condoms are made of polyurethane, latex rubber, and animal membranes ("skin"). Polyurethane condoms are thinner than latex condoms; however, they are more likely to break and to slip off than latex condoms. Using latex condoms definitely reduces the chances of contracting or passing on various sexually transmitted diseases. However, oil-based creams and lotions (petroleum jelly, massage oil, baby oil, and hand and body lotions, for example) should never be used with *latex* condoms (or diaphragms) (Warner et al., 2004). Within 60 seconds, these products can make microscopic holes in the rubber membrane that are large enough to allow passage of HIV and organisms produced by other sexually transmitted diseases. Water-based lubricants such as Astroglide or K-Y Warming Liquid do not cause this problem. Polyurethane condoms are impervious to oils. Skin condoms do *not* offer protection against sexually transmitted diseases.

In closing, we should mention emergency contraception. Women may seek emergency contraception in cases of sexual assault, contraceptive failure, or unprotected sex. Progestin pills (Plan B) are available from pharmacies without a prescription for women aged 18 and older (younger women must have a prescription) (Alan Guttmacher Institute, 2006). Plan B pills are 95% effective in preventing pregnancy if they are taken within 24 hours after intercourse (75% effective within 72 hours). The drug works like birth control pills, by preventing ovulation or fertilization and implantation of the fertilized egg into the uterine wall ("Condoms—Extra Protection," 2005). If the fertilized egg is already implanted into the wall of the uterus, progestin will not harm it. By contrast, mifepristone (RU 486) is a drug that can induce a miscarriage in the first seven weeks of a pregnancy (Stewart, Ellertson, & Cates, 2004). Prescribed by a physician, mifepristone is typically administered in the form of two pills taken several days apart. Although no substitute for regular birth control, the drug can be used after unprotected sex and is particularly helpful in cases of rape.

Sexually Transmitted Diseases

A *sexually transmitted disease* (STD) is a disease or infection that is transmitted primarily through sexual contact. When people think of STDs, they typically think of syphilis and gonorrhea, but these diseases are only the tip of the iceberg. There are actually around 25 sexually transmitted diseases. Some of them—for instance, pubic lice—are minor nuisances that can readily be treated. Others, however, are severe afflictions that are difficult to treat. For instance, if it isn't detected early, syphilis can cause heart failure, blindness, and brain damage, and AIDS is eventually fatal.

Prevalence and Transmission

No one is immune to sexually transmitted diseases. Even monogamous partners can develop some STDs (yeast infections, for instance). Health authorities estimate that about 19 million new cases occur in the United States each year (Alan Guttmacher Institute, 2006). The highest incidence of STDs occurs in the under-25 age group (Cates, 2004). About one person in four contracts an STD by age 21 (Feroli & Burstein, 2003).

The United States has seen a recent surge of HIV infections stemming from heterosexual transmission (Kaiser Family Foundation, 2007). And an estimated half of all new HIV infections occur in people under age 25. AIDS is increasing more rapidly among women than among men, especially among blacks and Latinas (Kaiser Family Foundation, 2007). Women whose sexual partners have multiple sex partners or who inject drugs are especially at risk. An increasing concern is that a woman's partner may be secretly having sex with other men and may deny that he is gay or bisexual (Kalb & Murr, 2006). Infected women are more likely to be poor and less likely to get treatment (Cowley & Murr, 2004). The rate of HIV infections is also up among young gay and bisexual men, especially blacks and Latinos (Kaiser Family Foundation, 2007).

Women suffer more severe long-term consequences of STDs than men, including chronic pelvic pain, infertility, and cervical cancer (Cates, 2004). Because of the transmission dynamics of sexual intercourse, they are also more likely to acquire an STD from any single sexual encounter. But women are less likely to seek treatment because more of their STDs are asymp-

Web Link 13.6 **AIDS HIV AEGIS**

This is the largest and probably most important web-based resource dealing with the human immunodeficiency virus (HIV) and acquired immune deficiency syndrome (AIDS). A simply extraordinary collection of information sources can be found here.

tomatic or not perceived to be serious. Human papillomavirus (HPV) infections cause about half of STDs diagnosed among 15- to 24-year-olds (Alan Guttmacher Institute, 2006). Certain types of HPV can lead to cervical cancer. In 2006, the U.S. Food and Drug Administration approved a vaccine (Gardisil) for use by females aged 9 to 26. It will prevent infection with the types of HPV that lead to cervical cancer.

The principal types of sexually transmitted diseases are listed in **Figure 13.16** on the next page, along with their symptoms and modes of transmission. Most of these infections are spread from one person to another through intercourse, oral-genital contact, or anal-genital contact. Concerning the transmission of STDs, seven points are worth emphasizing:

1. You should consider *any* activity that exposes you to blood (including menstrual blood), semen, vaginal secretions, urine, feces, or saliva as high-risk behavior *unless* you and your partner are in a mutual, sexually exclusive relationship and neither of you is infected.

2. The more sexual partners you have, the higher your chances of exposure to a sexually transmitted infection.

3. Having sexual contact with a male or female sex worker puts you at high risk for contracting an HIV infection.

4. Don't assume that the labels people attach to themselves (heterosexual or homosexual) accurately describe their actual sexual behavior. According to a government study based on a nationally representative sample of individuals aged 15 to 44, 6% of males and 11% of females reported that they had had at least one same-gender sexual experience in their lives (Mosher, Chandra, & Jones, 2005).

5. People can be carriers of sexually transmitted diseases without knowing it. For instance, in its early stages gonorrhea may cause no readily apparent symptoms in women, who may unknowingly transmit the infection to their partners.

6. Even when people know they have a sexually transmitted infection, they may fail to refrain from sex or inform their partners. Guilt and embarrassment cause many people to ignore symptoms of sexually transmitted diseases and continue their normal sexual activities. Many people will lie about homosexual activity, sex with prostitutes, drug use, and the number of sexual partners they have had. So don't assume that sexual partners will warn you that they may be contagious.

7. Engaging in anal intercourse (especially being the receiving partner) puts one at high risk for AIDS. Rectal tissues are delicate and easily torn, thus letting the virus pass through the membrane. Always use a condom during anal sex. Oral-genital sex may also transmit HIV, particularly if semen is swallowed.

Prevention

Abstinence is obviously the best way to avoid acquiring STDs. Of course, this is not an appealing or realistic option for most people. Short of abstinence, the best strategy is to engage in sexual activity only in the context of a long-term relationship, where partners have an opportunity to know each other reasonably well. Casual sex greatly increases the risk for STDs, including HIV.

We offer the following suggestions for safer sex (Crooks & Baur, 2008; King, 2005):

- Don't have sex with lots of people. You increase your risk of contracting STDs.
- Don't have sex with someone who has had lots of previous partners. People won't always be honest about their sexual history, so it's important to know whether you can trust a prospective partner's word.
- If you are not involved in a sexually exclusive relationship, always use latex condoms with spermicides. They have a good track record of preventing STDs and offer effective protection against the AIDS virus. (And never use oil-based lubricants with latex condoms; use water-based lubricants instead.)
- If there is any possibility that you or your partner has an STD, abstain from sex, always use condoms, or use other types of sexual expression such as hand-genital stimulation.
- Wash your genitals with soap and warm water before and after sexual contact.
- Urinate shortly after intercourse.
- Because HIV is easily transmitted through anal intercourse, it's a good idea to avoid this type of sex.
- Watch for sores, rashes, or discharge around the vulva or penis, or elsewhere on your body, especially the mouth. If you have cold sores, avoid kissing or oral sex.

Along with being judicious about sexual relations, you need to talk openly about safer sexual practices with your partner. But if you don't carry the process one step further and practice what you preach, you remain at risk. As we noted, many people engage in risky sexual behavior—a practice they can ill afford while we are in the grip of the deadly AIDS epidemic.

Unfortunately, the availability of new drug treatments for HIV seems to have increased risk taking among gay and bisexual men (Peterson & Bakeman, 2006). Although these new drugs are welcome news, they cost over $10,000 per year—well out of the reach of those without health insurance (Freedberg et al., 2001).

If you have any reason to suspect that you have an STD, find a good health clinic and get tested *as soon as possible.* It's normal to be embarrassed or afraid of getting bad news, but don't delay. Health professionals are in the business of helping people, not judging them. To be really sure, get tested twice. If both tests are negative,

Sexually Transmitted Diseases (STDs)		
STD	**Transmission**	**Symptoms**
Acquired immune deficiency syndrome (AIDS)	The AIDS virus is spread by coitus or anal intercourse. There is a chance the virus may also be spread by oral-genital sex, particularly if semen is swallowed. (AIDS can also be spread by nonsexual means: contaminated blood, contaminated hypodermic needles, and transmission from an infected woman to her baby during pregnancy or childbirth.)	Most people infected with the virus show no immediate symptoms; antibodies usually develop in the blood 2-8 weeks after infection. People with the virus may remain symptom-free for 5 years or more. No cure for the disease has yet been found. Common symptoms include fevers, night sweats, weight loss, chronic fatigue, swollen lymph nodes, diarrhea and/or bloody stools, atypical bruising or bleeding, skin rashes, headache, chronic cough, and a whitish coating on the tongue or throat.
Chlamydia infection	The *Chlamydia trichomatis* bacterium is transmitted primarily through sexual contact. It may also be spread by fingers from one body site to another.	In men, chlamydial infection of the urethra may cause a discharge and burning during urination. Chlamydia-caused epidydimitis may produce a sense of heaviness in the affected testicle(s), inflammation of the scrotal skin, and painful swelling at the bottom of the testicle. In women, pelvic inflammatory disease caused by chlamydia may disrupt menstrual periods, temperature, and cause abdominal pain, nausea, vomiting, headache, infertility, and ectopic pregnancy.
Human papillomavirus (HPV)	Virus is often on genital skin areas not covered by a condom (vulva, scrotum, etc.); virus is spread primarily through penile-vaginal, oral-genital, oral-anal, or genital-anal contact; transmission most often occurs by asymptomatic individuals.	Often asymptomatic; 10% of infections lead to contagious genital warts, which may appear 3 to 8 months after contact with infected person; HPV is associated with various cancers.
Gonorrhea ("clap")	The *Neisseria gonorrhoeae* bacterium (gonococcus) is spread through penile-vaginal, oral-genital, or genital-anal contact.	Most common symptoms in men are a cloudy discharge from the penis and burning sensations during urination. If the disease is untreated, complications may include inflammation of the scrotal skin and swelling at the base of the testicle. In women, some green or yellowish discharge is produced, but the disease commonly remains undetected. At a later stage, pelvic inflammatory disease may develop.
Herpes	The genital herpes virus (HSV-2) appears to be transmitted primarily by penile-vaginal, oral-genital, or genital-anal contact. The oral herpes virus (HSV-1) is transmitted primarily by kissing, or oral-genital contact.	Small red, painful bumps (papules) appear in the region of the genitals (genital herpes) or mouth (oral herpes). The papules become painful blisters that eventually rupture to form wet, open sores.
Pubic lice ("crabs")	*Phthirus pubis,* the pubic louse, is spread easily through body contact or through shared clothing or bedding.	Persistent itching. Lice are visible and may often be located in pubic hair or other body hair.
Syphilis	The *Treponema pallidum* bacterium (spirochete) is transmitted from open lesions during penile-vaginal, oral-genital, oral-anal, or genital-anal contact.	*Primary stage:* A painless chancre (sore) appears at the site where the spirochetes entered the body. *Secondary stage:* The chancre disappears and a generalized skin rash develops. *Latent stage:* There may be no observable symptoms. *Tertiary stage:* Heart failure, blindness, mental disturbance, and many other symptoms may occur. Death may result.
Trichomoniasis	The protozoan parasite *Trichomonas vaginalis* is passed through genital sexual contact or less frequently by towels, toilet seats, or bathtubs used by an infected person.	In women, white or yellow vaginal discharge with an unpleasant odor; vulva is sore and irritated. Men are usually asymptomatic.
Viral hepatitis	The hepatitis B virus may be transmitted by blood, semen, vaginal secretions, and saliva. Manual, oral, or penile stimulation of the anus is strongly associated with the spread of this virus. Hepatitis A seems to be spread primarily via the fecal-oral route. Oral-anal sexual contact is a common mode of sexual transmission for hepatitis A.	Vary from nonexistent to mild, flulike symptoms to an incapacitating illness characterized by high fever, vomiting, and severe abdominal pain.

Figure 13.16

Overview of common sexually transmitted diseases (STDs). This chart summarizes the symptoms and modes of transmission of nine STDs. Note that intercourse is not required to transmit all STDs—many can be contracted through oral-genital contact or other forms of physical intimacy. (Adapted from Carroll, 2007; Crooks & Baur, 2008; Hatcher et al., 2004) you can stop worrying. If you have several sexual partners in a year, you should have regular STD checkups. You will have to ask for them, as most doctors and health clinics won't perform them otherwise.

Remember that the symptoms of some STDs disappear as the infection progresses. If your test results are positive, it's essential to get the proper treatment *right away.* Notify your sexual partner(s) so they can be tested immediately, too. And avoid sexual intercourse and oral sex until you and your partner are fully treated and a physician or clinic says you are no longer infectious.

In the Application, we focus on enhancing sexual satisfaction and treating common sexual problems.

APPLICATION

Enhancing Sexual Relationships

LEARNING OBJECTIVES

- *List six general suggestions for enhancing sexual relationships.*
- *Discuss the nature, prevalence, and causes of common sexual dysfunctions.*
- *Describe the strategies for coping with erectile difficulties, premature ejaculation, orgasmic difficulties, and hypoactive sexual desire.*

Answer the following statements "true" or "false."

___ **1.** Sexual problems are unusual.

___ **2.** Sexual problems belong to couples rather than individuals.

___ **3.** Sexual problems are highly resistant to treatment.

___ **4.** Sex therapists sometimes recommend masturbation as a treatment for certain types of problems.

The answers are (1) false, (2) true, (3) false, and (4) true. If you missed several of these questions, you are by no means unusual. Misconceptions about sexuality are the norm rather than the exception. Fortunately, there is plenty of useful information on how to improve sexual relationships.

For the sake of simplicity, our advice is directed to heterosexual couples, but much of what we have to say is also relevant to same-gender couples. For advice aimed specifically at same-gender couples, we recommend *Permanent Partners: Building Gay and Lesbian Relationships That Last* by Betty Berzon (2004).

General Suggestions

Let's begin with some general ideas about how to enhance sexual relationships, drawn from several excellent books on sexuality (Carroll, 2007; Crooks & Baur, 2008; King, 2005). Even if you are satisfied with your sex life, these suggestions may be useful as "preventive medicine."

1. *Pursue adequate sex education.* A surprising number of people are ignorant about the realities of sexual functioning. So the first step in promoting sexual satisfaction is to acquire accurate information about sex. The shelves of most bookstores are bulging with popular books on sex, but many of them are loaded with inaccuracies. A good bet is to pick up a college textbook on human sexuality. The Recommended Readings in this chapter describe books that we think are excellent. Enrolling in a course on human sexuality is also a good idea. Most colleges offer such courses today.

2. *Review your sexual values system.* Many sexual problems stem from a negative sexual values system that associates sex with immorality. The guilt feelings caused by such an orientation can interfere with sexual functioning. Thus, sex therapists often encourage adults to examine the sources and implications of their sexual values.

3. *Communicate about sex.* As children, people often learn that they shouldn't talk about sex. Many people carry this edict into adulthood and have great difficulty discussing sex, even with their partner. Good communication is essential in a sexual relationship. **Figure 13.17** on the next page lists common problems in sexual relations. Many of these problems—such as choosing an inconvenient time, too little erotic activity before intercourse, and too little tenderness afterward—are traceable largely to poor communication. Your partner is not a mind-reader! You have to share your thoughts and feelings. Remember that both men and women say they want more instructions from their partner (refer back to **Figure 13.7**). If you are unsure about your partner's preferences, ask. And provide candid (but diplomatic) feedback when your partner asks for your reactions.

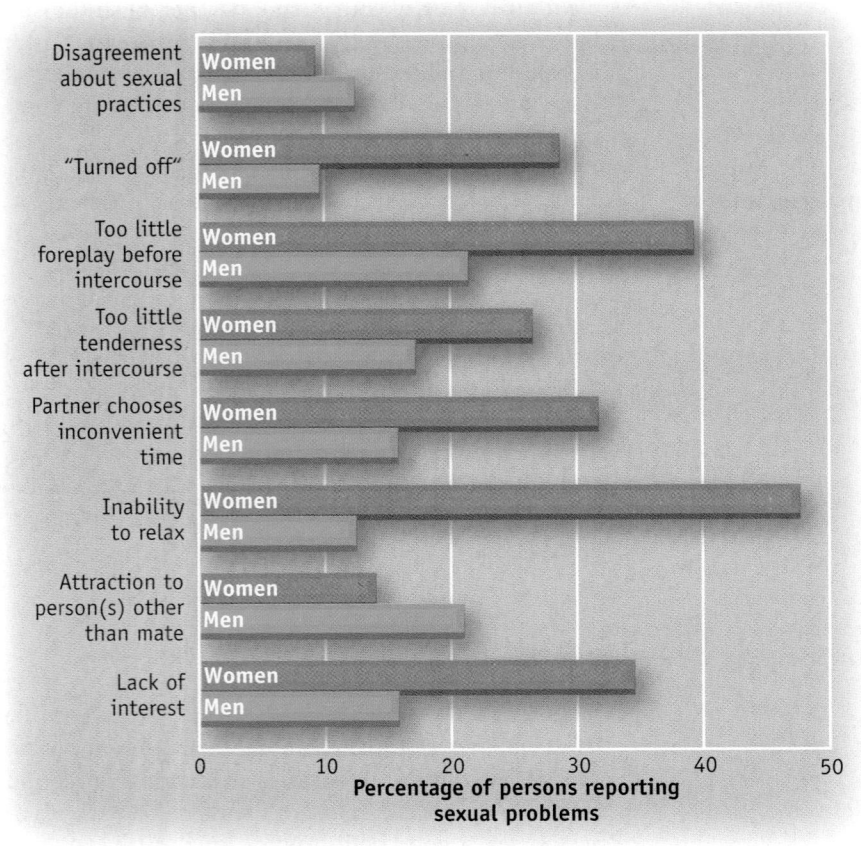

Figure 13.17

Common problems in sexual relations. The percentage of men and women reporting various types of problems in their sexual relationships is shown here, based on a sample of 100 couples. (Adapted from Frank, Anderson, & Rubenstein, 1978.)

4. *Avoid goal setting.* Sexual encounters are not tests or races. Sexual experiences are usually best when people relax and enjoy themselves. People get overly concerned about orgasms or about both partners reaching orgasm simultaneously. A grim determination to climax typically makes it harder to do so. This mental set can lead to disruptive habits like *spectatoring,* or stepping outside the sexual act to judge one's performance. It's better to adopt the philosophy that getting there is at least half the fun.

5. *Enjoy your sexual fantasies.* As we noted earlier, the mind is the ultimate erogenous zone. Although Freudian theory originally saw sexual fantasy as an unhealthy by-product of sexual frustration and immaturity, research shows that sexual fantasies are most common among those who have the fewest sexual problems (Leitenberg & Henning, 1995; Renaud & Byers, 2001). Men and women both report that their sexual fantasies increase their excitement. So don't be afraid to use fantasy to enhance your sexual arousal.

6. *Be selective about sex.* Sexual encounters generally work out better when you have privacy and a relaxed atmosphere, when you are well rested, and when you are enthusiastic. Of course, you can't count on (or insist on) having ideal situations all the time, but you should be aware of the value of being selective. If your heart just isn't in it, it may be wise to wait. Partners often differ about when, where, and how often they like to have sex. Such differences are normal and should not be a source of resentment. Couples simply need to work toward reasonable compromises—through open communication.

Understanding Sexual Dysfunction

Many people struggle with ***sexual dysfunctions*—impairments in sexual functioning that cause subjective distress.** **Figure 13.18** shows the prevalence of some of the most common sexual problems (Laumann et al., 1994).

Physical, psychological, and interpersonal factors can contribute to sexual problems. *Physical factors* include chronic illness, disabilities, some medications, alcohol, and drugs. *Individual psychological factors* include performance anxiety, negative attitudes about sexuality learned during childhood, spectatoring, fears of pregnancy and STDs, life stresses such as unemployment, and prior sexual abuse. *Interpersonal factors* include ineffective communication about sexual matters and unresolved relationship issues that fuel anger and resentment.

People commonly assume that a sexual problem resides in just one partner (physical or individual psychological factors). While this is sometimes the case, most sexual problems emerge out of partners' unique ways of relating to each other (interpersonal factors). Moreover, even in those cases where a problem may lie more with one partner than another, the couple needs to work together for an acceptable solution. In other words, sexual problems belong to couples rather than to individuals.

Now let's examine the symptoms and causes of four common sexual dysfunctions: erectile difficulties, premature ejaculation, orgasmic difficulties, and low sexual desire.

***Erectile difficulties* occur when a man is persistently unable to achieve or maintain an erection adequate for intercourse.** The traditional name for this problem is *impotence,* but sex therapists have discarded the term because of its demeaning connotation. A man who has never had an erection sufficient for intercourse is said to have *lifelong erectile difficulties.* A man who has had intercourse in the past but who is currently having problems achieving erections is said to have *acquired erectile difficulties.* The latter problem is more common and easier to overcome.

Some 30 million American men are estimated to suffer from erectile difficulties if a broad criterion (the inability to get an erection adequate for satisfactory sexual performance) is used (Levine, 2003). Erectile difficulties affect about 1 in 20 men age 40 and over, and about 1 in 4 over age 65.

Physical factors can play a role in erectile dysfunction. For example, experts estimate that as many as 25% of all cases may be the result of side effects from medication (Miller, 2000). A host of common diseases (such as diabetes) can produce erectile problems as a side effect. Many temporary conditions, such as fatigue, worry about work, an argument with one's partner, a depressed mood, or too much alcohol can cause such incidents. The most common psychological cause of erectile difficulties is anxiety about sexual performance. Anxiety may stem from doubts about virility or conflict about the morality of sexual desires. Interpersonal factors can enter in if one's partner turns an incident into a major catastrophe. If the man allows himself to get unduly concerned about his sexual response, the seeds of anxiety may be sown.

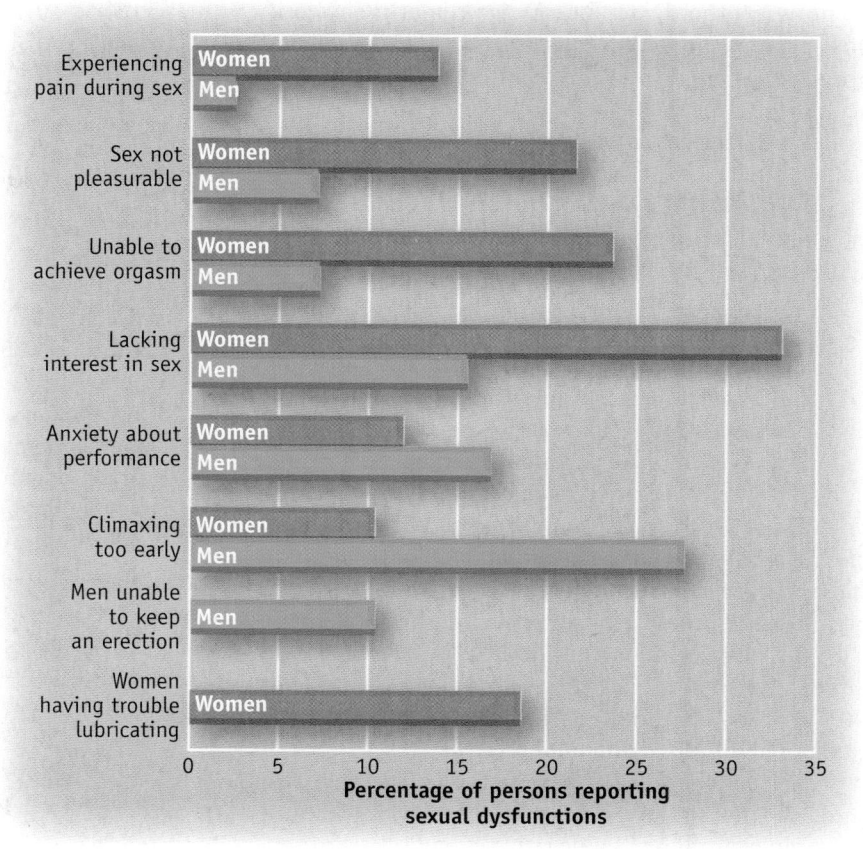

Figure 13.18

Sexual dysfunction in normal couples. This graph shows the prevalence of various sexual dysfunctions during a year in a probability sample of American men and women. The most common problems among men are premature ejaculation and anxiety about performance; in women, they are lack of interest in sex and orgasmic difficulties.

From Laumann, E. O., Gagnon, J. H., Michael, R. T., & Michaels, S. (1994). *The social organization of sexuality: Sexual practices in the United States.* Chicago: University of Chicago Press. Copyright © 1994 by University of Chicago Press. Reprinted by permission.

***Premature ejaculation* occurs when sexual relations are impaired because a man consistently reaches orgasm too quickly.** What is "too quickly"? Obviously, any time estimate is hopelessly arbitrary. The critical consideration is the subjective feelings of the partners. If either partner feels that the ejaculation is persistently too fast for sexual gratification, they have a problem. Approximately 29% of men repeatedly experience premature ejaculation (Laumann et al, 1994).

What causes premature ejaculation? Some men who have a lifelong history of quick ejaculation may have a neurophysiological predisposition to this condition (Metz & Pryor, 2000). But psychological factors are the typical cause. Some men simply don't exert much effort to prolong intercourse. Most of these men

© Marc Romanelli/The Image Bank/Getty Images

Unresolved sexual problems can be a source of tension and frustration in relationships. Physical, psychological, and interpersonal factors can contribute to sexual difficulties.

do not view their ejaculations as premature, even if their partners do. Other causes can include stress, depression, or anger at one's partner. Some therapists believe that early sexual experiences in which a rapid climax was advantageous can establish a habit of rapid ejaculation.

***Orgasmic difficulties* occur when people experience sexual arousal but have persistent problems in achieving orgasm.** When this problem occurs in men, it is often called *male orgasmic disorder.* The traditional name for this problem in women, *frigidity,* is no longer used because of its derogatory implications. Since this problem is much more common among women, we'll limit our discussion to them. A woman who has never experienced an orgasm through any kind of stimulation is said to have *generalized lifelong orgasmic difficulties.* Women who experience orgasms in some situations or only rarely are said to have *situational orgasmic difficulties.* This category includes women who experience orgasm only through noncoital techniques (oral, manual, and self-stimulation). Although lifelong orgasmic difficulties would seem to be the more severe problem, they are actually more responsive to treatment than situational orgasmic difficulties.

Physical causes of orgasmic difficulties are rare (medications can be a problem). One of the leading psychological causes is a negative attitude toward sex. Women who have been taught that sex is dirty or sinful are likely to approach it with shame and guilt. These feelings can undermine arousal, inhibit sexual expression, and impair orgasmic responsiveness. Arousal may also be inhibited by fear of pregnancy or excessive concern about achieving orgasm.

Some women have orgasmic difficulties because intercourse is too brief. Others fail to experience orgasms because their partners are unconcerned about their needs and preferences. But many couples simply need to explore sexual activities such as manual or oral stimulation of the clitoris that are more effective in producing female orgasm than sexual intercourse, alone (Bancroft, 2002b).

***Hypoactive sexual desire,* or the lack of interest in sexual activity,** seems to be on the rise. Individuals with this problem rarely initiate sex or tend to avoid sexual activities with their partner (Aubin & Heiman, 2004). It occurs in both men and women, but it is more common among women (see **Figure 13.18**). Many attribute the recent increases in this problem to the fast pace of contemporary life and to couples' heavy workloads both at home and the office. In men, low sexual desire is often related to embarrassment about erectile dysfunction (McCarthy, Bodnar, & Handal, 2004). In women, it is most often associated with relationship difficulties (Aubin & Heiman, 2004). Sometimes the problem arises when a person is trying to sort out his or her sexual orientation.

Coping with Specific Problems

© Bettmann/Corbis

William Masters and Virginia Johnson

With the advent of modern sex therapy, sexual problems no longer have to be chronic sources of frustration and shame. ***Sex therapy* involves the professional treatment of sexual dysfunctions.** Masters and Johnson reported high success rates for their treatments of specific problems, as **Figure 13.19** shows. Although some critics argue that the cure rates reported by Masters and Johnson are overly optimistic, there is a consensus that sexual dysfunctions can be overcome with regularity (McCarthy et al., 2004). The advent of medications to treat sexual problems (Viagra) has resulted in an increased emphasis on medical and individual treatments over relationship interventions (Aubin & Heiman, 2004; McHugh, 2006). Nonetheless, couple-based treatment approaches definitely have their place and are effective (O'Sullivan, McCrudden, & Tolman, 2006). If you're looking for a sex therapist, be sure to get someone who is qualified to work in this specialized field. One professional credential to look for is that provided by the American Association of Sex Educators, Counselors, and Therapists (AASECT).

Erectile Difficulties

Viagra, the much-touted pill for treating erectile disorders, is about 80% effective (Handy, 1998a). Still, it is not without its drawbacks—some of them life threatening. Cialis and Levitra are two similar pills that enhance erections over a longer time period (24 to 36 hours) than Viagra. To work effectively, these pills must be incorporated into the couple's lovemaking style (Rosen, 2000). The expectation that a pill alone will solve sexual problems that stem from relationship or psychological issues can set men up for additional sexual dysfunction (McCarthy et al., 2004).

To overcome psychologically-based erectile difficulties, the key is to decrease the man's performance anxiety. It is a good idea for a couple to discuss the problem openly. The woman should be reassured that the difficulty does not reflect lack of affection by her partner. Obviously, it is crucial for her to be emotionally supportive rather than hostile and demanding.

Masters and Johnson introduced an effective procedure for the treatment of erectile difficulties and other dysfunctions. ***Sensate focus* is an exercise in which partners take turns pleasuring each other while giving guided verbal feedback and in which certain kinds of stimulation are temporarily forbidden.** One partner stimulates the other, who simply lies back and enjoys it while giving instructions and feedback about what feels good. Initially, the partners are

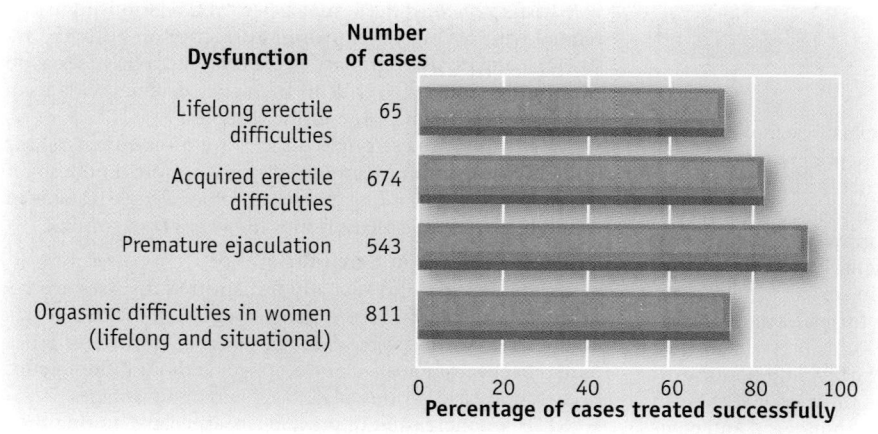

Figure 13.19

Success rates reported by Masters and Johnson in their treatment of sexual dysfunctions. This figure shows the success rates for cases treated between 1959 and 1985. Treatment was categorized as successful only if the change in sexual function was clear and enduring. The minimum follow-up period was two years, and in many cases follow-up was five years later.

Adapted from Masters, W. H., Johnson, V. E., & Kolodny, R. C. (1988). *Human sexuality* (3rd ed.). Boston: Allyn & Bacon. Copyright © 1988 by Pearson Education. Adapted by permission of the publisher.

not allowed to touch each other's genitals or to attempt intercourse. This prohibition should free the man from feelings of pressure to perform. Over a number of sessions, the couple gradually includes genital stimulation in their sensate focus, but intercourse is still banned. With the pressure to perform removed, many men spontaneously get erections. Repeated arousals should begin to restore the man's confidence in his sexual response. As his confidence returns, the couple can move on gradually to attempts at intercourse.

Premature Ejaculation

Men troubled by premature ejaculation range from those who climax almost instantly to those who cannot last the time that their partner requires. In the latter case, simply slowing down the tempo of intercourse may help. Sometimes the problem can be solved indirectly by discarding the traditional assumption that orgasms should come through intercourse. If the female partner enjoys oral or manual stimulation, these techniques can be used to provide her with an orgasm either before or after intercourse. This strategy can reduce the performance pressure for the male partner, and couples may find that intercourse starts to last longer.

For the problem of instant ejaculation, two treatments are very effective: the *stop-start method* (Semans, 1956) and the *squeeze technique* (Masters & Johnson, 1970). With both, the woman brings the man to the verge of orgasm through manual stimulation. Then, she either stops stimulating him (stop-start technique) or squeezes the base or the end of his penis firmly for 3–5 seconds (squeeze technique) until he calms down. She repeats this procedure three or four times before bringing him to orgasm. These exercises can help a man recognize preorgasmic sensations and teach him that he can delay ejaculation. Medication may also help (Renshaw, 2005).

Orgasmic Difficulties

Negative attitudes and embarrassment about sex are often at the root of women's orgasmic difficulties. Thus, therapeutic discussions are usually geared toward helping nonorgasmic women reduce their ambivalence about sexual expression, become more clear about their sexual needs, and become more assertive about them. Sex therapists often suggest that women who have never had an orgasm try to have one by first using a vibrator and then shifting to masturbation, as the latter more closely approximates stimulation by a partner (Crooks & Baur, 2008). Many women achieve orgasms in intercourse after an initial breakthrough with self-stimulation. To make this transition, it is essential that the woman express her sexual wishes to her partner. Sensate focus is also an effective technique for treating orgasmic difficulties (Heiman & Meston, 1997).

When a woman's orgasmic difficulties stem from not feeling close to her partner, treatment usually focuses on couples' relationship problems more than on sexual functioning per se. Therapists also focus on helping couples improve their communication skills.

Hypoactive Sexual Desire

Therapists consider reduced sexual desire the most challenging sexual problem to treat (Aubin & Heiman, 2004). This is because the problem usually has multiple causes, which can also be difficult to identify. If the problem is a result of fatigue from overwork, couples may be encouraged to allot more time to personal and relationship needs. Sometimes hypoactive sexual desire reflects relationship problems. Treatment for reduced sexual desire is usually more intensive than that for more specific sexual disorders, and it is usually multifaceted to deal with the multiple aspects of the problem.

Medications can be used for low sexual desire. For instance, some older men take supplemental testosterone to offset the age-related decline in this hormone (Crooks & Baur, 2008). And the medical and financial success of Viagra has stimulated pharmaceutical companies to work on developing drugs that will boost women's sexual desire (Diamond et al., 2006; Marshall, 2005). Still, drugs will not solve relationship problems. For these, couples therapy is needed.

KEY IDEAS

Becoming a Sexual Person

▶ One's sexual identity is made up of sexual orientation, body image, sexual values and ethics, and erotic preferences. Physiological factors such as hormones influence sexual differentiation, maturation, and anatomy more than they do sexual activity. Psychosocial factors appear to have more impact on sexual behavior. Sexual identity is shaped by families, peers, schools, and the media. Because of differences in sexual socialization, sexuality usually has different meanings for males and females.

▶ Experts believe that sexual orientation is best viewed as a continuum, with end points of heterosexuality and homosexuality. The determinants of sexual orientation are not yet known but appear to be a complex interaction of biological and environmental factors. Attitudes toward homosexuals are negative, but moving in a positive direction. Coming to terms with a homosexual orientation is a process. Recent evidence suggests that homosexuals are at greater risk for depression and suicide attempts than are heterosexuals, a phenomenon linked to their membership in a stigmatized group.

Interaction in Sexual Relationships

▶ Sexual motives can be grouped into approach and avoidance motives. One's motives for sex are linked to personal and relationship well-being. Men tend to be motivated more by physical gratification, whereas women are more likely to have emotional motives.

▶ Disparities between partners in sexual interest and erotic preferences lead to disagreements that require negotiation. Effective communication plays an important role in sexual and relationship satisfaction.

The Human Sexual Response

▶ The physiology of the human sexual response was described by Masters and Johnson. They analyzed the sexual response cycle into four phases: excitement, plateau, orgasm, and resolution. For a more complete view of this process, individuals' subjective experiences during sexual encounters also need to be factored in.

▶ Women reach orgasm in intercourse less consistently than men, usually because foreplay and intercourse are too brief and because of gender differences in sexual socialization.

Sexual Expression

▶ Sexual fantasies are normal and are an important aspect of sexual expression. Kissing and touching are important erotic activities, but their importance is often underestimated by heterosexual males. Despite the strongly negative attitudes about masturbation that are traditional in our society, this practice is quite common, even among married people. Oral-genital sex has become a common element in most couples' sexual repertoires.

▶ Coitus is the most widely practiced sexual act in our society. Four coital positions are commonly used, each with its advantages and disadvantages. Sexual activities between gay males include mutual masturbation, fellatio, and, less often, anal intercourse. Lesbians engage in mutual masturbation, cunnilingus, and tribadism.

Patterns of Sexual Behavior

▶ American sexual attitudes and behavior have become more liberal over the past 40 years, although this trend slowed in the 1990s. Teen pregnancy rates have declined recently, but they still remain high. STD rates are highest among young people. The incidence of sexually risky behavior among teens has declined sharply in recent years.

▶ Satisfaction with the sexual aspect of a relationship is correlated with overall relationship satisfaction in both gay and straight couples. Younger married couples tend to have sex about two or three times a week. This frequency declines with age in both heterosexual and same-gender couples.

▶ Most Americans strongly disapprove of extramarital sex. Infidelity is uncommon among married couples and lesbians and more common among gay male couples. People become involved in extradyadic relationships for a variety of reasons.

Practical Issues in Sexual Activity

▶ Contraception and sexually transmitted diseases are two practical issues that concern many couples. Many people who do not want to conceive a child fail to use contraceptive procedures effectively, if at all. Contraceptive methods differ in effectiveness and have various advantages and disadvantages.

▶ STDs are increasing in prevalence, especially among those under 25. The danger of contracting STDs is higher among those who have had more sexual partners. In the United States, the rates of HIV infections stemming from heterosexual sex are on the rise, particularly among women. HIV rates are also up among young gay and bisexual men. Using condoms decreases the risk of contracting STDs. Early treatment of STDs is important.

Application: Enhancing Sexual Relationships

▶ To enhance their sexual relationships, individuals need to have adequate sex education and positive values about sex. They also need to be able to communicate with their partners about sex and avoid goal setting in sexual encounters. Enjoying sexual fantasies and being selective about their sexual encounters are also important.

▶ Common sexual dysfunctions include erectile difficulties, premature ejaculation, orgasmic difficulties, and hypoactive sexual desire. Treatments for low sexual desire are less effective than those for more specific sexual problems.

KEY TERMS

Anal intercourse p. 422
Androgens p. 408
Bisexuals p. 407
Coitus p. 423
Cunnilingus p. 422
Erectile difficulties p. 434
Erogenous zones p. 421
Estrogens p. 408
Fellatio p. 422
Gonads p. 408
Heterosexuals p. 407
Homophobia p. 414
Homosexuals p. 407
Hypoactive sexual desire p. 436
Orgasm p. 419
Orgasmic difficulties p. 436
Premature ejaculation p. 435
Refractory period p. 419
Sensate focus p. 436
Sex therapy p. 436
Sexual dysfunction p. 434
Sexual identity p. 407
Sexually transmitted disease (STD) p. 430
Vasocongestion p. 418

KEY PEOPLE

Linda Garnets and Douglas Kimmel p. 415
Alfred Kinsey pp. 412–413
William Masters and Virginia Johnson pp. 418–419, 438–439
Letitia Anne Peplau p. 410

PRACTICE TEST

1. Young men typically feel _____ about sex; young women typically feel _____ about sex.
   a. positive; positive
   b. positive; negative
   c. ambivalent; ambivalent
   d. positive; ambivalent

2. Which of the following statements about sexual orientation is true?
   a. Heterosexuality and homosexuality are best viewed as two distinct categories.
   b. Heterosexuality and homosexuality are best viewed as end points on a continuum.
   c. Biological factors alone probably determine sexual orientation.
   d. Environmental factors alone probably determine sexual orientation.

3. Which of the following describes the correct order of the four phases of Masters and Johnson's sexual response cycle?
   a. Resolution, plateau, excitement, orgasm
   b. Plateau, excitement, orgasm, resolution
   c. Excitement, plateau, orgasm, resolution
   d. Excitement, orgasm, plateau, resolution

4. Sexual fantasies:
   a. are signs of abnormality.
   b. are quite normal.
   c. rarely include having sex with someone other than one's partner.
   d. are an excellent indication of what people want to experience in reality.

5. Which of the following characterizes teen sexual behavior in the "age of AIDS"?
   a. Fewer teens are engaging in risky sexual behavior now than 10 years ago.
   b. The teen pregnancy rate has increased since the early 90s.
   c. About 80 percent of sexually active teens use condoms regularly.
   d. The teen pregnancy rate in America is among the lowest in the world.

6. Regarding overall marital satisfaction and sexual satisfaction, research indicates there is:
   a. a strong relationship.
   b. a weak relationship.
   c. no relationship.
   d. a strong relationship, but only in the first year of marriage.

7. About what percent of Americans strongly disapprove of sexual infidelity?
   a. 10%
   b. 30%
   c. 60%
   d. 90%

8. Which of the following statements about condom use is false?
   a. It's okay to use oil-based lubricants with polyurethane condoms.
   b. It's okay to use oil-based lubricants with rubber condoms.
   c. Skin condoms do not protect against STDs.
   d. It's okay to use water-based lubricants with rubber or polyurethane condoms.

9. Sexually transmitted diseases:
   a. are all very serious.
   b. always cause symptoms right away.
   c. are most common among people under age 25.
   d. are most common among people between 26 and 40.

10. Which of the following is *not* one of the text's suggestions for enhancing your sexual relationships?
   a. Pursue adequate sex education.
   b. Review your sexual values system.
   c. Communicate about sex.
   d. Set clear goals for each sexual encounter.

Book Companion Website

Visit the Book Companion Website at **academic.cengage.com/psychology/weiten,** where you will find tutorial quizzes, flash cards, and web links for every chapter, a final exam, and more! You can also link to the Psychology Resource Center (accessible directly at **academic.cengage.com/login**) for a range of psychology-related resources.

Personal Explorations Workbook

The following exercises in your *Personal Explorations Workbook* may enhance your self-understanding in relation to issues raised in this chapter. **Questionnaire 13.1:** Sexuality Scale. **Personal Probe 13.1:** How Did You Acquire Your Attitudes About Sex? **Personal Probe 13.2:** Reflecting on the Place of Sexuality Throughout Your Life.

ANSWERS

1. d Pages 410, 412
2. b Pages 412–413
3. c Pages 418–419
4. b Pages 421–422
5. a Pages 423–424
6. a Pages 425–426
7. d Page 426
8. b Page 430
9. c Pages 430–431
10. d Pages 433–434

CHAPTER 14

Psychology and Physical Health

STRESS, PERSONALITY, AND ILLNESS
Personality, Emotions, and Heart Disease
LIVING IN TODAY'S WORLD *Coping with Traumatic Events*
Stress and Cancer
Stress and Other Diseases
Stress and Immune Functioning
Conclusions
HABITS, LIFESTYLES, AND HEALTH
Smoking
Drinking
Overeating
Poor Nutrition
Lack of Exercise
Behavior and AIDS
REACTIONS TO ILLNESS
The Decision to Seek Treatment
The Sick Role
Communicating with Health Providers
Adherence to Medical Advice
APPLICATION: UNDERSTANDING THE EFFECTS OF DRUGS
Drug-Related Concepts
Narcotics
Sedatives
Stimulants
Hallucinogens
Marijuana
Ecstasy (MDMA)
REVIEW
PRACTICE TEST

Janet is a fairly typical student. She carries a full course load, works a part-time job, and plans to pursue a challenging career in nursing. She hopes to work in a hospital for a few years until she enrolls in graduate school. Right now, however, her life is regulated by work: homework, her job, and more school-related work in the wards of the teaching hospital where she learns the science and practice of nursing. In a typical semester, Janet feels under control for the first few weeks, but then her work piles up: tests, papers, reading, appointments, labs, and so on. She feels anxious and stressed. Instead of getting eight full hours of sleep, she often does with much less. Fast food becomes a familiar and necessary comfort—she doesn't have time to prepare, let alone eat, healthy and well-balanced meals. Her regular exercise routine often gives way to other time commitments; she can't jog or get to the gym as much as she'd like. By the end of the term, she is anxious, stressed, tired, and run down. In fact, she usually celebrates the end of the semester by getting sick and ending up in bed for a few days instead of having some relaxing times with her friends and family.

Are you at all like Janet? How often do you become ill in a typical semester? Do you begin strong and healthy but feel worn out and frayed by the end? If you are like many students, your lifestyle has a close connection to your health and well-being. In the past few decades, research has demonstrateed quite clearly that health is affected by social and psychological factors as well as biological ones. In other words, health is affected not just by germs or viruses but also by the choices people make and the lives they lead.

This chapter focuses on the fact that more than any other time in history, people's health is more likely to be compromised by *chronic diseases*—conditions that develop across many years—rather than by *contagious diseases,* those caused by specific infectious agents (such as polio, smallpox, or malaria—see **Figure 14.1**). Moreover, lifestyle and stress play a much larger role in the development of chronic diseases than they do in contagious diseases. Today, the three leading chronic diseases (heart disease, cancer, and stroke) account for almost 60% of all deaths in the United States, and these mortality statistics reveal only the tip of the iceberg. Psychological and social factors also contribute to many other, less serious illnesses, such as headaches, backaches, skin disorders, asthma, and ulcers.

In light of these trends, it is not surprising that the way we think about illness is changing. Traditionally,

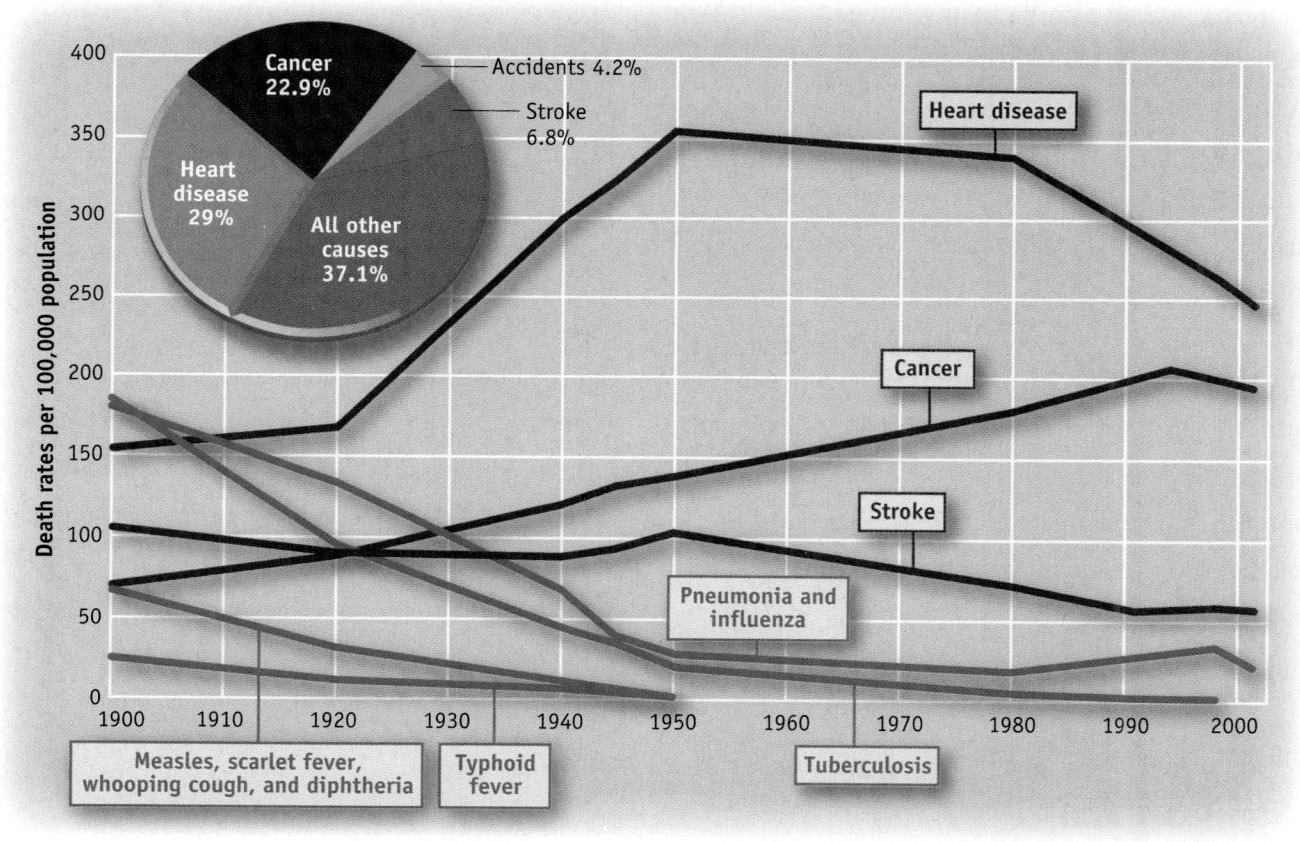

Figure 14.1

Changing patterns of illness. Trends in the death rates for various diseases during the 20th century reveal that contagious diseases (shown in blue) have declined as a threat to health. However, the death rates for stress-related chronic diseases (shown in red) have remained quite high. The pie chart (inset), which depicts the percentage of deaths caused by most of the leading killers today, shows the results of these trends: Three chronic diseases (heart disease, cancer, and stroke) account for almost 60% of all deaths.

illness has been thought of as a purely biological phenomenon produced by an infectious agent or some internal physical breakdown. However, the shifting patterns of disease and new findings relating stress to physical illness have rocked the foundation of this biological model. In its place a new model has gradually emerged (Suls & Rothman, 2004). The ***biopsychosocial model*** **holds that physical illness is caused by a complex interaction of biological, psychological, and sociocultural factors.** This model does not suggest that biological factors are unimportant. Rather, it simply asserts that biological factors operate in a psychosocial context that can also be highly influential. Medical and psychological professionals who adhere to the biopsychosocial model attend to additional factors, including cultural values, that can affect the ways individuals think about and deal with chronic illness, especially where interactions with health care providers and adherence to treatments are concerned (Sperry, 2006). Similarly, the reactions of family members introduce another level of concern, as illness not only affects the dynamics of how family members respond but also how they relate to the patient and to one another. **Figure 14.2** illustrates how the three factors in the biopsychosocial model affect one another and, in turn, health.

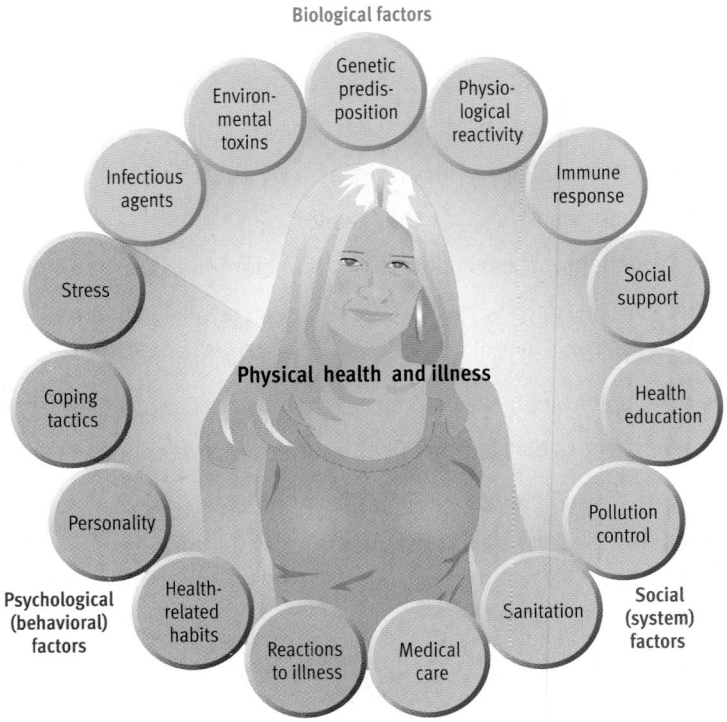

Figure 14.2

The biopsychosocial model. Whether one's health is good or bad, the biopsychosocial model assumes that health is not just attributable to biological processes. According to this increasingly influential view, one's physical health depends on interactions between biolgical factors, psychological factors, and social system factors. Some key factors in each category are depicted here.

The growing recognition that psychological factors influence physical health led to the development of a new specialty within psychology (Baum, Revenson, & Singer, 2001; Friedman & Adler, 2007). ***Health psychology*** **is concerned with how psychosocial factors relate to the promotion and maintenance of health and with the causation, prevention, and treatment of illness.** This specialty is relatively young, having emerged in the late 1970s. In this chapter we focus on the rapidly growing domain of health psychology. The chapter's first section analyzes the link between stress and illness. The second section examines common health-impairing habits, such as smoking and overeating. The third section discusses how people's reactions to illness can affect their health. The Application expands on one particular type of health-impairing habit: the use of recreational drugs.

Web Link 14.1 **healthfinder**

Through the U.S. Department of Health and Human Services, the government has opened an ambitious online gateway to consumer-oriented information about health in all its aspects. Annotated descriptions are available for all resources identified in no-cost searches of this database.

Stress, Personality, and Illness

LEARNING OBJECTIVES

- *Describe the Type A personality and evidence regarding its most toxic element.*
- *Discuss possible explanations for the link between hostility and heart disease.*
- *Summarize evidence relating emotional reactions and depression to heart disease.*
- *Describe the evidence linking stress and personality to cancer.*
- *Summarize evidence linking stress to a variety of diseases and immune functioning.*
- *Evaluate the strength of the relationship between stress and illness.*

As we noted in Chapter 3, during the 1970s health researchers began to uncover new links between stress and a variety of diseases previously believed to be purely physiological in origin. In this section, we'll look at the evidence on the apparent link between stress and physical illness and discuss how personality factors contribute to this relationship. What does it mean to say that personality can affect wellness? A guiding assumption is that a person's characteristic demeanor can influence his or her physical health. As noted in Chapter 2, personality is made up of the unique grouping of behavioral traits that a person exhibits consistently. Thus, an individual who is chronically grumpy, hostile toward others, and routinely frustrated is more likely to develop an illness and perhaps even to die earlier than someone who is emotionally open, who is friendly, and who leads a balanced life (Friedman, 2007). Of course, the link between personality and disease is somewhat more complex but nonetheless real. We begin with a look at heart disease, far and away the leading cause of death in North America.

Personality, Emotions, and Heart Disease

Heart disease accounts for nearly 30% of the deaths in the United States every year. ***Coronary heart disease* results from a reduction in blood flow through the coronary arteries, which supply the heart with blood.** This type of heart disease causes about 90% of heart-related deaths. Atherosclerosis is the principal cause of coronary disease. ***Atherosclerosis* is a gradual narrowing of the coronary arteries,** usually caused by a buildup of fatty deposits and other debris on the inner walls (see **Figure 14.3**). Atherosclerosis progresses slowly over many years. Narrowed coronary arteries may eventually lead to situations in which the heart is temporarily deprived of adequate blood flow, causing a condition known as *myocardial ischemia.* This ischemia may be accompanied by brief chest pain, called *angina.* If a coronary artery is blocked completely (by a blood clot, for instance), the abrupt interruption of blood flow can produce a full-fledged heart attack, or *myocardial infarction.* Atherosclerosis is more prevalent in men than women and tends to increase with age.

Other established risk factors for coronary disease include smoking, diabetes, high cholesterol levels, and high blood pressure (Greenland et al., 2003; Khot et al., 2003). Smoking and diabetes are somewhat stronger risk factors for women than for men (Stoney, 2003). Contrary to public perception, cardiovascular diseases kill women just as much as men, but these diseases tend to emerge in women about 10 years later than in men (Stoney, 2003).

Recently, attention has shifted to the possibility that inflammation may contribute to atherosclerosis and elevated coronary risk (Hackam & Anand, 2003). Evidence is mounting that inflammation plays a key role in the initiation and progression of atherosclerosis, as well as the acute complications that trigger heart attacks (Albert et al., 2002; Libby, Ridker, & Maseri, 2002). Fortunately, researchers have found a marker—levels of C-reactive protein (CRP) in the blood—that may help physicians estimate individuals' coronary risk more accurately than was possible previously (Ridker, 2001). **Figure 14.4** (on the next page) shows how combined levels of CRP and cholesterol appear to be related to coronary risk. CRP levels are also predictive of the development of high blood pressure, which suggests that hypertension may be part of an inflammatory syndrome (Sesso et al., 2003).

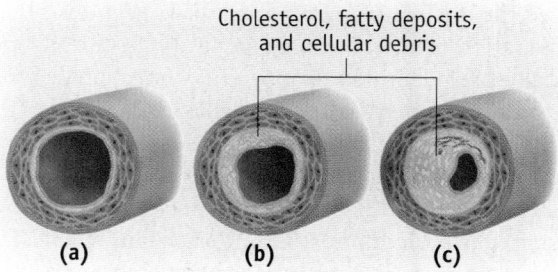

Figure 14.3

Atherosclerosis. Atherosclerosis, a narrowing of the coronary arteries, is the principal cause of coronary disease. **(a)** A normal artery. **(b)** Fatty deposits, cholesterol, and cellular debris on the walls of the artery have narrowed the path for blood flow. **(c)** Advanced atherosclerosis. In this situation, a blood clot might suddenly block the flow of blood through the artery.

Figure 14.4

The relationship of cholesterol and inflammation to coronary risk. Levels of C-reactive protein (CRP) in the blood appear to be a useful index of the inflammation that contributes to atherosclerosis (Ridker, 2001). This graph shows how increasing CRP levels and increasing cholesterol levels combine to elevate cardiovascular risk (for a heart attack or stroke). The relative risks shown are for successive quintiles on each measure (each quintile represents one-fifth of the sample, ordered from those who scored lowest to those who scored highest). The relative risks are in relation to those who fall in the lowest quintile on both measures.

Adapted from Ridker, P. M. (2001). High sensitivity C-reactive protein: Potential adjunct for global risk assessment in primary prevention of cardiovascular disease. *Circulation, 103,* 1813–1818. Copyright © 2001 American Heart Association. Adapted by permission of the publisher Lippincott Williams & Wilkins and the author.

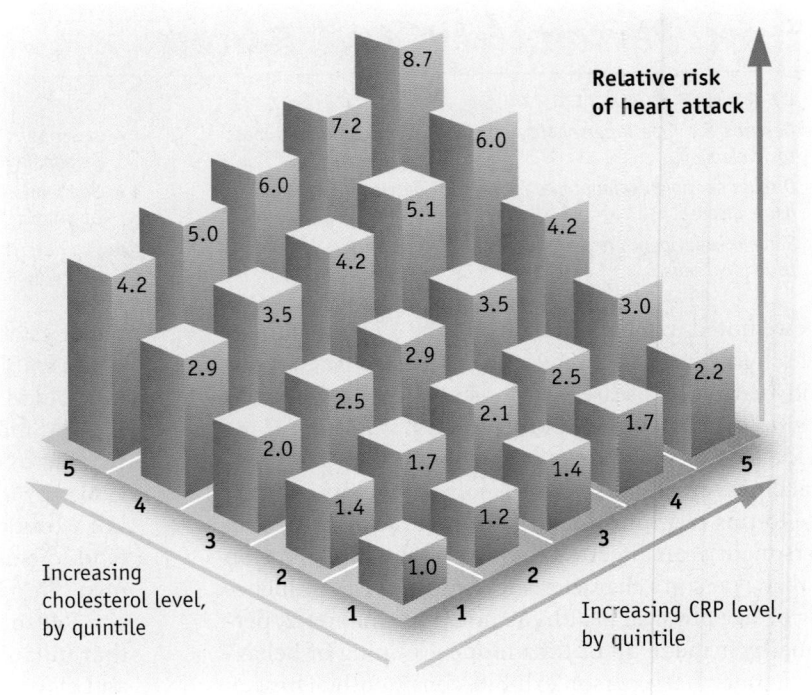

Hostility and Coronary Risk

In the 1960s and 1970s a pair of cardiologists, Meyer Friedman and Ray Rosenman (1974), were investigating the causes of coronary disease. Originally, they were interested in the usual factors thought to produce a high risk of heart attack: smoking, obesity, physical inactivity, and so forth. Although they found these factors to be important, they eventually recognized that a piece of the puzzle was missing. Many people who smoked constantly, got little exercise, and were severely overweight still managed to avoid the ravages of heart disease. Meanwhile, others who seemed to be in much better shape with regard to these risk factors experienced the misfortune of a heart attack. What was their explanation for these perplexing findings? Stress! Specifically, they identified an apparent connection between coronary risk and a pattern of behavior they called the *Type A personality,* which involves self-imposed stress and intense reactions to stress.

Friedman and Rosenman divided people into two basic types (Friedman, 1996; Rosenman, 1993). The ***Type A personality*** **includes three elements: (1) a strong competitive orientation, (2) impatience and time urgency, and (3) anger and hostility.** In contrast, the ***Type B personality*** **is marked by relatively relaxed, patient, easygoing, amicable behavior.** Type A's are ambitious, hard-driving perfectionists who are exceedingly time conscious. They routinely try to do several things at once. They fidget frantically over the briefest delays. They tend to be highly competitive, achievement-oriented workaholics who drive themselves with many deadlines. They are easily aggravated and get angry quickly. Type B's are less hurried, less competitive, and less easily angered than Type A's.

Decades of research uncovered a tantalizingly modest correlation between Type A behavior and increased coronary risk. More often than not, studies found an association between Type A personality and an elevated incidence of heart disease, but the findings were not as strong or as consistent as expected (Ragland & Brand, 1988; Smith & Gallo, 2001). However, in recent years, researchers have found a stronger link between personality and coronary risk by focusing on a specific component of the Type A personality: anger and hostility (Myrtek, 2007; Rozanski, Blumenthal, & Kaplan, 1999). ***Hostility*** **refers to a persistent negative attitude marked by cynical, mistrusting thoughts, feelings of anger, and overtly aggressive actions.** For example, in one study of almost 13,000 men and women who had no prior history of heart disease (Williams et al., 2000), investigators found an elevated incidence of heart attacks among participants who exhibited an angry temperament. The participants, who were followed for a median period of 4.5 years, were classified as being low (37.1%), moderate (55.2%), or high (7.7%) in anger. Among participants with normal blood pressure, the high-anger subjects experienced almost three times as many coronary events as the low-anger subjects (see **Figure 14.5**). In another study, CT scans were used to look for signs of atherosclerosis in a sample of 374

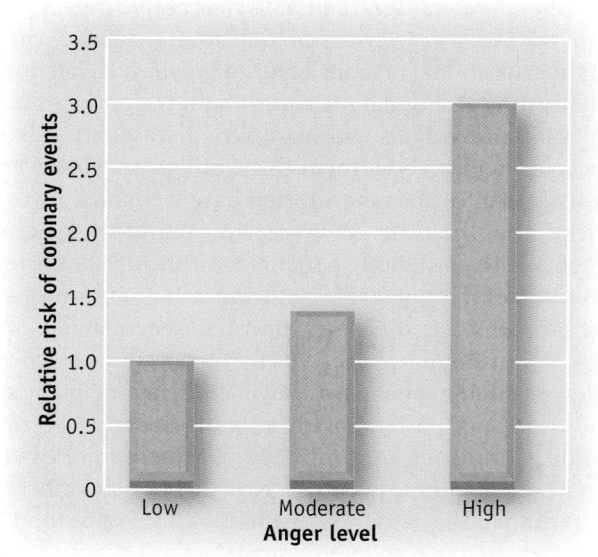

Figure 14.5

Anger and coronary risk. Working with a large sample of healthy men and women who were followed for a median of 4.5 years, Williams et al. (2000) found an association between trait anger and the likelihood of a coronary event. Among subjects who manifested normal blood pressure at the beginning of the study, a moderate anger level was associated with a 36% increase in coronary attacks, and a high level of anger nearly tripled participants' risk for coronary disease. (Based on data in Williams et al., 2000)

men and women whose cynical hostility had been assessed a decade earlier when they were 18 to 30 years old (Irabarren et al., 2000). Participants with above-average hostility scores were twice as likely to exhibit atherosclerosis as participants with below-average hostility scores.

Many other studies have also found an association between hostility and various aspects of cardiovascular disease (Eaker et al., 2004; Nelson, Franks, & Brose, 2005; Niaura et al, 2002), including CRP levels (Suarez, 2004). Thus, recent research trends suggest that hostility may be the crucial toxic element that accounts for the correlation between Type A behavior and heart disease. Interestingly, there is some evidence that hostility plays a greater role in cardiovascular risk for blacks than for whites. One recent study using a sample of healthy participants found that younger African Americans who exhibited high hostility showed a greater elevation in cardiovascular risk factors than a similar group of young white adults (Cooper & Waldstein, 2004). Another study found that African American men are at greater risk than African American women or white men (Scherwitz et al. 1991).

Why are anger and hostility associated with coronary risk? Research has uncovered a number of possible explanations (see **Figure 14.6**). First, anger-prone individuals appear to exhibit greater physiological reactivity than those who are lower in hostility (Smith & Gallo, 1999; Suarez et al., 1998). The frequent ups and downs in heart rate and blood pressure may create wear and tear in their cardiovascular systems.

Second, hostile people probably create additional stress for themselves (Smith, 2006; Smith & Gallo, 2001; Smith, Glazer, & Ruiz, 2004). For example, their quick anger may provoke many arguments and conflicts with others. Consistent with this line of thinking, Smith and colleagues (1988) found that subjects high in hostility reported more hassles, more negative life events, more marital conflict, and more work-related stress than subjects who were lower in hostility.

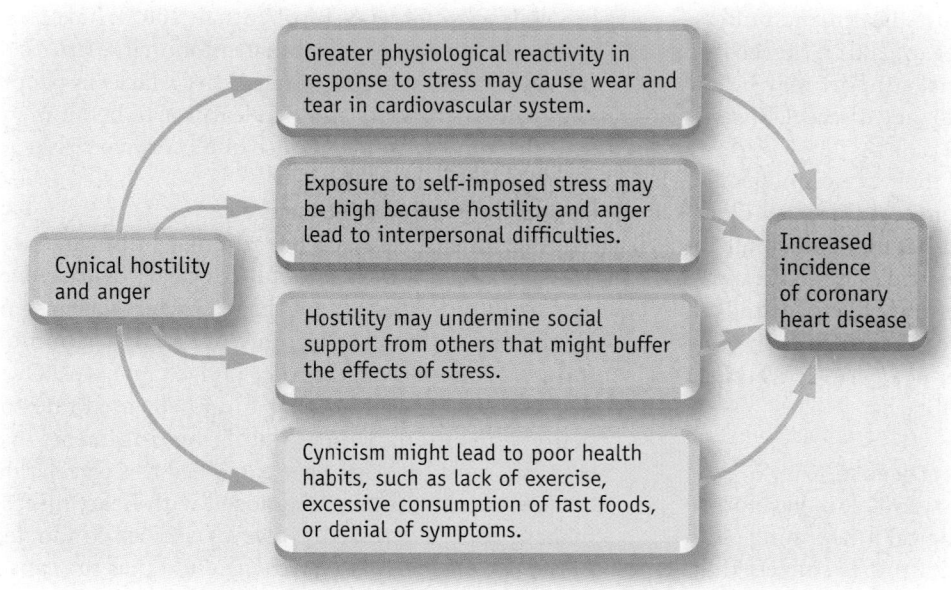

Figure 14.6

Mechanisms that may link hostility and anger to heart disease. Explanations for the apparent link between cynical hostility and heart disease are many and varied. Four widely discussed possibilities are summarized in the middle column of this diagram.

© Anabella Bluesky/Photo Researchers, Inc.

Research suggests that excessive anger and hostility are associated with an increased risk for various types of heart disease.

Third, thanks to their antagonistic ways of relating to others, hostile individuals tend to have less social support than others (Brummett et al., 2001; Chen, Gilligan, & Coups, 2005; Smith, 2003). Women who perceive little or no social support at home or at work are at greater risk for mortality due to a heart attack than other women (Kawachi et al., 1994). Living alone following a cardiac event actually increases a person's risk for a subsequent heart attack. Williams (1996), for example, found that single people or those who had no close friend with whom they could disclose private thoughts and concerns were three times more likely to die in a five-year period than those who had either a spouse or a close friend. As we noted in Chapter 3, research suggests that social support may be an important coping resource that promotes health and buffers the effects of stress (Wills & Fegan, 2001). Moreover, research indicates that low social support may be an independent risk factor for coronary disease (Rozanski, Blumenthal, & Kaplan, 1999).

Fourth, perhaps because of their cynicism, people high in anger and hostility seem to exhibit a higher prevalence of poor health habits that may contribute to the development of cardiovascular disease. For example, people high in hostility are more likely to smoke, drink alcohol and coffee, and be overweight than others (Everson et al., 1997; Siegler et al., 1992; Watkins, Ward, & Southard, 1992).

Emotional Reactions and Heart Disease

Although work on personality risk factors has dominated research on how psychological functioning contributes to heart disease, recent studies suggest that emotional reactions may also be critical. *One line of research has supported the hypothesis that transient mental stress and the resulting emotions that people experience can tax the heart.* Based on anecdotal evidence, cardiologists and laypersons have long voiced suspicions that strong emotional reactions might trigger heart attacks in individuals with coronary disease, but it has been difficult to document this connection. However, advances in cardiac monitoring have facilitated investigation of the issue. As suspected, laboratory experiments with cardiology patients have shown that brief periods of mental stress can trigger acute symptoms of heart disease, such as myocardial ischemia and angina (Gottdiener et al., 1994). Overall, the evidence suggests that mental stress can elicit ischemia in about 30%–70% of patients with ongoing heart problems (Kop, Gottdiener, & Krantz, 2001). Moreover, research indicates that these patients have a higher risk for heart attack than the cardiology patients who do not manifest ischemia in response to mental stress (Krantz et al., 2000).

Researchers have also examined the importance of emotional reactions by having patients keep a diary of their emotions while their cardiac functioning is monitored continuously as they go about their business. For example, Gullette and colleagues (1997) found that the likelihood of ischemia increased two- or threefold when people reported negative emotions, such as tension, frustration, and sadness. In another study, 660 patients who experienced a nonfatal myocardial infarction were subsequently interviewed about events that occurred in the 6 hours prior to the onset of their heart attack (Möller et al., 1999). The interviews suggested that episodes of anger were a frequent trigger for the participants' heart attacks. Consistent with this evidence, studies that have provided stress management training for coronary patients have shown promising results in efforts to reduce the likelihood of additional heart attacks (Claar & Blumenthal, 2003). Taken together, these studies suggest that emotional reactions to stressful events may precipitate heart attacks in people with coronary disease and that learning to better manage one's emotions may reduce one's coronary risk.

Depression and Heart Disease

Another line of research has recently implicated depression as a major risk factor for heart disease. *Depressive disorders,* which are characterized by persistent feelings of sadness and despair, are a fairly common form of psychological disorder (see Chapter 15). Over the years, many studies have found elevated rates of depression among patients suffering from heart disease, but most theorists have explained this correlation by asserting that being diagnosed with heart disease makes people depressed. However, studies conducted in the last decade or so have suggested that the causal relations may also flow in the opposite direction—*that the emotional dysfunction of depression may cause heart*

LIVING IN TODAY'S WORLD

Coping with Traumatic Events

A principal theme of this chapter is that stress can affect one's physical health. In today's world, a major new source of stress is living with the ominous threat of further terrorist attacks and the emotional fallout that results. Aware of these problems, a variety of health organizations have consulted their top experts and posted advice on the Internet about how to cope with terrorism-related anxiety and emotional reactions to traumatic events. The advice on these sites is fairly similar, with a great deal of overlap in content. The best overall list of suggested coping strategies, found at the website of the National Center for PTSD, is provided here. These strategies may be helpful in dealing with this new form of stress:

- Spend time with other people. Coping with stressful events is easier when people support each other.
- If it helps, talk about how you are feeling. Be willing to listen to others who need to talk about how they feel.
- Get back to your everyday routines. Familiar habits can be comforting.
- Take time to grieve and cry if you need to. To feel better in the long run, you need to let these feelings out instead of pushing them away or hiding them.
- Ask for support and help from your family, friends, church, or other community resources. Join or develop support groups.
- Eat healthy food and take time to walk, stretch, exercise, and relax, even if just for a few minutes at a time.
- Make sure you get enough rest and sleep. You may need more sleep than usual when you are highly stressed.
- Do something that just feels good to you, such as taking a warm bath, taking a walk, sitting in the sun, or petting your cat or dog.
- If you are trying to do too much, cut back by putting off or giving up a few things that are not absolutely necessary.
- If TV news reports get too distressing, turn them off and distract yourself by doing something you enjoy.

disease (Thomas, Kalaria, & O'Brien, 2004). For example, Pratt and colleagues (1996) examined a large sample of people 13 years after they were screened for depression. They found that participants who had been depressed at the time of the original study were four times more likely than others to experience a heart attack during the intervening 13 years. Because the participants' depressive disorders preceded their heart attacks, one cannot argue that their heart disease caused their depression. Overall, studies have found that depression roughly doubles one's chances of developing heart disease (Lett et al., 2004; Rudisch & Nemeroff, 2003). Moreover, depression also appears to influence how heart disease progresses, as it is associated with a worse prognosis among cardiology patients (Glassman et al., 2003). Although the new emphasis is on how depression contributes to heart disease, experts caution that the relationship between the two conditions is surely bidirectional and that heart disease also increases vulnerability to depression (Sayers, 2004).

Recent research suggests that the connection of depression to heart disease is more complex than previously realized. Anger, anxiety, and depression are all cited as predictors of cardiovascular disease, yet different researchers find different results. One explanation for the mixed findings involving these three emotional states is that how they are defined and measured involves considerable conceptual overlap. In other words, what looks like an effect attributable to anxiety in one study might be labeled anger or depression in another, and so on. A solution to this conceptual dilemma might be to explore how a general disposition towards negative emotions could be a better predictor of heart disease than any of the three variables alone (Suls & Bunde, 2005).

Stress and Cancer

If one single word can strike terror into most people's hearts, it is probably *cancer.* People generally view cancer as the most sinister, tragic, loathsome, and unbearable of diseases. In reality, cancer is actually a *collection* of over 200 related diseases that vary in their characteristics and amenability to treatment (Nezu et al., 2003). ***Cancer* refers to malignant cell growth, which may occur in many organ systems in the body.** The core problem in cancer is that cells begin to reproduce in a rapid, disorganized fashion. As this reproduction process lurches out of control, the teeming new cells clump together to form tumors. If this wild growth continues unabated, the spreading tumors cause tissue damage and begin to interfere with normal functioning in the affected organ systems.

It is widely believed by the general public that stress and personality play major roles in the development of cancer (McKenna et al., 1999). However, the research linking psychological factors to the *onset* of cancer is extremely weak. A few retrospective studies have found evidence that high stress precedes the development of cancer (Cohen, Kunkel, & Levenson, 1998; Katz & Epstein, 2005), but many others have failed to find any connection, and there is no convincing evidence that stress contributes to the causation of cancer (Newell, 1991; Petticrew, Fraser, & Regan, 1999).

Investigators have also attempted to determine whether there is a *cancer-prone personality* that might reflect unsuccessful patterns of coping with stress. The cancer-prone or "Type C" personality is described as someone who is very passive and rarely complains. Type C people are presumed to hold in their emotions to a great degree. This forced emotional inhibition is thought to be one reason such individuals are more likely to develop cancer than people who freely express their thoughts and feelings to others. Indeed, oncologists—physicians who specialize in the treatment of cancer—and other medical professionals have long observed that cancer patients tend to be "nice people"; perhaps their friendly or placid exteriors cover up considerable repressed emotion (Holland & Lewis, 1996). These studies have yielded some intriguing threads of consistency, but they must be viewed with great caution, given the possibility that someone's personality may change after discovering that he or she has cancer.

Although efforts to link psychological factors to the onset of cancer have largely failed, more convincing evidence has shown that stress and personality influence the *course* of the disease. The onset of cancer frequently sets off a chain reaction of stressful events (Andersen, Golden-Kreutz, & DiLillo, 2001). Patients typically have to grapple with fear of the unknown; difficult and aversive treatment regimens; nausea, fatigue, and other treatment side effects; dislocations in intimate relationships; career disruptions; job discrimination; and financial worries. Such stressors may often contribute to the progress of the disease, perhaps by impairing certain aspects of immune system functioning (Andersen, Kiecolt-Glaser, & Glaser, 1994). The impact of all this stress may depend in part on one's personality. Research suggests that mortality rates are somewhat higher among patients who respond with depression, repressive coping, and other negative emotions (Friedman, 1991). In contrast, prospects appear to be better for patients who can maintain their emotional stability and enthusiasm.

Stress and Other Diseases

The development of questionnaires to measure life stress has allowed researchers to look for correlations between stress and a variety of diseases. For example, Zautra and Smith (2001) found an association between life stress and the course of rheumatoid arthritis. Another study found an association between stressful life events and the emergence of lower back pain (Lampe et al., 1998). Other researchers have connected stress to the occurrence of asthmatic reactions (Ritz et al., 2000) and periodontal disease (Marcenes & Sheiham, 1992). Studies have also found an association between high stress and flareups of irritable bowel syndrome (Blanchard & Keefer, 2003) and peptic ulcers (Levenstein, 2002).

These are just a handful of representative examples of research relating stress to physical diseases. **Figure 14.7** provides a longer list of health problems that have been linked to stress. Many of these stress-illness connections are based on tentative or inconsistent findings, but the sheer length and diversity of the list is remarkable. Why should stress increase the risk for so many kinds of illness? A partial answer may lie in immune functioning.

Stress and Immune Functioning

The apparent link between stress and many types of illness probably reflects the fact that stress can undermine the body's immune functioning. **The *immune response* is the body's defensive reaction to invasion by bacteria, viral agents, or other foreign substances.** The human immune response works to protect the body from many forms of disease. Immune reactions are remarkably complex and multifaceted (Chiappelli & Liu, 2000). Hence, there are a great many ways to measure immune function in an organism, and these multiple measures can sometimes produce conflicting, confusing results in research.

Nonetheless, a wealth of studies indicate that experimentally induced stress can impair immune functioning *in animals* (Moynihan & Ader, 1996). That is, stressors such as crowding, shock, food restriction, and restraint reduce various aspects of immune reactivity in laboratory animals (Chiappelli & Hodgson, 2000). Of course, stress can affect animal immune function in natural settings, as well (Nelson & Demas, 2004).

Studies by Janice Kiecolt-Glaser and her colleagues have also related stress to suppressed immune activity *in humans* (Kiecolt-Glaser & Glaser, 1995). In one study, medical students provided researchers with

Health Problems That May Be Linked to Stress

Health Problem	Representative evidence
Common cold	Mohren et al. (2001)
Ulcers	Levenstein (2002)
Asthma	Lehrer et al. (2002)
Migraine headaches	Ramadan (2000)
Premenstrual distress	Stanton et al. (2002)
Vaginal infections	Williams & Deffenbacher (1983)
Herpes virus	Padgett & Sheridan (2000)
Skin disorders	Arnold (2000)
Rheumatoid arthritis	Keefe et al. (2002)
Chronic back pain	Lampe et al. (1998)
Diabetes	Landel-Graham, Yount, & Rudnicki (2003)
Complications of pregnancy	Dunkel-Schetter et al. (2001)
Hyperthyroidism	Yang, Liu, & Zang (2000)
Hemophilia	Buxton et al. (1981)
Stroke	Harmsen et al. (1990)
Appendicitis	Creed (1989)
Multiple sclerosis	Grant et al. (1989)
Periodontal disease	Marcenes & Sheiham (1992)
Hypertension	O'Callahan, Andrews, & Krantz (2003)
Cancer	Holland & Lewis (1993)
Coronary heart disease	Orth-Gomer et al. (2000)
AIDS	Ironson et al. (2000)
Inflammatory bowel disease	Searle & Bennett (2001)
Epileptic seizures	Kelly & Schramke (2000)

Figure 14.7

Stress and healh problems. The onset or progress of the health problems listed here *may* be affected by stress. Although the evidence is fragmentary in many instances, it's alarming to see the number and diversity of problems on this list.

blood samples so that their immune response could be assessed at various points (Kiecolt-Glaser et al., 1984). The students provided the baseline sample a month before final exams and contributed the "high-stress" sample on the first day of their finals. The subjects also responded to the Social Readjustment Rating Scale (SRRS; see Chapter 3) as a measure of recent stress. Reduced levels of immune activity were found during the extremely stressful finals week. Reduced immune activity was also correlated with higher scores on the SRRS. In another study, investigators exposed quarantined volunteers to respiratory viruses that cause the common cold and found that those under high stress were more likely to be infected by the viruses (Cohen, Tyrell, & Smith, 1993).

Courtesy, Janice Kiecolt-Glaser

Janice Kiecolt-Glaser

In a thorough review of 30 years of research on stress and immunity, Segerstrom and Miller (2004) conclude that chronic stress can reduce both *cellular immune responses* (which attack intracellular pathogens, such as viruses) and *humoral immune responses* (which attack extracellular pathogens, such as bacteria). They also report that the *duration* of a stressful event is a key factor determining its impact on immune function. Long-lasting stressors, such as caring for a seriously ill spouse or enduring unemployment for months, are associated with greater immune suppression than relatively brief stressors. Underscoring the importance of the link between stress and immune function, a recent study found evidence that chronic stress may produce *premature aging of immune system cells* (Epel et al., 2004). The study revealed that women who were dealing with heavy, long-term stress (caring for a child with a serious, chronic illness, such as cerebral palsy) had immune system cells that appeared to be a decade older than their chronological age, perhaps shedding light for the first time on why people under severe stress often look old and haggard. Unfortunately, evidence suggests that in the face of stress, people's immune systems do not fight off illness as well as they grow older (Graham, Christian, & Kiecolt-Glaser, 2006; Kiecolt-Glaser & Glaser, 2001). To summarize, scientists have assembled impressive evidence that stress can temporarily suppress human immune functioning, which can make people more vulnerable to infectious disease agents.

Conclusions

A wealth of evidence suggests that stress influences physical health. However, virtually all of the relevant research is correlational, so it cannot demonstrate conclusively that stress *causes* illness (Smith & Gallo, 2001; Watson & Pennebaker, 1989). The association between stress and illness could be due to a third variable. Perhaps some aspect of personality or some type of physiological predisposition makes people overly prone to

Web Link 14.2 **Centers for Disease Control and Prevention (CDC)**

The CDC is the federal agency charged with monitoring and responding to serious threats to the nation's health as well as taking steps to prevent illness. This site's "Health Information from A to Z" offers the public in-depth medical explanations of many health problems both common (flu, allergies) and unusual (fetal alcohol syndrome, meningitis).

Figure 14.8

The stress/illness correlation. Based on the evidence as a whole, most health psychologists would probably accept the assertion that stress often contributes to the causation of illness. However, some critics argue that the stress-illness correlation could reflect other causal processes. One or more aspects of personality, physiology, or memory might contribute to the correlation between high stress and a high incidence of illness (see Chapter 3 for additional discussion of this complex issue).

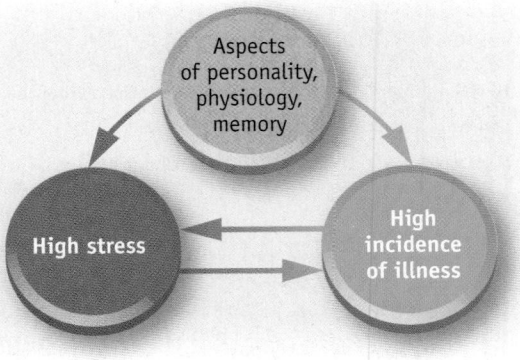

interpret events as stressful *and* overly prone to interpret unpleasant physical sensations as symptoms of illness (see **Figure 14.8**). For instance, in the Chapter 3 Application we discussed how neuroticism might increase individuals' sensitivity to both stress and illness. Moreover, critics of this research note that many of the studies used research designs that may have inflated the apparent link between stress and illness (Schwarzer & Schulz, 2003; Turner & Wheaton, 1995).

Despite methodological problems favoring inflated correlations, the research in this area consistently indicates that the *strength* of the relationship between stress and health is modest. The correlations typically fall in the .20s and .30s (Cohen, Kessler, & Gordon, 1995). Clearly, stress is not an irresistible force that produces inevitable effects on health. Actually, this fact should come as no surprise. As we saw in Chapter 3, some people handle stress better than others. Furthermore, stress is only one actor on a crowded stage. A complex network of biopsychosocial factors influence health, including genetic endowment, exposure to infectious agents and environmental toxins, nutrition, exercise, alcohol and drug use, smoking, use of medical care, and cooperation with medical advice. In the next section we look at some of these factors as we examine health-impairing habits and lifestyles.

Habits, Lifestyles, and Health

LEARNING OBJECTIVES

- *Give some reasons for why people develop health-impairing habits.*
- *Discuss the health effects of smoking and the dynamics of giving up smoking.*
- *Summarize data on patterns of alcohol use and the short-term risks of drinking.*
- *Describe the major long-term health risks and social costs of drinking.*
- *Discuss the health risks and determinants of obesity.*
- *Outline the key elements in effective weight loss efforts.*
- *Provide examples of links between nutrition and health and discuss the basis for poor nutrition.*
- *List three general goals intended to foster sound nutrition.*
- *Summarize evidence on the benefits and risks of exercise.*
- *List four guidelines for embarking on an effective exercise program.*
- *Describe AIDS and summarize evidence on the transmission of the HIV virus.*
- *Identify some common misconceptions about AIDS and discuss the prevention of AIDS.*

Some people seem determined to dig an early grave for themselves. They do precisely those things they have been warned are particularly bad for their health. For example, some people drink heavily even though they know they're corroding their liver. Others eat all the wrong foods even though they know they're increasing their risk for a heart attack. Unfortunately, health-impairing habits contribute to far more deaths than most people realize. In a recent analysis of the causes of death in the United States, Mokdad and colleagues (2004) estimate that unhealthy behaviors are responsible for about half of all deaths each year. The habits that account for the most premature mortality, by far, are smoking and poor diet/physical inactivity (see **Figure 14.9**). Other leading behavioral causes of death include alcohol consumption, unsafe driving, contracted sexually transmitted diseases, and illicit drug use.

It may seem puzzling that people behave in self-destructive ways. Why do they do it? Several factors are involved. First, many health-impairing habits creep up on people slowly. For instance, drug use may grow imperceptibly over years, or exercise habits may decline ever so gradually. Second, many health-impairing habits involve activities that are quite pleasant at the time. Actions such as eating favorite foods, smoking cigarettes, and getting "high" are potent reinforcing events. Third, the risks associated with most health-impairing habits are chronic diseases such as cancer that usually

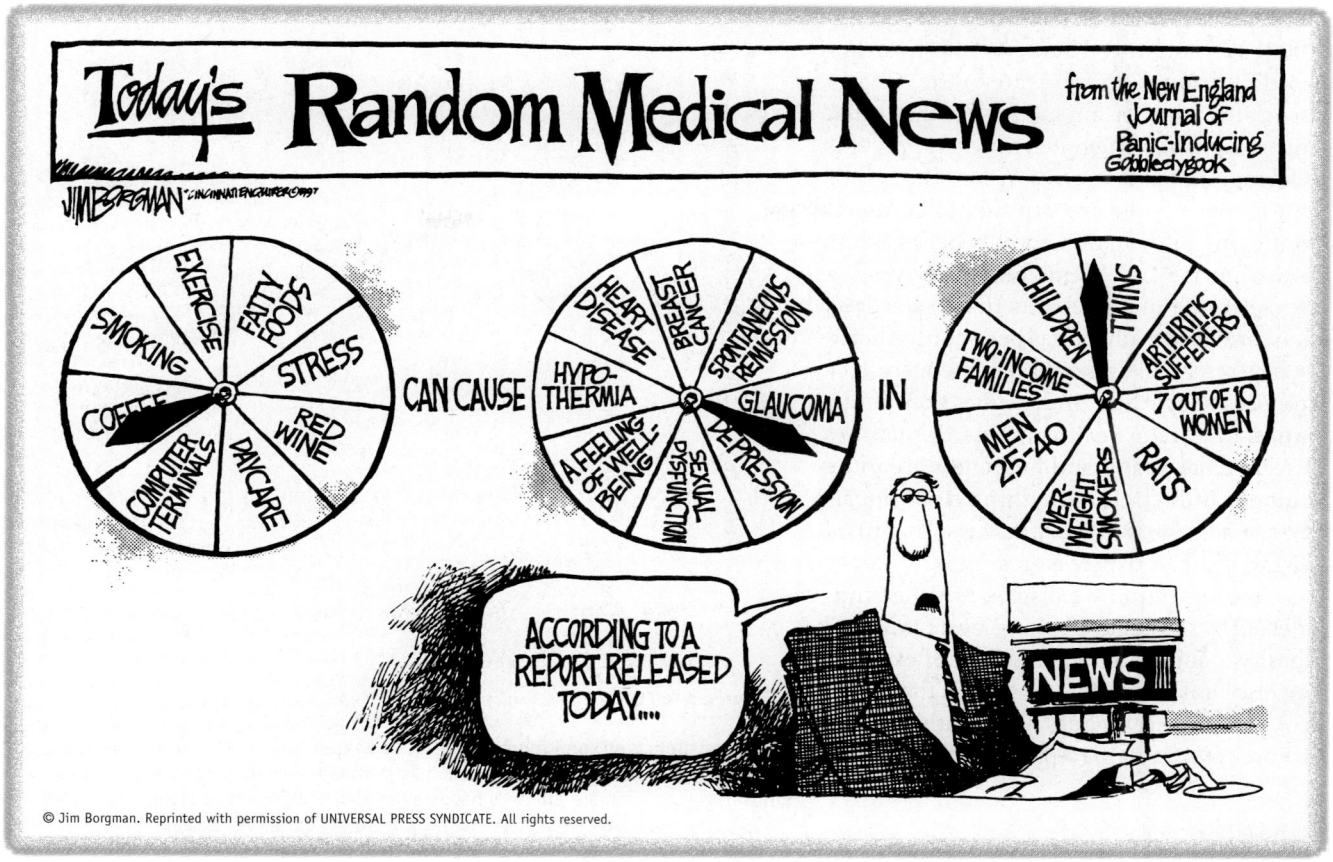

© Jim Borgman. Reprinted with permission of UNIVERSAL PRESS SYNDICATE. All rights reserved.

take 10, 20, or 30 years to develop. It is relatively easy to ignore risks that lie in the distant future. Fourth, it appears that *people have a tendency to underestimate the risks associated with their own health-impairing habits* while viewing the risks associated with others' self-destructive behaviors much more accurately (Weinstein,

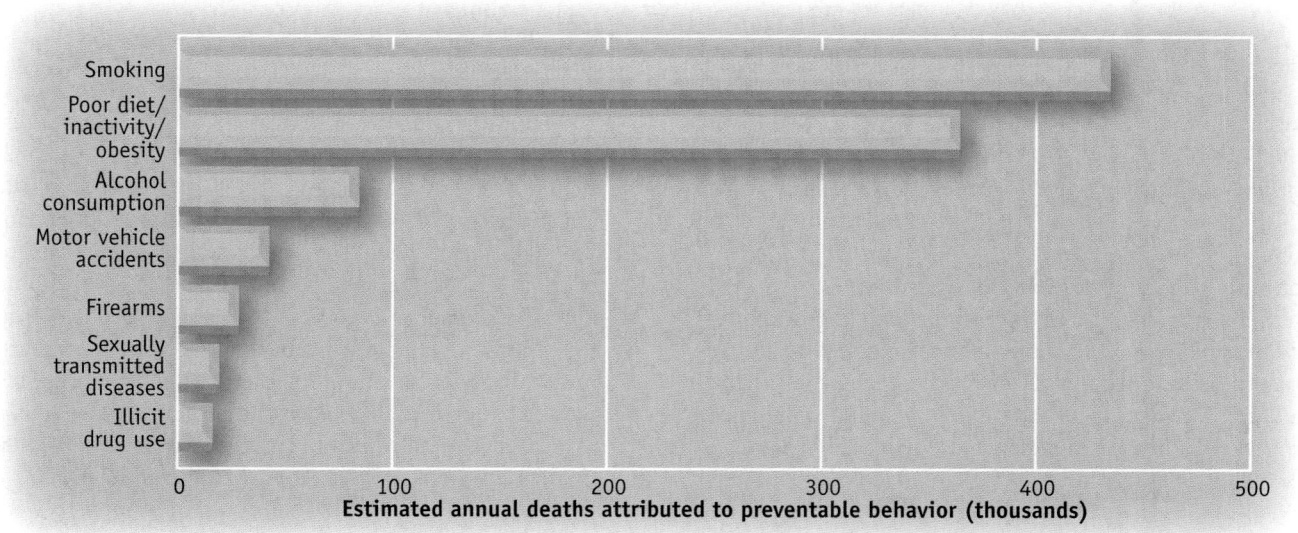

Figure 14.9

Mortality due to health-impairing behaviors. Synthesizing data from many sources, Mokdad and colleagues (2004) estimated the number of annual deaths in the United States attributable to various health-impairing behaviors in an article published in *The Journal of the American Medical Association.* As you can see, their calculations suggest that smoking and obesity are the leading causes of preventable mortality. However, their mortality estimate for obesity has proven controversial and is the subject of some debate (some experts argue that their estimate is too high). (Data from Mokdad et al., 2004)

2003; Weinstein & Klein, 1996). In other words, most people are aware of the dangers associated with certain habits, but they often engage in *denial* when it is time to apply this information to themselves. Yet another problem is that people are exposed to so much conflicting information about what's healthy and what isn't. It seems like every week a report in the media claims that yesterday's standard health advice has been contradicted by new research. This apparent inconsistency confuses people and undermines their motivation to pursue healthy habits. Sometimes it seems that health and happiness are more a matter of luck than anything else. In reality, the actions we take and the self-control we exercise can matter a great deal.

In this section we discuss how health is affected by smoking, drinking, overeating and obesity, poor nutrition, and lack of exercise. We also look at behavioral factors that relate to AIDS. The health risks of recreational drug use are covered in the Application.

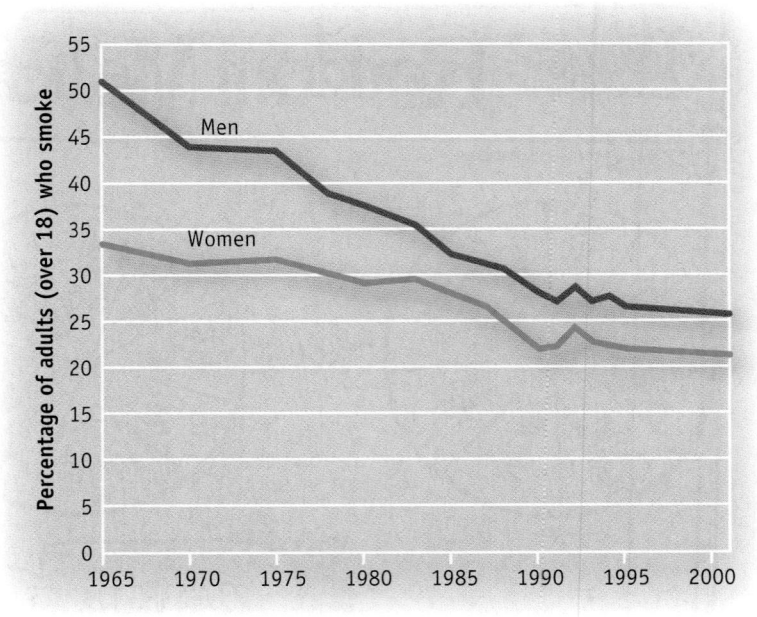

Figure 14.10

The prevalence of smoking in the United States. This graph shows how the percentage of U.S. adults who smoke has declined steadily since the mid-1960s. Although considerable progress has been made, smoking still accounts for about 435,000 premature deaths each year. (Data from Centers for Disease Control)

Smoking

The percentage of people who smoke has declined noticeably since the mid-1960s (see **Figure 14.10**). Nonetheless, about 25.7% of adult men and 21% of adult women in the United States continue to smoke regularly. Unfortunately, these percentages are slightly higher (28% for both sexes) among college students (Rigotti, Lee, & Wechsler, 2000). Moreover, smoking is even more common in many other societies.

Health Effects

Suspicions about the health risks associated with tobacco use were voiced in some quarters early in the 20th century. However, the risks of smoking were not widely appreciated until the mid-1960s. Since then, accumulating evidence has clearly shown that smokers face a much greater risk of premature death than nonsmokers. For example, the average smoker has an estimated life expectancy *13–14 years shorter* than that of a similar nonsmoker (Schmitz & Delaune, 2005). The overall risk is positively correlated with the number of cigarettes smoked and their tar and nicotine content. Cigar smoking, which has increased dramatically in recent years, elevates health risks almost as much as cigarette smoking (Baker et al., 2000).

Why are mortality rates higher for smokers? Smoking increases the likelihood of developing a surprisingly large range of diseases, as you can see in **Figure 14.11** (Schmitz & Delaune, 2005; Woloshin, Schwartz, & Welch, 2002). Lung cancer and heart disease kill the largest number of smokers. However, smokers also have an elevated risk for oral, bladder, and kidney cancer, as well as cancers of the larynx, esophagus, and pancreas; for atherosclerosis, hypertension, stroke, and other cardiovascular diseases; and for bronchitis, emphysema, and other pulmonary diseases. Most smokers know about the risks associated with tobacco use, but they tend to underestimate the actual risks as applied to themselves (Ayanian & Cleary, 1999) at the same time they overestimate the likelihood they can quit smoking when they want to (Weinstein, Slovic, & Gibson, 2004).

Web Link 14.3 **The QuitNet Community**

The Boston University School of Public Health sponsors an online community of individuals who seek to quit smoking and tobacco use. A range of excellent resources, including an online support "community" available 24 hours a day, can help make this behavioral health change a reality.

Giving Up Smoking

Studies show that if people can give up smoking, their health risks decline reasonably quickly (Williams et al., 2002). Five years after people stop smoking, their health risk is already noticeably lower than that for people who continue to smoke. The health risks for people who give up tobacco continue to decline until they reach a normal level after about 15 years (see

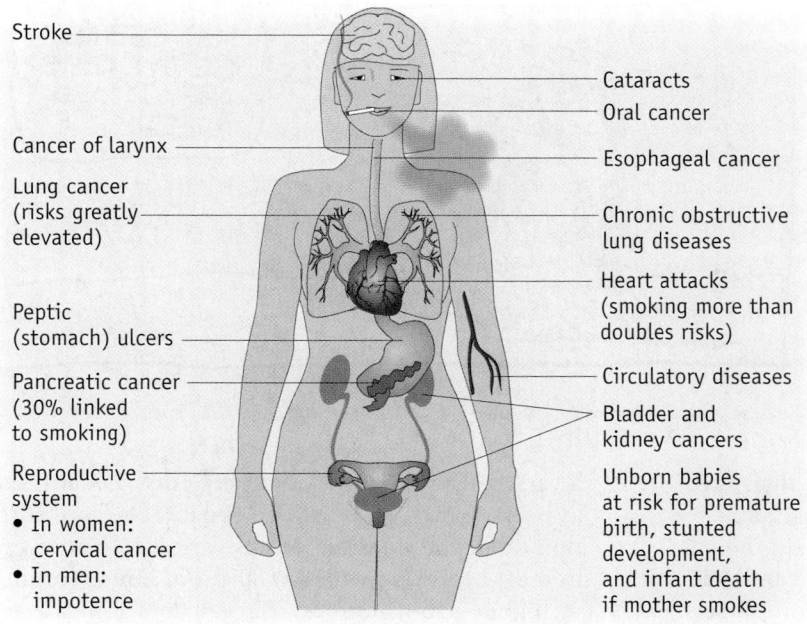

Figure 14.11

Health risks associated with smoking. This figure provides an overview of the various diseases that are more common among smokers than nonsmokers. As you can see, tobacco elevates one's vulnerability to a remarkably diverse array of diseases, including the three leading causes of death in the modern world—heart attack, cancer, and stroke.

Figure 14.12). Evidence suggests that 70% of smokers would like to quit, but they are reluctant to give up a major source of pleasure and they worry about craving cigarettes, gaining weight, becoming anxious and irritable, and feeling less able to cope with stress (Grunberg, Faraday, & Rahman, 2001).

There are nearly 40 million ex-smokers in the United States. Collectively, they clearly demonstrate that it is possible to give up smoking successfully. But many didn't succeed until their third, fourth, or fifth attempt, and most would testify that quitting isn't easy. Research shows that long-term success rates for efforts to quit smoking are in the vicinity of only 25% (Cohen et al., 1989). Light smokers are somewhat more successful at quitting than heavy smokers. Discouragingly, people who enroll in formal smoking cessation programs are only slightly more successful than people who try to quit on their own (Swan, Hudman, & Khroyan, 2003). In fact, it is estimated that the vast majority of people

Recommended READING

The Stop Smoking Workbook: The Definitive Step-by-Step Guide to Healthy Quitting
by Lori Stevic-Rust & Anita Maximin
(MJF Books, 1996)

The title says it all—this highly practical book is intended to help smokers through the challenging process of giving up tobacco. Written by two health psychologists, the book begins with a review of facts and myths about smoking, including a detailed review of the habit's physiological effects. Then the authors take the reader through a series of self-assessments intended to help them better understand when and why they smoke. The authors go on to outline strategies for setting a quit date and getting through the first few weeks. They also discuss how to deal with the urge to smoke and how to reduce the likelihood of relapse. The book is loaded with exercises and questionnaires that really make it something of a "workbook." The information is scientifically sound and the coverage of smoking-related issues is thorough.

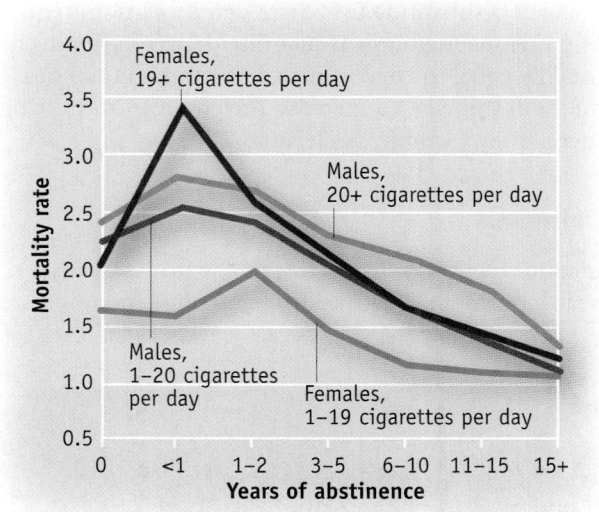

Figure 14.12

Quiting smoking and mortality. Research suggests that various types of health risks associated with smoking decline gradually after people give up tobacco. The data shown here, from the 1990 U.S. Surgeon General's report on smoking, illustrate the overall effects on mortality rates. The mortality rates on the vertical axis show how much death rates are elevated among smokers and ex-smokers in comparison to nonsmokers. For example, a mortality rate of 3.0 would mean that smokers' death rate was triple that of nonsmokers. (Data from U.S. Department of Health and Human Services, 1990)

© Tribune Media Services, Inc. All Rights Reserved. Reprinted with permission.

who successfully give up smoking quit on their own, without professional help (Niaura & Abrams, 2002).

In recent years attention has focused on the potential value of *nicotine substitutes,* which can be delivered via gum, skin patches, nasal sprays, or inhalers. The rationale for nicotine substitutes is that insofar as nicotine is addictive, using a substitute might be helpful during the period when the person is trying to give up cigarettes. Do these substitutes work? They do help. Controlled studies have demonstrated that nicotine substitutes increase long-term rates of quitting in comparison to placebos (Swan et al., 2003). However, the increases are modest and the success rates are still discouragingly low. Nicotine substitutes are not a magic bullet or a substitute for a firm determination to quit. The various methods of nicotine delivery seem to be roughly equal in effectiveness, but combining a couple methods appears to increase the chances of quitting successfully (Schmitz & Delaune, 2005).

Drinking

Alcohol rivals tobacco as one of the leading causes of health problems in Americans. Alcohol encompasses a variety of beverages containing ethyl alcohol, such as beers, wines, and distilled spirits. The concentration of alcohol in these drinks varies from about 4% in most beers up to 40% in 80-proof liquor (or more in higher-proof liquors). Survey data indicate that about half of adults in the United States drink. As **Figure 14.13** shows, per capita consumption of alcohol in the United States declined in the 1980s and 1990s, but this decrease followed decades of steady growth, and alcohol consumption remains relatively high, although certainly not the highest in the world.

Drinking is particularly prevalent on college campuses. When researchers from the Harvard School of Public Health (Wechsler et al., 2002) surveyed nearly 11,000 undergraduates at 119 schools, they found that 81% of the students drank. Moreover, 49% of the men and 41% of the women reported that they engage in binge drinking with the intention of getting drunk. Perhaps most telling, college students spend far more money on alcohol ($5.5 billion annually) than they do on their books.

© Topham/The Image Works

Overindulging in alcohol is particularly widespread among college students.

Why Do People Drink?

The effects of alcohol are influenced by the user's experience, relative size and weight, gender, motivation, and mood, as well as by the presence of food in the stomach, the proof of the beverage, and the rate of drinking. Thus, we see great variability in how alcohol affects different people on different occasions. Nonetheless, the central effect is a "Who cares?" brand of euphoria that temporarily boosts self-esteem as one's problems melt away. Negative emotions such as tension, worry, anxiety, and depression are dulled, and inhibitions may be loosened (Johnson & Ait-Daoud, 2005). Thus, when first-year college students are asked why they drink, they say it's to relax, to feel less tense in social situations, to keep friends company, and to forget their problems. Of course, many other factors are also at work (Wood, Vinson, & Sher, 2001). Families and peer groups often encourage alcohol use. Drinking is a widely endorsed and encouraged social ritual

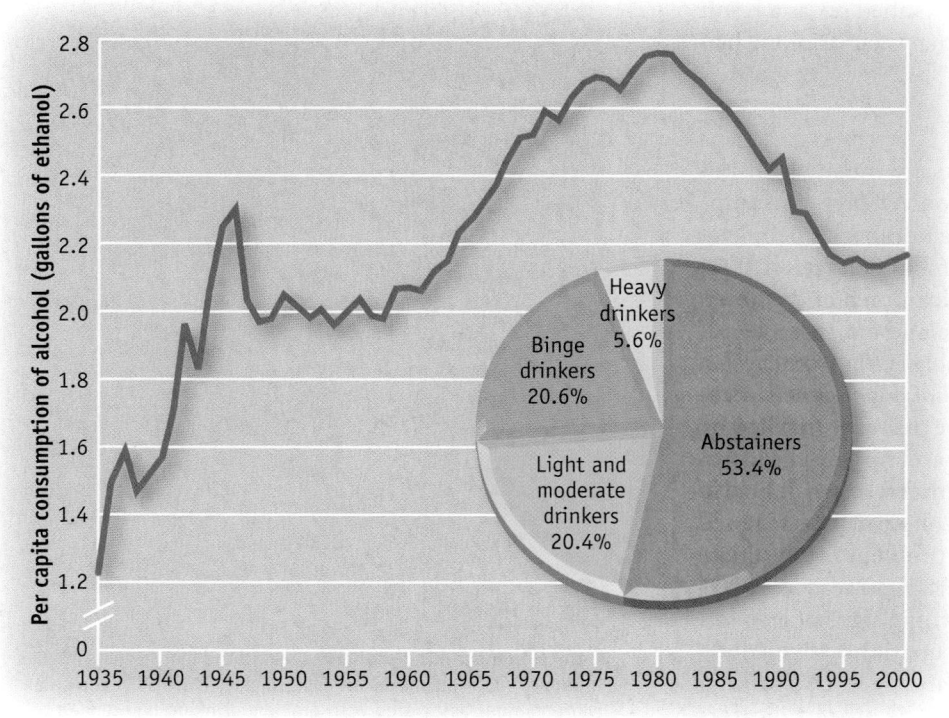

Figure 14.13

Drinking in America. Drinking in the United States, as indexed by per capita consumption (average consumed per person per year) of ethanol in gallons, rose steadily through most of the 20th century, although notable declines occurred during the 1980s and 1990s. The inset shows the percentage of American adults who are abstainers, light drinkers (one or two drinks on the same occasion in the past month), binge drinkers (people who have consumed five or more drinks on the same occasion at least once in the past month), and heavy drinkers (people who have consumed five or more drinks on the same occasion at least five times in the past month). The highest rates of binge drinking and heavy drinking are seen among young adults. (Data from National Institute on Alcohol Abuse and Alcoholism and U.S. Department of Health and Human Services)

in our culture. Its central role is readily apparent if you think about all the alcohol consumed at weddings, sports events, holiday parties, and so forth. Moreover, the alcohol industry spends hundreds of millions of dollars on advertising to convince us that drinking is cool, sexy, sophisticated, and harmless.

Short-Term Risks and Problems

Alcohol has a variety of side effects, including some that can be very problematic. To begin with, we have that infamous source of regret, the "hangover," which may include headaches, dizziness, nausea, and vomiting. In the constellation of alcohol's risks, however, hangovers are downright trivial. For instance, life-threatening overdoses are more common than most people realize. Although it's possible to overdose with alcohol alone, a more common problem is overdosing on combinations of alcohol and sedative or narcotic drugs.

In substantial amounts, alcohol has a decidedly negative effect on intellectual functioning and perceptual-motor coordination. The resulting combination of tainted judgment, slowed reaction time, and reduced coordination can be deadly when people attempt to drive after drinking. Depending on one's body weight, it may take only a few drinks for driving to be impaired. It's estimated that alcohol contributes to 30% of all automobile fatalities in the United States (Yi et al., 1999). Drunk driving is a major social problem and the leading cause of death in young adults. Alcohol is also implicated in many other types of accidents. Victims test positive for alcohol in 38% of fire fatalities, 49% of drownings, and 63% of fatal falls (Smith, Branas, & Miller, 1999).

With their inhibitions released, some drinkers become argumentative and prone to aggression. In the Harvard survey of undergraduates from 119 schools, 29% of the students who did *not* engage in binge drinking reported that they had been insulted or humiliated by a drunken student, 19% had experienced serious arguments, 9% had been pushed, hit, or assaulted, and 19.5% had been the target of unwanted sexual advances (Wechsler et al., 2002). Worse yet, alcohol appears to contribute to about 90% of student rapes and 95% of violent crime on campus. In society at large, alcohol is associated with a variety of violent crimes, including murder, assault, rape, child abuse, and intimate partner violence (Wood et al., 2001). The phrase "associated with" can also be interpreted literally: A recent study suggests that people become more aggressive when primed to think about alcohol and aggression in the absence of actual consumption (Bartholow & Heinze, 2006). In other words, people's perceptions about alcohol can matter as much as their consumption. Controlled research demonstrates alcohol can serve as a potential cue for aggression, especially among those people who subscribe to the cultural belief that drinking is linked to hostile behavior. Finally, alcohol can also contribute to reckless sexual behavior, which may have ramifications for one's health. In the Harvard survey, 21% of students who drank reported that they had unplanned sex as a result of drinking, and 10% indicated that their drinking had led to unprotected sex.

Long-Term Health Effects

Alcohol's long-term health risks are mostly (but not exclusively) associated with chronic, heavy consumption of alcohol. Estimates of the number of people at risk vary considerably. According to Schuckit (2000) approximately 5–10% of American men and women engage in chronic alcohol abuse and another 10% of men and 3–5% of women probably suffer from *alcohol dependence,* or *alcoholism.* ***Alcohol dependence (alcoholism)* is a chronic, progressive disorder marked by a growing compulsion to drink and impaired control over drinking that eventually interferes with health and social behavior.** Whether alcoholism is best viewed as a disease or as a self-control problem is the source of considerable debate, but experts have reached a reasonable consensus about the warning signs of alcoholism. These signs include preoccupation with alcohol, drinking to relieve uncomfortable feelings, gulping drinks, clandestine drinking, and the other indicators listed in **Figure 14.14**.

Alcoholism and problem drinking are associated with an elevated risk for a wide range of serious health problems, which are summarized in **Figure 14.15** (Mack, Franklin, & Frances, 2003; Moak & Anton, 1999). Although there is some thought-provoking evidence that moderate drinking may reduce one's risk for coronary disease (Chick, 1998; Mukamal et al., 2003), it is clear that heavy drinking increases the risk for heart disease, hypertension, and stroke. Excessive drinking is also correlated with an elevated risk for various types of cancer, including oral, stomach, pancreatic, colon, and

Warning Signs of Problem Drinking or Alcoholism

1. Gulping drinks.
2. Drinking to modify uncomfortable feelings.
3. Personality or behavioral changes after drinking.
4. Getting drunk frequently.
5. Experiencing "blackouts"—not being able to remember what happened while drinking.
6. Frequent accidents or illness as a result of drinking.
7. Priming—preparing yourself with alcohol before a social gathering at which alcohol is going to be served.
8. Not wanting to talk about the negative consequences of drinking (avoidance).
9. Preoccupation with alcohol.
10. Focusing social situations around alcohol.
11. Sneaking drinks or clandestine drinking.

Figure 14.14

Detecting a drinking problem. Facing the reality that one has a problem with alcohol is always difficult. This list of the chief warning signs associated with problem drinking is intended to help with this process.

Adapted from Edlin, G., & Golanty, E. (1992). *Health and wellness.* Boston: Jones & Bartlett. Copyright © 1992 Jones & Bartlett Publishers, Inc. Reprinted with permission.

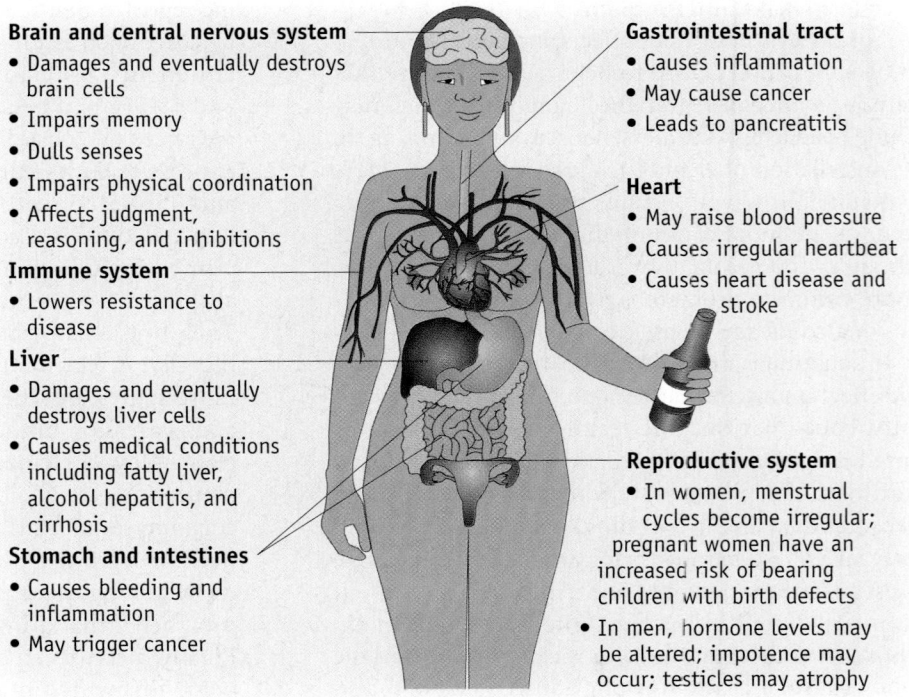

Figure 14.15

Health risks associated with drinking. This figure provides an overview of the various diseases that are more common among drinkers than abstainers. As you can see, alcohol elevates one's vulnerability to a remarkably diverse array of diseases.

Web Link 14.4 **National Institute on Alcohol Abuse and Alcoholism**

Just two of the many scientific research sources from this NIH agency include the entire collection of the bulletin *Alcohol Alert,* issued since 1988 on specific topics related to alcoholism (such as "Alcohol and Sleep" and "Youth Drinking") and the ETOH Database, a searchable repository of more than 100,000 records on alcoholism and alcohol abuse.

rectal cancer. Moreover, serious drinking problems can lead to cirrhosis of the liver, malnutrition, pregnancy complications, brain damage, and neurological disorders. Finally, alcoholism can produce severe psychotic states, characterized by delirium, disorientation, and hallucinations.

Overeating

Obesity is a common health problem. The criteria for obesity vary considerably. One simple, intermediate criterion is to classify people as obese if their weight exceeds their ideal body weight by 20%. If this criterion is used, 31% of men and 35% of women in the United States qualify as obese (Brownell & Wadden, 2000). Many experts prefer to assess obesity in terms of ***body mass index (BMI)*—weight (in kilograms) divided by height (in meters) squared (kg/m2).** This increasingly used index of weight controls for variations in height. A BMI of 25.0–29.9 is typically regarded as overweight, and a BMI over 30 is considered obese (Björntorp, 2002). Although American culture seems to be obsessed with slimness, recent surveys show surprisingly sharp increases in the incidence of obesity (Corsica & Perri, 2003). If a BMI over 25 is used as the cutoff, almost two-thirds of American adults are struggling with weight problems (Sarwer, Foster, & Wadden, 2004). Moreover, they have plenty of company from their children, as weight problems among children and adolescents have increased 15%–22% in recent decades (West et al., 2004).

Obesity is similar to smoking in that it exerts a relatively subtle impact on health that is easy for many people to ignore. Nevertheless, the long-range effects can be quite dangerous; obesity is a significant health problem that elevates one's mortality risk (Allison et al., 1999; Bender et al., 1999). In fact, obesity is probably responsible for the early deaths of well over a quarter of a million people in North America each year (DeAngelis, 2004). Overweight people are more vulnerable than others to heart disease, diabetes, hypertension, respiratory problems, gallbladder disease, stroke, arthritis, some cancers, muscle and joint pain, and back problems (Manson, Skerrett, & Willet, 2002; Pi-Sunyer, 2002). For example, **Figure 14.16** shows how the prevalence of diabetes, hypertension, coronary disease, and musculoskeletal pain are elevated as BMI increases.

Evolution-oriented researchers have a plausible explanation for the dramatic increase in the prevalence of obesity (Pinel, Assanand, & Lehman, 2000). They point out that over the course of history, most animals and humans have lived in environments in which there was fierce competition for limited, unreliable food resources and starvation was a very real threat. As a result, warm-blooded, foraging animals evolved a propensity to consume more food than immediately necessary when the opportunity presented itself because food might not be available later. Excess calories were stored in the body to prepare for food shortages. This approach to eating remains adaptive for most species of animals that continue to struggle with the ebb and flow of unpredictable food supplies. However, in today's modern, industrialized societies, the vast majority of humans live in environments that provide an abundant, reliable supply of tasty, high-calorie food. In these environments, humans' evolved tendency to overeat when food is plentiful leads most people down a pathway of chronic, excessive food consumption. According to this line of thinking, most people in food-replete environments tend to overeat in relation to their physiological needs, but because of variations in genetics, metabolism, and other factors only some become overweight.

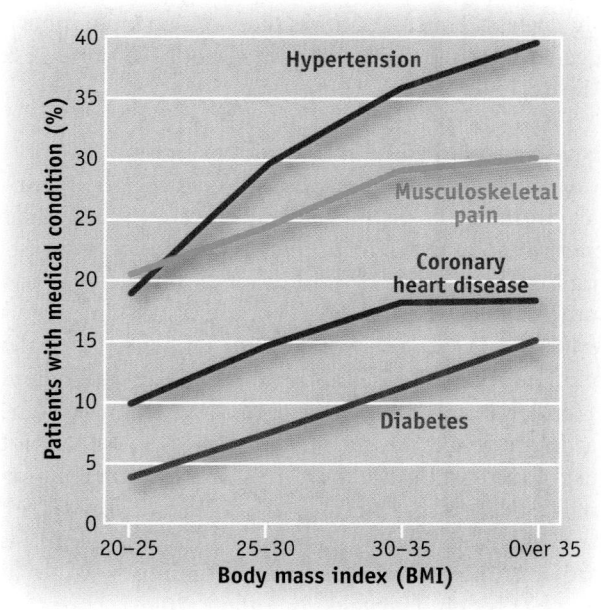

Figure 14.16

Weight and the prevalence of various diseases. This graph shows how obesity, as indexed by BMI, is related to the prevalence of four common types of illness. The prevalence of diabetes, heart disease, muscle pain, and hypertension increases as BMI goes up. Clearly, obesity is a significant health risk. (Data from Brownell & Wadden, 2000)

Determinants of Obesity

A few decades ago it was widely believed that obesity was a function of personality. Obesity was thought to occur mostly in depressed, anxious, compulsive people who overeat to deal with their negative emotions or in individuals who are lazy and undisciplined. However, research eventually showed that there is no such thing as an "obese personality" (Rodin, Schank, & Striegel-Moore, 1989). Instead, research showed that a complex network of interacting factors determine whether people develop weight problems.

Heredity. Chief among the factors contributing to obesity is *genetic predisposition* (Bouchard, 2002). In one influential study, adults raised by foster parents were compared with their biological and foster parents in regard to body mass index (Stunkard et al., 1986). The investigators found that the adoptees resembled their biological parents much more than their adoptive parents. In a subsequent *twin study,* Stunkard and associates (1990) found that identical twins reared apart were far more similar in body mass index than fraternal twins reared together (see Chapter 2 for a discussion of the logic underlying twin studies). Based on a study of over 4000 twins, Allison and colleagues (1994) estimate that genetic factors account for 61% of the variation in weight among men and 73% of the variation among women. These genetic factors probably explain why some people can eat constantly without gaining weight whereas other people grow chubby eating far less. Thus, it appears that some people inherit a genetic vulnerability to obesity (Cope, Fernandez, & Allison, 2004).

Excessive eating and inadequate exercise. The bottom line for overweight people is that their energy intake from food consumption chronically exceeds their energy expenditure from physical activities and resting metabolic processes. In other words, they eat too much in relation to their level of exercise (Wing & Polley, 2001). In modern America, the tendency to eat too much and to exercise too little is easy to understand (Henderson & Brownell, 2004). Tasty, caloric, high-fat foods are readily available nearly everywhere, not just in restaurants and grocery stores but in shopping malls, airports, gas stations, schools, and workplaces. And when people eat out, they tend to eat larger meals and consume more high-fat food than they would at home (French, Harnack, & Jeffery, 2000). Unfortunately, the increased availability of highly caloric food in America has been paralleled by declining physical activity. Modern conveniences, such as cars and elevators, and changes in the world of work, such as the shift to more desk jobs, have conspired to make American lifestyles more sedentary then ever before. Consider how much time the average person, child or adult, spends watching television, surfing the Internet, playing video games, or even chatting on the phone. Our private lives as well as our work lives promote sedentary comfort, so that many of the activities we engage in each day are more mental or physical. We work and play less with our bodies than past generations and a number of labor-saving devices improve our quality of life while they reduce the rate at which we obtain "natural" exercise that burns off calories.

Set point. People who lose weight on a diet have a rather strong (and depressing) tendency to gain back all the weight they lose. The reverse is also true: People who have to work to put weight on often have trouble keeping it on (Leibel, Rosenbaum, & Hirsch, 1995). According to Richard Keesey (1995), these observations suggest that each body may have a *set point,* or a natural point of stability in body weight. ***Set-point theory* proposes that the body monitors fat-cell levels to keep them (and weight) fairly stable.** When fat stores slip below a crucial set point, the body supposedly begins to compensate for this change (Keesey, 1993). This compensation apparently leads to increased hunger and decreased metabolism. Studies have raised some doubts about various details of set-point theory, leading some researchers to propose an alternative called *settling-point theory* (Pinel et al., 2000). ***Settling-point theory* proposes that weight tends to drift around the level at which the constellation of factors that determine food consumption and energy expenditure achieve an equilibrium.** According to this view, weight tends to remain stable as long as there are no durable changes in any of the factors that influence it (e.g., diet, exercise or the lack thereof, stress, sleep). Settling-point theory casts a much wider net than set-point theory, which attributes weight stability to specific physiological processes. Another difference is that set-point theory asserts that an obese person's body will initiate processes that actively defend an excessive weight, whereas settling-point theory suggests that if an obese person makes long-term changes in eating or exercise, that person's settling point will drift downward without active resistance. Thus, settling-point theory is a little more encouraging to those who hope to lose weight.

Socioeconomic factors. Obesity is caused by a combination of genetics, eating behavior, lifestyle issues, and a lack of exercise. What are the effects of social and economic factors, such as family characteristics, marital status, and education, on body weight? Regarding family factors separate from heredity, having obese relatives heightens one's risk for being overweight,. So does being married: single people, including those who were divorced or widowed, are less likely to have a weight problem (Kilicarslan et al., 2006). More years of education is associated with a lower incidence of obesity, while unemployment appears to be predictive of weight increases.

Losing Weight

Whether out of concern about their health or just old-fashioned vanity, an ever-increasing number of people are trying to lose weight. At any given time, about 21% of men and 39% of women are dieting (Hill, 2002). Research has provided some good news for those who need to lose weight. Studies have demonstrated that relatively modest weight reductions can significantly diminish many of the health risks associated with obesity. For example, a 10% weight loss is associated with reduced medical risks (Jeffery et al., 2000). Thus, the traditional objective of obesity treatment—reducing to one's ideal weight—has been replaced by more modest and realistic goals (Sarwer et al., 2004).

While many factors may contribute to obesity, there is only one way to lose weight. Individuals must change their ratio of energy intake (food consumption) to energy output (physical activities). To be quite specific, to lose one pound a person needs to burn up 3,500 more calories than he or she consumes. Those wanting to shed pounds have three options in trying to change their ratio of energy input to energy output: (1) sharply reduce food consumption, (2) sharply increase exercise output, or (3) simultaneously decrease food intake and step up exercise output in more moderate ways. Dieting alone is unlikely to be sufficient to lose weight and to maintain the loss (Jeffery et al., 2004). Virtually all experts recommend the third option. Brownell (1995) emphasizes that exercise is an essential ingredient of an effective weight-loss regimen. Exercise seems especially important for *maintaining* reduced weight, as it is the single best predictor of long-term weight loss (Curioni & Lourenco, 2005; Wing & Polley, 2001). Moreover, exercise can yield many other benefits, which we will discuss momentarily.

Weight Loss Through Persistence: Making Science Work for You
by Daniel S. Kirschenbaum
(New Harbinger, 1994)

If you want to lose weight, read this book. It is an excellent guide to weight reduction, written by a clinical psychologist affiliated with Northwestern University Medical School. The author knits together three of the themes emphasized in this chapter: the utility of behavioral control of overeating, the importance of having some rudimentary knowledge of nutrition, and the value of exercise. Kirschenbaum reviews some myths about the challenge of losing weight, then explains how people move through a series of stages of change along the way to successful persistence. A review of healthy eating strategies and sound nutritional principles is followed by a chapter on how to exercise effectively. Finally, Kirschenbaum outlines a plan for improved self-control and wraps up his coverage with a chapter on managing stress so that stress doesn't disrupt weight control efforts. A crucial theme throughout the book is that successful weight control is a lifetime project. This book, which is enlivened by an ample supply of case studies and exercises, is well written, scientifically sound, and extremely practical.

Self-modification techniques (see the Chapter 4 Application) can be helpful in achieving gradual weight loss. Indeed, behavior modification procedures represent the cornerstone of most reputable, professional weight-loss programs. Overall, the evidence on weight-loss programs suggests that they are moderately successful in the short term (the first 6 months), but in the long run the vast majority of people regain most of the weight that they lose (Jeffery et al., 2000).

CATHY Copyright © 1982 Cathy Guisewite. Reprinted with permission of UNIVERSAL PRESS SYNDICATE. All rights reserved.

Poor Nutrition

***Nutrition* is a collection of processes (mainly food consumption) through which an organism utilizes the materials (nutrients) required for survival and growth.** The term also refers to the *study* of these processes. Unfortunately, most of us don't study nutrition very much. Moreover, the cunning mass marketing of nutritionally worthless foods makes maintaining sound nutritional habits more and more difficult.

Nutrition and Health

Whether we like it or not, we are very much what we eat. Evidence is accumulating that patterns of nutrition influence susceptibility to a variety of diseases and health problems. For example, in a study of over 42,000 women, investigators found an association between a measure of overall diet quality and mortality. Women who reported poorer quality diets had elevated mortality rates (Kant et al., 2000). What are the specific links between diet and health? In addition to the problems associated with obesity, which we have already discussed, other possible connections between eating patterns and health include the following:

1. Heavy consumption of foods that elevate serum cholesterol level (eggs, cheeses, butter, shellfish, sausage, and the like) appears to increase the risk of cardiovascular disease (Stamler et al., 2000; see **Figure 14.17**). Eating habits are only one of several factors that influence serum cholesterol level, but they do make an important contribution.

2. Vulnerability to cardiovascular diseases may also be influenced by other dietary factors. For example, low-fiber diets may increase the likelihood of coronary disease (Ludwig et al., 1999; Wolk et al., 1999) and high intake of red and processed meats, sweets, potatoes, and refined grains is associated with increased cardiovascular risk (Hu & Willett, 2002). Recent research indicates that the omega 3 fatty acids found in fish and fish oils offer some protection against coronary disease (Din, Newby, & Flapan, 2004).

3. High salt intake is thought to be a contributing factor in the development of hypertension (Vollmer et al., 2001), although there is still some debate about its exact role.

4. High caffeine consumption may elevate one's risk for hypertension (James, 2004) and for coronary disease (Happonen, Voutilainen, Salonen, 2004), although the negative effects of caffeine appear relatively modest.

5. High-fat diets have been implicated as possible contributors to some forms of cancer, especially prostate cancer (Rose, 1997), colon and rectal cancer (Shike, 1999), and breast cancer (Wynder et al., 1997). Some studies also suggest that high-fiber diets may reduce one's risk for colon and rectal cancer (Reddy, 1999), but the evidence is not conclusive.

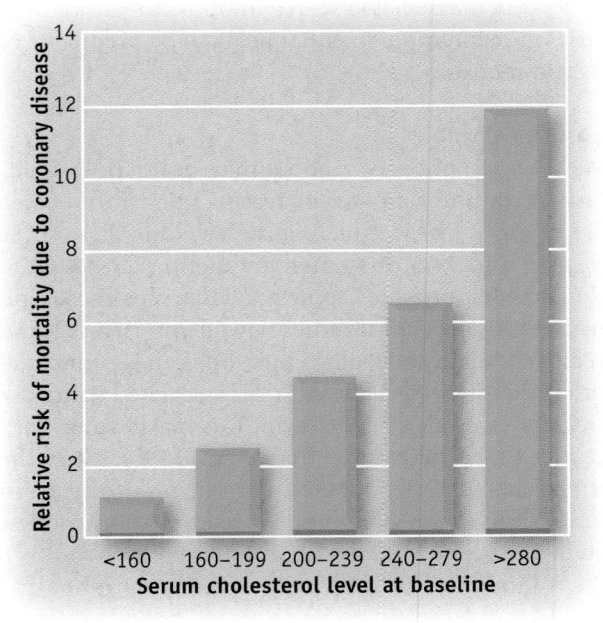

Figure 14.17

The link between cholesterol and coronary risk. In a review of several major studies, Stamler et al. (2000) summarize crucial evidence on the association between cholesterol levels and the prevalence of cardiovascular disease. This graph is based on a sample of over 11,000 men who were 18 to 39 at the beginning of the study (1967–1973) when their serum cholesterol level was measured. The data shown here depict participants' relative risk for coronary heart disease during the ensuing 25 years, as a function of their initial cholesterol level. (Data from Stamler et al., 2000)

6. Vulnerability to osteoporosis, an abnormal loss of bone mass observed most commonly in postmenopausal women, appears to be elevated by a lifelong pattern of inadequate calcium intake (Kalwarf, Khoury, Lanphear, 2003).

Of course, nutritional habits interact with other factors—genetics, exercise, environment, and so on—to determine whether someone will develop a particular disease. Nonetheless, the examples just described indicate that eating habits can influence physical health.

Web Link 14.5 **Go Ask Alice!**

One of the longest standing and most popular sources of frank information on the Net has been *Alice!* from Columbia University's Health Education Program. Geared especially to the needs of undergraduate students, *Alice!* offers direct answers to questions about relationships, sexuality and sexual health, fitness and nutrition, alcohol and drug consumption, emotional health, and general health.

The Basis for Poor Nutrition

Nutritional deficiencies are more widespread in the United States than most people realize. One study found that 70% of men and 80% of women consumed a diet deficient in at least one of 15 essential nutrients (Murphy et al., 1992). Another study found that young people from over 20 countries routinely ignore nutritional advice by consuming foods that are unhealthy (Wardle et al., 2004). For the most part, these deficiencies are not a result of low income or an inability to afford appropriate foods. Instead, most malnutrition in America is attributable to lack of knowledge about nutrition and lack of effort to ensure good nutrition (West et al., 2004).

In other words, our nutritional shortcomings are the result of ignorance and poor motivation. Americans are remarkably naive about the basic principles of nutrition. Schools tend to provide little education in this area, and most people are not highly motivated to make sure their food consumption is nutritionally sound. Instead, people approach eating very casually, guided not by nutritional needs but by convenience, palatability, and clever advertising.

For most people, then, the first steps toward improved nutrition involve changing attitudes and acquiring information. First and foremost, people need to recognize the importance of nutrition and commit themselves to making a real effort to regulate their eating patterns. Second, people should try to acquire a basic education in nutritional principles.

Nutritional Goals

The most healthful approach to nutrition is to follow well-moderated patterns of food consumption that ensure nutritional adequacy while limiting the intake of certain substances that can be counterproductive. Here are some general guidelines for achieving these goals:

1. *Consume a balanced variety of foods.* Food is made up of a variety of components, six of which are essential to your physical well-being. These six *essential nutrients* are proteins, fats, carbohydrates, vitamins, minerals, and fiber. Proteins, fats, and carbohydrates supply the body with its energy. Vitamins and minerals help release that energy and serve other important functions as well. Fiber provides roughage that facilitates digestion. Educational efforts to promote adequate intake of all essential nutrients have generally suggested that people should be guided by the classic food pyramid published by the U.S. Department of Agriculture (see **Figure 14.18**). Although the food pyramid remains a useful benchmark, it has been subjected to considerable criticism, and hotly debated revisions are under way (Norton, 2004). The principal

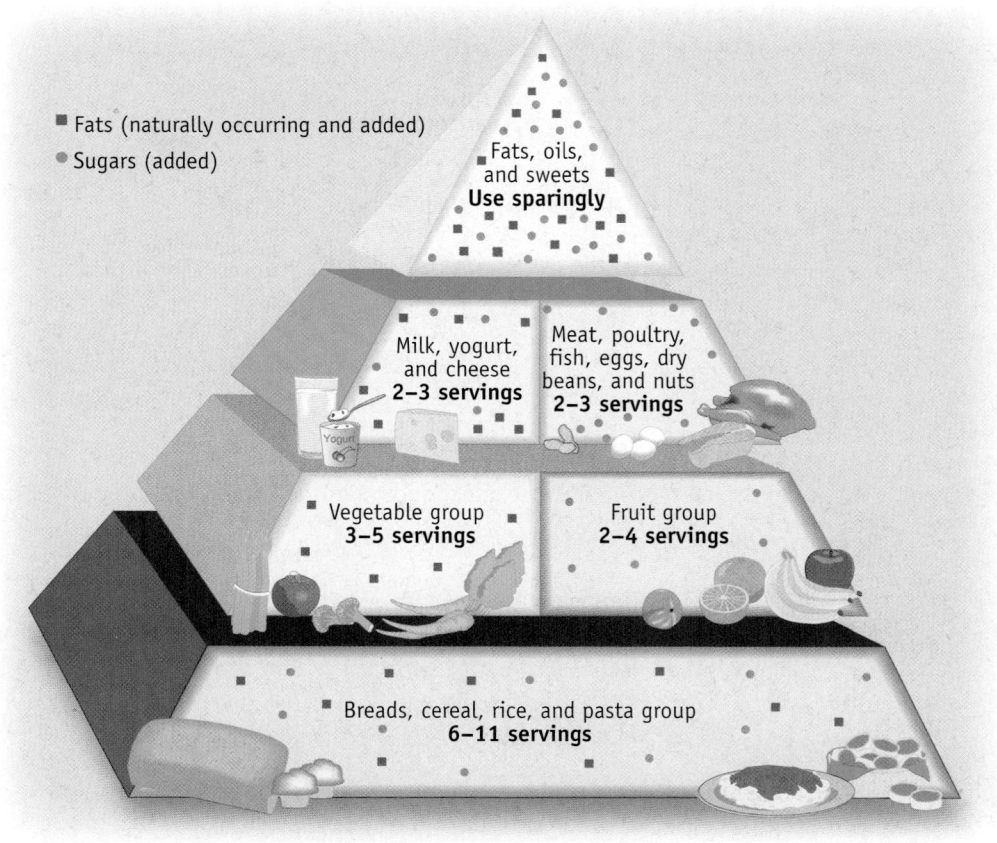

Figure 14.18

The food guide pyramid. The food pyramid, endorsed in 1992 by the U.S. Department of Agriculture, is intended to provide a simple and easy guide to nutritionally balanced eating. It identifies key categories of food and makes recommendations about how many daily servings one should have in each category. As your text explains, it has been subjected to criticism and currently is under revision.

Recommended READING

Eat, Drink, and Be Healthy: The Harvard Medical School Guide to Healthy Eating
by Walter C. Willett (Free Press, 2005)

Harvard Medical School professor Walter Willett is a renowned nutrition researcher who has written a superb book on healthy eating. Willett has been one of the more vocal critics of the food pyramid released by the U.S. Department of Agriculture in 1992. He asserts that "It was built on shaky scientific ground back in 1992. Since then it has been steadily eroded by new research from all parts of the globe" (pp. 15–16). Willett explains that the food pyramid was the product of extensive wrangling between scientists, bureaucrats, and special-interest lobbies, such as the meat, dairy, and sugar industries. Given all the compromises that were struck, it was never an optimal guide for healthy eating. Moreover, the food pyramid does not reflect many important, recent scientific findings on nutrition. Willett reviews these findings and their practical implications in an easy-to-understand, readable style. He sifts through the often contradictory evidence on nutrition and health and makes sense of it all. He describes an alternative healthy eating pyramid and then provides extensive advice on how to eat in a sensible manner.

problem with the food pyramid is its failure to distinguish between different types of fat, different forms of carbohydrates, and different sources of protein (Willett & Stampfer, 2003). For example, the current thinking is that monounsaturated and polyunsaturated fats are healthy, whereas saturated fats should be consumed sparingly. A revised food pyramid, which takes distinctions such as these into consideration, is shown in **Figure 14.19**.

2. *Avoid excessive consumption of saturated fats, cholesterol, refined-grain carbohydrates, sugar, and salt.* These commodities are all overrepresented in the typical American diet. It is particularly prudent to limit the intake of saturated fats by eating less beef, pork, ham, hot dogs, sausage, lunch meats, whole milk, and fried foods. Consumption of many of these foods should also be limited to reduce cholesterol intake, which influences vulnerability to heart disease. In particular, beef, pork, lamb, sausage, cheese, butter, and eggs are high in cholesterol. Refined-grain carbohydrates, such as white bread, pasta, and white rice, are problematic because they increase glucose levels in the blood too quickly. Refined (processed) sugar is believed to be grossly overconsumed. Hence, people should limit their dependence on soft drinks, chocolate, candy, pastries, and high-sugar cereals. Finally, many people should cut down on their salt intake. Doing so may require more than simply ignoring the salt shaker or passing

Figure 14.19

The healthy eating pyramid. This alternative food pyramid was developed by Walter Willett and colleagues at the Harvard Medical School. It corrects a variety of flaws that were apparent in the USDA food pyramid and incorporates recent scientific findings on healthy versus unhealthy fats and carbohydrates.

Adapted from Willett, W. C. (2001). *Eat, drink, and be healthy: The Harvard Medical School guide to healthy eating.* New York: Free Press. Copyright © 2001 by the President and Fellows at Harvard College. Adapted with permission of Simon & Schuster Adult Publishing Group.

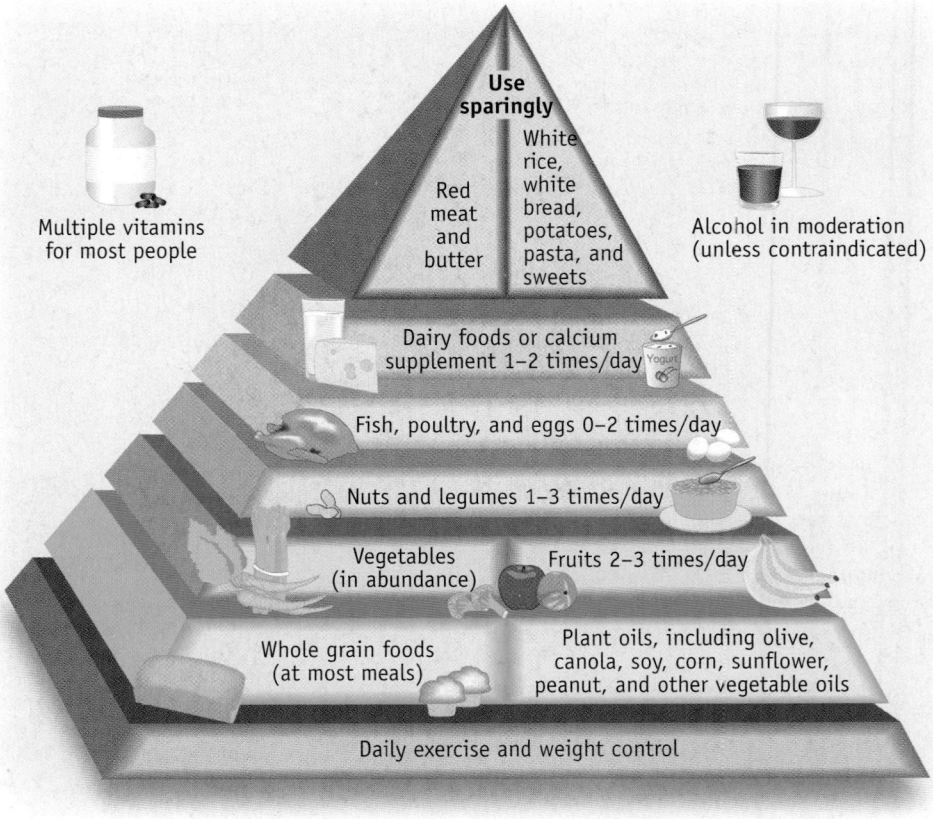

up the potato chips, since many prepackaged foods are loaded with salt.

3. *Increase consumption of polyunsaturated fats, whole-grain carbohydrates, natural sugars, and foods with fiber.* To substitute polyunsaturated fats for saturated ones, people can eat more fish, chicken, turkey, and veal; trim meats of fat more thoroughly; use skim (nonfat) milk; and switch to vegetable oils that are high in polyunsaturated fats. Healthy carbohydrates include whole-grain foods such as whole wheat bread, oatmeal, and brown rice, which are digested more slowly than refined-grain carbohydrates. Fruits and vegetables tend to provide natural sugars and ample fiber. Healthy sources of protein include fish, poultry, eggs, and nuts.

Web Link 14.6 **About.Com: Health and Fitness**

About.com is a commercial endeavor enlisting subject experts to edit topic-specific directories with annotated links and other information resources. More than 60 directories related to topics of health and fitness—including alcoholism, substance abuse, and smoking cessation—are now available at About.com.

Lack of Exercise

A great deal of evidence suggests that there is a link between exercise and health. Research indicates that regular exercise is associated with increased longevity (Lee & Skerrett, 2001). Moreover, you don't have to be a dedicated athlete to benefit from exercise. Even a moderate level of reasonably regular physical activity is associated with lower mortality rates (Richardson et al., 2004; see **Figure 14.20**). Unfortunately, physical fitness appears to be declining in the United States. Only 25% of American adults get an adequate amount of regular exercise (Dubbert et al., 2004).

Benefits and Risks of Exercise

Exercise is correlated with greater longevity because it promotes a diverse array of specific benefits. First, an appropriate exercise program can enhance cardiovascular fitness and thereby reduce one's susceptibility to cardiovascular problems (Caspersen et al., 1991). Fitness is associated with reduced risk for coronary disease, stroke, and hypertension (Blair, Cheng, & Holder, 2001; Lee et al., 2001). Second, regular physical activity can contribute to the avoidance of obesity (Corsica & Perri, 2003). Hence, fitness may indirectly reduce one's risk for a variety of obesity-related health problems, including diabetes, respiratory difficulties, arthritis, and back pain. Third, some recent studies suggest that physical fitness is also associated with a decreased risk for colon cancer and for breast and reproductive cancer in women (Thune & Furberg, 2001). The apparent link between exercise and reduced cancer risk has been a pleasant surprise for scientists, who are now scrambling to replicate the findings and figure out the physiological mechanisms underlying this association.

Fourth, exercise may serve as a buffer that reduces the potentially damaging effects of stress (Plante, Caputo, & Chizmar, 2000). This buffering effect may occur because people high in fitness show less physiological reactivity to stress than those who are less fit. Fifth, exercise may have a favorable impact on mental health, which in turn may have positive effects on physical health. Studies have found a consistent association between regular exercise over a period of at least eight weeks and reduced depression (Phillips, Kiernan, & King, 2001), which is important given the evidence that depression is correlated with increased vulnerability to heart disease. Sixth, successful participation in an exercise program can produce desirable personality changes that may promote physical wellness. Research suggests that fitness training can lead to improvements in one's mood, self-esteem, and work efficiency, as well as reductions in tension and anxiety (Dunn, Trivedi, & O'Neal, 2001; Hays, 1999; Sonstroem, 1997).

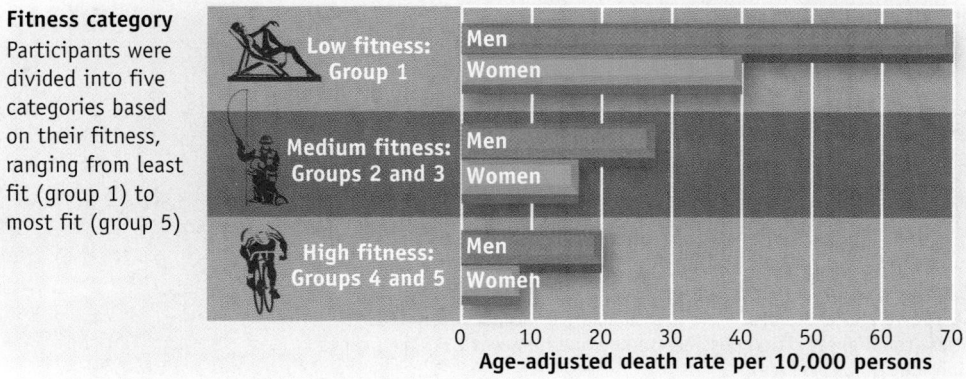

Figure 14.20

Physical fitness and mortality. Blair et al. (1989) studied death rates among men and women who exhibited low, medium, or high fitness. Even medium fitness was associated with lower mortality rates in both genders. The investigators note that one could achieve this level of fitness by taking a brisk half-hour walk each day. (Data from Blair et al., 1989)

Regular exercise has many physical and psychological benefits that promote increased longevity.

Devising an Exercise Program

Putting together a good exercise program is difficult for many people. Exercise is time consuming, and if you're out of shape, your initial attempts may be painful, aversive, and discouraging. People who do not get enough exercise cite lack of time, lack of convenience, and lack of enjoyment as the reasons (Jakicic & Gallagher, 2002). To circumvent these problems, it is wise to heed the following advice (Greenberg, 2002; Jakicic & Gallagher, 2002; Phillips et al., 2001):

1. *Look for an activity that you will find enjoyable.* You have a great many physical activities to choose from (see **Figure 14.21**). Shop around for one that you find intrinsically enjoyable. Doing so will make it much easier for you to follow through and exercise regularly.
2. *Increase your participation gradually.* Don't try to do too much too quickly. An overzealous approach can lead to frustration, not to mention injury. An exercise regimen should build gradually. If you experience injuries, avoid the common tendency to ignore them. Consult your physician to see whether continuing your exercise program is advisable.
3. *Exercise regularly without overdoing it.* Sporadic exercise will not improve your fitness. A widely cited rule of thumb is that you should plan on exercising for a minimum of 30 minutes three to five times a week, or you will gain little benefit from your efforts. At the other extreme, don't try to become fit overnight by

How Beneficial Is Your Favorite Sport?

Physical fitness	Jogging	Bicycling	Swimming	Skating (ice or roller)	Handball/ Squash	Skiing—Nordic	Skiing—Alpine	Basketball	Tennis	Calis-thenics	Walking	Golf	Softball	Bowling
Cardiorespiratory endurance (stamina)	21	19	21	18	19	19	16	19	16	10	13	8	6	5
Muscular endurance	20	18	20	17	18	19	18	17	16	13	14	8	8	5
Muscular strength	17	16	14	15	15	15	15	15	14	16	11	9	7	5
Flexibility	9	9	15	13	16	14	14	13	14	19	7	9	9	7
Balance	17	18	12	20	17	16	21	16	16	15	8	8	7	6
General well-being														
Weight control	21	20	15	17	19	17	15	19	16	12	13	6	7	5
Muscle definition	14	15	14	14	11	12	14	13	13	18	11	6	5	5
Digestion	13	12	13	11	13	12	9	10	12	11	11	7	8	7
Sleep	16	15	16	15	12	15	12	12	11	12	14	6	7	6
Total	**148**	**142**	**140**	**140**	**140**	**139**	**134**	**134**	**128**	**126**	**102**	**67**	**64**	**51**

Figure 14.21

A scorecard on the benefits of 14 sports and exercises. Here is a summary of how seven experts rated the value of 14 sports activities (the highest rating possible on any one item was 21). The ratings were based on vigorous participation four times per week.

Adapted from Conrad, C. C. (1976, May). How different sports rate in promoting physical fitness. *Medical Times,* pp. 45. Copyright 1976 by Romaine Pierson Publishers. Reprinted by permission.

working out too vigorously. One recent study found that people are more likely to stick to an exercise regimen consisting of more frequent workouts of moderate intensity than a regimen of less frequent but more intense workouts (Perri et al., 2002).

4. *Reinforce yourself for your participation.* To offset the inconvenience or pain that may be associated with exercise, it is a good idea to reinforce yourself for your participation. The behavior modification procedures discussed in Chapter 4 can be helpful in devising a viable exercise program.

5. *It's never too late to begin an exercise regimen.* Be forewarned: The number of people who engage in regular exercise declines with age (Phillips et al., 2001). Yet even modest regular exercise has pronounced health benefits, as has been shown in studies with participants well into their 70s, 80s, and 90s (Fiatrone et al., 1993; Raloff, 1996). As they age, people may believe that health declines are not only natural but inevitable (O'Brien & Vertinsky, 1991). A better and more apt belief is this one: Use it or lose it.

Behavior and AIDS

At present, some of the most problematic links between behavior and health may be those related to AIDS, a pandemic, or worldwide epidemic. AIDS stands for ***acquired immune deficiency syndrome,*** **a disorder in which the immune system is gradually weakened and eventually disabled by the human immunodeficiency virus (HIV).** Being infected with the HIV virus is *not* equivalent to having AIDS. AIDS is the final stage of the HIV infection process, typically manifested about 7–10 years after the original infection (Carey & Vanable, 2003). With the onset of AIDS, one is left virtually defenseless against a host of opportunistic infectious agents. The symptoms of AIDS vary widely depending on the specific constellation of diseases that one develops (Cunningham & Selwyn, 2005). Unfortunately, the worldwide prevalence of this deadly disease continues to increase at an alarming rate, especially in certain regions of Africa (De Cock & Janssen, 2002).

Prior to 1996–1997, the average length of survival for people after the onset of the AIDS syndrome was about 18 to 24 months. Encouraging advances in the treatment of AIDS with drug regimens referred to as *highly active antiretroviral therapy* hold out promise for *substantially* longer survival (Sande & Ronald, 2004). But these drugs are being rushed into service and their long-term efficacy is yet to be determined. Medical experts are concerned that the general public has gotten the impression that these treatments have transformed AIDS from a fatal disease to a manageable one, which is a premature conclusion. HIV strains are evolving, and many have developed resistance to the currently available antiretroviral drugs (Trachtenberg & Sande, 2002). Moreover, many patients do not respond well to the new drugs, and many who are responsive have difficulty sticking to the complicated drug administration regimens that often require people to take 20–30 pills daily and that often have adverse side effects (Catz & Kelly, 2001; Sorenson, Haug, & Batki, 2005). Another daunting problem is that these expensive new drugs remain largely unavailable in developing nations, which have not seen progress in treatment. In some African nations the impact of AIDS has reduced life expectancy to levels not seen for hundreds of years. In Botswana, for instance, projections suggest that life expectancy has declined from 66 to 33 years (Carey & Vanable, 2003).

Transmission

As mentioned in Chapter 13, the HIV virus is transmitted through person-to-person contact involving the exchange of bodily fluids, primarily semen and blood. The two principal modes of transmission in the United States have been sexual contact and the sharing of needles by intravenous (IV) drug users. In the United States, sexual transmission has occurred primarily among gay and bisexual men, but heterosexual transmission has increased in recent years (Catania et al., 2001). In the world as a whole, infection through heterosexual relations has been more common from the beginning. In heterosexual relations, male-to-female transmission is estimated to be about eight times more likely than female-to-male transmission (Ickovics, Thayaparan, & Ethier, 2001). The HIV virus can be found in the tears and saliva of infected individuals, but the concentrations are low, and there is no evidence that the infection can be spread through casual contact. Even most forms of noncasual contact, including kissing, hugging, and sharing food with infected individuals, appear safe (Kalichman, 1995).

Misconceptions

Misconceptions about AIDS are widespread. Ironically, the people who hold these misconceptions fall into two polarized camps. On the one hand, a great many people have unrealistic fears that AIDS can be readily transmitted through casual contact with infected individuals. These people worry unnecessarily about contracting AIDS from a handshake, a sneeze, or an eating utensil. They tend to be paranoid about interacting with homosexuals, thus fueling discrimination against gays. Some people also believe that it is dangerous to donate blood when, in fact, blood donors are at no risk whatsoever.

On the other hand, many young heterosexuals who are sexually active with a variety of partners foolishly downplay their risk for HIV, naively assuming that they are safe as long as they avoid IV drug use and sexual relations with gay or bisexual men. They greatly underestimate the probability that their sexual partners may have previously used IV drugs or had unprotected sex with an infected individual. They don't understand, for instance, that most bisexual men do not disclose their bisexuality to their female partners (Kalichman et al., 1998). Also, because AIDS is usually accompanied by discernible symptoms, many young people believe that prospective sexual partners who carry the HIV virus will exhibit telltale signs of illness. However, as we have already noted, having AIDS and being infected with HIV are not the same thing, and HIV carriers often remain healthy and symptom-free for many years after they are infected. In sum, many myths about AIDS persist, despite extensive efforts to educate the public about this complex and controversial disease. **Figure 14.22** contains a short quiz to test your knowledge of the facts about AIDS.

Prevention

The behavioral changes that minimize the risk of developing AIDS are fairly straightforward, although making the changes is often much easier said than done (Coates & Collins, 1998). In all groups, the more sexual partners a person has, the higher the risk that he or she will be exposed to the HIV virus. Thus, people can reduce their risk by having sexual contacts with fewer partners and by using condoms to control the exchange of semen. It is also important to curtail certain sexual practices (in particular, anal sex) that increase the probability of semen/blood mixing. The 1980s and early 1990s saw considerable progress toward wider use of safe sex practices and the evolution of prevention strategies (Wolitski, Henny, & Lyles, 2006), but new cohorts of young people appear to be much less concerned about the risk of HIV infection than the generation that witnessed the original emergence of AIDS (Catania et al., 2001). In particular, experts are concerned that recent advances in treatment may lead to more casual attitudes about risky sexual practices, a development that would not bode well for public health efforts to slow the spread of AIDS (Cabaj, 2006; Crepaz, Hart, & Marks, 2004). This false sense of security among young adults may have dire consequences in the long run unless they adopt prevention practices and an attitude of vigilance. Indeed, by the year 2015, fully half of all cases of HIV/AIDS in the United States are projected to be among adults who are 50 and older (Centers for Disease Control, 2006).

Figure 14.22

A quiz on knowledge of AIDS. Because misconceptions about AIDS abound, it may be wise to take this brief quiz to test your knowledge.

Adapted from Kalichman, S. C. (1995). *Understanding AIDS: A guide for mental health professionals.* Washington, DC: American Psychological Association. Copyright © 1995 by the American Psychological Association. Adapted with permission of the publisher and author.

AIDS Risk Knowledge Test

Answer the following "true" or "false."

T	F	**1.** The AIDS virus cannot be spread through kissing.
T	F	**2.** A person can get the AIDS virus by sharing kitchens and bathrooms with someone who has AIDS.
T	F	**3.** Men can give the AIDS virus to women.
T	F	**4.** The AIDS virus attacks the body's ability to fight off diseases.
T	F	**5.** You can get the AIDS virus by someone sneezing, like a cold or the flu.
T	F	**6.** You can get AIDS by touching a person with AIDS.
T	F	**7.** Women can give the AIDS virus to men.
T	F	**8.** A person who got the AIDS virus from shooting up drugs cannot give the virus to someone by having sex.
T	F	**9.** A pregnant woman can give the AIDS virus to her unborn baby.
T	F	**10.** Most types of birth control also protect against getting the AIDS virus.
T	F	**11.** Condoms make intercourse completely safe.
T	F	**12.** Oral sex is safe if partners "do not swallow."
T	F	**13.** A person must have many different sexual partners to be at risk for AIDS.
T	F	**14.** It is more important to take precautions against AIDS in large cities than in small cities.
T	F	**15.** A positive result on the AIDS virus antibody test often occurs for people who do not even have the virus.
T	F	**16.** Only receptive (passive) anal intercourse transmits the AIDS virus.
T	F	**17.** Donating blood carries no AIDS risk for the donor.
T	F	**18.** Most people who have the AIDS virus look quite ill.

Answers: 1. T 2. F 3. T 4. T 5. F 6. F 7. T 8. F 9. T 10. F 11. F 12. F 13. F 14. F 15. F 16. F 17. T 18. F

Reactions to Illness

LEARNING OBJECTIVES

- *Summarize evidence on patterns of treatment-seeking behavior.*
- *Explain the appeal of the "sick role."*
- *Identify the factors that tend to undermine doctor-patient communication and how to improve it.*
- *Discuss the prevalence of nonadherence to medical advice and its causes.*

So far we have emphasized the psychosocial aspects of maintaining health and minimizing the risk of illness. Health is also affected by how individuals respond to physical symptoms and illnesses. Some people engage in denial and ignore early-warning signs of developing diseases. Others engage in active coping efforts to conquer their diseases. In this section, we discuss the decision to seek medical treatment, the sick role, communication with health providers, and compliance with medical advice.

The Decision to Seek Treatment

Have you ever experienced nausea, diarrhea, stiffness, headaches, cramps, chest pains, or sinus problems? Of course you have; everyone experiences some of these problems periodically. However, whether you view these sensations as *symptoms* is a matter of individual interpretation. When two persons experience the same unpleasant sensations, one may shrug them off as a nuisance, while the other may rush to a physician (Leventhal, Cameron, & Leventhal, 2005; Martin & Leventhal, 2004). Studies suggest that those who are relatively high in anxiety and neuroticism tend to report more symptoms of illness than others do (Feldman et al., 1999). Those who are extremely attentive to bodily sensations and health concerns also report more symptoms than the average person (Barsky, 1988).

Variations in the perception of symptoms help explain why people vary so much in their readiness to seek medical treatment (Cameron, Leventhal, & Leventhal, 1993). Generally, people are more likely to seek medical care when their symptoms are unfamiliar, appear to be serious, last longer than expected, or disrupt their work or social activities (Bernard & Krupat, 1994; Martin et al., 2003). Another key consideration is how friends and family react to the symptoms. Medical consultation is much more likely when friends and family view symptoms as serious and encourage the person to seek medical care, although nagging a person about seeking care can sometimes backfire (Martin et al., 2003). Gender also influences decisions to seek treatment, as women are much more likely than men to utilize medical services (Bertakis et al., 2000). Finally, age matters: Young children (age 5 and under) and older adults (late middle age and beyond) are more likely to utilize health services (U.S. Department of Health and Human Services, 1995). These facts should not be surprising, especially in the case of young children, who often experience frequent illnesses and vaccinations and have parents or caregivers who take them for frequent checkups. As we already know, older folks seek medical attention for chronic health issues (see Chapter 11).

The process of seeking medical treatment can be divided into three stages of active, complex problem solving (Martin et al., 2003). First, people have to decide that their physical sensations *are* symptoms—that they are indicative of illness. Second, they have to decide that their apparent illness warrants medical attention. Third, they have to go to the trouble to make the actual arrangements for medical care, which can be complicated and time consuming. The task of checking insurance coverage, finding an appropriate doctor, negotiating an appointment, arranging to get off work or take care of children, and so forth can be a huge series of hassles.

Courtesy, Robin DiMatteo

Robin DiMatteo

Small wonder then, that the biggest problem in regard to treatment seeking is the tendency of many people to delay the pursuit of needed professional consultation. Delays can be important, because early diagnosis and quick intervention can facilitate more effective treatment of many health problems. Unfortunately, procrastination is the norm even when people are faced with a medical emergency, such as a heart attack (Martin & Leventhal, 2004). Why do people dawdle in the midst of a crisis? Robin DiMatteo (1991) mentions a number of reasons, noting that people delay because they often (1) misinterpret and downplay the significance of their symptoms, (2) fret about looking silly if the problem turns out to be nothing, (3) worry about "bothering" their physician, (4) are reluctant to disrupt their plans (to go out to dinner, see a movie, and so forth), and (5) waste time on trivial matters (such as taking a shower, gathering personal items, or packing clothes) before going to a hospital emergency room. In short, people must recognize that the symptoms are serious and then they must exert considerable effort to get medical attention. Regrettably, even minor events or distractions can impede their progress (Anderson, Cacioppo, & Roberts, 1995).

The Sick Role

Although many people tend to delay medical consultations, some people are actually eager to seek medical care. Given this reality, it is not surprising that up to 60% of patients' visits to their primary care physicians appear to have little medical basis (Ellington & Wiebe, 1999). Many of the people who are quick to solicit medical assistance probably have learned that there are potential benefits in adopting the "sick role" (Hamilton, Deemer, & Janata, 2003; Lubkin, 1990). For instance, the sick role absolves people from responsibility for their incapacity and can be used to exempt them from many of their normal duties and obligations (Segall, 1997). Fewer demands are placed on sick people, who can often be selective in deciding which demands to ignore. Illness can provide a convenient, face-saving excuse for one's failures (Wolinksky, 1988). Sick people may also find themselves receiving lots of attention (affection, concern, sympathy) from friends and relatives. This positive attention can be rewarding and can encourage the maintenance of symptoms (Walker, Claar, & Garber, 2002).

Thus, some people grow to *like* the sick role, although they may not be aware of it. Such people readily seek professional care, but they tend to behave in subtle ways that prolong their illness (Kinsman, Dirks, & Jones, 1982). For example, they may only pretend to go along with medical advice, a common problem that we discuss momentarily.

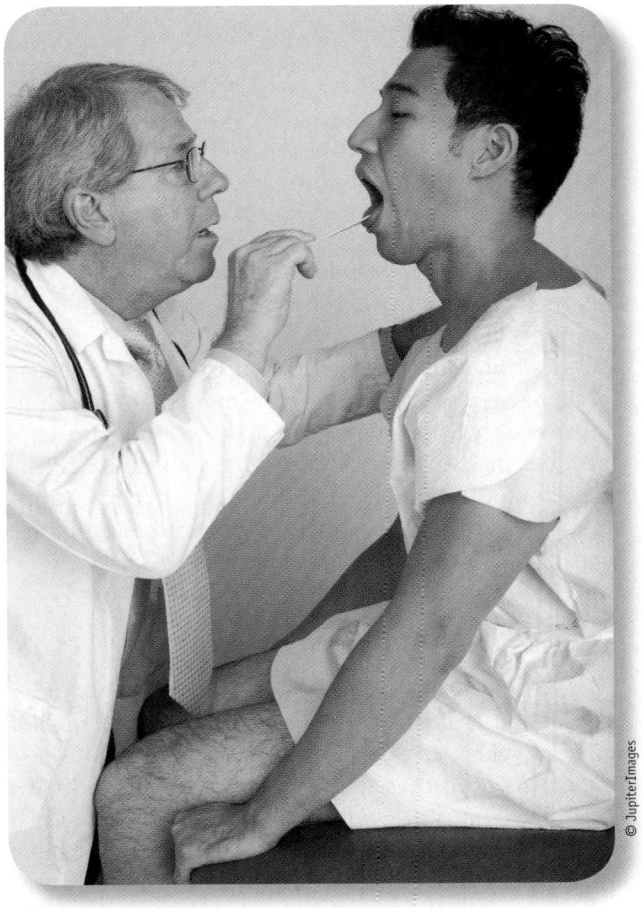

Communication between health care providers and patients tends to be far from optimal for a variety of reasons.

Communicating with Health Providers

When people seek help from physicians and other health care providers, many factors can undermine effective communication. A large portion of medical patients leave their doctors' offices not understanding what they have been told and what they are supposed to do (Johnson & Carlson, 2004). This situation is unfortunate, because good communication is a crucial requirement for sound medical decisions, informed choices about treatment, and appropriate follow-through by patients (Buckman, 2002; Gambone, Reiter, & DiMatteo, 1994).

There are many barriers to effective provider-patient communication (Beisecker, 1990; DiMatteo, 1997). Economic realities dictate that medical visits be generally quite brief, allowing little time for discussion. Illness and pain are subjective matters that may be difficult to describe. Many providers use too much medical jargon and overestimate their patients' understanding of technical terms. Some providers are uncomfortable being questioned and discourage their patients' information seeking. Patients who are upset and worried about their illness may simply forget to report some symptoms or to ask questions they meant to ask. Other patients are evasive about their real concerns because they fear a serious diagnosis. Many patients are reluctant to challenge doctors' authority and are too passive in their interactions with providers. Doctors and nurses often believe their explanations are clear; however, patient misunderstanding can be a common phenomenon, one posing particular problems for individuals whose instructions regarding diagnosis, treatment, and medication are complex (Parker, 2000).

Web Link 14.7 **MedFriendly**

Do you ever wonder what complicated medical terms really mean? Have you tried to read a medical report from a doctor and found yourself not knowing what the doctor was talking about? The MedFriendly site may be your answer in its often humorous, but always clear and helpful definitions of many terms, concepts, and abbreviations used in medicine and health care generally.

Adherence to Medical Advice

Many patients fail to adhere to the instructions they receive from physicians and other health care professionals. The evidence suggests that noncompliance with medical advice may occur 30% of the time when short-term treatments are prescribed for acute conditions and 50% of the time when long-term treatments are needed for chronic illness (Johnson & Carlson, 2004). Nonadherence takes many forms. Patients may fail to begin a treatment regimen, stop the regimen early, reduce or increase the levels of treatment that were prescribed, or be inconsistent and unreliable in following treatment procedures (Dunbar-Jacob & Schlenk, 2001). Nonadherence is a major problem that has been linked to increased sickness, treatment failures, and higher mortality (Christensen & Johnson, 2002; DiMatteo et al., 2002). Moreover, nonadherence wastes expensive medical visits and medications and increases hospital admissions, leading to enormous economic costs. Robin DiMatteo (2004b) speculates that in the United States alone, nonadherence may be a $300 billion a year drain on the health care system.

Why don't people comply with the advice that they've sought out from highly regarded health care professionals? Physicians tend to attribute noncompliance to patients' personal characteristics, but research indicates that personality traits and demographic factors are surprisingly unrelated to adherence rates (DiMatteo, 2004b). One factor that *is* related to adherence is patients' *social support.* Adherence is improved when patients have family members, friends, or co-workers who remind them and help them to comply with treatment requirements (DiMatteo, 2004a). Another factor is a sense of self-efficacy—patients will adhere to recommendations they believe in and believe they are capable of performing (DiMatteo, 1994). Here are some other considerations that influence the likelihood of adherence (Dunbar-Jacob & Schlenk, 2001; Johnson & Carlson, 2004):

1. *Frequently, noncompliance is due to patients simply forgetting instructions or failing to understand the instructions as given.* Highly trained professionals often forget that what seems obvious and simple to them may be obscure and complicated to many of their patients.

2. *Another key factor is how aversive or difficult the treatments are.* If the prescribed regimen is unpleasant, compliance will tend to decrease. For example, adherence is reduced when prescribed medications have many severe side effects. And the more that following instructions interferes with routine behavior, the less likely it is that the patient will cooperate successfully.

3. *If a patient has a negative attitude toward a physician, the probability of noncompliance will increase.* When patients are unhappy with their interactions with the doctor, they're more likely to ignore the medical advice provided.

In response to the noncompliance problem, researchers have investigated many methods of increasing patients' adherence to medical advice. Interventions have included simplifying instructions, providing more rationale for instructions, reducing the complexity of treatment regimens, helping patients with emotional distress that undermines adherence, and training patients in the use of behavior modification strategies. All of these interventions can improve adherence, although their effects tend to be modest (Christensen & Johnson, 2002; Roter et al., 1998).

APPLICATION

Understanding the Effects of Drugs

LEARNING OBJECTIVES

- *Explain the concepts of drug tolerance, physical and psychological dependence, and overdose.*
- *Summarize the main effects and risks of narcotics and sedatives.*
- *Summarize the main effects and risks of stimulant drugs and hallucinogens.*
- *Summarize the main effects and risks of marijuana and ecstasy (MDMA).*

Answer the following "true" or "false."

___ **1.** Smoking marijuana can make men impotent and sterile.

___ **2.** Overdoses caused by cocaine are relatively rare.

___ **3.** It is well documented that LSD causes chromosome damage.

___ **4.** Hallucinogens are addictive.

___ **5.** Ecstasy is a relatively harmless drug.

As you will learn in this Application, all of these statements are false. If you answered all of them accurately, you may already be well informed about drugs. If not, you *should* be. Intelligent decisions about drugs require an understanding of their effects and risks.

This Application focuses on the use of drugs for their pleasurable effects, commonly referred to as *drug abuse* or *recreational drug use.* Drug abuse reaches

Web Link 14.8 **National Institute on Drug Abuse (NIDA)**

This government-sponsored site houses a great deal of information on the medical consequences of abusing various drugs. It also is an excellent resource for statistics on trends in drug abuse.

into every corner of our society and is a problematic health-impairing habit. Although small declines appear to have occurred in the overall abuse of drugs in recent years, survey data show that illicit drug use has mostly been increasing since the 1960s (Winick & Norman, 2005).

Like other controversial social problems, recreational drug use often inspires more rhetoric than reason. For instance, a former president of the American Medical Association made headlines when he declared that marijuana "makes a man of 35 sexually like a man of 70." In reality, the research findings do not support this assertion. This influential physician later retracted his statement, admitting that he had made it simply to campaign against marijuana use (Leavitt, 1995). Unfortunately, such scare tactics can backfire by undermining the credibility of drug education efforts.

Recreational drug use involves personal, moral, political, and legal issues that are not matters for science to resolve. However, the more knowledgeable you are about drugs, the more informed your decisions and opinions about them will be. Accordingly, this Application is intended to provide you with nonjudgmental, realistic coverage of issues related to recreational drug use. We begin by reviewing key drug-related concepts. Then we examine the effects and risks of five types of widely abused drugs: narcotics, sedatives, stimulants, hallucinogens, and marijuana. We wrap up our coverage with a brief discussion of ecstasy (MDMA), which has stirred up controversy in recent years.

Drug-Related Concepts

The principal types of recreational drugs are described in **Figure 14.23**. This table lists representative drugs in each of the five categories and indicates how the drugs are taken, their principal medical uses, their desired effects, and their common side effects.

Most drugs produce tolerance effects. ***Tolerance* is a progressive decrease in a person's responsiveness to a drug with continued use.** Tolerance effects usually lead people to consume larger and larger doses of a drug to attain the effects they desire. Tolerance builds more rapidly to some drugs than to others. The first column in **Figure 14.24** indicates whether various categories of drugs tend to produce rapid or gradual tolerance.

In evaluating the potential problems associated with the use of specific drugs, a key consideration is the likelihood of either physical or psychological dependence. Although both forms of drug dependence have a physiological basis (Di Chiara, 1999; Self, 1998), important differences exist between the two syndromes. ***Physical dependence* exists when a person must continue to take a drug to avoid withdrawal ill-**

Recreational drug users come from all ages and all walks of life.

© Image 100/Alamy Images

Comparison of Major Categories of Abused Drugs

Drugs	Methods of administration	Principal medical uses	Desired effects	Short-term side effects
Narcotics (opiates) Morphine Heroin	Injected, smoked, oral	Pain relief	Euphoria, relaxation, anxiety reduction, pain relief	Lethargy, drowsiness, nausea, impaired coordination, impaired mental functioning, constipation
Sedatives Barbiturates (e.g., Seconal) Nonbarbiturates (e.g., Quaalude)	Oral, injected	Sleeping pill, anticonvulsant	Euphoria, relaxation, anxiety reduction, reduced inhibitions	Lethargy, drowsiness, severely impaired coordination, impaired mental functioning, emotional swings, dejection
Stimulants Amphetamines Cocaine	Oral, sniffed, injected, freebased, smoked	Treatment of hyperactivity and narcolepsy; local anesthetic (cocaine only)	Elation, excitement, increased alertness, increased energy, reduced fatigue	Increased blood pressure and heart rate, increased talkativeness, restlessness, irritability, insomnia, reduced appetite, increased sweating and urination, anxiety, paranoia, increased aggressiveness, panic
Hallucinogens LSD Mescaline Psilocybin	Oral		Increased sensory awareness, euphoria, altered perceptions, hallucinations, insightful experiences	Dilated pupils, nausea, emotional swings, paranoia, jumbled thought processes, impaired judgment, anxiety, panic reaction
Cannabis Marijuana Hashish THC	Smoked, oral	Treatment of glaucoma; other uses under study	Mild euphoria, relaxation, altered perceptions, enhanced awareness	Bloodshot eyes, dry mouth, reduced memory, sluggish motor coordination, sluggish mental functioning, anxiety

Figure 14.23

Major categories of abused drugs. This chart summarizes the methods of ingestion, chief medical uses, and principal effects of five major types of recreational drugs. Alcohol is covered in the main body of the chapter. (Based on Julien, 2001; Levinthal, 2002; Lowinson, et al., 2005)

ness (which occurs when drug use is terminated). The symptoms of withdrawal illness (also called abstinence syndrome) vary depending on the drug. Withdrawal from heroin and barbiturates can produce fever, chills, tremors, convulsions, seizures, vomiting, cramps, diarrhea, and severe aches and pains. The agony of withdrawal from these drugs virtually compels addicts to continue using them. Withdrawal from stimulants leads to a different and somewhat milder syndrome dominated by fatigue, apathy, irritability, depression, and disorientation.

Psychological dependence **exists when a person must continue to take a drug to satisfy intense mental and emotional craving for it.** Psychological dependence is more subtle than physical dependence, as it is not marked by a clear withdrawal reaction. However, psychological dependence can create a powerful, overwhelming need for a drug. The two types of dependence often coexist—that is, many people manifest both psychological and physical dependence on a specific drug. Both types of dependence are established gradually with repeated use of a drug. However, specific drugs vary greatly in their potential for creating dependence. The second and third columns in **Figure 14.24** provide estimates of the risk of each kind of dependence for the drugs covered in our discussion.

Risks Associated with Major Categories of Abused Drugs

Drugs	Tolerance	Risk of physical dependence	Risk of psychological dependence	Fatal overdose potential
Narcotics (opiates)	Rapid	High	High	High
Sedatives	Rapid	High	High	High
Stimulants	Rapid	Moderate	High	Moderate to high
Hallucinogens	Gradual	None	Very low	Very low
Cannabis	Gradual	None	Low to moderate	Very low

Figure 14.24

Specific risks for various categories of drugs. This chart shows estimates of the risk potential for tolerance, dependence, and overdose for the five major categories of drugs discussed in this Application.

An *overdose* is an excessive dose of a drug that can seriously threaten one's life. Any drug can be fatal if a person takes enough of it, but some drugs carry more risk of overdose than others. In **Figure 14.24**, column 4 estimates the risk of accidentally consuming a lethal overdose of various drugs. Drugs that are central nervous system (CNS) depressants—narcotics and sedatives—carry the greatest risk of overdose. It's important to understand that the effects of these drugs are additive. Many overdoses involve lethal *combinations* of CNS depressants. What happens when people overdose on these drugs? Their respiratory system usually grinds to a halt, producing coma, brain damage, and death within a brief period. In contrast, fatal overdoses with CNS stimulants (cocaine and amphetamines) usually involve a heart attack, stroke, or cortical seizure.

Now that our basic vocabulary is spelled out, we can begin to examine the effects and risks of major recreational drugs. Of course, we'll be describing the *typical* effects of each drug. Please bear in mind that the effects of any drug depend on the user's age, body weight, physiology, personality, mood, expectations, and previous experience with the drug. The dose and potency of the drug, the method of administration, and the setting in which the drug is taken also influence its effects (Leavitt, 1995). Our coverage is based largely on comprehensive books by Julien (2001), Levinthal (2002), and Lowinson and colleagues (2005), but we cite additional sources when discussing specific studies or controversial points.

Narcotics

***Narcotics* (or opiates) are drugs derived from opium that are capable of relieving pain.** In government regulations, the term *narcotic* is used in a haphazard way to refer to a variety of drugs besides opiates. The most widely abused opiates are heroin, morphine, and a relatively new painkiller called Oxycontin. However, less potent opiates, such as codeine, Demerol, and Vicodin, are also subject to misuse.

Effects

The most significant narcotics problem in modern, Western society is the use of heroin. Most users inject this drug intravenously with a hypodermic needle. The main effect is an overwhelming sense of euphoria. This "Who cares?" feeling makes the heroin high an attractive escape from reality. Common side effects include nausea, lethargy, drowsiness, constipation, and slowed respiration.

Risks

Narcotics carry a high risk for both *psychological and physical dependence* (Knapp, Ciraulo, & Jaffe, 2005). It is estimated that there are about 600,000 heroin addicts in the United States (Winick & Norman, 2005). Although heroin withdrawal usually isn't life threatening, it can be terribly unpleasant, so that "junkies" have a desperate need to continue their drug use. Once dependence is entrenched, users tend to develop a *drug-centered lifestyle* that revolves around the need to procure more heroin. This lifestyle occurs because the drug is expensive and available only through highly undependable black market channels. Obviously, it is difficult to lead a productive life if one's existence is dominated by a desperate need to "score" heroin. The inordinate cost of the drug forces many junkies to resort to criminal activities to support their habit.

Heroin is blamed for over 4,000 deaths annually in the United States, so *overdose* is a very real danger. Opiates are additive with other CNS depressants, and most narcotic overdoses occur in combination with the use of sedatives or alcohol. Junkies also risk *contracting infectious disease* because they often share hypodermic needles and tend to be sloppy about sterilizing them. The most common of these diseases used to be hepatitis, but in recent years AIDS has been transmitted at an alarming rate through the population of intravenous drug users (Des Jarlais, Hagan, & Friedman, 2005).

Sedatives

***Sedatives* are sleep-inducing drugs that tend to decrease central nervous system and behavioral activity.** In street jargon, they are often called "downers." Over the years, the most widely abused sedatives have been the barbiturates, which are compounds derived from barbituric acid. However, barbiturates have gradually become medically obsolete and diminished in availability, so sedative abusers have had to turn to drugs in the benzodiazepine family, such as Valium (Wesson et al., 2005).

Effects

People abusing sedatives generally consume larger doses than are prescribed for medical purposes. These overly large doses have a euphoric effect similar to that produced by drinking large amounts of alcohol (Wesson et al., 2005). Feelings of tension, anxiety, and depression are temporarily replaced by a relaxed, pleasant state of intoxication, in which inhibitions may be loosened. Sedatives carry a truckload of dangerous side effects. Motor coordination suffers badly, producing slurred speech and a staggering walk, among other things. Intellectual functioning also becomes sluggish, and judgment is impaired. One's emotional tone may become unstable, with feelings of dejection often intruding on the intended euphoric mood.

Risks

Sedatives have the potential to produce *both psychological and physical dependence.* They are also among the leading causes of *overdoses* in the United States because of their additive interactions with other CNS depressants (especially alcohol) and because of the degree to which they impair judgment. In their drug-induced haze, sedative abusers are likely to take doses they would ordinarily recognize as dangerous. Sedative users also elevate their risk for *accidental injuries* because these drugs can have significant effects on motor coordination. Many users trip down stairs, fall off bar stools, get into automobile accidents, and so forth.

Stimulants

***Stimulants* are drugs that tend to increase central nervous system and behavioral activity.** They range from mild, widely available forms, such as caffeine and nicotine, to stronger, carefully regulated stimulants, such as cocaine and amphetamines ("speed"). Here we focus on the latter two drugs.

Cocaine is an organic substance extracted from the coca shrub, which grows most prominently in South America. It is usually consumed as a crystalline powder that is snorted through the nasal cavities, although it can be consumed orally or intravenously. "Crack" is a processed variant of cocaine, consisting of little chips of cocaine that are usually smoked. Smoking crack tends to be more dangerous than snorting cocaine powder because smoking leads to a more rapid absorption of the drug into the bloodstream and more concentrated delivery of cocaine to the brain. That said, all the forms of cocaine and all the routes of administration can deliver highly toxic amounts of the drug to the brain (Repetto & Gold, 2005).

Synthesized in a pharmaceutical laboratory, amphetamines are usually consumed orally. However, speed is also sold as a crystalline powder (called "crank" or "crystal meth") that may be snorted or injected intravenously. A smokable form of methamphetamine, called "ice," is seen in some regions.

Effects

Amphetamines and cocaine have almost indistinguishable effects, except that cocaine produces a very brief high (20–30 minutes unless more is taken), while a speed high can last many hours (Gold, Miller, & Jonas, 1992). Stimulants produce a euphoria very different from that created by narcotics or sedatives. They produce a buoyant, elated, enthusiastic, energetic, "I can conquer the world!" feeling accompanied by increased alertness. Common side effects include increased blood pressure, muscle tension, sweating, and restlessness. Some users experience unpleasant feelings of irritability, anxiety, and paranoia.

Risks

Stimulants can cause physical dependence, but the physical distress caused by stimulant withdrawal is mild compared to that caused by narcotic or sedative withdrawal. Psychological dependence on stimulants is a more common problem. Cocaine can create an exceptionally *powerful psychological dependence* that compels the user to pursue the drug with a fervor normally seen only when physical dependence exists (Gold & Jacobs, 2005).

Both cocaine and amphetamines can suppress appetite and disrupt sleep. Thus, heavy use of stimulants may lead to poor eating, poor sleeping, and ultimately, a *deterioration in physical health.* Furthermore, stimulant use increases one's risk for stroke, heart attack, and other forms of cardiovascular disease, and crack smoking is associated with a host of respiratory problems (Gourevitch & Arnsten, 2005; Weaver & Schnoll, 1999).

Heavy stimulant use occasionally leads to the onset of a severe psychological disorder called *amphetamine* or *cocaine psychosis* (depending on the drug involved), which is dominated by intense paranoia (King & Ellinwood, 2005). All of the risks associated with stimulant use increase when more potent forms of the drugs (crack and ice) are used. Overdoses on stimulants used to be relatively infrequent (Kalant & Kalant, 1979). However, in recent years, *cocaine overdoses have increased sharply* as more people experiment with more dangerous modes of ingestion. In 2001, cocaine was the leading cause of drug-related emergency room visits (Gold & Jacobs, 2005).

Hallucinogens

***Hallucinogens* are a diverse group of drugs that have powerful effects on mental and emotional functioning, marked most prominently by distortions in sensory and perceptual experience.** The principal hallucinogens are LSD, mescaline, and psilocybin, which have similar effects, although they vary in potency. Mescaline comes from the peyote plant, psilocybin comes from a particular type of mushroom, and LSD is a synthetic drug. Common street names for hallucinogens include "acid," "mushrooms," "fry," and "blotter."

Effects

Hallucinogens intensify and distort perception in ways that are difficult to describe, and they temporarily impair intellectual functioning as thought processes become meteoric and jumbled. These drugs can produce awesome feelings of euphoria that sometimes include an almost mystical sense of "oneness" with the human race. This is why they have been used in religious ceremonies in various cultures. Unfortunately, at the other end of the emotional spectrum, they can also produce nightmarish feelings of anxiety, fear, and paranoia, commonly called a "bad trip."

Risks

There is no potential for physical dependence on hallucinogens, and no deaths attributable to overdose are known to have occurred. Psychological dependence has been reported but appears to be rare. Research reports that LSD increases chromosome breakage were based on poor methodology (Dishotsky et al., 1971). However, like most drugs, hallucinogens may be harmful to a fetus if taken by a pregnant woman.

Although the dangers of hallucinogens have probably been exaggerated in the popular press, there are some significant risks (Pechnick & Ungerleider, 2005). Emotion is highly volatile with these drugs, so users can never be sure that they won't experience *acute panic* from a terrifying bad trip. Generally, this disorientation subsides within a few hours, leaving no permanent emotional scars. However, in such a severe state of disorientation, *accidents and suicide* are possible. *Flashbacks* are vivid hallucinogenic experiences occurring months after the original drug ingestion. They do not appear to be a common problem, but repetitious flashbacks have proved troublesome for some individuals. In a small minority of users, hallucinogens may contribute to the emergence of a *variety of psychological disorders* (psychoses, depressive reactions, paranoid states) that may be partially attributable to the drug (Pechnick & Ungerleider, 2005).

Marijuana

***Cannabis* is the hemp plant from which marijuana, hashish, and THC are derived.** Marijuana (often called "pot," "weed," "reefer," or "grass") is a mixture of dried leaves, flowers, stems, and seeds taken from the plant, while hashish comes from the plant's resin. THC, the active chemical ingredient in cannabis, can be synthesized for research purposes (for example, to give to animals).

Effects

When smoked, cannabis has an almost immediate impact that may last several hours. The effects of the drug vary greatly, depending on the user's expectations and experience with it, the drug's potency, and the amount smoked. The drug has subtle effects on emotion, perception, and cognition (Grinspoon, Bakalar, & Russo, 2005). Emotionally, the drug tends to create a mild, relaxed state of euphoria. Perceptually, it enhances the impact of incoming stimulation, thus making music sound better, food taste better, and so on. Cannabis tends to produce a slight impairment in cognitive functioning (especially short-term memory) and perceptual-motor coordination while the user is high. However, there are huge variations among users.

Risks

Overdose and physical dependence are not problems with marijuana, but as with any other drug that produces pleasant feelings, it has the potential to produce *psychological dependence* (Grinspoon, Bakalar, & Russo, 2005). There is no solid evidence that cannabis causes psychological disorders. However, marijuana can cause *transient problems with anxiety and depression* in some people. Studies also suggest that cannabis may have a more *negative effect on driving* than has been widely believed (Ramaekers, Robbe, & O'Hanlon, 2000). Like tobacco smoke, marijuana smoke carries carcinogens and impurities into the lungs, thus increasing one's chances for *respiratory and pulmonary diseases, and probably lung cancer* (Stephens, 1999). However, the evidence on other widely publicized risks remains controversial. Here is a brief overview of the evidence on some of these controversies:

▶ *Does marijuana reduce one's immune response?* Research with animals clearly demonstrates that cannabis can suppress various aspects of immune system responding (Cabral & Pettit, 1998). However, infectious diseases do not *appear* to be more common among marijuana smokers than among nonsmokers. Hence, it is unclear whether marijuana increases susceptibility to infectious diseases in humans (Bredt et al., 2002; Klein, Friedman, & Specter, 1998).

▶ *Does marijuana lead to impotence and sterility in men?* In animal research, cannabis temporarily decreases testosterone levels and sperm production (Brown & Dobs, 2002). Citing these findings, the popular media have frequently implied that marijuana is likely to make men sterile and impotent. However, research with humans has yielded weak, inconsistent, and reversible effects on testosterone and sperm levels (Brown & Dobs, 2002). At present, the evidence suggests that marijuana has little lasting impact on male smokers' fertility or sexual functioning (Grinspoon, Bakalar, & Russo, 2005).

▶ *Does marijuana have long-term negative effects on cognitive functioning?* It has long been known that marijuana has a negative impact on attention and memory while users are high, but until recently studies had failed to find any permanent cognitive deficits attributable to cannabis use. However, a spate of recent studies using more elaborate and precise assessments of cognitive functioning *have* found an association between chronic, heavy marijuana use and measureable impairments in attention and memory (see **Figure 14.25**) that show up when users are not high (Ehrenreich et al., 1999; Solowij et al., 2002). That said, the cognitive deficits that have been observed are modest and certainly not disabling, and one study found that the deficits vanished after a month of marijuana abstinence (Pope, Gruber, & Yurgelun-Todd, 2001; Pope et al., 2001).

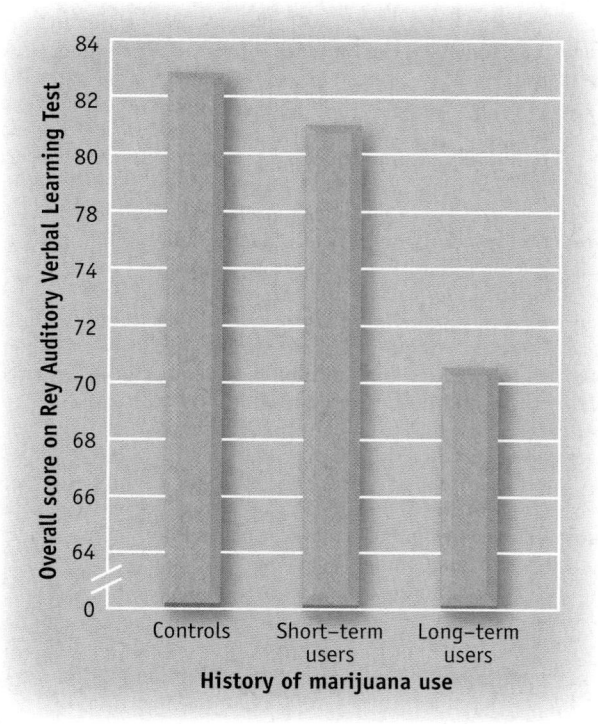

Figure 14.25

Chronic cannabis use and cognitive performance. Solowij and associates (2002) administered a battery of neuropsychological tests to 51 long-term cannabis users, who had smoked marijuana regularly for an average of 24 years; 51 short-term cannabis users, who had smoked marijuana regularly for an average of 10 years; and 33 control subjects who had little or no history of cannabis use. The cannabis users were required to abstain from smoking marijuana for a minimum of 12 hours prior to their testing. The study found evidence suggestive of subtle cognitive impairments among the long-term cannabis users on many of the tests. The graph shown here depicts the results observed for overall performance on the Rey Auditory Verbal Learning Test, which measures several aspects of memory functioning.

Ecstasy (MDMA)

The newest drug controversy in Western society centers on MDMA, better known as "ecstasy." MDMA was originally formulated in 1912 but was not widely used in the United States until the 1990s, when it became popular in the context of "raves" and dance clubs (Millman & Beeder, 1994). This compound is related to both amphetamines and hallucinogens, especially mescaline. It produces a high that typically lasts a few hours or more. Users report that they feel warm, friendly, euphoric, sensual, insightful, and empathetic, yet alert and energetic. Problematic side effects include increased blood pressure, muscle tension, sweating, blurred vision, insomnia, and transient anxiety.

Empirical research on ecstasy is still in its infancy, so assertions about its risks and dangers must be tentative and provisional. Data on adverse effects are also complicated by the fact that the vast majority of MDMA users ingest it in conjunction with many other drugs (Hammersley et al., 1999; Pedersen & Skrondal, 1999). Yet another complicating factor is that MDMA often contains potentially harmful impurities, contaminants, and toxic by-products introduced during its illicit manufacture (Grob & Poland, 2005).

MDMA does not appear to be especially addictive, but psychological dependence can clearly become a problem for some people. MDMA has been implicated in cases of stroke and heart attack, seizures, heat stroke, and liver damage, but its exact contribution is hard to gauge given all the other drugs that MDMA users typically consume (Burgess, O'Donohoe, & Gill, 2000; Grob & Poland, 2005). Chronic, heavy use of ecstasy appears to be associated with sleep disorders, depression, and elevated anxiety and hostility (Morgan, 2000). Moreover, studies of former MDMA users suggest that ecstasy may have subtle, long-term effects on cognitive functioning (Medina et al., 2005; Parrott, 2000). Quite a few studies have found memory deficits in former users (Bhattachary & Powell, 2001; Zakzanis & Young, 2001). Other studies have found decreased performance on laboratory tasks requiring attention and learning (Gouzoulis-Mayfrank et al., 2000). Thus, although more research is needed, there are many reasons to be concerned about the possible effects of ecstasy.

KEY IDEAS

Stress, Personality, and Illness

▶ The biopsychosocial model holds that physical health is influenced by a complex network of biological, psychological, and sociocultural factors. Stress is one of the psychological factors that can affect physical health. In particular, cynical hostility has been implicated as a contributing cause of coronary heart disease. A number of mechanisms may contribute to this connection.

▶ Emotional reactions may also influence susceptibility to heart disease. Recent research has suggested that transient mental stress and the negative emotions that result may tax the heart. Yet another line of research has identified the emotional dysfunction of depression as a risk factor for heart disease.

▶ The connection between psychological factors and the onset of cancer is not well documented, but stress and personality may influence the course of the disease. Researchers have found associations between stress and the onset of a variety of other diseases. Stress may play a role in a variety of diseases because it can temporarily suppress immune functioning. While there's little doubt that stress can contribute to the development of physical illness, the link between stress and illness is modest.

Habits, Lifestyles and Health

▶ People commonly engage in health-impairing habits and lifestyles. These habits creep up slowly, and their risks are easy to ignore because the dangers often lie in the distant future.

▶ Smokers have much higher mortality rates than nonsmokers because they are more vulnerable to a variety of diseases. Giving up smoking can reduce one's health risks, but doing so is difficult and relapse rates are high.

▶ Drinking rivals smoking as a source of health problems. In the short term, drinking can impair driving, cause various types of accidents, and increase the likelihood of aggressive interactions or reckless sexual behavior. In the long term, chronic, excessive alcohol consumption increases one's risk for numerous health problems, including cirrhosis of the liver, heart disease, hypertension, stroke, and cancer.

▶ Obesity elevates one's risk for many health problems. Body weight is influenced by genetic endowment, eating and exercise habits, and perhaps set point or settling point. Weight loss is best accomplished by decreasing caloric consumption while increasing exercise.

▶ Poor nutritional habits have been linked to many health problems, including cardiovascular diseases and some types of cancer, although some of the links are tentative. One's health can best be served by following balanced food consumption patterns while limiting the intake of saturated fats, cholesterol, refined carbohydrates, sugar, and salt.

▶ Lack of exercise is associated with elevated mortality rates. Regular exercise can reduce one's risk for cardiovascular disease, cancer, and obesity-related diseases; buffer the effects of stress; and lead to desirable personality changes.

▶ Although misconceptions abound, HIV is transmitted almost exclusively by sexual contact and the sharing of needles by intravenous drug users. One's risk for HIV infection can be reduced by avoiding IV drug use, having fewer sexual partners, using condoms, and curtailing certain sexual practices.

Reactions to Illness

▶ Variations in seeking treatment are influenced by the severity, duration, and disruptiveness of one's symptoms and by the reactions of friends and family. The biggest problem is the tendency of many people to delay needed medical treatment. At the other extreme, a minority of people learn to like the sick role because it earns them attention and allows them to avoid stress.

▶ Good communication is crucial to effective health services, but many factors undermine communication between patients and health providers, such as short visits, overuse of medical jargon, and patients' reluctance to ask questions.

▶ Noncompliance with medical advice is a major problem, which appears to occur 30%–50% of the time. The likelihood of nonadherence is greater when instructions are difficult to understand, when recommendations are difficult to follow, and when patients are unhappy with their doctor.

Application: Understanding the Effects of Drugs

▶ Recreational drugs vary in their potential for tolerance effects, psychological dependence, physical dependence, and overdose. The risks associated with narcotics use include both types of dependence, overdose, and the acquisition of infectious diseases.

▶ Sedatives can also produce both types of dependence, are subject to overdoses, and elevate the user's risk for accidental injuries. Stimulant use can lead to psychological dependence, overdose, psychosis, and a deterioration in physical health. Cocaine overdoses have increased greatly in recent years.

▶ Hallucinogens can in some cases contribute to accidents, suicides, and psychological disorders, and they can cause flashbacks. The risks of marijuana use include psychological dependence, impaired driving, transient problems with anxiety and depression, and respiratory and pulmonary diseases. Recent studies suggest that marijuana use may have some long-term negative effects on cognitive processes.

▶ More research is needed, but it appears that the use of ecstasy (MDMA) may contribute to a variety of acute and chronic physical maladies. MDMA may also have subtle, negative effects on cognitive functioning.

KEY TERMS

Acquired immune deficiency syndrome (AIDS) p. 465
Alcohol dependence p. 456
Alcoholism p. 456
Atherosclerosis p. 443
Biopsychosocial model p. 442
Body mass index (BMI) p. 457
Cancer p. 447
Cannabis p. 474
Coronary heart disease p. 443
Hallucinogens p. 473
Health psychology p. 442
Hostility p. 444
Immune response p. 448
Narcotics p. 472
Nutrition p. 460
Overdose p. 472
Physical dependence pp. 470–471
Psychological dependence p. 471
Sedatives p. 472
Set-point theory p. 458
Settling-point theory p. 458
Stimulants p. 473
Tolerance p. 470
Type A personality p. 444
Type B personality p. 444

KEY PEOPLE

Robin DiMatteo p. 467
Meyer Friedman and Ray Rosenman p. 444
Janice Kiecolt-Glaser pp. 448–449

PRACTICE TEST

1. The greatest threats to health in our society today are:
   - **a.** environmental toxins.
   - **b.** accidents.
   - **c.** chronic diseases.
   - **d.** contagious diseases caused by specific infectious agents.

2. Which of the following is *not* associated with elevated coronary risk?
   - **a.** Cynical hostility
   - **b.** Strong emotional reactions to transient mental stress
   - **c.** Obsessive-compulsive disorder
   - **d.** Depression

3. Why do people tend to act in self-destructive ways?
   - **a.** Because many health-impairing habits creep up on them
   - **b.** Because many health-impairing habits involve activities that are quite pleasant at the time
   - **c.** Because the risks tend to lie in the distant future
   - **d.** All of the above

4. Some short-term risks of alcohol consumption include all but which of the following?
   - **a.** Hangovers and life-threatening overdoses in combination with other drugs
   - **b.** Poor perceptual coordination and driving drunk
   - **c.** Increased aggressiveness and argumentativeness
   - **d.** Transient anxiety from endorphin-induced flashbacks

5. Twin studies and other behavioral genetics research suggest that:
   - **a.** genetic factors have little impact on people's weight.
   - **b.** heredity has scant influence on BMI but does influence weight.
   - **c.** heredity accounts for 60% or more of the variation in weight.
   - **d.** heredity is responsible for severe, morbid obesity but has little influence over the weight of normal people.

6. Which of the following has *not* been found to be a mode of transmission for AIDS?
   - **a.** Sexual contact among homosexual men
   - **b.** The sharing of needles by intravenous drug users
   - **c.** Sexual contact among heterosexuals
   - **d.** Sharing food

7. Regarding the seeking of medical treatment, the biggest problem is:
   - **a.** the tendency of many people to delay seeking treatment.
   - **b.** the tendency of many people to rush too quickly for medical care for minor problems.
   - **c.** not having enough doctors to cover peoples' needs.
   - **d.** the tendency of people in higher socioeconomic categories to exaggerate their symptoms.

8. In which of the following cases are people most likely to follow the instructions they receive from health care professionals?
   - **a.** When the instructions are complex and punctuated with impressive medical jargon
   - **b.** When they do not fully understand the instructions but still feel the need to do something
   - **c.** When they like and understand the health care professional
   - **d.** All of the above

9. Which of the following risks is *not* typically associated with narcotics use?
   - **a.** Overdose
   - **b.** Infectious disease
   - **c.** Physical dependence
   - **d.** Flashbacks

10. The use of sedatives may result in personal injury because they:
    - **a.** cause motor coordination to deteriorate.
    - **b.** enhance motor coordination too much, making people overconfident about their abilities.
    - **c.** suppress pain warnings of physical harm.
    - **d.** trigger hallucinations such as flying.

Book Companion Website

Visit the Book Companion Website at **academic.cengage.com/psychology/weiten,** where you will find tutorial quizzes, flash cards, and web links for every chapter, a final exam, and more! You can also link to the Psychology Resource Center (accessible directly at **academic.cengage.com/login**) for a range of psychology-related resources.

Personal Explorations Workbook

The following exercises in your *Personal Explorations Workbook* may enhance your self-understanding in relation to issues raised in this chapter. **Questionnaire 14.1:** Chronic Self-Destructiveness Scale. **Personal Probe 14.1:** How Do Your Health Habits Rate? **Personal Probe 14.2:** Examining Specific Health Habits.

ANSWERS

1. c Page 441
2. c Pages 443–447
3. d Pages 450–451
4. d Pages 455–456
5. c Page 458
6. d Page 465
7. a Page 467
8. c Pages 468–469
9. d Page 472
10. a Page 473

CHAPTER 15

Psychological Disorders

"The government of the United States was overthrown more than a year ago! I'm the president of the United States of America and Bob Dylan is vice president!" So said Ed, the author of a prominent book on journalism, who was speaking to a college journalism class, as a guest lecturer. Ed also informed the class that he had killed both John and Robert Kennedy, as well as Charles de Gaulle, the former president of France. He went on to tell the class that all rock music songs were written about him, that he was the greatest karate expert in the universe, and that he had been fighting "space wars" for 2000 years. The students in the class were mystified by Ed's bizarre, disjointed "lecture," but they assumed that he was putting on a show that would eventually lead to a sensible conclusion. However, their perplexed but expectant calm was shattered when Ed pulled a hatchet from the props he had brought with him and hurled the hatchet at the class! Fortunately, he didn't hit anyone, as the hatchet sailed over the students' heads. At that point, the professor for the class realized that Ed's irrational behavior was not a pretense. The professor evacuated the class quickly while Ed continued to rant and rave about his presidential administration, space wars, vampires, his romances with female rock stars, and his personal harem of 38 "chicks." (Adapted from Pearce, 1974)

ABNORMAL BEHAVIOR: CONCEPTS AND CONTROVERSIES
The Medical Model Applied to Abnormal Behavior
Criteria of Abnormal Behavior
Psychodiagnosis: The Classification of Disorders
The Prevalence of Psychological Disorders

ANXIETY DISORDERS
Generalized Anxiety Disorder
Phobic Disorder
Panic Disorder and Agoraphobia
Obsessive-Compulsive Disorder
Etiology of Anxiety Disorders

SOMATOFORM DISORDERS
Somatization Disorder
Conversion Disorder
Hypochondriasis
Etiology of Somatoform Disorders

DISSOCIATIVE DISORDERS
Dissociative Amnesia and Fugue
Dissociative Identity Disorder
Etiology of Dissociative Disorders

MOOD DISORDERS
Major Depressive Disorder
Bipolar Disorder

LIVING IN TODAY'S WORLD *Understanding and Preventing Suicide*
Etiology of Mood Disorders

SCHIZOPHRENIC DISORDERS
General Symptoms
Subtypes
Course and Outcome
Etiology of Schizophrenia

APPLICATION: UNDERSTANDING EATING DISORDERS
Types of Eating Disorders
History and Prevalence
Etiology of Eating Disorders

REVIEW

PRACTICE TEST

Clearly, Ed's behavior was abnormal. Even *he* recognized that when he agreed later to be admitted to a mental hospital, signing himself in as the "President of the United States of America." What causes such abnormal behavior? Does Ed have a mental illness, or does he just behave strangely? What is the basis for judging behavior as normal versus abnormal? How common are such disorders? These are just a few of the questions we address in this chapter as we discuss psychological disorders and their complex causes.

Abnormal Behavior: Concepts and Controversies

LEARNING OBJECTIVES

- *Describe and evaluate the medical model of abnormal behavior.*
- *Explain the most commonly used criteria of abnormality.*
- *Discuss the history of the DSM system, and describe the five axes of DSM-IV.*
- *Summarize data on the prevalence of various psychological disorders.*

Misconceptions about abnormal behavior are common. We therefore need to clear up some preliminary issues before we describe the various types of psychological disorders. In this section, we discuss (1) the medical model of abnormal behavior, (2) the criteria of abnormal behavior, (3) the classification of psychological disorders, and (4) the prevalence of such disorders.

The Medical Model Applied to Abnormal Behavior

In Ed's case, there's no question that his behavior was abnormal. But does it make sense to view his unusual and irrational behavior as an *illness*? This is a controversial question. **The *medical model* proposes that it is useful to think of abnormal behavior as a disease.** This point of view is the basis for many of the terms used to refer to abnormal behavior, including mental *illness,* psychological *disorder,* and psycho*pathology* (*pathology* refers to manifestations of disease). The medical model gradually became the dominant way of thinking about abnormal behavior during the 19th and 20th centuries, and its influence remains strong today.

The medical model clearly represented progress over earlier models of abnormal behavior. Prior to the 18th century, most conceptions of abnormal behavior were based on superstition. People who behaved strangely were thought to be possessed by demons, to be witches in league with the devil, or to be victims of God's punishment. Their disorders were "treated" with chants, rituals, exorcisms, and such. If the people's behavior was seen as threatening, they were candidates for chains, dungeons, torture, and death (see **Figure 15.1**).

The rise of the medical model brought improvements in the treatment of those who exhibited abnormal behavior. As victims of an illness, they were viewed with more sympathy and less hatred and fear. Although living conditions in early asylums were often deplorable, gradual progress was made toward more humane

Figure 15.1

Historical conceptions of mental illness. Throughout most of history, psychological disorders were thought to be caused by demonic possession, and the mentally ill were candidates for chains and torture.

care of the mentally ill. It took time, but ineffectual approaches to treatment eventually gave way to scientific investigation of the causes and cures of psychological disorders.

However, in recent decades, some critics have suggested that the medical model may have outlived its usefulness (Kiesler, 1999). A particularly vocal critic has been Thomas Szasz (1974, 1993). He asserts that "strictly speaking, disease or illness can affect only the body; hence there can be no mental illness. . . . Minds can be 'sick' only in the sense that jokes are 'sick' or economies are 'sick'" (1974, p. 267). He further argues that abnormal behavior usually involves a deviation from social norms rather than an illness. He contends that such deviations are "problems in living" rather than medical problems. According to Szasz, the medical model's disease analogy converts moral and social questions about what is acceptable behavior into medical questions.

© David Lees/Corbis

Thomas Szasz

Although Szasz's criticism has some merit, we'll take the position that the disease analogy continues to be useful, although you should keep in mind that it is *only* an analogy. Medical concepts such as *diagnosis, etiology,* and *prognosis* have proven valuable in the treatment and study of abnormality. ***Diagnosis* involves distinguishing one illness from another. *Etiology* refers to the apparent causation and developmental history of an illness. A *prognosis* is a forecast about the probable course of an illness.** These medically based concepts have widely shared meanings that permit clinicians, researchers, and the public to communicate more effectively in their discussions of abnormal behavior.

Criteria of Abnormal Behavior

If your next-door neighbor scrubs his front porch twice every day and spends virtually all his time cleaning and recleaning his house, is he normal? If your sister-in-law goes to one physician after another seeking treatment for ailments that appear imaginary, is she psychologically healthy? How are we to judge what's normal and what's abnormal? More important, who's to do the judging?

These are complex questions. In a sense, *all* people make judgments about normality in that they all express opinions about others' (and perhaps their own) mental health. Of course, formal diagnoses of psychological disorders are made by mental health professionals. In making these diagnoses, clinicians rely on a variety of criteria, the foremost of which are the following:

1. *Deviance.* As Szasz has pointed out, people are often said to have a disorder because their behavior deviates from what their society considers acceptable. What constitutes normality varies somewhat from one culture to another, but all cultures have such norms. When people ignore these standards and expectations, they may be labeled mentally ill. For example, *transvestic fetishism* is a sexual disorder in which a man achieves sexual arousal by dressing in women's clothing. This behavior is regarded as disordered because a man who wears a dress, brassiere, and nylons is deviating from our culture's norms. This example illustrates the arbitrary nature of cultural standards regarding normality, as the same overt behavior (cross-gender dressing) is acceptable for women yet deviant for men.

2. *Maladaptive behavior.* In many cases, people are judged to have a psychological disorder because their everyday adaptive behavior is impaired. This is the key criterion in the diagnosis of substance use (drug) disorders. In and of itself, alcohol and drug use is not terribly unusual or deviant. However, when the use of cocaine, for instance, begins to interfere with a person's social or occupational functioning, a substance use disorder exists. In such cases, it is the maladaptive quality of the behavior that makes it disordered.

3. *Personal distress.* Frequently, the diagnosis of a psychological disorder is based on an individual's re-

© AP Images/David Davies/PA

This man clearly exhibits a certain type of deviance, but does that mean that he has a psychological disorder? The criteria of mental illness are more subjective and complicated than most people realize, and to some extent, judgments of mental health represent value judgments.

port of great personal distress. This is usually the criterion met by people who are troubled by depression or anxiety disorders. Depressed people, for instance, may or may not exhibit deviant or maladaptive behavior. Such people are usually labeled as having a disorder when they describe their subjective pain and suffering to friends, relatives, and mental health professionals.

Although two or three criteria may apply in a particular case, people are often viewed as disordered when only one criterion is met. As you may have already noticed, diagnoses of psychological disorders involve *value judgments* about what represents normal or abnormal behavior (Sadler, 2005; Widiger & Sankis, 2000). The criteria of mental illness are not nearly as value-free as the criteria of physical illness. In evaluating physical diseases, people can usually agree that a weak heart or a malfunctioning kidney is pathological, regardless of their personal values. However, judgments about mental illness reflect prevailing cultural values, social trends, and political forces, as well as scientific knowledge (Kutchins & Kirk, 1997; Mechanic, 1999).

These realities are readily apparent if you consider how psychiatric views of homosexuality have changed over time. Homosexuality used to be listed as a sexual disorder in the American Psychiatric Association's diagnostic system (which we will discuss shortly). Because homosexuality was viewed as pathological, many gays were coaxed or coerced into therapeutic treatments for their "disorder" that often proved demeaning or harmful (Smith, Bartlett, & King, 2004). However, in 1973 a committee appointed by the American Psychiatric Association voted to delete homosexuality from the official list of psychological disorders. This action occurred for several reasons (Bayer, 1987; Forstein, 2004; Rothblum, Solomon, & Albee, 1986). First, attitudes toward homosexuality in our society had become more tolerant. Second, gay rights activists campaigned vigorously for the change. Third, research showed that gays and heterosexuals were indistinguishable on measures of psychological health. Although this long-overdue decision was informed by scientific findings, it was also influenced by political lobbying and shifts in social values.

Antonyms such as *normal* versus *abnormal* and *mental health* versus *mental illness* imply that people can be divided neatly into two distinct groups: those who are normal and those who are not. In reality, it is often difficult to draw a line that clearly separates normality from abnormality. On occasion, everyone experiences personal distress. Everybody acts in deviant ways once in a while. And everyone displays some maladaptive behavior. People are judged to have psychological disorders only when their behavior becomes *extremely* deviant, maladaptive, or distressing. Thus, normality and abnormality exist on a continuum. It's a matter of degree, not an either-or proposition (see **Figure 15.2**).

Web Link 15.1 **Psych Central**

The work of John Grohol, Psych Central is arguably the premier site on the web for all aspects of mental health, including psychological disorders and treatment, professional issues, and information for mental health care consumers. This site offers nearly 2,000 annotated listings to information sources.

Psychodiagnosis: The Classification of Disorders

Obviously, we cannot lump all psychological disorders together without giving up all hope of understanding them better. A sound taxonomy of mental disorders can facilitate empirical research and enhance communication among scientists and clinicians (First, 2003; Zimmerman & Spitzer, 2005). Hence, a great deal of effort has been invested in devising an elaborate system for classifying psychological disorders.

Guidelines for psychodiagnosis were extremely vague and informal prior to 1952, when the American Psychiatric Association unveiled its *Diagnostic and Statistical Manual of Mental Disorders* (Nathan & Langenbucher, 2003). This classification scheme described about 100 disorders. Revisions intended to improve the system were incorporated into the second edition (DSM-II) published in 1968, but the diagnostic guidelines were still pretty sketchy. However, the third edition (DSM-III), published in 1980, represented a

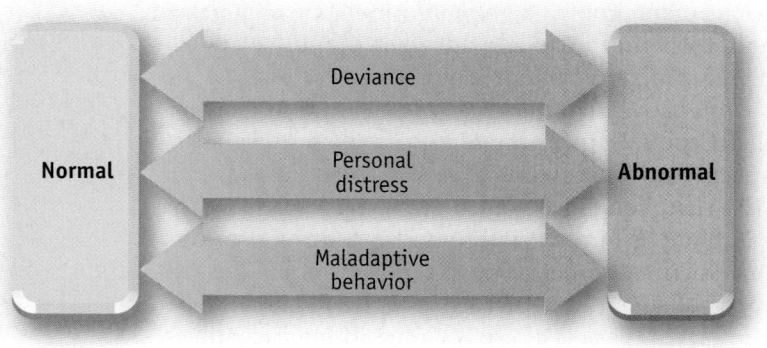

Figure 15.2

Normality and abnormality as a continuum. No sharp boundary divides normal and abnormal behavior. Behavior is normal or abnormal in degree, depending on the extent to which it is deviant, personally distressing, or maladaptive.

major advance, as the diagnostic criteria were made much more explicit, concrete, and detailed to facilitate more consistent diagnoses across clinicians (Blacker & Tsuang, 1999). The current, fourth edition (DSM-IV), released in 1994 and revised slightly in 2000, made use of intervening research to refine the criteria introduced in DSM-III. Each revision of the DSM system has expanded the list of disorders covered. The current version describes about three times as many types of psychological disorders as the original DSM (Houts, 2002).

The publication of DSM-III in 1980 introduced a new multiaxial system of classification, which asks for judgments about individuals on five separate dimensions, or "axes." **Figure 15.3** provides an overview of the entire system and the five axes. The diagnoses of disorders are made on Axes I and II. Clinicians record most types of disorders on Axis I. They use Axis II to list long-running personality disorders or mental retardation. People may receive diagnoses on both Axes I and II.

The remaining axes are used to record supplemental information. A patient's physical disorders are listed on Axis III (General Medical Conditions). On Axis IV (Psychosocial and Environmental Problems), the clinician makes notations regarding the types of stress experienced by the individual in the past year. On Axis V (Global Assessment of Functioning), estimates are made of the individual's current level of adaptive functioning (in social and occupational behavior, viewed as a whole) and of the individual's highest level of functioning in the past year. Most theorists agree that the multiaxial system is a step in the right direction because it recognizes the importance of information besides a traditional diagnostic label.

Work is currently underway to formulate the next edition (DSM-V) of the diagnostic system (e.g., Banzato, 2004; Spitzer, First, & Wakefield, 2007; Widiger & Simonsen, 2005), which is tentatively scheduled for publication in 2011. Clinical researchers are collecting data, holding conferences, and formulating arguments about whether various syndromes should be added, eliminated, or renamed. Should complicated grief reactions become a standard diagnostic option (Lichtenthal, Cruess, & Prigerson, 2004)? Should the diagnostic system use the term drug *dependence* or drug *addiction* (O'Brien, Volkow, & Li, 2006)? Should pathological gambling be lumped with impulse-control disorders or addictive disorders (Potenza, 2006)? Should the category of somatoform disorders (see pp. 489–491) be eliminated (Fava et al., 2007)? Should Internet addiction be added to the official list of disorders (Sandoz, 2004)? Vigorous debates about issues such as these will occupy clinical researchers in the upcoming years, and DSM-V may look somewhat different from its predecessors.

The Prevalence of Psychological Disorders

How common are psychological disorders? What percentage of the population is afflicted with mental illness? Is it 10%? Perhaps 25%? Could the figure range as high as 40% or 50%?

Such estimates fall in the domain of ***epidemiology*—the study of the distribution of mental or physical disorders in a population.** In epidemiology, ***prevalence* refers to the percentage of a population that exhibits a disorder during a specified time period.** In the case of mental disorders, the most interesting data are the estimates of *lifetime prevalence,* the percentage of people having a specific disorder at any time in their lives.

Studies published in the 1980s and early 1990s found psychological disorders in roughly *one-third* of the population (Regier & Kaelber, 1995; Robins, Locke, & Regier, 1991). Subsequent research, which focused on a somewhat younger sample (ages 18–54 instead of over age 18), suggested that about 44% of the adult population will struggle with some sort of psychological disorder at some point in their lives (Kessler & Zhao, 1999; Regier & Burke, 2000). The most recent large-scale epidemiological study estimated the lifetime risk of a psychiatric disorder to be 51% (Kessler et al., 2005a). Obviously, all these figures are *estimates* that depend to some extent on the sampling methods and assessment techniques used (Wakefield, 1999).

The progressively higher estimates in recent years have begun to generate some controversy in the field. Some experts believe that recent estimates are implausibly high and that they may trivialize psychiatric diagnoses (Wakefield & Spitzer, 2002). Characterizing someone as mentally ill doesn't mean much if the label is applicable to half of the population. The debate centers on where to draw the line between normal difficulties in functioning and full-fledged mental illness—that is, when do symptoms qualify as a disease (Regier, Narrow, & Rae, 2004)? Critics of the recent high estimates argue that they include many people whose problems have little clinical significance—in other words, their problems don't require treatment (Narrow et al., 2002). Those who defend the recent research argue that it

Web Link 15.2 **NAMI: The National Alliance for the Mentally Ill**

Professional and lay evaluators have consistently found NAMI among the most helpful and informative organizations dealing with the entire spectrum of mental disorders, including schizophrenia and depression. The NAMI site offers a particularly rich array of information on specific mental disorders and on how patients and their families can find support.

Axis I
Clinical Syndromes

1. *Disorders usually first diagnosed in infancy, childhood, or adolescence*
   This category includes disorders that arise before adolescence, such as attention deficit disorders, autism, mental retardation, enuresis, and stuttering.
2. *Organic mental disorders*
   These disorders are temporary or permanent dysfunctions of brain tissue caused by diseases or chemicals. Examples are delirium, dementia, and amnesia.
3. *Substance-related disorders*
   This category refers to the maladaptive use of drugs and alcohol. Mere consumption and recreational use of such substances are not disorders. This category requires a maladaptive pattern of use, as with alcohol abuse and cocaine dependence.
4. *Schizophrenia and other psychotic disorders*
   The schizophrenias are characterized by psychotic symptoms (for example, grossly disorganized behavior, delusions, and hallucinations) and by over 6 months of behavioral deterioration. This category also includes delusional disorder and schizoaffective disorder.
5. *Mood disorders*
   The cardinal feature is emotional disturbance. Patients may, or may not, have psychotic symptoms. These disorders include major depression, bipolar disorder, dysthymic disorder, and cyclothymic disorder.
6. *Anxiety disorders*
   These disorders are characterized by physiological signs of anxiety (for example, palpitations) and subjective feelings of tension, apprehension, or fear. Anxiety may be acute and focused (panic disorder) or continual and diffuse (generalized anxiety disorder).
7. *Somatoform disorders*
   These disorders are dominated by somatic symptoms that resemble physical illnesses. These symptoms cannot be accounted for by organic damage. There must also be strong evidence that these symptoms are produced by psychological factors or conflicts. This category includes somatization, conversion disorder, and hypochondriasis.
8. *Dissociative disorders*
   These disorders all feature a sudden, temporary alteration or dysfunction of memory, consciousness, identity, and behavior, as in dissociative amnesia and multiple personality.
9. *Sexual and gender-identity disorders*
   There are three basic types of disorders in this category: gender identity disorders (discomfort with identity as male or female), paraphilias (preference for unusual acts to achieve sexual arousal), and sexual dysfunctions (impairments in sexual functioning).

Axis II
Personality Disorders

These disorders are patterns of personality traits that are longstanding, maladaptive, and inflexible and involve impaired functioning or subjective distress. Examples include borderline, schizoid, and antisocial personality disorders.

Axis III
General Medical Conditions

Physical disorders or conditions are recorded on this axis. Examples include diabetes, arthritis, and hemophilia.

Axis IV
Psychosocial and Environmental Problems

Axis IV is for reporting psychosocial and environmental problems that may affect the diagnosis, treatment, and prognosis of mental disorders (Axes I and II). A psychosocial or environmental problem may be a negative life event, an environmental difficulty or deficiency, a familial or other interpersonal stress, an inadequacy of social support or personal resources, or another problem that describes the context in which a person's difficulties have developed.

Axis V
Global Assessment of Functioning (GAF) Scale

Code	Symptoms
100	Superior functioning in a wide range of activities
90	Absent or minimal symptoms, good functioning in all areas
80	Symptoms transient and expectable reactions to psychosocial stressors
70	Some mild symptoms or some difficulty in social, occupational, or school functioning, but generally functioning pretty well
60	Moderate symptoms or difficulty in social, occupational, or school functioning
50	Serious symptoms or impairment in social, occupational, or school functioning
40	Some impairment in reality testing or communication or major impairment in family relations, judgment, thinking, or mood
30	Behavior considerably influenced by delusions or hallucinations, serious impairment in communication or judgment, or inability to function in almost all areas
20	Some danger of hurting self or others, occasional failure to maintain minimal personal hygiene, or gross impairment in communication
10	Persistent danger of severely hurting self or others
1	

Figure 15.3

Overview of the DSM diagnostic system. Published by the American Psychiatric Association, the *Diagnostic and Statistical Manual of Mental Disorders* is the formal classification system used in the diagnosis of psychological disorders. It is a *multiaxial* system, which means that information is recorded on the five axes described here.

Adapted with permission from the *Diagnostic and Statistical Manual of Mental Disorders*, 4th ed. *Text revision*. Copyright © 2000 American Psychiatric Association.

makes sense to count people with mild disorders because mild disorders often progress into more severe disorders and this progression might be prevented by early diagnosis and intervention (Kessler et al., 2003). The outcome of this debate is difficult to predict, as both points of view have merit.

In any event, whether one goes with conservative or liberal estimates, the prevalence of psychological disorders is quite a bit higher than most people assume. The data that yielded the 44% estimate of total lifetime prevalence are summarized in **Figure 15.4**, which shows prevalence estimates for the most common classes of disorders. As you can see, the most common types of psychological disorders are (1) substance (alcohol and drugs) use disorders, (2) anxiety disorders, and (3) mood disorders.

We are now ready to start examining the specific types of psychological disorders. Obviously, we cannot cover all of the diverse disorders listed in DSM-IV. However, we will introduce most of the major categories of disorders to give you an overview of the many forms abnormal behavior takes. In discussing each set of disorders, we begin with brief descriptions of the specific syndromes or subtypes that fall in the category. Then we focus on the *etiology* of the disorders in that category. Although many paths can lead to specific disorders, some are more common than others. We highlight some of the common paths in order to enhance your understanding of the roots of abnormal behavior.

Recommended **READING**

The Burden of Sympathy: How Families Cope with Mental Illness
by David A. Karp
(Oxford University Press, 2001)

Although psychological disorders are quite common, they remain shrouded in mystery. Mental illness is not a topic that people want to talk about, and little advice is available for the families of people suffering from psychological disorders. Nevertheless, millions of people are troubled by severe disorders such as schizophrenia and bipolar disorder, so millions of families must struggle with these trying and difficult afflictions. This book thus fills an important need. Based on extensive interviews, Karp, a sociologist, discusses the devastating effects that mental illness can have on patients' families and how they deal with these effects. Although this is not a "how to" manual, it includes many useful insights about the mental health system and a good deal of concrete, realistic advice. Other worthwhile books intended for families of psychiatric patients include *How to Cope with Mental Illness in Your Family: A Self-Care Guide for Offspring and Parents* (Marsh & Dickens, 1997) and *When Someone You Love Has a Mental Illness: A Handbook for Family, Friends, and Caregivers* (Woolis, 1992).

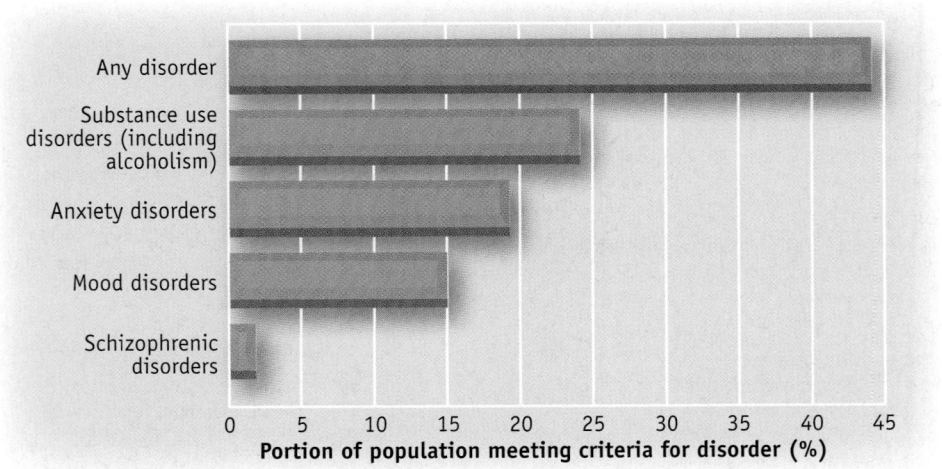

Figure 15.4

Lifetime prevalence of psychological disorders. The estimated percentage of people who have, at any time in their life, suffered from one of four types of psychological disorders or from a disorder of any kind (top bar) is shown here. Prevalence estimates vary somewhat from one study to the next, depending on the exact methods used in sampling and assessment. The estimates shown here are based on pooling data from Waves 1 and 2 of the Epidemiological Catchment Area studies and the National Comorbidity Study, as summarized by Regier and Burke (2000) and Dew, Bromet, and Switzer (2000). These studies, which collectively evaluated over 28,000 subjects, provide the best data to date on the prevalence of mental illness in the United States.

Anxiety Disorders

LEARNING OBJECTIVES

- *List and describe four types of anxiety disorders.*
- *Discuss the contribution of biological factors and conditioning to the etiology of anxiety disorders.*
- *Explain the contribution of cognitive factors and stress to the etiology of anxiety disorders.*

Everyone experiences anxiety from time to time. It is a natural and common reaction to many of life's difficulties. For some people, however, anxiety becomes a chronic problem. These people experience high levels of anxiety with disturbing regularity. ***Anxiety disorders* are a class of disorders marked by feelings of excessive apprehension and anxiety.** There are four principal types of anxiety disorders: generalized anxiety disorder, phobic disorder, obsessive-compulsive disorder, and panic disorder. They are not mutually exclusive, as many people who develop one anxiety syndrome often suffer from another at some point in their lives (Merikangas, 2005).

Generalized Anxiety Disorder

The *generalized anxiety disorder* is marked by a chronic, high level of anxiety that is not tied to any specific threat. People with this disorder worry constantly about yesterday's mistakes and tomorrow's problems. They worry excessively about minor matters related to family, finances, work, and personal illness (Sanderson & Barlow, 1990). In particular, they worry about how much they worry (Barlow et al., 2003). Their anxiety is frequently accompanied by physical symptoms, such as muscle tension, diarrhea, dizziness, faintness, sweating, and heart palpitations. Generalized anxiety disorder tends to have a gradual onset, has a lifetime prevalence of about 5%, and is seen more frequently in females than males (Brown, 1999; Merikangas, 2005).

Phobic Disorder

In a phobic disorder, an individual's troublesome anxiety has a specific focus. **A *phobic disorder* is marked by a persistent and irrational fear of an object or situation that presents no realistic danger.** Although mild phobias are extremely common, people are said to have a phobic disorder only when their fears seriously interfere with their everyday behavior. Phobic reactions tend to be accompanied by physical symptoms of anxiety, such as trembling and palpitations (Rapee & Barlow, 2001). The following case provides an example of a phobic disorder:

Hilda is 32 years of age and has a rather unusual fear. She is terrified of snow. She cannot go outside in the snow. She cannot even stand to see snow or hear about it on the weather report. Her phobia severely constricts her day-to-day behavior. Probing in therapy revealed that her phobia was caused by a traumatic experience at age 11. Playing at a ski lodge, she was buried briefly by a small avalanche of snow. She had no recollection of this experience until it was recovered in therapy. (Adapted from Laughlin, 1967, p. 227)

As Hilda's unusual snow phobia illustrates, people can develop phobic responses to virtually anything. Nonetheless, certain types of phobias are relatively common, as the data in **Figure 15.5** (on the next page) show. Particularly common are acrophobia (fear of heights), claustrophobia (fear of small, enclosed places), brontophobia (fear of storms), hydrophobia (fear of water), and various animal and insect phobias (Antony & McCabe, 2003). People troubled by phobias typically realize that their fears are irrational, but they still are unable to calm themselves when they encounter a phobic object.

Panic Disorder and Agoraphobia

A *panic disorder* is characterized by recurrent attacks of overwhelming anxiety that usually occur suddenly and unexpectedly. These paralyzing attacks are accompanied by physical symptoms of anxiety. After a number of anxiety attacks, victims often become apprehensive, wondering when their next panic attack will occur. Their concern about exhibiting panic in public sometimes escalates to the point where they are afraid to leave home. This creates a condition called *agoraphobia.*

***Agoraphobia* is a fear of going out to public places** (its literal meaning is "fear of the marketplace or open places"). Because of this fear, some people become prisoners confined to their homes, although many can venture out if accompanied by a trusted companion (Hollander & Simeon, 2003). As its name suggests, agoraphobia has traditionally been viewed as a phobic disorder. However, more recent evidence suggests that agoraphobia is mainly a complication of panic disorder. About two-thirds of people who suffer from panic disorder are female (Horwath & Weissman, 2000). The onset of panic disorder typically occurs during late adolescence or early adulthood (Pine & McClure, 2005a).

Figure 15.5

Common phobias. Frequently reported phobias are listed here, along with their typical age of onset and information on gender differences in phobias.

From Marks, I. M. (1969). *Fears and phobias.* San Diego: Academic Press. Copyright 1969 by Isaac Marks. Reprinted by permission.

Common Phobias

	Percent of all phobias	Gender difference	Typical age of onset
Agoraphobia (fear of places of assembly, crowds, open spaces)	10%–50%	Large majority are women	Early adulthood
Social phobia (fear of being observed doing something humiliating)	10%	Majority are women	Adolescence
Specific phobias *Animals* Cats (ailurophobia) Dogs (cynophobia) Insects (insectophobia) Spiders (arachnophobia) Birds (avisophobia) Horses (equinophobia) Snakes (ophidiophobia) Rodents (rodentophobia)	5%–15%	Vast majority are women	Childhood
Inanimate objects Dirt (mysophobia) Storms (brontophobia) Heights (acrophobia) Darkness (nyctophobia) Closed spaces (claustrophobia)	20%	None	Any age
Illness-injury (nosophobia) Death (thanatophobia) Cancer (cancerophobia) Venereal disease (venerophobia)	15%–25%	None	Middle age

Cartoon by Harris © 1990. Reprinted by permission of ScienceCartoonsPlus.com.

Obsessive-Compulsive Disorder

Obsessions are *thoughts* that repeatedly intrude on one's consciousness in a distressing way. Compulsions are *actions* that one feels forced to carry out. Thus, **an *obsessive-compulsive disorder (OCD)* is marked by persistent, uncontrollable intrusions of unwanted thoughts (obsessions) and urges to engage in senseless rituals (compulsions).** To illustrate, let's examine the bizarre behavior of a man once reputed to be the wealthiest person in the world:

The famous industrialist Howard Hughes was obsessed with the possibility of being contaminated by germs. This led him to devise extraordinary rituals to minimize the possibility of such contamination. He would spend hours methodically cleaning a single telephone. He once wrote a three-page memo instructing assistants on exactly how to open cans of fruit for him. The following is just a small portion of the instructions that Hughes provided for a driver who delivered films to his bungalow. "Get out of the car on the traffic side. Do not at any time be on the side of the car between the car and the curb. . . . Carry only one can of film at a time. Step over the gutter opposite the place where the sidewalk dead-ends into the curb from a point as far out into the center of the road as possible. Do not ever walk on the grass at all, also do not step into the gutter at all. Walk to the bungalow keeping as near to the center of the sidewalk as possible." (Adapted from Barlett & Steele, 1979, pp. 227–237)

Obsessions often center on fear of contamination, inflicting harm on others, suicide, or sexual acts. Compulsions usually involve stereotyped rituals that temporarily relieve anxiety. Common examples include constant handwashing; repetitive cleaning of things that are already clean; endless rechecking of locks, faucets, and such; and excessive arranging, counting, and hoarding of things (Pato, Eisen, & Phillips, 2003). Specific types of obsessions tend to be associated with specific types of compulsions. For example, obsessions about contamination tend to be paired with cleaning compulsions, and obsessions about symmetry tend to be paired with ordering and arranging compulsions (Leckman et al., 1997). Although many of us can be compulsive at times, full-fledged obsessive-compulsive disorders occur in roughly 2.5% of the population

Repetitive handwashing is an example of a common compulsive behavior.

(Turner et al., 2001). The typical age of onset for OCD is late adolescence, with most cases (75%) emerging before the age of 30 (Kessler et al., 2005a). OCD can be a particularly debilitating disorder, as it is often associated with severe social and occupational impairments (Torres et al., 2006).

Etiology of Anxiety Disorders

Like most psychological disorders, anxiety disorders develop out of complicated interactions among a variety of factors. Conditioning and learning appear especially important, but biological factors may also contribute to anxiety disorders.

Biological Factors

Recent studies suggest that there may be a weak to moderate genetic predisposition to anxiety disorders, depending on the specific type of disorder (Hettema, Neale, & Kendler, 2001; McMahon & Kassem, 2005). These findings are consistent with the idea that inherited differences in temperament might make some people more vulnerable than others to anxiety disorders. Kagan and his colleagues (1992) have found that about 15%–20% of infants display an *inhibited temperament,* characterized by shyness, timidity, and wariness, which appears to have a strong genetic basis. Research suggests that this temperament is a risk factor for the development of anxiety disorders (Coles, Schofield, & Pietrefesa, 2006).

One influential theory holds that *anxiety sensitivity* may make people vulnerable to anxiety disorders (McWilliams et al., 2007; Reiss, 1991; Schmidt, Zvolensky, & Maner, 2006). According to this notion, some people are very sensitive to internal physiological symptoms of anxiety and are prone to overreact with fear when they experience these symptoms. Anxiety sensitivity may fuel an inflationary spiral in which anxiety breeds more anxiety, which eventually spins out of control in the form of an anxiety disorder.

Recent evidence suggests that a link may exist between anxiety disorders and neurochemical activity in the brain. ***Neurotransmitters* are chemicals that carry signals from one neuron to another.** Therapeutic drugs (such as Valium) that reduce excessive anxiety appear to alter activity at synapses for a neurotransmitter called GABA. This finding and other lines of evidence suggest that disturbances in the neural circuits using GABA may play a role in some types of anxiety disorders (Skolnick, 2003). Abnormalities in other neural circuits using the transmitter serotonin have been implicated in panic and obsessive-compulsive disorders (Sullivan & Coplan, 2000). Thus, scientists are beginning to unravel the neurochemical bases for anxiety disorders.

Conditioning and Learning

Many anxiety responses may be *acquired through classical conditioning* and *maintained through operant conditioning* (see Chapter 2). According to Mowrer (1947), an originally neutral stimulus (the snow in Hilda's case, for instance) may be paired with a frightening event (the avalanche) so that it becomes a conditioned stimulus eliciting anxiety (see **Figure 15.6** on the next page). Once a fear is acquired through classical conditioning, the person may start avoiding the anxiety-producing stimulus. The avoidance response is negatively reinforced because it is followed by a reduction in anxiety. This process involves operant conditioning (also shown in **Figure 15.6**). Thus, separate conditioning processes may create and then sustain specific anxiety responses (Levis, 1989). Consistent with this view, studies find that a substantial portion of people suffering from phobias can identify a traumatic conditioning experience that probably contributed to their anxiety disorder (Antony & McCabe, 2003; King, Eleonora, & Ollendick, 1998).

The tendency to develop phobias of certain types of objects and situations may be explained by Martin Seligman's (1971) concept of *preparedness.* Like many theorists, Seligman believes that classical conditioning creates most phobic responses. *However, he suggests that people are biologically prepared by their evolutionary history to acquire some fears much more easily than*

Figure 15.6

Conditioning as an explanation for phobias. (1) Many phobias appear to be acquired through classical conditioning when a neutral stimulus is paired with an anxiety-arousing stimulus. **(2)** Once acquired, a phobia may be maintained through operant conditioning, because avoidance of the phobic stimulus leads to a reduction in anxiety, resulting in negative reinforcement.

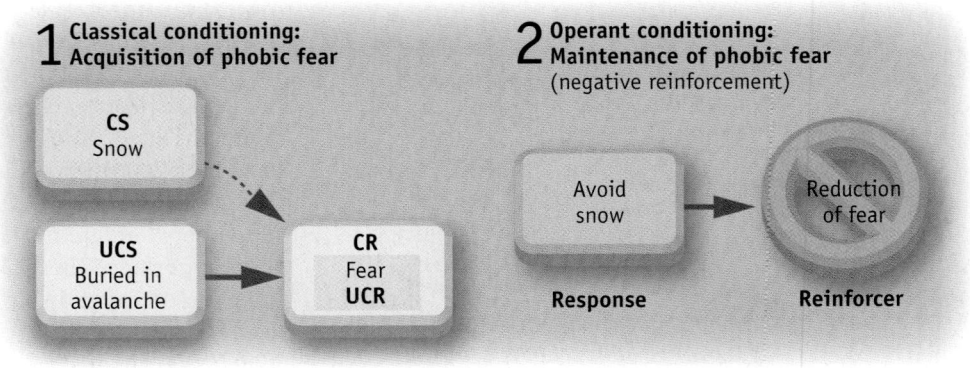

others. His theory would explain why people develop phobias of ancient sources of threat (such as snakes and spiders) much more readily than modern sources of threat (such as electrical outlets or hot irons). Some laboratory studies have yielded evidence consistent with the idea that we are wired by evolution to readily develop certain conditioned fears, but the evidence is inconsistent (Ohman & Mineka, 2003; Rapee & Barlow, 2001).

There are a number of problems with conditioning models of phobias (Rachman, 1990). For instance, many people with phobias cannot recall or identify a traumatic conditioning experience that led to their phobia. Conversely, many people endure extremely traumatic experiences that should create a phobia but do not. To provide better explanations for these complexities, conditioning models of anxiety disorders are currently being revised to include a larger role for cognitive factors (de Jong & Merckelbach, 2000).

Web Link 15.3 **National Institute of Mental Health: For the Public**

A wealth of information on psychological disorders is available at this subpage of the U.S. National Institute of Mental Health's massive website. Visitors will find detailed online booklets on generalized anxiety disorder, obsessive-compulsive disorder, panic disorder, depression, bipolar disorder, and so forth. Brief fact sheets, dense technical reports, and many other resources are also available.

Cognitive Factors

Cognitive theorists maintain that certain styles of thinking make some people particularly vulnerable to anxiety disorders. According to these theorists, some people are prone to suffer from problems with anxiety because they tend to (a) misinterpret harmless situations as threatening, (b) focus excessive attention on perceived threats, and (c) selectively recall information that seems threatening (Beck, 1997; McNally, 1994, 1996). In one intriguing test of the cognitive view, anxious and nonanxious subjects were asked to read 32 sentences that could be interpreted in either a threatening or a nonthreatening manner (Eysenck et al., 1991). For instance, one such sentence was "The doctor examined little Emma's growth," which could mean that the doctor checked her height or the growth of a tumor. As **Figure 15.7** shows, the anxious subjects interpreted the sentences in a threatening way more often than the nonanxious subjects did. Thus, the cognitive view holds that some people are prone to anxiety disorders because they see threat in every corner of their lives (Aikens & Craske, 2001; Riskind, 2005).

Figure 15.7

Cognitive factors in anxiety disorders. Eysenck and his colleagues (1991) compared how subjects with anxiety disorders and nonanxious subjects tended to interpret sentences that could be viewed as threatening or nonthreatening. Consistent with cognitive models of anxiety disorders, anxious subjects were more likely to interpret the sentences in a threatening light.

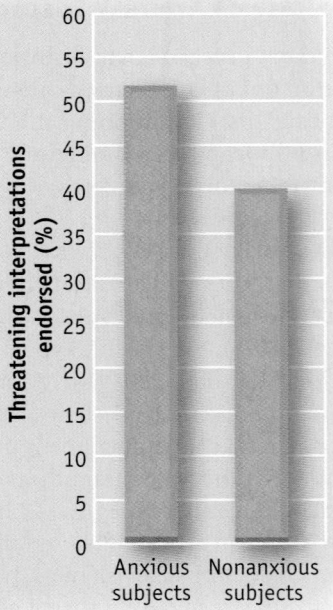

Stress

Finally, studies have supported the long-held suspicion that anxiety disorders are stress related (Sandin et al., 2004; Venturello et al., 2002). For instance, Faravelli and Pallanti (1989) found that patients with panic disorder had experienced a dramatic increase in stress in the month prior to the onset of their disorder. In another study, Brown et al. (1998) found an association between stress and the development of social phobia. Thus, there is reason to believe that high stress often helps precipitate the onset of anxiety disorders.

Somatoform Disorders

LEARNING OBJECTIVES

- *Describe three types of somatoform disorders.*
- *Summarize what is known about the causes of somatoform disorders.*

Chances are, you have met people who always seem to be complaining about aches, pains, and physical maladies of doubtful authenticity. When physical illness appears *largely* psychological in origin, people are said to suffer from somatoform disorders. ***Somatoform disorders* are physical ailments that cannot be fully explained by organic conditions and are largely due to psychological factors.** Although their symptoms are more imaginary than real, victims of somatoform disorders are *not* simply faking illness. Deliberate feigning of illness for personal gain is another matter altogether, called *malingering.*

People with somatoform disorders typically seek treatment from physicians practicing neurology, internal medicine, or family medicine, instead of from psychologists or psychiatrists. Making accurate diagnoses of somatoform disorders can be difficult, because the causes of physical ailments are sometimes hard to identify. In some cases, a problem is misdiagnosed as a somatoform disorder when a genuine organic cause for a person's physical symptoms goes undetected despite medical examinations and tests (Yutzy, 2003). Diagnostic ambiguities such as these have led some theorists to argue that the category of somatoform disorders should be eliminated in DSM-V (Mayou et al., 2005), but other theorists have expressed vigorous disagreement (Rief, Henningsen, & Hiller, 2006). In this section, we will look at three specific types of somatoform disorders: somatization disorder, conversion disorder, and hypochondriasis.

Somatization Disorder

Individuals with somatization disorders are often said to "cling to ill health." **A *somatization disorder* is marked by a history of diverse physical complaints that appear to be psychological in origin.** Somatization disorder occurs mostly in women (Guggenheim, 2000) and often coexists with depression or anxiety disorders (Gureje et al., 1997). Victims report an endless succession of minor physical ailments that seem to wax and wane in response to the stress in their lives (Servan-Schreiber, Kolb, & Tabas, 1999). They usually have a long and complicated history of medical treatment from many doctors. The distinguishing feature of this disorder is the diversity of victims' physical complaints. Over the years, they report a mixed bag of cardiovascular, gastrointestinal, pulmonary, neurological, and genitourinary symptoms. The unlikely nature of such a mixture of symptoms occurring together often alerts a physician to the possible psychological basis for the patient's problems. However, somatization patients are typically resistant to the suggestion that their symptoms might be the result of psychological distress (Hollifield, 2005).

Conversion Disorder

***Conversion disorder* is characterized by a significant loss of physical function with no apparent organic basis, usually in a single organ system.** Common symptoms include partial or complete loss of vision, partial or complete loss of hearing, partial paralysis, severe laryngitis or mutism, seizures, vomiting, and loss of feeling or function in limbs, such as that seen in the following case:

Mildred was a rancher's daughter who lost the use of both of her legs during adolescence. Mildred was at home alone one afternoon when a male relative attempted to assault her. She screamed for help, and her legs gave way as she slipped to the floor. She was found on the floor a few minutes later when her mother returned home. She could not get up, so she was carried to her bed. Her legs buckled when she made subsequent attempts to walk on her own. Due to her illness, she was waited on hand and foot by her family and friends. Neighbors brought her homemade things to eat or to wear. She became the center of attention in the household. (Adapted from Cameron, 1963, pp. 312–313)

People with conversion disorder are usually troubled by more severe ailments than people with somatization disorder. In some cases of conversion disorder, there are telltale clues about the psychological origins of the illness because the patient's symptoms are not consistent with medical knowledge about their apparent disease. For instance, the loss of feeling in one hand that is seen in "glove anesthesia" is inconsistent with the known facts of neurological organization (see **Figure 15.8**).

Hypochondriasis

Hypochondriacs constantly monitor their physical condition, looking for signs of illness. Any tiny alteration from their physical norm leads them to conclude that they have contracted a disease. ***Hypochondriasis* (more widely known as *hypochondria*) is characterized by excessive preoccupation with health concerns and incessant worry about developing physical illnesses.** The following case illustrates the nature of hypochondria:

Jeff is a middle-aged man who works as a clerk in a drug store. He spends long hours describing his health problems to anyone who will listen. Jeff is an avid reader of popular magazine articles on medicine. He can tell you all about the latest medical discoveries. He takes all sorts of pills and vitamins to ward off possible illnesses. He's the first to try every new product on the market. Jeff is constantly afflicted by new symptoms of illness. His most recent problems were poor digestion and a heartbeat that he thought was irregular. He frequently goes to physicians who can find nothing wrong with him physically. They tell him that he is healthy. He thinks they use "backward techniques." He suspects that his illness is too rare to be diagnosed successfully. (Adapted from Suinn, 1984, p. 236)

When hypochondriacs are assured by their physician that they do not have any real illness, they often are skeptical and disbelieving (Starcevic, 2001). As in Jeff's case, they frequently assume that the physician must be incompetent, and they go shopping for another doctor. Hypochondriacs don't subjectively suffer from physical distress as much as they overinterpret every conceivable sign of illness. Hypochondria frequently appears alongside other psychological disorders, especially anxiety disorders and depression (Iezzi, Duckworth, & Adams, 2001). For example, Howard Hughes's obsessive-compulsive disorder was coupled with profound hypochondria.

Etiology of Somatoform Disorders

Inherited aspects of physiological functioning that promote anxiety reactions may predispose some people to somatoform disorders, but genetic factors do *not* appear to make much of a contribution to the development of these disorders (Hollifield, 2005). The available evidence suggests that these disorders are largely a function of personality and learning.

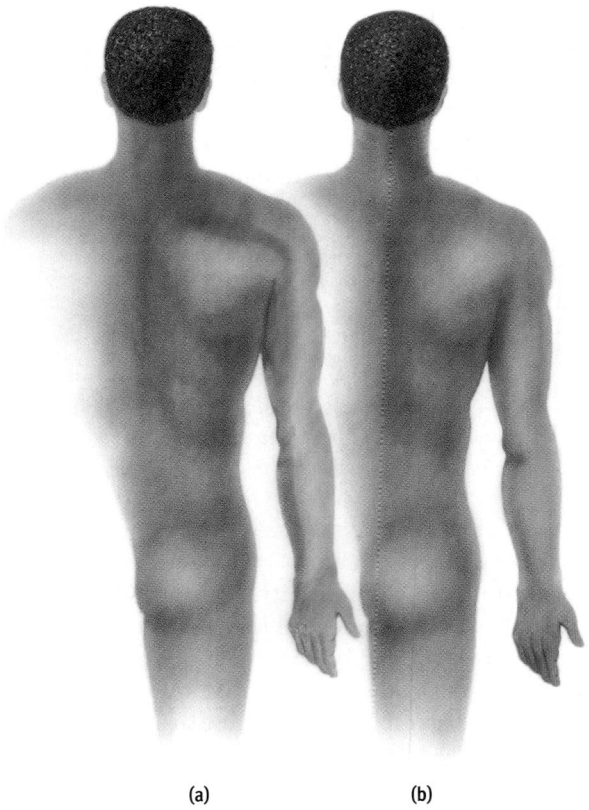

Figure 15.8

Glove anesthesia. In conversion disorders, the physical complaints are sometimes inconsistent with the known facts of physiology. Such is the case in *glove anesthesia,* in which the patient complains of losing feeling in a hand. Given the patterns of nerve distribution in the arm shown in **(a),** a loss of feeling in the hand exclusively as shown in **(b)** is a physical impossibility, indicating that the patient's problem is psychological in origin.

Personality Factors

People with certain types of personality traits seem to be particularly prone to develop somatoform disorders. The prime candidates appear to be people with *histrionic* personality characteristics (Nemiah, 1985; Slavney, 1990). The histrionic personality tends to be self-centered, suggestible, excitable, highly emotional, and overly dramatic. Such people thrive on the attention that they get when they become ill. The personality trait of *neuroticism* also seems to elevate individuals' susceptibility to somatoform disorders (Noyes et al., 2005). Research also suggests that the pathological care-seeking behavior seen in these disorders may be caused by *insecure attachment styles* (see Chapter 8)

that are rooted in early experiences with caregivers (Noyes et al., 2003).

Cognitive Factors

In recent years, theorists have devoted increased attention to how cognitive peculiarities might contribute to somatoform disorders. For example, Barsky (2001) asserts that some people focus excessive attention on their internal physiological processes and amplify normal bodily sensations into symptoms of distress, which lead them to pursue unnecessary medical treatment. Recent evidence suggests that people with somatoform disorders tend to draw catastrophic conclusions about minor bodily complaints (Salkovskis & Warwick, 2001). They also seem to apply a faulty standard of good health, equating health with a complete absence of symptoms and discomfort, which is unrealistic (Barsky et al., 1993).

The Sick Role

As we discussed in Chapter 14, some people grow fond of the role associated with being sick (Hotopf, 2004; Pilowsky, 1993). Their complaints of physical symptoms may be reinforced by indirect benefits derived from their illness (Schwartz, Slater, & Birchler, 1994). One payoff is that becoming ill is a superb way to avoid having to confront life's challenges. Many people with somatoform disorders are avoiding facing up to marital problems, career frustrations, family responsibilities, and the like. After all, when you're sick, others cannot place great demands on you. Another benefit is that physical problems can provide a convenient excuse when people fail, or worry about failing, in endeavors that are critical to their self-esteem (Organista & Miranda, 1991).

Attention from others is another payoff that may reinforce complaints of physical illness. When people become ill, they command the attention of family, friends, co-workers, neighbors, and doctors. The sympathy that illness often brings may strengthen the person's tendency to feel ill. This clearly occurred in Mildred's case of conversion disorder. Her illness paid handsome dividends in terms of attention, consolation, and kindhearted assistance from others.

Dissociative Disorders

LEARNING OBJECTIVES

- *Describe three types of dissociative disorders.*
- *Summarize what is known about the causes of dissociative disorders.*

Dissociative disorders are probably the most controversial set of disorders in the diagnostic system, sparking heated debate among normally subdued researchers and clinicians (Loewenstein & Putnam 2005). ***Dissociative disorders*** **are a class of disorders in which people lose contact with portions of their consciousness or memory, resulting in disruptions in their sense of identity.** Here we describe three dissociative syndromes—dissociative amnesia, dissociative fugue, and dissociative identity disorder—all of which are relatively uncommon.

Dissociative Amnesia and Fugue

Dissociative amnesia and fugue are overlapping disorders characterized by serious memory deficits. ***Dissociative amnesia*** **is a sudden loss of memory for important personal information that is too extensive to be due to normal forgetting.** Memory losses may occur for a single traumatic event (such as an automobile accident or home fire) or for an extended period of time surrounding the event. Cases of amnesia have been observed after people have experienced disasters, accidents, combat stress, physical abuse, and rape, or after they have witnessed the violent death of a parent, among other things (Arrigo & Pezdek, 1997; Loewenstein, 1996). **In *dissociative fugue,* people lose their memory for their sense of personal identity.** Having forgotten their name, their family, where they live, and where they work, these people typically wander away from their home area. In spite of this wholesale forgetting, they remember matters unrelated to their identity, such as how to drive a car and how to do math.

Dissociative Identity Disorder

Dissociative identity disorder (DID)* involves the coexistence in one person of two or more largely complete, and usually very different, personalities.** The name for this disorder used to be ***multiple personality disorder, which still enjoys informal usage. In dissociative identity disorder, the divergences in behavior go far beyond those that people normally display in adapting to different roles in life. People with "multiple personalities" feel that they have more than one identity. Each personality has his or her own name, memories, traits, and physical mannerisms. Although rare, this "Dr. Jekyll and Mr. Hyde" syndrome is frequently portrayed in novels, movies, and television shows. In popular media portrayals, the syndrome is often mistakenly called *schizophrenia.* As you will see later, schizophrenic disorders are entirely different and do not involve "split personality."

In dissociative identity disorder, the various personalities generally report that they are unaware of each other (Eich et al., 1997), although doubts have been raised about the accuracy of this assertion (Allen & Iacono, 2001). The alternate personalities commonly display traits that are quite foreign to the original personality. For instance, a shy, inhibited person might develop a flamboyant, extraverted alternate personality. Transitions between identities often occur suddenly. The disparities between identities can be bizarre, as personalities may assert that they are different in age, race, gender, and sexual orientation (Kluft, 1996). Dissociative identity disorder rarely occurs in isolation. Most DID patients also have a history of anxiety, mood, or personality disorders (Ross, 1999).

Starting in the 1970s, there was a dramatic increase in the diagnosis of multiple-personality disorder (Kihlstrom, 2001). Only 79 well-documented cases had accumulated up through 1970, but by the late-1990s about 40,000 cases were estimated to have been reported (Lilienfeld & Lynn, 2003). Some theorists believe that these disorders used to be underdiagnosed—that is, they often went undetected (Maldonado & Spiegel, 2003). However, other theorists argue that a handful of clinicians have begun overdiagnosing the condition and that some clinicians even *encourage and contribute* to the emergence of DID (McHugh, 1995; Powell & Gee, 1999). Consistent with this view, a survey of all the psychiatrists in Switzerland found that 90% of them had never seen a case of dissociative identity disorder, whereas three of the psychiatrists had each seen more than 20 DID patients (Modestin, 1992). The data from this study suggest that 6 psychiatrists (out of 655 surveyed) accounted for two-thirds of the dissociative identity disorder diagnoses in Switzerland.

Web Link 15.4 **International Society for the Study of Dissociation**

Dissociative disorders, including dissociative identity disorder, are the focus of this organization of research and clinical professionals. In addition to a selective bibliography and a set of treatment guidelines, the site provides an impressive set of links to other professional groups involved in studying and treating dissociation.

Etiology of Dissociative Disorders

Dissociative amnesia and fugue are usually attributed to excessive stress. However, relatively little is known about why this extreme reaction to stress occurs in a tiny minority of people but not in the vast majority who are subjected to similar stress. Some theorists speculate that certain personality traits—fantasy-proneness and a tendency to become intensely absorbed in personal experiences—may make some people more susceptible to dissociative disorders, but adequate evidence is lacking on this line of thought (Kihlstrom, Glisky, & Angiulo, 1994).

The causes of dissociative identity disorder are particularly obscure. Some skeptical theorists, such as Nicholas Spanos (1994, 1996) and others (Gee, Allen, & Powell, 2003; Lilienfeld et al., 1999), believe that people with multiple personalities are engaging in intentional role playing to use mental illness as a face-saving excuse for their personal failings. Spanos also argues that a small minority of therapists help create multiple personalities in their patients by subtly encouraging the emergence of alternate personalities. According to Spanos, dissociative identity disorder is a creation of modern North American culture, much as demonic possession was a creation of early Christianity. To bolster his argument, he discusses how DID patients' symptom presentations seem to have been influenced by popular media. For example, the typical patient with dissociative identity disorder used to report having two or three personalities, but since the publication of *Sybil* (Schreiber, 1973) and other books describing patients with many personalities, the average number of alternate personalities has climbed to about 15. In a similar vein, a dramatic upsurge occurred in the number of dissociative patients reporting that they were victims of ritual satanic abuse during childhood after the publication of *Michelle Remembers* (Smith & Pazder, 1980), a book about a DID patient who purportedly was tortured by a satanic cult.

In spite of these concerns, many clinicians are convinced that DID is an authentic disorder (Gleaves, May, & Cardena, 2001). They argue that there is no incentive for either patients or therapists to manufacture cases of multiple personalities, which are often greeted with skepticism and outright hostility. They maintain that most cases of DID are rooted in severe emotional trauma that occurred during childhood (Draijer & Langeland, 1999). A substantial majority of people with DID report a history of disturbed home life, beatings and rejection from parents, and sexual abuse (Scroppo et al., 1998; Foote et al., 2006). However, this abuse typically has not been independently verified (Lilienfeld & Lynn, 2003). Moreover, this link would not be unique to DID, as a history of child abuse elevates the likelihood of *many* disorders, especially among females (MacMillan et al., 2001). In the final analysis, very little is known about the causes of dissociative identity disorder, which remains a controversial diagnosis (Barry-Walsh, 2005). In one survey of American psychiatrists, only one-quarter of the respondents indicated that they felt there was solid evidence for the scientific validity of the DID diagnosis (Pope et al., 1999). Consistent with this finding, a more recent study found that scientific interest in DID has dwindled since the mid-1990s (Pope et al., 2006).

Mood Disorders

LEARNING OBJECTIVES

- *Describe the two major mood disorders and discuss their prevalence.*
- *Explain how biological factors may be related to the development of mood disorders.*
- *Discuss how cognitive processes may contribute to mood disorders.*
- *Explain how interpersonal behavior and stress may contribute to mood disorders.*

What might Abraham Lincoln, Leo Tolstoy, Marilyn Monroe, Vincent Van Gogh, Ernest Hemingway, Winston Churchill, Virginia Woolf, Janis Joplin, Irving Berlin, Kurt Cobain, Francis Ford Coppola, Carrie Fisher, Ted Turner, Sting, Mike Wallace, Larry Flynt, Jane Pauley, and Ben Stiller have in common? Yes, they all achieved great prominence, albeit in different ways at different times. But, more pertinent to our interest, they all suffered from severe mood disorders. Although mood disorders can be terribly debilitating, people with mood disorders may still achieve greatness, because such disorders tend to be *episodic.* In other words, emotional disorders often come and go. Thus, episodes of disturbance are interspersed among periods of normality. These episodes of disturbance can vary greatly in length, but they typically last 3 to 12 months (Akiskal, 2005).

Of course, we all have our ups and downs in terms of mood. Life would be dull indeed if emotional tone were constant. Everyone experiences depression occasionally and has other days that bring an emotional high. Such emotional fluctuations are natural, but some people are prone to extreme distortions of mood. ***Mood disorders* are a class of disorders marked by emotional disturbances that may spill over to disrupt physical, perceptual, social, and thought processes.**

© Steven Henry/Getty Images

© Tim Mosenfelder/Getty Images

© Elisabetta Villa/Getty Images

Mood disorders are common and have afflicted many successful, well-known people, such as Anne Rice, Sheryl Crow and Harrison Ford.

Figure 15.9

Episodic patterns in mood disorders. Episodes of emotional disturbance come and go unpredictably in mood disorders. People with unipolar disorders suffer from bouts of depression only, while people with bipolar disorders experience both manic and depressive episodes. The time between episodes of disturbance varies greatly.

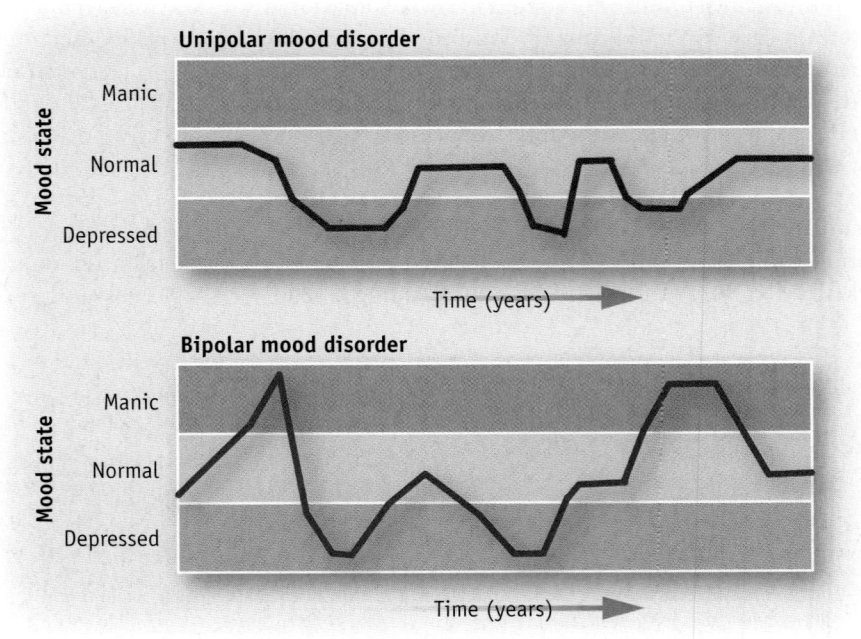

Mood disorders include two basic types: unipolar and bipolar (see **Figure 15.9**). People with *unipolar disorders* experience emotional extremes at just one end of the mood continuum—depression. People with *bipolar disorders* experience emotional extremes at both ends of the mood continuum, going through periods of both *depression* and *mania* (excitement and elation). The mood swings in bipolar disorders can be patterned in many ways.

Major Depressive Disorder

The line between normal and abnormal depression can be difficult to draw (Kendler & Gardner, 1998). Ultimately, a subjective judgment is required. Crucial considerations in this judgment include the duration of the depression and its disruptive effects. When a depression significantly impairs everyday adaptive behavior for more than a few weeks, there is reason for concern.

In *major depressive disorder* people show persistent feelings of sadness and despair and a loss of interest in previous sources of pleasure. **Figure 15.10** summarizes the most common symptoms of depressive disorders and compares them to the symptoms of mania. Negative emotions form the heart of the depressive syndrome, but many other symptoms may appear. Depressed people often give up activities that they used to find enjoyable. For example, a depressed person might quit going bowling or give up a favorite hobby like photography. Reduced appetite and insomnia are common. People with depression often lack energy. They tend to move sluggishly and talk slowly. Anxiety, irritability, and brooding are frequently observed. Self-esteem tends to sink as the depressed person begins to feel worthless. Depression plunges people into feelings of hopelessness, dejection, and boundless guilt. The severity of abnormal depression varies considerably. The onset of unipolar disorder can occur at

Figure 15.10

Common symptoms in manic and depressive episodes. The emotional, cognitive, and motor symptoms exhibited in manic and depressive illnesses are largely the opposite of each other.

From Sarason, I. G., & Sarason, B. R. (1987). *Abnormal psychology: The problem of maladaptive behavior* (5th ed., p. 283). Englewood Cliffs, NJ: Prentice-Hall. © 1987 Prentice-Hall. Reprinted by permission of Prentice-Hall, Inc.

Comparison of Manic and Depressive Symptoms

Characteristics	Manic episode	Depressive episode
Emotional	Elated, euphoric, very sociable, impatient at any hindrance	Gloomy, hopeless, socially withdrawn, irritable
Cognitive	Characterized by racing thoughts, flight of ideas, desire for action, and impulsive behavior; talkative, self-confident; experiencing delusions of grandeur	Characterized by slowness of thought processes, obsessive worrying, inability to make decisions, negative self-image, self-blame, and delusions of guilt and disease
Motor	Hyperactive, tireless, requiring less sleep than usual, showing increased sex drive and fluctuating appetite	Less active, tired, experiencing difficulty in sleeping, showing decreased sex drive and decreased appetite

any point in the life span, but a substantial majority of cases emerge before age 40 (Hammen, 2003). Depression occurs in children and adolescents, as well as adults (Gruenberg & Goldstein, 2003). The vast majority (75%–95%) of people who suffer from depression experience more than one episode over the course of their lifetime (Dubovsky, Davies, Dubovsky, 2003). The average number of depressive episodes is five to six, and the average length of these episodes is about six months (Akiskal, 2005).

How common are depressive disorders? Very common. A recent, large-scale study of a nationally representative sample of over 9000 adults found that the lifetime prevalence of depressive disorder was 16.2% (Kessler et al., 2003). That estimate suggests that over 30 million people in the United States have suffered from depression! That said, estimates of the prevalence of depression vary quite a bit from one study to another because of the previously mentioned difficulty in drawing a line between normal dejection and abnormal depression. Hence, researchers using different procedures and cutoff points obtain different estimates.

Evidence suggests that the prevalence of depression is increasing, as it is higher in more recent age cohorts (Rehm, Wagner, & Ivens-Tyndal, 2001). The factors underlying this rise in depression are not readily apparent, and researchers are scrambling to collect data that might shed light on this unanticipated trend. They have not ruled out the possibility that the increase may be somewhat artificial, reflecting more sensitive diagnostic criteria and greater willingness of people to acknowledge their depressive symptoms (Goodwin et al., 2006).

Researchers also find that the prevalence of depression is about twice as high in women as it is in men (Rihmer & Angst, 2005). The many possible explanations for this gender gap are the subject of considerable debate. The gap does *not* appear to be attributable to differences in genetic makeup or other biological factors (Kessler et al., 2003). Susan Nolen-Hoeksema (2001) argues that women experience more depression than men because they are far more likely to be victims of sexual abuse and somewhat more likely to endure poverty, harassment, and role constraints. In other words, she attributes the higher prevalence of depression among women to their experience of greater stress and adversity. Nolen-Hoeksema also believes that women have a greater tendency than men to *ruminate* about setbacks and problems. Evidence suggests that this tendency to dwell on one's difficulties elevates vulnerability to depression, as we will discuss momentarily.

Courtesy, Susan Nolen-Hoeksema

Susan Nolen-Hoeksema

Web Link 15.5 **Dr. Ivan's Depression Central**

Some might suggest that psychiatrist Ivan Goldberg's site would be better titled "Everything You Ever Wanted to Know About Depression . . ." He offers visitors a great depth of resources regarding depression and mood disorders.

Bipolar Disorder

***Bipolar disorder* (formerly known as *manic-depressive disorder*) is marked by the experience of both depressed and manic periods.** The symptoms seen in manic periods generally are the opposite of those seen in depression (see **Figure 15.10** for a comparison). In a manic episode, a person's mood becomes elevated to the point of euphoria. Self-esteem skyrockets as the person bubbles over with optimism, energy, and extravagant plans. People become hyperactive and may go for days without sleep. They talk rapidly and shift topics wildly as their minds race at breakneck speed. Judgment is often impaired. Some people in manic periods gamble impulsively, spend money frantically, or become sexually reckless. Like depressive disorders, bipolar disorders vary considerably in severity.

You may be thinking that the euphoria in manic episodes sounds appealing. If so, you are not entirely wrong. In their milder forms, manic states can seem attractive. The increases in energy, self-esteem, and optimism can be deceptively seductive. Because of the increase in energy, many bipolar patients report temporary surges of productivity and creativity (Goodwin & Jamison, 1990).

Although manic episodes may have some positive aspects, bipolar disorder ultimately proves to be troublesome for most victims. Manic periods often have a paradoxical negative undertow of uneasiness and irritability (Dilsaver et al., 1999). Moreover, mild manic

"Those? Oh, just a few souvenirs from my bipolar-disorder days."

© The New Yorker Collection 1996 Tom Cheney from cartoonbank.com. All rights reserved.

Understanding and Preventing Suicide

Suicide is the 11th leading cause of death in the United States, accounting for over 30,000 deaths annually. Official statistics may underestimate the scope of the problem, as many suicides are disguised as accidents, either by the suicidal person or by the survivors who try to cover up afterward. Experts estimate that suicide attempts may outnumber completed suicides by a ratio of as much as 20 to 1 (Sudak, 2005). Anyone might commit suicide, but some groups are at higher risk than others (Carroll-Ghosh, Victor, & Bourgeois, 2003). Evidence suggests that women *attempt* suicide three times more often than men. But men are more likely to actually kill themselves in an attempt, so they *complete* four times as many suicides as women. In regard to age, completed suicides peak in the 45–54 age bracket. Suicide rates have tripled among adolescents and young adults in the last several decades (see Chapter 11), but these rates still remain lower than those observed in older age groups (Sudak, 2005).

Some factors that are associated with an elevated risk of suicide include unemployment, serious health problems, social isolation, feelings of hopelessness, and a history of substance abuse, aggressive behavior, or past suicide attempts (Dawkins et al., 2003). With the luxury of hindsight, it is recognized that about 90% of the people who complete suicide suffer from some type of psychological disorder, although in some cases this disorder may not be readily apparent beforehand (Dawkins, Golden, & Fawcett, 2003). As you might expect, suicide rates are highest for people with mood disorders (Mann & Currier, 2006).

Myths About Suicide

Many false beliefs exist regarding the nature of suicidal behavior. Some common myths about suicide include the following (Fremouw, Perczel, & Ellis, 1990; Shneidman, 1985; Suicide Awareness Voices of Education, 2007):

Myth 1: People who talk about suicide don't actually commit suicide. Undoubtedly, there are many people who threaten suicide without ever going through with it. Nonetheless, there is no group at higher risk for suicide than those who openly discuss the possibility. Many people who kill themselves have a history of earlier threats that they did not carry out.

Myth 2: Suicide usually takes place with little or no warning. The vast majority of suicide attempts are preceded by some kind of warning. These warnings may range from clear threats to vague statements. For example, at dinner with friends the night before he committed suicide, one prominent attorney cut up his American Express card, saying, "I'm not going to need this anymore." The probability of an actual suicide attempt is greatest when a threat is clear, when it includes a detailed plan, and when the plan involves a relatively deadly method.

Myth 3: People who attempt suicide are fully intent on dying. It appears that only a small minority of those who attempt suicide definitely want to die. A substantial portion of suicide attempts are made by people who are highly ambivalent about dying! They only want to send out a dramatic distress signal. Thus, they arrange their suicide so that a rescue is relatively likely.

Myth 4: People who are suicidal remain so forever. Many people who become suicidal do so for a limited period of time. If they manage to ride through their crisis period, thoughts of suicide may disappear entirely. Apparently, time heals many wounds—if it is given the opportunity.

Preventing Suicide

As Sudak (2005, p. 2449) notes, "It is not possible to prevent all suicides or to totally and absolutely protect a given patient from suicide. What is possible is to reduce the likelihood of suicide." Hence, we will review some general advice that may be useful if you ever have to help someone through a suicidal crisis (American Association of Suicidology, 2007; American Foundation for Suicide Prevention, 2007; Maris, Berman, & Silverman, 2000; Rosenthal, 1988; Shneidman, Farberow, & Litman, 1994).

1. *Take suicidal talk seriously.* When people talk about suicide in vague generalities, it's easy to dismiss it as "idle talk" and let it go. However, people who talk about suicide are a high-risk group and their veiled threats should not be ignored. The first step in suicide prevention is to directly ask such people if they're contemplating suicide.

2. *Provide empathy and social support.* It is important to show the suicidal person that you care. People often contemplate suicide because they see the world around them as indifferent and uncaring. Hence, you must demonstrate to the suicidal person that you are genuinely concerned. Suicide threats are often a last-ditch cry for help. It is therefore imperative that you offer that help.

3. *Identify and clarify the crucial problem.* The suicidal person is often confused and feels lost in a sea of

Understanding and Preventing Suicide (continued)

frustration and problems. It is a good idea to try to help sort through this confusion. Encourage the person to try to identify the crucial problem. Once it is isolated, the problem may not seem quite so overwhelming.

4. *Do not promise to keep someone's suicidal ideation secret.* If you really feel like someone's life is in danger, don't agree to keep his or her suicidal plans secret to preserve your friendship.

5. *In an acute crisis, do not leave a suicical person alone.* Stay with the person until additional help is available. Try to remove any guns, drugs, sharp objects, and so forth that might provide an available means to commit suicide.

6. *Encourage professional consultation.* Most mental health professionals have some experience in dealing with suicidal crises. Many cities have suicide prevention centers with 24-hour hotlines. These centers are staffed with people who have been specially trained to deal with suicidal problems. It is important to try to get a suicidal person to seek professional assistance.

episodes usually escalate to higher levels that become scary and disturbing. Impaired judgment leads many victims to do things that they greatly regret later, as illustrated in the following case:

Robert, a dentist, awoke one morning with the idea that he was the most gifted dental surgeon in his tri-state area. He decided that he should try to provide services to as many people as possible, so that more people could benefit from his talents. Thus, he decided to remodel his two-chair dental office, installing 20 booths so that he could simultaneously attend to 20 patients. That same day he drew up plans for this arrangement, telephoned a number of remodelers, and invited bids for the work. Later that day, impatient to get going on his remodeling, he rolled up his sleeves, got himself a sledgehammer, and began to knock down the walls in his office. Annoyed when that didn't go so well, he smashed his dental tools, washbasins, and X-ray equipment. Later, Robert's wife became concerned about his behavior and summoned two of her adult daughters for assistance. The daughters responded quickly, arriving at the family home with their husbands. In the ensuing discussion, Robert—after bragging about his sexual prowess—made advances toward his daughters. He had to be subdued by their husbands. (Adapted from Kleinmuntz, 1980, p. 309)

Although not rare, bipolar disorder is much less common than unipolar depression. Bipolar disorder affects about 1%–2.5% of the population (Dubovsky et al., 2003). Unlike depressive disorder, bipolar disorder is seen equally in men and women (Rihmer & Angst, 2005). As **Figure 15.11** shows, the onset of bipolar disorders is age related, with the peak of vulnerability occurring between the ages of 20 and 29 (Goodwin & Jamison, 1990).

Etiology of Mood Disorders

We know quite a bit about the etiology of mood disorders, although the puzzle hasn't been assembled completely. There appear to be a number of routes into these disorders, involving intricate interactions between psychological and biological factors.

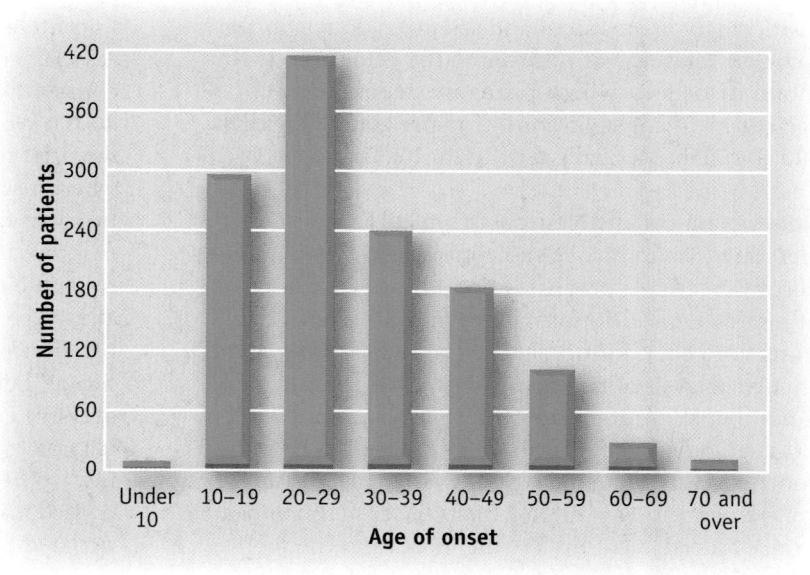

Figure 15.11

Age of onset for bipolar mood disorder. The onset of bipolar disorder typically occurs in adolescence or early adulthood. The data graphed here, which were combined from ten studies, show the distribution of age of onset for 1,304 bipolar patients. As you can see, bipolar disorder emerges most frequently during the 20s decade.

From Goodwin, F. K., & Jamison, K. R. (1990). *Manic-depressive illness.* New York: Oxford University Press. Copyright © 1990 Oxford University Press, Inc. Used by permission of Oxford University Press, Inc.

Genetic Vulnerability

The evidence strongly suggests that genetic factors influence the likelihood of developing major depression or a bipolar mood disorder (Kalidindi & McGuffin, 2003; Sullivan, Neale, & Kendler, 2000). In studies that assess the impact of heredity on psychological disorders, investigators look at *concordance rates.* **A *concordance rate* indicates the percentage of twin pairs or other pairs of relatives that exhibit the same disorder.** If relatives who share more genetic similarity show higher concordance rates than relatives who share less genetic overlap, this finding supports the genetic hypothesis. Twin studies, which compare identical and fraternal twins (see Chapter 2), suggest that genetic factors *are* involved in mood disorders (Kelsoe, 2005; Knowles, Kaufmann, & Rieder, 1999). Concordance rates average around 65%–72% for identical twins but only 14%–19% for fraternal twins, who share less genetic similarity. Thus, evidence suggests that heredity can create a *predisposition* to mood disorders. Environmental factors probably determine whether this predisposition is converted into an actual disorder. Research suggests that genetic vulnerability may play a larger role in women's depression than in men's (Kendler et al., 2006). The influence of genetic factors also appears to be stronger for bipolar disorders than for unipolar disorders (Kieseppa et al., 2004). Some promising results have been reported in *genetic mapping* studies that have attempted to pinpoint the specific genes that shape vulnerability to mood disorders (Caspi et al., 2003; Holmans et al., 2007). However, results have been disturbingly inconsistent and scientists do *not* appear to be on the verge of unraveling the genetic code for mood disorders, which probably depend on subtle variations in constellations of many genes (Kendler, 2005a, 2005b; Merikangas & Risch, 2003).

Neurochemical and Neuroanatomical Factors

Heredity may influence susceptibility to mood disorders by creating a predisposition toward certain types of neurochemical abnormalities in the brain. Correlations have been found between mood disorders and abnormal levels of two neurotransmitters in the brain: norepinephrine and serotonin (Sher & Mann, 2003), although other neurotransmitter disturbances may also contribute (Thase, Jindal, & Howland, 2002). The details remain elusive, but low levels of serotonin appear to be a crucial factor underlying most forms of depression (Flores et al., 2004). A variety of drug therapies are fairly effective in the treatment of severe mood disorders. Most of these drugs are known to affect the availability (in the brain) of the neurotransmitters that have been related to mood disorders (Dubovsky et al., 2003). Since this effect is unlikely to be a coincidence, it bolsters the plausibility of the idea that neurochemical changes produce mood disturbances. That said, after 40 years of enormous research effort, the neurochemical bases of mood disorders remain more mysterious than scientists would like (Delgado & Moreno, 2006).

Studies have also found some interesting correlations between mood disorders and a variety of structural abnormalities in the brain (Flores et al., 2004). Perhaps the best documented correlation is the association between depression and *reduced hippocampal volume* (Campbell et al, 2004; Videbech, 2006). The *hippocampus,* which is known to play a major role in memory (see **Figure 15.12**), tends to be about 8%–10% smaller in depressed subjects than in normal subjects (Videbech & Ravnkilde, 2004). A fascinating new theory of the biological bases of depression may be able to account for this finding. The springboard for this theory is the recent discovery that the human brain continues to generate new neurons in adulthood, especially in the hippocampal formation (Gage, 2002). This process is called *neurogenesis.* Evidence suggests that depression occurs when major life stress causes neurochemical reactions that suppress neurogenesis, resulting in reduced hippocampal volume (Jacobs, 2004; Warner-Schmidt & Duman, 2006). According to this view, the suppression of neurogenesis is the central cause of depression, and antidepressant drugs that relieve depression do so because they promote neurogenesis (Duman & Monteggia, 2006). A great deal of additional research will be required to fully test this innovative new model of the biological bases of depressive disorders.

Cognitive Factors

A variety of theories emphasize how cognitive factors contribute to depressive disorders (Abramson et al., 2002). We will discuss Aaron Beck's (1976, 1987) influential cognitive theory of depression in Chapter 16, where his approach to therapy is described. In this section, we examine Martin Seligman's *learned helplessness model* of depression (see Chapter 4) and its most recent descendant, *hopelessness theory.* Based largely on animal research, Seligman (1974) proposed that depression is caused by *learned helplessness*—passive "giving up" behavior produced by exposure to unavoidable aversive events (such as uncontrollable shock in the laboratory). He originally considered learned helplessness to be a product of conditioning but eventually revised his theory, giving it a cognitive slant. The reformulated theory of learned helplessness postulated that the roots of depression lie in how people explain the setbacks and other negative events that they experience (Abramson, Seligman, & Teasdale, 1978). According to Seligman (1990), people who exhibit a *pessimistic explanatory style* are especially vulnerable to depression (see Chapter 5). These people tend to attribute their setbacks to their personal flaws instead of situational

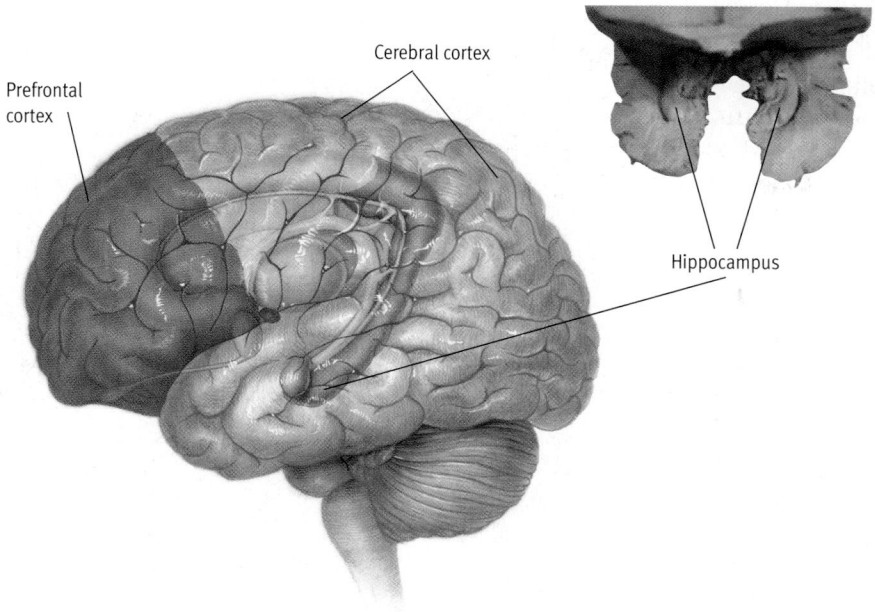

Figure 15.12

The hippocampus and depression. This graphic shows the hippocampus in blue. The photo inset shows a brain dissected to reveal the hippocampus in both the right and left hemispheres. It has long been known that the hippocampus plays a key role in memory, but its possible role in depression has only come to light in recent years. Research suggests that shrinkage of the hippocampal formation due to suppressed neurogenesis may be a key causal factor underlying depressive disorders. This graphic also shows the location of the *prefrontal cortex,* which will be discussed in our upcoming coverage of schizophrenic disorders (see p. 506).

factors, and they tend to draw global, far-reaching conclusions about their personal inadequacies based on these setbacks.

Hopelessness theory builds on these insights by postulating a sense of hopelessness as the "final pathway" leading to depression and by incorporating additional factors that may interact with explanatory style to foster this sense of hopelessness (Abramson, Alloy, & Metalsky, 1995). According to hopelessness theory, a pessimistic explanatory style is just one of several or more factors—along with high stress, low self-esteem, and so forth—that may contribute to hopelessness, and thus depression. Although hopelessness theory casts a wider net than the learned helplessness model, it continues to emphasize the importance of people's *cognitive reactions* to the events in their lives.

In accord with this line of thinking, Susan Nolen-Hoeksema (1991, 2000) has found that people who *ruminate* about their problems and setbacks have elevated rates of depression and tend to remain depressed longer than those who do not ruminate. People who tend to ruminate repetitively focus their attention on their depressing feelings, thinking constantly about how sad, lethargic, and unmotivated they are. According to Nolen-Hoeksema (1995), excessive rumination tends to extend and amplify episodes of depression. She believes that women are more likely to ruminate than men and that this disparity may be a major reason why depression is more prevalent in women.

In sum, cognitive models of depression maintain that negative thinking is what leads to depression in many people. The principal problem with cognitive theories is their difficulty in separating cause from effect (Rehm, Wagner, & Ivens-Tyndal, 2001). Does negative thinking cause depression? Or does depression cause negative thinking (see **Figure 15.13**)? A *clear* demonstration of a causal link between negative thinking and depression is not possible because it would require manipulating people's explanatory style (which is not easy to change) in sufficient degree to produce full-fledged depressive disorders (which would not be ethical). However, a study by Lauren Alloy and her colleagues (1999) provided impressive evidence consistent with a causal link between negative thinking and vulnerability to depression. They assessed the explanatory style of a sample of first-year college students who were

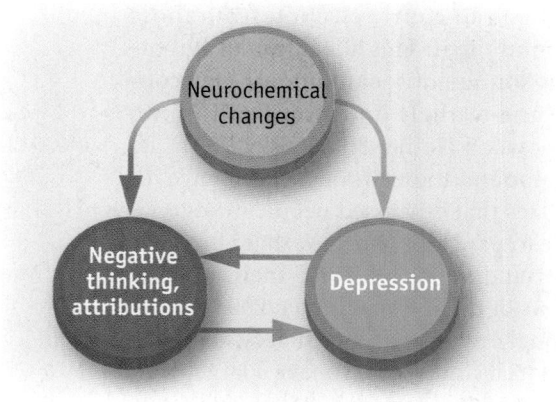

Figure 15.13

Interpreting the correlation between negative thinking and depression. Cognitive theories of depression assert that consistent patterns of negative thinking cause depression. Although these theories are highly plausible, depression could cause negative thoughts, or both could be caused by a third factor, such as neurochemical changes in the brain.

not depressed at the outset of the study. The students were characterized as being at high risk or low risk for depression based on whether they exhibited a negative cognitive style. The follow-up data over the ensuing two and a half years on students who had no prior history of depression showed dramatic differences between the two groups in vulnerability to depression. During this relatively brief period, a major depressive disorder emerged in 17% of the high-risk students in comparison to only 1% of the low-risk students (see **Figure 15.14**). These findings and other data from the study suggest that negative thinking makes people more vulnerable to depression.

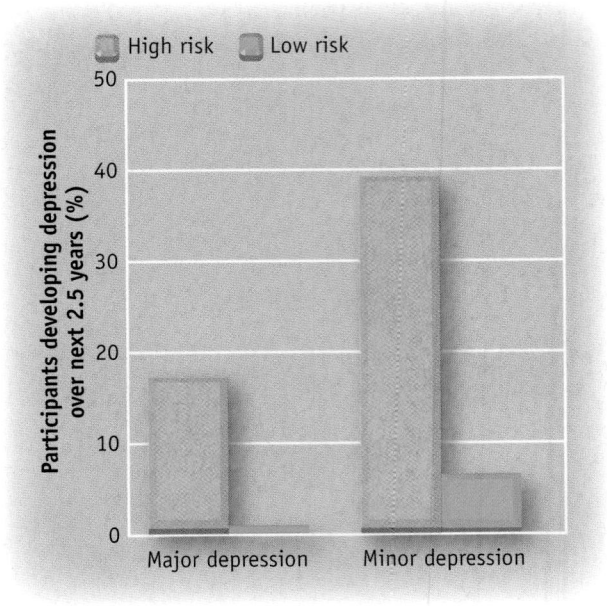

Figure 15.14

Negative thinking and prediction of depression. Alloy and colleagues (1999) measured the explanatory style of first-year college students and characterized them as being high risk or low risk for depression. This graph shows the percentage of these students who experienced major or minor episodes of depression over the next 2.5 years. As you can see, the high-risk students, who exhibited a negative thinking style, proved to be much more vulnerable to depression. (Data from Alloy et al., 1999)

Interpersonal Roots

Some theorists suggest that inadequate social skills put people on the road to depressive disorders (Coyne, 1999; Lewinsohn & Gotlib, 1995). According to this notion, depression-prone people lack the social finesse needed to acquire many important kinds of reinforcers, such as good friends, top jobs, and desirable spouses. This paucity of reinforcers could understandably lead to negative emotions and depression (see **Figure 15.15**). Consistent with this theory, researchers have indeed found correlations between poor social skills and depression (Petty, Sachs-Ericsson, & Joiner, 2004).

Another interpersonal factor is that depressed people tend to be depressing (Joiner & Katz, 1999). Individuals suffering from depression often are irritable and pessimistic. They complain a lot and aren't particularly enjoyable companions. They also alienate people by constantly asking for reassurances about their relationships and their worth (Burns et al., 2006). As a consequence, depressed people tend to court rejection from those around them. This alienation of important sources of social support may contribute to their downward spiral into depression (Joiner & Metalsky, 2001). To compound these problems, evidence indicates that depressed people may gravitate to partners who view them unfavorably and hence reinforce their negative views of themselves (Joiner, 2002). Interestingly, recent evidence suggests that lack of social support may make a larger contribution to depression in women than in men (Kendler, Myers, & Prescott, 2005).

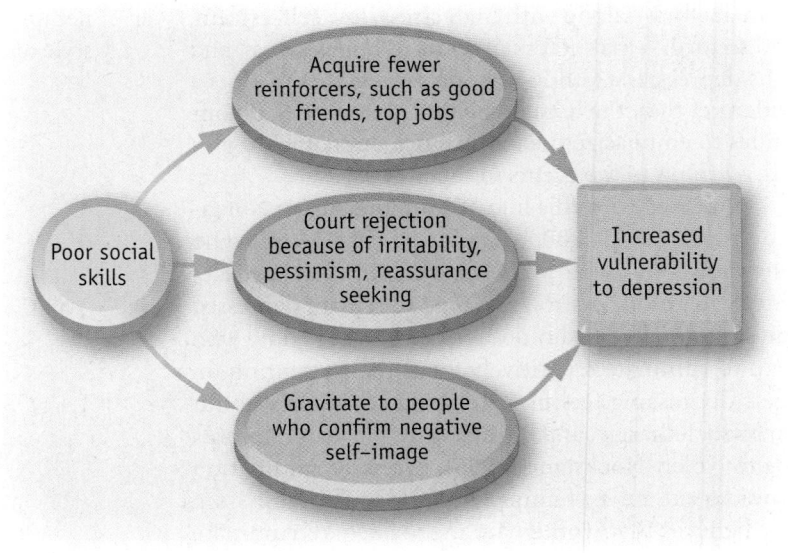

Figure 15.15

Interpersonal factors in depression. Interpersonal theories about the etiology of depression emphasize how inadequate social skills may contribute to the development of the disorder. Recent studies suggest that excessive reassurance-seeking may play a particularly critical role in the social dynamics promoting depression.

Precipitating Stress

Mood disorders sometimes appear mysteriously "out of the blue" in people who appear to be leading benign, nonstressful lives. For this reason, experts used to believe that mood disorders are relatively uninfluenced by stress. However, recent advances in the measurement of personal stress have altered this picture. The evidence available today suggests a moderately strong link between stress and the onset of mood disorders (Kendler, Kuhn, & Prescott, 2004; Kessler, 1997). Stress also appears to affect how people with mood disorders respond to treatment and whether they experience a relapse of their disorder (Monroe & Hadjiyannakis, 2002).

Of course, many people endure great stress without getting depressed. The impact of stress varies in part because different people have different degrees of *vulnerability* to mood disorders (Lewinsohn, Joiner, & Rohde, 2001). Variations in vulnerability appear to depend primarily on biological makeup. Similar interactions between stress and vulnerability probably influence the development of many kinds of disorders, including those that are next on our agenda: the schizophrenic disorders.

Schizophrenic Disorders

LEARNING OBJECTIVES

- *Describe the prevalence and general symptoms of schizophrenia.*
- *Describe the subtypes of schizophrenia and distinguish between positive and negative symptoms.*
- *Discuss the course and outcome of schizophrenia.*
- *Summarize how genetic vulnerability and neurochemical factors may contribute to the etiology of schizophrenia.*
- *Discuss evidence relating schizophrenia to structural abnormalities in the brain and neurodevelopmental insults to the brain.*
- *Summarize how expressed emotion and stress may contribute to schizophrenia.*

Literally, *schizophrenia* means "split mind." However, when Eugen Bleuler coined the term in 1911, he was referring to the fragmenting of thought processes seen in the disorder—not to a "split personality." Unfortunately, writers in the popular media often assume that the split-mind notion refers to the syndrome in which a person manifests two or more personalities. As you have already learned, this syndrome is actually called *dissociative identity disorder.* Schizophrenia is a much more common, and altogether different, type of disorder.

Schizophrenic disorders **are a class of disorders marked by disturbances in thought that spill over to affect perceptual, social, and emotional processes.** How common is schizophrenia? Prevalence estimates suggest that about 1% of the population may suffer from schizophrenic disorders (Lauriello, Bustillo, & Keith, 2005). That may not sound like much, but it means that in North American alone there may be several million people troubled by schizophrenic disturbances. Moreover, schizophrenia is an extremely costly disorder for society, because it is a severe, debilitating illness that tends to have an early onset and often requires lengthy hospital care. Because of these considerations, the financial impact of schizophrenia is estimated to exceed the costs of all types of cancers combined (Buchanan & Carpenter, 2005).

General Symptoms

Although there are a number of distinct schizophrenic syndromes, they share some general characteristics that we need to examine before looking at the subtypes. Many of these characteristics are apparent in the following case history (adapted from Sheehan, 1982).

Sylvia was first diagnosed as schizophrenic at age 15. She has been in and out of many types of psychiatric facilities since then. She has never been able to hold a job for any length of time. During severe flare-ups of her disorder, her personal hygiene deteriorates. She rarely washes, wears clothes that neither fit nor match, smears makeup on heavily but randomly, and slops food all over herself. Sylvia occasionally hears voices talking to her. Sylvia tends to be argumentative, aggressive, and emotionally volatile. Over the years, she has been involved in innumerable fights with fellow patients, psychiatric staff members, and strangers. Her thoughts can be highly irrational, as is apparent from the following quotation:

"Mick Jagger wants to marry me. If I have Mick Jagger, I don't have to covet Geraldo Rivera. Mick Jagger is St. Nicholas and the Maharishi is Santa Claus. I want to form a gospel rock group called the Thorn Oil, but Geraldo wants me to be the music critic on Eyewitness News, so what can I do? Got to listen to my boyfriend. Teddy Kennedy cured me of my ugliness. I'm pregnant with the son of God. I'm going to marry David Berkowitz and get it over with. Creedmoor is the headquarters of the American Nazi Party. They're eating the patients here. Archie Bunker wants me to play his niece on his TV show. I work for Epic Records. I'm Joan of Arc. I'm Florence Nightingale. The door between the ward and the porch is the dividing line between New York and California. Divorce isn't a piece of

paper, it's a feeling. Forget about Zip Codes. I need shock treatment." (Sheehan, 1982, pp. 104–105)

Sylvia's case clearly shows that schizophrenic thinking can be bizarre and that schizophrenia is a brutally serious, psychologically disfiguring disorder. Although no single symptom is inevitably present, the following symptoms are commonly seen in schizophrenia (Ho, Black, & Andreasen, 2003; Lindenmayer & Khan, 2006).

Irrational thought. Cognitive deficits and disturbed thought processes are the central, defining feature of schizophrenic disorders (Barch, 2003; Heinrichs, 2005). Various kinds of delusions are common. ***Delusions* are false beliefs that are maintained even though they clearly are out of touch with reality.** For example, one patient's delusion that he was a tiger (with a deformed body) persisted for 15 years (Kulick, Pope, & Keck, 1990). More typically, affected persons believe that their private thoughts are being broadcast to other people, that thoughts are being injected into their mind against their will, or that their thoughts are being controlled by some external force (Maher, 2001). In *delusions of grandeur,* people maintain that they are extremely famous or important. Sylvia expressed an endless array of grandiose delusions, such as thinking that Mick Jagger wanted to marry her, that she dictated the hobbit stories to Tolkien, and that she was going to win the Nobel Prize for medicine. In addition to delusions, the schizophrenic person's train of thought deteriorates. Thinking becomes chaotic rather than logical and linear. There is a "loosening of associations" as the schizophrenic shifts topics in disjointed ways. The quotation from Sylvia illustrates this symptom dramatically. The entire passage involves a wild "flight of ideas," but at one point (beginning with the sentence "Creedmoor is the headquarters . . .") she rattles off ten consecutive sentences that have no apparent connection to the preceding sentence.

Deterioration of adaptive behavior. Schizophrenia involves a noticeable deterioration in the quality of one's routine functioning in work, social relations, and personal care. Friends will often make remarks such as "Hal just isn't himself anymore." This deterioration is readily apparent in Sylvia's inability to get along with others or function in the work world. It's also apparent in her neglect of personal hygiene.

Distorted perception. A variety of perceptual distortions may occur in schizophrenia, with the most common being auditory hallucinations. ***Hallucinations* are sensory perceptions that occur in the absence of a real external stimulus or that represent gross distortions of perceptual input.** Schizophrenics frequently report that they hear voices of nonexistent or absent people talking to them. Sylvia, for instance, heard messages from Paul McCartney. These voices often provide an insulting running commentary on the person's behavior ("You're an idiot for shaking his hand"). The voices may be argumentative ("You don't need a bath"), and they may issue commands ("Prepare your home for visitors from outer space").

Disturbed emotion. Normal emotional tone can be disrupted in schizophrenia in a variety of ways. Although it may not be an accurate indicator of their underlying emotional experience (Kring, 1999), some victims show little emotional responsiveness, a symptom referred to as "blunted or flat affect." Others show inappropriate emotional responses that don't jell with the situation or with what they are saying. People with schizophrenia may also become emotionally volatile. This pattern was displayed by Sylvia, who often overreacted emotionally in erratic, unpredictable ways.

Surviving Schizophrenia: A Manual for Families, Consumers, and Providers
by E. Fuller Torrey (Harper, 1988, 1995)

E. Fuller Torrey, a prominent psychiatrist who specializes in the study and treatment of schizophrenia, has written a practical book intended for the lay public. Torrey points out that many myths surrounding schizophrenia have added to the anguish of families who have been victimized by this illness. He explains that schizophrenia is *not* caused by childhood trauma, domineering mothers, or passive fathers. He discusses how genetic vulnerability, flawed brain chemistry, and other factors contribute to the development of schizophrenic disorders. Torrey discusses the treatment of schizophrenia at great length. He also explains the various ways in which the disease can evolve. Some of the best material is found in chapters on what the patient needs and what the family needs.

Throughout the book, Torrey writes with clarity, eloquence, and conviction. He is not reluctant to express strong opinions. For instance, in an appendix he lists the ten worst readings on schizophrenia (along with the ten best), and his evaluations are brutal. He characterizes one book as "absurd drivel" and dismisses another by saying, "If a prize were to be given to the book which has produced the most confusion about schizophrenia over the past twenty years, this book would win going away." Scientists and academicians are usually reluctant to express such strong opinions, so Torrey's candor is remarkably refreshing.

Subtypes

Four subtypes of schizophrenic disorders are recognized, including a category for people who don't fit neatly into any of the first three categories (Ho et al., 2003; Kirkpatrick & Tek, 2005).

Paranoid Type

As its name implies, ***paranoid schizophrenia* is dominated by delusions of persecution, along with delusions of grandeur.** In this common form of schizophrenia, people come to believe that they have many enemies who want to harass and oppress them. They may become suspicious of friends and relatives, or they may attribute the persecution to mysterious, unknown persons. They are convinced that they are being watched and manipulated in malicious ways. To make sense of this persecution, they often develop delusions of grandeur. They believe that they must be enormously important people, often seeing themselves as great inventors or as great religious or political leaders. For example, in the case described at the beginning of the chapter, Ed's belief that he was president of the United States was a delusion of grandeur.

Catatonic Type

***Catatonic schizophrenia* is marked by striking motor disturbances, ranging from muscular rigidity to random motor activity.** Some catatonics go into an extreme form of withdrawal known as a catatonic stupor. They may remain virtually motionless and seem oblivious to the environment around them for long periods of time. Others go into a state of catatonic excitement. They become hyperactive and incoherent. Some alternate between these dramatic extremes. The catatonic subtype is not particularly common, and its prevalence seems to be declining.

Disorganized Type

In *disorganized schizophrenia,* a particularly severe deterioration of adaptive behavior is seen. Prominent symptoms include emotional indifference, frequent incoherence, and virtually complete social withdrawal. Aimless babbling and giggling are common. Delusions often center on bodily functions ("My brain is melting out my ears").

Web Link 15.6 **Doctor's Guide to the Internet: Schizophrenia**

Produced by a communications and medical education consulting company, the free Doctor's Guide site is updated frequently to provide a current overview of the state of research on schizophrenic disorders. A more detailed set of resources for physicians parallels this site, which is intended primarily for patients and their families.

Undifferentiated Type

People who are clearly schizophrenic but who cannot be placed into any of the three previous categories are said to have ***undifferentiated schizophrenia,* which is marked by idiosyncratic mixtures of schizophrenic symptoms.** The undifferentiated subtype is fairly common.

Positive Versus Negative Symptoms

Many theorists have raised doubts about the value of dividing schizophrenic disorders into these four subtypes (Sanislow & Carson, 2001). Critics note that the catatonic subtype is disappearing and that undifferentiated cases aren't a subtype so much as a hodgepodge of "leftovers." Critics also point out that the classic schizophrenic subtypes do not differ meaningfully in etiology, prognosis, or response to treatment. The absence of such differences casts doubt on the value of the current classification scheme.

Courtesy, Nancy Andreasen, M.D.

Nancy Andreasen

Because of such problems, Nancy Andreasen (1990) and others (Carpenter, 1992; McGlashan & Fenton, 1992) have proposed an alternative approach to subtyping. This scheme divides schizophrenic disorders into just two categories based on the predominance of negative versus positive symptoms (see **Figure 15.16** on the next page). *Negative symptoms* involve behavioral deficits, such as flattened emotions, social withdrawal, apathy, impaired attention, and poverty of speech. *Positive symptoms* involve behavioral excesses or peculiarities, such as hallucinations, delusions, bizarre behavior, and wild flights of ideas.

Theorists advocating this scheme hoped to find consistent differences between the two subtypes in etiology, prognosis, and response to treatment, and some progress along these lines *has* been made. For example, a predominance of positive symptoms is associated with better adjustment prior to the onset of schizophrenia and greater responsiveness to treatment (Fenton & McGlashan, 1994; Galderisi et al., 2002). However, the assumption that patients can be placed into discrete categories based on this scheme now seems untenable. Most patients exhibit both types of symptoms and vary only in the degree to which positive or negative symptoms dominate (Black & Andreasen, 1994). Moreover, there is some debate about which symptoms should be classified as positive and which as negative, and some theorists have proposed a third category of symptoms reflecting *disorganization* of

Figure 15.16

Examples of positive and negative symptoms in schizophrenia. Some theorists believe that schizophrenic disorders should be classified into just two types, depending on whether patients exhibit mostly positive symptoms (behavioral excesses) or negative symptoms (behavioral deficits). The percentages shown here, based on a sample of 111 schizophrenic patients studied by Andreasen (1987), provide an indication of how common each specific symptom is.

Positive and Negative Symptoms in Schizophrenia

Negative symptoms	Percent of patients	Positive symptoms	Percent of patients
Few friendship relationships	96	Delusions of persecution	81
Few recreational interests	95	Auditory hallucinations	75
Lack of persistence at work or school	95	Delusions of being controlled	46
Impaired grooming or hygiene	87	Derailment of thought	45
Paucity of expressive gestures	81	Delusions of grandeur	39
Social inattentiveness	78	Bizarre social, sexual behavior	33
Emotional nonresponsiveness	64	Delusions of thought insertion	31
Inappropriate emotion	63	Aggressive, agitated behavior	27
Poverty of speech	53	Incoherent thought	23

behavior (Toomey et al., 1997; Lindenmayer & Khan, 2006). Although it seems fair to say that the distinction between positive and negative symptoms is enhancing our understanding of schizophrenia, it has not yielded a classification scheme that can replace the traditional subtypes of schizophrenia.

Course and Outcome

Schizophrenic disorders usually emerge during adolescence or early adulthood, with 75% of cases manifesting by the age of 30 (Perkins, Miller-Anderson, & Lieberman, 2006). Those who develop schizophrenia usually have a long history of peculiar behavior and cognitive and social deficits, although most do not manifest a full-fledged psychological disorder during childhood (Walker et al., 2004). The emergence of schizophrenia may be sudden, but it usually is insidious and gradual. Once it clearly emerges, the course of schizophrenia is variable, but patients tend to fall into three broad groups. Some patients, presumably those with milder disorders, are treated successfully and enjoy a full recovery. Other patients experience a partial recovery so that they can return to independent living for a time. However, they experience regular relapses and are in and out of treatment facilities for much of the remainder of their lives. Finally, a third group of patients endure chronic illness that sometimes results in permanent hospitalization. Estimates of the percentage of patients falling in each category vary. Overall, it appears that about 15%–20% of schizophrenic patients enjoy a full recovery, although some long-term studies have yielded higher estimates (Modestin et al., 2003; Robinson et al., 2004).

Etiology of Schizophrenia

Most of us can identify, at least to some extent, with people who suffer from mood disorders, somatoform disorders, and anxiety disorders. You can probably imagine events that might leave you struggling with depression, grappling with anxiety, or worrying about your physical health. But what could possibly have led Ed to believe that he had been fighting space wars and vampires? What could account for Sylvia thinking that she was Joan of Arc, or that she had dictated the hobbit novels to Tolkien? As mystifying as these delusions may seem, you'll see that the etiology of schizo-

© Reuters/Corbis

John Nash, the Nobel prize–winning mathematician whose story was told in the film **A Beautiful Mind**, *has struggled with paranoid schizophrenia since 1959.*

phrenic disorders is not all that different from the etiology of other disorders.

Genetic Vulnerability

Evidence is plentiful that hereditary factors play a role in the development of schizophrenic disorders (Sullivan et al., 2006; Tsuang, Glatt, & Faraone, 2003). For instance, in twin studies, concordance rates for schizophrenia average around 48% for identical twins, in comparison to about 17% for fraternal twins (Gottesman, 1991, 2001). Studies also indicate that a child born to two schizophrenic parents has about a 46% probability of developing a schizophrenic disorder (as compared to the probability of about 1% for the population as a whole). These and other findings that demonstrate the genetic roots of schizophrenia are summarized in **Figure 15.17**. Overall, the picture is similar to that seen for mood disorders. Several converging lines of evidence indicate that people inherit a genetically transmitted *vulnerability* to schizophrenia (Riley & Kendler, 2005; Schneider & Deldin, 2001). Although genetic factors may account for more than two-thirds of the variability in susceptibility to schizophrenia, genetic mapping studies have made little progress in identifying the specific genes responsible (Crow, 2007; Owen & O'Donovan, 2003).

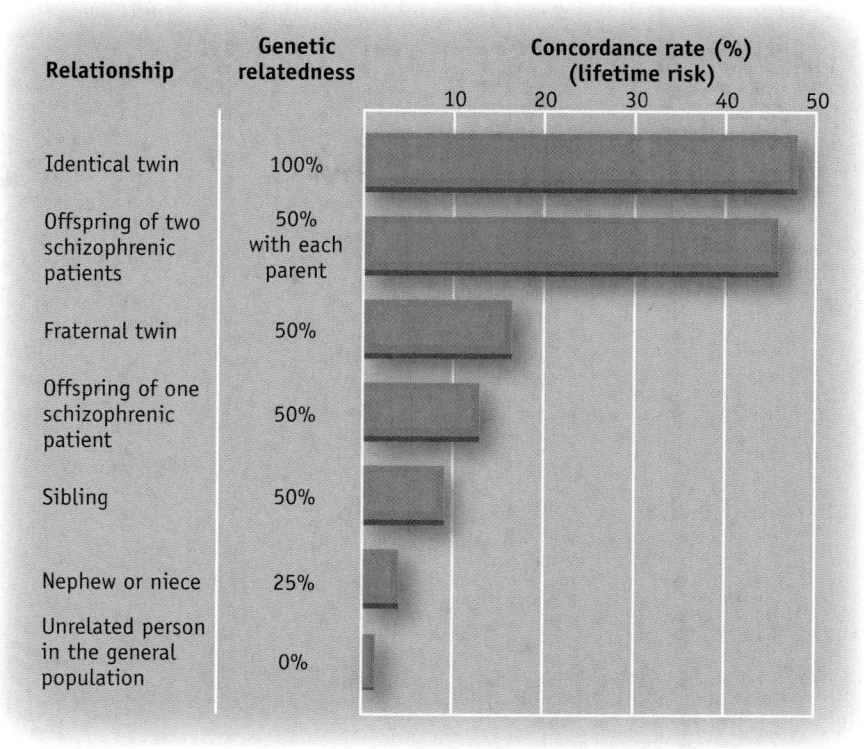

Figure 15.17

Genetic vulnerability to schizophrenic disorders. Relatives of schizophrenic patients have an elevated risk for schizophrenia. This risk is greater among closer relatives. Although environment also plays a role in the etiology of schizophrenia, the concordance rates shown here suggest that there must be a genetic vulnerability to the disorder. These concordance estimates are based on pooled data from 40 studies. (Data from Gottesman, 1991)

Neurochemical Factors

Like mood disorders, schizophrenic disorders appear to be accompanied by changes in the activity of one or more neurotransmitters in the brain (Patel, Pinals, Breier, 2003). Excess *dopamine* activity has been implicated as a likely cause of schizophrenia (Javitt & Laruelle, 2006). This hypothesis makes sense because most of the drugs that are useful in the treatment of schizophrenia are known to dampen dopamine activity in the brain (Tamminga & Carlsson, 2003). However, the evidence linking schizophrenia to high dopamine levels is riddled with inconsistencies, complexities, and interpretive problems (Abi-Dargham, 2004). Researchers are currently exploring how interactions between the dopamine, serotonin, and other neurotransmitter systems may contribute to schizophrenia (Patel et al., 2003). Recent research has also suggested that abnormalities in neural circuits using *glutamate* as a neurotransmitter may play a role in schizophrenic disturbance (Tibbo et al., 2004). Thus, investigators are gradually making progress in their search for the neurochemical bases of schizophrenia.

Structural Abnormalities in the Brain

For decades, studies have suggested that individuals with schizophrenia exhibit a variety of deficits in attention, perception, and information processing (Gold & Green, 2005; Keefe & Eesley, 2006). Impairments in working (short-term) memory are especially prominent (Silver et al., 2003). These cognitive deficits suggest that schizophrenic disorders may be caused by neurological defects. Until recent decades, however, this theory was based more on speculation than on actual research. However, advances in brain-imaging technology have yielded mountains of intriguing data since the mid-1980s. CT scans and MRI scans suggest an association between enlarged brain ventricles (the hollow, fluid-filled cavities in the brain depicted in **Figure 15.18** on the next page) and schizophrenic disturbance (Belger & Dichter, 2006). Enlarged ventricles are assumed to reflect either the degeneration or failure to develop of nearby brain tissue. The significance of

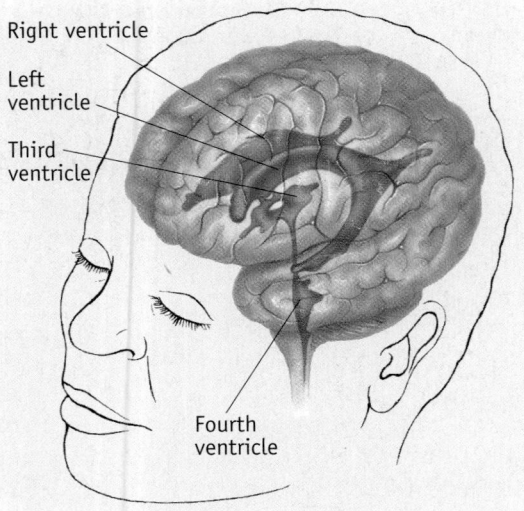

Figure 15.18

Schizophrenia and the ventricles of the brain. Cerebrospinal fluid (CSF) circulates around the brain and spinal cord. The hollow cavities in the brain filled with CSF are called *ventricles*. The four ventricles in the human brain are depicted here. Studies with modern brain-imaging techniques suggest that an association exists between enlarged ventricles in the brain and the occurrence of schizophrenic disturbance.

enlarged ventricles is hotly debated, however. Structural deterioration in the brain could be a contributing *cause* or a *consequence* of schizophrenia.

Brain-imaging studies have also uncovered structural and metabolic abnormalities in the frontal lobes of individuals with schizophrenia. Although the research results are not entirely consistent, schizophrenia appears to be associated with smaller size and reduced metabolic activity in specific areas of the *prefrontal cortex* (consult **Figure 15.12**; Fowles, 2003). Scientists are also intrigued by the fact that a major dopamine pathway runs through the area in the prefrontal cortex where metabolic abnormalities have been found. A connection may exist between the abnormal dopamine activity implicated in schizophrenia and the dysfunctional metabolic activity seen in this area of the prefrontal cortex (Conklin & Iacono, 2002). Although the research on the prefrontal cortex is intriguing, Ho, Black, and Andreasen (2003) caution that the neural correlates of schizophrenia are complex and that the disease is not likely to be caused by "a single abnormality in a single region of the brain" (p. 408).

The Neurodevelopmental Hypothesis

In recent years, several new lines of evidence have led to the emergence of the *neurodevelopmental hypothesis* of schizophrenia, which posits that schizophrenia is caused in part by various disruptions in the normal maturational processes of the brain before or at birth (Brown, 1999). According to this hypothesis, insults to the brain during sensitive phases of prenatal development or during birth can cause subtle neuorological damage that elevates individuals' vulnerability to schizophrenia years later in adolescence and early adulthood (see **Figure 15.19**). What are the sources of these early insults to the brain? Thus far, research has focused on viral infections or malnutrition during prenatal development and obstetrical complications during the birth process.

The evidence on viral infections has been building since Sarnoff Mednick and his colleagues (1988) discovered an elevated incidence of schizophrenia among the children of women who were in their second trimester of prenatal development during a 1957 influenza epidemic in Finland. Several subsequent studies in other locations have also found a link between exposure to influenza during pregnancy and increased prevalence of schizophrenia (Brown et al., 2004). Another study, which investigated the possible impact of prenatal malnutrition, found an elevated incidence

Figure 15.19

The neurodevelopmental hypothesis of schizophrenia. Research suggests that insults to the brain sustained during prenatal development or at birth may disrupt crucial maturational processes in the brain, resulting in subtle neurological damage that gradually becomes apparent as youngsters develop. This neurological damage is believed to increase both vulnerability to schizophrenia and the incidence of minor physical anomalies.

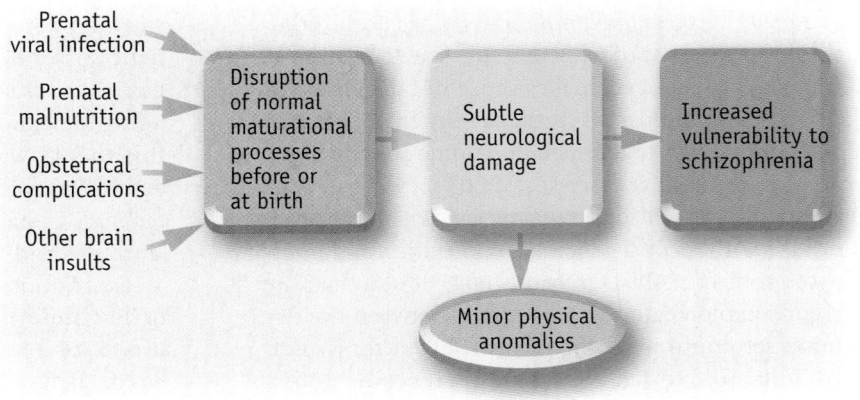

of schizophrenia in a cohort of people who were prenatally exposed to a severe famine in 1944–45 because of a Nazi blockade of food deliveries in the Netherlands during World War II (Susser et al., 1996). A follow-up study of some schizophrenic patients exposed to this famine found increased brain abnormalities among the patients, as the neurodevelopmental hypothesis would predict (Hulshoff et al., 2000). Other research has shown that schizophrenic patients are more likely than control subjects to have a history of obstetrical complications (Kelly et al., 2004; Murray & Bramon, 2005). Finally, research suggests that minor physical anomalies (slight anatomical defects of the head, hands, feet, and face) that would be consistent with prenatal neurological damage are more common among people with schizophrenia than in other people (McNeil, Cantor-Graae, & Ismail, 2000; Schiffman et al., 2002). Collectively, these diverse studies argue for a relationship between early neurological trauma and a predisposition to schizophrenia (Mednick et al., 1998).

Expressed Emotion

Studies of expressed emotion have primarily focused on how this element of family dynamics influences the *course* of schizophrenic illness after the onset of the disorder (Leff & Vaughn, 1985). *Expressed emotion (EE)* reflects the degree to which a relative of a schizophrenic patient displays highly critical or emotionally overinvolved attitudes toward the patient. Audio-taped interviews of relatives' communication are carefully evaluated for critical comments, hostility toward the patient, and excessive emotional involvement (overprotective, overconcerned attitudes) (Hooley, 2004).

Studies show that a family's expressed emotion is a good predictor of the course of a schizophrenic patient's illness (Hooley & Candela, 1999; Kavanaugh, 1992). After release from a hospital, patients who return to a family high in expressed emotion show relapse rates three or four times those of patients who return to a family low in expressed emotion. Part of the problem for patients returning to homes high in expressed emotion is that their families are probably sources of stress rather than of social support (Cutting & Docherty, 2000). However, Rosenfarb et al. (1995) caution against placing all the blame on the families high in expressed emotion. They found that patients returning to high-EE homes exhibited more odd and disruptive behavior than patients returning to low-EE homes. Thus, the more critical, negative attitudes experienced by patients in high-EE homes may be caused in part by their own behavior.

Precipitating Stress

Many theories of schizophrenia assume that stress plays a role in triggering schizophrenic disorders (Walker et al., 2004). According to this notion, various biological and psychological factors influence individuals' *vulnerability* to schizophrenia. High stress may then serve to precipitate a schizophrenic disorder in someone who is vulnerable (McGlashan & Hoffman, 2000).

APPLICATION

Understanding Eating Disorders

LEARNING OBJECTIVES

- *Describe the symptoms of anorexia nervosa, bulimia nervosa, and binge-eating disorder.*
- *Discuss the history, prevalence, and gender distribution of eating disorders.*
- *Explain how genetic factors, personality, and culture may contribute to eating disorders.*
- *Explain how family dynamics and disturbed thinking may contribute to eating disorders.*

Answer the following "true" or "false."

___ **1.** Although they have attracted attention only in recent years, eating disorders have a long history and have always been fairly common.

___ **2.** Eating disorders are universal problems found in virtually all cultures.

___ **3.** People with anorexia nervosa are much more likely to recognize their eating behavior as pathological than people suffering from bulimia nervosa.

___ **4.** The prevalence of eating disorders is twice as high in women as it is in men.

___ **5.** The binge-and-purge syndrome seen in bulimia nervosa is not common in anorexia nervosa.

All five of these statements are false, as you will see in this Application. The psychological disorders that we discussed in the main body of the chapter have largely been recognized for centuries and generally are found in one form or another in all cultures and societies. Eating disorders, however, present a sharp contrast to this picture: They have only been recognized in recent decades, and initially they were largely confined to affluent, Westernized cultures (Russell, 1995; Szmukler & Patton, 1995). In spite of these fascinating differences, eating disorders have much in common with traditional forms of pathology.

Types of Eating Disorders

***Eating disorders* are severe disturbances in eating behavior characterized by preoccupation with weight and unhealthy efforts to control weight.** The vast majority of cases consist of two sometimes overlapping syndromes: *anorexia nervosa* and *bulimia nervosa.* A third syndrome, called *binge-eating disorder,* is described in the appendix of DSM-IV as a potential new disorder, pending further study. We will devote our attention in this Application to the two established eating disorders, but we will briefly outline the symptoms of this new disorder.

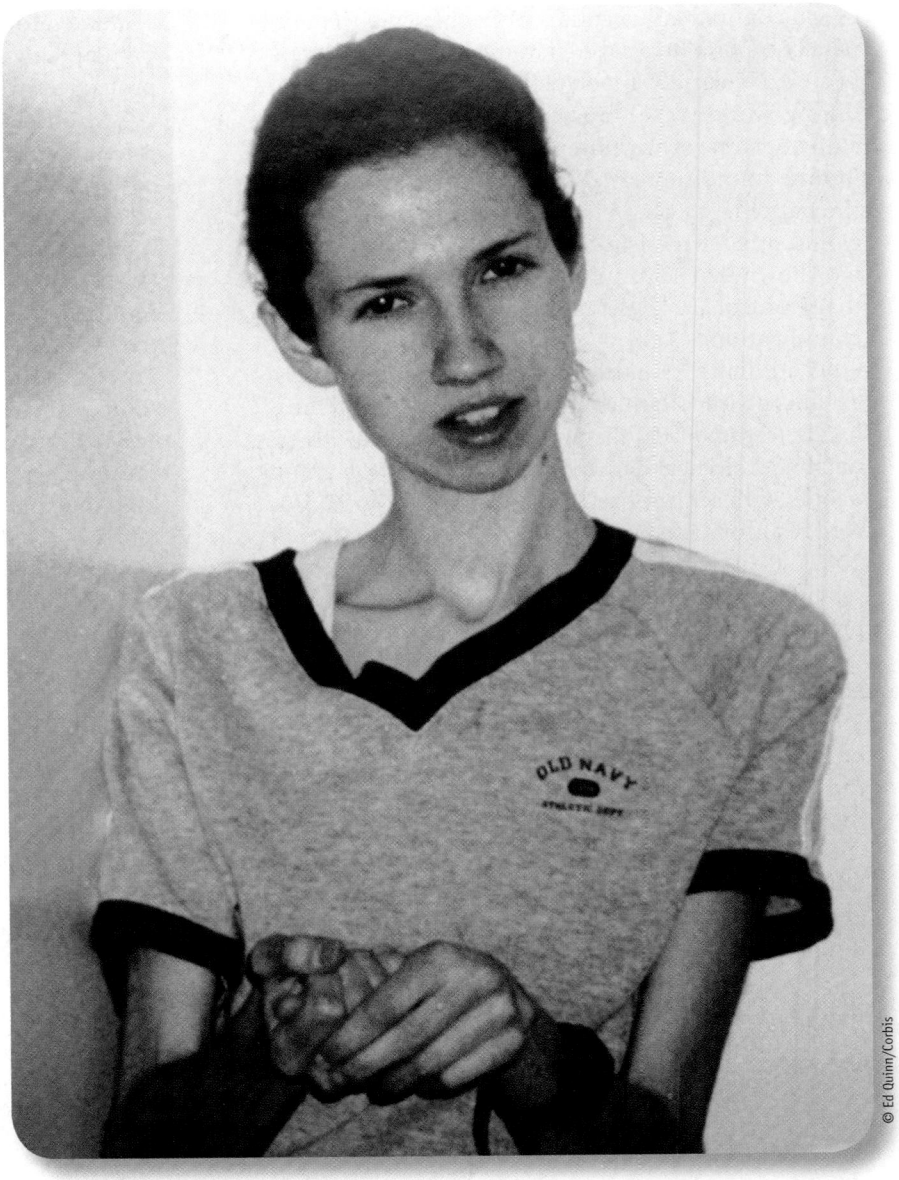

© Ed Quinn/Corbis

Eating disorders have become distressingly common among young women in Western cultures. No matter how frail they become, people suffering from anorexia insist that they are too fat.

Anorexia Nervosa

***Anorexia nervosa* involves intense fear of gaining weight, disturbed body image, refusal to maintain normal weight, and dangerous measures to lose weight.** Two subtypes have been distinguished (Herzog & Delinsky, 2001). In *restricting type anorexia nervosa,* people drastically reduce their intake of food, sometimes literally starving themselves. In *binge-eating/purging type anorexia nervosa,* victims attempt to lose weight by forcing themselves to vomit after meals, by misusing laxatives and diuretics, and by engaging in excessive exercise.

Both types entail a disturbed body image. No matter how frail and emaciated the victims become, they insist that they are too fat. Their morbid fear of obesity means that they are never satisfied with their weight. If they gain a pound or two, they panic. The only thing that makes them happy is to lose more weight. The common result is a relentless decline in body weight—in fact, patients entering treatment for anorexia nervosa are typically 25%–30% below their normal weight (Hsu, 1990). Because of their disturbed body image, people suffering from anorexia generally do *not* appreciate the maladaptive quality of their behavior and

Web Link 15.7 **The Alliance for Eating Disorders Awareness**

This site offers a great deal of information on eating disorders. Visitors can find statistics, suggested readings, information on symptoms and treatments, self-tests, success stories from people who have overcome their eating disorders, and links to other worthwhile websites.

rarely seek treatment on their own. They are typically coaxed or coerced into treatment by friends or family members who are alarmed by their appearance.

Anorexia nervosa eventually leads to a cascade of medical problems, including *amenorrhea* (a loss of menstrual cycles in women), gastrointestinal problems, low blood pressure, *osteoporosis* (a loss of bone density), and metabolic disturbances that can lead to cardiac arrest or circulatory collapse (Pomeroy & Mitchell, 2002; Walsh, 2003). Anorexia is a debilitating illness that leads to death in 5%–10% of patients (Steinhausen, 2002).

Bulimia Nervosa

***Bulimia nervosa* involves habitually engaging in out-of-control overeating followed by unhealthy compensatory efforts, such as self-induced vomiting, fasting, abuse of laxatives and diuretics, and excessive exercise.** The eating binges are usually carried out in secret and are followed by intense guilt and concern about gaining weight. These feelings motivate ill-advised strategies to undo the effects of the overeating. However, vomiting prevents the absorption of only about half of recently consumed food, and laxatives and diuretics have negligible impact on caloric intake, so people suffering from bulimia nervosa typically maintain a reasonably normal weight (Beumont, 2002; Kaye et al., 1993).

Medical problems associated with bulimia nervosa include cardiac arrythmias, dental problems, metabolic deficiencies, and gastrointestinal problems (Halmi, 2002, 2003). Bulimia often coexists with other psychological disturbances, including depression, anxiety disorders, and substance abuse (Hudson et al., 2007).

Obviously, bulimia nervosa shares many features with anorexia nervosa, such as a morbid fear of becoming obese, preoccupation with food, and rigid, maladaptive approaches to controlling weight that are grounded in naive all-or-none thinking. The close relationship between the disorders is demonstrated by the fact that many patients who initially develop one syndrome cross over to display the other syndrome (Tozzi et al., 2005). However, the syndromes also differ in crucial ways. First and foremost, bulimia is a less life-threatening condition. Second, although their weight and appearance usually is more "normal" than that seen in anorexia, people with bulimia are much more likely to recognize that their eating behavior is pathological and are more prone to recognize their need for treatment (Striegel-Moore, Silberstein, & Rodin, 1993; Guarda et al., 2007).

Binge-Eating Disorder

***Binge-eating disorder* involves distress-inducing eating binges that are not accompanied by the purging, fasting, and excessive exercise seen in bulimia.** Obviously, this syndrome resembles bulimia, but it is a less severe disorder. Still, this disorder creates great distress, as these people tend to be disgusted by their bodies and distraught about their overeating. People with binge-eating disorder are frequently overweight. Their excessive eating is often triggered by stress (Gluck, 2006). Research suggests that this comparatively mild syndrome may be more common than anorexia or bulimia (Hudson et al., 2007). A great deal of additional research is needed to determine whether this syndrome should be recognized as an independent disorder or perhaps a subtype of bulimia nervosa.

History and Prevalence

Historians have been able to track down descriptions of anorexia nervosa that date back centuries, so the disorder is not entirely new, but anorexia nervosa did not become a *common* affliction until the middle of the 20th century (Vandereycken, 2002). Although binging and purging have a long history in some cultures, they were not part of a pathological effort to control weight, and bulimia nervosa appears to be a new syndrome that emerged gradually in the middle of the 20th century and was first recognized in the 1970s (Russell, 1997; Vandereycken, 2002).

Both disorders are a product of modern, affluent Western culture, where food is generally plentiful and the desirability of being thin is widely endorsed. Until recently, these problems were not seen outside of Western cultures (Hoek, 2002). However, in recent years, advances in communication have exported Western culture to farflung corners of the globe, and eating disorders have started showing up in many non-Western societies, especially affluent Asian countries (Lee & Katzman, 2002).

A huge gender gap exists in the likelihood of developing eating disorders. About 90%–95% of individuals who are treated for anorexia nervosa and bulimia nervosa are female (Thompson & Kinder, 2003). This staggering discrepancy appears to be a result of cultural pressures rather than biological ones (Smolak & Murnen, 2001). Western standards of attractiveness emphasize being slender more for females than for males, and women generally experience heavier pressure to be physically attractive than men do (Sobal, 1995). The prevalence of eating disorders is also elevated in certain groups that place an undue emphasis on thinness, such as fashion models, dancers, actresses, and athletes. Eating disorders mostly afflict *young* women. The typical age of onset for anorexia is 14–18, and for bulimia it is 15–21 (see **Figure 15.20** on the next page).

How common are eating disorders in Western societies? The prevalence of these disorders has increased dramatically in recent decades, although this escalation may be leveling off (Steiger & Seguin, 1999). Studies of

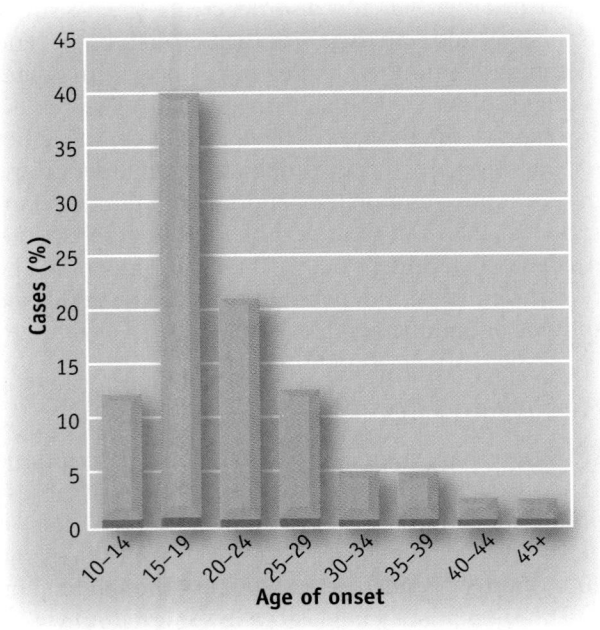

Figure 15.20

Age of onset for anorexia nervosa. Eating disorders emerge primarily during adolescence, as these data for anorexia nervosa show. This graph shows how age of onset was distributed in a sample of 166 female patients from Minnesota. As you can see, over half experienced the onset of their illness before the age of 20, with vulnerability clearly peaking between the ages of 15 and 19. (Data from Lucas, et al., 1991)

young women suggest that about 1% develop anorexia nervosa and about 2%–3% develop bulimia nervosa (Anderson & Yager, 2005). In some respects, these figures may only scratch the surface of the problem. Evidence suggests that as many as 20% of female college students may struggle with transient bulimic symptoms (Anderson & Yager, 2005). And recent community surveys suggest that there may be more undiagnosed eating disorders among men than generally appreciated (Hudson et al., 2007).

Etiology of Eating Disorders

Like other types of psychological disorders, eating disorders are caused by multiple determinants that work interactively. **Figure 15.21** provides an overview of the factors that contribute to the emergence of anorexia nervosa and bulimia nervosa.

Genetic Vulnerability

The scientific evidence is not nearly as strong or complete for eating disorders as it is for many other types of psychopathology (such as anxiety, mood, and schizophrenic disorders), but some people may inherit a genetic vulnerability to these problems (Slof-Op't Landt et al., 2005). Studies show that relatives of patients with eating disorders have elevated rates of anorexia nervosa and bulimia nervosa (Bulik, 2004). And studies of female twins report higher concordance rates for identical twins than fraternal twins, suggesting that a genetic predisposition may be at work (Steiger, Bruce, & Israël, 2003).

Personality Factors

Strober (1995) has suggested that genetic factors may exert their influence indirectly by fostering certain personality traits that make people more vulnerable to eating disorders. Although there are innumerable exceptions, victims of anorexia nervosa tend to be obsessive, rigid, neurotic, and emotionally restrained, whereas victims of bulimia nervosa tend to be impulsive, overly sensitive, and low in self-esteem (Anderluh, Tchanturia. & Rabe-Hesketh, 2003; Wonderlich, 2002). Recent research also suggests that perfectionism is a risk factor for anorexia (Bulik et al., 2003; Halmi et al., 2000).

Cultural Values

The contribution of cultural values to the increased prevalence of eating disorders can hardly be overestimated (Anderson-Fye & Becker, 2004; Stice, 2001). In Western society, young women are socialized to believe that they must be attractive, and to be attractive, they must be as thin as the actresses and fashion models that dominate the media (Levine & Harrison, 2004). Thanks to this cultural milieu, many young women are dissatisfied with their weight because the societal ideals promoted by the media are unattainable for most of them (Thompson & Stice, 2001). Unfortunately, in a small portion of these women, the pressure to be thin, in combination with genetic vulnerability, family pathology, and other factors, leads to unhealthy efforts to control weight.

The Role of the Family

Many theorists emphasize how family dynamics can contribute to the development of anorexia nervosa and bulimia nervosa in young women (Haworth-Hoeppner, 2000). Some theorists suggest that parents who are overly involved in their children's lives turn the normal adolescent push for independence into an unhealthy struggle (Minuchin, Rosman, & Baker, 1978). Needing to assert their autonomy, some adolescent girls seek extreme control over their bodies, leading to pathological patterns of eating (Bruch, 1978). Other theorists argue that parents of adolescents with eating disorders tend to define their children's needs for them instead of allowing them to define their own needs, thus making the youngsters insensitive to their internal needs (Bruch, 1973; Steiner et al., 1991). In contrast, Pike and Rodin (1991) maintain that some mothers contribute

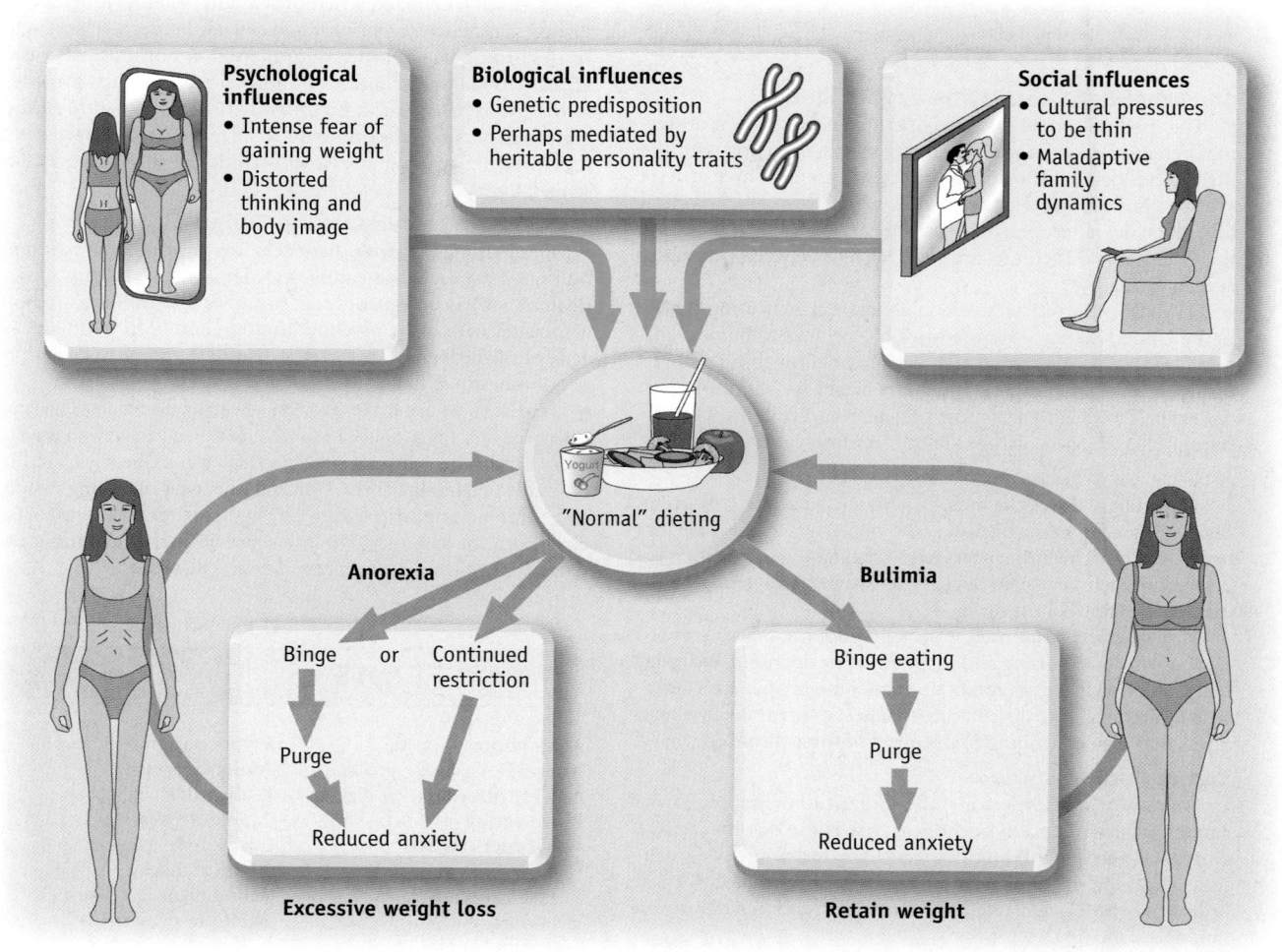

Figure 15.21

The etiology of eating disorders. The causes of eating disorders are complex and multifaceted. Psychological, biological, and social factors often lead people into "normal" dieting, which sometimes spins out of control. Maladaptive weight control efforts temporarily relieve individuals' pathological fear of gaining weight, but this reduced anxiety has a tremendous cost, as anorexia nervosa and bulimia nervosa are dangerous illnesses.

Graphic adapted from Barlow. D. H., & Durand, V. M. (1999). *Abnormal psychology: An integrative approach.* Belmont, CA: Wadsworth. Copyright © 1999 Wadsworth Publishing. Reprinted by permission.

to eating disorders simply by endorsing society's message that "you can never be too thin" and by modeling unhealthy dieting behaviors of their own. Although the hypotheses about the role of family dynamics in eating pathology are speculative, it does appear that families can contribute to eating disorders in a variety of ways.

Cognitive Factors

Many theorists emphasize the role of disturbed thinking in the etiology of eating disorders (Williamson et al., 2001). For example, anorexic patients' typical belief that they are fat when they are really wasting away is a dramatic illustration of how thinking goes awry. Patients with eating disorders display rigid, all-or-none thinking and many maladaptive beliefs, such as "I must be thin to be accepted," "If I am not in complete control, I will lose all control," and "If I gain one pound, I'll go on to gain enormous weight." Additional research is needed to determine whether distorted thinking is a *cause* or merely a *symptom* of eating disorders.

KEY IDEAS

Abnormal Behavior: Myths and Realities

▶ The medical model assumes that it is useful to view abnormal behavior as a disease. There are some problems with the medical model, but the disease analogy is useful. Three criteria are used in deciding whether people suffer from psychological disorders: deviance, personal distress, and maladaptive behavior. Often, it is difficult to draw a clear line between normality and abnormality.

▶ DSM-IV is the official psychodiagnostic classification system in the United States, although work has begun on the next edition (DSM-V). This system asks for information about patients on five axes. Psychological disorders are more common than widely believed, with a lifetime prevalence of roughly 44%, although there is some debate about recent prevalence estimates.

Anxiety Disorders

▶ The anxiety disorders include generalized anxiety disorder, phobic disorder, panic disorder, and obsessive-compulsive disorder (OCD). These disorders have been linked to genetic predisposition, temperament, anxiety sensitivity, and neurochemical abnormalities in the brain.

▶ Many anxiety responses, especially phobias, may be caused by classical conditioning and maintained by operant conditioning. Cognitive theorists maintain that some people are vulnerable to anxiety disorders because they see threat everywhere. Stress may also contribute to the onset of these disorders.

Somatoform Disorders

▶ Somatoform disorders include somatization disorder, conversion disorder, and hypochondriasis. These disorders often emerge in people with highly suggestible, histrionic personalities, who think irrationally about their health. Somatoform disorders may be learned avoidance strategies reinforced by attention and sympathy.

Dissociative Disorders

▶ Dissociative disorders include dissociative amnesia, dissociative fugue, and dissociative identity disorder (DID). These disorders appear to be uncommon, although there is some controversy about the prevalence of DID. Stress and childhood trauma may contribute to DID, but overall, the causes of dissociative disorders are not well understood.

Mood Disorders

▶ The principal mood disorders are major depressive disorder and bipolar disorder. People vary in their genetic vulnerability to mood disorders, which are accompanied by changes in neurochemical activity in the brain. Reduced hippocampal volume and suppressed neurogenesis may be factors in depression.

▶ Cognitive models posit that a pessimistic explanatory style, rumination, and other types of negative thinking contribute to depression. Depression is often rooted in interpersonal inadequacies, as people who lack social finesse often have difficulty acquiring life's reinforcers. Mood disorders are sometimes stress related.

Schizophrenic Disorders

▶ Schizophrenic disorders are characterized by deterioration of adaptive behavior, irrational thought, distorted perception, and disturbed mood. Schizophrenic disorders are classified as paranoid, catatonic, disorganized, or undifferentiated. The distinction between positive and negative symptoms has proven useful, but it has not yielded an effective new classification scheme.

▶ Research has linked schizophrenia to genetic vulnerability, changes in neurotransmitter activity, and enlarged ventricles in the brain. The neurodevelopmental hypothesis attributes schizophrenia to disruptions of normal maturational processes in the brain before or at birth. Patients who return to homes high in expressed emotion tend to have elevated relapse rates. Precipitating stress may also contribute to the emergence of schizophrenia.

Application: Understanding Eating Disorders

▶ The principal eating disorders are anorexia nervosa and bulimia nervosa. Binge-eating disorder is a new diagnostic syndrome that has been proposed. Anorexia and bulimia are both associated with other psychopathology, and both lead to a cascade of medical problems. Eating disorders appear to be a product of modern, affluent, Westernized culture.

▶ Females account for 90%–95% of eating disorders. The typical age of onset is roughly 15 to 20. There appears to be a genetic vulnerability to eating disorders, which may be mediated by heritable personality traits. Cultural pressures on young women to be thin clearly help foster eating disorders. Some theorists emphasize how family dynamics and disturbed thinking can contribute to the development of eating disorders.

KEY TERMS

Agoraphobia p. 485
Anorexia nervosa p. 508
Anxiety disorders p. 485
Binge-eating disorder p. 509
Bipolar disorder p. 495
Bulimia nervosa p. 509
Catatonic schizophrenia p. 503
Concordance rate p. 498
Conversion disorder p. 489
Delusions p. 502
Diagnosis p. 480
Disorganized schizophrenia p. 503
Dissociative amnesia p. 491
Dissociative disorders p. 491
Dissociative fugue p. 491
Dissociative identity disorder (DID) p. 492
Eating disorders p. 508
Epidemiology p. 482
Etiology p. 480
Generalized anxiety disorder p. 485
Hallucinations p. 502
Hypochondriasis p. 490
Major depressive disorder p. 494
Manic-depressive disorder p. 495
Medical model p. 479
Mood disorders p. 493
Multiple-personality disorder p. 492
Neurotransmitters p. 487
Obsessive-compulsive disorder (OCD) p. 486
Panic disorder p. 485
Paranoid schizophrenia p. 503
Phobic disorder p. 485
Prevalence p. 482
Prognosis p. 480
Schizophrenic disorders p. 501
Somatization disorder p. 489
Somatoform disorders p. 489
Undifferentiated schizophrenia p. 503

KEY PEOPLE

Nancy Andreasen p. 503
Susan Nolen-Hoeksema pp. 495, 499
Martin Seligman p. 498
Thomas Szasz p. 480

PRACTICE TEST

1. Sergio has just entered treatment for bipolar disorder and he is informed that most patients respond to drug treatment within a month. This information represents:
   a. a prognosis.
   b. an etiology.
   c. a histology.
   d. a concordance.

2. Although Sue always feels high levels of dread, worry, and anxiety, she still meets her daily responsibilities. Sue's behavior:
   a. should not be considered abnormal, since her adaptive functioning is not impaired.
   b. should not be considered abnormal, since everyone sometimes experiences worry and anxiety.
   c. can still be considered abnormal, since she feels great personal distress.
   d. both a and b.

3. Recent epidemiological studies have found that the most common types of psychological disorders are:
   a. mood disorders and anxiety disorders.
   b. anxiety disorders and schizophrenic disorders.
   c. substance-use disorders and anxiety disorders.
   d. substance-use disorders and somatoform disorders.

4. People who repeatedly perform senseless rituals to overcome their anxiety are said to have a(n):
   a. generalized anxiety disorder.
   b. manic disorder.
   c. obsessive-compulsive disorder.
   d. phobic disorder.

5. If a person has a paralyzed arm for which no organic basis can be found, she probably has:
   a. a conversion disorder.
   b. paralytic hypochondriasis.
   c. a dissociative disorder.
   d. a schizophrenic disorder.

6. After several months during which he was always gloomy and dejected, Mario has suddenly perked up. He feels elated and energetic and works around the clock on a writing project. He has also started to bet heavily on sporting events over the Internet, which he never did previously. Mario's behavior is consistent with:
   a. schizophrenia.
   b. obsessive-compulsive disorder.
   c. bipolar disorder.
   d. dissociative identity disorder.

7. A concordance rate indicates:
   a. the percentage of twin pairs or other relatives that exhibit the same disorder.
   b. the percentage of people with a given disorder that are currently receiving treatment.
   c. the prevalence of a given disorder in the general population.
   d. the rate of cure for a given disorder.

8. Which of the following would be a negative symptom of schizophrenia?
   a. Auditory hallucinations
   b. Delusions of persecution
   c. Having virtually no friendships
   d. Delusions of grandeur

9. Jamaal, who works as a projectionist at the local theater, is convinced that everyone is out to get him. He is sure that his phone is tapped by ruthless enemies. He thinks that most of the people in the theater each night are there to spy on him. Worse yet, he is sure people follow him home from work every night. Jamaal is probably suffering from:
   a. paranoid schizophrenia.
   b. catatonic schizophrenia.
   c. bipolar disorder.
   d. dissociative fugue.

10. About _____ % of patients with eating disorders are female.
   a. 40
   b. 50–60
   c. 75
   d. 90–95

Book Companion Website

Visit the Book Companion Website at **academic.cengage.com/psychology/weiten,** where you will find tutorial quizzes, flash cards, and web links for every chapter, a final exam, and more! You can also link to the Psychology Resource Center (accessible directly at **academic.cengage.com/login**) for a range of psychology-related resources.

Personal Explorations Workbook

The following exercises in your *Personal Explorations Workbook* may enhance your self-understanding in relation to issues raised in this chapter. **Questionnaire 15.1:** Manifest Anxiety Scale. **Personal Probe 15.1:** What Are Your Attitudes on Mental Illness? **Personal Probe 15.2:** Do You Think That We Are All Candidates for a Disorder?

ANSWERS

1. a Page 480
2. c Pages 480–481
3. c Pages 483–484
4. c Page 486
5. a Pages 489–490
6. c Page 495
7. a Page 498
8. c Pages 503–504
9. a Page 503
10. d Page 509

CHAPTER 16

Psychotherapy

What do you picture when you hear the term *psychotherapy*? If you're like most people, you probably envision a troubled patient lying on a couch in a therapist's office, with the therapist asking penetrating questions and providing sage advice. Typically, people believe that psychotherapy is only for those who are "sick" and that therapists have special powers that allow them to "see through" their clients. It is also widely believed that therapy requires years of deep probing into a client's innermost secrets. Many people further assume that therapists routinely tell their patients how to lead their lives. Like most stereotypes, this picture of psychotherapy is a mixture of fact and fiction, as you'll see in the upcoming pages.

In this chapter, we take a down-to-earth look at the process of *psychotherapy,* using the term in its broadest sense to refer to all the diverse approaches to the treatment of psychological problems. We start by discussing some general questions about the provision of treatment. Who seeks therapy? What kinds of professionals provide treatment? How many types of therapy are there? After considering these general issues, we examine some of the more widely used approaches to treating psychological maladies, analyzing their goals, techniques, and effectiveness. The Application at the end of the chapter focuses on practical issues involved in finding a therapist, in case you ever have to advise someone about seeking help.

THE ELEMENTS OF THE TREATMENT PROCESS
Treatments: How Many Types Are There?
Clients: Who Seeks Therapy?
Therapists: Who Provides Professional Treatment?

INSIGHT THERAPIES
Psychoanalysis
Client-Centered Therapy
Group Therapy
Evaluating Insight Therapies
Therapy and the Recovered Memories Controversy

BEHAVIOR THERAPIES
Systematic Desensitization
Aversion Therapy
Social Skills Training
Cognitive-Behavioral Treatments

LIVING IN TODAY'S WORLD *How Do Clinicians Treat Posttraumatic Stress Disorder?*
Evaluating Behavior Therapies

BIOMEDICAL THERAPIES
Treatment with Drugs
Electroconvulsive Therapy (ECT)

CURRENT TRENDS AND ISSUES IN TREATMENT
Grappling with the Constraints of Managed Care
Blending Approaches to Treatment
Increasing Multicultural Sensitivity in Treatment

APPLICATION: LOOKING FOR A THERAPIST
Where Do You Find Therapeutic Services?
Is the Therapist's Profession or Sex Important?
Is Therapy Always Expensive?
Is the Therapist's Theoretical Approach Important?
What Is Therapy Like?

REVIEW

PRACTICE TEST

The Elements of the Treatment Process

LEARNING OBJECTIVES

- *Identify the three major categories of therapy.*
- *Discuss why people do or do not seek psychotherapy.*
- *Describe the various types of mental health professionals involved in the provision of therapy.*

Today people have a bewildering array of psychotherapy approaches to choose from. In fact, the immense diversity of therapeutic treatments makes defining the concept of *psychotherapy* difficult. After organizing a landmark conference that brought together many of the world's leading authorities on psychotherapy, Jeffrey Zeig (1987) commented, "I do not believe there is any capsule definition of psychotherapy on which the 26 presenters could agree" (p. xix). In lieu of a definition, we can identify a few basic elements that the various approaches to treatment have in common. All psychotherapies involve a helping relationship (the treatment) between a professional with special training (the therapist) and another person in need of help (the client). As we look at each of these three elements, you'll see the diverse nature of modern psychotherapy.

Treatments: How Many Types Are There?

In their efforts to help people, mental health professionals use many methods of treatment, including discussion, emotional support, persuasion, conditioning procedures, relaxation training, role playing, drug therapy, biofeedback, and group therapy. Some therapists also use a variety of less conventional procedures, such as rebirthing, poetry therapy, and primal therapy. No one knows exactly how many approaches to treatment there are. One expert (Kazdin, 1994) estimates that there may be over 400 distinct types of psychotherapy! Fortunately, we can impose some order on this chaos. As varied as therapists' procedures are, approaches to treatment can be classified into three major categories:

1. *Insight therapies.* Insight therapy is "talk therapy" in the tradition of Freud's psychoanalysis. This is probably the approach to treatment that you envision when you think of psychotherapy. In insight therapies, clients engage in complex verbal interactions with their therapists. The goal in these discussions is to pursue increased insight regarding the nature of the client's difficulties and to sort through possible solutions. Insight therapy can be conducted with an individual or with a group.

2. *Behavior therapies.* Behavior therapies are based on the principles of learning and conditioning, which were introduced in Chapter 2. Instead of emphasizing personal insights, behavior therapists make direct efforts to alter problematic responses (phobic behaviors, for instance) and maladaptive habits (drug use, for instance). Behavior therapists work on changing clients' overt behaviors. They use different procedures for different kinds of problems.

3. *Biomedical therapies.* Biomedical approaches to therapy involve interventions into a person's physiological functioning. The most widely used procedures are drug therapy and electroconvulsive therapy. As the name bio*medical* therapies suggests, these treatments have traditionally been provided only by physicians with a medical degree (usually psychiatrists). This situation is changing, however, as psychologists have been campaigning for prescription privileges (Norfleet, 2002; Welsh, 2003). To date psychologists have obtained prescription authority in two states (New Mexico and Louisiana), and they have made legislative progress toward this goal in many other states (Long, 2005). Although some psychologists have argued against pursuing the right to prescribe medication (Heiby, 2002; Robiner et al., 2003), the movement is gathering momentum and seems likely to prevail.

In this chapter we examine approaches to therapy that fall into each of these three categories. Although different methods are used in each, the three major classes of treatment are not entirely incompatible. For example, a client being seen in insight therapy may also be given medication.

Clients: Who Seeks Therapy?

In the therapeutic triad (therapists, treatments, clients), the greatest diversity is seen among the clients. According to the 1999 U.S. Surgeon General's report on mental health (U.S. Department of Health and Human Services, 1999), about 15% of the U.S. population use mental health services in a given year. These people bring to therapy the full range of human problems: anxiety, depression, unsatisfactory interpersonal relations, troublesome habits, poor self-control, low self-esteem, marital conflicts, self-doubt, a sense of emptiness, and feelings of personal stagnation. The two most common presenting problems are excessive anxiety and depression (Narrow et al., 1993).

Interestingly, people often delay for many years before finally seeking treatment for their psychological problems (Kessler, Olfson, & Berglund, 1998). One recent large-scale study (Wang, Berglund, et al., 2005) found that the median delay in seeking treatment was 6 years for bipolar disorder and for drug dependence, 8 years for depression, 9 years for generalized anxiety disorder, and 10 years for panic disorder! **Figure 16.1** summarizes data from the same study on the percentage of people with various disorders who seek treatment within the first year after the onset of the disorder. As you can see, the figures are surprisingly low for most disorders.

A client in treatment does *not* necessarily have an identifiable psychological disorder. Some people seek professional help for everyday problems (career decisions, for instance) or vague feelings of discontent (Strupp, 1996). One surprising finding in recent research has been that only about half of the people who use mental health services in a given year meet the criteria for a full-fledged mental disorder (Kessler et al., 2005b).

People vary considerably in their willingness to seek psychotherapy. One study found that even when people perceive a need for professional assistance, only 59% actually seek professional help (Mojtabai, Olfson, & Mechanic, 2002). As you can see in **Figure 16.2**, women are more likely than men to receive treatment, and whites are more likely than blacks or Hispanics to obtain therapy. Treatment is also more likely when people have medical insurance and when they have more education (Olfson et al., 2002; Wang, Lane, et al, 2005). *Unfortunately, it appears that many people who need therapy don't receive it* (Kessler et al., 2005b). As **Figure 16.3** (on page 518) shows, only a portion of the people who need treatment get it. People who could benefit from therapy do not seek it for a variety of reasons. Lack of health insurance and cost concerns appear to be major barriers to obtaining needed care for many

A Consumer's Guide to Psychotherapy
by Larry E. Beutler, Bruce Bongar, and Joel N. Shurkin
(Oxford University Press, 2001)

This book is a serious, sophisticated work that may be more thoroughly grounded in scientific research than any of its competitors. The character of the book is consistent with the fact that Larry Beutler is one of the leading researchers on the efficacy of psychotherapy. That is *not* to say that this is a research treatise. It is a pragmatic, readable discussion of everyday issues, such as what to look for in choosing a therapist, what questions to ask when you have doubts about your therapy, what role you play in the success of your treatment, how to recognize and deal with unprofessional or unethical behavior on the part of a therapist, and how to recognize when therapy is not working. The greatest strength of the book is its analysis of what research says about the effectiveness of specific therapies for particular problems. The authors carefully summarize the findings on what works best with what problems.

Figure 16.1

Treatment seeking for various disorders. In a study of the extent to which people seek treatment for psychological disorders, Wang et al. (2005) found that only a minority of people promptly pursue treatment for their disorder. The data summarized here show the percentage of people who obtain professional treatment within the first year after the onset of various disorders. The percentages vary depending on the disorder, but all the figures are surprisingly low. (Data from Wang et al., 2005).

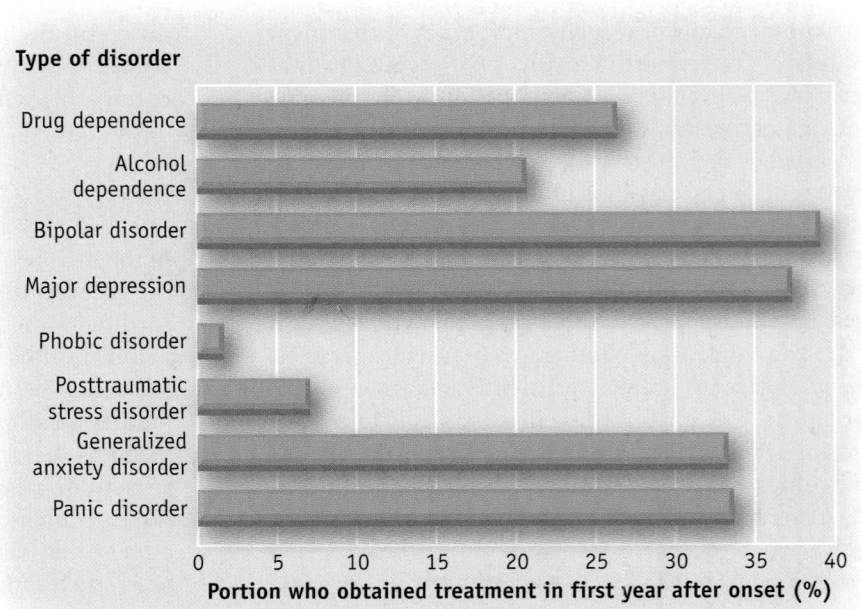

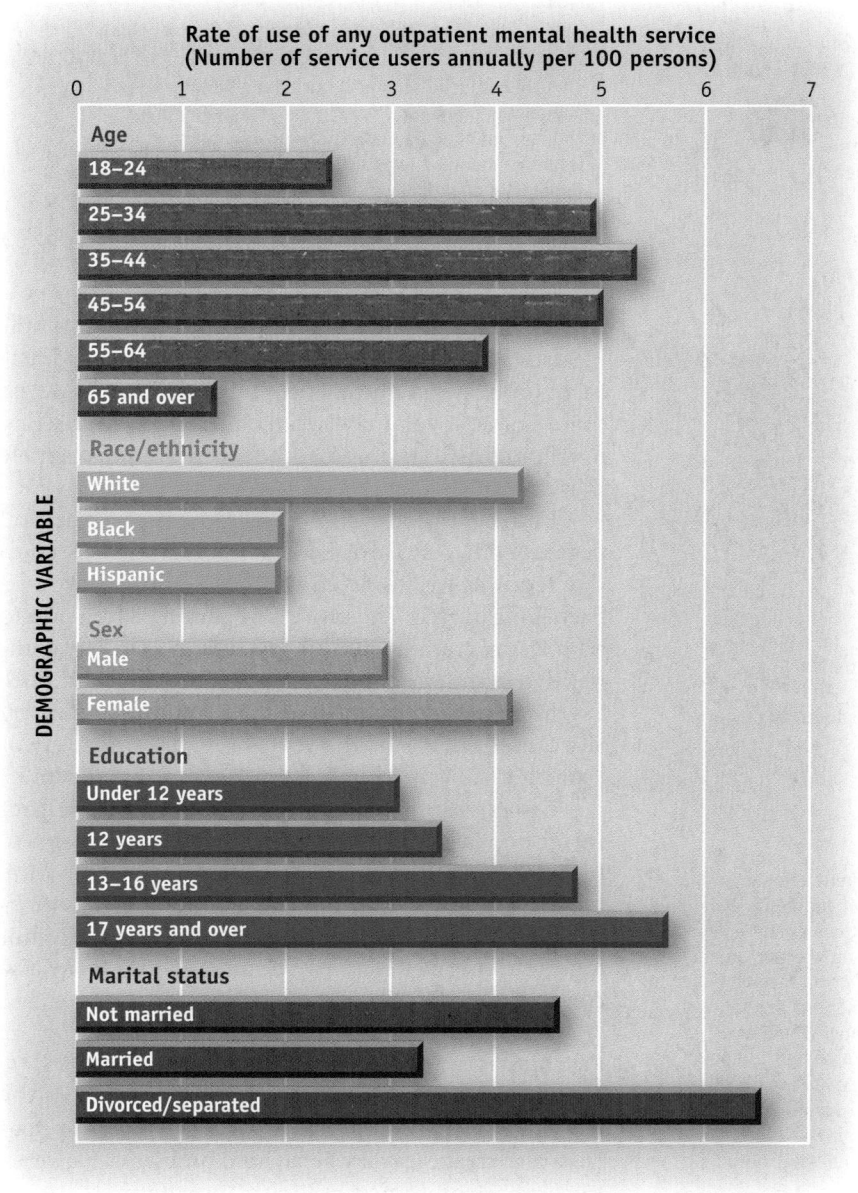

Figure 16.2

Therapy utilization rates. Olfson and colleagues (2002) gathered data on the use of nonhospital outpatient mental health services in the United States in relation to various demographic variables. In regard to marital status, utilization rates are particularly high among those who are divorced or separated. The use of therapy is greater among those who have more education and, in terms of age, utilization peaks in the 35–44 age bracket. Females are more likely to pursue therapy than males are, but utilization rates are extremely low among ethnic minorities. (Data from Olfson et al., 2002)

people. According to the Surgeon General's report, the biggest roadblock is the "stigma surrounding the receipt of mental health treatment." Unfortunately, many people equate seeking therapy with admitting personal weakness.

Therapists: Who Provides Professional Treatment?

Friends and relatives may provide excellent advice about personal problems, but their assistance does not qualify as therapy. Psychotherapy refers to *professional* treatment by someone with special training. However, a common source of confusion about psychotherapy is the variety of "helping professions" available to offer assistance. Psychology and psychiatry are the principal professions involved in psychotherapy, providing the lion's share of mental health care. However, therapy is also provided by social workers, psychiatric nurses, and counselors, as outlined in **Figure 16.4** (on the next page).

Psychologists

Two types of psychologists may provide therapy, although the distinction between them is more theoretical than real. ***Clinical psychologists* and *counseling psychologists* specialize in the diagnosis and treatment of psychological disorders and everyday behavioral problems.** In theory, the training of clinical psychologists emphasizes treatment of full-fledged

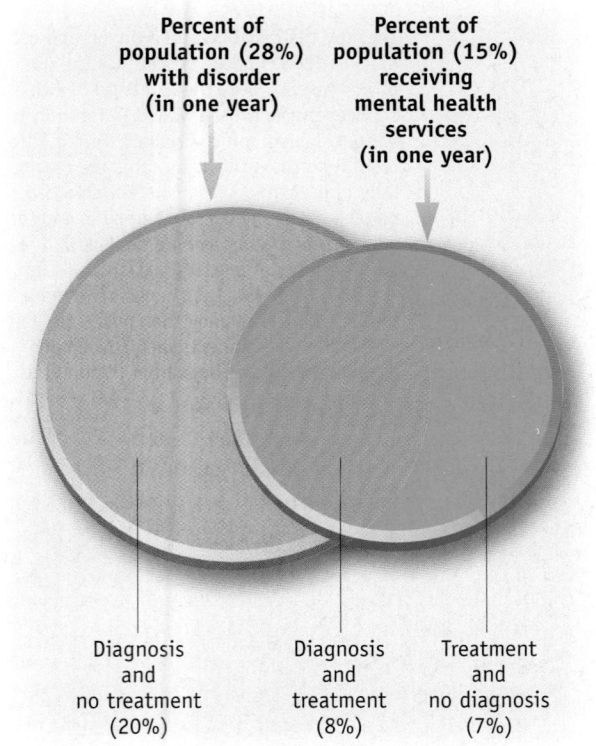

Figure 16.3

Psychological disorders and professional treatment. Not everyone who has a psychological disorder receives professional treatment, and not everyone who seeks treatment has a clear disorder. This graph, from the 1999 Surgeon General's report on mental health, shows that 15% of the adult population receive mental health treatment each year. Almost half of these people (7%) do not receive a psychiatric diagnosis, although some of them probably have milder disorders that are not assessed in epidemiological research. This graph also shows that over two-thirds of the people who *do* have disorders do *not* receive professional treatment. (Data from *Mental Health: A Report from the Surgeon General,* U.S. Department of Health and Human Services, 1999)

Web Link 16.1 **Online Dictionary of Mental Health**

This thematically arranged "dictionary" comprises diverse links involving many forms of psychotherapy, the treatment of psychological disorders, and general issues of mental health. It is sponsored by the Centre for Psychotherapeutic Studies at the University of Sheffield's Medical School in the UK.

disorders, whereas the training of counseling psychologists is slanted toward treatment of everyday adjustment problems in normal people. In practice, however, there is great overlap between clinical and counseling psychologists in training, in skills, and in the clientele they serve.

Both types of psychologists must earn a doctoral degree (Ph.D., Psy.D., or Ed.D.). A doctorate in psychology requires five to seven years of training beyond a bachelor's degree. The process of gaining admission to a Ph.D. program in clinical psychology is highly competitive (about as competitive as for medical school). Psychologists receive most of their training on university campuses, although they also serve a one- to two-year internship in a clinical setting, such as a hospital.

In providing therapy, psychologists use either insight or behavioral approaches. In comparison to psychiatrists, they are more likely to use behavioral techniques and less likely to use psychoanalytic methods. Clinical and counseling psychologists do psychological testing as well as psychotherapy, and many also conduct research.

Psychiatrists

***Psychiatrists* are physicians who specialize in the treatment of psychological disorders.** Many psychiatrists also treat everyday behavioral problems. However, in comparison to psychologists, psychiatrists devote

Figure 16.4

The principal mental health professions. Psychotherapists come from a variety of professional backgrounds. This chart provides an overview of various types of therapists' education and typical professional activities.

Types of Therapists

Title	Degree	Years beyond bachelor's degree	Typical roles and activities
Clinical or counseling psychologist	Ph.D. Psy.D. Ed.D.	5–7	Diagnosis, psychological testing, insight and behavior therapy
Psychiatrist	M.D.	8	Diagnosis; insight, behavior, and biomedical therapy
Social worker	M.S.W.	2	Insight and behavior therapy, family therapy, helping patients return to the community
Psychiatric nurse	B.S., B.A., M.A.	0–2	Inpatient care, insight and behavior therapy
Counselor	M.A., M.S.	2	Insight and behavior therapy, working primarily with everyday adjustment and marital and career issues

more time to relatively severe disorders (schizophrenia, mood disorders) and less time to everyday marital, family, job, and school problems. Psychiatrists have an M.D. degree. Their graduate training requires four years of course work in medical school and a four-year apprenticeship in a residency at an approved hospital. Their psychotherapy training occurs during their residency, since the required course work in medical school is essentially the same for all students, whether they are going into surgery, pediatrics, or psychiatry.

In their provision of therapy, psychiatrists increasingly emphasize drug therapies (Olfson et al., 2002). In comparison to psychologists, psychiatrists are more likely to use psychoanalysis and less likely to use group therapies or behavior therapies.

Other Mental Health Professionals

Several other mental health professions provide psychotherapy services. In hospitals and other institutions, *psychiatric social workers* and *psychiatric nurses* often work as part of a treatment team with a psychologist or psychiatrist. Psychiatric nurses, who may have a bachelor's or master's degree in their field, play a large role in hospital inpatient treatment. Psychiatric social workers generally have a master's degree and typically work with patients and their families to ease the patient's integration back into the community. Although social workers have traditionally worked in hospitals and social service agencies, many are licensed as independent, private practitioners who provide a wide range of therapeutic services.

Many kinds of *counselors* also provide therapeutic services. Counselors are usually found working in schools, colleges, and human service agencies (youth centers, geriatric centers, family planning centers, and so forth). Counselors typically have a master's degree. They often specialize in particular types of problems, such as vocational counseling, marital counseling, rehabilitation counseling, and drug counseling.

Although clear differences exist among the helping professions in education and training, their roles in the treatment process overlap considerably. In this chapter, we refer to psychologists or psychiatrists as needed, but otherwise we use the terms *clinician, therapist,* and *mental health professional* to refer to psychotherapists of all kinds, regardless of their professional degree.

Now that we have discussed the basic elements in psychotherapy, we can examine specific approaches to treatment in terms of their goals, procedures, and effectiveness. We begin with a few representative insight therapies.

Insight Therapies

LEARNING OBJECTIVES

- *Explain the logic of psychoanalysis and describe the techniques used to probe the unconscious.*
- *Discuss interpretation, resistance, and transference in psychoanalysis.*
- *Describe therapeutic climate and process in client-centered therapy.*
- *Describe how group therapy is generally conducted.*
- *Summarize evidence on the efficacy of insight therapies.*
- *Discuss the role of common factors in insight therapy.*
- *Review both sides of the recovered memories controversy.*

Many schools of thought exist as to how to do insight therapy. Therapists with different theoretical orientations use different methods to pursue different kinds of insights. What these varied approaches have in common is that ***insight therapies*** **involve verbal interactions intended to enhance clients' self-knowledge and thus promote healthful changes in personality and behavior.** Although there may be hundreds of insight therapies, the leading eight or ten approaches appear to account for the lion's share of treatment. In this section, we delve into psychoanalysis, client-centered therapy, and group therapy.

Psychoanalysis

Sigmund Freud worked as a psychotherapist for almost 50 years in Vienna. Through a painstaking process of trial and error, he developed innovative techniques for the treatment of psychological disorders and distress. His system of *psychoanalysis* came to dominate psychiatry for many decades. Although the dominance of psychoanalysis has eroded in recent decades, a diverse array of psychoanalytic approaches to therapy continue to evolve and remain influential today (McWilliams & Weinberger, 2003; Ursano & Silberman, 2003).

National Library of Medicine

Sigmund Freud

Psychoanalysis **is an insight therapy that emphasizes the recovery of unconscious conflicts, motives, and defenses through techniques such as free association, dream analysis, and transference.** To appreciate the logic of psychoanalysis, we have to look at

Freud's thinking about the roots of mental disorders. Freud treated mostly anxiety-dominated disturbances, such as phobic, panic, obsessive-compulsive, and conversion disorders, which were then called *neuroses.* He believed that neurotic problems are caused by unconscious conflicts left over from early childhood. As explained in Chapter 2, he thought that these inner conflicts involve battles among the id, ego, and superego, usually over sexual and aggressive impulses. Freud theorized that people depend on defense mechanisms to avoid confronting these conflicts, which remain hidden in the depths of the unconscious. However, he noted that defensive maneuvers often lead to self-defeating behavior. Furthermore, he asserted that defenses tend to be only partially successful in alleviating anxiety, guilt, and other distressing emotions. With this model in mind, let's take a look at the therapeutic procedures used in psychoanalysis.

Probing the Unconscious

Given Freud's assumptions, we can see that the logic of psychoanalysis is very simple. The analyst attempts to probe the murky depths of the unconscious to discover the unresolved conflicts causing the client's neurotic behavior. In a sense, the analyst functions as a psychological detective. In this effort to explore the unconscious, he or she relies on two techniques: free association and dream analysis.

In *free association,* clients spontaneously express their thoughts and feelings exactly as they occur, with as little censorship as possible. Clients lie on a couch so they will be better able to let their minds drift freely. In free associating, clients expound on anything that comes to mind, regardless of how trivial, silly, or embarrassing it might be. Gradually, most clients begin to let everything pour out without conscious censorship. The analyst studies these free associations for clues about what is going on in the unconscious.

In *dream analysis,* the therapist interprets the symbolic meaning of the client's dreams. For Freud, dreams were the "royal road to the unconscious," the most direct means of access to patients' innermost conflicts, wishes, and impulses. Clients are encouraged and trained to remember their dreams, which they describe in therapy. The therapist then analyzes the symbolism in these dreams to interpret their meaning.

To better illustrate these matters, let's look at an actual case treated through psychoanalysis (adapted from Greenson, 1967, pp. 40–41). Mr. N was troubled by an unsatisfactory marriage. He claimed to love his wife, but he preferred sexual relations with prostitutes. Mr. N reported that his parents also endured lifelong marital difficulties. His childhood conflicts about their relationship appeared to be related to his problems. Both dream analysis and free association can be seen in the following description of a session in Mr. N's treatment:

Mr. N reports a fragment of a dream. All that he can remember is that he is waiting for a red traffic light to change when he feels that someone has bumped into him from behind. . . . The associations led to Mr. N's love of cars, especially sports cars. He loved the sensation, in particular, of whizzing by those fat, old, expensive cars. . . . His father always hinted that he had been a great athlete, but he never substantiated it. . . . Mr. N doubted whether his father could really perform. His father would flirt with a waitress in a cafe or make sexual remarks about women passing by, but he seemed to be showing off. If he were really sexual, he wouldn't resort to that.

As is characteristic of free association, Mr. N's train of thought meanders about with little direction. Nonetheless, clues about his unconscious conflicts are apparent. What did Mr. N's therapist extract from this session? The therapist saw sexual overtones in the dream fragment, where Mr. N was bumped from behind. The therapist also inferred that Mr. N had a competitive orientation toward his father, based on the free association about whizzing by fat, old, expensive cars. As you can see, analysts must *interpret* their clients' dreams and free associations. This is a critical process throughout psychoanalysis.

Interpretation

***Interpretation* involves the therapist's attempts to explain the inner significance of the client's thoughts, feelings, memories, and behaviors.** Contrary to popular belief, analysts do not interpret everything, and they generally don't try to dazzle clients with startling revelations. Instead, analysts move forward inch by inch, offering interpretations that should be just out of the client's own reach (Samberg & Marcus, 2005).

© Bruce Ayres/Stone/Getty Images

In psychoanalysis, the therapist encourages the client to reveal thoughts, feelings, dreams, and memories that can then be interpreted in relation to the client's current problems.

Mr. N's therapist eventually offered the following interpretations to his client:

I said to Mr. N near the end of the hour that I felt he was struggling with his feelings about his father's sexual life. He seemed to be saying that his father was sexually not a very potent man. . . . He also recalls that he once found a packet of condoms under his father's pillow when he was an adolescent and he thought "My father must be going to prostitutes." I then intervened and pointed out that the condoms under his father's pillow seemed to indicate more obviously that his father used the condoms with his mother, who slept in the same bed. However, Mr. N wanted to believe his wish-fulfilling fantasy: mother doesn't want sex with father and father is not very potent. The patient was silent and the hour ended.

As you may already have guessed, the therapist has concluded that Mr. N's difficulties are rooted in an Oedipal complex (see Chapter 2). Mr. N has unresolved sexual feelings toward his mother and hostile feelings about his father. These unconscious conflicts, which are rooted in his childhood, are distorting his intimate relations as an adult.

Resistance

How would you expect Mr. N to respond to his therapist's suggestion that he was in competition with his father for the sexual attention of his mother? Obviously, most clients would have great difficulty accepting such an interpretation. Freud fully expected clients to display some resistance to therapeutic efforts. ***Resistance* involves largely unconscious defensive maneuvers intended to hinder the progress of therapy.** Resistance is assumed to be an inevitable part of the psychoanalytic process (Samberg & Marcus, 2005). Why do clients try to resist the helping process? Because they don't want to face up to the painful, disturbing conflicts that they have buried in their unconscious. Although they have sought help, they are reluctant to confront their real problems.

Resistance may take many forms. Patients may show up late for their sessions, merely pretend to engage in free association, or express hostility toward the therapist. For instance, Mr. N's therapist noted that after the session just described, "The next day he began by telling me that he was furious with me." Analysts use a variety of strategies to deal with their clients' resistance.

Web Link 16.2 **The American Psychoanalytic Association**

The site for this professional organization provides a great deal of useful information about psychoanalytic approaches to treatment. The resources include news releases, background information on psychoanalysis, an engine for literature searches, and a bookstore.

Often, a key consideration is the handling of *transference,* which we consider next.

Transference

***Transference* occurs when clients start relating to their therapists in ways that mimic critical relationships in their lives.** Thus, a client might start relating to a therapist as if the therapist were an overprotective mother, rejecting brother, or passive spouse. In a sense, the client *transfers* conflicting feelings about important people onto the therapist. For instance, in his treatment, Mr. N transferred some of the competitive hostility he felt toward his father onto his analyst.

Psychoanalysts often encourage transference so that clients begin to reenact relations with crucial people in the context of therapy. These reenactments can help bring repressed feelings and conflicts to the surface, allowing the client to work through them. The therapist's handling of transference is complicated and difficult because transference may arouse confusing, highly charged emotions in the client.

Undergoing psychoanalysis is not easy. It can be a slow, painful process of self-examination that routinely requires three to five years of hard work. It tends to be a lengthy process because patients need time to gradually work through their problems and genuinely accept unnerving revelations (Williams, 2005). Ultimately, if resistance and transference can be handled effectively, the therapist's interpretations should lead the client to profound insights. For instance, Mr. N eventually admitted, "The old boy is probably right, it does tickle me to imagine that my mother preferred me and I could beat out my father. Later, I wondered whether this had something to do with my own screwed-up sex life with my wife." According to Freud, once clients recognize the unconscious sources of their conflicts, they can resolve these conflicts and discard their neurotic defenses.

Although still available, classical psychoanalysis as done by Freud is not widely practiced anymore (Kay & Kay, 2003). Freud's psychoanalytic method was geared to a particular kind of clientele that he was seeing in Vienna a century ago. As his followers fanned out across Europe and America, many found that it was necessary to adapt psychoanalysis to different cultures, changing times, and new kinds of patients (Karasu, 2005). Thus, many variations on Freud's original approach to psychoanalysis have developed over the years. These descendants of psychoanalysis are collectively known as *psychodynamic approaches* to therapy.

Client-Centered Therapy

You may have heard of people going into therapy to "find themselves" or to "get in touch with their real feelings." These now-popular phrases emerged out of the human potential movement, which was stimulated in part by the work of Carl Rogers (1951, 1986). Taking a humanistic perspective, Rogers devised *client-centered therapy* (also known as *person-centered therapy*) in the 1940s and 1950s.

***Client-centered therapy* is an insight therapy that emphasizes providing a supportive emotional climate for clients, who play a major role in determining the pace and direction of their therapy.** You may wonder why the troubled, untrained client is put in charge of the pace and direction of the therapy. Rogers (1961) provides a compelling justification:

Courtesy, Carl Rogers Memorial Library

Carl Rogers

It is the client who knows what hurts, what directions to go, what problems are crucial, what experiences have been deeply buried. It began to occur to me that unless I had a need to demonstrate my own cleverness and learning, I would do better to rely upon the client for the direction of movement in the process. (pp. 11–12)

Rogers's theory about the principal causes of neurotic anxieties is quite different from the Freudian explanation. As discussed in Chapter 2, Rogers maintained that most personal distress is due to inconsistency, or "incongruence," between a person's self-concept and reality (see **Figure 16.5**). According to his theory, incongruence makes people prone to feel threatened by realistic feedback about themselves from others. For example, if you inaccurately viewed yourself as a hard-working, dependable person, you would feel threatened by contradictory feedback from friends or co-workers. According to Rogers, anxiety about such feedback often leads to reliance on defense mechanisms, distortions of reality, and stifled personal growth. Excessive incongruence is thought to be rooted in clients' overdependence on others for approval and acceptance.

Given Rogers's theory, client-centered therapists seek insights that are quite different from the repressed conflicts that psychoanalysts try to track down. Client-centered therapists help clients to realize that they do not have to worry constantly about pleasing others and winning acceptance. They encourage clients to respect their own feelings and values. They help people restructure their self-concept to correspond better to reality. Ultimately, they try to foster self-acceptance and personal growth.

Therapeutic Climate

In client-centered therapy, the *process* of therapy is not as important as the emotional *climate* in which the therapy takes place. According to Rogers, it is critical for the therapist to provide a warm, supportive, accepting climate in which clients can confront their shortcomings without feeling threatened. The lack of threat should reduce clients' defensive tendencies and thus help them to open up. To create this atmosphere of emotional support, Rogers believed that client-centered therapists must provide three conditions:

1. *Genuineness.* The therapist must be genuine with the client, communicating in an honest and spontaneous manner. The therapist should not be phony or defensive.
2. *Unconditional positive regard.* The therapist must also show complete, nonjudgmental acceptance of the client as a person. The therapist should provide warmth and caring for the client with no strings attached. This mandate does not mean that the therapist has to approve of everything that the client says or does. A therapist can disapprove of a particular behavior while continuing to value the client as a human being.

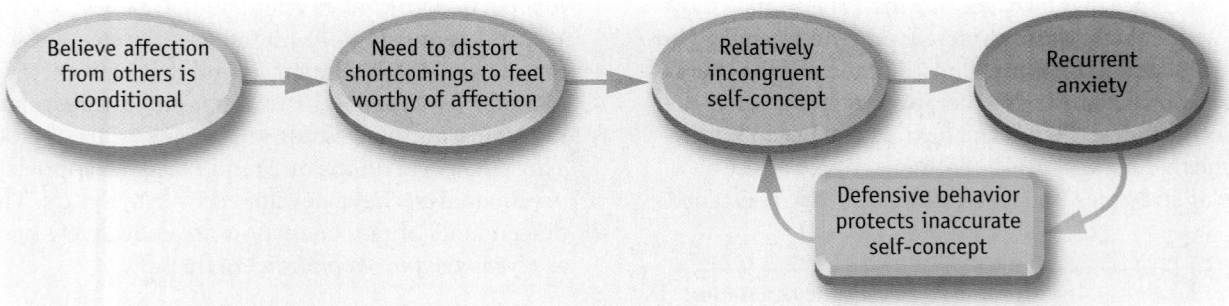

Figure 16.5

Rogers's view of the roots of disorders. Carl Rogers's theory posits that anxiety and self-defeating behavior are rooted in an incongruent self-concept that makes one prone to recurrent anxiety, which triggers defensive behavior, which fuels more incongruence.

3. *Empathy.* Finally, the therapist must provide accurate empathy for the client. This means that the therapist must understand the client's world from the client's point of view. Furthermore, the therapist must be articulate enough to communicate this understanding to the client.

Rogers firmly believed that a supportive emotional climate is the major force that promotes healthy changes in therapy. However, some client-centered therapists have begun to place more emphasis on the therapeutic process (Rice & Greenberg, 1992).

Therapeutic Process

In client-centered therapy, the client and therapist work together almost as equals. The therapist provides relatively little guidance and keeps interpretation and advice to a minimum. So, just what does the client-centered therapist do, besides creating a supportive climate? Primarily, the therapist provides feedback to help clients sort out their feelings. The therapist's key task is *clarification.* Client-centered therapists try to function like a human mirror, reflecting statements back to their clients, but with enhanced clarity. They help clients become more aware of their true feelings by highlighting themes that may be obscure in the clients' rambling discourse.

By working with clients to clarify their feelings, client-centered therapists hope to gradually build toward more far-reaching insights. In particular, they try to help clients become more aware of and comfortable about their genuine selves. Obviously, these are ambitious goals. Client-centered therapy resembles psychoanalysis in that both seek to achieve a major reconstruction of a client's personality.

Group Therapy

Although it dates back to the early part of the 20th century, group therapy came of age during World War II and its aftermath in the 1950s (Rosenbaum, Lakin, & Roback, 1992). During this period, the expanding demand for therapeutic services forced clinicians to use group techniques (Scheidlinger, 1993). ***Group therapy* is the simultaneous treatment of several or more clients in a group.** Most major insight therapies have been adapted for use with groups. In fact, the ideas underlying Rogers's client-centered therapy spawned the much-publicized encounter group movement. Although group therapy can be conducted in a variety of ways, we can provide a general overview of the process as it usually unfolds (see Alonso, Alonso, & Piper, 2003; Vinogradov, Cox, & Yalom, 2003; Wong, 2005).

Participants' Roles

A therapy group typically consists of 4 to 12 people, with 6 to 8 participants regarded as an ideal number (Vinogradov et al., 2003). The therapist usually screens the participants, excluding anyone who seems likely to be disruptive. Some theorists maintain that judicious selection of participants is crucial to effective group treatment (Salvendy, 1993). There is some debate about whether it is better to have a homogeneous group (people who are similar in age, gender, and presenting problem) rather than a heterogeneous one. Practical necessities usually dictate that groups be at least somewhat diversified.

In group treatment the therapist's responsibilities include selecting participants, setting goals for the group, initiating and maintaining the therapeutic

© Bruce Ayres/Stone/Getty Images

Group therapies have proven particularly helpful when members share similar problems, such as alcoholism, overeating, or depression.

process, and protecting clients from harm (Vinogradov et al., 2003). The therapist often plays a relatively subtle role, staying in the background and focusing mainly on promoting group cohesiveness. The therapist always retains a special status, but the therapist and clients are on much more equal footing in group therapy than in individual therapy. The leader in group therapy expresses emotions, shares feelings, and copes with challenges from group members. In other words, group therapists participate in the group's exchanges and "bare their own souls" to some extent.

In group therapy, participants essentially function as therapists for one another (Stone, 2003). Group members describe their problems, trade viewpoints, share experiences, and discuss coping strategies. Most important, they provide acceptance and emotional support for each other. In this supportive atmosphere, group members work at peeling away the social masks that cover their insecurities. Once their problems are exposed, members work at correcting them. As members come to value one another's opinions, they work hard to display healthy changes to win the group's approval.

Advantages of the Group Experience

Group therapies obviously save time and money, which can be critical in understaffed mental hospitals and other institutional settings (Vinogradov et al., 2003). Therapists in private practice usually charge less for group than individual therapy, making therapy affordable for more people. However, group therapy is *not* just a less costly substitute for individual therapy. For many types of patients and problems, group therapy can be just as effective as individual treatment (Alonso et al., 2003; Stone, 2003). Moreover, group therapy has unique strengths of its own. Irwin Yalom (1995), who has studied group therapy extensively, has described some of these advantages:

1. *In group therapy, participants often come to realize that their misery is not unique.* Clients often enter therapy feeling sorry for themselves. They think that they alone have a burdensome cross to bear. In the group situation, they quickly see that they are not unique. They are reassured to learn that many other people have similar or even worse problems.
2. *Group therapy provides an opportunity for participants to work on their social skills in a safe environment.* Many personal problems essentially involve difficulties in relating effectively to people. Group therapy can provide a workshop for improving interpersonal skills that cannot be matched by individual therapy.
3. *Certain kinds of problems are especially well suited to group treatment.* Specific types of problems and clients respond especially well to the social support that group therapy can provide. Peer self-help groups illustrate this advantage. In peer self-help groups, people who have a problem in common get together regularly to help one another out. The original peer self-help group was Alcoholics Anonymous. Today, similar groups are made up of former psychiatric patients, single parents, drug addicts, and so forth.

Whether treatment is conducted on a group or an individual basis, clients usually invest considerable time, effort, and money in insight therapies. Are they worth the investment? Let's look at the research evidence on the efficacy of insight therapies.

Evaluating Insight Therapies

Evaluating the effectiveness of any approach to treatment is a complex challenge (Hill & Lambert, 2004; Kendall, Holmbeck, & Verduin, 2004). This is especially true for insight therapies. If you were to undergo insight therapy, how would you judge its effectiveness? By how you felt? By looking at your behavior? By asking your therapist? By consulting your friends and family? What would you be looking for? Various schools of therapy pursue entirely different goals. And clients' ratings of their progress are likely to be slanted toward a favorable evaluation because they want to justify their effort, their heartache, their expense, and their time. Even evaluations by professional therapists can be highly subjective (Luborsky, Singer, & Luborsky, 1999). Moreover, people enter therapy with diverse problems of varied severity, creating huge confounds in efforts to assess the effectiveness of therapeutic interventions.

Despite these difficulties, thousands of outcome studies have been conducted to evaluate the effectiveness of insight therapy. These studies have examined a broad range of clinical problems and used diverse methods to assess therapeutic outcomes, including scores on psychological tests and ratings by family members, as well as therapists' and clients' ratings. These studies consistently indicate that insight therapy *is* superior to no treatment or to placebo treatment and that the effects of therapy are reasonably durable (Kopta et al., 1999; Lambert & Archer, 2006). Studies generally find the greatest improvement early in treatment (the first 13–18 weekly sessions) with further gains gradually diminishing over time (Lambert, Bergin, & Garfield, 2004). Overall, about 50% of patients show a clinically meaningful recovery within about 20 sessions and another 25% of patients achieve this goal after about 45 sessions (Lambert & Ogles, 2004; see **Figure 16.6**). Of course, these broad generalizations mask considerable variability in outcome, but the general trends are encouraging.

Although considerable evidence suggests that insight therapy produces positive effects for a sizable majority of clients, there is vigorous debate about the *mechanisms of action* underlying these positive effects. The advocates of various therapies tend to attribute the benefits of therapy to the particular methods and procedures used by each specific approach to therapy (Chambless & Hollon, 1998). In essence, they argue that different therapies achieve similar benefits through different processes. An alternative view espoused by many theorists is that the diverse approaches to therapy share certain common factors and that it is these common factors that account for much of the improvement experienced by clients (Frank & Frank, 1991). Evidence supporting the common factors view has mounted in recent years (Ahn & Wampold, 2001; Lambert & Barley, 2001).

What are the common denominators that lie at the core of diverse approaches to therapy? Although the models proposed to answer to this question vary considerably, there is some consensus. The most widely cited common factors include (1) the development of a therapeutic alliance with a professional helper, (2) the provision of emotional support and empathic understanding by the therapist, (3) the cultivation of hope and positive expectations in the client, (4) the provision of a rationale for the client's problems and a plausible method for ameliorating them, and (5) the opportunity to express feelings, confront problems, gain new insights, and learn new patterns of behavior (Grencavage & Norcross, 1990; Weinberger, 1995). How important are these common factors in therapy? Some theorists argue that common factors account for virtually *all* of the progress that clients make in therapy (Wampold, 2001). It seems more likely that the benefits of therapy represent the combined effects of common factors and specific procedures (Beutler & Harwood, 2002). Either way, it is clear that common factors play a significant role in insight therapy.

Therapy and the Recovered Memories Controversy

While debate about the efficacy of insight therapy has simmered for many decades, the 1990s brought an entirely new controversy to rock the psychotherapy profession like never before. This emotionally charged debate was sparked by a spate of reports of people recovering repressed memories of sexual abuse and other childhood trauma through therapy. You've no doubt read or seen media stories about people—including some celebrities—who recovered long-lost recollections of sexual abuse, typically with the help of their therapists. For example, in 1991 the comedian Roseanne suddenly recalled years of abuse by her parents, and a former Miss America remembered having been sexually assaulted by her father (Wielawski, 1991). Such recovered memories have led to a rash of lawsuits in which adult plaintiffs have sued their parents, teachers, neighbors, pastors, and so forth for alleged child abuse 20 or 30 years earlier (even the Archbishop of Chicago was sued, although the suit was soon dropped). For the most part, these parents, teachers, and neighbors have denied the allegations. Many of them have seemed genuinely baffled by the accusations, which have torn apart some previously happy families (Gudjonsson, 2001; Wylie, 1998). In an effort to make sense of the charges, many accused parents have argued that their children's

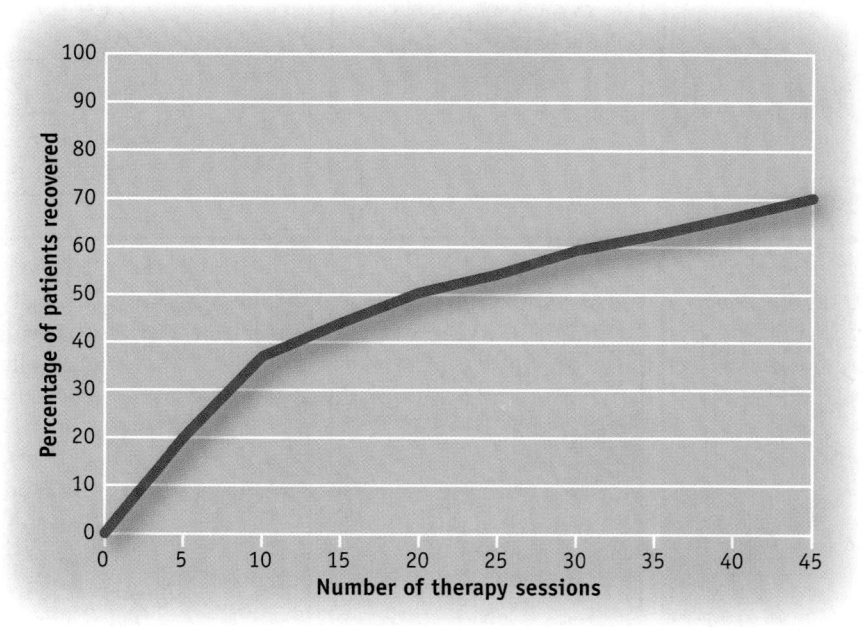

Figure 16.6

Recovery as a function of number of therapy sessions. Based on a national sample of over 6,000 patients, Lambert, Hansen, and Finch (2001) mapped out the relationship between recovery and the duration of treatment. These data show that about half of the patients had experienced a clinically significant recovery after 20 weekly sessions of therapy. After 45 sessions of therapy, about 70% had recovered.

Source: Adapted from Lambert, M. J., Hansen, N. B., & Finch, A. E. (2001). Patient-focused research: Using patient outcome data to enhance treatment effects. *Journal of Consulting and Clinical Psychology, 69,* 159–172. Copyright © 2001 by the American Psychological Association. Adapted by permission of the publisher and author.

recollections are false memories created inadvertently by well-intentioned therapists through the power of suggestion.

The crux of the debate is that child abuse usually takes place behind closed doors, and in the absence of corroborative evidence, there isn't any way to reliably distinguish genuine recovered memories from those that are false. A handful of recovered memories have been substantiated by independent witnesses or belated admissions of guilt from the accused (Brewin, 2003; Bull, 1999; Reisner, 1998; Shobe & Schooler, 2001). But in the vast majority of cases, the allegations of abuse have been vehemently denied, and independent corroboration has not been available. Recovered recollections of sexual abuse have become so common, a support group has been formed for accused people who feel that they have been victimized by "false memory syndrome."

Psychologists are sharply divided on the issue of recovered memories, leaving the public understandably confused. Many psychologists, especially therapists in clinical practice, accept most recovered memories at face value (Banyard & Williams, 1999; Briere & Conte, 1993; Gleaves & Smith, 2004; Skinner, 2001). They assert that it is common for patients to bury traumatic incidents in their unconscious (Del Monte, 2000; Wilsnack et al., 2002). Citing evidence that sexual abuse in childhood is far more widespread than most people realize (MacMillan et al., 1997), they argue that most repressed memories of abuse are probably genuine. They attribute the recent upsurge in reports of recovered memories to therapists' and clients' increased sensitivity to an issue that people used to be reluctant to discuss.

In contrast, many other psychologists, especially memory researchers, have expressed skepticism about the recovered memories phenomenon (Kihlstrom, 2004; Lindsay & Poole, 1995; Loftus, 1998, 2003; McNally, 2004). These psychologists do not argue that people are lying about their repressed memories. Rather, they maintain that some suggestible, confused people struggling to understand profound personal problems have been convinced by persuasive therapists that their emotional problems must be the result of abuse that occurred years ago. Critics blame a small minority of therapists who presumably have good intentions but operate under the dubious assumption that virtually all psychological problems are attributable to childhood sexual abuse (Lindsay & Read, 1994; Spanos, 1994). Using hypnosis, dream interpretation, and leading questions, they supposedly prod and probe patients until they inadvertently create the memories of abuse that they are searching for. Consistent with this view, Yapko (1994) reviewed evidence that some therapists

DOONESBURY © 1994 G. B. Trudeau. Reprinted with permission of UNIVERSAL PRESS SYNDICATE. All rights reserved.

are (1) overly prone to see signs of abuse where none has occurred, (2) unsophisticated about the extent to which memories can be distorted, and (3) naive about how much their expectations and beliefs can influence their patients' efforts to achieve self-understanding.

Psychologists who doubt the authenticity of repressed memories support their analysis by pointing to discredited cases of recovered memories (Brown, Goldstein, & Bjorklund, 2000). For example, with the help of a church counselor, one woman recovered memories of how her minister father repeatedly raped her, got her pregnant, and then aborted the pregnancy with a coat-hanger. However, subsequent evidence revealed that the woman was still a virgin and that her father had had a vasectomy years before (Loftus, 1997; Testa, 1996). The skeptics also point to published case histories that clearly involved suggestive questioning and to cases in which patients have recanted recovered memories of sexual abuse (see **Figure 16.7**) after realizing that these memories were implanted by their therapists (Loftus, 1994; Shobe & Schooler, 2001). Those who question recovered memories also point to several lines of carefully controlled laboratory research that demonstrate that it is not all that difficult to create "memories" of events that never happened (Hyman & Kleinnecht, 1999; Lindsay et al., 2004; Roediger & McDermott, 1995, 2000). Skepticism about the validity of recovered memories of abuse has also been fueled by the following observations and research findings:

► Many repressed memories of abuse have been recovered under the influence of hypnosis. However, an extensive body of research indicates that hypnosis tends to increase memory distortions while paradoxically making people feel more confident about their recollections (Lynn, Neuschatz, & Fite, 2002; Whitehouse et al., 1988).

© AP Images

Tom Rutherford (shown here with his wife, Joyce) received a $1 million settlement in a suit against a church therapist and a Springfield, Missouri, church in a false memory case. Under the church counselor's guidance, the Rutherfords' daughter, Beth, had "recalled" childhood memories of having been raped repeatedly by her minister father, gotten pregnant, and undergone a painful coat-hanger abortion. Her father lost his job and was ostracized. After he later revealed he'd had a vasectomy when Beth was age 4, and a physical exam revealed that at age 23 she was still a virgin, the memories were shown to be false.

► Many repressed memories of abuse have been recovered through therapists' dream interpretations. But dream interpretation depends on highly subjective guesswork that cannot be verified. Moreover, research shows that bogus dream interpretations can lead normal subjects to believe that they actually experienced the events suggested in the dream analyses (Loftus, 2000; Loftus & Mazzoni, 1998).

A Case History of Recovered Memories Recanted

Suffering from a prolonged bout of depression and desperate for help, Melody Gavigan, 39, a computer specialist from Long Beach, California, checked herself into a local psychiatric hospital. As Gavigan recalls the experience, her problems were just beginning. During five weeks of treatment there, a family and marriage counselor repeatedly suggested that her depression stemmed from incest during her childhood. While at first Gavigan had no recollection of any abuse, the therapist kept prodding. "I was so distressed and needed help so desperately, I latched on to what he was offering me," she says. "I accepted his answers."

When asked for details, she wrote page after page of what she believed were emerging repressed memories. She told about running into the yard after being raped in the bathroom. She incorporated into another lurid rape scene an actual girlhood incident, in which she had dislocated a shoulder. She went on to recall being molested by her father when she was only a year old—as her diapers were being changed—and sodomized by him at five. Following what she says was the therapist's advice, Gavigan confronted her father with her accusations, severed her relationship with him, moved away, and formed an incest survivors' group.

But she remained uneasy. Signing up for a college psychology course, she examined her newfound memories more carefully and concluded that they were false. Now Gavigan has begged her father's forgiveness and filed a lawsuit against the psychiatric hospital for the pain that she and her family suffered.

Figure 16.7

A case of recovered memories recanted. Recovered memories of sexual abuse are viewed with skepticism in some quarters. One reason is that some people who have recovered previously repressed recollections of childhood abuse have subsequently realized that their "memories" were the product of suggestion. A number of case histories, such as the one summarized here (from Jaroff, 1993), have demonstrated that therapists who relentlessly search for memories of abuse in their patients sometimes create the memories they are seeking.

From Jaroff, L. (1999, November 29). Lies of the mind. *Time*, pp. 52–59. Copyright © 1993 Time Inc. Reprinted by permission.

► Some recovered memories have described incidents of abuse that occurred before the victim reached age 3 and even when the victim was still in the womb (Taylor, 2004). However, when adults are asked to recall their earliest memories, their oldest recollections typically don't go back past age 2 or 3 (Bruce, Dolan, & Phillips-Grant, 2000; Eacott & Crawley, 1998).

Of course, psychologists who believe in recovered memories have mounted rebuttals to these arguments. For example, Kluft (1999) argues that a recantation of a recovered memory of abuse does not prove that the memory was false. Gleaves (1994) points out that individuals with a history of sexual abuse often vacillate between denying and accepting that the abuse occurred. Harvey (1999) argues that laboratory demonstrations showing how easy it is to create false memories have involved trivial memory distortions that are a far cry from the vivid, emotionally wrenching recollections of sexual abuse that have generated the recovered memories controversy. Olio (1994) concludes, "The possibility of implanting entire multiple scenarios of horror that differ markedly from the individual's experience, such as memories of childhood abuse in an individual who does not have a trauma history, remains an unsubstantiated hypothesis" (p. 442). Moreover, even if one accepts the assertion that therapists *can* create false memories of abuse in their patients, some critics have noted that there is virtually no direct evidence on how often this occurs and no empirical basis for the claim that there has been an *epidemic* of such cases (Berliner & Briere, 1999; Leavitt, 2001; Wilsnack et al., 2002).

So, what can we conclude about the recovered memories controversy? It seems pretty clear that therapists can unknowingly create false memories in their patients and that a significant portion of recovered memories of abuse are the product of suggestion. But it also seems likely that some cases of recovered memories are authentic (Brown, Scheflin, Whitfield, 1999). At this point, we don't have adequate data to estimate what proportion of recovered memories of abuse fall in each category (Gow, 1999; Lindsay & Read, 2001). Thus, the matter needs to be addressed with great caution. On the one hand, people should be extremely careful about accepting recovered memories of abuse in the absence of convincing corroboration. On the other hand, recovered memories of abuse cannot be summarily dismissed, and it would be tragic if the repressed memories controversy made people overly skeptical about the all-too-real problem of childhood sexual abuse.

Behavior Therapies

LEARNING OBJECTIVES

- *Summarize the general approach and principles of behavior therapies.*
- *Describe the three steps in systematic desensitization and the logic underlying the treatment.*
- *Describe the use of aversion therapy and social skills training.*
- *Discuss the logic, goals, and techniques of cognitive therapy.*
- *Summarize evidence on the efficacy of behavior therapies.*

Behavior therapy is different from insight therapy in that behavior therapists make no attempt to help clients achieve grand insights about themselves. Why not? Because behavior therapists believe that such insights aren't necessary in order to produce constructive change. Consider a client troubled by compulsive gambling. The behavior therapist doesn't care whether this behavior is rooted in unconscious conflicts or parental rejection. What the client needs is to get rid of the maladaptive behavior. Consequently, the therapist simply designs a program to eliminate the compulsive gambling. The crux of the difference between insight therapy and behavior therapy lies in how each views symptoms. Insight therapists treat pathological symptoms as signs of an underlying problem. In contrast, behavior therapists think that the symptoms *are* the problem. Thus, ***behavior therapies* involve the application of the principles of learning to direct efforts to change clients' maladaptive behaviors.**

Behaviorism has been an influential school of thought in psychology since the 1920s. But behaviorists devoted little attention to clinical issues until the 1950s, when behavior therapy emerged out of three independent lines of research fostered by B. F. Skinner (1953) and his colleagues in the United States, Hans Eysenck (1959) and his colleagues in Britain, and Joseph Wolpe (1958) and his colleagues in South Africa (Glass & Arnkoff, 1992). Since then, there has been an explosion of interest in behavioral approaches to psychotherapy.

Behavior therapies are based on two main assumptions assumptions (Berkowitz, 2003). *First, it is assumed that behavior is a product of learning.* No matter how self-defeating or pathological a client's behavior might be, the behaviorist believes that it is the result of past conditioning. *Second, it is assumed that what has been learned can be unlearned.* The same learning principles that explain how the maladaptive behavior was acquired can be used to get rid of it. Thus, behavior

Cartoon by Harris © 1990. Reprinted by permission of ScienceCartoonsPlus.com.

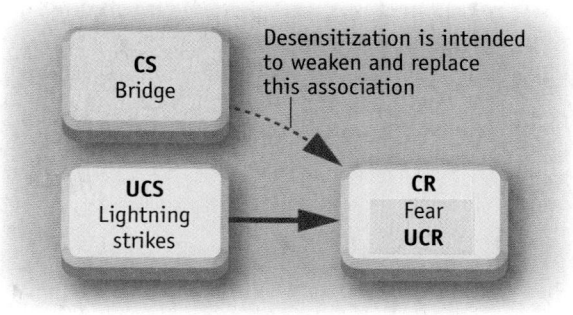

Figure 16.8

The logic underlying systematic desensitization. Behaviorists argue that many phobic responses are acquired through classical conditioning, as in the example diagrammed here. Systematic desensitization targets the conditioned associations between phobic stimuli and fear responses.

therapists attempt to change clients' behavior by applying the principles of classical conditioning, operant conditioning, and observational learning.

Behavior therapies are close cousins of the self-modification procedures described in the Chapter 4 Application. Both use the same principles of learning to alter behavior directly. In discussing *self-modification,* we examined some relatively simple procedures that people can apply to themselves to improve everyday self-control. In our discussion of *behavior therapy,* we examine more complex procedures used by mental health professionals in the treatment of more severe problems.

Systematic Desensitization

Courtesy, Joseph Wolpe

Joseph Wolpe

Devised by Joseph Wolpe (1958, 1987), systematic desensitization revolutionized psychotherapy by giving therapists their first useful alternative to traditional "talk therapy" (Fishman & Franks, 1992). ***Systematic desensitization* is a behavior therapy used to reduce clients' anxiety responses through counterconditioning.** The treatment assumes that most anxiety responses are acquired through classical conditioning (as we discussed in Chapter 15). According to this model, a harmless stimulus (for instance, a bridge) may be paired with a frightening event (lightning striking it), so it becomes a conditioned stimulus eliciting anxiety. The goal of systematic desensitization is to weaken the association between the conditioned stimulus (the bridge) and the conditioned response of anxiety (see **Figure 16.8**). Systematic desensitization involves three steps.

First, the therapist helps the client build an anxiety hierarchy. The hierarchy is a list of anxiety-arousing stimuli centering on the specific source of anxiety, such as flying, academic tests, or snakes. The client ranks the stimuli from the least anxiety arousing to the most anxiety arousing. This ordered list of related, anxiety provoking stimuli constitutes the anxiety hierarchy. An example of an anxiety hierarchy for one woman's fear of heights is shown in **Figure 16.9** (on the next page).

The second step involves training the client in deep muscle relaxation. This second phase may begin during early sessions while the therapist and client are still constructing the anxiety hierarchy. Different therapists use different relaxation training procedures. Whatever procedures are used, the client must learn to engage in deep and thorough relaxation on command from the therapist.

In the third step, the client tries to work through the hierarchy, learning to remain relaxed while imagining each stimulus. Starting with the least anxiety-arousing stimulus, the client imagines the situation as vividly as possible while relaxing. If the client experiences strong anxiety, he or she drops the imaginary scene and concentrates on relaxation. The client keeps repeating this process until he or she can imagine a scene with little or no anxiety. Once a particular scene is conquered, the client moves on to the next stimulus situation in the anxiety hierarchy. Gradually, over a number of therapy sessions, the client progresses through the hierarchy, unlearning troublesome anxiety responses.

As clients conquer *imagined* phobic stimuli, they may be encouraged to confront the *real* stimuli. Although desensitization to imagined stimuli *can* be effective by itself, contemporary behavior therapists usually follow it up with direct exposures to the real anxiety-arousing stimuli (Emmelkamp, 2004). Indeed, behavioral interventions emphasizing direct exposures to anxiety-arousing situations have become behavior therapists' treatment of choice for phobic and other anxiety disorders. Usually, these real-life confrontations prove harmless, and individuals' anxiety responses decline.

According to Wolpe (1958, 1990), the principle at work in systematic desensitization is simple. Anxiety

An Anxiety Hierarchy for Systematic Desensitization

Degree of fear	
5	I'm standing on the balcony of the top floor of an apartment tower.
10	I'm standing on a stepladder in the kitchen to change a light bulb.
15	I'm walking on a ridge. The edge is hidden by shrubs and treetops.
20	I'm sitting on the slope of a mountain, looking out over the horizon.
25	I'm crossing a bridge 6 feet above a creek. The bridge consists of an 18-inch-wide board with a handrail on one side.
30	I'm riding a ski lift 8 feet above the ground.
35	I'm crossing a shallow, wide creek on an 18-inch-wide board, 3 feet above water level.
40	I'm climbing a ladder outside the house to reach a second-story window.
45	I'm pulling myself up a 30-degree wet, slippery slope on a steel cable.
50	I'm scrambling up a rock, 8 feet high.
55	I'm walking 10 feet on a resilient, 18-inch-wide board, which spans an 8-foot-deep gulch.
60	I'm walking on a wide plateau, 2 feet from the edge of a cliff.
65	I'm skiing an intermediate hill. The snow is packed.
70	I'm walking over a railway trestle.
75	I'm walking on the side of an embankment. The path slopes to the outside.
80	I'm riding a chair lift 15 feet above the ground.
85	I'm walking up a long, steep slope.
90	I'm walking up (or down) a 15-degree slope on a 3-foot-wide trail. On one side of the trail the terrain drops down sharply; on the other side is a steep upward slope.
95	I'm walking on a 3-foot-wide ridge. The slopes on both sides are long and more than 25 degrees steep.
100	I'm walking on a 3-foot-wide ridge. The trail slopes on one side. The drop on either side of the trail is more than 25 degrees.

Figure 16.9

Example of an anxiety hierarchy. Systematic desensitization requires the construction of an anxiety hierarchy like the one shown here, which was developed for a woman with a fear of heights who had a penchant for hiking in the mountains.

and relaxation are incompatible responses. The trick is to recondition people so that the conditioned stimulus elicits relaxation instead of anxiety. This is *counterconditioning*—an attempt to reverse the process of classical conditioning by associating the crucial stimulus with a new conditioned response. Although Wolpe's explanation of how systematic desensitization works has been questioned, the technique's effectiveness in eliminating specific anxieties has been well documented (Spiegler & Guevremont, 2003).

Aversion Therapy

Aversion therapy is far and away the most controversial of the behavior therapies. It's not something that you would sign up for unless you were pretty desperate. Psychologists usually suggest it only as a treatment of last resort, after other interventions have failed. What's so terrible about aversion therapy? The client has to endure decidedly unpleasant stimuli, such as shocks or drug-induced nausea.

***Aversion therapy* is a behavior therapy in which an aversive stimulus is paired with a stimulus that elicits an undesirable response.** For example, alcoholics have had drug-induced nausea paired with their favorite drinks during therapy sessions (Landabaso et al., 1999). By pairing an *emetic drug* (one that causes vomiting) with alcohol, the therapist hopes to create a conditioned aversion to alcohol (see **Figure 16.10**).

Aversion therapy takes advantage of the automatic nature of responses produced through classical conditioning. Admittedly, alcoholics treated with aversion therapy know that they won't be given an emetic outside of their therapy sessions. However, their reflex response to the stimulus of alcohol may be changed so that they respond to it with nausea and distaste. Obviously, this response should make it much easier to resist the urge to drink.

Aversion therapy is not a widely used technique, and when it is used it is usually only one element in a larger treatment program. Troublesome behaviors treated successfully with aversion therapy have included drug and alcohol abuse, sexual deviance, gambling, shoplifting, stuttering, cigarette smoking, and overeating (Bordnick et al., 2004; Emmelkamp, 1994; Grossman & Ruiz, 2004; Maletzky, 2002).

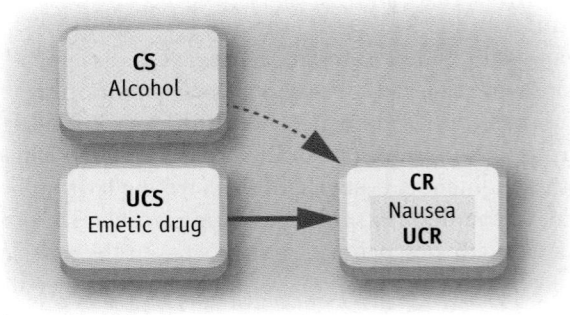

Figure 16.10

Aversion therapy. Aversion therapy uses classical conditioning to create an aversion to a stimulus that has elicited problematic behavior. For example, in the treatment of drinking problems, alcohol may be paired with a nausea-inducing drug to create a conditioned aversion to alcohol.

Social Skills Training

Many psychological problems grow out of interpersonal difficulties. Behavior therapists point out that humans are not born with social finesse. People acquire their social skills through learning. Unfortunately, some people have not learned how to be friendly, how to make conversation, how to express anger appropriately, and so forth. Social ineptitude can contribute to anxiety, feelings of inferiority, and various kinds of disorders. In light of these findings, therapists are increasingly using social skills training in efforts to improve clients' social abilities. This approach to therapy has yielded promising results in the treatment of social anxiety (Shear & Beidel, 1998), autism (Kransny et al., 2003), attention deficit disorder (Antshel & Remer, 2003), and schizophrenia (Bellack, Murdrt, & Gingerich, 2004).

Social skills training **is a behavior therapy designed to improve interpersonal skills that emphasizes shaping, modeling, and behavioral rehearsal.** This type of behavior therapy can be conducted with individual clients or in groups. Social skills training depends on the principles of operant conditioning and observational learning. The therapist makes use of *modeling* by encouraging clients to watch socially skilled friends and colleagues, so that the clients can acquire responses (eye contact, active listening, and so on) through observation.

In *behavioral rehearsal,* the client tries to practice social techniques in structured role-playing exercises. The therapist provides corrective feedback and uses approval to reinforce progress. Eventually, clients try their newly acquired skills in real-world interactions. Usually, they are given specific homework assignments. *Shaping* is used in that clients are gradually asked to handle more complicated and delicate social situations. For example, a nonassertive client may begin by working on making requests of friends. Only much later will the client be asked to tackle standing up to his or her boss.

Cognitive-Behavioral Treatments

In Chapter 3 we saw that people's cognitive interpretations of events make all the difference in the world in how well they handle stress. In Chapter 15 we learned that cognitive factors play a key role in the development of depression and other disorders. Citing the importance of findings such as these, behavior therapists started to focus more attention on their clients' cognitions in the 1970s (Arnkoff & Glass, 1992; Hollon & Beck, 2004). ***Cognitive-behavioral treatments*** **use varied combinations of verbal interventions and behavior modification techniques to help clients change maladaptive patterns of thinking.** Some of these treatments, such as Albert Ellis's (1973) *rational emotive behavior therapy* and Aaron Beck's (1976) *cognitive therapy* emerged out of an insight therapy tradition, whereas other treatments, such as the systems developed by Donald Meichenbaum (1977) and Michael Mahoney (1974) emerged from the behavioral tradition. Since we covered the main ideas underlying Ellis's approach in our discussion of coping strategies in Chapter 4, we focus on Beck's system of cognitive therapy here (Beck, 1987; Beck & Newman, 2005).

Cognitive therapy **uses specific strategies to correct habitual thinking errors that underlie various types of disorders.** In recent years cognitive therapy has been applied fruitfully to a wide range of disorders (Rush & Beck, 2000), but it was originally devised as a treatment for depression. According to cognitive therapists, depression is caused by "errors" in thinking (see **Figure 16.11**). They assert that depression-prone people tend to (1) blame their setbacks on personal inadequacies without considering circumstantial explanations, (2) focus selectively on negative events while

Figure 16.11

Beck's cognitive theory of depression. According to Aaron Beck (1976, 1987), depression is caused by certain patterns of negative thinking. This chart lists some of the particularly damaging cognitive errors that can foster depression.

Adapted from Beck, A. T. (1976). *Cognitive therapy and the emotional disorders.* New York: International Universities Press. Copyright © 1976 by International Universities Press, Inc. Adapted by permission of the publisher.

Cognitive Errors That Promote Depression

Cognitive error	Description
Overgeneralizing	If it is true in one case, it applies to any case that is even slightly similar.
Selective abstraction	The only events that matter are failures, deprivation, and so on. I should measure myself by errors, weaknesses, etc.
Excessive responsibility (assuming personal causality)	I am responsible for all bad things, failures, and so on.
Assuming temporal causality (predicting without sufficient evidence)	If it has been true in the past, then it is always going to be true.
Self-references	I am the center of everyone's attention, especially when it comes to bad performances or personal attributes.
"Catastrophizing"	Always think of the worst. It is most likely to happen to you.
Dichotomous thinking	Everything is either one extreme or another (black or white; good or bad).

LIVING IN TODAY'S WORLD

How Do Clinicians Treat Posttraumatic Stress Disorder?

As discussed in Chapter 3, *posttraumatic stress disorder (PTSD)* involves enduring psychological disturbance following the experience of a major traumatic event. Given the association between terrorist attacks and PTSD (DeRoma et al., 2003; Lating et al., 2004), interest has increased in clinical treatments for PTSD. Unfortunately, the research on the etiology and symptoms of PTSD has outstripped the research on its treatment, which remains in its infancy. This situation probably reflects the fact that PTSD wasn't widely recognized as an independent disorder until the 1980s. Nonetheless, PTSD has proven treatable (Livanou, 2001). As is the case with most other disorders, there is no consensus on a single, ideal approach to treating PTSD, and the probability of successful treatment depends on the severity of a particular person's disorder.

Recovery from PTSD tends to be a gradual process, and clients need to be realistic about their goals. Once individuals have been severely traumatized, they are likely to always have some emotional pain lurking beneath the surface. However, therapy for PTSD can lead to fewer and less intense emotional reactions and to enhanced coping skills that help clients manage their emotions more effectively (Ruzek, 2001). According to the National Center for PTSD, treatment generally includes the following four components:

- Educating trauma survivors and their families about how persons get PTSD, how PTSD affects survivors and their loved ones, and other problems that commonly come along with PTSD symptoms.
- Exposing survivors to the event via imagery that allows them to reexperience it in a safe, controlled environment, while also carefully examining their reactions and beliefs in relation to that event.
- Examining and resolving strong feelings, such as anger, shame, or guilt, that are common among survivors of trauma.
- Teaching the survivor to cope with posttraumatic memories, reminders, reactions, and feelings without becoming overwhelmed or emotionally numb.

Given these elements in the treatment process, a variety of specific approaches to treatment are used (Beckham, Davidson, & March, 2003; Schottenbauer et al., 2006). *Cognitive therapy* with a strong behavioral slant is often employed. The cognitive part of this approach focuses on changing clients' thoughts that trigger emotional reactions, while the behavioral component usually involves some form of guided exposure to the trauma-arousing event, similar to systematic desensitization. Brief *psychodynamic therapy* is also used with PTSD patients. Psychodynamic therapists usually help clients confront their traumatic memories and intense emotions. *Group therapy* is another common approach. Trauma survivors seem to benefit from the peer-to-peer sharing that takes place in group treatment. *Drug therapies* are frequently used as an adjunct to other approaches. Antianxiety and antidepressant medications can reduce many of the symptoms associated with PTSD (Artai-Otong, 2007; Davis et al., 2006). Among the various approaches to treating PTSD, cognitive-behavioral approaches have the greatest empirical support for their efficacy (Hembree & Foa, 2000).

ignoring positive ones, (3) make unduly pessimistic projections about the future, and (4) draw negative conclusions about their worth as a person based on insignificant events. For instance, imagine that you got a low grade on a minor quiz in a class. If you made the kinds of errors in thinking just described, you might blame the grade on your woeful stupidity, dismiss comments from a classmate that it was an unfair test, gloomily predict that you will surely flunk the course, and conclude that you are not genuine college material.

Courtesy, Aaron T. Beck

Aaron Beck

The goal of cognitive therapy is to change clients' negative thoughts and maladaptive beliefs. To begin, clients are taught to detect their automatic negative thoughts, the sorts of self-defeating statements that people are prone to make when analyzing problems. Examples might include "I'm just not smart enough," "No one really likes me," or "It's all my fault." Clients are then trained to subject these automatic thoughts to reality testing. The therapist helps them to see how unrealistically negative the thoughts are.

Cognitive therapy uses a variety of behavioral techniques, such as modeling, systematic monitoring of one's behavior, and behavioral rehearsal (Wright, Beck, & Thase, 2003), Clients are given "homework assignments" that focus on changing their overt behaviors. They may be instructed to engage in overt responses on their own, outside of the clinician's office. For example, one shy, insecure young man in cognitive therapy was told to go to a singles bar and engage three different women in conversations for up to five minutes each (Rush, 1984). He was instructed to record his thoughts before and after each of the conversations. This assignment revealed various maladaptive patterns of thought that gave the young man and his therapist plenty to work on in subsequent sessions.

Web Link 16.3 **The Beck Institute of Cognitive Therapy and Research**

This site offers a diverse array of materials relating to Aaron Beck's cognitive therapy. Resources found here include newsletters, a referral system, a bookstore, recommended readings for clients, and questions and answers about cognitive therapy.

Evaluating Behavior Therapies

Behavior therapists have historically placed more emphasis than insight therapists on the importance of measuring therapeutic outcomes. As a result, there is ample research on the effectiveness of behavior therapy (Jacob & Pelham, 2005). How does its effectiveness compare to that of insight therapy? In direct comparisons, the differences between the therapies are usually small. However, these modest differences tend to favor behavioral approaches for certain types of disorders. Of course, behavior therapies are not well suited to the treatment of some types of problems (vague feelings of discontent, for instance). Furthermore, it's misleading to make global statements about the effectiveness of behavior therapies, because they include a variety of procedures designed for different purposes. For example, the value of systematic desensitization for phobias has no bearing on the value of aversion therapy for sexual deviance.

For our purposes, it is sufficient to note that there is favorable evidence on the efficacy of most of the widely used behavioral interventions. Behavior therapies can make significant contributions to the treatment of anxiety problems, phobias, obsessive-compulsive disorders, sexual dysfunction, schizophrenia, drug-related problems, eating disorders, hyperactivity, autism, and mental retardation (Berkowitz, 2003; Emmelkamp, 2004).

Biomedical Therapies

LEARNING OBJECTIVES

- *Describe the principal drug therapies used in the treatment of psychological disorders and summarize evidence regarding their efficacy.*
- *Discuss some of the problems associated with drug therapies and drug research.*
- *Describe ECT and discuss its efficacy and risks.*

In the 1950s, a French surgeon was looking for a drug that would reduce patients' autonomic response to surgical stress. The surgeon noticed that chlorpromazine produced a mild sedation. Based on this observation, Delay and Deniker (1952) decided to give chlorpromazine to hospitalized schizophrenic patients to see whether it would have a calming effect on them. Their experiment was a dramatic success. Chlorpromazine became the first effective antipsychotic drug—and a revolution in psychiatry had begun. Hundreds of thousands of severely disturbed patients—patients who had appeared doomed to lead the remainder of their lives in mental hospitals—were gradually sent home thanks to the therapeutic effects of antipsychotic drugs (see **Figure 16.12** on the next page). Today, biomedical therapies, such as drug treatment, lie at the core of psychiatric practice.

***Biomedical therapies* are physiological interventions intended to reduce symptoms associated with psychological disorders.** These therapies assume that psychological disorders are caused, at least in part, by biological malfunctions. As we discussed in the previous chapter, this assumption clearly has merit for many disorders, especially the more severe ones. We will discuss two biomedical approaches to psychotherapy: drug therapy and electroconvulsive therapy.

Treatment with Drugs

***Psychopharmacotherapy* is the treatment of mental disorders with medication.** We will refer to this kind of treatment more simply as *drug therapy.* Therapeutic

Web Link 16.4 **Psychopharmacology Tips by Dr. Bob**

University of Chicago physician and pharmacology specialist Robert Hsiang provides both broad and specific references about the interface of drugs and the human mind, including a searchable archive of professional information and tips about the field.

Figure 16.12

The declining inpatient population in mental hospitals. The number of inpatients in public mental hospitals has declined dramatically since the late 1950s. In part, this drop has been due to "deinstitutionalization"—a philosophy that emphasizes outpatient care whenever possible. However, above all else, this decline was made possible by the development of effective antipsychotic medications.

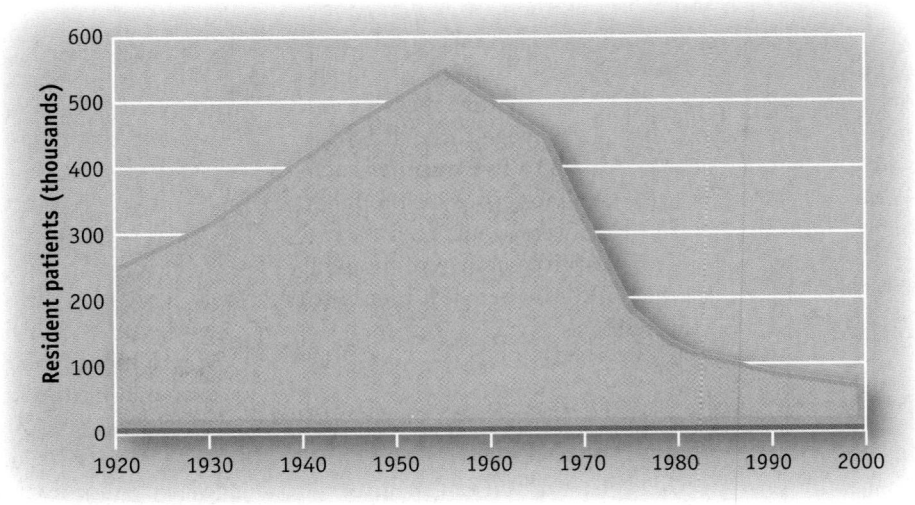

drugs for psychological problems fall into four major groups: antianxiety drugs, antipsychotic drugs, antidepressant drugs, and mood stabilizers.

Antianxiety Drugs

Most of us know someone who pops pills to relieve anxiety. The drugs involved in this common coping strategy are ***antianxiety drugs,* which relieve tension, apprehension, and nervousness.** The most popular of these drugs are Valium and Xanax, which are the trade names (the proprietary names that pharmaceutical companies use in marketing drugs) for diazepam and alprazolam, respectively.

Valium, Xanax, and other drugs in the benzodiazepine family are often called *tranquilizers.* These drugs are routinely prescribed for people with anxiety disorders. They are also given to millions of people who simply suffer from chronic nervous tension. In the mid-1970s, pharmacists in the United States were filling nearly *100 million* prescriptions each year for Valium and similar antianxiety drugs. Many critics characterized this level of use as excessive (Lickey & Gordon, 1991). However, since the 1990s, benzodiazepine prescriptions have declined noticeably (Raj & Sheehan, 2004).

Antianxiety drugs exert their effects almost immediately. They can be fairly effective in alleviating feelings of anxiety (Dubovsky, 2005). However, their effects are measured in hours, so their impact is relatively short-lived. Common side effects of antianxiety drugs include drowsiness, depression, nausea, and confusion. These drugs also have some potential for abuse, dependency, and overdose (Ballenger, 2000). Another drawback is that patients who have been on antianxiety drugs for a while often experience withdrawal symptoms when their drug treatment is stopped (Raj & Sheehan, 2004). Although some psychiatrists argue that the problems associated with the benzodiazepine drugs have been exaggerated, physicians have reduced their prescription of these drugs since the 1970s (Silberman, 1998).

A newer antianxiety drug called Buspar (buspirone), which does not belong to the benzodiazepine family, appears useful in the treatment of generalized anxiety disorder (Hudziak & Waterman, 2005). Unlike Valium, Buspar is slow acting, exerting its effects in one to three weeks, and has fewer sedative side effects (Ninan & Muntasser, 2004).

Antipsychotic Drugs

Antipsychotic drugs are used primarily in the treatment of schizophrenia. They are also given to people with severe mood disorders who become delusional. The trade names (and generic names) of some prominent drugs in this category are Thorazine (chlorpromazine), Mellaril (thioridazine), and Haldol (haloperidol). ***Antipsychotic drugs* are used to gradually reduce psychotic symptoms, including hyperactivity, mental confusion, hallucinations, and delusions.**

Studies suggest that antipsychotics reduce psychotic symptoms in about 70% of patients, albeit in varied degrees (Kane & Marder, 2005). When antipsychotic drugs are effective, they work their magic gradually, as shown in **Figure 16.13**. Patients usually begin to respond within one to three weeks, but considerable variability in responsiveness is seen (Emsley, Rabinowitz, & Medori, 2006). Further improvement may occur for several months. Many schizophrenic patients are placed on antipsychotics indefinitely because these drugs can reduce the likelihood of a relapse into an active schizophrenic episode (Marder & van Kammen, 2005).

Antipsychotic drugs undeniably make a major contribution to the treatment of severe mental disorders, but they are not without problems. They have many

"I think the dosage needs adjusting. I'm not nearly as happy as the people in the ads."

© The *New Yorker* Collection 2001 Barbara Smaller from cartoonbank.com. All rights reserved.

unpleasant side effects (Cohen, 1997; Wilkaitis, Mulvihill, & Nasrallah, 2004). Drowsiness, constipation, and cotton mouth are common. Patients may also experience tremors, muscular rigidity, and impaired coordination. After being released from a hospital, many schizophrenic patients, supposedly placed on antipsychotics indefinitely, discontinue their drug regimen because of the disagreeable side effects. Unfortunately, a relapse eventually occurs in most patients after they stop taking antipsychotic medication (Gitlin et al., 2001). In addition to minor side effects, antipsychotics may cause a severe and lasting problem called *tardive dyskinesia,* which is seen in about 20% of patients who receive long-term treatment with traditional antipsychotics (Miyamoto et al., 2003). ***Tardive dyskinesia* is a neurological disorder marked by chronic tremors and involuntary spastic movements.** Once this debilitating syndrome emerges, there is no cure, although spontaneous remission sometimes occurs after the discontinuation of antipsychotic medication (Pi & Simpson, 2000).

Psychiatrists are currently enthusiastic about a newer class of antipsychotic agents called *atypical antipsychotic drugs* (such as clozapine, olanzapine, and quetiapine). These drugs can help some patients who do not respond to conventional antipsychotic medications (Volavka et al., 2002). Moreover, the atypical antipsychotics produce fewer unpleasant side effects and carry less risk for tardive dyskinesia (Correll, Leucht, & Kane, 2004; Lieberman et al., 2003). Of course, like all powerful drugs, they are not without their risks, as they appear to increase patients' vulnerability to diabetes and cardiovascular problems (Meltzer et al., 2002). Although they are much more expensive than traditional antipsychotics, the atypical antipsychotics have become the first line of defense in the treatment of schizophrenia (van Kammen & Marder, 2005). However, recent research has generated some controversy regarding this trend. Studies have found that the newer antipsychotics aren't any more effective than the older medications in reducing symptoms and that the side effects of the newer drugs are only marginally less troublesome than those of the older drugs (Lieberman et al., 2005; Stroup, Kraus, & Marder, 2006). These findings raise vexing, complicated questions about the cost effectiveness of psychiatrists' reliance on the newer medications (Lieberman, 2006; Rosenheck, 2006).

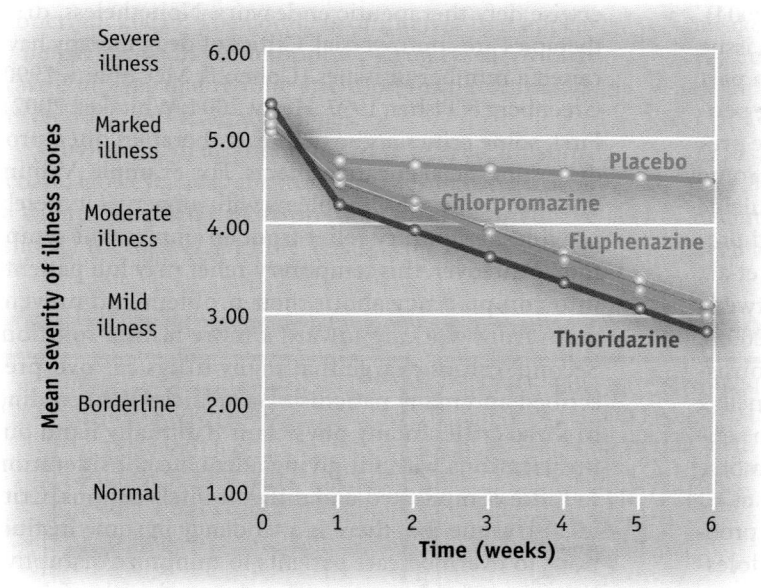

Figure 16.13

The time course of antipsychotic drug effects. Antipsychotic drugs reduce psychotic symptoms gradually, over a span of weeks, as graphed here. In contrast, patients given placebo pills show little improvement.

From Cole, J. O., Goldberg, S. C., & Davis, J. M. (1966). Drugs in the treatment of psychosis. In P. Solomon (Ed.), *Psychiatric drugs.* New York: Grune & Stratton. From data in the NIMH-PSC Collaborative Study I. Reprinted by permission of J. M. Davis.

Antidepressant Drugs

As their name suggests, ***antidepressant drugs* gradually elevate mood and help bring people out of a depression.** Prior to 1987, there were two principal classes of antidepressants: *tricyclics* (such as Elavil) and *MAO inhibitors* (such as Nardil). These two sets of drugs affect neurochemical activity in different ways and tend to work with different patients. Overall, they are beneficial for about two-thirds of depressed patients (Gitlin, 2002), form of therapy. Although only about 8% of psychiatrists administer ECT (Hermann et al., 1998), estimates suggest that about 100,000 people receive ECT treatments each year in the United States (Hermann et al., 1995). Some critics argue that ECT is overused because it is a lucrative procedure that boosts psychiatrists' income while consuming relatively little of their time in comparison to insight therapy (Frank, 1990). Conversely, some advocates argue that ECT is underutilized because the public harbors many misconceptions about its risks and side effects (McDonald et al., 2004). Although ECT was once considered appropriate for a wide range of disorders, in recent decades it has primarily been recommended for the treatment of depression.

Effectiveness of ECT

The evidence on the therapeutic efficacy of ECT is open to varied interpretations. Proponents of ECT maintain that it is a remarkably effective treatment for major depression (Prudic, 2005; Rudorfer, Henry, & Sackeim, 2003). Moreover, they note that many patients who do not benefit from antidepressant medication improve in response to ECT (Nobler & Sackeim, 2006). However, opponents of ECT argue that the available studies are flawed and inconclusive and that ECT is probably no more effective than a placebo (Rose et al., 2003). Overall, enough favorable evidence seems to exist to justify *conservative* use of ECT in treating severe mood disorders in patients who have not responded to medication (Carney & Geddes, 2003; Metzger, 1999). Unfortunately, relapse rates after ECT are distressingly high. Over 50% of patients relapse within 6 to 12 months, although relapse rates can be reduced by giving ECT patients antidepressant drugs (Sackeim et al., 2001).

The debate about whether ECT works does *not* make ECT unique among approaches to the treatment of psychological disorders. Controversies exist regarding the effectiveness of most therapies. However, this controversy is especially problematic because ECT carries some risks.

Risks Associated with ECT

Even ECT proponents acknowledge that memory losses, impaired attention, and other cognitive deficits are common short-term side effects of electroconvulsive therapy (Lisanby et al., 2000; Nobler & Sackeim, 2006). However, ECT proponents assert that these deficits are mild and usually disappear within a month or two (Glass, 2001). An American Psychiatric Association (2001) task force concluded that there is no objective evidence that ECT causes structural damage in the brain or that it has any lasting negative effects on the ability to learn and remember information. In contrast, ECT critics maintain that ECT-induced cognitive deficits are often significant and sometimes permanent (Breggin, 1991; Frank, 1990; Rose et al., 2003), although their evidence seems to be largely anecdotal. Given the concerns about the risks of ECT and the doubts about its efficacy, it appears that the use of ECT will remain controversial for some time to come.

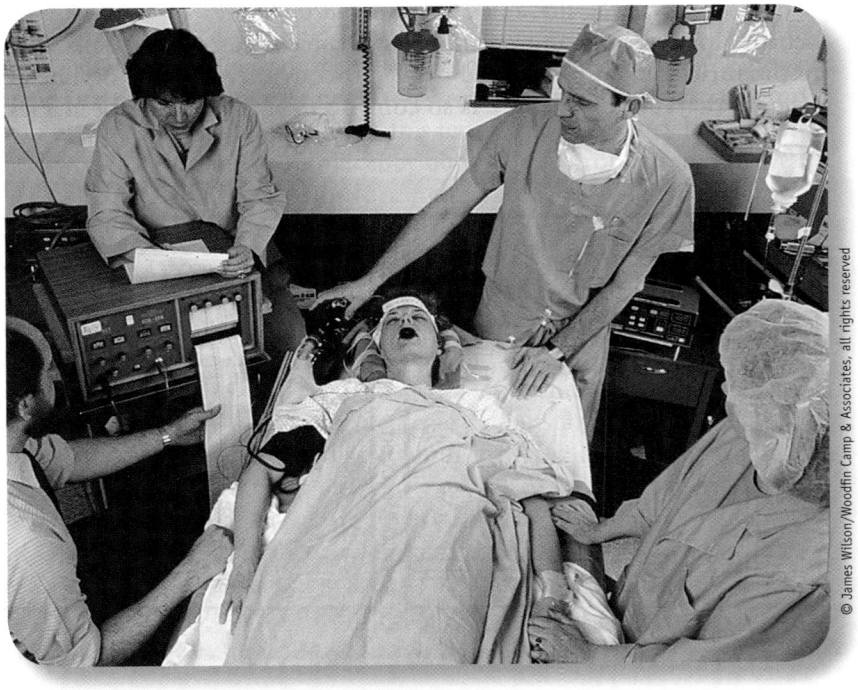
© James Wilson/Woodfin Camp & Associates, all rights reserved

This patient is being prepared for electroconvulsive therapy. The mouthpiece keeps the patient from biting her tongue during the electrically induced seizures.

© Janine Wiedel Photolibrary/Alamy

Cultural barriers have emerged in the psychotherapy process. A number of minority groups in the United States shy away from using professional services in this field. Those who do try it also tend to quickly terminate treatment more often than white Americans.

1. *Cultural barriers.* In times of psychological distress, some cultural groups are reluctant to turn to formal, professional sources of assistance. Given their socialization, they prefer to rely on informal assistance from family members, the clergy, respected elders, herbalists, acupuncturists, and so forth, who share their cultural heritage. Many members of minority groups have a history of frustrating interactions with American bureaucracies and are distrustful of large, intimidating, foreign institutions, such as hospitals and community mental health centers (Pierce, 1992).

2. *Language barriers.* Effective communication is crucial to the provision of psychotherapy, yet most hospitals and mental health agencies are not adequately staffed with therapists who speak the languages used by minority groups in their service areas. The resulting communication problems make it awkward and difficult for many minority group members to explain their problems and obtain the type of help they need.

3. *Institutional barriers.* Stanley Sue and Nolan Zane (1987) argue that the "single most important explanation for the problems in service delivery involves the inability of therapists to provide culturally responsive forms of treatment" (p. 37). The vast majority of therapists have been trained almost exclusively in the treatment of middle-class white Americans and are not familiar with the cultural backgrounds and unique characteristics of various ethnic groups. This culture gap often leads to misunderstandings and ill-advised treatment strategies (Hughes, 1993). Unfortunately, there is a grievous shortage of ethnic therapists to meet the needs of various ethnic groups (Mays & Albee, 1992).

What can be done to improve mental health services for American minority groups? Researchers in this area have offered a variety of suggestions (Hong, Garcia, & Soriano, 2000; Miranda et al., 2005; Pedersen, 1994; Sue & Zane, 1987; Yamamoto et al., 1993). Discussions of possible solutions usually begin with the need to recruit and train more ethnic minority therapists. Studies show that ethnic minorities are more likely to go to mental health facilities that are staffed by a higher proportion of people who share their ethnic background (Snowden & Hu, 1996; Sue, Zane, & Young, 1994). Furthermore, clients' satisfaction with therapy tends to be greater when they are treated by therapists from their own culture. Therapists can also be given special training to work more effectively with people from different cultural backgrounds. For example, Wade and Bernstein (1991) found that a cultural sensitivity training program for white therapists working with an African American clientele resulted in improved client satisfaction. Finally, most authorities urge further investigation of how traditional approaches to therapy can be modified and tailored to be more compatible with specific cultural groups' attitudes, values, norms, and traditions (Hwang, 2006).

APPLICATION

Looking for a Therapist

LEARNING OBJECTIVES

- *Discuss where to seek therapy.*
- *Evaluate the potential importance of a therapist's gender and professional background.*
- *Summarize the evidence on whether therapists' theoretical approaches influence their effectiveness.*
- *Discuss what one should expect from therapy.*

Answer the following "true" or "false."

___ **1.** Psychotherapy is an art as well as a science.

___ **2.** The type of professional degree that a therapist holds is relatively unimportant.

___ **3.** Psychotherapy can be harmful or damaging to a client.

___ **4.** Psychotherapy does not have to be expensive.

___ **5.** It is a good idea to shop around when choosing a therapist.

All of these statements are true. Do any of them surprise you? If so, you're in good company. Many people know relatively little about the practicalities of selecting a therapist. The task of finding an appropriate therapist is no less complex than shopping for any other major service. Should you see a psychologist or a psychiatrist? Should you opt for individual therapy or group therapy? Should you see a client-centered therapist or a behavior therapist? The unfortunate part of this decision process is that people seeking psychotherapy often feel overwhelmed by personal problems. The last thing they need is to be confronted by yet another complex problem.

Nonetheless, the importance of finding a good therapist cannot be overestimated. Therapy can sometimes have harmful rather than helpful effects. We have already discussed how drug therapies and ECT can sometimes be damaging, but problems are not limited to these interventions. Talking about your problems with a therapist may sound pretty harmless, but studies indicate that insight therapies can also backfire (Lambert & Ogles, 2004; McGlashan et al., 1990). Although a great many talented therapists are available, psychotherapy, like any other profession, has incompetent practitioners as well. Therefore, you should shop for a skilled therapist, just as you would for a good attorney or a good mechanic.

In this Application, we present some information that should be helpful if you ever have to look for a therapist for yourself or for a friend or family member (based on Beutler, Bongar, & Shurkin, 2001; Bruckner-Gordon, Gangi, & Wallman, 1988; Ehrenberg & Ehrenberg, 1994; Pittman, 1994).

Web Link 16.5 **Psychology Today: Therapy Center**

This subpage of the web site for *Psychology Today* magazine, offers a good deal of practical advice related to the challenge of finding a therapist. Topics covered include how to choose a therapist, the differences between various mental health professions, descriptions of many theoretical approaches to therapy, and tips on how to get medical insurance to cover psychotherapy services.

Where Do You Find Therapeutic Services?

Psychotherapy can be found in a variety of settings. Contrary to general belief, most therapists are not in

© Tom McCarthy/SKA

Finding the right therapist is no easy task. You need to take into account the therapist's training and orientation, fees charged, and personality. An initial visit should give you a good idea of what a particular therapist is like.

private practice. Many work in institutional settings such as community mental health centers, hospitals, and human service agencies. The principal sources of therapeutic services are described in **Figure 16.14**. The exact configuration of therapeutic services available will vary from one community to another. To find out what your community has to offer, it is a good idea to consult your friends, your local phone book, or your local community mental health center.

Is the Therapist's Profession or Sex Important?

Psychotherapists may be trained in psychology, psychiatry, social work, counseling, psychiatric nursing, or marriage and family therapy. Researchers have *not* found any reliable associations between therapists' professional background and therapeutic efficacy (Beutler et al., 2004), probably because many talented therapists can be found in all of these professions. Thus, the kind of degree that a therapist holds doesn't need to be a crucial consideration in your selection process.

Whether a therapist's sex is important depends on your attitude. If *you* feel that the therapist's sex is important, then for you it is. The therapeutic relationship must be characterized by trust and rapport. Feeling uncomfortable with a therapist of one sex or the other could inhibit the therapeutic process. Hence, you should feel free to look for a male or female therapist if you prefer to do so. This point is probably most relevant to female clients whose troubles may be related to the extensive sexism in our society (A. Kaplan, 1985). It is entirely reasonable for women to seek a therapist with a feminist perspective if that would make them feel more comfortable.

Speaking of sex, you should be aware that sexual exploitation is an occasional problem in the context of therapy. Studies indicate that a small minority of therapists take advantage of their clients sexually (Pope, Keith-Spiegel, & Tabachnick, 1986). These incidents almost always involve a male therapist making advances to a female client. The available evidence indicates that these sexual liaisons are usually harmful to clients

The Psychotherapy Maze
by Otto and Miriam Ehrenberg
(Aronson, 1994)

This book is billed as a "consumer's guide to the ins and outs of therapy." The Ehrenbergs provide a frank, down-to-earth discussion of practical issues relating to psychotherapy. Most books on therapy are devoted to explaining various theoretical approaches to therapy. The Ehrenbergs go far beyond that in this book. They tackle such practical issues as how to select a therapist, how to help make therapy work for you, and how to judge whether therapy is doing you any good. They also discuss mundane but important details such as fees, insurance, missed sessions, and emergency phone calls. The Ehrenbergs' goal is to make therapy less intimidating and mysterious. They succeed handsomely in this endeavor.

Principal Sources of Therapeutic Services

Source	Comments
Private practitioners	Self-employed therapists are listed in the Yellow Pages under their professional category, such as psychologists or psychiatrists. Private practitioners tend to be relatively expensive, but they also tend to be highly experienced therapists.
Community mental health centers	Community mental health centers have salaried psychologists, psychiatrists, and social workers on staff. The centers provide a variety of services and often have staff available on weekends and at night to deal with emergencies.
Hospitals	Several kinds of hospitals provide therapeutic services. There are both public and private mental hospitals that specialize in the care of people with psychological disorders. Many general hospitals have a psychiatric ward, and those that do not will usually have psychiatrists and psychologists on staff and on call. Although hospitals tend to concentrate on inpatient treatment, many provide outpatient therapy as well.
Human service agencies	Various social service agencies employ therapists to provide short-term counseling. Depending on your community, you may find agencies that deal with family problems, juvenile problems, drug problems, and so forth.
Schools and workplaces	Most high schools and colleges have counseling centers where students can get help with personal problems. Similarly, some large businesses offer in-house counseling to their employees.

Figure 16.14

Sources of therapeutic services. Therapists work in a variety of organizational settings. Foremost among them are the five described here.

INSIDE WOODY ALLEN by Stuart Hample. Reprinted by permission. © King Features Syndicate, Inc., 1977. World rights reserved.

(Gabbard, 1994; Williams, 1992). There are absolutely no situations in which therapist-client sexual relations are an ethical therapeutic practice. If a therapist makes sexual advances, a client should terminate treatment.

Is Therapy Always Expensive?

Psychotherapy does not have to be prohibitively expensive. Private practitioners tend to be the most expensive, charging between $25 and $140 per (50-minute) hour. These fees may seem high, but they are in line with those of similar professionals, such as dentists and attorneys. Community mental health centers and social service agencies are usually supported by tax dollars. Hence, they can charge lower fees than most therapists in private practice. Many of these organizations use a sliding scale, so that clients are charged according to how much they can afford. Thus, most communities have inexpensive opportunities for psychotherapy. Moreover, many health insurance plans provide at least partial reimbursement for the cost of treatment.

Is the Therapist's Theoretical Approach Important?

Logically, you might expect that the diverse approaches to therapy vary in effectiveness. For the most part, that is *not* what researchers find, however. After reviewing the evidence, Jerome Frank (1961) and Lester Luborsky and his colleagues (1975) both quote the dodo bird who has just judged a race in *Alice in Wonderland:* "Everybody has won, and *all* must have prizes." Improvement rates for various theoretical orientations usually come out pretty close in most studies (Lambert & Ogles, 2004; Luborsky et al., 2002; Wampold, 2001). In their landmark review of outcome studies, Smith and Glass (1977) estimated the effectiveness of many major approaches to therapy. As **Figure 16.15** shows, the estimates cluster together closely.

However, these findings are a little misleading, as they have been averaged across many types of patients and many types of problems. Most experts seem to think that *for certain types of problems, some approaches*

Figure 16.15

Efficacy of various approaches to therapy. Smith and Glass (1977) reviewed nearly 400 studies in which clients who were treated with a specific type of therapy were compared with a control group made up of people with similar problems who went untreated. The bars indicate the percentile rank (on outcome measures) attained by the average client treated with each type of therapy when compared to control subjects. The higher the percentile, the more effective the therapy was. As you can see, the different approaches were fairly close in their apparent effectiveness.

Adapted from Smith, M. L., & Glass, G. V. (1977). Meta-analysis of psychotherapy outcome series. *American Psychologist, 32,* 752–760. Copyright © 1977 by the American Psychological Association. Adapted by permission of the publisher and author.

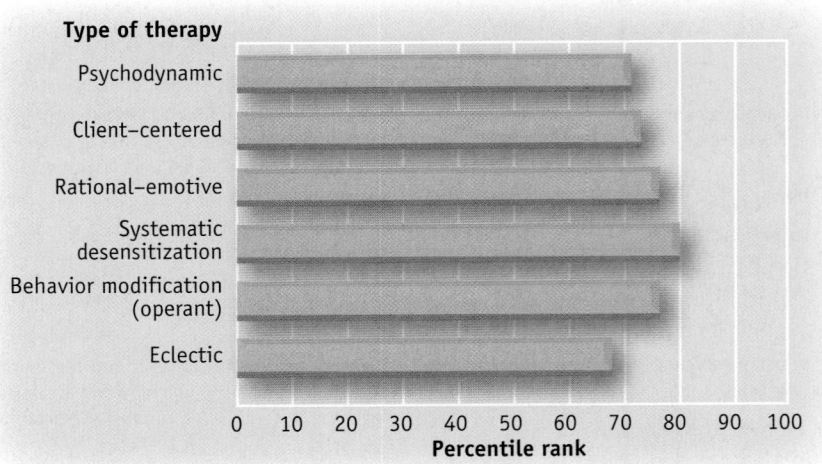

Therapy is both a science and an art. It is scientific in that practitioners are guided in their work by a huge body of empirical research. It is an art in that therapists often have to be creative in adapting their treatment procedures to individual patients and their idiosyncrasies.

to therapy are more effective than others (Beutler, 2002; Crits-Christoph, 1997; Norcross, 1995). For example, Martin Seligman (1995) asserts that panic disorders respond best to cognitive therapy, that specific phobias are most amenable to treatment with systematic desensitization, and that obsessive-compulsive disorders are best treated with behavior therapy or medication. Thus, for a specific type of problem, a therapist's theoretical approach *may* make a difference.

It is also important to point out that the finding that various approaches to therapy are roughly equal in overall efficacy does not mean that all *therapists* are created equal. Some therapists unquestionably are more effective than others. However, these variations in effectiveness appear to depend on individual therapists' personal skills rather than on their theoretical orientation (Beutler et al., 2004). Good, bad, and mediocre therapists are found within each school of thought.

The key point is that effective therapy requires skill and creativity. Arnold Lazarus (1989), who devised an approach to treatment called multimodal therapy, emphasizes that therapists "straddle the fence between science and art." Therapy is scientific in that interventions are based on extensive theory and empirical research (Forsyth & Strong, 1986). Ultimately, though, each client is a unique human being, and the therapist has to creatively fashion a treatment program that will help that individual.

What Is Therapy Like?

It is important to have realistic expectations about therapy, or you may be unnecessarily disappointed. Some people expect miracles. They expect to turn their life around quickly with little effort. Others expect their therapist to run their lives for them. These are unrealistic expectations.

Therapy is usually a slow process. Your problems are not likely to melt away quickly. Moreover, therapy is hard work, and your therapist is only a facilitator. Ultimately, *you* have to confront the challenge of changing your behavior, your feelings, or your personality. This process may not be pleasant. You may have to face up to some painful truths about yourself. As Ehrenberg and Ehrenberg (1994) point out, psychotherapy takes time, effort, and courage.

KEY IDEAS

The Elements of the Treatment Process

▶ Psychotherapy involves three elements: treatments, clients, and therapists. Approaches to treatment are diverse, but they can be grouped into three categories: insight therapies, behavior therapies, and biomedical therapies. People vary considerably in their willingness to seek psychotherapy, and many people who need therapy do not receive it.

▶ Therapists come from a variety of professional backgrounds. Clinical and counseling psychologists, psychiatrists, social workers, psychiatric nurses, and counselors are the principal providers of therapeutic services.

Insight Therapies

▶ Insight therapies involve verbal interactions intended to enhance self-knowledge. In psychoanalysis, free association and dream analysis are used to explore the unconscious. When an analyst's probing hits sensitive areas, resistance can be expected. The transference relationship may be used to overcome this resistance. Classical psychoanalysis is not widely practiced anymore, but Freud's legacy lives on in a rich diversity of modern psychodynamic therapies.

▶ Rogers pioneered client-centered therapy, which is intended to provide a supportive climate in which clients can restructure their self-concepts. This therapy emphasizes clarification of the client's feelings and self-acceptance. Most theoretical approaches to insight therapy have been adapted for use with groups. Group therapy has its own unique strengths and is not merely a cheap substitute for individual therapy.

▶ The weight of the evidence suggests that insight therapies can be effective. The benefits of insight therapies may be due in part to common factors. Repressed memories of childhood sexual abuse recovered through therapy are a new source of controversy in the mental health field. Although many recovered memories of abuse may be the product of suggestion, some probably are authentic.

Behavior Therapies

▶ Behavior therapies use the principles of learning in direct efforts to change specific aspects of behavior. Wolpe's systematic desensitization is a treatment for phobias. It involves the construction of an anxiety hierarchy, relaxation training, and step-by-step movement through the hierarchy.

▶ In aversion therapy, a stimulus associated with an unwanted response is paired with an unpleasant stimulus in an effort to eliminate the maladaptive response. Social skills training can improve clients' interpersonal skills through shaping, modeling, and behavioral rehearsal. Beck's cognitive therapy concentrates on changing the way clients think about events in their lives. Ample evidence shows that behavior therapies are effective.

Biomedical Therapies

▶ Biomedical therapies involve physiological interventions for psychological problems. Two examples of biomedical treatments are drug therapy and electroconvulsive therapy. A great variety of disorders are treated with drugs. The principal types of therapeutic drugs are antianxiety drugs, antipsychotic drugs, antidepressant drugs, and mood stabilizers.

▶ Drug therapies can be effective, but they have their pitfalls. Many drugs produce problematic side effects, and some are overprescribed. Critics are also concerned that the pharmaceutical industry has gained too much influence over drug testing research.

▶ Electroconvulsive therapy (ECT) is used to trigger a cortical seizure that is believed to have therapeutic value for depression. There is contradictory evidence and heated debate about the effectiveness of ECT and about possible risks associated with its use.

Current Trends and Issues in Treatment

▶ Many clinicians and their clients believe that managed care has restricted access to mental health care and undermined its quality. Managed care has also raised concerns about providers' autonomy and clients' confidentiality.

▶ Combinations of insight, behavioral, and biomedical therapies are often used fruitfully in the treatment of psychological disorders. Many modern therapists are eclectic, using ideas and techniques gleaned from a number of theoretical approaches.

▶ Because of cultural, language, and access barriers, therapeutic services are underutilized by ethnic minorities in America. However, the crux of the problem is the failure of institutions to provide culturally sensitive forms of treatment for ethnic minorities.

Application: Looking for a Therapist

▶ Therapeutic services are available in many settings, and such services do not have to be expensive. Excellent and mediocre therapists can be found in all of the mental health professions. Thus, therapists' personal skills are more important than their professional degree. In selecting a therapist, it is reasonable to insist on a therapist of one gender or the other.

▶ The various theoretical approaches to treatment appear to be fairly similar in overall effectiveness. However, for certain types of problems, some approaches to therapy may be more effective than others. Therapy requires time, hard work, and the courage to confront your problems.

KEY TERMS

Antianxiety drugs p. 534
Antidepressant drugs p. 535
Antipsychotic drugs p. 534
Aversion therapy p. 530
Behavior therapies p. 528
Biomedical therapies p. 533
Client-centered therapy p. 522
Clinical psychologists p. 517
Cognitive-behavioral treatments p. 531
Cognitive therapy p. 531
Counseling psychologists p. 517
Dream analysis p. 520
Electroconvulsive therapy (ECT) p. 537
Free association p. 520
Group therapy p. 523
Insight therapies p. 519
Interpretation p. 520
Mood stabilizers p. 536
Psychiatrists p. 518
Psychoanalysis p. 519
Psychopharmacotherapy p. 533
Resistance p. 521
Social skills training p. 531
Systematic desensitization p. 529
Tardive dyskinesia p. 535
Transference p. 521

KEY PEOPLE

Aaron Beck pp. 531–533
Sigmund Freud pp. 519–521
Carl Rogers pp. 522–523
Joseph Wolpe pp. 529–530

PRACTICE TEST

1. Which of the following approaches to psychotherapy is based on the theories of Sigmund Freud and his followers?
   a. Behavior therapies
   b. Client-centered therapy
   c. Biomedical therapies
   d. Psychoanalytic therapy

2. Miriam is seeing a therapist who encourages her to let her mind ramble and say whatever comes up, regardless of how trivial or irrelevant it may seem. The therapist explains that she is interested in probing the depths of Miriam's unconscious mind. This therapist appears to practice _____ and the technique in use is _____.
   a. psychoanalysis; transference
   b. psychoanalysis; free association
   c. cognitive therapy; free association
   d. client-centered therapy; clarification

3. Because Suzanne has an unconscious sexual attraction to her father, she behaves seductively toward her therapist. Suzanne's behavior is most likely a form of:
   a. resistance.
   b. transference.
   c. misinterpretation.
   d. spontaneous remission.

4. Client-centered therapy emphasizes:
   a. interpretation.
   b. probing the unconscious
   c. clarification.
   d. all of the above.

5. With regard to studies of the efficacy of various treatments, research suggests:
   a. insight therapy is superior to no treatment or placebo treatment.
   b. individual insight therapy is effective, but group therapy is not.
   c. group therapy is effective, but individual insight therapy rarely works.
   d. insight therapy is effective, but only if patients remain in therapy for at least three years.

6. According to behavior therapists, pathological behaviors:
   a. are signs of an underlying emotional or cognitive problem.
   b. should be viewed as the expression of an unconscious sexual or aggressive conflict.
   c. can be modified directly through the application of established principles of conditioning.
   d. both a and b.

7. A stimulus that elicits an undesirable response is paired with a noxious stimulus in:
   a. systematic desensitization.
   b. cognitive therapy.
   c. aversion therapy.
   d. psychoanalysis.

8. Bryce's psychiatrist has prescribed both Prozac and lithium for him. Bryce's diagnosis is probably:
   a. schizophrenia.
   b. obsessive-compulsive disorder.
   c. bipolar disorder.
   d. dissociative disorder.

9. Drug therapies have been criticized on the grounds that:
   a. they are ineffective in most patients.
   b. they temporarily relieve symptoms without addressing the real problem.
   c. many drugs are overprescribed and many patients are overmedicated.
   d. both b and c.

10. A therapist's theoretical approach is not nearly as important as his or her:
    a. age.
    b. appearance.
    c. personal characteristics and skills.
    d. type of professional training.

Book Companion Website

Visit the Book Companion Website at **academic.cengage.com/psychology/weiten,** where you will find tutorial quizzes, flash cards, and web links for every chapter, a final exam, and more! You can also link to the Psychology Resource Center (accessible directly at **academic.cengage.com/login**) for a range of psychology-related resources.

Personal Explorations Workbook

The following exercises in your *Personal Explorations Workbook* may enhance your self-understanding in relation to issues raised in this chapter. **Questionnaire 16.1:** Attitudes Toward Seeking Professional Psychological Help. **Personal Probe 16.1:** What Are Your Feelings about Therapy? **Personal Probe 16.2:** Thinking About Therapy.

ANSWERS

1. d Pages 519–521
2. b Pages 519–520
3. b Page 521
4. c Page 523
5. a Pages 524–525
6. c Pages 528–529
7. c Page 530
8. c Pages 535–536
9. d Pages 536–537
10. c Page 545

Glossary

acquired immune deficiency syndrome (AIDS) A disorder in which the immune system is gradually weakened and eventually disabled by the human immunodeficiency virus (HIV).

actor-observer effect The tendency to attribute one's own behavior to situational factors and others' behavior to personal factors.

acculturation Changing to adapt to a new culture.

acute stressors Threatening events that have a relatively short duration and a clear end point.

adjustment The psychological processes through which people manage or cope with the demands and challenges of everyday life.

aggression Any behavior intended to hurt someone, either physically or verbally.

agoraphobia A fear of going out to public places.

alcohol dependence *See* alcoholism

alcoholism A chronic, progressive disorder marked by a growing compulsion to drink and impaired control over drinking that eventually interfere with health and social behavior.

ambient stress Chronic environmental conditions that, although not urgent, are negatively valued and place adaptive demands on people.

anal intercourse The insertion of the penis into a partner's anus and rectum.

androcentrism The belief that the male is the norm.

androgens The principal class of male sex hormones.

androgyny The coexistence of both masculine and feminine personality traits in an individual.

anorexia nervosa An eating disorder characterized by intense fear of gaining weight, disturbed body image, refusal to maintain normal weight, and use of dangerous methods to lose weight.

antecedents In behavior modification, events that typically precede a target response.

antianxiety drugs Drugs that relieve tension, apprehension, and nervousness.

antidepressant drugs Drugs that gradually elevate mood and help to bring people out of a depression.

antipsychotic drugs Drugs used to gradually reduce psychotic symptoms, including hyperactivity, mental confusion, hallucinations, and delusions.

anxiety disorders A class of psychological disorders marked by feelings of excessive apprehension and anxiety.

approach-approach conflict A conflict in which a choice must be made between two attractive goals.

approach-avoidance conflict A conflict in which a choice must be made about whether to pursue a single goal that has both attractive and unattractive aspects.

archetypes Emotionally charged images and thought forms that have universal meaning.

assertiveness Acting in one's own best interest by expressing one's feelings and thoughts honestly and directly.

atherosclerosis A disease characterized by gradual narrowing of the coronary arteries.

attachment styles Typical ways of interacting in close relationships.

attitudes Beliefs and feelings about people, objects, and ideas.

attributions Inferences that people draw about the causes of events, others' behavior, and their own behavior.

autonomic nervous system (ANS) That portion of the peripheral nervous system made up of the nerves that connect to the heart, blood vessels, smooth muscles, and glands.

aversion therapy A behavior therapy in which an aversive stimulus is paired with a stimulus that elicits an undesirable response.

avoidance-avoidance conflict A conflict in which a choice must be made between two unattractive goals.

basking in reflected glory The tendency to enhance one's image by publicly announcing one's association with those who are successful.

battering Physical abuse, emotional abuse, and sexual abuse, especially in marriage or relationships.

behavior Any overt (observable) response or activity by an organism.

behavior modification A systematic approach to changing behavior through the application of the principles of conditioning.

behavior therapies The application of the principles of learning to direct efforts to change clients' maladaptive behaviors.

behavioral contract A written agreement outlining a promise to adhere to the contingencies of a behavior modification program.

behaviorism A theoretical orientation based on the premise that scientific psychology should study observable behavior.

bereavement The painful loss of a loved one through death.

binge-eating disorder An eating disorder that involves distress-inducing eating binges that are not accompanied by the purging, fasting, and excessive exercise seen in bulimia.

biomedical therapies Physiological interventions intended to reduce symptoms associated with psychological disorders.

biopsychosocial model The idea that physical illness is caused by a complex interaction of biological, psychological, and sociocultural factors.

bipolar disorders Psychological disorders marked by the experience of both depressed and manic periods.

bisexuals People who seek emotional-sexual relationships with members of both genders.

body mass index (BMI) Weight (in kilograms) divided by height (in meters) squared (kg/m2).

brainstorming Generating as many ideas as possible while withholding criticism and evaluation.

bulimia nervosa An eating disorder characterized by habitual out-of-control overeating followed by unhealthy compensatory efforts, such as self-induced vomiting, fasting, abuse of laxatives and diuretics, and excessive exercise.

burnout Physical, mental, and emotional exhaustion that is attributable to work-related stress.

bystander effect The social phenomenon in which individuals are less likely to provide needed help when others are present than when they are alone.

cancer Malignant cell growth, which may occur in many organ systems in the body.

cannabis The hemp plant from which marijuana, hashish, and THC are derived.

case study An in-depth investigation of an individual subject.

catastrophic thinking Unrealistic appraisals of stress that exaggerate the magnitude of one's problems.

catatonic schizophrenia A type of schizophrenia marked by striking motor disturbances, ranging from muscular rigidity to random motor activity.

catharsis The release of emotional tension.

cerebral hemispheres The right and left halves of the cerebrum, which is the convoluted outer layer of the brain.

channel The medium through which a message reaches the receiver.

chronic stressors Threatening events that have a relatively long duration and no readily apparent time limit.

classical conditioning A type of learning in which a neutral stimulus acquires the capacity to evoke a response that was originally evoked by another stimulus.

client-centered therapy An insight therapy that emphasizes providing a supportive emotional climate for clients, who play a major role in determining the pace and direction of their therapy.

clinical psychologists Psychologists who specialize in the diagnosis and treatment of psychological disorders and everyday behavioral problems.

clinical psychology The branch of psychology concerned with the diagnosis and treatment of psychological problems and disorders.

close relationships Relatively long-lasting relationships in which frequent interactions occur in a variety of settings and in which the impact of the interactions is strong.

cognitive therapy An insight therapy that emphasizes recognizing and changing negative thoughts and maladaptive beliefs.

cohabitation Living together in a sexually intimate relationship without the legal bonds of marriage.

coitus The insertion of the penis into the vagina and (typically) pelvic thrusting.

collective unconscious According to Jung, a storehouse of latent memory traces inherited from people's ancestral past that is shared with the entire human race.

collectivism Putting group goals ahead of personal goals and defining one's identity in terms of the groups to which one belongs.

commitment The decision and intent to maintain a relationship in spite of the difficulties and costs that may arise.

communication apprehension The anxiety caused by having to talk with others.

comparison level One's standard of what constitutes an acceptable balance of rewards and costs in a relationship.

comparison level for alternatives One's estimation of the available outcomes from alternative relationships.

compensation A defense mechanism characterized by efforts to overcome imagined or real inferiorities by developing one's abilities.

compliance Yielding to social pressure in one's public behavior, even though one's private beliefs have not changed.

concordance rate A statistic indicating the percentage of twin pairs or other pairs of relatives that exhibit the same disorder.

conditioned response (CR) A learned reaction to a conditioned stimulus that occurs because of previous conditioning.

conditioned stimulus (CS) A previously neutral stimulus that has, through conditioning, acquired the capacity to evoke a conditioned response.

confirmation bias The tendency to behave toward others in ways that confirm your expectations about them.

conflict The struggle that occurs when two or more incompatible motivations or behavioral impulses compete for expression.

conformity Yielding to real or imagined social pressure.

conscious According to Freud, whatever one is aware of at a particular point in time.

constructive coping Efforts to deal with stressful events that are judged to be relatively healthful.

context The environment in which communication takes place.

control group Subjects in an experiment who do not receive the special treatment given to the experimental group.

conversion disorder Psychological disorder characterized by a significant loss of physical function or by other physical symptoms (with no apparent organic basis), usually in a single organ system.

coping Active efforts to master, reduce, or tolerate the demands created by stress.

coronary heart disease A chronic disease characterized by a reduction in blood flow from the coronary arteries, which supply the heart with blood.

corpus callosum The band of fibers connecting the two hemispheres of the brain.

correlation The extent to which two variables are related to each other.

correlation coefficient A numerical index of the degree of relationship that exists between two variables.

counseling psychologists Psychologists who specialize in the treatment of everyday behavioral problems.

cunnilingus The oral stimulation of the female genitals.

date rape Forced and unwanted intercourse with someone in the context of dating.

death anxiety Fear and apprehension about one's own death.

death system The collection of rituals and procedures used by a culture to handle death.

defense mechanisms Largely unconscious reactions that protect a person from unpleasant emotions such as anxiety and guilt.

defensive attribution The tendency to blame victims for their misfortune, so that one feels less likely to be victimized in a similar way.

defensiveness An excessive concern wth protecting oneself from being hurt.

delusions False beliefs that are maintained even though they clearly are out of touch with reality.

dementia An abnormal condition marked by multiple cognitive defects that include memory impairment.

dependent variable In an experiment, the variable that is thought to be affected by manipulations of the independent variable.

diagnosis Distinguishing one illness from another.

discrimination Behaving differently, usually unfairly, toward members of a group.

disorganized schizophrenia A type of schizophrenia characterized by a particularly severe deterioration of adaptive behavior.

displaced workers Individuals who are unemployed because their jobs have disappeared.

displacement Diverting emotional feelings (usually anger) from their original source to a substitute target.

display rules Norms that govern the appropriate display of emotions.

dissociative amnesia A sudden loss of memory for important personal information that is too extensive to be due to normal forgetting.

dissociative disorders A class of psychological disorders characterized by loss of contact with portions of one's consciousness or memory, resulting in disruptions in one's sense of identity.

dissociative fugue A loss of memory for one's entire past life, along with one's sense of personal identity.

dissociative identity disorder Dissociative disorder involving the coexistence in one person of two or more largely complete, and usually very different, personalities. Also called multiple-personality disorder.

door-in-the-face technique Making a very large request that is likely to be turned down to increase the chance that people will agree to a smaller request later.

downward social comparison The defensive tendency to compare oneself with someone whose troubles are more serious than one's own.

dream analysis A psychotherapeutic technique in which the therapist interprets the symbolic meaning of the client's dreams.

dual-earner households Households in which both partners are employed.

eating disorders Severe disturbances in eating behavior characterized by preoccupation with weight and unhealthy efforts to control weight.

ego According to Freud, the decision-making component of personality that operates according to the reality principle.

elaboration likelihood model The idea that an individual's thoughts about a persuasive message (rather than the message itself) determine whether attitude change will occur.

electroconvulsive therapy (ECT) A biomedical treatment in which electric shock is used to produce a cortical seizure accompanied by convulsions.

electronically mediated communication Interpersonal communication that takes place via technology.

emotional intelligence The ability to monitor, assess, express, or regulate one's emotions; the capacity to identify, interpret, and understand others' emotions; and the ability to use this information to guide one's thinking and actions.

emotions Powerful, largely uncontrollable feelings, accompanied by physiological changes.

empathy Adopting another's frame of reference to understand his or her point of view.

empiricism The premise that knowledge should be acquired through observation.

endocrine system Glands that secrete chemicals called hormones into the bloodstream.

endogamy The tendency of people to marry within their own social group.

epidemiology The study of the distribution of mental or physical disorders in a population.

erectile difficulties The male sexual dysfunction characterized by the persistent inability to achieve or maintain an erection adequate for intercourse.

erogenous zones Areas of the body that are sexually sensitive or responsive.

estrogens The principal class of female sex hormones.

etiology The apparent causation and developmental history of an illness.

evolutionary psychology A field of psychology that examines behavioral processes in terms of their adaptive value for members of a species over the course of many generations.

experiment A research method in which the investigator manipulates an (independent) variable under carefully controlled conditions and observes whether there are changes in a second (dependent) variable as a result.

experimental group The subjects in an experiment who receive some special treatment in regard to the independent variable.

explanatory style The tendency to use similar causal attributions for a wide variety of events in one's life.

expressiveness A style of communication characterized by the ability to express tender emotions easily and to be sensitive to the feelings of others.

external attributions Ascribing the causes of behavior to situational demands and environmental constraints.

extinction The gradual weakening and disappearance of a conditioned response tendency.

factor analysis Technique of analyzing correlations among many variables to identify closely related clusters of variables.

family life cycle An orderly sequence of developmental stages that families tend to progress through.

fellatio The oral stimulation of the penis.

fight-or-flight response A physiological reaction to threat that mobilizes an organism for attacking (fight) or fleeing (flight) an enemy.

fixation In Freud's theory, a failure to move forward from one stage to another as expected.

foot-in-the-door technique Getting people to agree to a small request to increase the chances that they will agree to a larger request later.

free association A psychotherapeutic technique in which clients spontaneously express their thoughts and feelings exactly as they occur, with as little censorship as possible.

frustration The feelings that occur in any situation in which the pursuit of some goal is thwarted.

fundamental attribution error The tendency to explain others' behavior as a result of personal rather than situational factors.

games Manipulative interactions progressing toward a predictable outcome, in which people conceal their real motivations.

gender The state of being male or female.

gender identity The ability to correctly classify oneself as male or female.

gender-role identity A person's identification with the traits regarded as masculine or feminine.

gender-role transcendence perspective The idea that to be fully human, people need to move beyond gender roles as a way of organizing the world and of perceiving themselves and others.

gender roles Cultural expectations about what is appropriate behavior for each gender.

gender schemas Cognitive structures that guide the processing of gender-relevant information.

gender stereotypes Widely shared beliefs about males' and females' abilities, personality traits, and social behavior.

general adaptation syndrome A model of the body's stress response, consisting of three stages: alarm, resistance, and exhaustion.

generalized anxiety disorder A psychological disorder marked by a chronic high level of anxiety that is not tied to any specific threat.

glass ceiling An invisible barrier that prevents most women and ethnic minorities from advancing to the highest levels of an occupation.

gonads The sex glands.

group therapy The simultaneous treatment of several or more clients in a group.

hallucinations Sensory perceptions that occur in the absence of a real external stimulus or that represent gross distortions of perceptual input.

hallucinogens A diverse group of drugs that have powerful effects on mental and emotional functioning, marked most prominently by distortions in sensory and perceptual experience.

hardiness A personality syndrome marked by commitment, challenge, and control that is purportedly associated with strong stress resistance.

health psychology The subfield of psychology concerned with the relation of psychosocial factors to the promotion and maintenance of health, and with the causation, prevention, and treatment of illness.

hedonic adaptation The phenomenon that occurs when the mental scale that people use to judge the pleasantness and unpleasantness of their experiences shifts so that their neutral point, or baseline for comparison, is changed.

heritability ratio An estimate of the proportion of trait variability in a population that is determined by variations in genetic inheritance.

heterosexism The assumption that all individuals and relationships are heterosexual.

heterosexuals People whose sexual desires and erotic behaviors are directed toward the other gender.

hierarchy of needs A systematic arrangement of needs, according to priority, in which basic needs must be met before less basic needs are aroused.

hindsight bias The common tendency to mold one's interpretation of the past to fit how events actually turned out.

homogamy The tendency of people to marry others who have similar personal characteristics.

homophobia The intense fear and intolerance of homosexuality.

homosexuals People who seek emotional/sexual relationships with members of the same gender.

hormones Chemical substances released into the bloodstream by the endocrine glands.

hostility A persistent negative attitude marked by cynical, mistrusting thoughts, feelings of anger, and overtly aggressive actions.

humanism A theoretical orientation that emphasizes the unique qualities of humans, especially their free will and their potential for personal growth.

hypoactive sexual desire Lack of interest in sexual activity.

hypochondriasis (hypochondria) Excessive preoccupation with health concerns and incessant worry about developing physical illnesses.

id In Freud's theory, the primitive, instinctive component of personality that operates according to the pleasure principle.

identification Bolstering self-esteem by forming an imaginary or real alliance with some person or group.

identity A relatively clear and stable sense of who one is and what one stands for.

immune response The body's defensive reaction to invasion by bacteria, viral agents, or other foreign substances.

impression management Usually conscious efforts to influence the way others think of one.

incongruence The disparity between one's self-concept and one's actual experience.

independent variable In an experiment, a condition or event that an experimenter varies in order to see its impact on another variable.

individualism Putting personal goals ahead of group goals and defining one's identity in terms of personal attributes rather than group memberships.

industrial/organizational (I/O) psychology The study of human behavior in the workplace.

informational influence Pressure to conform that operates when people look to others for how to behave in ambiguous situations.

ingratiation Efforts to make oneself likable to others.

insight therapies A group of psychotherapies in which verbal interactions are intended to enhance clients' self-knowledge and thus promote healthful changes in personality and behavior.

instrumentality A style of communication that focuses on reaching practical goals and finding solutions to problems.

interdependence theory *See* social exchange theory

internal attributions Ascribing the causes of behavior to personal dispositions, traits, abilities, and feelings rather than to external events.

Internet addiction Spending an inordinate amount of time on the Internet and inability to control online use.

interpersonal communication An interactional process whereby one person sends a message to another.

interpersonal conflict Disagreement among two or more people.

interpretation A therapist's attempts to explain the inner significance of the client's thoughts, feelings, memories, and behaviors.

intimacy Warmth, closeness, and sharing in a relationship.

intimate violence Aggression toward those who are in close relationships to the aggressor.

investments Things that people contribute to a relationship that they can't get back if the relationship ends.

kinesics The study of communication through body movements.

labor force All people who are employed as well as those who are currently unemployed but are looking for work.

learned helplessness Passive behavior produced by exposure to unavoidable aversive events.

leisure Unpaid activities one chooses to engage in because they are personally meaningful.

life changes Any noticeable alterations in one's living circumstances that require readjustment.

loneliness The emotional state that occurs when a person has fewer interpersonal relationships than desired or when these relationships are not as satisfying as desired.

lowball technique Getting people to commit themselves to an attractive proposition before its hidden costs are revealed.

major depressive disorder Psychological disorder characterized by persistent feelings of sadness and despair and a loss of interest in previous sources of pleasure.

manic-depressive disorder *See* bipolar disorder.

marriage The legally and socially sanctioned union of sexually intimate adults.

matching hypothesis The idea that people of similar levels of physical attractiveness gravitate toward each other.

medical model The idea that it is useful to think of abnormal behavior as a disease.

meditation A family of mental exercises in which a conscious attempt is made to focus attention in a nonanalytical way.

menarche The first occurrence of menstruation.

menopause The cessation of menstruation.

mere exposure effect An increase in positive feelings toward a novel stimulus (such as a person) based on frequent exposure to it.

message The information or meaning that is transmitted from one person to another.

meta-analysis A statistical technique that evaluates the results of many studies on the same question.

midlife crisis A turbulent period of doubts and reappraisals of one's life.

mnemonic devices Strategies for enhancing memory.

monogamy The practice of having only one spouse at a time.

mood disorders A class of disorders marked by emotional disturbances that may spill over to disrupt physical, perceptual, social, and thought processes.

mood stabilizers Drugs used to control mood swings in patients with bipolar mood disorders.

mourning Formal practices of an individual and a community in response to a death.

multiple-personality disorder *See* dissociative identity disorder

narcissism The tendency to regard oneself as grandiosely self-important.

narcotics (opiates) Drugs derived from opium that are capable of relieving pain.

naturalistic observation An approach to research in which the researcher engages in careful observation of behavior without intervening directly with the subjects.

need for cognition The tendency to seek out and enjoy effortful thought, problem-solving activities, and in-depth analysis.

need for self-actualization The need to fulfill one's potential; the highest need in Maslow's motivational hierarchy.

negative reinforcement The strengthening of a response because it is followed by the removal of a (presumably) unpleasant stimulus.

neurons Individual cells that receive, integrate, and transmit information.

neuroticism A broad personality trait associated with chronic anxiety, insecurity, and self-consciousness.

neurotransmitters Chemicals that carry signals from one neuron to another.

noise Any stimulus that interferes with accurately expressing or understanding a message.

nonverbal communication The transmission of meaning from one person to another through means or symbols other than words.

nonverbal sensitivity The ability to accurately encode (express) and decode (understand) nonverbal cues.

normative influence Pressure to conform that operates when people conform to social norms for fear of negative social consequences.

nutrition A collection of processes (mainly food consumption) through which an organism uses the materials (nutrients) required for survival and growth.

obedience A form of compliance that occurs when people follow direct commands, usually from someone in a position of authority.

observational learning Learning that occurs when an organism's responding is influenced by observing others, who are called models.

obsessive-compulsive disorder (OCD) A psychological disorder marked by persistent uncontrollable intrusions of unwanted thoughts (obsessions) and by urges to engage in senseless rituals (compulsions).

occupational interest inventories Tests that measure one's interests as they relate to various jobs or careers.

Oedipal complex According to Freud, a child's erotically tinged desires for the other-sex parent, accompanied by feelings of hostility toward the same-sex parent.

operant conditioning A form of learning in which voluntary responses come to be controlled by their consequences.

optimism A general tendency to expect good outcomes.

orgasm The release that occurs when sexual arousal reaches its peak intensity and is discharged in a series of muscular contractions that pulsate through the pelvic area.

orgasmic difficulties Sexual disorders characterized by an ability to experience sexual arousal but persistent problems in achieving orgasm.

overcompensation Making up for frustration in one area by seeking overgratification in another area.

overlearning Continued rehearsal of material after one has first appeared to have mastered it.

overdose An excessive dose of a drug that can seriously threaten one's life.

panic disorder Recurrent attacks of overwhelming anxiety that usually occur suddenly and unexpectedly.

paralanguage All vocal cues other than the content of the verbal message itself.

paranoid schizophrenia A type of schizophrenia dominated by delusions of persecution, along with delusions of grandeur.

parasuicide Self-destructive behavior that is not fatal nor entirely intentional.

parental investment theory The idea that a species' mating patterns depend on what each sex has to invest—in the way of time, energy, and survival risk—to produce and nurture offspring.

passion The intense feelings (both positive and negative) experienced in love relationships, including sexual desire.

person perception The process of forming impressions of others.

personal space A zone of space surrounding a person that is felt to "belong" to that person.

personality An individual's unique constellation of consistent behavioral traits.

personality trait A durable disposition to behave in a particular way in a variety of situations.

persuasion The communication of arguments and information intended to change another person's attitudes.

phobic disorders Anxiety disorders marked by a persistent and irrational fear of an object or situation that presents no realistic danger.

physical dependence The need to continue to take a drug to avoid withdrawal illness.

polygamy Having more than one spouse at one time.

polygraph A device that records fluctuations in physiological arousal as a person answers questions.

positive reinforcement The strengthening of a response because it is followed by the arrival of a (presumably) pleasant stimulus.

possible self One's conceptions about the kind of person one might become in the future.

posttraumatic stress disorder (PTSD) Disturbed behavior that emerges sometime after a major stressful event is over.

preconscious According to Freud, material just beneath the surface of awareness that can be easily retrieved.

prejudice A negative attitude toward members of a group.

premature ejaculation Impaired sexual relations because a man consistently reaches orgasm too quickly.

pressure Expectations or demands that one behave in a certain way.

prevalence The percentage of a population that exhibits a disorder during a specified time period.

primacy effect The fact that initial information tends to carry more weight than subsequent information.

primary appraisal An initial evaluation of whether an event is (1) irrelevant to one, (2) relevant, but not threatening, or (3) stressful.

primary sex characteristics The structures necessary for reproduction.

procrastination The tendency to delay tackling tasks until the last minute.

prognosis A forecast about the probable course of an illness.

projection Attributing one's own thoughts, feelings, or motives to another person.

projective tests Personality tests that ask subjects to respond to vague, ambiguous stimuli in ways that may reveal the subjects' needs, feelings, and personality traits.

proxemics The study of people's use of interpersonal space.

proximity Geographic, residential, and other forms of spatial closeness.

psychiatrists Physicians who specialize in the treatment of psychological disorders.

psychoanalysis An insight therapy that emphasizes the recovery of unconscious conflicts, motives, and defenses through techniques such as free association, dream analysis, and transference.

psychodynamic theories All the diverse theories descended from the work of Sigmund Freud that focus on unconscious mental forces.

psychological dependence The need to continue to take a drug to satisfy intense mental and emotional craving for it.

psychological test A standardized measure of a sample of a person's behavior.

psychology The science that studies behavior and the physiological and mental processes that underlie it and the profession that applies the accumulated knowledge of this science to practical problems.

psychopharmacotherapy The treatment of mental disorders with medication.

psychosexual stages In Freud's theory, developmental periods with a characteristic sexual focus that leave their mark on adult personality.

psychosomatic diseases Genuine physical ailments caused in part by psychological factors, especially emotional distress.

puberty The stage during which sexual functions reach maturity and that marks the beginning of adolescence.

pubescence The two-year span preceding puberty during which the changes leading to physical and sexual maturity take place.

public self An image presented to others in social interations.

punishment The weakening (decrease in frequency) of a response because it is followed by the arrival of a (presumably) unpleasant stimulus.

rational-emotive therapy An approach to therapy that focuses on altering clients' patterns of irrational thinking to reduce maladaptive emotions and behavior.

rationalization Creating false but plausible excuses to justify unacceptable behavior.

reaction formation Behaving in a way that is exactly the opposite of one's true feelings.

receiver The person to whom a message is targeted.

reciprocal liking Liking those who show they like you.

reciprocity principle The rule that one should pay back in kind what one receives from others.

reference group A set of people who are used as a gauge in making social comparisons.

refractory period A time after orgasm during which males are unable to experience another orgasm.

regression A reversion to immature patterns of behavior.

relationship maintenance The actions and activities used to sustain the desired quality of a relationship.

reliability The measurement consistency of a test.

repression Keeping distressing thoughts and feelings buried in the unconscious.

resistance Largely unconscious defensive maneuvers intended to hinder the progress of therapy.

schizophrenic disorders A class of disorders marked by disturbances in thought that spill over to affect perceptual, social, and emotional processes.

secondary appraisal An evaluation of one's coping resources and options for dealing with stress.

secondary sex characteristics The physical features that distinguish one gender from the other but are not essential for reproduction.

sedatives Sleep-inducing drugs that tend to decrease central nervous system and behavioral activity.

self-actualization *See* need for self-actualization.

self-attributions Inferences that people draw about the causes of their own behavior.

self-concept A collection of beliefs about one's basic nature, unique qualities, and typical behavior.

self-defeating behaviors Seemingly intentional acts that thwart a person's self-interest.

self-disclosure The voluntary act of verbally communicating private information about oneself to another person.

self-discrepancy The mismatching of self-perceptions.

self-efficacy One's belief about one's ability to perform behaviors that should lead to expected outcomes.

self-enhancement The tendency to maintain positive views of oneself.

self-esteem One's overall assessment of one's worth as a person; the evaluative component of the self-concept.

self-fulfilling prophecy The process whereby expectations about a person cause the person to behave in ways that confirm the expectations.

self-handicapping The tendency to sabotage one's performance to provide an excuse for possible failure.

self-monitoring The degree to which people attend to and control the impressions they make on others.

self-regulation Directing and controlling one's behavior.

self-report inventories Personality scales that ask individuals to answer a series of questions about their characteristic behavior.

self-serving bias The tendency to attribute one's successes to personal factors and one's failures to situational factors.

self-verification theory The idea that people prefer to receive feedback from others that is consistent with their own self-views.

sender The person who initiates a message.

sensate focus A sex-therapy exercise in which partners take turns pleasuring each other with guided verbal feedback while certain kinds of stimulation are temporarily forbidden.

set-point theory The idea that there is a natural point of stability in body weight, thought to involve the monitoring of fat cell levels.

settling-point theory The idea that weight tends to drift around the level at which the constellation of factors that determine food consumption and energy expenditure achieve an equilibrium.

sex therapy The professional treatment of sexual dysfunctions.

sexism Discrimination against people on the basis of their sex.

sexual dysfunction An impairment in sexual functioning that causes subjective distress.

sexual harassment The subjection of individuals to unwelcome sexually oriented behavior.

sexual identity The complex of personal qualities, self-perceptions, attitudes, values, and preferences that guide one's sexual behavior.

sexual orientation A person's preference for emotional and sexual relationships with individuals of the same gender, the other gender, or either gender.

sexually transmitted disease (STD) An illness that is transmitted primarily through sexual contact.

shaping Modifying behavior by reinforcing closer and closer approximations of a desired response.

shyness Discomfort, inhibition, and excessive caution in interpersonal relations.

social clock A person's notion of a developmental schedule that specifies what the person should have accomplished by certain points in life.

social comparison theory The idea that people need to compare themselves with others in order to gain insight into their own behavior.

social constructionism The assertion that individuals construct their own reality based on societal expectations, conditioning, and self-socialization.

social exchange theory The idea that interpersonal relationships are governed by perceptions of the rewards and costs exchanged in interactions.

social role theory The assertion that minor gender differences are exaggerated by the different social roles that males and females occupy.

social skills training A behavior therapy designed to improve interpersonal skills that emphasizes shaping, modeling, and behavioral rehearsal.

social support Aid and succor provided by members of one's social networks.

socialization The process by which individuals acquire the norms and roles expected of people in a particular society.

somatization disorder A psychological disorder marked by a history of diverse physical complaints that appear to be psychological in origin.

somatoform disorders A class of psychological disorders involving physical ailments that have no authentic organic basis but are due solely to psychological factors.

source The person who initiates, or sends, a message.

spermarche An adolescent male's first ejaculation.

SQ3R A study system designed to promote effective reading that includes five steps: survey, question, read, recite, and review.

standardization The uniform procedures used to administer and score a test.

stereotypes Widely held beliefs that people have certain characteristics simply because of their membership in a particular group.

stimulants Drugs that tend to increase central nervous system and behavioral activity.

stress Any circumstances that threaten or are perceived to threaten one's well-being and thereby tax one's coping abilities.

subjective well-being Individuals' personal assessments of their overall happiness or life satisfaction.

superego According to Freud, the moral component of personality that incorporates social standards about what represents right and wrong.

surveys Structured questionnaires designed to solicit information about specific aspects of subjects' behavior.

systematic desensitization A behavior therapy used to reduce clients' anxiety responses through counterconditioning.

tardive dyskinesia A neurological disorder marked by chronic tremors and involuntary spastic movements.

test norms Statistics that provide information about where a score on a psychological test ranks in relation to other scores on that test.

token A symbol of all the members of a group.

token economy A system for doling out symbolic reinforcers that are exchanged later for a variety of genuine reinforcers.

tolerance A progressive decrease in responsiveness to a drug with continued use.

transference A phenomenon that occurs when clients start relating to their therapist in ways that mimic critical relationships in their lives.

twin studies A research method in which researchers assess hereditary influence by comparing the resemblance of identical twins and fraternal twins on a trait.

Type A personality A personality style marked by a competitive orientation, impatience and urgency, and anger and hostility.

Type B personality A personality style marked by relatively relaxed, patient, easy-going, amicable behavior.

unconditioned response (UCR) An unlearned reaction to an unconditioned stimulus that occurs without previous conditioning.

unconditioned stimulus (UCS) A stimulus that evokes an unconditioned response without previous conditioning.

unconscious According to Freud, thoughts, memories, and desires that are well below the surface of conscious awareness but that nonetheless exert great influence on our behavior.

undifferentiated schizophrenia A type of schizophrenia marked by idiosyncratic mixtures of schizophrenic symptoms.

validity The ability of a test to measure what it was designed to measure.

variables *See* dependent variable; independent variable.

vasocongestion Engorgement of blood vessels.

work An activity that produces something of value for others.

work-family conflict The feeling of being pulled in multiple directions by competing demands from job and family.

working memory The short-term, limited capacity memory store that people use to juggle information they are currently focusing on.

References

AAUW Educational Foundation (1992). *How schools shortchange girls.* Washington, DC: AAUW.

Abbey, A., Clinton-Sherrod, A. M., McAuslan, P., Zawacki, T., & Buck, P. O. (2003). The relationship between the quantity of alcohol consumed and the severity of sexual assaults committed by college men. *Journal of Interpersonal Violence, 18*(7), 813–833.

Abbey, A., McAuslan, P., Zawacki, T. , Clinton, A. M., & Buck, P. O. (2001a). Attitudinal, experimental, and situational predictors of sexual assault perpetration. *Journal of Interpersonal Violence, 16*(8), 784–807.

Abbey, A., Zawacki, T., Buck, P. O., Clinton, A. M., & McAuslan, P. (2001b). Alcohol and sexual assault. *Alcohol Research and Health, 25*(1), 43–51.

Abbey, A., Zawacki, T., Buck, P. O., Clinton, A. M., & McAuslan, P. (2004). Sexual assault and alcohol consumption: What do we know about their relationship and what types of research are still needed? *Aggression and Violent Behavior, 9*(3), 271–303.

Abdel-Khalek, A. M. (2006). Happiness, health, and religiosity: Significant relations. *Mental Health, 9*(1), 85–97.

Abel, M. H. (1998). Interaction of humor and gender in moderating relationships between stress and outcomes. *Journal of Psychology, 132,* 267–276.

Abel, M. H. (2002). Humor, stress, and coping strategies. *Humor: International Journal of Humor Research, 15*(4), 365–381.

Aber, J. L., Brown, J. L., & Jones, S. M. (2003). Developmental trajectories toward violence in middle childhood: Course, demographic differences, and response to school-based intervention. *Developmental Psychology, 39*(2), 324–348.

Abi-Dargham, A. (2004). Do we still believe in the dopamine hypothesis? New data bring new evidence. *International Journal of Neuropsychopharmacology, 7*(Suppl1), S1–S5.

Abi-Dargham, A., Gil, R., Krystal, J., Baldwin, R. M., Seibyl, J. P., Bowers, M., van Dyck, C. H., Charney, D. S., Innis, R. B., & Laruelle, M. (1998). Increased striatal dopamine transmission in schizophrenia: Confirmation in a second cohort. *American Journal of Psychiatry, 155,* 761–767.

Abma, J. C., & Martinez, G. M. (2006). Childlessness among older women in the United States: Trends and profiles. *Journal of Marriage and Family, 68,* 1045–1056.

Aboud, F. E., & Mendelson, M. J. (1996). Determinants of friendship selection and quality: Developmental perspectives. In W. M. Bukowski, A. F. Newcomb, & W. W. Hartup (Eds.), *The company they keep: Friendship in childhood and adolescence.* Cambridge, UK: Cambridge University Press.

Abrams, D., Viki, G. T., Masser, B., & Bohner, G. (2003). Perceptions of stranger acquaintance rape: The role of benevolent and hostile sexism in victim blame and rape proclivity. *Journal of Personality and Social Psychology, 84,* 111–125.

Abramson, L. Y., Alloy, L. B., Hankin, B. L., Haeffel, G. J., MacCoon, D. G., & Gibb, B. E. (2002). Cognitive vulnerability-stress models of depression in a self-regulatory and psychobiological context. In I. H. Gotlib & C. L. Hammen (Eds.), *Handbook of depression.* New York: Guilford.

Abramson, L. Y., Alloy, L. B., & Metalsky, J. I. (1995). Hopelessness depression. In J. N. Buchanan & M. E. P. Seligman (Eds.), *Explanatory style.* Hillsdale, NJ: Erlbaum.

Abramson, L. Y., Seligman, M. E. P., & Teasdale, J. D. (1978). Learned helplessness in humans: Critique and reformulation. *Journal of Abnormal Psychology, 87,* 49–74.

Ackerman, S., Zuroff, D. C., & Moskowitz, D. S. (2000). Generativity in midlife and young adults: Links to agency, communion, and subjective well-being. *International Journal of Aging and Human Development, 50*(1), 17–41.

Acock, A. C., & Demo, D. H. (1994). *Family diversity and well-being.* Thousand Oaks, CA: Sage.

ACSF investigators (1992, December). AIDS and sexual behaviour in France. *Nature, 360,* 407–409.

Adams, G., Anderson, S. L., & Adonu, J. K. (2004). The cultural grounding of closeness and intimacy. In D. J. Mashek & A. Aron (Eds.), *Handbook of closeness and intimacy.* Mahwah, NJ: Erlbaum.

Adcock, C. J. (1965). Thematic Apperception Test. In O. K. Buros (Ed.), *Sixth Mental Measurements Yearbook.* Highland Park, NY: Gryphon Press.

Addis, M. E., & Mahalik, J. R. (2003). Men, masculinity, and the contexts of help seeking. *American Psychologist, 58*(1), 5-14.

Adler, A. (1917). *Study of organ inferiority and its psychical compensation.* New York: Nervous and Mental Diseases Publishing.

Adler, A. (1927). *Practice and theory of individual psychology.* New York: Harcourt, Brace & World.

Adler, N. E., & Snibbe, A. C. (2003). The role of psychological processes in explaining the gradient between socioeconomic status and health. *Current Directions in Psychological Science, 12*(4), 119–123.

Adorno, T. W., Frenkel-Brunswik, E., Levinson, D. J., & Sanford, B. W. (1950). *The authoritarian personality.* New York: Harper & Row.

Ahn, H., & Wampold, B. E. (2001). Where oh where are the specific ingredients? A meta–analysis of component studies in counseling and psychotherapy. *Journal of Counseling Psychology, 48,* 251–257.

Ahrons, C. R. (1999). Divorce: An unscheduled family transition. In B. Carter & M. McGoldrick (Eds.), *The expanded family life cycle: Individual, family, and social perspectives* (3rd ed.). Boston: Allyn & Bacon.

Ai, A. L., Santangelo, L. K., & Cascio, T. (2006). The traumatic impact of the September 11, 2001, terrorist attacks and the potential protection of optimism. *Journal of Interpersonal Violence, 21,* 689–700.

Aikins, D. E., & Craske, M. G. (2001). Cognitive theories of generalized anxiety disorder. *Psychiatric Clinics of North America, 24,* 57–74.

Ainsworth, M. D. S., Blehar, M. C., Waters, E., & Wall, S. (1978). *Patterns of attachment: A psychological study of the strange situation.* Hillsdale, NJ: Erlbaum.

Akgun, S., & Ciarrochi, J. (2003). Learned resourcefulness moderates the relationship between academic stress and academic performance. *Educational Psychology, 23*(3), 287-294.

Akimoto, S. A., & Sanbonmatsu, D. M. (1999). Differences in self-effacing behavior between European and Japanese Americans: Effect on competence evaluations. *Journal of Cross-Cultural Psychology, 30,* 159–177.

Akiskal, H. S. (2005). Mood disorders: Clinical features. In B. J. Sadock & V. A. Sadock (Eds.), *Kaplan & Sadock's comprehensive textbook of psychiatry.* Philadelphia: Lippincott Williams & Wilkins.

Alan Guttmacher Institute. (2006). *Plan B decision by FDA a victory for common sense.* Retrieved June 24, 2007 from http://guttmacher.org/media/inthenews/2006/08/27/index.html.

Albert, C. M., Ma, J., Rifai, N., Stampfer, M. J., & Ridker, P. M. (2002). Prospective study of C-reactive protein, homocysteine, and plasma lipid levels as predictors of sudden cardiac death. *Circulation, 105,* 2595–2599.

Alberti, R. E., & Emmons, M. L. (2001). *Your perfect right.* San Luis Obispo, CA: Impact Publishers.

Alexander, C. N., Robinson, P., Orme-Johnson, D. W., Schneider, R. H., et al. (1994). The effects of transcendental meditation compared with other methods of relaxation and meditation in reducing risk factors, morbidity, and mortality. *Homeostasis in Health & Disease, 35,* 243–263.

Alicke, M. D. (1985). Global self-evaluation as determined by the desirability and controllability of trait adjectives. *Journal of Personality and Social Psychology, 49*(6), 1621–1630.

Alicke, M. D., Smith, R. H., & Klotz, J. L. (1986). Judgments of personal attractiveness: The role of faces and bodies. *Personality and Social Psychology Bulletin, 12,* 381–389.

Allen, J. J. B., & Iacono, W. G. (2001). Assessing the validity of amnesia in dissociative identity disorder: A dilemma for the DSM and the courts. *Psychology, Public Policy, and Law, 7,* 311–344.

Allen, K., Blascovich, J., & Mendes, W. B. (2002). Cardiovascular reactivity in the presence of pets, friends, and spouses: The truth about cats and dogs. *Psychosomatic Medicine, 64*(5), 727–739.

Allen, K. R., & Demo, D. H. (1995). The families of lesbians and gay men: A new frontier in family research. *Journal of Marriage and the Family, 57,* 111–127.

Allgood, W. P., Risko, V. J., Alvarez, M. C., & Fairbanks, M. M. (2000). Factors that influence study. In R. F. Flippo & D. C. Caverly (Eds.), *Handbook of college reading and study strategy research.* Mahwah, NJ: Erlbaum.

Allison, D. B., Fontaine, K. R., Manson, J. E., Stevens, J., & VanItallie, T. B. (1999). Annual deaths attributable to obesity in the United States. *Journal of the American Medical Association, 282*(16), 1530–1538.

Allison, D. B., Heshka, S., Neale, M. C., Lykken, D. T., & Heymsfield, S. B. (1994). A genetic analysis of relative weight among 4,020 twin pairs, with an emphasis on sex effects. *Health Psychology, 13,* 362–365.

Alloy, L. B., & Abramson, L. Y. (1988). Depressive realism: Four theoretical perspectives. In L. B. Alloy (Ed.), *Cognitive processes in depression.* New York: Guilford Press.

Alloy, L. B., Abramson, L. Y., Whitehouse, W. G., Hogan, M. E., Tashman, N. A., Steinberg, D. L., Rose, D. T., & Donovan, P. (1999). Depressogenic cognitive styles: Predictive validity, information processing and personality characteristics, and developmental origins. *Behavioral Research and Therapy, 37,* 503–531.

Allport, G. W. (1937). *Personality: A psychological interpretation.* New York: Holt.

Allport, G. W. (1961). *Pattern and growth in personality.* New York: Holt, Rinehart & Winston.

Alonso, A., Alonso, S., & Piper, W. (2003). Group psychotherapy. In G. Stricker, & T. A. Widiger (Eds.), *Handbook of psychology: Vol. 8. Clinical psychology.* New York: Wiley.

Altemeyer, B. (1988a). *Enemies of freedom: Understanding right-wing authoritarianism.* San Francisco: Jossey-Bass.

Altemeyer, B. (1988b). The good soldier, marching in step: A psychological explanation of state terror. *Sciences, March/April,* 30–38.

Altemeyer, B. (1996). *The authoritarian specter.* Cambridge, MA: Harvard University Press.

Altemeyer, B. (1998). The other "authoritarian personality." *Advances in Experimental Social Psychology, 30,* 47–92.

Alvarez, J., & Hunt, M. (2005). Risk and resilience in canine search and rescue handlers after 9–11. *Journal of Traumatic Stress, 133,* 584–600.

Alzate, H. (1990). Vaginal erogeneity, "female ejaculation," and the "Granfenberg spot." *Archives of Sexual Behavior, 19,* 607–611.

Amato, P. R. (1999). Children of divorced parents as young adults. In E. M. Hetheringon (Ed.), *Coping with divorce, single parenting, and remarriage: A risk and resiliency perspective.* Mahwah, NJ: Erlbaum.

Amato, P. R. (2001). The consequences of divorce for adults and children. In R. M. Milardo (Ed.), *Understanding families into the new millennium: A decade in review.* Minneapolis, MN: National Council on Family Relations.

Amato, P. R. (2003). Reconciling divergent perspectives: Judith Wallerstein, quantitative family research, and children of divorce. *Family Relations: Interdisciplinary Journal of Applied Family Studies, 52*(4), 332–339.

Amato, P. R. (2004a). Divorce in social and historical context: Changing scientific perspectives on children and marital dissolution. In M. Coleman & L. H. Ganong (Eds.), *Handbook of contemporary families: Considering the past, contemplating the future.* Thousand Oaks, CA: Sage.

Amato, P. R. (2004b). Tension between institutional and individual views of marriage. *Journal of Marriage and Family, 66,* 959–965.

Amato, P. R. (2007). Studying marriage and commitment with survey data. In S. L. Hofferth & L. M. Casper (Eds.), *Handbook of measurement issues in family research.* Mahwah, NJ: Erlbaum.

Amato, P. R., & DeBoer, D. D. (2001). The transmission of marital instability across generations: Relationship skills or commitment to marriage? *Journal of Marriage and Family, 63,* 1038–1051.

Amato, P. R., Johnson, D. R., Booth, A., & Rogers, S. J. (2003). Continuity and change in marital quality between 1980 and 2000. *Journal of Marriage and Family, 65,* 1–22.

Amato, P. R., & Previti, D. (2003). People's reasons for divorcing: Gender, social class, the life course, and adjustment. *Journal of Family Issues, 24*(5), 602–626.

Amato, P. R., & Rogers, S. J. (1997). A longitudinal study of marital problems and subsequent divorce. *Journal of Marriage and the Family, 59,* 612–624.

Ambady, N., LaPlante, D., Nguyen, T., Rosenthal, R., Chaumeton, N., & Levinson W. (2002). Surgeon's tone of voice: A clue to malpractice history. *Surgery, 132,* 5–9.

American Association of Suicidology. (2007). *Understanding and helping the suicidal individual.* Retrieved April 12, 2007 from http://www.suicidology.org/associations/1045/files/Understanding.pdf.

American Council on Education. (1997). Many college graduates participate in training courses to improve their job skills. *Higher Education and National Affairs, 46*(19), 3.

American Foundation for Suicide Prevention. (2007). *When you fear someone may take their own life.* Retrieved April 12, 2007 from http://www.afsp.org/index.cfm?page_id=F2F25092-7E90-9BD4-C4658F1D2B5D19A0.

American Psychiatric Association. (1994). *Diagnostic and statistical manual of mental disorders* (4th ed.). Washington, DC: Author.

American Psychiatric Association Task Force on Electroconvulsive Therapy. (2001). *The practice of electroconvulsive therapy: Recommendations for treatment* (2nd ed.). Washington, DC: American Psychiatric Association.

Ames, S. C., Jones, G. N., Howe, J. T., & Brantley, P. J. (2001). A prospective study of the impact of stress on quality of life: An investigation of low-income individuals with hypertension. *Annals of Behavioral Medicine, 23*(2), 112–119.

Anderluh, M. B., Tchanturia, K., & Rabe-Hesketh. (2003). Childhood obsessive-compulsive personality traits in adult women with eating disorders: Defining a broader eating disorder phenotype. *American Journal of Psychiatry, 160,* 242–247.

Andersen, B. L., Golden-Kreutz, D. M., & DiLillo, V. (2001). Cancer. In A. Baum, T. A. Revenson, & J. E. Singer (Eds.), *Handbook of health psychology.* Mahwah, NJ: Erlbaum.

Andersen, B. L., Kiecolt-Glaser, J. K., & Glaser, R. (1994). A biobehavioral model of cancer stress and disease course. *American Psychologist, 49,* 389–404.

Anderson, A. E., & Yager, J. (2005). Eating disorders. In B. J. Sadock & V. A. Sadock (Eds.), *Kaplan & Sadock's comprehensive textbook of psychiatry.* Philadelphia: Lippincott Williams & Wilkins.

Anderson, B. L., Cacioppo, J. T., & Roberts, D. C. (1995). Delay in seeking a cancer diagnosis: Delay stages and psychological comparison processes. *British Journal of Social Psychology, 34,* 33–52.

Anderson, C., John, O. P., Keltner, D., & Kring, A. M. (2001). Who attains social status? Effects of personality and physical attractiveness in social groups. *Journal of Personality and Social Psychology, 81*(1), 116–132.

Anderson, C. A. (2004). An update on the effects of playing violent video games. *Journal of Adolescence, 27*(1), 113–122.

Anderson, C. A., Berkowitz, L., Donnerstein, E., Huesmann, L. R., Johnson, J. D., Linz, D., Malamuth, N. M., & Wartella, E. (2003). The influence of media violence on youth. *Psychological Science in the Public Interest, 4*(3), 81–110.

Anderson, C. A., & Bushman, B. J. (2001). Effects of violent video games on aggressive behavior, aggressive cognition, aggressive affect, physiological arousal, and prosocial behavior: A meta-analytic review of the scientific literature. *Psychological Science, 12,* 353–359.

Anderson, C. A., & Huesmann, L. R. (2003). Human aggression: A social-cognitive view. In M. A. Hogg & J. Cooper (Eds.), *The Sage handbook of social psychology.* Thousand Oaks, CA: Sage Publications.

Anderson, C. A., Miller, R. S., Riger, A. L., Dill, J. C., & Sedikides, C. (1994). Behavioral and characterological attributional styles as predictors of depression and loneliness: Review, refinement, and test. *Journal of Personality and Social Psychology, 66,* 549–558.

Anderson, D. A., & Hamilton, M. (2005). Gender role stereotyping of parents in children's picture books: The invisible father. *Sex Roles, 52*(3–4), 145–151.

Anderson, K. J. (1990). Arousal and the inverted-U hypothesis: A critique of Neiss's "reconceptualizing arousal." *Psychological Bulletin, 107,* 96–100.

Anderson, S. C., & Chen, S. (2002). The relational self: An interpersonal social-cognitive theory. *Psychological Review, 109,* 619–645.

Anderson, S. E., Dallal, G. E., & Must, A. (2003). Relative weight and race influence average age at menarche: Results from two nationally representative surveys of U.S. girls studied 25 years apart. *Pediatrics, 111,* 844–850.

Anderson, S. M., Reznik, I., & Manzella, L. M. (1996). Eliciting facial affect, motivation, and expectancies in transference: Significant-other representations in social relations. *Journal of Personality and Social Psychology, 71,* 1108–1129.

Anderson, V. L., Levinson, E. M., Barker, W., & Kiewra, K. R. (1999). The effects of meditation on teacher-perceived occupational stress, state and trait anxiety and burnout. *School Psychology Quarterly, 14,* 3–25.

Anderson-Fye, E. P., & Becker, A. E. (2004). Sociocultural aspects of eating disorders. In J. K. Thompson (Ed.), *Handbook of eating disorders and obesity.* New York: Wiley.

Andreasen, N. C. (1987). The diagnosis of schizophrenia. *Schizophrenia Bulletin, 13,* 9–22.

Andreasen, N. C. (1990). Positive and negative symptoms: Historical and conceptual aspects. In N. C. Andreasen (Ed.), *Modern problems of pharmacopsychiatry: Positive and negative symptoms and syndromes.* Basel: Karger.

Andresen, J. (2000). Meditation meets behavioural medicine: The story of experimental research on meditation. *Journal of Consciousness Studies, 7*(11–12), 17–73.

Angell, M. (2000). Is academic medicine for sale? *New England Journal of Medicine, 342,* 1516–1518.

Angell, M. (2004). *The truth about the drug companies: How they decieve us and what to do about it.* New York: Random House.

Ankey, C. D. (1992). Sex differences in relative brain size: The mismeasure of woman, too? *Intelligence, 16,* 329–336.

Antai-Otong, D. (2007). Pharmacologic management of posttraumatic stress disorder. *Perspectives in Psychiatric Care, 43*(1), 55–59.

Anthony, D. (1999). Pseudoscience and minority religions: An evaluation of the brainwashing theories of Jean-Marie Abgrall. *Social Justice Research, 12,* 421–456.

Antoniou, A. G. (2005). Emotional intelligence and transformational leadership. In A. G. Antoniou & C. L. Cooper (Eds.), *Research companion to organizational health psychology.* Northampton, MA: Edward Elgar.

Antonucci, T., & Akiyama, H. (1997). Concern with others at midlife: Care, comfort, or compromise? In M. E. Lachman & J. B. James (Eds.), *Multiple paths of midlife development.* Chicago: University of Chicago Press.

Antonuccio, D. O., Danton, W. G., & McClanahan, T. M. (2003). Psychology in the presciption era: Building a firewall between marketing and science. *American Psychologist, 58*(12), 1028–1043.

Antony, M. M., & McCabe, R. E. (2003). Anxiety disorders: Social and specific phobias. In A. Tasman, J. Kay, & J. A. Lieberman (Eds.), *Psychiatry.* New York: Wiley.

Antshel, K. M., & Remer, R. (2003). Social skills training in children with attention deficit hyperactivity disorder: A randomized-controlled clinical trial. *Journal of Clinical Child & Adolescent Psychology, 32*(1), 153-165.

Apperloo, M. J. A., Van Der Stege, J. G., Hoek, A., & Weijmar Schultz, W. C. M. (2003). In the mood for sex: The value of androgens. *Journal of Sex and Marital Therapy, 29*(2), 87–102.

Aquilino, W. S. (1997). From adolescent to young adult: A prospective study of parent-child relations during the transition to adulthood. *Journal of Marriage and the Family, 59,* 670–686.

Arbona, C. (2005). Promoting the career development and academic achievement of at-risk youth: College access programs. In S. D. Brown & R. W. Lent (Eds.), *Career development and counseling: Putting theory and research to work.* New York: Wiley.

Archer, J. (1996). Sex differences in social behavior: Are the social role and evolutionary explanations compatible? *American Psychologist, 51,* 909–917.

Archer, J. (2005). Are women or men the more aggressive sex? In S. Fein, G. R. Goethals, & M. J. Sandstrom (Eds.), *Gender and aggression: Interdisciplinary perspectives.* Mahwah, NJ: Erlbaum.

Arendell, T. (2000). Conceiving and investigating motherhood: The decade's scholarship. *Journal of Marriage and the Family, 62*(4), 1192–1207.

Argyle, M. (1987). *The psychology of happiness.* London: Metheun.

Argyle, M. (1999). Causes and correlates of happiness. In D. Kahneman, E. Diener, & N. Schwarz (Eds.), *Well-being: The foundations of hedonic psychology.* New York: Sage.

Argyle, M. (2001). *The psychology of happiness* (2nd ed.). New York: Routledge.

Argyle, M., & Henderson, M. (1984). The rules of friendship. *Journal of Social and Personal Relationships, 1,* 211–237.

Aribsib, J. M., Cohen, G., & Nail, P. R. (1999). Self-affirmation theory: An update and appraisal. In E. Harmon-Jones & J. S. Mills (Eds.), *Cognitive dissonance: Progress on a pivotal theory in social psychology.* Washington, DC: American Psychological Association.

Ariely, D., & Wertenbroch, K. (2002). Procrastination, deadlines, and performance: Self-control by precommitment. *Psychological Science, 13*(3), 219–224.

Aries, E. (1998). Gender differences in interaction: A reexamination. In D. J. Canary & K. Dindia (Eds.), *Sex differences and similarities in communication: Critical essays and empirical investigations of sex and gender in interaction.* Mahwah, NJ: Erlbaum.

Arkowitz, H., & Lilienfeld, S. O. (2006). Do self-help books help? *Scientific American Mind, 17*(5), 78–79.

Armbruster, B. B. (2000). Taking notes from lectures. In R. F. Flippo & D. C. Caverly (Eds.), *Handbook of college reading and study strategy research.* Mahwah, NJ: Erlbaum.

Armour, S. (2004, May 4). Some moms quit as offices scrap family-friendliness. *USA Today,* pp. 1A–2A.

Arndt, J., Cook, A., & Routledge, C. (2004). The blueprint of terror management: Understanding the cognitive architecture of psychological defense against the awareness of death. In J. Greenberg, S. L. Koole, & T. Pyszczynski (Eds.), *Handbook of experimental existential psychology.* New York: Guilford.

Arndt, J., Goldenberg, J. L., Greenberg, J., Pyszczynski, T., & Solomon, S. (2000). Death can be hazardous to your health: Adaptive and ironic consequences of defenses against the terror of death. In P. R. Duberstein & J. M. Masling (Eds.), *Psychodynamic perspectives on sickness and health.* Washington, DC: American Psychological Association.

Arnett, J. J. (1999). Adolescent storm and stress, reconsidered. *American Psychologist, 54*(5), 317–326.

Arnett, J. J. (2000). Emerging adulthood: A theory of development from the late teens through the twenties. *American Psychologist, 55,* 469–480.

Arnett, J. J. (2004). *Emerging adulthood: The winding road from the late teens through the twenties.* New York: Oxford University Press.

Arnkoff, D. B., & Glass, C. R. (1992). Cognitive therapy and psychotherapy. In D. K. Freedheim (Ed.), *History of psychotherapy: A century of change.* Washington, DC: American Psychological Association.

Arnold, K. D. (1995). *Lives of promise: What becomes of high school valedictorians.* San Francisco: Jossey-Bass.

Arnold, L. M. (2000). Psychocutaneous disorders. In B. J. Sadock & V. A. Sadock (Eds.), *Kaplan and Sadock's comprehensive textbook of psychiatry* (7th ed.). Philadelphia: Lippincott/Williams & Wilkins.

Aron, A. (1988). The matching hypothesis reconsidered again: Comment on Kalick and Hamilton. *Journal of Personality and Social Psychology, 54,* 441–446.

Aron, A., Fisher, H. E., & Strong, G. (2006). Romantic love. In A. L. Vangelisti & D. Perlman (Eds.), *The Cambridge handbook of personal relationships.* New York: Cambridge University Press.

Aron, A., Norman, C. C., Aron, E. N., McKenna, C., & Heyman, R. E. (2000). Couples' shared participation in novel and arousing activities and experienced relationship quality. *Journal of Personality and Social Psychology, 78,* 273–284.

Aron, A., & Westbay, L. (1996). Dimensions of the prototype of love. *Journal of Personality and Social Psychology, 70,* 535–551.

Aronson, E. (2001). *Nobody left to hate: Teaching compassion after Columbine.* New York: Owl Books.

Aronson, E., & Patnoe, S. (1997). *Cooperation in the classroom: The jigsaw method.* New York: Longman.

Aronson, J. M., Cohen, G., & Nail, P. R. (1999). Self-affirmation theory: An update and appraisal. In E. Harmon-Jones & J. S. Mills (Eds.), *Cognitive dissonance: Progress on a pivotal theory in social psychology* (pp. 127–147). Washington, DC: American Psychological Association.

Arrigo, J. M., & Pezdek, K. (1997). Lessons from the study of psychogenic amnesia. *Current Directions in Psychological Science, 6,* 148–152.

Asch, S. E. (1955). Opinions and social pressures. *Scientific American, 193*(5), 31–35.

Asch, S. E. (1956). Studies of independence and conformity: A minority of one against a unanimous majority. *Psychological Monographs, 70* (9, Whole No. 416).

Asher, S., & Paquette, J. A. (2003). Loneliness and peer relations in childhood. *Current Directions in Psychological Science, 12*(3), 75–78.

Ashmore, R. D. (1990). Sex, gender, and the individual. In L. A. Pervin (Ed.), *Handbook of personality.* New York: Guilford Press.

Ashok, J., & Parkin, A. J. (1996). Things that go bump in your life: Explaining the reminiscence bump in autobiographical memory. *Psychology and Aging, 11,* 85–91.

Ashton, M. C., Lee, K., Perugini, M. , Szarota, P., de Vries, R. E., Di Blas, L., Boies, K., & De Raad, B. (2004). A six-factor structure of personality-descriptive adjectives: Solutions from psycholexical studies in seven languages. *Journal of Personality and Social Psychology, 86*(2), 356–366.

Aspinwall, L. G., Richter, L., & Hoffman R. R., III. (2001). Understanding how optimism works: An examination of optimists' adaptive moderation of belief and behavior. In E. C. Chang (Ed.), *Optimism and pessimism: Implications for theory, research, and practice.* Washington, DC: American Psychological Association.

Aspinwall, L. G., & Staudinger, U. M. (2003). A psychology of human strengths: Some central issues of an emerging field. In L. G. Aspinwall & U. M. Staudinger (Eds.), *A psychology of human strengths: Fundamental questions and future directions for a positive psychology.* Washington, DC: American Psychological Association.

Aspinwall, L. G., & Taylor, S. E. (1993). Effects of social comparison direction, threat, and self-esteem on affect, evaluation, and expected success. *Journal of Personality and Social Psychology, 64,* 708–722.

Atchley, R. C. (1999). *Continuity and adaptation in aging: Creating positive experiences.* Baltimore: John Hopkins University Press.

Athenstaedt, U., Haas, E., & Schwab, S. (2004). Gender role self-concept and gender-typed communication behavior in mixed-sex and same-sex dyads. *Sex Roles, 50*(1/2), 37–52.

Atwood, J. D., & Gagnon, J. H. (1987). Masturbatory behavior in college youth. *Journal of Sex Education and Therapy, 13(2),* 35–42.

Aubé, J., & Koestner, R. (1995). Gender characteristics and relationship adjustment: Another look at similarity-complementarity hypotheses. *Journal of Personality, 63,* 879–904.

Aubin, S., & Heiman, J. R. (2004). Sexual dysfunction from a relationship perspective. In J. H. Harvey, A. Wenzel, & S. Sprecher (Eds.), *The handbook of sexuality in close relationships.* Mahwah, NJ: Lawrence Erlbaum.

Aubrey, J. S. (2006). Exposure to sexually objectifying media and body self-perceptions among college women: An examination of the selective exposure hypothesis and the role of moderating variables. *Sex Roles, 55*(3/4), 159–172.

Aubrey, J. S., & Harrison, K. (2004). The gender-role content of children's favorite television programs and its links to their gender-related perceptions. *Media Psychology, 6,* 11–146.

Auerbach, S. M., & Gramling, S. E. (1998). *Stress management psychological foundations.* Upper Saddle River, NJ: Prentice-Hall.

Aunola, K., Leskinen, E., Lerkkanen, M., & Nurmi, J. (2004). Developmental dynamics of math performance from preschool to grade 2. *Journal of Educational Psychology, 96,* 699–713.

Ayanian, J. Z., & Cleary, P. D. (1999). Perceived risks of heart disease and cancer among cigarette smokers. *Journal of the American Medical Association, 281*(11), 1019–1021.

Ayar, A. A. (2006). Road Rage: Recognizing a psychological disorder. *Journal of Psychiatry & Law, 34,* 123–143.

Ayres, J., Hopf, T., & Ayres, D. M. (1994). An examination of whether imaging ability enhances the effectiveness of an intervention designed to reduce speech anxiety. *Communication Education, 43*(3), 252–258.

Ayres, J. J. B. (1998). Fear conditioning and avoidance. In W. O'Donohue (Ed.), *Learning and behavior therapy.* Boston, MA: Allyn and Bacon.

Aziz, S., & Zickar, M. J. (2006). A cluster analysis investigation of workaholism as a syndrome. *Journal of Occupational Health Psychology, 11*(1), 52–62.

Babcock, J. C., Green, C. E., & Robie, C. (2004). Does batterers' treatment work? A meta-analytic review of domestic violence treatment. *Clinical Psychology Review, 23*(8), 1023–1053.

Badgett, M. V. L. (2003). Employment and sexual orientation: Disclosure and discrimination in the workplace. In L. D. Garnets & D. C. Kimmel (Eds.), *Psychological perspectives on lesbian, gay, and bisexual experiences* (2nd ed,). New York: Columbia University Press.

Bailey, J. M. (2003). Biological perspectives on sexual orientation. In L. D. Garnets & D. C. Kimmel (Eds.), *Psychological perspectives on lesbian, gay, and bisexual experiences* (2nd ed.). New York: Columbia University Press.

Bailey, J. M., & Dawood, K. (1998). Behavior genetics, sexual orientation, and the family. In C. J. Patterson & A. R. D'Augelli (Eds.), *Lesbian, gay and bisexual identities in families: Psychological perspectives.* New York: Oxford University Press.

Bailey, J. M., Dunne, M. P., & Martin, N. G. (2000). Genetic and environmental influences on sexual orientation and its correlates in an Australian twin sample. *Journal of Personality and Social Psychology, 78*(3), 524–536.

Bailey, J. M., Kim, P. Y., Hills, A. , & Linsenmeier, J. A. W. (1997). Butch, femme, or straight acting? Partner preferences of gay men and lesbians. *Journal of Personality and Social Psychology, 73*(5), 960–973.

Bailey, J. M., & Pillard, R. C. (1991). A genetic study of male sexual orientation. *Archives of General Psychiatry, 48,* 1089–1096.

Bailey, J. M., Pillard, R. C., Neale, M. C., & Agyei, Y. (1993). Heritable factors influence sexual orientation in women. *Archives of General Psychiatry, 50,* 217–223.

Bailey, J. M., Willerman, L., & Parks, C. (1991). A test of maternal stress theory of human male homosexuality. *Archives of Sexual Behavior, 20,* 277–294.

Baird, B. M., Le, K., & Lucas, R. E. (2006). On the nature of intraindividual personality variability: Reliability, validity, and associations with well-being. *Journal of Personality and Social Psychology, 90,* 521–527.

Baker, F., Ainsworth, S. R., Dye, J. T., Crammer, C., Thun, M. J., Hoffmann, D., Repace, J. L., Henningfield, J. E., Slade, J., Pinney, J., Shanks, T., Burns, D. M., Connolly, G. N., & Shopland, D. R. (2000). Health risks associated with cigar smoking. *Journal of the American Medical Association, 284,* 735–740.

Baldessarini, R. J. (2001). Drugs and the treatment of psychiatric disorders: Depression and the anxiety disorders. In J. G. Hardman & L. E. Limbird (Eds.), *Goodman & Gilman's The pharmacological basis of therapeutics.* New York: McGraw-Hill.

Ballenger, J. C. (2000). Benzodiazepine receptor agonists and antagonists. In B. J. Sadock & V. A. Sadock (Eds.), *Kaplan and Sadock's comprehensive textbook of psychiatry.* Philadelphia: Lippincott/Williams & Wilkins.

Balsam, K. F., Beauchaine, T. P., Mickey, R. M., & Rothblum, E. D. (2005). Mental health of lesbian, gay, bisexual, and heterosexual siblings: Effects of gender, sexual orientation, and family. *Journal of Abnormal Psychology, 114,* 471–476.

Baltes, M., & Carstensen, L. L. (2003). The process of successful aging: Selection, optimization, and compensation. In U. Staudinger, & U. Lindenberger (Eds.), *Understanding human development: Dialogues with lifespan psychology.* Dordrecht, Netherlands: Kupler.

Bancroft, J. (2002a). Biological factors in human sexuality. *The Journal of Sex Research, 39*(1), 15–21.

Bancroft, J. (2002b). The medicalization of female sexual dysfunction: The need for caution. *Archives of Sexual Behavior, 31*(5), 451–455.

Bandura, A. (1973). *Aggression: A social learning analysis.* Englewood Cliffs, NJ: Prentice-Hall.

Bandura, A. (1977). *Social learning theory.* Englewood Cliffs, NJ: Prentice-Hall.

Bandura, A. (1986). *Social foundations of thought and action: A social-cognitive theory.* Englewood Cliffs, NJ: Prentice-Hall.

Bandura, A. (1993). Perceived self-efficacy in cognitive development and functioning. *Educational Psychologist, 28,* 117–148.

Bandura, A. (1997). *Self-efficacy: The exercise of control.* New York: W. H. Freeman.

Bandura, A. (1999a). A sociocognitive analysis of substance abuse: An agentic perspective. *Psychological Science, 10*(3), 214–217.

Bandura, A. (1999b). Social cognitive theory of personality. In L. A. Pervin & O. P. John (Eds.), *Handbook of personality: Theory and research* (2nd ed.). New York: Guilford Press.

Bandura, A. (2000). Social cognitive theory: An agentic perspective. *Annual Review of Psychology, 52,* 1–26.

Bandura, A. (2004). Health promotion by social cognitive means. *Health Education & Behavior, 31*(2), 143–164.

Bank, B. J., & Hansford, S. L. (2000). Gender and friendship: Why are men's best same-sex friendships less intimate and supportive? *Personal Relationships, 7*(1), 63–78.

Banks, A., & Gartrell, N. K. (1995). Hormones and sexual orientation: A questionable link. *Journal of Homosexuality, 28,* 247–268.

Banse, R. (2004). Adult attachment and maritial satisfaction: Evidence for dyadic configuration effects. *Journal of Social and Personal Relationships, 21,* 273–282.

Banse, R., & Scherer, K. R. (1996). Acoustic profiles in vocal emotion expression. *Journal of Personality and Social Psychology, 70*(3), 614636.

Banyard, V. L., & Williams, L. M. (1999). Memories for child sexual abuse and mental health functioning: Findings on a sample of women and implications for future research. In L. M. Williams & V. L. Banyard (Eds.), *Trauma & memory.* Thousand Oaks, CA: Sage.

Banzato, C. E. M. (2004). Classification in psychiatry: The move towards ICD-11 and DSM-V. *Current Opinion in Psychiatry, 17,* 497–501.

Barber, B. K. (1994). Cultural, family, and personal contexts of parent-adolescent conflict. *Journal of Marriage and the Family, 56,* 375–386.

Barber, B. L., & Demo, D. H. (2006). The kids are alright (at least, most of them): Links between divorce and dissolution and child well-being. In M. A. Fine & J. H. Harvey (Eds.), *Handbook of divorce and relationship resolution.* Mahwah, NJ: Erlbaum.

Barch, D. M. (2003). Cognition in schizophrenia: Does working memory work? *Current Directions in Psychological Science, 12*(4), 146–150.

Barden, J., Rucker, D., & Petty, R. E. (2005). "Saying one thing and doing another": Examining the impact of event order on hypocrisy judgments of others. *Personality and Social Psychology Bulletin, 31,* 1463–1474.

Bargh, J. A. (1997). The automaticity of everyday life. In R. S. Wyer Jr.(Ed.), *Advances in social cognition* (Vol. 10). Mahwah, NJ: Erlbaum.

Bargh, J. A. (1999). The cognitive monster: The case against the controllability of automatic stereotype effects. In S. Chaiken & Y. Trope (Eds.), *Dual process theories in social psychology.* New York: Guilford.

Bargh, J. A., & McKenna, K. Y. A. (2004). The Internet and social life. *Annual Review of Psychology, 55,* 573–590.

Bargh, J. A., McKenna, K. Y. A., & Fitzsimons, G. M. (2002). Can you see the real me? Activation and expression of the "true self" on the Internet. *Journal of Social Issues, 58*(1), 33–48.

Barker, E. T., Williams, R. L., & Galambos, N. L. (2006). Daily spillover to and from binge eating in first-year university females. *Eating Disorders: The Journal of Treatment and Prevention, 14,* 229–242.

Barlett, D. L., & Steele, J. B. (1979). *Empire: The life, legend and madness of Howard Hughes.* New York: Norton.

Barlow, D. H., Pincus, D. B., Heinrichs, N., & Choate, M. L. (2003). Anxiety disorders. In G. Stricker & T. A. Widiger (Eds.), *Handbook of psychology: Vol. 8. Clinical psychology.* New York: Wiley.

Barnes, M. L., & Buss, D. M. (1985). Sex differences in the interpersonal behavior of married couples. *Journal of Personality and Social Psychology, 48,* 654–661.

Barnes, V. A., Treiber, F., & Davis, H. (2001). The impact of Transcendental Meditation on cardiovascular function at rest and during acute stress in adolescents with high norspeed in old age. *Current Directions in Psychological Science, 6,* 163–169.

Barnett, H. L., Keel, P. K., & Conoscenti, L. M. (2001). Body type preferences in Asian and Caucasian college students. *Sex Roles, 45* (11–12), 867–878.

Barnett, O. W., & LaViolette, A. D. (1993). *It could happen to anyone: Why battered women stay.* Thousand Oaks, CA: Sage.

Barnett, R. C. (2005). Dual-earner couples: Good/bad for her and/or him? In D. F. Halpern & S. E. Murphy (Eds.), *From work-family balance to work-family interaction: Changing the metaphor.* Mahwah, NJ: Erlbaum.

Barnett, R. C., & Hyde, J. S. (2001). Women, men, work, and family: An expansionist theory. *American Psychologist, 56*(10), 781–796.

Baron, R. A., Neuman, J. H., & Geddes, D. (1999). Social and personal determinants of workplace aggression: Evidence for the impact of perceived injustice and the Type A behavior pattern. *Aggressive Behavior, 25*(4), 261–296.

Baron, R. S. (2000). Arousal, capacity, and intense indoctrination. *Personality and Social Psychology Review, 4*(3), 238–254.

Barry-Walsh, J. (2005). Dissociative identity disorder. *Australian & New Zealand Journal of Psychiatry, 39*(1–2), 109–110.

Barsky, A. J. (1988). The paradox of health. *New England Journal of Medicine, 318,* 414–418.

Barsky, A. J. (2001). Somatosensory amplification and hypochondriasis. In V. Starcevic & D. R. Lipsitt (Eds.), *Hypochondriasis: Modern perspectives on an ancient malady.* New York: Oxford University Press.

Barsky, A. J., Coeytaux, R. R., Sarnie, M. K., & Cleary, P. D. (1993). Hypochondriacal patients' beliefs about good health. *American Journal of Psychiatry, 150,* 1085–1090.

Bartholomew, K. (1990). Avoidance of intimacy: An attachment perspective. *Journal of Social and Personal Relationships, 7,* 47–178.

Bartholomew, K., & Horowitz, L. M. (1991). Attachment styles among young adults: A test of a four-category model. *Journal of Personality and Social Psychology, 61,* 226–244.

Bartholow, B. D., Bushman, B. J., & Sestir, M. A. (2006). Chronic violent video game exposure and desensitization to violence: Behavioral and event-related brain potential data. *Journal of Experimental Social Psychology, 42,* 532–539.

Bartholow, B. D., & Heinze, A. (2006). Alcohol and aggression without consumption: Alcohol cues, aggressive thoughts, and hostile perception bias. *Psychological Science, 17,* 30–37.

Baruch, G. K. (1984). The psychological well-being of women in the middle years. In G. K. Baruch & J. Brooks-Gunn (Eds.), *Women in midlife.* New York: Plenum.

Basow, S. A. (1992). *Gender stereotypes and roles* (3rd ed.). Pacific Grove, CA: Brooks/Cole.

Basow, S. A., & Rubenfeld, K. (2003). "Troubles Talk": Effects of gender and gender-typing. *Sex Roles, 48*(3/4), 183–187.

Baum, A., Revenson, T. A., & Singer, J. E. E. (2001). *Handbook of health psychology.* Mahwah, NJ: Erlbaum.

Baumbusch, J. L. (2004). Unclaimed treasures: Older women's reflections on lifelong singlehood. *Journal of Women & Aging, 16,* 105–121.

Baumeister, R. F. (1984). Choking under pressure: Self-consciousness and paradoxical effects of incentives on skillful performance. *Journal of Personality and Social Psychology, 46,* 610–620.

Baumeister, R. F. (1989). The optimal margin of illusion. *Journal of Social and Clinical Psychology, 8,* 176–189.

Baumeister, R. F. (1990). Suicide as escape from self. *Psychological Review, 97,* 90–113.

Baumeister, R. F. (1995). Disputing the effects of championship pressures and home audiences. *Journal of Personality and Social Psychology, 68,* 644–648.

Baumeister, R. F. (1997). Esteem threat, self-regulatory breakdown, and emotional distress as factors in self-defeating behavior. *Review of General Psychology, 1,* 145–174.

Baumeister, R. F. (1998). The self. In D. T. Gilbert, S. T. Fiske, & G. Lindzey (Eds.), *The handbook of social psychology.* Boston: Mcgraw-Hill.

Baumeister, R. F. (1999). The nature and structure of the self: An overview. In R. F. Baumeister (Ed.), *The self in social psychology.* Ann Arbor, MI: Edwards Bros.

Baumeister, R. F., & Bratslavsky, E. (1999). Passion, intimacy, and time: Passionate love as a function of change in intimacy. *Personality and Social Psychology Review, 3*(1), 49–67.

Baumeister, R. F., Bratslavsky, E., Muraven, M., & Tice, D. M. (1998). Ego depletion: Is the active self a limited resource? *Journal of Personality and Social Psychology, 74*(5), 1252–1265.

Baumeister, R. F., Bushman, B. J., & Campbell, W. K. (2000). Self-esteem, narcissism, and aggression: Does violence result from low self-esteem or from threatened egotism? *Current Directions in Psychological Science, 9*(1), 26–29.

Baumeister, R. F., Campbell, J. D., Krueger, J. I., & Vohs, K. D. (2003). Does high self-esteem cause better performance, interpersonal success, happiness, or healthier lifestyles? *Psychological Science in the Public Interest, 4*(1), 1–44.

Baumeister, R. F., Gailliot, M., DeWall, M., & Oaten, M. (2006). Self-regulation and personality: How interventions increase regulatory success, and how depletion moderates the effects of traits on behavior. *Journal of Personality, 74,* 1773–1801.

Baumeister, R. F., & Leary, M. R. (1995). The need to belong: Desire for interpersonal attachments as a fundamental human motivation. *Psychological Bulletin, 117*(3), 497–529.

Baumeister, R. F., Muraven, M., & Tice, D. M. (2000). Ego depletion: A resource model of volition, self-regulation, and controlled processing. *Social Cognition, 18*(2), 130–150.

Baumeister, R. F., & Scher, S. J. (1988). Self-defeating behavior patterns among normal individuals: Review and analysis of common self-destructive tendencies. *Psychological Bulletin, 104*(1), 3–22.

Baumeister, R. F., Smart, L., & Boden, J. M. (1996). Relation of threatened egotism to violence and aggression: The dark side of high self-esteem. *Psychological Review,* 103, 5–33.

Baumeister, R. F., & Sommer, K. L. (1997). What do men want? Gender differences and two spheres of belongingness: Comment on Cross and Madson (1997). *Psychological Bulletin, 122*(1), 38–44.

Baumeister, R. F., & Steinhilber, A. (1984). Paradoxical effects of supportive audiences on performance under pressure: The home field disadvantage in sports championships. *Journal of Personality and Social Psychology, 47,* 85–93.

Baumeister, R. F., & Twenge, J. M. (2003). The social self. In T. Millon & M. J. Lerner (Eds.) *Handbook of psychology: Vol. 5. Personality and social psychology.* New York: Wiley.

Baumeister, R. F., & Vohs, K. D. (2003). Self-regulation and the executive function of the self. In M.R. Leary & J. P. Tangney (Eds.), *Handbook of Self and Identity.* New York: Guilford.

Baumrind, D. (1964). Some thoughts on the ethics of reading Milgram's "Behavioral study of obedience." *American Psychologist, 19,* 421–423.

Baumrind, D. (1967). Child care practices anteceding three patterns of preschool behavior. *Genetic Psychology Monographs, 75,* 43–88.

Baumrind, D. (1971). Current patterns of parental authority. *Developmental Psychology Monographs, 4* (1, Part 2).

Baumrind, D. (1978). Parental disciplinary patterns and social competence in children. *Youth and Society, 9,* 239–276.

Baumrind, D. (1989). The permanence of change and the impermanence of stability. *Human Development, 32,* 187–195.

Baumrind, D. (1991). The influence of parenting style on adolescent competence and sustance abuse. *Journal of Early Adolescence, 11*(1), 56–95.

Baumrind, D., Larzelere, R. E., & Cowan, P. A. (2002). Ordinary physical punishment: Is it harmful? Comment on Gershoff (2002). *Psychological Bulletin, 128*(4), 580–589.

Bavelas, J. B., Coates, L., & Johnson, T. (2002). Listener responses as a collaborative process: The role of gaze. *Journal of Communication, 52*(3), 566–580.

Baxter, L. A. (1988). A dialectical perspective on communication strategies in relationship development. In S. Duck (Ed.), *Handbook of personal relationships.* New York: Wiley.

Bay-Cheng, L. Y., Zucker, A. N., Stewart, A. J., & Pomerleau, C. S. (2002). Linking femininity, weight concern, and mental health among Latina, black, and white women. *Psychology of Women Quarterly, 26*(1), 36–45.

Bayer, R. (1987). *Homosexuality and American psychiatry: The politics of diagnosis.* Princeton, NJ: Princeton University Press.

Beall, A. E., Eagly, A. H., & Sternberg, R. J. (2004). Introduction. In A. H. Eagly, A. E. Beall, & R. J. Sternberg (Eds.), *The psychology of gender.* New York: Guilford Press.

Beaudry, M., Bousvert, J., Simard, M., Parent, C., & Blais, M. (2004). Communication: A key component to meeting the challenges of stepfamilies. *Journal of Divorce & Remarriage, 42,* 85–104.

Beck, A. T. (1976). *Cognitive therapy and the emotional disorders.* New York: International Universities Press.

Beck, A. T. (1987). Cognitive therapy. In J. K. Zeig (Ed.), *The evolution of psychotherapy.* New York: Brunner/Mazel.

Beck, A. T. (1991). Cognitive therapy: A 30-year retrospective. *American Psychologist, 46,* 368–375.

Beck, A. T. (1997). Cognitive therapy: Reflections. In J. K. Zeig (Ed.), *The evolution of psychotherapy: The third conference* . New York: Brunner/Mazel.

Beck, A. T., & Newman, C. F. (2005). Cognitive therapy. In B. J. Sadock & V. A. Sadock (Eds.), *Kaplan and Sadock's comprehensive textbook of psychiatry.* Philadelphia: Lippincott Williams & Wilkins.

Becker, E. (1997). *The denial of death.* New York: Free Press.

Beckham, J. C., Davidson, J. R. T., & March, J. S. (2003). Anxiety disorders: Traumatic stress disorders. In A. Tasman, J. Kay, & J. A. Lieberman (Eds.), *Psychiatry.* New York: Wiley.

Beer, J. M., Arnold, R. D., & Loehlin, J. C. (1998). Genetic and environmental influences on MMPI factor scale: Joint model fitting to twin and adoption data. *Journal of Personality and Social Psychology, 74,* 818–827.

Behar, R. (1991, May 6). The thriving cult of greed and power. *Time,* pp. 50–77.

Beilock, S. L., Kulp, C. A., Holt, L. E., & Carr, T. H. (2004). More on the fragility of performance: Choking under pressure in mathematical problem solving. *Journal of Experimental Psychology, 133,* 584–600.

Beisecker, A. E. (1990). Patient power in doctor-patient communication: What do we know? *Health Communication, 2,* 105–122.

Bekelman, J. E., Li, Y., & Gross, C. P. (2003). Scope and impact of financial conflicts of interests in biomedical research. *Journal of the American Medical Association, 289,* 454–465.

Belger, A., & Dichter, G. (2006). Structural and functional neuroanatomy. In J. A. Liberman, T. S. Stroup, & D. O. Perkins (Eds.), *Textbook of schizophrenia.* Washington, DC: American Psychiatric Publishing.

Bell, A. P., & Weinberg, M. S. (1978). *Homosexualities: A study of diversity among men and women.* New York: Simon & Schuster.

Bell, A. P., Weinberg, M. S., & Hammersmith, K. S. (1981). *Sexual preference—Its development in men and women.* Bloomington: Indiana University Press.

Bell, R. A. (1991). Gender, friendship network density, and loneliness. *Journal of Social Behavior and Personality,6,* 45–56.

Bellack, A. S., Mueser, K. T., & Gingerich, J. A. (2004). *Social skills training for schizophrenics: A step-by-step guide* (2nd ed.). New York: The Guilford Press.

Beller, M., & Gafni, N. (1996). The 1991 international assessment of educational progress in mathematics and sciences: The gender differences perspective. *Journal of Educational Psychology, 88,* 365–377.

Belluck, P. (2000, April 21). States declare war on divorce rates before any I do's. *New York Times,* p. A1.

Belmore, S. M. (1987). Determinants of attention during impression formation. *Journal of Experimental Psychology: Learning, Memory, and Cognition, 13,* 480–489.

Belsky, J. (1992). Consequences of child care for children's development: A deconstructionist view. In A. Booth (Ed.), *Child care in the 1990s.* Hillsdale, NJ: Erlbaum.

Belsky, J. (2002). Quantity counts: Amount of child care and children's socioemotional development. *Journal of Developmental & Behavioral Pediatrics, 23,* 167–170.

Belsky, J. (2006). Early child care and early child development: Major findings of the NICHD study of Early Child Care. *European Journal of Developmental Psychology, 3,* 95–110.

Belsky, J., & Kelly, J. (1994). *The transition to parenthood.* New York: Dell.

Bem, D. J. (2000). Exotic becomes erotic: Interpreting the biological correlates of sexual orientation. *Archives of Sexual Behavior, 29*(6), 531–548.

Bem, S. L. (1975, September). Androgyny vs. the tight little lives of fluffy women and chesty men. *Psychology Today,* pp. 58–62.

Bem, S. L. (1983). Gender schema theory and its implications for child development: Raising gender-aschematic children in a gender-schematic society. *Signs, 8,* 598–616.

Bem, S. L. (1985). Androgyny and gender schema theory: A conceptual and empirical integration. In T. B. Sonderegger (Ed.), *Nebraska symposium on motivation 1984: Psychology and gender* (Vol. 32). Lincoln: University of Nebraska Press.

Bem, S. L. (1993). The lenses of gender: *Transforming the debate on sexual inequality.* New Haven, CT: Yale University Press.

Benbow, C. P. (1988). Sex differences in mathematical reasoning ability in intellectually talented preadolescents: Their nature, effects, and possible causes. *Behavioral and Brain Sciences, 11,* 169–232.

Bender, R., Jockel, K. H., Trautner, C., Spraul, M., & Berger, M. (1999). Effect of age on excess mortality in obesity. *Journal of the American Medical Association, 281,* 1498–1504.

Bendis, D. (1997, May). A dose of moral adrenaline from Dr. Laura. *The Christian Century,* 476–478.

Benedict, R. (1934). *Patterns of culture.* Boston: Houghton Mifflin.

Benet, V., & Waller, N. G. (1995). The big seven factor model of personality description: Evidence for its cross-cultural generality in a Spanish sample. *Journal of Personality and Social Psychology, 69,* 701–718.

Ben-Ezra, M. (2004). Trauma in antiquity: 4000-year-old post-traumatic reactions? *Stress and Health, 20,* 121–125.

Benjamin, L. T., Jr., Cavell, T. A., & Shallenberger, W. R., III. (1984). Staying with initial answers on objective tests: Is it a myth? *Teaching of Psychology, 11,* 133–141.

Ben-Porath, Y. S. (2003). Assessing personality and psychopathology with self-report inventories. In J. R. Graham & J. A. Naglieri (Eds.), *Handbook of psychology: Vol. 10. Assessment psychology.* New York: Wiley.

Benson, H. (1975). *The relaxation response* (1st ed.). New York: Morrow.

Benson, H., & Klipper, M. Z. (1988). *The relaxation response* (2nd ed.). New York: Avon.

Berdahl, J. L., & Moore, C. (2006). Workplace harassment: Double jeopardy for minority women. *Journal of Applied Psychology, 91,* 426–436.

Berger, J. M., Levant, R., McMillan, K. K., Kelleher, W., & Sellers, A. (2005). Impact of gender role conflict, traditional masculinity ideology, alexithymia, and age on men's attitudes toward psychological help seeking. *Psychology of Men and Masculinity, 6*(1), 73–78.

Berkman, C. S., & Gurland, B. J. (1998). The relationship between ethnoracial group and functional level in older persons. *Ethnicity and Health, 3*(3), 175–188.

Berkowitz, L. (1989). Frustration-aggression hypothesis: Examination and reformulation. *Psychological Bulletin, 106,* 59–73.

Berkowitz, L. (1993). *Aggression: Its causes, consequences, and control.* New York: McGraw-Hill.

Berkowitz, R. I. (2003). Behavior therapies. In R. E. Hales & S. C. Yudofsky (Eds.), *Textbook of clinical psychiatry.* Washington, DC: American Psychiatric Publishing.

Berliner, K., Jacob, D., & Schwartzberg, N. (1999). The single adult and the family life cycle. In B. Carter & M. McGoldrick (Eds.), *The expanded family life cycle: Individual, family, and social perspectives* (3rd ed.). Boston: Allyn & Bacon.

Berliner, L., & Briere, J. (1999). Trauma, memory, and clinical practice. In L. M. Williams & V. L. Banyard (Eds.), *Trauma & memory.* Thousand Oaks, CA: Sage.

Berman, J. J., Murphy-Berman, V., & Pachauri, A. (1988). Sex differences in friendship patterns in India and in the United States. *Basic and Applied Social Psychology, 9,* 61–71.

Bernard, L. C., & Krupat, E. (1994). *Health psychology: Biopsychosocial factors in health and illness.* Fort Worth, TX: Harcourt Brace.

Berne, E. (1964). *Games people play.* New York: Grove Press.

Berne, P. H., & Savary, L. M. (1993). *Building self-esteem in children.* New York: Continuum.

Berry, D. S. (2000). Attractiveness, attraction, and sexual selection: Evolutionary perspectives on the form and function of physical attractiveness. In M. P. Zanna (Ed.), *Advances in experimental social psychology.* New York: Academic Press.

Berry, D. S., Pennebaker, J. W., Mueller, J. S., & Hiller, W. S. (1997). Linguistic bases of social perception. *Personality and Social Psychology Bulletin, 23*(5), 526–537.

Berry, J. W., & Ataca, B. (2000). Cultural factors. In G. Fink (Ed.), *Encyclopedia of stress* (Vol. 1). San Diego: Academic Press.

Berscheid, E., Dion, K., Walster, E., & Walster, G. (1971). Physical attractiveness and dating choice: A test of the matching hypothesis. *Journal of Personality and Social Psychology, 7,* 173–189.

Berscheid, E., & Reis, H. T. (1998). Attraction and close relationships. In D. T. Gilbert, S. T. Fiske, & G. Lindzey (Eds.), *The handbook of social psychology* (Vol. 2). Boston: McGraw-Hill.

Berscheid, E., Snyder, M., & Omoto, A. M. (1989). The relationship closeness inventory: Assessing the closeness of interpersonal relationships. *Journal of Personality and Social Psychology, 57,* 792–807.

Berscheid, E., & Walster, E. (1978). *Interpersonal attraction.* Reading, MA: Addison-Wesley.

Bertakis, K. D., Azari, R., Helms, J. L., Callahan, E. J., & Robbins, J. A. (2000). Gender differences in the utilization of health care services. *Journal of Family Practice, 49*(2), 147–152.

Berzon, B. (2004). *Permanent partners: Building gay and lesbian relationships that last.* New York: The Penguin Group.

Best, D. L., & Thomas, J. J. (2004). Cultural diversity and cross-cultural perspectives. In A. H. Eagly, A. E. Beall, & R. J. Sternberg (Eds.), *The psychology of gender.* New York: Guilford Press.

Betz, N. E. (1993). Women's career development. In F. L. Denmark & M. A. Paludi (Eds.), *Psychology of women: A handbook of issues and theories.* Westport, CT: Greenwood Press.

Betz, N. E. (2005). Women's career development. In S. D. Brown & R. W. Lent (Eds.), *Career development and counseling: Putting theory and research to work.* New York: Wiley.

Betz, N. E. (2006). Women's career development. In J. Worell & C. D. Goodheart (Eds.), *Handbook of girls' and women's psychological health.* New York: Oxford University Press.

Betz, N. E., & Klein, K. L. (1996). Relationships among measures of career self-efficacy, generalized self-efficacy, and global self-esteem. *Journal of Career Assessment, 4*(3), 285–298.

Beumont, P. J. V. (2002). Clinical presentation of anorexia nervosa and bulimia nervosa. In C. G. Fairburn & K. D. Brownell (Eds.), *Eating disorders and obesity: A comprehensive handbook.* New York: Guilford.

Beutler, L. E. (2000). David and Goliath: When empirical and clinical standards of practice meet. *American Psychologist, 55*(9), 997–1007.

Beutler, L. E. (2002). The dodo bird is extinct. *Clinical Psychology: Science & Practice, 9*(1), 30–34.

Beutler, L. E., Bongar, B., & Shurkin, J. N. (2001). *A consumers guide to psychotherapy.* New York: Oxford University Press.

Beutler, L. E., & Harwood, T. M. (2002). What is and can be attributed to the therapeutic relationship? *Journal of Contemporary Psychotherapy, 32*(1), 25–33.

Beutler, L. E., Malik, M., Alimohamed, S., Harwood, T. M., Talebi, H., Noble, S., & Wong, E. (2004). Therapist variables. In M. J. Lambert (Ed.), *Bergin and Garfield's handbook of psychotherapy and behavior change.* New York: Wiley.

Bhattachary, S., & Powell, J. H. (2001). Recreational use of 3,4-methylenedioxymethamphetamine (MDMA) or "ecstasy": Evidence for cognitive impairment. *Psychological Medicine, 31*(4), 647–658.

Bianchi, S. (2000). Maternal employment and time with children: Dramatic change or surprising continuity? *Demography, 37,* 401–414.

Bianchi, S., & Casper, L. M. (2000). American families. *Population Bulletin* (Vol. 55, Chap. 4). Washington, DC: Population Reference Bureau.

Bianchi, S., Milkie, M. A., Sayer, L. C., & Robinson, J. P. (2000). Is anyone doing the housework? Trends in the gender division of household labor. *Social Forces, 79*(1), 191–228.

Bianchi, S., Subaiya, L., & Kahn, J. R. (1999). The gender gap in the economic well-being of nonresident fathers and custodial mothers. *Demography, 36,* 195–203.

Biernat, M., & Billings, L. S. (2001). Standards, expectancies and social comparison. In A. Tesser & N. Schwarz (Eds.), *Blackwell handbook of social psychology: Intraindividual processes.* Malden, MA: Blackwell.

Biernat, M., & Kobrynowicz, D. (1997). Gender- and race-based standards of competence: Lower minimum standards but higher ability standards for devalued groups. *Journal of Personality and Social Psychology, 72*(3), 544–557.

Bishop, S. R. (2002). What do we really know about mindfulness-based stress reduction? *Psychosomatic Medicine, 64*(1), 71–83.

Björntorp, P. (2002). Definition and classification of obesity. In C. G. Fairburn & K. D. Brownell (Eds.), *Eating disorders and obesity: A comprehensive handbook.* New York: Guilford.

Black, D. W., & Andreasen, N. C. (1994). Schizophrenia, schizophreniform disorder, and delusional (paranoid) disorder. In R. E. Hales, S. C. Yudofsky, & J. A. Talbott (Eds.), *The American Psychiatric Press textbook of psychiatry* (2nd ed.). Washington, DC: American Psychiatric Press.

Blacker, D., & Tsuang, M. T. (1999). Classification and DSM-IV. In A. M. Nicholi (Ed.), *The Harvard guide to psychiatry.* Cambridge, MA: Harvard University Press.

Blacker, L. (1999). The launching phase of the life cycle. In B. Carter & M. McGoldrick (Eds.), *The expanded family life cycle: Individual, family, and social perspectives* (3rd ed.). Boston: Allyn & Bacon.

Blaine, B., & Crocker, J. (1993). Self-esteem and self-serving biases in reaction to positive and negative events: An integrative review. In R. F. Baumeister (Ed.), *Self-esteem: The puzzle of low self-regard.* New York : Plenum.

Blair, S. N., Cheng, Y., & Holder, J. S. (2001). Is physical activity or physical fitness more important in defining health benefits? *Medicine and Science in Sports and Exercise, 33,* S379–S399.

Blair-Loy, M., & DeHart, G. (2003). Family and careeer trajectories among African American female attorneys. *Journal of Family Issues, 24,* 908–933.

Blaisure, K. R., & Geasler, M. J. (2006). Educational interventions for separating and divorcing parents and their children. In M. A. Fine & J. H. Harvey (Eds.), *Handbook of divorce and relationship resolution.* Mahwah, NJ: Erlbaum.

Blakemore, J. E. O. (2003). Children's beliefs about violating gender norms: Boys shouldn't look like girls, and girls shouldn't act like boys. *Sex Roles, 48*(9/10), 411–419.

Blanchard, E. B., & Keefer, L. (2003). Irritable bowel syndrome. In A. M. Nezu, C. M. Nezu, & P. A. Geller (Eds.), *Handbook of psychology: Vol. 9. Health psychology.* New York: Wiley.

Blanco, C., Laje, G., Olfson, M., Marcus, S. C., & Pincus, H. A. (2002). Trends in the treatment of bipolar disorder by outpatient psychiatrists. *American Journal of Psychiatry, 159,* 1005–1010.

Blanton, H., Buunk, B. P., Gibbons, F. X., & Kuyper, H. (1999). When better-than-others compare upward: Choice of comparison and comparative evaluation as independent predictors of academic performance. *Journal of Personality and Social Psychology, 76,* 420–430.

Blass, T. (1999). The Milgram paradigm after 35 years: Some things we now know about obedience to authority. *Journal of Applied Social Psychology, 29*(5), 955–978.

Blazer, D. G. (2000). Mood disorders: Epidemiology. In B. J. Sadock & V. A. Sadock (Eds.), *Kaplan and Sadock's Comprehensive textbook of psychiatry* (7th ed., Vol. 1). Philadelphia: Lippincott/Williams & Wilkins.

Bleier, R. (1984). *Science and gender: A critique of biology and its theories on women.* New York: Pergamon Press.

Block, J. H. (1973). Conceptions of sex role: Some cross-cultural and longitudinal perspectives. *American Psychologist, 28,* 512–526.

Block, J., & Robbins, R. W. (1993). A longitudinal study of consistency and change in self-esteem from early adolescence to early adulthood. *Child Development, 64,* 909–923.

Bloodworth, R. C. (1987). Major problems associated with marijuana abuse. *Psychiatric Medicine, 3,* 173–184.

Bloom, P. N., McBride, C. M., & Pollack, K. I. (2006). Recruiting teen smokers in shopping malls to a smoking cessation program using the foot-in-the-door technique. *Journal of Applied Social Psychology, 36,* 1129–1134.

Bloomfield, H. (2000). *Making peace with your past: The six essential steps to enjoying a great future.* New York: HarperCollins.

Blum, R. W., Beuhring, T., Shew, M. L., Bearinger, L. H., Sieving, R. E., & Resnick, M. D. (2000). The effect of race/ethnicity, income, and family structure on adolescent risk behavior. *American Journal of Public Health, 90,* 1879–1884.

Blumstein, P., & Schwartz, P. (1983). *American couples: Money, work, sex.* New York: Morrow.

Boase, J., & Wellman, B. (2006). Personal relationships: On and off the Internet. In A. L. Vangelisti & D. Perlman (Eds.), *The Cambridge handbook of personal relationships.* New York: Cambridge University Press.

Bobek, B. L., & Robbins, S. B. (2005). Counseling for career transition: Career pathing, job loss, and re-entry. In S. D. Brown & R. W. Lent (Eds.), *Career development and counseling: Putting theory and research to work.* New York: Wiley.

Bock, P. K. (2000). Culture and personality revisited. *American Behavioral Scientist, 44,* 32–40.

Bodenhausen, G. V. (1988). Stereotypic biases in social decision making and memory: Testing process models of stereotype use. *Journal of Personality and Social Psychology, 55,* 726–737.

Bodenhausen. G. V., Macrae, C. N., & Hugenberg, K. (2003). Social cognition. In T. Millon, & M. J. Lerner (Eds.) *Handbook of psychology: Vol. 5. Personality and social psychology.* New York: Wiley.

Bodenheimer, T. (2000). Uneasy alliance: Clinical investigators and the pharmaceutical industry. *New England Journal of Medicine, 342,*1539–1544.

Boelen, P. A., van den Bout, J., & van den Hout, M. A. (2003). The role of negative interpretations of grief reactions in emotional problems after bereavement. *Journal of Behavior Therapy and Experimental Psychiatry, 34,* 225–238.

Boen, F., Vabeselaere, N., & Feys, J. (2002). Behavioral consequences of fluctuating group success: An Internet study of soccer-team fans. *Journal of Social Psychology, 142,* 769–781.

Boerner, K., Wortman, C. B., & Bonanno, G. A. (2005). Resilient or at risk? A 4-year study of older adults who initially showed high or low distress following conjugal loss. *Journal of Gerontology, 60B,* 67–73.

Bogg, T., & Roberts, B. W. (2004). Conscientiousness and health-related behaviors: A meta-analysis of the leading behavioral contributors to mortality. *Psychological Bulletin, 130,* 887–919.

Boles, D. B. (2005). A large-sample study of sex differences in functional cerebral lateralization. *Journal of Clinical and Experimental Neuropsychology, 27,* 759–768.

Bolger, N. (1990). Coping as a personality process: A prospective study. *Journal of Personality and Social Psychology, 59,* 525–537.

Bolger, N., & Amarel, D. (2007). Effects of social support visibility on adjustment to stress: Experimental evidence. *Journal of Personality and Social Psychology , 92,* 458–475.

Bolger, N., Zuckerman, A., & Kessler, R. C. (2000). Invisible support and adjustment to stress. *Journal of Personality and Social Psychology, 79,* 953–961.

Bolles, R. N. (2007). *The 2007 what color is your parachute? A practical manual for job-hunters and career-changers.* Berkeley, CA: Ten Speed Press.

Bonanno, G. A. (1998). The concept of "working through" loss: A critical evaluation of the cultural, historical, and empirical evidence. In A. Maercker, M. Schuetzwohl, & Z. Solomon (Eds.), *Posttraumatic stress disorder: Vulnerability and resilience in the lifespan.* Göttingen, Germany: Hogrefe and Huber.

Bonanno, G. A. (2004). Loss, trauma, and human resilience: Have we underestimated the human capacity to thrive after extremely aversive events? *American Psychologist, 59*(1), 20–28.

Bonanno, G. A., Galea, S., Bucciarelli, A., & Vlahov, D. (2006). Psychological resilience after disaster: New York City in the aftermath of the September 11th terrorist attack. *Psychological Science, 17*(3), 181–186.

Bonanno, G. A., & Kaltman, S. (1999). Toward an integrative perspective on bereavement. *Psychological Bulletin, 125*(6), 760–776.

Bonanno, G. A., & Keltner, D. (1997). Facial expressions of emotion and the course of bereavement. *Journal of Abnormal Psychology, 106,* 126–137.

Bonanno, G. A., Wortman, C. B., Lehman, D. R., Tweed, R. G., Haring, M., Sonnega, J., Carr, D., & Nesse, R. M. (2002). Resilience to loss and chronic grief: A prospective study from preloss to 18-months postloss. *Journal of Personality and Social Psychology, 83*(5), 1150–1164.

Bond, C. F., Jr., & DePaulo, B. M. (2006). Accuracy of deception judgments. *Personality and Social Psychology Review, 10*(3), 214–234.

Bond, J. T., Galinsky, E., Kim, S. S., & Brownfield, E. (2005). *The 2005 national study of employers.* New York: Families and Work Institute.

Bond, J. T., Thompson, C., Galinsky, E., & Prottas, D. (2003). *The 2002 national study of the changing workforce.* New York: Families and Work Institute.

Bond, R., & Smith, P. B. (1996). Culture and conformity: A meta-analysis of studies using Asch's (1952b, 1956) line judgment task. *Psychological Bulletin, 119*(1), 111–137.

Bonebright, C. A., Clay, D. L., & Ankenmann, R. D. (2000). The relationship of workaholism with work-life conflict, life satisfaction, and purpose in life. *Journal of Counseling Psychology, 47,* 469–477.

Boneva, B., Kraut, R., & Frohlich, D. (2001). Using e-mail for personal relationships: The difference gender makes. *American Behavioral Scientist, 45,* 530–549.

Bongar, B. (2007). The psychology of terrorism: Defining the need and describing the goals. In B. Bongar, L. M. Brown, L. E. Beutler, J. N. Breckenridge, & P. G. Zimbardo (Eds.), *Psychology of terrorism.* New York: Oxford University Press.

Booth, A., & Amato, P. R. (1994). Parental gender role nontraditionalism and offspring outcomes. *Journal of Marriage and the Family, 56,* 865–877.

Booth, A., & Amato, P. R. (2001). Parental predivorce relations and offspring postdivorce well-being. *Journal of Marriage and Family, 63,* 197–212.

Bordnick, P. S., Elkins, R. L., Orr, T. E., Walters, P., & Thyer, B. A. (2004). Evaluating the relative effectiveness of three aversion therapies designed to reduce craving among cocaine abusers. *Behavioral Interventions, 19*(1), 1–24.

Borman, W. C., Klimoski, R. J., & Ilgen, D. R. (2003). Stability and change in industrial and organizational psychology. In W. C. Borman, D. R. Ilgen, & R. J. Klimoski (Eds.), *Handbook of psychology: Vol. 12. Industrial and organizational psychology.* New York: Wiley.

Bornstein, R. F. (2003). Psychodynamic models of personality. In T. Millon & M. J. Lerner (Eds.), *Handbook of psychology, Vol. 5: Personality and social psychology.* New York: Wiley.

Borys, S., & Perlman, D. (1985). Gender differences in loneliness. *Personality and Social Psychology Bulletin, 11,* 63–74.

Bossé, R., Spiro, A., & Kressin, N. R. (1996). The psychology of retirement. In R. T. Woods (Ed.), *Handbook of the clinical psychology of aging.* Chicester, UK: Wiley.

Bost, K. K., Cox, M. J., Burchinal, M. R., & Payne, C. (2002). Structural and supporting changes in couples' family and friendships networks across the transition to parenthood. *Journal of Marriage and the Family, 64,* 517–31.

Bouchard, C. (2002). Genetic influences on body weight. In C. G. Fairburn & K. D. Brownell (Eds.), *Eating disorders and obesity: A comprehensive handbook.* New York: Guilford.

Boudreaux, E., Carmack, C. L., Scarinci, I. C., & Brantley, P. J. (1998). Predicting smoking stage of change among a sample of low socioeconomic status, primary care outpatients: Replication and extension using decisional balance and self-efficacy theories. *International Journal of Behavioral Medicine, 5*(2), 148–165.

Bower, G. H. (1970). Organizational factors in memory. *Cognitive Psychology, 1,* 18–46.

Bower, S. A., & Bower, G. H. (1991). *Asserting yourself: A practical guide for positive change* (2nd ed.). Reading, MA: Addison-Wesley.

Bower, S. A., & Bower, G. H. (2004). *Asserting yourself: A practical guide for positive change* (updated ed.). Cambridge, MA: Da Capo Press/Perseus.

Bowers, J. W., Metts, S. M., & Duncanson, W. T. (1985). Emotion and interpersonal communication. In M. L. Knapp & G. R. Miller (Eds.), *Handbook of interpersonal communication.* Newbury Park, CA: Sage.

Bowes-Sperry, L., & Tata, J. (1999). A multiperspective framework of sexual harassment. In G. N. Powell (Ed.), *Handbook of gender and work.* Thousand Oaks, CA: Sage.

Bowins, B. (2004). Psychological defense mechanisms: A new perspective. *American Journal of Psychoanalysis, 64*(1), 1–26.

Bowlby, J. (1980). *Attachment and loss: Vol. 3. Loss: Sadness and depression.* New York: Basic Books.

Bradbury, T. N., & Fincham, F. D. (1990). Attributions in marriage: Review and critique. *Psychological Bulletin, 107,* 3–33.

Bradford, J., & Ryan, C. (1987). *National lesbian health care survey: Mental health implications.* Washington, DC: National Lesbian and Gay Health Foundation.

Brady, K. T., Back, S. E., & Coffey, S. F. (2004). Substance abuse and posttraumatic stress disorder. *Current Directions in Psychological Science, 13*(5), 206–209.

Bramlett, M. D., & Mosher, W. D. (2001). *First marriage dissolution, divorce, and remarriage: United States. Advance data from vital and health statistics, No. 323.* Hyattsville, MD: National Center for Health Statistics.

Branaman, T. F., & Gallagher, S. N. (2005). Polygraph testing in sex offender treatment: A review of limitations. *American Journal of Forensic Psychology, 23*(1), 45–64.

Brannon, L. (2005). *Gender: Psychological perspectives.* Boston: Allyn & Bacon.

Brannon, R. (1976). The male sex role: Our culture's blueprint of manhood, and what it's done for us lately. In D. David & R. Brannon (Eds.), *The forty-nine percent majority.* Reading, MA: Addison-Wesley.

Branscombe, N. R., Wann, D. L., Noel, J. G., & Coleman, J. (1993). In-group or out-group extremity: Importance of the threatened social identity. *Personality and Social Psychology Bulletin, 19,* 381–388.

Breckenridge, J. N., & Zimbardo, P. G. (2007). The strategy of terrorism and the psychology of mass-mediated fear. In B. Bongar, L. M. Brown, L. E. Beutler, J. N. Breckenridge, & P. G. Zimbardo (Eds.), *Psychology of terrorism.* New York: Oxford University Press.

Bredt, B. M., Higuera-Alhino, D., Hebert, S. J., McCune, J. M., & Abrams, D. I. (2002). Short-term effects of cannabinoids on immune phenotype and function in HIV-1-infected patients. *Journal of Clinical Pharmacology, 42,* 90S–96S.

Breggin, P. R. (1991). *Toxic psychiatry.* New York: St. Martin's Press.

Brehm, J. W. (1956). Postdecision changes in the desirability of alternatives. *Journal of Abnormal and Social Psychology, 52,* 384–389.

Brehm, J. W. (1966). *A theory of psychological reactance.* New York: Academic Press.

Brehm, S. S. (1992). *Intimate relationships* (2nd ed.). New York: McGraw-Hill.

Brehm, S. S., & Brehm, J. W. (1981). *Psychological reactance.* New York: Academic Press.

Brehm, S. S., & Kassin, S. M. (1993). *Social psychology* (2nd ed.). Boston: Houghton Mifflin.

Brehm, S. S., Kassin, S. M., & Fein, S. (2002). *Social psychology.* Boston: Houghton Mifflin.

Brennan, K. A., Clark, C. L., & Shaver, P. R. (1998). Self-report measurement of adult attachment: An integrative overview. In J. A. Simpson & W. S. Rholes (Eds.), *Attachment theory and close relationships.* New York: Guilford Press.

Breslin, F. C., & Mustard, C. (2003). Factors influencing the impact of unemployment on mental health among young and older adults in a longitudinal, population-based survey. *Scandinavian Journal of Work, Environment & Health, 29*(1), 5–14.

Brett, J. M. (1980). The effect of job transfer on employees and their families. In C. L. Cooper & R. Payne (Eds.), *Current concerns in occupational stress.* New York: Wiley.

Brettle, R. P., & Leen, L. S. (1991). The natural history of HIV and AIDS in women. *AIDS, 5,* 1283–1292.

Brewer, M. B. (1999). The psychology of prejudice: Ingroup love or outgroup hate? *Journal of Social Issues, 55,* 429–444.

Brewer, M. B., & Brown, R. J. (1998). Inter-group relations. In D. T. Gilbert, S. T. Fiske, & G. Lindzey (Eds.), *The handbook of social psychology* (4th ed., Vol. 2). New York: McGraw-Hill.

Brewin, C. R. (2003). *Posttraumatic stress disorder: Malady or myth.* New Haven: Yale University Press.

Brewster, K. L., & Padavic, I. (2000). Change in gender-ideology, 1977–1996: The contributions of intracohort change and population turn-over. *Journal of Marriage and the Family, 62,* 477–487.

Brewster, M. P. (2002). Domestic violence, theories, research, and practice implications. In A. R. Roberts (Ed.), *Handbook of domestic violence intervention strategies: Policies, programs, and legal remedies.* New York: Oxford University Press.

Brickman, P., Coates, D., & Janoff-Bulman, R. (1978). Lottery winners and accident victims: Is happiness relative? *Journal of Personality and Social Psychology, 36,* 917–927.

Bridges, K. R., & Roig, M. (1997). Academic procrastination and irrational thinking: A re-examination with context controlled. *Personality & Individual Differences, 22,* 941–944.

Briere, J., & Conte, J. R. (1993). Self-reported amnesia for abuse in adults molested as children. *Journal of Traumatic Stress, 6,* 21–31.

Brissette, I., Scheier, M. F., & Carver, C. S. (2002). The role of optimism in social network development, coping, and psychological adjustment during a life transition. *Journal of Personality and Social Psychology, 82*(1), 102–111.

Briton, N. J., & Hall, J. A. (1995). Beliefs about female and male nonverbal communication. *Sex Roles, 32*(1-2), 79–90.

Britton, B. K., & Tesser, A. (1991). Effects of time-management practices on college grades. *Journal of Educational Psychology, 83,* 405–410.

Brody, J. E. (1997, November 4). Girls and puberty: The crisis years. *The New York Times,* p. C9.

Brody, L. R. (2000). The socialization of gender differences in emotional expression: Display rules, infant temperament, and differentiation. In A. H. Fischer (Ed.), *Gender and emotion: Social psychological perspectives.* Cambridge, UK: Cambridge University Press.

Brody, L. R., & Hall, J. A. (1993). Gender and emotion. In M. Lewis & J. M. Haviland (Eds.), *Handbook of emotions.* New York: Guilford Press.

Broidy, L. M., Nagin, D. S., Tremblay, R. E., Bates, J. E., Brame, B., Dodge, K. A., Fergusson, D., Horwood, J. L., Loeber, R., Laird, R., Lynam, D. R., Moffitt, T. E., Pettit, G. S., & Vitaro, F. (2003). Developmental trajectories of childhood disruptive behaviors and adolescent delinquency: A six-site, cross-national study. *Developmental Psychology, 39*(2), 222–245.

Bromage, B. K., & Mayer, R. E. (1986). Quantitative and qualitative effects of repetition on learning from technical text. *Journal of Educational Psychology, 78,* 271–278.

Bromley, M., & Blieszner, R. (1997). Planning for long-term care: Filial behavior and relationship quality of adult children with independent parents. *Family Relations,* 155–162.

Brooks-Gunn, J. (1991). Maturational timing variations in adolescent girls, antecedents of. In R. M. Lerner, A. C. Petersen, & J. Brooks-Gunn (Eds.), *Encyclopedia of adolescence.* New York: Garland.

Broomhall, H. S., & Winefield, A. H. (1990). A comparison of the affective well-being of young and middle-aged unemployed men matched for length of employment. *British Journal of Medical Psychology, 63,* 43–52.

Brown, A. S. (1999). New perspectives on the neurodevelopmental hypothesis of schizophrenia. *Psychiatric Annals, 29*(3), 128–130.

Brown, A. S., Begg, M. D., Gravenstein, S., Schaefer, C. A., Wyatt, R. J., Bresnahan, M., Babulas, V. P., & Susser, E. S. (2004). Serologic evidence of prenatal influenza in the etiology of schizophrenia. *Archives of General Psychiatry, 61*(8), 774–780.

Brown, D. (2007). *Career information, career counseling, and career development.* Boston: Allyn & Bacon.

Brown, D., Scheflin, A. W., & Whitfield, C. L. (1999). Recovered memories: The current weight of the evidence in science and in the courts. *Journal of Psychiatry & Law, 27,* 5–156.

Brown, E. J., Juster, H. R., Heimberg, R. G., & Winning, C. D. (1998). Stressful life events and personality styles: Relation to impairment and treatment outcome in patients with social phobia. *Journal of Anxiety Disorders, 12*(3), 233–251.

Brown, J. D., & McGill, K. L. (1989). The cost of good fortune: When positive life events produce negative health consequences. *Journal of Personality and Social Psychology, 57,* 1103–1110.

Brown, L. M., Bradley, M. M., & Lang, P. J. (2006). Affective reactions to pictures of ingroup and outgroup members. *Biological Psychology, 71,* 303–311.

Brown, R., Maras, P., Masser, B., Vivian J., & Hewstone, M. (2001). Life on the ocean wave: Testing some intergroup hypotheses in a naturalistic setting. *Group Processes and Intergroup Relations, 4*(2), 81–97.

Brown, R. D., Goldstein, E., & Bjorklund, D. F. (2000). The history and zeitgeist of the repressed–false memory debate: Scientific and sociological perspectives on suggestibility and childhood memory. In D. F. Bjorklund (Ed.), *False-memory creation in children and adults.* Mahwah, NJ: Erlbaum.

Brown, S., & Booth, A. (1996). Cohabitation versus marriage: A comparison of relationship quality. *Journal of Marriage and the Family,* 668–678.

Brown, S. L., Nesse, R. M., Vinokur, A. D., & Smith, D. M. (2003). Providing social support may be more beneficial than receiving it: Results from a prospective study of mortality. *Psychological Science, 14*(4), 320–327.

Brown, S. L., Sanchez, L. A., Nock, S. L., & Wright, J. D. (2006). Links between premarital cohabitation and subsequent marital quality, stability, and divorce: A comparison of covenant versus standard marriages. *Social Science Research, 35,* 454–470.

Brown, T. A. (2001). Generalized anxiety disorder and obsessive-compulsive disorder. In T. Millon, P. H. Blaney, & R. D. Davis (Eds.), *Oxford textbook of psychopathology.* New York: Oxford University Press.

Brown, T. T., & Dobs, A. S. (2002). Endocrine effects of marijuana. *Journal of Clinical Pharmacology, 42,* 97S–102S.

Browne, A. (1993a). Family violence and homelessness: The relevance of trauma histories in the lives of homeless women. *American Journal of Orthopsychiatry, 63,* 370–384.

Browne, A. (1993b). Violence against women by male partners: Prevalence, outcomes, and policy implications. *American Psychologist, 48,* 1077–1087.

Brownell, K. D. (1995). Exercise in the treatment of obesity. In K. D. Brownell & C. G. Fairburn (Eds.), *Eating disorders and obesity: A comprehensive handbook.* New York: Guilford Press.

Brownell, K. D., & Wadden, T. A. (2000). Obesity. In B. J. Sadock, & V. A. Sadock (Eds.), *Kaplan and Sadock's comprehensive textbook of psychiatry* (7th ed.). Philadelphia: Lippincott/Williams & Wilkins.

Brubaker, T. (1990). Families in later life: A burgeoning research area. *Journal of Marriage and the Family, 52,* 959–982.

Bruce, D., Dolan, A., & Phillips-Grant, K. (2000). On the transition from childhood amnesia to the recall of personal memories. *Psychological Science, 11,* 360–364.

Bruch, H. (1973). *Eating disorders: Obesity, anorexia nervosa and the person within.* New York: Basic Books.

Bruch, H. (1978). *The golden cage: The enigma of anorexia nervosa.* Cambridge, MA: Harvard University Press.

Bruckner-Gordon, F., Gangi, B. K., & Wallman, G. U. (1988). *Making therapy work: Your guide to choosing, using, and ending therapy.* New York: HarperCollins.

Brummett, B. H., Babyak, M. A., Mark, D. B., Clapp-Channing, N. E., Siegler, I. C., & Barefoot, J. C. (2004). Prospective study of perceived stress in cardiac patients. *Annual Behavioral Medicine, 27*(1), 22–30.

Brummett, B. H., Barefoot, J. C., Siegler, I. C., Clapp-Channing, N. E., Lytle, B. L., Bosworth, H. B., Williams, R. B., & Mark, D. B. (2001). Characteristics of socially isolated patients with coronary artery disease who are at elevated risk for mortality. *Psychosomatic Medicine, 63*(2), 267–272.

Bryan, A. D., Aiken, L. S., & West, S. G. (1999). The impact of males proposing condom use on perceptions of an initial sexual encounter. *Personality and Social Psychology Bulletin, 25*(3), 275–286.

Bryant, R. A., & Guthrie, R. M. (2005). Maladaptive appraisals as a risk factor for posttraumatic stress: A study of trainee firefighters. *Psychological Science, 16,* 749–752.

Bryant, S., & Rakowski, W. (1992). Predictors of mortality among elderly African-Americans. *Research on Aging, 14,* 50–67.

Bryden, M. P. (1988). An overview of the dichotic listening procedure and its relation to cerebral organization. In K. Hugdahl (Ed.), *Handbook of dichotic listening.* Chichester, England: Wiley.

Bryer, K. B. (1979). The Amish way of death: A study of family support systems. *American Psychologist, 34,* 255–261.

Buchanan, R. W., & Carpenter, W. T. (2005). Concept of schizophrenia. In B. J. Sadock & V. A. Sadock (Eds.), *Kaplan & Sadock's comprehensive textbook of psychiatry.* Philadelphia: Lippincott Williams & Wilkins.

Buckingham, J. T., & Alicke, M. D. (2002). The influence of individual versus aggregate social comparison and the presence of others on self–evaluations. *Journal of Personality and Social Psychology, 83*(5), 1117–1130.

Buckman, R. (2002). Communications and emotions: Skills and effort are key. *British Medical Journal, 325,* 672.

Buehlman, K. T., Gottman, J. M., & Katz, L. F. (1992). How a couple views their past predicts their future: Predicting divorce from an oral history interview. *Journal of Family Psychology, 5,* 295–318.

Bulcroft, R., & Teachman, J. (2004). Ambiguous constructions: Development of a childless or childfree life course. In M. Coleman, & L. H. Ganong (Eds.), *Handbook of contemporary families: Considering the past, contemplating the future.* Thousand Oaks, CA: Sage.

Bulik, C. M. (2004). Genetic and biological risk factors. In J. K. Thompson (Ed.), *Handbook of eating disorders and obesity.* New York: Wiley.

Bulik, C. M., Tozzi, F., Anderson, C., Mazzeo, S. E., Aggen, S., & Sullivan, P. F. (2003). The relation between eating disorders and components of perfectionism. *American Journal of Psychiatry, 160,* 366-368.

Bull, D. L. (1999). A verified case of recovered memories of sexual abuse. *American Journal of Psychotherapy, 53,* 221–224.

Bumpass, L. L., & Acquilino, W. S. (1995). *A social map of midlife: Family and work over the middle life course.* Madison: University of Wisconsin-Madison Center for Demography and Ecology.

Bumpass, L. L., & Lu, H. H. (2000). Trends in cohabitation and implications for children's family contexts in the United States. *Population Studies, 54,* 29–41.

Bumpass, L. L., Raley, R. K., & Sweet, J. (1995). The changing character of stepfamilies: Implications of cohabitation and nonmarital childbearing. *Demography, 32,* 425–436.

Burger, J. M. (1999). The foot-in-the-door compliance procedure: A multiple-process analysis and review. *Personality and Social Psychology Review, 3*(4), 303–325.

Burger, J. M. (2000). *Personality* (5th ed.). Belmont, CA: Wadsworth.

Burger, J. M. (2004). *Personality.* Belmont, CA: Wadsworth.

Burger, J. M., & Caldwell, D. F. (2003). The effects of monetary incentives and labelling on the foot-in-the-door effect: Evidence for a self-perception process. *Basic and Applied Social Psychology, 25*(3), 235–241.

Burger, J. M., & Cornelius, T. (2003). Raising the price of agreement: Public commitment and the low-ball compliance procedure. *Journal of Applied Social Psychology, 33*(5), 923–934.

Burger, J. M., & Guadagno, R. E. (2003). Self-concept clarity and the foot-in-the-door procedure. *Basic and Applied Social Psychology, 25*(1), 79–86.

Burgess, C., O'Donohoe, A., & Gill, M. (2000). Agony and ecstasy: A review of MDMA effects and toxicity. *European Psychiatry, 15*(5), 287–294.

Burgess, E. O. (2004). Sexuality in midlife and later life couples. In J. H. Harvey & S. Sprecher (Eds.), *The handbook of sexuality in close relationships.* Mahwah, NJ: Lawrence Erlbaum.

Burgoon, J. K. (1994). Nonverbal signals. In M. L. Knapp & G. R. Miller (Eds.), *Handbook of interpersonal communication* (2nd ed.). Thousand Oaks, CA: Sage.

Burhans, K. K., & Dweck, C. S. (1995). Helplessness in early childhood: The role of contingent worth. *Child Development, 66,* 1719–1738.

Burke, R. J. (2000). Workaholism in organizations: Psychological and physical well-being. *Stress Medicine, 16*(1), 11–16.

Burke, R. J. (2001). Workaholism in organizations: The role of organizational values. *Personnel Review, 30,* 637–645.

Burn, S. M., & Ward, A. Z. (2005). Men's conformity to traditional masculinity and relationship satisfaction. *Psychology of Men and Masculinity, 6,* 254–263.

Burns, A. B., Brown, J. S., Plant, E. A., Sachs-Ericsson, N., & Joiner, T. E. Jr. (2006). On the specific depressotypic nature of excessive reassurance-seeking. *Personality and Individual Differences, 40*(1), 135–145.

Bursztajn, H. J., & Brodsky, A. (2002). Managed healthcare complications, liability risk, and clinical remedies. *Primary Psychiatry, 9*(4), 37–41.

Buscaglia, L. (1982). *Living, loving and learning.* Thorofare, NJ: Charles B. Slack.

Bushman, B. J. (2002). Does venting anger feed or extinguish the flame? Catharsis, rumination, distraction, anger, and aggressive responding. *Personality and Social Psychology Bulletin, 28,* 724–731.

Bushman, B. J., & Anderson, C. A. (2001). Media violence and the American public. *American Psychologist, 56,* 477–489.

Bushman, B. J., & Baumeister, R. F. (1998). Threatened egotism, narcissism, self-esteem, and direct and displaced aggression: Does self-love or self-hate lead to violence? *Journal of Personality and Social Psychology, 75*(1), 219–229.

Bushman, B. J., & Baumeister, R. F. (2002). Does self-love or self-hate lead to violence? *Journal of Research in Personality, 36*(6), 543–545.

Bushman, B. J., Baumeister, R. F., & Stack, A. D. (1999). Catharsis, aggression, and persuasive influence: Self-fulfilling or self-defeating prophecies? *Journal of Personality and Social Psychology, 76,* 367–376.

Bushman, B. J., Bonacci, A. M., van Dijk, M., & Baumeister, R. F. (2003). Narcissism, sexual refusal, and aggression: Testing a narcissistic reactance model of sexual coercion. *Journal of Personality and Social Psychology, 84,* 1027–1040.

Buss, D. M. (1988). The evolution of human intrasexual competition: Tactics of mate attraction. *Journal of Personality and Social Psychology, 54,* 616–628.

Buss, D. M. (1989). Sex differences in human mate preferences: Evolutionary hypotheses tested in 37 cultures. *Behavioral and Brain Sciences, 12,* 1–14.

Buss, D. M. (1991). Evolutionary personality psychology. *Annual Review of Psychology, 42,* 459–491.

Buss, D. M. (1994). Mate preferences in 37 cultures. In W. J. Lonner & R. S. Malpass (Eds.), *Psychology and culture.* Boston: Allyn & Bacon.

Buss, D. M. (1995). Evolutionary psychology: A new paradigm for psychological science. *Psychological Inquiry, 6,* 1–30.

Buss, D. M. (1996). The evolutionary psychology of human social strategies. In E. T. Higgins & A. W. Kruglanski (Eds.), *Social psychology: Handbook of basic principles.* New York: Guilford Press.

Buss, D. M. (1997). Evolutionary foundation of personality. In R. Hogan, J. Johnson, & S. Briggs (Eds.), *Handbook of personality psychology.* San Diego: Academic Press.

Buss, D. M., & Kenrick, D. T. (1998). Evolutionary social psychology. In D. T. Gilbert, S. T. Fiske, & G. Lindzey (Eds.), *The handbook of social psychology.* New York: McGraw-Hill.

Buss, D. M., Shackelford, T. K., Kirkpatrick, L. A., & Larsen, R. J. (2001). A half century of mate preferences: The cultural evolution of values. *Journal of Marriage and Family, 63,* 491–503.

Bussey, K., & Bandura, A. (1984). Influence of gender constancy and social power on sex-linked modeling. *Journal of Personality and Social Psychology, 47,* 1292–1302.

Bussey, K., & Bandura, A. (1999). Social cognitive theory of gender development and differentiation. *Psychological Review, 106*(4), 676–713.

Bussey, K., & Bandura, A. (2004). Social cognitive theory of gender development and functioning. In A. H. Eagly, A. E. Beall, & R. J. Sternberg (Eds.), *The psychology of gender.* New York: Guilford Press.

Butler, E. A., Egloff, B., Wlhelm, F. H., Smith, N. C., Erickson, E. A., & Gross, J. J. (2003). The social consequences of expressive suppression. *Emotion, 3*(1), 48–67.

Butler, J. L., & Baumeister, R. F. (1998). The trouble with friendly faces: Skilled performance with a supportive audience. *Journal of Personality and Social Psychology, 75*(5), 1213–1230.

Butler, R., & Lewis, M. (1982). *Aging and mental health* (3rd ed.). St. Louis: Mosby.

Buunk, A. P., & Dijkstra, P. (2006). Temptation and threat: Extradyadic relations and jealousy. In A. L. Vangelisti & D. Perlman (Eds.), *The Cambridge handbook of personal relationships.* New York: Cambridge University Press.

Buxton, M. N., Arkel, Y., Lagos, J., Deposito, F., Lowenthal, H., & Simring, S. (1981). Stress and platelet aggregation in hemophiliac children and their family members. *Research Communications in Psychology, Psychiatry and Behavior, 6,* 21–48.

Byrm, R. J., & Lenton, R. L. (2001). *Love online: A report on digital dating in Canada.* Retrieved April 30, 2007 from http://www.nelson.com/nelson/harcourt/sociology/newsociety3e/loveonline.pdf.

Byrne, A., & Carr, D. (2005). Caught in the cultural lag: The stigma of singlehood. *Psychological Inquiry, 16,* 84–141.

Byrne, D. (1971). *The attraction paradigm.* New York: Academic Press.

Byrne, D., & Clore, G. L. (1970). A reinforcement model of evaluative responses. *Personality: An International Journal, 1*(2), 103–128.

Byrne, D., Clore, G. L., & Smeaton, G. (1986). The attraction hypothesis: Do similar attitudes affect anything? *Journal of Personality and Social Psychology, 51,* 1167–1170.

Byrne, R. (2006). *The secret.* New York: Atria Books.

Byrnes, J. P. (2001). *Cognitive development and learning in instructional contexts* (2nd ed.). Needham Heights, MA: Allyn & Bacon.

Byrnes, J. P., Miller, D. C., & Schafer, W. D. (1999). Gender differences in risk-taking: A meta-analysis. *Psychological Bulletin, 125,* 367–383.

Cabaj, R. P. (2006). Review of barebacking: Psychosocial and public health approaches. *Sexuality Research & Social Policy: A Journal of the NSRC, 3,* 91–93.

Cabral, G. A., & Petit, D. A. D. (1998). Drugs and immunity: Cannabinoids and their role in decreased resistance to infectious disease. *Journal of Neuroimmunology, 83,* 116–123.

Cachelin, F. M., Phinney, J. S., Schug, R. A., & Striegel-Moore, R. H. (2006). Acculturation and eating disorders in a Mexican American community sample. *Psychology of Women Quarterly, 30,* 340–347.

Cacioppo, J. T., Petty, R. E., Feinstein, J., & Jarvis, B. (1996). Individual differences in cognitive motivation: The life and times of people varying in need for cognition. *Psychological Bulletin, 119,* 197–253.

Calhoun, L. G., & Tedeschi, R. G. (2001). Posttraumatic growth: The positive lessons of loss. In R. A. Neimeyer (Ed.), *Meaning reconstruction and the experience of loss.* Washington, DC: American Psychological Association.

Call, V., Sprecher, S., & Schwartz, P. (1995). The incidence and frequency of marital sex in a national sample. *Journal of Marriage and the Family, 57,* 639–650.

Cameron, L., Leventhal, E. A., & Leventhal, H. (1993). Symptom representations and affect as determinants of care seeking in a community-dwelling, adult sample population. *Health Psychology, 12,* 171–179.

Cameron, N. (1963). *Personality development and psychopathology.* Boston: Houghton Mifflin.

Campbell, J. D. (1990). Self-esteem and clarity of the self-concept. *Journal of Personality and Social Psychology, 59,* 538–549.

Campbell, J. D., Assanand, S., & DiPaula, A. (2000). Structural features of the self-concept and adjustment. In A. Tesser, R. B. Felson, & J. M. Suls (Eds.), *Psychological perspectives on self and identity.* Washington, DC: American Psychological Association.

Campbell, J. D., & Lavallee, L. F. (1993). Who am I? The role of self-concept confusion in understanding the behavior of people with low self-esteem. In R. Baumeister (Ed.), *Self-esteem: The puzzle of low self-regard.* New York: Plenum.

Campbell, L. F., & Smith, T. P. (2003). Integrating self-help books into psychotherapy. *Journal of Clinical Psychology, 59*(2), 177–186.

Campbell, R. J. (2000). Managed care. In B. J. Sadock & V. A. Sadock (Eds.), *Kaplan and Sadock's comprehensive textbook of psychiatry* (7th ed., Vol. 2). Philadelphia: Lippincott/Williams & Wilkins.

Campbell, S., Marriott, M., Nahmias, C., & MacQueen, G. M. (2004). Lower hippocampal volume in patients suffering from depression: A meta-analysis. *American Journal of Psychiatry, 161,* 598–607.

Campbell, W. K., Sedikides, C., Reeder, G. D., & Elliot A. J. (2000). Among friends? An examination of friendship and the self-serving bias. *British Journal of Social Psychology, 39*(2), 229–239.

Canary, D. J., & Dainton, M. (2006). Maintaining relationships. In A. L. Vangelisti & D. Perlman (Eds.), *The Cambridge handbook of personal relationships.* New York: Cambridge University Press.

Canary, D. J., & Stafford, L. (2001). Equity in the preservation of personal relationships. In J. H. Harvey & A. E. Wenzel (Eds.), *Close romantic relationships: Maintenance and enhancement.* Mahwah, NJ: Erlbaum.

Canary, D. J., Stafford, L., & Semic, B. A. (2002). A panel study of the associations between maintenance strategies and relational characteristics. *Journal of Marriage and Family, 64,* 395–406.

Canetto, S. S., & Sakinofsky, I. (1998). The gender paradox in suicide. *Suicide and Life-Threatening Behavior, 28,* 1–23.

Cannon, W. B. (1932). *The wisdom of the body.* New York: Norton.

Carbonell, D. M., Reinherz, H. Z., & Beardslee, W. R. (2005). Adaptation and coping in childhood and adolescence for those at risk for depression in emerging adulthood. *Child and Adolescent Social Work Journal, 22,*, 395–416.

Carducci, B. J. (1998). *The psychology of personality: Viewpoints, research, and applications.* Pacific Grove, CA: Brooks/Cole Publishing.

Carducci, B. J. (1999). *The pocket guide to making successful small talk.* New Albany, IN: Pocket Guide Publications.

Carey, M. P., & Vanable, P. A. (2003). AIDS/HIV. In A. M. Nezu, C. M. Nezu, & P. A. Geller (Eds.), *Handbook of psychology: Vol. 9. Health psychology.* New York: Wiley.

Carli, L. L., & Bukatko, D. (2000). Gender, communication, and social influence: A developmental perspective. In T. Eckes & H. M. Trautner (Eds.), *The developmental social psychology of gender.* Mahwah, NJ: Erlbaum.

Carlson, R. (1997). *Don't sweat the small stuff . . . and it's all small stuff: Simple ways to keep the little things from taking over your life.* New York: Hyperion.

Carnelley, K. B., Wortman, C. B., Bolger, N., & Burke, C. T. (2006). The time course of grief reactions to spousal loss: Evidence from a national probability sample. *Journal of Personality and Social Psychology, 91,* 476–492.

Carney, S., & Geddes, J. (2003). Electroconvulsive therapy. *British Medical Journal, 326,* 1343–1344.

Caron, S. L. (2007). *Sex matters for college students: FAQs in human sexuality.* Upper Saddle River, NJ: Prentice Hall.

Carpenter, W. T. (1992). The negative symptom challenge. *Archives of General Psychiatry, 49,* 236–237.

Carpenter, W. T. (2002). From clinical trial to prescription. *Archives of General Psychology, 59,* 282–285.

Carr, V. J. (2000). Stress effects of earthquakes. In G. Fink (Ed.), *Encyclopedia of stress* (Vol. 2). San Diego: Academic Press.

Carrington, P. (1993). Modern forms of meditation. In P. M. Lehrer & R. L. Woolfolk (Eds.), *Principles and practice of stress management* (2nd ed.). New York: Guilford Press.

Carroll, J. L. (2007). *Sexuality now: Embracing diversity.* Belmont, CA: Wadsworth.

Carroll, J. L., Volk, K. D., & Hyde, J. S. (1985). Differences between males and females in motives for engaging in sexual intercourse. *Archives of Sexual Behavior, 14,* 131–139.

Carroll-Ghosh, T., Victor, B. S., & Bourgeois, J. A. (2003). Suicide. In R. E. Hales & S. C. Yudofsky (Eds.), *Textbook of clinical psychiatry.* Washington, DC: American Psychiatric Publishing.

Carson, S. H., & Langer, E. J. (2006). Mindfulness and self-acceptance. *Journal of Rational-Emotive & Cognitive Behavior Therapy, 24,* 29–43.

Carstensen, L. L. (1995). Evidence for a life-span theory of socioemotional selectivity. *Current Directions in Psychological Science, 4*(5), 151–156.

Carter, B. (1999). Becoming parents: The family with young children. In B. Carter & M. McGoldrick (Eds.), *The expanded family life cycle: Individual, family, and social perspectives* (3rd ed.). Boston: Allyn & Bacon.

Carter, B., & McGoldrick, M. (1988). Overview: The changing family life cycle—A framework for family therapy. In E. A. Carter & M. McGoldrick (Eds.), *The changing family life cycle: A framework for family therapy* (2nd ed.). New York: Gardner Press.

Carter, B., & McGoldrick, M. (1999). Overview: The expanded family life cycle: Individual, family, and social perspectives. In B. Carter & M. McGoldrick (Eds.), *The expanded family life cycle: Individual, family, and social perspectives* (3rd ed.). Boston: Allyn & Bacon.

Carter, R. T., Williams, B., Juby, H. L., & Buckley, T. R. (2005). Racial identity as mediator of the relationship between gender role and conflict and severity of psychological symptoms in Black, Latino, and Asian men. *Sex Roles, 53,* 473–486.

Carton, J. S., Kessler, E. A., & Pape, C. L. (1999). Nonverbal decoding skills and relationship well-being in adults. *Journal of Nonverbal Behavior, 23*(1), 91–100.

Carver, C. S. (2007). Stress, coping, and health. In H. S. Friedman & R. C. Silver (Eds.), *Foundations of health psychology.* New York: Oxford University Press.

Carver, C. S., Pozo, C., Harris, S. D., Noriega, V., Scheier, M. F., Robinson, D. S., Ketcham, A. S.,

Moffat, F. L., Jr., & Clark, K. C. (1993). How coping mediates the effect of optimism on distress: A study of women with early-stage breast cancer. *Journal of Personality and Social Psychology, 65,* 375–390.

Carver, C. S., & Scheier, M. F. (1994). Situational coping and coping dispositions in a stressful transaction. *Journal of Personality and Social Psychology, 66,* 184–195.

Carver, C. S., & Scheier, M. F. (2002). Optimism. In C. R. Snyder & S. J. Lopez (Eds.), *Handbook of positive psychology.* New York: Oxford University Press.

Carver, C. S., & Scheier, M. F. (2005). Optimism. In C. R. Snyder & S. J. Lopez (Eds.), *Foundations of health psychology.* New York: Oxford University Press.

Carver, C. S., Scheier, M. F., & Weintraub, J. K. (1989). Assessing coping strategies: A theoretically based approach. *Journal of Personality and Social Psychology, 56,* 267–283.

Cascio, W. F., & Young, C. E. (2005). Work-family balance: Does the market reward firms that respect it? In D. F. Halpern & S. E. Murphy (Eds.), *From work-family balance to work-family interaction: Changing the metaphor.* Mahwah, NJ: Erlbaum.

Cashdan, E. (1998). Smiles, speech, and body posture: How women and men display sociometric status and power. *Journal of Nonverbal Behavior, 22,* 209–228.

Caspersen, C. J., Bloemberg, B. P., Saris, W. H., Merritt, R. K., & Kromhout, D. (1991). The prevalance of selected physical activities and their relation with coronary heart disease risk factors in elderly men: The Zutphen study, 1985. *American Journal of Epidemiology, 133,* 1078–1092.

Caspi, A., Sugden, K., Moffitt, T. E., Taylor, A., Craig, I. W., Harrington, H., McClay, J., Mill, J., Martin, J., Braithwaite, A., & Poulton, R. (2003). Influence of life stress on depression: Moderation by a polymorphism in the 5-HTT gene. *Science, 301,* 386–389.

Cassata, D. (2005, October 16). The decline of American civilization, or at least its manners. *Statesboro Herald,* p. 9A.

Cassel, R. N. (2000). Third force psychology and person-centered theory: From ego-status to ego-ideal. *Psychology: A Journal of Human Behavior, 37*(3), 44–48.

Castonguay, L. G., Reid Jr., J. J., Halperin, G. S., & Goldfried, M. R. (2003). Psychotherapy integration. In G. Stricker, & T. A. Widiger (Eds.), *Handbook of psychology: Vol. 8. Clinical psychology.* New York: Wiley.

Catalyst. (2007). *Catalyst releases 2006 census of women in Fortune 500 corporate officer and board positions.* Retrieved on June 5, 2007 from http://www.catalyst.org/pressroom/press_releases/2006_Census_Release.pdf.

Catania, J. A., Binson, D., Dolcini, M. M., Moskowitz, J. T., & van der Straten, A. (2001). In A. Baum, T. A. Revenson, & J. E. Singer (Eds.), *Handbook of health psychology.* Mahwah, NJ: Erlbaum.

Cate, R. M., & Lloyd, S. A. (1988). Courtship. In S. Duck (Ed.), *Handbook of personal relationships.* New York: Wiley.

Cates, W., Jr. (2004). Reproductive tract infections. In R. A. Hatcher, J. Trussell, F. H. Stewart, A. L. Nelson, W. Cates Jr., F. Guest, & D. Kowal (Eds.), *Contraceptive technology.* New York: Ardent Media.

Cattell, R. B. (1950). *Personality: A systematic, theoretical and factual study.* New York: McGraw-Hill.

Cattell, R. B. (1966). *The scientific analysis of personality.* Chicago: Aldine.

Cattell, R. B. (1990). Advances in Cattellian personality theory. In L. A. Pervin (Ed.), *Handbook of personality: Theory and research.* New York: Guilford.

Cattell, R. B., Eber, H. W., & Tatsuoka, M. M. (1970). *Handbook of the Sixteen Personality Factor Questionnaire* (16PF). Champaign, IL: Institute for Personality and Ability Testing.

Catz, S. L., & Kelly, J. A. (2001). Living with HIV disease. In A. Baum, T. A. Revenson, & J. E. Singer (Eds.), *Handbook of health psychology.* Mahwah, NJ: Erlbaum.

Cavanaugh, J. C. (1993). *Adult development and aging* (2nd ed.). Pacific Grove, CA: Brooks/Cole.

Cavanaugh, J. C. (2000). Metamemory from a social-cognitive perspective. In D. Park & N. Schwarz (Eds.), *Cognitive aging: A primer.* Philadelphia: Psychology Press.

Cavanaugh, J. C., Feldman, J. M., & Hertzog, C. (1998). Meta-memory as social cognition: A reconceptualization of what memory questionnaires assess. *Review of General Psychology, 2,* 48–65.

Caverly, D. C., Orlando, V. P., & Mullen, J. L. (2000). Textbook study reading. In R. F. Flippo & D. C. Caverly (Eds.), *Handbook of college reading and study strategy research.* Mahwah, NJ: Erlbaum.

Centers for Disease Control. (2002). Youth risk behavior surveillance—United States, 2001. *Morbidity and Mortality Weekly Report,* Retrieved March 19, 2007 from http://www.cdc.gov/mmwr/preview/mmwrhtml/ss5104a1.htm#top.

Centers for Disease Control. (2006). Update: Trends in AIDS incidence-United States. *MMWR, 46*(37), 861–867.

Centers for Disease Control. (2007). *A glance at the HIV/AIDS epidemic.* Retrieved June 24, 2007 from http://www.cdc.gov/hiv/resources/factsheets/pdf/at=a-glance.pdf.

Cerletti, U., & Bini, L. (1938). Un nuevo metodo di shockterapie "L'elettro-shock." Boll. Acad. Med. *Roma, 64,* 136–138.

Cetron, M. J., & Davies, O. (2003, March–April). Trends shaping the future: Technological, workplace, management, and institutional trends. *The Futurist,* pp. 30–43.

Chamberlin, J. (2007, March). Too much information. *GradPSYCH,* pp. 14–16.

Chambless, D. L., & Hollon, S. D. (1998). Defining empirically supported therapies. *Journal of Consulting & Clinical Psychology, 66*(1), 7–18.

Chambless, D. L., & Ollendick, T. H. (2001). Empirically supported psychological interventions: Controversies and evidence. *Annual Review of Psychology, 52,* 685–716.

Chambliss, C. H. (2000). *Psychotherapy and managed care: Reconciling research and reality.* Boston, MA: Allyn & Bacon.

Chan, R. W., Brooks, R. C., Raboy, B., & Patterson, C. J. (1998). Division of labor among lesbian and heterosexual parents: Associations with children's adjustment. *Journal of Family Psychology, 12,* 402–419.

Chandler, M. J., Lalonde, C. E., Sokol, B. W., & Hallett, D. (2003). Personal persistence, identity development, and suicide: A study of native and non-native North American adolescents. *Monographs of the Society for Research in Child Development, 68*(2), viii–130.

Chang, E. C. (1996). Cultural differences in optimism, pessimism, and coping: Predictors of subsequent adjustment in Asian American and Caucasian American college students. *Journal of Counseling Psychology, 43,* 113–123.

Chang, R. Y., & Kelly, P. K. (1993). *Step-by-step problem solving: A practical guide to ensure problems get (and stay) solved.* Irvine, CA: Richard Chang Associates.

Chaplin, W. F., Phillips, J. B., Brown, J. D., Clanton, N. R., & Stein, J. L. (2000). Handshaking, gender, personality, and first impressions. *Journal of Personality and Social Psychology, 79*(1), 110–117.

Charles, S. T., & Carstensen, L. L. (1999). The role of time in the setting of social goals across the life span. In T. M. Hess & F. Blanchard-Fields (Eds.), *Social cognition and aging.* San Diego: Academic Press.

Charlesworth, W. R., & Dzur, C. (1987). Gender comparisons of preschoolers' behavior and resource utilization in group problem-solving. *Child Development, 58,* 191–200.

Chartrand, T., Pinckert, S., & Burger, J. M. (1999). When manipulation backfires: The effects of time delay and requester on the foot-in-the-door technique. *Journal of Applied Social Psychology, 29*(1), 211–221.

Chemers, M. M., Hu, L., & Garcia, B. F. (2001). Academic self-efficacy and first-year college student performance and adjustment. *Journal of Educational Psychology, 93*(1), 55–64.

Chen, Y. Y., Gilligan, S., & Coups, E. J. (2005). Hostility and perceived social support: Interactive effects on cardiovascular reactivity to laboratory stressors. *Annals of Behavioral Medicine, 29,* 37–43.

Cheng, C. (2001). Assessing coping flexibility in real-life and laboratory settings: A multimethod approach. *Journal of Personality and Social Psychology, 80*(5), 814–833.

Cheng, C. (2003). Cognitive and motivational processes underlying coping flexibility: A dual-process model. *Journal of Personality and Social Psychology, 84,* 425–438.

Cheng, C., & Cheung, M. W. L. (2005). Cognitive processes underlying coping flexibility: Differentiation and integration. *Journal of Personality, 73,* 859–886.

Cherlin, A. J. (1999). Going to extremes: Family structure, children's well-being, and social science. *Demography, 36,* 421–428.

Cherlin, A. J. (2004). The deinstitutionalization of American marriage. *Journal of Marriage and Family, 66,* 848–861.

Chia, R. C., Moore, J. L., Lam, K. N., Chuang, C. J., & Cheng, B. S. (1994). Cultural differences in gender role attitudes between Chinese and American students. *Sex Roles, 31,* 23–29.

Chiappelli, F., & Hodgson, D. (2000). Immune suppression. In G. Fink (Ed.), *Encyclopedia of stress* (Vol. 2). San Diego: Academic Press.

Chiappelli, F., & Liu, Q. N. (2000). Immunity. In G. Fink (Ed.), *Encyclopedia of stress.* San Diego: Academic Press.

Chick, J. (1998). Alcohol, health, and the heart: Implications for clinicians. *Alcohol and Alcoholism, 33*(6), 576–591.

Chick, K. A., Heilman-Houserk, R. A., & Hunter, M. W. (2002). The impact of child care on gender role development and gender stereotypes. *Early Childhood Education Journal, 29*(3), 149–154.

Chiriboga, D. A. (1987). Personality in later life. In P. Silverman (Ed.), *The elderly as modern pioneers.* Bloomington: Indiana University Press.

Chiriboga, D. A. (1989). Mental health at the midpoint: Crisis, challenge, or relief? In S. Hunter & M. Sundel (Eds.), *Mid-life myths: Issues, findings, and practical implications.* Thousand Oaks, CA: Sage.

Choi, I., Dalal, R., Kim-Prieto, C., & Park, H. (2003). Culture and judgment of causal relevance. *Journal of Personality and Social Psychology, 84*(1), 46-59.

Choi, I., Nisbett, R. E., & Norenzayan, A. (1999). Causal attribution across cultures: Variation and universality. *Psychological Bulletin, 125*(1), 47–63.

Choice, P., & Lamke, L. K. (1997). A conceptual approach to understanding abused women's stay/leave decisions. *Journal of Family Issues, 18,* 290–314.

Chopra, D. (1993). *Ageless body, timeless mind.* New York: Crown.

Chopra, S. S. (2003). Industry funding of clinical trials: Benefit of bias? *JAMA, 290,* 113–114.

Chou, C., Condron, L., & Belland, J. C. (2005). A review of the research on Internet addiction. *Educational Psychology Review, 17,* 363–388.

Choudhry, N. K., Stelfox, H. T., & Detsky, A. S. (2002). Relationships between authors of clinical practice guidelines and the pharmaceutical industry. *Journal of the American Medical Association, 287*(5), 612–617.

Christensen, A., & Jacobson, N. S. (2000). *Reconcilable differences.* New York: Guilford Press.

Christensen, A. J., & Johnson, J. A. (2002). Patient adherence with medical treatment regimens: An interactive approach. *Current Directions in Psychological Science, 11*(3), 94–97.

Christensen, P., & Kashy, D. (1998). Perceptions of and by lonely people in initial social interaction. *Personality and Social Psychology Bulletin, 24*(3), 322–329.

Christoph, R. T., Schoenfeld, G. A., & Tansky, J. W. (1998). Overcoming barriers to training utilizing technology: The influence of self-efficacy factors on multimedia-based training receptiveness. *Human Resource Development Quarterly, 9*(1), 25–38.

Christophe, V., & Rime, B. (1997). Exposure to the social sharing of emotion: Emotional impact, listener responses and secondary social sharing. *European Journal of Social Psychology, 27,* 37–54.

Christopher, F. S., & Sprecher, S. (2000). Sexuality in marriage, dating, and other relationships: A decade review. *Journal of Marriage and the Family, 62,* 999–1017.

Chua, H. F., Leu, J., & Nisbett, R. E. (2005). Culture and diverging views of social events. *Personality and Social Psychology Bulletin, 31,* 925–934.

Chun, C., Moos, R. H., & Cronkite, R. C. (2006). Culture: A fundamental context for the stress and coping paradigm. In P. T. P. Wong & L. C. J. Wong (Eds.), *Handbook of multicultural perspectives on stress and coping.* New York: Springer.

Cialdini, R. B. (2001). *Influence: Science and practice* (4th ed.). Boston: Allyn & Bacon.

Cialdini, R. B. (2007). *Influence: Science and practice.* New York: HarperCollins.

Cialdini, R. B., Borden, R. J., Thorne, A., Walker, M. R., Freeman, S., & Sloan, L. R. (1976). Basking in reflected glory: Three (football) field studies. *Journal of Personality and Social Psychology, 34,* 366–375.

Cialdini, R. B., & Goldstein, N. J. (2004). Social Influence: Compliance and comformity. *Annual Review of Psychology, 55,* 591–621.

Ciarrochi, J., Dean, F. P., & Anderson, S. (2002). Emotional intelligence moderates the relationship between stress and mental health. *Personality & Individual Differences, 32,* 197–209.

Cicirelli, V. G. (1999). Personality and demographic factors in older adults' fear of death. *Gerontologist, 39*(5), 569–579.

Cicirelli, V. G. (2002). *Older adults' views on death.* New York: Springer.

Claar, R. L., & Blumenthal, J. A. (2003). The value of stress-management interventions in life-threatening medical conditions. *Current Directions in Psychological Science, 12*(4), 133–137.

Clark, D. (2005). *Loving someone gay.* Berkeley, CA: Celestial Arts.

Clark, M. S., & Grote, N. K. (2003). Close relationships. In T. Millon & M. J. Lerner (Eds.) *Handbook of psychology: Vol. 5. Personality and social psychology.* New York: Wiley.

Clark, M. S., & Mills, J. (1993). The difference between communal and exchange relationships: What it is and is not. *Journal of Personality and Social Psychology Bulletin, 19,* 684–691.

Clarke-Stewart, K. A., & Bailey, B. L. (1989). Adjusting to divorce: Why do men have it easier? *Journal of Divorce, 13,* 75–94.

Cleek, M. G., & Pearson, T. A. (1985). Perceived causes of divorce: An analysis of interrelationships. *Journal of Marriage and the Family, 47,* 179–183.

Clements, A. M., Rimrodt, S. L., Abel, J. R., Blankner, J. G., Mostofsky, S. H., Pekar, J. J., et al. (2006). Sex differences in cerebral laterality of language and visuospatial processing. *Brain and Language, 98*(2), 150–158.

Clements, M. L., Stanley, S. M., & Markman, H. J. (2004). Before they said "I do": Discriminating among marital outcomes over 13 years. *Journal of Marriage and Family, 66,* 613–626.

Cloitre, M., Morin, N. A., & Linares, O. (2004, January-February). Children's resilience in the face of trauma. *The New York University Child Study Letter.*

Clow, A. (2001). The physiology of stress. In F. Jones & J. Bright (Eds.), *Stress: Myth, theory and research.* Harlow, England: Pearson Education.

Coates, T. J., & Collins, C. (1998). Preventing HIV infection. *Scientific American, 279*(1), 96–97.

Cochran, S. D. (2001). Emerging issues in research on lesbians' and gay men's mental health: Does sexual orientation really matter? *American Psychologist, 56,* 931–947.

Cohan, C. L., & Kleinbaum, S. (2002). Toward a greater understanding of the cohabitation effect: Premarital cohabitation and marital communication. *Journal of Marriage and Family, 64,* 180–192.

Cohen, C. E. (1981). Person categories and social perception: Testing some boundaries of the processing effects of prior knowledge. *Journal of Personality and Social Psychology, 40,* 441–452.

Cohen, D. (1997). A critique of the use of neuroleptic drugs in psychiatry. In S. Fisher & R. P. Greenberg (Eds.), *From placebo to panacea: Putting psychiatric drugs to the test.* New York: Wiley.

Cohen, D., & McCubbin, M. (1990). The political economy of tardive dyskinesia: Asymmetries in power and responsibility. *The Journal of Mind and Behavior, 11,* 465–488.

Cohen, D. B. (1999). *Stranger in the nest: Do parents really shape their child's personality, intelligence, or character?* New York: Wiley.

Cohen, F. (1979). Personality, stress and the development of physical illness. In G. C. Stone, F. Cohen, N. E. Adler, & associates (Eds.), *Health psychology—A handbook.* San Francisco: Jossey-Bass.

Cohen, F., Solomon, S., Maxfield, M., Pyszczynski, T., & Greenberg, J. (2004). Fatal attraction: The effects of mortality salience on evaluations of charismatic, task-oriented, and relationship-oriented leaders. *Psychological Science, 15,* 846–851.

Cohen, M. J. M., Kunkel, E. S., & Levenson, J. L. (1998). Associations between psychosocial stress and malignancy. In J. R. Hubbard & E. A. Workman (Eds.), *Handbook of stress medicine: An organ system approach.* Boca Raton: CRC Press.

Cohen, S., Doyle, W. J., Turner, R., Alper, C. M., & Skoner, D. P. (2003). Sociability and susceptibility to the common cold. *Psychological Science, 14*(5), 389–395.

Cohen, S., Evans, G. W., Krantz, D. S., & Stokols, D. (1980). Physiological, motivational, and cognitive effects of aircraft noise on children: Moving from the laboratory to the field. *American Psychologist, 35,* 231–243.

Cohen, S., Hamrick, N., Rodriguez, M. S., Feldman, P. J., Rabin, B. S., & Manuck, S. B. (2002). Reactivity and vulnerability to stress-associated risk for upper respiratory illness. *Psychosomatic Illness, 64,* 302–310.

Cohen, S., Kessler, R. C., & Gordon, L. U. (1995). Strategies for measuring stress in studies of psychiatric and physical disorders. In S. Cohen, R. C. Kessler, & L. U. Gordon (Eds.), *Measuring stress: A guide for health and social scientists.* New York: Oxford University Press.

Cohen, S., Lichtenstein, E., Prochaska, J. O., Rossi, J. S., Gritz, E. R., Carr, C. R., Orleans, C. T., Schoenbach, V. J., Biener, L., Abrams, D., DiClemente, C., Curry, S., Marlatt, G. A., Cummings, K. M., Emont, S. L., Giovino, A., & Ossip-Klein, D. (1989). Debunking myths about self-quitting: Evidence from 10 prospective studies of persons who attempt to quit smoking by themselves. *American Psychologist, 44,* 1355–1365.

Cohen, S., Tyrrell, D. A., & Smith, A. P. (1993). Negative life events, perceived stress, negative affect, and susceptibility to the common cold. *Journal of Personality and Social Psychology, 64,* 131–140.

Cohen-Bendahan, C. C. C., van de Beek, C., & Berenbaum, S. A. (2005). Prenatal sex hormone effects on child and adult sex-typed behavior: Methods and findings. *Neuroscience & Biobehavioral Reviews, 29,* 353–384.

Colder, C. R. (2001). Life stress, physiological and subjective indexes of negative emotionality and coping reasons for drinking: Is there evidence for a self-medication model of alcohol use? *Psychology of Addictive Behaviors, 15*(3), 237–245.

Cole, S. W., Kemeny, M. E., Taylor, S. E., & Visscher, B. R. (1996). Elevated physical health risk among gay men who conceal their homosexual identity. *Health Psychology, 15,* 243–251.

Coles, M. E., Schofield, C. A., & Pietrefesa, A. S. (2006). Behavioral inhibition and obsessive-compulsive disorder. *Journal of Anxiety Disorders, 20,* 1118–1132.

Collaer, M. L., & Hines, M. (1995). Human behavioral sex differences: A role for gonadal hormones during early development? *Psychological Bulletin, 118,* 55–107.

College Entrance Examination Board. (2004). *Writing: a Ticket to Work. . . . Or a Ticket Out: A Survey of Business Leaders.* Retrieved September 4, 2007 from http://www.writingcommission.org/prod_downloads/writingcom/writing-ticket-to-work.pdf

Colley, A., & Todd, Z. (2002). Gender-linked differences in the style and content of e-mails to friends. *Journal of Language and Social Psychology, 21*(4), 380–392.

Colligan, T. W., & Higgins, E. M. (2005). Workplace stress: Etiology and consequences. *Journal of Workplace Behavioral Health, 21*(2), 89–97.

Collins, N. L., & Feeney, B. C. (2004). An attachment theory perspective on closeness and intimacy. In D. J. Mashek & A. Aron (Eds.), *Handbook of closeness and intimacy.* Mahwah, NJ: Erlbaum.

Collins, N. L., & Miller, L. C. (1994). Self-disclosure and liking: A meta-analytic review. *Psychological Bulletin, 116,* 457–475.

Collins, R. L. (1996). For better or worse: The impact of upward social comparison on self-evaluations. *Psychological Bulletin, 119*(1), 51–69.

Collins, W. A., & Madsen, S. D. (2006). Personal relationships in adolescence and early adulthood. In A. L. Vangelisti & D. Perlman (Eds.), *The Cambridge handbook of personal relationships.* New York: Cambridge University Press.

Collins, W. A., Maccoby, E. E., Steinberg, L., Hetherington, E. M., & Bornstein, M. H. (2000). Contemporary research in parenting: The case for nature and nurture. *American Psychologist, 55,* 218–232.

Coltrane, S. (2001). Marketing the marriage "solution": Misplaced simplicity in the politics of fatherhood. *Sociological Perspectives, 44*(4), 387–418.

Coltrane, S., & Adams, M. (2003). The social construction of the divorce "problem": Morality, child victims, and the politics of gender. *Family Relations: Interdisciplinary Journal of Applied Family Studies, 52*(4), 363–372.

Colvin, C. R., & Block, J. (1994). Do positive illusions foster mental health? An examination of the Taylor and Brown formulation. *Psychological Bulletin, 116,* 3–20.

Colvin, C. R., Block, J., & Funder, D. C. (1995). Overly positive self-evaluations and personality: Negative implications for mental health. *Journal of Personality and Social Psychology, 68,* 1152–1162.

Comas-Diaz, L. (1987). Feminist therapy with mainland Puerto Rican women. *Psychology of Women Quarterly, 11,* 461–474.

Condoms—extra protection. (2005, February). *Consumer Reports,* pp. 34–38.

Condon, J. W., & Crano, W. D. (1988). Inferred evaluation and the relation between attitude similarity and interpersonal attraction. *Journal of Personality and Social Psychology, 54*(5), 789–797.

Conklin, H. M., & Iacono, W. G. (2002). Schizophrenia: A neurodevelopmental perspective. *Current Directions in Psychological Science, 11,* 33–37.

Connidis, I. A., & McMullin, J. A. (1999). Permanent childlessness: Perceived advantages and disadvantages among older persons. *Canadian Journal on Aging, 18,* 447–465.

Contrada, R. J., Ashmore, R. D., Gary, M. L., Coups, E., Egeth, J. D., Sewell, A., Ewell, K., Goyal, T. M., & Chasse, V. (2000). Ethnicity-related sources of stress and their effects on well-being. *Current Directions in Psychological Science, 9*(4), 136–139.

Coontz, S. (1997, November 17). Divorcing reality. *The Nation,* pp. 21–24.

Coontz, S. (2000). *The way we never were: American families and the nostalgia trap.* New York: Basic Books.

Cooper, A. (2002). *Sex and the Internet.* Philadelphia: Brunner-Routledge.

Cooper, A., Boies, S., Maheu, M., & Greenfield, D. (2000). Sexuality and the Internet: The next sexual revolution. In L. T. Szuchman & F. Muscarella (Eds.), *Psychological perspectives on human sexuality.* New York: Wiley.

Cooper, A., & Griffin-Shelley, E. (2002). A quick tour of online sexuality: Part 1. *Annals of the American Psychotherapy Association, 5*(6), 11–13.

Cooper, A., Morahan-Martin, J., Mathy, R. M., & Maheu, M. (2002). Toward an increased understanding of user demographics in online sexual activities. *Journal of Sex and Marital Therapy, 28,* 105–129.

Cooper, A., & Sportolari, L. (1997). Romance in cyberspace: Understanding online attraction. *Journal of Sex Education and Therapy, 22,* 7–14.

Cooper, A., Safir, M. P., & Rosenmann, A. (2006). Workplace worries: A preliminary look at online sexual activities at the office—Emerging issues for clinicians and employers. *CyberPsychology & Behavior, 9*(1), 22–29.

Cooper, C. L., & Dewe, P. (2004). *Stress: A brief history.* Malden, MA: Blackwell Publishing.

Cooper, D. C., & Waldstein, S. R. (2004). Hostility differentially predicts risk factors in African American and White young adults. *Journal of Psychosomatic Research, 57,* 491–497.

Cooper, L., & Bright. J. (2001). Individual differences in reactions to stress. In F. Jones & J. Bright (Eds.), *Stress: Myth, theory and research.* Harlow, England: Pearson Education.

Cooper, M. L. (2006). Does drinking promote risky sexual behavior? A complex answer to a simple question. *Current Directions in Psychological Science, 15*(1), 19–23.

Cooper, M. L., Albino, A. W., Orcutt, H. K., & Williams, N. (2004). Attachment styles and intrapersonal adjustment: A longitudinal study from adolescence into young adulthood. In W. S. Rholes & J. A. Simpson (Eds.), *Adult attachment: Theory, research, and clinical implications.* New York: Guilford.

Cooper, M. L., Shapiro, C. M., & Powers, A. M. (1998). Motivations for sex and risky sexual behavior among adolescents and young adults: A functional perspective. *Journal of Personality and Social Psychology, 75,* 1528–1558.

Cooper, P. J. (1995). Eating disorders and their relationship to mood and anxiety disorders. In K. D. Brownell & C. G. Fairburn (Eds.), *Eating disorders and obesity: A comprehensive handbook.* New York: Guilford Press.

Cope, M. B., Fernández, J. R., & Allilson, D. B. (2004). Genetic and biological risk factors. In J. K. Thompson (Ed.), *Handbook of eating disorders and obesity.* New York: Wiley.

Cordova, J. V., Gee, C. B., & Warren, L. Z. (2005). Emotional skillfulness in marriage: Intimacy as a mediator of the relationship between emotional skillfulness and marital satisfaction. *Journal of Social and Clinical Psychology, 24,* 218–235.

Cornell, D. G. (1997). Post hoc explanation is not prediction. *American Psychologist, 52,* 1380.

Corr, C. A. (1993). Coping with dying: Lessons that we should and should not learn from the work of Elisabeth Kübler-Ross. *Death Studies, 17*(1), 69–83.

Correia, I., Vala, J., & Aguiar, P. (2007). Victim's innocence, social categorization, and the threat to the belief in a just world. *Journal of Experimental Social Psychology, 43,* 31–38.

Correll, C. U., Leucht, S., & Kane, J. M. (2004). Lower risk for tardive dyskinesia associated with second-generation antipsychotics: A systematic review of 1-year studies. *American Journal of Psychiatry, 161,* 414–425.

Corsica, J. A., & Perri, M. G. (2003). Obesity. In A. M. Nezu, C. M. Nezu, & P. A. Geller (Eds.), *Handbook of psychology: Vol. 9. Health psychology.* New York: Wiley.

Costa, P. T., Jr., & McCrae, R. R. (1985). *NEO Personality Inventory.* Odessa, FL: Psychological Assessment Resources.

Costa, P. T., Jr., & McCrae, R. R. (1988). Personality in adulthood: A six-year longitudinal study of self-reports and spouse ratings on the NEO Personality Inventory. *Journal of Personality and Social Psychology, 54,* 853–863.

Costa, P. T., Jr., & McCrae, R. R. (1992). *Revised NEO Personality Inventory: NEO PI and NEO Five-Factor Inventory (Professional Manual).* Odessa, FL: Psychological Assessment Resources.

Costa, P. T., Jr., & McCrae, R. R. (1994). Set like plaster? Evidence for the stability of adult personality. In T. F. Heatherton & J. L. Weinberger (Eds.), *Can personality change?* Washington, DC: American Psychological Association.

Costa, P. T., Jr., & McCrae, R. R. (1997). Longitudinal stability of adult personality. In R. Hogan, J. Johnson, & S. Briggs (Eds.), *Handbook of personality psychology.* San Diego: Academic Press.

Cotter, D. A., Hermsen, J. M., Ovadia, S., & Vanneman, R. (2001). The glass ceiling effect. *Social Forces, 80,* 655–682.

Courtenay, W. H. (2000). Behavioral factors associated with disease, injury, and death among men: Evidence and implications for prevention. *Journal of Men's Studies, 9*(1), 81–142.

Covey, S. R. (1989). *The seven habits of highly effective people.* New York: Simon & Schuster.

Cowan, C. P., & Cowan, P. A. (1997). Working with couples during stressful transitions. In S. Dreman (Ed.), *The family on the threshold of the 21st century.* Mahwah, NJ: Erlbaum.

Cowan, C. P., & Cowan, P. A. (2000). *When partners become parents.* Mahwah, NJ: Erlbaum.

Cowley, J., & Murr, A. (2004, December 6). The new face of AIDS. *Newsweek,* pp. 76–78.

Cox, M. J., Paley, B., Burchinal, M., & Payne, C. C. (1999). Marital perceptions and interactions across the transition to parenthood. *Journal of Marriage and the Family, 61,* 611–625.

Coyne, J. C. (1999). Thinking interactionally about depression: A radical restatement. In T. E. Joiner & J. C. Coyne (Eds.), *Interpersonal processes in depression.* Washington, DC: American Psychological Association.

Coyne, S. M., Archer, J., & Eslea, M. (2006). "We're not friends anymore! Unless . . .": The frequency and harmfulness of indirect, relational, and social aggression. *Aggressive Behavior, 32,* 294–307.

Craik, F. I. M., & Tulving, E. (1975). Depth of processing and the retention of words in episodic memory. *Journal of Experimental Psychology. General, 104,* 268–294.

Cramer, P. (2000). Defense mechanisms in psychology today: Further processes for adaptation. *American Psychologist, 55*(6), 637–646.

Crawford, M., & Popp, D. (2003). Sexual double standards: A review and methodological critique of two decades of research. *Journal of Sex Research, 40*(1), 13–26.

Creed, F. (1989). Appendectomy. In G. W. Brown & T. O. Harris (Eds.), *Life events and illness.* New York: Guilford Press.

Creed, P., Prideaux, L., & Patton, W. (2005). Antecedents and consequences of career decisional states in adolescence. *Journal of Vocational Behavior, 67,* 397–412.

Crepaz, N., Hart, T. A., & Marks, G. (2004). Highly active antiretroviral therapy and sexual risk behavior. *Journal of the American Medical Association, 292*(2), 224–236.

Crews, F. (2006). *Follies of the wise: Dissenting essays.* Emeryville, CA: Shoemaker Hoard.

Crick, N. R., Casas, J. F., & Nelson, D. A. (2002). Toward a more comprehensive understanding of peer maltreatment: Studies of relational victimization. *Current Directions in Psychological Science, 11*(3), 98–101.

Crimmins, E. M., & Ingegneri, D. G. (1990). Interaction and living arrangements of older parents and their children. *Research on Aging, 12,* 3–35.

Crisp, R. J., & Hewastone, M. E. (2006). *Multiple social categorization: Processes, models, and applications.* New York: Psychology Press.

Critelli, J. W., & Ee, J. S. (1996). Stress and physical illness: Development of an integrative model. In T. W. Miller (Ed.), *Theory and assessment of stressful life events.* Madison, CT: International Universities Press.

Crits-Christoph, P. (1997). Limitations of the dodo bird verdict and the role of clinical trials in psychotherapy research: Comment on Wampold, et al. (1997). *Psychological Bulletin, 122,* 216–220.

Crocker, J., & Luhtanen, R. (1990). Collective self-esteem and ingroup bias. *Journal of Personality and Social Psychology, 58,* 60–67.

Crocker, J., & McGraw, K. M. (1984). What's good for the goose is not good for the gander: Solo status as an obstacle to occupational achievement for males and females. *American Behavioral Scientist, 27,* 357–370.

Crocker, J., & Nuer, N. (2004). Do people need self-esteem? Comment on Pyszczynski et al. *Psychological Bulletin, 130,* 469–472.

Crocker, J., & Park, L. E. (2004). The costly pursuit of self-esteem. *Psychological Bulletin, 130,* 392–414.

Crohan, S. E. (1992). Marital happiness and spousal consensus on beliefs about marital conflict: A longitudinal investigation. *Journal of Social and Personal Relationships, 9,* 89–102.

Crooks, R., & Baur, K. (2008). *Our sexuality.* Belmont, CA: Wadsworth.

Crosby, F. J., & Sabattini, L. (2006). Family and work balance. In J. Worrell & C. D. Goodheart (Eds.), *Handbook of girls' and women's psychological health.* New York: Oxford University Press.

Crosby, O., & Moncarz, R. (2006, Fall). The 2004–14 job outlook for college graduates. *Occupational Outlook Quarterly,* pp. 42–57.

Crosby, O., Iyer, A., Clayton, S., & Downing, R. A. (2003). Affirmative action: Psychological data and the policy debates. *American Psychologist, 58*(1), 93–115.

Cross, C. K., & Hirschfeld, R. M. A. (1986). Epidemiology of disorders in adulthood: Suicide. In G. L. Klerman, M. M. Weissman, P. S. Appelbaum, & L. H. Roth (Eds.), *Psychiatry: Vol. 5. Social, epidemiologic, and legal psychiatry.* New York: Basic Books.

Cross, P. (1977). Not can but will college teaching be improved? *New Directions for Higher Education, 17,* 1–15.

Cross, S. E., Bacon, P. L., & Morris, M. L. (2000). The relational-interdependent self-construal and relationships. *Journal of Personality and Social Psychology, 78*(4), 791–808.

Cross, S. E., & Gore, J. S. (2003). Cultural models of the self. In M.R. Leary & J. P. Tangney (Eds.), *Handbook of self and identity.* New York: Guilford.

Cross, S. E., & Madson, L. (1997). Models of the self: Self-construal and gender. *Psychological Bulletin, 122*(1), 5–37.

Cross, S. E., & Markus, H. (1991). Possible selves across the life span. *Human Development, 34*(4), 230–255.

Cross, S. E., & Markus, H. R. (1999). The cultural constitution of personality. In L. A. Pervin & O. P. John (Eds.), *Handbook of personality: Theory and research* (2nd ed.). New York: Guilford Press.

Crouter, A. C., & Bumpus, M. F. (2001). Linking parents' work stress to children's and adolescents' psychological adjustment. *Current Directions in Psychological Science, 10*(5), 156–159.

Crouter, A. C., Bumpus, M. F., Maguire, M. C., & McHale, S. M. (1999). Linking parents' work pressure and adolescents' well-being: Insights into dynamics in dual-earner families. *Developmental Psychology, 35,* 1453–1461.

Crow, T. J. (2007). How and why genetic linkage has not solved the problem of psychosis: Review and hypothesis. *American Journal of Psychiatry, 164,* 13–21.

Crowell, J. A., Treboux, D., & Waters, E. (2002). Stability of attachment representations: The transition to marriage. *Developmental Psychology, 38,* 467–479.

Crowley, A. E., & Hoyer, W. D. (1994). An integrative framework for understanding two-sided persuasion. *Journal of Consumer Research, 20,* 561–574.

Crowley, B. J., Hayslip, B. Jr., & Hobdy, J. (2003). Psychological hardiness and adjustment to life events in adulthood. *Journal of Adult Development, 10*(4), 237–248.

Cullen, L. T. (2007, February 22). It's a wrap. You're hired! *Time,* p. 57.

Culpepper, L., Davidson, J. R. T., Dietrich, A. J., Goodman, W. K., Kroenke, K., & Schwenk, T. L. (2004). Suicidality as a possible effect of antidepressant treatment. *Journal of Clinical Psychiatry, 65*(6), 742–749.

Cummings, E. M., Braungart-Rieker, J. M., & du Rocher-Schudlich, T. (2003). Emotion and personality development in childhood. In R. M. Lerner, M. A. Easterbrooks, & J. Mistry (Eds.), *Handbook of psychology: Vol. 6. Developmental psychology.* New York: Wiley.

Cunningham, C. O., & Selwyn, P. A. (2005). HIV-related medical complications and treatment. In J. H. Lowinson, P. Ruiz, R. B. Millman, & J. G. Langrod (Eds.), *Substance abuse: A comprehensive textbook.* Philadelphia: Lippincott/Williams & Wilkins.

Cunningham, M. (2001). The influence of parental attitudes and behaviors on children's attitudes toward gender and household labor in early adulthood. *Journal of Marriage and the Family, 63*(1), 111–122.

Cunningham, M. R., Barbee, A. P., & Pike, C. L. (1990). What do women want? Facialmetric assessment of multiple motives in the perception of male facial physical attractiveness. *Journal of Personality and Social Psychology, 59,* 61–72.

Cunningham, M. R., Druen, P. B., & Barbee, A. P. (1997). Angels, mentors, and friends: Trade-offs among evolutionary, social, and individual variables in physical appearance. In J. A. Simpson & D. T. Kenrick (Eds.), *Evolutionary Social Psychology.* Mahwah, NJ: Erlbaum.

Cunningham, M. R., Roberts, A. R., Barbee, A. P., Druen, P. B., & Wu, C., (1995). "Their ideas of beauty are, on the whole, the same as ours": Consistency and variability in the cross-cultural perception of female physical attractiveness. *Journal of Personality and Social Psychology, 68,* 261–279.

Curioni, C. C., & Lourenco, P. M. (2005). Long-term weight loss after diet and exercise: A systematic review. *International Journal of Obesity, 29,* 1168–1174.

Curtis, R. C., & Miller, K. (1986). Believing another likes or dislikes you: Behaviors making the beliefs come true. *Journal of Personality and Social Psychology, 51,* 284–290.

Cutrona, C. E. (1982). Transition to college: Loneliness and the process of social adjustment. In L. A. Peplau & D. Perlman (Eds.), *Loneliness: A sourcebook of current theory, research, and therapy.* New York: Wiley.

Cutting, L. P., & Docherty, N. M. (2000). Schizophrenia outpatients' perceptions of their parents: Is expressed emotion a factor? *Journal of Abnormal Psychology, 109*(2), 266–272.

Dabbs, J. M., with Dabbs, M. G. (2000). *Heroes, rogues, and lovers: Testosterone and behavior.* New York: McGraw-Hill.

Dainton, M. (2000). Maintenance behaviors, expectations for maintenance, and satisfaction: Linking comparison levels to relational maintenance strategies. *Journal of Social and Personal Relationships, 17*(6), 827–842.

Dallman, M. F., Bhatnagar, S., & Viau, V. (2000). Hypothalamo-pituitary-adrenal axis. In G. Fink (Ed.), *Encyclopedia of stress* (Vol. 2). San Diego: Academic Press.

D'Amico, M. L. (1998). Internet has become a necessity, U.S. poll shows. *CNNinteractive* [Internet magazine],1.

Danieli, Y., Engdahl, B., & Schlenger, W. E. (2004). The psychological aftermath of terrorism. In F. M. Moghaddam & A. J. Marsella (Eds.), *Understanding terrorism: Psychological roots, consequences, and interventions.* Washington, D.C.: American Psychological Association.

Daniels, K., Hartley, R., & Travers, C. J. (2006). Beliefs about stressors alter stressors' impact: Evidence from two experience-sampling studies. *Human Relations, 59,* 1261–1285.

Dantzer, R., & Mormede, P. (1995). Psychoneuroimmunology of stress. In B. E. Leonard & K. Miller (Eds.), *Stress, the immune system and psychiatry.* New York: Wiley.

Das, E. H. H. J., de Wit, J. B. F., & Stroebe, W. (2003). Fear appeals motivate acceptance of action recommendations: Evidence for a positive bias in the processing of persuasive messages. *Personality and Social Psychology Bulletin, 29*(5), 650–664.

D'Augelli, A. R., & Hershberger, S. L. (1993). Lesbian, gay, and bisexual youth in community settings: Personal challenges and mental health problems. *American Journal of Community Psychology, 21,* 421–448.

David, D. H., & Lyons-Ruth, K. (2005). Differential attachment responses of male and female infants to frightening maternal behavior: Tend or befriend versus fight of flight? *Infant Mental Health Journal, 26*(1), 1–18.

Davidson, M. J., & Fielden, S. (1999). Stress and the working woman. In G. N. Powell (Ed.), *Handbook of gender and work.* Thousand Oaks, CA: Sage.

Davies, A. P. C., & Shackelford, T. K. (2006). An evolutionary psychological perspective on gender similarities and differences. *American Psychologist, 32,* 640–641.

Davies, L. (1995). A closer look at gender and distress among the never married. *Women and Health, 23,* 13–30.

Davila, J., & Cobb, R. J. (2003). Predicting change in self-reported and interviewer-assessed adult attachment: Tests of the individual difference and life stress models of attachment change. *Personality and Social Psychology Bulletin, 29,* 859–870.

Davila, J., & Sargent, E. (2003). The meaning of life (events) predicts changes in attachment security. *Personality and Social Psychology Bulletin, 29,* 1383–1395.

Davis, J. L., & Rusbult, C. E. (2001). Attitude alignment in close relationships. *Journal of Personality and Social Psychology, 81*(1), 65–84.

Davis, K. L., Mohs, R. C., Marin, D., Purohit, D. P., Perl, D. P., Lantz, M., Austin, G., & Haroutunian, V. (1999). Cholinergic markers in elderly patients with early signs of Alzheimer's disease. *Journal of the American Medical Association, 281,* 1401–1406.

Davis, L. L., Frazier, E. C., Williford, R. B., & Newell, J. M. (2006). Long-term pharmacotherapy for post-traumatic stress disorder. *CNS Drugs, 20,* 465–476.

Davis, M. H., Morris, M. M., & Kraus, L. A. (1998). Relationship-specific and global perceptions of social support: Associations with well-being and attachment. *Journal of Personality and Social Psychology, 74,* 468–481.

Davis, R. A. (2001). A cognitive-behavioral model of pathological Internet use. *Computers in Human Behavior, 17*(2), 187–195.

Dawkins, K., Golden, R. N., & Fawcett, J. A. (2003). Therapeutic management of the suicidal patient. In A. Tasman, J. Kay, & J. A. Lieberman (Eds.), *Psychiatry.* New York: Wiley.

Dean, L. R., Carroll, J. S., & Yang, C. (2007). Materialism, perceived financial problems, and marital satisfaction. *Family and Consumer Sciences Research Journal, 35,* 260–281.

DeAngelis, T. (2001, December). Are men emotional mummies? *Monitor on Psychology,* pp. 40–41.

DeAngellis, T. (2004). What's to blame for the surge in super-size Americans? *Monitor on Psychology, 35*(1), 46, 62.

Deaux, K., & Hanna, R. (1984). Courtship in the personals column: The influence of gender and sexual orientation. *Sex Roles, 11,* 363–375.

Deaux, K., & Lewis, L. L. (1983). Components of gender stereotypes. *Psychological Documents, 13,* Ms. No. 2583.

Deaux, K., & Lewis, L. L. (1984). Structure of gender stereotypes: Interrelationships among components and gender label. *Journal of Personality and Social Psychology, 46,* 991–1004.

DeCarvalho, R. J. (1991). *The founders of humanistic psychology.* New York: Praeger.

De Cock, K. M., & Janssen, R. S. (2002). An unequal epidemic in an unequal world. *Journal of the American Medical Association, 288*(2), 236–238.

DeFrain, J., & Olson, D. H. (1999). Contemporary family patterns and relationships. In M. B. Sussman, S. K. Steinmetz, & G. W. Peterson (Eds.), *Handbook of marriage and the family.* New York: Plenum Press.

DeGroot, T., & Motowidlo, S. (1999). Why visual and vocal interview cues can affect interviewers' judgments and predict job performance. *Journal of Applied Psychology, 84,* 986–993.

de Jong, P. J., & Merckelbach, H. (2000). Phobia-relevant illusory correlations: The role of phobic responsivity. *Journal of Abnormal Psychology, 109,* 597–601.

de Jong Gierveld, J., van Tilburg, T., & Dykstra, P. A. (2006). Loneliness and social isolation. In A. L. Vangelisti & D. Perlman (Eds.), *The Cambridge handbook of personal relationships.* New York: Cambridge University Press.

de Kloet, E. R., Joels, M., & Holsboer, F. (2005). Stress and the brain: From adaptation to disease. *Nature Reviews Neuroscience, 6,* 463–474.

Delay, J., & Deniker, P. (1952). *Trente-huit cas de psychoses traitees par la cure prolongee et continue de 4560 RP.* Paris: Masson et Cie.

De Leo, D., Bille-Brahe, U., Kerkhof, A., & Schmidke, A. (Eds.). (2004). *Suicidal behavior: Theories and research findings.* Cambridge, MA: Hogrefe & Huber.

Delgado, P. L., & Moreno, F. A. (2006). Neurochemistry of mood disorders. In D. J. Stein, D. J. Kupfer, & A. F. Schatzberg (Eds.), *Textbook of mood disorders.* Washington, DC: American Psychiatric Publishing.

Del Monte, M. M. (2000). Retrieved memories of childhood sexual abuse. *British Journal of Medical Psychology, 73,* 1–13.

DeLongis, A., Folkman, S., & Lazarus, R. S. (1988). The impact of daily stress on health and mood: Psychological and social resources as mediators. *Journal of Personality and Social Psychology, 54,* 486–495.

DeMaris, A., & Swinford, S. (1996). Female victims of spousal violence: Factors influencing their level of fearfulness. *Family Relations, 45*(1), 98–106.

DeMaris, A., Benson, M. L., Fox, G. L., Hill, T., & Van Wyk, J. (2003). Distal and proximal factors in domestic violence: A test of an integrated model. *Journal of Marriage and Family, 65,* 652–667.

Demerouti, E., & Geurts, S. (2004). Towards a typology of work-home interaction. *Community, Work, & Family, 7,* 285–309.

Demo, D. H. (1992). Parent-child relations: Assessing recent changes. *Journal of Marriage and the Family, 54,* 104–117.

Dempster, F. N. (1996). Distributing and managing the conditions of encoding and practice. In E. L. Bjork & R. A. Bjork (Eds.), *Memory.* San Diego: Academic Press.

Denisoff, E., & Endler, N. S. (2000). Life experiences, coping, and weight preoccupation in young adult women. *Canadian Journal of Behavioural Science, 32*(2), 97–103.

Dennerstein, L., Dudley, E., & Guthrie, J. (2002). Empty nest or revolving door? A prospective study of women's quality of life in midlife during the phase of children leaving and re-entering the home. *Psychological Medicine, 32*(3), 545–550.

Dennis, C., & Ross, L. (2005). Relationships among infant sleep patterns, maternal fatigue, and development of depressive symptomatology. *Birth, 32,* 187–193.

Dennis, W. (1966). Creative productivity between the ages of 20 and 80 years. *Journal of Gerontology, 21,* 1–8.

DePaulo, B. M. (1994). Spotting lies: Can humans learn to do better? *Current Directions in Psychological Science, 3(3),* 83–86.

DePaulo, B. M., & Friedman, H. (1998). Nonverbal communication. In D. T. Gilbert, S. T. Fiske, &

G. Lindzey (Eds.), *The handbook of social psychology* (Vol. 2). Boston: McGraw-Hill.

DePaulo, B. M., LeMay, C. S., & Epstein, J. A. (1991). Effects of importance of success and expectations for success on effectiveness at deceiving. *Personality and Social Psychology Bulletin, 17,* 14–24.

DePaulo, B. M., Lindsay, J. J., Malone, B. E., Muhlenbruck, L., Charlton, K., & Cooper, H. (2003). Cues to deception. *Psychological Bulletin, 129*(1), 74–118.

DePaulo, B. M., & Morris, W. L. (2005). Singles in society and in science. *Psychological Inquiry, 16,* 57–83.

DePaulo, B. M., & Morris, W. L. (2006). The unrecognized stereotyping and discrimination against singles. *Current Directions in Psychological Science, 15,* 251–254.

DePaulo, B. M., Stone, J., & Lassiter, G. D. (1985). Deceiving and detecting deceit. In B. R. Schlenker (Ed.), *The self and social life.* New York: McGraw-Hill.

Derlega, V. J., Winstead, B. A., Wong, P. T. P., & Hunter, S. (1985). Gender effects in an initial encounter: A case where men exceed women in disclosure. *Journal of Social and Personal Relationships, 2,* 25–44.

Derogatis, L. R. (1982). Self-report measures of stress. In L. Goldberger & S. Breznitz (Eds.), *Handbook of stress: Theoretical and clinical aspects.* New York: Free Press.

DeRoma, V., Saylor, C., Swickert, R. , Sinsi, C., Marable, T. B., & Vickery, P. (2003). College students' PTSD symptoms, coping, and perceived benefits following media exposure to 9/11. *Journal of College Student Psychotherapy, 18*(1), 49–64.

Des Jarlais, D. C., Hagan, H., & Friedman, S. R. (2005). Epidemiology and emerging public heath perspectives. In J. H. Lowinson, P. Ruiz, R. B. Millman, & J. G. Langrod (Eds.), *Substance abuse: A comprehensive textbook.* Philadelphia: Lippincott/Williams & Wilkins.

Desert, M., & Leyens, J. (2006). Social comparisons across cultures I: Gender stereotypes in high and low power distance cultures. In S. Guimond (Ed.), *Social Comparison and Social Psychology: Understanding cognition, intergroup relations, and culture.* New York: Cambridge University Press.

DeSpelder, L. A., & Strickland, A. L. (1983). *The last dance: Encountering death and dying.* Palo Alto, CA: Mayfield.

Dessler, W. A. (2000). Indigenous societies. In G. Fink (Ed.), *Encyclopedia of stress* (Vol. 1). San Diego: Academic Press.

de St. Aubin, E., McAdams, D. P., & Kim, T. (2004). *The generative society: Caring for future generations.* Washington, DC: American Psychological Association.

Deutsch, M., & Gerard, H. B. (1955). A study of normative and informational social influences upon individual judgment. *Journal of Abnormal and Social Psychology, 51,* 629–636.

Devine, P. G. (1989). Stereotypes and prejudice: Their automatic and controlled components. *Journal of Personality and Social Psychology, 56,* 5–18.

de Vries, B. (1996). The understanding of friendship: An adult life course perspective. In C. Magai & S. H. McFadden (Eds), *Handbook of emotion, adult development, and aging.* San Diego, CA: Academic Press.

Dew, M. A., Bromet, E. J., & Switzer, G. E. (2000). Epidemiology. In M. Hersen & A. S. Bellack (Eds.), *Psychopathology in adulthood.* Boston: Allyn & Bacon.

de Wilde, E. J., Kienhorst, I. C. W. M., Diekstra, R. F. W., & Wolters, W. H. G. (1992). The relationship between adolescent suicidal behavior and life events in childhood and adolescence. *American Journal of Psychiatry, 149,* 45–51.

Dey, J. G., & Hill, C. (2007). *Behind the pay gap.* Washington, DC: American Association of University Women Educational Foundation.

Diamond, L. E. (2003). Was it a phase? Young women's relinquishment of lesbian/bisexual identities over a 5-year period. *Journal of Personality and Social Psychology, 84,* 352–364.

Diamond, L. E., Earle, D. C., Heiman, J. R., Rosen, R. C., Perelman, M. A., & Harning, R. (2006). An effect on the subjective sexual response in premenopausal women with sexual arousal disorder by Bremelanotide (PT-141), a melanocortin receptor agonist. *Journal of Sexual Medicine, 3,* 628–638.

Diamond, L. M. (2006). The intimate same-sex relationships of sexual minorities. In A. L. Vangelisti & D. Perlman (Eds.), *The Cambridge handbook of personal relationships.* New York: Cambridge University Press.

Diamond, L. M., & Dubé, E. M. (2002). Friendship and attachment among heterosexual and sexual-minority youths: Does the gender of your friend matter? *Journal of Youth and Adolescence, 31,* 155–166.

Di Chiara, G. (1999). Drug addiction as dopamine-dependent associative learning disorder. *European Journal of Pharmacology, 375,* 13–30.

Dick, D. M., Rose, R. J., Pulkkinen, L., & Kaprio, J. (2001). Measuring puberty and understanding its impact: A longitudinal study of adolescent twins. *Journal of Youth and Adolescence, 30,* 385–399.

DiClemente, C. C., Fairhurst, S. K., & Piotrowski, N. A. (1995). Self-efficacy and addictive behaviors. In J. E. Maddux (Ed.), *Self-efficacy, adaptation, and adjustment: Theory, research and application.* New York: Plenum Press.

DiClemente, R. J., Hansen, W. B., & Ponton, L. E. (1995). *Handbook of adolescent health risk behavior.* New York: Plenum Press.

Diekman, A. B., & Eagly, A. H. (2000). Stereotypes as dynamic constructs: Women and men of the past, present, and future. *Personality and Social Psychology Bulletin, 26*(10), 1171–1188.

Diekman, A. B., & Murnen, S. K. (2004). Learning to be little women and little men: The inequitable gender equality of nonsexist children's literature. *Sex Roles, 50*(5/6), 373–385.

Diekstra, R. F. W. (1995). Depression and suicidal behaviors in adolescence: Sociocultural and time trends. In M. Rutter (Ed.), *Psychosocial disturbances in young people: Challenges for prevention.* New York: Cambridge University Press.

Diekstra, R. F. W., Kienhorst, C. W., & de Wilde, E. J. (1996). Suicide and suicidal behavior among adolescents. In M. Rutter & D. J. Smith (Eds.), *Psychosocial disorders in young people: Time trends and their causes.* New York: Wiley.

Diener, E. (1984). Subjective well-being. *Psychological Bulletin, 93,* 542–575.

Diener, E., & Diener, C. (1996). Most people are happy. *Psychological Science, 7,* 181–185.

Diener, E., Gohm, C. L., Suh, E., & Oishi, S. (2000). Similarity of the relations between marital status and subjective well-being across cultures. *Journal of Cross-Cultural Psychology, 31,* 419–436.

Diener, E., Lucas, R. E., & Scollon, C. N. (2006). Beyond the hedonic treadmill: Revising the adaptation theory of well-being. *American Psychologist, 61,*, 305–314.

Diener, E., & Oishi, S. (2005). The nonobvious social psychology of happiness. *Psychological Inquiry, 16*(4), 162–167.

Diener, E., Sandvik, E., Seidlitz, L., & Diener, M. (1993). The relationship between income and subjective well-being: Relative or absolute? *Social Indicators Research, 28,* 195–223.

Diener, E., & Seligman, M. E. P. (2002). Very happy people. *Psychological Science, 13,* 80–83.

Diener, E., & Seligman, M. E. P. (2004). Beyond money: Toward an economy of well-being. *Psychological Science in the Public Interest, 5*(1), 1–31.

Diener, E., Suh, E. M., Lucas, R. E. , & Smith, H. L. (1999). Subjective well-being: Three decades of progress. *Psychological Bulletin, 125*(2), 276–302.

Diener, E., Wolsic, B., & Fujita, F. (1995). Physical attractiveness and subjective well-being. *Journal of Personality and Social Psychology, 69,* 120–129.

Dilsaver, S. C., Chen, Y. R., Shoaib, A. M., & Swann, A. C. (1999). Phenomenology of mania: Evidence for distinct depressed, dysphoric, and euphoric presentations. *American Journal of Psychiatry, 156,* 426–430.

Dilworth, J. E. L. (2004). Predictors of negative spillover from family to work. *Journal of Family Issues, 25,* 241–261.

DiMatteo, M. R. (1991). *The psychology of health, illness, and medical care: An individual perspective.* Pacific Grove, CA: Brooks/Cole.

DiMatteo, M. R. (1994). Enhancing patient adherence to medical recommendations. *Journal of the American Medical Association, 271,* 79–83.

DiMatteo, M. R. (1997). Health behaviors and care decisions: An overview of professional-patient communication. In D. S. Gochman (Ed.), *Handbook of health behavior research II: Provider determinants.* New York: Plenum Press.

DiMatteo, M. R. (2004a). Social support and patient adherence to medical treatment: A meta-analysis. *Health Psychology, 23*(2), 207–218.

DiMatteo, M. R. (2004b). Variations in patients' adherence to medical recommendations: A quantitative review of 50 years of research. *Medical Care, 42*(3), 200–209.

DiMatteo, M. R., Giordani, P. J., Lepper, H. S., & Croghan, T. W. (2002). Patient adherence and medial treatment outcomes: A meta-analysis. *Medical Care, 40*(9), 794–811.

Din, J. N., Newby, D. E., & Flapan, A. D. (2004). Omega 3 fatty acids and cardiovascular disease—fishing for a natural treatment. *British Medical Journal, 328,* 30–35.

Dindia, K., & Allen, M. (1992). Sex differences in self-disclosure: A meta-analysis. *Psychological Bulletin, 112,* 106–124.

Dinges, D. F., Rogers, N. J., & Baynard, M. D. (2005). Chronic sleep deprivation. In M. H. Kryger, T. Roth, & W. C. Dement (Eds.), *Principles and practice of sleep medicine.* Philadelphia: Elsevier Saunders.

Dion, K. K., Berscheid, E., & Walster, E. (1972). What is beautiful is good. *Journal of Personality and Social Psychology, 24,* 285–290.

Dion, K. K., & Dion, K. L. (1993). Individualistic and collectivistic perspectives on gender and the cultural context of love and intimacy. *Journal of Social Issues, 49,* 53–69.

Dion, K. L. (2003). Prejudice, racism and discrimination. In T. Millon & M. J. Lerner (Eds.), *Handbook of psychology: Vol. 5. Personality and social psychology.* New York: Wiley.

Dion, K. L., & Dion, K. K. (1988). Romantic love: Individual and cultural perspectives. In R. J. Sternberg & M. L. Barnes (Eds.), *The psychology of love.* New Haven, CT: Yale University Press.

Dishotsky, N. I., Loughman, W. D., Mogar, R. E., & Lipscomb, W. R. (1971). LSD and genetic damage: Is LSD chromosome damaging, carcinogenic, mutagenic, or teratogenic? *Science, 172,* 431–440.

DiTommaso, E., Brannen-McNulty, C., Ross, L., & Burgess, M. (2003). Attachment styles, social skills and loneliness in young adults. *Personality and Individual Differences, 35*(2), 303–312.

Dixon, L., & Browne, K. (2003). The heterogeneity of spouse abuse: A review. *Aggression and Violent Behavior, 8*(1), 107–130.

Dixon, R. A., & Cohen, A. (2003). Cognitive development in adulthood. In R. M. Lerner, M. A. Easterbrooks, & J. Mistry (Eds.), *Handbook of psychology: Vol. 6. Developmental psychology.* New York: Wiley.

Dohrenwend, B. P., Raphael, K. G., Schwartz, S., Stueve, A., & Skodol, A. (1993). The structured event probe and narrative rating method for measuring stressful life events. In L. Goldberger & S. Breznitz (Eds.), *Handbook of stress: Theoretical and clinical aspects* (2nd ed.). New York: Free Press.

Dolby, S. K. (2005). *Self-help books: Why Americans keep reading them.* Urbana: University of Illinois Press.

Dollard, J., Doob, L. W., Miller, N. E., Mowrer, O. H., & Sears, R. R. (1939). *Frustration and aggression.* New Haven, CT: Yale University Press.

Domar, A. D., & Dreher, H. (2000). *Self-nurture: Learning to care for yourself as effectively as you care for everyone else.* New York: Viking.

Donahue, E. M., Robins, R. W., Roberts, B. W., & John, O. P. (1993). The divided self: Concurrent and longitudinal effects of psychological adjustment and social roles on self-concept differentiation. *Journal of Personality and Social Psychology, 64,* 834–846.

Donnellan, M. B., Trzesniewski, K. H., Robins, R. W., Moffitt, T. E., & Caspi, A. (2005). Low self-esteem is related to aggression, antisocial behavior, and delinquency. *Psychological Science, 16,* 328–335.

Donovan, R. L., & Jackson, B. L. (1990). Deciding to divorce: A process guided by social exchange, attachment and cognitive dissonance theories. *Journal of Divorce, 13,* 23–35.

Dougall, A. L., & Baum, A. (2000). Three Mile Island, stress effects of. In G. Fink (Ed.), *Encyclopedia of stress* (Vol. 3). San Diego: Academic Press.

Dougall, A. L., & Baum, A. (2001). Stress, health, and illness. In A. Baum, T. A. Revenson, & J. E. Singer (Eds.), *Handbook of health psychology.* Mahwah, NJ: Erlbaum.

Dougherty, T. W., Turban, D. B., & Callender, J. C. (1994). Confirming first impressions in the employment interview: A field study of interview behavior. *Journal of Applied Psychology, 79*(5), 659–665.

Douglass, M. E., & Douglass, D. N. (1993). *Manage your time, your work, yourself.* New York: American Management Association.

Dovidio, J. F., Ellyson, S. L., Keating, C. F., Heltman, K., & Brown, C. E. (1988). The relationship of social power to visual display of dominance between men and women. *Journal of Personality and Social Psychology, 54,* 233–242.

Dovidio, J. F., & Gaertner, S. L. (1996). Affirmative action, unintentional racial biases, and intergroup relations. *Journal of Social Issues, 52,* 51–75.

Dovidio, J. F., & Gaertner, S. L. (1999). Reducing prejudice: Combating intergroup biases. *Current Directions in Psychological Science, 8,* 101–105.

Dovidio, J. F., & Gaertner, S. L. (2004). Aversive racism. In M. P. Zanna (Ed.), *Advances in experimental social psychology.* San Diego: Elsevier.

Dovidio, J. F., Gaertner, S. L., Esses, V. M., & Brewer, M. B. (2003). Social conflict, harmony, and integration. In T. Millon & M. J. Lerner (Eds.) *Handbook of psychology: Vol. 5. Personality and social psychology.* New York: Wiley.

Dovidio, J. F., Gaertner, S. L., & Pearson, A. R. (2005). On the nature of prejudice: The psychological foundations of hate. In R. J. Sternberg (Ed.), *The psychology of hate.* Washington, DC: American Psychological Association.

Downey, L., & van Willigen, M. (2005). Enviromental stressors: The mental health impacts of living near industrial activity. *Journal of Health and Social Behavior, 46,* 289–305.

Doyle, J. A. (1989). *The male experience.* Dubuque, IA: William C. Brown.

Drago, R. W. (2007). *Striking a balance: Work, family, life.* Boston: Dollars & Sense.

Draijer, N., & Langeland, W. (1999). Childhood trauma and perceived parental dysfunction in the etiology of dissociative symptoms in psychiatric inpatients. *American Journal of Psychiatry, 156,* 379–385.

Dresser, N. (2005). *Multicultural manners: Essential rules of etiquette for the 21st century.* Hoboken, NJ: Wiley.

Drew, J. (2003). The myth of female sexual dysfunction and its medicalization. *Sexualities, Evolution and Gender, 5*(2), 89–96.

Drigotas, S. M., Rusbult, C. E., Wieselquist, J., & Whitton, S. W. (1999). Close partner as sculptor of the ideal self: Behavioral affirmation and the Michelangelo phenomenon. *Journal of Personality and Social Psychology, 77*(2), 293–323.

Driskell, J. E., Willis, R. P., & Copper, C. (1992). Effect of overlearning on retention. *Journal of Applied Psychology, 77,* 615–622.

Driver, J., Tabares, A., Shapiro, A. , Nahm, E. Y., & Gottman, J. M. (2003). Interactional patterns in marital success and failure: Gottman laboratory studies. In F. Walsh (Ed.), *Normal family processes: Growing diversity and complexity.* New York: Guilford.

Driver, J. L., & Gottman, J. M. (2004). Daily marital interactions and positive affect during marital conflict among newlywed couples. *Family Processes, 43,* 301–314.

Drum, D. J., & Sekel, A. (2003). Health care marketplace in the United States. In G. Stricker & T. A. Widiger (Eds.), *Handbook of psychology, Vol. 8. Clinical psychology.* New York: Wiley.

Dubbert, P. M., King, A. C., Marcus, B. H., & Sallis, J. F. (2004). Promotion of physical activity through the life span. In J. M. Raczynski & L. C. Leviton (Eds.), *Handbook of clinical health psychology: Vol. 2. Disorders of behavior and health.* Washington, DC: American Psychological Association.

Dubovsky, S. L. (2005). Benzodiazepine receptor agonists and antagonists. In B. J. Sadock & V. A. Sadock (Eds.), *Kaplan and Sadock's comprehensive textbook of psychiatry.* Philadelphia: Lippincott Williams & Wilkins.

Dubovsky, S. L., Davies, R., & Dubovsky, A. N. (2003). Mood disorders. In R. E. Hales, & S. C. Yudofsky (Eds.), *Textbook of clinical psychiatry.* Washington, DC: American Psychiatric Publishing.

Duck, S. (1994). *Meaningful relationships: Talking, sense, and relating.* Thousand Oaks, CA: Sage.

Duck, S., Pond, K., & Leatham, G. (1995). Loneliness and the evaluation of relational events. *Journal of Social and Personal Relationships, 11,* 253–276.

Duckworth, K., & Borus, J. F. (1999). Population-based psychiatry in the public sector and managed care. In A. M. Nicholi, Jr. (Ed.), *The Harvard guide to psychiatry.* Cambridge, MA: Harvard University Press.

Duffy, S. M., & Rusbult, C. E. (1986). Satisfaction and commitment in homosexual and heterosexual relationships. *Journal of Homosexuality, 12,* 1–23.

DuFrene, D. D., & Lehman, C. M. (2002). Persuasive appeal for clean language. *Business Communication Quarterly, 65*(1), 48–56.

Duggan, E. S., & Brennan, K. A. (1994). Social avoidance and its relation to Bartholomew's adult attachment typology. *Journal of Social and Personal Relationships, 11,* 147–153.

Duman, R. S., & Monteggia, L. M. (2006). A neurotrophic model for stress-related mood disorders. *Biological Psychiatry, 59,* 1116–1127.

Dunbar-Jacob, J., & Schlenk, E. (2001). Patient adherence to treatment regimen. In A. Baum, T. A. Revenson, & J. E. Singer (Eds.), *Handbook of health psychology.* Mahwah, NJ: Erlbaum.

Dunkel, C. S., Kelts, D., & Coon, B. (2006). Possible selves as mechanisms of change in therapy. In C. Dunkel & J. Kerpelman (Eds.), *Possible selves: Theory, research, and applications.* Hauppague, NY: Nova Science Publishers.

Dunkel-Schetter, C., Gurung, R. A. R., Lobel, M., & Wadhwa, P. D. (2001). Stress processes in pregnancy and birth: Psychological, biological, and sociocultural influences. In A. Baum, T. A. Revenson, & J. E. Singer (Eds.), *Handbook of health psychology.* Mahwah, NJ: Erlbaum.

Dunn, A. L., Trivedi, M. H., & O'Neal, H. A. (2001). Physical activity dose-response effects on outcomes of depression and anxiety. *Medicine and Science in Sports and Exercise, 33,* S587–S597.

Dunn, D. S., & Wilson, T. D. (1990). When the stakes are high: A limit to the illusion-of-control effect. *Social Cognition, 8,* 305–323.

Dunning, D., Heath, C., & Suls, J. M. (2004). Flawed self-assessment: Implications for health, education, and the workplace. *Psychological Science in the Public Interest, 5*(3), 69–106.

Dunning, D., & Sherman, D. A. (1997). Stereotypes and tacit inference. *Journal of Personality and Social Psychology, 73*(3), 459–471.

Dweck, C. S. (2007). Is math a gift? Beliefs that put females at risk. In S. J. Ceci & W. M. Williams (Eds.), *Why aren't more women in science: Top researchers debate the evidence.* Washington, DC: American Psychological Association.

Dyer, W. W. (1976). *Your erroneous zones.* New York: Crowell.

Eacott, M. J., & Crawley, R. A. (1998). The offset of childhood amnesia: Memory for events that occurred before age three. *Journal of Experimental Psychology: General, 127,* 22–23.

Eagly, A. H. (1987). *Sex differences in social behavior: A social-role interpretation.* Hillsdale, NJ: Erlbaum.

Eagly, A. H., Ashmore, R. D., Makhijani, M. G., & Longo, L. C. (1991). What is beautiful is good, but . . . : A meta-analytic review of research on the physical attractiveness stereotype. *Psychology Bulletin, 110,* 107–128.

Eagly, A. H., & Chaiken, S. (1998). Attitude structure and function. In D. T. Gilbert, S. T. Fiske, & G. Lindzey (Eds.), *Handbook of social psychology.* New York: McGraw-Hill.

Eagly, A. H., & Karau, S. J. (2002). Role congruity theory of prejudice toward female leaders. *Psychological Review, 109*(3), 573–598.

Eagly, A. H., & Wood, W. (1999). The origins of sex differences in human behavior: Evolved dispositions versus social roles. *American Psychologist, 54*(6), 408–423.

Eagly, A. H., Wood, W., & Diekman, A. B. (2000). Social role theory of sex differences and similarities: A current appraisal. In T. Eckes & H. M. Trautner (Eds.), *The developmental social psychology of gender.* Mahwah, NJ: Erlbaum.

Eaker, E. D., Sullivan, L. M., Kelly-Hayes, M., D'Agostino, R. B., & Benjamin, E. J. (2004). Anger and hostility predict the development of atrial fibrillation in men in the Framingham Offspring Study. *Circulation, 109*(10), 1267–1271.

Eals, M., & Silverman, I. (1994). The hunter-gatherer theory of spatial sex differences: Proximate factors mediating the female advantage in recall of object arrays. *Ethology and Sociobiology, 15,* 95–115.

Earley, P. (2006). *Crazy: A father's search through America's mental health madness.* New York: G. P. Putnam's Sons.

Easterbrook, G. (2003). *The progress paradox: How life gets better while people feel worse.* New York: Random House.

Easterlin, B. L., & Cardena, E. (1999). Cognitive and emotional differences between short- and long-term Vipassana meditators. *Imagination, Cognition and Personality, 18*(1), 68–81.

Ebbinghaus, H. (1885/1964). *Memory: A contribution to experimental psychology.* (H. A. Ruger & E. R. Bussemius, Trans.). New York: Dover. (Original work published 1885)

Eccles, J. S. (2001). Achievement. In J. Worrell (Ed.), *Encyclopedia of women and gender.* San Diego: Academic Press.

Eccles, J. S., Early, D., Frasier, K., Belansky, E., & McCarthy, K. (1997). The relation of connection, regulation, and support for autonomy to adolescents' functioning. *Journal of Adolescent Research, 12,* 263–286.

Eccles, J. S., Wigfield, A., & Byrnes, J. (2003). Cognitive development in adolescence. In R. M. Lerner, M.A. Easterbrooks, & J. Mistry (Eds.), *Handbook of psychology: Vol. 6. Developmental psychology.* New York: Wiley.

Eckert, P., & McConnell-Ginet, S. (2003). *Language and gender.* Cambridge, UK: Cambridge University Press.

Edlin, G., & Golanty, E. (1992). *Health and wellness: A holistic approach.* Boston: Jones and Bartlett.

Edwards, C., Dunham, D. N., Ries, A., & Barnett, J. (2006). Symptoms of traumatic stress and substance use in a non-clinical sample of young adults. *Addictive Behaviors, 31,* 2094–2104.

Edwards, K., & Smith, E. E. (1996). A disconfirmation bias in the evaluation of arguments. *Journal of Personality and Social Psychology, 71,* 5–24.

Edwards, R., & Hamilton, M. A. (2004). You need to understand my gender role: An empirical test of Tannen's model of gender and communication. *Sex Roles, 50*(7/8), 491–504.

Edwards, S. (2006). Physical exercise and psychological well-being. *South African Journal of Psychology, 36,* 357–373.

Egan, T. (2000, October 23). Technology sent Wall Street into market for pornography. *New York Times,* pp. 1–20.

Egeci, I. S., & Gençöz, T. (2006). Factors associated with relationship satisfaction: Importance of communication skills. *Contemporary Family Therapy: An International Journal, 28,* 383–391.

Ehrenberg, O., & Ehrenberg, M. (1994). *The psychotherapy maze: A consumer's guide to getting in and out of therapy.* Northvale, NJ: Jason Aronson.

Ehrenreich, H., Rinn, T., Kunert, H. J., Moeller, M. R., Poser, W., Schilling, L., Gigerenzer, G., & Hoehe, M. R. (1999). Specific attentional dysfunction in adults following early start of cannabis use. *Psychopharmacology, 142,* 295–301.

Eich, E., Macaulay, D., Loewenstein, R. J., & Dihle, P. H. (1997). Memory, amnesia, and dissociative identity disorder. *Psychological Science, 8,* 417–422.

Einstein, G. O., & McDaniel, M. A. (2004). *Memory fitness: A guide for successful aging.* New Haven, CT: Yale University Press.

Eisenberger, N. I., Kemeny, M. E., & Wyatt, G. E. (2003). Psychological inhibition and CD4 T-cell levels in HIV-seropositive women. *Journal of Psychosomatic, 54,* 213–224.

Eisler, R. M., & Ragsdale, K. (1992). Masculine gender role and midlife transition in men. In V. B. Van Hasselt & M. Hersen (Eds.), *Handbook of social development: A lifespan perspective.* New York: Plenum.

Ekman, P. (1972). Universals and cultural differences in facial expressions of emotion. In J. Cole (Ed.), *Nebraska symposium on motivation, 1971.* Lincoln, NE: University of Nebraska Press.

Ekman, P. (1975, September). The universal smile: Face muscles talk every language. *Psychology Today,* pp. 35–39.

Ekman, P. (1994). Strong evidence for universals in facial expressions: A reply to Russell's mistaken critique. *Psychological Bulletin, 115,* 268–287.

Ekman, P., & Friesen, W. V. (1974). Detecting deception from the body or face. *Journal of Personality and Social Psychology, 29*(3), 288–298.

Ekman, P., & Friesen, W. V. (1984). *Unmasking the face.* Palo Alto, CA: Consulting Psychologists Press.

Ekman, P., & O'Sullivan, M. (1991). Who can catch a liar? *American Psychologist, 44*(9), 913–920.

Ekman, P., O'Sullivan, M., & Frank, M. G. (1999). A few can catch a liar. *Psychological Science, 10*(3), 263–266.

Elfenbein, H. A., & Ambady, N. (2003). Universals and cultural differences in recognizing emotions of a different cultural group. *Current Directions in Psychological Science, 12*(5), 159–164.

Elias, M. F., Elias, J. W., & Elias, P. K. (1990). Biological and health influences on behavior. In J. E. Birren & K. W. Schaie (Eds.), *Handbook of the psychology of aging.* San Diego: Academic Press.

Elkind, D. (1978). *A sympathetic understanding of the child: Birth to sixteen.* Boston: Allyn and Bacon.

Ellington, L., & Wiebe, D. J. (1999). Neuroticism, symptom presentation, and medical decision making. *Health Psychology, 18*(6), 634–643.

Elliot, A. J., & Church, M. A. (2003). A motivational analysis of defensive pessimism and self-handicapping. *Journal of Personality, 71,* 369–393.

Elliot, L., & Brantley, C. (1997). *Sex on campus.* New York: Random House.

Ellis, A. (1973). *Humanistic psychotherapy: The rational-emotive approach.* New York: Julian Press.

Ellis, A. (1977). *Reason and emotion in psychotherapy.* Seacaucus, NJ: Lyle Stuart.

Ellis, A. (1985). *How to live with and without anger.* New York: Citadel Press.

Ellis, A. (1987). The evolution of rational-emotive therapy (RET) and cognitive behavior therapy (CBT). In J. K. Zeig (Ed.), *The evolution of psychotherapy.* New York: Brunner/Mazel.

Ellis, A. (1989). Rational-emotive therapy. In R. J. Corsini & D. Wedding (Eds.), *Current Psychotherapies.* Itasca, IL: Peacock.

Ellis, A. (1993). The advantages and disadvantages of self-help therapy materials. *Professional Psychology: Research and Practice, 24,* 335–339.

Ellis, A. (1994). *Reason and emotion in psychotherapy.* Seacaucus, NJ: Birch Lane Press.

Ellis, A. (1995). Thinking processes involved in irrational beliefs and their disturbed consequences. *Journal of Cognitive Psychotherapy, 9,* 105–116.

Ellis, A. (1996). How I learned to help clients feel better and get better. *Psychotherapy, 33,* 149–151.

Ellis, A. (1999). *How to make yourself happy and remarkably less disturbable.* Atascadero, CA: Impact Publishers.

Ellis, A. (2001a). *Feeling better, getting better, staying better: Profound self-help therapy for your emotions.* Atascadero, CA: Impact Publishers.

Ellis, A. (2001b). *Overcoming destructive beliefs, feelings, and behaviors: New directions for Rational Emotive Behavior Therapy.* Amherst, NY: Prometheus Books.

Ellis, A. (2003). *Ask Albert Ellis: Straight answers and sound advice from America's best-known psychologist.* Atascadero, CA: Impact Publishers.

Ellis, A. (2004). Expanding the ABCs of rational emotive behavior therapy. In A. Freeman, M. J. Mahoney, P. Devito, & D. Martin (Eds.), *Cognition and psychotherapy.* New York: Springer Publishing.

Ellis, J. (2006, January 28). "IM-speak" struggle for teachers. *Statesboro Herald,* pp. 1A, 14A.

Ellison, N., Heino, R., & Gibbs, J. (2006). Managing impressions online: Self-presentation processes in the online dating environment. *Journal of Computer-Mediated Communication, 11,* 415–441.

Emanuel, H. M. (1987). Put time on your side. In A. D. Timpe (Ed.), *The management of time.* New York: Facts On File.

Emavardhana, T., & Tori, C. D. (1997). Changes in self-concept, ego defense mechanisms, and religiosity following seven-day Vipassana meditation retreats. *Journal for the Scientific Study of Religion, 36,* 194–206.

Emmelkamp, P. M. G. (1994). Behavior therapy with adults. In A. E. Bergin & S. L. Garfield (Eds.), *Handbook of psychotherapy and behavior change* (4th ed.). New York: Wiley.

Emmelkamp, P. M. G. (2004). In M. J. Lambert (Ed.), *Bergin and Garfield's handbook of psychotherapy and behavior change.* New York: Wiley.

Emmons, R. A. (2003). Personal goals, life meaning, and virtue: Wellsprings of a positive life. In C. L. M. Keyes & J. Haidt (Eds.), *Flourishing: Positive psychology and the life well-lived.* Washington, DC: American Psychological Association.

Employers bemoan workers' writing skills. (2004, September 15). *The Statesboro Herald,* p. 9.

Emsley, R., Rabinowitz, J., & Medori, R. (2006). Time course for antipsychotic treatment response in first-episode schizophrenia. *American Journal of Psychiatry, 163,* 743–745.

Epel, E. S., Blackburn, E. H., Lin, J., Dhabhar, F. S., Adler, N. E., Morrow, J. D., & Cawthon, R. M. (2004). Accelerated telomere shortening in response to life stress. *Proceedings of the National Academy of Sciences, 101,* 17312–17315.

Epstein, R. (2001). Physiologist Laura. *Psychology Today, 34* (4), 5.

Epstein, R. (2007, February–March). The truth about online dating. *Scientific American Mind, 18,* pp. 28–35.

Erdelyi, M. H. (2001). Defense processes can be conscious or unconscious. *American Psychologist, 56*(9), 761–762.

Erikson, E. H. (1963). *Childhood and society.* New York: Norton.

Erikson, E. H. (1968). *Identity: Youth and crisis.* New York: Norton.

Ernst, C., & Angst, J. (1983). Birth order: Its influence on personality. *Behavioral and Brain Sciences, 10*(1), 55.

Esping-Andersen, G. (2007). Sociological explanations of changing income distributions. *American Behavioral Scientist, 50,* 639–658.

Espiritu, D. A. V., Rashid, H., Mast, B. T., Fitzgerald, J., Steinberg, J., & Lichtenberg, P. A. (2001). Depression, cognitive impairment and function in Alzheimer's disease. *International Journal of Geriatric Psychiatry, 16*(11), 1098–1103.

Esterling, B. A., Kiecolt-Glaser, J. K., Bodnar, J. D., & Glaser, R. (1994). Chronic stress, social support, and persistent alterations in the natural killer cell response to cytokines in older adults. *Health Psychology, 13,* 291–298.

Esterson, A. (1993). *Seductive mirage: An exploration of the work of Sigmund Freud.* Chicago: Open Court.

Esterson, A. (2001). The mythologizing of psychoanalytic history: Deception and self-deception in Freud's accounts of the seduction theory episode. *History of Psychiatry, 7,* 329–352.

Etaugh, C. (1993). Maternal employment: Effects on children. In J. Frankel (Ed.), *The employed mother and the family context.* New York: Springer.

Evans, G. W. (2001). Environmental stress and health. In A. Baum, T. A. Revenson, & J. E. Singer (Eds.), *Handbook of health psychology.* Mahwah, NJ: Erlbaum.

Evans, G. W., Hygge, S., & Bullinger, M. (1995). Chronic noise and psychological stress. *Psychological Science, 6,* 333–338.

Evans, G. W., & Stecker, R. (2004). Motivational consequences of environmental stress. *Journal of Environmental Psychology, 24*(2), 143–165.

Evans, G. W., & Wener, R. E. (2006). Rail commuting duration and passenger stress. *Health Psychology, 25,* 408–412.

Evans, G. W., Lepore, S. J., & Schroeder, A. (1996). The role of interior design elements in human responses to crowding. *Journal of Personality and Social Psychology, 70,* 41–46.

Evans, R. G., & Dinning, W. D. (1982). MMPI correlates of the Bem Sex Role Inventory and Extended Personal Attributes Questionnaire in a male psychiatric sample. *Journal of Clinical Psychology, 38,* 811–815.

Everly, G. S., Jr., & Mitchell, J. T. (2001). America under attack: The "10 commandments" of responding to mass terrorist attacks. *International Journal of Emergency Mental Health, 3,* 133–135.

Everson, S. A., Kauhanen, J., Kaplan, G. A., Goldberg, D. E., Julkunen, J., Tuomilehto, J., & Salonen, J. T. (1997). Hostility and increased risk of mortality and acute myocardial infarction: The mediating role of behavioral risk factors. *American Journal of Epidemiology, 146*(2), 142–152.

Ewart, C. K., & Suchday, S. (2002). Discovering how urban poverty and violence affect health: Development and validation of a neighborhood stress index. *Health Psychology, 21*(3), 254–262.

Exline, J. J., Baumeister, R. F., Bushman, B. J., Campbell, W. K., & Finkel, E. J. (2004). Too proud to let go: Narcissistic entitlement as a barrier to forgiveness. *Journal of Personality and Social Psychology, 87,* 894–912.

Eysenck, H. J. (1959). Learning theory and behaviour therapy. *Journal of Mental Science, 195,* 61–75.

Eysenck, H. J. (1967). *The biological basis of personality.* Springfield, IL: Charles C Thomas.

Eysenck, H. J. (1982). *Personality, genetics and behavior: Selected papers.* New York: Praeger.

Eysenck, H. J. (1991). Dimensions of personality: 16, 5, or 3?—Criteria for a taxonomic paradigm. *Personality and Individual Differences, 12,* 773–790.

Eysenck, H. J. (1993a). Forty years on: The outcome problem in psychotherapy revisited. In T. R. Giles (Ed.), *Handbook of effective psychotherapy.* New York: Plenum.

Eysenck, H. J. (1993b). Prediction of cancer and coronary heart disease: Mortality by means of a personality inventory: Results of a 15-year follow-up study. *Psychological Reports, 72,* 499–516.

Eysenck, M. W., Mogg, K., May, J., Richards, A., & Mathews, A. (1991). Bias in interpretation of ambiguous sentences related to threat in anxiety. *Journal of Abnormal Psychology, 100,* 144–150.

Faber R. J. (2003). Self- control and compulsive buying. In T. Kasser, & A. D. Kanner (Eds.), *Psychology and consumer culture: The struggle for a good life in a materialistic world.* Washington, DC: American Psychological Association.

Fabian, G. (2002). Sequential request and organ donation. *Journal of Social Psychology, 22,* 171–178.

Fagot, B. I., & Hagan, R. (1991). Observations of parent reactions to sex-stereotyped behaviors: Age and sex effects. *Child Development, 62,* 617–628.

Fagot, B. I., Hagan, R., Leinbach, M. D., & Kronsberg, S. (1985). Differential reactions to assertive and communicative acts of toddler boys and girls. *Child Development, 56,* 1499–1505.

Fairbank, J. A., Ebert, L., & Caddell, J. M. (2001). Posttraumatic stress disorder. In P. B. Sunker & H. E. Adams (Eds.), *Comprehensive handbook of psychopathology* (3rd ed.). New York: Kluwer Academic/Plenum Publishers.

Fairbrother, K., & Warn, J. (2003). Workplace dimensions, stress, and job satisfaction. *Journal of Managerial Psychology, 18*(1), 8–21.

Falk, P. (1994). The gap between psychological assumptions and empirical research in lesbian-mother child custody cases. In A. E. Gottfried & A. W. Gottfried (Eds.), *Redefining families: Implications for children's development.* New York: Plenum.

Falsetti, S. A., & Ballenger, J. C. (1998). Stress and anxiety disorders. In J. R. Hubbard & E. A. Workman (Eds.), *Handbook of stress medicine: An organ system approach.* New York: CRC Press.

Families and Work Institute. (2004). *Generation and gender in the workplace.* New York: Families and Work Institute.

Fancher, R. E. (1979). *Pioneers of psychology.* New York: Norton.

Farah, A. (1997). An overview of ECT. *Primary Psychiatry, 4,* 58–62.

Faravelli, C., & Pallanti, S. (1989). Recent life events and panic disorders. *American Journal of Psychiatry, 146,* 622–626.

Farina, A., Burns, G. L., Austad, C., Bugglin, C., & Fischer, E. H. (1986). The role of physical attractiveness in the readjustment of discharged psychiatric patients. *Journal of Abnormal Psychology, 95,* 139–143.

Fassler, D. (2001). *Talking to children about war and terrorism: 20 tips for parents.* Retrieved November 20, 2001 from American Psychiatric Association Web site: http://www.psych.org/disaster/20tipsparents11801.cfm.

Faulkner, G., & Carless, D. (2006). Physical activity in the process of psychiatric rehabilitation: Theoretical and methodological issues. *Psychiatric Rehabilitation Journal, 29,* 258–265.

Faust, K. A., & McKibben, J. N. (1999). Marital dissolution: Divorce, separation, annulment, and widowhood. In M. B. Sussman, S. K. Steinmetz, & G. W. Peterson (Eds.), *Handbook of marriage and the family.* New York: Plenum Press.

Fausto-Sterling, A. (1992). *Myths of gender: Biological theories about women and men* (2nd ed.). New York: Basic Books.

Fava, G. A., Fabbri, S., Sirri, L., & Wise, T. N. (2007). Psychological factors affecting medical condition: A new proposal for DSM-V. *Psychosomatics: Journal of Consultation Liaison Psychiatry, 42*(2), 103–111.

Federal Interagency Forum on Aging-Related Statistics. (2004). *Older Americans 2004: Key indicators of well-being.* Washington, DC: Government Printing Office.

Feeney, J. A. (2004). Adult attachment and relationship functioning under stressful conditions: Understanding partners' responses to conflict and challenge. In W. S. Rholes & J. A. Simpson (Eds.), *Adult attachment: Theory, research, and clinical implications.* New York: Guilford.

Feeney, J. A., & Noller, P. (1990). Attachment style as a predictor of adult romantic relationships. *Journal of Personality and Social Psychology, 58,* 281–291.

Fehr, B. (1996). *Friendship processes.* Thousand Oaks, CA: Sage.

Fehr, B. (2000). The life cycle of friendship. In C. Hendrick & S. S. Hendrick (Eds.), *Close relationships: A sourcebook.* Thousand Oaks, CA: Sage.

Fehr, B. (2004). Intimacy expectations in same-sex friendships: A prototype interaction-pattern model. *Journal of Personality and Social Psychology, 86*(2), 265–284.

Fein, S. (1996). Effects of suspicion on attributional thinking and the correspondence bias. *Journal of Personality and Social Psychology, 70,* 1164–1184.

Feingold, A. (1988). Matching for attractiveness in romantic partners and same-sex friends: A meta-analysis and theoretical critique. *Psychological Bulletin, 104,* 226–235.

Feingold, A. (1992a). Gender differences in mate selection preferences: A test of the parental investment model. *Psychological Bulletin, 112,* 125–139.

Feingold, A. (1992b). Good-looking people are not what we think. *Psychological Bulletin, 111,* 304–341.

Feiring, C., & Lewis, M. (1987). The child's social network: Sex differences from three to six years. *Sex Roles, 17,* 621–636.

Feldman, P. J., Cohen, S., Doyle, W. J., Skoner, D. P., & Gwaltney, J. M., Jr. (1999). The impact of personality on the reporting of unfounded symptoms and illness. *Journal of Personality and Social Psychology, 77*(2), 370–378.

Feldman-Barrett, L., & Swim, J. K. (1998). Appraisals of prejudice and discrimination. In J. K. Swim & C. Stangor (Eds.), *Prejudice: The target's perspective.* New York: Academic Press.

Felker, B., & Hubbard, J. R. (1998). Influence of mental stress on the endocrine system. In J. R. Hubbard & E. A. Workman (Eds.), *Handbook of stress medicine: An organ system approach.* New York: CRC Press.

Felmlee, D. H., Sprecher, S., & Bassin, E. (1990). The dissolution of intimate relationships: A hazard model. *Social Psychology Quarterly,* 513–30.

Felmlee, D. H. (1995). Causes and consequences of women's employment discontinuity, 1967–1973. *Work and Occupation, 22,* 167–187.

Felson, R. B. (1989). Parents and the reflected appraisal process: A longitudinal analysis. *Journal of Personality and Social Psychology, 56,* 965–971.

Felson, R. B. (1992). Coming to see ourselves: Social sources of self-appraisals. *Advances in Group Processes, 9,* 185–205.

Fenton, W. S., & McGlashan, T. H. (1994). Antecedents, symptom progression, and long-term outcome of the deficit syndrome in schizophrenia. *American Journal of Psychiatry, 151,* 351–356.

Fenwick, P. (1987). Meditation and the EEG. In M. A. West (Ed.), *The psychology of meditation.* Oxford: Clarendon Press.

Ferguson, J. M. (2001). SSRI antidepressant medications: Adverse effects and tolerability. *Primary Care Companion Journal of Clinical Psychiatry, 3,* 22–27.

Feroli, K., & Burstein, G. (2003). Adolescent sexually transmitted diseases. *American Journal of Maternal/Child Nursing, 28,* 113–118.

Ferrari, J. R. (1992). Psychometric validation of two adult measures of procrastination: Arousal and avoidance measures. *Journal of Psychopathology & Behavioral Assessment, 14,* 97–100.

Ferrari, J. R. (2001). Getting things done on time: Conquering procrastination. In C. R. Snyder (Ed.), *Coping with stress: Effective people and processes.* New York: Oxford University Press.

Ferrari, J. R., Johnson, J. L., & McCown, W. G. (1995). *Procrastination and task avoidance: Theory research and treatment.* New York: Plenum Press.

Ferriss, A. L. (2002). Religion and the quality of life. *Journal of Happiness Studies, 3,* 199–215.

Festinger, L. (1954). A theory of social comparison processes. *Human Relations, 7,* 117–140.

Fiatrone, M. A., O'Neill, E. F., Doyle, N., Clements, K. M., Roberts, S. B., Kehayias, J. J., Lipsitz, L. A., & Evans, W. J. (1993). The Boston FICSIT study: The effects of resistance training and nutritional supplementation on physical frailty in the oldest old. *Journal of the American Geriatrics Society, 41,* 333–337.

Fiedler, K., Schmid, J., & Stahl, T. (2002). What is the current truth about polygraph lie detection? *Basic & Applied Social Psychology, 24,* 313–324.

Fiese, B. H., & Skillman, G. (2000). Gender differences in family stories: Moderating influence of parent gender role and child gender. *Sex Roles, 43*(5–6), 267–283.

Figueredo, A. J., Sefcek, J. A., Vasquez, G., Brumbach, B. H., King, J. E., & Jacobs, W. J. (2005). Evolutionary personality psychology. In D. M. Buss (Ed.), *The handbook of evolutionary psychology.* New York: Wiley.

Fincham, F. D. (2001). Attributions in close relationships: From Balkanization to integration. In G. J. O. Fletcher, & M. S. Clark (Eds.), *Blackwell handbook of social psychology: Vol. 2. Interpersonal processes.* Oxford: Blackwell.

Fincham, F. D. (2003). Marital conflict: Correlates, structure, and context. *Current Directions in Psychological Science, 12*(1), 23–27.

Fincham, F. D., & Beach, S. R. H. (2006). Relationship satisfaction. In A. L. Vangelisti & D. Perlman (Eds.), *The Cambridge handbook of personal relationships.* New York: Cambridge University Press.

Fine, R. (1990). *The history of psychoanalysis.* New York: Continuum.

Finkelhor, D., Mitchell, K., & Wolak, J. (2000). *Online victimization: A report on the nation's youth.* Washington, DC: National Center for Missing and Exploited Children.

Finkenauer, C., & Hazam, H. (2000). Disclosure and secrecy in marriage: Do both contribute to marital satisfaction? *Journal of Social and Personal Relationships, 17*(2), 245–263.

First, M. B. (2003). Psychiatric classification. In A. Tasman, J. Kay, & J. A. Lieberman (Eds.), *Psychiatry.* New York: Wiley.

Fischer, K. W., & Bidell, T. R. (1998). Dynamic development of psychological structures in action and thought. In R. M. Lerner (Ed.), *Handbook of child psychology: Vol. 1. Theoretical models of human development.* New York: Wiley.

Fischer, P., Greitemeyer, T., & Pollozek, F. (2006). The unresponsive bystander: Are bystanders more responsive in dangerous emergencies? *European Journal of Social Psychology, 36,* 267–278.

Fisher, E. B., Brownson, R. C., Heath, A. C., Luke, D. A., & Sumner II, W. (2004). Cigarette smoking. In J. M. Raczynski & L. C. Leviton (Eds.), *Handbook of clinical health psychology: Vol. 2. Disorders of behavior and health.* Washington, DC: American Psychological Association.

Fisher, S., & Greenberg, R. P. (1996). *Freud scientifically reappraised: Testing the theories and therapy.* New York: Wiley.

Fishman, D. B., & Franks, C. M. (1992). Evolution and differentiation within behavior therapy: A theoretical epistemological review. In D. K. Freedheim (Ed.), *History of psychotherapy: A century of change.* Washington, DC: American Psychological Association.

Fiske, S. T. (1993). Social cognition and social perception. *Annual Review of Psychology, 44,* 155–194.

Fiske, S. T. (1998). Stereotyping, prejudice, and discrimination. In D. T. Gilbert, S. T. Fiske, & G. Lindzey (Eds.), *The handbook of social psychology.* New York: McGraw-Hill.

Fiske, S. T. (2002). What we know now about bias and intergroup conflict, the problem of the century. *Current Directions in Psychological Science, 11*(4), 123–128.

Fiske, S. T. (2004). *Social beings: A core motives approach to social psychology.* New York: Wiley.

Fiske, S. T., Harris, L. T., & Cuddy, A. J. C. (2004). Why ordinary people torture enemy prisoners. *Science, 36,* 1482–1483.

Fiske, S. T., & Ruscher, J. B. (1993). Negative interdependence and prejudice: Whence the affect? In D. M. Mackie & D. L. Hamilton (Eds.), *Affect, cognition, and stereotyping: Interactive processes in group perception.* New York: Academic.

Fiske, S. T., & Taylor, S. E. (1991). *Social cognition.* New York: McGraw-Hill.

Fitch, S. A., & Adams, G. R. (1983). Ego identity and intimacy status: Replication and extension. *Developmental Psychology, 19,* 839–845.

Fitness, J., Fletcher, G., & Overall, N. (2007). Interpersonal attraction and intimate relationships. In M. A. Hogg & J. Cooper (Eds.), *The Sage handbook of social psychology.* Los Angeles: Sage.

Flaks, D. K., Ficher, I., Masterpasqua, M., & Joseph, G. (1995). Lesbians choosing motherhood: A comparative study of lesbians and heterosexual parents and their children. *Developmental Psychology, 31,* 105–114.

Flannagan, D., & Perese, S. (1998). Emotional references in mother-daughter and mother-son dyads' conversations about school. *Sex Roles, 39*(5–6), 353–367.

Flannery, R. B., Jr. (1999). Psychological trauma and posttraumatic stress disorder: A review. *International Journal of Mental Health, 1*(2), 135–140.

Flavell, J. H., Miller, P. H., & Miller, S. A. (2001). *Cognitive development.* Upper Saddle River, NJ: Prentice-Hall.

Flavin, C., & Dunn, S. (1999). Reinventing the energy system. In L. R. Brown, C. Flavin, H. French, J. Abramovitz, S. Dunn, G. Gardner, A. Mattoon, A. P. McGinn, M. O'Meara, M. Renner, D. Roodman, P. Sampat, L. Starke, & J. Tuxill (Eds.), *State of the world 1999.* New York: Norton.

Fleeson, W. (2004). Moving personality beyond the person-situation debate: The challenge and the opportunity of within-person variability. *Current Directions in Psychological Science, 13*(2), 83–87.

Fleeson, W., Malanos, A. B., & Achille, N. M. (2002). An intraindividual process approach to the relationship between extraversion and positive affect: Is acting extraverted as "good" as being extraverted? *Journal of Personality and Social Psychology, 83*(6), 1409–1422.

Fletcher, G. (2002). *The new science of intimate relationships.* Malden, MA: Blackwell Publishers.

Fletcher, G. J. O., Overall, N. C., & Friesen, M. D. (2006). Social cognition in intimate relationships. In A. L. Vangelisti & D. Perlman (Eds.), *The Cambridge handbook of personal relationships.* New York: Cambridge University Press.

Fletcher, G. J. O., & Thomas, G. (2000). Behavior and on-line cognition in marital interaction. *Personal Relationships, 7*(1), 111–130.

Fletcher, G. J. O., Tither, J. M., O'Loughlin, C., Friesen, M., & Overall, N. (2004). Warm and homely or cold and beautiful? Sex differences in trading off traits in mate selection. *Personality and Social Psychology Bulletin, 30,* 659–672.

Fletcher, G. J. O., & Ward, C. (1988). Attribution theory and processes: A cross-cultural perspective. In M. H. Bond (Ed.), *The cross-cultural challenge to social psychology.* Newbury Park, CA: Sage.

Flett, G. L., Hewitt, P. L., & Martin, T. R. (1995). Dimensions of perfectionism and procrastination. In J. R. Ferrari, J. L. Johnson, & W. G. McCown (Eds.), *Procrastination and task avoidance: Theory, research, and treatment.* New York: Plenum Press.

Flippen, C., & Tienda, M. (2000). Pathways to retirement: Patterns of labor force participation and labor market exit among pre-retirement population by race, Hispanic orgin, and sex . *Journals of Gerontology: Series B: Psychological Sciences and Social Sciences, 55B*(1), S14–S27.

Flores, B. H., Musselman, D. L., DeBattista, C., Garlow, S. J., Schatzberg, A. F., & Nemeroff, C. B. (2004). Biology of mood disorders. In A. F. Schatzberg & C. B. Nemeroff (Eds.), *Textbook of psychopharmacology.* Washington, DC: American Psychiatric Publishing.

Floyd, F. J., & Bakeman, R. (2006). Coming-out across the life course: Implications of age and historical context. *Archives of Sexual Behavior, 35,* 287–297.

Floyd, M. (2003). Bibliotherapy as an adjunct to psychotherapy for depression in older adults. *Journal of Clinical Psychology, 59*(2), 187–195.

Flynn, F. J., Reagans, R. E., Amanatullah, E. T., & Ames, D. R. (2006). Helping one's way to the top: Self-monitors achieve status by helping others and knowing who helps whom. *Journal of Personality and Social Psychology, 91,* 1123–1137.

Foa, E. B. (1998). Rape and posttraumatic stress disorder. In E. A. Blechman & K. D. Brownell (Eds.), *Behavioral medicine and women: A comprehensive handbook.* New York: Guilford Press.

Foa, E. B., Hembree, E. A., Riggs, D., Rauch, S., & Franklin, M. (2001). *Common reactions to trauma.* Retrieved November 21, 2001 from U.S. Department of Veterans Affairs National Center for PTSD Web site: http:www.ncptsd.org/facts/disasters/fs_foa_handout.html.

Folkman, S. (1997). Positive psychological states and coping with severe stress. *Social Science and Medicine, 45,* 1207–1221.

Folkman, S., & Moskowitz, J. T. (2000). Positive affect and the other side of coping. *American Psychologist, 55*(6), 647–654.

Folkman, S., Moskowitz, J. T., Ozer, E. M., & Park, C. L. (1997). Positive meaningful events and coping in the context of HIV/AIDS. In B. H. Gottlieb (Ed.), *Coping with chronic stress.* New York: Plenum.

Foote, B., Smolin, Y., Kaplan M., Legatt, M. E., & Lipschitz, D. (2006). Prevalence of dissociative disorders in psychiatric outpatients. *American Journal of Psychiatry, 163,* 623–629.

Forbes, G. B., Adams-Curtis, L. E., & White, K. B. (2004). First- and second-generation measures of sexism, rape, myths and related beliefs, and hostility toward women: Their interrelationships and associations with college students' experience with dating aggression and sexual coercion. *Violence Against Women, 10*(3), 236–261.

Formicelli, L. (2001, March/April). Baby blues. *Psychology Today,* p. 24.

Forrest, J. A., & Feldman, R. S. (2000). Detecting deception and judge's involvement: Lower task involvement leads to better lie detection. *Personality and Social Psychology Bulletin, 26*(1), 118–125.

Forstein, M. (2004). The pseudoscience of sexual orientation change therapy. *BMJ USA, 4,* 143–144.

Forsyth, D. R., & Strong, S. R. (1986). The scientific study of counseling and psychotherapy: A unificationist view. *American Psychologist, 41,* 113–119.

Foster, J. D., Kuperminc, G. P., & Price, A. W. (2004). Gender differences in posttraumatic stress related symptoms among inner-city minority youth exposed to community violence. *Journal of Youth and Adolescence, 33,* 59–69.

Fouad, N. A. (2007). Work and vocational psychology: Theory, Research, and applications. *Annual Review of Psychology, 58,* 543–564.

Fouad, N. A., & Mohler, C. J. (2004). Cultural validity of Holland's theory and the Strong Interest Inventory for five racial/ethnic groups. *Journal of Career Assessment, 12,* 423–439.

Fouts, G., & Burggraf, K. (1999). Television situation comedies: Female body images and verbal reinforcements. *Sex Roles, 40*(5/6), 473–481.

Fouts, G., & Vaughan, K. (2002). Television situation comedies: Male weight, negative references, and audience reactions. *Sex Roles, 46*(11/12), 439–442.

Fowers, B. J. (2000). *Beyond the myth of marital happiness: How embracing the virtues of loyalty, generosity, justice, and courage can strengthen your relationship.* San Francisco: Jossey-Bass.

Fowers, B. J., Applegate, B., Olson, D. H., & Pomerantz, B. (1994). Marital conventionalization as a measure of marital satisfaction: A confirmatory factor analysis. *Journal of Family Psychology, 8,* 98–103.

Fowers, B. J., Lyons, E., Montel, K. H., & Shaked, N. (2001). Positive illusions about marriage among married and single individuals. *Journal of Family Psychology, 15*(1), 95–109.

Fowles, D. C. (2003). Schizophrenia spectrum disorders. In G. Stricker & T. A. Widiger (Eds.), *Handbook of psychology: Vol. 8. Clinical psychology.* New York: Wiley.

Fox, G. L., & Chancey, D. (1998). Sources of economic distress: Individual and family outcomes. *Journal of Family Issues, 19,* 725–749.

Fox, G. L., Bruce, C., & Combs-Orme, T. (2000). Parenting expectations and concerns of fathers and mothers of newborn infants. *Family Relations, 49*(2), 123–131.

Fox, R. (1996). Bisexuality in perspective: A review of theory and research. In B. Firestein (Ed.), *Bisexuality: The psychology and politics of an invisible minority.* Thousand Oaks, CA: Sage.

Fraley, R. C. (2002). Attachment stability from infancy to adulthood: Meta-analysis and dynamic modeling of developmental mechanisms. *Personality and Social Psychology Review, 6*(2), 123–151.

Fraley, R. C., & Brumbaugh, C. C. (2004). A dynamical systems approach to conceptualizing and studying stability and change in attachment security. In W. S. Rholes & J. A. Simpson (Eds.), *Adult attachment: Theory, research, and clinical implications.* New York: The Guilford.

Frank, E., Anderson, C., & Rubinstein, D. (1978). Frequency of sexual dysfunction in "normal" couples. *New England Journal of Medicine, 299,* 111–115.

Frank, J. D. (1961). *Persuasion and healing.* Baltimore: John Hopkins University Press.

Frank, J. D., & Frank, J. B. (1991). *Persuasion and healing: A comparison study of psychotherapy.* Baltimore: Johns Hopkins University Press.

Frank, L. R. (1990). Electroshock: Death, brain damage, memory loss, and brainwashing. *The Journal of Mind and Behavior, 11,* 489–512.

Frank, M. G., & Ekman, P. (1997). The ability to detect deceit generalizes different types of high-stake lies. *Journal of Personality and Social Psychology, 72,* 1429–1439.

Frank, R. H. (1999). *Luxury fever: Why money fails to satisfy in an era of excess.* New York: Free Press.

Frankel, F. H. (1993). Adult reconstruction of childhood events in the multiple personality literature. *American Journal of Psychiatry, 150,* 954–958.

Franzoi, S. L., & Herzog, M. E. (1987). Judging personal attractiveness: What body aspects do we use? *Personality and Social Psychology Bulletin, 13,* 19–33.

Frasure-Smith, N., Lesperance, F., & Talajic, M. (1995). The impact of negative emotions on prognosis following myocardial infarction: Is it more than depression? *Health Psychology, 14,* 388–398.

Frazier, P. A., Mortensen, H., & Steward, J. (2005). Coping strategies as mediators of the relations among perceived control and distress in sexual assault survivors. *Journal of Counseling Psychology, 52,* 267–278.

Frederick, S., & Loewenstein, G. (1999). Hedonic adaptation. In D. Kahneman, E. Diener, & N. Schwarz (Eds.), *Well-being: The foundations of hedonic psychology.* New York: Sage.

Fredrickson, B. L. (1998). What good are positive emotions? *Review of General Psychology, 2,* 300–319.

Fredrickson, B. L. (2001). The role of positive emotions in positive psychology: The broaden-and-build theory of positive emotions. *American Psychologist, 56,* 218–226.

Fredrickson, B. L. (2006). The broaden-and-build theory of positive emotions. In M. Csikszentmihalyi & I. S. Csikszentmihalyi (Eds.), *A life worth living: Contributions to positive psychology.* New York: Oxford University Press.

Fredrickson, B. L., & Branigan, C. (2005). Positive emotions broaden the scope of attention and thought-action repertoires. *Cognition and Emotion, 19,* 313–332.

Fredrickson, B. L., & Losada, M. F. (2005). Positive affect and the complex dynamics of human flourishing. *American Psychologist, 60,* 678–686.

Fredrickson, B. L., Roberts, T., Noll, S. M., Quinn, D. M., & Twenge, J. M. (1998). That swimsuit becomes you: Sex differences in self-objectification, restrained eating, and math performance. *Journal of Personality and Social Psychology , 75,* 269–284.

Fredrickson, B. L., Tugade, M. M., Waugh, C. E., & Larkin, G. R. (2003). What good are positive emotions in crises? A prospective study of resilience and emotions following the terrorist attacks on the United States on September 11th, 2001. *Journal of Personality and Social Psychology, 84*(2), 365–376.

Freedberg, K., Losina, E., Weinstein, M., Paltiel, A., Cohen, C., Seage, G., Craven, D., Zhang, H., Kimmel, A., & Goldie, S. (2001). The cost effectiveness of combination antiretroviral therapy for HIV disease. *New England Journal of Medicine,* 824–831.

Freedman, J. L., & Fraser, S. C. (1966). Compliance without pressure: The foot-in-the-door technique. *Journal of Personality and Social Psychology, 4,* 195–202.

Freeman, E., Bloom, D., & McGuire, E. (2001). A brief history of testosterone. *Journal of Urology, 165,* 371–373.

Freese, J., Powell, B., & Steelman, L. C. (1999). Rebel without a cause or effect: Birth order and social attitudes. *American Sociological Review, 64,* 207–231.

Fremouw, W. J., de Perczel, M., & Ellis, T. E. (1990). *Suicide risk: Assessment and response guidelines.* New York: Pergamon.

French, S. A., Harnack, L., & Jeffrey, R. W. (2000). Fast food restaurant use among women in the Pound of Prevention study: Dietary, behavioral and demographic correlates. *International Journal of Obesity, 24,* 1353–1359.

Freud, S. (1901/1960). *The psychopathology of everyday life* (Standard ed., Vol. 6.) London: Hogarth. (Original work published 1901)

Freud, S. (1920/1924). *A general introduction to psychoanalysis.* New York: Boni and Liveright. (Original work published 1920)

Freud, S. (1923). *The ego and the id* (Standard ed., Vol. 19.) London: Hogarth.

Freud, S. (1935). *A general introduction to psychoanalysis* (J. Rivere, Trans.). New York: Liveright.

Frey, B. S., & Stutzer, A. (2002). What can economists learn from happiness research? *Journal of Economic Literature, 40,* 402–435.

Fried, S. B., & Schultis, G. A. (1995). *The best self-help and self-awareness books: A topic-by-topic guide to quality information.* Chicago: American Library Association.

Friedan, B. (1964). *The feminine mystique.* New York: Dell.

Friedman, H. S. (1991). *The self-healing personality: Why some people achieve health and others succumb to illness.* New York: Holt.

Friedman, H. S. (2007). Personality, disease, and self-healing. In H. S. Friedman & R. C. Silver (Eds.), *Foundations of health psychology.* New York: Oxford University Press.

Friedman, H. S., & Adler, N. E. (2007). The history and background of health psychology. In H. S. Friedman & R. C. Silver (Eds.), *Foundations of health psychology.* New York: Oxford University Press.

Friedman, J. (1989). The impact of homophobia on male sexual development. *Siecus Report, 17,* 8–9.

Friedman, M. (1996). *Type A behavior: Its diagnosis and treatment.* New York: Plenum Press.

Friedman, M., & Rosenman, R. F. (1974). *Type A behavior and your heart.* New York: Knopf.

Friedman, M. J. (2006). Posttraumatic stress disorder among military returnees from Afghanistan and Iraq. *American Journal of Psychiatry, 163,* 586-593.

Friedrich, M. J. (2004). To "E" or not to "E," vitamin E's role in health and disease is the question. *Journal of the American Medical Association, 292*(6), 671–673.

Friend, R., Rafferty, Y., & Bramel, D. (1990). A puzzling misinterpretation of the Asch "conformity" study. *European Journal of Social Psychology, 20,* 29–44.

Fromholt, P., & Bruhn, P. (1998). Cognitive dysfunction and dementia. In I. H. Nordus, G. R. VandenBos, S. Berg, & P. Fromholt (Eds.), *Clinical geropsychology.* Washington, DC: American Psychological Association.

Fromm, E. (1963). *Escape from freedom.* New York: Holt.

Fromm, E. (1981). *Sane society.* New York: Fawcett.

Fuligni, A. J., & Eccles, J. S. (1993). Perceived parent-child relationships and early adolescents' orientation toward peers. *Developmental Psychology, 29,* 622–632.

Fullerton, C. S., Ursano, R. J., & Wang, L. (2004). Acute stress disorder, posttraumatic stress disorder, and depression in disaster or rescue workers. *American Journal of Psychiatry, 161,* 1370–1376.

Fullerton, H. N., Jr. (1997). Labor force 2006: Slowing down and changing composition. *Monthly Labor Review, 120,* 23–38.

Funder, D. C. (2001). Personality. *Annual Review of Psychology, 52,* 197–221.

Furman, E. (1984). Children's patterns in mourning the death of a loved one. In H. Wass & C. A. Corr (Eds.), *Childhood and death.* Washington, DC: Hemisphere.

Furnham, A., & Cheng, H. (2000). Perceived parental behavior, self-esteem and happiness. *Social Psychiatry and Psychiatric Epidemiology, 35*(10), 463–470.

Furnham, A., & Mak, T. (1999). Sex-role stereotyping in television commercials: A review and comparison of fourteen studies done on five continents over 25 years. *Sex Roles, 41,* 413–437.

Furnham, A., & Procter, E. (1989). Belief in a just world: Review and critique of the individual difference literature. *British Journal of Social Psychology, 28*(4), 365–384.

Furstenberg, F. F., Jr. (2001). The sociology of adolescence and youth in the 1990s: A critical commentary. In R. M. Milardo (Ed.), *Understanding families into the new millennium: A decade in review.* Minneapolis, MN: National Council on Family Relations.

Furstenberg, F. F., Jr., & Kiernan, K. E. (2001). Delayed parental divorce: How much do children benefit? *Journal of Marriage and Family, 63,* 446–457.

Fyer, A. J. (2000). Anxiety disorders: Genetics. In B. J. Sadock & V. A. Sadock (Eds.), *Kaplan and Sadock's comprehensive textbook of psychiatry* (7th ed., Vol. 1). Philadelphia: Lippincott/Williams & Wilkins.

Gabbard, G. O. (1994). Reconsidering the American Psychological Association's policy on sex with former patients: Is it justifiable? *Professional Psychology: Research and Practice, 25,* 329–335.

Gable, S. L., Gonzaga, G. C., & Strachman, A. (2006). Will you be there for me when things go right? Supportive responses to positive event disclosures. *Journal of Personality and Social Psychology, 91,* 904–917.

Gabrel, C. S. (2000). *Advance data from Vital and Health Statistics of the Centers for Disease Control and Prevention.* Washington, DC: U.S. Department of Health and Human Services.

Gabriel, S., & Gardner, W. L. (1999). Are there "his" and "hers" types of interdependence? The implications of gender differences in collective versus relational interdependence for affect, behavior, and cognition. *Journal of Personality and Social Psychology, 77*(3), 642–655.

Gaertner, S. L., & Dovidio, J. F. (1986). The aversive form of racism. In J. F. Dovidio & S. L. Gaertner (Eds.), *Prejudice, discrimination, and racism: Theory and research.* Orlando, FL: Academic Press.

Gaertner, S. L., & Dovidio, J. F. (2005). Understanding and addressing contemporary racism: From aversive racism to the common ingroup identity model. *Journal of Social Issues, 61,* 615–639.

Gaertner, S. L., Dovidio, J. F., & Banker, B. S. (2000). Reducing intergroup conflict: From superordinate goals to decategorization, and mutual differentiation. *Group Dynamics: Theory, Research and Practice, 4,* 98–114.

Gage, F. H. (2002). Neurogenesis in the adult brain. *Journal of Neuroscience, 22,* 612–613.

Galambos, N. L., Barker, E. T., & Krahn, H. J. (2006). Depression, self-esteem, and anger in emerging adulthood: Seven-year trajectories. *Developmental Psychology, 42,* 350–365.

Galderisi, S., Maj, M., Mucci, A., Cassano, G. B., Invernizzi, G., Rossi, A., Vita, A., Dell'Osso, L., Daneluzzo, E., & Pini, S. (2002). Historical, psychopathological, neurological, and neuropsychological aspects of deficit schizophrenia: A multicenter study. *American Journal of Psychiatry, 159,* 983–990.

Galinsky, E., Bond, J. T., Kim, S. S., Backon, L., Brownfield, E., & Sakai, K. (2005). *Overwork in America.* New York: Families and Work Institute.

Gall, T. L., Evans, D. R., & Howard, J. (1997). The retirement adjustment process: Changes in the well-being of male retirees across time. *Journal of Gerontology: Psychological Sciences, 52,* 110–117.

Gallagher, R., & Chase, A. (2002). *Building resilience in children in the face of fear and tragedy.* Retrieved January 11, 2005 From the New York University Child Study Center Website: Http://www.About-ourkids.Org/Aboutour/Articles/Crisis_Resilience.html.

Gambone, J. C., Reiter, R. C., & DiMatteo, M. R. (1994). *The PREPARED provider: A guide for improved patient communication.* Beaverton, OR: Mosybl Great Performance.

Gana, K., Alaphilippe, D., & Bailly, N. (2004). Positive illusions and mental and physical health in later life. *Aging and Mental Health, 8*(1), 58–64.

Ganahl, D. J., Prinsen, T. J., & Netzley, S. B. (2003). A content analysis of prime time commercials: A contextual framework of gender representation. *Sex Roles, 49,* 545–551.

Gangestad, S. W. (1993). Sexual selection and physical attractiveness: Implications for mating dynamics. *Human Nature, 4,* 205–235.

Gangestad, S. W., & Snyder, M. (2000). Self-monitoring appraisal and reappraisal. *Psychological Bulletin, 126*(4), 530–555.

Gantt, W. H. (1975, April 25). Unpublished lecture, Ohio State University. Cited in D. Hothersall (1984), *History of psychology.* New York: Random House.

Gao, G. (2001). Intimacy, passion and commitment in Chinese and U.S. American romantic relationships. *International Journal of Intercultural Relations, 25*(3), 329–342.

Garb, H. N., Florio, C. M., & Grove, W. M. (1998). The validity of the Rorschach and the Minnesota Multiphasic Personality Inventory: Results from meta-analysis. *Psychological Science, 9,* 402–404.

Garland, A. F., & Zigler, E. (1993). Adolescent suicide prevention: Current research and social policy implications. *American Psychologist, 48,* 169–182.

Garnets, L. D., & Kimmel, D. C. (1991). Lesbian and gay male dimensions in the psychological study of human diversity. In J. D. Goodchilds (Ed.), *Psychological perspectives on human diversity in America.* Washington, DC: American Psychological Association.

Garnets, L. D., & Kimmel, D. C. (2003a). Identity development and stigma management. In L. D. Garnets & D. C. Kimmel (Eds.), *Psychological perspectives on lesbian, gay, and bisexual experiences.* New York: Columbia University Press.

Garnets, L. D., & Kimmel, D. C. (2003b). Lesbian, gay male, and bisexual dimensions in the psychological study of human diversity. In L. D. Garnets & D. C. Kimmel (Eds.), *Psychological perspectives on lesbian, gay and bisexual experiences.* New York: Columbia University Press.

Gartrell, N., Banks, A., Hamilton, J., Reed, N., Bishop, H., & Rodas, C. (1999). The national lesbian family study: Interviews with mothers of toddlers. *American Journal of Orthopsychiatry, 69,* 362–369.

Gates, G. J., & Sell, R. (2007). Measuring gay and lesbian couples. In S. L. Hofferth & L. M. Casper (Eds.), *Handbook of measurement issues in family research.* Mahwah, NJ: Erlbaum.

Gatz, M., & Smyer, M. A. (2001). Mental health and aging at the outset of the twenty-first century. In J. E. Birren & K. W. Schaie (Eds.), *Handbook of the psychology of aging.* San Diego, CA: Academic Press.

Gaunt, R. (2006). Couple similarity and marital satisfaction: Are similar spouses happier? *Journal of Personality, 74,* 1401–1420.

Gavin, L. E., Black, M. M., Minor, S., Abel, Y., & Bentley, M. E. (2002). Young, disadvantaged fathers' involvement with their infants: An ecological perspective. *Journal of Adolescent Health, 31,* 266–276.

Ge, X., Conger, R. D., & Elder, G. H. Jr. (1996). Coming of age too early: Pubertal influences on girls' vulnerability to psychological distress. *Child Development, 67,* 3386–3400.

Ge, X., Conger, R. D., & Elder, G. H. Jr. (2001). The relation between puberty and psychological distress in adolescent boys. *Journal of Research on Adolescence, 11*(1), 49–70.

Ge, X., Kim, I. J., Brody, G. H., Conger, R. D., Simons, R. L., & Gibbons, F. X. (2003). It's about timing and change: Pubertal transition effects on symptoms of major depression among African American youth. *Developmental Psychology, 39,* 430–439.

Gecas, V., & Schwalbe, M. L. (1986). Parental behavior and adolescent self-esteem. *Journal of Marriage and the Family, 48,* 37–46.

Gecas, V., & Seff, M. A. (1990). Families and adolescents: A review of the 1980s. *Journal of Marriage and the Family, 52,* 941–958.

Geddes, J. R., Burgess, S., Hawton, K., Jamison, K., & Goodwin, G. M. (2004). Long-term lithium therapy for bipolar disorder: Systematic review and meta-analysis of randomized controlled trials. *American Journal of Psychiatry, 161,* 217–222.

Gee, T., Allen, K., & Powell, R. A. (2003). Questioning premorbid dissociative symptomatology in dissociative identity disorder. *Professional Psychology: Research & Practice, 34*(1), 114–116.

Geen, R. G. (1998). Aggression and antisocial behavior. In D. T. Gilbert, S. T. Fiske, & G. Lindzey (Eds.), *The handbook of social psychology* (4th ed., Vol. 2). Boston: McGraw-Hill.

Geeraert, N. Y., Yzerbyt, V. Y., Corneille, O., & Wigboldus, D. (2004). The return of dispositionalism: On the linguistic consequences of dispositional suppression. *Journal of Experimental Social Psychology, 40,* 264–272.

Geller, A. (2003, October 23). Employers looking for places to trim worker flexibility programs. *Statesboro Herald.*

Gelles, R. J. (1996). *The book of David: How preserving families can cost children's lives.* New York: Basic Books.

George, S. A. (2002). The menopause experience: A woman's perspective. *Journal of Obstetric, Gynecologic, and Neonatal Nursing, 31,* 71–85.

Gershoff, E. T. (2002). Corporal punishment by parents and associated child behaviors and experiences: A meta-analytic and theoretical review. *Psychological Bulletin, 128*(4), 539–579.

Gervey, B., Igou, E. R., & Trope, Y. (2005). Positive mood and future-oriented self-evaluation. *Motivation and Emotion, 29,* 269–296.

Gibbons, J. L. (2000). Gender development in cross-cultural perspective. In T. Eckes & H. M. Trautner (Eds.), *The developmental social psychology of gender.* Mahwah, NJ: Erlbaum.

Gibbons, R. D., Hur, K., Bhaumik, D. K., & Mann, J. J. (2006). The relationship between antidepressant prescription rates and rate of early adolescent suicide. *American Journal of Psychiatry, 163,* 1898–1904.

Gibbs, J. L., Ellison, N. B., & Heino, R. D. (2006). Self-presentation in online personals: The role of anticipated future interaction, self-disclosure, and perceived success in Internet dating. *Communication Research, 33*(2), 152–177.

Giddens, A. (2001). The global revolution in family and personal life. In A. S. Skolnick, & J. H. Skolnick (Eds.), *Families in Transition.* Boston: Allyn & Bacon.

Gierveld, J., van Tilburg, & Dykstra, P. A. (2006). Loneliness and social isolation. In A. L. Vangelisti & D. Perlman (Eds.). *The Cambridge handbook of personal relationships* (pp. 485–499). New York: Cambridge University Press.

Gilbert, D. T. (2002). Inferential correction. In T. Gilovich, D. W. Griffin, & D. Kahneman (Eds.), *Heuristics and biases: The psychology of intuitive judgment.* New York: Cambridge University Press.

Gilbert, D. T. (2006). *Stumbling on happiness.* New York: Alfred A. Knopf.

Gilbert, D. T., & Malone, P. S. (1995). The correspondence bias. *Psychological Bulletin, 117,* 21–38.

Giles, T. R., & Marafiote, R. A. (1998). Managed care and the practitioner: A call for unity. *Clinical Psychology: Science & Practice, 5,* 41–50.

Gilham, J. E., Shatté, A. J., Reivich, K. J., & Seligman, M. E. P. (2001). Optimism, pessimism, and explanatory style. In E. C. Chang (Ed.), *Optimism & pessimism: Implications for theory, research, and practice.* Washington, DC: American Psychological Association.

Gill, D. S., Christensen, A., & Fincham, F. D. (1999). Predicting marital satisfaction from behavior: Do all roads really lead to Rome? *Personal Relationships, 6,* 369–387.

Gilovich, T., Kruger, J., & Medvec, V. H. (2002). The spotlight effect revisited: Overestimating the manifest variability of our actions and appearance. *Journal of Experimental Social Psychology, 38,* 93–99.

Gitlin, M. (2002). Pharmacological treatment of depression. In I. H. Gotlib & C. L. Hammen (Eds.), *Handbook of depression.* New York: Guilford.

Gitlin, M., Nuechterlein, K., Subotnik, K. L., Ventura, J., Mintz, J., Fogelson, D. L., Bartzokis, G., & Aravagiri, M. (2001). Clinical outcome following neuroleptic discontinuation in patients with remitted recent-onset schizophrenia. *American Journal of Psychiatry, 158,* 1835–1842.

Glascock, J. (2001). Gender roles on prime-time network television: Demographics and behaviors. *Journal of Broadcasting and Electronic Media, 45*(4), 656–669.

Glaser, R., Kiecolt-Glaser, J. K., Bonneau, R. H., Malarkey, W., Kennedy, S., & Hughes, J. (1992). Stress-induced modulation of the immune response to recombinant Hepatitis B vaccine. *Psychosomatic Medicine, 54,* 22–29.

Glass, C. R., & Arnkoff, D. B. (1992). Behavior therapy. In D. K. Freedheim (Ed.), *History of psychotherapy: A century of change.* Washington, DC: American Psychological Association.

Glass, R. M. (2001). Electroconvulsive therapy. *Journal of the American Medical Association, 285*(10), 1346–1348.

Glass, R. M. (2004). Treatment of adolescents with major depression: Contributions of a major trial. *Journal of the American Medical Association, 292*(7), 861–863.

Glassman, A., Shapiro, P. A., Ford, D. E., Culpepper, L., Finkel, M. S., Swenson, J. R., Bigger, J. T., Rollman, B. L., & Wise, T. N. (2003). Cardiovascular health and depression. *Journal of Psychiatric Practice, 9*(6), 409–421.

Glazer, M. P., & Glazer, P. M. (1990). *The whistleblowers: Exposing corruption in government and industry.* New York: Basic Books.

Gleason, J. B., & Ely, R. (2002). Gender differences in language development. In A. McGillicuddy-DeLisi & R. DeLisi (Eds.), *Biology, society, and behavior: The development of sex differences in cognition. Advances in applied developmental psychology, 21.* Westport, CT: Ablex.

Gleaves, D. H. (1994). On "the reality of repressed memories." *American Psychologist, 49,* 440–441.

Gleaves, D. H., May, M. C., & Cardena, E. (2001). An examination of the diagnostic validity of dissociative identity disorders. *Clinical Psychology Review, 21,* 577–608.

Gleaves, D. H., Miller, K. J., Williams, T. J., & Summers, S. A. (2000). Eating disorders: An overview. In K. J. Miller & J. S. Mizes (Eds.), *Comparative treatments for eating disorders.* New York: Springer.

Gleaves D. H., & Smith. S. M. (2004). False and recovered memories in the laboratory and clinic: A review of experimental and clinical evidence. *Clinical Psychology: Science and Practice, 11*(1), 2–28.

Glenn, N. D. (1998). The course of marital success and failure in five American 10-year marriage cohorts. *Journal of Marriage and the Family, 60,* 569–576.

Gluck, M. E. (2006). Stress response and binge eating disorder. *Appetite, 46*(1), 26–30.

Godfrey, J. R. (2004). Toward optimal health: The experts discuss therapeutic humor. *Journal of Women's Health, 13,* 474–479.

Goeders, N. E. (2004). Stress, motivation, and drug addiction. *Current Directions in Psychological Science, 13*(1), 33–35.

Goetting, A. (1986). Parental satisfaction: A review of research. *Journal of Family Issues, 7,* 83–109.

Goffman, E. (1959). *The presentation of self in everyday life.* Garden City, NJ: Doubleday.

Gold, J. M., & Green, M. F. (2005). Schizophrenia: Cognition. In B. J. Sadock & V. A. Sadock (Eds.), *Kaplan & Sadock's comprehensive textbook of psychiatry.* Philadelphia: Lippincott Williams & Wilkins.

Gold, M. S., & Jacobs, W. S. (2005). Cocaine and crack: Clinical aspects. In J. H. Lowinson, P. Ruiz, R. B. Millman, & J. G. Langrod (Eds.), *Substance abuse: A comprehensive textbook.* Philadelphia: Lippincott/Williams & Wilkins.

Gold, M. S., Miller, N. S., & Jonas, J. M. (1992). Cocaine (and crack): Neurobiology. In J. H. Lowinson, P. Ruiz, & R. B. Millman (Eds.), *Substance abuse: A comprehensive textbook* (2nd ed.). Baltimore: Williams & Wilkins.

Goldberg, A. E., & Perry-Jenkins, M. (2004). Division of labor and working-class women's well-being across the transition to parenthood. *Journal of Family Psychology, 18*(1), 225–236.

Goldberg, C., & Zhang, L. (2004). Simple and joint effects of gender and self-esteem on responses to same-sex sexual harrassment. *Sex Roles, 50*(11/12), 823–833.

Goldberger, L. (1993). Sensory deprivation and overload. In L. Goldberger & S. Breznitz (Eds.), *Handbook of stress: Theoretical and clinical aspects* (2nd ed.). New York: Free Press.

Goldenberg, J. L. (2005). The body stripped down: An existential account of the threat posed by the physical body. *Current Directions in Psychological Science, 14*(4), 224–228.

Goldenberg, J. L., Cox, C. R., Pyszczynski, T., Greenberg, J., & Solomon, S. (2002). Understanding human ambivalence about sex: The effects of stripping sex of meaning. *Journal of Sex Research, 39,* 310–320.

Goldfried, M. R. (2001). Integrating gay, lesbian, and bisexual issues into mainstream psychology. *American Psychologist, 56*(11), 977–988.

Golding, J. M. (1996). Sexual assault history and women's reproductive and sexual health. *Psychology of Women Quarterly, 20,* 101–121.

Goldscheider, F. K., & Goldscheider, C. (1998). The effects of childhood family structure on leaving and returning home. *Journal of Marriage and the Family, 60,* 745–756.

Goldsmith, T. D., & Shapira, N. A. (2006). Problematic Internet use. In E. Hollander & D. J. Stein (Eds.), *Clinical manual of impulse-control disorders.* Washington, DC: American Psychiatric Publishing.

Goldzweig, C. L., Balekian, T. M., Rolon, C., Yano, E. M., & Shekelle, P. G. (2006). The state of women veterans' health research: Results of a systematic literature review. *Journal of General Internal Medicine, 21*(Suppl 3), S82–S92.

Golombok, S., Perry, B., Burnston, A., Murray, C., Money-Somers, J., Stevens, M., & Golding, J. (2003). Children with lesbian parents: A community study. *Developmental Psychology, 39,* 20–33.

Gonsiorek, J. C. (1991). The empirical basis for the demise of the illness model of homosexuality. In J. Gonsiorek & J. Weinrich (Eds.), *Homosexuality:*

Research implications for public policy. Newbury Park, CA: Sage.

Gonsiorek, J. C., & Weinrich, J. D. (1991). The definition and scope of sexual orientation. In J. C. Gonsiorek & J. D. Weinrich (Eds.), *Homosexuality: Research implications for public policy.* Newbury Park, CA: Sage.

Goodall, K. (1972, November). Field report: Shapers at work. *Psychology Today,* pp. 53–63, 132–138.

Gooden, A. M., & Gooden, M. A. (2001). Gender representation in notable children's picture books: 1995–1999. *Sex Roles, 45*(1/2), 89–101.

Goodrick, G. K., Pendleton, V. R., Kimball, K. T., Poston, W. S., Carlos, R., Rebecca, S., & Foreyt, J. P. (1999). Binge eating severity, self-concept, dieting self-efficacy and social support during treatment of binge eating disorder. *International Journal of Eating Disorders, 26*(3), 295–300.

Goodwin, F. K., & Jamison, K. R. (1990). *Manic-depressive illness.* New York: Oxford University Press.

Goodwin, R. D., Jacobi, F., Bittner, A., & Wittchen, H. (2006). Epidemiology of mood disorders. In D. J. Stein, D. J. Kupfer, & A. F. Schatzberg (Eds.), *Textbook of mood disorders.* Washington, DC: American Psychiatric Publishing.

Gordon, P. A. (2003). The decision to remain single: Implications for women across cultures. *Journal of Mental Health Counseling, 25*(1), 33–44.

Gordon, R. A. (1996). Impact of ingratiation on judgments and evaluations: A meta-analytic investigation. *Journal of Personality and Social Psychology, 71*(1), 54–70.

Gordon, R. M. (2005). The doom and gloom of divorce research: Comment on Wallerstein and Lewis (2004). *Psychoanalytic Psychology, 22,* 450–451.

Gordon, V. M. (2006). *Career advising: An academic advisor's guide.* San Francisco: Jossey-Bass.

Gottdiener, J. S., Krantz, D. S., & Howell, R. H., Hecht, G. M., Klein, J., Falconer, J. J., & Rozanski, A. (1994). Induction of silent myocardial ischemia with mental stress testing: Relationship to the triggers of ischemia during daily life activities and to ischemic functional severity. *Journal of the American College of Cardiology, 24,* 1645–1651.

Gottesman, I. I. (1991). *Schizophrenia genesis: The origins of madness.* New York: Freeman.

Gottesman, I. I. (2001). Psychopathology through a life span–genetic prism. *American Psychologist, 56,* 867–878.

Gottman, J. M. (1993). The roles of conflict engagement, escalation, and avoidance in marital interaction: A longitudinal view of five types of couples. *Journal of Consulting and Clinical Psychology, 61*(1), 6–15.

Gottman, J. M. (with Silver, N.). (1994). *Why marriages succeed or fail . . . And how you can make yours last.* New York: Simon & Schuster.

Gottman, J. M., Coan, J., Carrere, S., & Swanson, C. (1998). Predicting marital happiness and stability from newlywed interactions. *Journal of Marriage and the Family, 60,* 5–22.

Gottman, J. M., Gottman, J. S., & DeClaire, J. (2006). *Ten lessons to transform your marriage.* Crown Publishers: New York, NY.

Gottman, J. M., Ryan, K. D., Carrére, S., & Erley, A. M. (2002). Toward a scientifically based marital therapy. In H. Liddle & D. Santisteban (Eds.), *Family psychology: Science-based interventions.* Washington, DC: American Psychological Association.

Gould, R. L. (1978). *Transformations: Growth and change in adult life.* New York: Simon & Schuster.

Gourevitch, M. N., & Arnsten, J. H. (2005). Medical complications of drug use. In J. H. Lowinson, P. Ruiz, R. B. Millman, & J. G. Langrod (Eds.), *Substance abuse: A comprehensive textbook.* Philadelphia: Lippincott/Williams & Wilkins.

Gouzoulis-Mayfrank, E., Daumann, J., Tuchtenhagen, F., Pelz, S., Becker, S., Kunert, H.-J., Fimm, B., & Sass, H. (2000). Impaired cognitive performance in drug-free users of recreational ecstasy (MDMA). *Journal of Neurology, Neurosurgery, and Psychiatry, 68*(6), 719–725.

Gow, K. M. (1999). Recovered memories of abuse: Real, fabricated, or both? *Australian Journal of Clinical & Experimental Hypnosis, 27*(2), 81–97.

Graber, J. A., Lewinsohn, P. M., Seeley, J. R., & Brooks-Gunn, J. (1997). Is psychopathology associated with the timing of pubertal development? *Journal of the American Academy of Child and Adolescent Psychiatry, 36,* 1768–1776.

Graber, J. A., Petersen, A. C., & Brooks-Gunn, J. (1996). Pubertal processes: Methods, measures, and models. In J. A. Graber, J. Brooks-Gunn, & A. C. Petersen (Eds.), *Transitions through adolescence.* Mahwah, NJ: Erlbaum.

Graber, J. A., Seeley, J. R., Brooks-Gunn, J., & Lewinsohn, P. M. (2004). Is pubertal timing associated with psychopathology in young adulthood? *Journal of American Academy of Child and Adolescent Psychiatry, 43*(6), 718–726.

Graham, J. E., Christian, L. M., & Kiecolt-Glaser, J. K. (2006). Stress, age, and immune function: Toward a lifespan approach. *Journal of Behavioral Medicine, 29,* 389–400.

Graig, E. (1993). Stress as a consequence of the urban physical environment. In L. Goldberger & S. Breznitz (Eds.), *Handbook of stress: Theoretical and clinical aspects* (2nd ed.). New York: Free Press.

Grant, I., McDonald, W. I., Patterson, T., & Trimble, M. R. (1989). Multiple sclerosis. In G. W. Brown & T. O. Harris (Eds.), *Life events and illness.* New York: Guilford Press.

Grasha, A. F., & Kirschenbaum, D. S. (1986). *Adjustment and competence: Concepts and applications.* St. Paul, MN: West Publishing.

Grau, R., Salanova, M., & Peiro, J. M. (2001). Moderator effects of self-efficacy on occupational stress. *Psychology in Spain, 5*(1), 63–74.

Gray, J. (1992). *Men are from Mars, women are from Venus: A practical guide for improving communication and getting what you want in your relationship.* New York: HarperCollins.

Gray-Little, B., & Hafdahl, A. R. (2000). Factors influencing racial comparisons of self-esteem: A quantitative review. *Psychological Bulletin, 126,* 26–54.

Graziano, W. G., & Eisenberg, N. H. (1997). Agreeableness: A dimension of personality. In R. Hogan, J. Johnson, & S. Briggs (Eds), *Handbook of personality psychology.* San Diego, CA: Academic Press.

Green, J. D., & Sedikides, C. (2001). When do self-schemas shape social perception? The role of descriptive ambiguity. *Motivation and Emotion, 25,* 67–83.

Green, L. R., Richardson, D. S., Lago, T., & Schatten-Jones, E. C. (2001). Network correlates of social and emotional loneliness in young and older adults. *Personality and Social Psychology Bulletin, 27*(3), 281–288.

Greenberg, J. S. (2002). *Comprehensive stress management: Health and human performance.* New York: McGraw-Hill.

Greenberg, J., Pyszczynski, T., Solomon, S., Rosenblatt, A., Veeder, M., & Kirkland, S. (1990). Evidence for terror management theory II: The effects of mortality salience on reactions to those who threaten or bolster the cultural worldview. *Journal of Personality and Social Psychology, 58,* 308–318.

Greenberg, J., Solomon, S., & Pyszczynski, T. (1997). Terror management theory of self-esteem and cultural worldviews: Empirical assessments and conceptual refinements. *Advances in Experimental Social Psychology, 29,* 61–139.

Greenberg, J., Solomon, S., Pyszczynski, T., Rosenblatt, A., Burling, J., Lyon, D., Simon, L., Pinel, E. (1992). Why do people need self-esteem? Converging evidence that self-esteem serves an anxiety-buffering function. *Journal of Personality and Social Psychology, 63*(6), 913–922.

Greenberg, R. P., & Fisher, S. (1997). Mood-mending medicines: Probing drug, psychotherapy and placebo solutions. In S. Fisher & R. P. Greenberg (Eds.), *From placebo to panacea: Putting psychiatric drugs to the test.* New York: Wiley.

Greene, K., Derlega, V. J., & Mathews, A. (2006). Self-disclosure in personal relationships. In A. L. Vangelisti & D. Perlman (Eds.), *The Cambridge handbook of personal relationships.* New York: Cambridge University Press.

Greene, R. L. (1992). *Human memory: Paradigms and paradoxes.* Hillsdale, NJ: Erlbaum.

Greenfield, D. N. (1999). Psychological characteristics of compulsive Internet use: A preliminary analysis. *CyberPsychology and Behavior, 2*(5), 403–412.

Greenhaus, J. H. (2003). Career dynamics. In W. C. Borman, D. R. Ilgen, & R. J. Klimoski (Eds.), *Handbook of psychology: Vol. 12. Industrial and organizational psychology.* New York: Wiley.

Greenland, P., Knoll, M. D., Stamler, J., Neaton, J. D., Dyer, A. R., Garside, D. B., & Wilson, P. W. (2003). Major risk factors as antecedents of fatal and nonfatal coronary heart disease events. *Journal of the American Medical Association, 290,* 891–897.

Greenson, R. R. (1967). *The technique and practice of psychoanalysis* (Vol. 1). New York: International Universities Press.

Greenwald, A. G., & Banaji, M. R. (1995). Implicit social cognition: Attitudes, self-esteem, and stereotypes. *Psychological Review, 102*(1), 4–27.

Greenwood, G. L., Relf, M. V., Huang, B., Pollack, L. M., Canchola, J. A., & Catania, J. A. (2002). Battering victimization among a probability-based sample of men who have sex with men. *American Journal of Public Health, 92*(12), 1964–1969.

Gregory, R. J., Schwer Canning, S., Lee, T. W., & Wise, J. C. (2004). Cognitive bibliotherapy for depression: A meta-analysis. *Professional Psychology: Research and Practice, 35*(3), 275–280.

Greitemeyer, T. (2006). What do men and women want in a partner? Are educated partners always more desirable? *Journal of Experimental Social Psychology, 43,* 180–194.

Grencavage, L. M., & Norcross, J. C. (1990). Where are the commonalities among the therapeutic factors? *Professional Psychology: Research and Practice, 21,* 372–378.

Griffith, K. H., & Hebl, M. R. (2002). The disclosure dilemma for gay men and lesbians: "Coming out" at work. *Journal of Applied Psychology, 87*(6), 1191–1199.

Grinspoon, L., Bakalar, J. B., & Russo, E. (2005). Marihuana: Clinical aspects. In J. H. Lowinson, P. Ruiz, R. B. Millman, & J. G. Langrod (Eds.), *Substance abuse: A comprehensive textbook.* Philadelphia: Lippincott/Williams & Wilkins.

Grob, C. S., & Poland, R. E. (2005). MDMA. In J. H. Lowinson, P. Ruiz, R. B. Millman, & J. G. Langrod (Eds.), *Substance abuse: A comprehensive textbook.* Philadelphia: Lippincott/Williams & Wilkins.

Groesz, L. M., Levine, M. P., & Murnen, S. K. (2002). The effect of experimental presentation of thin media images on body satisfaction: A meta-analytic review. *International Journal of Eating Disorders, 31,* 1–16.

Gross, J. J. (2001). Emotion regulation in adulthood: Timing is everything. *Current Directions in Psychological Science, 10,* 214–219.

Grossbaum, M. F., & Bates, G. W. (2002). Correlates of psychological well-being at midlife: The role of generativity, agency and communion, and narrative themes. *International Journal of Behavioral Development, 26*(2), 120–127.

Grossi, G., Perski, A., Evengard, B. , Blomkvist, V., & Orth-Gromer, K. (2003). Physiological correlates of burnout among women. *Journal of Psychosomatic Research, 55,* 309–316.

Grossman, J. B., & Ruiz, P. (2004). Shall we make a leap-of-faith to disulfiram (Antabuse)? *Addictive Disorders & Their Treatment, 3*(3), 129–132.

Groth-Marnat, G. (1997). *Handbook of psychological assessment.* New York: Wiley.

Grothues, C. A., & Marmion, S. L. (2006). Dismantling the myths about intimate violence against women. In P. K. Lundberg-Love & S. L. Marmion (Eds.), *"Intimate" violence against women: When spouses, partners, or lovers attack.* Westport, CT: Praeger Publishers.

Gruber, J. E. (1990). Methodological problems and policy implication in sexual harassment research. *Population Research and Policy Review, 9,* 235–254.

Gruenberg, A. M., & Goldstein, R. D. (2003). Mood disorders: Depression. In A. Tasman, J. Kay, & J. A. Lieberman (Eds.), *Psychiatry.* New York: Wiley.

Grunberg, N. E., Faraday, M. M., & Rahman, M. A. (2001). The psychobiology of nicotine self-administration. In A. Baum, T. A. Revenson, & J. E. Singer (Eds.), *Handbook of health psychology.* Mahwah, NJ: Erlbaum.

Grundy, E., & Henretta, J. C. (2006). Between elderly parents and adult children: A new look at the intergenerational care provided by the "sandwich generation." *Ageing & Society, 26,* 707–722.

Guarda, A. S., Pinto, A. M., Coughlin, J. W., Hussain, S., Haug, N. A., & Heinberg, L. J. (2007). Perceived coercion and change in perceived need for admission in patients hospitalized for eating disorders. *American Journal of Psychiatry, 164,* 108–114.

Gudjonsson, G. H. (2001). Recovered memories: Effects upon the family and community. In G. M. Davies & T. Dalgleish (Eds.), *Recovered memories: Seeking the middle ground.* Chichester, England: Wiley.

Gueguen, N. (2003). Fundraising on the web: The effect of an electronic door-in-the-face technique on compliance to a request. *CyberPsychology & Behavior, 6,* 189–193.

Guest, F. (2004). HIV/AIDS and reproductive health. In R. A. Hatcher, J. Trussell, F. H. Stewart, A. L. Nelson, W. Cates Jr., F. Guest, & D. Kowal (Eds.), *Contraceptive technology.* New York: Ardent Media.

Guggenheim, F. G. (2000). Somatoform disorders. In B. J. Sadock & V. A. Sadock (Eds.), *Kaplan and Sadock's comprehensive textbook of psychiatry* (7th ed., Vol. 1). Philadelphia: Lippincott/Williams & Wilkins.

Gullette, E. C. D., Blumenthal, J. A., Babyak, M., Jiang, W., Waugh, R. A., Frid, D. J., O'Connor, C. M., Morris, J. J., & Krantz, D. S. (1997). Effects of mental stress on myocardial ischema during daily life. *Journal of the American Medical Association, 277,* 1521–1526.

Gunnel, D., & Ashby, D. (2004). Antidepressants and suicide: What is the balance of benefit and harm? *British Medical Journal, 329,* 34–38.

Gupta, G. R. (1992). Love, arranged marriage, and the Indian social structure. In J. J. Macionis & N. V. Benokraitis (Eds.), *Seeing ourselves: Classic, contemporary and cross-cultural reading in sociology.* Englewood Cliffs, NJ: Prentice-Hall.

Gupta, U., & Singh, P. (1982). Exploratory study of love and liking type of marriages. *Indian Journal of Applied Psychology, 19,* 92–97.

Gureje, O., Simon, G. E., Ustun, T. B., & Goldberg, D. P. (1997). Somatization in cross-cultural perspective: A world health organization study in primary care. *American Journal of Psychiatry, 154,* 989–995.

Gurland, B. J., Wilder, D. E., Lantigua, R., Stern, Y., Chen, J., Killeffer, E. H., & Mayeux, R. (1999). Rates of dementia in three ethnoracial groups. *International Journal of Geriatric Psychiatry, 14,* 481–493.

Gurung, R. A. R., Taylor, S. E., & Seeman, T. (2003). Accounting for changes in social support among married older adults: Insight from the MacArthur studies of successful aging. *Psychology and Aging, 18,* 487–496.

Gutek, B. A. (1993). Responses to sexual harassment. In S. Oskamp & M. Costanzo (Eds.), *Gender issues in contemporary society.* Newbury Park, CA: Sage.

Haan, N., Millsap, R., & Hartka, E. (1986). As time goes by: Change and stability in personality over 50 years. *Psychology of Aging, 1,* 220–232.

Haas, A., & Haas, K. (1993). *Understanding sexuality.* St. Louis: Times Mirror/Mosby.

Haas, L. (1999). Families and work. In M. B. Sussman, S. K. Steinmetz, & G. W. Peterson *Handbook of marriage and the family.* New York: Plenum Press.

Hackam, D. G., & Anand, S. S. (2003). Emerging risk factors for atherosclerotic vascular disease: A critical review of the evidence. *Journal of the American Medical Association, 290*(7), 932–940.

Hackstaff, K. B. (1999). *Marriage in a culture of divorce.* Philadelphia: Temple University Press.

Haden, S. C., Scarpa, A., Jones, R. T., & Ollendick, T. H. (2007). Posttraumatic stress disorder symptoms and injury: The modeling role of perceived social support and coping for young adults. *Personality and Individual Differences, 42,* 1187–1198.

Hadjistavropoulos, H., Dash, H., Hadjistavropoulos, T., & Sullivan, T. (2007). Recurrent pain among university students: Contributions of self-efficacy and perfectionism to the pain experience. *Personality and Individual Differences, 42,* 1081–1091.

Hafer, C. L. (2000). Do innocent victims threaten the belief in a just world? Evidence from a modified Stroop task. *Journal of Personality and Social Psychology, 79*(2), 165–173.

Hagerty, M. R. (2000). Social comparisons of income in one's community: Evidence from national surveys of income and happiness. *Journal of Personality and Social Psychology, 78,* 746–771.

Haidt, J. (2006). *The happiness hypothesis: Finding modern truths in ancient wisdom.* New York: Basic Books.

Haidt, J., & Algoe, S. (2004). Moral amplification and the emotions that attach us to saints and demons. In J. Greenberg, S. L. Koole, & T. Pyszczynski (Eds.), *Handbook of experimental existential psychology.* New York: Guilford.

Hall, D. R. (1996). Marriage as a pure relationship: Exploring the link between premarital cohabitation and divorce in Canada. *Journal of Comparative Family Studies, 27,* 1–12.

Hall, E. T. (1966) *The hidden dimension.* Garden City, NY: Doubleday.

Hall, G. S. (1904). *Adolescence.* New York: Appleton.

Hall, J. A. (1984). *Nonverbal sex differences: Communication accuracy and expressive style.* Baltimore: Johns Hopkins University Press.

Hall, J. A. (1990). *Nonverbal sex differences: Communication accuracy and expressive style* (2nd ed.). Baltimore: Johns Hopkins University Press.

Hall, J. A. (1998). How big are nonverbal sex differences? The case of smiling and sensitivity to nonverbal cues. In D. J. Canary & K. Dindia (Eds.), *Sex differences and similarities in communication: Critical essays and empirical investigations of sex and gender in interaction.* Mahwah, NJ: Erlbaum.

Hall, J. A., Coats, E. J., & LeBeau, L. S. (2005). Nonverbal behavior and the vertical dimension of social relations: A meta-analysis. *Psychological Bulletin, 131,* 898–924.

Halmi, K. A. (2002). Physiology of anorexia nervosa and bulimia nervosa. In C. G. Fairburn & K. D. Brownell (Eds.), *Eating disorders and obesity: A comprehensive handbook.* New York: Guilford.

Halmi, K. A. (2003). Eating disorders: Anorexia nervosa, bulimia nervosa, and obesity. In R. E. Hales & S. C. Yudofsky (Eds.), *Textbook of clinical psychiatry.* Washington, DC: American Psychiatric Publishing.

Halmi, K. A., Sunday, S. R., Strober, M., Kaplan, A., Woodside, D. B., Fichter, M., Treasure, J., Berrettini, W. H., & Kaye, W. H. (2000). Perfectionism in anorexia nervosa: Variation by clinical subtype, obsessionality, and pathological eating behavior. *American Journal of Psychiatry, 157,* 1799–1805.

Halpern, C. T., Udry, J. R., Campbell, B., & Suchindran, C. (1999). Effects of body fat on weight concerns, dating, and sexual activity: A longitudinal analysis of black and white adolescent girls. *Developmental Psychology, 35*(3), 721–736.

Halpern, C. T., Udry, J. R., Suchindran, C., & Campbell, B. (2000). Adolescent males' willingness to report masturbation. *Journal of Sex Research, 37,* 327–335.

Halpern, D. F. (1997). Sex differences in intelligence: Implications for education. *American Psychologist, 52,* 1091–1102.

Halpern, D. F. (2000). *Sex differences in cognitive abilities* (3rd ed.). Mahwah, NJ: Erlbaum.

Halpern, D. F. (2004). A cognitive-process taxonomy for sex differences in cognitive abilities. *Current Directions in Psychological Science, 13*(4), 135–139.

Halpern, D. F. (2005). Psychology at the intersection of work and family: Recommendations for employers, working families, and policymakers. *American Psychologist, 60,* 397–409.

Halpern, D. F. (2006). Girls and academic success: Changing patterns of academic achievement. In J. Worrell & C. D. Goodheart (Eds.), *Handbook of girls' and women's psychological health.* New York: Oxford University Press.

Halpern-Felsher, B. L., Cornell, J. L., Kropp, R. Y., & Tschann, J. M. (2005). Oral versus vaginal sex among adolescents: Perceptions, attitudes, and behavior. *Pediatrics, 115,* 845–851.

Halverson, A. M., Hallahan, M., Hart, A. J., & Rosenthal, R. (1997). Reducing the biasing effects of judges' nonverbal behavior with simplified jury instruction. *Journal of Applied Social Psychology, 82*(4), 590–598.

Hamilton, A. (1999). You've got mail! *Time,* 83.

Hamilton, J. C., Deemer, H. N., & Janata, J. W. (2003). Feeling sad but looking good: Sick role features that lead to favorable interpersonal judgments. *Journal of Social & Clinical Psychology, 22*(3), 253–274.

Hammen, C. (2003). Mood disorders. In G. Stricker & T. A. Widiger (Eds.), *Handbook of psychology: Vol. 8. Clinical psychology.* New York: Wiley.

Hammersley, R., Ditton, J., Smith, I., & Short, E. (1999). Patterns of ecstasy use by drug users. *British Journal of Criminology, 39*(4), 625–647.

Hampson, E., van Anders, S. M., & Mullin, L. I. (2006). A female advantage in the recognition of emotional facial expressions: Test of an evolutionary hypothesis. *Evolution and Human Behavior, 27,* 401–416.

Han, W., Waldfogel, J., & Brooks-Gunn, J. (2001). The effects of early maternal employment on later cognitive and behavioral outcomes. *Journal of Marriage and the Family, 63,* 336–354.

Hancock, D. R. (2001). Effects of test anxiety and evaluative threat on students' achievement and motivation. *Journal of Educational Research, 94*(5), 284–290.

Hancock, P. A., & Ganey, H. C. N. (2003). From the inverted-U to the extended-U: The evolution of a law of psychology. *Journal of Human Performance in Extreme Environment, 7*(1), 5–14.

Handy, B. (1998a, May 4). The Viagra craze. *Time,* 50–57.

Handy, B. (1998b, August 31). How we really feel about fidelity. *Time,* 52–54.

Hanna, S. L., Suggett, R., & Radtke, D. (2008). *Person to person: Positive relationships don't just happen.* Upper Saddle River, NJ: Pearson/Prentice Hall.

Hansen, J. C. (2005). Assessment of interests. In S. D. Brown & R. W. Lent (Eds.), *Career development and counseling: Putting theory and research to work.* Hoboken, NJ: Wiley.

Happonen, P., Voutilainen, S., & Salonen, J. T. (2004). Coffee drinking is dose dependently related to the risk of acute coronary events in middle-aged men. *Journal of Nutrition, 134*(9), 2381–2386.

Harber, K. D., Zimbardo, P. G., & Boyd, J. N. (2003). Participant self-selection bias as a function of individual differences in time perspective. *Basic and Applied Social Psychology, 25,* 255–264.

Haring, M., Hewitt, P. L., & Flett, G. L. (2003). Perfectionism, coping, and quality of intimate relationships. *Journal of Marriage & Family, 65*(1), 143–158.

Harmsen, P., Rosengren, A., Tsipogianni, A., & Wilhelmsen, L. (1990). Risk factors for stroke in middle-aged men in Goteborg, Sweden. *Stroke, 21,* 23–29.

Harpaz, I., & Snir, R. (2003). Workaholism: Its definition and nature. *Human Relations, 56*(3), 291–319.

Harper, G. W., Jernewall, N., & Zea, M. C. (2004). Giving voice to emerging science and theory for lesbian, gay, and bisexual people of color. *Cultural Diversity and Ethnic Minority Psychology, 10*(3), 187–199.

Harrigan, J. A., Lucic, K. S., Kay, D., McLaney, A., & Rosenthal, R. (1991). Effect of expresser role and type of self-touching on observers' perceptions. *Journal of Applied Psychology, 21,* 585–609.

Harris, J. R. (1998). *The nurture assumption: Why children turn out the way they do.* New York: Free Press.

Harris, J. R. (2000). Context-specific learning, personality, and birth order. *Current Directions in Psychological Science, 9*(5), 174–177.

Harris, M. B. (1996). Aggressive experiences and aggressiveness: Relationship to ethnicity, gender, and age. *Journal of Applied Social Psychology, 26*(10), 843–870.

Harris, P. R. (1985). Asch's data and the "Asch Effect": A critical note. *British Journal of Social Psychology, 24,* 229–230.

Harris, T. (1967). *I'm OK—You're OK.* New York: HarperCollins.

Harrison, J. A., & Wells, R. B. (1991). Bystander effects on male helping behavior: Social comparison and diffusion of responsibility. *Representative Research in Social Psychology, 19*(1), 53–63.

Harrison, K. (2003). Television viewers' ideal body proportions: The case of the curvaceously thin woman. *Sex Roles, 48*(5/6), 255–264.

Harter, S. (1998). The development of self-representations. In N. Eisenberg (Ed.), *Handbook of child psychology: Vol. 3. Social, emotional, and personality development.* New York: Wiley.

Harter, S. (2003). The development of self-representations during childhood and adolescence. In M. R. Leary & J. P. Tangney (Eds.), *Handbook of self and identity.* New York: Guilford.

Harter, S. (2006). Developmental and individual difference perspectives on self-esteem. In D. K. Mroczek & T. D. Little (Eds.), *Handbook of personality development.* Mahwah, NJ: Erlbaum.

Hartley, A. A., & McKenzie, C. R. M. (1991). Attentional and perceptual contributions to the identification of extrafoveal stimuli: Adult age comparisons. *Journal of Gerontology, 46,* P202–P206.

Hartup, W. W., & Stevens, N. (1999). Friendships and adaptation across the life span. *Current Directions in Psychological Science, 8*(3), 76–79.

Harvard Crimson. (2005, January 14). Full transcript: President Summers' remarks at the National Bureau of Economic Research. *Harvard Crimson,* Retrieved April 26, 2007 from http://www.thecrimson.com/article.aspx?ref=505844.

Harvey, E. (1999). Short-term and long-term effects of parental employment on children of the National Longitudinal Survey of Youth. *Developmental Psychology, 35,* 445–459.

Harvey, J. H., & Omarzu, J. (1997). Minding the close relationship. *Personality and Social Psychology Review, 1*(3), 224–240.

Harvey, J. H., & Wenzel, A. (2006). Theoretical perspectives in the study of close relationships. In A. L. Vangelisti & D. Perlman (Eds.), *The Cambridge handbook of personal relationships.* New York: Cambridge University Press.

Harvey, M. H. (1999). Memory research and clinical practice: A critique of three paradigms and a framework for psychotherapy with trauma survivors. In L. M. Williams, & V. L. Banyard (Eds.), *Trauma & memory.* Thousand Oaks, CA: Sage.

Hass, D. M., & Stafford, L. (1998). An initial examination of maintenance behaviors in gay and lesbian relationships. *Journal of Social and Personal Relationships, 15*(6), 846–855.

Hatcher, R. A., Trussell, J., Stewart, F. H., Nelson, A. L., Cates, W. Jr., Guest, F., & Kowal, D. (2004). *Contraceptive Technology.* New York: Ardent Media.

Hatfield, E., & Rapson, R. L. (1993). *Love, sex, and intimacy: Their psychology, biology, and history.* New York: HarperCollins.

Hawkins, A. J., Nock, S. L., Wilson, J. C., Sanchez, L., & Wright, J. D. (2002). Attitudes about covenant marriage and divorce: Policy implications from a three-state comparison. *Family Relations, 51,* 166–75.

Hawkins, D. N., & Booth, A. (2005). Unhappily ever after: Effects of long-term, low-quality marriages on well-being. *Social Forces, 84,* 451–471.

Hawkley, L. C., & Cicioppo, J. T. (2003). Loneliness and pathways to disease. *Brain, Behavior and Immunity, 17*(1), S98–S105.

Haworth-Hoeppner, S. (2000). The critical shapes of body image: The role of culture and family in the production of eating disorders. *Journal of Marriage and the Family, 62,* 212–227.

Hays, K. F. (1999). *Working it out: Using exercise in psychotherapy.* Washington, DC: American Psychological Association.

Hazan, C., & Shaver, P. (1986). *Parental caregiving style questionnaire.* Unpublished questionnaire.

Hazan, C., & Shaver, P. (1987). Romantic love conceptualized as an attachment process. *Journal of Personality and Social Psychology, 52,* 511–524.

Healy, D. (2004). *Let them eat Prozac: The unhealthy relationship between the pharmaceutical industry and depression.* New York: NYU Press.

Healy, D., & Whitaker, C. (2003). Antidepressants and suicide: Risk-benefit conundrums. *Journal of Psychiatry & Neuroscience, 28*(5), 340–347.

Heatherton, T. F., & Polivy, J. (1991). Development and validation of a scale for measuring state self-esteem. *Journal of Personality and Social Psychology, 60,* 895–910.

Heaton, T. B. (2002). Factors contributing to increasing marital stability in the United States. *Journal of Family Issues, 23,* 392–409.

Heaton, T. B., Jacobson, C. K. & Holland, K. (1999). Persistence and change in decisions to remain childless. *Journal of Marriage and the Family, 61,* 531–539.

Heavey, C. L., Christensen, A., & Malamuth, N. M. (1995). The longitudinal impact of demand and withdrawal during marital conflict. *Journal of Consulting and Clinical Psychology, 63*(5), 797–801.

Hebl, M. R., & Mannix, L. M. (2003). The weight of obesity in evaluating others: A mere proximity effect. *Personality and Social Psychology, 29*(1), 28–38.

Heckhausen, J. (2001). Adaptation and resilience in midlife. In M. E. Lachman (Ed.), *Handbook of midlife development.* New York: Wiley.

Hedges, L. V., & Nowell, A. (1995). Sex differences in mental test scores, variability, and numbers of high-scoring individuals. *Science, 269,* 41–45.

Hegarty, P., & Buechel, C. (2006). Androcentric reporting of gender differences in APA journals: 1965–2004. *Review of General Psychology, 10,* 377–389.

Heiby, E. M. (2002). It is time for a moratorium on legislation enabling prescription privileges for psychologists. *Clinical Psychology: Science & Practice, 9,* 256–258.

Heider, F. (1958). *The psychology of interpersonal relations.* New York: Wiley.

Heiman, J. R., & Meston, C. M. (1997). Empirically validated treatment for sexual dysfunction. *Annual Review of Sex Research, 8,* 148–194.

Heine, S. J., & Renshaw, K. (2002). Interjudge agreement, self-enhancement, and liking: Cross-cultural divergences. *Personality and Social Psychology Bulletin, 28*(5), 578–587.

Heine, S. J., Kitayama, S., Lehman, D. R., Takata, T., Ide, E., Leung, C., & Matsumoto, H. (2001). Divergent consequences of success and failure in Japan and North America: An investigation of self-improving motivations and malleable selves. *Journal of Personality and Social Psychology, 81,* 599–615.

Heinrichs, R. W. (2005). The primacy of cognition in schizophrenia. *American Psychologist, 60,* 229–242.

Helgeson, V. S. (1994). Relation of agency and communion to well-being: Evidence and potential explanations. *Psychological Bulletin, 116,* 412–428.

Helgeson, V. S., & Mickelson, K. D. (1995). Motives for social comparison. *Personality and Social Psychology Bulletin, 21,* 1200–1209.

Helgeson, V. S., Reynolds, K. A., & Tomich, P. L. (2006). A meta-analytic review of benefit finding and growth. *Journal of Consulting and Clinical Psychology, 74,* 797–816.

Hellström, A., & Tekle, J. (1994). Person perception through facial photographs: Effects of glasses, hair, and beard on judgments of occupation and personal qualities. *European Journal of Social Psychology, 24*(6), 693–705.

Helson, R., Mitchell, V., & Moane, G. (1984). Personality and patterns of adherence and nonadherence to the social clock. *Journal of Personality and Social Psychology, 46,* 1079–1096.

Helson, R., & Moane, G. (1987). Personality change in women from college to midlife. *Journal of Personality and Social Psychology, 53,* 176–186.

Helweg-Larsen, M., & Shepperd, J. A. (2001). Do moderators of the optimistic bias affect personal or target risk estimates? A review of the literature. *Personality & Social Psychology Review, 5*(1), 74–95.

Hembree, E. A., & Foa, E. (2000). Posttraumatic stress disorder: Psychological factors and psychosocial interventions. *Journal of Clinical Psychiatry, 61*(7), 33–39.

Hemenover, S. H. (2003). The good, the bad, and the healthy: Impacts of emotional disclosure of trauma on resilient self-concept and psychological distress. *Personality and Social Psychology Bulletin, 29*(10), 1236–1244.

Henderson, K. E., & Brownell, K. D. (2004). The toxic environment and obesity: Contribution and cure. In J. K. Thompson (Ed.), *Handbook of eating disorders and obesity.* New York: Wiley.

Hendrick, S. S., Hendrick, C., & Adler, N. L. (1988). Romantic relationships: Love, satisfaction, and staying together. *Journal of Personality and Social Psychology, 54,* 980–988.

Henley, N. M. (1986). *Body politics: Power, sex, and nonverbal communication* (2nd ed.). New York: Simon & Schuster.

Henley, N. M., & Freeman, J. (1995). The sexual politics of interpersonal behavior. In J. Freeman (Ed.), *Women: A feminist perspective* (5th ed.). Mountain View, CA: Mayfield.

Hennessy, D. A., & Wiesenthal, D. L. (1999). Traffic congestion, driver stress, and driver aggression. *Aggressive Behavior, 25*(6), 409–423.

Henry, R. G., Miller, R. B., & Giarrusso, R. (2005). Difficulties, disagreements, and disappointments in late-life marriages. *International Journal of Aging and Human Development, 61,* 243–264.

Heppner, P. P., & Lee, D. (2002). Problem-solving appraisal and psychological adjustment. In C. R. Snyder & S. J. Lopez (Eds.), *Handbook of positive psychology.* New York: Oxford University Press.

Heppner, P. P., & Lee, D. (2005). Problem-solving appraisal and psychological adjustment. In C. R. Snyder & S. J. Lopez (Eds.), *Handbook of positive psychology.* New York: Oxford University Press.

Herek, G. M. (2000). The psychology of sexual prejudice. *Current Directions in Psychological Science, 9,* 19–22.

Herek, G. M. (2002). Gender gaps in public opinion about lesbians and gay men. *Public Opinion Quarterly, 66*(2), 40–66.

Herek, G. M. (2003). The psychology of sexual prejudice. In L. D. Garnets & D. C. Kimmel (Eds.), *Psychological perspectives on lesbian, gay, and bisexual experiences.* New York: Columbia University Press.

Herek, G. M. (2006). Legal recognition of same-sex relationships in the United States: A social science perspective. *American Psychologist, 61,* 607–621.

Herek, G. M., & Capitanio, J. (1996). "Some of my best friends": Intergroup contact concealable stigma, and heterosexuals' attitudes toward gay men and lesbians. *Personality and Social Psychology Bulletin, 22,* 412–424.

Herek, G. M., Cogan, J. C., & Gillis, J. R. (2002). Victim experiences in hate crimes based on sexual orientation. *Journal of Social Issues, 58*(2), 319–339.

Heres, S., Davis, J., Maino, K., Jetzinger, E., Kissling, W., & Leucht, S. (2006). Why olanzapine beats risperidone, risperdone beats quetiapine, and quetiapine beats olanzapine: An exploratory analysis of head-to-head comparison studies of second-generation antipsychotics. *American Journal of Psychiatry, 163,* 185–194.

Hermann, D., Raybeck, D., & Gruneberg, M. (2002). *Improving memory and study skills: Advances* *in theory and practice.* Ashland, OH: Hogrefe & Huber.

Hermann, R. C., Dorwart, R. A., Hoover, C. W., & Brody, J. (1995). Variation in ECT use in the United States. *American Journal of Psychiatry, 152,* 869–875.

Hermann, R. C., Ettner, S. L., Dorwart, R. A., Hoover, C. W., & Yeung, E. (1998). Characteristics of psychiatrists who perform ECT. *American Journal of Psychiatry, 155,* 889–894.

Herrett-Skjellum, J., & Allen, M. (1996). Television programming and sex stereotyping: A meta-analysis. In B. Burleson (Ed.), *Communication Yearbook 1995.* Thousand Oaks, CA: Sage.

Hershberger, S. L., & D'Augelli, A. R. (2000). Issues in counseling lesbian, gay, and bisexual adolescents. In R. M. Perez, K. A. DeBord, & K. J. Bieschke (Eds.), *Handbook of counseling and psychotherapy with lesbian, gay, and bisexual clients.* Washington, DC: American Psychological Association.

Herzog, D. B., & Delinski, S. S. (2001). Classification of eating disorders. In R. H. Striegel-Moore & L. Smolak (Eds.), *Eating disorders.* Washington, DC: American Psychological Association.

Hess, N. H., & Hagen, E. H. (2006). Sex differences in indirect aggression: Psychological evidence from young adults. *Evolution and Human Behavior, 27,* 231–245.

Hetherington, E. M. (1993). An overview of the Virginia longitudinal study of divorce and remarriage with a focus on early adolescence. *Journal of Family Psychology, 7,* 1–18.

Hetherington, E. M. (1999). Should we stay together for the sake of the children? In E. M. Hetherington (Ed.), *Coping with divorce, single parenting, and remarriage: A risk and resiliency perspective.* Mahwah, NJ: Erlbaum.

Hetherington, E. M. (2003). Intimate pathways: Changing patterns in close personal relationships across time. *Family Relations: Interdisciplinary Journal of Applied Family Studies, 52*(4), 318–331.

Hetherington, E. M., Reiss, D., & Plomin, R. (1994). *Separate social worlds of siblings: The impact of nonshared environment on development.* Hillsdale, NJ: Erlbaum.

Hettema, J. M., Neale, M. C., & Kendler, K. S. (2001). A review and meta-analysis of the genetic epidemiology of anxiety disorders. *American Journal of Psychiatry, 158,* 1568–1578.

Hettich, P. I. (1998). *Learning skills for college and career.* Pacific Grove, CA: Brooks/Cole.

Hewstone, M. (1990). The ultimate attribution error? A review of the literature on intergroup causal attribution. *European Journal of Social Psychology, 20,* 311–335.

Heymann, J., Earle, A., Simmons, S., Breslow, S., & Kuehnhoff, A. (2004). *The work, family, and equity index: Where does the United States stand globally?* Boston: Harvard School of Public Health.

Hicks, T. V., & Leitenberg, H. (2001). Sexual fantasies about one's partner versus someone else: Gender differences in incidence and frequency. *Journal of Sex Research, 38*(1), 43–50.

Hiedemann, B., Suhomlinova, O., & O'Rand, A. M. (1998). Economic independence, economic status, and empty nest in midlife marital disruption. *Journal of Marriage and the Family, 60,* 219–231.

Higgins, E. T. (1987). Self-discrepancy: A theory relating self and affect. *Psychological Review, 94*(3), 319–340.

Higgins, E. T., Shah, J., & Friedman, R. (1997). Emotional responses to goal attainment: Strength of regulatory focus as a moderator. *Journal of Personality and Social Psychology, 72*(3), 515–525.

Hill, A. J. (2002). Prevalence and demographics of dieting. In C. G. Fairburn & K. D. Brownell (Eds.), *Eating disorders and obesity: A comprehensive handbook.* New York: Guilford.

Hill, C. E., & Lambert, M. J. (2004). Methodological issues in studying psychotherapy processes and outcomes. In M. J. Lambert (Ed.), *Bergin and Garfield's handbook of psychotherapy and behavior change.* New York: Wiley.

Hill, C. T., Rubin, Z., & Peplau, L. A. (1976). Breakups before marriage: The end of 103 affairs. *Journal of Social Issues, 32,* 147–168.

Hill, J. L., Waldfogel, J., Brooks-Gunn, J., & Han, W. (2005). Maternal employment and child development: A fresh look using newer methods. *Developmental Psychology, 41,* 833–850.

Hines, M. (1982). Prenatal gonadal hormones and sex differences in human behavior. *Psychological Bulletin, 92,* 56–80.

Hines, M. (1990). Gonadal hormones and human cognitive development. In J. Balthazart (Ed.), *Hormones, brain and behavior in vertebrates: 1. Sexual differentiation, neuroanatomical aspects, neurotransmitters and neuropeptides.* Basel: Karger.

Hines, M. (2004). Androgen, estrogen, and gender: Contributions of the early hormone environment to gender-related behavior. In A. H. Eagly, A. E. Beall, & R. J. Sternberg (Eds.), *The psychology of gender.* New York: Guilford Press.

Hiroto, D. S., & Seligman, M. E. P. (1975). Generality of learned helplessness in man. *Journal of Personality and Social Psychology, 31,* 311–327.

Hirt, E. R., Zillman, D., Erikson, G. A., & Kennedy, C. (1992). Costs and benefits of allegiance: Changes in fans' self-ascribed competence after team victory versus defeat. *Journal of Personality and Social Psychology, 63,* 724–738.

Ho, B., Black, D. W., & Andreasen, N. C. (2003). Schizophrenia and other psychotic disorders. In R. E. Hales & S. C. Yudofsky (Eds.), *Textbook of clinical psychiatry.* Washington, DC: American Psychiatric Publishing.

Hobfoll, S. E., & Vaux, A. (1993). Social support: Resources and context. In L. Goldberger & S. Breznitz (Eds.), *Handbook of stress: Theoretical and clinical aspects* (2nd ed.). New York: Free Press.

Hobson, C. J., & Delunas, L. (2001). National norms and life-event frequencies for the revised Social Readjustment Rating Scale. *International Journal of Stress Management, 8*(4), 299–314.

Hochschild, A. R. (1989). *The second shift.* New York: Viking.

Hochschild, A. R. (2001). *The time bind.* New York: Owl Books.

Hock, M. F., Deshler, D. D., & Schumaker, J. B. (2006). Enhancing student motivation through the pursuit of possible selves. In C. Dunkel & J. Kerpelman (Eds.), *Possible selves: Theory, research, and applications.* Hauppague, NY: Nova Science Publishers.

Hodge, B. (2002, March). PCs and the healthy office. *Smart Computing,* pp. 64–67.

Hoek, H. W. (2002). Distribution of eating disorders. In C. G. Fairburn & K. D. Brownell (Eds.), *Eating disorders and obesity: A comprehensive handbook.* New York: Guilford.

Hoffman, E. (1994). *The drive for self: Alfred Adler and the founding of individual psychology.* Reading, MA: Addison-Wesley.

Hoffnung, M. (2004). Wanting it all: Career, marriage, and motherhood during college-educated women's 20s. *Sex Roles, 50*(9/10), 711–723.

Hofstede, G. (1980). *Culture's consequences: International differences in work-related values.* Newbury Park, CA: Sage.

Hofstede, G. (1983). Dimensions of national cultures in fifty countries and three regions. In J. Deregowski, S. Dzuirawiec, & R. Annis (Eds.), *Explications in cross-cultural psychology.* Lisse: Swets and Zeitlinger.

Hogan, J., & Ones, D. S. (1997). Conscientiousness and integrity at work. In R. Hogan, J. Johnson, & S. Briggs (Eds), *Handbook of personality psychology.* San Diego: Academic Press.

Hogan, M. F., & Morrison, A. K. (2003). Organization and financing of mental health care. In A. Tasman, J. Kay, & J. A. Lieberman (Eds.), *Psychiatry.* New York: Wiley.

Holahan, C. J., & Moos, R. H. (1990). Life stressors, resistance factors, and improved psychological functioning: An extension of the stress resistance paradigm. *Journal of Personality and Social Psychology, 58,* 909–917.

Holahan, C. J., & Moos, R. H. (1994). Life stressors and mental health: Advances in conceptualizing stress resistance. In W. R. Avison & I. H. Gotlib (Eds.), *Stress and mental health: Contemporary issues and prospects for the future.* New York: Plenum.

Holahan, C. J., Moos, R. H., Holahan, C. K., Brennan, P. L., & Schutte, K. K. (2005). Stress generation, avoidance coping and depressive symptoms: A 10-year model. *Journal of Consulting and Clinical Psychology, 73,* 658–666.

Holden, C. (2004). FDA weighs suicide risk in children on antidepressants. *Science, 303,* 745.

Holen, A. (2000). Posttraumatic stress disorder, delayed. In G. Fink (Ed.), *Encyclopedia of stress* (Vol. 3). San Diego: Academic Press.

Holland, J. C., & Lewis, S. (1993). Emotions and cancer: What do we really know? In D. Goleman & J. Gurin (Eds.), *Mind/body medicine: How to use your mind for better health.* Yonkers, NY: Consumer Reports Books.

Holland, J. L. (1985). *Making vocational choices: A theory of vocational personalities and work environments.* Englewood Cliffs, NJ: Prentice-Hall.

Holland, J. L. (1996). Exploring careers with a typology: What we have learned and some new directions. *American Psychologist, 51,* 397–406.

Holland, R. W., Roeder, U., van Baaren, R. B., Brandt, A. C., & Hannover, B. (2004). Don't stand so close to me: The effects of self-construal on interpersonal closeness. *Psychological Science, 15,* 237–242.

Hollander, E., & Allen, A. (2006). Is compulsive buying a real disorder, and is it really compulsive? *American Journal of Psychiatry, 163,* 1670–1672.

Hollander, E., & Simeon, D. (2003). Anxiety disorders. In R. E. Hales & S. C. Yudofsky (Eds.), *Textbook of clinical psychiatry.* Washington, DC: American Psychiatric Publishing.

Hollifield, M. A. (2005). Somatoform disorders. In B. J. Sadock & V. A. Sadock (Eds.), *Kaplan & Sadock's comprehensive textbook of psychiatry.* Philadelphia: Lippincott Williams & Wilkins.

Hollon, S. D., & Beck, A. T. (2004). Cognitive and cognitive behavioral therapies. In M. J. Lambert (Ed.), *Bergin and Garfields handbook of psychotherapy and behavior change.* New York: Wiley.

Holmans, P., Weissman, M. M., Zubenko, G. S., Scheftner, W. A., Crowe, R. R., DePaulo, J. R., et al. (2007). Genetics of recurrent early-onset major depression (GenRED): Final genome scan report. *American Journal of Psychiatry, 164,* 248–258.

Holmes, T. H., & Rahe, R. H. (1967). The Social Readjustment Rating Scale. *Journal of Psychosomatic Research, 11,* 213–218.

Holt, T., Greene, L., & Davis, J. (2003). *National Survey of adolescents and young adults: Sexual health knowledge, attitudes, and experiences.* Menlo Park, CA: Henry J. Kaiser Family Foundation.

Hong, G. K., Garcia, M., & Soriano, M. (2000). Responding to the challenge: Preparing mental health professionals for the new millennium. In I. Cuellar & F. A. Paniagua (Eds.), *Handbook of multicultural mental health: Assessment and treatment of diverse populations.* San Diego: Academic Press.

Honts, C. R., Raskin, D. C., & Kircher, J. C. (2002). The scientific status of research on polygraph testing. In D. L. Faigman, D. H. Kaye, M. J. Saks, & J. Sanders (Eds.), *Modern scientific evidence: The law and science of expert testimony* (Vol. 2). St. Paul, MN: West Publishing.

Hoobler, J. M., & Brass, D. J. (2006). Abusive supervision and family undermining as displaced aggression. *Journal of Applied Psychology, 91,* 1125–1133.

Hood, K. E., Draper, P., Crockett, L. J., & Petersen, A. C. (1987). The ontogeny and phylogeny of sexual differences in development: A biopsychosocial synthesis. In B. Carter (Ed.), *Current conceptions of sex roles and sex typing: Theory and research.* New York: Praeger.

Hooker, E. (1957). The adjustment of the male overt homosexual. *Journal of Projective Techniques, 21,* 18–31.

Hooley, J. M. (2004). Do psychiatric patients do better clinically if they live with certain kinds of families? *Current Directions in Psychological Science, 13*(5), 202–205.

Hooley, J. M., & Candela, S. F. (1999). Interpersonal functioning in schizophrenia. In T. Millon, P. H. Blaney, & R. D. Davis (Eds.), *Oxford textbook of psychopathology.* New York: Oxford University Press.

Hopper, J. (2001). The symbolic origins of conflict in divorce. *Journal of Marriage and Family, 63,* 430–445.

Horstmann, G. (2003). What do facial expressions convey: Feeling states, behavioral intentions, or action requests? *Emotion, 3*(2), 150–166.

Horvath, M., & Ryan, A. M. (2003). Antecedents and potential moderators of the relationship between attitudes and hiring discrimination on the basis of sexual orientation. *Sex Roles, 48*(3/4), 115–130.

Horwath, E., & Weissman, M. M. (2000). Anxiety disorders: Epidemiology. In B. J. Sadock & V. A. Sadock (Eds.), *Kaplan and Sadock's comprehensive textbook of psychiatry* (7th ed., Vol. 1). Philadelphia: Lippincott/Williams & Wilkins.

Hotopf, M. (2004). Preventing somatization. *Psychological Medicine, 34,* 195–198.

Houts, A. C. (2002). Discovery, invention, and the expansion of the modern *Diagnostic and Statistical Manuals of Mental Disorders.* In L. E. Beutler & M. L. Malik (Eds.), *Rethinking the DSM.* Washington, DC: American Psychological Association.

Howard, G. S. (2000). Adapting human lifestyles for the 21st century. *American Psychologist, 55*(5), 509–515.

Howard, K. I., Moras, K., Brill, P. L., Martinovich, Z., & Lutz, W. (1996). Evaluation of psychotherapy: Efficacy, effectiveness, and patient progress. *American Psychologist, 51,* 1059–1064.

Hsee, C. K., & Hastie, R. (2006). Decision and experience: Why don't we choose what makes us happy? *Trends in Cognitive Sciences, 10*(1), 31–37.

Hsu, L. K. G. (1990). *Eating disorders.* New York: Guilford Press.

Hu, F. B., & Willett, W. C. (2002). Optimal diets for prevention of coronary heart disease. *Journal of the American Medical Association, 288*(20), 2569–2578.

Hu, Y., Zhang, R., & Li, W. (2005). Relationships among jealousy, self-esteem and self-efficacy. *Chinese Journal of Clinical Psychology, 13*(2), 165–166, 172.

Hubbard, J. A., & Coie, J. D. (1994). Emotional correlates of social competence in children's peer relationships. *Merrill-Palmer Quaterly, 40,* 1–20.

Hudson, J. I., Hiripi, E., Pope, H. G., & Kessler, R. C. (2007). The prevelance and correlates of eating disorders in the national comorbidity survey replication. *Biological Psychiatry, 61,* 348–358.

Hudziak, J., & Waterman, G. S. (2005). Buspirone. In B. J. Sadock & V. A. Sadock (Eds.), *Kaplan and Sadock's comprehensive textbook of psychiatry.* Philadelphia: Lippincott Williams & Wilkins.

Huesmann, L. R., Moise-Titus, J., Podolski, C.-L., & Eron, L. D. (2003). Longitudinal relations between children's exposure to TV violence and their aggressive and violent behavior in young adulthood: 1977–1992. *Developmental Psychology, 39,* 201–221.

Hughes, C. C. (1993). Culture in clinical psychiatry. In A. C. Gaw (Ed.), *Culture, ethnicity, and mental illness.* Washington, DC: American Psychiatric Press.

Hull, J. G., & Young, R. D. (1983). Self-consciousness, self-esteem, and success-failure as determinants of alcohol consumption in male social drinkers. *Journal of Personality and Social Psychology, 44,* 1097–1109.

Hull, J. G., Young, R. D. & Jouriles, E. (1986). Applications of the self-awareness model of alcohol consumption: Predicting patterns of use and abuse. *Journal of Personality and Social Psychology, 51,* 790–796.

Hulshoff, H. E., Hoek, H. W., Susser, E., Brown, A. S., Dingemans, A., Schnack, H. G., van Haren, N. E. M., Ramos, L. M. P., Gispen-de Wied, C. C., & Kahn, R. S. (2000). Prenatal exposure to famine and brain morphology in schizophrenia. *American Journal of Psychiatry, 157,* 1170–1172.

Hultin, M. (2003). Some take the glass escalator, some hit the glass ceiling? Career consequences of occupational sex segregation. *Work and Occupations, 30*(1), 30–61.

Hunsley, J., Lee, C. M., & Wood, J. M. (2003). Controversial and questionable assessment techniques. In S. O. Lilienfeld, S. J. Lynn, & J. M. Lohr (Eds.), *Science and pseudoscience in clinical psychology.* New York: Guilford.

Hunt, M. (1974). *Sexual behavior in the 1970s.* Chicago: Playboy Press.

Hunter, E. (1998). Adolescent attraction to cults. *Adolescence, 33,* 709–714.

Huntsinger, E. T., & Luecken, L. J. (2004). Attachment relationships and health behavior: The mediational role of self-esteem. *Psychology & Health, 19,* 515–526.

Huston, A. C., Donnerstein, E., Fairchild, H., Feshbach, N. D., Katz, P. A., Murray, J. P., Rubinstein, E. A., Wilcox, B. L., & Zuckerman, D. (1992). *Big world, small screen: The role of television in American society.* Lincoln: University of Nebraska Press.

Huston, A. C., & Wright, J. C. (1998). Mass media and children's development. In W. Damon (Series Ed.), *Handbook of child psychology* (Vol. 4). New York: Wiley.

Huston, T. L., & Melz, H. (2004). The case for (promoting). *Journal of Marriage and Family, 66,* 943–958.

Huston, T. L., Niehuis, S., & Smith, S. E. (2001). The early marital roots of conjugal distress and divorce. *Current Directions in Psychological Science, 10*(4), 116–119.

Hwang, W. (2006). The psychotherapy adaptation and modification framework: Application to Asian Americans. *American Psychologist, 61,* 702–715.

Hyde, J. S. (1994a). *Understanding human sexuality* (5th ed.). New York: McGraw-Hill.

Hyde, J. S. (1994b). Can meta-analysis make feminist transformations in psychology? *Psychology of Women Quarterly, 18,* 451–462.

Hyde, J. S. (1996). Where are the gender differences? Where are the gender similarities? In D.M. Buss & N. M. Malamuth (Eds.), *Sex, power, conflict: Evolutionary and feminist perspectives.* New York: Oxford University Press.

Hyde, J. S. (2004). *Half the human experience: The psychology of women.* Boston: Houghton Mifflin.

Hyde, J. S. (2005). The gender similarities hypothesis. *American Psychologist, 60,* 581–592.

Hyde, J. S., & DeLamater, J. D. (2003). *Understanding human sexuality.* New York: McGraw-Hill.

Hyde, J. S., & Frost, L. A. (1993). Meta-analysis in the psychology of women. In F. L. Denmark & M. A. Paludi (Eds.), *Psychology of women: A handbook of issue and theories.* Westport, CT: Greenwood Press.

Hyde, J. S., & Kling, K. C. (2001). Women, motivation, and achievement. *Psychology of Women Quarterly, 25,* 364–378.

Hyde, J. S., & Oliver, M. B. (2000). Gender differences in sexuality: Results from meta-analysis. In C. B. Travis & J. W. White (Eds.), *Sexuality, society, and feminism.* Washington, DC: American Psychological Association.

Hygge, S., Evans, G. W., & Bullinger, M. (2002). A prospective study of some effects of aircraft noise on cognitive performance in school children. *Psychological Science, 13*(5), 469–474.

Hyman, I. E., & Kleinknecht, E. E. (1999). False childhood memories: Research, theory, and applications. In L. M. Williams & V. L. Banyard (Eds.), *Trauma & memory.* Thousand Oaks, CA: Sage.

Hynes, K. H., & Clarkberg, M. (2005). Women's employment patterns during early parenthood: A group-based trajectory analysis. *Journal of Marriage and Family, 67,* 222–239.

Iaccino, J. F. (1996). A further examination of the bizarre imagery mnemonic: Its effectiveness with mixed context and delayed testing. *Perceptual & Motor Skills, 83,* 881–882.

Ickes, W. (1993). Traditional gender roles: Do they make and then break our relationships? *Journal of Social Issues, 3,* 71–85.

Ickes, W., Patterson, M. L., Rajecki, D. W., & Tanford, S. (1982). Behavioral and cognitive consequences of reciprocal versus compensatory responses to preinteraction expectancies. *Social Cognition, 1,* 160–190.

Ickovics, J. R., Thayaparan, B., & Ethier, K. A. (2001). Women and AIDS: A contextual analysis. In A. Baum, T. A. Revenson, & J. E. Singer (Eds.), *Handbook of health psychology.* Mahwah, NJ: Erlbaum.

Iezzi, T., Duckworth, M. P., & Adams, H. E. (2001). Somatoform and factitious disorders. In P. B. Sutker & H. E. Adams (Eds.), *Comprehensive handbook of psychopathology* (3rd ed.). New York: Kluwer Academic/Plenum Publishers.

Ilgen, D. R. (1990). Health issues at work: Opportunities for industrial/organization psychology. *American Psychologist, 45,* 252–261.

Impett, E. A., & Peplau, L. A. (2006). "His" and "her" relationships? A review of the empirical evidence. In A. L. Vangelisti & D. Perlman (Eds.), *The Cambridge handbook of personal relationships.* New York: Cambridge University Press.

Impett, E. A., Peplau, L. A., & Gable, S. L. (2005). Approach and avoidance sexual motives: Implications for personal and interpersonal well-being. *Personal Relationships, 12,* 465–482.

Infante, J. R., Torres-Avisbal, M., Pinel, P., Vallejo. J. A., Peran, F., Gonzalez, F., Contreras, P., Pacheco, C., Roldan, A., & Latre, J. M. (2001). Catecholamine levels in practitioners of the transcendental meditation technique. *Physiology & Behavior, 72*(1-2), 141–146.

Inglehart, R. (1990). *Culture shift in advanced industrial society.* Princeton, NJ: Princeton University Press.

Ingoldsby, B. B. (1995). Mate selection and marriage. In B. B. Ingoldsby & S. Smith (Eds.), *Families in multicultural perspective.* New York: Guilford Press.

Innocenti, G. M. (1994). Some new trends in the study of the corpus callosum. *Behavioral and Brain Research, 64,* 1–8.

Inskeep, S. (2005). *Women CEOs still rare among Fortune 500.* Retrieved May 7, 2007 from http://www.npr.org/templates/story/story.php?storyId=4509605.

Insko, C. A., Smith, R. H., Alicke, M. D., Wade, J., & Taylor, S. (1985). Conformity and group size: The concern with being right and the concern with being liked. *Personality and Social Psychology Bulletin, 11,* 41–50.

International Labour Office. (2002). *Key indicators of the labour market, 2001–2002.* Geneva: United Nations International Labour Office.

Internet World Stats. (2007). Internet usage statistics—the big picture. Retrieved June 18, 2007 from http://www.internetworldstats.com/stats.htm.

Ippolito, J., Adler, A. B., Thomas, J. L., Litz, B. T., & Holzl, R. (2005). Extending and applying the demand-control model: The role of soldier's coping on a peacekeeping deployment. *Journal of Occupational Health Psychology, 10,* 452–464.

Ironson, G., Wynings, C., Sschneiderman, N., Baum, A., Rodriguez, M., Greenwood, D., Benight, C., Antoni, M., LaPerriere, A., Huang, H. S., Klimas, N., & Fletcher, M. A. (1997). Post-traumatic stress symptoms, intrusive thoughts, loss, and immune function after Hurricane Andrew. *Psychosomatic Medicine, 59,* 128–141.

Ito, T. A., Chiao, K. W., Devine, P. G., Lorig, T., & Cacioppo, J. T. (2006). The influence of facial feedback on race bias. *Psychological Science, 17,* 256–261.

Ivancevich, J. M., Matteson, M. T., Freedman, S. M., & Phillips, J. S. (1990). Worksite stress management interventions. *American Psychologist, 45,* 252–261.

Iwao, S. (1993). *The Japanese woman: Traditional image and changing reality.* New York: Free Press.

Iwasaki, Y. (2003). Roles of leisure in coping with stress among university students: A repeated-assessment field study. *Anxiety, Stress & Coping: An International Journal, 16*(1), 31–57.

Iwasaki, Y., Mackay, K. J., Mactavish, J. B., Ristock, J., & Bartlett, J. (2006). Voices from the margins: Stress, active living, and leisure as a contributor to coping with stress. *Leisure Sciences, 28,* 163–180.

Izard, C., Fine, S., Schultz, D., Mostow, A., Ackerman, B., & Youngstrom, E. (2001). Emotion knowledge as a predictor of social behavior and academic competence in children at risk. *Psychological Science, 12*(1), 18–23.

Jackicic, J., & Gallagher, K. I. (2002). Physical activity considerations for management of body weight. In D. H. Bessesen, & R. Kushner (Eds.), *Evaluation & Management of Obesity.* Philadelphia: Hanley & Belfus.

Jackson, L. A., & McGill, O. D. (1996). Body type preferences and body characteristics associated with attractive and unattractive bodies by African Americans and Anglo Americans. *Sex Roles, 35*(5–6), 295–307.

Jackson, M. (2005). The limits of connectivity: Technology and 21st-century life. In D. F. Halpern & S. E. Murphy (Eds.), *From work-family balance to work-family interaction: Changing the metaphor.* Mahwah, NJ: Erlbaum.

Jackson, T., Fritch, A., Nagasaka, T., & Gunderson, J. (2002). Towards explaining the association between shyness and loneliness: A path analysis with American college students. *Social Behavior and Personality, 30*(3), 263–270.

Jacob, R. G., & Pelham, W. E. (2005). Behavior therapy. In B. J. Sadock & V. A. Sadock (Eds.), *Kaplan and Sadock's comprehensive textbook of psychiatry.* Philadelphia: Lippincott Williams & Wilkins.

Jacobs, B. L. (2004). Depression: The brain finally gets into the act. *Current Directions in Psychological Science, 13*(3), 103–106.

Jacobs, H. S. (2001). Idea of male menopause is not useful. *Medical Crossfire, 3,* 52–55.

Jacobs, J. E., Lanza, S., Osgood, D. W., Eccles, J. S., & Wigfield, A. (2002). Changes in children's self-competence and values: Gender and domain differences across grades one through twelve. *Child Development, 73,* 509–527.

Jacques, R. (1997). The unbearable whiteness of being: Reflections of a pale, stale male. In P. Prasad, A. Mills, M. Elmes, & A. Prasad (Eds.), *Managing the organizational melting pot: Dilemmas of workplace diversity.* Thousand Oaks, CA: Sage.

Jahoda, M. (1958). *Current concepts of positive mental health.* New York: Basic Books.

Jakupcak, M., Salters, K., Gratz, K. L., & Roemer, L. (2003). Masculinity and emotionality: An investigation of men's primary and secondary emotional responding. *Sex Roles, 49*(3/4), 111–120.

James, J. E. (2004). Critical review of dietary caffeine and blood pressure: A relationship that should be taken more seriously. *Psychosomatic Medicine, 66*(1), 63–71.

Janis, I. L. (1958). *Psychological stress.* New York: Wiley.

Janis, I. L. (1993). Decision making under stress. In L. Goldberger & S. Breznitz (Eds.), *Handbook of stress: Theoretical and clinical aspects* (2nd ed.). New York: Free Press.

Jankowiak, W. R., & Fischer, E. F. (1992). A cross-cultural perspective on romantic love. *Ethnology, 31,* 149–155.

Janoff-Bulman, R. (2004). Posttraumatic growth: Three explanatory models. *Psychological Inquiry, 15*(1), 30–34.

Jansz, J. (2000). Masculine identity and restrictive emotionality. In A. H. Fischer (Ed.), *Gender and emotion: Social psychological perspectives.* Cambridge, UK: Cambridge University Press.

Jaroff, L. (1993, November 29). Lies of the mind. *Time,* pp. 52–59.

Javitt, D. C., & Laruelle, M. (2006). Neurochemical theories. In J. A. Liberman, T. S. Stroup, & D. O. Perkins (Eds.), *Textbook of schizophrenia.* Washington, DC: American Psychiatric Publishing.

Jefferson, J. W., & Greist, J. H. (2005). Lithium. In B. J. Sadock & V. A. Sadock (Eds.), *Kaplan and Sadock's comprehensive textbook of psychiatry.* Philadelphia: Lippincott Williams & Wilkins.

Jeffery, R. W. (2001). Public health strategies for obesity treatment and prevention. *American Journal of Health Behavior, 25*(3), 252–259.

Jeffery, R. W., Epstein, L. H., Wilson, G. T., Drewnowski, A., Stunkard, A. J., Wing, R. R., & Hill, D. R. (2000). Long-term maintenance of weight loss: Current status. *Health Psychology, 19*(1), 5–16.

Jeffery, R. W., Kelly, K. M., Rothman, A. J., Sherwood, N. E., & Boutelle, K. N. (2004). The weight-loss experience: A descriptive analysis. *Annals of Behavioral Medicine, 27,* 100–106.

Jeffries, S., & Konnert, C. (2002). Regret and psychological well-being among voluntarily and involuntarily childless women and mothers. *International Journal of Aging and Human Development, 54,* 89–106.

Jellinger, K. A., Schmidt, R., & Windisch, M. E. (2002). *Ageing and dementia: Current and future concepts.* Vienna: Springer-Verlag.

Jemmott, J. B., III, & Magloire, K. (1988). Academic stress, social support, and secretory Immunoglobin A. *Journal of Personality and Social Psychology, 55,* 803–810.

Jeney-Gammon, P., Daugherty, T. K., Finch, A. J., Belter, R. W., & Foster K. Y. (1993). Children's coping styles and report of depressive symptoms following a natural disaster. *Journal of Genetic Psychology, 154,* 259–267.

Jepsen, L. K., & Jepsen, C. A. (2002). An empirical analysis of the matching patterns of same-sex and opposite-sex couples. *Demography, 39,* 435–453.

Jex, S. M., Bliese, P. D., Buzzell, S., & Primeau, J. (2001). The impact of self-efficacy on stressor-strain relations: Coping style as an explanatory mechanism. *Journal of Applied Psychology, 86,* 401–409.

Jeynes, W. H. (2006). The impact of parental remarriage on children: A meta-analysis. *Marriage & Family Review, 40,* 75–102.

Jick, H., Kaye, J. A., & Jick, S. S. (2004). Antidepressants and the risk of suicidal behaviors. *Journal of the American Medical Association, 292*(3), 338–343.

John, O. P., & Srivastava, S. (1999). The big five trait taxonomy: History, measurement, and theoretical perspectives. In L. A. Pervin & O. P. John (Eds.), *Handbook of personality: Theory and research* (2nd ed.). New York: Guilford Press.

Johnson, A. M., Wadsworth, J., Wellings, K., Bradshaw, S., & Field, J. (1992). Sexual lifestyles and HIV risk. *Nature, 360,* 410–412.

Johnson, B. A., & Ait-Dauod, N. (2005). Alcohol: Clinical aspects. In J. H. Lowinson, P. Ruiz, R. B. Millman, & J. G. Langrod (Eds.), *Substance abuse: A comprehensive textbook.* Philadelphia: Lippincott/Williams & Wilkins.

Johnson, I. M., Crowley, J., & Sigler, R. T. (1992). Agency response to domestic violence: Services provided to battered women. In E. C. Viano (Ed.), *Intimate violence: Interdisciplinary perspectives.* Washington, DC: Hemisphere.

Johnson, M. P. (2000). Conflict and control: Images of symmetry and asymmetry in domestic violence. In A. Booth, A. C. Crouter, & M. Clements (Eds.), *Couples in conflict.* Hillsdale, NJ: Erlbaum.

Johnson, M. P., & Ferraro, K. J. (2001). Research on domestic violence in the 1990's: Making distinctions. In R. M. Milardo (Ed.), *Understanding families into the new millennium: A decade in review.* Minneapolis, MN: National Council on Family Relations.

Johnson, S. B., & Carlson, D. N. (2004). Medical regimen adherence: Concepts, assessment, and interventions. In J. M. Raczynski, & L. C. Leviton (Eds.), *Handbook of clinical health psychology: Vol. 2. Disorders of behavior and health.* Washington, DC: American Psychological Association.

Johnson, T. W., & Colucci, P. (1999). Lesbians, gay men, and the family life cycle. In B. Carter & M. McGoldrick (Eds.), *The expanded family life cycle: Individual, family, and social perspectives* (3rd ed.). Boston: Allyn & Bacon.

Johnson, W., & Krueger, R. F. (2006). How money buys happiness: Genetic and environmental processes linking finances and life satisfaction. *Journal of Personality and Social Psychology, 90,* 680–691.

Joiner, T. E. (2002). Depression in its interpersonal context. In I. H. Gotlib & C. L. Hammen (Eds.), *Handbook of depression.* New York: Guilford.

Joiner, T. E., & Katz, J. (1999). Contagion of depressive symptoms and mood: Meta-analytic review and explanations from cognitive, behavioral, and interpersonal viewpoints. *Clinical Psychology: Science and Practice, 6,* 149–164.

Joiner, T. E., & Metalsky, G. I. (1995). A prospective test of an integrative interpersonal theory of depression: A naturalistic study of college students. *Journal of Personality and Social Psychology, 69,* 778–788.

Joiner, T. E., & Metalsky, G. I. (2001). Excessive reassurance-seeking: Delineating a risk factor involved in the development of depressive symptoms. *Psychological Science, 12,* 371–378.

Jones, C. M., Braithwaite, V. A., & Healy, S. D. (2003). The evolution of sex differences in spatial ability. *Behavioral Neuroscience, 117,* 403–411.

Jones, D. (1995). Sexual selection, physical attractiveness, and facial neotony: Cross-cultural evidence and implications. *Current Anthropology, 36,* 723–748.

Jones, E. E. (1990). *Interpersonal perception.* New York: Freeman.

Jones, E. E., & Davis, K. (1965). From acts to dispositions: The attribution process in person perception. In L. Berkowitz (Ed.), *Advances in experimental social psychology* (Vol. 2). New York: Academic Press.

Jones, F., & Kinman, G. (2001). Approaches to studying stress. In F. Jones & J. Bright (Eds.), *Stress: Myth, theory and research*. Harlow, England: Pearson Education.

Jones, R. A., & Brehm, J. W. (1970). Persuasiveness of one- and two-sided communications as a function of awareness there are two sides. *Journal of Experimental Social Psychology, 6,* 47–56.

Jordan, C. H., Spencer, S. J., & Zanna, M. P. (2003). "I love me . . . I love me not": Implicit self-esteem, explicit self-esteem, and defensiveness. In S. J. Spencer, S. Fein, M. P. Zanna, & J. M. Olson (Eds.), *Motivated social perception: The Ontario symposium.* Mahwah, NJ: Erlbaum.

Jordan, C. H., Spencer, S. J., Zanna, M. P., Hoshino-Browne, E., & Correll, J. (2003). Secure and defensive high self-esteem. *Journal of Personality and Social Psychology, 85,* 969–978.

Jorgensen, R. S., Johnson, B. T., Kolodziej, M. E., & Schreer, G. E. (1996). Elevated blood pressure and personality: A meta-analytic review. *Psychological Bulletin, 120,* 293–320.

Josselson, R. L. (1988). The embedded self: I and thou revisited. In D. K. Lapsley & F. C. Power (Eds.), *Self, ego, and identity.* New York: Springer-Verlag.

Joung, I. M. A., Stronks, K., Van De Mheen, H., Van Poppel, F. W. A., Van Der Meer, J. B. W., & Mackenbach, J. P. (1997). The contribution of intermediary factors to marital status differences in self-reported health. *Journal of Marriage and the Family, 59,* 476–490.

Jourard, S. M., & Landsman, T. (1980). *Healthy personality: An approach from the viewpoint of humanistic psychology.* New York: Macmillan.

Joyner, T. (1999, November 14). All-work is American way: Atlanta poll finds 21 percent work 50-plus hours a week. *The Atlanta Journal-Constitution,* pp. R1, R5.

Joyner, T. (2001, May 27). Why can't we enjoy a vacation? Americans getting tired, and it shows at work. *The Atlanta Journal-Constitution,* pp. D1, D3.

Judge, T. A., & Bono, J. E. (2000). Five-factor model of personality and transformational leadership. *Journal of Applied Psychology, 85,* 751–765.

Julien, R. M. (2001). *A primer of drug action.* New York: Freeman.

Jung, C. G. (1921). Psychological types. In *Collected Works* (Vol. 6). Princeton, NJ: Princeton University Press.

Jung, C. G. (1933). *Modern man in search of a soul.* New York: Harcourt, Brace & World.

Jussim, L., & Harber, K. D. (2005). Teacher-expectations and self-fulfilling prophecies: Knowns and unknowns, resolved and unresolved controversies. *Personality and Social Psychology Review, 9,* 131–155.

Justman, S. (2005). *Fool's paradise: The unreal world of pop psychology.* Chicago: Ivan R. Dee.

Kagan, J. (1998). Biology and the child. In W. Damon (Ed.), *Handbook of child psychology (Vol. 3): Social, emotional, and personality development.* New York: Wiley.

Kagan, J., Snidman, N., & Arcus, D. M. (1992). Initial reactions to unfamiliarity. *Current Directions in Psychological Science, 1,* 171–174.

Kahn, A. S., & Andreoli Mathie, V. (1999). Sexuality, society, and feminism: Psychological perspectives on women. In C. B. Travis & J. W. White (Eds.), *Sexuality, society, and feminism: Psychological perspectives on women.* Washington, DC: American Psychological Association.

Kahneman, D. (1999). Objective happiness. In D. Kahneman, E. Diener, & N. Schwarz (Eds.), *Well-being: The foundations of hedonic psychology.* New York: Sage.

Kahneman, D., Krueger, A. B., Schkade, D., Schwarz, N., & Stone, A. A. (2006). Would you be happier if you were richer? A focusing illusion. *Science, 312,* 1908–1910.

Kaiser, A., Kuenzli, E., Zappatore, E., & Nitsch, C. (2007). On females' lateral and males' bilateral activation during language production: A fMRI study. *International Journal of Psychophysiology, 63,* 192–198.

Kaiser, C. R., Vick, B. S., & Major, B. (2004). A prospective investigation of the relationship between just-world beliefs and the desire for revenge after September 11, 2001. *Psychological Science, 15,* 503–506.

Kaiser Family Foundation. (2004). *Sex education in America: Principals' survey.* Menlo Park, CA: Henry J. Kaiser Family Foundation.

Kaiser Family Foundation. (2007). *HIV/AIDS policy fact sheet.* Retrieved June 24, 2007 from http://www.kff.org/hivaids/us.cfm.

Kalant, H., & Kalant, O. J. (1979). Death in amphetamine users: Causes and rates. In D. E. Smith (Ed.), *Amphetamine use, misuse and abuse.* Boston: G. K. Hall.

Kalb, C., & Murr, A. (2006, May 16). Battling a black epidemic. *Newsweek,* pp. 42–48.

Kalichman, S. C. (1995). *Understanding AIDS: A guide for mental health professionals.* Washington, DC: American Psychological Association.

Kalichman, S. C., Roffman, R. A., Picciano, J. F., & Bolan, M. (1998). Risk for HIV infection among bisexual men seeking HIV-prevention services and risks posed to their female partners. *Health Psychology, 17,* 320–327.

Kalidindi, S., & McGuffin, P. (2003). The genetics of affective disorders: Present and future. In R. Plomin, J. C. Defries, I. W. Craig, & P. McGuffin (Eds.), *Behavioral genetics in the postgenomic era.* Washington, DC: American Psychological Association.

Kalmijn, M. (1998). Intermarriage and homogamy: Causes, patterns, trends. *Annual Review of Sociology, 24,* 395–421.

Kalwarf, H. J., Khoury, J. C., & Lanphear, B. P. (2003). Milk intake during childhood and adolescence, adult bone density, and osteoporotic fractures in U.S. women. *American Journal of Clinical Nutrition, 77,* 257–265.

Kamp Dush, C. M., Cohan, C. L., & Amato, P. R. (2003). The relationship between cohabitation and marital quality and stability: Change across cohorts? *Journal of Marriage and Family, 65,* 539–549.

Kandell, J. J. (1998). Internet addiction on campus: The vulnerability of college students. *CyberPsychology and Behavior, 1*(1), 11–17.

Kane, E. W. (2000). Racial and ethnic variations in gender-related attitudes. *Annual review of sociology, 26,* 419–439.

Kane, J. M., & Marder, S. R. (2005). Schizophrenia: Somatic treatment. In B. J. Sadock & V. A. Sadock (Eds.), *Kaplan and Sadock's comprehensive textbook of psychiatry.* Philadelphia: Lippincott Williams & Wilkins.

Kane, T. D., Marks, M. A., Zaccaro, S. J., & Blair, V. (1996). Self-efficacy, personal goals, and wrestlers' self-regulation. *Journal of Sport & Exercise Psychology, 18*(1), 36–48.

Kanner, A. D., Coyne, J. C., Schaefer, C., & Lazarus, R. S. (1981). Comparison of two modes of stress measurement: Daily hassles and uplifts versus major life events. *Journal of Behavioral Medicine, 4,* 1–39.

Kanner, A. D., & Soule, R. G. (2004). Globalization, corporate culture, and freedom. In T. Kasser & A. D. Kanner (Eds.), *Psychology and consumer culture: The struggle for a good life in a materialistic world.* Washington, DC: American Psychological Association.

Kant, A. K., Schatzkin, A., Graubard, B. I., & Schairer, C. (2000). A prospective study of diet quality and mortality in women. *Journal of the American Medical Association, 283,* 2109–02115.

Kapinus, C. A., & Johnson, M. P. (2003). The utility of family life cycle as a theoretical and empirical tool: Commitment and family life-cycle stage. *Journal of Family Issues, 24,* 155–184.

Kaplan, A. G. (1985). Female or male therapists for women patients: New formulations. *Psychiatry, 48,* 111–121.

Kaplan, D. S., Liu, R. X., & Kaplan, H. B. (2005). School-related stress in early adolescence and academic performance three years later: The conditional influence of self expectation. *Social Psychology of Education, 8,* 3–17.

Kaplan, H. I. (1989). History of psychosomatic medicine. In H. I. Kaplan & B. J. Sadock (Eds.), *Comprehensive textbook of psychiatry/V* (Vol. 2) (5th ed.). Baltimore: Williams & Wilkins.

Kaplan, H. S. (1979). *Disorders of sexual desire.* New York: Simon & Schuster.

Karasek, R. A., Jr. (1979). Job demands, job decision latitude, and mental strain: Implications for job redesign. *Administrative Science Quarterly, 24,* 285–308.

Karasek, R. A., Jr., Baker, D., Marxer, F., Ahlbom, A., & Theorell, T. (1981). Job decision latitude, job demands, and cardiovascular disease: A prospective study of Swedish men. *American Journal of Public Health, 71,* 694–705.

Karasek, R. A., Jr., & Theorell, T. (1990). *Healthy work: Stress, productivity, and the reconstruction of working life.* New York: Basic Books.

Karasu, T. B. (2005). Psychoanalysis and psychoanalytic psychotherapy. In B. J. Sadock & V. A. Sadock (Eds.), *Kaplan and Sadock's comprehensive textbook of psychiatry.* Philadelphia: Lippincott Williams & Wilkins.

Kardiner, A., & Linton, R. (1945). *The individual and his society.* New York: Columbia University Press.

Karney, B. R., & Bradbury, T. N. (2000). Attributions in marriage: State or trait? A growth curve analysis. *Journal of Personality and Social Psychology, 78*(2), 295–309.

Kassel, J. D., Stroud, L. R., & Paronis, C. A. (2003). Smoking, stress, and negative affect: Correlation, causation, and context across stages of smoking. *Psychological Bulletin, 129*(2), 270–304.

Kasser, T. (2002). *The high prices of materialism.* Cambridge, MA: MIT Press.

Kasser, T. (2004). The good life or the goods life? Positive psychology and personal well-being in the culture of consumption. In P. A. Linley & S. Joseph (Eds.), *Positive psychology in practice.* New York: Wiley.

Kasser, T., Ryan, R. M., Couchman, C. E., & Sheldon, K. M. (2004). Materialistic values: Their causes and consequences. In T. Kasser & A. D. Kanner (Eds.), *Psychology and consumer culture: The struggle for a good life in a materialistic world.* Washington, DC: American Psychological Association.

Kastenbaum, R. J. (1999). Dying and bereavement. In J. C. Cavanaugh & S. K. Whitbourne (Eds.), *Gerontology: An interdisciplinary perspective* . New York: Oxford University Press.

Kastenbaum, R. J. (2001). *Death, society, and human experience* (7th ed.). Boston: Allyn & Bacon.

Katigbak, M. S., Church, A. T., Guanzon-Lapena, M. A., Carlota, A. J. & del Pilar, G. H. (2002). Are indigenous personality dimensions culture specific? Philippine inventories and the five-factor model. *Journal of Personality and Social Psychology, 82,* 89–101.

Katz, L. S., & Epstein, S. (2005). The relation of cancer-prone personality to exceptional recovery from cancer: A preliminary study. *Advances in Mind-Body Medicine, 21,* 6–20.

Kaufman, G., & Taniguchi, H. (2006). Gender and marital happiness in later life. *Journal of Family Issues, 27,* 735–757.

Kaufman, G., & Uhlenberg, P. (1998). Effects of life course transitions on the quality of relationships between adult children and their parents. *Journal of Marriage & the Family, 60,* 924–938.

Kausler, D. H. (1994). *Learning and memory in normal aging.* San Diego: Academic Press.

Kavanagh, D. J. (1992). Recent developments in expressed emotion in schizophrenia. *British Journal of Psychiatry, 160,* 601–620.

Kavesh, L., & Lavin, C. (1988). *Tales from the front.* New York: Doubleday.

Kawachi, I., Colditz, G. A., Stampfer, M. J., Willett, W. C., Manson, J. E., Rosner, B., & et al. (1994). Smoking cessation and time course of decreased risks of coronary heart disease in middle-aged women. *Archives of Internal Medicine, 154,* 169–175.

Kay, J., & Kay, R. L. (2003). Individual psychoanalytic psychotherapy. In A. Tasman, J. Kay, & J. A. Lieberman (Eds.), *Psychiatry.* New York: Wiley.

Kaye, W. H., Weltzin, T. E., Hsu, L. K. G., McConaha, C. W., & Bolton, B. (1993). Amount of calories retained after binge eating and vomiting. *American Journal of Psychiatry, 150,* 969–971.

Kazdin, A. E. (1982). History of behavior modification. In A. S. Bellack, M. Hersen, & A. E. Kazdin (Eds.), *International handbook of behavior modification and behavior therapy.* New York: Plenum.

Kazdin, A. E. (1994). Methodology, design, and evaluation in psychotherapy research. In A. E. Bergin & S. L. Garfield (Eds.), *Handbook of psychotherapy and behavior change* (4th ed.). New York: Wiley.

Kazdin, A. E. (2001). *Behavior modification in applied settings.* Belmont, CA: Wadsworth.

Kazdin, A. E., & Benjet, C. (2003). Spanking children: Evidence and issues. *Current Directions in Psychological Science,* 99–103.

Keck, P. E. Jr., & McElroy, S. L. (2006). Lithium and mood stabilizers. In D. J. Stein, D. J. Kupfer, & A. F. Schatzberg (Eds.), *Textbook of mood disorders.* Washington, DC: American Psychiatric Publishing.

Keefe, F. J., Smith, S. J., Buffington, A. L. H., Gibson, J., Studts, J. L., & Caldwell, D. S. (2002). Recent advances and future directions in the biopsychosocial assessment and treatment of arthritis. *Journal of Consulting & Clinical Psychology, 70*(3), 640–655.

Keefe, R. S. E., & Eesley, C. E. (2006). Neurocognitive impairments. In J. A. Liberman, T. S. Stroup, & D. O. Perkins (Eds.), *Textbook of schizophrenia.* Washington, DC: American Psychiatric Publishing.

Keesey, R. E. (1993). Physiological regulation of body energy: Implications for obesity. In A. J. Stunkard & T. A. Wadden (Eds.), *Obesity: Theory and therapy.* New York: Raven Press.

Keesey, R. E. (1995). A set-point model of body weight regulation. In K. D. Brownell & C. G. Fairburn (Eds.), *Eating disorders and obesity: A comprehensive handbook.* New York: Guilford Press.

Kegan, R. (1994). *In over our heads: The mental demands of modern life.* Cambridge, MA: Harvard University Press.

Keinan, G. (1987). Decision making under stress: Scanning of alternatives under controllable and uncontrollable threats. *Journal of Personality and Social Psychology, 52,* 639–644.

Keita, G. P., & Hurrell, J. J., Jr. (1994). *Job stress in a changing workforce.* Washington, DC: American Psychological Association.

Keith, J. (1990). Age in social and cultural context: Anthropological perspectives. In R. H. Binstock & L. K. George (Eds.), *Handbook of midlife development.* San Diego: Academic Press.

Keller, S. N., & Brown, J. D. Media interventions to promote responsible sexual behavior. *The Journal of Sex Research, 39*(1), 67–72.

Kelley, H. H. (1950). The warm-cold dimension in first impressions of persons. *Journal of Personality, 18,* 431–439.

Kelley, H. H. (1967). Attribution theory in social psychology. In D. Levine (Ed.), *Nebraska Symposium on Motivation* (Vol. 15). Lincoln: University of Nebraska Press.

Kelley, H. H., & Thibaut, J. W. (1978). *Interpersonal relations: A theory of interdependence.* New York: Wiley-Interscience.

Kellogg, J. S., Hopko, D. R., & Ashcraft, M. H. (1999). The effects of time pressure on arithmetic performance. *Journal of Anxiety Disorders, 13*(6), 591–600.

Kelly, B. D., Feeney, L., O'Callaghan, E., Browne, R., Byrne, M., Mulryan, N., Scully, A., Morris, M., Kinsella, A., Takei, N., McNeil, T., Walsh, D., & Larkin, C. (2004). Obstetric adversity and age at first presentation with schizophrenia: Evidence of a dose-response relationship. *American Journal of Psychiatry, 161,* 920–922.

Kelly, J. B., & Emery, R. E. (2003). Children's adjustment following divorce: Risk and resilience perspectives. *Family Relations: Interdisciplinary Journal of Applied Family Studies, 52*(4), 352–362.

Kelly, K. M., & Schramke, C. J. (2000). Epilepsy. In G. Fink (Ed.), *Encyclopedia of stress.* San Diego: Academic Press.

Kelly, K. R., & Cobb, S. J. (1991). A profile of the career development characteristics of young gifted adolescents: Examining gender and multicultural differences. *Roeper Review, 13,* 202–206.

Kelman, H. C., & Hamilton, V. L. (1989). *Crimes of obedience: Toward a social psychology of authority and responsibility.* New Haven, CT: Yale University Press.

Kelsey, J. E. (2005). Selective serotonin reuptake inhibitors. In B. J. Sadock & V. A. Sadock (Eds.), *Kaplan and Sadock's comprehensive textbook of psychiatry.* Philadelphia: Lippincott Williams & Wilkins.

Kelsoe, J. (2005). Mood disorders: Genetics. In B. J. Sadock & V. A. Sadock (Eds.), *Kaplan & Sadock's comprehensive textbook of psychiatry.* Philadelphia: Lippincott Williams & Wilkins.

Kemeny, M. E. (2003). The psychobiology of stress. *Current Directions in Psychological Science, 12*(4), 124–129.

Kemeny, M. E. (2007). Psychoneuroimmunology. In H. S. Friedman & R. C. Silver (Eds.), *Foundations of health psychology.* New York: Oxford University Press.

Kemeny, M. E., Weiner, H., Duran, R., Taylor, S. E., Visscher, B., & Fahey, J. L. (1995). Immune system changes after the death of a partner in HIV-positive gay men. *Psychosomatic Medicine, 57,* 547–554.

Kendall, A. R., Mahue-Giangreco, M., Carpenter, C. L., Ganz, P. A., & Bernstein, L. (2005). Influence of exercise activity on quality of life in long-term breast cancer survivors. *Quality of Life Research, 14,* 361–371.

Kendall, P. C., Holmbeck, G., & Verduin, T. (2004). Methodology, design, and evaluation in psychotherapy research. In M. J. Lambert (Ed.), *Bergin and Garfield's handbook of psychotherapy and behavior change.* New York: Wiley.

Kendler, K. S. (2000). Schizophrenia: Genetics. In B. J. Sadock & V. A. Sadock (Eds.), *Kaplan and Sadock's comprehensive textbook of psychiatry* (7th ed.). Philadelphia: Lippincott/Williams & Wilkins.

Kendler, K. S. (2005a). "A gene for . . . ?": The nature of gene action in psychiatric disorders. *American Journal of Psychiatry, 162,* 1243–1252.

Kendler, K. S. (2005b). Psychiatric genetics: A methodologic critique. *American Journal of Psychiatry, 162,* 3–11.

Kendler, K. S., & Gardner, C. O., Jr. (1998). Boundaries of major depression: An evaluation of DSM-IV criteria. *American Journal of Psychiatry, 155,* 172–177.

Kendler, K. S., Gatz, M., Gardner, C. O., & Pedersen, N. L. (2006). A Swedish national twin study of lifetime major depression. *American Journal of Psychiatry, 163,* 109–114.

Kendler, K. S., Kuhn, J., & Prescott, C. A. (2004). The interrelationship of neuroticism, sex, and stressful life events in the prediction of episodes of major depression. *American Journal of Psychiatry, 161,* 631–636.

Kendler, K. S., Myers, J., & Prescott, C. A. (2005). Sex differences in the relationship between social support and risk for major depression: A longitudinal study of opposite-sex twin pairs. *American Journal of Psychiatry, 162,* 250–256.

Kendler, K. S., Thornton, L. M., Gilman, S. E., & Kessler, R. C. (2000). Sexual orientation in a U.S. national sample of twin and nontwin sibling pairs. *American Journal of Psychiatry, 157*(11), 1843–1846.

Kennedy, S. H., Holt, A., & Baker, G. B. (2005). Monoamine oxidase inhibitors. In B. J. Sadock & V. A. Sadock (Eds.), *Kaplan and Sadock's comprehensive textbook of psychiatry.* Philadelphia: Lippincott Williams & Wilkins.

Kenrick, D. T., Sadalla, E. K., Groth, G., & Trost, M. R. (1990). Evolution, traits, and the stages of human courtship: Qualifying the parental investment model. *Journal of Personality, 58,* 97–116.

Kenrick, D. T., & Trost, M. R. (1993). The evolutionary perspective. In A. E. Beall & R. J. Sternberg (Eds.), *The psychology of gender.* New York: Guilford Press.

Kenrick, D. T., Trost, M. R., & Sundie, J. M. (2004). Sex roles as adaptations: An evolutionary perspective on gender differences and similarities. In A. H. Eagly, A. E. Beall, & R. J. Sternberg (Eds.), *The psychology of gender.* New York: Guilford Press.

Keogh, E., Bond, F. W., French, C. C., Richards, A., & Davis, R. E. (2004). Test anxiety, susceptibility to distraction and examination performance. *Anxiety, Stress and Coping: An International Journal, 17*(3), 241–252.

Kernis, M. H. (2003a). Optimal self-esteem and authenticity: Separating fantasy from reality. *Psychological Inquiry, 14*(1), 83–89.

Kernis, M. H. (2003b). Toward a conceptualization of optimal self-esteem. *Psychological Inquiry, 14*(1), 1–26.

Kernis, M. H., & Goldman, B. M. (2003). Stability and variability in self-concept and self-esteem. In M. R. Leary and J. P. Tangney (Eds.), *Handbook of self and identity.* New York: Guilford.

Kernis, M. H., & Paradise, A. W. (2002). Distinguishing between secure and fragile forms of high self-esteem. In E. L. Deci, & R. M. Ryan (Eds.), *Handbook of self-determination research.* Rochester, NY: University of Rochester Press.

Kessler, R. C. (1997). The effects of stressful life events on depression. *Annual Review of Psychology, 48,* 191–214.

Kessler, R. C. (2002). Epidemiology of depression. In I. H. Gotlib, & C. L. Hammen (Eds.), *Handbook of depression.* New York: Guilford.

Kessler, R. C., Berglund, P., Demler, O., Jin, R., Koretz, D., Merikangas, K. R., Rush, A. J., Walters, E. E., & Wang, P. S. (2003a). The epidemiology of major depressive disorder: Results from the national comorbidity survey replication (NCS-R). *The Journal of the American Medical Association, 289*(23), 3095–3105.

Kessler, R. C., Berglund, P., Demler, O., Jin, R., & Walters, E. E. (2005a). Lilfetime prevalence and age-of-onset distributions of DSM-IV disorders in the national comorbidity survey replication. *Archives of General Psychiatry, 62,* 593–602.

Kessler, R. C., Demier, O., Frank, R. G., Olfson, M., Pincus, H. A., Walters, E. E., Wang, P., Wells, K. B., & Zaslavsky, A. M. (2005b). Prevalence and treatment of mental disorders. 1990–2003. *New England Journal of Medicine, 352,* 2515–2523.

Kessler, R. C., Merikangas, K. R., Berglund, P., Eaton, W. W., Koretz, D. S., & Walters, E. E. (2003b). Mild disorders should not be eliminated from the DSM-V. *Archives of General Psychiatry, 60,* 1117–1122.

Kessler, R. C., Olfson, M., & Berglund, P. A. (1998). Patterns and predictors of treatment contact after first onset of psychiatric disorders. *American Journal of Psychiatry, 155,* 62–69.

Kessler, R. C., & Zhao, S. (1999). The prevalence of mental illness. In A. V. Horvitz & T. L. Scheid (Eds.), *A handbook for the study of mental health: Social contexts, theories, and systems.* New York: Cambridge University Press.

Keysar, B., & Henly, A. S. (2002). Speakers' overestimation of their effectiveness. *Psychological Science, 13,* 207–212.

Khot, U. N., Khot, M. B., Bajzer, C. T., Sapp, S. K., Ohman, E. M., Brener, S. J., Ellis, S. G., Lincoff, M. A., & Topol, E. J. (2003). Prevalence of conventional risk factors in patients with coronary heart disease. *Journal of the American Medical Association, 290,* 898–904.

Kiecolt-Glaser, J. K., & Glaser, R. (1995). Measurement of immune response. In S. Cohen, R. C. Kessler, & L. U. Gordon (Eds.), *Measuring stress: A guide for health and social scientists.* New York: Oxford University Press.

Kiecolt-Glaser, J. K., Garner, W., Speicher, C., Penn, G. M., Holliday, J., & Glaser, R. (1984). Psychosocial modifiers of immunocompetence in medical students. *Psychosomatic Medicine, 46,* 7–14.

Kiecolt-Glaser, J. K., & Glaser, R. (2001). Stress and immunity: Age enhances the risks. *Current Directions in Psychological Science, 10*(1), 18–21.

Kieffer, K. M., Cronin, C., & Gawet, D. L. (2006). Test and study worry and emotionality in the prediction of college students' reason for drinking: An exploratory investigation. *Journal of Alcohol and Drug Addiction, 50*(1), 57–81.

Kierein, N. M., & Gold, M. A. (2000). Pygmalion in work organizations: A meta-analysis. *Journal of Organizational Behavior, 21*(8), 913–928.

Kiernan, K. (2004). Redrawing the boundaries of marriage. *Journal of Marriage and Family, 66,* 980–987.

Kieseppa, T., Partonen, T., Huakka, J., Kaprio, J., & Lonnqvist, J. (2004). High concordance of bipolar 1 disorder in a nationwide sample of twins. *American Journal of Psychiatry, 161,* 1814–1821.

Kiesler, C. A. (2000). The next wave of change for psychology and mental health services in the health care revolution. *American Psychologist, 55*(5), 481–487.

Kiesler, D. J. (1999). *Beyond the disease model of mental disorders.* New York: Praeger.

Kihlstrom, J. F. (1998). Exhumed memory. In S. J. Lynn & K. M. McConkey (Eds.), *Truth in memory.* New York: Guilford Press.

Kihlstrom, J. F. (2001). Dissociative disorders. In P. B. Sutker & H. E. Adams (Eds.), *Comprehensive handbook of psychopathology* (3rd ed.). New York: Kluwer Academic/Plenum Publishers.

Kihlstrom, J. F. (2004). An unbalanced balancing act: Blocked, recovered, and false memories in the laboratory and clinic. *Clinical Psychology: Science & Practice, 11*(1), 34–41.

Kihlstrom, J. F., Glisky, M. L., & Angiulo, M. J. (1994). Dissociative tendencies and dissociative disorders. *Journal of Abnormal Psychology, 103,* 117–124.

Kilby, R. W. (1993). *The study of human values.* Lanham, MD: University Press of America.

Killicarslan, A., Isildak, M., Guven, G. S., Oz, S. G., Tannover, M. D., Duman, A. E., Saracbasi, O., & Sozen, T. (2006). Demographic, socioeconomic and educational aspects of obesity in an adult population. *Journal of the National Medical Association, 98,* 1313–1317.

Kilmartin, C. T. (2000). *The masculine self* (2nd ed.). Boston: McGraw-Hill.

Kilmartin, C. T. (2007). *The masculine self.* Cornwall-on-Hudson, NY: Sloan Publishing.

Kim, H. S., Sherman, D. K., Ko, D., & Taylor, S. E. (2006). Pursuit of comfort and pursuit of harmony: Culture, relationships, and social support seeking. *Personality and Social Psychology Bulletin, 32,*1595–1607.

Kim, H., & Markus, H. R. (1999). Deviance or uniqueness, harmony or conformity? A cultural analysis. *Journal of Personality and Social Psychology, 77*(4), 785–800.

Kim, J. E., & Moen, P. (2001). Moving into retirement: Preparations and transitions in late midlife. In M. E. Lachman (Ed.), *Handbook of midlife development.* New York: Wiley.

Kimura, D., & Hampson, E. (1993). Neural and hormonal mechanisms mediating sex differences in cognition. In P. A. Vernon (Ed.), *Biological approaches to the study of human intelligence.* Norwood, NJ: Ablex.

King, B. M. (2005). *Human sexuality today.* Upper Saddle River, NJ: Pearson Prentice Hall.

King, C. A. (1997). Suicidal behavior in adolescence. In R. W. Maris, M. M. Silverman, & S. S. Canetto (Eds.), *Review of suicidology.* New York: Guilford Press.

King, G. R., & Ellinwood Jr., E. H. (2005). Amphetamines and other stimulants. In J. H. Lowinson, P. Ruiz, R. B. Millman, & J. G. Langrod (Eds.), *Substance abuse: A comprehensive textbook.* Philadelphia: Lippincott/Williams & Wilkins.

King, J. L. (2004). *On the down low: A journey into the lives of "straight" black men who sleep with men.* New York: Broadway Books.

King, L. A., & Emmons, R. A. (1990). Conflict over emotional expression: Psychological and physical correlates. *Journal of Personality and Social Psychology, 58,* 864–877.

King, L. A., & Emmons, R. A. (1991). Psychological, physical, and interpersonal correlates of emotional expressiveness, conflict and control. *European Journal of Personality, 5,* 131–150.

King, L. A., King, D. W., Fairbank, J. A., Keane, T. M., & Adams, G. A. (1998). Resilience-recovery factors in post-traumatic stress disorder among female and male Vietnam veterans: Hardiness, postwar social support, and additional stressful life events. *Journal of Personality and Social Psychology, 74,* 420–434.

King, N. J., Eleonora, G., & Ollendick, T. H. (1998). Etiology of childhood phobias: Current status of Rachman's three pathways theory. *Behaviour Research and Therapy, 36,* 297–309.

Kinsey, A. C., Pomeroy, W. B., & Martin, C. E. (1948). *Sexual behavior in the human male.* Philadelphia: Saunders.

Kinsey, A. C., Pomeroy, W. B., Martin, C. E., & Gebhard, P. H. (1953). *Sexual behavior in the human female.* Philadelphia: Saunders.

Kinsman, R. A., Dirks, J. F., & Jones, N. F. (1982). Psychomaintenance of chronic physical illness: Clinical assessment of personal styles affecting medical management. In T. Millon, C. Green, & R. Meagher (Eds.), *Handbook of clinical health psychology.* New York: Plenum.

Kinsman, S. B., Romer, D., Furstenberg, F. F., & Schwarz, D. F. (1998). Early sexual initiation: The role of peer norms. *Pediatrics, 102,* 1185–1192.

Kirby, D. (2001). *Emerging answers: Research findings on programs to reduce teen pregnancy.* Washington, DC: National Campaign to Prevent Teenage Pregnancy.

Kirkpatrick, B., & Tek, C. (2005). Schizophrenia: Clinical features and psychopathology concepts. In B. J. Sadock & V. A. Sadock (Eds.), *Kaplan & Sadock's comprehensive textbook of psychiatry.* Philadelphia: Lippincott Williams & Wilkins.

Kirkpatrick, L. A. (2005). *Attachment, evolution, and the psychology of religion.* New York: Guilford.

Kirkpatrick, L. A., & Davis, K. E. (1994). Attachment style, gender, and relationship stability: A longitudinal analysis. *Journal of Personality and Social Psychology, 66,* 502–512.

Kirkpatrick, L. A., & Hazan, C. (1994). Attachment styles and close relationships: A four-year prospective study. *Personal Relationships, 1,* 123–142.

Kitson, G. C. (1992). *Portrait of divorce: Adjustment to marital breakdown.* New York: Guilford Press.

Klag, S., & Bradley, G. (2004). The role of hardiness in stress and illness: An exploration of the effect of negative affectivity and gender. *British Journal of Health Psychology, 9*(2), 137–161.

Klass, D. (1996). The deceased child in the psychic and social worlds of bereaved parents during the resolution of grief. In D. Klass, P. R. Silverman, & S. L. Nickman (Eds.), *Continuing bonds: New understandings of grief.* Washington, DC: Taylor and Francis.

Klassen, M. (1987). How to get the most out of your time. In A. D. Timpe (Ed.), *The management of time.* New York: Facts on File.

Klein, D. N., & Rubovits, D. R. (1987). The reliability of subjects' reports of life events inventories: A longitudinal study. *Journal of Behavioral Medicine, 10,* 501–512.

Klein, F., Sepekoff, B., & Wolf, T. J. (1985). Sexual orientation: A multivariable dynamic process. *Journal of Homosexuality, 11,* 35–49.

Klein, T. W., Friedman, H., & Specter, S. (1998). Marijuana, immunity and infection. *Journal of Neuroimmunology, 83,* 102–115.

Kleinke, C. L. (1986). Gaze and eye contact: A research review. *Psychological Bulletin, 100,* 78–100.

Kleinke, C. L., Meeker, F. B., & Staneski, R. A. (1986). Preference for opening lines: Comparing ratings by men and women. *Sex Roles, 15,* 585–600.

Kleinmuntz, B. (1980). *Essentials of abnormal psychology.* San Francisco: Harper & Row.

Kline, D. W., Kline, T. J. B., Fozard, J. L., Kosnik, W., Schieber, F., & Sekuler, R. (1992). Vision, aging, and driving: The problems of older drivers. *Journal of Gerontology, 42,* P27–P34.

Kline, G. H., Pleasant, N. D., Whitton, S. W., & Markman, H. J. (2006). Understanding couple conflict. In A. L. Vangelisti & D. Perlman (Eds.), *The Cambridge handbook of personal relationships.* New York: Cambridge University Press.

Kline, P. (1995). A critical review of the measurement of personality and intelligence. In D. H. Saklofske & M. Zeidner (Eds.), *International handbook of personality and intelligence.* New York: Plenum Press.

Klinesmith, J., Kasser, T., & McAndrew, F. T. (2006). Guns, testosterone, and aggression: An experimental test of a mediational hypothesis. *Psychological Science, 17,* 568–571.

Kling, K. C., Hyde, J. S., Showers, C. J., & Buswell, B. N. (1999). Gender differences in self-esteem: A meta-analysis. *Psychological Bulletin, 125*(4), 470–500.

Klohnen, E. C., & Luo, S. (2003). Interpersonal attraction and personality: What is attractive—self similarity, ideal similarity, complementarity, or attachment security? *Journal of Personality and Social Psychology , 85,* 709–722.

Klonoff, E. A., & Landrine, H. (1999). Cross-validation of the schedule of racist events. *Journal of Black Psychology, 25*(2), 231–254.

Klose, M., & Jacobi, F. (2004). Can gender differences in the prevalence of mental disorders be explained by sociodemographic factors? *Archives of Women's Mental Health, 7,* 133–148.

Kluckhohn, C., & Murray, H. A. (1948). *Personality in nature, society and culture.* New York: Knopf.

Kluft, R. P. (1996). Dissociative identity disorder. In L. K. Michelson & W. J. Ray (Eds.), *Handbook of dissociation: Theoretical, empirical, and clinical perspectives.* New York: Plenum.

Kluft, R. P. (1999). True lies, false truths, and naturalistic raw data: Applying clinical research findings to the false memory debate. In L. M. Williams & V. L. Banyard (Eds.), *Trauma & memory.* Thousand Oaks, CA: Sage.

Klumb, P. L., & Baltes, M. M. (2004). Adverse life events in late life: Their manifestation and management in daily life. *International Journal of Stress Management, 11*(1), 3–20.

Knapp, C. M., Ciraulo, D. A., & Jaffe, J. (2005). Opiates: Clinical aspects. In J. H. Lowinson, P. Ruiz, R. B. Millman, & J. G. Langrod (Eds.), *Substance abuse: A comprehensive textbook.* Philadelphia: Lippincott/Williams & Wilkins.

Knapp, D. E., Faley, R. H., Ekeberg, W. C., & Dubois, C. L. Z. (1997). Determinants of target responses to sexual harassment: A conceptual framework. *Academy of Management Review, 22*(3), 687–729.

Knaus, W. (2000). Procrastination, blame, and change. *Journal of Social Behavior and Personality, 15,* 153–166.

Knickmeyer, N., Sexton, K., & Nishimura, N. (2002). The impact of same-sex friendships on the well-being of women: A review of the literature. *Women and Therapy, 25*(1), 37–59.

Knowles, J. A., Kaufmann, C. A., & Rieder, R. O. (1999). Genetics. In R. E. Hales, S. C. Yudofsky, & J. A. Talbott (Eds.), *American Psychiatric Press textbook of psychiatry.* Washington, DC: American Psychiatric Press.

Knowles, R. B., Wyart, C., Buldyrev, S. V., Cruz, L., Urbanc, B., Hasselmo, M. E., Stanley, H. E., & Hyman, B. T. (1999). Plaque-induced neurite abnormalities: Implications of disruption of neuronal networks in Alzheimer's disease. *Proceedings of the National Academy of Sciences, 96,* 5274–5279.

Knox, D. (2000). *The divorced dad's survival book: How to stay connected to your kids.* New York: Perseus.

Kobasa, S. C. (1979). Stressful life events, personality, and health: An inquiry into hardiness. *Journal of Personality and Social Psychology, 37,* 1–11.

Kobasa, S. C. (1984, September). How much stress can you survive? *American Health,* pp. 64–77.

Konrad, A. M. (2003). Family demands and job attribute preferences: A 4-year longitudinal study of women and men. *Sex Roles, 49*(1–2), 35–46.

Koopman, C., Classen, C., & Spiegel, D. (1994). Predictors of posttraumatic stress symptoms among survivors of the Oakland/Berkeley, Calif., firestorm. *American Journal of Psychiatry, 151,* 888–894.

Kop, W. J., Gottdiener, J. S., & Krantz, D. S. (2001). Stress and silent ischemia. In A. Baum, T. A. Revenson, & J. E. Singer (Eds.), *Handbook of health psychology.* Mahwah, NJ: Erlbaum.

Kopta, S. M., Lueger, R. J., Saunders, S. M., & Howard, K. I. (1999). Individual psychotherapy outcome and process research: Challenges leading to greater turmoil or a positive transition? *Annual Review of Psychology, 50,* 441–469.

Koran, L. M., Faber, R. J., Aboujaoude, E., Large, M. D., & Serpe, R. T. (2006). Estimated prevalence of compulsive buying behavior in the United States. *American Journal of Psychiatry, 163,* 1806–1812.

Koren, D., Arnon, I., & Klein, E. (1999). Acute stress response and posttraumatic stress disorder in traffic accident victims: A one-year prospective, follow-up study. *American Journal of Psychiatry, 156*(3), 367–373.

Koriat, A., & Bjork, R. A. (2005). Illusions of competence in monitoring one's knowledge during study. *Journal of Experimental Psychology: Learning, Memory, and Cognition, 31,* 187–194.

Kornspan, A. S., & Etzel, E. F. (2001). The relationship of demographic and psychological variables to career maturity of junior college student-athletes. *Journal of College Student Development, 42*(2), 122–132.

Koss, M. P., & Cook, S. I. (1993). Facing the facts: Date and acquaintance rape are significant problems for women. In R. J. Gelles, & D. R. Losede (Eds.), *Current controversies on family violence.* Thousand Oaks, CA: Sage.

Koss, M. P., Goodman, L. A., Browne, A., Fitzgerald, L. F., Keita, G. P., & Russo, N. F. (1994). *No safe haven: Male violence against women at home, at work, and in the community.* Washington, DC: American Psychological Association.

Kouzma, N. M., & Kennedy, G. A. (2004). Self-reported sources of stress in senior high school students. *Psychological Reports, 94,* 314–316.

Kozlowski, S. W. J., & Bell, B. S. (2003). Work groups and teams in organizations. In W. C. Borman, D. R. Ilgen, & R. J. Klimoski (Eds.), *Handbook of psychology: Vol. 12. Industrial and organizational psychology.* New York: Wiley.

Kraaij, V., & Garnefski, N. (2006). The role of intrusion, avoidance, and cognitive coping strategies more then 50 years after war. *Anxiety, Stress, & Coping, 19*(1), 1–14.

Kramer, P. D. (2006). *Freud: Inventor of the modern mind.* New York: HarperCollins.

Kransny, L., Williams, B. J., Provencal, S., & Ozonoff, S. (2003). Social skills interventions for the autism spectrum: Essential ingredients and a model curriculum. *Child and Adolescent Psychiatric Clinics of North America, 12*(1), 107–122.

Krantz, D. S., Sheps, D. S., Carney, R. M., & Natelson, B. H. (2000). Effects of mental stress in patients with coronary artery disease. *Journal of the American Medical Association, 283*(14), 1800–1802.

Kreider, R. M. (2005). *Number, timing, and duration of marriages and divorces: 2001. U.S. Census Bureau, Household Economic Studies.* Washington DC: Department of Commerce.

Kring, A. M. (1999). Emotion in schizophrenia: Old mystery, new understanding. *Current Directions in Psychological Science, 8,* 160–163.

Kring, A. M., & Gordon, A. H. (1998). Sex differences in emotion: Expression, experience, and physiology. *Journal of Personality and Social Psychology, 74*(3), 686–703.

Kroger, J. (1997). Gender and identity: The intersection of structure, content, and context. *Sex Roles, 36*(11/12), 747–770.

Krueger, W. C. F. (1929). The effect of overlearning on retention. *Journal of Experimental Psychology, 12,* 71–78.

Kübler-Ross, E. (1969). *On death and dying.* New York: Macmillan.

Kübler-Ross, E. (1970). The dying patient's point of view. In O. G. Brim, Jr., H. E. Freeman, S. Levine, & N. A. Scotch (Eds.), *The dying patient.* New York: Sage.

Kudo, E. (2003). Explicit and direct self-serving bias in Japan: Examination of self-serving bias for success and failure. *Journal of Cross-Cultural Psychology, 34,* 511–521.

Kulick, A. R., Pope, H. G., & Keck, P. E. (1990). Lycanthropy and self-identification. *Journal of Nervous and Mental Disease, 178,* 134–137.

Kulik, L. (2000). Jobless men and women: A comparative analysis of job search intensity, attitudes toward unemployment and related responses. *Journal of Occupational and Behavioral Psychology, 73*(4), 487–500.

Kunkel, D., Eyal, K., Finnerty, K., Biely, E., & Donnerstein, E. (2005a). *Sex on TV 4: Executive Summary.* Retrieved June 16, 2007 from http://www.kff.org/entmedia/upload/sex-on-TV-4-Executive-Summary.pdf.

Kunkel, D., Eyal, K., Finnerty, K., Biely, E., & Donnerstein, E. (2005b). *Sex on TV 4: Full report.* Retrieved June 16, 2007 from http://www.kff.org/entmedia/upload/sex-on-TV-4-full-report.pdf.

Kurdek, L. A. (1991). Sexuality in homosexual and heterosexual couples. In K. McKinney & S. Sprecher (Eds.), *Sexuality in close relationships.* Hillside, NJ: Erlbaum.

Kurdek, L. A. (1994). The nature and correlates of relationship quality in gay, lesbian, and heterosexual cohabiting couples. In B. Greene & G. M. Herek (Eds.), *Lesbian and gay psychology.* Thousand Oaks, CA: Sage.

Kurdek, L. A. (1998). Relationship outcomes and their predictors: Longitudinal evidence from heterosexual married, gay cohabiting, and lesbian cohabiting couples. *Journal of Marriage and the Family, 30,* 553–568.

Kurdek, L. A. (2004). Gay men and lesbians: The family context. In M. Coleman & L. H. Ganong (Eds.), *Handbook of contemporary families: Considering the past, contemplating the future.* Thousand Oaks, CA: Sage.

Kurdek, L. A. (2005). What do we know about gay and lesbian couples? *Current Directions in Psychological Science, 14*(5), 251–254.

Kurdek, L. A. (2006). Differences between partners from heterosexual, gay, and lesbian cohabiting couples. *Journal of Marriage and Family, 68,* 509–528.

Kurdek, L. A., & Schmitt, J. P. (1986a). Early development of relationship quality in heterosexual married, heterosexual cohabiting, gay, and lesbian couples. *Developmental Psychology, 22,* 305–309.

Kurdek, L. A., & Schmitt, J. P. (1986b). Interaction of sex role self-concept with relationship quality and relationship beliefs in married, heterosexual cohabiting, gay, and lesbian couples. *Journal of Personality and Social Psychology, 51,* 365–370.

Kutcher, E. J., & Bragger, J. D. (2004). Selection interviews of overweight job applicants: Can structure reduce the bias? *Journal of Applied Social Psychology, 34,* 1993–2022.

Kutchins, H., & Kirk, S. A. (1997). *Making us crazy: DSM—The psychiatric Bible and the creation of mental disorders.* New York: Free Press.

Lachman, M. E. (2004). Development in midlife. *Annual Review of Psychology, 55,* 305–331.

Lachman, M. E. (2006). Perceived control over aging-related declines: Adaptive beliefs and behaviors. *Current Directions in Psychological Science, 15,* 282–286.

Lachman, M. E., & Bertrand, R. M. (2001). Personality and the self in midlife. In M. E. Lachman (Ed.), *Handbook of midlife development.* New York: Wiley.

Lachman, M. E., & Firth, K. M. (2004). The adaptive value of feeling in control during midlife. In C. D. R. Brim & R. C. Kessler (Eds.), *How healthy are we? A national study of well-being at midlife.* Chicago: University of Chicago Press.

LaFrance, M., Hecht, M. A., & Paluck, E. L. (2003). The contingent smile: A meta-analysis of sex differences in smiling. *Psychological Bulletin, 129,* 305–334.

La Greca, A. M. (2000). Posttraumatic stress disorder in children. In G. Fink (Ed.), *Encyclopedia of stress* (Vol. 3). San Diego: Academic Press.

Lakein, A. (1996). *How to get control of your time and your life.* New York: New American Library.

Lam, L. T., & Kirby, S. L. (2002). Is emotional intelligence an advantage? An exploration of the impact of emotional and general intelligence on individual performance. *Journal of Social Psychology, 142,* 133–143.

Lambert, A. J., Burroughs, T., & Nguyen, T. (1999). Perceptions of risk and the buffering hypothesis: The role of just world beliefs and right wing authoritarianism. *Personality and Social Psychology Bulletin, 25,* 643–656.

Lambert, M. J., & Archer, A. (2006). Research findings on the effects of psychotherapy and their implications for practice. In C. D. Goodheart, A. E. Kazdin, & R. J. Sternberg (Eds.), *Evidence-based psychotherapy: Where practice and research meet.* Washington, DC: American Psychological Association.

Lambert, M. J., & Barley, D. E. (2001). Research summary on the therapeutic relationship and psychotherapy outcome. *Psychotherapy: Theory, Research, Practice, Training, 38,* 357–361.

Lambert, M. J., & Bergin, A. E. (1994). The effectiveness of psychotherapy. In A. E. Bergin & S. L. Garfield (Eds.), *Handbook of psychotherapy and behavior change* (4th ed.). New York: Wiley.

Lambert, M. J., Bergin, A. E., & Garfield, S. L. (2004). Introduction and historical overview. In M. J. Lambert (Ed.), *Bergin and Garfield's handbook of psychotherapy and behavior change.* New York: Wiley.

Lambert, M. J., & Ogles, B. M. (2004). The efficacy and effectiveness of psychotherapy. In M. J. Lambert (Ed.), *Bergin and Garfield's handbook of psychotherapy and behavior change.* New York: Wiley.

Lambert, T. A., Kahn, A. S., & Apple, K. J. (2003). Pluralistic ignorance and hooking up. *Journal of Sex Research, 40*(2), 129–133.

Lamborn, S. D., Mounts, N. S., Steinberg, L., & Dornbusch, S. M. (1991). Patterns of competence and adjustment among adolescents from authoritative, authoritarian, indulgent, and neglectful families. *Child Development, 62,* 1049–1065.

Lammers, C., Ireland, M., Resnick, M., & Blum, R. (2000). Influences on adolescents' decisions to postpone onset of sexual intercourse: A survival analysis of virginity among youths ages 13 to 18 years. *Journal of Adolescent Health, 26,* 42–48.

Lampe, A., Soellner, W., Krismer, M., Rumpold, G., Kantner-Rumplmair, W., Ogon, M., & Rathner, G. (1998). The impact of stressful life events on exacerbation of chronic low-back pain. *Journal of Psychosomatic Research, 44*(5), 555–563.

Landabaso, M. A., Iraurgi, I., Sanz, J., Calle, R., Ruiz de Apodaka, J., Jimenez-Lerma, J. M., & Gutierrez-Fraile, M. (1999). Naltrexone in the treatment of alcoholism. Two-year followup results. *European Journal of Psychiatry, 13,* 97–105.

Landau, M. J., Goldenberg, J. L., Greenberg, J., Gillath, O., Solomon, S., Cox, C., Martens, A., & Pyszczynski, T. (2006a). The siren's call: Terror management and the threat of men's sexual attraction to women. *Journal of Personality and Social Psychology, 90*(1), 129–146.

Landau, M. J., Greenberg, J., Solomon, S., Pyszczynski, T., & Martens, A. (2006b). Windows into nothingness: Terror management, meaninglessness, and negative reactions to modern art. *Journal of Personality and Social Psychology, 90,* 879–892.

Landel-Graham, J., Yount, S. E., & Rudnicki, S. R. (2003). Diabetes mellitus. In A. M. Nezu, C. M. Nezu, & P. A. Geller (Eds.), *Handbook of psychology: Vol. 9. Health psychology.* New York: Wiley.

Lane, C. J., & Zelinski, E. M. (2003). Hierarchical linear models of the memory functioning questionnaire. *Psychology and Aging, 18,* 38–53.

Langer, E. J. (1975). The illusion of control. *Journal of Personality and Social Psychology, 32*(2), 311–328.

Langer, E. J. (1989). *Mindfulness.* New York: Addison-Wesley.

Langer, E. J. (2002). Well-being: Mindfulness versus positive evaluation. In C. R. Snyder & S. J. Lopez (Eds.), *Handbook of positive psychology.* New York: Oxford University Press.

Langlois, J. H., Kalakanis, L., Rubenstein, A. J., Larson, A., Hallam, M., & Smoot, M. (2000). Maxims or myths of beauty? A meta-analytic and theoretical review. *Psychological Bulletin, 126*(3), 390–423.

Lansford, J. E., Sherman, A. M., & Antonucci, T. C. (1998). Satisfaction with social networks: An examination of socioemotional selectivity theory across cohorts. *Psychology and Aging, 13*(4), 544–552.

Lanza, S. T., & Collins, L. M. (2002). Pubertal timing and the onset of substance use in females during early adolescence. *Prevention Science, 3*(1), 69–82.

LaPiere, R. T. (1934). Attitudes vs. actions. *Social Forces, 13,* 230–237.

LaPierre, Y. D. (2003). Suicidality with selective serotonin reuptake inhibitors: Valid claim? *Journal of Psychiatry & Neuroscience, 28*(5), 340–347.

Larson, R. W. (2002). Globalization, societal change, and new technologies: What they mean for the future of adolescence. *Journal of Research on Adolescence, 12,* 1–30.

Larson, R. W., Richards, M. H., Monera, G., Holmbeck, G., & Duckett, E. (1996). Changes in adolescents' daily interactions with their families from ages 10–18: Disengagement and transformation. *Developmental Psychology, 32,* 744–754.

Larson, R., & Pleck, J. (1998). Hidden feelings: Emotionality in boys and men. In *Gender and motivation* (Vol. 45). Lincoln: University of Nebraska Press.

Larson, R., & Richards, M. H. (1994). *Divergent realities: The emotional lives of mothers, fathers, and adolescents.* New York: Basic Books.

Larzelere, R. E. (2000). Child outcomes of nonabusive and customary physical punishment by parents: An updated literature review. *Clinical Child and Family Psychology Review, 3*(4), 199–221.

Laskoff, M. B. (2004). *Landing on the right side of your ass: A survival guide for the recently unemployed.* New York: Three Rivers Press.

Lating, J. M., Sherman, M. F., Everly, G. S., Lowry, J. L., & Peragine, T. F. (2004). PTSD reactions and functioning of American Airlines flight attendants in the wake of September 11. *Journal of Nervous & Mental Disease, 192*(6), 435–441.

Lauer, J., & Lauer, R. (1985, June). Marriages made to last. *Psychology Today,* pp. 22–26.

Laughlin, H. (1967). *The neuroses.* Washington, DC: Butterworth.

Laughlin, H. (1979). *The ego and its defenses.* New York: Aronson.

Laumann, E. O., Gagnon, J. H., Michael, R. T., & Michaels, S. (1994). *The social organization of sexuality: Sexual practices in the United States.* Chicago: University of Chicago Press.

Laurenceau, J. P., Barrett, L. F., & Pietromonaco, P. R. (1998). Intimacy as an interpersonal process: The importance of self-disclosure, partner disclosure, and perceived partner responsiveness in interpersonal exchanges. *Journal of Personality and Social Psychology, 74*(5), 1238–1251.

Laurenceau, J., Barrett, L. F., & Rovine, M. J. (2005). The interpersonal process model of intimacy in marriage: A daily-diary and multilevel modeling approach. *Journal of Family Psychology, 19,* 314–323.

Laurenceau, J. P., & Kleinman, B. M. (2006). Intimacy in personal relationships. In A. L. Vangelisti & D. Perlman (Eds.), *The Cambridge handbook of personal relationships.* New York: Cambridge University Press.

Lauriello, J., Bustillo, J. R., & Keith, S. J. (2005). Schizophrenia: Scope of the problem. In B. J. Sadock & V. A. Sadock (Eds.), *Kaplan & Sadock's comprehensive textbook of psychiatry.* Philadelphia: Lippincott Williams & Wilkins.

Laursen, B., Coy, K. C., & Collins, W. A. (1998). Reconsidering changes in parent-child conflict across adolescence: A meta-analysis. *Child Development, 69,* 817–832.

Lauzen, M. M., & Dozier, D. M. (2002). You look mahvelous: An examination of gender and appearance comments in the 1999–2000 prime-time season. *Sex Roles, 46*(11/12), 429–437.

Lavine, H., Sweeney, D., & Wagner, S. H. (1999). Depicting women as sex objects in television advertising: Effects on body dissatisfaction. *Personality and Social Psychology Bulletin, 25*(8), 1049–1058.

Lay, C. H. (1992). Trait procrastination and the perception of person-task characteristics. *Journal of Social Behavior and Personality, 7,* 483–494.

Lay, C. H. (1995). Trait procrastination, agitation, dejection, and self-discrepancy. In J. R. Ferrari, J. L. Johnson, & W. G. McCown (Eds.), *Procrastination and task avoidance: Theory, research, and treatment.* New York: Plenum.

Lay, C. H., Edwards, J. M., Parker, J. D. A., & Endler, N. S. (1989). An assessment of appraisal anxiety, coping, and procrastination during an examination period. *European Journal of Personality, 3,* 195–208.

Lazarus, A. A. (1989). Multimodal therapy. In R. J. Corsini & D. Wedding (Eds.), *Current psychotherapies.* Itasca, IL: F. E. Peacock.

Lazarus, R. S. (1991). *Emotion and adaptation.* New York: Oxford.

Lazarus, R. S. (1993). Why we should think of stress as a subset of emotion. In L. Goldberger & S. Breznitz (Eds.), *Handbook of stress: Theoretical and clinical aspects* (2nd ed.). New York: Free Press.

Lazarus, R. S., & Folkman, S. (1984). *Stress, appraisal and coping.* New York: Springer.

Le, B., & Agnew, C. R. (2003). Commitment and its theorized determinants: A meta-analysis of the investment model. *Personal Relationships, 10*(1), 37–57.

Leahy, J. M. (1993). A comparison of depression in women bereaved of a spouse, a child, or a parent. *Omega, 26,* 207–217.

Leana, C. R., & Feldman, D. C. (1991). Gender differences in responses to unemployment. *Journal of Vocational Behavior, 38,* 65–77.

Leaper, C. R., Breed, L., Hoffman, L., & Perlman, C. A. (2002). Variations in the gender-stereotyped content of children's television cartoons across genres. *Journal of Applied Social Psychology, 32,* 1653–1662.

Leary, M. R. (2004). The function of self-esteem in terror management theory and sociometer theory: Comment on Pyszczynski et al. (2004). *Psychological Bulletin, 130*(3), 478–482.

Leary, M. R., & Baumeister, R. F. (2000). The nature and function of self-esteem: Sociometer theory. In M. P. Zanna (Ed.), *Advances in experimental social psychology* (Vol. 32). San Diego, CA: Academic Press.

Leary, M. R., Tambor, E. S., Terdal, S. K., & Downs, D. L. (1995). Self-esteem as an interpersonal monitor: The sociometer hypothesis. *Journal of Personality and Social Psychology, 68*(3), 519–530.

Leavitt, F. (1995). *Drugs and behavior* (3rd ed.). Thousand Oaks, CA: Sage.

Leavitt, F. (2001). Iatrogenic recovered memories: Examining the empirical evidence. *American Journal of Forensic Psychology, 19*(2), 21–32.

LeBlanc, M. M., & Barling, J. (2004). Workplace aggression. *Current Directions in Psychological Science, 13*(1), 9–12.

LeBoeuf, M. (1980, February). Managing time means managing yourself. *Business Horizons,* pp. 41–46.

Leckman, J. F., Grice, D. E., Boardman, J., Zhang, H., Vitale, A., Bondi, C., Alsobrook, J., Peterson, B. S., Cohen, D. J., Rasmussen, S. A., Goodman, W. K., McDougle, C. J., & Pauls, D. L. (1997). Symptoms of obsessive-compulsive disorder. *American Journal of Psychiatry, 154,* 911–917.

Lee, F. R. (2006, March 28). "Big love": Real polygamists look at HBO polygamists and find sex. *New York Times.*

Lee, G. R. (1988). Marital satisfaction in later life: The effects of nonmarital roles. *Journal of Marriage and the Family, 50,* 775–783.

Lee, G. R., Willetts, M. C., & Seccombe, K. (1998). Widowhood and depression. *Research on Aging, 20,* 611–630.

Lee, I.-M., Rexrode, K. M., Cook, N. R., Manson, J. E., & Buring, J. E. (2001). Physical activity and coronary heart disease in women: Is "no pain, no gain" passé? *Journal of the American Medical Association, 285,* 1447–1454.

Lee, I.-M., & Skerrett, P. J. (2001). Physical activity and all-cause mortality. What is the dose-response relation? *Medicine and Science in Sports and Exercise, 33,* S459–S471.

Lee, R. M., & Ramirez, M. (2000).The history, current status, and future of multicultural psychotherapy. In I. Cuellar & F. A. Paniagua (Eds.), *Handbook of multicultural mental health: Assessment and treatment of diverse populations.* San Diego: Academic Press.

Lee, S., & Katzman, M. A. (2002). Cross-cultural perspectives on eating disorders. In C. G. Fairburn & K. D. Brownell (Eds.), *Eating disorders and obesity: A comprehensive handbook.* New York: Guilford.

Lee, Y. T., & Seligman, M. E. P. (1997). Are Americans more optimistic than the Chinese? *Personality and Social Psychology Bulletin, 23,* 32–40.

Lefcourt, H. M. (2001). The humor solution. In C. R. Snyder (Ed.), *Coping with stress: Effective people and processes.* New York: Oxford University Press.

Lefcourt, H. M. (2005). Humor. In C. R. Snyder & S. J. Lopez (Eds.), *Handbook of positive psychology.* New York: Oxford University Press.

Lefcourt, H. M., Davidson, K., Shepherd, R., Phillips, M., Prkachin, K., & Mills, D. (1995). Perspective-taking humor: Accounting for stress moderation. *Journal of Social and Clinical Psychology, 14,* 373–391.

Leff, J., & Vaughn, C. (1985). *Expressed emotion in families.* New York: Guilford Press.

Lefkowitz, E. S., & Zeldow, P. B. (2006). Masculinity and femininity predict optimal mental health: A belated test of the androgyny hypothesis. *Journal of Personality Assessment, 87,* 95–101.

Lehrer, P., Feldman, J., Giardino, N., Song, H., & Schmaling, K. (2002). Psychological aspects of asthma. *Journal of Consulting & Clinical Psychology, 70*(3), 691–711.

Lehrer, P. M., & Woolfolk, R. L. (1984). Are stress reduction techniques interchangeable, or do they have specific effects? A review of the comparative empirical literature. In R. L. Woolfolk & P. M. Lehrer (Eds.), *Principles and practice of stress management.* New York: Guilford Press.

Lehrer, P. M., & Woolfolk, R. L. (1993). Specific effects of stress management techniques. In P. M. Lehrer & R. L. Woolfolk (Eds.), *Principles and practice of stress management* (2nd ed.). New York: Guilford Press.

Leibel, R. L., Rosenbaum, M., & Hirsch, J. (1995). Changes in energy expenditure resulting from altered body weight. *New England Journal of Medicine, 332,* 621–629.

Leigh, G. K., Holman, T. B., & Burr, W. R. (1984). An empirical test of sequence in Murstein's SVR Theory of mate selection. *Family Relations, 33* 225–231.

Leigh, G. K., Holman, T. B., & Burr, W. R. (1987). Some confusions and exclusions of the SVR theory of dyadic pairing: A response to Murstein. *Journal of Marriage and the Family, 49,* 933–937.

Leitenberg, H., Detzer, M. J., & Srebnik, D. (1993). Gender differences in masturbation and the relation of masturbation experience in preadolescence and/or early adolescence to sexual behavior and sexual adjustment in young adulthood. *Archives of Sexual Behavior, 22,* 87–98.

Leitenberg, H., & Henning, K. (1995). Sexual fantasy. *Psychological Bulletin, 117,* 469–496.

Leiter, M. P., & Maslach, C. (2001). Burnout and health. In A. Baum, T. A. Revenson, & J. E. Singer (Eds.), *Handbook of health psychology.* Mahwah, NJ: Erlbaum.

Lemelle, A. J. Jr., & Battle, J. (2004). Black masculinity matters in attitudes toward gay males. *Journal of Homosexuality, 47,* 39–51.

Lemieux, R., & Hale, J. L. (2002). Cross-sectional analysis of intimacy, passion, and commitment: Testing the assumptions of the triangular theory of love. *Psychological Reports, 90,* 1009–1014.

Lemme, B. H. (1999). *Development in adulthood.* Boston: Allyn & Bacon.

L'Engle, K. L., Brown, J. D., & Kenneavy, K. (2006). The mass media are an important context for adolescents' sexual behavior. *Journal of Adolescent Health, 38*(3), 186–192.

Lengua, L. J., Long, A. C., & Meltzoff, A. N. (2006). Pre-attack stress-load, appraisals, and coping in children's responses to the 9/11 terrorist attacks. *Journal of Child Psychology and Psychiatry, 47,* 1219–1227.

Leo, J. (1987, January 12). Exploring the traits of twins. *Time,* p. 63.

Lerman, H. (1986). *A mote in Freud's eye: From psychoanalysis to the psychology of women.* New York: Springer.

Lerner, M. J. (1980). *The belief in a just world: A fundamental decision.* New York: Plenum.

Lerner, M. J. (1998). The two forms of belief in a just world: Some thoughts on why and how people care about justice. In L. Montada & M. J. Lerner (Eds.), *Responses to victimizations and belief in a just world: Critical issues in social justice.* New York: Plenum Press.

Letherby, G., & Williams, C. (1999). Non-motherhood: Ambivalent autobiographies. *Feminist Studies, 25,* 719–728.

Lett, H. S., Blumenthal, J. A., Babyak, M. A., Sherwood, A., Strauman, T., Robins, C., & Newman, M. F. (2004). Depression as a risk factor for coronary artery disease: Evidence, mechanisms, and treatment. *Psychosomatic Medicine, 66*(3), 305–315.

Levant, R. F. (1996). The new psychology of men. *Professional Psychology: Research and Practice, 27,* 259–265.

Levant, R. F. (2003, Fall). Why study boys and men? *Nova Southeastern University Center for Psychological Studies Newsletter,* pp. 12–13.

Levant, R. F., Barbanel, L., & DeLeon, P. H. (2004). Psychology's response to terrorism. In F. M. Moghaddam & A. J. Marsella (Eds.), *Understanding terrorism: Psychological roots, consequences, and interventions.* Washington, DC: American Psychological Association.

LeVay, S. (1996). *Queer science: The use and abuse of research into homosexuality.* Cambridge, MA: The MIT Press.

Levenson, J. L., McDaniel, J. S., Moran, M. G., & Stoudemire, A. (1999). Psychological factors affecting medical conditions. In R. E. Hales, S. C. Yudofsky, & J. A. Talbott (Eds.), *Textbook of psychiatry* (3rd ed.). Washington, DC: American Psychiatric Press, Inc.

Levenstein, S. (2002). Psychosocial factors in peptic ulcer and inflammatory bowel disease. *Journal of Consulting & Clinical Psychology, 70*(3), 739–750.

Leventhal, H., Cameron, L., & Leventhal, E. A. (2005). Do messages from your body, your friends, your doctor, or the media shape your health behavior? In T. C. Brock & M. C. Green (Eds.), *Persuasion: Psychological insights and perspectives.* Thousand Oaks, CA: Sage.

Lever, J. (1994, August 24). Sexual revelations. *The Advocate,* 17–24.

Levin, S., van Laar, C., & Sidanius, J. (2003). The effects of ingroup and outgroup friendship on ethnic attitudes in college: A longitudinal study. *Group Processes and Intergroup Relations, 6*(1), 76–92.

Levine, M. P., & Harrison, K. (2004). Media's role in the perpetuation and prevention of negative body image and disordered eating. In J. K. Thompson (Ed.), *Handbook of eating disorders and obesity.* New York: Wiley.

LeVine, R. A. (2001). Culture and personality studies, 1918–1960. *Journal of Personality, 69,* 803–818.

Levine, R. V., Sato, S., Hashimoto, T., & Verma, J. (1995). Love and marriage in eleven cultures. *Journal of Cross-Cultural Psychology, 26*(5), 554–571.

Levine, S. B. (2003). Erectile dysfunction: Why drug therapy isn't always enough. *Cleveland Clinic Journal of Medicine, 70*(3), 241–246.

Levinson, D. J., Darrow, C. M., Klein, E. G., Levinson, M. H., & McKee, B. (1978). *The seasons of a man's life.* New York: Knopf.

Levinthal, C. E. (2002). *Drugs, behavior, and modern society.* Boston: Allyn & Bacon.

Levis, D. J. (1989). The case for a return to a two-factor theory of avoidance: The failure of non-fear interpretations. In S. B. Klein & R. R. Bowrer (Eds.), *Contemporary learning theories: Pavlovian conditioning and the status of traditional learning theory.* Hillsdale, NJ: Erlbaum.

Levitt, J. G. (2006). *Your career: How to make it happen.* Mason, OH: South-Western.

Levy, S. R., Stroessner, S. J., & Dweck, C. S. (1998). Stereotype formation and endorsement: The role of implicit theories. *Journal of Personality and Social Psychology, 74*(6), 1421–1436.

Lewandowski, C. A. (2003). Organizational factors contributing to worker frustration: The precursor to burnout. *Journal of Sociology and Social Welfare, 30*(4), 175–185.

Lewin, E. (2004). Does marriage have a future? *Journal of Marriage and Family, 66,* 1000–1006.

Lewin, K. (1935). *A dynamic theory of personality.* New York: McGraw-Hill.

Lewinsohn, P. M., & Gotlib, I. H. (1995). Behavioral theory and treatment of depression. In E. E. Beckham & W. R. Leber (Eds.), *Handbook of depression* (2nd ed.). New York: Guilford Press.

Lewinsohn, P. M., Joiner, T. E. Jr., & Rohde, P. (2001). Evaluation of cognitive diathesis-stress models in predicting major depressive disorder in adolescents. *Journal of Abnormal Psychology, 110*(2), 203–215.

Lewis, B. P., & Linder, D. E. (1997). Thinking about choking? Attentional processes and paradoxical performance. *Personality and Social Psychology Bulletin, 23,* 937–944.

Lewis, R. A., & Lin, L.-W. (1996). Adults and their midlife parents. In N. Vanzetti & S. Duck (Eds.), *A lifetime of relationships.* Pacific Grove, CA: Brooks/Cole.

Lewis, R. J., Derlega, V. J., Clarke, E. G., & Kuang, J. C. (2006). Stigma consciousness, social constraints, and lesbian well-being. *Journal of Counseling Psychology, 53,* 48–56.

Libby, P., Ridker, P. M., & Maseri, A. (2002). Inflammation and atherosclerosis. *Circulation, 105,* 1135–1143.

Licata, N. (2002). Should premarital counseling be mandatory as a requisite to obtaining a marriage license? *Family Court Review, 40,* 518–532.

Lichtenthal, W. G., Cruess, D. G., & Prigerson, H. G. (2004). A case for establishing complicated grief as a distinct mental disorder in DSM-V. *Clinical Psychology Review, 24,* 637–662.

Lichter, D. T., Batson, C. D., & Brown, J. B. (2004). Welfare reform and marriage promotion: The marital expectations and desires of single and cohabiting mothers. *Social Service Review, 78*(1), 2–25.

Lichter, D. T., & Crowley, M. L. (2004). Welfare reform and child poverty: Effects of maternal employment, marriage, and cohabitation. *Social Science Research, 33,* 385–408.

Lickey, M. E., & Gordon, B. (1991). *Medicine and mental illness: The use of drugs in psychiatry.* New York: Freeman.

Lieberman, J. A. (2006). Comparative effectiveness of antipsychotic drugs. *Archives of General Psychiatry, 63*(10), 1069–1072.

Lieberman, J. A., Stoup, T. S., McEvoy, J. P., Swartz, M. S., Rosenheck, R. A., Perkins, D. O., Keefe, R. S. E., Davis, S. M., Davis, C. E., Lebowitz, D. B., Severe, J. , Hsiao, J. K., & CATIE Investigators Group. (2005). Effectiveness of antipsychotic drugs in patients with chronic schizophrenia. *New England Journal of Medicine, 353,* 1209–1223.

Lieberman, J. A., Tollefson, G., Tohen, M., Green, A. I., Gur, R. E., Kahn, R., McEvoy, J., Perkins, D., Sharma, T., Zipursky, R., Wei, H., Hamer, R. M., & HGDH Study Group. (2003). Comparative efficacy and safety of atypical and conventional antipsychotic drugs in first-episode psychosis: A randomized double-blind trial of olanzapine versus haloperidol. *American Journal of Psychiatry, 160,* 1396–1404.

Lieberman, M. D., Gaunt, R., Gilbert, D. T., & Trope, Y. (2004). Reflection and reflexion: A social cognitive neuroscience approach to attributional inference. In M. P. Zanna (Ed.), *Advances in experimental social psychology* (Vol. 34). San Diego, CA: Academic Press.

Liebert, R. M., & Liebert, L. L. (1998). *Liebert & Spiegler's personality strategies and issues.* Pacific Grove: Brooks/Cole.

Lilienfeld, S. O., & Lynn, S. J. (2003). Dissociative identity disorder: Multiple personalities, multiple controversies. In S. O. Lilienfeld, S. Lynn, S. Jay, & J. M. Lohr (Eds.), *Science and pseudoscience in clinical psychology.* New York: Guilford Press.

Lilienfeld, S. O., Lynn, S. J., Kirsch, I., Chaves, J. F., Sarbin, T. R., Ganaway, G. K., & Powell, R. A. (1999). Dissociative identity disorder and the sociocognitive model: Recalling the lessons of the past. *Psychological Bulletin, 125*(5), 507–523.

Lilienfeld, S. O., Wood, J. M., & Garb, H. N. (2000). The scientific status of projective tests. *Psychological Science in the Public Interest, 1*(2), 27–66.

Lim, G. Y., & Roloff, M. E. (1999). Attributing sexual consent. *Journal of Applied Communication Research, 27*(1), 1–23.

Lin, Y., & Huang, C. (2006). The process of transforming daily social interactions to relationship intimacy: A longitudinal study. *Chinese Journal of Psychology, 48*(1), 35–52.

Linde, J. A., Rothman, A. J., Baldwin, A. S., & Jeffery, R. W. (2006). The impact of self-efficacy on behavior change and weight change among overweight participants in a weight loss trial. *Health Psychology, 25,* 282–291.

Lindenberger, U., & Baltes, P. (1997). Intellectual functioning in old and very old age: Cross-sectional results from the Berlin aging study. *Psychology and Aging, 12,* 410–432.

Lindenmayer, J. P., & Khan, A. (2006). Psychopathology. In J. A. Liberman, T. S. Stroup, & D. O. Perkins (Eds.), *Textbook of schizophrenia.* Washington, DC: American Psychiatric Publishing.

Lindgren, H. C. (1969). *The psychology of college success: A dynamic approach.* New York: Wiley.

Lindsay, D. S., Hagen, L., Read, J. D., Wade, K. A., & Garry, M. (2004). True photographs and false memories. *Psychological Science, 15*(3), 149–154.

Lindsay, D. S., & Poole, D. A. (1995). Remembering childhood sexual abuse in therapy: Psychotherapists' self-reported beliefs, practices, and experiences. *Journal of Psychiatry & Law, 23,* 461–476.

Lindsay, D. S., & Read, J. D. (1994). Psychotherapy and memories of childhood sexual abuse: A cognitive perspective. *Applied Cognitive Psychology, 8,* 281–338.

Lindsay, S. D., & Read, J. D. (2001). The recovered memories controversy: Where do we go from here. In G. M. Davies & T. Dalgleish (Eds.), *Recovered memories: Seeking the middle ground.* Chichester, England: Wiley.

Linley, P. A., & Joseph, S. (2004). Positive change following trauma and adversity: A review. *Journal of Traumatic Stress, 17*(1), 11–21.

Lipkus, I. M., Dalbert, C., & Siegler, I. C. (1996). The importance of distinguishing the belief in a just world for self versus for others: Implications for psychological well-being. *Personality and Social Psychology Bulletin, 22,* 666–677.

Lippa, R. A. (2005). *Gender, nature, and nurture.* Mahwah, NJ: Erlbaum.

Lippa, R. A. (2006). The gender reality hypothesis. *American Psychologist, 61,* 639–640.

Lips, H. M. (2005). *Sex and gender.* New York: McGraw-Hill.

Lisanby, S. H., Maddox, J. H., Prudic, J., Devanand, D. P., & Sackeim, H. A. (2000). The effects of electroconvulsive therapy on memory of autobiographical and public events. *General Psychiatry, 57,* 581–590.

Litzinger, S., & Gordon, K. C. (2005). Exploring relationships among communication, sexual satisfaction, and marital satisfaction. *Journal of Sex & Marital Therapy, 31,* 409–424.

Livanou, M. (2001). Psychological treatments for post-traumatic stress disorder: An overview. *International Review of Psychiatry, 13*(3), 181–188.

Liverant, G. I., Hofmann, S. G., & Litz, B. T. (2004). Coping and anxiety in college students after the September 11th terrorist attacks. *Anxiety, Stress, & Coping, 17*(2), 127–139.

Livesley, W. J., Jang, K. L., & Vernon, P. A. (2003). Genetic basis of personality structure. In T. Millon, & M. J. Lerner (Eds.), *Handbook of psychology: Vol. 5. Personality and social psychology.* New York: Wiley.

Lock, R. D. (2005a). *Taking charge of your career direction: Career planning guide, Book 1.* Belmont, CA: Wadsworth.

Lock, R. D. (2005b). *Job Search: Career Planning Guide, Book 2.* Belmont, CA: Wadsworth.

Lockwood, P. (2002). Could it happen to you? Predicting the impact of downward social comparisons on the self. *Journal of Personality and Social Psychology, 82,* 343–358.

Loehlin, J. C. (1992). *Genes and environment in personality development.* Newbury Park, CA: Sage.

Loewenstein, R. (1996). Dissociative amnesia and dissociative fugue. In L. K. Michelson & W. J. Ray (Eds.), *Handbook of dissociation: Theoretical, empirical, and clinical perspectives.* New York: Plenum Press.

Loewenstein, R., & Putnam, F. W. (2005). Dissociative disorders. In B. J. Sadock & V. A. Sadock (Eds.), *Kaplan & Sadock's comprehensive textbook of psychiatry.* Philadelphia: Lippincott Williams & Wilkins.

Loftus, E. F. (1994). The repressed memory controversy. *American Psychologist, 49,* 443–445.

Loftus, E. F. (1997). Creating false memories. *Scientific American,* 71–75.

Loftus, E. F. (1998). Remembering dangerously. In R. A. Baker (Ed.), *Child sexual abuse and false memory syndrome.* Amherst, NY: Prometheus Books.

Loftus, E. F. (2000). Remembering what never happened. In E. Tulving (Ed.), *Memory, consciousness, and the brain: The Tallinn conference.* Philadelphia: Psychology Press.

Loftus, E. F. (2003). Make-believe memories. *American Psychologist, 58,* 864–873.

Loftus, E. F., & Mazzoni, G. A. L. (1998). Using imagination and personalized suggestion to change people. *Behavior Therapy, 29,* 691–706.

Long, J. E., Jr. (2005). Power to prescribe: The debate over prescription privileges for psychologists and the legal issues implicated. *Law & Psychology, 29,* 243–260.

Longman, D. G., & Atkinson, G. W. (2005). *Class: College learning and study skills.* Belmont, CA: Wadsworth.

Lopes, P. N., Brackett, M. A., Nezlek, J. B., Schutz, A., Sellin, I., & Salovey, P. (2004). Emotional intelligence and social interaction. *Personality and Social Psychology Bulletin, 30*(8), 1018–1034.

Lopez, D. J. (2005). Race-related stress and sociocultural orientation among Latino students during their transition into a predominately white, highly selective institution. *Journal of Hispanic Higher Education, 4,* 354–365.

Loving, T. J., Heffner, K. L., & Kiecolt-Glaser, J. K. (2006). Physiology and interpersonal relationships. In A. L. Vangelisti & D. Perlman (Eds.), *The Cambridge handbook of personal relationships.* New York: Cambridge University Press.

Lowinson, J. H., Ruiz, P., Millman, R. B., & Langrod, J. G. (2005). *Substance abuse: A comprehensive textbook.* Philadelphia: Lippincott/Williams & Wilkins.

Lozano, B. E., Stephens, R. S., & Roffman, R. A. (2006). Abstinence and moderate use goals in the treatment of marijuana dependence. *Addiction, 101,* 1589–1597.

Lubkin, I. M. (1990). Illness roles. In I. M. Lubkin (Ed.), *Chronic illness: Impact and interventions* (2nd ed.). Boston: Jones and Bartlett.

Luborsky, L., Rosenthal, R., Diguer, L., Andrusyna, T. P., Berman, J. S., Levitt, J. T., Seligman, D. A., & Krause, E. D. (2002). The dodo bird verdict is alive and well—mostly. *Clinical Psychology: Science & Practice, 9,* 2–12.

Luborsky, L., Singer, B., & Luborsky, L. (1975). Comparative studies of psychotherapies: Is it true that everyone has won and all must have prizes? *Archives of General Psychiatry, 32,* 995–1008.

Lucas, A. R., Beard, C. M., O'Fallon, W. M., & Kurland, L. T. (1991). 50-year trends in the incidence of anorexia nervosa in Rochester, Minn.: A population-based study. *American Journal of Psychiatry, 148,* 917–922.

Lucas, J. W., & Lovaglia, M. J. (2005). Self-handicapping: Gender, race, and status. *Current Research in Social Psychology, 10*(16) [electronic journal].

Lucas, R. E. (2005). Time does not heal all wounds: A longitudinal study of reaction and adaptation to divorce. *Psychological Science, 16,* 945–950.

Lucas, R. E., Clark, A. E., Georgellis, Y., & Diener, E. (2003). Reexamining adaptation and set point model of happiness: Reactions to changes in marital status. *Journal of Personality and Social Psychology, 84*(3), 527–539.

Lucas, R. E., Clark, A. E., Georgellis, Y., & Diener, E. (2004). Unemployment alters the set point for life satisfaction. *Psychological Science, 15*(1), 8–13.

Lucas, R. E., Diener, E., & Suh, E. (1996). Discriminant validity of well-being measures. *Journal of Personality and Social Psychology, 71,* 616–628.

Ludwig, D. S., Pereira, M. A., Kroenke, C. H., Hilner, J. E., Van Horn, L., Slattery, M. L., & Jacobs, D. R. Jr. (1999). Dietary fiber, weight gain, and cardiovascular disease risk factors in young adults. *Journal of the American Medical Association, 282*(16), 1539–1546.

Luecke-Aleska, D., Anderson, D. R., Collins, P. A., & Schmitt, K. L. (1995). Gender constancy and television viewing. *Developmental Psychology, 31,* 773–780.

Luhtanen, R., & Crocker, J. (1992). A collective self-esteem scale: Self-evaluation of one's social identity. *Personality and Social Psychology Bulletin, 18,* 302–318.

Lulofs, R. S. (1994). *Conflict: From theory to action.* Scottsdale, AZ: Gorsuch Scarisbuck Publishers.

Lulofs, R. S., & Cahn, D. D. (2000). *Conflict: From theory to action* (2nd ed.). Boston: Allyn & Bacon.

Lundberg, U. (2000). Catecholamines. In G. Fink (Ed.), *Encyclopedia of stress* (Vol. 1). San Diego: Academic Press.

Lundberg-Love, P. K., & Wilkerson, D. K. (2006). Battered women. In P. K. Lundberg-Love & S. L. Marmion (Eds.), *"Intimate" violence against women: When spouses, partners, or lovers attack.* Westport, CT: Praeger.

Lundeburg, K., Stith, S. M., Penn, C. E., & Ward, D. B. (2004). A comparison of nonviolent, psychologically violent, and physically violent male college daters. *Journal of Interpersonal Violence, 19*(10), 1191–1200.

Luo, S., & Klohnen, E. C. (2005). Assortative mating and marital quality in newlyweds: A couple-centered approach. *Journal of Personality and Social Psychology, 88,* 304–326.

Lurie, P., Almeida, C. M., Stine, N., Stine, A. R., & Wolfe, S. M. (2006). Financial conflict of interest disclosure and voting patterns at food and drug administration drug advisory committee meetings. *JAMA, 295,* 1921–1928.

Lutz, C. J., & Ross, S. R. (2003). Elaboration versus fragmentation: Distinguishing between self-complexity and self-concept differentiation. *Journal of Social and Clinical Psychology, 22*(5), 537–559.

Lye, D. N., & Biblarz, T. J. (1993). The effects of attitudes toward family life and gender roles on marital satisfaction. *Journal of Family Issues, 14,* 157–188.

Lykken, D. (1999). *Happiness: The nature and nurture of joy and contentment.* New York: St. Martin's.

Lykken, D., McGue, M., Tellegen, A., & Bouchard, T. J., Jr. (1992). Emergenesis: Genetic traits that may not run in families. *American Psychologist, 47*(12), 1565–1577.

Lykken, D., & Tellegen, A. (1996). Happiness is a stochastic phenomenon. *Psychological Science, 7,* 186–189.

Lynch, D. J., McGrady, A., Alvarez, E., & Forman, J. (2005). Recent life changes and medical utilization in an academic family practice. *Journal of Nervous and Mental Disease, 193,* 633–635.

Lyness, K. S., & Heilman, M. E. (2006). When fit is fundamental: Performance evaluations and promotions of upper-level female and male managers. *Journal of Applied Psychology, 91,* 777–785.

Lynn, D. J., & Vaillant, G. E. (1998). Anonymity, neutrality, and confidentiality in the actual methods of Sigmund Freud: A review of 43 cases, 1907–1939. *American Journal of Psychiatry, 155,* 163–171.

Lynn, M., & Shurgot, B. A. (1984). Responses to lonely hearts advertisements: Effects of reported physical attractiveness, physique, and coloration. *Personality and Social Psychology Bulletin, 10,* 349–357.

Lynn, S. J., Neuschatz, J., & Fite, R. (2002). Hypnosis and memory: Implications for the courtroom and psychotherapy. In M. L. Eisen (Ed.), *Memory and suggestibility in the forensic interview.* Mahwah, NJ: Erlbaum.

Lytton, H., & Romney, D. M. (1991). Parents' differential socialization of boys and girls: A meta-analysis. *Psychological Bulletin, 109,* 267–296.

Lyubomirsky, S., King, L., & Diener, E. (2005). The benefits of frequent positive affect: Does happiness lead to success? *Psychological Bulletin, 131,* 803–855.

Lyubomirsky, S., Sheldon, K. M., & Schkade, D. (2005). Pursuing happiness: The architecture of sustainable change. *Review of General Psychology, 9*(2), 111–131.

Lyubomirsky, S., Tkach, C., & DiMatteo, R. M. (2006). What are the differences between happiness and self-esteem? *Social Indicators Research, 78,* 363–404.

Maccoby, E. E. (1990). Gender and relationships: A developmental account. *American Psychologist, 45,* 513–520.

Maccoby, E. E. (1998). *The two sexes: Growing up apart, coming together.* Cambridge, MA: Belknap Press.

Maccoby, E. E. (2000). Parenting and its effects on children: On reading and misreading behavior genetics. *Annual Review of Psychology, 51,* 1–27.

Maccoby, E. E. (2002). Gender and group processes: A developmental perspective. *Current Direction in Psychological Science, 11*(2), 54–58.

Maccoby, E. E., & Martin, J. A. (1983). Socialization in the context of the family: Parent-child interaction. In P. H. Mussen (Series Ed.) & E. M. Hetherington (Vol. Ed.), *Handbook of child psychology: Vol. 4. Socialization, personality, and social development.* New York: Wiley.

MacDonald, G., Saltzman, J. L., & Leary, M. R. (2003). Social approval and trait self-esteem. *Journal of Research in Personality, 37*(2), 23–40.

MacGeorge, E. L., Graves, A. R., Feng, B., Gillihan, S. J., & Burleson, B. R. (2004). The myth of gender cultures: Similarities outweigh differences in men's and women's provision of and responses to supportive communication. *Sex Roles, 50*(3/4), 143–175.

Macionis, J. J. (1997). *Sociology* (6th ed.). Upper Saddle River, NJ: Prentice Hall.

Mack, A. H., Franklin Jr., J. E., & Frances, R. J. (2003). Substance use disorders. In R. E. Hales & S. C. Yudofsky (Eds.), *Textbook of clinical psychiatry.* Washington, DC: American Psychiatric Publishing.

MacKenzie, R. A. (1997). *The time trap.* New York: AMACOM.

Mackie, D. M., Worth, L. T., & Asuncion, A. G. (1990). Processing of persuasive in-group messages. *Journal of Personality and Social Psychology, 58,* 812–822.

MacMillan, H. L., Fleming, J. E., Streiner, D. L., Lin, E., Boyle, M. H., Jamieson, E., Duku, E. K., Walsh, C. A., Wong, M. Y. Y., & Beardslee, W. R. (2001). Childhood abuse and lifetime psychopathology in a community sample. *American Journal of Psychiatry, 158,* 1878–1883.

Macmillan, M. (1991). *Freud evaluated: The completed arc.* Amsterdam: North-Holland.

MacMillian, H. L., Fleming, J. E., Trocme, N., Boyle, M. H., Wong, M., Racine, Y. A., Beardslee, W. R., & Offord, D. R. (1997). Prevalence of child physical and sexual abuse in the community: Results from the Ontario health supplement. *Journal of the American Medical Association, 278,* 131–135.

Madden, M., & Lenhart, A. (2006). *Online dating.* Retrieved April 29, 2007 from http://www.pewinternet.org/pdfs/PIP_Online_Dating.pdf.

Maddi, S. R. (2002). The story of hardiness: Twenty years of theorizing, research, and practice. *Consulting Psychology Journal: Practice and Research, 54*(3), 175–185.

Maddi, S. R. (2006). Hardiness: The courage to grow from stresses. *Journal of Positive Psychology, 1*(3), 160–168.

Maddi, S. R., & Hightower, M. (1999). Hardiness and optimism as expressed in coping patterns. *Consulting Psychology Journal: Practice and Research, 51*(2), 95–105.

Maddox, G. L. (2001). Housing and living arrangements. In R. H. Binstock & L. K. George (Eds.), *Handbook of aging and the social sciences.* San Diego: Academic Press.

Maddux, J. E., & Gosselin, J. T. (2003). Self-efficacy. In M. R. Leary & J. P. Tangney (Eds.), *Handbook of self and identity.* New York: Guilford.

Maguen, S., & Armistead, L. (2006). Abstinence among female adolescents: Do parents matter above and beyond the influence of peers? *American Journal of Orthopsychiatry, 76,* 260–264.

Maher, B. A. (2001). Delusions. In P. B. Sutker & H. E. Adams (Eds.), *Comprehensive handbook of psychopathology* (3rd ed.). New York: Kluwer Academic/Plenum Publishers.

Maheu, M., & Subotnik, R. (2001). *Infidelity and the Internet: Virtual relationships and real betrayal.* New York: Sourcebooks.

Mahoney, M. J. (1974). *Cognition and behavior modification.* Cambridge, MA: Ballinger.

Mahoney, M. J. (1979). *Self-change: Strategies for solving personal problems.* New York: Norton.

Maisey, D. S., Vale, E. L. E., Cornelissen, P. L., & Tovee, M. J. (1999). Characteristics of male attractiveness for women. *Lancet, 353,* 1500.

Major, B., Barr, L., Zubeck, J., & Babey, S. H. (1999). Gender and self-esteem: A meta-analysis. In W. B. Swann, Jr., J. H. Langlois, & L. A. Gilbert (Eds.), *Sexism and stereotypes in modern society: The gender science of Janet Taylor Spence.* Washington, DC: American Psychological Association.

Major, B., Schmidlin, A. M., & Williams, L. (1990). Gender patterns in social touch: The impact of setting and age. *Journal of Personality and Social Psychology, 58,* 634–643.

Maldonado, J. R., & Spiegel, D. (2003). Dissociative disorders. In R. E. Hales & S. C. Yudofsky (Eds.), *Textbook of clinical psychiatry.* Washington, DC: American Psychiatric Publishing.

Malefo, V. (2000). Psycho-social factors and academic performance among African women students at a predominantly white university in South Africa. *South African Journal of Psychology, 30*(4), 40–45.

Maletzky, B. M. (2002). The paraphilias: Research and treatment. In P. E. Nathan & J. M. Gorman (Eds), *A guide to treatments that work.* London: Oxford University Press.

Malina, R. M. (1990). Physical growth and performance during the transitional years (9–16). In G. R. Adams & T. P. Gullota (Eds.), *From childhood to adolescence: A transitional period?* Newbury Park, CA: Sage.

Malle, B. F. (2004). *How the mind explains behavior: Folk explanations, meaning, and social interaction.* Cambridge, MA: MIT Press.

Malle, B. F., & Knobe, J. (1997). Which behaviors do people explain? A basic actor-observer asymmetry. *Journal of Personality and Social Psychology, 72,* 288–304.

Mallen, M. J., Day, S. X., & Green, M. A. (2003). Online versus face-to-face conversations: An examination of relational and discourse variable. *Psychotherapy: Theory, Research, Practice, Training, 40*(1–2), 155–163.

Maltz, D. N., & Borker, R. A. (1983). A cultural approach to male-female miscommunication. In J. A. Gumperz (Ed.), *Language and social identity.* New York: Cambridge University Press.

Mandler, G. (1993). Thought, memory, and learning: Effects of emotional stress. In L. Goldberger & S. Breznitz (Eds.), *Handbook of stress: Theoretical and clinical aspects* (2nd ed.). New York: Free Press.

Mann, J. J., & Currier, D. (2006). Understanding and preventing suicide. In D. J. Stein, D. J. Kupfer, & A. F. Schatzberg (Eds.), *Textbook of mood disorders.* Washington, DC: American Psychiatric Publishing.

Manning, W. D. (2004). Children and the stability of cohabiting couples. *Journal of Mariage and Family, 66,* 674–689.

Manson, J. E., Skerrett, P. J., & Willett, W. C. (2002). Epidemiology of health risks associated with obesity. In C. G. Fairburn & K. D. Brownell (Eds.), *Eating disorders and obesity: A comprehensive handbook.* New York: Guilford.

Maracek, J. (2001). Disorderly constructs: Feminist frameworks for clinical psychology. In R. K. Unger (Ed.), *Handbook of women and gender.* New York: Wiley.

Marcenes, W. G., & Sheiham, A. (1992). The relationship between work stress and oral health status. *Social Science and Medicine, 35,* 1511.

Marcia, J. E. (1980). Identity in adolescence. In J. Adelson (Ed.), *Handbook of adolescent psychology.* New York: Wiley.

Marcia, J. E. (1991). Identity and self-development. In R. M. Lerner, A. C. Petersen, & J. Brooks-Gunn (Eds.), *Encyclopedia of adolescence* (Vol. 1). New York: Garland.

Marcia, J. E., Waterman, A. S., Matteson, D. R., Archer, S. L., & Orlofsky, J. L. E. (1993). *Ego identity: A handbook for psychosocial research.* New York: Springer-Verlag.

Marcus-Newhall, A., Pedersen, W. C., Carlson, M., & Miller, N. (2000). Displaced aggression is alive and well: A meta-analytic review. *Journal of Personality and Social Psychology, 78*(4), 670–689.

Marder, S. R., & van Kammen, D. P. (2005). Dopamine receptor antagonists (typical antipsychotics). In B. J. Sadock & V. A. Sadock (Eds.), *Kaplan and Sadock's comprehensive textbook of psychiatry.* Philadelphia: Lippincott Williams & Wilkins.

Mariani, M. (2001, Summer). Distance learning in post-secondary education. *Occupational Outlook Quarterly,* pp. 2–10.

Maris, R. W., Berman, A. L., & Silverman, M. M. (2000). *Comprehensive textbook of suicidology.* New York: The Guilford Press.

Marker, N. F. (1996). Flying solo at midlife: Gender, marital status, and psychological well-being. *Journal of Marriage and the Family, 58,* 917–932.

Markey, P. M. (2000). Bystander intervention in computer-mediated communication. *Computers in Human Behavior, 16*(2), 183–188.

Markides, K. S., & Krause, N. (1985). Intergenerational solidarity and psychological well-being among older Mexican Americans: A three-generations study. *Journal of Gerontology, 40,* 390–392.

Markman, A. B., & Maddox, W. T. (2006). Choking and excelling under pressure. *Psychological Science, 17,* 944–948.

Marks, M. J., & Fraley, R. C. (2006). Confirmation bias and the sexual double standard. *Sex Roles, 54,* 19–26.

Marks, N. F., Lambert, J. D., & Choi, H. (2002). Transitions to caregiving, gender, and psychological well-being: A prospective U. S. national study. *Journal of Marriage and Family, 64,* 657–667.

Markus, H., & Kitayama, S. (1991). Culture and the self: Implications for cognition, emotion, and motivation. *Psychological Review, 98,* 224–253.

Markus, H., & Kitayama, S. (2004). Models of agency: Sociocultural diversity in the construction of action. In V. Murphy-Berman & J. Berman (Eds.), *Nebraska Symposium on Motivation. Cross-cultural differences in perspectives on the self.* Lincoln: University of Nebraska Press.

Markus, H., & Nurius, P. (1986). Possible selves. *American Psychologist, 41,* 954–969.

Markus, H., & Wurf, E. (1987). The dynamic self-concept: A social psychological perspective. *Annual Review of Psychology, 38,* 299–337.

Marsella, A. J. (2004). Reflections on international terrorism: Issues, concepts, and directions. In F. M. Moghaddam & A. J. Marsella (Eds.), *Understanding terrorism: Psychological roots, consequences, and interventions.* Washington, DC: American Psychological Association.

Marshall, B. L. (2006). The new virility: Viagra, male ageing, and sexual function. *Sexualities, 9,* 345–362.

Marshall, L. (2005, February 25). Sex, romance and a patch. *Statesboro Herald,* p. 6A.

Marshall, S. J., Gorely, T., & Biddle, S. J. H. (2006). A descriptive epidemiology of screen-based media use in youth: A review and critique. *Journal of Adolescence, 29*(3), 333–349.

Martimportugues-Goyenechea, C., & Gomez-Jacinto, L. (2005). Simultaneous multiple stressors in the enviroment: Physiological stress reactions, performance, and stress evaluation. *Psychological Reports, 97,* 867–874.

Martin, A. J., Marsh, H. W., Williamson, A., & Debus, R. L. (2003). Self-handicapping, defensive pessimism, and goal orientation: A qualitative study of university students. *Journal of Educational Psychology, 95,* 617–628.

Martin, C. L., & Ruble, D. (2004). Children's search for gender cues: Cognitive perspectives on gender development. *Current Direction in Psychological Science, 13*(2), 67–70.

Martin, C. L., Ruble, D., & Szkrybalo, J. (2002). Cognitive theories of early gender development. *Psychological Bulletin, 128*(6), 903–933.

Martin, R. A. (1996). The situational humor response questionnaire (SHRQ) and coping humor scale (CHS): A decade of research findings. *Humor: International Journal of Humor Research, 9,* 251–272.

Martin, R. A. (2002). Is laughter the best medicine? Humor, laughter, and physical health. *Current Directions in Psychological Science, 11*(6), 216–220.

Martin, R. A., & Lefcourt, H. M. (1983). Sense of humor as a moderator of the relation between stressors and moods. *Journal of Personality and Social Psychology, 45,* 1313–1324.

Martin, R., & Leventhal, H. (2004). Symptom perception and health care–seeking behavior. In J. M. Raczynski & L. C. Leviton (Eds.), *Handbook of clinical health psychology: Vol. 2. Disorders of behavior and health.* Washington, DC: American Psychological Association.

Martin, R., Rothrock, N., Leventhal, H., & Leventhal, E. (2003). Common sense models of illness: Implications for symptom perception and health-related behaviors. In J. Suls & K. A. Wallston (Eds.), *Social psychological foundations of health and illness.* Malden, MA: Blackwell Publishing.

Martin, T. C., & Bumpass, L. L. (1989). Recent trends in marital disruption. *Demography, 26,* 37–51.

Martin-Krumm, C. P., Sarrazin, P. G., Peterson, C., & Famose, J. (2003). Explanatory style and resilience after sports failure. *Personality and Individual Differences, 35*(7), 1685–1695.

Martino, S. C., Collins, R. L., Elliott, M. N., Strachman, A., Kanouse, D. E., & Berry, S. H. (2006). Exposure to degrading versus nondegrading music lyrics and sexual behavior among youth. *Pediatrics, 118,* e430–e441.

Martins, Y., Tiggemann, M., & Kirkbride, A. (2007). Those speedos become them: The role of self-objectification in gay and heterosexual men's body image. *Personality and Social Psychology Bulletin, 33,* 634–647.

Masheter, C. (1997). Healthy and unhealthy friendship and hostility between ex-spouses. *Journal of Marriage and the Family, 59,* 463–475.

Masi, L., & Bilezikian, J. P. (1997). Osteoporosis: New hope for the future. *International Journal of Fertility and Women's Medicine, 42,* 245–254.

Maslach, C. (2003). Job burnout: New directions in research and intervention. *Current Directions in Psychological Science, 12*(5), 189–192.

Maslach, C. (2005). Understanding burnout: Work and family issues. In D. F. Halpern & S. E. Murphy (Eds.), *From work-family balance to work-family interaction: Changing the metaphor.* Mahwah, NJ: Erlbaum.

Maslach, C., & Leiter, M. P. (1997). *The truth about burnout.* San Francisco: Jossey-Bass.

Maslach, C., & Leiter, M. P. (2000). Burnout. In G. Fink (Ed.), *Encyclopedia of stress* (Vol. 1). San Diego: Academic Press.

Maslow, A. (1968). *Toward a psychology of being.* New York: Van Nostrand.

Maslow, A. (1970). *Motivation and personality.* New York: Harper & Row.

Mason, M. A. (1998). The modern American stepfamily: Problems and possibilities. In M. A. Mason, A. Skolnick, & S. D. Sugarman (Eds.), *All our families: New policies for a new century.* New York: Oxford University Press.

Masten, A. S. (2001). Ordinary magic: Resilience processes in development. *American Psychologist, 56*(3), 227–238.

Masters, W. H., & Johnson, V. E. (1966). *Human sexual response.* Boston: Little, Brown.

Masters, W. H., & Johnson, V. E. (1970). *Human sexual inadequacy.* Boston: Little, Brown.

Masters, W. H., Johnson, V. E., & Kolodny, R. C. (1988). *Human sexuality.* Glenview, IL: Scott, Foresman.

Masuda, T., & Nisbett, R. E. (2006). Culture and change blindness. *Cognitive Science, 30,* 381–399.

Matlin, M. W. (2004). *The psychology of women* (5th ed.). Belmont, CA: Wadsworth.

Matsumoto, D. (1994). *People: Psychology from a cultural perspective.* Pacific Grove, CA: Brooks/Cole.

Mattanah, J. F. (2005). Authoritative parenting and the encouragement of children's autonomy. In P. A. Cowan et al. (Eds.), *The family context of parenting in elementary school.* Mahwah, NJ: Erlbaum.

Matthews, K. A. (1992). Myths and realities of menopause. *Psychosomatic Medicine, 54,* 1–9.

Maume, D. J., Jr. (1999). Glass ceilings and glass escalators: Occupational segregation and race and sex differences in managerial promotions. *Work and Occupations, 26*(4), 483–509.

Maume, D. J., Jr. (2004). Is the glass ceiling a unique form of inequality? Evidence from a random-effects model of managerial attainment. *Work and Occupation, 31,* 250–274.

Maurer, L. (1999). Transgressing sex and gender: Deconstruction zone ahead? *SIECUS Report, 27,* 14–21.

Mayer, J. D., Salovey, P., & Caruso, D. R. (2002). *Mayer-Salovey-Caruso Emotional Intelligence Test (MSCEIT): User's manual.* Toronto, Canada: Multi-Health Systems.

Mayer, J. D., Perkins, D. M., Caruso, D. R., & Salovey, P. (2001). Emotional intelligence and giftedness. *Roeper Review, 23,* 131–137.

Mayou, R., Kirmayer, L. J., Simon, G., Kroenke, K., & Sharpe, M. (2005). Somatoform disorders: Time for a new approach in DSM-V. *American Journal of Psychiatry, 162,* 847–855.

Mays, V. M., & Albee, G. W. (1992). Psychotherapy and ethnic minorities. In D. K. Freedheim (Ed.), *History of psychotherapy: A century of change.* Washington, DC: American Psychological Association.

Mazzuca, J. (2003, March 25). *Open dialogue: Parents talk to teens about sex.* Retrieved January 25, 2005 from http://www.Gallup.Com/Poll/Content/?Ci=8047.

McAdams, D. P. (1988). *Power, intimacy, and the life story.* New York: Guilford Press.

McAdams, D. P. (1997). *The stories we live by: Personal myths and the making of the self.* New York: Guilford.

McCarthy, B. W., Bodnar, L. E., & Handal, M. (2004). Integrating sex therapy and couple therapy. In J. H. Harvey, A. Wenzel, & S. Sprecher (Eds.), *The handbook of sexuality in close relationships.* Mahwah, NJ: Lawrence Erlbaum.

McCarty, R., & Pacak, K. (2000). Alarm phase and general adaptation syndrome. In G. Fink (Ed.), *Encyclopedia of stress* (Vol. 1). San Diego: Academic Press.

McCauley, C. (2007). Psychological issues in understanding terrorism and the response to terrorism. In B. Bongar, L. M. Brown, L. E. Beutler, J. N. Breckenridge, & P. G. Zimbardo (Eds.), *Psychology of terrorism.* New York: Oxford University Press.

McCoy, S. K., & Major, B. (2003). Group identification moderates emotional responses to perceived prejudice. *Personality and Social Psychology Bulletin, 29,* 1005–1017.

McCrae, R. R. (1984). Situational determinants of coping responses: Loss, threat and challenge. *Journal of Personality and Social Psychology, 46,* 919–928.

McCrae, R. R. (1996). Social consequences of experimental openness. *Psychological Bulletin, 120,* 323–337.

McCrae, R. R. (2005). Personality structure. In V. A. Derlega, B. A. Winstead, & W. H. Jones (Eds.), *Personality: Contemporary theory and research.* Belmont, CA: Wadsworth.

McCrae, R. R., & Costa, P. T., Jr. (1984). *Emerging lives, enduring dispositions: Personality in adulthood.* Boston: Little, Brown.

McCrae, R. R., & Costa, P. T., Jr. (1987). Validation of the five-factor model of personality across instruments and observers. *Journal of Personality and Social Psychology, 52,* 81–90.

McCrae, R. R., & Costa, P. T., Jr. (1990). *Personality in adulthood.* New York: Guilford Press.

McCrae, R. R., & Costa, P. T., Jr. (1997). Personality trait structure as a human universal. *American Psychologist, 52,* 509–516.

McCrae, R. R., & Costa, P. T., Jr. (1999). A five-factor theory of personality. In L. A. Pervin, & O. P. John (Eds.), *Handbook of personality: Theory and research* (2nd ed.). New York: The Guilford Press.

McCrae, R. R., & Costa, P. T., Jr. (2003). *Personality in adulthood: A five-factor theory perspective.* New York: Guilford.

McCrae, R. R., & Terracciano, A. (2006). National character and personality. *Current Direction in Psychological Science, 15*(4), 156–161.

McCrae, R. R., Terracciano, A., & 78 members of the Personality Profiles of Cultures Project. (2005a). Universal features of personality traits from the observer's perspective: Data from 50 cultures. *Journal of Personality and Social Psychology, 88,* 547–561.

McCrae, R. R., Terracciano, A., et al. (2005b). Personality profiles of cultures: Aggregate personality traits. *Journal of Personality and Social Psychology, 89,* 407–425.

McCullough, M. E. (2001). Forgiving. In C. R. Snyder (Ed.), *Coping with stress: Effective people and processes.* New York: Oxford University Press.

McCullough, M. E., Bellah, C. G., Kilpatrick, S. D., & Johnson, J. L. (2001). Vengefulness: Relationships with forgiveness, rumination, well-being, and the Big Five. *Personality and Social Psychology Bulletin, 27*(5), 601–610.

McCullough, M. E., & Witvliet, C. V. (2002). The psychology of forgiveness. In C. R. Synder & S. J. Lopez (Eds.), *Handbook of positive psychology.* New York: Oxford University Press.

McCullough, M. E., & Witvliet, C. V. (2005). The psychology of forgiveness. In C. R. Snyder & S. J. Lopez (Eds.), *Handbook of positive psychology.* New York: Oxford University Press.

McDaniel, M. A., Waddill, P. J., & Shakesby, P. S. (1996). Study strategies, interest, and learning from text: The application of material appropriate processing. In D. J. Herrmann, C. McEvoy, C. Hertzog, P. Hertel, & M. K. Johnson (Eds.), *Basic and applied memory research: Theory in context* (Vol. 1). Mahwah, NJ: Erlbaum.

McDonald, W. M., Thompson, T. R., McCall W. V., & Zormuski, C. F. (2004). In A. F. Schatzberg, & C. B. Nemeroff (Eds.), *Textbook of psychopharmacology.* Washington, DC: American Psychiatric Publishing.

McDougle, L. G. (1987). Time management: Making every minute count. In A. D. Timpe (Ed.), *The management of time.* New York: Facts on File.

McEwen, B. S. (2000). Stress, definitions and concepts of. In G. Fink (Ed.), *Encyclopedia of stress* (Vol. 3). San Diego: Academic Press.

McEwen, B. S., & Lasley, E. N. (2002). *The end of stress as we know it.* Washington, DC: Joseph Henry Press.

McFarlane, M., Bull, S. S., & Rietmeijer, C. A. (2000). The Internet as a newly emerging risk environment for sexually transmitted diseases. *Journal of the American Medical Association, 284,* 443–446.

McGee, M. (2005). *Self-help, Inc.: Makeover culture in American life.* New York: Oxford University Press.

McGee-Cooper, A., & Trammell, D. (1994). *Time management for unmanageable people.* New York: Bantam Books.

McGlashan, T. H., & Fenton, W. S. (1992). The positive-negative distinction in schizophrenia: Review of natural history validators. *Archives of General Psychiatry, 49,* 63–72.

McGlashan, T. H., & Hoffman, R. E. (2000). Schizophrenia: Psychodynamic to neurodynamic theories. In B. J. Sadock & V. A. Sadock (Eds.), *Kaplan and Sadock's comprehensive textbook of psychiatry* (7th ed., Vol. 1). Philadelphia: Lippincott/Williams & Wilkins.

McGlashan, T. H., Mohr, D. C., Beutler, L. E., Engle, D., Shoham-Salomon, V., Bergan, J., Kaszniak, A. W., & Yost, E. B. (1990). Identification of patients at risk for nonresponse and negative outcome in psychotherapy. *Journal of Consulting and Clinical Psychology, 58,* 622–628.

McGoldrick, M. (1999). Becoming a couple. In B. Carter & M. McGoldrick (Eds.), *The expanded family life cycle: Individual, family, and social perspectives* (3rd ed.). Boston: Allyn & Bacon.

McGraw, L. A., & Walker, A. J. (2004). The more things change, the more they stay the same. In M. Coleman & L. H. Ganong (Eds.), *Handbook of contemporary families: Considering the past, contemplating the future.* Thousand Oaks, CA: Sage.

McGraw, P. C. (1999). *Life strategies: Doing what works, doing what matters.* New York: Hyperion Press.

McGregor, H. A., Lieberman, J. D., Greenberg, J., Solomon, S., Arndt, J., Simon, L., & Pyszczynski, T. (1998). Terror management and aggression: Evidence that mortality salience motivates aggression against worldview-threatening others. *Journal of Personality and Social Psychology, 74*(3), 590–605.

McGuire, W. J., & Padawer-Singer, A. (1978). Trait salience in the spontaneous self-concept. *Journal of Personality and Social Psychology, 33,* 743–754.

McHugh, M. C. (2006). What do women want? A new view of women's sexual problems. *Sex Roles, 54,* 361–369.

McHugh, P. R. (1995). Dissociative identity disorder as a socially constructed artifact. *Journal of Practical Psychiatry and Behavioral Health, 1,* 158–166.

McKay, A., & Holoway, P. (1997). Sexual health education: A study of adolescents' opinions, self-perceived needs, and current and preferred sources of information. *Canadian Journal of Human Sexuality, 6,* 29–38.

McKay, M., Davis, M., & Fanning, P. (1995). *Messages: The communication skills book.* Oakland, CA: New Harbinger.

McKay, M., & Fanning, P. (2000). *Self-esteem* (3rd ed.). Oakland, CA: New Harbinger.

McKeever, V. M., & Huff, M. E. (2003). A diathesis-stress model of posttraumatic stress disorder: Ecological, biological and residual stress pathways. *Review of General Psychology, 7*(3), 237–250.

McKenna, K. Y. A., & Bargh, J. A. (2000). Plan 9 from cyberspace: The implications of the Internet for personality and social psychology. *Personality and Social Psychology Review, 4*(1), 57–75.

McKenna, K. Y. A., Green, A., & Gleason, M. (2002). Relationship formation on the Internet: What's the big attraction? *Journal of Social Issues, 58,* 9–31.

McKenna, M. C., Zevon, M. A., Corn, B., & Rounds, J. (1999). Psychosocial factors and the development of breast cancer: A meta-analysis. *Health Psychology, 18*(5), 520–531.

McLean, D. E., & Link, B. G. (1994). Unraveling complexity: Strategies to refine concepts, measures, and research designs in the study of life events and mental health. In W. R. Avison & I. H. Gotlib (Eds.), *Stress and mental health: Contemporary issues and prospects for the future.* New York: Plenum Press.

McMahon, F. J., & Kassem, L. (2005). Anxiety disorders: Genetics. In B. J. Sadock & V. A. Sadock (Eds.), *Kaplan & Sadock's comprehensive textbook of psychiatry.* Philadelphia: Lippincott Williams & Wilkins.

McManus, P. A., & DiPrete, T. (2001). Losers and winners: Financial consequences of separation and divorce for men. *American Sociological Review, 66,* 246–268.

McNally, R. J. (1994). Cognitive bias in panic disorder. *Current Directions in Psychological Science, 3,* 129–132.

McNally, R. J. (1996). *Panic disorder: A critical analysis.* New York: Guilford Press.

McNally, R. J. (2004). Is traumatic amnesia nothing but psychiatric folklore? *Cognitive Behaviour Therapy, 33*(2), 97–101.

McNeil, T. F., Cantor-Graae, E., & Ismail, B. (2000). Obstetrics complications and congenital malformation in schizophrenia. *Brain Research Reviews, 31,* 166–178.

McPherson, M., Smith-Lovin, L., & Brashears, M. E. (2006). Social isolation in America: Changes in core discussion networks over two decades. *American Sociological Review, 71,* 353–375.

McPherson, M., Smith-Lovin, L., & Cook, J. M. (2001). Birds of a feather: Homophily in social networks. *Annual Review of Sociology, 27,* 415–444.

McWhirter, B. T. (1990). Loneliness: A review of current literature, with implications for counseling and research. *Journal of Counseling and Development, 68,* 417–422.

McWilliams, L. A., Becker, E. S., Margraf, J., Clara, I. P., & Vriends, N. (2007). Anxiety disorder specificity of anxiety sensitivity in a community sample of young women. *Personality and Individual Differences, 42,* 345–354.

McWilliams, N., & Weinberger, J. (2003). Psychodynamic psychotherapy. In G. Stricker & T. A. Widiger (Eds.), *Handbook of psychology: Vol. 8. Clinical psychology.* New York: Wiley.

Mead, M. (1950). *Sex and temperament in three primitive societies.* New York: Mentor Books.

Mechanic, D. (1999). Mental health and mental illness. In A. V. Horvitz & T. L. Scheid (Eds.), *A handbook for the study of mental health: Social contexts, theories, and systems.* New York: Cambridge University Press.

Medina, K. L., Shear, P. K., & Corcoran, K. (2005). Ecstasy (MDMA) exposure and neuropsychological functioning: A poly drug perspective. *Journal of the International Neurological Society, 11,* 753–765.

Mednick, S. A., Machon, R. A., Huttunen, M. O., & Bonett, D. (1988). Adult schizophrenia following prenatal exposure to an influenza epidemic. *Archives of General Psychiatry, 45,* 189–192.

Mednick, S. A., Watson, J. B., Huttunen, M., Cannon, T. D., Katila, H., Machon, R., Mednick, B., Hollister, M., Parnas, J., Schulsinger, F., Sajaniemi, N., Voldsgaard, P., Pyhala, R., Gutkind, D., & Wang, X. (1998). A two-hit working model of the etiology of schizophrenia. In M. F. Lenzenweger & R. H. Dworkin (Eds.), *Origins and development of schizophrenia: Advances in experimental psychopathology.* Washington DC: American Psychological Association.

Medora, N. P., Larson, J. H., Hortacsu, N., & Dave, P. (2002). Perceived attitudes towards romanticism: A cross-cultural study of American, Asian-Indian, and Turkish young adults. *Journal of Comparative Family Studies, 33*(2), 155–178.

Meece, J. L., & Scantlebury, K. (2006). Gender and schooling: Progress and persistent barriers. In J. Worrell & C. D. Goodheart (Eds.), *Handbook of girls' and women's psychological health.* New York: Oxford University Press.

Meehan, P. J., Lamb, J. A., Saltzman, L. E., & O'Carroll, P. W. (1992). Attempted suicide among young adults: Progress toward a meaningful estimate of prevalence. *American Journal of Psychiatry, 149,* 41–44.

Meeus, W. (1996). Studies on identity development in adolescence: An overview of research and some new data. *Journal of Youth and Adolescence, 25*(5), 569–598.

Meichenbaum, D. (1977). *Cognitive-behavior modification.* New York: Plenum.

Meichenbaum, D. (1993). Stress inoculation training: A 20-year update. In P. M. Lehrer & R. L. Woolfolk (Eds.), *Principles and practice of stress management* (2nd ed.). New York: Guilford Press.

Meijer, A. M., & van den Wittenboer, G. L. H. (2007). Contribution of infants' sleep and crying to marital relationship of first-time parent couples in the 1st year after childbirth. *Journal of Family Psychology, 21,* 49–57.

Mellers, B. A., Richards, V., & Birnbaum, M. H. (1992). Distributional theories of impression formation. *Organizational Behavior and Human Decision Processes, 51,* 313–343.

Meltzer, H. Y., Davidson, M., Glassman, A. H., & Vieweg, V. R. (2002). Assessing cardiovascular risks versus clinical benefits of atypical antipsychotic drug treatment. *Journal of Clinical Psychiatry, 63*(9), 25–29.

Menec, V. H. (2003). The relation between everyday activities and successful aging: A 6-year longitudinal study. *Journal of Gerontology, 58,* 74–82.

Merikangas, K. R. (2005). Anxiety disorders: Epidemiology. In B. J. Sadock & V. A. Sadock (Eds.), *Kaplan & Sadock's comprehensive textbook of psychiatry.* Philadelphia: Lippincott Williams & Wilkins.

Merikangas, K. R., & Risch, N. (2003). Will the genomics revolution revolutionize psychiatry? *American Journal of Psychiatry, 160,* 625–635.

Merrill, S. S., & Verbrugge, L. M. (1999). Health and disease in midlife. In S. L. Willis & J. D. Reid (Eds.), *Life in the middle: Psychological and social development in middle age.* San Diego: Academic Press.

Merton, R. (1948). The self-fulfilling prophecy. *Antioch Review, 8,* 193–210.

Metz, M. E., & Pryor, J. L. (2000). Premature ejaculation: A psychological approach for assessment and management. *Journal of Sex and Marital Therapy, 26,* 293–320.

Metzger, E. D. (1999). Electroconvulsive therapy. In A. M. Nicholi (Ed.), *The Harvard guide to psychiatry.* Cambridge, MA: Harvard University Press.

Meyer, I. H. (2003). Minority stress and mental health in gay men. In L. D. Garnets & D. C. Kimmel (Eds.), *Psychological perspectives on lesbian, gay, and bisexual experiences.* New York: Columbia University Press.

Meyers, S. A., & Landsberger, S. A. (2002). Direct and indirect pathways between adult attachment style and marital satisfaction. *Personal Relationships, 9*(2), 159–172.

Michaels, S. (1996). The prevalence of homosexuality in the United States. In R. P. Cabaj & T. S. Stein (Eds.), *Textbook of homosexuality and mental health.* Washington, DC: American Psychiatric Press.

Michaud, S. L., & Warner, R. M. (1997). Gender differences in self-reported response to troubles talk. *Sex Roles, 37*(7–8), 527–540.

Mickelson, K. D., Kessler, R. C., & Shaver, P. R. (1997). Adult attachment in a nationally representative sample. *Journal of Personality and Social Psychology, 73,* 1092–1106.

Mikulincer, M. (2006). Attachment, caregiving, and sex within romantic relationships: A behavioral systems perspective. In M. Mikulincer & G. S. Goodman (Eds.), *Dynamics of romantic love: Attachment, caregiving, and sex.* New York: The Guilford Press.

Mikulincer, M., Florian, V., & Tolmacz, R. (1990). Attachment styles and fear of personal death: A case study of affect regulation. *Journal of Personality and Social Psychology, 58,* 273–280.

Mikulincer, M., & Shaver, P. R. (2003). The attachment behavioral system in adulthood: Activation, psychodynamics, and interpersonal processes. In Mark P. Zanna (Ed.), *Advances in Experimental Social Psychology* (Vol. 35). San Diego: Academic Press.

Milgram, N., Marshevsky, S., & Sadeh, C. (1995). Correlates of academic procrastination: Discomfort, task aversiveness, and task capability. *Journal of Psychology, 129,* 145–155.

Milgram, S. (1963). Behavioral study of obedience. *Journal of Abnormal and Social Psychology, 67,* 371–378.

Milgram, S. (1974). *Obedience to authority.* New York: Harper & Row.

Milkie, M. A., & Peltola, P. (1999). Playing all the roles: Gender and the work-family balancing act. *Journal of Marriage and the Family, 61,* 476–490.

Miller, D. T., & Ross, M. (1975). Self-serving biases in the attribution of causality: Fact or fiction? *Psychological Bulletin, 82,* 213–225.

Miller, G. P. (1978). *Life choices: How to make the critical decisions—about your education, career, marriage, family, life style.* New York: Thomas Y. Crowell.

Miller, I. J. (1996). Managed care is harmful to outpatient mental health services: A call for accountability. *Professional Psychology: Research and Practice, 27,* 349–363.

Miller, J. G. (1984). Culture and the development of everyday social explanation. *Journal of Personality and Social Psychology, 46,* 961–978.

Miller, N. E. (1944). Experimental studies of conflict. In J. McV. Hunt (Ed.), *Personality and the behavior disorders* (Vol. 1). New York: Ronald.

Miller, N. E. (1959). Liberalization of basic S-R concepts: Extension to conflict behavior, motivation, and social learning. In S. Koch (Ed.), *Psychology: A study of a science.* (Vol. 2). New York: McGraw-Hill.

Miller, R. B., Yorgason, J. B., Sandberg, J. G., & White, M. B. (2003). Problems that couples bring to therapy: A view across the life cycle. *American Journal of Family Therapy, 31,* 395–407.

Miller, R. S., Perlman, D., & Brehm, S. S. (2007). *Intimate relationships.* Boston: McGraw-Hill.

Miller, T. (2000). Diagnostic evaluation of erectile dysfunction. *American Family Physician, 61,* 95–104.

Millett, K. (1970). *Sexual politics.* Garden City, NY: Doubleday.

Millman, R. B., & Beeder, A. B. (1994). The new psychedelic culture: LSD, ecstasy, "rave" parties and the Grateful Dead. *Psychiatric Annals, 24*(3), 148–150.

Mills, J., & Clark, M. C. (2001). Viewing close romantic relationships as communal relationships: Implications for maintenance and enhancement. In J. H. Harvey & A. Wenzel (Eds.), *Close romantic relationships: Maintenance and enhancement.* Mahwah, NJ: Erlbaum.

Mino, I., Profit, W. E., & Pierce, C. M. (2000). Minorities and stress. In G. Fink (Ed.), *Encyclopedia of stress* (Vol. 1). San Diego: Academic Press.

Minuchin, S., Rosman, B. L., & Baker, L. (1978). *Psychosomatic families: Anorexia nervosa in context.* Cambridge, MA: Harvard University Press.

Miranda, J., Bernal, G., Lau, A., Kohn, L., Hwang, W., & LaFromboise, T. (2005). State of the science on psychosocial interventions for ethnic minorities. *Annual Review of Clinical Psychology, 1,* 113–142.

Mischel, W. (1973). Toward a cognitive social learning conceptualization of personality. *Psychological Review, 80,* 252–283.

Mischel, W. (1990). Personality dispositions revisited and revised: A view after three decades. In L. A. Pervin (Ed.), *Handbook of personality: Theory and research.* New York: Guilford Press.

Mischel, W., & Mischel, H. N. (1976). A cognitive social learning approach to morality and self-regulation. In T. Lickona (Ed.), *Moral development and behavior: Theory, research and social issues.* New York: Holt, Rinehart & Winston.

Mischel, W., & Morf, C. C. (2003). The self as a psycho-social dynamic processing system: A meta-perspective on a century of the self in psychology. In M. R. Leary & J. P. Tangney (Eds.), *Handbook of self and identity.* New York: Guilford.

Mischel, W., Shoda, Y., & Peake, P. K. (1988). The nature of adolescent competencies predicted by preschool delay of gratification. *Journal of Personality and Social Psychology, 54,* 687–696.

Misra, R., & Castillo, L. G. (2001). Academic stress among college students: Comparison of American and international students. *International Journal of Stress Management, 11*(2), 132–148.

Mitchell, B. A. (2006). *The boomerang age: Transitions to adulthood in families.* New Brunswick, NJ: Aldine Transaction.

Mitchell, V. F. (1987). Rx for improving staff effectiveness. In A. D. Timpe (Ed.), *The management of time.* New York: Facts on File.

Miyamoto, S., Lieberman, J. A., Fleischhacker, W. W., Aoba, A., & Marder, S. R. (2003). Antipsychotic drugs. In A. Tasman, J. Kay, & J. A. Lieberman (Eds.), *Psychiatry.* New York: Wiley.

Miyamoto, Y., & Kitayama, S. (2002). Cultural variation in correspondence bias: The critical role of attitude diagnosticity of socially constrained behavior. *Journal of Personality and Social Psychology, 83*(5), 1239–1248.

Miyamoto, Y., Nisbett, R. E., & Masuda, T. (2006). Culture and the physical environment: Holistic versus analytic perceptual affordances. *Psychological Science, 17,* 113–119.

Moak, D. H., & Anton, R. F. (1999). Alcohol. In B. S. McCrady & E. E. Epstein (Eds.), *Addictions: A comprehensive guidebook.* New York: Oxford University Press.

Modestin, J. (1992). Multiple personality disorder in Switzerland. *American Journal of Psychiatry, 149,* 88–92.

Modestin, J., Huber, A., Satirli, E. , Malti, T., & Hell, D. (2003). Long-term course of schizophrenic illness: Bleuler's study reconsidered. *American Journal of Psychiatry, 160,* 2202–2208.

Moe, A., & De Bini, R. (2004). Studying passages with the loci method: Are subject-generated more effective than experimenter-supplied loci pathways? *Journal of Mental Imagery, 28*(3–4), 75–86.

Moen, P., & Wethington, E. (1999). Midlife development in a life course context. In S. L. Willis, & J. D. Reid (Eds.), *Life in the middle: Psychological and social development in middle age.* San Diego: Academic Press.

Mohren, D. C. L., Swaen, G. M. H., Borm, P. J. A., Bast, A., & Galama, J. M. D. (2001). Psychological job demands as a a risk factor for common cold in a Dutch working population. *Journal of Psychomatic Research, 50*(1), 21–27.

Mojtabai, R., Olfson, M., & Mechanic, D. (2002). Perceived need and help-seeking in adults with mood, anxiety, or substance use disorder. *Archives of General Psychiatry, 59*(, 77–84.

Mokdad, A. H., Marks, J. S., Stroup, D. F., & Gerberding, J. L. (2004). Actual causes of death in the United States, 2000. *Journal of the American Medical Association, 291,* 1238–1245.

Möller, J., Hallqvist, J., Diderichsen, F., Theorell, T., Reuterwall, C., & Ahlbom, A. (1999). Do episodes of anger trigger myocardial infarction? A case-crossover analysis in the Stockholm heart epidemiology program (SHEEP). *Psychosomatic Medicine, 61,* 842–849.

Moncrieff, J. (2001). Are antidepressants overrated? A review of methodological problems in antidepressant trials. *Journal of Nervous and Mental Disorders, 189,* 288–295.

Monroe, S. M., & Hadjiyannakis, K. (2002). The social environment and depression: Focusing on severe life stress. In I. H. Gotlib & C. L. Hammen (Eds.), *Handbook of depression.* New York: Guilford.

Monroe, S. M., & Kelley, J. M. (1995). Measurement of stress appraisal. In S. Cohen, R. C. Kessler, & L. U. Gordon (Eds.), *Measuring stress: A guide for health and social scientists.* New York: Oxford University Press.

Monroe, S. M., & McQuaid, J. R. (1994). Measuring life stress and assessing its impact on mental health. In W. R. Avison & I. H. Gotlib (Eds.), *Stress and mental health: Contemporary issues and prospects for the future.* New York: Plenum.

Montepare, J. M., & Lachman, M. (1989). "You're only as old as you feel": Self-perceptions of age, fears of aging, and life satisfaction from adolescence to old age. *Psychology and Aging, 4*(1), 73–78.

Moore, D. W. (2001, August 31). Most American workers satisfied with their job: One-third would be happier in another job. [On-line]. The Gallup Organization. Available: www.gallup.com/poll/releases/pr010831.asp. Retrieved 1/19/2002.

Moore, D. W. (2003, January 3). Family, health, most important aspects of life. Retrieved January 20, 2005, from http://www.Gallup.Com/Poll/Content/?Ci=7504.

Moore, D. W. (2004, May 20). Modest rebound in public acceptance of homosexuals. Retrieved January 31, 2005 from http://www.Gallup.Com/Poll/Content/?Ci=11755.

Moore, M. K. (1992). An empirical investigation of the relationship between religiosity and death concern. *Dissertation Abstracts International, 53,* 527.

Moore, N. B., & Davidson, J. K. (1997). Guilt about first intercourse: An antecedent of sexual dissatisfaction among college women. *Journal of Sex and Marital Therapy, 23,* 29–46.

Moos, R. H., & Billings, A. G. (1982). Conceptualizing and measuring coping resources and processes. In L. Goldberger & S. Breznitz (Eds.), *Handbook of stress: Theoretical and clinical aspects.* New York: Free Press.

Moos, R. H., & Schaefer, J. A. (1993). Coping resources and processes: Current concepts and measures. In L. Goldberger & S. Breznitz (Eds.), *Handbook of stress: Theoretical and clinical aspects* (2nd ed.). New York: Free Press.

Moradi, B., & Risco, C. (2006). Perceived discrimination experiences and mental health of Latina/o American persons. *Journal of Counseling Psychology, 53,* 411–421.

Morahan-Martin, J., & Schumacher, P. (2000). Incidence and correlates of pathological Internet use among college students. *Computers in Human Behavior, 16*(1), 13–29.

Morahan-Martin, J., & Schumacher, P. (2003). Loneliness and social uses of the Internet. *Computers in Human Behavior, 19*(6), 659–671.

Moray, N. (1959). Attention in dichotic listening: Affective cues and the influence of instructions. *Quarterly Journal of Experimental Psychology, 11,* 56–60.

Morell, C. (2000). Saying no: Women's experiences with reproductive refusal. *Feminism & Psychology, 10,* 313–322.

Moretti, M. M., & Higgins, E. T. (1990). Relating self-discrepancy to self-esteem: The contribution of discrepancy beyond actual-self ratings. *Journal of Experimental Social Psychology, 26,* 108–123.

Morgan, H. J., & Janoff-Bulman, R. (1994). Victims' responses to traumatic life events: An unjust world or an uncaring world? *Social Justice Research, 7,* 47–68.

Morgan, M. J. (2000). Ecstasy (MDMA): A review of its possible persistent psychological effects. *Psychopharmacology, 152*(3), 230–248.

Morgenstern, J. (2000). *Time management from the inside out.* New York: Holt.

Morley, J. E. (2001). Male menopause is underdiagnosed and undertreated. *Medical Crossfire, 3*(1), 46–47, 51.

Morley, J. E., & Perry H. M. (2003). Androgens and women at the menopause and beyond. *The Journal of Gerontology, 58*(5), 409–416.

Morris, M. W., & Peng, K. (1994). Culture and cause: American and Chinese attributions for social and physical events. *Journal of Personality and Social Psychology, 67,* 949–971.

Morrison, D. R., & Cherlin, A. J. (1995). The divorce process and young children's well-being: A prospective analysis. *Journal of Marriage and the Family, 57,* 800–812.

Morrison, D. R., & Coiro, M. J. (1999). Parental conflict and marital disruption: Do children benefit when high-conflict marriages are dissolved? *Journal of Marriage and the Family, 61,* 626–637.

Morrison, T. G., Morrison, M. A., & Hopkins, C. (2003). Striving for bodily perfection? An exploration of the drive for masculinity in Canadian men. *Psychology of Men and Masculinity, 4*(2), 111–120.

Mortenson, S. T. (2006). Cultural differences and similarities in seeking support as a response to academic failure: A comparison of American and Chinese college students. *Communication Education, 55*(2), 127–146.

Moseman, S. E., Freeman, M. P., Misiaszek, J., & Gelenberg, A. J. (2003). Mood stabilizers. In A. Tasman, J. Kay, & J. A. Lieberman (Eds.), *Psychiatry.* New York: Wiley.

Mosher, D. L. (1991). Macho men, machismo, and sexuality. *Annual Review of Sex Research, 2,* 199–248.

Mosher, W. D., Chandra, A., & Jones, J. (2005). *Sexual behavior and selected health measures: Men and women 15–44 years of age, United States, 2002.* Hyattsville, MD: National Center for Health Statistics.

Moskowitz, D. S. (1994). Cross-situational generality and the interpersonal circumplex. *Journal of Personality and Social Psychology, 66,* 921–933.

Mowrer, O. H. (1947). On the dual nature of learning: A reinterpretaton of "conditioning" and "problem-solving." *Harvard Educational Review, 17,* 102–150.

Moynihan, J. A., & Ader, R. (1996). Psychoneuroimmunology: Animal models of disease. *Psychosomatic Medicine, 58,* 546–558.

Mroczek, D. K., & Almeida, D. M. (2004). The effect of daily stress, personality, and age on daily negative affect. *Journal of Personality, 72,* 355–378.

Muehlenhard, C. L., & McCoy, M. L. (1991). Double standard/double bind: The sexual double standard and women's communication about sex. *Psychology of Women Quarterly, 15,* 447–461.

Mukamal, K. J., Conigrave, K. M., Mittleman, M. A., Camargo, C. A., Stampfer, M. J., Willet, W. C., & Rimm, E. B. (2003). Roles of drinking pattern and type of alcohol consumed in coronary heart disease in men. *New England Journal of Medicine, 348*(2), 109–118.

Munck, A. (2000). Corticosteroids and stress. In G. Fink (Ed.), *Encyclopedia of stress* (Vol. 1). San Diego: Academic Press.

Muris, P. (2002). Relationships between self-efficacy and symptoms of anxiety disorders and depression in a normal adolescent sample. *Personality and Individual Differences, 32,* 337–348.

Murphy, M., Glaser, K., & Grundy, E. (1997). Marital status and long-term illness in Great Britain. *Journal of Marriage and the Family, 59,* 156–164.

Murphy, S. E., & Zagorski, D. A. (2005). Enhancing work-family and work-life interaction: The role of management. In D. F. Halpern & S. E. Murphy (Eds.), *From work-family balance to work-family interaction: Changing the metaphor.* Mahwah, NJ: Erlbaum.

Murphy, S. P., Rose, D., Hudes, M., & Viteri, F. E. (1992). Demographic and economic factors associated with dietary quality for adults in the 1987–88 nationwide food consumption theory. *Journal of the American Diet Association, 92,* 1352–1357.

Murray, C. (2001). *Family formation.* Washington, DC: American Enterprise Institute.

Murray, R. M., & Bramon, E. (2005). Developmental model of schizophrenia. In B. J. Sadock & V. A. Sadock (Eds.), *Kaplan & Sadock's comprehensive textbook of psychiatry.* Philadelphia: Lippincott Williams & Wilkins.

Murrell, A. J., Dietz-Uhler, B. L., Dovidio, J. F., Gaertner, S. L., & Drout, E. (1994). Aversive racism and resistance to affirmative action: Perceptions of justice are not necessarily color blind. *Basic and Applied Social Psychology, 17*(1–2), 71–86.

Murrell, A. J., & James, E. H. (2001). Gender and diversity in organizations: Past, present, and future directions. *Sex Roles, 45*(5/6), 243–257.

Murstein, B. I. (1976). *Who will marry whom? Theories and research in marital choice.* New York: Springer.

Murstein, B. I. (1986). *Paths to marriage.* Newbury Park, CA: Sage.

Mutchler, J. E., Burr, J. A., Pienta, A. M., & Massagli, M. P. (1997). Pathways to labor force exit: Work transitions and work instability. *Journal of Gerontology, 52,* 4–12.

Myers, D. G. (1980). *Inflated self: Human illusions and the biblical call to hope.* New York: Seabury Press.

Myers, D. G. (1992). *The pursuit of happiness: Who is happy—and why.* New York: Morrow.

Myers, D. G. (1999). Close relationships and quality of life. In D. Kahneman, E. Diener, & N. Schwarz (Eds.), *Well-being: The foundations of hedonic psychology.* New York: Sage.

Myers, D. G. (2000). *The American paradox: Spiritual hunger in an age of plenty.* New Haven, CT: Yale University Press.

Myers, D. G. (2001, December). Do we fear the right things? *American Psychological Society Observer, 14*(10), 3.

Myers, D. G., & Diener, E. (1995). Who is happy? *Psychological Science, 6,* 10–19.

Myers, D. G., & Diener, E. (1997). The pursuit of happiness. *Scientific American, Special Issue 7,* 40–43.

Myrtek, M. (2007). Type A behavior and hostility as independent risk factors for coronary heart disease. In J. Jochen, B. Barde, & A. M. Zeiher (Eds.), *Contributions toward evidence-based psychocardiology: A systematic review of the literature.* Washington, DC: American Psychological Association.

Nabi, R. L., & Sullivan, J. L. (2001). Does television viewing relate to engagement in protective action against crime? A cultivation analysis from a theory of reasoned action perpective. *Communication Research, 28*(6), 802–825.

Nakonezny, P. A., Reddick, R., & Rodgers, J. L. (2004). Did divorces decline after the Oklahoma City bombing? *Journal of Marriage and Family, 66,* 90–100.

Nalwa, K., & Anand, A. P. (2003). Internet addiction in students: A cause of concern. *CyberPsychology and Behavior, 6*(6), 653–656.

Narrow, W. E., Rae, D. S., Robins, L. N., & Regier, D. A. (2002). Revised prevalence based estimates of mental disorders in the United States: Using a clinical significance criterion to reconcile 2 surveys' estimates. *Archives of General Psychology, 59*(2), 115–123.

Narrow, W. E., Regier, D. A., Rae, D. S., Manderscheid, R. W., & Locke, B. Z. (1993). Use of services by persons with mental and addictive disorders: Findings from the National Institute of Mental Health Epidemiologic Catchment Area Program. *Archives of General Psychiatry, 50,* 95–107.

Nash, M. (1997). Gift of love. *Time,* 80–82.

Nathan, P. E., & Langenbucher, J. (2003). Diagnosis and classification. In G. Stricker & T. A. Widiger (Eds.), *Handbook of psychology: Vol. 8. Clinical psychology.* New York: Wiley.

National Center for Health Statistics. (2006). *National Vital Statistics Reports,* Vol. 54, No. 14, pp. 34–35.

National Institute of Mental Health. (2001). *Helping children and adolescents cope with violence and disasters.* Bethesda, MD: National Institute of Mental Health.

Naveh-Benjamin, M., Lavi, H., McKeachie, W. J., & Lin, Y. (1997). Individual differences in students' retention of knowledge and conceptual structures learned in university and high school courses: The case of test anxiety. *Applied Cognitive Psychology, 11,* 507–526.

Naylor, T. H., Willimon, W. H., & Naylor, M. R. (1994). *The search for meaning.* Nashville: Abingdon Press.

Neese, R. M., & Young, E. A. (2000). Evolutionary origins and functions of the stress response. In G. Fink (Ed.), *Encyclopedia of stress* (Vol. 2). San Diego: Academic Press.

Neimeyer, R. A., & Van Brunt, D. (1995). Death anxiety. In H. Wass & R. A. Neimeyer (Eds.), *Dying: Facing the facts* (3rd ed.). Washington, DC: Taylor & Francis.

Neiss, R. (1988). Reconceptualizing arousal: Psychobiological states in motor performance. *Psychological Bulletin, 103,* 345–366.

Neiss, R. (1990). Ending arousal's reign of error: A reply to Anderson. *Psychological Bulletin, 107,* 101–105.

Nelson, C., & Demas, G. E. (2004). Seasonal patterns of stress, disease, and sickness responses. *Current Directions in Psychological Science, 13,* 198–201.

Nelson, R. J., Franks, S., & Brose, A. (2005). The influence of hostility and family history of cardiovascular disease on autonomic activation in response to controllable versus uncontrollable stress, anger imagery reduction, and relaxation therapy. *Journal of Behavioral Medicine, 28,* 213–221.

Nemiah, J. C. (1985). Somatoform disorders. In H. I. Kaplan & B. J. Sadock (Eds.), *Comprehensive textbook of psychiatry/IV.* Baltimore: Williams & Wilkins.

Nettle, D. (2006). The evolution of personality variation in humans and other animals. *American Psychologist, 61*(6), 622–631.

Neupert, S. D., Almeida, D. M., Mroczek, D. K., & Spiro, A. (2006). Daily stressors and memory failures in a naturalistic setting: Findings from the VA normative aging study. *Psychology and Aging, 21,* 424–429.

Newcomb, M. D. (1990). Social support and personal characteristics: A developmental and interactional perspective. *Journal of Social and Clinical Psychology, 9,* 54–68.

Newell, G. R. (1991, May). Stress and cancer. *Primary Care and Cancer,* 29–30.

Newman, M., & Berkowitz, B. (1976). *How to be awake and alive.* Westminster, MD: Ballantine.

Nezu, A. M., Nezu, C. M., Felgoise, S. H., & Zwick, M. L. (2003). Psychosocial oncology. In A. M. Nezu, C. M. Nezu, & P. A. Geller (Eds.), *Handbook of psychology: Vol. 9. Health psychology.* New York: Wiley.

Ng, D. M., & Jeffery, R. W. (2003). Relationships between perceived stress and health behaviors in a sample of working adults. *Health Psychology, 22,* 638–642.

Niaura, R., & Abrams, D. B. (2002). Smoking cessation: Progress, priorities, and prospectus. *Journal of Consulting & Clinical Psychology, 70*(3), 494–509.

Niaura, R., Todaro, J. F., Stroud, L., Spiro, A., Ward, K. D., & Weiss, S. (2002). Hostility, the metabolic syndrome, and incident coronary heart disease. *Health Psychology, 21*(16), 588–593.

NICHD Early Child Care Research Network. (1997). The effects of infant child care on infant-mother attachment security: Results of the NICHD Study of Early Child Care. *Child Development, 68,* 860–879.

Nichols, B. (2006). Violence against women: The extent of the problem. In P. K. Lundberg-Love & S. L. Marmion (Eds.), *"Intimate" violence against women: When spouses, partners, or lovers attack.* Westport, CT: Praeger.

Nicholson, C. (2006). Freedom and choice, culture, and class. *APS Observer, 19*(8), 31, 45.

Nickerson, C., Schwarz, N., Diener, E., & Kahneman, D. (2003). Zeroing in on the dark side of the American dream: A closer look at the negative consequences of the goal for financial success. *Psychological Science , 14*(6), 531–536.

Nickerson, R. S. (1998). Confirmation bias: A ubiquitous phenomenon in many guises. *Review of General Psychology, 2,* 175-220.

Nie, N. H., & Erbring, L. (2002). Internet and society: A preliminary report. *IT & Society, 1*(1), 275–283.

Niederhoffer, K. G., & Pennebaker, J. W. (2005). Sharing one's story: On the benefits of writing or talking about emotional experience. In C. R. Snyder & S. J. Lopez (Eds.), *Handbook of positive psychology.* New York: Oxford University Press.

Nielsen Media Research. (2005). *Nielsen reports Americans watch TV at record levels.* Retrieved May 3, 2007 from http://www.nielsenmedia.com.

Nielsen Media Research. (2006). *Nielsen media research reports television's popularity is still growing.* Retrieved May 3, 2007 from http://www.nielsenmedia.com/nc/portal/site.Public/menuitem.55dc65b4a.

Nielsen, J. M. (1990). *Sex and gender in society: Perspective on stratification* (2nd ed.). Prospect Heights, IL: Waveland.

Niemann, Y. F., Jennings, L., Rozelle, R. M., Baxter, J. C., & Sullivan, E. (1994). Use of free responses and cluster analysis to determine stereotypes of eight groups. *Personality and Social Psychology Bulletin, 20,* 379–390.

Ninan, P. T., & Muntasser, S. (2004). Buspiron and gepirone. In A. F. Schatzberg & C. B. Nemeroff (Eds), *Textbook of psychopharmacology.* Washington, DC: American Psychiatric Publishing.

Nisbett, R. E., & Miyamoto, Y. (2005). The influence of culture: Holistic versus analytic perception. *Trends in Cognitive Science, 9,* 467–473.

Nisbett, R. E., Peng, K., Choi, I., & Norenzayan, A. (2001). Culture and systems of thought: Holistic versus analytic cognition. *Psychological Review, 108*(2), 291–310.

Nobler, M. S., & Sackeim, H. A. (2006). Electroconvulsive therapy and transcranial magnetic stimulation. In D. J. Stein, D. J. Kupfer, & A. F. Schatzberg (Eds.), *Textbook of mood disorders.* Washington, DC: American Psychiatric Publishing.

Nobre, P. J., & Pinto-Gouveia, J. (2006). Dysfunctional sexual beliefs as vulnerability factors for sexual dysfunction. *Journal of Sex Research, 43*(1), 68–75.

Nock, S. L. (1995). A comparison of marriages and cohabitating relationships. *Journal of Family Issues, 13,* 53–76.

Nolen-Hoeksema, S. (1991). Responses to depression and their effects on the duration of depressive episodes. *Journal of Abnormal Psychology, 100,* 569–582.

Nolen-Hoeksema, S. (1995). Gender differences in coping with depression across the lifespan. *Depression, 3,* 81–90.

Nolen-Hoeksema, S. (2000). The role of rumination in depressive disorders and mixed anxiety/depressive symptoms. *Journal of Abnormal Psychology, 109*(3), 504–511.

Nolen-Hoeksema, S. (2001). Gender differences in depression. *Current Directions in Psychological Science, 10,* 173–176.

Nolen-Hoeksema, S. (2002). Gender differences in depression. In I. H. Gotlib & C. L. Hammen (Eds.), *Handbook of depression.* New York: Guilford.

Nolen-Hoeksema, S., & Davis, C. G. (2005). Positive responses to loss: Perceiving benefits and growth. In C. R. Snyder & S. J. Lopez (Eds.), *Handbook of positive psychology.* New York: Oxford University Press.

Nolen-Hoeksema, S., & Keita, G. P. (2003). Women and depression: An introduction. *Psychology of Women Quarterly, 27,* 89–90.

Noller, P. (1985). Negative communications in marriage. *Journal of Social and Personal Relationships, 2,* 289–301.

Noller, P. (1987). Nonverbal communication in marriage. In D. Perlman & S. Duck (Eds.), *Intimate relationships: Development, dynamics, and deterioration.* Newbury Park, CA: Sage.

Noller, P. (2006). Bringing it all together: A theoretical approach. In A. L. Vangelisti & D. Perlman (Eds.), *The Cambridge handbook of personal relationships.* New York: Cambridge University Press.

Noller, P., & Fitzpatrick, M. A. (1990). Marital communication in the eighties. *Journal of Marriage and the Family, 52,* 832–843.

Noller, P., & Gallois, C. (1988). Understanding and misunderstanding in marriage: Sex and marital adjustment differences in structured and free interaction. In P. Noller & M. A. Fitzpatrick (Eds.), *Perspectives on marital interaction.* Clevedon, England: Multilingual Matters.

Nomaguchi, K. M. (2006). Maternal employment, nonparental care, mother-child interactions and child outcomes during preschool years. *Journal of Marriage and Family, 68,* 1341–1369.

Nomaguchi, K. M., & Milkie, M. A. (2003). Costs and rewards of children: The effects of becoming a parent on adults' lives. *Journal of Marriage and Family, 65,* 356–374.

Noom, M. J., Dekovic, M., & Meeus, W. (2001). Conceptual analysis and measurement of adolescent autonomy. *Journal of Youth and Adolescence, 30,* 577–595.

Norcross, J. C. (1995). Dispelling the dodo bird verdict and the exclusivity myth in psychotherapy. *Psychotherapy, 32,* 500–504.

Norcross, J. C., Santrock, J. W., Campbell, L. F., Smith, T. P., Sommer, R., & Zuckerman, E. L. (2003). *Authoritative guide to self-help resources in mental health.* New York: Guilford.

Norem, J. K. (1989). Cognitive strategies as personality: Effectiveness, specificity, flexibility, and chance. In D. M. Buss & N. Cantor (Eds.), *Personal-*

ity psychology: Recent trends and emerging directions. New York : Springer-Verlag.

Norem, J. K. (2001). *The positive power of negative thinking: Using defensive pessimism to manage anxiety and perform at your peak.* New York: Basic Books.

Norem, J. K. (2002). Defensive self-deception and social adaptation among optimists. *Journal of Research in Personality, 36,* 549–555.

Norem, J. K., & Smith, S. (2006). Defensive pessimism: Positive past, anxious present, and pessimistic future. In L. J. Sanna & E. C. Chang (Eds.), *Judgments over time: The interplay of thoughts, feelings, and behaviors.* New York: Oxford University Press.

Norenzayan, A., Choi, I., & Nisbett, R. E. (2002). Cultural similarities and differences in social inference: Evidence from behavioral predictions and lay theories of behavior. *Personality and Social Psychology Bulletin, 28,* 109–120.

Norfleet, M. A. (2002). Responding to society's needs: Prescription privileges for psychologists. *Journal of Clinical Psychology, 58,* 599–610.

Norman, C., & Aron, A. (2003). Aspects of possible self that predict motivation to achieve or avoid it. *Journal of Experimental Social Psychology, 39,* 500–507.

Norris, F. H., & Kaniasty, K. (1996). Received and perceived social support in times of stress: A test of the social support deterioration deterrence model. *Journal of Personality and Social Psychology, 71*(3), 498–511.

Norton, P. G. W. (2004, February 1). Low-fat foods helped fuel obesity epidemic. *Family Practice News,* p. 22.

Norton, S. (2002). Women exposed: Sexual harrassment and female vulnerability. In L. Diamant & J. Lee (Eds.), *The psychology of sex, gender, and jobs.* Westport, CT: Praeger.

Notarius, C., & Markman, H. (1993). *We can work it out: Making sense of marital conflict.* New York: G. P. Putnam's Sons.

Nowell, A., & Hedges, L. V. (1998). Trends in gender differences in academic achievement from 1960–1994: An analysis of differences in mean, variance, and extreme scores. *Sex Roles, 39*(1/2), 21–43.

Noyes, R. Jr., Stuart, S. P., Lanbehn, D. R., Happel, R., Longley, S. L., Muller, B. A., & Yagla, S. J. (2003). Test of an interpersonal model of hypochondriasis. *Psychosomatic Medicine, 65,* 292–300.

Noyes, R. Jr., Watson, D. B., Letuchy, E. M., Longley, S. L., Black, D. W., Carney, C. P., & Doebbeling, B. N. (2005). Relationship between hypochondriacal concerns and personality dimensions and traits in a military population. *Journal of Nervous and Mental Disease, 193*(2), 110–118.

Nurminen, E., Malmivaara, A., Ilmarinen, J., Ylöstalo, P., Mutanen, P., Ahonen, G., & Aro, T. (2002). Effectiveness of a worksite exercise program with respect to perceived work ability and sick leaves among women with physical work. *Scandinavian Journal of Work, Environment and Health, 28*(2), 85–93.

Nurnberger, J. I., & Zimmerman, J. (1970). Applied analysis of human behavior: An alternative to conventional motivational inferences and unconscious determination in therapeutic programming. *Behavior Therapy, 1,* 59–69.

Oakes, P. (2001). The root of all evil in intergroup relations? Unearthing the categorization process. In R. Brown & S. L. Gaertner (Eds.), *Blackwell handbook of social psychology: Intergroup processes.* London: Blackwell.

Oaten, M., & Cheng, K. (2005). Academic examination stress impairs self-control. *Journal of Social and Clinical Psychology, 24,* 254–279.

Oaten, M., & Cheng, K. (2006). Longitudinal gains in self-regulation from regular physical exercise. *British Journal of Health Psychology, 11,* 717–733.

O'Brien, B. (1996). Economic evaluation of pharmaceuticals. *Medical Care, 34,* 99–108.

O'Brien, C. P., Volkow, N., & Li, T.-K. (2006). What's in a word? Addiction versus dependence in DSM-V. *American Journal of Psychiatry, 163,* 764–765.

O'Brien, S. J., & Vertinsky, P. A. (1991). Unfit survivors: Exercise as a resource for aging women. *The Gerontologist, 31,* 347–357.

O'Callahan, M., Andrews, A. M., & Krantz, D. S. (2003). Coronary heart disease and hypertension. In A. M. Nezu, C. M. Nezu, & P. A. Geller (Eds.), *Handbook of psychology: Vol. 9. Health psychology.* New York: Wiley.

Ocon, R. (2006). *Issues on gender and diversity in management.* Lanham, MD: University Press of America.

O'Donohue, W., & Crouch, J. L. (1996). Marital therapy and gender-linked factors in communication. *Journal of Marital and Family Therapy, 22,* 87–101.

Oesterman, K., Bjoerkqvist, K., Lagerspetz, K. M. J., Kaukiainen, A., Landau, S. F., Fraczek, A., & Caprara, G. V. (1998). Cross-cultural evidence of female indirect aggression. *Aggressive Behavior, 24*(1), 1–80.

Oettingen, G., & Gollwitzer, P. M. (2001). Goal setting and goal striving. In A. Tesser & N. Schwarz. (Eds.), *Blackwell handbook of social psychology: Intraindividual processes.* Malden, MA: Blackwell.

Offer, D., Ostrov, E., & Howard, K. I. (1981). *The adolescent.* New York: Basic Books.

Ohman, A., & Mineka, S. (2003). The malicious serpent: Snakes as a prototypical stimulus for an evolved module of fear. *Current Directions in Psychological Science, 12,* 5–9.

O'Keefe, D. J., & Hale, S. L. (2001). An odds-ratio based meta-analysis of research on the door-in-the-face influence strategy. *Communication Reports, 14*(1), 31–38.

Olff, M., Langeland, W., Draijer, N., & Gersonons, B. P. R. (2007). Gender differences in posttraumatic stress disorder. *Psychological Bulletin, 133,* 183–204.

Olfson, M., Marcus, S. C., Druss, B. , & Pincus, H. A. (2002). National trends in the use of outpatient psychotherapy. *American Journal of Psychiatry, 159,* 1914–1920.

Olfson, M., Shaffer, D., Marcus, S. C., & Greenberg, T. (2003). Relationship between antidepressant medication treatment and suicide in adolescents. *Archives of General Psychiatry, 60*(10), 978–982.

Olio, K. (1994). Truth in memory. *American Psychologist, 49,* 442–443.

Olivardia, R., Pope, H. G., & Phillips, K. A. (2000). *The Adonis complex: The secret crisis of male body obsession.* New York: Free Press.

Oliver, M. B., & Hyde, J. S. (1993). Gender differences in sexuality: A meta-analysis. *Psychological Bulletin, 114,* 29–51.

O'Neil, J. M., & Egan, J. (1992). Men's and women's gender role journeys: A metaphor for healing, transition, and transformation. In B. Wainrib (Ed.), *Gender issues across the life cycle.* New York: Springer.

O'Neill, N., & O'Neill, G. (1972). *Open marriage.* New York: Evans.

Ong, A. D., Bergeman, C. S., Bisconti, T. L., & Wallace, K. A. (2006). Psychological resilience, positive emotions, and successful adaptation to stress in later life. *Journal of Personality and Social Psychology, 91,* 730–749.

Ono, H. (1998). Husbands' and wives' resources and marital dissolution. *Journal of Marriage and the Family, 60,* 674–689.

Ono, H. (2006). Homogamy among the divorced and never married on marital history in recent decades: Evidence from vital statistics data. *Social Science Research, 35,* 356–383.

Orenstein, P. (1994). *School girls: Young women, self-esteem, and the confidence gap.* New York: Doubleday.

Organista, P. B., & Miranda, J. (1991). Psychosomatic symptoms in medical outpatients: An investigation of self-handicapping theory. *Health Psychology, 10,* 427–431.

Orlofsky, J. L., Marcia, J. E., & Lesser, I. M. (1973). Ego identity status and the intimacy versus isolation crisis of young adulthood. *Journal of Personality and Social Psychology, 27,* 211–219.

Orth-Gomer, K., Wamala, S. P., Horsten, M., Schenck-Gustafsson, K., Schneiderman, N., & Mittleman, M. A. (2000). Marital stress worsens prognosis in women with coronary heart disease: The Stockholm female coronary risk study. *Journal of the American Medical Association, 284*(23), 3008–3014.

Oskamp, S. (2000). A sustainable future for humanity? How psychology can help. *American Psychologist, 55*(5), 496–508.

Osman, S. L. (2003). Predicting men's rape perceptions based on the belief that "no" really means "yes." *Journal of Applied Social Psychology, 33*(4), 683–692.

O'Sullivan, L. F., McCrudden, M. C., & Tolman, D. L. (2006). To your sexual health! Incorporating sexuality into the health perspective. In J. Worrell & C. D. Goodheart (Eds.), *Handbook of girls' and women's psychological health.* New York: Oxford University Press.

Otto, M. W., Pollack, M. H., Jenike, M. A., & Rosenbaum, J. F. (1999). Anxiety disorders and their treatment. In A. M. Nicholi (Ed.), *The Harvard guide to psychiatry* (3rd ed.). Cambridge, MA: Harvard University Press.

Ouellette, S. C. (1993). Inquiries into hardiness. In L. Goldberger & S. Breznitz (Eds.), *Handbook of stress: Theoretical and clinical aspects* (2nd ed.). New York: Free Press.

Ouellette, S. C., & DiPlacido, J. (2001). Personality's role in the protection and enhancement of health: Where the research has been, where it is stuck, how it might move. In A. Baum, T. A. Revenson, & J. E. Singer *Handbook of health psychology.* Mahwah, NJ: Erlbaum.

Owen, M. J., & O'Donovan, M. C. (2003). Schizophrenia and genetics. In R. Plomin, J. C. Defries, I. W. Craig & P. McGuffin (Eds.), *Behavioral genetics in the postgenomic era.* Washington, DC: American Psychological Association.

Oyserman, D., Bybee, D., & Terry, K. (2006). Possible selves and academic outcomes: How and when possible selves impel action. *Journal of Personality and Social Psychology, 91,* 188–204.

Ozer, D. J., & Reise, S. P. (1994). Personality assessment. *Annual Review of Psychology, 45,* 357–388.

Ozer, E. J., Best, S. R., Lipsey, T. L., & Weiss, D. S. (2003). Predictors of posttraumatic stress disorder and symptoms in adults: A meta-analysis. *Psychological Bulletin, 129*(1), 52–73.

Ozer, E. J., & Weiss, D. S. (2004). Who develops posttraumatic stress disorder? *Current Directions in Psychological Science, 13,* 169–172.

Ozer, E. M., & Bandura, A. (1990). Mechanisms governing empowerment effects: A self-efficacy analysis. *Journal of Personality and Social Psychology, 58,* 472–486.

Padgett, D. A., & Sheridan, J. F. (2000). Herpesviruses. In G. Fink (Ed.), *Encyclopedia of stress.* San Diego: Academic Press.

Paivio, A. (1986). *Mental representations: A dual coding approach.* New York: Oxford University Press.

Papalia, D. E., & Olds, C. W. (1995). *Human Development* (6th ed.). New York: McGraw-Hill.

Papp, L. M., Cummings, E. M., & Schermerhorn, A. C. (2004). Pathways among marital distress, parental symptomatology, and child adjustment. *Journal of Marriage and Family, 66,* 368–384.

Park, C. W., & Young, S. M. (1986). Consumer response to television commercials: The impact of involvement and background music on brand attitude formation. *Journal of Marketing Research, 23* 11–24.

Park, K. (2005). Choosing childlessness: Weber's typology of action and motives of the voluntarily childless. *Sociological Inquiry, 75,* 372–402.

Parker, R. (2000). Health literacy: A challenge for American patients and their health care providers. *Health Promotion International, 15,* 277–283.

Parrott, A. C. (2000). Human research on MDMA (3,4-Methylenedioxymethamphetamine) neurotoxicity: Cognitive and behavioural indices of change. *Neuropsychobiology, 42*(1), 17–24.

Parrott, D. J., & Zeichner, A. (2006). Effect of psychopathy on physical aggression toward gay and heterosexual men. *Journal of Interpersonal Violence, 21,* 390–410.

Parsons, T., & Bales, R. F. (1995). *Family, socialization, and interaction process.* Glencoe, IL: Free Press.

Pasley, K., & Moorefield, B. S. (2004). Stepfamilies: Changes and challenges. In M. Coleman, & L. H. Ganong (Eds.), *Handbook of contemporary families: Considering the past, contemplating the future.* Thousand Oaks, CA: Sage.

Pasterski, V. L., Geffner, M. E., Brain, C., Hindmarsh, P., Brook, C., & Hines, M. (2005). Prenatal hormones and postnatal socialization by parents as determinants of male-typical toy play in girls with congenital adrenal hyperplasia. *Child Development, 76,* 264–278.

Patel, J. K., Pinals, D. A., & Breier, A. (2003). Schizophrenia and other psychoses. In A. Tasman, J. Kay, & J. A. Lieberman (Eds.), *Psychiatry.* New York: Wiley.

Pato, M. T., Eisen, J. L., & Phillips, K. A. (2003). Obsessive-compulsive disorder. In A. Tasman, J. Kay, & J. A. Lieberman (Eds.), *Psychiatry.* New York: Wiley.

Patterson, C. J. (2001). Family relationships of lesbians and gay men. In R. M. Milardo (Ed.), *Understanding families into the new millennium: A decade in review.* Minneapolis: National Council on Family Relations.

Patterson, C. J. (2003). Children of lesbian and gay parents. In L. D. Garnets & D. C. Kimmel (Eds.), *Psychological perspectives on lesbian, gay, and bisexual experiences.* New York: Columbia University Press.

Patterson, C. J. (2006). Children of lesbian and gay parents. *Current Directions in Psychological Science, 15,* 241–254.

Patterson, C. J., & Redding, R. E. (1996). Lesbian and gay families with children: Implications of social science research for policy. *Journal of Social Issues, 52*(3), 29–50.

Patterson, G. R., DeBaryshe, B. D., & Ramsey, E. (1989). A developmental perspective on antisocial behavior. *American Psychologist, 44*(2), 329–335.

Patterson, M. L. (1988). Functions of nonverbal behavior in close relationships. In S. Duck (Ed.), *Handbook of personal relationships: Theory, research, and interventions.* New York: Wiley.

Paul, A. M. (2001). Self-help: Shattering the myths. *Psychology Today, 34*(2), 60.

Paul, E. L., McManus, B., & Hayes, A. (2000). "Hookups": Characteristics and correlates of college students' spontaneous and anonymous sexual experiences. *Journal of Sex Research, 37*(1), 76–88.

Paulhus, D. L. (1991). Measurement and control of response bias. In J. P. Robinson, P. Shaver, & L. S. Wrightsman (Eds.), *Measures of personality and social psychological attitudes.* San Diego: Academic Press.

Paulhus, D. L., Fridhandler, B., & Hayes, S. (1997). Psychological defense: Contemporary theory and research. In R. Hogan, J. Johnson, & S. Briggs (Eds), *Handbook of personality psychology.* San Diego: Academic Press.

Paulhus, D. L., Trapnell, P. D., & Chen, D. (1999). Birth order effects on personality and achievement within families. *Psychological Science, 10,* 482–488.

Paunonen, S. V. (1998). Hierarchical organization of personality and prediction of behavior. *Journal of Personality and Social Psychology, 74*(2), 538–556.

Paunonen, S. V. (2003). Big five factors of personality and replicated predictions of behavior. *Journal of Personality and Social Psychology, 84,* 411–424.

Paunonen, S. V., & Ashton, M. C. (1998). The structured assessment of personality across cultures. *Journal of Cross-Cultural Psychology, 29,* 150–170.

Pavlov, I. P. (1906). The scientific investigation of psychical faculties or processes in the higher animals. *Science, 24,* 613–619.

Paxton, S. J., Norris, M., Wertheim, E. H., Durkin, S. J., & Anderson, J. (2005). Body dissatisfaction, dating, and importance of thinness to attractiveness in adolescent girls. *Sex Roles, 53,* 663–675.

Payne, B. K. (2006). Weapon bias: Split-second decisions and unintended sterotyping. *Current Directions in Psychological Science, 15,* 287–291.

Payne, D. G., & Wenger, M. J. (1996). Practice effects in memory: Data, theory, and unanswered questions. In D. J. Herrmann, C. McEvoy, C. Hertzog, P. Hertel, & M. K. Johnson (Eds.), *Basic and applied memory research: Practical applications* (Vol. 2). Mahwah, NJ: Erlbaum.

Pearce, L. (1974). Duck! It's the new journalism. *New Times, 2,* 40–41.

Pearson, P. (1998). *When she was bad: Violent women and the myth of innocence.* New York: Viking.

Pearson, Q. M. (1998). Job satisfaction, leisure satisfaction, and psychological health. *Career Development Quarterly, 46*(4), 416–426.

Pechacek, T. F., & Babb, S. (2004). Commentary: How acute and reversible are the cardiovascular risks of secondhand smoke? *British Medical Journal, 328,* 980–983.

Pechnick, R. N., & Ungerleider, T. J. (2005). Hallucinogens. In J. H. Lowinson, P. Ruiz, R. B. Millman, & J. G. Langrod (Eds.), *Substance abuse: A comprehensive textbook.* Philadelphia: Lippincott/Williams & Wilkins.

Pedersen, P. (1994). A culture-centered approach to counseling. In W. J. Lonner & R. Malpass (Eds.), *Psychology and culture.* Boston: Allyn & Bacon.

Pedersen, W., & Skrondal, A. (1999). Ecstasy and new patterns of drug use: A normal population study. *Addiction, 94*(11), 1695–1706.

Pegula, S., & Marsh, S. M. (2007). Fatal occupational injuries—United States, 2005. *Journal of the American Medical Association, 297,* 2193–2194.

Peirce, R. S., Frone, M. R., Russell, M., & Cooper, M. L. (1996). Financial stress, social support, and alcohol involvement: A longitudinal test of the buffering hypothesis in a general population survey. *Health Psychology, 15,* 38–47.

Peladeau, N., Forget, J., & Gagne, F. (2003). Effect of paced and unpaced practice on skill application and retention: How much is enough? *American Educational Research Journal, 40,* 769–801.

Pennebaker, J. W. (1997). *Opening up: The healing power of expressing emotions.* New York: Guilford.

Pennebaker, J. W., Colder, M., & Sharp, L. K. (1990). Accelerating the coping process. *Journal of Personality and Social Psychology, 58,* 528–537.

Peplau, L. A. (1988). Research on homosexual couples: An overview. In J. P. De Cecco (Ed.), *Gay relationships.* New York: Harrington Park Press.

Peplau, L. A. (1991). Lesbian and gay relationships. In J. C. Gonsiorek & J. D. Weinrich (Eds.), *Homosexuality: Research implications for public policy.* Newbury Park, CA: Sage.

Peplau, L. A. (2003). Human sexuality: How do men and women differ? *Current Directions in Psychological Science, 12*(2), 37–40.

Peplau, L. A., & Cochran, S. D. (1990). A relational perspective on homosexuality. In D. P. McWhirter, S. A. Sanders, & J. M. Reinisch (Eds.), *Homosexuality/heterosexuality: Concepts of sexual orientation.* New York: Oxford University Press.

Peplau, L. A., & Fingerhut, A. W. (2007). The close relationships of lesbians and gay men. *Annual Review of Psychology, 58,* 405–424.

Peplau, L. A., Fingerhut, A., & Beals, K. P. (2004). Sexuality in the relationships of lesbians and gay men. In J. H. Harvey, A. Wenzel, & S. Sprecher (Eds.), *The handbook of sexuality in close relationships.* Mahwah, NJ: Lawrence Erlbaum.

Peplau, L. A., & Garnets, L. D. (2000). A new paradigm for understanding women's sexuality and sexual orientation. *Journal of Social Issues, 56*(2), 329–350.

Peplau, L. A., & Gordon, S. L. (1985). Women and men in love: Gender differences in close heterosexual relationships. In V. E. O'Leary, R. K. Unger, & B. S. Wallston (Eds.), *Women, gender, and social psychology.* Hillsdale, NJ: Erlbaum.

Peplau, L. A., Hill, C. T., & Rubin, Z. (1993). Sex role attitudes in dating and marriage: A 15-year follow-up of the Boston couples study. *Journal of Social Issues, 49,* 31–52.

Peplau, L. A., & Spalding, L. R. (2000). The close relationships of lesbians, gay men, and bisexuals. In C. Hendrick & S. S. Hendrick (Eds.), *Close relationships: A sourcebook.* Thousand Oaks, CA: Sage.

Peplau, L. A., & Spalding, L. R. (2003). The close relationships of lesbians, gay men, and bisexuals. In L. D. Garnets & D. C. Kimmel (Eds.), *Psychological perspectives on lesbian, gay, and bisexual experiences.* New York: Columbia University Press.

Peretti, P. O., & Abplanalp, R. R., Jr. (2004). Chemistry in the college dating process: Structure and function. *Social Behavior and Personality, 32*(2), 147–154.

Perkins, D. F., & Borden, L. M. (2003). Positive behaviors, problem behaviors, and resiliency in adolescence. In R. M. Lerner, M.A. Easterbrooks, & J. Mistry (Eds.), *Handbook of psychology: Vol. 6. Developmental psychology.* New York: Wiley.

Perkins, D. O., Miller-Anderson, L., & Lieberman, J. A. (2006). Natural history and predictors of clinical course. In J. A. Liberman, T. S. Stroup, & D. O. Perkins (Eds.), *Textbook of schizophrenia.* Washington, DC: American Psychiatric Publishing.

Perlis, R. H., Perlis, C. S., Wu, Y. , Hwang, C., Joseph, M., & Nierenberg, A. A. (2005). Industry sponsorship and financial conflict of interest in the reporting of clinical trials in psychiatry. *American Journal of Psychiatry, 162,* 1957–1960.

Perloff, R. M. (1993). *The dynamics of persuasion.* Hillsdale, NJ: Erlbaum.

Perreault, S., & Bourhis, R. Y. (1999). Ethnocentrism, social identification, and discrimination. *Personality and Social Psychology Bulletin, 25*(1), 92–103.

Perrett, D. I., Lee, K. J., Penton-Voak, I., Rowland, D., Yoshikawa, S., Burt, D. M., Henzi, S. P., Castles, D. L., & Akamatsu, S. (1998). Effects of sexual dimorphism on facial attractiveness. *Nature, 394,* 884–887.

Perri, M. G., Anton, S. D., Durning, P. E., Ketterson, T. U., Sydeman, S. J., Berlant, N. E., Kanasky Jr., W. F., Newton Jr., R. L., Llimacher, M. C., & Martin, A. D. (2002). Adherence to exercise prescriptions: Effects of prescribing moderate versus higher levels of intensity and frequency. *Health Psychology, 21*(5), 452–458.

Perry-Jenkins, M., Repetti, R. L., & Crouter, A. C. (2001). Work and family in the 1990s. In R. M. Milardo (Ed.), *Understanding families into the new millennium: A decade in review.* Minneapolis, MN: National Council on Family Relations.

Perry-Jenkins, M., & Turner, E. (2004). Jobs, marriage, and parenting: Working it out in dual-earner families. In M. Coleman, & L. H. Ganong (Eds.), *Handbook of contemporary families: Considering the past, contemplating the future.* Thousand Oaks, CA: Sage.

Person, E. S. (1990). The influence of values in psychoanalysis: The case of female psychology. In C. Zanardi (Ed.), *Essential papers in psychoanalysis.* New York: New York University Press.

Pervin, L. A. (1994). Personality stability, personality change, and the question of process. In T. F. Heatherton & J. L. Weinberger (Eds.), *Can personality change?* Washington, DC: American Psychological Association.

Pervin, L. A., & John, O. P. (2001). *Personality: Theory and research.* New York: Wiley.

Petersen, A. C. (1987, September). Those gangly years. *Psychology Today,* pp. 28–34.

Petersen, A. C. (1988). Adolescent development. *Annual Review of Psychology, 39,* 583–607.

Petersen, R. C., Ed. (2003). *Mild cognitive impairment.* Oxford, England: Oxford University Press.

Peterson, B. E., & Lane, M. D. (2001). Implications of authoritarianism for young adulthood: Longitudinal analysis of college experiences and future goals. *Personality and Social Psychology Bulletin, 27*(6), 678–690.

Peterson, C., & Bossio, L. M. (2001). Optimism and physical well-being. In E. C. Chang (Ed.), *Optimism and pessimism: Implications for theory, research, and practice.* Washington, DC: American Psychological Association.

Peterson, C., Maier, S. F., & Seligman, M. E. P. (1993). *Learned helplessness: A theory for the age of personal control.* New York: Oxford University Press.

Peterson, C., & Seligman, M. E. P. (2004). *Character strengths and virtues: A handbook and classification.* Washington, DC: American Psychological Association/New York: Oxford University Press.

Peterson, C., & Vaidya, R. S. (2001). Explanatory style, expectations, and depressive symptoms. *Personality and Individual Differences, 31,* 1217–1223.

Peterson, C., Seligman, M. E. P., & Vaillant, G. E. (1988). Pessimistic explanatory style is a risk factor for physical illness: A thirty-five-year longitudinal study. *Journal of Personality and Social Psychology, 55,* 23–27.

Peterson, C., Seligman, M. E. P., Yurko, K. H., Martin, L. R., & Friedman, H. S. (1998). Castastrophizing and untimely death. *Psychological Science, 9,* 127–130.

Peterson, J. L., & Bakeman, R. (2006). Impact of beliefs about HIV treatment and peer condom norms on risky sexual behavior among gay and bisexual men. *Journal of Community Psychology, 34*(1), 37–46.

Peterson, N., & González, R. (2005). *The role of work in people's lives: Applied career counseling and vocational psychology.* Belmont, CA: Wadsworth.

Petit, J. W., & Joiner, T. E. (2006). *Chronic depression: Interpersonal sources, therapeutic solutions.* Washington, DC: American Psychological Association.

Petras, R., & Petras, K. (1993). *The 776 stupidest things ever said.* New York: Doubleday.

Petrill, S. A. (2005). Behavioral genetics and intelligence. In O. Wilhelm & R. W. Engle (Eds.), *Handbook of understanding and measuring intelligence.* Thousand Oaks, CA: Sage Publications.

Petticrew, M., Fraser, J. M., & Regan, M. F. (1999). Adverse life-events and risk of breast cancer: A meta-analysis. *British Journal of Health Psychology, 4,* 1–17.

Pettigrew, T. F. (2001). The ultimate attribution error: Extending Allport's cognitive analysis of prejudice. In M. A. Hogg & D. Abrams (Eds.), *Intergroup relations: Essential readings.* New York: Psychology Press.

Pettigrew, T. F., & Tropp, L. R. (2000). Does intergroup contact reduce prejudice: Recent meta-analytic findings. In S. Oskamp (Ed.), *Reducing prejudice and discrimination.* Mahwah, NJ: Erlbaum.

Pettigrew, T. F., & Tropp, L. R. (2006). A meta-analytic test of intergroup contact theory. *Journal of Personality and Social Psychology, 90,* 751–783.

Petty, R. E., & Cacioppo, J. T. (1986). The elaboration likelihood model of persuasion. In L. Berkowitz (Ed.), *Advances in experimental social psychology* (Vol. 19). Orlando, FL: Academic Press.

Petty, R. E., & Cacioppo, J. T. (1990). Involvement and persuasion: Tradition versus integration. *Psychological Bulletin, 107,* 367–374.

Petty, R. E., Fleming, M. A., Priester, J. R., & Feinstein, A. H. (2001). Individual versus group interest violation: Surprise as a determinant of argument scrutiny and persuasion. *Social Cognition, 19*(4), 418–442.

Petty, R. E., Priester, J. R., & Wegener, D. T. (1994). Cognitive processes in attitude change. In R. S. Wyer & T. K. Srull (Eds.), *Handbook of social cognition* (Vol. 2). Hillsdale, NJ: Erlbaum.

Petty, R. E., & Wegener, D. T. (1998). Attitude change: Multiple roles for persuasion variables. In D. T. Gilbert, S. T. Fiske, & G. Lindzey (Eds.), *The handbook of social psychology* (4th ed., Vol. 1). New York: McGraw-Hill.

Petty, R. E., Wegener, D. T., & Fabrigar, L. R. (1997). Attitudes and attitude change. *Annual Review of Psychology, 48,* 609–647.

Petty, S. C., Sachs-Ericsson, N., & Joiner, T. E., Jr. (2004). Interpersonal functioning deficits: Temporary or stable characteristics of depressed individuals. *Journal of Affective Disorders, 81*(2), 115–122.

Phillips, W. T., Kiernan, M., & King, A. C. (2001). The effects of physical activity on physical and psychological health. In A. Baum, T. A. Revenson, & J. E. Singer (Eds.), *Handbook of health psychology.* Mahwah, NJ: Erlbaum.

Pi, E. H., & Simpson, G. M. (2001). Medication-induced movement disorders. In B. J. Sadock & V. A. Sadock (Eds.), *Kaplan and Sadock's comprehensive textbook of psychiatry* (7th ed., Vol. 2). Philadelphia: Lippincott/ Williams & Wilkins.

Pierce, C. M. (1992). Contemporary psychiatry: Racial perspectives on the past and future. In A. Kales, C. M. Pierce, & M. Greenblatt (Eds.), *The mosaic of contemporary psychiatry in perspective.* New York: Springer-Verlag.

Pietromonaco, P. R., Greenwood, D., & Barrett, L. F. (2004). Conflict in adult close relationships: An attachment perspective. In W. S. Rholes & J. A. Simpson (Eds.), *Adult attachment: Theory, research, and clinical implications.* New York: Guilford.

Piferi, R. L., & Lawler, K. A. (2006). Social support and ambulatory blood pressure: An examination of both receiving and giving. *International Journal of Psychophysiology, 62,* 328–336.

Pike, A., Manke, B., Reiss, D., & Plomin, R. (2000). A genetic analysis of differential experiences of adolescent siblings across three years. *Social Development, 9,* 96–114.

Pike, K. M., & Rodin, J. (1991). Mothers, daughters, and disordered eating. *Journal of Abnormal Psychology, 100,* 198–294.

Pillow, D. R., Zautra, A. J., & Sandler, I. (1996). Major life events and minor stressors: Identifying mediational links in the stress process. *Journal of Personality and Social Psychology, 70,* 381–394.

Pilowsky, I. (1993). Aspects of abnormal illness behaviour. *Psychotherapy and Psychosomatics, 60,* 62–74.

Pine, D. S., & McClure, E. B. (2005a). Anxiety disorders: Clinical features. In B. J. Sadock & V. A. Sadock (Eds.), *Kaplan & Sadock's comprehensive textbook of psychiatry.* Philadelphia: Lippicott Williams & Wilkins.

Pine, D. S., & McClure, E. B. (2005b). Anxiety disorders: Genetics. In B. J. Sadock & V. A. Sadock (Eds.), *Kaplan & Sadock's comprehensive textbook of psychiatry.* Philadelphia: Lippincott Williams & Wilkins.

Pinel, J. P. J., Assanand, S., & Lehman, D. R. (2000). Hunger, eating, and ill health. *American Psychologist, 55,* 1105–1116.

Pines, A. M. (1993). Burnout. In L. Goldberger & S. Breznitz (Eds.), *Handbook of stress: Theoretical and clinical aspects* (2nd ed.). New York: Free Press.

Pink, D. H. (2001). *Free agent nation: The future of working for yourself.* New York: Warner Business Books.

Pinquart, M. (2003). Loneliness in married, widowed, divorced, and never-married older adults. *Journal of Social and Personal Relationships, 20*(1), 31–53.

Pinquart, M., & Sorensen, S. (2001). Influences on loneliness in older adults: A meta-analysis. *Basic and Applied Social Psychology, 23,* 245–266.

Pipher, M. (1994). *Reviving Ophelia: Saving the selves of adolescent girls.* New York: Ballantine.

Pi-Sunyer, F. X. (2002). Medical complications of obesity in adults. In C. G. Fairburn & K. D. Brownell (Eds.), *Eating disorders and obesity: A comprehensive handbook.* New York: Guilford.

Pittman, F., III. (1994, January/February). A buyer's guide to psychotherapy. *Psychology Today,* pp. 50–53, 74–81.

Piver, S. (2000). *The hard questions: 100 questions to ask before you say "I do."* New York: Jeremy P. Tarcher/Putnam.

Planalp, S., Fitness, J., & Fehr, B. (2006). Emotion in theories of close relationships. In A. L. Vangelisti & D. Perlman (Eds.), *The Cambridge handbook of personal relationships.* New York: Cambridge University Press.

Plante, T. G. (2005). *Contemporary clinical psychology.* New York: Wiley.

Plante, T. G., Caputo, D., & Chizmar, L. (2000). Perceived fitness and responses to laboratory induced stress. *International Journal of Stress Management, 7*(1), 61–73.

Pleck, J. H. (1981). *The myth of masculinity.* Cambridge, MA: MIT Press.

Pleck, J. H. (1995). The gender role strain paradigm: An update. In R. F. Levant & W. S. Pollack (Eds.), *A new psychology of men.* New York: Basic Books.

Plomin, R. (1994). Nature, nurture, and development. In R. J. Sternberg (Ed.), *Encyclopedia of human intelligence.* New York: Macmillan.

Plomin, R., & Caspi, A. (1999). Behavioral genetics and personality. In L. A. Pervin & O. P. John (Eds.), *Handbook of personality: Theory and research* (2nd ed.). New York: Guilford Press.

Plomin, R., & Spinath, F. M. (2004). Intelligence: Genetics, genes, and genomics. *Journal of Personality & Social Psychology, 86,* 112–129.

Plous, S. L., & Zimbardo, P. G. (2004, September 10). How social science can reduce terrorism. *The Chronicle of Higher Education,* pp. B9–B10.

Polivy, J., & Herman, C. P. (2002). Causes of eating disorder. *Annual Review of Psychology, 53,* 187–213.

Pollak, L. (2007). *Getting from college to career: 90 things to do before you join the real world.* New York: HarperCollins.

Pomeroy, C., & Mitchell, J. E. (2002). Medical complications of anorexia nervosa and bulimia nervosa. In C. G. Fairburn & K. D. Brownell (Eds.), *Eating disorders and obesity: A comprehensive handbook.* New York: Guilford.

Pope, E., & Shouldice, M. (2001). Drugs and sexual assault: A review. *Trauma Violence and Abuse, 2*(1), 51–55.

Pope, H. G., Barry, S., Bodkin, A., & Hudson, J. I. (2006). Tracking scientific interest in the dissociative disorders: A study of scientific publication output 1984–2003. *Psychotherapy and Psychosomatics, 75,* 19–24.

Pope, H. G., Gruber, A. J., Hudson, J. I., Huestis, M. A., & Yurgelun- Todd, D. (2001). Neuropsychological performance in long-term cannabis users. *Archives of General Psychiatry, 58,* 909–915.

Pope, H. G., Gruber, A. J., & Yurgelun-Todd, D. (2001). Residual neuropsychologic effects of cannabis. *Current Psychiatry Report, 3,* 507–512.

Pope, H. G., Oliva, P. S., Hudson, J. I., Bodkin, J. A., & Gruber, A. J. (1999). Attitudes toward DSM-IV dissociative disorders diagnoses among board-certified American psychiatrists. *American Journal of Psychiatry, 156*(2), 321–323.

Pope, K. S., Keith-Spiegel, P., & Tabachnick, B. G. (1986). Sexual attraction to clients. *American Psychologist, 41,* 147–158.

Popenoe, D. (1993). American family decline, 1960–1990: A review and appraisal. *Journal of Marriage and the Family, 55,* 527–555.

Popenoe, D. (1999). *Life without father: Compelling new evidence that fatherhood and marriage are indispensable for the good of children and society.* Cambridge, MA: Harvard University Press.

Potenza, M. N. (2006). Should addictive disorders include non–substance-related conditions? *Addiction, 101*(Suppl 1), 142–151.

Potter, W. Z., Padich, R. A., Rudorfer, M. V., & Krishnan, K. R. R. (2006). Tricyclics, tetracyclics, and monoamine oxidase inhibitors. In D. J.Stein, D. J. Kupfer, & A. F. Schatzberg (Eds.), *Textbook of mood disorders.* Washington, DC: American Psychiatric Publishing.

Powell, J. L., & Drucker, A. D. (1997). The role of peer conformity in the decision to ride with an intoxicated driver. *Journal of Alcohol and Drug Education, 43*(1), 1–7.

Powell, R. A., & Gee, T. L. (1999). The effects of hypnosis on dissociative identity disorder: A reexamination of the evidence. *Canadian Journal of Psychiatry, 44,* 914–916.

Pratt, L. A., Ford, D. E., Crum, R. M., Armenian, H. K., Gallo, J. J., & Eaton, W. W. (1996). Depression, psychotropic medication, and risk of myocardial infarction: Prospective data from the Baltimore ECA follow-up. *Archives of Internal Medicine, 94,* 3123–3129.

Pratto, F., Sidanius, J., Stallworth, L. M., & Malle, B. F. (1994). Social dominance orientation: A personality variable predicting social and political attitudes. *Journal of Personality and Social Psychology, 67,* 741–763.

Pratto, F., & Walker, A. (2004). The bases of gendered power. In A. H. Eagly, A. E. Beall, & R. J. Sternberg (Eds.), *The psychology of gender.* New York: Guilford Press.

Presser, H. B. (2000). Nonstandard work schedules and marital instability. *Journal of Marriage and the Family, 62,* 93–110.

Pressman, S. (1993). *Outrageous betrayal: The real story of Werner Erhard, EST and the Forum.* New York: St. Martin's Press.

Preto, N. G. (1999). Transformation of the family system during adolescence. In B. Carter & M. McGoldrick (Eds.), *The expanded family life cycle: Individual, family, and social perspectives* (3rd ed.). Boston: Allyn & Bacon.

Pruchno, R., & Rosenbaum, J. (2003). Social relationships in adulthood and old age. In R. M. Lerner, M. A. Easterbrooks, & J. Mistry (Eds.), *Handbook of psychology: Vol. 6. Developmental psychology.* New York: Wiley.

Prudic, J. (2005). Electroconvulsive therapy. In B. J. Sadock & V. A. Sadock (Eds.), *Kaplan and Sadock's comprehensive textbook of psychiatry.* Philadelphia: Lippincott Williams & Wilkins.

Pryor, F. L., & Schaffer, D. (1997, July). Wages and the university educated: A paradox resolved. *Monthly Labor Review,* 3–14.

Pryor, J. B., Giedd, J. L., & Williams, K. B. (1995). A social psychological model for predicting sexual harassment. *Journal of Social Issues, 51,* 69–84.

Puetz, T. W., O'Connor, P. J., & Dishman, R. K. (2006). Effects of chronic exercise on feelings of energy and fatigue: A quantitative synthesis. *Psychological Bulletin, 132,* 866–876.

Putnam, R. D. (1996). The strange disappearance of civic America. *The American Prospect, 24,* 34–46.

Pyszczynski, T., Greenberg, J., & Goldenberg, J. L. (2003). Freedom versus fear: On the defense, growth, and expansion of the self. In M. R. Leary & J. P. Tangney (Eds.), *Handbook of self and identity.* New York: Guilford.

Pyszczynski, T., Greenberg, J., & Solomon, S. (1999). A dual-process model of defense against conscious and unconscious death-related thoughts: An extension of terror management theory. *Psychological Review, 106*(4), 835–845.

Pyszczynski, T., Greenberg, J., Solomon, S., Arndt, J., & Schimel, J. (2004). Why do people need self-esteem? A theoretical and empirical review. *Psychological Bulletin, 130*(3), 435–468.

Pyszczynski, T., Solomon, S., & Greenberg, J. (2003a). Giving peace a chance. In T. Pyszczynski, S. Solomon, & J. Greenberg (Eds.), *In the wake of 9/11: The psychology of terror.* Washington, DC: American Psychological Association.

Pyszczynski, T., Solomon, S., & Greenberg, J. (2003b). *In the wake of 9/11: The psychology of terror.* Washington, DC: American Psychological Association.

Quinn, K. A., Macrae, C. N., & Bodenhausen, G. V. (2003). Stereotyping and impression formation: How categorical thinking shapes person perception. In M. A. Hogg & J. Cooper (Eds.), *The Sage handbook of social psychology.* Thousand Oaks, CA: Sage Publications.

Rabkin, J. G. (1993). Stress and psychiatric disorders. In L. Goldberger & S. Breznitz (Eds.), *Handbook of stress: Theoretical and clinical aspects* (2nd ed.). New York: Free Press.

Rachman, S. J. (1990). *Fear and courage.* New York: Freeman.

Rachman, S. J. (1992). Behavior therapy. In L. R. Squire (Ed.), *Encyclopedia of learning and memory.* New York: Macmillan.

Ragins, B. R., Cornwell, J. M., & Miller, J. S. (2003). Heterosexism in the workplace: Do race and gender matter? *Group & Organization Management, 28*(1), 45–74.

Ragland, D. R., & Brand, R. J. (1988). Type A behavior and mortality from coronary heart disease. *The New England Journal of Medicine, 318,* 65–69.

Rahe, R. H., & Arthur, R. H. (1978). Life change and illness studies. *Journal of Human Stress, 4,* 3–15.

Rahe, R. H., Veach, T. L., Tolles, R. L., & Murakami, K. (2000). The stress and coping inventory: An educational and research instrument. *Stress Medicine, 16,* 199–208.

Rahim, M. A., & Magner, N. R. (1995). Confirmatory factor analysis of the styles of handling interpersonal conflict: First-order factor model and its invariance across groups. *Journal of Applied Psychology, 80,* 122–132.

Rahman, Q. (2005). Fluctuating asymmetry, second to fourth finger length and human sexual orientation. *Psychoneuroendocrinology, 30,* 382–391.

Raines, L. (2006, June 4). For interviews, rein in your fashion freedom. *Atlanta Journal/Constitution,* p. 3.

Raj, A., & Sheehan, D. (2004). Benzodiazepines. In A. F. Schatzberg & C. B. Nemeroff (Eds.), *Textbook of psychopharmacology.* Washington, DC: American Psychiatric Publishing.

Raloff, J. (1996). Breakfast trends. *Science News, 150,* 90–91.

Ramadan, N. M. (2000). Migraine. In G. Fink (Ed.), *Encyclopedia of stress.* San Diego: Academic Press.

Ramaekers, J. G., Robbe, H. W. J., & O'Hanlon, J. F. (2000). Marijuana, alcohol and actual driving performance. *Human Psychopharmacology Clinical & Experimental, 15*(7), 551–558.

Randhawa, B. S., & Hunter, D. M. (2001). Validity of performance assessment in mathematics for early adolescents. *Canadian Journal of Behavioral Science, 33,* 14–24.

Rank, M. R. (2004). The disturbing paradox of poverty in American families: What we have learned over the past four decades. In M. Coleman & L. H. Ganong (Eds.), *Handbook of contemporary families: Considering the past, contemplating the future.* Thousand Oaks, CA: Sage.

Ransome, P. (2005). *Work, consumption and culture: Affluence and social change in the twenty-first century.* Thousand Oaks, CA: SAAR.

Rapee, R. M., & Barlow, D. H. (2001). Generalized anxiety disorders, panic disorders, and phobias. In P. B. Sutker & H. E. Adams (Eds.), *Comprehensive handbook of psychopathology* (3rd ed.). New York: Kluwer Academic/Plenum Publishers.

Raphael, B., & Dobson, M. (2000). Effects of public disasters. In G. Fink (Ed.), *Encyclopedia of stress* (Vol. 1). San Diego: Academic Press.

Raskin, P. M. (1986). The relationship between identity and intimacy in early adulthood. *Journal of Genetic Psychology, 147,* 167–181.

Ray, G. E., Cohen, R., Secrist, M. E., & Duncan, M. K. (1997). Relating aggressive and victimization behaviors to children's sociometric status and friendships. *Journal of Social and Personal Relationships, 14*(1), 95–108.

Read, C. R. (1991). Achievement and career choices: Comparisons of males and females. *Roeper Review, 13* 188–193.

Reddy, B. S. (1999). Role of dietary fiber in colon cancer: An overview. *American Journal of Medicine, 106*(1A), 16S–19S.

Reed, G. M., Kemeny, M. E., Taylor, S. E., & Visscher, B. R. (1999). Negative HIV-specific expectancies and AIDS-related bereavement as predictors of symptom onset in asymptomatic HIV-positive gay men. *Health Psychology, 18,* 354–363.

Rees, C. J., & Metcalfe, B. (2003). The faking of personality questionnaire results: Who's kidding whom. *Journal of Managerial Psychology, 18,* 156–165.

Regan, P. C. (2003). *The mating game: A primer on love, sex, and marriage.* Thousand Oaks, CA: Sage Publications.

Regan, P. C., & Berscheid, E. (1997). Gender differences in characteristics desired in potential sexual and marriage partners. *Journal of Psychology and Human Sexuality, 9*(1), 25–37.

Regier, D. A., & Burke, J. D. (2000). Epidemiology. In B. J. Sadock & V. A. Sadock (Eds.), *Kaplan and Sadock's comprehensive textbook of psychiatry.* Philadelphia: Lippincott/Williams & Wilkins.

Regier, D. A., Narrow, W. E., & Rae, D. S. (2004). For DSM-V, It's the "disorder threshold," stupid. *Archives of General Psychiatry, 61,* 1051.

Rehm, L. P., Wagner, A., & Ivens-Tyndal, Co. (2001). Mood disorders: Unipolar and bipolar. In P. B. Sutker & H. E. Adams (Eds.), *Comprehensive handbook of psychopathology* (3rd ed.). New York: Kluwer Academic/Plenum.

Reibel, D. K., Greeson, J. M., Brainard, G. C., & Rosenzweig, S. (2001). Mindfulness-based stress reduction and health-related quality of life in a heterogeneous patient population. *General Hospital Psychiatry, 23*(4), 183–192.

Reid, M., Miller, W., & Kerr, B. (2004). Sex-based glass ceilings in U. S. state-level bureaucracies, 1987-1997. *Administration and Society, 36,* 377–405.

Reid, P. T., & Paludi, M. A. (1993). Developmental psychology of women: Conception to adolescence. In F. L. Denmark & M. A. Paludi (Eds.), *Psychology of women: A handbook of issues and theories.* Westport, CT: Greenwood Press.

Reimann, R. (1997). Does biology matter?: Lesbian couples' transition to parenthood and their division of labor. *Qualitative Sociology, 20*(2), 153–185.

Reinisch, J. M. (1990). *The Kinsey Institute new report on sex: What you must know to be sexually literate.* New York: St. Martin's.

Reis, H. T. (1998). Gender differences in intimacy and related behaviors: Context and processes. In D. Canary & K. Dindia (Eds.), *Sex and gender in communication: Similarities and differences.* Mahwah, NJ: Erlbaum.

Reis, H. T., & Patrick. B. C. (1996). Attachment and intimacy: Component processes. In E. T. Higgins & A. Kruglanski (Eds.), *Social psychology: Handbook of basic principles.* New York: Guilford.

Reis, H. T., & Shaver, P. (1988). Intimacy as an interpersonal process. In S. W. Duck (Ed.), *Handbook of personal relationships.* New York: Wiley.

Reis, H. T., & Wheeler, L. (1991). Studying social interaction with the Rochester Interaction Record. *Advances in Experimental Social Psychology, 24,* 269–318.

Reis, T. J., Gerrard, M., & Gibbons, F. X. (1993). Social comparison and the pill: Reactions to upward and downward comparison of contraceptive behavior. *Personality and Social Psychology Bulletin, 19,* 13–21.

Reisner, A. D. (1998). Repressed memories: True and false. In R. A. Baker (Ed.), *Child sexual abuse and false memory syndrome.* Amherst, NY: Prometheus Books.

Reiss, S. (1991). Expectancy model of fear, anxiety and panic. *Clinical Psychology Review, 11,* 141–154.

Reissman, C., Aron, A., & Bergen, M. R. (1993). Shared activities and marital satisfaction: Causal direction and self-expansion versus boredom. *Journal of Social and Personal Relationships, 10,* 243–254.

Renaud, C. A., & Byers, E. S. (2001). Positive and negative sexual cognitions: Subjective experience and relationships to sexual adjustment. *Journal of Sex Research, 38*(3), 252–262.

Rennie, D., & Luft, H. S. (2000). Making them transparent, making them credible. *Journal of the American Medical Association, 283,* 2516–2521.

Rennison, C. M., & Welchans, S. (2000). *Intimate partner violence.* Washington, DC: U.S. Department of Justice, Office of Justice Programs, Bureau of Justice Statistics.

Renshaw, D. C. (2005). Premature ejaculation revisited–2005. *Family Journal, 13,* 150–152.

Renzetti, C. (1995). Violence in gay and lesbian relationships. In R. J. Gelles (Ed.), *Vision 2010: Families and violence, abuse and neglect.* Minneapolis: National Council on Family Relations.

Repetto, M., & Gold, M. S. (2005). Cocaine and crack: Neurobiology. In J. H. Lowinson, P. Ruiz, R. B. Millman, & J. G. Langrod (Eds.), *Substance abuse: A comprehensive textbook.* Philadelphia: Lippincott/Williams & Wilkins.

Rhodewalt, F., Sanbonmatsu, D. M., Tschanz, B., Feick, D. L., & Waller, A. (1995). Self-handicapping and interpersonal trade-offs: The effects of claimed self-handicaps on observers' performance evaluations and feedback. *Personality and Social Psychology Bulletin, 21,* 1042–1050

Rhodewalt, F., Tragakis, M. W., & Finnerty, J. (2006). Narcissism and self-handicapping: Linking self-aggrandizement to behavior. *Journal of Research in Personality, 40,* 573–597.

Riba, M. B., & Miller, R. R. (2003). Combined therapies: Psychotherapy and pharmacotherapy. In A. Tasman, J. Kay, & J. A. Lieberman (Eds.), *Psychiatry.* New York: Wiley.

Rice, J. K., & Else-Quest, N. (2006). The mixed messages of motherhood. In J. Worrell & C. D. Goodheart (Eds.), *Handbook of girls' and women's psychological health.* New York: Oxford University Press.

Rice, L. N., & Greenberg, L. S. (1992). Humanistic approaches to psychotherapy. In D. K. Freedheim (Ed.), *History of psychotherapy: A century of change.* Washington, DC: American Psychological Association.

Richardson, C. R., Kriska, A. M., Lantz, P. M., & Hayword, R. A. (2004). Physical activity and mortality across cardiovascular disease risk groups. *Medicine and Science in Sports and Exercise, 36*(11), 1923–1929.

Richardson, J. G., & Simpson, C. H. (1982). Children, gender and social structure: An analysis of the contents of letters to Santa Claus. *Child Development, 53* 429–436.

Richmond, V. P., & McCroskey, J. C. (1995). *Communication: Apprehension, avoidance, and effectiveness* (5th ed.). Boston: Allyn & Bacon.

Richter, H. (2007, May 7). Lights, camera, hired! *Newsweek,* p. 65.

Ridge, S. R., & Feeney, J. A. (1998). Relationship history and relationship attitudes in gay males and lesbians: Attachment style and gender differences. *Australian and New Zealand Journal of Psychiatry, 32*(6), 848–859.

Ridgeway, C. L., & Bourg, C. (2004). Gender as status: An expectation states theory approach. In A. H. Eagly, A. E. Beall, & R. J. Sternberg (Eds.), *The psychology of gender.* New York: Guilford Press.

Ridker, P. M. (2001). High-sensitivity C-reactive protein: Potential adjunct for global risk assessment in the primary prevention of cardiovascular disease. *Circulation, 103,* 1813–1818.

Rief, W., Henningsen, P., & Hiller, W. (2006). Classification of somatoform disorders. *American Journal of Psychiatry, 163,* 746–747.

Riemann, R., Angleitner, A., & Strelau, J. (1997). Genetic and environmental influences on personality: A study of twins reared together using the self- and peer report NEO-FFI scales. *Journal of Personality, 65,* 449–476.

Rierdan, J., & Koff, E. (1991). Depressive symptomatology among very early maturing girls. *Journal of Youth and Adolescence, 20,* 415–425.

Rifkin, J. (1989). *Time wars: The primary conflict in human history.* New York: Simon & Schuster.

Rigotti, N. A., Lee, J. E., & Wechsler, H. (2000). U.S. college students' use of tobacco products: Results of a national survey. *Journal of the American Medical Association, 284,* 699–705.

Rihmer, Z. (2003). Do SSRI's increase the risk of suicide among depressives even if they are only taking placebo? *Psychotherapy & Psychosomatics, 72*(6), 357–358.

Rihmer, Z., & Angst, J. (2005). Mood disorders: Epidemiology. In B. J. Sadock & V. A. Sadock (Eds.), *Kaplan & Sadock's comprehensive textbook of psychiatry.* Philadelphia: Lippicott Williams & Wilkins.

Riis, J., Loewenstein, G., Baron, J. , Jepson, C., Fagerlin, A., & Ubel, P. A. (2005). Ignorance of hedonic adaptation to hemodialysis: A study using ecological momentary assessment. *Journal of Experimental Psychology: General, 134,* 3–9.

Riley, B. P., & Kendler, K. S. (2005). Schizophrenia: Genetics. In B. J. Sadock & V. A. Sadock (Eds.), *Kaplan & Sadock's comprehensive textbook of psychiatry.* Philadelphia: Lippincott Williams & Wilkins.

Riley, L. D., & Bowen, C. (2005). The sandwich generation: Challenges and coping strategies of multigenerational families. *Family Journal: Counseling and Therapy for Couples and Families, 13,* 52–58.

Rimal R. N. (2001). Longitudinal influences of knowledge and self-efficacy on exercise behavior: Tests of a mutual reinforcement model. *Journal of Health Psychology, 6,* 31–46.

Rindfuss, R. R. (1991). The young adult years: Diversity, structural change, and fertility. *Demography, 28,* 493–512.

Riskey, D. R., & Birnbaum, M. H. (1974). Compensatory effects in moral judgment: Two rights don't make up for a wrong. *Journal of Experimental Psychology, 103,* 171–173.

Riskind, J. H. (2005). Cognitive mechanisms in generalized anxiety disorder: A second generation of theoretical perspectives. *Cognitive Therapy & Research, 29*(1), 1–5.

Riso, L. P., du Toit, P. L., Blandino, J. A., Penna, S., Dacey, S., Duin, J. S., Pacoe, E. M., Grant, M. M., & Ulmer, C. S. (2003). Cognitive aspects of chronic depression. *Journal of Abnormal Psychology, 112*(1), 72–80.

Ritskes, R., Ritskes-Hoitinga, M., Stodkilde-Jorgensen, H., Baerentsen, K. , & Hartman, T. (2003). MRI scanning during Zen meditation: The picture of enlightenment. *Constructivism in the Human Sciences, 8*(1), 85–90.

Ritz, T., Steptoe, A., DeWilde, S., & Costa, M. (2000). Emotions and stress increase respiratory resistance in asthma. *Psychosomatic Medicine, 62*(3), 401–412.

Rivas-Vazquez, R. A. (2001). Antidepressants as first-line agents in the current pharmacotherapy of anxiety disorders. *Professional Psychology: Research & Practice, 32*(1), 101–104.

Robbins, A., & Wilner, A. (2001). *Quarterlife crisis: The unique challenges of life in your twenties.* New York: Putnam.

Roberts, A. R. (2002). Myths, facts, and realities regarding battered women and their children: An overview. In A. R. Roberts (Ed.), *Handbook of domestic violence intervention strategies: Policies, programs, and legal remedies.* New York: Oxford University Press.

Roberts, B. W., & DelVecchio. W. F. (2000). The rank-order consistency of personality traits from childhood to old age: A quantitative review of the longitudinal studies. *Psychological Bulletin, 126,* 3–25.

Roberts, B. W., & Pomerantz, E. M. (2004). On traits, situations, and their integration: A developmental perspective. *Personality and Social Psychology Review, 8*(4), 402–416.

Roberts, D. F., Foehr, U. G., Rideout, V. J., & Vrodie, M. (1999). Kids and media @ the new millennium. Menlo Park, CA: Kaiser Family Foundation.

Roberts, L. J. (2000). Fire and ice in marital communication: Hostile and distancing behaviors as predictors of marital distress. *Journal of Marriage and the Family, 62,* 693–707.

Roberts, L. J., & Krokoff, L. J. (1990). A time series analysis of withdrawal, hostility, and displeasure in satisfied and dissatisfied marriages. *Journal of Marriage and the Family, 52,* 95–105.

Roberts, P., & Newton, P. M. (1987). Levinsonian studies of women's adult development. *Psychology and Aging, 2,* 154–163.

Roberts, S. (2006, October 15). It's official: To be married means to be outnumbered. *New York Times.*

Robertson, J. M., Lin, C., Woodford, J., Danos, K. K., & Hurst, M. A. (2001). The (un)emotional male: Physiological, verbal and written correlates of expressiveness. *Journal of Men's Studies, 9,* 393–412.

Robiner, W. N., Bearman, D. L., Berman, M., Grove, W. M., Colon, E., Armstrong, J., Mareck, S., & Tanenbaum, R. L. (2003). Prescriptive authority for psychologists: Despite deficits in education and knowledge. *Journal of Clinical Psychology in Medical Settings, 10*(3), 211–212.

Robins, L. N., Locke, B. Z., & Regier, D. A. (1991). An overview of psychiatric disorders in America. In L. N. Robins & D. A. Regier (Eds.), *Psychiatric disorders in America: The epidemiologic catchment area study.* New York: Free Press.

Robins, R. W., & Trzesniewski, K. H. (2005). Self-esteem development across the lifespan. *Current Direction in Psychological Science, 14,* 158–162.

Robinson, B., Frye, E. M., & Bradley, L. J. (1997). Cult affiliation and disaffiliation: Implications for counseling. *Counseling and Values, 41,* 166–173.

Robinson, B. E., Flowers, C., & Ng, K. (2006). The relationship between workaholism and marital disaffection: Husband's perspective. *Family Journal: Counseling and Therapy for Couples and Families, 14,* 213–220.

Robinson, D. G., Woerner, M. G., McMeniman, M., Mendelowitz, A., & Bilder, R. M. (2004). Symptomatic and functional recovery from a first episode of schizophrenia or schizoaffective disorder. *American Journal of Psychiatry, 161,* 473–479.

Robinson, F. P. (1970). *Effective study* (4th ed.). New York: HarperCollins.

Robinson, J. P., & Godbey, G. (1997). *Time for life: The surprising ways Americans use their time.* University Park, PA: Pennsylvania State University Press.

Robinson, M. D., Johnson, J. T., & Shields, S. A. (1995). On the advantages of modesty: The benefits of a balanced self-presentation. *Communication Research, 22,* 575–591.

Robles, T. F., Glaser, R., & Kiecolt-Glaser, J. K. (2005). Out of balance: A new look at chronic stress, depression, and immunity. *Current Directions in Psychological Science, 14,* 111–115.

Rodger, C. (2004). Aging male syndrome, andropause, androgen decline or mid-life crisis? *Journal of Men's Health & Gender, 1,* 55–59.

Rodin, J., Schank, D., & Striegel-Moore, R. H. (1989). Psychological features of obesity. *Medical Clinics of North America, 73* 47–66.

Rodrigues, A. E., Hall, J. H., & Fincham, F. D. (2006). What predicts divorce and relationship dissolution. In M. A. Fine & J. H. Harvey (Eds.), *Handbook of divorce and relationship resolution.* Mahwah, NJ: Erlbaum.

Roediger, H. L., III, & McDermott, K. B. (1995). Creating false memories: Remembering words not presented in lists. *Journal of Experimental Psychology: Learning, Memory, and Cognition, 21,* 803–814.

Roediger, H. L., III, & McDermott, K. B. (2000). Tricks of memory. *Current Directions in Psychological Science, 9,* 123–127.

Rogers, C. R. (1951). *Client-centered therapy: Its current practice, implications, and theory.* Boston: Houghton Mifflin.

Rogers, C. R. (1961). *On becoming a person: A therapist's view of psychotherapy.* Boston: Houghton Mifflin.

Rogers, C. R. (1977). *Carl Rogers on personal power.* New York: Delacorte.

Rogers, C. R. (1980). *A way of being.* Boston: Houghton Mifflin.

Rogers, C. R. (1986). Client-centered therapy. In I. L. Kutash & A. Wolf (Eds.), *Psychotherapist's casebook.* San Francisco: Jossey-Bass.

Rogers, M. P., Fricchione, G., & Reich, P. (1999). Psychosomatic medicine and consultation-liaison psychiatry. In A. M. Nicholi (Ed.), *The Harvard guide to psychiatry* (3rd ed.). Cambridge, MA: Harvard University Press.

Rogers, R. W., & Prentice-Dunn, S. (1997). Protection motivation theory. In D. Gochman (Ed.), *Handbook of health behavior research* (Vol. 1). New York: Plenum.

Rogers, S. J., & White, L. K. (1998). Satisfaction with parenting: The role of marital happiness, family structure, and parents' gender. *Journal of Marriage and the Family, 60,* 293–308.

Rogge, R. D., Bradbury, T. N., Hahlweg, K., Engl, J., & Thurmaier, F. (2006). Predicting marital distress and dissolution: Refining the two-factor hypothesis. *Journal of Family Psychology, 20,* 156–159.

Rohde, P. A., Atzwanger, K., Butovskayad, M., Lampert, A., Mysterud, I., Sanchez-Andres, A., & Sulloway, F. J. (2003). Perceived parental favoritism, closeness to kin and the rebel of the family: The effects of birth order and sex. *Evolution & Human Behavior, 24,* 261–276.

Rohner, R. P., & Veneziano, R. A. (2001). The importance of father love: History and contemporary evidence. *Review of General Psychology, 5*(4), 382–405.

Rohrer, D., Taylor, K., Pashler, H., Wixted, J. T., & Capeda, N. J. (2005). The effect of overlearning on long-term retention. *Applied Cognitive Psychology, 19,* 361–374.

Rojewski, J. W. (2005). Occupational aspirations: Constructs, meanings, and application. In S. D. Brown & R. W. Lent (Eds.), *Career development and counseling: Putting theory and research to work.* New York: Wiley.

Rokach, A. (2000). Perceived causes of loneliness in adulthood. *Journal of Social Behavior and Personality, 15,* 67–84.

Rollie, S. S., & Duck, S. (2006). Divorce and dissolution of romantic relationships. In M. A. Fine & J. H. Harvey (Eds.), *Handbook of divorce and relationship resolution.* Mahwah, NJ: Erlbaum.

Rook, K. S. (1998). Investigating the positive and negative sides of personal relationships: Through a lens darkly? In B. H. Spitzberg & W. R. Cupach (Eds.), *The dark side of close relationships.* Mahwah, NJ: Lawrence Erlbaum.

Rook, K. S., & Pietromonaco, P. (1987). Close relationships: Ties that heal or ties that bind? In W. H. Jones & D. Perlman (Eds.), *Advances in personal relationships.* Greenwich, CT: JAI Press.

Rose, D., Wykes, T., Leese, M., Bindman, J., & Fleischmann, P. (2003). Patient's perspectives on electroconvulsive therapy: Systematic review. *British Medical Journal, 326,* 1363–1365.

Rose, D. P. (1997). Dietary fatty acids and cancer. *American Journal of Clinical Nutrition, 66*(4), 998S–1003S.

Rosen, D. H. (1974). *Lesbianism: A study of female homosexuality.* Springfield, IL: Charles C Thomas.

Rosen, E., Ackerman, L., & Zosky, D. (2002). The sibling empty nest syndrome: The experience of sadness as siblings leave the family home. *Journal of Human Behavior in the Social Environment, 6,* 65–80.

Rosen, G. M. (1993). Self-help or hype? Comments on psychology's failure to advance self-care. *Professional Psychology: Research and Practice, 24,* 340–345.

Rosen, G. M., Glasgow, R. E., & Moore, T. E. (2003). Self-help therapy: The science and business of giving psychology away. In S. O. Lilienfeld, S. J. Lynn, & J. M. Lohr (Eds.), *Science and pseudoscience in clinical psychology.* New York: Guilford Press.

Rosen, R. (2000). Medical and psychological interventions for erectile dysfunction. In S. Leiblum & R. Rosen (Eds.), *Principles and practice of sex therapy.* New York: Guilford.

Rosen, R. D. (1977). *Psychobabble.* New York: Atheneum.

Rosenbaum, M., Lakin, M., & Roback, H. B. (1992). Psychotherapy in groups. In D. K. Freedheim (Ed.), *History of psychotherapy: A century of change.* Washington, DC: American Psychological Association.

Rosenberg, M. (1956). *Society and the adolescent self-image.* Princeton, NJ: Princeton University Press.

Rosenblatt, A., Greenberg, J., Solomon, S., Pyszczynski, T., & Lyon, D. (1989). Evidence for terror management theory: I. The effects of mortality salience on reactions to those who violate or uphold cultural values. *Journal of Personality and Social Psychology, 57,* 681–690.

Rosenbluth, S. C. (1997). Is sexual orientation a matter of choice? *Psychology of Women Quarterly, 21,* 595–610.

Rosenfarb, I. S., Goldstein, M. J., Mintz, J., & Nuechterlein, K. H. (1995). Expressed emotion and subclinical psychopathology observable within the transactions between schizophrenic patients and their family members. *Journal of Abnormal Psychology, 104,* 259–267.

Rosenfield, S. (1999). Splitting the difference: Gender, the self and mental health. In C. S. Aneshensel & J. C. Phelan (Eds.), *Handbook of the sociology of mental health.* New York: Kluwer Academic.

Rosenheck, R. A. (2006). Outcomes, costs, and policy caution. *Archives of General Psychiatry, 63,* 1074–1076.

Rosenman, R. H. (1993). Relationships of the Type A behavior pattern with coronary heart disease. In L. Goldberger & S. Breznitz (Eds.), *Handbook of stress: Theoretical and clinical aspects* (2nd ed.). New York: Free Press.

Rosenthal, H. (1988). *Not with my life I don't: Preventing suicide and that of others.* Muncie, IN: Accelerated Development.

Rosenthal, R. (1985). From unconscious experimenter bias to teacher expectancy effects. In J. B. Dusek, V. C. Hall & W. J. Meyer (Eds.), *Teacher expectancies.* Hillsdale, NJ: Erlbaum.

Rosenthal, R. (2003). Covert communication in laboratories, classrooms, and the truly real world. *Current Directions in Psychological Science, 12*(5), 151–154.

Rosier, K. B., & Feld, S. L. (2000). Covenant marriage: A new alternative for traditional families. *Journal of Comparative Family Studies, 31,* 385–394.

Ross, C. A. (1999). Dissociative disorders. In T. Millon, P. H. Blaney, & R. D. Davis (Eds.), *Oxford textbook of psychopathology.* New York: Oxford University Press.

Ross, C. E., & Van Willigen, M. (1997). Education and the subjective quality of life. *Journal of Health & Social Behavior, 38,* 275–297.

Ross, L. D. (1977). The intuitive psychologist and his shortcomings: Distortions in the attribution process. In L. Berkowitz (Ed.), *Advances in experimental social psychology* (Vol. 10). New York: Academic Press.

Ross, L., & Nisbett, R. E. (1991). *The person and the situation: Perspectives of social psychology.* New York: McGraw-Hill.

Ross, L., & Ward, A. (1996). Naive realism: Implications for social conflict and misunderstanding. In T. Brown, E. Reed, & E. Turiel (Eds.), *Values and knowledge.* Hillsdale, NJ: Erlbaum.

Ross, M., & Conway, M. (1986). Remembering one's own past: The construction of personal histories. In R. M. Sorrentino & E. T. Higgins (Eds.), *Handbook of motivation and cognition: Foundations of social behavior.* New York: Guilford Press.

Ross, M., & Wilson, A. E. (2002). It feels like yesterday: Self-esteem, valence of personal past experiences, and judgments of subjective distance. *Journal of Personality and Social Psychology, 82,* 792–803.

Ross, M. W. (2005). Typing, doing, and being: Sexuality and the Internet. *Journal of Sex Research, 42,* 342–352.

Roter, D. L., Hall, J. A., Merisca, R., Nordstrom, B., Cretin, D., & Svarstad, B. (1998). Effectiveness of interventions to promote patient compliance. *Medical Care, 36,* 1138–1161.

Rothblum, E. D., Solomon, L. J., & Albee, G. W. (1986). A sociopolitical perspective on DSM-III. In T. Million & G. L. Klerman (Eds.), *Contemporary directions in psychopathology: Toward the DSM-IV.* New York: Guilford Press.

Rotter, J. B. (1982). *The development and application of social learning theory.* New York: Praeger.

Roughton, B. (2001, May 27). In Europe, workers time off adds up. *The Atlanta Journal-Constitution,* pp. D1–D2.

Rowe, D. (1994). *The limits of family influence: Genes, experience, and behavior.* New York: Guilford.

Rowe, D., & van den Oord, E. J. C. G. (2005). Genetic and environmental influences. In V. A. Derlega, B. A. Winstead, & W. H. Jones (Eds.), *Personality: Contemporary theory and research.* Belmont, CA: Wadsworth.

Rozanski, A., Blumenthal, J. A., & Kaplan, J. (1999). Impact of psychological factors on the pathogenesis of cardiovascular disease and implications for therapy. *Circulation, 99*(16), 2192–2197.

Rozee, P. D., Bateman, P., & Gilmore, T. (1991). The personal perspective of acquaintance rape prevention: A three-tier approach. In A. Parrot & L. Bechhofer (Eds.), *Acquaintance rape: The hidden crime.* New York: Wiley.

Rubenstein, C. M., & Shaver, P. (1982). The experience of loneliness. In L. A. Peplau & D. Perlman (Eds.), *Loneliness: A sourcebook of current theory, research and therapy.* New York: Wiley.

Rubin, R. H. (2001). Alternative lifestyles revisited, or whatever happened to swingers, group marriages, and communes? *Journal of Family Issues, 22,* 711–726.

Rubin, Z., Peplau, L. A., & Hill, C. T. (1981). Loving and leaving: Sex differences in romantic attachments. *Sex Roles, 7,* 821–835.

Rudisch, B., & Nemeroff, C. B. (2003). Epidemiology of comorbid coronary artery disease and depression. *Biological Psychiatry, 54*(3), 227–240.

Rudorfer, M. V., Henry, M. E., & Sackeim, H. A. (2003). Electroconvulsive therapy. In A. Tasman, J. Kay, & J. A. Lieberman (Eds.), *Psychiatry.* New York: Wiley.

Rush, A. J. (1984). Cognitive therapy. In T. B. Karasu (Ed.), *The psychiatric therapies.* Washington, DC: American Psychiatric Association.

Rush, A. J., & Beck, A. T. (2000). Cognitive therapy. In B. J. Sadock & V. A. Sadock (Eds.), *Kaplan and Sadock's comprehensive textbook of psychiatry* (7th ed., Vol. 1). Philadelphia: Lippincott/Williams & Wilkins.

Russell, G. F. M. (1995). Anorexia nervosa through time. In G. Szmukler, C. Dare, & J. Treasure (Eds.), *Handbook of eating disorders: Theory, treatment, and research.* New York: Wiley.

Russell, G. F. M. (1997). The history of bulimia nervosa. In D. M. Garner & P. E. Garfinkel (Eds.), *Handbook of treatment for eating disorders* (2nd ed.). New York: Guilford Press.

Russo, N. F. (1979). Overview: Sex roles, fertility, and the motherhood mandate. *Psychology of Women Quarterly, 4,* 7–15.

Rutledge, T., & Hogan, B. E. (2002). A quantitative review of prospective evidence linking psychological factors with hypertension development. *Psychosomatic Medicine, 64,* 758–766.

Ruzek, J. (2001). *Coping with PTSD and recommended lifestyle changes for PTSD patients.* Retrieved November 28, 2001 from U.S. Department of Veterans Affairs National Center for PTSD Website: http://www.ncptsd.org/facts/treatment/fs_coping.html.

Ryan, C., & Futterman, D. (1997). Lesbian and gay youth: Care and counseling. *Adolescent Medicine, 8,* 221.

Ryan, R. M., & Deci, E. L. (2001). On happiness and human potentials: A review of research on hedonic and eudaimonic well-being. *Annual Review of Psychology, 52,* 141–166.

Rye, M. S., Folck, C. D., Heim, T. A., Olszewski, B. T., Traina, E. (2004). Forgiveness of an ex-spouse: How does it relate to mental health following a divorce? *Journal of Divorce and Remarriage, 41,* 31–51.

Saad, L. (1999, September 3). *American workers generally satisfied, but indicate their jobs leave much to be desired.* Princeton, NJ: Gallup News Service.

Saad, L. (2007). *Americans rate the morality of 16 social issues.* Retrieved June 23, 2007 from http://www.galluppoll.com/content/?ci=27757&p=1.

Sabatelli, R. M., & Ripoll, K. (2004). Variations in marriage over time: An ecological/exchange perspective. In M. Coleman & L. H. Ganong (Eds.), *Handbook of contemporary families: Considering the past, contemplating the future.* Thousand Oaks, CA: Sage.

Sackeim, H. A., Haskett, R. F., Mulsant, B. H., Thase, M. E., Mann, J. J., Pettinati, H. M., Greenberg, R. M., Crowe, R. R., Cooper, T. B., & Prudic, J. (2001). Continuation pharmacotherapy in the prevention of relapse following electroconvulsive therapy: A randomized controlled trial. *Journal of the American Medical Association, 285*(10), 1299–1307.

Sadker, M., & Sadker, D. (1994). *Failing at fairness: How America's schools cheat girls.* New York: Scribners.

Sadler, J. Z. (2005). *Values and psychiatric diagnosis.* New York: Oxford University Press.

Sagiv, L., Roccas, S., & Hazan, O. (2004). Value pathways to well-being: Healthy values, valued goal attainment, and environmental congruence. In P. A. Linley & S. Joseph (Eds.), *Positive psychology in practice.* New York: Wiley.

Sagrestano, L. M., Heavey, C. L., & Christensen, A. (2006). Individual differences versus social structural approaches to explaining demand-withdraw and social influence behaviors. In K. Dindia, & D. J. Canary (Eds.), *Sex differences and similarities in communication.* Mahwah, NJ: Erlbaum.

Saks, A. M. (2006). Multiple predictions and criteria of job search success. *Journal of Vocational Behavior, 68,* 400–415.

Salerno, S. (2005). *Sham: How the self-help movement made America helpless.* New York: Crown Publishers.

Salkovskis, P. M., & Warwick, H. M. C. (2001). Meaning, misinterpretations, and medicine: A cognitive-behavioral approach to understanding health anxiety and hypochondriasis. In V. Starcevic & D. R. Lipsitt (Eds.), *Hypochondriasis: Modern perspectives on an ancient malady.* New York: Oxford University Press.

Salovey, P., & Mayer, J. D. (1990). Emotional intelligence. *Imagination, Cognition, and Personality, 9,* 185–211.

Salovey, P., Mayer, J. D., & Caruso, D. (2002). The positive psychology of emotional intelligence. In C. R. Synder & S. J. Lopez (Eds.), *Handbook of positive psychology.* New York: Oxford University Press.

Salovey, P., Mayer, J. D., & Caruso, D. (2005). The positive psychology of emotional intelligence. In C. R. Snyder & S. J. Lopez (Eds.), *Handbook of positive psychology.* New York: Oxford University Press.

Salovey, P., Rothman, A. J., Detweiler, J. B., & Steward, W. T. (2000). Emotional states and physical health. *American Psychologist, 55*(1), 110–121.

Salthouse, T. A. (2000). Steps toward the explanation of adult age differences in cognition. In T. Perfect & E. Maylor (Eds.), *Theoretical debate in cognitive aging.* Oxford, UK: Oxford University Press.

Salthouse, T. A. (2004). What and when of cognitive aging. *Current Directions in Psychological Science, 13*(4), 140–144.

Salvendy, J. T. (1993). Selection and preparation of patients and organization of the group. In H. I. Kaplan & B. J. Sadock (Eds.), *Comprehensive group psychotherapy.* Baltimore: Williams & Wilkins.

Samberg, E., & Marcus, E. R. (2005). Process, resistance, and interpretation. In E. S. Person, A. M. Cooper, & G. O. Gabbard (Eds.), *Textbook of psychoanalysis.* Washington, DC: American Psychiatric Publishing.

Samovar, L. A., & Porter, R. E. (2004). *Communication between cultures.* Belmont, CA: Wadsworth.

Samovar, L. A., Porter, R. E., & McDaniel, E. R. (2007). *Communication between cultures.* Belmont, CA: Wadsworth.

Samovar, L. A., Porter, R. E., & Stefani, L. A. (1998). *Communication between cultures* (2nd ed.). Belmont, CA: Wadsworth.

Sampson, R. (2003). *Acquaintance rape of college students. Problem-oriented guides for police: Problem specific guides series, No. 17.* Washington, DC: U.S. Department of Justice.

Sanchez, L. M., & Turner, S. M. (2003). Practicing psychology in the era of managed care: Implications for practice and training. *American Psychologist, 58*(2), 116–129.

Sande, M. A., & Ronald, A. (2004). Treatment of HIV/AIDS: Do the dilemmas only increase? *Journal of the American Medical Association, 292*(2), 224–236.

Sanders, G. (2000). Men together: Working with gay couples in contemporary times. In P. Papp (Ed.), *Couples on the fault line.* New York: Guilford Press.

Sanderson, W. C., & Barlow, D. H. (1990). A description of patients diagnosed with DSM-III-R generalized anxiety disorder. *Journal of Nervous and Mental Disease, 178,* 588–591.

Sandin, B., Chorot, P., Santed, M. A., & Valiente, R. M. (2004). Differences in negative life events between patients with anxiety disorders, depression and hypochondriasis. *Anxiety, Stress & Coping: An International Journal, 17*(1), 37–47.

Sandnabba, N. K., & Ahlberg, C. (1999). Parents' attitudes and expectations about children's cross-gender behavior. *Sex Roles, 40*(3–4), 249–263.

Sandoz, J. (2004). Internet addiction. *Annals of the American Psychotherapy Association, 7*(1), 34.

Sanislow, C. A., & Carson, R. C. (2001). Schizophrenia: A critical examination. In P. B. Sutker & H. E. Adams (Eds.), *Comprehensive handbook of psychopathology* (3rd ed.). New York: Kluwer Academic/Plenum.

Santelli, J. S., Morrow, B., Anderson, J. E., & Lindberg, L. D. (2006). Contraceptive use and pregnancy risk among U. S. high school students, 1991–2003. *Perspectives on Sexual and Reproductive Health, 38*(2), 106–111.

Sanz de Acedo, M. L., & Garcia Ganuza, J. M. (2003). Improvement of mental rotation in girls and boys. *Sex Roles, 49*(5–6), 277–286.

Sapolsky, R. M. (2004). *Why zebras don't get ulcers: The acclaimed guide to stress, stress-related diseases, and coping.* New York: Holt.

Sarason, I. G., Johnson, J. H., & Siegel, J. M. (1978). Assessing the impact of life changes: Development of the Life Experiences Survey. *Journal of Consulting and Clinical Psychology, 46,* 932–946.

Sarason, I. G., Pierce, G. R., & Sarason, B. R. (1994). General and specific perceptions of social support. In W. R. Avison & I. H. Gotlib (Eds.), *Stress and mental health: Contemporary issues and prospects for the future.* New York: Plenum.

Sarwer, D. B., Foster, G. D., & Wadden, T. A. (2004). Treatment of obesity I: Adult obesity. In J. K. Thompson (Ed.), *Handbook of eating disorders and obesity.* New York: Wiley.

Savin-Williams, R. C. (2001). *Mom, dad. I'm gay.* Washington, D. C.: American Psychological Association.

Savin-Williams, R. C. (2006). Who's gay? Does it matter? *Current Directions in Psychological Science, 15,* 40–44.

Saxena, S., van Ommeren, M., Tang K. C., & Armstrong, T. P. (2005). Mental health benefits of physical activity. *Journal of Mental Health, 14,* 445–451.

Sayer, L. C. (2005). Gender, time, and inequality: Trends in women's and men's paid work, unpaid work, and free time. *Social Forces, 84,* 285–303.

Sayer, L. C. (2006). Economic aspects of divorce and relationship dissolution. In M. A. Fine & J. H. Harvey (Eds.), *Handbook of divorce and relationship resolution.* Mahwah, NJ: Erlbaum.

Sayers, S. L. (2004). Depression and heart disease: The interrelationship between these two common disorders is complex and requires careful diagnostic and treatment methods. *Psychiatric Annals, 34*(4), 282–288.

Scanzoni, J. (2004). Household diversity: The starting point for healthy families in the new century. In M. Coleman & L. H. Ganong (Eds.), *Handbook of contemporary families: Considering the past, contemplating the future.* Thousand Oaks, CA: Sage.

Schaalma, H. P., Abraham, C., Gillmore, M. R., & Kok, G. (2004). Sex education as health promotion: What does it take? *Archives of Sexual Behavior, 33,*, 259–269.

Schachner, D. A., Shaver, P. R., & Mikulincer, M. (2005). Patterns of nonverbal behavior and sensitivity in the context of attachment relations. *Journal of Nonverbal Behavior, 29*(3), 141–169.

Schachter, S. (1959). *The psychology of affiliation.* Stanford, CA: Stanford University Press.

Schaie, K. W. (1994). The course of adult development. *American Psychologist, 49*(4), 304–313.

Schaninger, C. M., & Buss, W. C. (1986). A longitudinal comparison of consumption and finance handling between happily married and divorced couples. *Journal of Marriage and the Family, 48,* 129–136.

Scheidlinger, S. (1993). History of group psychotherapy. In H. I. Kaplan & B. J. Sadock (Eds.), *Comprehensive group psychotherapy.* Baltimore: Williams & Wilkins.

Scheier, M. F., & Carver, C. S. (1985). Optimism, coping, and health: Assessment and implications of generalized outcome expectancies. *Health Psychology, 4,* 219–247.

Scheier, M. F., Carver, C. S., & Bridges, M. W. (2001). Optimism, pessimism, and psychological well-being. In E. C. Chang (Ed.), *Optimism and pessimism: Implications for theory, research, and practice.* Washington, DC: American Psychological Association.

Scheier, M. F., Matthews, K. A., Owens, J. F., Magovern, G. J., Sr., Lefebvre, R. C., Abbott, R. A., & Carver, C. S. (1989). Dispositional optimism and recovery from coronary artery bypass surgery: The beneficial effects on physical and psychological well-being. *Journal of Personality and Social Psychology, 57,* 1024–1040.

Scherwitz, L., Perkins, L., Chesney, M., & Hughes, G. (1991). Cook-Medley Hostility Scale and subsets: Relationship to demographic and psychosocial characteristics in young adults in the CARDIA study. *Psychosomatic Medicine, 53,* 36–49.

Schiappa, E., Gregg, P. B., & Hewes, D. E. (2006). Can one TV show make difference? Will & Grace and the parasocial contact hypothesis. *Journal of Homosexuality, 51*(4), 15–37.

Schiffman, J., Ekstrom, M., LaBrie, J., Schulsinger, F., Sorenson, H., & Mednick, S. (2002). Minor physical anomalies and schizophrenia spectrum disorders: A prospective investigation. *American Journal of Psychiatry, 159,* 238–243.

Schilit, W. K. (1987). Thinking about managing your time. In A. D. Timpe (Ed.), *The management of time.* New York: Facts On File.

Schimel, J., Simon, L., Greenberg, J., Pyszczynski, T., Solomon, S., Waxmonsky, J., & Arndt, J. (1999). Stereotypes and terror management: Evidence that mortality salience enhances stereotypic thinking and preferences. *Journal of Personality and Social Psychology, 77*(5), 905–926.

Schirmer, L. L., & Lopez, F. G. (2001). Probing the social support and work strain relationship among adult workers: Contributions of adult attachment orientations. *Journal of Vocational Behavior, 59*(1), 17–33.

Schlegel, A., & Barry, H., III. (1991). *Adolescence: An anthropological inquiry.* New York: Free Press.

Schlenger, W. E., Kulka, R. A., Fairbank, J. A., Hough, R. L., et al. (1992). The prevalence of post-traumatic stress disorder in the Vietnam generation: A multimethod, multisource assessment of psychiatric disorder. *Journal of Traumatic Stress, 5,* 333–363.

Schlenker, B. R. (2003). Self-presentation. In M.R. Leary & J. P. Tangney (Eds.), *Handbook of self and identity.* New York: Guilford.

Schlenker, B. R., & Pontari, B. A. (2000). The strategic control of information: Impression management and self-presentation in daily life. In A. Tesser, R. B. Felson, & J. M. Suls (Eds.), *Psychological perspectives on self and identity.* Washington, DC: American Psychological Association.

Schmidt, N. B., Zvolensky, M. J., & Maner, J. K. (2006). Anxiety sensitivity: Prospective prediction of panic attacks and Axis I pathology. *Journal of Psychiatric Research, 40,* 691–699.

Schmitz, J. M., & DeLaune, K. A. (2005). Nicotine. In J. H. Lowinson, P. Ruiz, R. B. Millman, & J. G. Langrod (Eds.), *Substance abuse: A comprehensive textbook.* Philadelphia: Lippincott/Williams & Wilkins.

Schneider, D. J. (2004). *The psychology of stereotyping.* New York: Guilford.

Schneider, F., & Deldin, P. J. (2001). Genetics and schizophrenia. In P. B. Sutker & H. E. Adams (Eds.), *Comprehensive handbook of psychopathology* (3rd ed.) New York: Kluwer Academic/Plenum.

Schneider, J. P. (2003). The impact of compulsive cybersex behaviors on the family. *Sexual and Relationship Therapy, 18*(3), 329–354.

Schneider, T. R. (2004). The role of neuroticism on psychological and physiological stress responses. *Journal of Experimental Social Psychology, 40,* 795–804.

Schooler, D., Ward, L. M., Merriwether, A., & Caruthers, A. (2004). Who's that girl: Television's role in the body image development of young white and black women. *Psychology of Women Quarterly, 28,* 38–47.

Schoon, I., & Parsons, S. (2002). Teenage aspirations for future careers and occupational outcomes. *Journal of Vocational Behavior, 60*(2), 262–288.

Schottenbauer, M. A., Arnkoff, D. B., Glass, C. R., & Gray, S. H. (2006). Psychotherapy for PTSD in the community: Reported prototypical treatments. *Clinical Psychology & Psychotherapy, 13*(2), 108–122.

Schramm, D. G., Marshall, J. P., Harris, V. W., & Lee, T. R. (2005). After "I do": The newlywed transition. *Marriage & Family Review, 38,* 45–67.

Schraw, G., Wadkins, T., & Olafson, L. (2007). Doing the things we do: A grounded theory of academic procrastination. *Journal of Educational Psychology, 99*(1), 12–25.

Schreiber, F. R. (1973). *Sybil.* New York: Warner.

Schroeder, D. H., & Costa, P. T., Jr. (1984). Influence of life events stress on physical illness: Substantive effects or methodological flaws? *Journal of Personality and Social Psychology, 46,* 853–863.

Schuckit, M. A. (2000). Alcohol-related disorders. In B. J. Sadock & V. A. Sadock (Eds.), *Kaplan and Sadock's comprehensive textbook of psychiatry* (7th ed.). Philadelphia: Lippincott/Williams & Wilkins.

Schunk, D. H. (2003). Self-efficacy for reading and writing: Influence of modeling, goal setting, and self-evaluation. *Reading and Writing Quarterly: Overcoming Learning Difficulties, 19*(2), 159–172.

Schutte, N. S., Malouff, J. M., Thorsteinsson, E. B., Bhullar, N., & Rooke, S. E. (2007). A meta-analytic investigation of the relationship between emotional intelligence and health. *Personality and Individual Differences, 42,* 921–933.

Schwartz, B. (2004). *The paradox of choice: Why more is less.* New York: Ecco.

Schwartz, J. E., Neale, J., Marco, C., Shiffman, S. S., & Stone, A. A. (1999). Does trait coping exist? A momentary assessment approach to the evaluation of traits. *Journal of Personality and Social Psychology, 77*(2), 360–369.

Schwartz, J. P., Waldo, M., & Higgins, A. J. (2004). Attachment styles: Relationship to masculine gender role conflict in college men. *Psychology of Men & Masculinity, 5*(2), 143–146.

Schwartz, L., Slater, M. A., & Birchler, G. R. (1994). Interpersonal stress and pain behaviors in patients with chronic pain. *Journal of Consulting and Clinical Psychology, 62,* 861–864.

Schwarz, N., & Strack, F. (1999). Reports of subjective well-being: Judgmental processes and their methodological implications. In D. Kahneman, E. Diener, & N. Schwarz (Eds.), *Well-being: The foundations of hedonic psychology.* New York: Russell Sage Foundation.

Schwarzer, R., & Schulz, U. (2003). Stressful life events. In A. M. Nezu, C. M. Nezu, & P. A. Geller (Eds.), *Handbook of psychology: Vol. 9. Health psychology.* New York: Wiley.

Scroppo, J. C., Drob, S. L., Weinberger, J. L., & Eagle, P. (1998). Identifying dissociative identity disorder: A self-report and projective study. *Journal of Abnormal Psychology, 107,* 272–284.

Scully, J. A., Tosi, H., & Banning, K. (2000). Life event checklists: Revisiting the social readjustment rating scale after 30 years. *Educational & Psychological Measurement, 60*(6), 864–876.

Seabrook, R., Brown, G. D. A., & Solity, J. E. (2005). Distributed and massed practice: From laboratory to classroom. *Applied Cognitive Psychology, 19*(1), 107–122.

Searle, A., & Bennett, P. (2001). Psychological factors and inflammatory bowel disease: A review of a decade of literature. *Psychology, Health and Medicine, 6*(2), 121–135.

Seccombe, K. (1987). Children: Their impact on the elderly in declining health. *Research on Aging, 9,* 312–326.

Seccombe, K. (2001). Families in poverty in the 1990s: Trends, causes, consequences, and lessons learned. In R. M. Milardo (Ed.), *Understanding families into the new millennium: A decade in review.* Minneapolis: National Council on Family Relations.

Sedikides, C. (1993). Assessment, enhancement, and verification determinants of the self-evaluation process. *Journal of Personality and Social Psychology, 65*(2), 317–338.

Sedikides, C. (1995). Central and peripheral self-conceptions are differently influenced by mood: Tests of the differential sensitivity hypothesis. *Journal of Personality and Social Psychology, 69,* 759–777.

Sedikides, C., & Strube, M. J. (1997). Self-evaluation: To thine own self be good, to thine own self be sure, to thine own self be true, and to thine own self be better. In M. P. Zanna (Ed.), *Advances in experimental social psychology* (Vol. 29). New York: Academic Press.

Segal, M. W. (1974). Alphabet and attraction: An unobtrusive measure of the effect of propinquity in a field setting. *Journal of Personality and Social Psychology, 30,* 654–657.

Segall, A. (1997). Sick role concepts and health behavior. In D. S. Gochman (Ed.), *Handbook of health behavior research I: Personal and social determinants.* New York : Plenum Press.

Segerstrom, S. C., Taylor, S. E., Kemeny, M. E., & Fahey, J. L. (1998). Optimism is associated with mood, coping and immune change in response to stress. *Journal of Personality and Social Psychology, 74,* 1646–1655.

Self, D. W. (1998). Neural substrates of drug craving and relapse in drug addiction. *Annals of Medicine, 30,* 379–389.

Seligman, M. E. P. (1971). Phobias and preparedness. *Behavior Therapy, 2,* 307–321.

Seligman, M. E. P. (1974). Depression and learned helplessness. In R. J. Friedman & M. M. Katz (Eds.), *The psychology of depression: Contemporary theory and research.* New York: Wiley.

Seligman, M. E. P. (1990). *Learned optimism: How to change your mind and your life.* New York: Pocket Books.

Seligman, M. E. P. (1991). *Learned optimism.* New York: Alfred A. Knopf.

Seligman, M. E. P. (1992). *Helplessness: On depression, development, and death.* New York: Freeman.

Seligman, M. E. P. (1994). *What you can change and what you can't.* New York: Knopf.

Seligman, M. E. P. (1995). The effectiveness of psychotherapy. *American Psychologist, 50,* 965–974.

Seligman, M. E. P. (2003). The past and future of positive psychology. In C. L. M. Keyes & J. Haidt (Eds.), *Flourishing: Positive psychology and the life well-lived.* Washington, DC: American Psychological Association.

Seligman, M. E. P., & Csikszentmihalyi, M. (2000). Positive psychology: An introduction. *American Psychologist, 55*(1), 5–14.

Seligman, M. E. P., & Isaacowitz, D. M. (2000). Learned helplessness. In G. Fink (Ed.), *Encyclopedia of stress* (Vol. 2). San Diego: Academic Press.

Seligman, M. E. P., & Levant, R. F. (1998). Managed care policies rely on inadequate science. *Professional Psychology: Research and Practice, 29,* 211–212.

Seligman, M. E. P., Schulman, P., DeRubeis, R. J., & Hollon, S. D. (1999). The prevention of depression and anxiety. *Prevention and Treatment,* http://journals.apa.org/prevention/volume2/pre0020008a.html

Sellers, R. M., Copeland-Linder, N., Martin, P. P., & Lewis, R. L. (2006). Racial identity matters: The relationship between racial discrimination and psychological functioning in African American adolescents. *Journal of Research on Adolescence, 16,* 187–216.

Seltzer, J. A. (2001). Families formed outside of marriage. In R. M. Milardo (Ed.), *Understanding families into the new millennium: A decade in review.* Minneapolis: National Council on Family Relations.

Seltzer, J. A. (2004). Cohabitation and family change. In M. Coleman & L. H. Ganong (Eds.), *Handbook of contemporary families: Considering the past, contemplating the future.* Thousand Oaks, CA: Sage.

Selye, H. (1936). A syndrome produced by diverse nocuous agents. *Nature, 138,* 32.

Selye, H. (1956). *The stress of life.* New York: McGraw-Hill.

Selye, H. (1974). *Stress without distress.* New York: Lippincott.

Selye, H. (1982). History and present status of the stress concept. In L. Goldberger & S. Breznitz (Eds.), *Handbook of stress: Theoretical and clinical aspects.* New York: Free Press.

Semans, J. H. (1956). Premature ejaculation: A new approach. *Journal of Southern Medicine, 79,* 353–361.

Senecal, C., Lavoie, K., & Koestner, R. (1997). Trait and situational factors in procrastination: An interactional model. *Journal of Social Behavior and Personality, 12,* 889–903.

Serido, J., Almeida, D. M., & Wethington, E. (2004). Chronic stressors and daily hassles: Unique and interactive relationships with psychological distress. *Journal of Health and Social Behavior, 45,* 17–33.

Servan-Schreiber, D., Kolb, R., & Tabas, G. (1999). The somatizing patient. *Primary Care, 26*(2), 225–242.

Servin, A., Nordenstrom, A., Larsson, A., & Bohlin, G. (2003). Prenatal androgens and gender-typed behavior: A study of girls with mild and server forms of congenital hyperplasia. *Developmental Psychology, 39,* 440–450.

Sesso, H. D., Buring, J. E., Rifai, N., Blake, G. J., Gaziano, J. M., & Ridker, P. M. (2003). C-reactive protein and the risk of developing hypertension. *Journal of the American Medical Association, 290*(22), 2945–2951.

Seta, J. J., Seta, C. E., & McElroy, T. (2002). Strategies for reducing the stress of negative life experiences: An averaging/summation analysis. *Personality and Social Psychology Bulletin, 28*(11), 1574–1585.

Settersten, R. A., & Hagestad, G. (1996). What's the latest? Cultural deadlines for educational and work transitions. *Gerontologist, 36,* 602–613.

Settles, I. H., Cortina, L. M., Malley, J., & Stewart, A. J. (2006). The climate for women in academic science: The good, the bad, and changeable. *Psychology of Women Quarterly, 30,* 47–58.

Shaffer, D. R. (1989). *Developmental psychology: Childhood and adolescence.* Pacific Grove, CA: Brooks/Cole.

Shah, J., & Higgins, E. T. (2001). Regulatory concerns and appraisal efficiency: The general impact of promotion and prevention. *Journal of Personality and Social Psychology, 80,* 693–705.

Shalev, A. Y. (2001). Posttraumatic stress disorder. *Primary Psychiatry, 8*(10), 41–46.

Shapira-Berman, O. (2004). Why do married mothers choose to do all house tasks? Re-examining feminist agenda and its implications for therapy. *Journal of Feminist Family Therapy, 16*(3), 51–70.

Shapiro, A. F., Gottman, J. M., & Carrère. (2000). The baby and marriage: Identifying factors that buffer against decline in marital satisfaction after the first baby arrives. *Journal of Family Psychology, 14*(1), 59–70.

Shapiro, D. H., Jr. (1984). Overview: Clinical and physiological comparison of meditation with other self-control strategies. In D. H. Shapiro, Jr. & R. N. Walsh (Eds.), *Meditation: Classic and contemporary perspectives.* New York: Aldine.

Shapiro, S. L., Schwartz, G. E. R., & Santerre, C. (2002). Meditation and positive psychology. In C. R. Snyder & S. J. Lopez (Eds.), *Handbook of positive psychology.* New York: Oxford University Press.

Shavelson, R. J., Hubner, J. J., & Stanton, G. C. (1976). Self-concept: Validation of construct interpretations. *Review of Educational Research, 46,* 407–411.

Shaver, P. R., & Brennan, K. A. (1992). Attachment styles and the "Big Five" personality traits: Their connections with each other and with romantic relationship outcomes. *Personality and Social Psychology Bulletin, 18,* 536–545.

Shaver, P. R., & Hazan, C. (1993). Adult attachment: Theory and research. In W. Jones & D. Perlman (Eds.), *Advances in personal relationships* (Vol. 4). London: Jessica Kingsley.

Shaver, P. R., & Mikulincer, M. (2006). Attachment theory, individual psychodynamics, and relationship functioning. In A. L. Vangelisti & D. Perlman (Eds.), *The Cambridge handbook of personal relationships.* New York: Cambridge University Press.

Shaver, P. R., Wu, S., & Schwartz, J. C. (1991). Cross-cultural similarities and differences in emotion and its representation: A prototype approach. In M. S. Clark (Ed.), *Review of personality and social psychology* (Vol. 13). Newbury Park, CA: Sage.

Shaw, L. H., & Gant, L. M. (2002). In defense of the Internet: The relationship between Internet communication and depression, loneliness, self-esteem, and perceived social support. *CyberPsychology, 5*(2), 157–171.

Shear, M. K., & Beidel, D. C. (1998). Psychotherapy in the overall management strategy for social anxiety disorder. *Journal of Clinical Psychiatry, 59,* 39–46.

Sheehan, S. (1982). *Is there no place on earth for me?* Boston: Houghton Mifflin.

Sheese, B. E., Brown, E. L., & Graziano, W. G. (2004). Emotional expression in cyberspace: Searching for moderators of the Pennebacker disclosure effect via e-mail. *Health Psychology, 23,* 457–464.

Sheldon, J. P. (2004). Gender stereotypes in educational software for young children. *Sex Roles, 51,* 433–444.

Sheldon, K. M., & Kasser, T. (2001a). Getting older, getting better? Personal strivings and psychological maturity across the life span. *Developmental Psychology, 37*(4), 491–501.

Sheldon, K. M., & Kasser, T. (2001b). Goals, congruence, and positive well-being: New empirical support for humanistic theories. *Journal of Humanistic Psychology, 41*(1), 30–50.

Shelton, R. C., & Lester, N. (2006). Selective serotonin reuptake inhibitors and newer antidepressants. In D. J. Stein, D. J. Kupfer, & A. F. Schatzberg (Eds.), *Textbook of mood disorders.* Washington, DC: American Psychiatric Publishing.

Shepperd, J. A., & McNulty, J. K. (2002). The affective consequences of expected and unexpected outcomes. *Psychological Science, 13,* 85–88.

Sher, L. (2003). Daily hassles, cortisol, and depression. *Australian and New Zealand Journal of Psychiatry, 37*(3), 383–384.

Sher, L., Kandel, I., & Merrick, J. (2006). Editorial: Alcohol and suicidal behavior in adolescents: A medical and social problem. *International Journal of Adolescent Medicine and Health, 18,* 1–2.

Sher, L., & Mann, J. J. (2003). Psychiatric pathophysiology: Mood disorders. In A. Tasman, J. Kay, & J. A. Lieberman (Eds.), *Psychiatry.* New York: Wiley.

Sher, T. G., & Baucom, D. H. (1993). Marital communication: Differences among maritally distressed, depressed, and nondistressed-nondepressed couples. *Journal of Family Psychology, 7,* 148–153.

Sherif, M. (1936). *The psychology of social norms.* New York: Harper.

Sherman, A. M., de Vries, B., & Lansford, J. E. (2000). Friendship in childhood and adulthood: Lessons across the life span. *International Journal of Aging and Human Development, 51*(1), 31–51.

Shike, M. (1999). Diet and lifestyle in the prevention of colorectal cancer: An overview. *American Journal of Medicine, 106*(1A), 11S–15S, 50S–51S.

Shiota, M. N. (2006). Silver linings and candles in the dark: Differences among positive coping strategies in predicting subjective well-being. *Emotion, 6,* 335–339.

Shneidman, E. S. (1985). *At the point of no return.* New York: Wiley.

Shneidman, E. S., Farberow, N. L., & Litman, R. E. (1994). *The psychology of suicide: A clinician's guide to evaluation and treatment.* Northvale, NJ: J. Aronson.

Shobe, K. K., & Schooler, J. W. (2001). Discovering fact and fiction: Case-based analyses of authentic and fabricated discovered memories of abuse. In G. M. Davies & T. Dalgleish (Eds.), *Recovered memories: Seeking the middle ground.* Chichester, England: Wiley.

Shoda, Y., Mischel, W., & Peake, P. K. (1990). Predicting adolescent cognitive and self-regulatory competencies from preschool delay of gratification: Identifying diagnostic conditions. *Developmental Psychology, 26,* 978–986.

Shors, T. J. (2004). Learning during stressful times. *Learning and Memory, 11*(2), 137–144.

Shotland, R. L., & Hunter, B. A. (1995). Women's "token resistant" and compliant sexual behaviors are related to uncertain sexual intentions and rape. *Personality and Social Psychology Bulletin, 21,* 226–236.

Shuchter, S. R., & Zisook, S. (1993). The course of normal grief. In M. S. Stroebe, W. Stroebe, & R. O. Hansson (Eds.), *Handbook of bereavement: Theory, research, and intervention.* Cambridge, England: Cambridge University Press.

Shulman, R. B. (2001). Response versus remission in the treatment of depression: Understanding residual symptoms. *Primary Psychiatry, 8*(5), 28–30, 34.

Shuval, J. T. (1993). Migration and stress. In L. Goldberger & S. Breznitz (Eds.), *Handbook of stress: Theoretical and clinical aspects* (2nd ed.). New York: Free Press.

Sidanius, J., & Pratto, P. (1999). *Social dominance: An intergroup theory of social hierarchy and oppression.* New York: Cambridge University Press.

Sidanius, J., & Pratto, P. (2004). Ethnic enclaves and the dynamics of social identity on the college campus: The good, the bad, and the ugly. *Journal of Personality and Social Psychology, 87,* 96–110.

Sidanius, J., Van Laar, C., & Levin, S. (2004). Ethnic enclaves and the dynamics of social identity on the college campus: The good, the bad, and the ugly. *Journal of Personality and Social Psychology, 87,* 96–110.

Siddiqui, R. N., & Pandey, J. (2003). Coping with environmental stressors by urban slum dwellers. *Enviroment and Behavior, 35,* 589–604.

Siebert, A. (1995). *Student success: How to succeed in college and still have time for your friends.* Fort Worth, TX: Harcourt Brace.

SIECUS. (2004, Fall). SIECUS Fact Sheet: Public support for comprehensive sexuality education. Retrieved January 25, 2005 from http://63.73.227.69/Pubs/Fact/Fact0017.html.

Siegel, O. (1982). Personality development in adolescence. In B. B. Wolman (Ed.), *Handbook of developmental psychology.* Englewood Cliffs, NJ: Prentice-Hall.

Siegler, I. C., & Brummett, B. H. (2000). Associations among NEO personality assessments and well-being at mid-life: Facet-level analyses. *Psychology & Aging, 15,* 710–714.

Siegler, I. C., Bosworth, H. B., & Poon, L. W. (2003). Disease, health and aging. In R. M. Lerner, M.A. Easterbrooks, & J. Mistry (Eds.), *Handbook of psychology: Vol. 6. Developmental psychology.* New York: Wiley.

Siegler, I. C., Peterson, B. L., Barefoot, J. C., & Williams, R. B. (1992). Hostility during late adolescence predicts coronary risk factors at mid-life. *American Journal of Epidemiology, 136*(2), 146–154.

Signorielli, N., & Bacue, A. (1999). Recognition and respect: A content analysis of prime-time television characters. *Sex Roles, 40*(7/8), 527–544.

Silberman, E. K. (1998). Psychiatrists' and internists' beliefs. *Primary Psychiatry, 5,* 65–71.

Silke, A. (2003). *Terrorists, victims, and society: Psychological perspectives on terrorism and its consequences.* New York: Wiley.

Silver, H., Feldman, P., Bilker, W., & Gur, R. C. (2003). Working memory deficit as a core neuropsychological dysfunction in schizophrenia. *American Journal of Psychiatry, 160,* 1809–1816.

Silver, M. (2002, June 10). What they're seeing. *U.S. News & World Report,* p. 41.

Silverman, P. R., & Worden, J. M. (1992). Children's reactions in the early months after the death of a parent. *American Journal of Orthopsychiatry, 62,* 93–104.

Simmons, T., & Dye, J. L. (2004). What has happened to the median age at first marriage data? Paper presented at the meeting of the American Sociological Association, San Francisco, CA.

Simmons, T., & O'Connell, M. (2003). *Married-couple and unmarried-partner households: 2000. U.S. Census Bureau, Census 2000 Special Reports.* Washington, DC: U.S. Department of Commerce.

Simon, G. E., Savarino, J., Operskalski, B., & Wang, P. S. (2006). Suicide risk during antidepressant treatment. *American Journal of Psychiatry, 163,* 41–47.

Simonton, D. K. (1997). Creative productivity: A predictive and explanatory model of career trajectories and landmarks. *Psychological Review, 104*(1), 66–89.

Sinclair, R. C., Mark, M. M., & Clore, G. L. (1994). Mood-related persuasion depends on (mis)attributions. *Social Cognition, 12,* 309–326.

Singer, A. R., Cassin, S. E., & Dobson, K. S. (2005). The role of gender in the career aspirations of professional psychology graduates: Are there more similarities than differences? *Canadian Psychology, 46*(4), 215–222.

Singh, D. (1993). Adaptive significance of female physical attractiveness: Role of waist-to-hip ratio. *Journal of Personality and Social Psychology, 65,* 293–307.

Singh, D. (1995). Female judgment of male attractiveness and desirability for relationships: Role of waist-to-hip ratio and financial status. *Journal of Personality and Social Psychology, 69,* 1089–1101.

Sinkkonen, J., Anttila, R., & Siimes, M. A. (1998). Pubertal maturation and changes in self-image in early adolescent Finnish boys. *Journal of Youth and Adolescence, 27,* 209–218.

Sinnott, J. D. (1989). A model for solution of ill-structured problems: Implications for everyday and abstract problem solving. In J. D. Sinnott (Ed.), *Everyday problem solving: Theory and application.* New York: Praeger.

Sirois, F. M., Melia-Gordon, M. L., & Pychyl, T. A. (2003). "I'll look after my health, later": An investigation of procrastination and health. *Personality and Individual Differences, 35*(5), 1167–1184.

Skinner, A. E. G. (2001). Recovered memories of abuse: Effects on the individual. In G. M. Davies & T. Dalgleish (Eds.), *Recovered memories: Seeking the middle ground.* Chichester, England: Wiley.

Skinner, B. F. (1953). *Science and human behavior.* New York: Macmillan.

Skinner, B. F. (1974). *About behaviorism.* New York: Knopf.

Skinner, B. F. (1987). Whatever happened to psychology as the science of behavior? *American Psychologist, 42,* 780–786.

Skinner, B. F. (1990). Can psychology be a science of mind? *American Psychologist, 45,* 1206–1210.

Skinner, E. A., Edge, K., Altman, J., & Sherwood, H. (2003). Searching for the structure of coping: A review and critique of category systems for classifying ways of coping. *Psychological Bulletin, 129,*216–269.

Skinner, N. F. (2003). Birth order effects in dominance: Failure to support Sulloway's view. *Psychological Reports, 92,* 387–388.

Skinner, P. H., & Shelton, R. L. (1985). *Speech, language, and hearing: Normal processes and disorders* (2nd ed.). New York: Wiley.

Skolnick, P. (2003). Psychiatric pathophysiology: Anxiety disorders. In A. Tasman, J. Kay, & J. A. Lieberman (Eds.), *Psychiatry.* New York: Wiley.

Skowronski, J. J., & Carlston, D. E. (1989). Negativity and extremity biases in impression formation: A review of explanation. *Psychological Review, 105,* 131–142.

Skowronski, J. J., & Carlston, D. E. (1992). Caught in the act: When impressions are based on highly diagnostic information behaviours are resistant to contradiction. *European Journal of Social Psychology, 22,* 435–452.

Slashinki, M. J., Coker, A. L., & Davis, K. E. (2003). Physical aggression, forced sex, and stalking victimization by a dating partner: An analysis of the National Violence Against Women Survey. *Violence & Victims, 18*(6), 595–617.

Slaski, M., & Cartwright, S. (2003). Emotional intelligence training and its implications for stress, health and performance. *Stress and Health: Journal of the International Society for the Investigation of Stress, 19*(4), 233–239.

Slavney, P. R. (1990). *Perspectives on hysteria.* Baltimore: John Hopkins University Press.

Sloan, D. M., & Marx, B. P. (2004). A closer examination of the structured written disclosure procedure. *Journal of Consulting and Clinical Psychology, 72*(2), 165–175.

Slof-Op't Landt, M. C. T., van Furth, E. F., Meulenbelt, I., Slagboom, P. E., Bartels, M., Boomsma, D. I., & Bulik, C. M. (2005). Eating disorders: From twin studies to candidate genes and beyond. *Twin Research and Human Genetics, 8,* 467–482.

Slonim-Nevo, V., & Al-Krenawi, A. (2006). Success and failure among polygamous families: The experience of wives, husbands, and children. *Family Process, 45,* 311–330.

Slovic, P., Fischhoff, B., & Lichtenstein, S. (1982). Facts versus fears: Understanding perceived risk. In D. Kahneman, P. Slovic, & A. Tversky (Eds.), *Judgment under uncertainty: Heuristics and biases.* Cambridge, England: Cambridge University Press.

Smiler, A. P. (2004). Thirty years after the discovery of gender: Psychological concepts and measures of masculinity. *Sex Roles, 50*(1–2), 15–26.

Smith, A. K. (2000, November 6). Charting your own course. *U.S. News & World Report,* 56–60, 62, 64–65.

Smith, C. A., & Lazarus, R. S. (1993). Appraisal components, core relational themes, and the emotions. *Cognition and Emotion, 7,* 233–269.

Smith, D. A. (1999). The end of theoretical orientations? *Applied & Preventative Psychology, 8,* 269–280.

Smith, D. M., & Gates, G. J. (2001) *Gay and lesbian families in the United States: Same-sex unmarried partner households: Preliminary analysis of 2000 U.S. census data, a human rights campaign report* [Web Page]. URL www.hrc.org.

Smith, D. M., Langa, K. M., Kabeto, M. U., & Ubel, P. A. (2005). Health, wealth, and happiness: Financial resources buffer subjective well-being after the onset of a disability. *Psychological Science, 16,* 663–666.

Smith, G., Bartlett, A., & King, M. (2004). Treatments of homosexuality in Britain since the 1950s—an oral history: The experience of patients. *BMJ USA, 4,* 143–144.

Smith, G. S., Branas, C. C., & Miller, T. R. (1999). Fatal nontraffic injuries involving alcohol: A meta-analysis. *Annals of Emergency Medicine, 33*(6), 659–668.

Smith, J. C. (1975). Meditation and psychotherapy: A review of the literature. *Psychological Bulletin, 32,* 553–564.

Smith, M., & Pazder, L. (1980). *Michelle remembers.* New York: Pocket Books.

Smith, M. L., & Glass, G. V. (1977). Meta-analysis of psychotherapy outcome studies. *American Psychologist, 32,* 752–760.

Smith, P. B., & Bond, M. H. (1999). *Social psychology across cultures.* Boston: Allyn & Bacon.

Smith, R. E. (1989). Effects of coping skills training on generalized self-efficacy and locus of control. *Journal of Personality and Social Psychology, 56,* 228–233.

Smith, T. W. (1999). *The emerging 21st century American family.* University of Chicago: National Opinion Research Center.

Smith, T. W. (2003). Hostility and health: Current status of a psychosomatic hypothesis. In P. Salovey & A. J. Rothman (Eds.), *Social psychology of health.* New York: Psychology Press.

Smith, T. W. (2006). Personality as risk and resilience in physical health. *Current Directions in Psychological Science, 15,* 227–231.

Smith, T. W., & Gallo, L. C. (1999). Hostility and cardiovascular reactivity during marital interaction. *Psychosomatic Medicine, 61,* 436–445.

Smith, T. W., & Gallo, L. C. (2001). Personality traits as risk factors for physical illness. In A. Baum, T. A. Revenson, & J. E. Singer (Eds.), *Handbook of health psychology.* Mahwah, NJ: Erlbaum.

Smith, T. W., Glazer, K., & Ruiz, J. M. (2004). Hostility, anger, aggressiveness, and coronary heart disease: An interpersonal perspective on personality, emotion, and health. *Journal of Personality, 72,* 1217–1270.

Smith, T. W., Pope, M. K., Sanders, J. D., Allred, K. D., & O'Keefe, J. L. (1988). Cynical hostility at home and work: Psychosocial vulnerability across domains. *Journal of Research in Personality, 22,* 525–548.

Smith, W. P., Compton, W. C., & West, W. B. (1995). Meditation as an adjunct to a happiness enhancement program. *Journal of Clinical Psychology, 51,* 269–273.

Smock, P. J. (2000). Cohabitation in the United States: An appraisal of research themes, findings, and implications. *Annual Review of Sociology, 26,* 1–20.

Smock, P. J., Manning, W. D., & Gupta, S. (1999). The effect of marriage and divorce on women's economic well-being. *American Sociological Review, 64,* 794–812.

Smolak, L. (2006). Body image. In J. Worrell & C. D. Goodheart (Eds.), *Handbook of girls' and women's psychological health.* New York: Oxford University Press.

Smolak, L., & Murnen, S. K. (2001). Gender and eating problems. In R. H. Striegel-Moore & L. Smolak (Eds.), *Eating disorders: Innovative directions in research and practice.* Washington, DC: American Psychological Association.

Smoll, F. L., & Schutz, R. W. (1990). Quantifying gender differences in physical performance: A developmental perspective. *Developmental Psychology, 26,* 360–369.

Smyth, J., Litcher, L., Hurewitz, A., & Stone, A. (2001). Relaxation training and cortisol secretion in adult asthmatics. *Journal of Health Psychology, 6*(2), 217–227.

Smyth, J. M., & Pennebaker, J. W. (1999). Sharing one's story: Translating emotional experiences into words as a coping tool. In C. R. Snyder (Ed.), *Coping: The psychology of what works.* New York: Oxford Univer-sity Press.

Smyth, J. M., & Pennebaker, J. W. (2001). What are the health effects of disclosure? In A. Baum, T. A. Revenson, & J. E. Singer (Eds.), *Handbook of health psychology.* Mahwah, NJ: Erlbaum.

Snowden, L. R., & Yamada, A. (2005). Cultural differences in access to care. *Annual Review of Clinical Psychology, 1,* 143–166.

Snowdon, D. (2001). *Aging with grace: What the nun study teaches us about leading longer, healthier, and more meaningful lives.* New York: Bantam Books.

Snyder, M. (1979). Self-monitoring processes. In L. Berkowitz (Ed.), *Advances in experimental social psychology* (Vol. 12). New York: Academic Press.

Snyder, M. (1986). *Public appearances/Private realities: The psychology of self-monitoring.* New York: Freeman.

Snyder, M., & Swann, W. B., Jr. (1978). Hypothesis testing processes in social interaction. *Journal of Personality and Social Psychology, 36*(11), 1202–1212.

Sobal, J. (1995). Social influences on body weight. In K. D. Brownell & C. G. Fairburn (Eds.), *Eating disorders and obesity: A comprehensive handbook.* New York: Guilford Press.

Solberg, E. C., Diener, E., & Robinson, M. (2004). Why are materialists less satisfied? In T. Kasser & A. D. Kanner (Eds.). *Psychology and consumer culture: The struggle for a good life in a materialistic world.* Washington, DC: American Psychological Association.

Solberg, E. C., Diener, E., Wirtz, D., Lucas, R. E., & Oishi, S. (2002). Wanting, having, and satisfaction: Examining the role of desire discrepancies in satisfaction with income. *Journal of Personality and Social Psychology, 83*(3), 725–734.

Solms, M. (2004). Freud returns. *Scientific American, 290*(5), 83–88.

Solomon, S., Greenberg, J. L., & Pyszczynski, T A. (1991). A terror management theory of social behavior: The psychological functions of self-esteem and cultural worldviews. In M. Zanna (Ed.), *Advances in experimental social psychology* (Vol. 24). Orlando, FL: Academic Press.

Solomon, S., Greenberg, J., & Pyszczynski, T. (2004a). The cultural animal: Twenty years of terror management. In J. Greenberg, S. L. Koole, & T. Pyszczynski (Eds.), *Handbook of experimental existential psychology.* New York: Guilford Press.

Solomon, S., Greenberg, J., & Pyszczynski, T. (2004b). Lethal consumption: Death-denying materialism. In T. Kasser, & A. D. Kanner (Eds.), *Psychology and consumer culture: The struggle for a good life in a materialistic world.* Washington, DC: American Psychological Association.

Solomon, S. E., Rothblum, E. D., & Balsam, K. F. (2004). Pioneers in partnership: Lesbian and gay male couples in civil unions compared with those not in civil unions and married heterosexual siblings. *Journal of Family Psychology, 18,* 275–286.

Solowij, N., Stephens, R. S., Roffman, R. A., Babor, T., Kadden, R., Miller, M., Christiansen. K., McRee, B., & Vendetti, J. (2002). Cognitive functioning of long-term heavy cannabis users seeking treatment. *Journal of the American Medical Association, 287,* 1123–1131.

Sommer, B. R., Hoff, A. L., & Costa, M. (2003). Folic acid supplementation in dementia: A preliminary report. *Journal of Geriatric Psychiatry and Neurology, 16,* 156–159.

Sommers-Flanagan, R., Sommers-Flanagan, J., & Davis, B. (1993). What's happening on music television? A gender-role content analysis. *Sex Roles, 28,* 745–753.

Son Hing, L. S., Bobocel, D. R., & Zanna, M. P. (2007). Authoritarian dynamics and unethical decision making: High social dominance orientation leaders and high right wing authoritarianism followers. *Journal of Personality and Social Psychology, 92,* 67–81.

Son Hing, L. S., Li, W., & Zanna, M. P. (2002). Inducing hypocrisy to reduce prejudicial responses among aversive racists. *Journal of Experimental Social Psychology, 38,* 71–78.

Sonnentag, S., & Frese, M. (2003). Stress in organizations. In W. C. Borman , D. R. Ilgen, & R. J. Klimoski (Eds.), *Handbook of psychology: Vol. 12. Industrial and organizational psychology.* New York: Wiley.

Sonstroem, R. J. (1997). Physical activity and self-esteem. In W. P. Morgan (Ed.), *Physical activity and mental health.* Washington, DC: Taylor & Francis.

Sorensen, J. L., Haug, N. A., & Batki, S. L. (2005). Psychosocial issues of HIV/AIDS among drug users in treatment. In J. H. Lowinson, P. Ruiz, R. B. Millman, & J. G. Langrod (Eds.), *Substance abuse: A comprehensive textbook.* Philadelphia: Lippincott/Williams & Wilkins.

Sotiriou, P. E. (2002). *Integrating college study skills: Reasoning in reading, listening, and writing.* Belmont, CA: Wadsworth.

South, S. J. (1993). Racial and ethnic differences in the desire to marry. *Journal of Marriage and the Family, 55,* 357–370.

South, S. J., Bose, S., & Trent, K. (2004). Anticipating divorce: Spousal agreement, predictive accuracy, and effects on labor supply and fertility. *Journal of Divorce and Remarriage, 40*(3–4), 1–22.

South, S. J., & Lloyd, K. M. (1995). Spousal alternatives and marital dissolution. *American Sociological Review, 60,* 21–35.

Spada, M. M., & Wells, A. (2006). Metacognitions about alcohol use in problem drinkers. *Clinical Psychology & Psychotherapy, 13*(2), 138–143.

Spanos, N. P. (1994). Multiple identity enactments and multiple personality disorder: A sociocognitive perspective. *Psychological Bulletin, 116,* 143–165.

Spanos, N. P. (1996). *Multiple identities and false memories.* Washington, DC: American Psychological Association.

Spector, I., & Carey, M. (1990). Incidence and prevalence of the sexual dysfunctions: A critical review of the empirical literature. *Archives of Sexual Behavior, 19,* 389–408.

Spelke, E. S. (2005). Sex differences in intrinsic aptitude for mathematics and science? *American Psychologist, 60,* 950–958.

Spence, J. T. (1983). Comment on Lubinski, Tellegen, and Butcher's "Masculinity, femininity, and androgyny viewed and assessed as distinct concepts." *Journal of Personality and Social Psychology, 44,* 440–446.

Spence, J. T., & Buckner, C. E. (2000). Instrumental and expressive traits, trait stereotypes, and sexist attitudes. *Psychology of Women Quarterly, 24,* 44–62.

Spence, J. T., & Robbins, A. S. (1992). Workaholism: Definition, measurement, and preliminary results. *Journal of Personality Assessment, 58,* 160–178.

Spencer, P. T. (1990). Exercise as psychotherapy. *Counseling Psychology Quarterly, 3*(3), 291–293.

Sperry, L. (2006). *Psychological treatment of chronic illness: The biopsychosocial therapy approach.* Washington, DC: American Psychological Association.

Sperry, R. W. (1982). Some effects of disconnecting the cerebral hemispheres. *Science, 217,* 1223–1226, 1250.

Spiegel, D., Bloom, J. R., Kraemer, H. C., & Gottheil, E. (1989). Psychological support for cancer patients. *Lancet, 2,* 1447.

Spiegler, M. D., & Guevremont, D. C. (1998). *Contemporary behavior therapy.* Pacific Grove, CA: Brooks/Cole.

Spiegler, M. D., & Guevremont, D. C. (2003). *Contemporary behavior therapy.* Belmont, CA: Wadsworth.

Spitzberg, B. H. (1999). An analysis of empirical estimates of sexual aggression victimization and perpetration. *Violence and Victims, 14*(3), 241–260.

Spitzer, R. L., First, M. B., & Wakefield, J. C. (2007). Saving PTSD from itself in DSM-V. *Journal of Anxiety Disorders, 21,* 233–241.

Spokane, A. R., & Cruza-Guet, M. C. (2005). Holland's theory of vocational personalities in work environments. In S. D. Brown & R. W. Lent (Eds.), *Career development and counseling: Putting theory and research to work.* New York: Wiley.

Sporer, S. L., & Schwandt, B. (2007). Moderators of nonverbal indicators of deception: A meta-analytic synthesis. *Psychology, Public Policy, and Law, 13,* 1–34.

Sprecher, S. (1994). Two sides to the breakup of dating relationships. *Personal Relationships, 1,* 199–222.

Sprecher, S. (2002). Sexual satisfaction in premarital relationships: Associations with satisfaction, love, commitment, and stability. *The Journal of Sex Research, 39*(3), 190–196.

Sprecher, S., & Cate, R. M. (2004). Sexual satisfaction and sexual expression as predictors of relationship satisfaction and stability. In J. H. Harvey, A. Wenzel, & S. Sprecher (Eds.), *The handbook of sexuality and close relationships.* Mahwah, NJ: Lawrence Erlbaum.

Sprecher, S., Christopher, F. S., & Cate, R. (2006). Sexuality in close relationships. In A. L. Vangelisti & D. Perlman (Eds.), *The Cambridge handbook of personal relationships.* New York: Cambridge University Press.

Sprecher, S., & Duck, S. (1994). Sweet talk: The importance of perceived communication for romantic and friendship attraction experienced during a get-acquainted date. *Personality and Social Psychology Bulletin, 20*(4), 391–400.

Sprecher, S., & Regan, P. C. (1998). Passionate and companionate love in courting and young married couples. *Sociological Inquiry, 68*(2), 163–185.

Sprecher, S., Sullivan, Q., & Hatfield, E. (1994). Mate selection preferences: Gender differences examined in a national sample. *Journal of Personality and Social Psychology, 66,* 1074–1080.

Springen, K. (2004, November 1). Under the knife. *Newsweek,* pp. 59–60.

Springer, S. P., & Deutsch, G. (1998). *Left brain, right brain.* New York: Freeman.

Stack, S. (1998). Marriage, family and loneliness: A cross-national study. *Sociological Perspectives, 41,* 415–432.

Stack, S., & Eshleman, J. R. (1998). Marital status and happiness: A 17-nation study. *Journal of Marriage and the Family, 60,* 527–536.

Stafford, L., & Canary, D. J. (1991). Maintenance strategies and romantic relationship type, gender and relational characteristics. *Journal of Social and Personal Relationships, 8,* 217–242.

Stajkovic, A. D., & Luthans, F. (1998). Self-efficacy and work-related performance: A meta-analysis. *Psychological Bulletin, 124*(2), 240–261.

Stamler, J., Daviglus, M. L., Garside, D. B., Dyer, A. R., Greenland, P., & Neaton, J. D. (2000). Relationship of baseline serum cholesterol levels in 3 large cohorts of younger men to long-term coronary, cardiovascular, and all-cause mortality and to longevity. *Journal of the American Medical Association, 284,* 311–318.

Stanley, S. M., Whitton, S. W., & Markman, H. J. (2004). Maybe I do? Interpersonal commitment and premarital or nonmarital cohabitation. *Journal of Family Issues, 25,* 496–519.

Stanton, A. L., Lobel, M., Sears, S. , & DeLuca, R. S. (2002). Psychosocial aspects of selected issues in women's reproductive health: Current status and future directions. *Journal of Consulting & Clinical Psychology, 70*(3), 751–770.

Starcevic, V. (2001). Clinical features and diagnosis of hypochondriasis. In V. Starcevic & D. R. Lipsitt (Eds.), *Hypochondriasis: Modern perspectives on an ancient malady.* New York: Oxford University Press.

Starker, S. (1990). Self-help books: Ubiquitous agents of health care. *Medical Psychotherapy: An International Journal, 3* 187–194.

Starker, S. (1992). Characteristics of self-help book readers among VA medical outpatients. *Medical Psychotherapy: An International Journal, 5,* 89–93.

Starrels, M. E., Ingersoll-Dayton, B., Dowler, D. W., & Neal, M. B. (1997). The stress of caring for a parent: Effects of the elder's impairment on an employed adult child. *Journal of Marriage and the Family, 59,* 860–872.

Statt, D. A. (1994). *Psychology and the world of work.* New York: New York University Press.

Stattin, H., & Magnusson, D. (1990). *Pubertal maturation in female development.* Hillsdale, NJ: Erlbaum.

Staudinger, U. M., & Bluck, S. (2001). A view on midlife development from a life-span theory. In M. E. Lachman (Ed.), *Handbook of midlife development.* New York: Wiley.

Steel, P. (2007). The nature of procrastination: A meta-analytic and theoretical review of quintessential self-regulatory failure. *Psychological Bulletin, 133*(1), 65–94.

Steele, C. M. (1988). The psychology of self-affirmation: Sustaining integrity of the self. In L. Berkowitz (Ed.), *Advances in experimental social psychology.* New York: Academic Press.

Steele, C. M. (1997). A threat in the air: How stereotypes shape intellectual identity and performance. *American Psychologist, 52,* 613–629.

Steiger, H., Bruce, K. R., & Israël, M. (2003). Eating disorders. In G. Stricker & T. A. Widiger (Eds.), *Handbook of psychology: Vol. 8. Clinical psychology.* New York: Wiley.

Steiger, H., & Seguin, J. R. (1999). Eating disorders: Anorexia nervosa and bulimia nervosa. In T. Millon, P. H. Blaney, & R. D. Davis (Eds.), *Oxford textbook of psychopathology.* New York: Oxford University Press.

Stein, M. B., Forde, D. R., Anderson, G., & Walker, J. R. (1997a). Obsessive-compulsive disorder in the community: An epidemiologic survey with clinical reappraisal. *American Journal of Psychiatry, 154,* 1120–1126.

Stein, M. B., Walker, J. R., Hazen, A. L., & Forde, D. R. (1997b). Full and partial posttraumatic stress disorder: Findings from a community survey. *American Journal of Psychiatry, 154,* 1114–1119.

Stein, N., Marshall, N. L., & Tropp, L. R. (1993). *Secrets in public: Sexual harassment in our schools.* Wellesley, MA: Center for Research on Women at Wellesley College and the NOW Legal Defense and Education Fund.

Stein, P. J. (1975). Singlehood: An alternative to marriage. *Family Coordinator, 24,* 489–503.

Stein, P. J. (1976). *Single.* Englewood Cliffs, NJ: Prentice-Hall.

Stein, R. J., O'Byrne, K. K., Suminski, R. R., & Haddock, C. K. (1999). Etiology and treatment of obesity in adults and children: Implications for the addiction model. *Drugs and Society, 15*(1–2), 103–121.

Steinberg, L. (2001). We know some things: Parent-adolescent relationships in retrospect and prospect. *Journal of Research on Adolescence, 11*(1), 1–19.

Steinberg, L. (2004). *The ten basic principles of good parenting.* New York: Simon & Schuster.

Steinberg, L., Blatt-Eisengart, I., & Cauffman, E. (2006). Patterns of competence and adjustment among adolescents from authoritative, authoritarian, indulgent, and neglectful homes: A replication in a sample of serious juvenile offenders. *Journal of Research on Adolescence, 16,* 47–58.

Steinberg, L., & Levine, A. (1997). *You and your adolescent: A parents' guide for ages 10 to 20.* New York: Harper Perennial.

Steiner, H., Smith, C., Rosenkranz, R. T., & Litt, I. (1991). The early care and feeding of anorexics. *Child Psychiatry and Human Development, 21,* 163–167.

Steinhausen, H. (2002). The outcome of anorexia nervosa in the 20th century. *American Journal of Psychiatry, 159,* 1284–1293.

Steinmetz, H., Staiger, J. F., Schluag, G., Huang, Y., & Jancke, L. (1995). Corpus callosum and brain volume in women and men. *Neuroreport, 3,* 1002–1004.

Stephens, R. S. (1999). Cannabis and hallucinogens. In B. S. McCrady, & E. E. Epstein (Eds.), *Addictions: A comprehensive guidebook.* New York: Oxford University Press.

Sternberg, R. J. (1986). A triangular theory of love. *Psychological Review, 93* 119–135.

Sternberg, R. J. (1988). Triangulating love. In R. J. Sternberg & M. L. Barnes (Eds.), *The psychology of love.* New Haven, CT: Yale University Press.

Sternberg, R. J., Grigorenko, E. L., & Kidd, K. K. (2005). Intelligence, race, and genetics. *American Psychologist, 60,* 45–69.

Stevens, D. P., Minnotte, K. L., Mannon, S. E., & Kiger, G. (2007). Examining the "neglected side of the work-family interface": Antecedents of positive and negative family-to-work spillover. *Journal of Family Issues, 28,* 242–262.

Stewart, A. J., & Ostrove, J. M. (1998). Women's personality in middle age: Gender, history, and midcourse corrections. *American Psychologist, 53,* 1185–1194.

Stewart, A. J., Ostrove, J. M., & Helson, R. (2001). Middle aging in women: Patterns of personality change from the 30's to the 50's. *Journal of Adult Development, 8*(1), 23–37.

Stewart, F. H., Ellertson, C., & Cates, W. Jr. (2004). Abortion. In R. A. Hatcher, J. Trussell, F. H. Stewart, A. L. Nelson, W. Cates Jr., F. Guest, & D. Kowal (Eds.), *Contraceptive technology* (18th rev. ed.). New York: Ardent Media.

Stice, E. (2001). Risk factors for eating pathology: Recent advances and future directions. In R. H. Striegel-Moore & L. Smolak (Eds.), *Eating disorders: Innovative directions in research and practice.* Washington, DC: American Psychological Association.

Stice, E., Spangler, D., & Agras, W. S. (2001). Exposure to media-portrayed thin-ideal images adversely affects vulnerable girls: A longitudinal experiment. *Journal of Social and Clinical Psychology, 20,* 270–288.

Stillion, J. M. (1995). Death in the lives of adults: Responding to the tolling of the bell. in H. Wass & R. A. Neimeyer (Eds.), *Dying: Facing the facts.* New York: Taylor & Francis.

Stith, S. M., Rosen, K. H., Middleton, K. A., Busch, A. L., Lundeberg, K., & Carlton, R. P. (2000). The intergenerational transmission of spouse abuse: A meta-analysis. *Journal of Marriage and the Family, 62,* 640–654.

Stith, S. M., Smith, D. B., Penn, C. E., Ward, D. B., & Tritt, D. (2004). Intimate partner physical abuse perpetration and victimization risk factors: A meta-analytic review. *Aggression and Violent Behavior, 10,* 65–98.

Stoffer, G. R., Davis, K. E., & Brown, J. B., Jr. (1977). The consequences of changing initial answers on objective tests: A stable effect and a stable misconception. *Journal of Educational Research, 70,* 272–277.

Stoll, B. M., Arnaut, G. L., Fromme, D. K., & Felker-Thayer, J. A. (2005). Adolescents in stepfamilies: A qualitative analysis. *Journal of Divorce & Remarriage, 44,* 177–189.

Stone, L. (1977). *The family, sex and marriage in England 1500–1800.* New York: Harper & Row.

Stone, P., & Lovejoy, M. (2004, November). Fast-track women and the "choice" to stay home. *Annals of the American Academy of Political and Social Science, 596,* 62–83.

Stone, W. N. (2003). Group psychotherapy. In A. Tasman, J. Kay, & J. A. Lieberman (Eds.), *Psychiatry.* New York: Wiley.

Stoney, C. M. (2003). Gender and cardiovascular disease: A psychobiological and integrative approach. *Current Directions in Psychological Science, 12*(4), 129–133.

Strauman, T. J., Vookles, J., Berenstein, V., Chaiken, S., & Higgins, E. T. (1991). Self-discrepancies and vulnerability to body dissatisfaction and disordered eating. *Journal of Personality and Social Psychology, 61,* 946–956.

Strickland, C. J. (1997). Suicide among American Indian, Alaskan Native, and Canadian Aboriginal youth: Advancing the research agenda. *International Journal of Mental Health, 25,* 11–32.

Striegel-Moore, R. H., McMahon, R. P., Biro, F. M., Schreiber, G., Crawford, P. B., & Voorhees, C. (2001). Exploring the relationship between timing of menarche and eating disorder symptoms in black and white adolescent girls. *International Journal of Eating Disorders, 30*(4), 421–433.

Striegel-Moore, R. H., Silberstein, L. R., & Rodin, J. (1993). The social self in bulimia nervosa: Public self-consciousness, social anxiety, and perceived fraudulence. *Journal of Abnormal Psychology, 102,* 297–303.

Strober, M. (1995). Family-genetic perspectives on anorexia nervosa and bulimia nervosa. In K. D. Brownell & C. G. Fairburn (Eds.), *Eating disorders and obesity: A comprehensive handbook.* New York: Guilford Press.

Stroebe, K., Lodewijkx, H. F. M., & Spears, R. (2005). Do unto others as they do unto you: Reciprocity and social identification as determinants of ingroup favoritism. *Personality and Social Psychology Bulletin, 31,* 831–845.

Stroebe, W., Stroebe, M., Abakoumkin, G., & Schut, H. (1996). The role of loneliness and social support in adjustment to loss: A test of attachment versus stress theory. *Journal of Personality and Social Psychology, 70*(6), 1241–1249.

Stroup, T. S., Kraus, J. E., & Marder, S. R. (2006). Pharmacotherapies. In J. A. Lieberman, T. S. Stroup, & D. O. Perkins (Eds.), *Textbook of schizophrenia.* Washington, DC: American Psychiatric Publishing.

Strupp, H. H. (1996). The tripartite model and the *Consumer Reports* study. *American Psychologist, 51,* 1017–1024.

Stuart, P. (1992). Murder on the job. *Personnel Journal, 71,* 72–84.

Stubbe, J. H., Posthuma, D., Boomsma, D. I., & De Geus, E. J. C. (2005). Heritability of life satisfaction in adults: A twin-family study. *Psychological Medicine, 35,* 1581–1588.

Stunkard, A. J., Harris, J. R., Pederson, N. L., & McClearn, G. E. (1990). The body-mass index of twins who have been reared apart. *New England Journal of Medicine, 322,* 1483–1487.

Stunkard, A. J., Sorensen, T., Hanis, C., Teasdale, T. W., Chakraborty, R., Schull, W. J., & Schulsinger, F. (1986). An adoption study of human obesity. *New England Journal of Medicine, 314,* 193–198.

Suarez, E. C. (2004). C-reactive protein is associated with psychological risk factors of cardiovascular disease in apparently healthy adults. *Psychosomatic Medicine, 66*(5), 684–691.

Suarez, E. C., Kuhn, C. M., Schanberg, S. M., Williams, R. B., Jr., & Zimmermann, E. A. (1998). Neuroendocrine, cardiovascular, and emotional responses of hostile men: The role of interpersonal challenge. *Psychosomatic Medicine, 60*(1), 78–88.

Suarez-Orozco, C., & Suarez-Orozco, M. M. (1995). *Transformation: Immigration, family life, and achievement motivation among Latino adolescents.* Stanford, CA: Stanford University Press.

Suchday, S., Kapur, S., Ewart, C. K., & Friedberg, J. P. (2006). Urban stress and health in developing countries: Development and validation of a neighborhood stress index for India. *Behavioral Medicine, 32*(3), 77–86.

Sudak, H. S. (2005). Suicide. In B. J. Sadock & V. A. Sadock (Eds.), *Kaplan & Sadock's comprehensive textbook of psychiatry.* Philadelphia: Lippincott Williams & Wilkins.

Sue, D. (1979). Erotic fantasies of college students during coitus. *Journal of Sex Research, 15,* 299–305.

Sue, S., & Zane, N. (1987). The role of culture and cultural techniques in psychotherapy: A critique and reformulation. *American Psychologist, 42,* 37–45.

Sue, S., Zane, N., & Young, K. (1994). Research on psychotherapy with culturally diverse populations. In A. E. Bergin & S. L. Garfield (Eds.), *Handbook of psychotherapy and behavior change* (4th ed.). New York: John Wiley.

Suicide Awareness Voices of Education. (2007). *Someone you know is suicidal.* Retrieved April 12, 2007 from http://www.save.org/prevention/someone_you_know.html.

Suinn, R. M. (1984). *Fundamentals of abnormal psychology.* Chicago: Nelson-Hall.

Sullivan, G. M., & Coplan, J. D. (2000). Anxiety disorders: Biochemical aspects. In B. J. Sadock & V. A. Sadock (Eds.), *Kaplan and Sadock's comprehensive textbook of psychiatry,* (7th ed., Vol. 1). Philadelphia: Lippincott/Williams & Wilkins.

Sullivan, P. F., Neale, M. C., & Kendler, K. S. (2000). Genetic epidemiology of major depression: Review and meta-analysis. *American Journal of Psychiatry, 157,* 1552–1562.

Sullivan, P. F., Owen, M. J., O'Donovan, M. C., & Freedman, R. (2006). Genetics. In J. A. Liberman, T. S. Stroup, & D. O. Perkins (Eds.), *Textbook of schizophrenia.* Washington, DC: American Psychiatric Publishing.

Sulloway, F. J. (1991). Reassessing Freud's case histories: The social construction of psychoanalysis. *ISIS, 82,* 245–275.

Sulloway, F. J. (1995). Birth order and evolutionary psychology: A meta-analytic overview. *Psychological Inquiry, 6,* 75–80.

Sulloway, F. J. (1996). *Born to rebel: Birth order, family dynamics, and creative lives.* New York: Pantheon Books.

Sullum, J., Clark, M. M., & King, T. K. (2000). Predictors of exercise relapse in a college population. *Journal of American College Health, 48,* 175–180.

Suls, J., & Bunde, J. (2005). Anger, anxiety, and depression as risk factors for cardiovascular disease: The problems and implications of overlapping affective dispositions. *Psychological Bulletin, 131,* 260–300.

Suls, J., & Rothman, A. (2004). Evolution of the biopsychosocial model: Prospects and challenges for health psychology. *Health Psychology, 23*(2), 119–125.

Summers, G., & Feldman, N. S. (1984). Blaming the perpetrator: An attributional analysis of spouse abuse. *Journal of Social and Clinical Psychology, 2,* 339–347.

Super, D. E. (1957). *The psychology of careers.* New York: HarperCollins.

Super, D. E. (1985). Career and life development. In D. Brown & L. Brooks (Eds.), *Career choice and development.* San Francisco: Jossey-Bass.

Super, D. E. (1988). Vocational adjustment: Implementing a self-concept. *The Career Development Quarterly, 36,* 351–357.

Surra, C. A., Gray, C. R., Boettcher, T. M. J., Cottle, N. R., & West, A. R. (2006). From courtship to universal properties: Research on dating and mate selection, 1950 to 2003. In A. L. Vangelisti & D. Perlman (Eds.), *The Cambridge handbook of personal relationships.* New York: Cambridge University Press.

Susman, E. J., Dorn, L. D., & Schiefelbein, V. L. (2003). Puberty, sexuality, and health. In R. M. Lerner, M.A. Easterbrooks, & J. Mistry (Eds.), *Handbook of psychology: Vol. 6. Developmental psychology.* New York: Wiley.

Susser, E., Neugebauer, R., Hoek, H. W., Brown, A. S., Lin, S., Labovitz, D., & Gorman, J. M. (1996). Schizophrenia after prenatal famine: Further evidence. *Archives of General Psychiatry, 53,* 25–31.

Sutherland, V. J. (2000). Understimulation/boredom. In G. Fink (Ed.), *Encyclopedia of stress* (Vol. 3). San Diego: Academic Press.

Swan, G. E., Hudmon, K. S., & Khroyan, T. V. (2003). Tobacco dependence. In A. M. Nezu, C. M. Nezu , & P. A. Geller (Eds.), *Handbook of psychology: Vol. 9. Health psychology.* New York: Wiley.

Swan, S. C., & Snow, D. L. (2006). The development of a theory of women's use of violence in intimate relationships. *Violence Against Women, 12,* 1026–1045.

Swanger, N. (2006). Visible body modification (VBM): Evidence from human resource managers and recruiters and the effects on employment. *International Journal of Hospitality Management, 25*(1), 154–158.

Swann, W. B., Rentfrow, P. J., & Guinn, J. S. (2003). Self-verification: The search for coherence. In M. R. Leary & J. P. Tangney (Eds.), *Handbook of self and identity.* New York: Guilford.

Swann, W. B., Stein-Seroussi, A., & Giesler, R. B. (1992). Why people self-verify. *Journal of Personality and Social Psychology, 62,* 392–401.

Swann, W. B., Stein-Seroussi, A., & McNulty, S. E. (1992). Outcasts in a white-lie society: The enigmatic worlds of people with negative self-conceptions. *Journal of Personality and Social Psychology, 62,* 618–624.

Swanson, J. L., & D'Achiardi, C. (2005). Beyond interests, needs/values, and abilities: Assessing other important career constructs over the life span. In S. D. Brown & R. W. Lent (Eds.), *Career development and counseling: Putting theory and research to work.* New York: Wiley.

Swap, W. C. (1977). Interpersonal attraction and repeated exposure to rewarders and punishers. *Personality and Social Psychology Bulletin, 3,* 248–251.

Swim, J. K., Aikin, K. J., Hall, W. S., & Hunter, B. A. (1995). Sexism and racism: Old-fashioned and modern prejudices. *Journal of Personality and Social Psychology, 68,* 199–214.

Sygnatur, E. F., & Toscano, G. A. (2000, Spring). Work-related homicides: The facts. *Compensation and Working Conditions,* 3–8.

Szasz, T. S. (1974). *The myth of mental illness.* New York: HarperCollins.

Szasz, T. S. (1993). *A lexicon of lunacy: Metaphoric malady, moral responsibility, and psychiatry.* New Brunswick, NJ: Transaction.

Szmukler, G. I., & Patton, G. (1995). Sociocultural models of eating disorders. In G. Szmukler, C. Dare, & J. Treasure (Eds.), *Handbook of eating disorders: Theory, treatment and research.* New York: Wiley.

Tajfel, H. (1982). *Social identity and intergroup relations.* London: Cambridge University Press.

Takanishi, R. (1993). The opportunities of adolescence—Research, interventions, and policy. *American Psychologist, 48,* 85–87.

Tamminga, C. A., & Carlsson, A. (2003). Psychiatric pathophysiology: Schizophrenia. In A. Tasman, J. Kay, & J. A. Lieberman (Eds.), *Psychiatry.* New York: Wiley.

Tang, M. (2002). A comparison of Asian American, Caucasian American, and Chinese college students: An initial report. *Journal of Multicultural Counseling and Development, 30*(2), 124–134.

Tannen, D. (1990). *You just don't understand: Women and men in conversation.* New York: Ballantine.

Tannen, D. (1998). *The argument culture: Moving from debate to dialogue.* New York: Random House.

Tanner, J. M. (1990). *Fetus into man: Physical growth from conception to maturity.* Cambridge, MA: Harvard University Press.

Tashiro, T., Frazier, P., & Berman, M. (2006). Stress-related growth following divorce and relationship dissolution. In M. A. Fine & J. H. Harvey (Eds.), *Handbook of divorce and relationship resolution.* Mahwah, NJ: Erlbaum.

Tasker, F. (2005). Lesbian mothers, gay fathers, and their children: A review. *Journal of Developmental & Behavioral Pediatrics, 26,* 224–240.

Tavris, C. (1982). *Anger: The misunderstood emotion.* New York: Simon & Schuster.

Tavris, C. (1989). *Anger: The misunderstood emotion* (2nd ed.). New York: Simon & Schuster.

Taylor, D. A., & Altman, I. (1987). Communication in interpersonal relationships: Social penetration processes. In M. E. Roloff & G. R. Miller (Eds.), *Interpersonal processes: New directions in communication research.* Newbury Park, CA: Sage.

Taylor, E. (2001). Positive psychology and humanistic psychology: A reply to Seligman. *Journal of Humanistic Psychology, 41*(1), 13–29.

Taylor, L. D. (2005). Effects of visual and verbal sexual television content and perceived realism on attitudes and beliefs. *Journal of Sex Research, 42*(2), 130–137.

Taylor, M. C. (1995). White backlash to workplace affirmative action: Peril or myth? *Social Forces, 73,* 1385–1414.

Taylor, R. J., Chatters, L. M., Tucker, M. B., & Lewis, E. (1990). Developments in research on black families: A decade review. *Journal of Marriage and the Family, 52,* 993–1014.

Taylor, S. (2004). Amnesia, folklore and folks: Recovered memories in clinical practice. *Cognitive Behaviour Therapy, 33*(2), 105–108.

Taylor, S. E. (1981a). A categorization approach to stereotyping. In D. H. Hamilton (Ed.), *Cognitive processes in stereotyping and intergroup relations.* Hillsdale, NJ: Erlbaum.

Taylor, S. E. (1981b). The interface of cognitive and social psychology. In J. Harvey (Ed.), *Cognition, social behavior, and the environment.* Hillsdale, NJ: Erlbaum.

Taylor, S. E. (2006). Tend and befriend: Biobehavioral bases of affiliation under stress. *Current Directions in Psychological Science, 15*(6), 273–277.

Taylor, S. E. (2007). Social support. In H. S. Friedman & R. C. Silver (Eds.), *Foundations of health psychology.* New York: Oxford University Press.

Taylor, S. E., & Brown, J. D. (1988). Illusion and well-being: A social psychological perspective on mental health. *Psychological Bulletin, 103,* 193–210.

Taylor, S. E., & Brown, J. D. (1994). Positive illusions and well-being revisited: Separating fact from fiction. *Psychological Bulletin, 116,* 21–27.

Taylor, S. E., Klein, L. C., Lewis, B. P., Gruenewald, T. L., Gurung, R. A. R., & Updegraff, J. A. (2000). Biobehavioral responses to stress in females: Tend-and-befriend, not fight-or-flight. *Psychological Review, 107*(3), 411–429.

Taylor, S. E., Lerner, J. S., Sherman, D. K., Sage, R. M., & McDowell, N. K. (2003). Are self-enhancing cognitions associated with healthy or unhealthy biological profiles? *Journal of Personality and Social Psychology, 85*(4), 605–615.

Taylor, S. E., Sherman, D. K., Kim, H. S., Jarcho, J., Takagi, K., & Dunagan, M. S. (2004). Culture and social support: Who seeks it and why? *Journal of Personality, 87,* 354–362.

Teachman, J. D. (2003). Premarital sex, premarital cohabitation, and the risk of subsequent marital dissolution among women. *Journal of Marriage and Family, 65,* 444–445.

Teachman, J. D., Polonko, K. A., & Scanzoni, J. (1999). Demography and families. In M. B. Sussman, S. K. Steinmetz, & G. W. Peterson (Eds.), *Handbook of marriage and the family.* New York: Plenum.

Teachman, J. D., Tedrow, L. M., & Crowder, K. D. (2001). The changing demography of America's families. In R. M. Milardo (Ed.), *Understanding families into the new millennium: A decade in review.* Minneapolis: National Council on Family Relations.

Teachman, J., Tedrow, L., & Hall, M. (2006). The demographic future of divorce and dissolution. In M. A. Fine & J. H. Harvey (Eds.), *Handbook of divorce and relationship resolution.* Mahwah, NJ: Erlbaum.

Tedeschi, R. G., & Calhoun, L. G. (1996). The traumatic growth inventory: Measuring the positive legacy of trauma. *Journal of Traumatic Stress, 9,* 455–471.

Tedeschi, R. G., & Calhoun, L. G. (2004). Posttraumatic growth: Conceptual foundations and empirical evidence. *Psychological Inquiry, 15*(1), 1–18.

Tellegen, A., Lykken, D. T., Bouchard, T. J., Jr., Wilcox, K. J., Segal, N. L., & Rich, S. (1988). Personality similarity in twins reared apart and together. *Journal of Personality and Social Psychology, 54,* 1031–1039.

Tennen, H., & Affleck, G. (2002). Benefit-finding and benefit-reminding. In C. R. Synder & S. J. Lopez (Eds.), *Handbook of positive psychology.* New York: Oxford University Press.

Tennen, H., & Affleck, G. (2005). Benefit-finding and benefit-reminding. In C. R. Snyder & S. J. Lopez (Eds.), *Handbook of positive psychology.* New York: Oxford University Press.

Terracciano, A., Abdel-Khalak, A. M., Adam, N., Adamovova, L., Ahn, C., Ahn, H., & et al. (2005). National character does not reflect mean personality trait levels in 49 cultures. *Science, 310,* 96–100.

Terracciano, A., Costa, P. T., & McCrae, R. R. (2006). Personality plasticity after age 30. *Personality and Social Psychology Bulletin, 32,* 999–1009.

Tesch, S. A., & Whitbourne, S. K. (1982). Intimacy and identity status in young adults. *Journal of Personality and Social Psychology, 43,* 1041–1051.

Tesser, A. (2001). Self-esteem. In A. Tesser & N. Schwarz (Eds.), *Blackwell handbook of social psychology: Intraindividual processes.* Malden, MA: Blackwell.

Testa, K. (1996). Church to pay $1 million in false-memory case. *San Jose Mercury News,* 8A.

Thase, M. E., Jindal, R., & Howland, R. H. (2002). Biological aspects of depression. In I. H. Gotlib & C. L. Hammen (Eds.), *Handbook of depression.* New York: Guilford.

Theisen, T. (2002, March 17). Too many are lying to get the job. *Atlanta Journal-Constitution,* p. R5.

Thibaut, J. W., & Kelley, H. H. (1959). *The social psychology of groups.* New York: Wiley.

Thomas, A. J., Kalaria, R. N., & O'Brien, J. T. (2004). Depression and vascular disease: What is the relationship? *Journal of Affective Disorders, 79*(1–3), 81–95.

Thomas, K. M. (2005). *Diversity dynamics in the workplace.* Belmont, CA: Wadsworth.

Thompkins, C. D., & Rando, R. A. (2003). Gender role conflict and shame in college men. *Psychology of Men and Masculinity, 4*(1), 79–81.

Thompson, J. K., & Kinder, B. (2003). Eating disorders. In M. Hersen & S. Turner (Eds.), *Handbook of adult psychopathology.* New York: Plenum Press.

Thompson, J. K., & Stice, E. (2001). Thin-ideal internalization: Mounting evidence for a new risk factor for body-image disturbance and eating pathology. *Current Directions in Psychological Science, 10*(5), 181–183.

Thompson, T., & Massat, C. R. (2005). Experiences of violence, post-traumatic stress, academic achievement and behavior problems of urban African-American children. *Child and Adolescent Social Work Journal, 22,* 367–393.

Thompson, T. L., & Zerbinos, E. (1995). Gender roles in animated cartoons: Has the picture changed in 20 years? *Sex Roles, 32,* 651–673.

Thornton, A., & Young-DeMarco, L. (2001). Four decades of trends in attitudes toward family issues in the United States: The 1960s through the 1990s. *Journal of Marriage and Family, 63,* 1009–1037.

Thorson, J. A., & Powell, F. C. (2000). Death anxiety in younger and older adults. In A. Tomer (Ed.), *Death attitudes and the older adult: Theories, concepts, and applications.* Philadelphia: Brunner-Routledge.

Thune, I., & Furberg, A. (2001). Physical activity and cancer risk: Dose-response and cancer, all sites and site specific. *Medicine and Science in Sports and Exercise, 33*(6), S530–S550.

Tibbo, P., Hanstock, C., Valiakalayil, A., & Allen, P. (2004). 3-T proton MRS investigation and glutamine in adolescents at high genetic risk for schizophrenia. *American Journal of Psychiatry, 161,* 1116–1118.

Tice, D. M., & Baumeister, R. F. (1997). Longitudinal study of procrastination, performance, stress, and health: The cost and benefits of dawdling. *Psychological Science, 8,* 454–458.

Tice, D. M., Bratslavsky, E., & Baumeister, R. F. (2001). Emotional distress regulation takes precedence over impulse control: If you feel bad, do it! *Journal of Personality and Social Psychology, 80*(1), 53–67.

Tice, D. M., Butler, J. L., Muraven M. B., & Stillwell A. M. (1995). When modesty prevails: Differential favorability of self-presentation to friends and strangers. *Journal of Personality and Social Psychology, 69,* 1120–1138.

Tice, D. M., & Wallace, H. M. (2003). The reflected self: Creating yourself as (you think) others see you. In M. R. Leary & J. P. Tangney (Eds.), *Handbook of self and identity.* New York: Guilford.

Tigner, R. B. (1999). Putting memory research to good use: Hints from cognitive psychology. *College Teaching, 47*(4), 149–151.

Titsworth, B. S., & Kiewra, K. A. (2004). Spoken organizational lecture cues and student notetaking as facilitators of student learning. *Contemporary Educational Psychology, 29,* 447–461.

Tjaden, P., & Thoennes, N. (2000). Prevalence and consequences of male-to-female and female-to-male intimate partner violence as measured by the National Violence Against Women Survey. *Violence Against Women, 6,* 142–161.

Toffler, A. (1970). *Future shock.* New York: Random House.

Toffler, A. (1980). *The third wave.* New York: Bantam Books.

Tolin, D. F., & Foa, E. B. (2006). Sex differences in trauma and posttraumatic stress disorder: A quantitative review of 25 years of research. *Psychological Bulletin, 132,* 959–992.

Tolman, D. L. (2002). *Dilemmas of desire: Teenage girls talk about sexuality.* Cambridge, MA: Harvard University Press.

Toomey, R., Kremen, W. S., Simpson, J. C., Samson, J. A., Seidman, L. J., Lyons, M. J., Faraone, S. V., & Tsuang, M. T. (1997). Revisiting the factor structure for positive and negative symptoms: Evidence from a large heterogeneous group of psychiatric patients. *American Journal of Psychology, 154,* 371–377.

Torres, A. R., Prince, M. J., Bebbington, P. E., Bhugra, D., Brugha, T. S., Farrell, M., Jenkins, R., Lewis, G., Meltzer, H., & Singleton, N. (2006). Obsessive-compulsive disorder: Prevalence, comorbidity, impact, and help-seeking in the British national psychiatric morbidity survey of 2000. *American Journal of Psychiatry, 163,* 1978–1985.

Torrey, E. F. (1992). *Freudian fraud: The malignant effect of Freud's theory on American thought and culture.* New York: Harper Perennial.

Torrey, E. F., Bowler, A. E., Taylor, E. H., & Gottesman, I. I. (1994). *Schizophrenia and manic-depressive disorder.* New York: Basic Books.

Toufexis, A. (1990, December 17). Drowsy America. *Time,* pp. 78–85.

Tozzi, F., Thornton, L. M., Klump, K. L., Fichter, M. M., Halmi, K. A., Kaplan, A. S., Strober, M., Woodside, D. B., Crow, S., Mitchell, J., Rotondo, A., Mauri, M., Cassano, G., Keel, P., Plotnicov, K. H., Pollice, C., Lilenfeld, L. R., Berrettini, W. H., Bulik, C. M., & Kaye, W. H. (2005). Symptom fluctuation in eating disorders: Correlates of diagnostic crossover. *American Journal of Psychiatry, 162,* 732–740.

Trachtenberg, J. D., & Sande, M. A. (2002). Emerging resistance to nonnucleoside reverse transcriptase inhibitors: A warning and a challenge. *Journal of the American Medical Association, 288*(2), 239–241.

Travis, F. (2001). Autonomic and EEG patterns distinguish transcending from other experiences during Transcendental Meditation practice. *International Journal of Psychophysiology, 42,* 1–9.

Travis, L. A., Bliwise, N. G., Binder, J. L., & Horne-Moyer, H. L. (2001). Changes in clients' attachment style over the course of time-limited dynamic psychotherapy. *Psychotherapy: Theory, Research, Practice, Training, 38*(2), 149–159.

Treas, J., & Lawton, L. (1999). Family relations in adulthood. In M. B. Sussman, S. K. Steinmetz, & G. W. Peterson (Eds.), *Handbook of marriage and the family.* New York: Plenum Press.

Triandis, H. C. (1994). *Culture and social behavior.* New York: McGraw-Hill.

Triandis, H. C. (2001). Individualism-collectivism and personality. *Journal of Personality, 69*(6), 907–924.

Trope, Y. (1983). Self-assessment in achievement behavior. In J. Suls & A. Greenwald (Eds.), *Psychological perspectives* (Vol. 2). Hillsdale, NJ: Erlbaum.

Trope, Y. (1986). Self-enhancement and self-assessment in achievement behavior. In R. Sorrentino & E. T. Higgins (Eds.), *Handbook of motivation and cognition* (Vol. 2). New York: Guilford Press.

Trope, Y., & Gaunt, R. (2003). Attribution and person perception. In M. A. Hogg & J. Cooper (Eds.), *The Sage handbook of social psychology.* Thousand Oaks, CA: Sage Publications.

Troy, A. B., Lewis-Smith, J., & Laurenceau, J. (2006). Interracial and intraracial romantic relationships: The search for differences in satisfaction, conflict, and attachment style. *Journal of Social & Personal Relationships, 23,* 65–80.

Trussell, J. (2004). Contraceptive efficacy. In R. A. Hatcher, J. Trussell, F. H. Stewart, A. L. Nelson, W. Cates Jr., F. Guest, & D. Kowal *Contraceptive technology.* New York: Ardent Media.

Trussell, J., Brown, S., & Hogue, C. (2004). Adolescent sexual behavior, pregnancy, and childbearing. In R. A. Hatcher, J. Trussell, F. H. Stewart, A. L. Nelson, W. Cates Jr., F. Guest, & D. Kowal (Eds.), *Contraceptive technology.* New York: Ardent Media.

Trzesniewski, K. H., Donnellan, M. B., & Robins, R. W. (2003). Stability of self-esteem across the life span. *Journal of Personality and Social Psychology, 84*(1), 205–220.

Tsai, M., & Uemera, A. (1988). Asian Americans: The struggles, the conflicts, and the successes. In P. Bronstein & K. Quina (Eds.), *Teaching a psychology of people.* Washington, DC: American Psychological Association.

Tsuang, M. T., Glatt, S. J., & Faraone, S. V. (2003). Genetics and genomics in schizophrenia. *Primary Psychiatry, 10*(3), 37–40, 50.

Tugade, M. M., & Fredrickson, B. L. (2004). Resilient individuals use positive emotions to bounce back from negative emotional experiences. *Journal of Personality and Social Psychology, 86*(2), 320–333.

Turkheimer, E., & Waldron, M. (2000). Nonshared environment: A theoretical, methodological, and quantitative review. *Psychological Bulletin, 126,* 78–108.

Turner, J. C. (1987). *Rediscovering the social group: A self-categorization theory.* Oxford, England: Basil Blackwell.

Turner, J. C., & Reynolds, K. J. (2004). The social identity perspective in intergroup relations: Theories, themes, and controversies. In M. B. Brewer & M. Hewstone (Eds.), *Self and social identity.* Malden, MA: Blackwell.

Turner, J. R., & Wheaton, B. (1995). Checklist measurement of stressful life events. In S. Cohen, R. C. Kessler, & L. U. Gordon (Eds.), *Measuring stress: A guide for health and social scientists.* New York: Oxford University Press.

Turner, S. M., Beidel, D. C., Stanley, M. A., & Heiser, N. (2001). Obsessive-compulsive disorder. In P. B. Sutker & H. E. Adams (Eds.), *Comprehensive textbook of psychiatry* (3rd ed.). New York: Kluwer Academic/Plenum.

Turner-Bowker, D. M. (2001). How can you pull yourself up by your bootstraps if you don't have boots? Work appropriate clothing for women. *Journal of Social Issues, 57,* 311–322.

Twenge, J. M. (2000). The age of anxiety? Birth cohort change in anxiety and neuroticism, 1952–1993. *Journal of Personality and Social Psychology, 79*(6), 1007–1021.

Twenge, J. M., & Campbell W. K. (2003). Isn't it fun to get the respect that we're going to deserve? Narcissism, social rejection, and aggression. *Personality and Social Psychology, 29*(2), 261–272.

Twenge, J. M., Campbell, W. K., & Foster, C. A. (2003). Parenthood and marital satisfaction: A meta-analytic review. *Journal of Marriage and Family, 65,* 574–83.

Twenge, J. M., & Crocker, J. (2002). Race and self-esteem: Meta-analyses comparing whites, blacks, Hispanics, Asians, and American Indians and comment on Gray-Little and Hafdahl (2000). *Psychological Bulletin, 128*(3), 371–408.

Uchino, B. N., Cacioppo, J. T., & Kiecolt-Glaser, J. K. (1996). The relationship between social support and physiological processes: A review with emphasis on underlying mechanisms and implications for health. *Psychological Bulletin, 119,* 488–531.

Uhlmann, E., & Swanson, J. (2004). Exposure to violent video games increases automatic aggressiveness. *Journal of Adolescence, 27,* 41–52.

Uleman, J. S., Hon, A., Roman, R. J., & Moskowitz, G. B. (1996). Online evidence for spontaneous trait inferences at encoding. *Personality and Psychology Bulletin, 22*(4), 377–394.

Ullman, S. E. (2004). Sexual assualt victimization and suicidal behavior in women: A review of the literature. *Aggression and Violent Behavior, 9*(4), 331–351.

Ulrich, M., & Weatherall, A. (2000). Motherhood and infertility: Viewing motherhood through the lens of infertility. *Feminism & Psychology, 10,* 323–336.

Umberson, D., Wortman, C. B., & Kessler, R. C. (1992). Widowhood and depression: Explaining long-term gender differences in vulnerability. *Journal of Health and Social Behavior, 33,* 10–24.

Unger, R. (2006). Untangling the web: Threat, ideology, and political behavior. In P. R. Kimmel & C. E. Stout (Eds.), *Collateral damage: The psychological consequences of America's war on terrorism.* Westport, CT: Praeger.

Ursano, R. J., Fullerton, C. S., Vance, K., & Kao, T. C. (1999). Posttraumatic stress disorder and identification in disaster workers. *American Journal of Psychiatry, 156,* 353–359.

Ursano, R. J., & Silberman, E. K. (2003). Psychoanalysis, psychoanalytic psychotherapy, and supportive psychotherapy. In R. E. Hales & S. C. Yudofsky (Eds.), *Textbook of clinical psychiatry.* Washington, DC: American Psychiatric Publishing.

U.S. Bureau of Labor Statistics. (1998). *Occupational outlook handbook: 1998–1999.* Washington, DC: U.S. Government Printing Office.

U.S. Bureau of Labor Statistics. (2003). Highlight of women's earnings in 2002. Retrieved December 12, 2004 from http://www.bls.gov/cps/cpswom2002.pdf.

U.S. Bureau of Labor Statistics. (2004). *Occupational outlook handbook: 2004–2005.* Washington, DC: U.S. Government Printing Office.

U.S. Bureau of Labor Statistics. (2005). *Workers on flexible and shift schedules in 2004 summary.* Retrieved June 4, 2007 from http://www.bls.gov/news.release/flex.nr0.htm.

U.S. Bureau of Labor Statistics. (2006). *Occupational outlook handbook, 2006–2007 edition.* Washington, D.C.: U. S. Government Printing Office.

U.S. Bureau of Labor Statistics. (2007). *Employment characteristics of families in 2006.* Washington, D.C: Department of Labor.

U.S. Bureau of the Census. (2000). *Statistical abstract of the United States: 2000.* Washington, DC: U.S. Government Printing Office.

U.S. Bureau of the Census. (2003). *Statistical abstract of the United States: 2003.* Washington, DC: U.S. Government Printing Office.

U.S. Bureau of the Census. (2004a). *Statistical abstract of the United States: 2004–2005.* Washington, DC: U.S. Government Printing Office.

U.S. Bureau of the Census. (2004b). *America's families and living arrangements: 2003.* Washington, DC: U.S. Government Printing Office.

U.S. Bureau of the Census. (2005). *Occupation by sex and median earnings in the past 12 months.* Retrieved May 7, 2007 from http://factfinder.census.gov.servlet/STTable?_bm=y&-geo.

U.S. Bureau of the Census. (2006a). *Americans marrying older, living alone more, see households shrinking, Census Eureau reports* (CB06-83). Retrieved May 15, 2007 from http://www.census.gov/Press-Release/www/releases/archives/families_households/006840.html.

U.S. Bureau of the Census. (2006b). *Statistical abstract of the United States: 2007.* Washington, DC: U.S. Government Printing Office.

U.S. Department of Health and Human Services. (1990). *The health benefits of smoking cessation: A report of the surgeon general.* Washington, DC: U.S. Government Printing Office.

U.S. Department of Health and Human Services. (1995). *Healthy people 2000 review, 1994.* Washington, DC: U.S. Government Printing Office.

U.S. Department of Health and Human Services. (1999). *Mental health: A report of the Surgeon General.* Washington, DC: U.S. Government Printing Office.

U.S. Department of Health and Human Services. (2002, June 10). Preventing teenage pregnancy. Retrieved January 30, 2005 From http://www.Hhs.Gov/News/Press/2002pres/Teenpreg.html.

U.S. Department of Health and Human Services. (2003). *Profile of older Americans: 2003.* Washington, DC: U.S. Government Printing Office.

U.S. Department of Health and Human Services. (2006a). Trends in sexual risk behaviors among high school students--United States, 1991–2005. *Morbidity and Mortality Weekly Report, 55,* 851–854.

U.S. Department of Health and Human Services. (2006b). Youth risk behavior surveillance—United States, 2006. *Morbidity and Mortality Weekly Report, 55*(SS-5), 1–112.

U.S. Department of Health and Human Services. (2007). *Impacts of four Title V, Section 510 abstinence education programs, final report.* Retrieved June 16, 2007 from http://aspe.hhs.gov/hsp/abstinence07/index.htm.

U.S. Department of Justice. (2003). *Crime in the United States— 2003: Uniform crime reports.* Washington, DC: U.S. Government Printing Office.

U.S. Department of Justice. (2007). *Criminal offenders statistics.* Retrieved April 22, 2007 from http://www.ojp.usdoj.gov/bjs/crimoff.htm.

U.S. Department of Labor. (1992). *Pipelines of progress: An update on the glass ceiling initiative.* Washington, DC: U.S. Government Printing Office.

U.S. Department of Labor. (2000, Summer). Futurework: Trends and challenges for work in the 21st century. *Occupational Outlook Quarterly,* pp. 31–36.

U.S. Department of Labor. (2003). *Facts on women workers.* Washington, DC: U.S. Government Printing Office.

U.S. Department of Labor. (2006). High-paying occupations with many job openings, projected 2004–14. *Occupational Outlook Quarterly* (Spring), p. 56.

U.S. Equal Employment Opportunity Commission. (2007). *Occupational employment in private industry by race/ethnic group/sex, and by industry, United States, 2005.* Retrieved June 4, 2007 from http://www.eeoc.gov/stats/jobpat/2005/national.html.

U.S. General Accounting Office. (2003). *Women's earnings: Work patterns partially explain difference between men's and women's earnings.* Washington, DC: General Accounting Office.

U.S. Small Business Administration. (2006). *Women in business, 2006: A demographic review of women's business ownership.* Retrieved June 4, 2007 from http://www.sba.gov/advo/research/rs280tot.pdf.

Vaillant, G. E. (2000). Adaptive mental mechanisms: Their role in a positive psychology. *American Psychologist, 55*(1), 89–98.

Valent, P. (2000). Disaster syndrome. In G. Fink (Ed.), *Encyclopedia of stress* (Vol. 1). San Diego: Academic Press.

Vallone, R. P., Ross, L., & Lepper, M. R. (1985). The hostile media phenomenon: Biased perception and perceptions of bias in coverage of the Beirut massacre. *Journal of Personality and Social Psychology, 50,* 482–491.

Van Boven, L. (2005). Experientialism, materialism, and the pursuit of happiness. *Review of General Psychology, 9*(2), 132–142.

Vandenberg, S. G. (1987). Sex differences in mental retardation and their implications for sex differences in ability. In J. M. Reinisch, L. A. Rosenblum, & S. A. Sanders (Eds.), *Masculinity/Femininity: Basic perspectives.* New York: Oxford University Press.

Vandereycken, W. (2002). History of anorexia nervosa and bulimia nervosa. In C. G. Fairburn & K. D. Brownell (Eds.), *Eating disorders and obesity.* New York: Guilford Press.

Vandewater, E. A., Bickham, D. S., Lee, J. H., Cummings, H. M., Wartella, E. A., & Rideout, V. J. (2005). When the television is always on. *American Behavioral Scientist, 48,* 562–577.

van Griensven, F., Chakkraband, M. L. S., Thienkrua, W., Pengjuntr, W., Cardozo, B. L., Tantipiwatanaskul, P., & et al. (2007). Mental health problems among adults in tsunami-affected areas in Southern Thailand. *JAMA, 296,* 537–548.

van Kammen, D. P., & Marder, S. R. (2005). Serotonin-dopamine antagonists (atypical or second-generation antipsychotics). In B. J. Sadock & V. A. Sadock (Eds.), *Kaplan and Sadock's comprehensive textbook of psychiatry.* Philadelphia: Lippincott Williams & Wilkins.

van Wel, F., Linssen, H., & Abma, R. (2000). The parental bond and the well-being of adolescents and young adults. *Journal of Youth and Adolescence, 29,* 307–318.

Vartanian, L. R., Giant, C. L., & Passino, R. M. (2001). "Ally McBeal vs. Arnold Schwarzenegger": Comparing mass media, interpersonal feedback and gender as predictors of satisfaction with body thinness and masculinity. *Social Behavior and Personality, 29*(7), 711–723.

Vazire, S., & Gosling, S. D. (2004). e-Perceptions: Personality impressions based on personal websites. *Journal of Personality and Social Psychology, 87*(1), 123–132.

Veenhoven, R. (1993). *Happiness in nations.* Rotterdam, Netherlands: Risbo.

Veevers, J. E., Gee, E. M., & Wister, A. V. (1996). Homeleaving age norms: Conflict or consensus? *International Journal of Aging and Human Development, 43*(4), 277–295.

Vega, W. A., Kolody, B., Aguilar-Gaxiola, S., & Catalano, R. (1999). Gaps in service utilization by Mexican Americans with mental health problems. *American Journal of Psychiatry, 156,* 928–934.

Venturello, S., Barzega, G., Maina, G., & Bogetto, F. (2002). Premorbid conditions and precipitating events in early-onset panic disorder. *Comprehensive Psychiatry, 43,* 28–36.

Verderber, K. S., Verderber, R. F., & Berryman-Fink, C. (2007). *Inter-Act: Interpersonal communication concepts, skills, and contexts.* New York: Oxford University Press.

Verderber, R. F., & Verderber, K. S. (2004). *Inter-Act: Interpersonal communication concepts, skills, and contexts.* New York: Oxford University Press.

Verderber, R. F., Verderber, K. S., & Berryman-Fink, C. (2008). *Communicate.* Belmont, CA: Wadsworth.

Verona, E., & Curtin, J. J. (2006). Gender differences in the negative affective priming of aggressive behavior. *Emotion, 6*(1), 115–124.

Vgontzas, A. N., Bixler, E. O., & Kales, A. K. (2000). Sleep, sleep disorders, and stress. In G. Fink (Ed.), *Encyclopedia of stress* (Vol. 3, p. 449–457). San Diego: Academic Press.

Videbech, P. (2006). Hippocampus and unipolar depression. *Directions in Psychiatry, 26*(3), 183–194.

Videbech, P., & Ravnkilde, B. (2004). Hippocampal volume and depression: A meta-analysis of MRI studies. *American Journal of Psychiatry, 161,* 1957–1966.

Viglione, D. J., & Rivera, B. (2003). Assessing personality and psychopathology with projective methods. In J. R. Graham, & J. A. Naglieri (Eds.), *Handbook of psychology: Vol. 10. Assessment psychology.* New York: Wiley.

Vinogradov, S., Cox, P. D., & Yalom, I. D. (2003). Group therapy. In R. E. Hales & S. C. Yudofsky (Eds.), *Textbook of clinical psychiatry.* Washington, DC: American Psychiatric Publishing.

Vinokur, A. D., Price, R. H., & Caplan, R. D. (1996). Hard times and hurtful partners: How financial strain affects depression and relationship satisfaction of unemployed persons and their spouses. *Journal of Personality and Social Psychology, 71,* 166–179.

Vittengl, J. R., & Holt, C. S. (2000). Getting acquainted: The relationship of self-disclosure and social attraction to positive affect. *Journal of Social and Personal Relationships, 17*(1), 53–56.

Volavka, J., Czobor, P., Sheitman, B., Lindenmayer, J. P., Citrome, L., McEvoy, J. P., Cooper, T. B. , Chakos, M., & Lieberman, J. A. (2002). Clozapine, olanzapine, risperidone, haloperidol in the treatment of patients with chronic schizophrenia and schizoaffective disorder. *American Journal of Psychiatry, 159,* 255–262.

Vollmer, W. M., Sacks, F. M., Ard, J., Appel, L. J., Bray, G. A., Simons-Morton, D. G., & et al. (2001). Effects of diet and sodium intake on blood pressure: Subgroup analysis of the DASH-sodium trial. *Annals of Internal Medicine, 18,* 1019–1028.

Von Baeyer, C. L., Sherk, D. L., & Zanna, M. P. (1981). Impression management in the job interview: When the female applicant meets the male (chauvinist) interviewer. *Personality and Social Psychology Bulletin, 7,* 45–51.

Vonk, R. (1993). The negativity effect in trait rating and in open-ended descriptions of persons. *Personality and Social Psychology Bulletin, 19,* 269–278.

Vorauer, J. D., Cameron, J. J., Holmes, J. G., & Pearce, D. G. (2003). Invisible overtures: Fears of rejection and the signal amplification bias. *Journal of Personality and Social Psychology, 84*(4), 793–812.

Voydanoff, P. (2005). Consequences of boundary-spanning demands and resources for work-to-family conflict and perceived stress. *Journal of Occupational Health Psychology, 10,* 491–503.

Voydanoff, P., & Donnelly, B. W. (1999). Multiple roles and psychological distress: The intersection of the paid worker, spouse, and parent roles with the role of the adult child. *Journal of Marriage and the Family, 61,* 725–738.

Voyer, D., & Hou, J. (2006). Type of items and the magnitude of gender differences on the mental rotations test. *Candian Journal of Experimental Psychology, 60*(2), 91–100.

Vrugt, A., & Luyerink, M. (2000). The contribution of bodily posture to gender stereotypical impressions. *Social Behavior and Personality, 28*(1), 91–103.

Wachtel, P. L. (1989). *The poverty of affluence: A psychological portrait of the American way of life.* Philadelphia: New Society.

Wade, C., & Tavris, C. (1990). *Learning to think critically: A handbook to accompany psychology.* New York: HarperCollins.

Wade, P., & Bernstein, B. (1991). Culture sensitivity training and counselor's race: Effects on black female clients' perceptions and attrition. *Journal of Counseling Psychology, 38,* 9–15.

Wagner, D. M. (1998, Feb 1). Divorce reform: New directions. *Current,* pp. 7–10.

Waite, L. (2000). Trends in men's and women's well-being in marriage. In L. J. Waite (Ed.), *The ties that bind.* New York: Aldine de Gruyter.

Waite, L. J. (1995). Does marriage matter? *Demography, 32,* 483–507.

Waite, L., & Gallagher, M. (2000). *The case for marriage: Why married people are happier, healthier, and better off financially.* New York: Doubleday.

Wakabayashi, C., & Donato, K. M. (2006). Does caregiving increase poverty among women in later life? Evidence from health and retirement survey. *Journal of Health and Social Behavior, 47,* 258–274.

Wakefield, J. C. (1999). The measurement of mental disorder. In A. V. Horvitz & T. L. Scheid (Eds.), *A handbook for the study of mental health: Social contexts, theories, and systems.* New York: Cambridge University Press.

Wakefield, J. C., & Spitzer, R. L. (2002). Lowered estimates—but of what? *Archives of General Psychiatry, 59*(2), 129–130.

Waldrop, D., Lightsey, O. R., Ethington, C. A., Woemmel, C. A., & Coke, A. L. (2001). Self-efficacy, optimism, health competence, and recovery from orthopedic surgery. *Journal of Counseling Psychology, 48,* 233–238.

Walker, E., Kestler, L., Bollini, A., & Hochman, K. M. (2004). Schizophrenia: Etiology and course. *Annual Review of Psychology, 55,* 401–30.

Walker, K. (1994). Men, women, and friendship: What they say, what they do. *Gender & Society, 8,* 246–265.

Walker, L. S., Claar, R. L., & Garber, J. (2002). Social consequences of children's pain: When do they encourage symptoms of maintenance? *Journal of Pediatric Psychology, 27*(8), 689–698.

Wallace, H. M., Baumeister, R. F., & Vohs, K. D. (2005). Audience support and choking under pressure: A home disadvantage? *Journal of Sports Sciences, 23,* 429–438.

Waller, M. R., & McLanahan, S. S. (2005). "His" and "her" marriage expectations: Determinants and consequences. *Journal of Marriage and Family, 67,* 53–67.

Wallerstein, J. S. (2005). Growing up in the divorced family. *Clinical Social Work Journal, 33,* 401–418.

Wallerstein, J. S., & Blakeslee, S. (1989). *Second chances: Men, women, and children a decade after divorce.* Boston: Houghton Mifflin.

Wallerstein, J. S., & Kelly, J. B. (1980). *Surviving the breakup: How children and parents cope with divorce.* New York: Basic Books.

Wallerstein, J. S., Lewis, J. M., & Blakeslee, S. (2000). *The unexpected legacy of divorce: A 25-year landmark study.* New York: Hyperion.

Wallis, C. (2003, December 15). Does kindergarten need cops? *Time,* pp. 52–53.

Wallis, C. (2004, March 22). The case for staying home. *Time,* pp. 51–59.

Walsh, B. T. (2003). Eating disorders. In A. Tasman, J. Kay, & J. A. Lieberman (Eds.), *Psychiatry.* New York: Wiley.

Walsh, F. (1999). Families in later life: Challenges and opportunities. In B. Carter & M. McGoldrick (Eds.), *The expanded family life cycle: Individual, family, and social perspectives* (3rd ed.). Boston: Allyn & Bacon.

Walsh, J. K., Dement, W. C., & Dinges, D. F. (2005). Sleep medicine, public safety, and public health. In M. H. Kryger, T. Roth, & W. C. Dement (Eds.), *Principles and practice of sleep medicine.* Philadelphia: Elsevier Saunders.

Walster, E., Aronson, E., Abrahams, D., & Rottman, L. (1966). Importance of physical attractiveness in dating behavior. *Journal of Personality and Social Psychology, 4,* 508–516.

Walter, C. A. (2000). The psychosocial meaning of menopause: Women's experiences. *Journal of Women and Aging, 12*(3–4), 117–131.

Wampold, B. E. (2001). *The great psychotherapy debate.* Mahwah, NJ: Erlbaum.

Wang, H., & Amato, P. R. (2000). Predictors of divorce adjustment: Stressors, resources, and definitions. *Journal of Marriage and the Family, 62,* 655–668.

Wang, P. S., Berglund, P., Olfson, M., Pincus, H. A., Wells, K. B., & Kessler, R. C. (2005). Failure and delay in initial treatment contact after first onset of mental disorders in the National Comorbidity Survey Replication. *Archives of General Psychiatry, 62,* 603–613.

Wang, P. S., Lane, M., Olfson, M., Pincus, H. A., Wells, K. B., & Kessler, R. C. (2005). Twelve-month use of mental health services in the United States: Results from the National Comorbidity Survey Replication. *Archives of General Psychiatry, 62,* 629–640.

Wannamethee, G., Shaper, A. G., & MacFarlane, P. W. (1993). Heart rate, physical activity, and mortality from cancer and other noncardiovascular disease. *American Journal of Epidemiology, 137,* 735–748.

Ward, A., & Brenner, L. (2006). Accentuate the negative: The positive effects of negative acknowledgement. *Psychological Science, 17,* 959–962.

Ward, C. N., & Lundberg-Love, P. K. (2006). Sexual abuse of women. In P. K. Lundberg-Love & S. L. Marmion (Eds.), *"Intimate" violence against women: When spouses, partners, or lovers attack.* Westport, CT: Praeger.

Wardle, J., Robb, K. A., Johnson, F., Griffith, J., et al. (2004). Socioeconomic variations in attitudes to eating and weight in female adolescents. *Health Psychology, 23,* 275–282.

Warner, L., Hatcher, R. A., & Steiner, M. J. (2004). Male condoms. In R. A. Hatcher, J. Trussell, F. H. Stewart, A. L. Nelson, W. Cates Jr., F. Guest, & D. Kowal (Eds.), *Contraceptive technology* (18th rev. ed.). New York: Ardent Media.

Warner-Schmidt, J. L., & Duman, R. S. (2006). Hippocampal neurogenesis: Opposing effects of stress and antidepressant treatment. *Hippocampus, 16,* 239–249.

Warr, P. (1999). Well-being and the workplace. In D. Kahneman, E. Diener, & N. Schwarz (Eds.), *Well-being: The foundations of hedonic psychology.* New York: Sage.

Warren, R. (2002). *The purpose driven life: What on Earth am I here for?* Grand Rapids, MI: Zondervan.

Waters, E., Merrick, S., Treboux, D., Crowell, J., & Albersheim, L. (2000). Attachment security in infancy and early adulthood: A twenty-year longitudinal study. *Child Development, 71*(3), 684–689.

Watkins, P. L., Ward, C. H., & Southard, D. R. (1992). The Type A belief system: Relationship to hostility, social support, and life stress. *Behavioral Medicine, 18,* 27–32.

Watson, D., & Clark, L. A. (1997). Extraversion and its positive emotional core. In R. Hogan, J. Johnson, & S. Briggs (Eds), *Handbook of personality psychology.* San Diego: Academic Press.

Watson, D., David, J. P., & Suls, J. (1999). Personality, affectivity, and coping. In C. R. Snyder (Ed.), *Coping: The psychology of what works.* New York: Oxford University Press.

Watson, D., Klohnen, E. C., Casillas, A., Nus Simms, E., Haig, J., & Berry, D. S. (2004). Match makers and deal breakers: Analyses of assortative mating in newlywed couples. *Journal of Personality, 72,* 1029–1068.

Watson, D., & Pennebaker, J. W. (1989). Health complaints, stress, and distress: Exploring the central role of negative affectivity. *Psychological Review, 96,* 234–254.

Watson, D., Suls, J., & Haig, J. (2002). Global self-esteem in relation to structural models of personality and affectivity. *Journal of Personality and Social Psychology, 83,* 185–197.

Watson, D. L., & Tharp, R. G. (2007). *Self-directed behavior: Self-modification for personal adjustment.* Belmont, CA: Wadsworth.

Watson, J. B. (1913). Psychology as the behaviorist views it. *Psychological Review, 20,* 158–177.

Weaver, A. D., & Byers, E. S. (2006). The relationships among body image, body mass index, exercise, and sexual functioning in heterosexual women. *Psychology of Women Quarterly, 30,* 333–339.

Weaver, M. F., & Schnoll, S. H. (1999). Stimulants: Amphetamines and cocaine. In B. S. McCrady & E. E. Epstein (Eds.), *Addictions: A comprehensive guidebook.* New York: Oxford University Press.

Weber, L. J. (2006). *Profits before people?* Bloomington, IN: Indiana University Press.

Webster, D. M. (1993). Motivated augmentation and reduction of the overattribution bias. *Journal of Personality and Social Psychology, 65,* 261–271.

Webster, D. M., Richter, L., & Kruglanski, A. W. (1996). On leaping to conclusions when feeling tired: Mental fatigue effects on impressional primacy. *Journal of Experimental Social Psychology, 32,* 181–195.

Wechsler, H., Lee, J. E., Kuo, M., Seibring, M., Nelson, T. F., & Lee, H. (2002). Trends in college binge drinking during a period of increased prevention efforts. *Journal of American College Health, 50*(5), 203–217.

Wegener, D. T., & Petty, R. E. (1994). Mood management across affective states: The hedonic contingency hypothesis. *Journal of Personality and Social Psychology, 66,* 1034–1048.

Weil, M. M., & Rosen, L. D. (1997). *TechnoStress: Coping with technology @ home @ work @ play.* New York: Wiley.

Weimer, B. L., Kerns, K. A., & Oldenburg, C. M. (2004). Adolescents' interactions with a best friend: Associations with attachment style. *Journal of Experimental Child Psychology, 88*(1), 102–120.

Weinberg, C. (1979). *Self-creation.* New York: Avon.

Weinberger, D. A. (1990). The construct validity of the repressive coping style. In J. L. Singer (Ed.), *Repression and dissociation.* Chicago: University of Chicago Press.

Weinberger, J. (1995). Common factors aren't so common: The common factors dilemma. *Clinical Psychology: Science and Practice, 2,* 45–69, 1915–1933.

Weiner, B. (1986). *An attribution theory of emotion and motivation.* New York: Springer-Verlag.

Weiner, B. (1994). Integrating social and personal theories of achievement striving. *Review of Educational Research, 64,* 557–573.

Weiner, B. (2006). *Social motivation, justice, and the moral emotions: An attributional approach.* Mahwah, NJ: Erlbaum.

Weinfield, N., Sroufe, L. A., & Egeland, B. (2000). Attachment from early infancy to early adulthood in a high-risk sample: Continuity, discontinuity, and their correlates. *Child Development, 71*(3), 695–702.

Weinstein, N. D. (1980). Unrealistic optimism about future life events. *Journal of Personality and Social Psychology, 39,* 806–820.

Weinstein, N. D. (1982). Unrealistic optimism about susceptibility to health problems. *Journal of Behavioral Medicine, 5,* 441–460.

Weinstein, N. D. (2003). Exploring the links between risk perceptions and preventive health behavior. In J. Suls & K. A. Wallston (Eds.), *Social psychological foundations of health and illness.* Malden, MA: Blackwell Publishing.

Weinstein, N. D., & Klein, W. M. (1996). Unrealistic optimism: Present and future. *Journal of Social and Clinical Psychology, 15*(1), 1–8.

Weinstein, N. D., Slovic, P., & Gibson, G. (2004). Accuracy and optimism in smokers' beliefs about quitting. *Nicotine & Tobacco Research, 6*(Suppl3), 375–380.

Weisaeth, L. (1993). Disasters: Psychological and psychiatric aspects. In L. Goldberger & S. Breznitz (Eds.), *Handbook of stress: Theoretical and clinical aspects* (2nd ed.). New York: Free Press.

Weisler, R. H., Barbee, J. G., & Townsend, M. H. (2007). Mental health and recovery in the Gulf Coast after Hurricanes Katrina and Rita. *JAMA, 296,* 585–588.

Weiss, E. M., Kemmler, G., Deisenhammer, E. A., Fleischhacker, W. W., & Delazer, M. (2003). Sex differences in cognitive functions. *Personality and Individual Differences, 35,* 863–875.

Weiss, R. (1973). *Loneliness: The experience of emotional and social isolation.* Cambridge, MA: MIT Press.

Weiss, R. S. (1975). *Marital separation.* New York: Basic Books.

Weisz, J. R., Rothbaum, F. M., & Blackburn, T. C. (1984). Standing out and standing in: The psychology of control in America and Japan. *American Psychologist, 39,* 955–969.

Weiten, W. (1988). Pressure as a form of stress and its relationship to psychological symptomatology. *Journal of Social and Clinical Psychology, 6,* 127–139.

Weiten, W. (1998). Pressure, major life events, and psychological symptoms. *Journal of Social Behavior and Personality, 13,* 51–68.

Weiten, W., Guadagno, R. E., & Beck, C. A. (1996). Students' perceptions of textbook pedagogical aids. *Teaching of Psychology, 23,* 105–107.

Weitzman, L. (1996). The economic consequences of divorce are still unequal: Comment on Peterson. *American Sociological Review, 61,* 537–538.

Wells, K., Klap, R., Koike, A., & Sherbourne, C. (2001). Ethnic disparities in unmet need for alcoholism, drug abuse, and mental health care. *American Journal of Psychiatry, 158,* 2027–2032.

Welsh, R. S. (2003). Prescription priveleges: Pro or con. *Clinical Psychology: Science & Practice, 10,* 371–372.

Wessely, S., & Kerwin, R. (2004). Suicide risk and the SSRI's. *Journal of the American Medical Association, 292*(3), 379–381.

Wesson, D. R., Smith, D. E., Ling, W., & Seymour, R. B. (2005). Sedatives–hypnotics. In J. H. Lowinson, P. Ruiz, R. B. Millman, & J. G. Langrod (Eds.), *Substance abuse: A comprehensive textbook*. Philadelphia: Lippincott/Williams & Wilkins.

West, D. S., Harvey-Berino, J., & Raczynski, J. M. (2004). Behavioral aspects of obesity, dietary intake, and chronic disease. In J. M. Raczynski & L. C. Leviton (Eds.), *Handbook of clinical health psychology: Vol. 2. Disorders of behavior and health.* Washington, DC: American Psychological Association.

Westefeld, J. S., Maples, M. R., Buford, B., & Taylor, S. (2001). Gay, lesbian, and bisexual college students: The relationship between sexual orientation and depression, loneliness and suicide. *Journal of College Student Psychotherapy, 15*(3), 71–82.

Westen, D. (1998). The scientific legacy of Sigmund Freud: Toward a psychodynamically informed psychological science. *Psychological Bulletin, 124*(3), 333–371.

Westen, D., & Gabbard, G. O. (1999). Psychoanalytic approaches to personality. In L. A. Pervin & O. P. John (Eds.), *Handbook of personality: Theory and research* (2nd ed.). New York: Guilford Press.

Wester, S. R., Pionke, D. R., & Vogel, D. L. (2005). Male gender role conflict, gay men, and same-sex romantic relationships. *Psychology of Men and Masculinity, 6,* 195–208.

Wester, S. R., Vogel, D. L., Wei, M., & McLain, R. (2006). African American men, gender role conflict, and psychological distress: The role of racial identity. *Journal of Counseling & Development, 84,* 419–429.

Wethington, E. (2002). The relationship of turning points at work to perceptions of psychological growth and change. In R. A. Settersten & T. J. Owens (Eds.), *New frontiers in socialization.* Amsterdam: JAI.

Wethington, E., Kessler, R., & Pixley, J. (2004). Turning points in adulthood. In O. G. Brim, C. D. Ryff, & R. Kessler (Eds.), *How healthy are we: A national study of well-being in midlife.* Chicago: University of Chicago Press.

Wheaton, B. (1994). Sampling the stress universe. In W. R. Avison & I. H. Gotlib (Eds.), *Stress and mental health: Contemporary issues and prospects for the future.* New York: Plenum Press.

Wheeler, L., Koestner, R., & Driver, R. (1982). Related attributes in the choice of comparison others: It's there, but it isn't all there is. *Journal of Experimental Social Psychology, 18,* 489–500.

Wheeler, L., & Suls, J. (2005). Social comparison and self-evaluations of competence. In A. J. Elliot & C. S. Dweck (Eds.), *Handbook of competence and motivation.* New York: Guilford.

Whipple, B. (2000). Beyond the G spot. *Scandinavian Journal of Sexology, 3*(2), 35–42.

Whiston, S. C., & Keller, B. K. (2004). The influences of the family of origin on career development: A review and analysis. *Counseling Psychologist, 32*(4), 493–568.

Whitaker, R. (2002). *Mad in America: Bad science, bad medicine, and the enduring mistreatment of the mentally ill.* New York: Perseus Publishing.

Whitbourne, S. K. (1996). *The aging individual: Physical and psychological perspectives.* New York: Springer.

Whitbourne, S. K. (2001). The physical aging process in midlife: Interactions with psychological and sociocultural factors. In M. E. Lachman (Ed.), *Handbook of midlife development.* New York: Wiley.

Whitbourne, S. K. (2002). *The aging individual: Physical and psychological perspectives.* New York: Springer.

Whitbourne, S. K., Zuschlag, M. K., Elliot, L. B., & Waterman, A. S. (1992). Psychosocial development in adulthood: A 22-year sequential study. *Journal of Personality and Social Psychology, 63,* 260–271.

White, L. K., & Edwards, J. N. (1990). Emptying the nest and parental well-being: An analysis of national panel data. *American Sociological Review, 55*(2), 235–242.

White, L. K., & Rogers, S. J. (1997). Strong support but uneasy relationships: Coresident and adult children's relationships with their parents. *Journal of Marriage and the Family, 59,* 62–76.

White, L. K., & Rogers, S. J. (2001). Economic circumstances and family outcomes: A review of the 1990s. In R. M. Milardo (Ed.), *Understanding families into the new millennium: A decade in review.* Minneapolis: National Council on Family Relations.

White, O. K. Jr., & White, D. (2005). Polygamy and Mormon identity. *Journal of American Culture, 28,* 165–177.

Whitehead, B. D., & Popenoe, D. (2001). *The state of our unions: The social health of marriage in America, 2001.* Piscataway, NJ: The National Marriage Project.

Whitehouse, W. G., & Dinges, D. F., Orne, E. C., & Orne, M. T. (1988). Hypnotic hyperamnesia: Enhanced memory accessibility or report bias? *Journal of Abnormal Psychology, 97,* 298–295.

Whiteman, S. D., McHale, S. M., & Crouter, A. C. (2003). What parents learn from experience: The first child as a first draft? *Journal of Marriage and Family, 65,* 608–621.

Whitley, B. E. (1999). Right-wing authoritarianism, social dominance orientation, and prejudice. *Journal of Personality and Social Psychology, 77*(1), 126–134.

Whitley, B. E. (2001). Gender-role variables and attitudes toward homosexuality. *Sex Roles, 45,* 691–721.

Whitley, B. E.., & Kite, M. E. (2006). *The psychology of prejudice and discrimination.* Belmont, CA: Wadsworth.

Whitty, M. T. (2005). The realness of cybercheating: Men's and women's representations of unfaithful internet relationships. *Social Science Computer Review, 23*(1), 57–67.

Whybrow, P. C. (2005). *American mania: When more is not enough.* New York: Norton.

Wickrama, K. A. S., Lorenz, F. O., Conger, R. D., & Elder, G. H. (1997). Marital quality and physical illness: A latent growth curve analysis. *Journal of Marriage and Family, 59,* 143–155.

Widiger, T. A., & Sankis, L. M. (2000). Adult psychopathology: Issues and controversies. *Annual Review of Psychology, 51,* 377–404.

Widiger, T. A., & Simonsen, E. (2005). Introduction to the special section: The American psychiatric association's research agenda for the DSM-V. *Journal of Personality Disorders, 19*(2), 103–109.

Wiederman, M. W. (1993). Evolved gender differences in mate preferences: Evidence from personal advertisements. *Ethology and Sociobiology, 14,* 331–352.

Wiederman, M. W. (1997). Extramarital sex: Prevalence and correlates in a national survey. *Journal of Sex Research, 34,* 167–174.

Wiederman, M. W. (2004). Methodological issues in studying sexuality in close relationships. In J. H. Harvey, A. Wenzel, & S. Sprecher (Eds.), *The handbook of sexuality in close relationships.* Mahwah, NJ: Lawrence Erlbaum.

Wielawski, I. (1991, October 3). *Unlocking the secrets of memory.* Los Angeles Times, p. 1.

Wilfong, J. D. (2006). Computer anxiety and anger: The impact of computer use, computer experience, and self-efficacy beliefs. *Computers in Human Behavior, 22,* 1001–1011.

Wilgosh, L. (2001). Enhancing gifts and talents of women and girls. *High Ability Studies, 12*(1), 45–59.

Wilkaitis, J., Mulvhill, T., & Nasrallah, H. A. (2004). Classic antipsychotic medications. In A. F. Schatzberg & C. B. Nemeroff (Eds), *Textbook of psychopharmacology.* Washington, DC: American Psychiatric Publishing.

Willets, M. C., Sprecher, S., & Beck, F. D. (2004). Overview of sexual practices and attitudes within relationship contexts. In J. H. Harvey, A. Wenzel, & S. Sprecher (Eds.), *The handbook of sexuality in close relationships.* Mahwah, NJ: Lawrence Erlbaum.

Willett, W. C., & Stampfer, W. J. (2003). Rebuilding the food pyramid. *Scientific American, 288*(1), 64–71.

Williams, C. G., Gagne, M., Ryan, R. M., & Deci, E. L. (2002). Facilitating autonomous motivation for smoking cessation. *Health Psychology, 21,* 40–50.

Williams, C. L. (1998). The glass escalator: Hidden advantages for men in the female professions. In M. S. Kimmel & M. A. Messner (Eds.), *Men's lives.* Boston: Allyn & Bacon.

Williams, J. E., & Best, D. L. (1982). *Measuring sex stereotypes: A thirty-nation study.* Newbury Park, CA: Sage.

Williams, J. E., & Best, D. L. (1990). *Measuring sex stereotypes: A multination study* (Rev. ed.). Newbury Park, CA: Sage Publications.

Williams, J. E., Paton, C. C., Siegler, I. C., Eigenbrodt, M. L., Neito, F. J., & Tyroler, H. A. (2000). Anger proneness predicts coronary heart disease risk. *Circulation, 101,* 2034–2039.

Williams, J. E., Satterwhite, R. C., & Best, D. L. (1999). Pancultural gender stereotypes revisited: The five-factor model. *Sex Roles, 40,* 513–526.

Williams, J. M. G., Watts, F. N., MacLeod, C., & Mathews, A. (1997). *Cognitive psychology and emotional disorders* (2nd ed.). Chichester, UK: Wiley.

Williams, K. B., Radefeld, P. S., Binning, J. F., & Sudak, J. R. (1993). When job candidates are "hard-" versus "easy-to-get": Effects of candidate availability on employment decisions. *Journal of Applied Social Psychology, 23*(3), 169–198.

Williams, K. E., & Bond, M. J. (2002). The roles of self-efficacy, outcome expectancies and social support in the self-care behaviors of diabetics. *Psychology, Health & Medicine, 7*(2), 127–141.

Williams, M. H. (1992). Exploitation and inference: Mapping the damage from therapist-patient sexual involvement. *American Psychologist, 47,* 412–421.

Williams, N. A., & Deffenbacher, J. L. (1983). Life stress and chronic yeast infections. *Journal of Human Stress, 9,* 26–31.

Williams, P. (2005). What is psychoanalysis? What is a psychoanalyst? In E. S. Person, A. M. Cooper, & G. O. Gabbard (Eds.), *Textbook of psychoanalysis.* Washington, DC: American Psychiatric Publishing.

Williams, R. B. (1996). Hostility and the heart. In D. Goleman & J. Gurin (Eds.), *Mind-body medicine: How to use your mind for better health.* Yonkers, NY: Consumer Reports Books.

Williams, R. B. (2001). Hostility (and other psychosocial risk factors): Effects on health and the potential for successful behavioral approaches to prevention and treatment. In A. Baum, T. A. Revenson, & J. E. Singer (Eds.), *Handbook of health psychology.* Mahwah, NJ: Erlbaum.

Williams, R. B., & Williams, V. P. (1993). *Anger kills: Seventeen strategies for controlling the hostility that can harm your health.* New York: Times Books/ Random House.

Williams, R. L., & Eggert, A. (2002). Notetaking predictors of test performance. *Teaching of Psychology, 29,* 234–237.

Williams, S. L. (1995). Self-efficacy, anxiety, and phobic disorders. In J. E. Maddux (Ed.), *Self-efficacy, adaptation, and adjustment: Theory, research, and application.* New York: Plenum Press.

Williamson, D. A., Zucker, N. L., Martin, C. K., & Smeets, M. A. M. (2001). Etiology and management of eating disorders. In P. B. Sutker & H. E. Adams (Eds.), *Comprehensive handbook of psychopathology* (3rd ed.). New York: Kluwer Academic/Plenum.

Willis, S. L., & Reid, J. E. E. (1999). *Life in the middle: Psychological and social development in middle age.* San Diego: Academic Press.

Wills, T. A., & Fegan, M. (2001). Social networks and social support. In A. Baum, T. A. Revenson, & J. E. Singer (Eds.), *Handbook of health psychology.* Mahwah, NJ: Erlbaum.

Wilpert, B. (1995). Organizational behavior. *Annual review of psychology, 46,* 59–90

Wilsnack, S. C., Wonderlich, S. A., Kristjanson, A. F., Vogeltanz-Holm, N. D., & Wilsnack, R. W. (2002). Self-reports of forgetting and remembering childhood sexual abuse in a nationally representative sample of U.S. women. *Child Abuse and Neglect, 26*(2), 139–147.

Wilson, A. E., & Ross, M. (2000). The frequency of temporal-self and social comparisons in people's personal appraisals. *Journal of Personality and Social Psychology, 78,* 928–942.

Wilson, J. P., Drozdek, B., & Turkovic, S. (2006). Posttraumatic shame and guilt. *Trauma, Violence and Abuse, 7*(2), 122–141.

Wilson, R. S., & Bennett, D. A. (2003). Cognitive activity and the risk of Alzheimer's disease. *Current Directions in Psychological Science, 12*(3), 87–91.

Wilson, T. D. (2002). *Strangers to ourselves: Discovering the adaptive unconscious.* Cambridge: Belknap Press.

Wilson, T. D., & Gilbert, D. T. (2005). Affective forecasting: Knowing what to want. *Current Directions in Psychological Science, 14*(3), 131–134.

Wing, J. F., Schette, N. S., & Byrne, B. (2006). The effect of positive writing on emotional intelligence and life satisfaction. *Journal of Clinical Psychology, 62,* 1291–1302.

Wing, R. R., & Polley, B. A. (2001). Obesity. In A. Baum, T. A. Revenson, & J. E. Singer (Eds.), *Handbook of health psychology.* Mahwah, NJ: Erlbaum.

Winick, C., & Norman, R. L. (2005). Epidemiology. In J. H. Lowinson, P. Ruiz, R. B. Millman, & J. G. Langrod (Eds.), *Substance abuse: A comprehensive textbook.* Philadelphia: Lippincott/Williams & Wilkins.

Winter, D. D. N. (2004). Shopping for sustainability: Psychological solutions to overconsumption. In T. Kasser & A. D. Kanner (Eds.), *Psychology and consumer culture: The struggle for a good life in a materialistic world.* Washington, DC: American Psychological Association.

Winzelberg, A. J., & Luskin, F. M. (1999). The effect of a meditation training in stress levels in secondary school teachers. *Stress Medicine, 15,* 69–77.

Wise, D., & Rosqvist, J. (2006). Explanatory style and well-being. In J. C. Thomas, D. L. Segal, & M. Hersen (Eds.), *Comprehensive handbook of personality and psychopathology: Personality and everyday functioning.* Hoboken, NJ: Wiley.

Wissink, I. B., Dekovic, M., & Meijer, A. M. (2006). Parenting behavior, quality of the parent-adolescent functioning in four ethnic groups. *Journal of Early Adolescence, 26,* 133–159.

Wittenberg, M. T., & Reis, H. T. (1986). Loneliness, social skills, and social perception. *Personality and Social Psychology Bulletin, 12,* 121–130.

Witvliet, C., Ludwig, T. E., & Vander Laan, K. L. (2001). Granting forgiveness or harboring grudges: Implications for emotion, physiology, and health. *Psychological Science, 121*(2), 117–123.

Wolfe, J. B., & Betz, N. E. (2004). The relationship of attachment variables to career decision-making self-efficacy and fear of commitment. *Career Development Quarterly, 52,* 363–369.

Wolfinger, N. H. (2005). *Understanding the divorce cycle: The children of divorce in their own marriages.* New York: Cambridge University Press.

Wolinsky, F. D. (1988). Sick role legitimation. In D. S. Gochman (Ed.), *Health behavior: Emerging research perspectives.* New York: Plenum Press.

Wolitski, R. J., Henny, K. D., & Lyles, C. M. (2006). Evolution of HIV/AIDS prevention programs—United States, 1981–2006. *Journal of the American Medical Association, 296,* 760–762.

Wolk, A., Manson, J. E., Stampfer, M. J., Colditz, G. A., Hu, F. B., Speizer, F. E., Hennekens, C. H., & Willett, W. C. (1999). Long-term intake of dietary fiber and decreased risk of coronary heart disease among women. *Journal of the American Medical Association, 281*(21), 1998–2004.

Woloshin, S., Schwartz, L. M., & Welch, H. G. (2002). Risk charts: Putting cancer in context. *Journal of the National Cancer Institute, 94,* 799–804.

Wolpe, J. (1958). *Psychotherapy by reciprocal inhibition.* Stanford, CA: Stanford University Press.

Wolpe, J. (1987). The promotion of scientific therapy: A long voyage. In J. K. Zeig (Ed.), *The evolution of psychotherapy.* New York: Brunner/Mazel.

Wolpe, J. (1990). *The practice of behavior therapy.* Elmsford, NY: Pergamon.

Women clerics find sexual harassment. (1990, December 1). *Washington Post, C12.*

Wonderlich, S. A. (2002). Personality and eating disorders. In C. G. Fairburn & K. D. Brownell (Eds.), *Eating disorders and obesity: A comprehensive handbook.* New York: Guilford.

Wong, N. (2005). Group psychotherapy and combined individual and group psychotherapy. In B. J. Sadock & V. A. Sadock (Eds.), *Kaplan and Sadock's comprehensive textbook of psychiatry.* Philadelphia: Lippincott Williams & Wilkins.

Wong, Y. J., & Rochlen, A. B. (2005). Demystifying men's emotional behavior: New directions and implications for counseling and research. *Psychology of Men and Masculinity, 6*(1), 62–72.

Wood, E., Desmarais, S., & Gugula, S. (2002). The impact of parenting experience on gender stereotyped toy play of children. *Sex Roles, 47*(1–2), 39–49.

Wood, J. V. (1989). Theory and research concerning social comparisons of personal attributes. *Psychological Bulletin, 106,* 231–248.

Wood, J. V., & Wilson, A. E. (2003). How important is social comparison? In M. R. Leary , & J. P. Tangney (Eds.), *Handbook of self and identity.* New York: Guilford.

Wood, M. D., Vinson, D. C., & Sher, K. J. (2001). Alcohol use and misuse. In A. Baum, T. A. Revenson, & J. E. Singer (Eds.), *Handbook of health psychology.* Mahwah, NJ: Erlbaum.

Wood, N., & Cowan, N. (1995). The cocktail party phenomenon revisited: How frequent are attention shifts to one's name in an irrelevant auditory channel? *Journal of Experimental Psychology: Learning, Memory, and Cognition, 21,* 255–260.

Wood, W., Conway, M., Pushkar, D., & Dugas, M. J. (2005). People's perceptions of women's and men's worry about life issues: Worrying about love, accomplishment, or money? *Sex Roles, 53,* 545–551.

Wood, W., & Eagly, A. H. (2002). A cross-cultural analysis of the behavior of women and men: Implications for the origins of sex differences. *Psychological Bulletin, 128*(5), 699–727.

Wood, W., & Kallgren, C. A. (1988). Communicator attributes and persuasion: Recipients' access to attitude-relevant information in memory. *Personality and Social Psychology Bulletin, 14,* 172–182.

Wood, W., & Quinn, J. M. (2003). Forewarned and forearmed? Two meta-analytic syntheses of forewarnings of influence appeals. *Psychological Bulletin, 129*(1), 119–138.

Woodhill, B. M., & Samuels, C. A. (2003). Positive and negative androgyny and their relationship with psychological health and well-being. *Sex Roles, 48,* 555–565.

Woodhill, B. M., & Samuels, C. A. (2004). Desirable and undesirable androgyny: A prescription for the twenty-first century. *Journal of Gender Studies, 13*(1), 15–28.

Woodzicka, J. A., & LaFrance, M. (2005). The effects of subtle sexual harassment on women's performance in a job interview. *Sex Roles, 53,* 67–77.

Worthen, J. B. (1997). Resiliency of bizarreness effects under varying conditions of verbal and imaginal elaboration and list composition. *Journal of Mental Imagery, 21,* 167–194.

Worthington, E. L. Jr., & Scherer, M. (2004). Forgiveness is an emotion-focused coping strategy that can reduce health risks and promote health resilience: Theory, review, and hypotheses. *Psychology and Health, 19*(3), 385–405.

Worthington, R. L., Flores, L. Y., & Navarro, R. L. (2005). Career development in context: Research with people of color. In S. D. Brown & R. W. Lent (Eds.), *Career development and counseling: Putting theory and research to work.* New York: Wiley.

Wortman, C. B., & Boerner, K. (2007). Beyond the myths of coping with loss: Assumptions versus scientific evidence. In H. S. Friedman & R. C. Silver (Eds.), *Foundations of health psychology.* New York: Oxford University Press.

Wortman, C. B., & Silver, R. C. (1990). Successful mastery of bereavement and widowhood: A life-course perspective. In P. B. Baltes & M. M. Baltes (Eds.), *Successful aging.* Cambridge, MA: Cambridge University Press.

Wortman, C. B., Wolff, K., & Bonanno, G. A. (2004). Loss of an intimate partner through death. In D. J. Mashek & A. Aron (Eds.), *Handbook of closeness and intimacy.* Mahwah, NJ: Erlbaum.

Wright, J. H., Beck, A. T., & Thase, M. E. (2003). Cognitive therapy. In R. E. Hales & S. C. Yudofsky (Eds.), *Textbook of clinical psychiatry.* Washington, DC: American Psychiatric Publishing.

Wright, P. H. (2006). Toward an expanded orientation to the comparative study of women's and men's same-sex friendships. In K. Dindia & D. J. Canary (Eds.), *Sex differences and similarities in communication.* Mahwah, NJ: Erlbaum.

Wright, R. A., & Contrada, R. J. (1986). Dating selectivity and interpersonal attraction: Toward a better understanding of the "elusive phenomenon." *Journal of Social and Personal Relationships, 3,* 131–148.

Wright, S. C., & Taylor, D. M. (2003). The social psychology of cultural diversity: Social stereotyping, prejudice, and discrimination. In M. A. Hogg & J. Cooper (Eds.), *The Sage handbook of social psychology.* Thousand Oaks, CA: Sage Publications.

Wrosch, C., Heckhausen, J., & Lachman, M. E. (2006). Goal management across adulthood and old age: The adaptive value of primary and secondary control. In D. K. Mroczek & T. D. Little (Eds.), *Handbook of personality development.* Mahwah, NJ: Erlbaum.

Wu, Z., & Hart, R. (2002). The effects of marital and nonmarital union transition on health. *Journal of Marriage and Family, 64,* 430–432.

Wylie, M. S. (1998). The shadow of a doubt. In R. A. Baker (Ed.), *Child sexual abuse and false memory syndrome.* Amherst, NY: Prometheus Books.

Wynder, E. L., Cohen, L. A., Muscat, J. E., Winters, B., Dwyer, J. T., & Blackburn, G. (1997). Breast cancer: Weighing the evidence for a promoting role of dietary fat. *Journal of the National Cancer Institute, 89*(11), 766–775.

Xiaohe, X., & Whyte, M. K. (1990). Love matches and arranged marriages: A Chinese replication. *Journal of Marriage and the Family, 52,* 709–722.

Yager, J. (1999). *Friendshifts: The power of friendship and how it shapes our lives.* Stamford, CT: Hannacroix Creek Books.

Yalom, I. D. (1995). *The theory and practice of group psychotherapy* (4th ed.). New York: Basic Books.

Yamamoto, J., Silva, J. A., Justice, L. R., Chang, C. Y., & Leong, G. B. (1993). Cross-cultural psychotherapy. In A. C. Gaw (Ed.), *Culture, ethnicity, and mental illness.* Washington, DC: American Psychological Press.

Yang, H., Liu, T., & Zang, D. (2000). A study of stressful life events before the onset of hypothyroidism. *Chinese Mental Health Journal, 14*(3), 201–202.

Yapko, M. D. (1994). *Suggestions of abuse: True and false memories of childhood sexual trauma.* New York: Simon & Schuster.

Yate, M. (2006). *Knock 'em dead: The ultimate job search guide.* Avon, MA: Adams Media.

Yehuda, R. (2003). Changes in the concept of PTSD and trauma. *Psychiatric Times, 20*(4), 35–40.

Yi, H., Stinson, F. S., Williams, G. D., & Dufour, M. C. (1999). *Surveillance report #53: Trends in alcohol-related fatal traffic crashes, United States, 1977–1998.* Rockville, MD: National Institute on Alcohol Abuse and Alcoholism.

Ying, Y., & Han, M. (2006). The contribution of personality, acculturative stressors, and social affiliation to adjustment: A longitudinal study of Taiwanese students in the United States. *International Journal of Intercultural Relations, 30,* 623–635.

Yoder, J. D., & Kahn, A. S. (2003). Making gender comparisons more meaningful: A call for more attention to social context. *Psychology of Women Quarterly, 27,* 281–290.

Yost, M. R., & Zurbriggen, E. L. (2006). Gender differences in the enactment of sociosexuality: An examination of implicit social motives, sexual fantasies, coercive sexual attitudes, and aggressive sexual behavior. *Journal of Sex Research, 43,* 163–173.

Young, J. E. (1982). Loneliness, depression and cognitive therapy: Theory and application. In L. A. Peplau & D. Perlman (Eds.), *Loneliness: A sourcebook of current theory, research and therapy.* New York: Wiley.

Young, K. S. (1998). *Caught in the net: How to recognize the signs of Internet addiction—and a winning strategy for recovery.* New York: Wiley.

Young, R., & Sweeting, H. (2004). Adolescent bullying, relationships, psychological well-being, and gender-atypical behavior: A gender diagnosticity approach. *Sex Roles, 50,* 525–537.

Younkin, S. L., & Betz, N. E. (1996). Psychological hardiness: A reconceptualization and measurement. In T. W. Miller (Ed.), *Theory and assessment of stressful life events.* Madison, CT: International Universities Press.

Yuen, C. N., & Lavin, M. J. (2004). Internet dependence in the collegiate population: The role of shyness. *CyberPsychology & Behavior, 7*(4), 379–383.

Yum, Y., & Schenck-Hamlin, W. (2005). Reactions to 9/11 as a function of terror management and perspective taking. *Journal of Social Psychology, 145,* 265–286.

Yutzy, S. H. (2003). Somatoform disorders. In R. E. Hales & S. C. Yudofsky (Eds.), *Textbook of clinical psychiatry.* Washington, DC: American Psychiatric Publishing.

Zaalberg, R., Manstead, A. S. R., & Fischer, A. H. (2004). Relations between emotions, display rules, social motives, and facial behaviour. *Cognition & Emotion, 18,* 183–207.

Zajonc, R. B. (1968). Attitudinal effects of mere exposure. *Journal of Personality and Social Psychology, 9,* 1–27.

Zakzanis, K. K., & Young, D. A. (2001). Memory impairment in abstinent MDMA ("Ecstasy") users: A longitudinal investigation. *Neurology, 56,* 966–969.

Zammichieli, M. E., Gilroy, F. D., & Sherman, M. F. (1988). Relation between sex-role orientation and marital satisfaction. *Personality and Social Psychology Bulletin, 14,* 747–754.

Zane, N., Hall, G. C. N., Sue, S., Young, K., & Nunez, J. (2004). Research on psychotherapy with culturally diverse populations. In M. J. Lambert (Ed.), *Bergin and Garfield's handbook of psychotherapy and behavior change.* New York: Wiley.

Zatzick, D. F. (1999). Managed care and psychiatry. In R. E. Hales, S. C. Yudofsky, & J. A. Talbott (Eds.), *American Psychiatric Press textbook of psychiatry.* Washington, DC: American Psychiatric Press.

Zautra, A. J., & Smith, B. W. (2001). Depression and reactivity to stress in older women with rheumatoid arthritis and osteoarthritis. *Psychosomatic Medicine, 63*(4), 687–696.

Zebrowitz, L. A., & Montepare, J. M. (2000). "Too young, too old": Stigmatizing adolescents and elders. In T. F. Heatheron et al. (Eds.), *The social psychology of stigma.* New York: Guilford.

Zechmeister, E. B., & Nyberg, S. E. (1982). *Human memory: An introduction to research and theory.* Pacific Grove, CA: Brooks/Cole.

Zeig, J. K. (1987). Introduction: The evolution of psychotherapy—Fundamental issues. In J. K. Zeig (Ed.), *The evolution of psychotherapy.* New York: Brunner/Mazel.

Zemishlany, Z., Aizenberg, D., & Weizman, A. (2001). Subjective effects of MDMA ("Ecstasy") on human sexual function. *European Psychiatry, 16*(2), 127–130.

Zimbardo, P. G. (1977). *Shyness: What it is, what to do about it.* Reading, MA: Addison-Wesley.

Zimbardo, P. G. (1990). *Shyness.* Reading, MA: Addison-Wesley.

Zimbardo, P. G. (1992). Cults in everyday life: Dependency and power. *Contemporary Psychology, 37,* 1187–1189.

Zimbardo, P. G. (2002). Mind control: Psychological reality or mindless rhetoric. *Cultic Studies Review, 1,* 309–311.

Zimmerman, B. J. (1995). Self-efficacy and educational development. In A. Bandura (Ed.), *Self-efficacy in changing societies.* New York: Cambridge University Press.

Zimmerman, M., & Spitzer, R. L. (2005). Psychiatric classification. In B. J. Sadock & V. A. Sadock (Eds.), *Kaplan & Sadock's comprehensive textbook of psychiatry.* Philadelphia: Lippincott Williams & Wilkins.

Zittleman, K., & Sadker, D. (2002). Gender bias in teacher education texts: New (and old) lessons. *Journal of Teacher Education, 53*(2), 168–180.

Zuckerman, M. (1979). *Sensation seeking: Beyond the optimal level of arousal.* Hillsdale, NJ: Erlbaum.

Zuckerman, M. (1995). Good and bad humors: Biochemical bases of personality and its disorders. *Psychological Science, 6,* 325–332.

Zuckerman, M., Kieffer, S. C., & Knee, C. R. (1998). Consequences of self-handicapping: Effects of coping, academic performance, and adjustment. *Journal of Personality and Social Psychology, 74*(6), 1619–1628.

Zuckerman, M., & Tsai, F. (2005). Costs of self-handicapping. *Journal of Social Psychology, 73,* 411–442.

Zuo, J., & Tang, S. (2000). Breadwinner status and gender ideologies of men and women regarding family roles. *Sociological Perspectives, 43*(1), 29–43.

Zvonkovic, A. M., Solomon, C. R., Humble, A. M., & Monoogian, M. (2005). Family work and relationships: Lessons from families of men whose jobs require travel. *Family Relations, 54,* 411–422.

Zvonkovic, A. N., Greaves, K. M., Schmiege, C. J., & Hall, L. D. (1996). The marital construction of gender through work and family decisions: A qualitative analysis. *Journal of Marriage and the Family, 58, 1,* 91–100.

Credits

Photo Credits

This page constitutes an extension of the copyright page. We have made every effort to trace the ownership of all copyrighted material and to secure permission from copyright holders. In the event of any question arising as to the use of any material, we will be pleased to make the necessary corrections in future printings. Thanks are due to the following authors, publishers, and agents for permission to use the material indicated.

Table of Contents

xix: © Bruce Ayres/Stone/Getty Images **xxi:** bottom: © Spencer Grant/PhotoEdit . **xxii:** bottom, © Richard Flood/DK Stock/Getty Images **xxiv:** bottom, © Matthew McVay/Corbis Saba **xxv:** bottom, © Paul Wood/Alamy **xxvi:** top, © Hill Street Studios/Blend Images/Getty Images **xxvii:** © Yellow Dog Productions/Stone/Getty Images **xxviii:** © Mario Tama/Getty Images **xxxi:** © Bruce Ayres/Stone/Getty Images

Chapter 1

2: © AP Images/Suzanne Plunkett **3:** © Carlos Spottorno/Taxi/Getty Images **5:** left, © Christopher J. Morris/Corbis **5:** right, © Reuters/HO **7:** bottom, © AP Images/Stephen Chernin **18:** inset, © David Young-Wolff/Photo Edit **23:** left, © Anderson Ross/Digital Vision/Getty Images **23:** right, © Javier Pierini/Taxi/Getty Images **24:** © Dana White/PhotoEdit **26:** © JFB/Stone/Getty Images

Chapter 2

35: right, National Library of Medicine **35:** bottom, © Peter Aprahamian/Corbis **40:** © Creatas/Jupiter Images **41:** left, © Bettmann/Corbis **41:** right, © Bettmann/Corbis **44:** © Bettmann/Corbis **46:** Courtesy of B. F. Skinner **47:** © Big Shots/Digital Vision/Getty Images **48:** Courtesy, Albert Bandura **51:** Carl Rogers Memorial Library **52:** Courtesy, Abraham Maslow **55:** right, Courtesy, Hans Eysenck, photo by Mark Gerson **55:** bottom right, © Michael Nichols/Magnum Photos **55:** bottom left, © Michael Nichols/Magnum Photos **61:** right, © Joe Raedle/Getty Images **61:** left, © Jack Carey/Alamy

Chapter 3

71: Courtesy, Richard Lazarus **73:** left, © AP Images/Reed Saxon **73:** right, © Richard Lord/PhotoEdit **76:** Courtesy, Neal Miller **79:** left, © Allen Birnbach/Masterfile **79:** right, © Kelvin Murray/Stone/Getty Images **82:** Courtesy, Susan Folkman **84:** © Bettmann/Corbis **90:** © AP Images/Ben Sklar **94:** right, Courtesy, Suzanne C. Ouelette **95:** © Paula Bronstein/Getty Images **97:** Courtesy, Eleanor Holmes Williams

Chapter 4

106: Courtesy, Dr. Martin Seligman **108:** © Paul Thomas/The Image Bank/Getty Images **111:** © Rachel Epstein/The Images Works **113:** Courtesy, Shelley Taylor **115:** Courtesy, Albert Ellis Institute **119:** left, © Radhika Chalasani/Getty Images **123:** © Bruce Ayres/Stone/Getty Images **128:** © Altrendo Images/Getty Images **129:** © Acey Harper/Time Life Pictures/Getty Images **134:** © Nicola Sutton/Life File/Photodisc Green/Getty Images **137:** © Mark Richards/PhotoEdit

Chapter 5

141: Stanford University News Service, photo by L. A. Cicero **144:** © Zigzag Images/Alamy **145:** © Pat Bruno/Positive Images **146:** © David Young-Wolff/Photo Edit **148:** Courtesy, Roy Baumeister **153:** © Blend Images/Alamy **159:** © GDT/Stone/Getty Images **162:** Courtesy, Albert Bandura **163:** © Mary Kate Denny/Photo Edit **164:** © Marc Vaughn/Masterfile **167:** Courtesy, Mark Snyder **168:** © Jo Hale/Getty Images

Chapter 6

174: bottom, Courtesy, Susan Fiske **174:** top, © Spencer Grant/PhotoEdit **180:** © Andrew Holbrooke/The Image Works **185:** © Bill Aaron/PhotoEdit **190:** © Mychal Watts/WireImage/Getty Images **191:** bottom, Courtesy, John T. Cacioppo **191:** top, Courtesy, Richard E. Petty **192:** © David McNew/Getty Images **193:** © Royalty Free-Masterfile **195:** right, © 1981 Eric Kroll, courtesy of Alexandra Milgram **196:** inset, Photos copyright 1965 by Stanley Milgram. From the film *Obedience*, distributed by The Pennsylvania State University. Obedience, distributed by The Pennsylvania State University. Reprinted by permission of Alexandra Milgram. **198:** Courtesy, Robert Cialdini **200:** © Bob Daemmrich/PhotoEdit **201:** © Tony Freeman/Photo Edit

Chapter 7

207: © Richard Flood/DK Stock/Getty Images **209:** © AP Images/Ron Edmonds **210:** © AP Images/Greg Baker **211:** Photos from *Unmasking the Face*, © 1975 by Paul Ekman, photographs courtesy of Paul Ekman **212:** right, © Tony Freeman/Photo Edit **212:** left, © Walter Hodges/Corbis **213:** © Bob Daemmrich/The Image Works **214:** Courtesy, Bella DePaulo **215:** © Bob Daemmrich/The Image Works **219:** © Mary Kate Denny/PhotoEdit **221:** © Dana Hursey/Masterfile **223:** © Michael Newman/Photo Edit **225:** © Radius Images/Alamy **226:** Photo by Sara Barrett, courtesy of Random House

Chapter 8

237: top, © Earl & Nazima Kowalt/Corbis **237:** bottom, © Royalty-Free/Masterfile **239:** © David Young-Wolff/PhotoEdit **243:** © Ephraim Ben-Shimon/Corbis **244:** Courtesy of David M. Buss **245:** © Hepp/Stone/Getty Images **253:** right, Michael Marsland/Yale University **253:** © AP Images/Winslow Townson **254:** Photo by Bill Warren/*Ithaca Journal* **255:** Photo provided by Philip Shaver **260:** © Ronnie Kaufman/Corbis **262:** © Royalty-Free/Masterfile

Chapter 9

272: © Michael Newman/PhotoEdit **277:** © AP Images/Susan Walsh **283:** Photo by Sharon M. Fentiman **285:** © Matthew McVay/Corbis Saba **288:** Courtesy, E. Mavis Hetherington **289:** right, © David Young-Wolff/Photo Edit **292:** © Ron Chapple/Thinkstock/Alamy **295:** © AP Images/Ben Margot **297:** © AP Images/Ed Andriesky

Chapter 10

303: Courtesy, Janet Shibley Hyde **310:** Courtesy, Alice Eagly **312:** Wadsworth Collection **314:** © David W. Hamilton/Alamy **315:** © Hill Street Studios/Blend/Getty Images **316:** © Michelle D. Bridwell/Photo Edit **327:** © Paul Wood/Alamy **328:** Courtesy, Sandra Bem **330:** Photo by Sara Barrett, courtesy of Random House

Chapter 11

339: © David Young-Wolff/Photographer's Choice/Getty Images **341:** © Ted Streshinsky/Corbis **343:** © Peter Byron/PhotoEdit **346:** © Red Chopsticks/Getty Images **351:** © Jutta Klee/Stone/Getty Images **352:** © Hill Street Studios/Blend Images/Getty Images **353:** Courtesy, Susan Whitbourne **357:** © Siphiwe Sibeko/Reuters **360:** © Ken Ross **362:** © AP Images/Evan Vucci **363:** © Arko Datta/Reuters/Corbis **364:** Courtesy, Diana Baumrind **365:** © David Young-Wolff/Photo Edit **367:** Courtesy, Laurence Steinberg

Chapter 12

375: left, © AP Images/Richard Drew **375:** right, © Bonnie Kamin/PhotoEdit **377:** © Bill Aron/PhotoEdit **379:** top, Columbia University Archives-Columbiana Library **381:** © Yellow Dog Productions/Stone/Getty Images **384:** © Peter Macdiarmid/Getty Images **387:** © AP Images/Steve Ruark **390:** © AP Images/Gregory Bull **403:** © JupiterImages/Creatas/Alamy

Chapter 13

410: Courtesy, Letitia Anne Peplau **412:** right, © AP Images/HO **412:** left, © Michael Newman/Photo Edit **414:** © AP Images/Reed Saxon **415:** bottom left, Courtesy, Douglas C Kimmel **415:** top left, Courtesy, Linda Doris Garnets **415:** right, © AP Images/Chris Pizzello **424:** © Mario Tama/Getty Images **426:** © AP Images/Seth Wenig **435:** © Marc Romanelli/The Image Bank/Getty Images **436:** © Bettmann/Corbis

Chapter 14

446: © Annabella Bluesky/Photo Researchers, Inc. **449:** Courtesy, Janice Kiecott-Glaser **454:** © Topham/The Image Works **464:** © Jim Cummings/Taxi/Getty Images **467:** Courtesy, M. Robin DiMatteo **468:** © JupiterImages **470:** © image100/Alamy Images

Chapter 15

480: © AP Images/David Davies/PA **480:** top, © David Lees/Corbis **487:** top right, © Jeffrey MacMillan/*U.S. News & World Report* **493:** right, © Elisabetta Villa/Getty Images **493:** left, © Steven Henry/Getty Images. **493:** center, © Tim Mosenfelder/Getty Images **495:** Courtesy of Susan Nolen-Hoeksema **503:** Courtesy, Nancy Andreasen, M.D. **504:** © Reuters/Corbis **508:** © Ed Quinn/Corbis

Chapter 16

519: National Library of Medicine **520:** © Bruce Ayres/Stone/Getty Images **522:** Courtesy, Carl Rogers Memorial Library **523:** © Bruce Ayres/Stone/Getty Images **527:** © AP/Wide World Photos **529:** Courtesy, Joseph Wolpe **532:** Courtesy, Aaron T. Beck **538:** © James Wilson/Woodfin Camp & Associates, all rights reserved **541:** © Janine Wiedel Photolibrary/Alamy **542:** Tom McCarthey/SKA **545:** © PhotoTake, Inc/Alamy

Text Credits

Table of Contents

xix: (figure) Adapted from Martin, R. A., and Lefcourt, H. M. (1983) "Sense of Humor as a Moderator of the Relation Between Stressors and Moods," *Journal of Personality and Social Psychology, 45* (6), 1313–1324. Copyright © 1983 by the American Psychological Association. Adapted by permission of the publisher and author. **xix:** (photo) © Bruce Ayres/Stone/Getty Images **xx:** (top figure) Adapted from Sharon S. Brehm and Saul M. Kassin, (1993), *Social Psychology,* 2nd Edition. Copyright © 1993 Houghton-Mifflin Company. Adapted by permission. **xxi:** (photo) Courtesy, Susan Fiske **xxi:** (figure) Adapted from Sharon S. Brehm and Saul M. Kassin, *Social Psychology, Second Edition.* Copyright © 1993 by Houghton Mifflin Company. Adapted with permission. **xxii:** (figure): "Where friends touch each other," page 89, [adapted] from *Eye to Eye: How People Interact,* by Peter Marsh. Copyright © 1988 by Andromeda Oxford Ltd. Reprinted by permission of HarperCollins, Publishers, Inc. and Andromeda Oxford Ltd. **xxii:** (photo) © Richard Flood/DK Stock/Getty Images **xxiii:** (bottom figure) From Sternberg, R. J. (1986) "A triangular theory of love," *Psychological Review, 93,* 119–135. Copyright © 1986 by the American Psychological Association. Reprinted by permission of the publisher and author. **xxiv:** (photo) © Matthew McVay/Corbis Saba **xxv:** (photo) © Paul Wood/Alamy **xxvi:** (figure) Adapted from Montepare, J. and Lachman, M. (1989) "You're only as old as you feel: Self-perceptions of age, fears of aging, and life satisfaction," *Psychology and Aging, 4,* 73–78. Copyright © 1989 American Psychological Association. Adapted by permission of the publisher and author. **xxvi:** (photo) © Hill Street Studios/Blend Images/Getty Images **xxvii:** (photo) © Yellow Dog Productions/Stone/Getty Images **xxviii:** (figure) From Laumann, E. O. Gagnon, J. H. Michael, R. T. and Michaels, S. (1994), *The Social Organization of Sexuality: Sexual Practices in the United States,* 1994. Copyright © 1994 University of Chicago Press. Reprinted by permission. **xxviii:** (photo) © Mario Tama/Getty Images **xxxi:** (photo) © Bruce Ayres/Stone/Getty Images

Chapter 1

6: Cartoon: Copyright © 2000. Used by permission. tomtomorrow@ix.netcom.com **8:** Cartoon DOONESBURY© 1978 G. B. Trudeau. Reprinted with permission of UNIVERSAL PRESS SYNDICATE. All rights reserved. **10:** CALVIN AND HOBBES © 1993 Watterson. Reprinted with permission of UNIVERSAL PRESS SYNDICATE. All rights reserved. **11:** Figure 1.1: From Wade, Carol; Tavris, Carole, *Learning* to *Think Critically: A Handbook for Psychology, 2nd Edition.* Copyright © 1990 Harper & Row. Reprinted by permission of Pearson Education, Inc., Upper Saddle River, N. J. Used by permission. **22:** Figure 1.11: Adapted from Myers, D. G., (1999) "Close relationships and quality of life," Figure 19.1. *In Well-Being: The Handbook of Hedonic Psychology* by Daniel Kahneman, Edward Diener and Norbert Schwarz, (Eds.) 1999. Copyright © 1999 Russell Sage Foundation, 112 East 64th Street, New York, NY 10021. Reprinted with permission. **28:** Cartoon DOONESBURY© G. B. Trudeau. Reprinted with permission of UNIVERSAL PRESS SYNDICATE. All rights reserved. **29:** Figure 1.15: Adapted from Bower, G. H., (1970) "Analysis of a mnemonic device," *American Scientist* (September-October), 58, 496–499. Copyright © 1970 by American Scientist. Reprinted by permission of the publisher and the author.

Chapter 2

37: top left, Cartoon ScienceCartoonsPlus.com © 1999 by Sidney Harris **42:** Figure 2.6 Adapted from *Psychology,* Second Edition, by C. R. Lefrancois. Copyright © 1983 by Wadsworth, Inc. Reprinted by permission of Brooks/Cole Publishing Company. **53:** Cartoon PEANUTS © United Feature Syndicate, Inc. **54:** Figure 2.16: Adapted from *Personality: Theory, Research and Application,* by C. R. Potkay and B. P. Allen, p. 246. Copyright © 1986 by Wadsworth, Inc. **56:** Figure 2.17: From Eysenck, H. J. (1967) *The Biological Basis of Personality (1st Edition*), p. 36. Copyright © 1967 by and Courtesy of Charles C. Thomas, Publisher, Springfield, IL. **57:** Figure 2.18: Based on Plomin, R. and Caspi, A. (1999) "Behavioral genetics and personality." In L. A. Pervin, & O. P. John (Eds.), *Handbook of Personality: Theory and Research.* Copyright © The Guilford Press. Adapted by permission. **63:** Figure 2.20 Based on McCrae, R. R. & Terracciano, A. (2005), "National character and personality," *Current Directions in Psychological Science, 15 (4),* 156–161. Blackwell Publishing. **65:** Figure 2.22: Reprinted by permission of Daniel S. Kirschenbaum from page 101 of *Adjustment and Competence: Concepts and Applications,* by A. F. Grasha & D. S. Kirschenbaum, © 1986. West Publishing Company. **66:** Figure 2.23: From Cattell, R. B. (1973) "Personality pinned down," in *Psychology Today,* July 1973, 40–46. Reprinted with permission from Psychology Today Magazine. Copyright © 1973 (Sussex Publishers, LLC.). **67:** Figure 2.24 Reprinted by permission of the publishers from Henry A. Murray, *Thematic Apperception Test,* Cambridge, Mass.: Harvard University Press, Copyright © 1943 by The President and Fellows of Harvard College, © 1971 by Henry A. Murray.

Chapter 3

73: Figure 3.2: Adapted from Evans, G. W., Hygge, S. and Bullinger, M. (1995) "Chronic noise and psychological stress" *Psychological Science, Vol. 6,* p. 333–338, figure 3.2. Oxford: Blackwell Publishers **77:** top, Cartoon BLONDIE © 2001. Reprinted with special permission of King Features Syndicate **78:** Figure 3.4: Reprinted from *Journal of Psychosomatic Research,* 11 (12) by Holmes, T. H. and Rahe, R. H. (1967) in "The Social Readjustment Rating Scale," 213–218, Copyright © 1967 with permission from Elsevier. **87:** Cartoon DILBERT © Scott Adams/Dist. by United Features Syndicate, Inc. **91:** Figure 3.15 Adapted from Overmier, J. B. & Murison, R., (2005). "Trauma and resulting sensitization effects are modulated by psychological factors," *Psychoneuroendocrinology, 30 (10),* 965–973, Table 2. Copyright © 2005 Elsevier Lt.d. Adapted by permission. All rights reserved. **96:** Cartoon CALVIN AND HOBBES © Watterson. Reprinted with permission of Universal Press Syndicate. All rights reserved. **96:** Figure 3.17: Adapted from Scheier, M.F. and Carver, C. S. (1985) "Optimism, coping, and health: Assessment and implications of generalized outcome expectancies," *Health Psychology, 4,* 219–247. Copyright © 1985 Lawrence Erlbaum & Associates. Adapted by permission and author. **99–101:** Figure 3.19: From Sarason, I. G. Johnson, J. H. and Siegel, J. M. (1978) "Assessing the impact of life changes," *Journal of Consulting and Clinical Psychology, 46,* 932–946. Copyright © 1978 by the American Psychological Association. Reprinted by permission of the publisher and author. **101:** Figure 3.20: From Sarason, I. G. Johnson, J. H. and Siegel, J. M. (1978) "Assessing the impact of life changes," *Journal of Consulting and Clinical Psychology, 46,* 932–946. Copyright © 1978 by the American Psychological Association. Reprinted by permission of the publisher and author.

Chapter 4

105: Figure 4.1: From Carver, C. S. Scheier, M. F. and Weintraub, J. K. (1989) "Assessing coping strategies: A theoretically based approach," *Journal of Personality and Social Psychology, 56(2),* 267–283. Copyright © 1989 American Psychological Association. Reprinted by permission of the publisher and author. **107:** Figure 4.2 Adapted from Liverant, G. I., Hofmann, S. G. & Litz, B. T. (2004), "Coping and anxiety in college students after the September 11th terrorist attacks," *Anxiety, Stress & Coping, 17 (2),* 127–139, Table III. Copyright © 2004 by Routledge. Adapted by permission of Taylor & Francis. **109:** bottom, Cartoon CATHY © Cathy Guisewite Reprinted with permission of UNIVERSAL PRESS SYNDICATE. All rights reserved **109:** Figure 4.3: Adapted from Bushman, B. J. & Anderson, C. A. (2001), "Media violence and the American public: Scientific facts versus media misinformation," *American Psychologist, 56,* 477–489. Copyright © 2001 American Psychological Association. Reprinted by permission of the publisher and author. **110:** Figure 4.4: From Young, K. S. (1998) *Caught in the net: How to recognize the signs of Internet addiction—and a winning strategy for recovery,* copyright © 1998 John Wiley & Sons, Inc. Reprinted with permission of John Wiley & Sons, Inc. **112:** Figure 4.5: Adapted From Carson, Robert C., Butcher, J. N., & Coleman, J. C. (1988), *Abnormal Psychology and Modern Life, 8th Edition,* pp 64–65. Published by Allyn and Bacon, Boston, MA, Copyright © 1988 by Pearson Education. Adapted by permission of the publisher. **112:** Cartoon CALVIN AND HOBBES © Watterson. Reprinted with permission of UNIVERSAL PRESS SYNDICATE. All rights reserved. **115:** Cartoon SALLY FORTH Copyright © 1984 News Group Chicago, reprinted by permission of North America Syndicate. **119:** Figure 4.8: Adapted from Martin, R. A. and Lefcourt, H. M. (1983) "Sense of humor as a moderator of the relation between stressors and moods," *Journal of Personality and Social Psychology, 45 (6),* 1313–1324. Copyright © 1983 by the American Psychological Association. Adapted by permission of the publisher and author. **119:** Cartoon Copyright © by Dan Piraro. Reprinted by permission of King Features Syndicate. **122:** Figure 4.10: From M. LeBoeuf, "Managing Time Means Managing Yourself," Questionnaire, p. 45. Reprinted from *Business Horizons Magazine,* February 1980. Copyright by the Foundation for the School of Business at Indiana University. Used with permission from Elsevier. **129:** Figure 4.14: Excerpt from "Sharing One's Story," [J. M. Smyth and J. W. Pennebaker,] pg. 84 from *Coping: The Psychology of What Works,* edited by C. R. Snyder, copyright © 1999 by Oxford University Press. Inc.. Used by permission of Oxford University Press, Inc. **131:** Figure 4.15: Page 114–115 from *The Relaxation Response* by Herbert Benson, M.D. with Miriam Z. Klipper. Copyright © 1975 by William Morrow & Company, Inc. Reprinted by permission of HarperCollins Publishers, Inc. **134:** Figure 4.18: From D. L. Watson & R. L. Tharp, *Self-Directed Behavior: Self-Modification for Personal Adjustment, Fourth Edition,* pp. 213–214. Copyright © 1972, 1977, 1981, 1985, 1993 by Brooks/Cole Publishing Company.

Chapter 5

144: Figure 5.3: From Hull J. G. and Young, R. D. (1983) "Self-consciousness, self-esteem, and success-failure as determinants of alcohol consumption in male social drinkers," *Journal of Personality and Social Psychology, 44 (6),* 1097–1109. Copyright © 1983 American Psychological Association. Reprinted by permission of the publisher and author. **147:** Figure 5.5: Adapted from Markus, H. R. and Kitayama, S. (1991) "Culture and the self: Implications for cognition, emotion, and motivation," *Psychological Review, 98 (2)* 224–253. Copyright © 1991 American Psychological Association. Adapted by permission of the publisher and author. **149:** Figure 5.7 Adapted from Rosenberg, M. (1965), Society and the adolescent self-image, Princeton University Press. Copyright © 1965 by Princeton University Press. http://www.bsos.umd.edu/socy/grad/socpsy_rosenberg.html **150:** Figure 5.8: Adapted from Sharon S. Brehm and Saul M. Kassin, (1993), *Social Psychology, 2nd Edition.* Copyright © 1993 Houghton-Mifflin Company. Adapted by permission. **158:** Cartoon PEANUTS © United Feature Syndicate, Inc. **160:** Figure 5.13 Adapted from Norem, J. K. (2001), *The Positive Power of Negative Thinking: Using Defensive Pessimism to Manage Anxiety and Perform at Your Peak.* Copyright © 2001 by Julie K. Norem. Reprinted by permission of Basic Books, a member of Perseus Book Group. **166:** Figure 5.17: Based on Jones, E. E. (1990) *Interpersonal Perception,* Table 703, p. 198. W. H. Freeman & Company. **169:** Cartoon FRANK & ERNEST Thaves/Dist. by Newspaper Enterprise Association, Inc.

Chapter 6

175: Figure 6.1: Adapted from Sharon S. Brehm and Saul M. Kassin, *Social Psychology,* Second Edition. Copyright © 1993 by HoughtonMifflin Company. Adapted with permission. **176:** Cartoon DILBERT © Scott Adams/Dist. by United Feature Syndicate, Inc **177:** Figure 6.3: Adapted from Smith, E. R. and Mackie, D. M. (1995) *Social Psychology,* p. 103. Copyright © 1995 Worth Publishing. Reprinted by permission. **179:** Figure 6.4: Data from 1999, September 15: Americans Agree That Being Attractive is a Plus in American Society. Taken from 2001, June 10, from http://gallup.com/poll/releases/pr990915. **183:** Figure 6.8: Statements from Swim, J. K. Aikin, K. J., Hall, W. S. & Hunter, B. A. (1995) "Sexism and racism: Old-fashioned and modern prejudices," *Journal of Personality and Social Psychology, 68 (2),* 199–214 (adapted from McConahay, J. B. (1986) "Modernism, ambivalence, and the Modern-Racism-Scale." In J. F. Dovidio & S. L. Gaerther (Eds.), Prejudice, discrimination, and racism (pp. 91–25). Academic Press). Copyright © 1995 American Psychological Association. Reprinted by permission of the publisher and author. **184:** Figure 6.9: Adapted from Pratto, F. Sidanius, J. Stallworth, L. M., & Mlle, B. F. (1994), "Social dominance orientation: A personality variable predicting social and political attitudes," *Journal of Personality and Social Psychology, 67,* 741–763 Copyright © 1994 by the American Psychological Association. Adapted by permission of the publisher and author. **187:** Figure 6.10: Adapted from Sharon S. Brehm and Saul M. Kassin, *Social Psychology,* Second Edition. Copyright © 1993 by Houghton Mifflin Company. Adapted with permission. **193:** Figure 6.13: Adapted from an illustration by Sarah Love on p. 35, *Scientific American, November 1955,* from "Opinion and Social Pressure," by Solomon Asch. Copyright © 1955 by Scientific American, Inc. All rights reserved. **194:** Figure 6.14: Adapted from an illustration by Sarah Love on p. 32, *Scientific American, November 1955,* from "Opinion and Social Pressure," by Solomon Asch. Copyright © 1955 by Scientific American, Inc. All rights reserved. **195:** Cartoon ZITS © Jerry Scott and Jim Borgman. Reprinted by permission of King Features Syndicate. **200:** Cartoon CALVIN AND HOBBES © Watterson. Reprinted with permission of UNIVERSAL PRESS SYNDICATE. All rights.

Chapter 7

207: Figure 7.2 Copyright © 1994–2006. NetLingo# The Internet Dictionary at http://www.netlingo.com **213:** Figure 7.7: "Where friends touch each other," page 89, [adapted] from *Eye to Eye: How People Interact,* by Peter Marsh. Copyright © 1988 by Andromeda Oxford Ltd. Reprinted by permission of HarperCollins, Publishers, Inc. and Andromeda Oxford Ltd. **218:** Cartoon DAVE © 1993 Dave Miller. Reprinted with permission of the artist. All rights reserved. **221:** Cartoon DILBERT © 2004 Scott Adams. Reprinted by permission of United Features Syndicate, Inc **231:** Excerpts from *Asserting Yourself: A Practical Guide for Positive Change* by Sharon Anthony Bower and Gordon H. Bower, pp 8, 9, 11. Copyright © 2004, 1991 by Sharon Anthony Bower and Gordon H. Bower. Reprinted by permission of Perseus DA CAPO PRESS, a member of Perseus Books. **231:** Cartoon by Marlette: KUDZU © Tribune Media Services, Inc. All Rights Reserved. Reprinted with permission. **232:** Figure 7.13: From *Asserting Yourself: A Practical Guide for Positive Change* by Sharon Anthony Bower and Gordon H. Bower. Copyright © 2004, 1991 by Sharon Anthony Bower and Gordon H. Bower, p. 100. Reprinted by permission of DA CAPO PRESS, a member of Perseus Books. **233:** Figure 7.14: From *Asserting Yourself: A Practical Guide for Positive Change* by Sharon Anthony Bower and Gordon H. Bower, p. 68. Copyright © 2004, 1991 by Sharon Anthony Bower and Gordon H. Bower. Reprinted by permission of DA CAPO PRESS, a member of Perseus Books.

Chapter 8

238: Figure 8.1: Adapted from R. Levine, S. Sato, T. Hashimoto, J. Verma, "Love and marriage in eleven cultures," 1995, *Journal of Cross-Cultural Psychology 26(5),* 561, 564. Copyright © 1995 by Sage Publications, Inc. Adapted by permission of Sage Publications. **239:** Figure 8.1 Adapted from Madden, M. & Lenhart, A. (2006), "Online dating," retrieved April 29, 2007 from http://www.pewinternet.org/pdfs/PIP_Online_Dating.pdf (Dating-Related Activities Online table, p. 5. Reprinted by permission of PEW Internet & American Life Project. Washington, D.C. **241:** Cartoon CATHY © 1993 by Cathy Guisewite. Reprinted with permission of UNIVERSAL PRESS SYNDICATE. All rights reserved. **242:** Figure 8.3: From Buss, D. M. (1989) "Sex differences in human mate preferences: Evolutionary hypotheses tested in 37 cultures," 1989, *Behavioral and Brain Sciences, 12,* 1–14. Copyright © 1989 by Cambridge University Press. Reprinted with the permission of Cambridge University Press and the author. **244:** Figure 8.4: Adapted from Buss,

D. M. (1988) "The evolution of human intrasexual competition: Tactics of mate attraction," *Journal of Personality and Social Psychology, 54(4),* 616–628. Copyright © 1988 by the American Psychological Association. Adapted by permission of the publisher and author. **246:** Cartoon BIZARRO © Dan Piraro. Reprinted by permission of King Features Syndicate. **247:** Figure 8.7: Adapted from Gonzales, M. H. Davis, J. M. Loeny, G. L. Lukens, C. K. & Junghans, C. H. (1983) "Interactional approach to interpersonal attraction," *Journal of Personality and Social Psychology, 44,* 1191–1197. Copyright © 1983 by the American Psychological Association. Adapted by permission of the publisher and author. **247:** Figure 8.8: Based on Regan, P.C. & Berscheid, E. "Gender differences in characteristics desired in a potential sexual marriage partner," 1997, *Journal of Psychology and Human Sexuality, 9,* Table 1, p. 32. Haworth Press, Inc. **249:** Figure 8.10: Adapted from Sharon S. Brehm and Saul M. Kassin, *Social Psychology, Second Edition.* Copyright © 1993 by Houghton Mifflin Company. Reprinted with permission. **254:** Figure 8.12: From Sternberg, R. J. (1986) "A triangular theory of love," *Psychological Review, 93,* 119–135. Copyright © 1986 by the American Psychological Association. Reprinted by permission of the publisher and author. **258:** Cartoon FOR BETTER OR FOR WORSE® © Lynn Johnston Productions, Inc./Distributed by Universal Press Syndicate. Reprinted with permission. All rights reserved. **259:** Figure 8.16: Adapted from Hill, C. T. Rubin, Z. & Peplau, L. A. (1976) "Breakups before marriage: The end of 103 affairs," *Journal of Social Issues, 32,* 147–168. © Society for the Psychological Study of Social Issues. Adapted by permission of the author. All rights reserved. **263:** Figure 8.18: From *Shyness: What Is It, What To Do About It,* by Philip Zimbardo. Copyright © 1977 by Philip Zimbardo, Inc. Reprinted by permission of DA CAPO PRESS, a member of Perseus Books. **264:** Figure 8.19: From a paper presented at the annual convention of the American Psychological Association, 9/2/79. An expanded version of this paper appears in *New Directions in Cognitive Therapy,* edited by Emery, Hollan, and Bedrosian, Guilford Press, 1981 and in *Loneliness: A Sourcebook of Current Theory, Research and Therapy,* by L. A. Peplau and D. Perlman (Eds.). Copyright © 1982 by John Wiley & Sons, Inc., and Jeffrey Young. **265:** Figure 8.20 Based on Shaver, P. & Rubenstein, C. (1980). "Childhood attachment experience and adult loneliness." In L. Wheeler (Ed.), *Review of Personality and Social Psychology, Vol. 1,* pp. 42–73. Thousand Oaks, CA: Sage Publications.

Chapter 9

271: Figure 9.3: Adapted from Peter J. Stein, "Singlehood: An alternative to marriage," *The Family Coordinator, 24(4),* 500. Copyrighted © 1975 by the National Council on Family Relations, 3989 Central Ave. N. E., Suite 550, Minneapolis, MN 55421. Reprinted by permission. **278:** Cartoon CATHY © 1994 by Cathy Guisewite. Reprinted with permission of UNIVERSAL PRESS SYNDICATE. All rights reserved. **280:** Cartoon SALLY FORTH © by Howard and Mac. Reprinted with special permission of King Features Syndicate. **284:** Cartoon CATHY © 1996 Cathy Guisewite. Reprinted with permission of UNIVERSAL PRESS SYNDICATE. All rights reserved. **287:** Cartoon © 1992 The New Yorker Collection 1992 Michael Maslin from cartoonbank.com. All rights reserved. **293:** Figure 9.13: From Peplau, L. A. "What homosexuals want," March 1981, *Psychology Today, 3,* 28–38. Reprinted with permission from Psychology Today Magazine. Copyright © 1981 (Sussex Publishers, LLC.). **297:** Figure 9.14: From I. M. Johnson, J. Crowley, and R. T. Sigler, "Agency response to domestic violence: Services provided to battered women," 1992. In E. C. Viano (Ed.), *Intimate Violence: Interdisciplinary Perspectives,* pp. 191–202 (Table on p. 199). Copyright © 1992 Hemisphere Publishing. Reprinted with permission of Taylor & Francis, Inc.

Chapter 10

304: Figure 10.2: Adapted from Ruble, T. L. (1983) "Sex stereotypes: Issues of change in the 70s," *Sex Roles, 9,* 397–402. Copyright © 1983 Plenum Publishing Co. Adapted by permission of Springer Science and *Business Media* and the author. **304:** Cartoon CATHY © 1986 Cathy Guisewite. Reprinted with permission of UNIVERSAL PRESS SYNDICATE. All rights reserved. **305:** Cartoon Six Chix © by Isabella Bannerman, Margaret Shulock, Rina Piccolo, Ann C. Telnaes, Kathryn LeMieux and Stephanie Piro. Reprinted by permission of King Features Syndicate. **307:** Figure 10.4: Adapted from Shepard, R. N. and Metzler, J. N. (1971) "Mental rotation of three-dimensionl objects," *Science, 171,* 701–703. Copyright © 1971 by American Association for the Advancement of Science. Adapted by permission of the publisher and author. **309:** Figure 10.6: Adapted from Kring, A. M., and Gordon, A. H. (1998) "Sex differences in emotions: Expression, experience and physiology," *Journal of Personality and Social Psychology, 74 (3),* 686–703. Copyright © 1998 American Psychological Association. Adapted by permission of the publisher and author. **315:** Figure 10.8: Adapted from Richardson, J. G., & Simpson, C. H. (1982) "Children, gender and social structure: An analysis of the contents of letters to Santa Claus," *Child Development, 53,* 429–436. Copyright © 1982 by the Society for Research in Child Development, Inc. Adapted by permission. **317:** Figure 10.9: Adapted from Robert M. Liebert & Joyce Sprafkin, *The Early Window: Effects of Television on Children and Youth, 3/e.* Published by Allyn and Bacon, Boston, Ma. Copyright © 1988 by Pearson Education. Adapted by permission of the publisher. **319:** Cartoon © The New Yorker Collection, Robert Weber 2002 from cartoonbank.com. All rights reserved. **322:** Cartoon DOONSBURY © 1975 G. B. Trudeau. Reprinted with permission of UNIVERSAL PRESS SYNDICATE. All rights reserved. **326:** Figure 10.13: Adapted from Stein, N., Marshall, N. L., and Tropp, L. R. (1993) *Secrets in Public: Sexual Harassment in Our Schools,* p. 4. Copyright © 1993 Center for Research on Women at Wellesley College and the NOW Legal Defense and Education Fund. Adapted by permission. **333:** Figure 10.15: Based on insights from *You Just Don't Understand: Women and Men in Conversation,* by Deborah Tannen, 1990. New York: William Morrow & Company, Inc.

Chapter 11

339: Cartoon *FOR BETTER OR FOR WORSE®* cartoon © 1988 Lynn Johnston Productions, Inc./Distributed by Universal Press Syndicate. Reprinted with permission. All rights reserved. **340:** Figure 11.2: Adapted from Tobin-Richards, M. H., Boxer, A. M., and Petersen, A. C. (1983) from "The psychological significance of pubertal change: Sex differences in perceptions of self during early adolescence." In J. Brooks-Gunn and A. C. Petersen (Eds.), *Girls at Puberty: Biological and Psychosocial Perspectives,* p. 137. Copyright © 1983 Plenum Publishing Inc. Adapted by permission of Springer Science and Business Media and the author. **341:** Figure 11.3: Figure [adapted] of Erikson's "Stages of Personality Development," from *Childhood and Society* by Erik H. Erikson. Copyright 1950 © 1963 by W. W. Norton & Co. Inc., renewed © 1978, 1991 by Erik H. Erikson. Used by permission of W. W. Norton & Company, Inc. Further permission from Hogarth Press (UK distribution). Reprinted by permission of The Random House Group Ltd. **342:** Figure 11.4: Adapted from Marcia, J. E. (1980) "Identity in Adolescence." In J. Adelson (Ed.), *Handbook of Adolescent Psychology,* pp. 159–210. Copyright © 1980 by John Wiley & Sons, Inc. Adapted by permission of John Wiley & Sons, Inc. **344:** Figure 11.5: Based on American Foundation for Suicide Prevention: When You Fear Someone May Take Their Life 9n.d.) Retrieved January 10, 2005 from http://www.afsp.org/about/whattodo.htm **349:** Figure 11.8: Adapted from Montepare, J., and Lachman, M. (1989) "You're only as old as you feel: Self-perceptions of age, fears of aging, and life satisfaction," *Psychology and Aging, 4,* 73–78. Copyright © 1989 American Psychological Association. Adapted by permission of the publisher and author. **349:** Cartoon ZITS © Jerry Scott and Jim Borgman. Reprinted by permission of King Features Syndicate. **350:** Cartoon CATHY © Cathy Guisewite. Reprinted with permission of UNIVERSAL PRESS SYNDICATE. All rights reserved. **357:** Figure 11.10. Reprinted from "Intellectual development in adulthood," by K. W. Schaie in *Handbook of the Psychology of Aging, Third Edition,* edited by J. E. Birren and K. W. Schaie, copyright © 1990 (Academic Press) reproduced with permission of Elsevier. **358:** Figure 11.11 Based on data from Dennis, W. (1966) "Creative productivity between the ages of 20 and 80 years." *Journal of Gerontology, 2(1),* 1–8. **365:** Figure 11.13: Based on data from "Socialization determinants of personal agency," a paper presented at the biennial meeting of the Society for Research in Child Development, New Orleans, 1977. **368:** Figure 11.14: Data from Lamborn, S. D., Mounts, N. S., Steinberg, L. &

Dornbusch, S. M. (1991), "Patterns of competence and adjustment among adolescents from authoritative, authoritarian, indulgent, and neglectful families." *Child Development, 62,* p 1060. Copyright © 1991 by the Society for Research in Child Development, Inc. Used with permission of SRCD.

Chapter 12

378: Figure 12.2: From John L. Holland, *Making Vocational Choices: A Theory of Vocational Personalities and Work Environments (2nd ed.).* © 1985, pp. 19–23, 36–40. Adapted by permission of Prentice-Hall, Inc. Englewood Cliffs, NJ. **379:** Figure 12.3: Adapted from J. Zaccaria, *Theories of Occupational Choice and Vocational Development,* pp. 51–52. Houghton Mifflin. Copyright © 1970 by Time Share Corporation, New Hampshire. **385:** Figure 12.7: Adapted from Maume, D. J. (2004), "Is the glass ceiling a unique form of inequality?," *Work and Occupations, 31(2),* 250–274. Copyright © 2004 by Sage Publications, Inc. Adapted by permission of Sage Publications. **387:** Cartoon CATHY copyright © 2001Cathy Guisewite. Reprinted with permission of UNIVERSAL PRESS SYNDICATE. All rights reserved. **388:** Figure 12.8: Adapted from Landy, F. J. (1989) *Psychology of Work Behavior (4th ed.),* p. 638. Copyright © 1989 by Wadsworth, Inc. Reprinted by permission of Brooks/Cole Publishing Company. **389:** Cartoon SALLY FORTH © Reprinted with special permission of King Features Syndicate. **389:** Figure 12.9: Redrawn from Karasek, R. A., Baker, D. Marxer, F., Ahlbom, A., Theorell, T. (1981), "Job decision latitude, job demands, and cardiovascular disease: A prospective study of Swedish men," *American Journal of Public Health, 71,* 694–705. Reprinted with permission from the American Public Heath Association. **391:** Figure 12.10: From Bowes-Sperry, L., and Tata, J. (1999) "A Multi-perspective framework of sexual harassment," in G. N. Powell (Ed.), *Handbook of Gender and Work,* pp. 263–280. © 1999 by Sage Publications. Reprinted with permission of Sage Publications, Inc. **395:** Cartoon DILBERT © 2005 Scott Adams/Dist. by United Feature Syndicate, Inc. **396:** Figure 12.12: From Table 4 on page 10 in Families and Work Institute (2004 October). Generation and gender in the workplace. New York: Author **396:** Figure 12.13: Adapted from Lawrence Mishel, Jared Bernstein, John Schmitt, and Economic Policy Institute, *The State of Working America 2000–2001,* p. 401. Copyright © 2001 by Cornell University. Adapted by permission of the publisher, Cornell University Press. **400:** Figure 12.15: Adapted from Lock, R. D. (2005) *Job search: Career Planning Guidebook, Book II.* Belmont, CA: Brooks/Cole Publishing Company. **400:** Cartoon DILBERT © 2006 Scott Adams/Dist. by United Feature Syndicate, Inc.

Chapter 13

409: Figure 13.1: Adapted from Holt, T., Greene, L., & Davis, J. (2003) "National survey of adolescents and young adults: Sexual health knowledge, attitudes, and experience," Kaiser Family Foundation, Question 2, p. 97. Henry J. Kaiser Family Foundation. **410:** Figure 13.2: From Kunkel, D., Eyal, K., Finnerty, K., Biely, E. & Donnerstein, E. (2005), A Biennial Report of the Kaiser Family Foundation: Sex on TV 4, Executive Summary," (#7399), The Henry J. Kaiser Family Foundation, November 2005. This information was reprinted with permission the Henry J. Kaiser Family Foundation. The Kaiser Family Foundation, based in Menlo Park, California, is a nonprofit, independent national health care philanthropy and is not associated with Kaiser Permanente or Kaiser Industries. **418:** Figure 13.7: From Elaine Hatfield and Richard L. Rapson, *Love, Sex and Intimacy: Their Psychology, Biology and History,* Table 3.10, p. 92. Published by Allyn and Bacon, Boston, MA. Copyright © 1997 by Pearson Education. Reprinted by permission of the publisher. **420:** Figure 13.9: From Laumann, E. O. Gagnon, J. H. Michael, R. T. and Michaels, S. (1994), *The Social Organization of Sexuality: Sexual Practices in the United States,* 1994. Copyright © 1994 University of Chicago Press. Reprinted by permission. **421:** Figure 13.10: From David Sue, "The Erotic fantasies of college students during coitus," 1979, *The Journal of Sex Research, 15,* p. 303. Copyright © 1979 Society for the Scientific Study of Sexuality. Reprinted by permission. **425:** Figure 13.12: From Lambert, T. A., Kahn, A. S. & Apple, K. J., (2003), "Pluralistic ignorance and hooking up," *The Journal of Sex Research,* 40(2) 129–133. Copyright © 1979 Society for the Scientific Study of Sexuality. Reprinted by permission. **425:** Figure 13.13: From *Sex in America* by Robert T. Michael, John H. Gagnon, Edward D. Laumann, and Gina Kolata. Copyright © 1994 by CSG Enterprises, Inc., Edward O. Lauman, Robert T. Michael, and Gina Kolata. By permission of Little, Brown & Co., Publishers, and Brockman, Inc. **427:** Figure 13.14: From Handy, B. (1998), "How We Really Feel About Infidelity," *Time,* August 3, 1998, pp. 52–53. Copyright © 1998 Time Inc. Reprinted by permission. **428:** Cartoon by Wasserman © 1986 Tribune Media Services, Inc. All Rights Reserved. Reprinted with permission. **434:** Figure 13.17: Adapted from Frank, E., Anderson, C., & Rubenstein, D. (1978) "Frequency of sexual dysfunction in 'normal' couples," *The New England Journal of Medicine, 299,* 111–115. **435:** Figure 13.18: From Laumann, E. O., Gagnon, J. H., Michael, R. T., and Michaels, S. (1994), *The Social Organization of Sexuality: Sexual Practices in the United States,* p. 369. Copyright © 1994 University of Chicago Press. Reprinted by permission. **437:** Figure 13.19: Adapted from William H. Masters, Virginia E. Johnson, and Robert C. Kolodny, *Human Sexuality, 3rd Edition* © 1988, p. 527. Published by Allyn and Bacon, Boston, MA. Copyright © 1998 by Pearson Education. Adapted by permission of the publisher.

Chapter 14

444: Figure 14.4: Adapted from Ridker, P. M. (2002). "High sensitivity C-reactive protein: Potential adjunct for global risk assessment in primary prevention of cardiovascular disease," *Circulation, 103,* 1813–1818. Copyright © 2002 American Heart Association. Adapted by permission of the publisher Lippincott Williams & Willams and the author. **451:** Cartoon © Jim Borgman. Reprinted with permission of UNIVERSAL PRESS SYNDICATE. All rights reserved **453:** Figure 14.11 Data from *Smoking and Health* (1990). Rockville, MD: Health and Human Services; Graph from *Healthy for Life: Wellness and the Art of Living* by B. K. Williams and S. M. Knight, p. 4.12, Brooks/Cole Publishing Company, 1994. **453:** Figure 14.11: Adapted from Hafen, B. Q., and Hoeger, W. W. K. (1998) *Wellness: Guidelines for a Healthy Lifestyle.* Copyright © 1998 by Morton Publishing Company. **454:** Cartoon © Roger Bollen **456:** Figure 14.14: From Edlin G., and Golanty, E., *Health and Wellness, Third Edition,* p. 294. Copyright © 1992, Jones & Bartlett Publishers, Sudbury, MA. www.jbpub.com. Reprinted with permission. **459:** Cartoon CATHY copyright © 1982 Cathy Guisewite. Reprinted with permission of UNIVERSAL PRESS SYNDICATE. All rights reserved. **461:** Figure 14.18: From Hales, D. *Invitation to Health, 9/e* p. 169. Copyright © 2000 by Wadsworth Publishing. **462:** Figure 14.19: Reprinted (adapted) with the permission of Simon & Schuster Adult Publishing Group from *Eat, Drink, and Be Healthy* by Walter C. Willett, M.D. Copyright © 2001, 2006 by President and Fellows at Harvard College. **464:** Figure 14.21: Adapted from Conrad, C. C., "How different sports rate in promoting physical fitness," *Medical Times, May 1976,* 4–5. Copyright © 1976 by Romaine Pierson Publishers. Reprinted by permission. **466:** Figure 14.22: Adapted from Kalichman, S. C. (1995) Understanding AIDS: A Guide for Mental Health Professionals, Appendix C, pp. 391–392. Copyright © 1995 by the American Psychological Association. Adapted with permission of the publisher and author.

Chapter 15

483: Figure 15.3: Adapted with permission from the *Diagnostic and Statistical Manual of Mental Disorders, Fourth Edition,* Text Revision Copyright © 2000 American Psychiatric Association. **486:** Figure 15.5: From I. M. Marks, *Fears & Phobias,* 1969, Academic Press. Copyright © 1969 by Isaac Marks. Reprinted by permission. **486:** Cartoon by Harris © 1990 ScienceCartoonsPlus.com **491:** Cartoon © Egar Argo. Reprinted by permission. **494:** Figure 15.10: From I. G. Sarason and B. R. Sarason, *Abnormal Psychology: The Problem of Maladaptive Behavior (5th Ed.),* © 1987, p. 283. Reprinted by permission of Prentice-Hall, Inc., Englewood Cliffs, NJ. **495:** Cartoon © The New Yorker Collection Cheney 1996. All rights reserved. From *The New Yorker,* Feb. 12, 1996. **497:** Figure 15.11: From Figure 6-1 (p. 132) "Age of onset for bipolar mood disorder," from *Manic-Depressive Illness,* by Frederick K. Goodwin and Kay R. Jamison, copyright © 1990 by Oxford University Press, Inc. Used by permission of Oxford University Press, Inc.

Chapter 16

525: Figure 16.6: Adapted from Lambert, M. J., Hansen, N. B., & Finch A. E. (2001), "Patient-focused research: Using patient outcome data to enhance treatment effects," *Journal of Consulting and Clinical Psychology, 69,* 159–172. Copyright © 2001 by the American Psychological Association. Adapted by permission of the publisher and author. **527:** Figure 16.7: From "Lies of the Mind" *Time,* 11/29/93. Copyright © 1993 Time Inc. Reprinted by permission **526:** Cartoon DOONESBURY © 1994 G. B. Trudeau. Reprinted with permission of UNIVERSAL PRESS SYNDICATE. All rights reserved. **529:** Cartoon © ScienceCartoonsPlus.com **530:** Figure 16.9: From K. E. Rudestam, *Methods of Self-Change: An ABC Primer,* pp. 42–43, 1980. Brooks/Cole Publishing Company. Copyright © 1980 by Wadsworth, Inc. **531:** Figure 16.11: Adapted from Beck, A. T. (1976) *Cognitive Therapy and the Emotional Disorders,* International Universities Press. Copyright © 1976 by International Universities Press, Inc. Adapted by permission of the publisher. **535:** Cartoon © The New Yorker Collection 2001, Barbara Smaller from cartoonbank.com. All rights reserved. **535:** Figure 16.13: From data in NIMH-PSC Collaborative Study I and reported in "Drugs in the Treament of Psychosis," by Cole, J. O., Goldberg, S. C., and Davis, J. M. (1966). In P. Solomon (Ed.) *Psychiatric Drugs,* Grune & Stratton. Additional data added from J. M. Davis, 1985. By permission of the author. **537:** Cartoon DILBERT © Scott Adams/Dist. by United Feature Syndicate, Inc. **544:** Figure 16.15: Adapted from Smith, M. L., & Glass, G. V. (1977), "Meta analysis of psychotherapy outcome series," *American Psychologist, 32 (September),* 752–760. Copyright © 1977 by the American Psychological Association. Adapted by permission of the publisher and author. **544:** Cartoon INSIDE WOODY ALLEN by Stuart Hample. Reprinted by permission. © King Features Syndicate, Inc., 1977. World rights reserved.

Name Index

A

Abbey, A., 297, 298
Abdel-Khalek, A. M., 21
Abel, M. H., 119
Aber, J. L., 226
Abi-Dargham, A., 505
Abma, J. C., 276
Aboud, F. E., 242
Abplanalp, R. R., Jr., 241, 272
Abrams, D., 180
Abrams, D. B., 454
Abramson, L. Y., 107, 498, 499
Achille, N. M., 22
Ackerman, L., 350
Ackerman, S., 348
Acock, A. C., 289
Acton, G. S., 311
Adams, G., 237
Adams, G. R., 347
Adams, H. E., 490
Adams, M., 288
Adams-Curtis, L. E., 298
Addis, M. E., 320
Ader, R., 448
Adler, A., 41–42
Adler, L., 254
Adler, N. E., 291, 442
Adonu, J. K., 237
Adorno, R., 184
Affleck, G., 120
Agnew, C. R., 249
Agras, W. S., 243
Aguiar, P., 180
Ahlberg, C., 314
Ahn, H., 525
Ahrons, C. R., 287
Ai, A. L., 96
Aiken, L. S., 428
Aikens, D. E., 488
Ainsworth, M., 255–256
Ait-Daoud, N., 454
Akgun, S., 91
Akimoto, S. A., 159
Akishkal, H. S., 493, 495
Akiyama, H., 345
Alaphilippe, D., 113
Albee, G. W., 481, 541
Albert, C. M., 443
Alberti, R. E., 228, 230, 233
Alexander, C. N., 131
Algoe, S., 152
Alicke, M. D., 158, 242
Al-Krenawi, A., 272
Allen, A., 1
Allen, J. J. B., 492
Allen, K., 94, 492
Allen, K. R., 294
Allen, M., 253, 318
Allgood, W. P., 25
Allison, D. B., 457, 458
Alloy, L. B., 499, 500
Allport, G., 33
Almeida, D. M., 34, 72
Alonso, A., 523, 524
Alonso, S., 523
Altemeyer, B., 184, 415
Altman, I., 218, 220
Altobelli, J., 291
Alvarez, J., 91
Alzate, H., 419
Amarel, D., 251
Amato, P. R., 269, 273, 285, 286, 287, 288, 291
Ambady, N., 177, 211
Ames, S. C., 98
Anand, A. P., 265
Anand, S. S., 443
Anderluh, M. B., 510
Andersen, B. L., 448
Andersen, S. C., 176
Andersen, S. M., 175
Anderson, A. E., 510
Anderson, B. L., 467
Anderson, C. A., 108, 109, 226, 264
Anderson, D. A., 316
Anderson, K. J., 82
Anderson, M., 342
Anderson, S., 127
Anderson, S. E., 338
Anderson, S. L., 237
Anderson, V. L., 130
Anderson-Fye, E. P., 510
Andreasen, N. C., 502, 503, 504, 506
Andresen, J., 130
Andrews, A. M., 449
Andreoli Mathie, V., 297
Angell, M., 537
Angiulo, M. J., 492
Angleitner, A., 57
Angst, J., 42, 495, 497
Ankenmann, R. D., 395
Antai-Otong, D., 532
Anton, R. F., 456
Antoniou, A. G., 127
Antonucci, T., 345, 353
Antonuccio, D. O., 537
Antony, M. M., 45, 485, 487
Antshel, K. M., 531
Anttila, R., 339
Apperloo, M. J. A., 408
Apple, K. J., 424
Aqilino, W. S., 278
Arbona, C., 374
Archer, A., 524
Archer, J., 273, 308, 311
Archer, R. L., 332
Arendell, T., 321
Argyle, M., 21, 22, 23, 250
Ariely, D., 124
Aries, E., 309
Arkowitz, H., 6, 8
Armbruster, B. B., 27
Armistead, L., 409
Armour, S., 395
Arndt, J., 61
Arnett, J. J., 343, 346, 349
Arnkoff, D. B., 528, 531
Arnold, K., 322
Arnold, K. D., 382
Arnold, L. M., 449
Arnold, R. D., 57
Arnon, L., 90
Arnsten, J. H., 473
Aron, A., 142, 244, 246, 254, 257, 260
Aronson, E., 188, 189
Arrigo, J. M, 491
Asch, S. E., 182, 192–194
Ashby, D., 536
Ashcraft, M. H., 88
Asher, S., 262
Ashmore, R. D., 309
Ashok, J., 358
Ashton, M. C., 34, 62
Aspinwall, L. G., 92, 97, 145
Assanand, S., 141, 457
Asuncion, A. G., 189
Ataca, B., 74
Atchley, R. C., 353
Athenstaedt, U., 220, 309
Atwood, J. H., 422
Aubé, J., 246
Aubin, S., 436, 437
Aubrey, J. S., 243, 317
Auerbach, S. M., 394
Aunola, K., 307
Ayanian, J. Z., 452
Ayar, A. A., 107
Ayres, D. M., 223
Ayres, J., 223
Ayres, J. J. B., 46
Aziz, S., 395

B

Babcock, J. C., 296
Back, S. E., 91
Bacue, A., 317, 318
Badgett, M. V. L., 384, 387
Bailey, B. L., 287
Bailey, J. M., 242, 294, 413, 414
Bailey, M., 413
Bailly, N., 113
Baird, B. M., 164
Bakalar, J. B., 474
Bakeman, R., 415, 431
Baker, F., 452
Baker, G. B., 536
Baldessarini, R. J., 536
Baldwin, D., 91
Bales, R. F., 304
Ballenger, J. C., 534, 91
Balsam, K. F., 252, 294, 416
Baltes, M. M., 71, 353, 354
Banaji, M. R., 178
Bancroft, J., 313, 420, 436
Bandura, A., 48–49, 162–163, 314
Bank, B. J., 252
Banks, A., 413
Banning, K., 77
Banse, R., 214, 257
Banyard, V. L., 526
Banzato, C. E. M., 482
Barbanel, L., 2
Barbee, A. P., 242
Barbee, J. G., 71
Barber, B. K., 277
Barber, B. L., 288
Barber, R. L., 286
Barch, D. M., 502
Barden, J., 182
Bargh, J. A., 155, 178, 207, 208, 219, 238, 239, 264, 265
Barker, E. T., 110, 308
Barlett, D. L., 486
Barley, D. E., 525
Barling, J., 392
Barlow, D. H., 485, 488, 511
Barnes, M. L., 332
Barnes, V. A., 131
Barnett, H. L., 323
Barnett, O. W., 296
Barnett, R. C., 281, 396
Baron, R. S., 4
Barrett, L. F., 219
Barrett, S., 8
Barry, H., III, 337
Barry-Walsh, J., 493
Barsky, A. J., 467, 491
Bartholomew, K., 256, 262
Bartholow, B. D., 108, 455
Bartlett, A., 481
Baruch, G. K., 351
Basow, S. A., 313, 331

Bassin, E., 259
Bates, G. W., 348
Batki, S. L., 465
Batson, C. D., 291
Battle, J., 293
Baucom, D. H., 283
Baum, A., 73, 75, 92, 97, 442
Baumbusch, J. L., 291
Baumeister, R. F., 87, 108, 109, 113, 124, 146, 148, 150, 151, 152, 160, 161, 162, 163, 165, 168, 236, 260, 344
Baumrind, D., 153, 197, 364–365, 367, 369
Baur, K., 407, 420, 425, 429, 431, 432, 433 437
Bavelas, J. B., 211
Baxter, L. A., 220
Bay-Cheng, L. Y., 323
Bayer, R., 481
Baynard, M. D., 1
Beach, S. R. H., 260
Beall, A. E., 305
Beals, K. P., 417
Beardslee, W. R., 106
Beaudry, M. 289
Beck, A., 111, 488, 498, 531–532
Beck, F. D., 424
Becker, A. E., 510
Becker, E., 359
Beckham, J. C., 532
Beeder, A. B., 475
Beer, J. M., 57
Behar, R., 4
Beidel, D. C., 531
Beilock, S. L., 88
Beisecker, A. E., 468
Bekelman, J. E., 537
Belger, A., 505
Bell, A. P., 413, 416
Bell, B. S., 374
Bell, R. A., 263
Bellack, A. S., 531
Belland, J. C., 111
Beller, M., 311
Belmore, S. M., 182
Belsky, J., 277, 282
Bem, D., 199, 413
Bem, S. L., 305, 315, 328–329
Benbow, C. P., 307
Bender, R., 457
Benedict, R., 62
Benet, V., 34
Ben-Ezra. M., 81
Benjamin, L. T., Jr., 16
Bennett, D. A., 355
Bennett, P., 449
Ben-Porath, Y. S., 66
Benson, H., 131
Berdahl, J. L., 326
Berenbaum, S. A., 413
Berg, J. H., 332
Bergen, M. R., 260
Berger, J. M., 320
Bergin, A. E., 524, 540
Berglund, P. A., 516
Berkman, C. S., 356
Berkowitz, B., 6
Berkowitz, L., 107, 369
Berkowitz, R. I., 528, 533
Berliner, K., 290
Berliner, L., 528
Berman, A. L., 309, 343, 496
Berman, M., 287
Bernard, L. C., 467
Berne, E., 224
Berne, P. H., 146
Bernstein, B., 541
Bernstein, J., 396
Berry, D. S., 173
Berry, J. W., 74
Berryman-Fink, C., 225
Berscheid, E., 178, 237, 241, 246, 247
Bertakis, K. D., 467
Bertrand, R. M., 351
Berzon, B., 433
Best, D. L., 178, 304, 305, 315, 317
Betz, N. E., 95, 162, 317, 322, 326, 347, 373, 380, 387
Beumont, P. J. V., 509
Beutler, L. E., 516, 525, 542, 543, 544
Bhatnagar, S., 85
Bhattachary, S., 475
Bianchi, S. M., 269, 270, 279, 280, 282, 286, 287
Biblarz, T. J., 279
Bidell, T. R., 340
Biernat, M., 157., 319
Bilezikian, J. P., 356
Billings, A. G., 109, 114
Billings, L. S., 157
Bini, L., 537
Birchler, G. R., 491
Birnbaum, M. H., 174, 182
Bishop, S. R., 131
Bixler, E. O., 91
Bjork, R. A., 28
Bjorklund, D. F., 527
Björntorp, P., 457
Black, D. W., 502, 503, 506
Blackburn, T. C., 180
Blacker, D., 482
Blacker, L., 278
Blaine, B., 148
Blair, S. N., 463
Blair-Loy, M., 380
Blaisure, K. R., 288
Blakemore, J. E. O., 316
Blakeslee, S., 288
Blanchard, E. B., 448
Blanco, C., 536
Blanton, H., 145
Blascovich, J., 94
Blass, T., 197
Blatt-Eisengard, I., 367
Bleier, R., 312
Bleuler, E., 501
Blieszner, R., 277
Block, J., 113, 148
Block, J. H., 331
Bloom, D., 408
Bloom, P. N., 198
Bloomfield, H., 6
Bluck, S., 349
Blum, R. W., 340
Blumenthal, J. A., 444, 446
Blumstein, D., 426
Blumstein, P., 274, 279
Bly, R., 320
Boase, J., 239
Bobek, B. L., 392, 393
Bobocel, D. R., 184
Bock, P. K., 62
Boden, J. M., 151
Bodenhausen, G. V., 178, 179, 186
Bodenheimer, T., 537
Bodnar, L. E., 436
Boelen, P. A., 72
Boen, F., 159, 160
Boeree, C. G., 51
Boerner, K., 362, 363
Bogg, T., 34
Boles, D. B., 312
Bolger, N., 113, 251
Bolles, R. N., 399, 401, 402
Bonanno, G. A., 91, 361, 362, 363
Bond, C. F., Jr., 214, 395
Bond, J. T., 320, 347, 382, 390, 396
Bond, M. H., 159
Bond, M. J., 49
Bond, R., 194
Bonebright, C. A., 395
Boneva, B., 220
Bongar, B., 2, 516, 542
Bono, J. E., 34
Booth, A., 286, 287, 288, 289, 291
Bordnick, P., 530
Bordon, L. M., 343
Borker, R. A., 331
Borman, W. C., 372
Bornstein, R. F., 42
Borus, J. F., 539
Borys, S., 262
Bose, S., 287
Bossé, R., 352
Bossio, L. M., 97
Bost, K. K., 276
Bosworth, H. B., 355
Bouchard, C., 458
Bouchard, G., 274
Boudreaux, E., 49
Bourg, C., 304
Bourgeois, J. A., 496
Bourhis, R., 187
Bowen, C., 277
Bower, G. H., 29, 230–233
Bower, S. A., 230–233
Bowers, J. W., 219
Bowes-Sperry, L., 391
Bowins, B., 113
Bowlby, J., 255, 361
Boxer, A. A., 340
Boyd, J. N., 124
Bradbury, T. N., 175, 329
Bradford, J., 415
Bradley, G., 95
Bradley, L. J., 4
Bradley, M. M., 177
Brady, K. T., 91
Bragger, J. D., 403
Braithwaite, V. A., 311
Bramel, D., 194
Bramlett, M. D., 274, 285, 289
Bramon, E., 507
Branaman, T. F., 215
Branas, C. C., 455
Brand, R. J., 444
Branigan, C., 82
Brannon, L., 385
Brannon, R., 318, 319
Branscombe, N. R., 187
Brantley, C., 420
Brashears, M. E., 262
Brass, D. J., 108
Bratslavsky, E., 109, 260
Braungart-Rieker, J. M., 367
Breckenridge, J. N., 2
Bredt, B. M., 474
Breggin, P., 538
Brehm, J. W., 76, 190, 201
Brehm, S. S., 150, 175, 201, 216, 249, 257, 332
Breier, A., 505
Brennan, K. A., 256, 257, 262
Brenner, L., 166
Breslin, F. C., 392
Brett, J. M., 78
Brewer, M. B., 177, 187
Brewster, K. L., 269
Brewster, M. P., 296
Brickman, P., 22
Bridges, K. R., 124
Bridges, M. W., 96
Briere, J., 526., 528
Bright, J., 72
Brissette, I., 250
Briton, N. J., 212
Britton, B. K, 124
Brodsky, A., 539
Brody, J. E., 307
Brody, L. R., 309, 320
Broidy, L. M., 226

Bromage, B. K., 28
Bromet, E. J., 484
Bromley, M., 277
Brooks-Gunn, J., 282, 338
Broomhall, H. S., 393
Brose, A., 445
Brown, A. S., 485, 506
Brown, D., 376, 528
Brown, D. G. A., 28
Brown, E. L., 219
Brown, E. J. P., 489
Brown, J., 113
Brown, J. B., 16, 291
Brown, J. D., 78, 145, 409, 409
Brown, J. L., 226
Brown, L. M., 177
Brown, R. D., 527
Brown, R. J., 17, 1867, 187
Brown, S., 289, 291, 423
Brown, S. L., 94, 286
Brown, T. T., 474
Browne, A., 296
Browne, K., 296
Brownell, K. D., 457, 458
Brubaker, T., 278
Bruce, C., 276
Bruce, D., 528
Bruce, K. R., 510
Bruch, H., 510
Bruckner-Gordon, F., 542
Bruhn, P., 355
Brumbaugh, C. C., 257
Brummett, B. H., 34, 92, 446
Bryan, A. D., 428
Bryant, R. A., 116
Bryant, S., 353
Bryden, M. P., 312
Bryer, K. B., 360
Buchanan, R. W., 501
Buckingham, J. T., 158
Buckman, R., 468
Buckner, C. E., 304
Buechel, C., 305
Buehlman, K. T., 283
Bukatko, D., 309
Bulcroft, R., 270, 276, 347
Bulik, C. M., 510
Bull, D. L., 526
Bull, S. S., 411
Bullinger, M., 72, 73
Bumpass, L. L., 285, 291
Bumpus, M. F., 281
Bunde, J., 447
Burger, J. M., 54, 198, 199
Burgess, C., 475
Burgess, E. O., 426
Burggraf, K., 318
Burgoon, J. K., 214
Burhans, K. K., 146
Burke, J. D., 482, 484
Burke, R. J., 394, 395
Burn, S. M., 320, 328
Burns, A. B., 500
Burr, W. R., 273
Burroughs, T., 180
Burstein, G., 430
Bursztajn, H. J., 539
Buscaglia, L., 6
Bushman, B. J., 108, 109, 151
Buss, D., 58, 241, 242, 243, 244, 245, 258, 259, 272, 273, 311, 332, 417
Buss, W. C., 283
Bussey, K., 49, 314
Bustillo, J. R., 501
Butcher, J. N., 112
Butler, E. A., 127
Butler, J. L., 87
Butler, R., 361
Buunk, A. P., 427
Buxton, M. N., 449
Bybee, D., 142
Byers, E. S., 434
Byrm, R. J., 240
Byrne, A., 290
Byrne, B., 127
Byrne, D., 247
Byrne, R., 7
Byrnes, J., 340

C

Cabaj, R. P., 466
Cabral, G. A., 474
Cachelin, F. M., 243
Cacioppo, J. T., 93, 191, 251, 467
Caddell, M., 91
Cahn, D. D., 227
Caldwell, D. F., 199
Calhoun, L. G., 92
Call, B., 258
Call, V., 426
Callander, J. C., 176, 402
Cameron, L., 467
Cameron, N., 489
Campbell, J. D., 141, 148
Campbell, L. F., 6
Campbell, R. J., 539
Campbell, S., 498
Campbell, S. M., 329
Campbell, W. K.,151, 159, 276
Canary, D. J., 248
Candela, S. F., 507
Canetto, S. S., 344
Cannon, W., 82–83
Cantor-Graae, E., 507
Capitanio, J., 250, 414, 415
Caplan, R. D., 394
Caputo, D., 463
Carbonell, D. M., 106
Cardena, E., 131, 492
Carducci, B. J., 54, 217
Carey, M., 420
Carey, M. P., 465
Carless, D., 130
Carli, L. L., 309
Carlson, D. N., 468, 469
Carlson, R., 6
Carlsson, A., 505
Carlston, D. E., 174
Carnelley, K. B., 363
Carney, S., 538
Caron, S. L., 408
Carpenter, W. T., 501, 503, 537
Carr, D., 290
Carr, V. J., 73
Carrère, 277
Carrington, P., 130
Carroll, J. L., 417, 421, 422, 428, 429, 432, 433
Carroll, J. S., 283
Carroll-Ghosh, T., 496
Carson, R. C., 112, 503
Carson, S. H., 155
Carstensen, L. L., 353
Carter, B., 275, 276
Carter, E. A., 287
Carter, R. T., 319
Carton, J. S., 216
Cartwright, S., 127
Caruso, D. R., 127
Carver, C. S., 71, 96, 97, 105, 106, 107, 250
Casas, J. F., 308
Cascio, T., 96
Cascio, W. F., 390
Cashdan, E., 212
Casper, L. M., 269, 270, 286
Caspi, A., 57, 498
Cassata, D., 226
Cassel, R. N., 50
Cassin, S. E., 324
Castillo, R. G., 79
Castongguay, L. G., 540
Catania, J. A., 465, 466
Cate, R., 274, 425, 409
Cates, W., Jr., 430
Cattell, R., 33, 66
Catz, S. L., 465
Cauffman, E., 367
Cavanaugh, J. C., 354, 358
Cavell, T. A., 16
Caverly, D. C., 26, 27
Cerletti, U., 537
Cetron, M. J., 381
Chaiken, S., 188, 189
Chamberlin, J., 400
Chambless, D. L., 525
Chambliss, C. H., 539
Chan, R. W., 294
Chancey, D., 282
Chandler, M. J., 341
Chandra, A., 431
Chang, E. C., 97
Chang, R. Y., 120
Chaplin. W. F., 403
Charles, S. T., 353
Charlesworth, W. R., 331
Chartrand, T., 198
Chase, A., 366
Chemers, M. M., 49
Chen, D., 42
Chen, S., 176
Chen, Y. Y., 446
Cheng, C., 106
Cheng, H., 153
Cheng, K., 130
Cheng, Y., 463
Cherlin, A. J., 269, 287, 288
Cheung, M. W. L., 106
Chia, R. C., 315
Chiapelli, F., 86, 448
Chick, J., 456
Chick, K. A., 315
Chiriboga, D. A., 345, 351
Chizmar, L., 463
Choi, H., 278
Choi, I., 179, 180
Choice, P., 296
Chopra, D., 6
Chopra, S. S., 537
Chou, C., 111
Chouldhry, N. K., 537
Christensen, A., 224, 260, 281, 283, 469
Christensen, P., 263
Christian, L. M., 449
Christoph, R. T., 49
Christophe, B., 219
Christopher, F. S., 18, 409, 423
Chua, H. F., 180
Chun, C., 74
Church, M. A., 160
Cialdini, R. B., 159, 193, 194, 198, 199, 200, 201
Ciarrochi, J., 91, 127
Cicirelli, V. G., 360
Ciraulo, D. A., 472
Claar, R. L., 446, 468
Clark, C. L., 256
Clark, D., 416
Clark, L. A., 34
Clark, M. M., 130
Clark, M. S., 224, 250
Clarkberg, M., 380
Clarke-Stewart, K. A., 287
Classen, C., 90
Clay, D. L., 395
Cleary, P. D., 452
Cleek, M. G., 283
Clements, A. M., 312
Clements, M. L., 274

Cloitre, M., 366
Clore, G. L., 191, 247
Clow, A., 85
Coates, D., 22
Coates, L., 211
Coates, T. J., 466
Coats, E. J., 216
Cobb, R. J., 257
Cobb, S. J., 322
Cochran, S. D., 294, 416
Coffey, S. F., 91
Cogan, J. C., 293
Cohan, C. L., 291
Cohen, A., 358
Cohen, C. E., 176
Cohen, D., 534, 536
Cohen, D. B., 57
Cohen, F., 61, 97
Cohen, M. J. M., 448
Cohen, S., 72, 94, 251, 449, 450, 453
Cohen-Bendahan. C. C. C., 413
Coie, J. D., 216
Coiro, M. J., 288
Coker, A. L., 297
Colder, C. R., 91
Colder, M., 128
Cole, S. W., 128
Coleman, J. C., 112
Coleman, M., 289
Coles, M. E., 487
Collaer, M. L., 313
Colley, A., 252
Colligin, T. W.,, 388
Collins, C., 466
Collins, L. M., 339
Collins, N. L., 219
Collins, R. L., 157
Collins, W. A., 251, 343
Colluci, P., 294
Coltrane, S., 280, 286, 288
Colvin, C. R., 113
Comas-Diaz, L., 315
Combs-Orme, T., 276
Compton, W. C., 131
Condon, J. W., 247
Condron, L., 111
Conger, R. D., 339
Conklin, H. M., 506
Connidis, I. A., 276
Conoscenti, L. M., 323
Conrad, C. C., 464
Conte, J. R., 526
Contrada, R. J., 74, 246
Conway, M., 157
Cook, A., 61
Cook, J. M., 272
Cook, S. I., 297
Coon, B., 141
Coontz, S., 270, 286
Cooper, A., 17, 18, 411, 426
Cooper, C. L., 71
Cooper, D. C., 445
Cooper, L., 72
Cooper, M. L., 257, 416, 428
Cooper, P. J., 91
Cooper. C. L., 84
Cope, M. B., 458
Coplan, J. D., 487
Copper, C., 28
Cordova, J. V., 207, 283
Cornelius, T., 199
Cornell, D. G., 58
Cornwell, J. M., 384
Corr, C. A., 361
Correia, I., 180
Correll, C. U., 535
Corsica, J. A., 457, 463
Costa, P. T., Jr., 33–34, 66, 97, 351, 359
Cotter, D. A., 385
Coups, E. J., 446
Courtenay, W. H., 323
Covey, S. R., 6
Cowan, C. P., 276, 347
Cowan, N., 155
Cowan, P. A., 276, 347, 369
Cowley, J., 430
Cox, M. J., 277
Cox, P. D., 523
Coy, K. C,, 343
Coyne, J. C., 500
Coyne, S. M., 308
Craik, F. I. M., 28
Cramer, P., 111
Crano, W. D., 247
Craske, M.G., 488
Crawford, M., 424
Crawley, R. A., 528
Creed, F., 449
Creed, P., 380
Crepaz, N., 466
Crews, F., 42
Crick, N. R., 308
Crimmins, E. M., 353
Crisp, R. J., 177
Critelli, J. W., 92, 98
Crits-Christoph. P., 545
Crocker, J., 148, 151, 152, 154, 178, 186, 308
Crohan, S. E., 283
Cronin, C., 79
Cronkite, R. C., 74
Crooks, R., 407, 420, 425, 429, 431, 432, 433, 437
Crosby, F. J., 390
Crosby, O., 375, 386
Cross, C. K., 343
Cross, P., 158
Cross, S. E., 141, 147, 148
Crouter, A. C., 277, 281, 347
Crow, T. J., 505
Crowder, K. D., 290
Crowell, J. A., 274
Crowley, A. E., 190
Crowley, B. J., 95
Crowley, J., 297
Crowley, M. L., 282
Cruess, D. G., 482
Cruza-Guet, M. C., 376, 378
Csikszentmihalyi, M., 92
Cuddy, A. J. C, 181
Cullen, L. T., 400, 401
Culpepper, L., 536
Cummings, E. M., 288, 367
Cunningham, C. O., 465
Cunningham, M., 316
Cunningham, M. R., 242
Curioni, C. C., 459
Currier, D., 496
Curtin, J. J., 75
Curtis, R. C., 246
Cutrona, C. E., 262
Cutting, L. P., 507

D

D'Achiardi, C., 374
D'Amico, M. L., 239
D'Augelli, A. R., 344
Dainton, M. 248
Dalbert, C., 180
Dallal, G. E., 338
Dallman, M. F., 85
Danieli, Y., 2, 89
Daniels, K., 72
Danton, W. G., 537
Dantzer, R., 86
Das, E. H. H., 190
David, D. H., 84
David, J. P., 98
David, M., 217
Davidson, J. R. T., 532
Davidson, M. J., 391, 392
Davies, A. P. C., 306
Davies, L., 290
Davies, O., 381
Davies, R., 495, 497
Davila, J., 257
Davis, B., 318
Davis, C. G., 120
Davis, H., 131
Davis, J. L., 247
Davis, K., 155, 175
Davis, K. E., 258, 297
Davis, K. F., 16
Davis, K. L., 354
Davis, L. L., 532
Davis, M., 212
Davis, M. N., 93
Davis, R. A., 110
Dawkins, K., 496
Dawood, K., 294
Day, S. X., 240
Dean, F. P., 127
Dean, L. R., 283
DeAngelis, T., 309, 457
Deaux, K., 242, 305
DeBaryshe, B. D., 367
De Beni, R., 29
DeBoer, D. D., 273
DeCarvalho, R. J., 50
Deci, E. L., 20
De Cock, K. M., 465
Deemer, H. N., 468
Deffenbacher, J. L., 449
DeFrain, J., 269, 275, 290
DeGroot, T., 403
DeHart, G., 380
de Jong, P. J P., 488
de Kloet, E. R., 86
Dekovic, M., 153, 341
Del Monte, M. M., 526
DeLamater, J. D., 324, 414
Delaune, K. A., 452, 454
Delay, J., 533
Deldin, P. G., 505
De Leo, D., 343
DeLeon, P. H., 2
Delgado, P. L., 498
DeLillo, V., 448
Delinsky, S. S., 508
Delongis, A., 71
Delunas, L., 77, 98
DelVecchio, W. F., 359
DeMaris, A., 296, 296
Demas, G. E., 448
Dement, W., 1
Demerouti, E., 281
Demo, D. H., 276, 286, 288, 289, 294, 349
Dempster, F. N., 28
Deniker, P., 533
Denisoff, E., 98
Dennerstein, L., 278, 350
Dennis, C., 276
Dennis, W., 358
DePaulo, B. M., 173, 209, 214, 215, 290
Derlega, V. J., 218, 220, 259
Derogatis, L. R., 97
DeRoma, V., 532
Desert, M., 304
Deshler, D. D., 141
Des Jarlais, D. C., 472
Desmarais, S., 315
DeSpelder, L. A., 360
Dessler, W. A., 74
de St. Aubin, E., 348
Detsky, A. S., 537
Detzer, M. J., 422
Deutsch, G., 312

Deutsch, M., 194
Devine, P. G., 178, 187
DeVries, B. , 250, 353
Dew, M. A., 484
Dewe, P., 71, 84
de Wilde, E. J., 343, 344
DeWit, J. B. F., 190
Dey, J. G., 380
Diamond, L., 252, 253, 411, 412, 420, 437
Dichter, G., 505
Dick, D. M., 338
DiClemente, C. C., 162
DiClemente, R. J., 340
Diekman, A. B, 316, 317., 304
Diekstra, R. F. W., 343, 344
Diener, C., 19
Diener, E., 2, 19, 20, 21, 22, 23, 251, 286
Dijkstra, P., 427
Dikel, M. F., 398
Dilsaver, S. C., 495
Dilworth, J. E. L., 281
DiMatteo, R. M., 23, 467, 468, 469
Din, J. N., 460
Dindia, K., 253
Dinges, D. F., 1
Dinning, W. D., 328
Dion, K. K., 178, 184, 238, 253
DiPaula, A., 141
DiPlacido, J., 95
DiPrete, T., 287
Dirks, J. F., 468
Dishman, R. K., 130
Dishotsky, N. L., 474
DiTomasso, E., 265
Dixon, L., 296
Dixon, R. A., 358
Dobs, A. S., 474
Dobson, K. S., 324
Dobson, M., 71
Docherty, N. M., 507
Dohrenwend, B. P., 98
Dolan, A., 528
Dolby, S. K., 4
Dollard, J., 107
Domar, A. D., 6
Donahue, E. M., 164
Donato, K. M., 278
Donnellan, M. B., 148, 151
Donnelly, B. W., 278
Donovan, R. L., 287
Dorn, L. D., 338
Dougall, A. L., 73, 75, 92, 97
Dougherty, T. W., 176, 402
Douglass, D. N., 124
Douglass, M. E., 124
Dovidio, J. F., 74, 183, 184, 185, 186, 212
Downey, L., 73
Doyle, J. A., 321
Dozier, D. M., 318
Drago, R. W., 382, 395
Draijer, N., 493
Dreher, H., 6
Dresser, N., 206
Drew, J., 324
Drigotas, S. M., 146
Driskell, J. E., 28
Driver, J. L., 274, 283
Driver, R., 145
Drozdek, B., 89
Drucker, A. D., 197
Druen, P. B., 242
Drum, D. J., 539
Du Chiara, G., 470
Dubbert, P. M., 463
Dubé, E. M., 252
Dubovsky, A. N., 495
Dubovsky, S. L., 495, 498, 534
Duck, S., 242, 244, 263, 287
Duckworth, K., 539
Duckworth, M. P., 490
Dudley, E., 278, 350
Duffy, S. M., 249
DuFrene, D. D., 226
Duggan, E. S., 262
Duman, R. S., 498
Dunbar-Jacobs, J., 469
Duncanson, W. T., 219
Dunkel, C. S., 141
Dunkel-Schetter, C., 449
Dunn, A. L., 463
Dunn, D. S., 158
Dunn, S., 3
Dunne, M. P., 413
Dunning, D., 157, 178
Durand, V. M., 511
duRocher-Schudlich, T., 367
Dweck, C. S., 146, 185, 307
Dyer, W. W., 6
Dzur, C., 331

E

Eacott, M. J., 528
Eagly, A. H., 178, 188, 245, 253, 304, 305, 310, 325
Eaker, E. D., 445
Eals, M., 311
Earley, P., 540
Easterbrook, G., 1
Easterlin, B. L., 131
Ebbinghaus, H., 2728
Eber, H. W., 66
Ebert, L., 91
Eccles, J. S., 322, 340, 343, 364
Eckert, S., 309
Edlin, G., 456
Edwards, C., 91
Edwards, J. N., 278
Edwards, K., 191
Edwards, R., 331
Edwards, S., 130
Ee, J. S., 92, 98
Eesley, C. E., 505
Egan, J., 329
Egan, T., 411
Egeci, I. S., 207
Egeland, B., 257
Eggert, A., 27
Ehreinreich, H., 475
Ehrenberg, M., 542, 543, 545
Ehrenberg, O., 542, 543, 545
Eich, E., 492
Einstein, G. O., 28
Eisen, J. L., 486
Eisenberg, N. H., 34
Eisenberger, N. I., 128
Eisler, R. M., 351
Ekman, P., 173, 209, 210, 211, 214, 215
Elder, G. H., Jr., 339
Eleonara, G., 487
Elfenbein, H. A., 211
Elias, J. W., 354
Elias, M. F., 354
Elias, P. K., 354
Elkind, D., 340, 342
Ellertson, C., 430
Ellington, L., 468
Ellinwood, E. H., Jr., 473
Elliot, A. J., 160
Elliott, L., 420
Ellis, A., 8, 111, 115–118, 168, 531
Ellis, J., 206
Ellis, T. E., 496
Ellison, N. B., 240
Else-Quest, N., 321
Ely, R., 309
Emavardhana, T., 131
Emery, R. E., 288
Emmanuel, H. M., 123
Emmelkamp, P. M. G., 529, 530, 533
Emmons, M. L., 228, 230, 233
Emmons, R., 76
Emmons, R. A., 4
Emsley, R., 534
Endler, N. S., 98
Engdalh, B., 2, 89
Epel, E. S., 449
Epstein, J. A., 209
Epstein, R., 5, 240
Epstein, S., 448
Erbring, L., 207
Erdelyi, M. H., 113
Erikson, E. H., 341, 342, 346–347, 348, 351–352
Ernst, C., 42
Eshleman, J. R., 290, 291
Eslea, M., 308
Esping-Anderson, G., 282
Espiritu, D. A. V., 355
Esterling, B. A., 86
Esterson, A., 43
Etaugh, C., 282
Ethier, K. A., 465
Etzel, E. F., 380
Evans, D. R., 352
Evans, G. W., 72, 73, 75, 107
Evans, R. G., 328
Everly, G. S., Jr., 117
Everson., S. A., 446
Ewart, C. K., 73
Exline, J. J., 130
Eysenck, H. J., 55–56, 488, 528

F

Faber, R. J., 1
Fabian, G., 198
Fabrigar, L. R., 189
Fagot, B. I., 314, 317
Fairbank, J. A., 91
Fairbrother, K., 387
Fairhurst, S. L., 162
Falk, P., 294
Falsetti, S. A., 91
Fancher, R. E., 44
Fanning, P., 168, 212, 217
Faraday, M. M., 453
Faraone, S. V., 505
Faravelli, C P., 489
Farberow, L., 496
Farina, A., 17
Farmer, K., 527
Farrell, R., 320
Faulkner, G., 130
Faust, K. A., 285
Fausto-Sterling, A., 311, 312, 313
Fava, G. A., 482
Fawcett, J. A., 496
Feeney, J. A., 256, 257
Fegan, M., 93, 94, 121, 446
Fehr, B., 220, 242, 251, 252
Fein, S., 179, 178
Feingold, A., 178, 243
Feiring, C., 330
Feld, S. L., 286
Feldman, D. C., 393
Feldman, J. M., 358
Feldman, N. S., 180
Feldman, P. J., 467
Feldman, R. S., 173
Feldman-Barrett, l., 74
Felker, B., 85
Felmlee, D., 259
Felson, R. B., 146, 153
Fenchel, M., 340

Fennema, E., 306
Fenton, W. S., 503
Fenwick, P., 130
Ferguson, T., 536
Fernandez, J. R., 458
Feroli, K., 430
Ferrari, J. R., 123, 124
Ferraro, J. K., 296
Ferriss, A. L., 21
Festinger, L., 144
Feys, J., 159, 160
Fiatrone, M. A., 465
Fielden, S., 391
Fielder, K., 215
Fiese, B. H., 316
Figueredo, A. J., 58
Finch, A. E., 525
Fincham, F. D., 224, 260, 279, 280, 283, 329
Fine, M., 289
Fine, R., 43
Fingerhut, A. W., 241, 246, 249, 252, 253, 412, 417, 426, 427
Finkelhor, D., 410
Finkenauer, C., 220
Finnerty, J., 161
First, M., B., 481, 482
Firth, K. M., 350
Fischer, A. H., 211
Fischer, E. F., 237
Fischer, K. W., 340
Fischer, P., 195
Fischhoff, B., 117
Fisher, S., 43, 536
Fisher, H. E., 246
Fishman, D. B., 529
Fiske, S. T., 174, 176, 177, 178, 181, 182, 186, 187
Fitch, S. A., 347
Fite, R., 527
Fitness, J., 220, 241
Fitzpatrick, M. A., 283
Fitzsimons, G. M., 239
Flaks, D. K., 294
Flannagan, D., 316
Flannery, R. B., Jr., 89, 91
Flapan, A. D., 460
Flavell, J. H., 340
Flavin, C., 3
Fleeson, W., 22, 50
Fletcher, G. J. O., 159, 175, 241, 244, 244, 273
Flett, G. L., 124, 274
Flippen, C., 352
Flores, B. H., 498
Flores, L. Y., 376
Florian, V., 256
Florio, C. M., 67
Flowers, C., 395
Floyd, F. J., 415
Floyd, M., 6
Flynn, F. J., 167
Foa, E. B., 89, 297, 309, 532
Folkman, S., 71, 72, 81, 82, 85, 92
Foote, B., 493
Forbes, G. B., 298
Forget, J., 28
Formicelli, L., 276
Forrest, J. A., 173
Forstein, M., 481
Forsyth, D. R., 545
Foster, C. A., 276
Foster, G. D., 457
Foster, J. D., 73
Fouad, N. A., 373, 378
Fouts, G., 318
Fowers, B. J., 273, 285
Fowles, D. C., 506
Fox, G. L., 276, 282
Fox, R., 416
Fraley, R. C., 176, 257
Frances, R. J., 456
Frank, E., 434
Frank, J., 544
Frank, J. B., 525
Frank, J. D., 525
Frank, L. R., 538
Frank, M. G., 214
Frank, R. H., 1
Frank. N. G., 173
Franklin, J. E., Jr., 456
Franks, C. M., 529
Franks, S., 445
Franzoi, S. L., 242
Fraser, J. M., 448
Fraser, S. C., 198
Frazier, P., 111, 287
Frederick, S., 24
Frederickson, B. L., 81, 82, 119, 243
Freedberg, K., 431
Freedman, J. L., 198
Freeman, E., 408
Freeman, J., 213
Freese, J., 42
Fremouw, W. J., 496
French, S. A., 458
Frese, M., 388, 389
Freud, S., 35–41, 43, 347, 413, 519–521
Frey, B. S., 20
Fricchione, G., 92
Fridhandler, B., 38
Fried, S. B., 6
Friedan, B., 322
Friedman, H. S., 173, 215, 442, 443, 448, 474
Friedman, J., 321
Friedman, M., 444
Friedman, M. J., 90, 532
Friedman, R., 143
Friedman, S. R., 472
Friend, R., 194, 194
Friesen, M. D., 244
Friesen, W. V., 210, 215
Frohlich, D., 220
Fromholt, P., 355
Fromm, E., 4
Frost, L. A., 329
Frustenberg, F. F., Jr., 288
Frye, E. M., 4
Fujita, F., 21
Fulgini, A. J., 343
Fullerton, C. S., 91
Funder, D. C., 58, 113
Furberg, A., 463
Furman, E., 363
Furnham, A., 153, 181, 317, 318
Furstenberg, F. F., Jr., 278
Futterman, D., 415

G

Gabbard, G. O., 42, 43, 544
Gable, S. L., 274, 416
Gabrel, C. S., 356
Gabriel, S., 148
Gaertner, S. L., 74, 183, 184
Gafni, N., 311
Gage, F. H., 498
Gagne, F., 28
Gagnon, J. H., 422
Galambos, N. L., 110, 308
Galderisi, S., 503
Galinsky, E., 386, 395
Gall, T. L., 352
Gallagher, K. I., 464
Gallagher, M., 286, 287
Gallagher, R., 366
Gallagher, S., 142
Gallagher, S. N., 215
Gallo, L. C., 444, 445, 449
Gallois, C., 283
Gambone, J. C., 468
Gana, K., 113
Ganahl, D. J., 318
Ganey, H. C. N., 82
Gangestad, S. W., 167, 211, 245
Gangi, B. K., 542
Ganong, L., 289
Gant, L. M., 265
Gantt, W. H., 44
Gao, G., 254
Garb, H. N., 67
Garber, J., 468
Garcia, B. E., 49
Garcia, M., 541
Garcia Ganuza, J. M., 307
Gardner, C. O., Jr., 494
Gardner, W. L., 148
Garfield, S. L., 524, 540
Garland, A. F., 344
Garnefski, N., 111
Garnets, L. D., 293, 345, 413, 414, 415
Gartrell, N., 294, 413
Gates, G. J., 292
Gatz, M., 354
Gaunt, R., 173, 175, 272
Gavin, L. E., 277
Gawet, D. L., 79
Ge, X., 339
Geasler, M. J., 288
Gecas, V., 277
Geddes, J. R., 536, 538
Gee, C. B., 207, 283
Gee, E. M., 278
Gee, T., 492
Geen, R. G., 308
Geeraert, N. Y., 179
Geisler, R. B., 157
Gelles, R. J., 286
Gençöz, T., 207
George, S. A., 356
Gerard, H. B., 194
Gerrard, M., 158
Gershoff, E. T., 368
Geruts, S., 281
Giant, C. L., 243, 323
Giarrusso, R., 279
Gibbons, F. X., 158
Gibbons, J. L., 314
Gibbons, R. D., 536
Gibbs, J. L., 240
Gibson, G., 452
Giddens, A., 285
Giedd, J. L., 391
Giesen, D., 427
Gilbert, D. T., 23, 179
Giles, T. R., 539
Gill, D. S., 224
Gill, M., 475
Gillham, J. E., 97
Gilligan, S., 446
Gillis, J. R., 293
Gilovich, T., 164
Gingerich, J., 531
Gitlin, M., 535
Glascock, J., 317
Glaser, K., 291
Glaser, R., 251, 448, 449
Glasgow, R. E., 8
Glass, C. R., 528, 531
Glass, G. V., 544
Glass, R. M., 537, 538, 540
Glassman, A., 447
Glatt, S. J., 505
Glazer, K., 445
Glazer, M. P., 197
Glazer, P. M., 197
Gleason, J. B., 309

Gleason, M. E. J., 239
Gleaves, D. H., 323, 492, 526, 528
Glenn, N. D., 347, 350
Glisky, M. L., 492
Gluck, M. E., 509
Godbey, G., 1
Godfrey, H. M., 119
Goeders, N. E., 91, 110
Goeting, A., 276
Goffman, E., 165
Golanty, E., 456
Gold, J. M., 505
Gold, M. A., 177
Gold, M. S., 473
Goldberg, A. E., 324
Goldberg, C., 390
Goldberg, I., 495
Goldberger, L., 93
Golden, R. N., 496
Goldenberg, J. L., 61
Golden-Kreutz, D. M., 448
Goldfried, M. C., 344
Golding, J. M., 297
Goldman, B. M., 149
Goldscheider, C., 278
Goldscheider, F. K., 278
Goldsmith, T. D., 111
Goldstein, E., 527
Goldstein, R. D., 495
Goldzweig, C. L., 391
Goleman, D., 127
Gollwitzer, P. M., 157
Golombok, S., 294
Gomez-Jacinto, L., 73
Gonsiorek, J. C., 292, 416
Gonzaga, G. C., 274
Gonzales, M. H., 247
Gonzales, R., 347
Goodall, K., 132
Gooden, A. M., 316
Gooden, M. A., 316
Goodrick, G. K., 162
Goodwin, F. K., 495, 497
Gordon, A. H., 309
Gordon, B., 534
Gordon, K. C., 283
Gordon, L. U., 450
Gordon, P. A., 321
Gordon, R. A., 165
Gordon, R. M., 288
Gordon, S. L., 253
Gordon, V. M., 375
Gore, J. S., 147, 148
Gosselin, J. T., 162
Gotlib, I. H., 500
Gottdiener, J. S., 446
Gottesman, I. I., 505
Gottman, J. M., 260, 274, 277, 283, 284
Gould, R., 351
Gourevitch, M. N., 473
Gouzoulis-Mayfrank, E., 475
Gow, K. M., 528
Graber, J. A., 338, 339
Graham, J. E., 449
Graig, E., 75
Gramling, S. E., 394
Grant, I., 449
Gray, J., 6
Gray-Little, B., 154
Graziano, W. G., 34, 219
Green, A. S., 239
Green, C. E., 296
Green, J. D., 141
Green, K., 259
Green, L. R., 261
Green, M. A., 240
Green, M. F., 505
Greenberg, J. L., 59–60, 61, 62, 152, 181
Greenberg, J. S., 464
Greenberg, L. S., 523
Greenberg, R. P., 43, 536
Greene, K., 218
Greene, R. L., 28
Greenfield, D. N., 110
Greenhaus, J. H., 382
Greenland, P., 443
Greenson, R. R., 520
Greenwald, A. G., 178
Greenwood, D. L., 296
Gregg, P. B., 414
Gregory, R. J., 6
Greitmeyer, T., 195, 272
Grencavage, L. M., 525
Griest, J. H., 536
Griffin-Shelley, E., 426
Griffith, K. H., 384
Grinspoon, L., 474
Grob, C. S., 475
Groesz, L. M., 243
Grohol, J., 481
Gross, C. P., 537
Gross, J. J., 127
Grossbaum, M. F., 348
Grossi, G., 88
Grossman, J. B., 530
Grote, N. K., 224, 250
Groth-Marnat, G., 67
Grothues, C. A., 296
Grove, W. M., 67
Gruber, A. J., 475
Gruber, J. E., 391
Gruenberg, A. M., 495
Grunberg, N. E., 453
Grundy, E., 277, 291
Guadagno, R. E., 199
Guarda, A. S., 509
Gudjonsson, G. H., 525
Gueguen, N., 200
Guest, F., 422
Guevremont, D. C., 530
Guggenheim, F. G., 489
Gugula, S., 315
Guinn, I. S., 157
Gullette, E. C. D., 446
Gunnell, D., 536
Gupta, G. R., 237
Gupta, S., 287
Gupta, U., 238
Gureje, O., 489
Gurland, B. J., 354, 356
Gurung, R. A. R., 353
Gutek, B. A., 391
Guthrie, J., 278, 350
Guthrie, R. M., 116

H

Haan, N., 359
Haas, D. M., 248
Haas, E., 220, 309
Haas, L., 279, 280, 281, 282
Hackam, D. G., 443
Hackstaff, K. B., 286
Haden, S. C., 251
Hadjistavropoulos, H., 49
Hadjiyannakis, K., 501
Hafdahl, A. R., 154
Hafer, C. L., 180
Hagan, H., 472
Hagan, R., 314
Hagen, E. H., 308
Hagerty, M. R., 23
Hagestad, G., 345
Haidt, J., 142, 152
Haig, J., 34
Hale, J. L., 254
Hale, S. L., 200
Hall, A. H., 280
Hall, D. R., 291
Hall, E. T., 209, 210
Hall, G. S., 342–343
Hall, J. A., 209, 212, 213, 216, 309, 332
Hall, M. 274
Halmi, K, A., 509, 510
Halpern, C. T., 243
Halpern, D. F., 269, 270, 306, 307, 310, 311, 317, 338
Halpern-Felsher, B. L., 422
Halverson, A. M., 177
Hamilton, A., 240
Hamilton, J. C., 468
Hamilton, M., 316
Hamilton, M. A., 331
Hamilton, T. E., III, 244
Hamilton, V. L., 197
Hammen, C., 495
Hammersley, R., 475
Hammersmith, K. S., 413
Hampson, E., 309, 312
Hamsen, P., 449
Han, M., 74
Han, W., 282
Hancock, D. R., 82
Hancock, P. A., 82
Handal, M., 436
Handy, B., 427, 436
Hanna, R., 242
Hanna, S. L., 218
Hansen, J. C., 376
Hansen, N. B., 525
Hansen, W. B., 340
Hansford, S. L., 252
Happonen, P., 460
Harber, K. D., 124, 177
Haring, M., 274
Harnack, L., 458
Harpaz, I., 394
Harper, G. W., 415
Harrigan, J. A., 212
Harris, J. R., 42, 57
Harris, L. T., 181
Harris, M., 360
Harris, M. B., 308
Harris, P. R., 194
Harris, T., 6
Harrison, J. A., 195
Harrison, K., 317, 323
Harrison, K., 510
Hart, R., 290
Hart, T. A., 466
Harter, S., 146, 151, 153
Hartka, E., 359
Hartley, A. A., 357
Hartley, R., 72
Hartup, W. W., 250
Harvey, J. H., 248, 250, 274
Harvey, M. H., 282, 528
Harwood, T. M., 525
Hastie, R., 23
Hatcher, R. A., 429, 430, 432
Hatfield, E., 237, 245, 247, 418
Haug, N. A., 465
Hawkins, A. J., 286
Hawkins, D. N., 286, 287
Haworth-Hoeppner, S., 510
Hayes, A., 424
Hayes, S., 38
Hays, K. F., 463
Hayskip, B., Jr., 95
Hazam, H., 220
Hazan, C., 254–257
Hazan, O., 4
Healy, D., 536, 537
Healy, S. D., 311
Heath, C., 157
Heatherton, T. F., 148
Heaton, T. B., 272, 276
Heavey, C. L., 260, 283
Hebl, M. R., 243, 384
Hecht, M. A., 209, 211

Heckhausen, J., 350, 351
Hedges, L. V., 306
Heffner, K. L., 236
Hegarty, P., 305
Heiby, E. M., 515
Heider, F., 155
Heilman, M. E., 325
Heilman-Houserk, R. A., 315
Heiman, J. R., 436, 437
Heine, S. J., 159
Heino, R. D., 240
Heinrichs, R. W., 502
Heinze, A., 455
Helgeson, V. S., 93, 144, 328
Hellstrom, A., 173
Helson, R., 345, 348, 359
Helweg-Larsen, M., 158
Hembree, E. A., 532
Hemenover, S. H., 128
Henderson, K. E., 458
Henderson, M., 250
Hendrick, C., 254
Hendrick, S. S., 254, 259
Henley, N. M., 210, 211, 213, 216
Hennessy, D. A., 75
Henning, K., 434
Henningsen, P., 489
Henny, K. D., 466
Henretta, J. C., 277
Henry, M. E., 538
Henry, R., G., 279
Heppner, P. P., 120
Herek, G. M., 250, 293, 294, 321, 414, 415
Heres, S., 537
Herman, C. P., 243, 323
Hermann, D., 29
Hermann, R. C., 538
Herrett-Skjellum, J., 318
Hershberger, S. L., 344
Hertzog, C., 358
Herzog, D. B., 508
Herzog, M. E., 242
Hess, N. H., 308
Hetherington, E. M., 57, 287, 288
Hettema, J. M., 487
Hettich, P. I., 26
Hewes, D. E., 414
Hewitt, P. L., 124, 274
Hewstone, M., 185
Hewstone, S., 177
Heymann, J., 386
Hicks, T. V., 421
Hiedelmann, B., 285
Higgins, A. J., 257
Higgins, E. M., 388
Higgins, E. T., 142
Hightower, M., 95
Hill, A. J., 315, 316, 459
Hill, C., 380
Hill, C. E., 524
Hill, C. T., 253, 257, 258
Hill, J. L., 282
Hiller, W., 489
Hines, M., 312, 313
Hiroto, D. S., 106
Hirsch, J., 458
Hirschfeld, R. M. A., 343
Hirschl, T. A., 291
Hirt, E. R., 148
Ho, B., 502, 503, 506
Hobdy, J., 95
Hobfoll, S. E., 94
Hobson, C. J., 77, 98
Hochschild, A. R., 281, 347
Hock, M. F., 141
Hodge, B., 386
Hodgson, D., 86, 448
Hoek, J. W., 509
Hoffman, E., 42
Hoffman, R. E., 91, 97, 507
Hoffnung, M., 323, 324
Hofmann, S. G., 107
Hofstede, G., 147
Hogan, J., 34
Hogan, M. F., 539
Hogue., C. 423
Holahan, C. J., 93, 113
Holden, C., 536
Holder, J. S., 463
Holen, A., 90
Holland, J. C., 448, 449
Holland, J. L., 377–378
Holland, K., 276
Holland, R. W., 209, 210
Hollander, E., 1, 485
Hollifield, M. A., 489, 490
Hollon, S. D., 525, 531
Holman, T. B., 273
Holmans, P., 498
Holmbeck, G., 524
Holmes, T. H., 77–78, 95, 97
Holoway, P., 409
Holsboer, F., 86
Holt, A., 536
Holt, C. S., 218
Hong, G. K., 541
Honts, C. R., 215
Hoobler, J. M., 108
Hood, K. E., 312
Hooker, E., 416
Hooley, J. M., 507
Hopf, T, 223
Hopkins, C., 323
Hopko, D. R., 88
Hopper, J., 288
Horowitz, L. M., 256
Horvath, M., 384
Horwath, E., 485
Hotopf, M., 491
Hou, J., 307
Houts, A. C., 482
Howard, G. S., 3
Howard, J., 352
Howard, K. I., 343
Howland, R. H., 498
Hoyer, W. D., 190
Hsee, C. K., 23
Hsu, L. K. G., 508
Hu, F. B., 460
Hu, L., 49
Hu, T. W., 541
Hu, Y., 49
Huang, C., 220
Hubbard, J. A., 216
Hubbard, J. R., 85
Hubner, J. J., 149
Hudman, K. S., 453
Hudson, J. I., 509, 510
Hudziak, J., 534
Huesmann, L. R., 226
Huff, M. E., 91
Hugenberg, K., 178
Hughes, C. C., 541
Hull, J. G., 143, 144
Hulshoff, H. E., 507
Hultin, M., 325
Hunsley, J., 67
Hunt, M., 18., 91
Hunter, B. A., 298
Hunter, D. M., 307
Hunter, E., 5
Hunter, M., 315
Huntsinger, E. T., 257
Hurrell, J., 387
Huston, A. C., 226, 227
Huston, T. L., 285, 286
Hwang, W., 541
Hyde, J. S., 281, 303, 306, 307, 308, 310, 322, 324, 329, 330, 338, 396, 410, 412, 413, 417
Hyes, K. H., 380
Hygge, S., 72, 73
Hyman, I. E., 527

I

Iaccino, J. F., 29
Iacono, W. G., 492, 506
Iawao, S., 237
Ickes, W. J., 186, 328
Ickovics, J. R., 465
Iezzi, T., 490
Ilgen, D. R., 372, 390
Impett, E. A., 410, 413, 416, 417, 420, 425
Infante, J. R., 131
Ingegneri, D. G., 353
Inglehart, R., 20
Ingoldsby, B. B., 271
Innocenti, G. M., 312
Inskeep, S., 325
Insko, C. A., 194
Ippolito, J., 388
Irabarren, C., 445
Ironson, G., 449
Isaacowitz, D. M., 107
Ismail, B., 507
Israël, M., 510
Ito, T. A., 179
Ivancevich, J. M., 389
Ivens-Tyndal, C. O., 91, 495, 499
Iwasaki, Y., 397, 398
Izard, C., 216

J

Jackson, B. L., 287
Jackson, L. A., 242
Jackson, M., 394
Jackson, T., 263
Jacob, D., 290
Jacob, R. G., 533
Jacobi, F., 309
Jacobs, B. L., 498
Jacobs, H. S., 356
Jacobs, J. E., 343
Jacobs, W. S., 473
Jacobson, C. K., 276
Jacobson, N. S., 281
Jacques, R., 386
Jaffe, J., 472
Jahoda, M., 113
Jakicici, J., 464
Jakupcak, M., 320
James, E. H., 386
James, J. E., 460
Jamison, K. R., 495, 497
Janata, J. W., 468
Jang, K. L., 56
Janis, I. L., 72, 82
Jankowiak, W. R., 237
Janoff-Bulman, R., 22, 93, 141
Janssen, R. S., 465
Jansz, J., 319, 320
Jaroff, L., 527
Javitt, D. C., 505
Jefferson, J. W., 536
Jeffrey, R. W., 110, 458, 459
Jeffries, S., 276
Jellinger, K. A., 355
Jemmott, J. B., III, 93
Jeney-Gammon, P., 111
Jepsen, C. A., 272
Jepsen, L. K., 272
Jernewall, N., 415
Jex, S. M., 49
Jeynes, W. H., 289
Jick, H., 536
Jick, S. S., 536
Jindal, K., 498
Joels, M., 86
John, O. P., 34, 50

Johnson, A. M., 412
Johnson, B. A., 454
Johnson, I. M., 297
Johnson, J. A., 469
Johnson, J. H., 99, 101
Johnson, J. L., 124
Johnson, J. T., 166
Johnson, M. P., 275, 295, 296
Johnson, S. B., 468, 469
Johnson, T., 211
Johnson, T. W., 294
Johnson, V. E., 418–420, 436, 437
Johnson, W., 19, 20
Joiner, T. E., 157, 500, 501
Jonas, J. M., 473
Jones, C. M., 311
Jones, D., 242
Jones, E. E., 155, 165, 166, 175, 179
Jones, F., 77
Jones, J., 431
Jones, N. F., 468
Jones, R. A., 190
Jones, S. M., 226
Jordan, C. H., 150
Jorgensen, R. S., 127
Joseph, S., 120
Josselson, R. L., 341
Joung, I. M. A., 290, 291
Jourard, S. M., 113
Joyner, T., 394, 396
Judge, T. A., 34
Julien, R. M., 471, 472
Jung, C. G., 41
Jussim, L., 177
Justman, S., 8

K

Kaelber, C. T., 482
Kagan, J., 487
Kahn, A. S., 297, 310
Kahn, A. S., 424
Kahn, J. R., 287
Kahneman, D., 20, 24
Kaiser, A., 312
Kaiser, C. R., 181
Kalant, H., 473
Kalant, O. J., 473
Kalaria, R. N., 447
Kalb, C., 430
Kales, A. K., 91
Kalichman, S. C., 465, 466
Kalick, S. M., 244
Kalidindi, S., 498
Kallgren, C. A., 189
Kalmijn, M., 246, 272
Kaltman, S., 361
Kalwarf, H. J., 460
Kamp Dush, C. M., 291
Kandel, I., 344
Kandell, J. J., 110
Kane, E. W., 305
Kane, J. M., 534, 535
Kane, T. O., 49
Kaniasty, K., 251
Kanner, A. D., 1
Kanner, A. D., 71
Kant, A. K., 460
Kapinus, C. A., 275
Kaplan, A. G., 543
Kaplan, D. S., 79
Kaplan, H. B., 79
Kaplan, H. I., 92
Kaplan, H. S., 420
Kaplan, J., 444, 446
Karasek, R. A., Jr., 388, 389
Karasu, T. B., 521
Karau, S. J., 325
Kardiner, A., 62
Karney, B. R., 175
Karp, D. A., 484
Kashy, D., 263
Kasper, H. T., 381
Kassel, J. D., 110
Kassem, L., 487
Kasser, T., 1–2, 4, 54, 313, 352
Kassin, S. M., 150, 175, 249
Kastenbaum, R. J., 359, 360
Katigbak, M. S., 62
Katz, J., 500
Katz, L. F., 283
Katz, L. G., 151
Katz, L. S., 448
Katzman, M. A., 509
Kaufman, C. A., 498
Kaufman, G., 262, 279
Kausler, D. H., 357, 358
Kavanaugh, D. J., 507
Kavesh, L., 279
Kawachi, I., 446
Kay, J., 521
Kay, R. L., 521
Kaye, J. A., 536
Kaye, W. H., 509
Kazdin, A. E., 132, 515
Keck, P. E., 502, 536
Keefe, F. J., 449
Keefe, R. S. E., 505
Keefer, L., 448
Keel, P. K., 323
Keen, S., 320
Keesey, R. E., 458
Kegan, R., 4
Keicolt-Glaser, J. K., 251
Keinan, G., 88
Keita, G. P., 309, 387
Keith, J., 345
Keith, S. J., 501
Keith-Spiegel, P., 543
Keller, B. K., 374
Keller, S. N., 409
Kelley, H. H., 155, 175, 248
Kellogg, J. S., 88
Kelly, B. D., 507
Kelly, H. H., 182
Kelly, J., 277
Kelly, J. A., 465
Kelly, J. B., 288
Kelly, J. M., 72
Kelly, K. M., 449
Kelly, K. R., 322
Kelly, P. K., 120
Kelman, H. C., 197
Kelsey, J. E., 536
Kelsoe, J., 498
Keltner, D., 362
Kelts, D., 141
Kemeny, M. E., 85, 86, 128
Kendall, A. R., 130
Kendall, P. C., 524
Kendler, K. S., 309, 413, 487, 494, 498, 498, 500, 501, 505
Kenneavy, K., 409
Kennedy, G. A., 79
Kennedy, S. H., 536
Kenrick, D. T., 253, 273, 311
Keough, E., 82
Kernis, M. H., 149, 150, 151
Kerns, K. A., 257
Kerr, B., 325
Kerwin, R., 536
Kessler, E. A., 216
Kessler, R. C., 3, 6, 251, 256, 351, 353, 450, 482, 484, 487, 495, 501, 516
Keysar, B., 216
Khan, A., 502, 504
Khot, U. N., 443
Khoury, J. C., 460
Khroyan, T. V., 453
Kiecolt-Glazer, J. K., 93, 236, 448–449
Kieffer, K. M., 79
Kieffer, S. C., 161
Kienhorst, C. W., 343
Kierein, N. M., 177
Kiernan, K. E., 288, 291
Kiernan, M., 463
Kieseppa, T., 498
Kiesler, C. A., 480, 539
Kiewra, K. A., 27
Kihlstrom, J. F., 492, 492, 526
Kilby, R. W., 272
Kilicarslan, A., 458
Kilmartin, C., 211, 220, 252, 319, 320, 321, 410
Kim, H. S., 121, 191
Kim, J. E., 352
Kimmel, D. C., 293, 345, 413, 414, 415
Kimura, D., 312
Kinder, B., 509
Kindlon, D., 320
King, A. C., 463
King, B. M., 422, 433
King, C. A., 344
King, G. R., 473
King, J. L., 431
King, L., 76, 286
King, L. A., 93
King, M., 481
King, N. J., 487
King, T. K., 130
Kinman, G., 77
Kinsey, A., 412, 413, 420
Kinsman, R. A., 468
Kinsman, S. B., 409
Kirby, D., 410
Kirby, S. L., 127
Kircher, J. C., 215
Kirk, S. A., 481
Kirkbride, A., 242, 407
Kirkpatrick, L. A., 257, 258, 503
Kirschenbaum, D. S., 459
Kitayama, S., 147, 159, 179
Kite, M. E., 385, 403
Kitson, G. C., 287
Klag, S., 95
Klass, D., 363
Klassen, M., 126
Klein, D. N., 98
Klein, E., 90
Klein, F., 412
Klein, K. L., 162
Klein, T. W., 474
Klein, W. M., 452
Kleinbaum, S., 291
Kleinke, C. L., 211, 217
Kleinman, B. M., 218
Kleinmuntz, B., 497
Kleinnecht, E. E., 527
Klimoski, R. J., 372
Kline, D. W., 354
Kline, G. H., 224, 229, 259
Kline, P., 66
Klinesmith, J., 313
Kling, K. C., 154., 306, 307
Klipper, M. Z., 131
Klohnen, E. C., 246–247, 272
Klonoff, E. A., 74
Klose, M., 309
Klotz, J. L., 242
Kluckhohn, C., 62
Kluft, R. P., 492, 528
Klumb, P. L., 71
Knapp, C. M., 472
Knapp, D. E., 391
Knaus, W., 123
Knee, C. R., 161
Knickmeyer, N., 250
Knobe, J., 175
Knowles, J. A., 498
Knowles, R. B., 354
Knox, D., 288

Ko, D., 121
Kobasa, S. C., 94–95
Kobrynowicz, D., 319
Koestner, R., 123, 145, 246
Koff, E., 339
Kolb, R., 489
Kolodny, R. C., 437
Konnert, C., 276
Konrad, A. M., 321
Koopman, C., 90
Kop, W. J., 446
Kopta, S. M., 524
Koran, L. M., 1
Koren, D., 90
Koriat, A., 28
Kornspan, A. S., 380
Koss, M. P., 296, 297, 298
Kouzma, N. M., 79
Kowalski, R. M., 321
Kozlowski, S. W. J., 374
Kraaij, V., 111
Krahn, H. J., 308
Kramer, P. D., 43
Kransny, L., 531
Krantz, D. S., 446, 449
Kraus, J. E., 535
Kraus, L. A., 93
Krause, N., 353
Kraut, R., 220
Kreider, R. M., 285, 289
Kressin, M. R., 352
Kring, A. M., 309, 502
Kroger, J., 342
Krokoff, L. J., 260
Krueger, R. F., 19, 20
Krueger, W. C. F., 28
Kruger, J., 164
Kruglanski, A. W., 182
Krupat, E., 467
Kübler-Ross, E., 360–361, 393
Kudo, E., 159
Kuhn, J., 501
Kulick, A. R., 502
Kulik, L., 392
Kunkel, D., 409, 410
Kunkel, E. S., 448
Kuperminc, G. P., 73
Kurdek, L. A., 207, 249, 252, 253, 257, 285, 293, 294, 329, 396, 426, 427
Kutcher, E. J., 403
Kutchins, H., 481

L

L'Engle, K. L., 409
Lachman, M. E., 349, 350, 351
LaFrance, M., 211
Lakein, A., 123, 124, 125, 25
Lakin, M., 523
Lam, L. T., 127
Lambert, J. D., 278
Lambert, M. J., 180, 524, 525, 540, 542, 544
Lambert, T. A., 424, 425
Lamborn, S. D., 368
Lamke, L. K., 296
Lammers, C., 424
Lamon, S. J., 306
Lampe, A., 448, 449
Lanares, O., 366
Landabaso, M. A., 530
Landau, M. J., 61
Landrine, H., 74
Landsberger, S. A., 257
Landsman, T., 113
Lane, C. J., 358
Lane, M., 516
Lane, M. D., 184
Lang, P. J., 177
Langeland, W., 493
Langenbucher, J., 481
Langer, E., 154–155, 158, 187
Langlois, J. H., 178, 242
Lanphear, B. P., 460
Lansford, J. E., 353
Lanza, S. T., 339
LaPiere, R. T., 183
LaPierre, Y. D., 536
Larson, R., 332, 343
Laruelle, M., 505
Larzelere, R. E., 369
Laskoff, M. B., 393
Lasley, E. N., 92
Lassiter, G. D., 214
Latané, B., 195
Lating, J. M., 532
Lauer, J., 259
Lauer, R., 259
Laughlin, H., 112, 485
Laumann, E. O., 412, 420, 422, 423, 426, 434, 435
Laurenceau, J. P., 218, 219, 272
Lauriello, J., 501
Laursen, B., 343
Lauzen, M. M., 318
Lavalle, L. F., 148
Lavin, C., 270
Lavin, M. J., 265
Lavine, H., 323
La Violette, A. D., 296
Lavoie, K., 123
Lawler, K. A., 94
Lawton, L., 278
Lay, C. H., 124
Lazarus, A., 545
Lazarus, R. S., 71, 72, 81, 85
Le, B., 249
Le, K., 164
Leahy, J. M., 363
Leana, C. R., 393
Leaper, C., 317
Leary, M. R., 150, 152, 153, 236
Leatham, G., 263
Leavitt, F., 470, 472, 528
LeBeau, L. S., 216
LeBlanc, M. M., 392
Le Boeuf, M., 122
Leckman, J. F., 486
Lee, C. M., 67
Lee, D., 120
Lee, F. R., 271, 272
Lee, G. R., 278, 353
Lee, I.-M., 463
Lee, J. E., 452
Lee, R. M., 540
Lee, S., 509
Lee, Y. T., 159
Lefcourt, H. M., 119, 120
Leff, J., 507
Lefkowitz, E. S., 329
Lehman, C. M., 226
Lehman, D., 457
Lehrer, P., 449
Lehrer, R. M., 131
Leibel, R. L., 458
Leigh, G. K., 273
Leitenberg, H., 421, 434
Leiter, M. P., 88
Lemack, G. E., 91
LeMay, C. S., 209
Lemelle, A. J., Jr., 293
Lemieux, R., 254
Lemme, B. H., 351
Lengua, L. J., 72
Lenhart, A., 239
Lenton, R. L., 240
Leo, J., 55
LePore, S. J., 73
Lepper, M. R., 186
Lerman, H., 43
Lerner, M. J., 180
Letherby, G., 276
Lett, H. S., 447
Leu, J., 180
Leucht, S., 535
Levant, R. F., 2, 318, 319, 320, 539
Le Vay, S., 292
Levenson, J. L., 92, 448
Levenstein, S., 448, 449
Leventhal, E. A., 467
Leventhal, H., 467
Lever, J., 423
Levin, S., 186, 250
Levine, A., 277
Levine, M. P., 243, 510
LeVine, R. A., 62
Levine, R. V., 195, 237, 238
Levine, S. B., 435
Levinson, D., 350–351
Levinthal, C. E., 471, 472
Levis, D. J., 487
Levitt, J. G., 376
Levy, S. R., 185
Lewandowski, C. A., 75
Lewin, E., 269
Lewin, K., 76
Lewinsohn, P. M., 500, 501
Lewis, B. P., 87
Lewis, J. M., 288
Lewis, L. L., 305
Lewis, M., 330, 361
Lewis, R. A., 350
Lewis, R. J., 74
Lewis, S., 448, 449
Lewis-Smith, J., 272
Leyens, J., 304
Li, T.-K., 482
Li, W., 49, 184
Li, Y., 537
Libby, P., 443
Licata, N., 286
Lichtenstein, S., 117
Lichtenthal, W.G., 482
Lichter, D. T., 282, 291
Lickey, M. E., 534
Lieberman, J. A., 504, 535
Lieberman, M. D., 179
Liebert, L. L., 50
Liebert, R. M., 50, 317
Lilienfeld, S. O., 6, 8, 67, 492, 493
Lim, G. Y., 298
Lin, L. W., 350
Lin, Y., 220
Linde, J. A., 49
Lindenberger, U, 354
Lindenmayer, J. P., 502, 504
Linder, D. E., 87
Lindren, H. C., 27
Lindsay, D. S., 526, 527, 528
Link, B. G., 77, 98
Linley, P. A., 120
Linton, R., 62
Lipkus, I. M., 180
Lippa, R. A., 306, 311, 312, 314, 316, 318
Lisanby, S. H., 538
Litman, R. E., 496
Litz, B. T., 107
Litzinger, S., 283
Liu, Q. N., 448
Liu, R. X., 79
Liu, T., 449
Livanou, M., 532
Liverant, G. I., 107
Livesley, W. J., 56
Lloyd, K. M., 259, 282
Lloyd, M., 375
Lloyd, S. A., 274
Lock, R. D., 381, 383, 393, 400, 401, 403
Locke, B. Z., 482
Lockwood, P., 145
Lodewijkx, H. F. M., 187
Loehlin, J. C., 56, 57

Loewenstein, G., 24
Loewenstein, R. J., 491
Loftus, E. F., 526, 527
Long, J. E., Jr., 515
Longman, D. G., 27
Lopes, P. N., 127
Lopez, D. J., 74
Lopez, F. G., 257
Losada, M. F., 82
Lourenco, P. M., 459
Lovaglia, M. J., 161
Lovejoy, M., 395
Loving, T. J., 236, 251, 264
Lowinson, J. H., 471, 472
Lozano, B. E., 162
Lu, H. H., 291
Lubkin, I. M., 468
Luborsky, L., 524, 544
Lucas, A. R., 510
Lucas, J. W., 161
Lucas, R. E., 22, 23, 24, 164, 288
Ludwig, D. S, 460
Ludwig, T. E., 130
Luecke-Aleksa, D., 317
Luecken, L. J., 257
Luft, H. S., 537
Luhtanen, R., 186
Lulofs, R. S., 224, 227
Lundberg, U., 85
Lundberg-Love, P. K., 295, 296, 298
Lundeberg, K., 298
Luo, S., 247, 272
Lurie, P., 537
Luskin, F. M., 131
Lussier, Y., 274
Luthans, F., 49, 162
Lutz, C. J., 164
Luyerink, M., 212
Lye, D. N., 279
Lykken, D., 20, 21, 22, 55
Lyles, C. M., 466
Lynch, D. J., 77
Lyness, K. S., 325
Lynn, D. J., 43
Lynn, M., 242
Lynn, S. J., 492, 493, 527
Lyons-Ruth, K., 84
Lytton, H., 314, 315, 316
Lyubomirsky, S., 22, 23, 286

M

Maccoby, E. E., 57, 153, 314, 316, 331, 364, 367
MacDonald, G., 153
MacGeorge, E. L., 330, 331
Macionis, J. J., 246
Mack, A. H., 456
Mackenzie, R. A., 122–123, 124
Mackie, D. M., 177, 189
MacMillan, H. L., 493, 526
Macmillan, M., 43
Macrae, C. N., 178, 179
Madden, M., 239
Maddi, S. R., 95
Maddox, G. I., 356
Maddox, W. T., 88
Maddux, J. E., 162
Madsen, S. D., 251
Madson, L., 148
Magloire, K., 93
Magner, N. R., 227
Magnusson, D., 339
Maguen, S., 409
Mahalik, J. R., 320
Maher, B. A., 502
Maheu, M., 411
Mahoney, M. J., 120
Mahoney. M., 531
Maier, S. F., 157
Maisey, D. S., 323
Major, B., 181, 187, 213, 307, 308
Mak, T., 317, 318
Malamuth, N. M., 283
Malanos, A. B., 22
Maldonado, J. R., 492
Malefo, V., 98
Maletzky, B. M., 530
Malina, R. M., 337
Malle, B. F., 175
Mallen, M. J., 240
Malone, P. S., 179
Maltz, D. N., 331
Mandler, G., 82
Maner, J. K., 487
Manktelow, J., 121
Mann, J. J., 496, 498
Manning, W. D., 287, 291
Mannix, L. M., 243
Manson, J. E., 457
Manstead, A. S. R., 211
Manzella, L. M., 175
Marafiote, R. A., 539
Marcenes, W. G., 448
March, J. S., 532
Marcia, J. E., 341–342
Marcus, E. R., 520, 521
Marcus-Newhall, A., 108
Marder, S. R., 534, 535
Marecek, J., 310
Mariani, M., 381
Maris, R. W., 309, 343, 496
Mark, M. M., 191
Marker, N. F., 290
Markey, P. M., 195
Markides, K. S., 353
Markman, A. B., 88
Markman, H. J., 229, 274, 291
Marks, G., 466
Marks, I. M., 486
Marks, M. J., 176
Marks, N. F., 278
Markus, H. R., 141, 147, 159, 191
Marmion, S. L., 296
Marsella, A. J., 2
Marsh, P., 213
Marsh, S. M., 394
Marshall, B. L., 356, 437
Marshall, N. L., 326
Marshevsky, S., 123
Martimportugués-Goyenechea, C., 73
Martin, C. L., 314, 315
Martin, J. A., 153, 364, 367
Martin, N. G., 413
Martin, R., 160., 467
Martin, R. A., 119, 120
Martin, T. R., 124
Martinez, G. M., 276
Martin-Krumm, C. P., 157
Martino, S. C., 410
Martins, Y., 242, 243, 407
Marx, B. P., 219
Maseri, A., 443
Masheter, C., 287
Masi, L., 356
Maslach, C., 88, 388, 395
Maslow, A., 52–54
Mason, M. A., 289
Massat, C. R., 73
Masten, A. S., 367
Masters, W. H., 418–420, 436, 437
Masuda, T., 180
Mathews, A., 218
Matlin, M. W., 329
Matsumoto, D., 216, 332
Mattanah, J. F., 367
Matthews, A., 259
Matthews, C. A., 272
Matthews, K. A., 356
Maume, D. J., 385
Maurer, L., 321
Maximin, A., 453
May, M. C., 492
Mayer, J. D., 127
Mayer, R. E., 28
Mayou, R., 489
Mays, V. M., 541
Mazzoni, G. A. L., 527
Mazzuca, J., 409
McAdams, D. P., 348, 351
McAndrew, F. T., 313
McBride, C. M., 198
McCabe, R. E., 45, 485, 487
McCarthy, R. W., 436
McCarty, R., 85
McClanahan, T. M., 537
McClure, E. B., 485
McConnell-Ginet, S., 309
McCoullough, M. E., 129, 130
McCown, W. G., 124
McCoy, M. L., 298
McCoy, S. K., 187
McCrae, R. R., 33–34, 62, 63, 66, 119, 351, 359
McCroskey, J. C., 222
McCrudden, M. C., 436
McCubbin, M., 536
McDaniel, E. R., 208
McDaniel, M. A., 28
McDermott, K. B., 527
McDougle, L. G., 123
McElroy, S. L., 536
McElroy, T., 71
McEwen, B. S., 71, 92
McFarlane, M., 411
McGee, M., 4, 6, 8
McGee-Cooper, A., 125
McGill, K. L., 78
McGill, O. D., 242
McGlashan, T. H., 91, 503, 507, 542
McGoldrick, M., 275, 276, 287
McGraw, K. M., 178
McGraw, L. A., 269, 270
McGraw, P. C., 6
McGregor, H. A., 61
McGuffin, P., 498
McGuire, E., 408
McGuire, W. J., 141
McHale, S. M., 277
McHugh, M. C., 436
McHugh, P. R., 492
McKay, A., 409
McKay, M., 168, 212, 217
McKeever, V. M., 91
McKenna, K. Y. A., 207, 208, 219, 238, 239, 240, 264, 265
McKenna, M. C., 448
McKenzie, C. R. M., 357
McKibben, J. N., 285
McLean, D. E., 77, 98
McMahon, F. J., 487
McManus, B., 424
McManus, P. A., 287
McMullin, J. A., 276
McNally, R. J., 488, 526
McNeil, T. F., 507
McNulty, J. K., 23
McPherson, M., 262, 272
McQuaid, J. R., 77, 98, 101
McWhirter, B. T., 264
McWilliams, L. A., 487
McWilliams, N., 519
Mead, M., 314
Mechanic, D., 481, 516
Mednick, S. A., 506, 507
Medora, N. P., 237
Medori, R., 534
Meduna, L., 537
Medvec, V. H., 165
Meece, J. L., 316, 317
Meehan, P. J., 343
Meeker, L. B., 217

Meeus, W., 341, 342
Meichenbaum, D., 9, 531
Meijer, A. M., 153, 276
Melia-Gordon, M. L., 124
Mellers, B. A., 182
Meltzer, H, Y., 535
Melz, H., 286
Mendelson, M. J., 242
Mendes, W. B., 94
Menec, V. H., 398
Merckelbach, H P., 488
Merikangas, K. R., 485, 498
Merrick, J., 344
Merrill, S. S., 349
Merton, R., 177
Messina, C. M., 216
Messina, J. J., 216
Meston, C. M., 437
Metalsky, G. I., 500
Metalsky, J. I., 499
Metcalf, B., 66
Metts, S. M., 219
Metz, M. E., 435
Metzger, E. D., 538
Metzler, J. N., 307
Meyer, I. H., 416
Meyers, S. A., 257
Michael, R. T., 425
Michaels, S., 292, 293, 412
Michaud, S. L., 331
Michelson, K. D., 144, 256
Mikulincer, M., 216, 256, 257
Milgram, N., 123
Milgram, S., 195–197
Milkie, M. A., 276, 281
Miller, D. C., 340
Miller, D. T., 159
Miller, G. E., 449
Miller, G. P., 120
Miller, I. J., 539
Miller, J. G., 180
Miller, J. S., 384
Miller, L., 246
Miller, L. C., 219, 332
Miller, N. E., 76
Miller, N. S., 473
Miller, R. B., 275, 279
Miller, R. R., 540
Miller, R. S., 216, 257, 258
Miller, S. A., 340
Miller, T., 435
Miller, T. R., 455
Miller, W., 325
Miller-Anderson, L., 504
Millett, K., 322
Millman, R. B., 475
Mills, J., 250
Millsap, R., 359
Mineka, S P., 488
Mino, I., 74
Miranda, J., 491
Mischel, H. N., 49
Mischel, W., 48, 49, 50, 141, 162
Mishel, L., 396
Misra, R., 79
Mitchell, B. A., 278
Mitchell, J. E., 509
Mitchell, J. T., 117
Mitchell, K., 410
Mitchell, V., 123, 345, 359
Miyamato, Y., 179, 180
Miyamoto, S., 535
Moak, D. H., 456
Moane, G., 345, 359
Modestin, J., 492, 504
Moe, A., 29
Moen, P., 348., 352
Mohler, C. J., 378
Mohren, D. C. L., 449
Mojtabai, R., 516
Mokdad, A. H., 450, 451
Möller, J., 446
Moncarz, R., 375
Moncrieff, J., 537
Monroe, S. M., 72, 77, 98., 101, 501
Monteggia, L. M., 498
Montepare, J. M., 349
Moore, C., 326
Moore, D. W., 372, 373, 396
Moore, M. K., 360
Moore, T. E., 8
Moorefield, B. S., 289
Moos, R. H., 74, 86, 93, 109, 114
Moradi, B., 74
Morahan-Martin, J., 110, 265
Moray, N., 155
Morell, C., 276
Moreno, F. A., 498
Moretti, M. M., 142
Morf, C. C., 141
Morgan, H. J., 141
Morgan, M. J., 475
Morgenstern, J., 124
Morin, N. A., 366
Morley, J. E., 356, 408
Mormede, P., 86
Morris, M. M., 93
Morris, M. W., 180
Morris, W. L., 290
Morrison, A. K., 539
Morrison, D. R., 287, 288
Morrison, M. A., 323
Morrison, T. G., 323
Mortensen, H., 111
Mortenson, J., 122
Moseman, S. E., 536
Mosher, D. L., 328
Mosher, W. D., 274, 285, 289, 431
Moskowitz, D. S., 146, 348
Moskowitz, J., 82, 92
Motowidlo, S., 403
Mowrer, O. H., 487
Moynihan, J. A., 448
Mroczek, D. K., 34
Muehlenhard, C. L., 298
Mueser, K. T., 531
Mukamal, K. J., 456
Mullen, J. L., 26, 27
Mullin, L. I., 309
Mulvihill, T., 535
Munck, A., 86
Muntasser, S., 534
Muraven, M., 161
Muris, P., 49
Murnen, S. K., 243, 316, 317, 509
Murphy, M., 291
Murphy, S. E., 390, 394
Murphy, S. P., 461
Murr, A., 430
Murray, C., 286
Murray, H. A., 62, 67
Murray, R. M., 507
Murrell, A. H., 386
Murrell, A. J., 184
Murstein, B., 273
Must, A., 338
Mustard, C., 392
Mutchler, J. E., 352
Myers, D. G., 1, 19, 20, 21, 22, 117, 145
Myers, J., 309, 500
Myrtek, M., 44

N

Nabi, R. L., 226
Nakonezny, P. A., 152
Nalwa, K., 265
Narrow, W. E., 482, 515
Nash, M., 355
Nasrallah, H. A., 535
Nathan, P. E., 481
Navarro, R. L., 376
Naveh-Benjamin, M., 82
Naylor, M. R., 4
Naylor, T. H., 4
Neale, M. C., 487, 498
Neese, R. M., 84
Neimeyer, R. A., 360
Neiss, R., 82
Nelson, C., 448
Nelson, D. A., 308
Nelson, R. J., 445
Nemeroff, C. B., 447
Nemiah, J. C., 490
Nettle, D., 58
Neupert, S. D., 88
Neuschatz, J., 527
Newby, D. E., 460
Newcomb, M. D., 121
Newell, G. R., 448
Newman, C. F., 531
Newman, M., 6
Newport, F., 179
Newton, P. M., 351
Nezu, A. M., 447
Ng, D. M., 110
Ng, K., 395
Nguyen, T., 180
Niaura, R., 445, 454
Nichols, B., 295
Nicholson, C., 147
Nickerson, C., 20
Nickerson, R. S., 176
Nida, S. A., 195
Niderhoffer, K. G., 128
Nie, N. H., 207
Niehuis, S., 285
Nielsen, J. M., 327
Niemann, Y. F., 305
Ninan, P. T., 534
Nisbett, R. E., 173, 179, 180
Nishimura, N., 250
Nobler, M. S., 538
Nobre, P. J., 407
Nock, S. L., 291
Nolen-Hoeksema, S., 20, 120, 309, 495, 499
Noller, P., 216., 249, 256, 283, 332
Nomaguchi, K. M., 276, 282
Noom, M. J., 341
Norcross, J. C., 6, 7, 525, 545
Norem, J. K., 160
Norenzayan, A., 179, 180
Norfleet, M. A., 515
Norman, C., 142
Norman, R. L., 470, 472
Norns, F. H., 251
Norton, P. G. W., 461
Norton, S., 391
Notarius, C, 229
Nowell, A., 306
Noyes, R., Jr., 490, 491
Nuer, N., 152
Nurius, P., 141
Nurminen, E., 389
Nurnberger, J. L., 135
Nyberg, S. E., 28
Nye, R. D., 52

O

Oakes, P., 177
Oaten, M., 130
O'Brien, B., 537
O'Brien, C. P., 482
O'Brien, S. J., 465
O'Brien, J. T., 447
O'Callahan, M., 449
Ocon, R., 386
O'Connell, M., 272
O'Connor, P. J., 130

O'Donohoe, A., 475
O'Donovan, M. C., 505
Oesterman, K., 308
Oettingen, G., 157
Offer, D., 343
Ogles, B. M., 524, 542, 544
O'Hanlon, J. F., 474
Ohman, A. P., 488
Oishi,S., 24
O'Keefe, D. J., 200
Oldenburg, C. M., 257
Olds, C. W., 350
Olff, M., 310
Olfson, M., 516, 517, 519, 536, 540
Olio, K., 528
Olivardia, R., 323
Oliver, M. B., 308
Ollendick, T. H., 487
Olson, D. H., 269, 275, 290
Olver, M. B., 410
Omarzu, J., 274, 248
Omoto, A. M., 237
O'Neal, H. A., 463
O'Neil, J., 329
O'Neill, G., 426
O'Neill, N., 426
Ones, D. S., 34
Ong, A. D., 81
Ono, H., 272, 282
O'Rand, A. M., 285
Orenstein, P., 154, 307
Organista, P. B., 491
Orlando, V. P., 26, 27
Orlofsky, J., 346–347
Orth-Gomer, K., 449
Oskamp, S., 3
Osman, S. L., 298
Ost, M. R., 308
Ostrov, E., 343
Ostrove, J. M., 348, 351
O'Sullivan, L. F., 436
O'Sullivan, M., 211, 214
Oulette, S., 94–95
Overall, N. C., 241, 244
Owen, M. J., 505
Oyserman, D., 142
Ozer, D. J., 34
Ozer, E. J., 91
Ozer, E. M., 162

P

Pacak, K., 85
Padavic, I., 269
Padgett, D. A., 449
Paivio, A., 29
Pallanti, S P., 489
Paluck, E. L., 211
Paludi, M. A., 316
Pandey, J., 73
Papalia, D. E., 350
Pape, C. L., 216
Papp, L. M., 288
Paquette, J. A., 262
Paradise, A. W., 150
Park, C. W., 190
Park, J., 254
Park, K. 276
Park, L. E., 151
Parker, R., 468
Parkin, A. J., 358
Paronis, C. A., 110
Parrott, A. C., 475
Parrott, D. J., 415
Parsons, S., 374
Parsons, T., 304
Pasley, K., 289
Passino, R. M., 243, 323
Pasterski, V. L., 313
Patel, J. K., 505
Patnoe, S., 188
Pato, M. T., 486
Patrick, B. C., 220, 259
Patterson, C. J., 294., 396, 413, 416
Patterson, G. R., 367
Patterson, M. L., 211
Patton, G., 508
Patton, W., 380
Paul, A. M., 8
Paul, E. L., 424
Paulhus, D. L., 38, 42., 66
Paunonen, S. V., 34, 62
Pavlov, I., 44–45
Pawader-Singer, A., 141
Paxton, S. J., 243
Payne, D. G., 28
Pazder, L., 492
Peake, P. K., 162
Pearce, L., 478
Pearson, A. R., 184
Pearson, P., 295, 398
Pearson, T. A., 283
Pechnick, R. N., 474
Pedersen, P., 541
Pederson, W., 475
Pegula, S., 394
Peirce, R. S., 93
Peladeau, N., 28
Pelham, W. H., 533
Peltola, P., 281
Peng, K., 180
Pennebaker, J. W., 128, 129, 219, 449
Peplau, L. A., 241, 242, 246, 249, 252, 253, 257, 258, 293, 294, 308–309, 347, 410, 412, 413, 416, 417, 420, 425, 426, 427
Perczel, M., 496
Perese, S., 316
Peretti, P. O., 241, 272
Perkins, D. F., 343
Perkins, D. O., 504
Perlis, R. H., 537
Perlman, D., 216, 257, 262
Perloff, R. M., 190
Perreault, S., 187
Perrett, D. L., 242
Perri, M. G., 457, 463, 465
Perry, B., 365
Perry, H. M., 408
Perry-Jenkins, M., 281, 282, 324, 347
Person, E. S., 43
Pervin, L. A., 50, 359
Petersen, A., 338, 343
Petersen, R. E., 340
Peterson, B. E., 184
Peterson, C., 92, 96–97, 157
Peterson, J. L., 431
Peterson, N., 347
Petit, D. A. D., 474
Petit, J. W., 157
Petras, K., 206
Petras, R., 206
Petrill, S. A., 56
Petrocelli, W., 392
Petticrew, M., 448
Pettigrew, T. F., 185, 188
Petty, R. E., 182, 189, 190, 191, 192
Petty, S. C., 500
Pezedek, K., 491
Phillips, K. A., 323, 486
Phillips, W. T., 463, 464, 465
Phillips-Grant, K., 528
Pi, E. H., 535
Pierce, C. M., 74, 541
Pierce, G. R., 93
Pietrefesa, A. S., 487
Pietromonaco, P., 237
Piferi, R. L., 94
Pike, A., 57
Pike, C. L., 242
Pike, K. M., 510
Pillard, R. C., 413, 414
Pillow, D. R., 71
Pilowsky, I., 491
Pinals, D. A., 505
Pinckert, S., 198
Pine, D. S., 485
Pinel, J. P. J., 457, 458
Pines, A. M., 88
Pink, D. H., 381–382, 383
Pinquart, M., 262
Pinto-Gouvenia, J., 407
Pionke, D. R., 294
Piotrowski, N. A., 162
Piper, W., 523
Pipher, M., 154
Pi-Sunyer, F. X., 457
Pittman, F., III, 542
Piver, S., 260
Pixley, J., 351
Planalp, S., 220
Plante, T. G., 463, 539
Pleck, J. H., 318, 319, 328, 332
Plomin, R., 56, 57
Plous, S., 175, 181
Poland, R. E., 475
Polivy, J., 148, 243, 323
Pollack, K. I., 198
Pollack, L., 376, 402
Pollack, W., 320
Polley, B. A., 458, 459
Pollozek, F., 195
Polonko, K. A., 269, 347
Pomerantz, E. M., 50
Pomeroy, C., 509
Pond, K., 263
Pontari, B. A., 157
Ponton, L. E., 340
Poole, D. A., 526
Poon, L. W., 355
Pope, E., 298
Pope, H. G., 323, 475, 493, 502
Pope, K. S., 543
Popenoe, D., 270, 285, 286
Popp, D., 424
Poppas, D. P., 91
Porter, R. E., 208, 212
Potenza, M. N., 482
Potter, W. Z., 536
Powell, B., 42
Powell, F. C., 360
Powell, J. A., 197
Powell, J. H., 475
Powell, R. A., 492
Powers, A., 416
Pratkanis, A. R., 188, 189
Pratt, L. A., 447
Pratto, F., 184, 325
Prentice-Dunn, S., 190
Prescott, C. A., 309, 500, 501
Presser, H. B., 281
Pressman, S., 4
Preto, N. G., 277
Previti, D., 285
Price, A. W., 73
Price, R. H., 394
Prideaux, L., 380
Priester, J. R., 192
Prigerson, H.G., 482
Procter, E., 181
Profit, W. E., 74
Pruchno, R., 353
Prudic, J., 538
Pryor, F. L., 383
Pryor, J. B., 391
Pryor, J. L., 435
Puetz, T. W., 130
Putnam, F. W., 491
Putnam, R. D., 262
Pychyl, T. A., 124
Pyszczynski, T. A., 59–60, 61, 62, 152, 181

Q
Quinn, J. M., 191
Quinn, K. A., 179

R
Rabe-Hesketh, 510
Rabinowitz, J., 534
Rabkin, J. G., 97
Rachman, S. J., 132, 488
Radel, J., 222
Radtke, D., 220
Rae, D. S., 482
Rafferty, Y., 194
Ragins, B. R., 384
Ragland, D. R., 444
Ragsdale, K., 351
Rahe, R. H., 77–78, 95, 97, 98
Rahim, M. A., 227
Rahman, M. A., 453
Rahman, Q., 413
Raines, L., 402
Raj, A., 534
Rakowski, W., 353
Raley, R. K., 285
Ramadan, N. M., 449
Ramaekers, J. G., 474
Ramirez, M., 540
Ramsey, E., 367
Randhawa, B. S., 307
Rando, R. A., 319
Rank, M. R., 282, 291
Ransome, P., 1
Rapee, R. M., 485, 488
Raphael, B., 71
Rapson, R. L., 237, 247, 418
Raskin, D. C., 215
Raskin, P. M., 347
Ravnkilde, B., 498
Ray, G. E., 262
Read, C. R., 317
Read, J. D., 526, 528
Reddick, R., 152
Redding, R. E., 416
Reddy, B. S., 460
Reed, G. M., 113
Rees, C. J., 66
Regan, M. F., 448
Regan, P. C., 243, 247, 258
Regier, D. A., 482, 484
Rehm, L. P., 91, 499
Reibel, D. K., 131
Reich, P., 92
Reid, J. E. E., 348
Reid, M., 325
Reid, P. T., 316
Reimann, R., 294
Reinherz, H. Z., 106
Reinisch, J. M., 417, 427
Reis, H. T., 218, 220, 241, 252, 259, 263
Reis, T. J., 158
Reise, S. P., 34
Reisner, A. D., 526
Reiss, D., 57
Reiss, S., 487
Reissman, C., 260
Reiter, R. C., 468
Reitmeijer, C. A., 411
Remer, R., 531
Renaud, C. A., 434
Rennie, D., 537
Rennison, C. M., 296
Renshaw, D. C., 437
Renshaw, K., 159
Rentfrow, P. J., 157
Renzetti, C., 296
Repa, B. K., 392
Repetti, R. L., 281, 347
Repetto, M., 473
Revelle, W., 53
Revenson, T. A., 442
Reynolds, K. A., 93
Reynolds, K. J., 186
Reznik, I., 175
Rhem, L. P., 495
Rhodes, K., 201
Rhodewalt, F., 161
Riba, M. B., 540
Rice, J. K., 321
Rice, L. N., 523
Richards, M. H., 343
Richards, V., 182
Richardson, C. R., 463
Richardson, J. G., 315
Richmond, V. P., 222
Richter, H., 401
Richter, L., 97, 182
Ridge, S. R., 256
Ridgeway, C. L., 304
Ridker, P. M., 443, 444
Rieder, R. O., 498
Rief, W., 489
Riemann, R., 57
Rierdan, J., 339
Rifkin, J., 1
Rigotti, N. A., 452
Rihmer, Z., 495, 497, 536
Riis, J., 21
Riley, B. P., 505
Riley, L. D., 277
Rimal, R. N., 49
Rime, B., 219
Rindfuss, R. R., 345
Ripoll, K., 285
Risch, N., 498
Risco, C., 74
Riskey, D. R., 174
Riskind, J. H., 488
Riso, L. P., 155
Ritz, T., 448
Rivas-Vazquez, R. A., 536
Rivera, B., 67
Roback, H. B., 523
Robbe, H. W., 474
Robbins, A., 351, 395
Robbins, S. B., 392, 393
Roberts, A. R., 296
Roberts, B. W., 34, 50, 359
Roberts, D. C., 467
Roberts, D. F., 317
Roberts, L. J., 260, 283
Roberts, P., 351
Roberts, S., 269, 291
Robertson, J. M., 320
Robie, C., 296
Robins, L. N., 482
Robins, R. W., 148
Robins, W. A., 152
Robinson, B., 4
Robinson, B. E., 395
Robinson, D. G., 504
Robinson, F. P., 26–27
Robinson, J. P., 1
Robinson, M., 2
Robinson, M. D., 166
Roccas, S., 4
Rochlen, A. B., 320
Rodger, C., 356
Rodgers, J. L., 152
Rodin, J., 458, 509, 510
Rodrigues, A. E., 280, 285
Roediger, H. L., III, 527
Roffman, R. A., 162
Rogers, C. R., 50–52, 168, 522–523
Rogers, M. P., 92
Rogers, N. J., 1
Rogers, R. W., 190
Rogers, S. J., 277, 278, 282, 285, 350
Rogge, R. D., 274, 283
Rohde, P. A., 42, 501
Rohner, R. P., 320
Rohrer, D., 28
Roig, M., 124
Rojewski, J. W., 374
Rokach, A., 262
Rollie, S.S., 287
Roloff, M. E., 298
Romney, D. M., 314, 315, 316
Ronald, A., 465
Rook, K, S., 237
Rose, D., 538
Rosemann, A., 411
Rosen, D. H., 416
Rosen, E., 350
Rosen, G. M., 8
Rosen, L. D., 1
Rosen, R., 436
Rosen, R. D., 7
Rosenbaum, J., 353
Rosenbaum, M., 458, 523
Rosenberg, M., 149
Rosenblatt, A., 61
Rosenbluth, S. C., 294
Rosenfarb, I. S., 507
Rosenfeld, L. B., 242
Rosenheck, R. A., 535
Rosenman, R. H., 444
Rosenthal, H., 496
Rosenthal, M. A., 177
Rosenthal, R., 177
Rosier, K. B., 286
Rosqvist, J., 107, 157
Ross, C. A., 492
Ross, C. E., 21
Ross, L., 173, 179, 186, 276
Ross, M., 144, 157, 159
Ross, M. W., 411
Ross, S. R., 164
Roter, D. L., 472
Rothbaum, F. M., 180
Rothblum, E. D., 252, 294, 481
Rothman, A., 442
Rotter, J., 48
Roughton, B., 396
Routledge, C., 61
Rovine, M. J., 219
Rowe, D. C., 56, 57
Rozanski, A., 444, 446
Rozee, P. D., 299
Rubenfeld, K., 331
Rubenstein, C. M., 263, 265
Rubin, R. H., 426
Rubin, Z., 253, 257, 258
Ruble, D. N., 314, 315
Ruble, T. L., 304
Rubovits, D. R., 98
Rucker, D., 182
Rudisch, B., 447
Rudorfer, M. V., 538
Ruiz, J. M., 445
Ruiz, P., 530
Rusbult, C. E., 247, 249
Ruscher, J. B., 186
Rush, A. J., 531, 533
Russell, G. F. M., 508, 509
Russo, E., 474
Russo, N. F., 321
Ruzek, J., 532
Ryan, A. M., 384
Ryan, C., 415
Ryan, R. M., 20

S
Saad, L., 375, 426
Sabatelli, R. M., 285
Sabattini, L., 390
Sabourin, S., 274
Sachs-Ericsson, N., 500
Sackeim, H. A., 538

Sadeh, C., 123
Sadker, D., 316, 317
Sadker, M., 316, 317
Sadler, J. Z., 481
Safir, M. P., 411
Sagiv, L., 4
Sagrestano, L. M., 260
Sakinofsky, I., 344
Saks, A. M., 49
Salerno, S., 4
Salkovskis, P. M., 491
Salonen, J. T., 460
Salovey, P., 82, 127
Salthouse, T. A., 357
Saltzman, J. L., 153
Salvendy, J. T., 523
Samberg, E., 520, 521
Samovar, L. A., 208, 209, 212, 213, 220, 224, 228, 230
Sampson, R., 297
Samuels, C. A., 329
San de Acedo, M. L., 307
Sanbonmatsu, D. M., 159
Sanchez, L. M., 539
Sande, M. A., 465
Sanders, G., 426
Sanderson, W. C., 485
Sandin, B., 489
Sandler, I., 71
Sandnabba, N. K., 314
Sandoz, J., 482
Sandy, J. M., 120
Sanislaw, C. A., 503
Sankis, L. M., 481
Santangelo, L. K., 96
Santelli, J. S., 428
Santerre, C., 130, 131
Sapolsky, R. M., 95, 130
Sarason, B. R., 93, 494
Sarason, I. G., 93, 98, 99, 101, 494
Sarwer, D. B., 457, 459
Satterwhite, R. C., 304
Savary, L. M., 146
Savin-Williams, R. C., 292, 415
Saxena, S., 130
Sayer, L. C., 280, 281, 287
Sayers, S. L., 447
Scantlebury, K., 316, 317
Scanzoni, J., 269, 286, 347
Schaalma, H. P., 409
Schachner, D. A., 216
Schachter, S., 13
Schaefer, J. B., 86
Schafer, W. D., 340
Schaffer, D., 383
Schaie, K. W., 357
Schaninger, C. M., 283
Schank, D., 458
Scheflin, A. W., 528
Scheidlinger, S., 523
Scheier, M. F., 96, 97, 105, 250
Schenck-Hamlin, W., 152
Scher, S. J., 163
Scherer, K. R., 214
Scherer, M., 129
Schermerhorn, A. C., 288
Scherwitz, L., 445
Schiappa, E., 414
Schiefelbein, V. L., 338
Schiffman, J., 507
Schilit, W. K., 126
Schimel, J., 61, 152
Schirmer, L. L., 257
Schkade, D., 22
Schlegel, A., 337
Schlenger, W. E., 2, 89, 90
Schlenk, E., 469
Schlenker, B. R., 157, 164, 165
Schmid, J., 215
Schmidlin, A. M., 213
Schmidt, N. B., 487
Schmidt, R., 355
Schmitt, J. P., 329, 396
Schmitz, J. M., 452, 454
Schneider, D. J., 72, 185
Schneider, F., 505
Schneider, J. P., 411
Schnoll, S. H., 473
Schoenfeld, G. A., 49
Schofield, C. A., 487
Schooler, J. W., 526, 527
Schoon, L., 374
Schottenbauer, M. A., 532
Schramke, C. J., 449
Schramm, D. G., 276
Schraw, G., 124
Schreiber, F. R., 492
Schroeder, A., 73
Schroeder, D. H., 97
Schuchter, S. R., 361
Schuckit, M.. A., 456
Schultis, G. A., 6
Schulz, U., 450
Schumacher, P., 110, 265
Schumaker, J. B., 141
Schunk, D. H., 162
Schutte, N. S., 127
Schutz, R. W., 339
Schwab, S., 220, 309
Schwandtd, B., 209
Schwartz, B., 2, 3, 7
Schwartz, G. E. R., 130, 131
Schwartz, J. C., 238
Schwartz, J. E., 106
Schwartz, J. P., 257
Schwartz, L., 491
Schwartz, L. M., 452
Schwartz, P., 258, 274, 279, 426
Schwartzberg, N., 290
Schwarz, N., 23
Schwarzer, R., 450
Scollon, C. N., 24
Scroppo, J. C., 493
Scully, J. A., 77
Seabrook, R., 28
Searle, A., 449
Seccombe, K., 282, 353
Sedikides, C., 141, 146, 157, 158
Seeman, T., 353
Seff, M. A., 277
Segal, M. W., 241
Segall, A., 468
Segerstrom, S. C., 96, 449
Seguin, J. R., 509
Sekel, A., 539
Self, D. W., 470
Seligman, M. E. P., 10, 20, 22, 92, 96–97, 106–107, 156–157, 487–488, 498–499, 539
Sell, R., 292
Sellers, R. M., 74
Seltzer, J. A., 291
Selwyn, P. A., 465
Selye, H., 84–85
Semans, J. H., 437
Semic, B. A., 248
Senecal, C., 123
Sepekoff, B., 412
Serido, J., 72
Servan-Schreiber, D., 489
Servin, A., 313
Sesso, H. D., 443
Sestir, M. A., 108
Seta, C. E., 71
Seta, J. J., 71
Settersten, R. A., 345
Settles, I. H., 326
Sexton, K., 250
Shackelford, T. K., 306
Shaffer, D. R., 255
Shah, J., 143
Shakesby, P. S., 28
Shallenberger, W. R., III, 16
Shapira, N. A., 111
Shapira-Berman, O., 324
Shapiro, A. F., 277
Shapiro, C. M., 416
Shapiro, D. H., Jr., 131
Shapiro, S. L., 130
Sharp, L. K., 128
Shavelson, R. J., 149
Shaver, P. R., 216 218, 238, 254–257, 263, 265
Shaw, L. H., 265
Shear, M. K., 531
Sheehan, D., 534
Sheehan, S., 501, 502
Sheese, B. E., 219
Sheiham, A., 448
Sheldon, J. P., 318
Sheldon, K., 352
Sheldon, K. M., 22, 54
Shelton, R. L., 306
Sheperd, R. N., 307
Shepperd, J. A., 23, 158
Sher, K. J., 454
Sher, L., 71, 344, 498
Sher, T. G., 283
Sheridan, J. F., 449
Sherif, M., 186, 194
Sherk, D. L., 165
Sherman, A. M., 353
Sherman, D. A., 178
Sherman, D. K., 121
Shields, S. A., 166
Shike, M., 460
Shiota, M. N., 105, 119
Shneidman, E. S., 496
Shobe, K. K., 526, 527
Shoda, Y., 162
Shors, T. J., 88
Shotland, R. L., 298
Shouldice, M., 298
Shulman, R. B., 536
Shurgot, B. A., 242
Shurkin, J. N., 516, 542
Shuval, J. T., 78
Sidanius, J., 184, 186, 250
Siddiqui, R. N., 73
Siebert, A., 25
Siegel, J. M., 99, 101
Siegel, O., 339
Siegler, I. C., 34, 180, 355, 446
Sigler, R. T., 297
Signorielli, N., 317, 318
Silberman, E. K., 519, 534
Silberstein, L. R., 509
Silke, A., 181
Silver, H., 505
Silver, M., 409
Silver, R. C., 363
Silverman, I., 311
Silverman, M. M., 309, 343, 496
Silverman, P. R., 363
Simeon, D., 485
Simes, M. A., 339
Simmons, T., 272
Simon, G. E., 536
Simonsen, E., 482
Simonton, D. T., 358
Simpson, C. H., 315
Simpson, G. M., 535
Sinclair, R. C., 191
Singer, A. R., 324
Singer, B., 524
Singer, J. E. E., 442
Singh, D., 242
Singh, P., 238
Sinkkonen, J., 339
Sinnott, J. D., 357
Sirois, F. M., 124
Skerrett, P. J., 457, 463

Skillman, G., 316
Skinner, A. E. G., 526
Skinner, B. F., 46–47, 48, 528
Skinner, E. A., 105
Skinner, N. F., 42
Skinner, P. H., 306
Skolnick, P., 487
Skowronski, J. J., 174
Skrondal, A., 475
Slashinski, M. J., 297
Slaski, M., 127
Slater, M. A., 491
Slavney, P. R., 490
Sloan, D. M., 219
Slof-Op't Landt, M. C. T., 510
Slonin-Nevo, V., 272
Slovic, P., 117., 452
Smart, L., 151
Smeaton, G., 247
Smiler, A. P., 319
Smith, A. K., 381
Smith, A. P., 449
Smith, B. W., 448
Smith, C. A., 81
Smith, D., 540
Smith, D. M., 20, 292
Smith, E. E., 191
Smith, E. R., 177, 178
Smith, G., 481
Smith, G. S., 455
Smith, J. C., 131
Smith, M., 492
Smith, M. L., 544
Smith, P. B., 159, 194
Smith, R. E., 162
Smith, R. H., 242
Smith, S., 160
Smith, S. E., 285
Smith, S. M., 526
Smith, T. P., 6
Smith, T. W., 276, 444, 445, 446, 449
Smith, W. P., 131
Smith-Lovin, L., 262, 272
Smock, P. J., 269, 287, 291
Smolak, L., 318, 323, 509
Smoll, F. L., 339
Smyer, M. A., 354
Smyth, J. M., 128, 129, 131
Snibbe, A. C., 291
Snir, R., 394
Snow, D. L., 296
Snowden, L. R., 540, 541
Snowdon, D., 355, 354
Snyder, M., 167, 176, 211, 237
Sobal, J., 509
Solberg, E. C., 2, 20
Solity, J. E., 28
Solomon, L. J., 481
Solomon, S., 59–60, 61, 62, 152, 181, 252, 294
Solowij, N., 475
Sommer, K. L., 148
Sommers-Flanagan, J., 318
Sommers-Flanagan, R., 318
Son Hing, L. S., 184
Sonnenberg, S., 388, 389
Sonstroem, R. J., 463
Sorensen, S., 262
Sorenson, J. L., 465
Soriano, M., 541
Sotiriou, P. E., 27
Soule, R. G., 1
South, S. J., 259, 272, 282, 287, 291
Southward, D. R., 446
Spada, M. M., 110
Spangler, D., 243
Spanos, N. P., 492–492, 526
Spaulding, L. R., 241. 242, 249, 252, 347, 416
Spears, R., 187
Specter, S., 474
Spector, L., 420
Spelke, E. S., 306
Spence, J. T., 304, 329, 395
Spencer, P. T., 130
Spencer, S. J., 150
Sperry, L., 442
Sperry, R. W., 312
Spiegel, D., 90, 251, 492
Spiegler, M. D., 530
Spinath, F. M., 56
Spiro, A., 352
Spitzberg, B. H., 297
Spitzer, R. L., 481, 482
Spokane, A. R., 376, 378
Sporer, S. L., 209
Sportolari, L., 411
Sprafkin, J. N., 317
Sprecher, S., 18, 242, 245, 258, 259, 409, 417, 423, 424, 425, 426
Springen, K., 243., 323, 407
Springer, S. P., 312
Srebnik, D., 422
Srivastava, S., 34
Sroufe, L. A., 257
Stack, A. D., 108
Stack, S., 262, 290, 291
Stafford, L., 248
Stahl, T., 215
Stajkovic, A. D., 49, 162
Stamler, J., 460
Stampfer, W. J., 462
Staneski, R. A., 217
Stanley, S. M., 274, 291
Stanton, A. L., 449
Stanton, G. C., 149
Starcevic, V., 490
Starker, S., 6
Starrels, M. E., 277
Stattin, H., 339
Staudinger, U. M., 92, 349
Stecker, R., 107
Steel, P., 49., 123
Steele, C. M., 74, 144
Steele, J. B., 486
Steelman, L. C., 42
Steiger, H., 509, 510
Stein, M. B., 90
Stein, N., 326
Stein, P. J., 271
Steinberg, L., 277, 349, 367–368, 369
Steiner, J., 510
Steiner, M. J., 430
Steinhausen, H., 509
Steinhilber, A., 87
Steinmetz, H., 312
Stein-Seroussi, A., 157
Stelfox, H. T., 537
Stephens, R. S., 162, 474
Sternberg, R. J., 58, 253–254, 257–258, 305
Stevens, D. P., 281
Stevens, N., 250
Stevic-Rust, L., 453
Steward, T., 111
Stewart, A., 348, 351
Stewart, F. H., 430
Stice, E., 243, 510
Stillion, J. M., 363
Stith, S. M., 296
Stoffer, G. R., 16, 17
Stone, J., 214
Stone, L., 237
Stone, P., 395
Stone, W. N., 523, 524
Stoney, C. M., 443
Strachman, A, 274
Strack, F., 23
Strauman, T. J., 143
Strelau, J., 57
Strickland, A. L., 360
Strickland, C. J., 344
Striegel-Moore, R. H., 339, 458, 509
Stroebe, K., 187
Stroebe, W., 190, 261, 363
Stroessner, S. J., 185
Strong, G., 246
Strong, S. R., 545
Stroud, L. R., 110
Stroup, T. S., 535
Strube, M. J., 157
Strupp, H. H., 519
Stuart, P., 393
Stubbs, J. H., 22
Stunkard, A. J., 458
Stutzer, A., 20
Suarez, E. C., 445
Suarez-Orozco, C., 343
Suarez-Orozco, M. M., 343
Subaiya, L., 287
Subotnik, R., 411
Suchday, S., 73
Sudak, H. S., 496
Sue, D., 421
Sue, S., 543, 541
Suggett, R., 220
Suh, E., 23
Suhomlinova, O., 285
Suinn, R. M., 490
Sullivan, G. M., 487
Sullivan, J. C., 226
Sullivan, P. F., 498, 505
Sullivan, Q., 245
Sulloway, F., 42, 43
Sullum, J., 130
Suls, J., 34, 98, 144, 157, 442, 447
Summers, G., 180
Summers, L. H., 302
Sundie, J. M., 311
Super, D. E., 347., 378–380
Surra, C. A., 246
Susman, E. J., 338
Susser, E., 507
Sutherland, V. J., 93
Swan, G. E., 453, 454
Swanger, N., 402
Swann, S. C., 295
Swann, W. B., 157, 176
Swanson, J., 108, 374
Swap, W. C., 241
Sweeney, D., 323
Sweet, J., 285
Sweeting, H., 316
Swim, J. K., 74, 183
Swinford, S., 296
Switzer, G. E., 484
Sygnatur, E. F., 393
Szasz, T., 480
Szkrybalo, J., 314
Szmukler, G. L., 508

T

Tabachnick, B. G., 543
Tabas, G., 489
Tajfel, H., 186
Takanishi, R., 343
Tamminga, C. A., 505
Tang, M., 374
Tang, S., 269
Taniguchi, H., 279
Tannen, D., 225, 226, 330–333
Tanner, J. M., 339
Tansky, J. W., 49
Tashiro, Y., 287
Tasker, F., 294, 416
Tata, J., 391
Tatsuoka, M. M., 66
Tavris, C., 11, 108, 324
Taylor, D., 409
Taylor, D. A., 220
Taylor, D. M., 183, 185
Taylor, E., 54

Taylor, M. C., 386
Taylor, R. J., 353
Taylor, S. E., 84, 93, 94, 113, 121, 145, 154, 176, 353, 528
Taylor, T. A., 218
Tchanturia, K., 510
Teachman, J. D., 269, 270, 274, 276, 290, 291, 347
Teasdale, J. D., 107, 498
Tedeschi, R. G., 92
Tedrow, L., 274, 290
Tekle, J., 173
Tellegen, A., 22, 57
Tennen, H., 120
Terracciano, A., 62, 63, 359
Terry, K., 142
Tesch, S. A., 347
Tesser, A., 124, 144
Testa, K., 527
Tharp, R. G., 132, 134
Thase, M. E., 498., 531
Thayaparan, B., 465
Theisen, T., 400
Theorell, T., 388
Thibaut, J. W., 248
Thoennes, N., 295
Thomas, A. J., 447
Thomas, G., 175
Thomas, J. J., 305., 315, 317
Thomas, K. M., 385, 386., 388
Thompkins, C. D., 319
Thompson, J. K., 509, 510
Thompson, M., 320
Thompson, T., 73
Thornton, A., 269
Thorson, J. A., 360
Thune, I., 463
Tibbo, P., 505
Tice, D. M., 109, 124, 146, 161, 166
Tienda, M., 352
Tiggeman, M., 242, 407
Titstworth, B. S., 27
Tjaden, P., 295
Tkach, C., 23
Tobin-Richards, M. H., 340
Todd, Z., 252
Toffler, A., 4
Tolin, D. F., 309
Tolmacz, R., 256
Tolman, D. L., 324., 436
Tomich, P. L., 93
Toomey, R., 504
Tori, C. D., 131
Torres, A. R., 487
Torrey, E. F., 43, 502
Toscano, G. A., 393
Tosi, H., 77
Toufexis, A., 1
Townsend, M. H., 71
Tozzi, F., 509
Tractenberg, M. A., 465
Tragakis, M. W., 161
Trammell, D., 125
Trapnell, P. D., 42
Travers, C. J., 72
Travis, C. B., 257
Travis, F., 130
Treas, J., 278, 427
Trebou, D., 274
Treiber, F., 131
Trent, K., 287
Triandis, H. C., 147., 237, 238
Trivedi, M. H., 463
Trochim, B., 15
Trope, Y., 157., 173, 175
Tropp, L. R., 188, 326
Trost, M. R., 311
Troy, A. B., 272
Trussell, J., 423, 428
Trzesniewski, K. H., 148., 152
Tsai, F., 161
Tsai, M., 316
Tsuang, M. T., 482., 505
Tucker-Ladd, C. E., 5
Tugade, M. M., 81., 119
Tulving, E., 28
Turban, D. B., 176, 402
Turkheimer, E., 57
Turkle-Bowker, D. M., 173
Turkovic, S., 89
Turner, E., 281
Turner, J. C., 186
Turner, J. R., 77, 97, 98, 450
Turner, S. M., 487, 539
Twenge, J. M., 3, 6, 146, 151, 154, 165, 276, 308
Tyrrell, D. A., 449

U

Uchino, B. N., 93, 251
Uemera, A., 316
Uhlenberg, P., 262
Uhlmann, F., 108
Uleman, J. S., 178
Ullman, S. E., 297
Ulrich, M., 276
Umberson, D., 353
Unger, R., 181
Ungerleider, T. J., 474
Ursano, R. J., 91, 519
Uzzo, R. G., 91

V

Vaidya, R. S., 157
Vaillant, G. E., 43, 97, 106
Vala, J., 180
Valent, P., 88
Valone, R. P., 186
Vanable, P. A., 465
van Anders, S. M., 309
Vanbeselaere, N., 159, 160
Van Boven, L., 20
Van Brunt, D., 360
van de Beek, C., 413
Vandenberg, S. G., 306
van den Bout, J., 72
van den Hout, 72
van den Ooord, 56, 57
van den Wittenboer, G. L. H., 276
Vander Laan, K. L., 130
Vandereycken, W., 509
Vandewater, E. A., 317
van Griensven, F., 71
van Kammen, D. P., 534, 535
van Laar, C., 186, 250
van Willigen, M., 21, 73
Vartanian, L. R., 243, 323
Vaughan, K., 318
Vaughn, C., 507
Vaux, A., 94
Veccia, E. M., 213
Veenhoven, R., 19, 20
Veevers, J. E., 278
Vega, W. A., 540
Veneziano, R. A., 320
Venturello, S., 489
Verbruggle, L. M., 349
Verderber, K. S., 207, 225, 228, 229
Verderber, R. F., 206, 207, 221, 225
Verduin, T., 524
Vernberg, E. M., 90
Vernon, P. A., 56
Verona, E., 75
Vertinsky, P. A., 465
Vgontzas, A. N., 91
Viau, V., 85
Vick, B. S., 181
Victor, B. S., 496
Videbech, P., 498
Viglione, D. J., 67
Vinogradov, S., 523, 524
Vinokur, A. D., 394
Vinson, D. C., 454
Vittengl, R., 218
Vogel, D. L., 294
Vohs, K. D., 87, 161
Volk, K., D., 417
Volkow, N., 482
Vollmer, W. M., 460
Volvavka, J., 535
Von Baeyer, C. L., 165
Vonk, R., 174
Vorauer, J. D., 263
Voutilainen, S., 460
Voydanhoff, P., 278, 281
Voyer, D., 307
Vrugt, A., 212

W

Wachtel, P., 1
Wadden, T. A., 457
Waddill, P. J., 28
Wade, C., 11
Wade, P., 541
Wagner, A., 91, 495, 499
Wagner, D. M., 286
Wagner, S. H., 323
Waite, L., 286, 287, 290
Wakabayashi, C., 278
Wakefield, J. C., 482
Waldfogel, J., 282
Waldo, M., 257
Waldron, M., 57
Waldrop, D., 49
Waldstein, S. R., 445
Walker, A., 325
Walker, A. J., 269, 270
Walker, E., 504, 507
Walker, K., 251
Walker, L. S., 468
Wallace, H. M., 87, 146
Waller, N. G., 34
Wallis, C., 324
Wallman, G. Y., 542
Wallterstein, J. S., 288
Walsh, B. T., 509
Walsh, F., 279
Walsh, J. K., 1
Walsh, L., 26
Walster, E., 178, 242, 246
Walter, C. A., 356
Wampold, B. E., 525, 544
Wang, H., 287
Wang, L., 91
Wang, P. S., 516
Ward, A., 166, 179
Ward, A. Z., 320., 328
Ward, C., 159
Ward, C. H., 446
Ward. C. N., 298
Wardle, J., 461
Warn, J., 387
Warner, L., 430
Warner, R. M., 331
Warner-Schmidt, J. L., 498
Warr, P., 22
Warren, L. Z., 207, 283
Warren, R., 6
Warwick, H. M. C., 491
Waterman, G. S., 534
Waters, E., 257, 274
Watkins, P. L., 446
Watson, D., 34, 98, 246, 449
Watson, D. L., 132, 134
Watson, J. B., 43, 48
Weatherall, A., 276

Weaver, M. F., 473
Weber, L. J., 537
Webster, D. M., 179, 182
Wechsler, H., 452, 454, 455
Wegener, D. T., 189, 190, 191, 192
Weil, M. M., 1
Weimer, B. L., 257
Weinberg, C., 6
Weinberg, M. S., 413, 416
Weinberger, D. A., 113
Weinberger, J., 519., 525
Weiner, B., 155, 156, 175
Weinfield, N., 257
Weinrich, J. D., 292
Weinstein, N. D., 158, 451, 452
Weintraub, J. K., 105
Weisaeth, L., 88
Weisler, R. H., 71
Weiss, D. S., 91
Weiss, E. M., 306
Weiss, R. S., 261, 268, 284
Weissman, M. M., 485
Weisz, J. R., 180
Weiten, W., 79
Weitzman, L., 382
Welch, H. G., 452
Welchans, S., 296
Wellman, B., 239
Wells, A., 110
Wells, L., 540
Wells, R. B., 195
Welsh, R. S., 515
Wener, R. E., 75
Wenger, M. J., 28
Wenzel, A., 250
Wertenbroch, K., 124
Wessely, S., 536
Wesson, D. R., 472
West, D. S., 457, 461
West, S. G., 428
West, W. B., 131
Westbay, L., 254
Westefeld, J. S., 262
Westen, D., 42, 43
Wester, S. R., 294, 319
Wethington, E., 72, 348, 351
Wheaton, B., 77, 97, 98, 450
Wheeler, L., 144, 145, 220
Whipple, B., 419
Whiston, S. C., 374
Whitaker, C., 536
Whitaker, R., 536
Whitbourne, S. K., 347, 349, 351, 353–354, 359
White, D., 271
White, K. B., 298
White, L. K., 277, 278, 282., 350
White, M. K., 237
White, O. K., Jr., 271
Whitehead, B. D., 285
Whitehouse, W. G., 527
Whiteman, S. D., 277
Whitfield, C. L., 528
Whitley, B. E., 321, 328, 385, 403, 415
Whitton, S. W., 291
Whitty, M. T., 411
Whybrow, P., 1
Wickrama, K. A. S., 287
Widiger, T. A., 481, 482
Wiebe, D. J., 468
Wiederman, M. W., 244, 407, 426
Wielawski, I., 525
Wiesenthal, D. L., 75
Wigfield, A., 340
Wilfong, J. D., 162
Wilgosh, L., 322
Wilis, R. P., 28
Wilkatis, J., 535
Wilkerson, D. K., 295, 296
Willett, W. C., 457, 460, 462
Willetts, M. C., 353, 424, 427
Williams, C., 276
Williams, C. D., 452
Williams, C. L., 325
Williams, J. E., 178, 304, 305, 444, 445
Williams, K. B., 391
Williams, K. E., 49
Williams, K. N., 201
Williams, L., 213
Williams, L. M., 526
Williams, M. H., 544
Williams, N. A., 449
Williams, P., 521
Williams, R. B., 129
Williams, R. L., 27, 110, 162, 129
Williamson, D. A., 511
Willimon, W. H., 4
Willis, S. L., 348
Wills, T. A., 93, 94, 120, 121, 446
Wilner, A., 351
Wilpert, B., 389
Wilsnack, S. C., 526, 528
Wilson, A. E., 144, 155
Wilson, J. P., 89
Wilson, R. S., 355
Wilson, T. D., 23, 143, 158
Windlisch, M. E., 355
Winefield, A. H., 393
Wing, J. F., 127
Wing, R. R., 458, 459
Winick, C., 470, 472
Winter, D. D. N., 3
Winzelberg, A. J., 130
Wise, D., 107, 157
Wissink, I. B., 153
Wister, A. V., 278
Wittenberg, M. T., 263
Witvliet, C. V., 129, 130
Wolak, J., 410
Wolfe, J. B., 373
Wolff, K., 362
Wolff, T. J., 412
Wolfinger, N. H., 273
Wolinksy, F. O., 468
Wolitski, R. J., 466
Wolk, A., 460
Woloshin, S., 452
Wolpe, J., 528, 529–530
Wolsic, B., 21
Wonderlich, S. A., 510
Wong, N., 523
Wong, Y. J., 320
Wood, E., 315
Wood, J. M., 67
Wood, J. V., 144, 155, 158
Wood, M. D., 454, 455
Wood, N., 155
Wood, W., 189, 191, 245, 253, 304, 320
Woodhill, B. M., 329
Woolfolk, R. L., 131
Worden, J. M., 363
Worth, L. T., 189
Worthen, J. B., 29
Worthington, E. L., Jr., 129
Worthington, R. L., 376, 384
Wortman, C. B., 353, 362, 363
Wright, J. C., 227
Wright, J. H., 531
Wright, P. H., 220, 251
Wright, R. A., 246
Wright, S. C., 183, 185
Wrosch, C., 350
Wu, S., 238
Wu, Z., 290
Wurf, E., 141
Wyatt, G. E., 128
Wylie, M. S., 525
Wynder, E. L., 460

X

Xiaohe, G., 237

Y

Yager, J., 250, 262, 510
Yalom, I. D., 523, 524
Yamada, A., 540
Yamamoto, J., 541
Yang, C., 283
Yang, H., 449
Yapko, M. D., 526
Yate, M., 403
Yehuda, R., 89
Yi, H., 455
Ying, Y., 74
Yoder, J. D., 310
Young, C. E., 390
Young, D. A., 475
Young, E. A., 84
Young, J, E. 264, 261
Young, K., 543
Young, K. S., 110
Young, R., 316
Young, R. D., 143, 144
Young, S. M., 190
Young-DeMarco, L., 269
Younkin, S. L., 95
Yuen, C. N., 265
Yum, Y., 152
Yurgelun-Todd, D., 475
Yutzy, S. H., 489

Z

Zaalberg, R., 211
Zacaria, J., 379
Zagorski, D. A., 390, 394
Zajonc, R. B., 241
Zakzanis, K. K., 475
Zane, N., 540, 541
Zang, D., 449
Zanna, M. P., 150, 165, 184
Zatzick, D. F., 539
Zautra, A. J., 71, 448
Zea, M. C., 415
Zebrowitz, L. A., 349
Zechmeister, E. B., 28
Zeichner, A., 415
Zeig, J., 515
Zeldow, P. B., 329
Zelinski, E. M., 358
Zhang, L., 390
Zhang, R., 49
Zhao, S., 482
Zickar, M. J., 395
Zigler, E., 344
Zimbardo, P. G., 2, 5, 124, 168, 181, 197, 263, 264
Zimmerman, B. J., 49
Zimmerman, J., 135
Zimmerman, M., 481
Zisook, S., 361
Zittleman, K., 317
Zosky, D., 350
Zuckerman, A., 251
Zuckerman, M., 65, 161
Zuo, J., 269
Zurbriggen, E. L., 308
Zuroff, D. C., 348
Zvolensky, M. J., 487
Zvonkovic, A. M., 279, 281

Subject Index

A

ability-achievement gap, 322–323
abnormal behavior
  criteria of, 480–481
  medical model of, 479–480
  see also psychological disorders
abstinence-only programs, 409
Abu Ghraib incident, 181, 197
abuse, partner, 295–296
academic performance
  improving, 24–29
  pressure and, 79
  self-efficacy and, 162
  self-esteem and, 150
  stress and, 91
  teachers' expectations of, 177
acceptance
  of dying, 361
  need for, 228
  parental, 364
  by therapist, 522
accidents
  drunk driving, 455
  job-related, 388
  sedative use and, 473
accommodating style, 228
acculturation, 74
achievement, self-esteem and, 150
acquired immune deficiency syndrome. *See* AIDS
acronyms, 29
acrophobia, 485
acrostics, 29
ACTH, 86
active listening, 27, 221
activity schedule, 26
actor-observer effect, 259–260
actual self, 142–143
adaptational outcomes, 87
addiction
  drug, 470–471
  Internet, 111
adjustment, defined, 12
adolescence, 337–344
  cognitive changes in, 340
  development of self-esteem in, 151, 153
  eating disorders in, 510
  personality changes in, 340–343
  physical changes in, 337–340
  pregnancy in, 428
  search for identity in, 341–343
  self-concept of, 146
  sexual identity in, 409
  suicide in, 343–344, 496
  turmoil in, 342–343
adolescent growth spurt, 337, 338
adolescents
  homosexual, 343–344, 415
  occupational choices of, 379
  parenting of, 277–278, 367
  sexual activity of, 422, 423, 424
adrenal glands, 85, 86, 338
adultery, 426
adulthood
  development in, 345
  early, 345–347
  emerging, 346
  late, 351–353
  middle, 348–351
adversarial culture, 226–227
advertising, 189
  gender stereotypes in, 318
aerobic exercise, 130
affiliation, need for, 13, 14
affirmative action, 386
affluence, 1
African Americans
  divorce rate for, 285
  elder care by, 356
  eye contact by, 212
  gender roles for, 316
  heart disease in, 445
  male role among, 319
  preferred body types of, 242
  social support networks of, 353
  stereotypes of, 178–179, 305
  stresses for, 74
  in workforce, 384
age
  at marriage, 273–274
  cognitive changes with, 356–359
  happiness and, 20
  personality and, 359
  physical changes with, 353–356
  stereotypes based on, 178
  subjectivity of, 349
Age of Propaganda (Pratkanis and Aronson), 189
aggression
  against partner, 295–296
  alcohol consumption and, 455
  as coping response, 107–108
  ego threats and, 151
  evolutionary origin of, 311
  Freud's view of, 37–38
  gender differences in, 308, 311, 313
  indirect, 308
  modeling of, 49
  relational, 308
  sexual, 296–299
  sexuality and, 410
  terror management and, 61
  toward females, 325–326
  vengeful, 1181
  verbal, 226
aggressive communication, 230
aging, 353–359
  cognitive changes and, 356–359
  dealing with, 348–349
  personality changes and, 359
  physical changes and, 353–356
  sexual behavior and, 426
aging parents, care of, 277–278
Aging with Grace (Snowdon), 355
agoraphobia, 485, 486
agreeableness, 34, 57, 58, 62, 274
AIDS, 423, 430, 431, 432, 465–466
  misconceptions about, 465–466
  partners of men with, 81
  prevention of, 466
  symptoms of, 465
  transmission of, 465
  treatment for, 465
air traffic controllers, 382, 387
alarm reaction, 84
alcohol, 454–457
  consumption patterns for, 455
  dependence on, 456
alcohol use/abuse, 163–164, 451
  for blunting self-awareness, 143–144
  as coping strategy, 110
  date rape and, 298
  health effects of, 456–457
  stress and, 91
  suicide and, 344
Alcoholics Anonymous, 524
alcoholism, 456
  aversion therapy for, 530
altruism, 34, 60
Alzheimer's disease, 354–355
ambient stress, 72
amenorrhea, 509
American Academy of Child and Adolescent Psychiatry (AACAP), 277
American Association of Sex Educators, Counselors, and Therapists, 436
American Civil Liberties Union, 185
American Geriatric Society, 352
American Institute of Stress, 84
American Medical Association, 470
American Psychiatric Association, 481
American Psychoanalytic Association, 521
American Psychological Association, 65, 80, 347, 374, 417, 481
amnesia, dissociative, 491, 492
amphetamines, 471, 473
Amway Corporation, 200–201
anal sex, 422–423, 431, 466
anal stage, 39, 40
analytic approach, 180
analytical psychology, 41
androcetrism, 305
androgens, 313, 408
androgyny, 328–329
anger, 81, 107, 108, 320
  heart disease and, 444, 445, 446
  managing, 129
  as response to traumatic events, 89
Anger: The Misunderstood Emotion (Tavris), 108
angina, 443, 446
animal research, 50
annoyance, 81
anonymity, in online relationships, 240
anorexia nervosa, 508–509
answer changing, on tests, 16, 17
antecedents, 133, 135
antianxiety drugs, 487, 534
antidepressant drugs, 498, 535–536
antipsychotic drugs, 533, 534–535
anxiety, 81
  affiliation need and, 13, 14
  avoidance behavior and, 47
  buffers for, 60, 61
  conditioned, 45, 46
  coping strategies and, 107
  death-related, 59, 61, 62, 360
  defense mechanisms and, 38, 112
  low self-esteem and, 151
  meditation and, 131
  modern, 3
  psychoanalysis for, 520
  in public speaking, 222–223
  as response to traumatic events, 89
  Rogers's view of, 51–52, 522
  self-discrepancies and, 143
  about sexual performance, 435
  terrorist threats and, 152
anxiety disorders, 483, 484, 485–489
  biological factors in, 487
  cognitive factors in, 488
  conditioning of, 487
  drug treatment for, 534
  etiology of, 487–489
  gender differences in, 309
  seeking treatment for, 516
  stress and, 91
  systematic desensitization for, 529–530
  types of, 485–487
anxiety hierarchy, 529, 530
anxiety sensitivity, 487
anxious-ambivalent attachment style, 255–256

appeals, emotional, 190
appearance. *See* physical appearance
appearance pressure, 323
appraisals, of stressful events, 72, 98, 116
apprehension, 81
approach-approach conflict, 76
approach-avoidance conflict, 76
aptitudes, 373–374
archetypes, 41
Argument Culture, The (Tannen), 225
arguments, one- versus two-sided, 190
arousal
  emotional, 82
  optimal level of, 82, 83
  physiological, 56, 215
  sexual, 418, 420, 421
art, terror management and, 61
arthritis, stress and, 92, 448
Asian Americans, 74, 154, 384
Asserting Yourself (Bower & Bower), 231
assertiveness, 229–233
assertiveness training, 230–232
asthma, stress and, 448
asylums, 479–480
atherosclerosis, 443, 444–445
attachment, love as, 254–257
attachment styles, 255
attention
  aging and, 357
  during lectures, 27
  selective, 223
  to speaker, 220, 221–222
  task performance and, 87–88
attitude change, elaboration likelihood model of, 191–192
attitudes, 188
  changing, 188–192
  racist, 183
  sexual, 409, 417–418
  similarity in, 247
attraction
  interpersonal, 240–247
  tactics of, 243, 244
attractiveness. *See* physical attractiveness
attributions, 174–175
  controllability of, 156
  defensive, 180, 181, 186
  errors in, 179–180, 185–186
  internal vs. external, 155, 175
  self, 155-156
  self-defeating, 263–264, 265
  stable vs. unstable, 155
atypical antipsychotic drugs, 535
authoritarian parenting, 153, 364, 365, 367
authoritarianism, 184–185
authoritative parenting, 153, 364, 365, 367
authority, obedience to, 195–197
autoeroticism, 422
automatic processing, 154, 187
autonomic arousal, 215
autonomic nervous system (ANS), 83–84
availability heuristic, 117
aversion therapy, 520
aversive racism, 184
aversive stimuli, 47
avoidance, 47, 359
  of conflict, 227–228
  as response to traumatic events, 89
avoidance-avoidance conflict, 76
avoidant attachment style, 255–256
awareness, levels of, 36–37

B

back pain, stress and, 448
barbiturates, 471, 472
baseline data, 133
basking in reflected glory (BIRG), 159–160
battering, 295–296
Beautiful Mind, A, 504
beauty, 241–242
behavior, defined, 11
behavior modification, 25, 132–137, 544
behavior therapies, 515, 528–533
  effectiveness of, 544
  systematic desensitization, 529–530
  assumptions of, 526–527
  aversive, 530
  cognitive, 531–533
  effectiveness of, 533
  rational emotive, 531
  social skills training, 531
behavioral contract, 136, 137
behavioral disengagement, 107
behavioral perspectives, on personality, 43–50
behavioral rehearsal, 531, 532
behaviorism, 43, 526
belief in a just world (BJW), 180, 181
beliefs, 188
belligerence, 284
benefit finding, 120
benzodiazepine, 534
bereavement, 361–362
bereavement overload, 363
better-than-average effect, 158
Beyonce, 168
bias, racial, 178–179
Big Five personality traits, 33–34, 42, 359
  culture and, 62
  heritability of, 56–57
  testing for, 66
Big Love, 271–272
binge-eating disorder, 509
biomedical therapies, 515, 535–538
biopsychosocial model, of health, 442
bipolar disorder, 494, 495, 497
  drug therapy for, 536
  seeking treatment for, 516
birth control, 427–430
birth order, 42d, 57
bisexuality, 252 412, 407
  AIDS and, 432, 465, 466
blaming, of victims, 180, 181, 186
blood pressure, 443, 445
  emotional suppression and, 127
  meditation and, 131
body image, 407
  attractiveness and, 243
  eating disorders and, 508
  ideal, 323
body language, 212–213
body mass index (BMI), 457
body weight, 457–458
  aging and, 354
  appearance pressure and, 323
  dieting and, 459
  obsession with, 508–509
boomerang generation, 278
Boston Couples Study, 258–259
brain
  aging and, 354
  gender differences and, 311-312
  mood disorders and, 498
  schizophrenic disorders and, 505–506
brain-imaging studies, 505–506
brainstorming, 121
breast cancer, exercise and, 130
breast cancer patients, social support for, 251
Brockovich, Erin, 197
brontophobia, 485
Bryant, Kobe, 189, 297
bulimia nervosa, 509
Burden of Sympathy (Karp), 484
burnout, 75, 88, 388
Bush, George W., 209
Buspar, 534
Byrne, Rhonda, 7
bystander effect, 195

C

caffeine, 460, 473
calories, 459
Canadian National Longitudinal Survey of Children and Youth, 282
cancer
  contraceptives and, 428–429
  diet and, 460
  exercise and, 463
  mortality rates for, 441
  smoking and, 452
  stress and, , 92 447–448
cancer-prone personality, 448
cannabis, 471
carbohydrates, 461, 462, 463
cardiovascular disease. *See* heart disease
cardiovascular fitness, 463
career advancement, 385
career change, 380
career choice, 373–376
  important considerations in, 376
  models of, 377–380
career counseling, 317
career development, 347
career patterns, in midlife years, 350
careers
  gender and, 281, 322–323, 325, 380
  interest inventories for, 376
caregiving, for elderly parents, 277–278
Carter, Jimmy, 357
cartoons, gender stereotypes in, 317
case studies, 16–17, 351
catastrophic thinking, 111, 115–116, 118, 157, 531
catastrophizing, 491
catatonic schizophrenia, 503
catecholamines, 85
catharsis, 108
causation
  correlation and, 18
  experimental method and, 15
cell phones, 206–207
Centers for Disease Control, 449
cerebral hemispheres, 312
cervical cap, 429
change, as source of stress, 76–78
channels, of communication, 188, 205–206
chat rooms, 206, 207, 219
child abuse, recovered memories of, 525–528
child care, 279, 282, 324, 347
  in workplace, 390
childlessness, 270, 276
childrearing, 364–369
  see also parenting
children
  adolescent, 277–278
  adult, 278, 350
  arrival of, 347
  attachment styles in, 255–256
  delaying having, 270
  development of self-esteem in, 151, 153
  divorce and, 286, 288
  effect on parents, 21
  exposure to TV aggression, 226–227
  of gay parents, 294
  gender-role learning in, 330
  grief in, 363
  launching into adult world, 278
  observational learning by, 49
  occupational choices of, 379
  parents' work and, 281–282
  posttraumatic stress disorder in, 90

children *(continued)*
psychosexual stages in, 39–41
remarriage and, 289
resilience in, 366
school performance of, 367, 368
self-concept in, 51, 146
sexual identity in, 413
sexual socialization of, 408–410, 412
young, 276–277
children's books, 316
China, 238
chlamydia, 432
chlorpromazine, 533, 534, 525
choices, overload of, 2–3
cholesterol
heart disease and, 443, 444
in diet, 460, 462
chronic diseases, 441
Cialis, 436
cigarette smoking, 452–454
City Stress Inventory (CSI), 73
civil unions, 414
clarification
in active listening, 221
in client-centered therapy, 523
class attendance, grades and, 27
classical conditioning, 43–46
of anxiety, 487, 529
claustrophobia, 485, 486
client-centered therapy, 544
clinical psychologists, 517–518
clinical psychology, 12
Clinton, Bill, 390
clitoris, 418, 420
close relationships. *See* relationships
clozapine, 535
cocaine, 471, 473
cocktail party effect, 155
cognition
conditioning and, 49
need for, 191
cognitive abilities
in adolescence, 340
aging and, 356–359
gender differences in, 306–307, 312
self-esteem and, 154–155
cognitive distortions, 177–180, 185–186
cognitive misers, 154, 179
cognitive restructuring, 223
cognitive therapy, 265, 545
cognitive-behavioral therapy, 157
cohabitation, 269, 291, 426
coitus, 423
collaborating, 228
collective unconscious, 41
collectivism/collectivist cultures, 154, 220
assertiveness and, 230
attribution errors and, 179–180
conflict and, 224
marriage and, 237–238
self-concept and, 147
social support and, 121–122
college degree
earnings and, 382–383
jobs and, 375
college students
drinking by, 454
sexual activity of, 424–425
commitment
love and, 254, 258, 259
in marriage, 269
communal relationships, 250
communication, 205
about sex, 417–418
adjustment and, 207
aggressive, 230
assertive, 229–233
electronically mediated, 206–207, 208
face-to-face, 207, 208, 239
with health service providers, 468, 541
problems in, 222–224
sexual, 433
submissive, 230
see also interpersonal communication; nonverbal communication
communication apprehension, 222–223
communication process, 205–206
communication style, gender differences in, 309, 330–333
community mental health centers, 543, 544
companionate love, 254, 258
comparison level, 249
comparison level for alternatives, 249
comparisons, positive, 120
compensation, 41, 42
competition, effects of, 186
competitive style, 228
compliance, 194, 198
compliments, giving, 165
compromising, 228
compulsions, 411, 486
compulsive buying syndrome, 1
concordance rates
for mood disorders, 498
for schizophrenic disorders, 505
conditionability, 56
conditioned reflex, 44–45
conditioned response (CR), 44, 45, 46, 529
conditioned stimulus (CS), 44, 45, 46, 487, 488, 529
conditioning
of anxiety disorders, 487
Bandura's view of, 48
classical, 43-46
operant, 43-46, 132–136
condoms, 428, 429, 430, 466
confidence, 148
confiding in others, 129
confirmation bias, 175–176, 179, 402
conflict(s)
avoiding, 224
constructive approach to, 228–229
Freud's view of, 37
gender-role, 319
in marriage, 274, 279, 283–284
internal, 37–38, 42, 76
interpersonal, 224–229
managing, 260
parent-adolescent, 277, 343, 349
relationships and, 259
as source of stress, 75–76
styles of dealing with, 227–228
types of, 225–227
work-family, 395
unconscious, 519–520
conformity, 192–195
resisting, 194–195
conformity pressure, 79
congenital adrenal hyperplasia, 313
congruence, 51
conscientiousness, 34, 57, 58, 62, 274
conscious, Freud's view of, 36–37
conservatives, 184
consistency
in person perception, 182
in personality, 33, 50
consistency principle, 198–199
constraint, in personality, 34
Consumer's Guide to Psychotherapy (Beutler, Bongar, & Shurkin), 516
consumerism, 1
consummate love, 254
contagious diseases, 441
contempt, 284
context, for communication, 206
contraception, 427–430
control
illusion of, 158
parental, 364
control group, 14
controlled processing, 154–155, 187
conversation skills, 217–218
conversations
in married couples, 274
between friends, 251–252
mixed-gender, 330–333
conversion disorder, 489–490
coping, 86, 105
appraisal-focused, 114, 115–120
constructive, 114–131
defensive, 111–113
emotion-focused, 126–131
flexibility in, 106
optimism and, 97
with job loss, 393
with loss, 363
positive emotions and, 82
problem-focused, 114, 120–126
self-esteem and, 150
with traumatic events, 447
coping strategies
adaptive value of, 106
classifying, 105–106
counterproductive, 106–114
coronary heart disease, 443
corpus callosum, 312
correlation
causation and, 18
comparison of, 109
positive vs. negative, 15, 16
strength of, 16
stress-illness, 450
correlation coefficient, 15
correlational research, 15–18
correspondence bias, 179
corticosteroids, 86
cortisol, 86
cosmetic surgery, 243, 323
counseling psychologists, 517–518
counselors, 518, 519
counterconditioning, 529, 530
courtship, 273, 274
covenant marriage, 286
crack cocaine, 473
cramming, 28
Crazy: A Father's Search Through America's Mental Health Madness (Earley), 540
C-reactive protein, 443, 444
credibility, of source, 189
crimes, violent, 308, 455
crises, resilience and, 81
critical thinking, 10, 11
cross-purpose communication, 332
Crow, Sheryl, 493
crowding, as source of stress, 72–73, 74
crystal meth, 473
cults, 4–5
cultural background, communication and, 206
cultural differences
in adolescence, 337
in assertiveness, 230
in attachment styles, 256
in attribution errors, 179–180
in close relationships, 237–238
in eating disorders, 509, 510
in eye contact, 212
in gender roles, 313–314, 316
in grieving, 361
in handling conflict, 224
in mate selection, 242-243
in mental health services, 540–541

in nonverbal communication, 209
in self-disclosure, 220
in self-esteem, 154
in workplace, 386
cultural worldviews, 59, 60, 61
culture
adversarial, 226–227
emotional expression and, 211
personality and, 62–63
self-concept and, 147–148
social support and, 121–122
as source of stress, 74
cunnilingus, 422
cutting off reflected failure (CORF), 159–160
cybersex, 411
cynicism, 88, 446

D

date rape, 296–299
dating
course of, 258
love and, 254
marriage and, 260
online, 238–240
role of physical attractiveness in, 242
sexual behavior and, 425
day care, 382
death
attitudes about, 359–360
fear of, 152
inevitability of, 59, 60
death anxiety, 360
death rates, for diseases, 441
death system, 359
deception, 211
detecting, 214–215
in online communications, 240
on projective tests, 67
on self-report inventories, 66
decision control, 388
decision making, 154
in marriage, 279
decoding, 205
defense mechanisms, 38–39, 42, 111–113, 520, 522
defensive attribution, 180, 181, 186
defensive illusions, 113
defensive pessimism, 160–161
Defensive Pessimism Questionnaire, 160
defensiveness
in communication, 223, 284
Rogers's view of, 51–52
DeGeneres, Ellen, 414
dejection, 81, 142
delaying tactics, 124
delusions, 502, 503
delusions of grandeur, 502, 503
demand control model, 388
demand withdrawal pattern, 260
dementia, 354
demonic possession, 479
denial, 112, 113, 360, 452
dependent variables, 13–14
Depo-Provera, 428, 429
depressants, 472
depression
exercise and, 463
hopelessness and, 498–499
learned helplessness and, 107
loss and, 362, 363
negative thinking and, 499–500
pessimistic style and, 157
postpartum, 276
as response to traumatic events, 89
spousal death and, 362
stress and, 91
depressive disorder(s), 494–495
causes of, 497–501
cognitive therapy for, 531–533
electroconvulsive therapy for, 538
gender differences in, 20–21, 309
heart disease and, 446–447
prevalence of, 3
seeking treatment for, 516
terror management and, 61
see also mood disorders
Desperate Housewives, 426
development, Erikson's stages of, 341, 346, 348, 351–352
deviance, 480
diabetes, 92, 443, 457
diagnosis, 480
Diagnostic and Statistical Manual of Mental Disorders (DSM), 481–484
diaphragm, 429
diazepam, 534
diet, health and, 460
dieting, 459
disagreements, 224–227
disasters
posttraumatic stress disorder following, 90
probability of, 117, 366
risk areas for, 73
discipline, parental, 48, 365, 368–369
disconfirmation bias, 191
discrimination, 182–183
employment, 384, 385
gender-based, 324–325
ingroups and, 187
modern, 183–184
subjective perception of, 74
in workplace, 387
diseases. *See* illness; specific diseases
disengagement, behavioral, 107
disobedience, 197
disorganized schizophrenia, 503
displaced workers, 392
displacement, 38, 39, 108
display rules, 211
dissociative amnesia, 491, 492
dissociative disorders, 483, 491–493
dissociative experiences, in posttraumatic stress disorder, 91
dissociative fugue, 491, 492
dissociative identity disorder (DID), 492–493
distance, interpersonal, 209, 210
distance education, 381
distinctiveness, personality and, 33
distributed practice, 28
diversity, in workforce, 383–385
diversity training, 386
division of labor
in family, 394
gender roles and, 327
in marriage, 280
divorce, 284–288
adjusting to, 287
causes for, 283
cohabitation and, 291
deciding to, 287
effects on children, 286, 288
factors in, 273
financial problems and, 282
infidelity and, 427
loneliness and, 262
predicting likelihood of, 283
waiting period for, 286
divorce rates, 269, 285–286, 380
childlessness and, 277
culture and, 238
for second marriages, 289
door-in-the-face technique, 199, 200
dopamine, 506
double standard, sexual, 176, 298, 407, 424
downsizing, 381, 392
downward social comparison, 145, 158
Dr. Laura, 4, 5
Dr. Phil, 4
dream analysis, 41, 520, 527
drinking, 454–457
drives, basic, 53
driving, drunk, 455
drug abuse, 451, 469–475
stress and, 91
drug companies, 537
drug therapy, 515, 533–537
drug use/abuse, 469–470
drugs (recreational)
dependence on, 470–471
effects of, 471, 472, 473
overdose potential of, 471, 472, 473
risks of, 471, 472, 473, 474
tolerance for, 470, 471
drunk driving, 455
DSM-IV, 482, 483
dual-earner couples, 281, 347, 382, 395
dying, process of, 360–361

E

Eat, Drink, and Be Healthy (Willett), 462
eating
as response to stress, 109–110
oral fixation and, 40
eating disorders, 91, 243, 309, 323, 507–511
eating habits, 460–463
eclecticism, in therapy, 540, 544
ecstasy, 475
education, occupational earnings and, 382–383
effectiveness, time management and, 124
efficiency
in person perception, 181
time management and, 124, 126
ego, 36, 38
ego-based conflicts, 227
ego-depletion model, 82, 161–162
ego integrity, 351
ego threats, 151
ejaculation, 338, 418
premature, 435-436, 437
elaboration likelihood model, 191–192
Elavil, 535
elderly. *See* aging
electroconvulsive therapy (ECT), 537–538
electronically mediated communication, 206–207, 208
e-mail, 206, 207, 214, 219
Emerging Adulthood (Arnett), 346
emetic drugs, 530
emoticons, 214
emotional arousal, interpretation of, 163
emotional expression, gender differences in, 309
emotional intelligence, 127
Emotional Intelligence (Goleman), 127
emotions, 80
in adolescence, 343
agitation-related, 143
appraisal of stress and, 81
arousal of, 82
conditioning of, 45, 46
dejection-related, 142
Ellis's view of, 115–116
expressing, 127–129
facial expression of, 211
heart disease and, 446
masculinity and, 320
negative, 81, 129–130, 446
nonverbal communication of, 208–209
paralanguage and, 214
physiological indicators of, 215
positive, 81, 119

emotions *(continued)*
recognizing, 309
release of, 108
repressed, 448
in schizophrenic disorders, 502
suppression of, 127–128, 320
empathy, 216
in therapy, 523
empiricism, 12–13
employee benefits, 395
employees
diversity of, 383–385
flexible schedules for, 390, 395
job stress and, 386–390
sexual harassment of, 390
employers
background checks by, 400
researching, 401–402
employment. *See* occupations; work
empty nest, 278, 350
encoding, 205
encouragement, 163
End of Stress as We Know It (McEwan & Lasley), 92
endocrine system, 85, 86, 312, 338, 356
endogamy, 272
Enron, 197
environment
for communication, 206
heredity and, 58
personality and, 57
stress in, 72–73, 74
environmental problems, 3
Epidemiological Catchment Area, 484
epidemiology, 482
erectile difficulties, 356, 434–435, 436, 437
erogenous zones, 421
erotic preferences, 408
est training, 7
estrogen, 356, 408
ethics
of experimental research, 15
sexual, 407
ethnic minorities
stresses for, 74
therapeutic services for, 540–541
in workforce, 384
stereotypes of, 178
ethnicity
gender-role attitudes and, 316
self-esteem and, 154
etiology, 480
euphoria
from alcohol, 454
in bipolar disorder, 495
from hallucinogens, 473
from stimulants, 472
evolutionary perspective
evaluation of, 58, 311
on flight-or-flight response, 84
on gender differences, 311
on mate selection, 244–245, 273
on obesity, 457
on personality, 57-58
on romance, 253
exams
anxiety and, 82
changing answers on, 16, 17
cramming for, 28
exchange relationships, 250
exchange theory, 248–249
exemplification, 165
exercise
benefits of, 130, 398, 463
lack of, 458463
for weight loss, 459
exercise program, 464–465
exhaustion stage, of general adaptation syndrome, 84–85
expectations
happiness and, 23
for parenthood, 277
perceiver, 175–180, 182
prejudice and, 186
experimental group, 14
experimental research, 13–15
expertise, of source, 189
explanatory style, 156–157, 498–499
expressed emotion, 507
expressive style, 331–332
expressiveness, 304
extinction
in classical conditioning, 46
in operant conditioning, 47–48
extradyadic sex, 426–427
extraversion, 22, 33-34, 41, 56, 57, 58, 62
eye contact, 211–212, 220

F

facial expression, 210–211, 309
fact-based conflict, 225
factor analysis, 33, 62
failure
handling, 162
as source of stress, 75
faith, happiness and, 21
false memory syndrome, 526
familiarity, as factor in attraction, 241
family
balancing work with, 395–396
eating disorders and, 510–511
expressed emotion in, 507
of homosexuals, 294
obesity and, 458–459
occupation and, 374
sexual socialization from, 408–409
family environment, personality and, 57
family life cycle, 274–279
family structures, 270
fantasy
as defense mechanism, 112, 113
sexual, 421–422, 434
fat, in diet, 460, 461, 462, 463
fat cells, 458
fatalism, 107
fathers
divorce and, 287
role of, 320
see also parenting
fatigue, 88
favors, doing, 165
fear, 81
as response to traumatic events, 89
conditioned, 45, 487, 488
irrational, 485
fear appeals, 190
Federline, Kevin, 189–190
fellatio, 422
female role, 321–326
femininity, 304, 328
feminist movement, 322
fertility control, 429
fiber, in diet, 460, 461, 462, 463
fight-or-flight response, 82–84
financial problems, in marriage, 282–283
firefighters, 387
firstborns, 42
fitness, physical, 463
fixation, 39–40
flashbacks, from LSD, 474
flexible work schedules, 390, 395
fluphenazine, 535
food. *See* eating; nutrition
food pyramid, 461–462
foot-in-the-door technique, 198–199
Ford, Harrison, 493
Foreman, George, 189
foreplay, 420
forewarning, of persuasive messages, 191
forgetting, 491
forgiveness, 129–130
Foundation for Critical Thinking, 10
Frank, Ann, 178
fraternal twins, 56
Free Agent Nation (Pink), 383
free agents, 382
free association, 520
Friendshifts (Yager), 250
friendships, 250–252
attraction in, 240–247
in late adulthood, 353
self-disclosure in, 220
touching in, 213
Friendster, 238
frigidity, 436
frustration, as source of stress, 75
frustration-aggression hypothesis, 107
fundamental attribution error, 179–180, 185–186
fundamentalism, 152

G

GABA, 487
galvanic skin response (GSR), 215
game playing, 224
games, as leisure activity, 397
gay marriage, 414
gays. *See* homosexuals; homosexuality
gaze, 211
gender, 303
gender bias
in children's books, 316
in occupational interest inventories, 376
on television, 318
gender differences, 303
in aggression, 308, 311, 313
in anxiety disorders, 485
in attraction tactics, 243, 244
biological origins of, 311–313
in body language, 212
in cognitive abilities, 306–307
in communication style, 309, 330–333
in depression, 20–21, 495
in eating disorders, 509
in emotional expression, 309
environmental origins of, 313–318
evolutionary perspective on, 311
in eye contact, 212
in facial expression, 211
in friendships, 251–252, 353
as group differences, 310
in happiness, 20–21
in hooking up, 424, 425
in mate selection, 242, 245, 272–273
in motives for infidelity, 427
in nonverbal communication, 216, 332
in online sexual activities, 17
in patterns of orgasm, 420
in personal space, 209
in personality traits, 307–309
in phobias, 486
in psychological disorders, 309–310
in responding to threat, 84
in romanticism, 253
in seeking treatment, 467
in self-disclosure, 220
in self-esteem, 154
in self-views, 148
in sexual attitudes, 417
in sexual socialization, 410, 412
in sexuality, 308–309, 313, 320–321, 324
in singlehood, 290
in STD effects, 430–431

in suicides, 496
in use of therapy, 517
in wages, 325, 326
gender identity, 303
gender-identity disorders, 483
gender-role expectations, 252, 318
for females, 321–326
for males, 318–321
traditional, 328
gender-role identity, 303, 328
gender-role socialization, 313–314
by media, 317–318
by parents, 315–316
by peers, 316
processes in, 314–315
by schools, 316–317
gender-role transcendence, 329
gender roles, 303, 313–314
alternatives to, 328–329
changing, 4, 327
friendships and, 251–252
in homosexual relationships, 294
in marriage, 269
rmodeling of, 49
gender schemas, 315
gender similarities hypothesis, 306
gender stereotypes, 178, 303–305
appearance pressure and, 323
in children's books, 316
in media, 317–318
in textbooks, 316–317
general adaptation syndrome, 84–85
generalized anxiety disorder, 485
generativity versus stagnation, 348
genetic mapping, 498, 505
genetic predisposition
to anxiety disorders, 487
to eating disorders, 510
to obesity, 458
to mood disorders, 498
to schizophrenic disorders, 505
genetics
behavioral, 56–48
sexual orientation and, 413, 414
genital herpes, 432
genital stage, 39, 40–41
genitals
oral stimulation of, 422
at puberty, 338
during sex, 418–420
gestures, 213
Getting from College to Career (Pollack), 402
giving up, 106–107, 498
glass ceiling, 325, 385
glass escalator, 325
globalization, 392
glove anesthesia, 490
glutamate, 505
goals, unrealistic, 168–169
gonads, 338, 408
gonorrhea, 431, 432
gratification, delaying, 161–162
Grave Matters (Harris), 360
Gray, John, 4
Green, Reg and Maggie, 129
grief, 81, 89
grief work, 362
grieving process, 361–362
group norms, 179–180
group therapy, 523–524
groups
competition between, 186
conformity in, 194
evolutionary value of, 58
reference, 144–145
growth needs, 53
growth spurt, adolescent, 337, 338
guilt, 81, 112, 143
reaction formation and, 38
as response to traumatic events, 89
sexual, 412
superego and, 36

H

habits, health-impairing, 450–466
Haldol, 534
hallucinations, 502
hallucinogens, 471, 473
hangovers, 455
happiness, 19–24
age and, 20
attractiveness and, 21
gender and, 20–21
health and, 21
heredity and, 22
intelligence and, 21
love and, 22
marriage and, 22, 291
money and, 1–2, 19–20
parenthood and, 21
personality and, 22–23
religion and, 21
self-esteem and, 150
social activity, 21
subjectivity of, 23
work and, 22
hard to get, playing, 246
hardiness, 94–95
Harvard University, 302
hashish, 471, 474
hassles, routine, 71
hate speech, 226
health
biopsychosocial model of, 442
happiness and, 21
health care, aging and, 356
health-impairing habits, 450–466
health maintenance organizations (HMOs), 539
health-protective behaviors, terror management and, 61
health providers, communicating with, 468
health psychology, 442
hearing, aging and, 354
heart attack, 443, 444, 446
heart disease
alcohol and, 456
depression and, 446–447
diet and, 460
job stress and, 389
mortality rates for, 441
obesity and, 457
personality and, 443–447
smoking and, 452
stress and, 92
Heaven's Gate, 4
hedonic adaptation, 24
hedonic treadmill, 24
hemispheric lateralization, 312
hepatitis B, 432
heredity
environment and, 58, 311
happiness and, 22
homosexuality and, 413
obesity and, 458
mood disorders and, 498
personality and, 55, 56–57
see also genetic predisposition
heritability ratios, 56, 58
heroes, need for, 60
heroin, 471, 472
herpes, genital, 432
heterosexism, 252, 384
heterosexual success, 321–322
heterosexuals, 252, 407
hidden agenda, 216
hierarchy of needs, Maslow's, 52–53
High Price of Materialism, The (Kasser), 1
Hill, Anita, 390
hindsight bias, 58
hippocampus, 498, 499
Hispanic Americans, 154
gender roles for, 316
male role among, 319
stresses for, 74
in workforce, 384
histrionic personality, 490
Hitler, Adolf, 195
HIV infection, 423, 430, 431, 432, 465
hobbies, 397
holistic approach, 180
homicides, in workplace, 394
homogamy, 272
homophobia, 293, 321, 414–415
homosexuality, 412–416
attitudes toward, 414–415
causes of, 413–414
development of, 415
marriage and, 414
prevalence of, 292–293, 412
as psychological disorder, 481
reaction formation and, 38
homosexuals, 252, 407
AIDS and, 432, 465
children of, 416
dating challenges for, 241
friendships and, 252
gay subculture, 243
infidelity among, 426–427
parents of, 415
romantic relationships of, 291–294, 347
sexual activity of, 423, 426
teenage, 343–344
in workforce, 384, 385, 387
honesty, in interpersonal communication, 216–217, 229
"hooking up,"424
hopelessness theory, 498–499
hormone-based contraceptives, 428–429
hormones, 85, 86, 312
aging and, 355–356
homosexuality and, 413
puberty and, 338
sex, 408
stress and, 72, 73
hostile work environment, 390
hostility
ego threats and, 151
heart disease and, 444–446
intergroup, 187
managing, 129–130
public, 226
household chores, 279–280, 281, 316, 323, 347
How to Stubbornly Refuse to Make Yourself Miserable About Anything (Ellis), 118
Hughes, Howard, 486, 490
human immunodeficiency virus. *See* HIV infection
human nature, 50, 54
human papillomavirus (PV), 431, 432
human potential movement, 521
humanism, 50
humanistic theories
evaluation of, 54
Maslow's, 52–54
Rogers', 50–52
humor, as stress reducer, 118–120
hunting-and-gathering societies, 311, 327
Hurricane Katrina, 89, 118
Hurried Child, The (Elkind), 342
hydrophobia, 485
hypertension, 443
alcohol and, 456
caffeine and, 460

hypertension *(continued)*
obesity and, 457
hypnosis, for recovering repressed memories, 526, 527
hypoactive sexual desire, 436, 437
hypochondriasis, 490
hypothalamus, 85, 86
hypothesis, 13

I

id, 36, 38
ideal self, 142–143, 240
identical twins, 56
identification, 39
identity, 341
gender-role, 328
from job, 373
loss of, 491
search for, 341–343
sexual, 407–408
identity crisis, 341, 347
identity statuses, 341–342, 347
illness
job stress and, 388–389
life changes and, 77
reactions to, 467–469
stress and, 85, 91–92
see also specific illnesses
illusion of control, 158
imitation
in observational learning, 49
of gender roles, 314
immune functioning
AIDS and, 465
emotional disclosure and, 128
humor and, 119
marijuana use and, 474
optimism and, 96
positive emotions and, 82
social support and, 93
stress and, 86, 448–449
Implanon, 429
impression formation, 173–182
in job interviews, 402–403
see also person perception
impression management, 164–167
impressions
first, 182
negative, 174, 182
impulse control, 109
In the Wake of 9/11 (Pyszczynski, Solomon, & Greenberg), 60
income
education and, 383
happiness and, 19–20
job identity and, 373
marriage and, 282
incongruence, 51, 522
independent variables, 13–14
independent view of self, 147–148
India, 73, 237
individualism/individualistic cultures, 154, 220
assertiveness and, 230
attribution errors and, 179–180
conflict and, 224
marriage and, 237–238
self-concept and, 147
self-serving bias and, 159
social support and, 121–122
indulgence, as coping strategy, 109–111
industrial/organizational (I/O) psychology, 372
infants, attachment styles in, 255–256
infectious diseases, 441
inferiority complex, 41, 42
infidelity, 426–427
inflammation, heart disease and, 443, 444
Influence (Cialdini), 193, 198
information, retention of, 28
information influence, 194–195
information processing, aging and, 358
ingratiation, 165
ingroup favoritism, 187
ingroups, 177–178, 184, 185
insecure attachment style, 262
insecurity, 274
insight therapies, 515, 519–525, 542
client-centered, 521–523
effectiveness of, 524–525, 544
group, 523–524
psychoanalysis, 519–521
insomnia, stress and, 91
instant messaging, 206
instrumental style, 331–332
instrumentality, 304
integrity vs. despair, 351-352
intellectualization, 112
intelligence
aging and, 356–357
emotional, 127
happiness and, 21
heritability of, 56
occupation and, 373
intercourse, sexual, 420, 421, 423, 424
interdependence theory, 248–249
interdependent view of self, 147–148
interest inventories, 376
Internet
close relationships and, 238–240
communicating via, 207
for overcoming loneliness, 264–265
sexual content on, 410, 411
sexual pursuits on, 17, 18
surfing, 397
Internet addiction, 110–111, 265, 411
interpersonal communication, 205
barriers to, 223–224
improving, 216–222, 333
in marriage, 283
premarital, 274
problems in, 222–224
about sex, 417–418
technology and, 206–207
interpersonal relationships
development of, 245–250
homosexual, 252–253, 291–294
interpretation, in psychoanalysis, 520–521
interruptions, 126
interviews, job, 165, 402–403
intimacy
isolation vs., 346–347
love and, 253, 257, 259
self-disclosure and, 220
sex and, 321, 410
intimacy statuses, 346–347
intimate violence, 295–299
intimidation, 166
intrauterine device (IUD), 428, 429
intravenous drug use, 465, 472
introducing oneself, 217
introversion, 41, 56
inverted-U hypothesis, 82
investments, in relationships, 249
irrational assumptions, 111, 116–118
irrational thinking, 169, 264, 502
irritability, as response to traumatic events, 89
irritable bowel syndrome, stress and, 448
ischemia, 443, 446

J

Japan, 159, 220, 361
jigsaw classroom, 188
Jim twins, 55
job interviews, 165, 402–403
job loss, 392–394
job openings, 401–402
job performance
self-efficacy and, 162
self-esteem and, 150
job satisfaction, 280, 281
interest inventories and, 376
leisure satisfaction and, 398
personality fit and, 389
job search, 398–403
job security, 381
job skills, 381
job stress, 386–390
dealing with, 389–390
demand control model of, 388
effects of, 388–389
jobs, information about, 374–375
judgment, withholding, 216
judgments, snap vs. systematic, 174, 191
junkies, 472
just world, belief in, 180, 181

K

Kaiser Family Foundation, 422
kinesics, 212
kissing, 422

L

labor force, 383–386
see also workforce
language, 205
latency stage, 40–41
Lay, Ken, 197
learned helplessness, 106–107, 498
learning
via classical conditioning, 43–46
lifelong, 381
observational, 48–49
via operant conditioning, 46–48
studying and, 25
lectures, getting more from, 27
LEGO career, 382
leisure, 396–398
income and, 20
lesbians, 252, 294, 407, 412–416
friendships and, 252
sexual activity of, 420
sexual satisfaction of, 426
see also homomsexuality; homosexuals
leukemia, stress and, 92
Levitra, 436
LGBT individuals, 407, 415
liberals, 184
lice, pubic, 432
lie detector, 215
life changes, 77–78
life expectancy, 348
smoking and, 452
Life Experience Survey (LES), 98–101
Life Orientation Test, 96
lifelong learning, 381
likability, of source, 189
link method, 29
liquor, 454
listening, 205
during lectures, 27
effective, 220–222
in mixed-gender conversations, 332–333
LISTSERVs, 206
lithium, 536
liver, alcohol and, 456
locus of control, internal, 181
loneliness, 261–265
causes of, 262–263
overcoming, 264–265
prevalence of, 261–262
shyness and, 263

loss
as source of stress, 75
coping with, 363
of job, 393
of spouse, 362–363
love
as attachment, 254–257
course of, 257–258
cultural differences in, 238
happiness and, 22
romantic, 252–258
sex and, 417
triangular theory of, 253–254
unconditional, 51
Loving Someone Gay, 416
lowball technique, 199
LSD, 471, 473
lung cancer, smoking and, 452
lying, 214–215
in online communications, 240
see also deception

M

macho sexual image, 321
mailing lists, 206
makeover culture, 4
maladaptive behavior, 480
male role, 319–321
malingering, 489
malnutrition, 461
managed care health plans, 539
Mandela, Nelson, 357
mania, 494, 495, 497
manipulation, 230
MAO inhibitors, 535–536
marijuana, 471, 474
marital bliss, 276
marital satisfaction
in early years, 276
in later years, 278–279, 350
predictors of, 248
sexual satisfaction and, 18, 425
work and, 280, 281
marital success, predictors of, 273–274
marriage, 269
abuse in, 295–296
adjusting to, 347
age at first, 273–274, 347
alternatives to, 290–294
arranged, 237, 238
based on romantic love, 237
communication problems in, 283–284
conflict in, 274, 278, 283–284
covenant, 286
cultural differences in, 237–238
division of labor in, 280
financial problems in, 282–283
gay, 414
government promotion of, 286
happiness and, 22
health benefits of, 290–291
infidelity in, 426–427
interracial, 272
masturbation in, 422
motivation for, 271
moving toward, 270–274
open, 426
postponing, 275
sex before, 424–425
sexual activity in, 425–426
trends in, 269–270
see also divorce
marriage mandate, 321
marriage squeeze, 272
Masculine Self, The (Kilmartin), 320
masculinities, 319
masculinity, 304, 328
masturbation, 420, 422
matching hypothesis, 243–244
mate selection, 271–273
cultural differences in, 242–243
materialism, 1-2, 4, 20, 61
mathematical abilities, gender differences in, 306–307
Mating Game, The (Regan), 258
Mayer-Salovey-Caruso Emotional Intelligence Test, 127
MDMA, 475
"me first" philosophy, 8
meaning, search for, 4
media
aggression in, 226
for messages, 188
health information in, 452
sexual content of, 409–410
as source of gender-role socialization, 317–318
violence in, 108, 109
medical advice, adherence to, 468–469
Medical College Admissions Test (MCAT), 113
medical treatment, seeking, 467
meditation, 130–131
Mellaril, 534
memorization, 28, 29
memory
aging and, 355, 358–359
improving, 27–29
loss of, 491
marijuana use and, 475
recovered, 525–528
stress and, 88
menarche, 338
menopause, 355–356
menstruation, 338, 412
mental abilities/processes
aging and, 356–359
behavioral perspective on, 43
study of, 11
mental health professions, 517–519
mental health services, 539, 541, 543
mental hospitals, declining populations in, 533, 534
mental illness. *See* psychological disorders
mentoring, 348
mentors, 386
mere exposure effect, 241
mescaline, 47, 4731
messages, 205
persuasive, 188, 190
Messages: The Communication Skills Book (McKay, Davis, & Fanning), 217
meta-analysis, 306
methamphetamine, 473
method of loci, 29
Michelle Remembers (Smith & Pazder), 492
midlife crisis, 350–351
mifepristone, 430
mindfulness, 155, 187
minding, of relationships, 248
mindlessness, 155, 187, 191
minerals, 461
Minnesota Multiphasic Personality Inventory (MMPI), 65
minorities
discrimination against, 183
stresses for, 74
use of psychotherapy by, 517
therapeutic services for, 540–541
in workforce, 384, 385
workplace harassment of, 326
miscommunication, 206
Mismeasure of Woman (Tavris), 324
mnemonics, 29
mobility, geographic, 77–78
modal personality, 62
modeling (models), 162
of assertive communication, 232
of gender roles, 314
in observational learning, 48–49
in social skills training, 531
money
happiness and, 19–20
as marital problem, 282–283
monogamy, 271–272
mood disorders, 483, 484, 493–501
biological causes of, 498
cognitive factors in, 498–499
drug therapy for, 535–536
etiology of, 497–501
gender differences in, 309
interpersonal roots of, 500
prevalence of, 495
seeking treatment for, 516
stress and, 500–501
suicide and, 496
types of, 494–497
mood stabilizers, 536
moods, in adolescence, 343
Morgan Stanley, 385
Mormon Church, 271–272
morphine, 471, 472
mortality
acknowledging, 349
from health-impairing behaviors, 450, 451
obesity and, 457
physical fitness and, 463
mortality rates
for diseases, 441
for smokers, 452, 453
mortality salience, 60, 61, 152
motherhood mandate, 321
mothers, in workforce, 323–324
motivational distortion, 223
motives
guiding self-understanding, 147
sexual, 416–417
motor vehicle accidents, 451
multiaxial system of classification, 482, 483
Multicultural Manners (Dresser), 206
multimodal therapy, 545
multiple-choice tests, changing answers on, 16, 17
multiple sclerosis, stress and, 92
multiple-personality disorder, 492–493
Mundugamor, 314
murder
of spouse, 296
in workplace, 392
music videos, 318, 410
mutual gaze, 211
My Lai incident, 197
myocardial infarction, 443
myocardial ischemia, 443, 446
MySpace, 238

N

narcissism, 151
narcotics, 471, 472
Nardil, 535
Nash, John, 504
National Alliance for the Mentally Ill, 482
National Business Employment Weekly, 401
national character, 62–63
National Comorbidity Study, 484
National Council on Family Relations, 281
National Institute on Drug Abuse, 470
nations, subjective well-being of, 19, 20
Native Americans, 230
health of, 356
suicide by, 344
natural resources, depletion of, 3
natural selection, 58, 244, 311
naturalistic observation, 16
Nazi war crimes, 197

needs
gratification of, 40
hierarchy of, 52-53
negative emotionality, 34
negative reinforcement, 47, 48
negative thinking, 531
depression and, 499–500
neglectful parenting, 153, 365, 367
NEO Personality Inventory, 66
netlingo, 206, 207
networking, social, 238
neurodevelopmental hypothesis, 506–507
neurogenesis, 498
neurons, 354
neuroses, 520
neuroticism, 34, 490, 57, 58, 62
illness and, 450
stress and, 98
neurotransmitters, 487, 498, 505
newlyweds, 276
nicotine, 473
nicotine substitutes, 454
night shifts, 281
noise
in communication process, 206, 223
as stressful, 72
nonverbal communication, 205
elements of, 209–214
gender differences in, 332
in job interviews, 403
in self-disclosure, 218, 219
significance of, 216
as source of information, 173
nonverbal cues
in assertive communication, 231
in effective listening, 220, 221–222
nonverbal sensitivity, 216
norepinephrine, 498
normality, 480, 481
normative influences, 194
note taking, from lectures, 27
NovaRing, 429
Now That You Know (Fairchild & Hayward), 416
nuclear family, 270
Nun Study, 355
nursing homes, 356
nutrients, essential, 461
nutrition, 460–463

O

obedience, 195–197
obesity, 457–458, 463
observation, naturalistic, 16
observational learning, 48–49
in gender-role socialization, 314
obsessions, 486
obsessive-compulsive disorder, 486–487, 545, 536
occupation, choosing, 373–376
occupational development, 378–380
occupational interest inventories, 375–376
Occupational Outlook Handbook, 374
occupations
high-growth, 382
researching, 374–375
for women, 325
see also careers
Oedipal complex, 40, 413
Oklahoma City bombing, 152
olanzapine, 535
omega 3 fatty acids, 460
open marriage, 426
openness to experience, 34, 57, 58, 62
operant conditioning, 46–48, 132–136, 487
opiates, 472
optimal level of arousal, 82, 83
optimal margin of illusion, 113
optimism, 95–97, 161
in children, 367
happiness and, 23
unrealistic, 158
optimistic explanatory style, 96–97, 156–157
oral contraceptives, 428–429
oral presentations, 222
oral sex, 422
oral stage, 39, 40
orgasm, 419, 420
faking, 420
orgasmic difficulties, 436, 437
osteoporosis, 460
ought self, 142–143
outcomes, in social exchanges, 248–249
outgroup derogation, 187
outgroups, 177–178, 184, 185
outlining, of textbooks, 28
outsourcing, 381
overcommunication, 222
overcompensation, 112
overdose, alcohol, 455
overeating, 163–164, 457–458
control of, 133–137
overlearning, 28
Oxycontin, 472

P

panic disorder, 485, 487, 489, 545
drug therapy for, 536
seeking treatment for, 516
Paradox of Choice (Schwartz), 7
paradox of close relationships, 237
paralanguage, 213
paranoid schizophrenia, 503
paraphrasing, 221
parasuicide, 343–344
parasympathetic nervous system, 83–84
parental investment theory, 244–245
parenthood, 276–277
happiness and, 21
parenting
in adversarial culture, 226–227
inferiority complex and, 41
in middle age, 349
self-esteem development and, 153
parenting styles, 153, 364–365, 367, 368
attachment and, 255–256
occupation and, 374
parents, 408–409
adult children living with, 278, 350
conflicts with adolescent children, 343, 349
elderly, 277–278
feedback from, 146
gay, 294
of gay children, 415
as source of gender-role socialization, 315-316
paroxetine, 536
partner abuse, 295–296, 455
passion, 253–254, 257–258
passive aggression, 230
patriotism, 60
peers
adolescents' influence by, 277
self-esteem and, 153
sex information from, 409
as source of gender-role socialization, 316
penis, 418–420, 422, 423, 430
penis envy, 40, 43
peptic ulcer, stress and, 448
perception, distorted, 502
perfectionism, 123, 274, 510
performance pressure, 79, 87, 88, 387
on minorities, 385
periodontal disease, stress and, 448
Permanent Partners (Berzon), 433
permissive parenting, 153, 365, 367
person-centered theory, Rogers's, 50–52
person-centered therapy, 522
person-environment fit model, 377–378
person perception, 173–182
attribution processes in, 174–175
cognitive distortions in, 177–180
expectations and, 175–180
key themes in, 181–182
process of, 174, 175
sources of information for, 173–174
personal space, 209–210
personal unconscious, 41
personality, 33
Adler's view of, 41–42
aging and, 359
Bandura's view of, 49
behavioral perspectives on, 43–50
biological perspectives on, 55–58
cancer-prone, 448
consistency in, 50
culture and, 62–63
evolutionary perspective on, 57–58
Eysenck's view of, 56
family environment and, 57
five-factor model of, 33–34
Freud's theory of, 36–41
gender differences in, 307–309
happiness and, 22–23
healthy, 53–54
heart disease and, 443–447
heritability of, 57
humanistic theories of, 50–54
Jung's view of, 41
marital success and, 274
Maslow's view of, 52–54
psychodynamic theories of, 35–43
self-monitoring and, 167
similarity in, 246–247
Skinner's view of, 46–47
somatization disorders and, 490
stability of, 359
personality development
Adler's view of, 42
behavioral perspectives on, 43, 44
Freud's psychosexual stages of, 39–41
Rogers's view of, 51
Skinner's view of, 46–47
personality structure
Eysenck's view of, 56
Freud's view of, 36–37
Rogers's view of, 51
personality tests, 63–67
personality traits, 33
Big Five, 33–34, 42, 359
cultural differences in, 62
desirable, 247
hierarchy of, 56
personality types, career choice and, 377–378
persuasion, 188–192
defined, 199
peripheral vs. central routes to, 191–192
process of, 188–189
pessimism, defensive, 160–161
pessimistic explanatory style, 96, 107, 156–157, 498–499
Peterson, Laci, 295
phallic stage, 39, 40
pharmaceutical industry, 537
phobias, 545
common, 485, 486
conditioning of, 45, 46, 487–488
systematic desensitization for, 529–530
physical appearance, 173
physical attractiveness
aging and, 354
eating disorders and, 509, 410
evolutionary perspective on, 244–245
as factor in attraction, 241–245
happiness and, 21

ideals for, 323
of job applicants, 402
of persuader, 189
psychiatric patients' readjustment and, 17
stereotypes of, 178
physique, desirable, 242–243, 323
pineal gland, 85
pink-collar ghetto, 325
pituitary gland, 85, 86, 338
placebo effects, with meditation, 131
planning, of time, 125–126
play activities, gender roles and, 315, 316, 331
pleasure principle, 36
poker face, 211
policy conflicts, 227
politics
authoritarianism and, 184
terror management and, 61
polygamy, 271–272
polygraph, 215
polyunsaturated fats, 463
pornography, 410
positive emotionality, 22
Positive Power of Negative Thinking, The (Norem), 160
positive psychology movement, 54
positive regard, unconditional, 522
positive reinforcement, 46
positive reinterpretation, 120
Positively Gay (Berzon), 416
postpartum depression, 276
posttraumatic growth, 92
posttraumatic stress disorder, 88–91, 93, 251
cognitive therapy for, 532
following rape, 297
gender differences in, 309–310
treatment for, 532
posture, 212
poverty, 1, 20, 73
preconscious, 37
prefrontal cortex, 499, 506
pregnancy, 338
fear of, 412
influenza during, 506
preventing, 427–430
pregnancy rates, 423, 428
prejudice, 182–188
causes of, 184–187
combating, 250
competition and, 186
reducing, 187–188
self-esteem and, 154
as source of stress, 74
terror management and, 61
in workplace, 386
premarital sex, 424
prenatal development
gender differentiation in, 312–313
homosexuality and, 413
schizophrenic disorders and, 506
sexual differentiation in, 408
preparedness, 487–488
pressure, 87
as source of stress, 78–79
to succeed, 319–320
primacy effect, 182, 403
primary process thinking, 36
primary sex characteristics, 338, 408
problem drinking, 456
problem solving
in adolescence, 340
aging and, 357–358
systematic, 120–121
problems, confronting, 114
problems in living, 480
procrastination, 123, 124, 164
in seeking treatment, 467
productivity, aging and, 358
progestin pills, 430
prognosis, 480
progress, paradox of, 1–4
projection, 38, 39
projective tests, 66–67
pro-marriage movement, 286
Promise Keepers, 319
protein, 461, 462
proxemics, 209
proximity, as factor in attraction, 241
Prozac, 536
pseudoconflict, 225
pseudostupidity, 340
psilocybin, 471, 473
psychiatric patients, postrelease adjustment of, 17
psychiatrists, 515, 518–519
psychoanalysis, 35, 519–521
psychoanalytic theory, 35–41
psychobabble, 7–8
psychodiagnosis, 481–484
psychodynamic theories
Adler's 41–42
evaluation of, 42–43
Freud's, 36–41
Jung's, 41
psychodynamic therapy, 544
psychological disorders
classification of, 481–484
Freud's view of, 41
gender differences in, 309–310
homosexuality as, 416
prevalence of, 482, 484, 485, 495, 501
Rogers's view of, 52
stress and, 91
see also specific disorders
psychological tests, 63–67
for career decisions, 375–376
psychologists, clinical, 517–518
psychology, 11
careers in, 374–375, 382
as profession, 12
as science, 11–12
psychopathology, 479
psychopharmacotherapy, 533
psychosexual stages, 39–41
psychosocial stages, 341, 346, 348, 351–352
psychosomatic diseases, 92
psychotherapy. *See* therapy
Psychotherapy Maze, The (Ehrenberg and Ehrenberg), 543
psychotic disorders, 483
puberty, 40, 338, 408
timing of, 338–340
pubescence, 337–338
pubic lice, 432
public self, 164
public speaking, 222
punishment
disciplinary, 48, 368–369
in gender-role socialization, 314
in operant conditioning, 48, 134
Pursuit of Happiness (Myers), 21
put-downs, responses to, 232
puzzle solving, 397

Q

Quaalude, 471
Queer Eye for the Straight Guy, 415
quetiapine, 535

R

racial profiling, 185
racial stereotypes, 178, 185
racism, 183–184
as source of stress, 74
in workplace, 387
Raelian UFO cult, 5
rage, 81
rape, 296–299, 455
rational emotive behavior therapy, 115, 531, 544
rational outness, 415
rationalization, 38, 39
reactance, 201
reaction formation, 38, 39
reading
for pleasure, 397
methods for improving, 25–27
reality principle, 36
receiver, of message, 188, 190–191, 205
receptivity, of audience, 190–191
reciprocal liking, 246
reciprocity, in self-disclosure, 219
reciprocity principle, 199–201
Reconcilable Differences (Christensen & Jacobson), 281
recovered memories controversy, 525–528
reference groups, 144-145
refractory period, 418
regression, 38, 39
rehearsal, of assertive communication, 232
reinforcement, 46–47, 135, 248
of gender roles, 314
reinforcement contingencies, 134
reinforcers, 134
rejection
depression and, 500
low self-esteem and, 169
rejection anxiety, 263
relational aggression, 308
relationship maintenance, 247–248
relationships, 237–240
abusive, 295–296
cohabiting,269, 291
communicating in, 216–222
communicating about sex in, 417–418
development of, 245–250
exchange theory of, 248–249
homosexual, 291–294, 347
minding, 248
See also friendship; marriage; romantic relationships
relaxation techniques, 131, 529, 530
reliability, of psychological tests, 64
religion, happiness and, 21
remarriage, 289
repression, 38, 39, 113
reproductive fitness, 58, 311
rescue workers, posttraumatic stress disorder in, 90
research methods, 13–18
resignation, 107
resilience, 81–82, 92
death of spouse and, 362–363
resistance, in psychoanalysis, 521
resistance stage, of general adaptation syndrome, 84–85
response tendencies, 43, 44, 48
responsibility, delegating, 123
résumé, preparing, 399–401
retirement, 352, 380
rewards
as reinforcement, 46, 134
in relationships, 248
rhymes, as mnemonics, 29
rhythm method, 429
Rice, Anne, 493
risky behavior, in adolescence, 340, 343, 344
ritual kin, 353
road rage, 107
Robbers' Cave, 186
Robbins, Tony, 4
rohypnol, 298
role expectations, for marriage, 269, 279–280
see also gender-role expectations
role models, 48–49, 162, 314

role playing, 232
roles
in early adulthood, 345
juggling multiple, 323–324, 396
romantic love, 252–258
romantic relationships, 237
attraction in, 240–247
breakup of, 258–259
course of, 257–258
maintaining, 259–260
self-disclosure in, 218–220
self-esteem and, 150
Rorschach test, 66
Rosenberg Self-Esteem Scale, 149
RU 486, 430
rudeness, 226
rumination, depression and, 495, 499
Rutherford, Tom, 527

S

sadness, 81, 142–143
safe sex, 431
salary
career choice and, 376
education and, 382–383
gender gap in, 380
negotiating, 403
salt, in diet, 460, 462
sandwich generation, 277
satanic abuse, 492
saturated fats, 462
scarcity principle, 201
schedules
making, 125–126
for time management, 25, 26
work, 390, 395
schizophrenic disorders, 483, 484, 501–507
biological causes of, 505–506
course and outcome of, 504
drug therapy for, 534–535
etiology of, 504–507
expressed emotion and, 507
neurodevelopmental hypothesis of, 506
positive vs. negative symptoms in, 503–504
prevalence of, 501
stress and, 507
subtypes of, 503
symptoms of, 500–502, 503–504
vulnerability to, 507
Schlessinger, Laura, 4, 5
schools
as source of gender-role socialization, 316
sex education in, 409
sexual harassment in, 326
scientific approach, 12–18
Seconal, 471
secondary sex characteristics, 338, 408
Secret, The (Byrne), 7
secrets, telling, 219
secure attachment style, 255–256
sedatives, 471, 472
segregation, job, 385
selective attention, 155, 223
selective serotonin reuptake inhibitors (SSRIs), 536
selectivity, in person perception, 182
self
independent vs. interdependent view of, 147–148
public, 164
self-actualization, need for, 53
self-assessment motive, 157
self-attributions, 155–156
self-awareness, 143–144
self-blame, 81, 111, 150, 169
self-cognition, 155
self-concept, 54, 141–148
culture and, 147–148
defense mechanisms and, 113
factors shaping, 144–148
gender and, 315
occupational development and, 378
Rogers's view of, 51, 522
stress and, 92
self-concept confusion, 148
self-consciousness, 87
self-consistency, 157
self-control, 132–137, 161, 364, 452
Self-Creation (Weinberg), 6
self-deception, 112–113
defense mechanisms and, 38–39
self-defeating attributional style, 263–264, 265
self-defeating behavior, 163–164
self-destructive behavior, 343–344, 450
Self-Directed Search (SDS), 376, 378
self-disclosure, 218–220
computer-mediated, 219
emotional, 128, 218
in friendships, 252
in marriage, 274, 283
in online relationships, 240
in relationship maintenance, 248, 259
risks of, 219
of sexual orientation, 415
written, 219
self-discrepancies, 142–144
self-effacing bias, 159
self-efficacy, 49, 162–163
adherence to medical advice and, 469
burnout and, 88
career choice and, 373
exercise and, 130
self-enhancement, 157–161
self-esteem, 148–154
anxiety buffering and, 152
defined, 148
depressive disorder and, 494
development of, 151, 153
divorce and, 287
ethnicity and, 154
exercise and, 130
gender differences in, 307–308
gender roles and, 328
happiness and, 23
identification and, 39
importance of, 150–151
improving, 167–169
measurement of, 149
parenting and, 364
punishment and, 369
secure vs. defensive, 150–151
structure of, 149
terror management and, 59, 60, 61
threats to, 186
trait vs. state, 148
Self-Esteem (McCay & Fanning), 168
self-fulfilling prophecies, 177, 179, 246, 358, 413
self-handicapping, 160–161, 164
self-help books, 5–9
self-help groups, 524
self-image, distortions in, 145–146
self-improvement, 157
self-indulgence, 109–111
self-modification programs, 459, 527
self-monitoring, 167, 211
self-perception, 154–166, 199
self-preoccupation, 223
self-presentation, 164–167
self-preservation instinct, 59
self-promotion, 165
self-realization programs, 4
self-regulation, 161–164
self-report inventories, 65–66
self-righteousness, 184
self-schemas, 141
self-serving bias, 158–159
self-socialization, 314–315
self-stimulation, 422, 437
self-talk, negative, 111, 118, 169, 264
self-verification motive, 157
sender, of message, 205
senility, 354
sensate focus, 436–437
sensation seeking scale, 65
sensitivity training, 541
September 11 attacks
aftermath of, 60
comparison effect and, 158
emotional responses to, 81
revenge motives and, 181
self-esteem and, 152
stress and, 72
serotonin, 487, 498, 505, 536
sertraline, 536
service occupations, 382, 387–388
set-point theory, 458
setting-point theory, 458
sex
casual, 424–425
communicating about, 417–418, 433
gender and, 303
Internet and, 410, 411
sex chromosomes, 312
sex education, 409, 433
sex hormones, 408
Sex Matters for College Students (Caron), 408
sex research, 406–407, 418
sex therapy, 436–437
love and, 417
sexism, 43, 183, 324–326
sexual abuse, 295
repressed memories of, 525–528
sexual activity
aging and, 355
motives for, 416–417
on Internet, 17, 18
sexual assault, 298
sexual desire
hormones and, 313
hypoactive, 436, 437
sexual differentiation, prenatal, 408
sexual dysfunctions, 434–437
sexual harassment, 325–326, 386, 390–392
prevalence of, 391
responses to, 391
Sexual Harassment on the Job (Petrocelli & Repa), 392
sexual identity, 407–408
development of, 415
influences on, 408–410
sexual impulses, Freud's view of, 37–38
sexual intercourse, 420, 421, 422, 423
in adolescence, 340
sexual maturation, 338, 292, 303, 407, 412–416
in early adulthood, 345
love and, 252–253
physical attractiveness and, 242
sexual prejudice, 414–415
sexual problems, 434–437
male role and, 320–321
stress and, 91
sexual relationships, 416–418
enhancing, 433–434
sexual response cycle, 418–420
sexual satisfaction, 420
marital satisfaction and, 18
Sexuality Now (Carroll), 421
sexuality
ambivalence about, 324, 437
gender differences in, 308–309, 313, 320–321, 324
terror management and, 61
sexually transmitted diseases (STDs), 422, 423, 430–433
prevalence of, 430
prevention of, 431, 433

principal types, 432
transmission of, 431, 432, 465
shame, as response to traumatic events, 89
shaping, 135, 232, 531
Shields, Brooke, 276, 277
shyness, 164
Shyness (Zimbardo), 264
sick role, 468, 491
SIECUS, 409
Silkwood, Karen, 197
similarity
as factor in attraction, 246
in married couples, 272
singlehood, 269, 271, 290–291
single-parent households, 270, 382
Sixteen Personality Factor Questionnaire (16 PF), 66
skills, mastering, 162
sleep deprivation, 1
smoking, 40, 110, 163–164, 443, 451, 452–454
snap judgments, 174, 191
sociability, 94
social activity, happiness and, 21
social categorization, 177–178, 185
social clock, 345, 350
social cognitive theory, 48-49, 50, 314
social comparison, 158
social comparison theory, 144–145, 168
social constructionism, 310
social context, 146–147
social dominance orientation (SDO), 184–185
social exchange theory, 248–249
social identity, threats to, 186–187
social identity theory, 186–187
social influence, strategies of, 4–5, 198–201
social isolation, 236, 262, 353
social networking, 238, 248
social norms, 194
social phobia, 486, 489
social pressure, 192–197
Social Readjustment Rating Scale (SRRS), 77, 78, 449
problems with, 97–98
social role theory, 310
social skills
learning, 524
occupation and, 374
poor, 263, 500
social skills training, 265, 531
social support
adherence to medical advice and, 469
disobedience to authority and, 197
from friends, 251
heart attack risk and, 446
from Internet groups, 238
lack of, 500
in late adulthood, 352–353
positive emotions and, 82
providing, 94
seeking, 121–122
stress tolerance and, 93–94
social workers, psychiatric, 518, 519
socialization, 313
gender-role, 313–318
sexual, 408–410, 412
socioeconomic status
career aspirations and, 374
gender expectations and, 316
self-esteem and, 308
sociometer theory, 150
somatization disorder, 489
somatoform disorders, 483, 489–491
source, of message, 188, 189–190
spanking, 368
spatial abilities, gender differences in, 307, 311
speaking, 205, 213–214
public, 222
rate of, 220
sperm production, aging and, 356
spermarche, 338
spermicides, 429
sports, 397
for exercise, 464
sports teams, performance pressure on, 87
spotlight effect, 165
spouse, death of, 362–363
SQ3R, 26
stagnation, 348
standardization, of tests, 64
Stanford Prison Simulation, 197
staring, 211
state self-esteem, 148
status
eye contact and, 212
in interpersonal communication, 217
personal space and, 209–210
posture and, 212
touch and, 213
stepfamilies, 289
stereotypes, 61, 178–179, 185
combating, 187
gender, 303–305
of national character, 63
racial, 74
self-concept and, 148
stereotypical confirmation, 74
steroids, 323
stimulants, 471, 472, 473
stimulation, need for, 93
stimulus-value-role theory, 273
stoicism, 319
stonewalling, 284
Stop Smoking Workbook, The (Stevic-Rust & Maximin), 453
stress management, 446
stress, 71
anxiety disorders and, 487
appraisal of, 72, 98, 116
behavioral responses to, 80, 86–87
brain-body pathways in, 85–86
cancer and, 447–448
chronic, 75, 84, 91
cognitive reactions to, 81
coping with, 105–131
cultural influences on, 74
disease and, 443, 448, 449
dissociative disorders and, 492
divorce as source of, 287
effects of, 87–93
emotional responses to, 80–82
environmental sources of, 72–73, 74
as everyday event, 71
exercise and, 130, 463
humor and, 118–120
immune functioning and, 448–449
leisure activities and, 398
major types of, 75–79
meditation and, 130–131
monitoring of, 97–101
mood disorders and, 500–501
nature of, 71–74
origin of term, 84
physical illness and, 91–92, 443, 448, 449
physiological responses to, 80, 82–86
positive effects of, 92–93
prolonged, 84–85, 388
psychological disorders and, 91
schizophrenic disorders and, 507
severe, 88
social support and, 251
subjective nature of, 72
tolerance of, 93–97
work-related, 88, 281, 386–390
stroke, 92, 441, 456
Strong Interest Inventory (SII), 376
study skills, 24–29
subjective well-being, 19–24
submissive communication, 230
substance use disorders, 483, 484
success ethic, 319
sugar, in diet, 462
suicide, 496–497
adolescent, 343–344
gender differences in, 309
preventing, 344, 496–497
SSRIs and, 536
Summers, Lawrence, 302
superego, 36, 38
superiority, striving for, 41, 42
superordinate goals, 187
surveys, 17
Surviving Schizophrenia (Torrey), 502
supplication, 166
swingers, 426
Sybil (Schreiber), 492
sympathetic nervous system, 83–84, 85
symptoms, interpretation of, 467
syphilis, 432
systematic desensitization, 223, 529–530, 544, 545
systematic judgments, 174
systematic relaxation, 131

T

tardive dyskinesia, 535
task performance
arousal and, 82, 83
pressure and, 87, 88
procrastination and, 124
Tchambuli, 314
teachers, as source of gender-role socialization, 317
technology
as contributor to loneliness, 262
interpersonal communication and, 206–207
job search process and, 401
job stress and, 388
progress and, 1–4
workplace changes and, 381
teenagers. *See* adolescence
television
as source of gender-role socialization, 317–318
sexual content of, 409–410
violence on, 226–227
television viewing habits, 317
temperament, anxiety disorders and, 487
Ten Basic Principles of Good Parenting (Steinberg), 369
"tend and befriend," 84
terror management theory, 59–62, 152
terrorism
emotional reactions to, 60, 89
modern, 152
threat of, 2, 117
terrorists, 181
test anxiety, 82
test norms, 64
testosterone, 313, 408
marijuana use and, 474
tests, personality, 63–67
text messaging, 206
textbooks
gender-role stereotypes in, 316–317
outlining, 28
reading, 27
THC, 471, 474
Thematic Apperception Test (TAT), 66, 67
therapist(s)
in client-centered therapy, 522–523
effectiveness of, 545
false memory syndrome and, 525–528
finding, 542–545
in group therapy, 524
for minority group clients, 541
in psychoanalysis, 520–521

therapist(s) *(continued)*
role in dissociative identity disorder, 492
sexual exploitation by, 543
theoretical approach of, 544–555
types of, 517–519, 543
therapy
aversion, 530
behavioral, 528–533
blending approaches to, 540
client-centered, 521–523
clients for, 515–516
cognitive, 531–533
common factors approach to, 525
cost of, 544
delays in seeking, 516–517
drug, 533–537
effectiveness of, 525, 544
electroconvulsive, 537–538
elements of, 515–519
group, 523-524
process of, 545
psychoanalysis, 519–521
psychodynamic approach to, 521
settings for, 542–543
types of, 515
utilization rates for, 517
thinking, irrational, 502
in adolescence, 340
catastrophic, 111, 115–116, 118, 157, 531
critical, 10, 11
irrational, 169, 264, 502
negative, 499–500, 531
thinness, emphasis on, 243
thioridazine, 534, 535
Thomas, Clarence, 390
Thorozine, 534
threats, responding to, 82–84
Three Psychologies (Nye), 52
thyroid, 85
time
lack of, 1
wasting of, 123
time fatigue, 1
time log, 125
time management, 122–126
studying and, 25
suggestions for, 124–126
Time Management from the Inside Out (Morgenstern), 122
tobacco smoking, 452–454
toilet training, 40
token economies, 134–135
tokens, in workforce, 385
tolerance
anxiety and, 60
drug, 470
touching, 213, 422
toy preference, gender and, 315
tradeoffs, 163–164
trait self-esteem, 148
tranquilizers, 534
transactional analysis, 224
transcendental meditation, 130
transference, in psychoanalysis, 521
transgender, 307
transvestic fetishism, 480
traumatic events
children's reactions to, 366
coping with, 447
likelihood of, 117, 366
prevalence of, 90
rational thinking about, 117
reactions to, 89
recovered memories of, 525–526
travel, 397
treatment, seeking, 467, 516–517
triangular theory of love, 253–254
tricyclics, 535–536
trustworthiness, of source, 189
tsunamis, 90, 363
tuberculosis, stress and, 92
twin studies, 55, 56–57
of homosexuality, 413
of mood disorders, 498
of obesity, 458
of schizophrenic disorders, 505
Type A personality, 444
Type B personality, 444
Type C personality, 448

U

ultimate attribution error, 186
unconditional positive regard, 522
unconditioned response (UCR), 44, 45, 46
unconditioned stimulus (UCS), 44, 45, 46
unconscious
Freud's view of, 36, 37, 520
Jung's view of, 41
underemployment, 383
undifferentiated schizophrenia, 503
undoing, 112
unemployment, 392–394
unipolar disorder, 494
University of Minnesota, 55, 57
upward social comparison, 145
urbanization, 74
U.S. Department of Agriculture, 461
U.S. Department of Labor, 382

V

vacations, paid, 396
vacillation, 76
vagina, 418–420, 423
validity, of psychological tests, 64–65
Valium, 472, 487, 534
valproate, 536
values
conflicts over, 227
sexual, 407, 433
work-related, 374
variables, 13–14
clusters of, 33
correlations between, 15–16
vasocongestion, 418
vengeance, 181
ventricles, of brain, 505–506
verbal abilities, gender differences in, 306
veterans
Iraq war, 90
Vietnam, 88, 93
Viagra, 356, 436
victims
blaming of, 180, 181, 186
of date rape, 297–299
of partner abuse, 295–296, 297
Victorian era, 35
video games, 318
videoconferencing, 206
Vienna Psychoanalytic Society, 41
Vietnam veterans, 88, 93
violence
community, 73
intimate, 295–299
in media, 108, 109
on television, 226–227
violent crimes, 308
on college campuses, 455
vision, aging and, 354
visual dominance, 212
visual imagery, as memory aid, 29
visualization, 223
vitamins, 461
vocal cues, 213
volunteer activities, 397
vomiting, 509
vulnerability, as response to traumatic events, 89

W

Wal-Mart, 385
Watkins, Sherron, 197
wealth, happiness and, 20
websites
dating, 239
sexually explicit, 17, 18
weight loss programs, 133–137
Weight Loss Through Persistence (Kirschenbaum), 459
weight problems, 457–458
well-being, subjective, 19-24
wellness programs, workplace, 389
What Color Is Your Parachute? (Bolles), 398, 399
"what is beautiful is good" stereotype, 178
What You Can Change and What You Can't (Seligman), 10
whistleblowers, 197
Why Marriages Succeed or Fail (Gottman), 282
Why Zebras Don't Get Ulcers (Sapolsky), 95
widowhood, 352, 362–363
willpower, 132
withdrawal
from conflict, 227–228
social, 265
withdrawal illness, 471
women
career development of, 347, 380
occupations for, 325
sexism and, 324–326
in workforce, 269, 270, 281, 282, 321–322, 323–324, 383–384, 385, 395–396
see also gender differences; gender roles
work, 381
from home, 382
generational differences in, 396
happiness and, 22
marriage and, 280, 281
in midlife years, 350
time management and, 1
see also career, job; occupation
work environment
hostile, 390
personality and, 377–378
work-family balance, 275, 281, 347, 395
workaholism, 394–395
workforce
demographic changes in, 383–384
women in, 269, 270, 281, 282, 321–322, 323–324, 383–384, 385, 395–396
working memory, 88, 358
workplace
harassment in, 326, 390–392
male bias in, 305
trends in, 380–386
violence in, 392, 394
workweek, 386, 396
World War II, 12
worldviews, cultural, 59, 60, 61
writing, about emotional experiences, 129

XYZ

Xanax, 534
yoga, 130
You Just Don't Understand (Tannen), 331
Zen, 130
Zoloft, 536

TO THE OWNER OF THIS BOOK

We hope that you have found *Psychology Applied to Modern Life,* Ninth Edition useful. So that this book can be improved in a future edition, would you take the time to complete this sheet and return it? Thank you.

School and address: _____

_____

Department: _____

Instructor's name: _____

1. What I like most about this book is: _____

_____

_____

2. What I like least about this book is: _____

_____

_____

3. My general reaction to this book is: _____

_____

_____

4. The name of the course in which I used this book is: _____

_____

5. Were all of the chapters of the book assigned for you to read? _____

   If not, which ones weren't? _____

6. In the space below, or on a separate sheet of paper, please write specific suggestions for improving this book and anything else you'd care to share about your experience in using this book.

_____

_____

_____

_____

_____

_____

_____

DO NOT STAPLE.
TAPE HERE

FOLD HERE

WADSWORTH
CENGAGE Learning™

NO POSTAG
NECESSAR
IF MAILED
IN THE
UNITED STA

BUSINESS REPLY MAIL

FIRST-CLASS MAIL PERMIT NO. 34 BELMONT CA

POSTAGE WILL BE PAID BY ADDRESSEE

Attn: Michele Sordi, Psychology Editor

Wadsworth Cengage Learning
10 Davis Dr
Belmont CA 94002-98001

FOLD HERE

OPTIONAL:

Your name: _____ Date _____

May we quote you, either in promotion for *Psychology Applied to Modern Life,* Ninth Edition, or in future publishing ventures?

Yes: _____ No: _____

DO NOT STAPLE.
TAPE HERE